PEARSON

COMMON CORE Literature

GRADE 9

PEARSON

HOBOKEN, NEW JERSEY • BOSTON, MASSACHUSETTS
CHANDLER, ARIZONA • GLENVIEW, ILLINOIS

COVER: Filip Fuxa/Shutterstock.com

Acknowledgments appear in the back of this book, and constitute an extension of this copyright page.

ISBN-13: 978-0-13-326820-1
ISBN-10: 0-13-326820-9
8 9 10 11 12 13 V057 18 17 16 15 14

PEARSON

COMMON CORE Literature

GRADE 9

PEARSON

HOBOKEN, NEW JERSEY • BOSTON, MASSACHUSETTS
CHANDLER, ARIZONA • GLENVIEW, ILLINOIS

Contributing Authors

The contributing authors guided the direction and philosophy of Pearson Common Core Literature. *They helped to build the pedagogical integrity of the program by contributing content expertise, knowledge of the Common Core State Standards, and support for the shifts in instruction the Common Core will bring. Their knowledge, combined with classroom and professional experience, ensures* Pearson Common Core Literature *is relevant for both teachers and students.*

William G. Brozo, Ph.D., is a Professor of Literacy in the Graduate School of Education at George Mason University in Fairfax, Virginia. He earned his bachelor's degree from the University of North Carolina and his master's and doctorate from the University of South Carolina. He has taught reading and language arts in the Carolinas and is the author of numerous articles on literacy development for children and young adults. His books include *To Be a Boy, To Be a Reader: Engaging Teen and Preteen Boys in Active Literacy; Readers, Teachers, Learners: Expanding Literacy Across the Content Areas; Content Literacy for Today's Adolescents: Honoring Diversity and Building Competence; Supporting Content Area Literacy with Technology* (Pearson); and *Setting the Pace: A Speed, Comprehension, and Study Skills Program*. His newest book is *RTI and the Adolescent Reader: Responsive Literacy Instruction in Secondary Schools*. As an international consultant, Dr. Brozo has provided technical support to teachers from the Balkans to the Middle East, and he is currently a member of a European Union research grant team developing curriculum and providing adolescent literacy professional development for teachers across Europe.

Diane Fettrow spent the majority of her teaching career in Broward County, Florida, teaching high school English courses and serving as department chair. She also worked as an adjunct instructor at Broward College, Nova Southeastern University, and Florida Atlantic University. After she left the classroom, she served as Secondary Language Arts Curriculum Supervisor for several years, working with more than 50 of the district's high schools, centers, and charter schools. During her time as curriculum supervisor, she served on numerous local and state committees; she also served as Florida's K–12 ELA content representative to the PARCC Model Content Frameworks Rapid Response Feedback Group and the PARCC K–12 and Upper Education Engagement Group. Currently she presents workshops on the Common Core State Standards and is working with Pearson on aligning materials to the CCSS.

Kelly Gallagher is a full-time English teacher at Magnolia High School in Anaheim, California, where he has taught for twenty-seven years. He is the former co-director of the South Basin Writing Project at California State University, Long Beach, and the author of *Reading Reasons: Motivational Mini-Lessons for Middle and High School; Deeper Reading: Comprehending Challenging Texts, 4–12; Teaching Adolescent Writers;* and *Readicide: How Schools Are Killing Reading and What You Can Do About It*. He is also a principal author of *Prentice Hall Writing Coach* (Pearson, 2012). Kelly's latest book is *Write Like This* (Stenhouse). Follow Kelly on Twitter @KellyGToGo, and visit him at www.kellygallagher.org.

Elfrieda "Freddy' Hiebert, Ph.D., is President and CEO of TextProject, a nonprofit organization that provides resources to support higher reading levels. She is also a research associate at the University of California, Santa Cruz. Dr. Hiebert received her Ph.D. in Educational Psychology from the University of Wisconsin-Madison. She has worked in the field of early reading acquisition for 45 years, first as a teacher's aide and teacher of primary-level students in California and, subsequently, as a teacher educator and researcher at the universities of Kentucky, Colorado-Boulder, Michigan, and California-Berkeley. Her research addresses how fluency, vocabulary, and knowledge can be fostered through appropriate texts. Professor Hiebert's research has been published in numerous scholarly journals, and she has authored or edited nine books. Professor Hiebert's model of accessible texts for beginning and struggling readers—TExT—has been used to develop numerous reading programs that are widely used in schools. Dr. Hiebert is the 2008 recipient of the William S. Gray Citation of Merit, awarded by the International Reading Association; is a member of the Reading Hall of Fame; and has chaired a group of early childhood literacy experts who served in an advisory capacity to the CCSS writers.

Donald J. Leu, Ph.D., is the John and Maria Neag Endowed Chair in Literacy and Technology and holds a joint appointment in Curriculum and Instruction and Educational Psychology in the Neag School of Education at the University of Connecticut. Don is an international authority on literacy education, especially the new skills and strategies required to read, write, and learn with Internet technologies and the best instructional practices that prepare students for these new literacies. He is a member of the Reading Hall of Fame, a Past President of the National Reading Conference, and a former member of the Board of Directors of the International Reading Association. Don is a Principal Investigator on a number of federal research grants, and his work has been funded by the U.S. Department of Education, the National Science Foundation, and the Bill and Melinda Gates Foundation, among others. He recently edited the *Handbook of Research on New Literacies* (Erlbaum, 2008).

Ernest Morrell, Ph.D., is a professor of English Education at Teachers College, Columbia University, and the president-elect of the National Council of Teachers of English (NCTE). He is also the Director of Teachers College's Harlem-based Institute for Urban and Minority Education (IUME). Dr. Morrell was an award-winning high school English teacher in California, and he now works with teachers and schools across the country to infuse multicultural literature, youth popular culture, and media production into standards-based literacy curricula and after-school programs. He is the author of nearly 100 articles and book chapters as well as five books, including *Critical Media Pedagogy: Achievement, Production, and Justice in City Schools* and *Linking Literacy and Popular Culture*. In his spare time he coaches youth sports and writes poems and plays.

Karen Wixson, Ph.D., is Dean of the School of Education at the University of North Carolina, Greensboro. She has published widely in the areas of literacy curriculum, instruction, and assessment. Dr. Wixson has been an advisor to the National Research Council and helped develop the National Assessment of Educational Progress (NAEP) reading tests. She is a former member of the IRA Board of Directors and co-chair of the IRA Commission on RTI. Recently, Dr. Wixson served on the English Language Arts Work Team that was part of the Common Core State Standards Initiative.

Grant Wiggins, Ed.D., is the President of Authentic Education in Hopewell, New Jersey. He earned his Ed.D. from Harvard University and his B.A. from St. John's College in Annapolis. Grant consults with schools, districts, and state education departments on a variety of reform matters; organizes conferences and workshops; and develops print materials and Web resources on curricular change. He is perhaps best known for being the co-author, with Jay McTighe, of *Understanding by Design* and *The Understanding by Design Handbook,* the award-winning and highly successful materials on curriculum published by ASCD.

INTRODUCTORY UNIT Contents

COMMON CORE FOUNDATIONS

COMMON CORE STATE STANDARDS

The following standards are introduced in this unit and revisited throughout the program.

Reading Literature

2. Determine a theme or central idea of a text and analyze in detail its development over the course of the text, including how it emerges and is shaped and refined by specific details; provide an objective summary of the text.

10. By the end of grade 9, read and comprehend literature, including stories, dramas, and poems, in the grades 9–10 text complexity band proficiently, with scaffolding as needed at the high end of the range.

Reading Informational Text

2. Determine a central idea of a text and analyze its development over the course of the text, including how it emerges and is shaped and refined by specific details; provide an objective summary of the text.

8. Delineate and evaluate the argument and specific claims in a text, assessing whether the reasoning is valid and the evidence is relevant and sufficient; identify false statements and fallacious reasoning.

Writing

1. Write arguments to support claims in an analysis of substantive topics or texts, using valid reasoning and relevant and sufficient evidence.

2. Write informative/explanatory texts to examine and convey complex ideas, concepts, and information clearly and accurately through the effective selection, organization, and analysis of content.

5. Develop and strengthen writing as needed by planning, revising, editing, rewriting, or trying a new approach, focusing on addressing what is most significant for a specific purpose and audience.

7. Conduct short as well as more sustained research projects to answer a question (including a self-generated question) or solve a problem; narrow or broaden the inquiry when appropriate; synthesize multiple sources on the subject, demonstrating understanding of the subject under investigation.

8. Gather relevant information from multiple authoritative print and digital sources, using advanced searches effectively; assess the usefulness of each source in answering the research question; integrate information in the text selectively to maintain the flow of ideas, avoiding plagiarism and following a standard format for citation.

9. Draw evidence from literary or informational texts to support analysis, reflection, and research.

Additional standards addressed in these workshops:

Reading Informational Text
6, 9, 10

Writing
1.a, 1.b, 1.e, 2.a, 2.b, 2.d, 2.e, 6

Language
1, 2, 2.c, 3, 3.a, 6

UNIT 1 Is conflict necessary?

PART 1 SETTING EXPECTATIONS

PART 2 TEXT ANALYSIS GUIDED EXPLORATION

FACING CONFLICT

PART 3
TEXT SET DEVELOPING INSIGHT

CONFORMITY

PART 4
DEMONSTRATING INDEPENDENCE

DIGITAL ASSETS KEY

These digital resources, as well as audio and the Online Writer's Notebook, can be found at **pearsonrealize.com**.

- Interactive Whiteboard Activities
- Virtual Tour
- Close Reading Notebook
- Video
- Close Reading Tool for Annotating Texts
- Grammar Tutorials
- Online Text Set

UNIT 1 Unit at a Glance

READ

Text Analysis
Internal and External Conflict
Situational Irony
Direct and Indirect Characterization
Plot
Comparing Points of View
Symbolism
Voice
Supporting Evidence
Diction
Description

Comprehension
Make Inferences
Analyze Cause and Effect
Make Predictions

Language Study
Latin Suffix *-esque*
Latin Prefix *de-*
Latin Root *-bene-*
Latin Suffix *-tion*

Conventions
Parts of Speech
Simple and Perfect Tenses
Subjects and Predicates
Active and Passive Voice

Language Study Workshop
Using a Dictionary and Thesaurus

DISCUSS

Presentation of Ideas
Oral Presentation
Debate

Comprehension and Collaboration
Retelling

Responding to Text
Group Discussion
Partner Discussion
Class Discussion

Speaking and Listening Workshop
Evaluating a Speech

RESEARCH

Research and Technology
Informational Brochure

Investigate the Topic: Conformity
Cultural Attitudes
Learning English
Ethics
Nonconformist Achievers
Prodigies

WRITE

Writing to Sources
Comparison-and-Contrast Essay
News Report
Written Presentation
Critique
Explanatory Essay
Response to Literature
Informational Essay
Argumentative Essay
Position Paper
Autobiographical Narrative
Short Story

Writing Process Workshop
Argument: Response to Literature
Word Choice: Perfecting Your Word Choice
Conventions: Using Quotations

UNIT VOCABULARY

Academic Vocabulary appears in *blue.*

Introducing the Big Question *amicably, antagonize, appreciate, argument, articulate, battle, compete, competition, controversy, cooperate, differences, equity, grievance, issue, mediate, survival, war*

The Most Dangerous Game *palpable, scruples, indolently, grotesque, naive, futile*

The Gift of the Magi *instigates, cascade, faltered, prudence, discreet, depreciate*

Rules of the Game *pungent, retort, prodigy, malodorous, concessions, benevolently*

The Cask of Amontillado *precluded, afflicted, explicit, recoiling, subsided, retribution*

Checkouts; The Girl Who Can *reverie, dishevelment, perverse, fertile, comprehension, humble, character, context, differentiate, perspective*

The Scarlet Ibis *imminent, infallibility, precariously, effective, detract, pervade*

Much Madness is divinest Sense— *discerning, prevail, emphasize, contradictory*

My English *bilingual, enumerated, accentuated, illustrate, noteworthy, barrier*

The Case for Fitting In *prejudice, solidarity, credentials, distinction, critical, consult*

***from* The Geeks Shall Inherit the Earth** *allegedly, monotonous, squelching, characterize, analyze, evidence*

***from* Blue Nines and Red Words** *prime, calculating, symmetrical, findings, progression, vivid*

Cartoon *from* The New Yorker *literal, implied, depicts*

COMMON CORE STATE STANDARDS

For the full wording of the standards, see the standards charts following the Contents pages.

Reading Literature

RL.9-10.1, RL.9-10.2, RL.9-10.3, RL.9-10.4, RL.9-10.5, RL.9-10.6, RL9-10.10

Reading Informational Text

RI.9-10.1, RI.9-10.2, RI.9-10.3, RI.9-10.4, RI.9-10.5, RI.9-10.6, RI.9-10.8, RI.9-10.10

Writing

W.9-10.1, W.9-10.1.a–e, W.9-10.2, W.9-10.2.a–d, W.9-10.2.f, W.9-10.3, W.9-10.3.a–e, W.9-10.4, W.9-10.5, W.9-10.6, W.9-10.7, W.9-10.8, W.9-10.9, W.9-10.9.a–b, W.9-10.10

Speaking and Listening

SL.9-10.1, SL.9-10.1.a–d, SL.9-10.2, SL.9-10.3, SL.9-10.4, SL.9-10.5

Language

L.9-10.1, L.9-10.1.a, L.9-10.2, L.9-10.2.b–c, L.9-10.3, L.9-10.3.a, L.9-10.4, L.9-10.4.a–d, L.9-10.5, L.9-10.5.a-b, L.9-10.6

UNIT 2 Is knowledge the same as understanding?

PART 1 SETTING EXPECTATIONS

PART 2 TEXT ANALYSIS GUIDED EXPLORATION

CHANGING PERSPECTIVES

PART 3
TEXT SET DEVELOPING INSIGHT

THE GREAT DEPRESSION

PART 4
DEMONSTRATING INDEPENDENCE

DIGITAL ASSETS KEY

These digital resources, as well as audio and the Online Writer's Notebook, can be found at **pearsonrealize.com.**

- Interactive Whiteboard Activities
- Virtual Tour
- Close Reading Notebook
- Video
- Close Reading Tool for Annotating Texts
- Grammar Tutorials
- Online Text Set

UNIT 2 Unit at a Glance

READ

Text Analysis
- Author's Style
- Expository Essay
- Persuasive Essay
- Persuasive Speech
- Comparing Themes
- Persuasive Appeals
- Metaphor
- Author's Perspective
- Reportage

Comprehension
- Main Idea
- Evaluate Persuasion

Language Study
- Latin Root *-dur-*
- Latin Root *-temp-*
- Latin Root *-sum-*
- Latin Root *-cred-*

Conventions
- Direct and Indirect Objects
- Predicate Nominatives and Predicate Adjectives
- Colons, Semicolons, Ellipsis Points
- Independent and Dependent Clauses

Language Study Workshop
- Etymology: Word Origins and Modern Meanings

DISCUSS

Presentation of Ideas
- Panel Discussion
- Radio News Report

Responding to Text
- Debate
- Group Discussion
- Partner Discussion
- Class Discussion

Speaking and Listening Workshop
- Delivering a Persuasive Speech

RESEARCH

Research and Technology
- Journal Entry
- Persuasive Speech

Investigate the Topic: The Great Depression
- Banks and the Great Depression
- Action During a Crisis
- The Dust Bowl
- The Value of Money

WRITE

Writing to Sources
- Analysis
- Expository Essay
- Abstract
- Proposal
- Reflective Essay
- Persuasive Essay
- Argumentative Essay
- Fictional Narrative
- Explanatory Essay
- Explanatory Caption

Writing Process Workshop
- Explanatory Text: Cause-and-Effect Essay
  - Voice: Setting Your Tone
  - Conventions: Revising to Correct Faulty Subject-Verb Agreement

UNIT VOCABULARY

Academic Vocabulary appears in *blue.*

Introducing the Big Question *ambiguous, clarify, comprehend, concept, connection, fact, feeling, information, insight, instinct, interpret, research, senses, sensory, sources, statistics*

On Summer *aloofness, melancholy, bias, duration, pretentious, apex*

The News *compensation, temporal, medium, imposition, revered, daunting*

Libraries Face Sad Chapter *volumes, presumed, curtailed, medium, duration, emulate*

"I Have a Dream" *momentous, defaulted, hallowed, degenerate, creed, oppression*

***from* Silent Spring ; "If I Forget Thee, Oh Earth…"** *blight, maladies, moribund, purged, perennial, argument, circumstance, determine, interpretation*

First Inaugural Address *candor, feasible, arduous, trace, signaled, accentuate*

***from* Nothing to Fear: Lessons in Leadership from FDR** *provocative, obscures, inevitable, visionary, asserts, critique*

***from* Americans in the Great Depression** *disproportionately, solicitude, prevalence, illuminate, establish, devastation*

Women on the Breadlines *exodus, privations, futility, interaction, subjective, articulate*

Bread Line, New York City, 1932 *composition, elevated, objective*

COMMON CORE STATE STANDARDS

For the full wording of the standards, see the standards charts following the Contents pages.

Reading Literature

RL.9-10.1, RL.9-10.2, RL.9-10.10

Reading Informational Text

RI.9-10.1, RI.9-10.2, RI.9-10.3, RI.9-10.4, RI.9-10.5, RI.9-10.6, RI.9-10.7, RI.9-10.8, RI.9-10.9, RI.9-10.10

Writing

W.9-10.1, W.9-10.1.a–e, W.9-10.2, W.9-10.2.a–f, W.9-10.3, W.9-10.3.a–e, W.9-10.4, W.9-10.5, W.9-10.7, W.9-10.8, W.9-10.9, W.9-10.9.b, W.9-10.10

Speaking and Listening

SL.9-10.1, SL.9-10.1.a–d, SL.9-10.2, SL.9-10.3, SL.9-10.4, SL.9-10.5, SL.9-10.6

Language

L.9-10.1, L.9-10.1.a–b, L.9-10.2, L.9-10.2.a–c, L.9-10.3, L.9-10.3.a, L.9-10.4, L.9-10.4.a, L.9-10.4.c, L.9-10.4.d, L.9-10.5, L.9-10.5.a–b, L.9-10.6

UNIT 3 How does communication change us?

PART 1
SETTING EXPECTATIONS

PART 2
TEXT ANALYSIS GUIDED EXPLORATION

THE RIGHT WORDS

DIGITAL ASSETS KEY

These digital resources, as well as audio and the Online Writer's Notebook, can be found at **pearsonrealize.com**.

- Interactive Whiteboard Activities
- Virtual Tour
- Close Reading Notebook
- Video
- Close Reading Tool for Annotating Texts
- Grammar Tutorials
- Online Text Set

UNIT 3 Unit at a Glance

READ

Text Analysis

Figurative Language
Sound Devices
Narrative Poetry
Rhyme and Meter
Comparing Poetic Forms
Alliteration
Memoir
Historical Context
Parallelism

Comprehension

Read Fluently
Paraphrase

Language Study

Latin Root *-fer-*
Greek Prefix *mono-*
Latin Prefix *pre-*
Latin Suffix *-ment*

Conventions

Prepositions and Prepositional Phrases
Participles and Participle Phrases; Gerunds and Gerund Phrases
Appositive and Absolute Phrases
Infinitives and Infinitive Phrases

Language Study Workshop

Words With Multiple Meanings

DISCUSS

Presentation of Ideas

Speech
Dialogue
Panel Discussion

Comprehension and Collaboration

Illustrated Presentation

Responding to Text

Group Discussion
Partner Discussion
One-on-One Discussion

Speaking and Listening Workshop

Oral Interpretation of Literature

RESEARCH

Investigate the Topic: The Kennedy Assassination

The World's Reaction
First Ladies and their Causes
Media and the Kennedy Assassination
Presidential Speeches
Americans Remember: Oral History

WRITE

Writing to Sources

Description of a Scene
Editorial
Poem
Explanatory Essay
Expository Essay
Character Analysis
Analytical Essay
Historical Narrative
Magazine Article
Memoir
Argumentative Essay

Writing Process Workshop

Argument: Problem-and-Solution Essay
- Ideas: Expressing Your Ideas
- Sentence Fluency: Revising to Combine Choppy Sentences

UNIT VOCABULARY

Academic Vocabulary appears in *blue*.

Introducing the Big Question *aware, communication, comprehension, discuss, empathy, exchange, illuminate, informed, interpretation, meaning, react, relationship, resolution, respond, understanding*

Poetry Collection 1 *deferred, fester, barren, paradoxical, abash*

Poetry Collection 2 *voluminously, endeavor, palpitating, monotone, disgrace, metaphysical, jibed*

Poetry Collection 3 *demure, pallor, preceded, multitude, writhing, defiance, pondered, beguiling, respite*

Poetry Collection 4 *diverged, bafflement, depravity, rifled, disclosed, woeful, treble, oblivion, warp*

I Hear America Singing; Women; Three Haiku; Sonnet 30 *intermission, stout, woes, wail, articulate, concept, interpretation, unique*

The Assassination of John F. Kennedy/Instead of an Elegy *delirium, antic, requiem, resolution, counteract, implicit*

***from* A White House Diary** *confines, poignant, immaculate, intimate, conduct, advocate*

American History *profound, vigilant, dilapidated, disseminating, forum, pose*

Address Before a Joint Session of the Congress *fortitude, formidable, eulogy, stirs, concise, articulated*

Images of a Tragedy *caption, consider, crystallize*

COMMON CORE STATE STANDARDS

For the full wording of the standards, see the standards charts following the Contents pages.

Reading Literature

RL.9-10.1, RL.9-10.2, RL.9-10.3, RL.9-10.4, RL.9-10.5, RL.9-10.7, RL.9-10.10

Reading Informational Text

RI.9-10.1, RI.9-10.2, RI.9-10.3, RI.9-10.4, RI.9-10.5, RI.9-10.6, RI.9-10.7, RI.9-10.9, RI.9-10.10

Writing

W.9-10.1, W.9-10.1.a–e, W.9-10.2, W.9-10.2.a–b, W.9-10.2.f, W.9-10.3, W.9-10.3.a–e, W.9-10.4, W.9-10.5, W.9-10.6, W.9-10.7, W.9-10.8, W.9-10.9, W.9-10.9.a–b, W.9-10.10

Speaking and Listening

SL.9-10.1, SL.9-10.1.a–d, SL.9-10.2, SL.9-10.3, SL.9-10.4, SL.9-10.5, SL.9-10.6

Language

L.9-10.1, L.9-10.1.a–b, L.9-10.2.a–c, L.9-10.3, L.9-10.4, L.9-10.4.a, L.9-10.4.c, L.9-10.4.d, L.9-10.5, L.9-10.5.a–b, L.9-10.6

UNIT 4 Do our differences define us?

PART 1
SETTING EXPECTATIONS

PART 2
TEXT ANALYSIS GUIDED EXPLORATION

TRAGIC ROMANCES

PART 3
TEXT SET DEVELOPING INSIGHT

ASPIRATION

PART 4
DEMONSTRATING INDEPENDENCE

DIGITAL ASSETS KEY

These digital resources, as well as audio and the Online Writer's Notebook, can be found at **pearsonrealize.com.**

- Interactive Whiteboard Activities
- Virtual Tour
- Close Reading Notebook
- Video
- Close Reading Tool for Annotating Texts
- Grammar Tutorials
- Online Text Set

UNIT 4 Unit at a Glance

READ

Text Analysis

Dialogue and Stage Directions
Blank Verse
Dialogue and Dramatic Speeches
Dramatic Irony
Tragedy and Motive
Comparing Archetypal Themes
Satire
Situational Irony
Anecdote
Evidence
Connotations

Comprehension

Summarize
Read in Sentences
Paraphrase
Break Down Long Sentences
Analyze Cause and Effect

Language Study

Latin Prefix *trans-*
Latin Suffix *-able*
Latin Root *-loque-*
Latin Prefix *en-*
Latin Prefix *ambi-*

Conventions

Parallelism

Language Study Workshop

Connotation and Denotation

DISCUSS

Comprehension and Collaboration

Staged Performance
Mock Trial

Responding to Text

Group Discussion
Partner Discussion
Panel Discussion

Speaking and Listening Workshop

Multimedia Presentation of a Research Report

RESEARCH

Research and Technology

Annotated Flowchart
Film Review
Multimedia Presentation

Investigate the Topic: Aspiration

Victorian Society
Social Structures in 19th Century France
Social Change Movements
Social Media
Grave Goods

WRITE

Writing to Sources

Editorial
Persuasive Letter
Persuasive Speech
Explanatory Essay
Character Analysis
Expository Essay
Advice Column
Critical Response
Persuasive Essay
Short Story
Personal Narrative

Writing Process Workshop

Explanatory Text: Comparison-and-Contrast Essay
- Organization: Getting Organized
- Sentence Fluency: Revising to Combine Sentences With Phrases

UNIT VOCABULARY

Academic Vocabulary appears in *blue.*

Introducing the Big Question *accept, assimilated, background, conformity, culture, determine, differences, differentiate, discriminate, individuality, similarity, understanding, unique, values*

The Tragedy of Romeo and Juliet:

Act I *pernicious, adversary, augmenting, grievance, oppression, transgression*

Act II *procure, predominant, intercession, sallow, lamentable, unwieldy*

Act III *gallant, fray, martial, exile, eloquence, fickle*

Act IV *pensive, vial, enjoined, wayward, dismal, loathsome*

Act V *remnants, penury, disperse, haughty, ambiguities, scourge*

Pyramus and Thisbe; *from* A Midsummer Night's Dream *lament, inevitable, enamored, enthralled, articulate, character, illuminate, standard*

***from* The Importance of Being Earnest** *demonstrative, ignorance, indiscretion, ideals, status, ancestry*

The Necklace *dejection, disheveled, profoundly, estimation, class, elaborate*

New Directions *amicably, balmy, ominous, strategy, emulate, exemplifies*

***from* Fragile Self-Worth** *discrepancy, empirical, realm, compensation, assertions, compelling*

My Possessions Myself *domestic, aggregate, embellishes, insights, reasoning, minimize*

Cartoon *from* The New Yorker *incongruity, depicted*

COMMON CORE STATE STANDARDS

For the full wording of the standards, see the standards charts following the Contents pages.

Reading Literature

RL.9-10.1, RL.9-10.2, RL.9-10.3, RL.9-10.4 RL.9-10.5, RL.9-10.6, RL.9-10.9, RL.9-10.10

Reading Informational Text

RI.9-10.1, RI.9-10.2, RI.9-10.3, RI.9-10.4, RI.9-10.5, RI.9-10.6, RI.9-10.8, RI.9-10.10

Writing

W.9-10.1, W.9-10.1.a–c, W.9-10.1.e, W.9-10.2, W.9-10.2.a–f, W.9-10.3, W.9-10.3.a–e, W.9-10.4, W.9-10.5, W.9-10.6, W.9-10.7, W.9-10.8, W.9-10.9, W.9-10.9.a, W.9-10.10

Speaking and Listening

SL.9-10.1, SL.9-10.1.a–d, SL.9-10.2, SL.9-10.4, SL.9-10.5

Language

L.9-10.1.a–b, L.9-10.2.c, L.9-10.3, L.9-10.3.a, L.9-10.4, L.9-10.4.a, L.9-10.4.c, L.9-10.4.d, L.9-10.5, L.9-10.5.a–b, L.9-10.6

UNIT 5 Do heroes have responsibilities?

PART 1 SETTING EXPECTATIONS

PART 2 TEXT ANALYSIS GUIDED EXPLORATION

PERILOUS JOURNEYS

PART 3
TEXT SET DEVELOPING INSIGHT

DEFINING HEROISM

PART 4
DEMONSTRATING INDEPENDENCE

DIGITAL ASSETS KEY

These digital resources, as well as audio and the Online Writer's Notebook, can be found at **pearsonrealize.com.**

- Interactive Whiteboard Activities
- Virtual Tour
- Close Reading Notebook
- Video
- Close Reading Tool for Annotating Texts
- Grammar Tutorials
- Online Text Set

UNIT 5 Unit at a Glance

READ

Text Analysis
- Epic Hero
- Epic Simile
- Comparing Contemporary Interpretations
- Archetype
- The Hero's Quest
- Characterization
- Archetypal Narrative Patterns
- Argumentation
- Structure

Comprehension
- Historical and Cultural Context

Language Study
- Old English Prefix *be-*
- Latin Prefix *dis-*

Conventions
- Simple and Compound Sentences
- Complex and Compound-Complex Sentences

Language Study Workshop
- Idioms, Technical Terms, and Jargon

DISCUSS

Comprehension and Collaboration
- Conversation
- Debate

Responding to Text
- Write and Discuss
- Group Discussion
- Partner Discussion
- Debate
- Write and Share

Speaking and Listening Workshop
- Comparing Media Coverage

RESEARCH

Investigate the Topic: Defining Heroism
- Rama as Hero
- Greek Mythological Heroes
- Fleeing Persecution
- Origin Stories
- False Heroes
- 9/11 Relief Efforts
- Blood Banks

WRITE

Writing to Sources
- Retelling
- Biography
- Explanatory Essay
- Comparison-and-Contrast Essay
- Response to Literature
- Short Story
- Persuasive Essay
- Definition Essay
- Article/Blog Post
- Reflective Essay
- Argumentative Essay

Writing Process Workshop
- Narration: Autobiographical Narrative
  - Sentence Fluency: Revising to Combine Sentences Using Adverb Clauses
  - Sentence Fluency: Varying Sentence Structure and Length

UNIT VOCABULARY

Academic Vocabulary appears in *blue.*

Introducing the Big Question *character, choices, hero, honesty, identify, imitate, intentions, involvement, justice, morality, obligation, responsibility, serve, standard, wisdom*

***from the* Odyssey, Part 1** *plundered, bereft, dispatched, assuage, ardor, insidious*

***from the* Odyssey, Part 2** *dissemble, incredulity, bemusing, equity, maudlin, contempt*

An Ancient Gesture; Siren Song; *Prologue and Epilogue from* the Odyssey; Ithaca *authentic, picturesque, siege, lofty, defrauded, circumstance, discuss, interpret, perspective*

***from* Ramayana** *intolerable, benediction, obstinate, chaos, rationality, embodiment*

Perseus *kindred, mortified, revelry, universal, rife*

The Washwoman *rancor, atonement, pious, exemplify, align, emigration*

***from* The Hero's Adventure** *elixir, psyche, motif, colloquial, stance*

***from* My Hero's Hero** *embody, surmount, recalcitrant, ultimately, underscore, ambiguity*

Of Altruism, Heroism and Nature's Gifts in the Face of Terror *altruism, indomitable, accrued, comprise, establish, prevalent*

American Blood Donation *distinct, underscores, implicitly*

COMMON CORE STATE STANDARDS

For the full wording of the standards, see the standards charts following the Contents pages.

Reading Literature

RL.9-10.1, RL.9-10.2, RL.9-10.3, RL.9-10.4, RL.9-10.5, RL.9-10.6, RL.9-10.7, RL.9-10.9, RL.9-10.10

Reading Informational Text

RI.9-10.1, RI.9-10.2, RI.9-10.3, RI.9-10.4, RI.9-10.5, RI.9-10.6, RI.9-10.7, RI.9-10.8, RI.9-10.10

Writing

W.9-10.1, W.9-10.1.a–e, W.9-10.2, W.9-10.2.a–c, W.9-10.2.f, W.9-10.3, W.9-10.3.a–e, W.9-10.4, W.9-10.5, W.9-10.6, W.9-10.7, W.9-10.8, W.9-10.9, W.9-10.9.a, W.9-10.10

Speaking and Listening

SL.9-10.1, SL.9-10.1.a–d, SL.9-10.3, SL.9-10.4, SL.9-10.5, SL.9-10.6

Language

L.9-10.1, L.9-10.1.b, L.9-10.2.c, L.9-10.3, L.9-10.3.a, L.9-10.4.a, L.9-10.4.c–d, L.9-10.5.a

Range of Reading

Literature

STORIES

DRAMA

POETRY

Epics

Lyric Poems

Narrative and Dramatic Poems

ONLINE LITERATURE LIBRARY

Highlighted selections are found in the **Online Literature Library** (OLL) in the Online Student Edition.

Range of Reading

Reflective Essays

MEDIA

LITERATURE IN CONTEXT—READING IN CONTENT AREAS

ONLINE LITERATURE LIBRARY

Highlighted selections are found in the **Online Literature Library** (OLL) in the Online Student Edition.

Features and Workshops

COMPARING TEXTS

Comparing Points of View

Comparing Themes

Comparing Poetic Forms

Comparing Archetypal Themes

Comparing Contemporary Interpretations

LANGUAGE STUDY

SPEAKING AND LISTENING

WRITING PROCESS

ONLINE TEXT SETS

These selections can be found in the **Online Literature Library** in the Online Student Edition.

Unit 1

POEM
All Watched Over by Machines of Loving Grace
Richard Brautigan

SCIENCE ARTICLE
Careers in Robotics
NASA Robotic Education Project

SCIENCE ARTICLE
Team Builds "Sociable" Robot
Elizabeth A. Thompson

Unit 2

SPEECH EXEMPLAR TEXT
***from* State of the Union Address (1941)**
Franklin Delano Roosevelt

SHORT STORY
The Golden Kite, the Silver Wind
Ray Bradbury

BIOGRAPHY
***from* A Lincoln Preface**
Carl Sandburg

Unit 3

POEM
The Writer
Richard Wilbur

SHORT STORY EXEMPLAR TEXT
***from* I Stand Here Ironing**
Tillie Olson

PERSUASIVE ESSAY
Carry Your Own Skis
Lian Dolan

Unit 4

POEM
The Horses
Edwin Muir

REFLECTIVE ESSAY
A Celebration of Grandfathers
Rudolfo A. Anaya

REFLECTIVE ESSAY
Desiderata
Elizabeth McCracken

Unit 5

SPEECH
There Is a Longing
Chief Dan George

SHORT STORY
The Man to Send Rain Clouds
Leslie Marmon Silko

POEM
There Is No Word for Goodbye
Mary Tall Mountain

State Standards Overview

The Common Core State Standards will prepare you to succeed in college and your future career. They are separated into four sections—Reading (Literature and Informational Text), Writing, Speaking and Listening, and Language. Beginning each section, the College and Career Readiness Anchor Standards define what you need to achieve by the end of high school. The grade-specific standards that follow define what you need to know by the end of your current grade level.

Common Core Reading Standards

College and Career Readiness Anchor Standards for Reading

Key Ideas and Details

1. Read closely to determine what the text says explicitly and to make logical inferences from it; cite specific textual evidence when writing or speaking to support conclusions drawn from the text.
2. Determine central ideas or themes of a text and analyze their development; summarize the key supporting details and ideas.
3. Analyze how and why individuals, events, and ideas develop and interact over the course of a text.

Craft and Structure

4. Interpret words and phrases as they are used in a text, including determining technical, connotative, and figurative meanings, and analyze how specific word choices shape meaning or tone.
5. Analyze the structure of texts, including how specific sentences, paragraphs, and larger portions of the text (e.g., a section, chapter, scene, or stanza) relate to each other and the whole.
6. Assess how point of view or purpose shapes the content and style of a text.

Integration of Knowledge and Ideas

7. Integrate and evaluate content presented in diverse formats and media, including visually and quantitatively, as well as in words.
8. Delineate and evaluate the argument and specific claims in a text, including the validity of the reasoning as well as the relevance and sufficiency of the evidence.
9. Analyze how two or more texts address similar themes or topics in order to build knowledge or to compare the approaches the authors take.

Range of Reading and Level of Text Complexity

10. Read and comprehend complex literary and informational texts independently and proficiently.

State Standards Overview

mmon Core State Standards will prepare you to succeed in college and ture career. They are separated into four sections—Reading (Literature and ational Text), Writing, Speaking and Listening, and Language. Beginning each , the College and Career Readiness Anchor Standards define what you need eve by the end of high school. The grade-specific standards that follow define ou need to know by the end of your current grade level.

mon Core Reading Standards

ege and Career Readiness Anchor Standards for Reading
deas and Details
ead closely to determine what the text says explicitly and to make logical nferences from it; cite specific textual evidence when writing or speaking to upport conclusions drawn from the text.
etermine central ideas or themes of a text and analyze their development; ummarize the key supporting details and ideas.
nalyze how and why individuals, events, and ideas develop and interact over he course of a text.
and Structure
nterpret words and phrases as they are used in a text, including determining echnical, connotative, and figurative meanings, and analyze how specific vord choices shape meaning or tone.
nalyze the structure of texts, including how specific sentences, paragraphs, nd larger portions of the text (e.g., a section, chapter, scene, or stanza) relate o each other and the whole.
ssess how point of view or purpose shapes the content and style of a text.
ration of Knowledge and Ideas
ntegrate and evaluate content presented in diverse formats and media, ncluding visually and quantitatively, as well as in words.
elineate and evaluate the argument and specific claims in a text, including he validity of the reasoning as well as the relevance and sufficiency of the evidence.
nalyze how two or more texts address similar themes or topics in order to uild knowledge or to compare the approaches the authors take.
e of Reading and Level of Text Complexity
ead and comprehend complex literary and informational texts independently nd proficiently.

ONLINE LITERATURE LIBRARY

Highlighted selections are found in the **Online Literature Library** (OLL) in the Online Student Edition.

Features and Workshops

COMPARING TEXTS

Comparing Points of View

Comparing Themes

Comparing Poetic Forms

Comparing Archetypal Themes

Comparing Contemporary Interpretations

LANGUAGE STUDY

SPEAKING AND LISTENING

WRITING PROCESS

ONLINE TEXT SETS

These selections can be found in the **Online Literature Library** in the Online Student Edit

Grade 9 Reading Standards for Literature

Key Ideas and Details

1. Cite strong and thorough textual evidence to support analysis of what the text says explicitly as well as inferences drawn from the text.
2. Determine a theme or central idea of a text and analyze in detail its development over the course of the text, including how it emerges and is shaped and refined by specific details; provide an objective summary of the text.
3. Analyze how complex characters (e.g., those with multiple or conflicting motivations) develop over the course of a text, interact with other characters, and advance the plot or develop the theme.

Craft and Structure

4. Determine the meaning of words and phrases as they are used in the text, including figurative and connotative meanings; analyze the cumulative impact of specific word choices on meaning and tone (e.g., how the language evokes a sense of time and place; how it sets a formal or informal tone).
5. Analyze how an author's choices concerning how to structure a text, order events within it (e.g., parallel plots), and manipulate time (e.g., pacing, flashbacks) create such effects as mystery, tension, or surprise.
6. Analyze a particular point of view or cultural experience reflected in a work of literature from outside the United States, drawing on a wide reading of world literature.

Integration of Knowledge and Ideas

7. Analyze the representation of a subject or a key scene in two different artistic mediums, including what is emphasized or absent in each treatment (e.g., Auden's "Musée des Beaux Arts" and Breughel's *Landscape with the Fall of Icarus*).
8. (Not applicable to literature)
9. Analyze how an author draws on and transforms source material in a specific work (e.g., how Shakespeare treats a theme or topic from Ovid or the Bible or how a later author draws on a play by Shakespeare).

Range of Reading and Level of Text Complexity

10. By the end of grade 9, read and comprehend literature, including stories, dramas, and poems, in the grades 9–10 text complexity band proficiently, with scaffolding as needed at the high end of the range.

State Standards Overview

Grade 9 Reading Standards for Informational Text

Key Ideas and Details

1. Cite strong and thorough textual evidence to support analysis of what the text says explicitly as well as inferences drawn from the text.
2. Determine a central idea of a text and analyze its development over the course of the text, including how it emerges and is shaped and refined by specific details; provide an objective summary of the text.
3. Analyze how the author unfolds an analysis or series of ideas or events, including the order in which the points are made, how they are introduced and developed, and the connections that are drawn between them.

Craft and Structure

4. Determine the meaning of words and phrases as they are used in a text, including figurative, connotative, and technical meanings; analyze the cumulative impact of specific word choices on meaning and tone (e.g., how the language of a court opinion differs from that of a newspaper).
5. Analyze in detail how an author's ideas or claims are developed and refined by particular sentences, paragraphs, or larger portions of a text (e.g., a section or chapter).
6. Determine an author's point of view or purpose in a text and analyze how an author uses rhetoric to advance that point of view or purpose.

Integration of Knowledge and Ideas

7. Analyze various accounts of a subject told in different mediums (e.g., a person's life story in both print and multimedia), determining which details are emphasized in each account.
8. Delineate and evaluate the argument and specific claims in a text, assessing whether the reasoning is valid and the evidence is relevant and sufficient; identify false statements and fallacious reasoning.
9. Analyze seminal U.S. documents of historical and literary significance (e.g., Washington's Farewell Address, the Gettysburg Address, Roosevelt's Four Freedoms speech, King's "Letter from Birmingham Jail"), including how they address related themes and concepts.

Range of Reading and Level of Text Complexity

10. By the end of grade 9, read and comprehend literary nonfiction in the grades 9–10 text complexity band proficiently, with scaffolding as needed at the high end of the range.

Common Core Writing Standards

College and Career Readiness Anchor Standards for Writing
Text Types and Purpose **1.** Write arguments to support claims in an analysis of substantive topics or texts, using valid reasoning and relevant and sufficient evidence. **2.** Write informative/explanatory texts to examine and convey complex ideas and information clearly and accurately through the effective selection, organization, and analysis of content. **3.** Write narratives to develop real or imagined experiences or events using effective technique, well-chosen details, and well-structured event sequences.
Production and Distribution of Writing **4.** Produce clear and coherent writing in which the development, organization, and style are appropriate to task, purpose, and audience. **5.** Develop and strengthen writing as needed by planning, revising, editing, rewriting, or trying a new approach. **6.** Use technology, including the Internet, to produce and publish writing and to interact and collaborate with others.
Research to Build and Present Knowledge **7.** Conduct short as well as more sustained research projects based on focused questions, demonstrating understanding of the subject under investigation. **8.** Gather relevant information from multiple print and digital sources, assess the credibility and accuracy of each source, and integrate the information while avoiding plagiarism. **9.** Draw evidence from literary or informational texts to support analysis, reflection, and research.
Range of Writing **10.** Write routinely over extended time frames (time for research, reflection, and revision) and shorter time frames (a single sitting or a day or two) for a range of tasks, purposes, and audiences.

Grade 9 Writing Standards

Text Types and Purposes

1. Write arguments to support claims in an analysis of substantive topics or texts, using valid reasoning and relevant and sufficient evidence.

a. Introduce precise claim(s), distinguish the claim(s) from alternate or opposing claims, and create an organization that establishes clear relationships among claim(s), counterclaims, reasons, and evidence.

b. Develop claim(s) and counterclaims fairly, supplying evidence for each while pointing out the strengths and limitations of both in a manner that anticipates the audience's knowledge level and concerns.

c. Use words, phrases, and clauses to link the major sections of the text, create cohesion, and clarify the relationships between claim(s) and reasons, between reasons and evidence, and between claim(s) and counterclaims.

d. Establish and maintain a formal style and objective tone while attending to the norms and conventions of the discipline in which they are writing.

e. Provide a concluding statement or section that follows from and supports the argument presented.

2. Write informative/explanatory texts to examine and convey complex ideas, concepts, and information clearly and accurately through the effective selection, organization, and analysis of content.

a. Introduce a topic; organize complex ideas, concepts, and information to make important connections and distinctions; include formatting (e.g., headings), graphics (e.g., figures, tables), and multimedia when useful to aiding comprehension.

b. Develop the topic with well-chosen, relevant, and sufficient facts, extended definitions, concrete details, quotations, or other information and examples appropriate to the audience's knowledge of the topic.

c. Use appropriate and varied transitions to link the major sections of the text, create cohesion, and clarify the relationships among complex ideas and concepts.

d. Use precise language and domain-specific vocabulary to manage the complexity of the topic.

e. Establish and maintain a formal style and objective tone while attending to the norms and conventions of the discipline in which they are writing.

f. Provide a concluding statement or section that follows from and supports the information or explanation presented (e.g., articulating implications or the significance of the topic).

3. Write narratives to develop real or imagined experiences or events using effective technique, well-chosen details, and well-structured event sequences.

a. Engage and orient the reader by setting out a problem, situation, or observation, establishing one or multiple point(s) of view, and introducing a narrator and/or characters; create a smooth progression of experiences or events.

b. Use narrative techniques, such as dialogue, pacing, description, reflection, and multiple plot lines, to develop experiences, events, and/or characters.
c. Use a variety of techniques to sequence events so that they build on one another to create a coherent whole.
d. Use precise words and phrases, telling details, and sensory language to convey a vivid picture of the experiences, events, setting, and/or characters.
e. Provide a conclusion that follows from and reflects on what is experienced, observed, or resolved over the course of the narrative.

Production and Distribution of Writing

4. Produce clear and coherent writing in which the development, organization, and style are appropriate to task, purpose, and audience.

5. Develop and strengthen writing as needed by planning, revising, editing, rewriting, or trying a new approach, focusing on addressing what is most significant for a specific purpose and audience.

6. Use technology, including the Internet, to produce, publish, and update individual or shared writing products, taking advantage of technology's capacity to link to other information and to display information flexibly and dynamically.

Research to Build and Present Knowledge

7. Conduct short as well as more sustained research projects to answer a question (including a self-generated question) or solve a problem; narrow or broaden the inquiry when appropriate; synthesize multiple sources on the subject, demonstrating understanding of the subject under investigation.

8. Gather relevant information from multiple authoritative print and digital sources, using advanced searches effectively; assess the usefulness of each source in answering the research question; integrate information into the text selectively to maintain the flow of ideas, avoiding plagiarism and following a standard format for citation.

9. Draw evidence from literary or informational texts to support analysis, reflection, and research.

a. Apply *grades 9–10 Reading standards* to literature (e.g., "Analyze how an author draws on and transforms source material in a specific work [e.g., how Shakespeare treats a theme or topic from Ovid or the Bible or how a later author draws on a play by Shakespeare]").
b. Apply *grades 9–10 Reading standards* to literary nonfiction (e.g., "Delineate and evaluate the argument and specific claims in a text, assessing whether the reasoning is valid and the evidence is relevant and sufficient; identify false statements and fallacious reasoning").

Range of Writing

10. Write routinely over extended time frames (time for research, reflection, and revision) and shorter time frames (a single sitting or a day or two) for a range of tasks, purposes, and audiences.

Common Core Speaking and Listening Standards

College and Career Readiness Anchor Standards for Speaking and Listening
Comprehension and Collaboration **1.** Prepare for and participate effectively in a range of conversations and collaborations with diverse partners, building on others' ideas and expressing their own clearly and persuasively. **2.** Integrate and evaluate information presented in diverse media and formats, including visually, quantitatively, and orally. **3.** Evaluate a speaker's point of view, reasoning, and use of evidence and rhetoric.
Presentation of Knowledge and Ideas **4.** Present information, findings, and supporting evidence such that listeners can follow the line of reasoning and the organization, development, and style are appropriate to task, purpose, and audience. **5.** Make strategic use of digital media and visual displays of data to express information and enhance understanding of presentations. **6.** Adapt speech to a variety of contexts and communicative tasks, demonstrating command of formal English when indicated or appropriate.

Grade 9 Speaking and Listening Standards

Comprehension and Collaboration

1. Initiate and participate effectively in a range of collaborative discussions (one-on-one, in groups, and teacher-led) with diverse partners on *grades 9–10 topics, texts, and issues,* building on others' ideas and expressing their own clearly and persuasively.

a. Come to discussions prepared, having read and researched material under study; explicitly draw on that preparation by referring to evidence from texts and other research on the topic or issue to stimulate a thoughtful, well-reasoned exchange of ideas.

b. Work with peers to set rules for collegial discussions and decision-making (e.g., informal consensus, taking votes on key issues, presentation of alternate views), clear goals and deadlines, and individual roles as needed.

c. Propel conversations by posing and responding to questions that relate the current discussion to broader themes or larger ideas; actively incorporate others into the discussion; and clarify, verify, or challenge ideas and conclusions.

d. Respond thoughtfully to diverse perspectives, summarize points of agreement and disagreement, and, when warranted, qualify or justify their own views and understanding and make new connections in light of the evidence and reasoning presented.

2. Integrate multiple sources of information presented in diverse media or formats (e.g., visually, quantitatively, orally) evaluating the credibility and accuracy of each source.

3. Evaluate a speaker's point of view, reasoning, and use of evidence and rhetoric, identifying any fallacious reasoning or exaggerated or distorted evidence.

Presentation of Knowledge and Ideas

4. Present information, findings, and supporting evidence clearly, concisely, and logically such that listeners can follow the line of reasoning and the organization, development, substance, and style are appropriate to purpose, audience, and task.

5. Make strategic use of digital media (e.g., textual, graphical, audio, visual, and interactive elements) in presentations to enhance understanding of findings, reasoning, and evidence and to add interest.

6. Adapt speech to a variety of contexts and tasks, demonstrating command of formal English when indicated or appropriate. (See grades 9–10 Language standards 1 and 3 for specific expectations.)

State Standards Overview

Common Core Language Standards

College and Career Readiness Anchor Standards for Reading

Conventions of Standard English

1. Demonstrate command of the conventions of standard English grammar and usage when writing or speaking.
2. Demonstrate command of the conventions of standard English capitalization, punctuation, and spelling when writing.

Knowledge of Language

3. Apply knowledge of language to understand how language functions in different contexts, to make effective choices for meaning or style, and to comprehend more fully when reading or listening.

Vocabulary Acquisition and Use

4. Determine or clarify the meaning of unknown and multiple-meaning words and phrases by using context clues, analyzing meaningful word parts, and consulting general and specialized reference materials, as appropriate.
5. Demonstrate understanding of figurative language, word relationships, and nuances in word meanings.
6. Acquire and use accurately a range of general academic and domain-specific words and phrases sufficient for reading, writing, speaking, and listening at the college and career readiness level; demonstrate independence in gathering vocabulary knowledge when considering a word or phrase important to comprehension or expression.

Grade 9 Language Standards

Conventions of Standard English

1. Demonstrate command of the conventions of standard English grammar and usage when writing or speaking.
   a. Use parallel structure.
   b. Use various types of phrases (noun, verb, adjectival, adverbial, participial, prepositional, absolute) and clauses (independent, dependent; noun, relative, adverbial) to convey specific meanings and add variety and interest to writing or presentations.

2. Demonstrate command of the conventions of standard English capitalization, punctuation, and spelling when writing.
   a. Use a semicolon (and perhaps a conjunctive adverb) to link two or more closely related independent clauses.
   b. Use a colon to introduce a list or quotation.
   c. Spell correctly.

Knowledge of Language

3. Apply knowledge of language to understand how language functions in different contexts, to make effective choices for meaning or style, and to comprehend more fully when reading or listening.
   a. Write and edit work so that it conforms to the guidelines in a style manual (e.g., *MLA Handbook,* Turabian's *Manual for Writers*) appropriate for the discipline and writing type.

Vocabulary Acquisition and Use

4. Determine or clarify the meaning of unknown and multiple-meaning words and phrases based on *grades 9–10 reading and content,* choosing flexibly from a range of strategies.
   a. Use context (e.g., the overall meaning of a sentence, paragraph, or text; a word's position or function in a sentence) as a clue to the meaning of a word or phrase.
   b. Identify and correctly use patterns of word changes that indicate different meanings or parts of speech (e.g., *analyze, analysis, analytical; advocate, advocacy*).
   c. Consult general and specialized reference materials (e.g., dictionaries, glossaries, thesauruses), both print and digital, to find the pronunciation of a word or determine or clarify its precise meaning, its part of speech, or its etymology.
   d. Verify the preliminary determination of the meaning of a word or phrase (e.g., by checking the inferred meaning in context or in a dictionary).

5. Demonstrate understanding of figurative language, word relationships, and nuances in word meanings.
   a. Interpret figures of speech (e.g., euphemism, oxymoron) in context and analyze their role in the text.
   b. Analyze nuances in the meaning of words with similar denotations.

6. Acquire and use accurately general academic and domain-specific words and phrases, sufficient for reading, writing, speaking, and listening at the college and career readiness level; demonstrate independence in gathering vocabulary knowledge when considering a word or phrase important to comprehension or expression.

COMMON CORE WORKSHOPS

- BUILDING ACADEMIC VOCABULARY
- WRITING AN OBJECTIVE SUMMARY
- COMPREHENDING COMPLEX TEXTS
- ANALYZING ARGUMENTS
- CONDUCTING RESEARCH

Common Core State Standards

Reading Literature 2, 10
Reading Informational Text 2, 6, 8, 9, 10
Writing 1.a, 1.b, 1.e, 2, 2.a, 2.b, 2.d, 2.e, 5, 6, 7, 8, 9
Language 1, 2, 2.c, 3, 3.a, 6

Common Core Workshop

INTRODUCTORY UNIT

BUILDING ACADEMIC VOCABULARY

Academic vocabulary is the language you encounter in textbooks and on standardized tests and other assessments. Understanding these words and using them in your classroom discussions and writing will help you communicate your ideas clearly and effectively.

There are two basic types of academic vocabulary: general and domain-specific. **General academic vocabulary** includes words that are not specific to any single course of study. For example, the general academic vocabulary word *analyze* is used in language arts, math, social studies, art, and so on. **Domain-specific academic vocabulary** includes words that are usually encountered in the study of a specific discipline. For example, the words *factor* and *remainder* are most often used in mathematics classrooms and texts.

Common Core State Standards

Language

6. Acquire and use accurately general academic and domain-specific words and phrases, sufficient for reading, writing, speaking, and listening at the college and career readiness level; demonstrate independence in gathering vocabulary knowledge when considering a word or phrase important to comprehension or expression.

General Academic Vocabulary

Word	Definition	Related Words	Word in Context
ambiguous (am BIHG yoo uhs) *adj.*	having more than one meaning; unclear	ambiguity ambiguously	The story's uncertain ending was **ambiguous.**
appreciate (uh PREE shee ayt) *v.*	be aware of the value of	appreciative appreciating	Once I read Frost's poem, I learned to **appreciate** his use of symbols.
argument (AHR gyuh muhnt) *n.*	persuasive message	argue argumentation argumentative	The **argument** in the essay is well supported.
articulate (ahr TIHK yuh layt) *v.*	express an idea clearly	articulating articulated	The writer was able to **articulate** his ideas clearly.
articulate (ahr TIHK yuh liht) *adj.*	able to express clearly	articulately inarticulate	It is important to be **articulate** when giving a speech.
assumption (uh SUHMP shuhn) *n.*	something taken for granted	assume assuming	My **assumption** that the character was telling the truth proved wrong.
character (KAR ihk tuhr) *n.*	qualities that make a person unique	characteristic characteristically	Jenny's **character** became clear through her actions and words.
circumstance (SUR kuhm stans) *n.*	situation; event	circumstantial	In that **circumstance,** I would have done the same thing as that character.

Ordinary Language: I **like** poems with strong rhymes and rhythms.

Academic Language: I **appreciate** poems with strong rhymes and rhythms.

Word	Definition	Related Words	Word in Context
clarify (KLAR uh fy) *v.*	make something more clear or understandable	clarification	More details were needed to **clarify** the writer's ideas about pollution.
compete (kuhm PEET) *v.*	battle against; try to win	competition competitor	The two characters **compete** in a battle of wits.
competition (kom puh TIHSH uhn) *n.*	rivalry; act of competing	compete competitor	There seemed to be a **competition** between the mother and daughter.
comprehend (kom prih HEHND) *v.*	understand	comprehensible comprehension	It was easy to **comprehend** the character's motives.
comprehension (kom prih HEHN shuhn) *n.*	act of understanding something	comprehend comprehensible	My **comprehension** of the poem was hampered by the use of archaic language.
concept (KON sehpt) *n.*	idea; notion	conceive conceptualize	The **concept** of freedom is explored in this essay.
context (KON tehkst) *n.*	surrounding text; situation	contextual	In this **context,** the word *democracy* takes on new meaning.
controversy (KON truh vuhr see) *n.*	discussion of a question in which opposing opinions clash	controversial controversially noncontroversial	The essayist explores the **controversy** that brewed in the heartland.
convince (kuhn VIHNS) *v.*	persuade by argument or evidence	convincing convincingly	The writer tries to **convince** her audience to change their ways.
credible (KREHD uh buhl) *adj.*	believable	credibility incredible	I found the story's plot to be **credible.**
defend (dih FEHND) *v.*	protect against attack	defense defensive	The writer tries to **defend** his notions about fairness.
determine (dih TUR muhn) *v.*	cause something to happen in a certain way	determined determination	The character's actions **determine** his fate.
differentiate (dihf uh REHN shee ayt) *v.*	see or express what makes two or more things different from each other	differ different	In this essay, the writer **differentiates** between students and scholars.

Word	Definition	Related Words	Word in Context
discriminate (dihs KRIHM uh nayt) *v.*	see the differences between things; act against someone because of prejudice	discrimination discriminatory	The character was unable to **discriminate** loyal friends from disloyal ones.
discuss (dihs KUHS) *v.*	talk about; write about	discussion	**Discuss** your ideas in your response.
identify (Y DEHN tuh fy) *v.*	say who someone or something is	identifiable identification	I will **identify** three key factors in the story's success.
illuminate (ih LOO muh nayt) *v.*	light up; make something clearer	illumination	Here is my attempt to **illuminate** my ideas.
imitate (IHM uh tayt) *v.*	copy the actions of another	imitation imitator imitative	The poet uses onomatopoeia to **imitate** the sounds of a rooster.
informed (ihn FAWRMD) *v.*	gave someone information	inform information informative	The character **informed** his teacher that he had finished his test.
interpret (ihn TUR priht) *v.*	understand or explain the meaning of something	interpreter interpretation interpretive	How do you **interpret** the title of this poem?
interpretation (ihn tur pruh TAY shuhn) *n.*	explanation of the meaning of something	intepret interpreter interpretive	My **interpretation** of the theme differs from that of my friend.
involvement (ihn VOLV muhnt) *n.*	state of being included in something	involve	The character's **involvement** in sports propels the plot.
perspective (puhr SPEHK tihv) *n.*	point of view		The story is told from the **perspective** of a three-year-old.
speculate (SPEHK yuh layt) *v.*	think about or make up theories about a subject; guess at	speculation speculative	**Speculate** about the author's reasons for setting this story in the tundra.
standard (STAN duhrd) *n.*	idea or thing to which other things are compared	nonstandard standardize	Shakespeare sets the **standard** by which many playwrights are judged.
standard (STAN duhrd) *adj.*	normal; average	standardize substandard	It is **standard** practice for stories to center on conflict.
unique (yoo NEEK) *adj.*	one of a kind	uniquely uniqueness	The poet has a **unique** style.
verify (VEHR uh fy) *v.*	make sure something is true; confirm	verification unverified	You should **verify** the facts before you accept them.

Ordinary Language: In this essay, I will **talk about** the story's theme.

Academic Language: In this essay, I will **discuss** the story's theme.

Practice

Examples of various kinds of domain-specific academic vocabulary appear in the charts below. On a separate piece of paper, create your own domain-specific academic vocabulary charts for each domain in which you enter new academic vocabulary words as you learn them.

Social Studies: Domain-Specific Academic Vocabulary

Word	Definition	Related Words	Word in Context
entrepreneurship (ahn truh pruh NOOR shihp) *n.*	willingness to assume the risk and responsibility of starting a business	entrepreneur entrepreneurial	The scholarship rewards **entrepreneurship.**
sovereignty (SOV ruhn tee) *n.*	independence and self-government	sovereign	The country fought for its **sovereignty**.
capitalism (KAP uht l ihz uhm) *n.*	economic system based on private investment and ownership	capital capitalist	With **capitalism,** private individuals or corporations control the wealth.
populist (POP yuh lihst) *adj.*	favoring common people over the wealthy and elite	populism	The politician tried to sway **populist** groups.
impeach (ihm PEECH) *v.*	accuse a public official of misconduct in office	impeached impeachment	The people will **impeach** a corrupt official.

Create a chart for these social studies academic vocabulary words: *enterprise, landmass, ecosystem, market,* and *opportunity.*

Mathematics: Domain-Specific Academic Vocabulary

Word	Definition	Related Words	Word in Context
theorem (THEE uh ruhm) *n.*	assertion that can be proved true using the rules of logic		The scientist worked hard to prove her **theorem.**
permutation (puhr myoo TAY shuhn) *n.*	ordered arrangement of a set of objects	permute permuting	The teacher formed a **permutation** by rearranging the letters.
congruent (KON groo uhnt) *adj.*	exactly equal in size and shape	congruity congruous	The triangles are **congruent.**
logarithm (LAWG uh rihth uhm) *n.*	power to which a constant must be raised to equal a specified number	logarithmic	The teacher said that 2 is the **logarithm** of 100 to the base 10.
inverse (ihn VURS) *adj.*	containing terms of which an increase in one causes a decrease in another	inversion invert	The **inverse** functions mirrored each other.

Create a chart for these mathematics academic vocabulary words: *graph, slope, triangle, quadrilateral,* and *diagram.*

Science: Domain-Specific Academic Vocabulary

Word	Definition	Related Words	Word in Context
meiosis (my OH sihs) *n.*	process of cell division that halves the number of chromosomes	meiotic	The biology video included a section about **meiosis.**
ion (Y uhn) *n.*	atom or a group of atoms that has an electric charge	ionic ionize	An **ion** can carry a positive or negative charge.
catalyst (KAT uh lihst) *n.*	substance that starts or speeds up a chemical reaction	catalytic	The chemical served as a **catalyst** in the experiment.
power (POW uhr) *n.*	rate at which work is done, or energy expended, per unit of time	powered powerful	The work done per second is called the **power.**
work (wurk) *n.*	product of the force applied to a body and the resulting distance the body moves	worked working	How much **work** needs to be done to pick up the box?

Create a chart for these science academic vocabulary words: *glacier, tsunami, atomic, tectonic,* and *fracture.*

Art: Domain-Specific Academic Vocabulary

Word	Definition	Related Words	Word in Context
abstract (ab STRAKT) *adj.*	not depicting recognizable scenes or objects	abstraction abstractly	The artist was known for his **abstract** paintings.
tone (tohn) *n.*	slight modification of a given color	tonal tonality	He chose a **tone** that matched the color of the leaves.
monochrome (MON uh krohm) *adj.*	in the shades of a single color	monochromatic	The painter uses a **monochrome** palette of blue.
complementary (kom pluh MEHN tuh ree) *adj.*	perceived as enhancing each other or another	complement complementariness	The colors in the painting are **complementary.**
proportion (pruh PAWR shuhn) *n.*	relation between parts	proportional proportioned	The figures are drawn in correct **proportion.**

Create a chart for these art academic vocabulary words: *outline, still life, sketch, contrast,* and *repetition.*

Technology: Domain-Specific Academic Vocabulary

Word	Definition	Related Words	Word in Context
byte (byt) *n.*	unit of computer information consisting of eight bits	megabyte gigabyte	The storage device can hold many **bytes.**
processor (PROS ehs uhr) *n.*	electronic device that responds to instructions that drive a computer	process processing	The computer **processor** quickly performs calculations.
pixel (PIHK suhl) *n.*	any of a number of very small picture elements that make up a picture	pixelated	I could see a single **pixel** in the magnified picture.
application (ap lih KAY shuhn) *n.*	software designed to help a user perform specific tasks	apply	The computer **application** will track the information.
streaming (STREE mihng) *n.*	technique for transferring data as a continuous stream	stream	The presenter was live **streaming** a video.

Create a chart for these technology academic vocabulary words: *graphic, format, copyright, scanner,* and *browser.*

Increasing Your Word Knowledge

Increase your word knowledge and chances of success by taking an active role in developing your vocabulary. To own a word, follow these steps:

Steps to Follow	Model
1. Learn to identify the word and its basic meaning.	The word *examine* means "to look at closely."
2. Take note of the word's spelling.	*Examine* begins and ends with an *e*.
3. Practice pronouncing the word so that you can use it in conversation.	The e on the end of the word is silent. Its second syllable gets the most stress.
4. Visualize the word and illustrate its key meaning.	"When I think of the word *examine*, I visualize a doctor checking a patient's health."
5. Learn the various forms of the word and its related words.	*Examination* and *exam* are forms of the word *examine*.
6. Compare the word with similar words.	*Examine*, *peruse*, and *study* are synonyms.
7. Contrast the word with similar words.	*Examine* suggests a more detailed study than *read* or *look at*.
8. Use the word in various contexts.	"I'd like to *examine* the footprints more closely." "I will *examine* the use of imagery in this poem."

Building Your Speaking Vocabulary

Language gives us the ability to express ourselves. The more words you know, the easier it will be to get your points across. There are two main aspects of language: reading and speaking. Using the steps above will help you to acquire a rich vocabulary. Follow these steps to help you learn to use this rich vocabulary in discussions, speeches, and conversations:

Steps to Follow	Tip
1. Practice pronouncing the word.	Become familiar with pronunciation guides that allow you to sound out unfamiliar words. Listening to audio books as you read the text will help you learn pronunciations of words.
2. Learn word forms.	Dictionaries often list forms of words following the main word entry. Practice saying word families aloud: "generate," "generated," "generation," "regenerate," "generator."
3. Translate your thoughts.	Restate your own thoughts and ideas in a variety of ways—to inject formality or to change your tone, for example.
4. Hold discussions.	With a classmate, practice using academic vocabulary words in discussions about the text. Choose one term to practice at a time, and see how many statements you can create using that term.
5. Record yourself.	Analyze your word choices by listening to yourself objectively. Note places your word choice could be strengthened or changed.

WRITING AN OBJECTIVE SUMMARY

The ability to write objective summaries is key to success in college and in many careers. Writing an effective objective summary involves recording the key ideas of a text while demonstrating your understanding.

What Is an Objective Summary?

An effective objective summary is a concise, complete, and accurate overview of a text. Following are key elements of an objective summary:

- A good summary focuses on the main theme or central idea of a text and specific, relevant details that support that theme or central idea, leaving out unnecessary supporting details.
- Effective summaries are brief, although the writer must take care not to misrepresent the text by leaving out key elements.
- A summary should accurately capture the essence of the longer text it is describing.
- Finally, the writer must take care to remain objective, or to refrain from inserting his or her own opinions, reactions, or personal connections into the summary.

What to Avoid in an Objective Summary

- Avoid simply copying a collection of sentences or paragraphs from the original source.
- An objective summary should also not be a long recounting of every event, detail, or point in the original text.
- Finally, a good summary does not include evaluative comments, such as the reader's overall opinion of or reaction to the piece. An objective summary is not the reader's interpretation or critical analysis of the work.

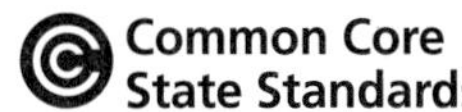

Literature

2. Determine a theme or central idea of a text and analyze in detail its development over the course of the text, including how it emerges and is shaped and refined by specific details; provide an objective summary of the text.

INFORMATIONAL TEXT

Model Objective Summary

Note the elements of an effective objective summary, called out in the yellow sidenotes. Then, write an objective summary of a text you have recently read. Review your summary, and delete any unnecessary details, opinions, or evaluations.

Summary of "Thank You, M'am"

"Thank You, M'am" by Langston Hughes is a~~n amusing~~ story of a young boy who tries to steal a large purse from Mrs. Luella Bates Washington Jones, but he gets more than he expected.

A one-sentence synopsis highlighting the theme or central idea of the story can be an effective start to a summary.

The adjective *amusing* marks an opinion and should not be included in an objective summary.

The story begins with a description of a large woman with a heavy purse walking alone at night. A boy tries to snatch her purse, but the weight of the purse causes him to fall on the ground. The woman kicks the boy and then grabs his shirt, picking him up off the ground.

Relating the development of the text in chronological order makes a summary easy to follow.

Then, the woman asks the boy if he will run if she lets go. He says yes, so she doesn't let go. The boy tells her he is sorry, and the woman responds by stating that his face is dirty. She begins to drag him down the street, declaring that his face will be washed this evening. ~~The boy looks to be fourteen years old.~~

Unnecessary details should be eliminated.

The boy tells the woman that he just wants to be let go, and the woman responds that he put himself in contact with her, and that contact is going to last awhile. She tells him that he will remember Mrs. Luella Bates Washington Jones.

The boy begins to struggle, but Mrs. Jones pins his arm up and drags him to her room. She asks the boy his name, and he tells her: Roger. She lets go of Roger and commands him to go wash his face. Even though the door is open, he goes to the sink.

Not using the names of the woman and the boy until this point maintains the essence of the story.

Mrs. Jones then asks if Roger tried to steal her purse because he was hungry. He explains that he wanted a pair of blue suede shoes. Mrs. Jones tells him he didn't have to snatch her purse for shoes, but that he could have asked her.

After a long pause, during which Roger once again thinks of running away, Mrs. Jones reveals that she once wanted things she could not get, and she had done things she would not talk about. Mrs. Jones leaves Roger alone with her purse as she goes behind a screen to prepare food. Roger wants her to trust him, so he moves to where she can see him.

After dinner, she gives him ten dollars to buy blue suede shoes and tells him not to steal anymore.

A key phrase at the end of the story is included in the summary.

Mrs. Jones then walks him to the door and wishes him good night. Roger is unable to say anything, even "Thank you, M'am," before Mrs. Jones shuts the door. ~~Mrs. Jones was right: the unexpected kindness she showed him means Roger will never forget Mrs. Luella Bates Washington Jones.~~

The writer's interpretations should not appear in an objective summary.

COMPREHENDING COMPLEX TEXTS

Over the course of your academic years, you will be required to read increasingly complex texts as preparation for college and the workplace. A complex text can be loosely described as a text that contains challenging vocabulary; long, complex sentences; figurative language; multiple levels of meaning; or unfamiliar settings and situations.

The selections in this textbook provide you with a range of readings, from short stories to autobiographies, poetry, drama, myths, and even science and social studies texts. Some of these will fall within your comfort zone; others will most likely be more challenging.

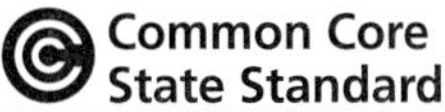

Literature

10. By the end of grade 9, read and comprehend literature, including stories, dramas, and poems, in the grades 9–10 text complexity band proficiently, with scaffolding as needed at the high end of the range.

Informational Text

10. By the end of grade 9, read and comprehend literary nonfiction in the grades 9–10 text complexity band proficiently, with scaffolding as needed at the high end of the range.

Strategy 1: **Multidraft Reading**

Good readers develop the habit of revisiting texts in order to comprehend them completely. Just as a musician returns over and over again to a song in order to master it, good readers return to texts to more fully enjoy and comprehend them. To fully understand a text, try this multidraft reading strategy:

First Reading

The first time you read a text, read to gain the basic meaning. If you are reading a narrative text, look for some of the story's basics: who did what to whom. If the text is nonfiction, look for the main ideas. If you are reading poetry, read first to get a sense of who the speaker is. Also take note of the setting and situation.

Second Reading

During your second reading of a text, focus on the artistry or effectiveness of the writing. Look for text structures, and think about why the author chose those organizational patterns. Then, examine the author's creative uses of language and the effects of that language. For example, has the author used rhyme, figurative language, or words with negative connotations?

Third Reading

After your third reading, compare and contrast the text with others of its kind you have read. For example, if you read a poem in sonnet form, think of other sonnets you have read, and think of ways the poems are alike or different. Evaluate the text's overall effectiveness and its central idea or theme.

Independent Practice

As you read this poem, practice the multidraft reading strategy by completing a chart like the one below.

"Memory" by Margaret Walker

I can remember wind-swept streets of cities
on cold and blustery nights, on rainy days;
heads under shabby felts and parasols
and shoulders hunched against a sharp concern;
seeing hurt bewilderment on poor faces,
smelling a deep and sinister unrest
these brooding people cautiously caress;
hearing ghostly marching on pavement stones
and closing fast around their squares of hate.
I can remember seeing them alone,
at work, and in their tenements at home.
I can remember hearing all they said:
their muttering protests, their whispered oaths,
and all that spells their living in distress.

Multidraft Reading Chart

	My Understanding
First Reading Look for key ideas and details that unlock the basic meaning.	
Second Reading Read for deeper meanings. Look for ways in which the author used text structures and language to create effects.	
Third Reading Read to integrate your knowledge and ideas. Connect the text to others of its kind and to your own experience.	

Strategy 2: **Close Read the Text**

Complex texts require close reading: a careful analysis of the words, phrases, and sentences. When you close read, use the following tips to comprehend the text:

Tips for Close Reading
1. **Break down long sentences** into parts. Look for the subject of the sentence and its verb. Then, identify which parts of the sentence modify, or give more information about, its subject.
2. **Reread passages** to confirm that you understand their meaning.
3. **Look for context clues,** such as **a.** restatement of an idea. For example, in this sentence, "utter defeat" restates the noun *rout.* The rugby team celebrated its **rout,** its utter defeat, of its arch rival. **b.** definition of sophisticated words. In this sentence, the underlined information defines the word *fealty.* **Fealty** is a pledge of support and allegiance between one person and another. **c.** examples of concepts and topics. In the following passage, the underlined text provides examples of the adjective *serendipitous.* Discovering a treasure when cleaning out an attic or bumping into an old friend when taking shelter from a rain storm—these **serendipitous** events never fail to bring a smile to one's face. **d.** contrasts of ideas and topics. **Altruism,** unlike selfishness, is a rare quality.
4. **Identify pronoun antecedents.** If long sentences contain pronouns, reread the text to make sure you know to whom or to what the pronouns refer.
5. **Look for conjunctions,** such as *and, or,* and *yet,* to understand relationships between ideas.
6. **Paraphrase,** or restate in your own words, passages of difficult text in order to check your understanding. Remember that a paraphrase is a restatement of an original text; it is not a summary.

INFORMATIONAL TEXT

Close Reading Model

As you read this document, take note of the sidenotes that model ways to unlock meaning in the text.

from *The Federalist* No. 2 by John Jay

To the People of the State of New York:

WHEN the people of America reflect that they are now called upon to decide a question, which, in its consequences, must prove one of the most important that ever engaged their attention, the propriety of their taking a very comprehensive, as well as a very serious, view of it, will be evident.

Break down this long sentence into parts. The text highlighted in yellow conveys the basic meaning of the sentence. The text highlighted in blue provides additional information.

Nothing is more certain than the indispensable necessity of government, and it is equally undeniable, that whenever and however it is instituted, the people must cede to it some of their natural rights in order to vest it with requisite powers. It is well worthy of consideration therefore, whether it would conduce more to the interest of the people of America that they should, to all general purposes, be one nation, under one federal government, or that they should divide themselves into separate confederacies, and give to the head of each the same kind of powers which they are advised to place in one national government.

Look for antecedents. In this sentence, the noun *government* is replaced by the pronoun *it*.

The conjunction *or* indicates that two options are being presented.

It has until lately been a received and uncontradicted opinion that the prosperity of the people of America depended on their continuing firmly united, and the wishes, prayers, and efforts of our best and wisest citizens have been constantly directed to that object. But politicians now appear, who insist that this opinion is erroneous, and that instead of looking for safety and happiness in union, we ought to seek it in a division of the States into distinct confederacies or sovereignties. However extraordinary this new doctrine may appear, it nevertheless has its advocates; and certain characters who were much opposed to it formerly, are at present of the number. Whatever may be the arguments or inducements which have wrought this change in the sentiments and declarations of these gentlemen, it certainly would not be wise in the people at large to adopt these new political tenets without being fully convinced that they are founded in truth and sound policy.

Search for context clues. The words in blue are context clues that help you figure out the meanings of the words in yellow.

Strategy 3: **Ask Questions**

Be an attentive reader by asking questions as you read. Throughout this textbook, we have provided questions for you following each selection. These questions are sorted into three basic categories that build in sophistication and lead you to a deeper understanding of the texts you read.

Here is an example from this book:

Some questions are about **Key Ideas and Details** in the text. To answer these questions, you will need to locate and cite explicit information in the text or draw inferences from what you have read.

Some questions are about **Craft and Structure** in the text. To answer these questions, you will need to analyze how the author developed and structured the text. You will also look for ways in which the author artfully used language and how those word choices affected the meaning and tone of the work.

The Jade Peony **Close Reading Activities**

Read

Comprehension: **Key Idea and Details**

1. **(a)** Citing details from the story, explain who gave the grandmother her first wind chime. **(b) Analyze Cause and Effect:** Using this information, explain why the making of wind chimes is so important to the grandmother in her later years.
2. **(a)** What is the main conflict between the grandmother and her family? **(b) Interpret:** How is this conflict resolved?
3. **(a) Compare and Contrast:** How do Sek-Lung's reactions to his grandmother's activities differ from those of other family members? **(b) Analyze:** How do you account for these differences? Cite details from the story to support your ideas.
4. **Summarize:** Write a brief, objective summary of the story. Describe the important characters, events, and details but do not state your opinion.

Text Analysis: **Craft and Structure**

5. **(a)** Who is the narrator of this story? **(b) Analyze:** How does the narrator's point of view shape what you, the reader, learn about the characters and events? Explain, citing specific passages from the story.
6. **(a) Describe:** How does the narrator describe the grandmother's physical appearance? Cite specific details. **(b) Interpret:** How does the physical description of the grandmother contribute to your understanding of her character?
7. **(a) Describe:** How does the narrator describe aspects of the setting, such as the grandmother's bedroom? Cite specific details. **(b) Interpret:** In what ways do details in the setting help to develop the characters?
8. **(a)** At what points in the story does the author introduce flashbacks? **(b) Distinguish:** Identify the mechanism—such as a memory or a dream—the author uses to introduce each flashback. **(c) Analyze:** What information does each flashback provide?

Connections: **Integration of Knowledge and Ideas**

Discuss

Conduct a **small-group discussion** about the use of symbols in this story. For example, consider the symbolic meanings of the jade peony or the white cat.

Research

Wayson Choy was influenced by the traditional Chinese tales he heard as a boy. Briefly research the types of stories Choy probably heard as he grew up. In particular, consider the following story elements:

Write

A good story will often express more than one theme. For example, one theme of "The Jade Peony" relates to mortality while another addresses the power of love. Write an **essay** in which you identify a key theme expressed in this story and explain how that theme is developed throughout the text. Cite details from the story to support your analysis.

Some questions are about the **Integration of Knowledge and Ideas**. These questions ask you to evaluate a text in many different ways, such as comparing texts, analyzing arguments in the text, and using many other methods to think critically about a text's ideas.

Preparing to Read Complex Texts

Attentive Reading As you read literature on your own, bring your imagination and questions to the text. The questions shown below and others that you ask as you read will help you learn and enjoy literature even more.

Common Core State Standards

Reading Literature/ Informational Text
10. By the end of grade 9, read and comprehend literature, including stories, dramas, poems, and literary nonfiction in the grades 9–10 text complexity band proficiently, with scaffolding as needed at the high end of the range.

When reading narratives, ask yourself...

Comprehension: **Key Ideas and Details**

- Who is the story's main character? Who are the other characters and how do they relate to the main character?
- What problems do the characters face? How do they react to these problems?
- Which characters do I like or admire? Which do I dislike? How do my reactions to the characters make me feel about the work as a whole?
- Is the setting of the story—the place, time, and society—believable and interesting? Why or why not?
- What happens in the story? Why do these events happen?

Text Analysis: **Craft and Structure**

- Who is the narrator? Is this voice part of the story or is it an outside observer?
- Do I find the narrator's voice interesting and engaging? Why or why not?
- Is there anything ... structured?

As you read independently, ask similar types of questions to ensure that you fully enjoy and comprehend texts you read for school and for pleasure. We have provided sets of questions for you on the Independent Reading pages at the end of each unit.

INFORMATIONAL TEXT

Model

Following is an example of a complex text. The sidenotes show sample questions that an attentive reader might ask while reading.

from "Farewell Address" by General Douglas MacArthur

. . . I have just left your fighting sons in Korea. . . . It was my constant effort to preserve them and end this savage conflict honorably and with the least loss of time and a minimum sacrifice of life. . . . Those gallant men will remain often in my thoughts and in my prayers always.

I am closing my fifty-two years of military service. . . . The world has turned over many times since I took the oath on the plain at West Point . . . But I still remember the refrain of one of the most popular barracks ballads of that day which proclaimed most proudly that old soldiers never die; they just fade away. And like the old soldier of that ballad, I now close my military career and just fade away—an old soldier who tried to do his duty as God gave him the light to see that duty. Good-bye.

Sample questions:

Integration of Knowledge and Ideas

What do I know about the Korean War? What can I learn from the general's comments?

Key Ideas and Details

What ideas are introduced in the first paragraph? How is the second paragraph different in topic? How are the two paragraphs related?

Craft and Structure

How is the last paragraph a good conclusion? How does the general feel about the Korean War? How does he feel about his career?

INFORMATIONAL TEXT

Independent Practice

Write three to five questions you might ask yourself as you read this passage from a speech delivered by President Andrew Johnson shortly after the death of President Abraham Lincoln.

from "State of the Union Address" by President Andrew Johnson

. . . To express gratitude to God in the name of the people for the preservation of the United States is my first duty in addressing you. Our thoughts next revert to the death of the late President by an act of parricidal treason. The grief of the nation is still fresh. It finds some solace in the consideration that he lived to enjoy the highest proof of its confidence by entering on the renewed term of the Chief Magistracy to which he had been elected; that he brought the civil war substantially to a close; that his loss was deplored in all parts of the Union, and that foreign nations have rendered justice to his memory. His removal cast upon me a heavier weight of cares than ever devolved upon any one of his predecessors. To fulfill my trust I need the support and confidence of all who are associated with me in the various departments of Government and the support and confidence of the people.

ANALYZING ARGUMENTS

The ability to evaluate an argument, as well as to make one, is an important skill for success in college and in the workplace.

What Is an Argument?

When you think of the word *argument,* you might think of a disagreement between two people, but an argument is more than that. An argument is a logical way of presenting a belief, conclusion, or stance. A good argument is supported with logical reasoning and relevant evidence.

Purposes of an Argument

There are three main purposes for writing a formal argument:

- to change the reader's mind
- to convince the reader to accept what is written
- to motivate the reader to take action based on what is written

Elements of Argument
Claim (assertion)—what the writer is trying to prove or the call to action *Example: Harold would make a good student council president.*
Grounds (evidence)—the support used to convince the reader *Example: He participates in several extracurricular activities, volunteers locally, and earns good grades.*
Justification—the link between the grounds and the claim; why the grounds are credible *Example: School and community involvement suggest he knows his school and town well; good grades indicate intelligence.*

Addressing the Opposition

While it might be tempting to ignore the opposing side of an issue or viewpoints with which you disagree, it is important to present a balanced argument. You can make your position more credible and your argument stronger by refuting the opposition's claim or by demonstrating that you understand it—perhaps even accept some aspects of it. When calling your reader to action, it is important to address barriers to that action or to point out ways in which the reader may have already moved in that direction.

Common Core State Standards

Informational Text

6. Determine an author's point of view or purpose in a text and analyze how an author uses rhetoric to advance that point of view or purpose.

8. Delineate and evaluate the argument and specific claims in a text, assessing whether the reasoning is valid and the evidence is relevant and sufficient; identify false statements and fallacious reasoning.

9. Analyze seminal U.S. documents of historical and literary significance (e.g., Washington's Farewell Address, the Gettysburg Address, Roosevelt's Four Freedoms speech, King's "Letter from Birmingham Jail"), including how they address related themes and concepts.

Language

6. Acquire and use accurately general academic and domain-specific words and phrases; gather vocabulary knowledge when considering a word or phrase important to comprehension or expression.

INFORMATIONAL TEXT

Model Argument

The excerpted speech includes the common elements of arguments.

from "Remarks on East-West Relations at the Brandenburg Gate in West Berlin," June 12, 1987 by President Ronald Reagan

. . . Behind me stands a wall that encircles the free sectors of this city, part of a vast system of barriers that divides the entire continent of Europe. From the Baltic, south, those barriers cut across Germany in a gash of barbed wire, concrete, dog runs, and guardtowers. Farther south, there may be no visible, no obvious wall. But there remain armed guards and checkpoints all the same—still a restriction on the right to travel, still an instrument to impose upon ordinary men and women the will of a totalitarian state. . . .

The first part of the argument describes the setting and context for the call to action.

. . . Yet I do not come here to lament. For I find in Berlin a message of hope, even in the shadow of this wall, a message of triumph. . . .

. . . Where four decades ago there was rubble, today in West Berlin there is the greatest industrial output of any city in Germany—busy office blocks, fine homes and apartments, proud avenues, and the spreading lawns of park land. Where a city's culture seemed to have been destroyed, today there are two great universities, orchestras and an opera, countless theaters, and museums. Where there was want, today there's abundance—food, clothing, automobiles. . . .

. . . From devastation, from utter ruin, you Berliners have, in freedom, rebuilt a city that once again ranks as one of the greatest on Earth. . . .

. . . In the 1950s, Khrushchev predicted: "We will bury you." But in the West today, we see a free world that has achieved a level of prosperity and well-being unprecedented in all human history. In the Communist world, we see failure, technological backwardness, declining standards of health, even want of the most basic kind—too little food. Even today, the Soviet Union still cannot feed itself. After these four decades, then, there stands before the entire world one great and inescapable conclusion: Freedom leads to prosperity. . . .

Grounds: The free West achieved prosperity, while the Communist East remained in decline.

Justification: A country achieves prosperity when its people have economic freedom. (The grounds support this idea with the example of the free West vs. the Communist East.)

And now the Soviets themselves may, in a limited way, be coming to understand the importance of freedom. We hear much from Moscow about a new policy of reform and openness. Some political prisoners have been released. Certain foreign news broadcasts are no longer being jammed. Some economic enterprises have been permitted to operate with greater freedom from state control. Are these the beginnings of profound changes in the Soviet state?. . .

The opposition's claim is refuted; later, the opposition is acknowledged for the steps they have already taken.

There is one sign the Soviets can make that would be unmistakable, that would advance dramatically the cause of freedom and peace. General Secretary Gorbachev, . . . if you seek prosperity for the Soviet Union and Eastern Europe . . . Come here to this gate! Mr. Gorbachev, open this gate! Mr. Gorbachev, tear down this wall!

The speaker gives a specific call to action.

Claim: The wall dividing West and East Berlin should be torn down.

THE ART OF ARGUMENT: RHETORICAL DEVICES AND PERSUASIVE TECHNIQUES

Rhetorical Devices

Rhetoric is the art of using language in order to make a point or to persuade listeners. Rhetorical devices such as the ones listed below are accepted elements of argument. Their use does not invalidate or weaken an argument. Rather, the use of rhetorical devices is regarded as a key part of an effective argument.

Rhetorical Devices	Examples
Repetition The repeated use of certain words, phrases, or sentences	What we long for is freedom: freedom to work and freedom to learn.
Parallelism The repeated use of similar grammatical structures	Good writing entertains; great writing inspires.
Rhetorical Question Calling attention to an issue by implying an obvious answer	Is there no reasonable solution to this problem?
Sound Devices The use of alliteration, assonance, rhyme, or rhythm	The path before them was dark, dangerous, and daunting.
Simile and Metaphor Comparison of two like things or asserting that one thing is another	We are caged birds, unable to fly free.

Persuasive Techniques

The persuasive techniques below are often found in advertisements and in other forms of informal persuasion. Although techniques like the ones below are sometimes found in formal arguments, these techniques are usually avoided.

Persuasive Techniques	Examples
Bandwagon Approach/Anti-Bandwagon Approach Appeals to a person's desire to belong/Encourages or celebrates individuality	You have to buy one; everyone has one. Be yourself; don't give in to peer pressure.
Emotional Appeal Capitalizes on people's fear, anger, or desire	Without a home security system, your family is in danger.
Endorsement/Testimony Employs a well-known person to promote a product or an idea	I use this product every time before I compete, and it has helped me win.
Loaded Language Uses words charged with emotion	They live in abject squalor, their hovels not fit for human habitation.
"Plain Folks" Appeal Shows a connection to everyday, ordinary people	I grew up in a hard-working community just like this one.
Hyperbole Exaggerates to make a point	There are a thousand reasons why I'm right.

EXEMPLAR TEXT

Model Speech

The excerpted speech below includes examples of rhetorical devices and persuasive techniques.

from "Remarks to the Senate in Support of a Declaration of Conscience" by Senator Margaret Chase Smith

Mr. President:

I would like to speak briefly and simply about a serious national condition. It is a national feeling of fear and frustration that could result in national suicide and the end of everything that we Americans hold dear. . . .

This emotional language appeals to national pride.

. . . The United States Senate has long enjoyed worldwide respect as the greatest deliberative body in the world. But recently that deliberative character has too often been debased to the level of a forum of hate and character assassination sheltered by the shield of congressional immunity. . . .

. . . I think that it is high time for the United States Senate and its members to do some soul-searching—for us to weigh our consciences—on the manner in which we are performing our duty to the people of America—on the manner in which we are using or abusing our individual powers and privileges. I think that it is high time that we remembered that we have sworn to uphold and defend the Constitution. I think that it is high time that we remembered that the Constitution, as amended, speaks not only of the freedom of speech but also of trial by jury instead of trial by accusation.

The repetition of the first few words in each sentence gives the speech rhythm.

Whether it be a criminal prosecution in court or a character prosecution in the Senate, there is little practical distinction when the life of a person has been ruined.

Those of us who shout the loudest about Americanism in making character assassinations are all too frequently those who, by our own words and acts, ignore some of the basic principles of Americanism:

The right to criticize;

The right to hold unpopular beliefs;

The right to protest;

The right of independent thought.

The exercise of these rights should not cost one single American citizen his reputation or his right to a livelihood nor should he be in danger of losing his reputation or livelihood merely because he happens to know someone who holds unpopular beliefs. Who of us doesn't? Otherwise none of us could call our souls our own. Otherwise thought control would have set in. . . .

The rhetorical question assumes that all people listening would answer in the same way.

. . . The American people are sick and tired of seeing innocent people smeared and guilty people whitewashed. . . .

The parallelism created by repeated grammatical structures adds to the rhythm of the speech.

COMPOSING AN ARGUMENT

Choosing a Topic

Choose a topic that matters to people—and to you. Brainstorm for topics you would like to write about; then, choose the topic that most interests you.

Once you have chosen a topic, check to make sure you can make an arguable claim. Ask yourself:

1. What am I trying to prove?
2. Are there people who would disagree with my claim?
3. Do I have evidence to support my claim?

If you are able to put into words what you want to prove and answered yes to questions 2 and 3, you have an arguable claim.

Introducing the Claim and Establishing Its Significance

Before you begin writing, consider your audience and how much you think they already know about the topic you have chosen to explore. Then, provide only as much background information as necessary. Remember that you are not writing a summary of the issue—you are crafting an argument.

Once you have provided context for your argument, clearly state your claim, or thesis. A written argument's claim often appears in the first paragraph.

Developing Your Claim With Reasoning and Evidence

Now that you have made your claim, support it with evidence, or grounds. A good argument should have at least three solid pieces of evidence to support the claim.

Evidence can range from personal experience to researched data or expert opinion. Knowing your audience's knowledge level, concerns, values, and possible biases can help inform your decision on what kind of evidence will have the strongest impact. Make sure your evidence is up to date and comes from a credible source, and don't forget to credit your sources. *(See pages lxxiii and lxxviii–lxxix for guidelines on citing sources.)*

Also address the opposing counterclaim within the body of your argument. Consider points you have made or evidence you have provided that a person might challenge. Decide how best to respond to these counterclaims.

Writing a Concluding Statement or Section

Restate your claim in the conclusion (not necessarily word for word) and synthesize the evidence you have provided. Make your conclusion compelling enough to be memorable and to leave the reader with something to think about.

Writing

1.a. Introduce precise, claim(s), distinguish the claim(s) from alternate or opposing claims, and create an organization that establishes clear relationships among claim(s), counterclaims, reasons, and evidence.

1.b. Develop claim(s) and counterclaims fairly, supplying evidence for each while pointing out the strengths and limitations of both in a manner that anticipates the audience's knowledge level and concerns.

1.e. Provide a concluding statement or section that follows from and supports the argument presented.

Practice

Complete an outline like the one below to help you plan your own argument.

Brainstorming for Topics:

____

____

The topic that most interests me is ______________________________ because

____

Arguable Claim (Thesis): ______________________________

What I Already Know About the Issue: ______________________________

What I Need to Find Out About the Issue:

____

Who Is My Audience, and How Much Does My Audience Know About the Issue?

____

Possible Sources of Evidence: ______________________________

Grounds to Support My Claim (at least three strong pieces of evidence):

1. ______________________________
2. ______________________________
3. ______________________________

Justifications for My Grounds (why my grounds are allowed to stand as evidence):

1. ______________________________
2. ______________________________
3. ______________________________

Opposing Viewpoints to Consider: ______________________________

CONDUCTING RESEARCH

We are lucky to live in an age when information is plentiful. However, not all information is equally useful, or even accurate. Strong research skills will help you locate and evaluate information.

Short-Term Research

You will often need to conduct **short-term research** to answer specific questions about a text or extend your understanding of an idea. These strategies can help you find appropriate information quickly and efficiently:

Target Your Goal Decide what information you need to find before you begin your research. Drafting a specific question can help you avoid time-wasting digressions. For example, instead of simply hunting for information about Mark Twain, you might ask, "What jobs other than writing did Mark Twain have?" or, "Which of Twain's books was most popular during his lifetime?"

Use Online Search Engines Efficiently Finding information on the Internet can be both easy and challenging. Type a word or phrase into a general search engine and you will probably get hundreds—or thousands—of results. However, those results are not guaranteed to be relevant or accurate. Using quotation marks can help you focus a search. Place a phrase in quotation marks to find pages that include exactly that phrase. Add several phrases in quotation marks to narrow your results.

Scan search results before you click on them. The first result isn't always the most relevant. Read the text and consider the domain before making a choice.

Consult Multiple Sources It is always a good idea to check for answers in more than one source. This strategy helps you be sure that the information you find is accurate. Be wary if you read the exact same phrases in more than one source—there is a good chance that someone simply cut and pasted details from one site and failed to check their validity.

Common Core State Standards

Writing

5. Develop and strengthen writing as needed by planning, revising, editing, rewriting, or trying a new approach, focusing on addressing what is most significant for a specific purpose and audience.

7. Conduct short as well as more sustained research projects to answer a question (including a self-generated question) or solve a problem; narrow or broaden the inquiry when appropriate.

8. Gather relevant information from multiple authoritative print and digital sources, using advanced searches effectively; assess the usefulness of each source in answering the research question.

Evaluating Internet Domains

Not everything you read on the Internet is true, so you have to evaluate sources carefully. The last three letters of an Internet URL identify the site's domain, which can help you evaluate information on the site.

- .gov — Government sites are sponsored by a branch of the United States federal government, such as the Census Bureau, Supreme Court, or Congress. These sites are considered reliable.
- .edu — Education domains include schools from kindergartens to universities. Information from an educational research center or department is likely to be carefully checked. However, education domains can also include student pages that are not edited or monitored.
- .org — Organizations are nonprofit groups and usually maintain a high level of credibility. Keep in mind that some organizations may express strong biases.
- .com — Commercial sites exist to make a profit. Information might be biased to show a product or service in a good light. The company may be providing information to encourage sales or to promote a positive image.

Long-Term Research

Long-term research allows you to dive into a topic and conduct a detailed, comprehensive investigation. Your final goal could be a formal research report or a media presentation. An organized research plan will help you gather and synthesize information from multiple sources.

Long-term research is a flexible process—you will constantly adjust your research plan based on your findings and your growing understanding of the topic. Throughout your investigation, you might decide to return to an earlier stage to refocus your thesis, gather more information, or reflect on what you have learned.

The Research Process

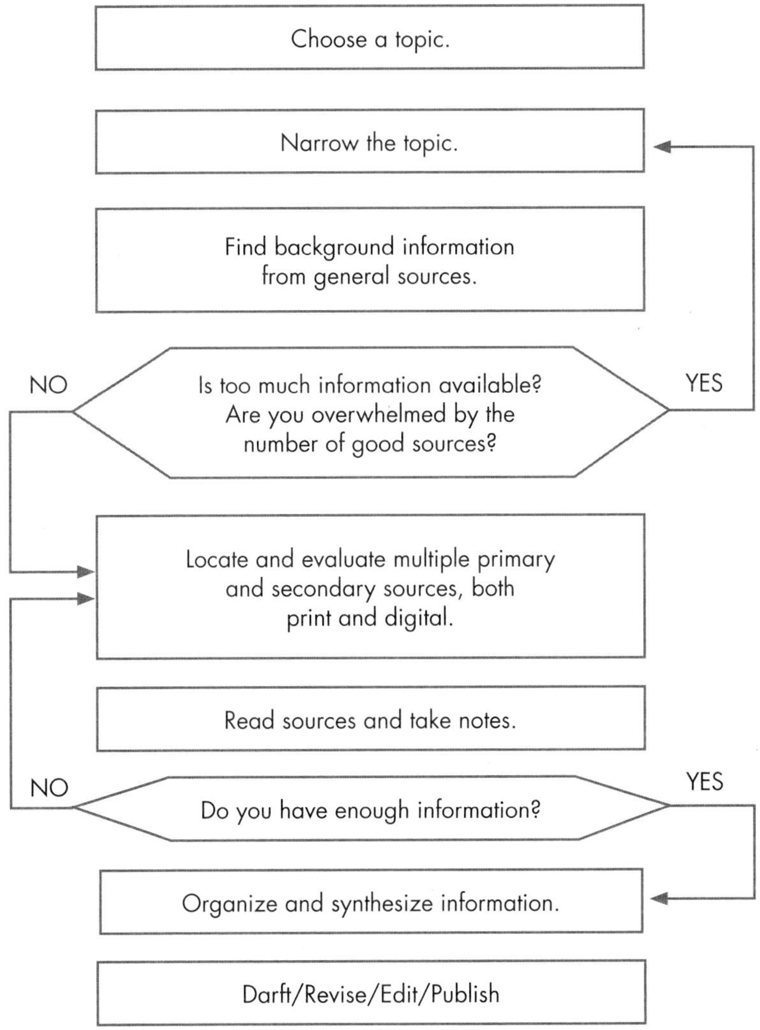

Consult the Research Process Workshop (pages lxiii–lxxii) for more details about the steps in this flowchart.

RESEARCH PROCESS WORKSHOP

Research Writing: Research Report

A **research report** presents and interprets information gathered through the extensive study of a subject. You might apply the elements of research writing in lab reports, documentaries, annotated bibliographies, histories, and persuasive essays.

Elements of a Research Report

- a thesis statement that is clearly expressed
- factual support from a variety of reliable, credited sources
- a clear introduction, body, and conclusion
- a bibliography or Works Cited list that provides a complete listing of research sources formatted in an approved style
- error-free grammar, formal style, and objective tone

PREWRITING/PLANNING STRATEGIES

A successful research report should focus on a topic that is both interesting and manageable. It is unlikely that you will be able to do justice to a broad subject, such as World War II or robotics, in the scope of a relatively brief paper. To avoid scope problems, first conduct background research. This will help you learn enough to choose a specific topic that you can then explore in greater depth.

After you finish your background research, create a plan to guide your investigation. Include these parts:

Research Question Compose a question about your topic. This question will help focus your research and prevent you from gathering details that are too broad for your purpose. As your research teaches you more about your topic, you may find it necessary to change, refocus, or adapt your original question.

Source List Create a list of sources to consult. Plan to use a variety of sources, and add new sources to your plan as you discover them. Place a check next to sources you have located and then underline sources you have consulted thoroughly.

Search Terms Write down terms you plan to investigate using online search engines. Making these decisions before you go online can help you avoid digressions that take you away from your topic.

Deadlines Break a long-term project into short-term goals in order to stay on track and prevent last-minute stress.

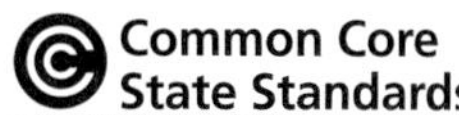

Writing

2.e. Establish and maintain a formal style and objective tone while attending to the norms and conventions of the discipline in which they are writing.

5. Develop and strengthen writing as needed by planning, revising, editing, rewriting, or trying a new approach, focusing on addressing what is most significant for a specific purpose and audience.

7. Conduct short as well as more sustained research projects to answer a question (including a self-generated question) or solve a problem; narrow or broaden the inquiry when appropriate.

8. Gather relevant information from multiple authoritative print and digital sources, using advanced searches effectively; assess the usefulness of each source in answering the research question.

SAMPLE RESEARCH QUESTIONS

What was Edgar Allan Poe's childhood like?

What was Franklin Delano Roosevelt's greatest achievement?

What artwork was inspired by Homer's Odyssey*?*

READING-WRITING CONNECTION

To get a feel for research writing, read the selection from *Nothing to Fear* by Alan Axelrod on page 294.

GATHERING DETAILS THROUGH RESEARCH

Use multiple sources. An effective research report combines information from several sources, and avoids relying too heavily on just one source. The creativity and originality of your research depends on how you combine ideas from many sources. Plan to include a variety of the following types of resources:

- **Primary and Secondary Sources:** To get a full view of your topic, use primary sources (firsthand or original accounts, such as interview transcripts and newspaper articles) and secondary sources (accounts that are not original, such as encyclopedia entries).
- **Print and Digital Sources:** The Internet allows fast access to data, but print resources are often edited more carefully. Plan to include both print and digital resources in order to guarantee that your work is accurate.
- **Media Sources:** You can find valuable information in media resources such as documentaries, television programs, podcasts, and museum exhibitions. Public lectures by experts also offer opportunities to hear authoritative opinions on many different topics.
- **Original Research:** Depending on your topic, you may wish to conduct original research to include among your sources. For example, you might interview experts or eyewitnesses or conduct a survey to find out about opinions or situations in your community.

Locate information. You can find sources of specific information through an online search, a card catalog, or the use of more advanced tools:

- **Databases:** Access databases of information to find appropriate sources. For example, the Modern Language Association (MLA) database indexes articles on topics within the humanities.
- **Indexes:** Locate magazine or newspaper articles by consulting the *Readers' Guide to Periodical Literature.*

Sample *Readers' Guide* Entry

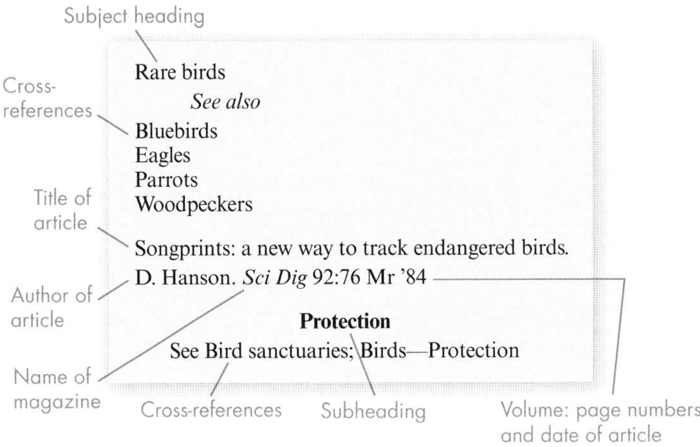

GATHERING DETAILS THROUGH RESEARCH (CONTINUED)

Evaluate sources. Apply evaluative criteria to make sure that your sources are appropriate to the purpose of your report and your audience. You may find the information you need to answer your research question in specialized resources, such as almanacs (for social, cultural, and natural statistics), government publications (for law, government programs, and subjects such as agriculture), and information services. Also, consider consumer, workplace, and public documents. Consult your librarian on the best sources to use.

Record and organize information. Take notes as you locate and connect pertinent information from multiple sources, and keep a reference list of every source you use. This will help you to make distinctions between the relative value and significance of specific data, facts, and ideas.

- **Source Cards:** For each source you consult, create a card that identifies its author, title, publisher, city, and date of publication. Note the page numbers on which you found relevant information.

  For Internet sources, record the name and Web address of the site, and the date you accessed the information.
- **Notecards:** For each item of information, create a separate notecard that includes the fact or idea, its source, and the page number on which you found the information.

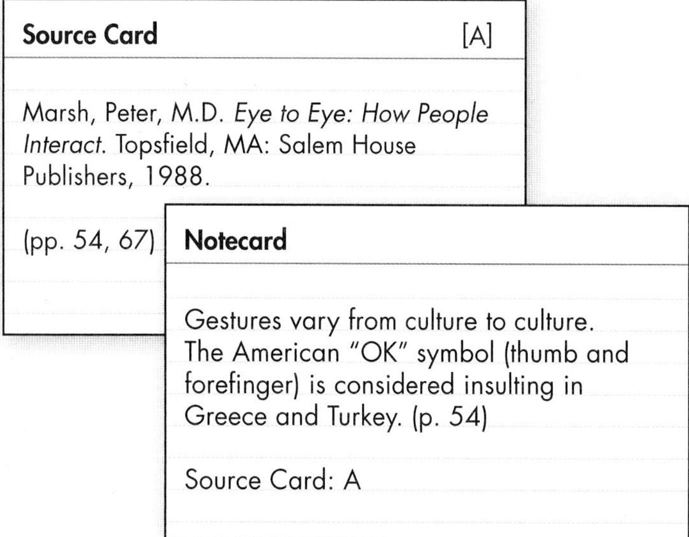

Source Card [A]

Marsh, Peter, M.D. *Eye to Eye: How People Interact.* Topsfield, MA: Salem House Publishers, 1988.

(pp. 54, 67)

Notecard

Gestures vary from culture to culture. The American "OK" symbol (thumb and forefinger) is considered insulting in Greece and Turkey. (p. 54)

Source Card: A

Quote accurately. Responsible research begins with the first note you take. Be sure to quote and paraphrase your sources accurately so you can identify these sources later. In your notes, circle all quotations and paraphrases to distinguish them from your own comments. When photocopying from a source, include the copyright information. Also, remember to include the Web addresses of printouts from online sources.

Common Core State Standards

Writing

9. Draw evidence from literary or informational texts to support analysis, reflection, and research.

Reliability Checklist

Ask yourself these questions about sources you find.

AUTHORITY

- Is the author well-known?
- What are the author's credentials?
- Does the tone of the writing inspire confidence? Why or why not?

BIAS

- Does the author have any obvious biases?
- What is the author's purpose for writing?
- Who is the target audience?

CURRENCY

- When was the work created? Has it been revised?
- Is there more current information available?

DRAFTING STRATEGIES

Propose a thesis statement. Write a sentence in which you take a position that can be supported by most of your research. A thesis statement is a controlling idea that gives your essay coherence.

- **Sample Thesis Statement:** *Claude Monet's use of light in his water lily paintings typifies Impressionist techniques.*

Choose a text structure. Use your thesis statement and knowledge of your audience to choose an organizational structure. Consider these options:

- **Chronological Order:** Present events in the order in which they occur. This is ideal for reporting a subject's history.
- **Order of Importance:** Present details in order of increasing or decreasing significance. This is ideal for building an argument.
- **Comparison and Contrast:** Present similarities and differences. This is ideal for addressing two or more subjects.

Write an outline. Review your notecards and build a road map that shows your plan for integrating and presenting key information. In an outline, use headings to identify the main idea in each section, and order these ideas so they flow logically. Use this outline to develop your draft.

Make direct references to sources. Use the following methods to incorporate the facts, examples, and quotations you have found:

- **Direct Quotation:** Enclose a writer's exact words in quotation marks. Omissions should not alter the intent of the passage. Indicate omitted words with **ellipses,** or dots.
- **Paraphrase:** Restate a writer's specific ideas in your own words, accurately reflecting the writer's meaning.
- **Summary:** Condense an extended idea into a brief statement in your own words to introduce background information or review key ideas.

Credit your sources. To avoid **plagiarism**—presenting another's work as your own—include documentation every time you use another writer's ideas. Note the author's last name and the page numbers of material used. Later, use these notes to create formal citations in a bibliography or Works Cited list at the end of your paper.

Plan for visuals. You may include visual aids, such as charts, maps, and graphs, to organize and display information in your report. Whenever you include additional information—whether it is visuals or quotations—be sure to make a clear link from your thesis to the data you include and reference.

Writing

2. Write informative/explanatory texts to examine and convey complex ideas, concepts, and information clearly and accurately through the effective selection, organization, and analysis of content.

2.a. Introduce a topic; organize complex ideas, concepts, and information to make important connections and distinctions; include formatting, graphics, and multimedia when useful to aiding comprehension.

2.b. Develop the topic with well-chosen, relevant, and sufficient facts, extended definitions, concrete details, quotations, or other information and examples appropriate to the audience's knowledge of the topic.

7. Conduct short as well as more sustained research projects to answer a question or solve a problem; synthesize multiple sources on the subject, demonstrating understanding of the subject under investigation.

REVISING STRATEGIES

Evaluate your sources. Underline any fact in your draft that may not have a trustworthy source. For example, you may have found information from a newspaper or a Web site known for sensationalizing or exaggerating events. Confirm this information through a more reliable source, such as an established encyclopedia, a scholarly Web site, or a reputable newspaper.

Model: Evaluating Sources
A good way for people to convey a positive message is to avoid certain movements. ~~When people cross their arms it is always a sign of panic.~~

The writer found that this claim was supported by only one source. Since it was not important to her basic argument, she chose to delete it.

Revise to vary word choice. Except for specific terminology required by your topic, avoid overuse of particular words and expressions. Review your draft to identify words that you may have overused. For each, use a dictionary and thesaurus to generate a list of possible synonyms, and substitute them as appropriate.

Example Synonym Banks

invention: innovation, development, contrivance, device

theory: belief, policy, system, position, idea, supposition

Peer Review

Exchange drafts with a partner. As you read each other's reports, circle or highlight words that recur repeatedly. Working together, identify replacements to improve word variety in the writing.

Revise to follow a consistent research format. As you finalize your report, be sure that it meets your teacher's criteria for length, format, and documentation of sources. The Modern Language Association (MLA) requires standardized parenthetical citations of sources and a Works Cited list that includes only the sources used in the report.

To credit sources within a research paper, include direct documentation in the form of footnotes, endnotes, or parenthetical citations. At the end of your paper, provide a reference list giving complete bibliographic information. If possible, use the footnoting function in a word processing program to aid your efforts.

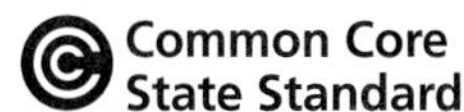

Common Core State Standards

Writing

2.d. Use precise language and domain-specific vocabulary to manage the complexity of the topic.

5. Develop and strengthen writing as needed by planning, revising, editing, rewriting, or trying a new approach, focusing on addressing what is most significant for a specific purpose and audience.

6. Use technology, including the Internet, to produce, publish, and update individual or shared writing products, taking advantage of technology's capacity to link to other information and to display information flexibly and dynamically.

Language

3. Apply knowledge of language to understand how language functions in different contexts, to make effective choices for meaning or style, and to comprehend more fully when reading or listening.

3.a. Write and edit work so that it conforms to the guidelines in a style manual appropriate for the discipline and writing type.

DOCUMENTING SOURCES

Writing

8. Gather relevant information from multiple authoritative print and digital sources, avoiding plagiarism and following a standard format for citation.

Language

3.a. Write and edit work so that it conforms to the guidelines in a style manual appropriate for the discipline and writing type.

Citing Sources in the Body of a Report You must give proper credit to the people whose ideas and words you have borrowed. When citing sources within the body of your report, follow a specific format. Modern Language Association (MLA) style calls for citations in parentheses directly following the material being cited.

- For print works, provide the author's or editor's name followed by a page number. If the work does not have an author, use a keyword or phrase from the title.

  Citing a Print Work: . . . body language makes up approximately 65 percent of human communication (Aylesworth 3).

- For Web sources, give the author's name (if it is available), the title of the article, or the title of the site.

  Citing a Web Source: Mysterydreams.org describes a lottery winner whose dreams reveal a winning ticket ("Dreaming of the Lottery").

Citing Sources at the End of a Report At the end of your report, give complete information for each source you cited in your paper. MLA style calls for an alphabetical Works Cited list.

- For books, provide the author's name—last name first—followed by the title of the work, the city of publication, the name of the publisher, the year of publication, and the medium of publication (e.g., Print).

  Entry for a Book: Aylesworth, Thomas G. *Understanding Body Talk.* New York: F. Watts, 1979. Print.

- For articles from periodicals, give the author's name—last name first—followed by the title of the article, the name of the magazine, the date of the issue, the volume and issue number, the pages of the article, and the format. Abbreviate any month with more than four letters by using the first three letters followed by a period. If the article is continued on a later, nonconsecutive page, give the number of the first page, followed by a plus sign.

  Entry for a Periodical Article: Kreisler, Kristin V. "Why We Dream What We Dream." *Reader's Digest.* Feb. 1995: 28. Print.

- For Web sites, give any of the following information that is available, in this order: author's name, page title, site title, date of last update, medium of publication (e.g., Web), and name of the sponsoring organization. Give the date you consulted the site.

  Entry for a Web Site: "Dreaming of the Lottery." Mystery Dreams Home Page. 2013. Web. 11 March 2014.

For more information on citing sources using MLA style, see page lxxviii.

EDITING AND PROOFREADING

Review your draft to correct factual and citation errors, as well as mistakes in format, grammar, and spelling.

Check your facts. Be sure that the facts you have included in your report are accurate. Errors sometimes occur during note-taking, drafting, and revising. To fact-check your report, place an open square next to each fact. Then, refer to your original sources to make sure you have stated each fact clearly and correctly. When you have confirmed a fact, place a check in the box and move on to the next one.

Review citations. Check that you have given credit for any ideas that are not your own. You might have unintentionally included exact phrases from one of your sources. To avoid plagiarism, give credit for all of those ideas. Try reading your draft aloud. Listen for words and phrases that do not sound familiar or do not have your own voice. Chances are good that those elements came from one of your sources. Either provide an accurate citation or paraphrase to include the idea in your own words.

Focus on format. Follow the manuscript requirements by including an appropriate title page, pagination, spacing and margins, and citations. Make sure you have used the preferred system for crediting sources in your paper and for bibliographical sources at the end. Double-check all punctuation and capitalization.

Proofread. Carefully reread your draft to find and correct spelling errors. Also check to be sure that you have used quotation marks correctly and that each open quotation mark has a corresponding closing quotation mark.

Writing

5. Develop and strengthen writing as needed by planning, revising, editing, rewriting, or trying a new approach, focusing on addressing what is most significant for a specific purpose and audience.

8. Gather relevant information from multiple authoritative print and digital sources; integrate information into the text selectively to maintain the flow of ideas, avoiding plagiarism and following a standard format for citation.

Language

1. Demonstrate command of the conventions of standard English grammar and usage when writing.

2. Demonstrate command of the conventions of standard English capitalization, punctuation, and spelling when writing.

2.c. Spell correctly.

Publishing and Presenting

Consider one of the following ways to share your writing:

Deliver an oral presentation. Read your research report aloud to your classmates, or consider re-creating the report as a multimedia presentation using presentation software. Add appropriate visual aids as needed, such as charts, maps, and graphs.

Organize a panel discussion. If several of your classmates have written on a similar topic, plan a discussion to compare and contrast your findings. Speakers can summarize their research before opening the panel to questions from the class.

MODEL: RESEARCH PAPER

As you read this student's completed research report, notice how she supports a thesis statement and integrates relevant research. Parenthetical citations within each paragraph refer to sources detailed in the Works Cited list at the end of the report. Marginal notes highlight elements that make this paper effective.

Student Model: Lyndsey Regan, Canyon Country, CA

Body Language

When we speak to other people, they are not only listening to our actual words, but sensing our facial expression, tone of voice, gestures, level of eye contact, posture, and movements as well. Nonverbal communication, or body language, makes up approximately 65 percent of human communication (Aylesworth 3). Body language has a major impact on how others perceive what we say. It can also be a tool for miscommunication when the speaker and listener are from different cultures or are communicating through technology that deprives them of visual cues. In fact, we often realize the importance of body language only when we cannot interpret someone else's body language correctly.

The opening line captures the reader's attention by presenting a surprising perspective.

Lyndsey expresses her thesis statement clearly and concisely.

In *Eye to Eye: How People Interact,* Dr. Peter Marsh explains that before we speak, our gestures, posture, and facial expressions are already broadcasting messages to those around us. While we are speaking, these gestures continue to communicate messages—usually clarifying what we are saying, but sometimes contradicting us in telltale ways (Marsh 116–119).

Lyndsey smoothly introduces a research source and explains the ideas it provided.

Often, body language is an unconscious act that triggers the most developed senses in other people—hearing and sight (Aylesworth 18). That is why body language is such a great way to emphasize words and ideas. Many people take advantage of this. Advertisers, for example, cast actors in their commercials who use body language that appeals to viewers.

Studies have shown that people's body language changes when they are not telling the truth (Vrij, Edward, Roberts, and Bull 239–263). If someone's body language is inconsistent with what he or she is saying, people tend to believe what the body is telling them. A good way for people to convey a positive message is to avoid certain movements, like fidgeting or letting your eyes wander. Instead, good communicators maintain steady eye contact, nod in agreement, and smile. You may notice that people on television, like hosts of infomercials and talk-shows, generally display this positive body language when speaking (Ruesch and Kees).

MODEL: RESEARCH PAPER (continued)

Body language is usually learned, but it can also be inherited. It is affected by age, gender, background, and situation. The meaning of body language can change depending on cultural context. According to Dr. Marsh, each culture has developed its own repertoire of symbolic gestures, many with original associations that have now long been forgotten (Marsh 53–54). This sometimes causes people to be alarmed by foreign visitors or nervous around people when they visit new countries.

In the United States, people have a wide variety of regional influences because the country is a melting pot of diverse cultures. A gesture that means the same thing throughout the Unite States is the "OK" sign made with the thumb and forefinger. This gesture is interpreted similarly in some European countries, but if you were to perform this sign in Greece or Turkey, it would be considered very insulting (Marsh 54).

Whenever Lyndsey presents a specific piece of evidence that is not her own idea or common knowledge, she cites it using the appropriate format.

There are other cultural differences in body language within Europe. In Germany, body language often reflects social status, and Germans often use body language for emphasis. Italian gestures are often passionate, emotional expressions communicated with the face, arms, and shoulders. Italians often use body language to clarify themselves or to express urgency. In France, people tend to use more formal gestures. They are generally not as expressive or insistent as Italians. The body language of the French is not nearly as casual as we are used to in America (Ruesch and Kees 23–25). As you can see by exploring a few examples from different cultures, there are many differences in body language. Therefore, when you communicate with people from other countries, take special care in your use of body language.

Technological advancements in our society affect the way we communicate. For example, when we speak on the telephone, we are unable to see the person on the other end of the line. The message that a person may be trying to convey may be misinterpreted without the additional visual information provided by his or her body language. With electronic mail, there is no visual or verbal communication whatsoever. As a result, people cannot completely understand the meaning of what is being communicated. Therefore, people using e-mail should be careful about what they write. To avoid miscommunication, communicating the old-fashioned way—in person—may be the best approach.

Lyndsey's organizational structure is logical and clear. First, she discusses how body language is used in a variety of cultures. Next, she gives examples of what happens when we do not have body language to guide us.

In conclusion, body language is a significant component of communication, even though we are often not aware of it. Body language, like facial expression and gestures, frequently enables people to clearly understand one another, but we must remember that people cannot always be read like a book. With cultural differences, body language can take on different meanings, and this allows for potential miscommunication (Smith, 2014). Changes in technology present a different kind of problem, but with a similar result. When body language cannot be seen, people may misinterpret the meaning of the communicator, making them angry or confused. As you can see, the additional information we provide with our body language plays a major role in how we communicate our thoughts and ideas.

Works Cited

Aylesworth, Thomas G. *Understanding Body Talk.* New York: F. Watts, 1979. Print.

Marsh, Peter, M.D. *Eye to Eye: How People Interact.* Topsfield, MA: Salem House Publishers, 1988. Print.

Ruesch, Jurgen, and Weldon Kees. *Nonverbal Communication: Notes on the Visual Perception of Human Relations.* Berkeley, CA: University of California Press, 1969. Print.

Vrij, Aldert, Katherine Edward, Kim P. Roberts, and Ray Bull. "Detecting Deceit via Analysis of Verbal and Nonverbal Behavior." *Journal of Nonverbal Behavior,* Winter 2000: 239–263.

Smith, John. "Analyzing Body Language." *Nonverbal Communication Studies.* 2014. Web. 10 February 2015.

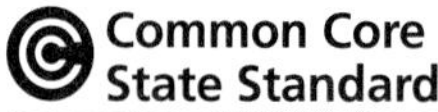

Common Core State Standards

Language

3.a. Write and edit work so that it conforms to the guidelines in a style manual appropriate for the discipline and writing type.

After her conclusion, Lyndsey presents the complete information for the works cited in her report using MLA format, a common style for citation.

CITING SOURCES

In research writing, cite your sources. In the body of your paper, provide a footnote, an endnote, or a parenthetical citation, identifying the sources of facts, opinions, or quotations. At the end of your paper, provide a bibliography or a Works Cited list, a list of all the sources you cite. Follow an established format, such as Modern Language Association (MLA) Style.

Works Cited List (MLA Style)

A works cited list must contain accurate information sufficient to enable a reader to locate each source you cite. The basic components of an entry are as follows:

- Name of the author, editor, translator, or group responsible for the work
- Title of the work
- Place and date of publication
- Publisher

For print materials, the information required for a citation generally appears on the copyright and title pages of a work. For the format of works cited list entries, consult the examples at right and in the chart on page lxxix.

Parenthetical Citations (MLA Style)

A parenthetical citation briefly identifies the source from which you have taken a specific quotation, factual claim, or opinion. It refers the reader to one of the entries on your works cited list. A parenthetical citation has the following features:

- It appears in parentheses.
- It identifies the source by the last name of the author, editor, or translator, or by the title (for a lengthy title, list the first word only).
- It gives a page reference, identifying the page of the source on which the information cited can be found.

Punctuation A parenthetical citation generally falls outside a closing quotation mark but within the final punctuation of a clause or sentence. For a long quotation set off from the rest of your text, place the citation at the end of the excerpt without any punctuation following.

Special Cases

- If the author is an organization, use the organization's name, in a shortened version if necessary.
- If you cite more than one work by the same author, add the title or a shortened version of the title.

Sample Works Cited Lists (MLA 7th Edition)

Carwardine, Mark, Erich Hoyt, R. Ewan Fordyce, and Peter Gill. *The Nature Company Guides: Whales, Dolphins, and Porpoises.* New York: Time-Life, 1998. Print.

"Discovering Whales." *Whales on the Net.* 1998. Whales in Danger Information Service. Web. 18 Oct. 2015.

Neruda, Pablo. "Ode to Spring." *Odes to Opposites.* Trans. Ken Krabbenhoft. Ed. and illus. Ferris Cook. Boston: Little, 1995. Print.

The Saga of the Volsungs. Trans. Jesse L. Byock. London: Penguin, 1990. Print.

List an anonymous work by title.

List both the title of the work and the collection in which it is found.

Sample Parenthetical Citations

It makes sense that baleen whales such as the blue whale, the bowhead whale, the humpback whale, and the sei whale (to name just a few) grow to immense sizes (Carwardine, Hoyt, and Fordyce 19–21). The blue whale has grooves running from under its chin to partway along the length of its underbelly. As in some other whales, these grooves expand and allow even more food and water to be taken in (Ellis 18–21).

Authors' last names

Page numbers where information can be found

Works Cited List or Bibliography

Provide full source information in either a Works Cited list or a bibliography. A Works Cited list includes only those sources you paraphrased or quoted directly in your paper. By contrast, a bibliography lists all the sources you consulted during research—even those you did not cite.

MLA Style for Listing Sources

Book with one author	Pyles, Thomas. *The Origins and Development of the English Language.* 2nd ed. New York: Harcourt, 1971. Print.
Book with two or three authors	McCrum, Robert, William Cran, and Robert MacNeil. *The Story of English.* New York: Penguin, 1987. Print.
Book with an editor	Truth, Sojourner. *Narrative of Sojourner Truth.* Ed. Margaret Washington. New York: Vintage, 1993. Print.
Book with more than three authors or editors	Donald, Robert B., et al. *Writing Clear Essays.* Upper Saddle River: Prentice, 1996. Print.
Single work in an anthology	Hawthorne, Nathaniel. "Young Goodman Brown." *Literature: An Introduction to Reading and Writing.* Ed. Edgar V. Roberts and H. E. Jacobs. Upper Saddle River: Prentice, 1998. 376–385. Print. [Indicate pages for the entire selection.]
Introduction to a work in a published edition	Washington, Margaret. Introduction. *Narrative of Sojourner Truth.* By Sojourner Truth. Ed. Washington. New York: Vintage, 1993. v–xi. Print.
Signed article from an encyclopedia	Askeland, Donald R. "Welding." *World Book Encyclopedia.* 1991 ed. Print.
Signed article in a weekly magazine	Wallace, Charles. "A Vodacious Deal." *Time* 14 Feb. 2000: 63. Print.
Signed article in a monthly magazine	Gustaitis, Joseph. "The Sticky History of Chewing Gum." *American History* Oct. 1998: 30–38. Print.
Newspaper	Thurow, Roger. "South Africans Who Fought for Sanctions Now Scrap for Investors." *Wall Street Journal* 11 Feb. 2000: A1+. Print. [For a multipage article that does not appear on consecutive pages, write only the first page number on which it appears, followed by the plus sign.]
Unsigned editorial or story	"Selective Silence." Editorial. *Wall Street Journal* 11 Feb. 2000: A14. Print. [If the editorial or story is signed, begin with the author's name.]
Signed pamphlet or brochure	[Treat the pamphlet as though it were a book.]
Work from a library subscription service	Ertman, Earl L. "Nefertiti's Eyes." *Archaeology* Mar.–Apr. 2008: 28–32. *Kids Search.* EBSCO. New York Public Library. Web. 18 June 2008. [Indicate the date you accessed the information.]
Filmstrips, slide programs, videocassettes, DVDs, and other audiovisual media	*The Diary of Anne Frank.* Dir. George Stevens. Perf. Millie Perkins, Shelley Winters, Joseph Schildkraut, Lou Jacobi, and Richard Beymer. 1959. Twentieth Century Fox, 2004. DVD.
CD-ROM (with multiple publishers)	Simms, James, ed. *Romeo and Juliet.* By William Shakespeare. Oxford: Attica Cybernetics; London: BBC Education; London: Harper, 1995. CD-ROM.
Radio or television program transcript	"Washington's Crossing of the Delaware." *Weekend Edition Sunday.* Natl. Public Radio. WNYC, New York. 23 Dec. 2013. Print. Transcript.
Internet Web page	"Fun Facts About Gum." NACGM site. 1999. National Association of Chewing Gum Manufacturers. Web. 19 Dec. 2015. [Indicate the date you accessed the information.]
Personal interview	Smith, Jane. Personal interview. 10 Feb. 2015.

All examples follow the style given in the *MLA Handbook for Writers of Research Papers,* seventh edition, by Joseph Gibaldi.

UNIT 1

THE BIG ? Is conflict necessary?

UNIT PATHWAY

PART 1
SETTING EXPECTATIONS

- INTRODUCING THE BIG QUESTION
- CLOSE READING WORKSHOP

PART 2
TEXT ANALYSIS GUIDED EXPLORATION

FACING CONFLICT

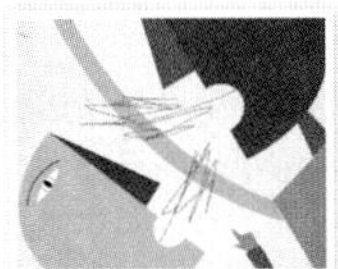

PART 3
TEXT SET DEVELOPING INSIGHT

CONFORMITY

PART 4
DEMONSTRATING INDEPENDENCE

- INDEPENDENT READING
- ONLINE TEXT SET

CLOSE READING TOOL

Use this tool to practice the close reading strategies you learn.

STUDENT eTEXT

Bring learning to life with audio, video, and interactive tools.

ONLINE WRITER'S NOTEBOOK

Easily capture notes and complete assignments online.

Find all Digital Resources at **pearsonrealize.com**

Introducing the Big Question

Is conflict necessary?

A conflict is a struggle between opposing forces. A conflict might be as small as an argument between friends or as large as a war between nations. It might also involve just one person who faces a personal challenge or a hard decision. Conflicts occur frequently in literature and in life, but are they necessary? Conflicts can be difficult for the people involved in them, but can a conflict also have a positive outcome?

Exploring the Big Question

Collaboration: Group Discussion Start thinking about the Big Question by identifying different types of conflicts and the consequences they can have. Make a list of a variety of conflicts you have either read about or experienced. Describe one specific example of each of the following:

- An argument or a disagreement between friends
- A contest or competition between teams
- A struggle to make a decision
- A controversy in the news
- A problem that must be solved

Share your examples with a group. Talk about both the causes and the effects of each conflict. Consider the positive and negative effects that each conflict might have for each person involved.

Before you begin the discussion, establish rules that will allow you to manage conflicts within your own group. For example, agree upon specific goals you want to achieve, how you will handle disagreements, and timeframes for completing your objectives. Write down the rules and refer to them as needed as you conduct your discussion. As you contribute your ideas, use the conflict-related words listed on the page at right.

Connecting to the Literature Each reading in this unit will give you additional insight into the Big Question. After you read each selection, pause to consider the conflicts it presents. Decide how these conflicts affect the lives of the characters, and whether they could or should have been avoided.

Vocabulary

Acquire and Use Academic Vocabulary The term "academic vocabulary" refers to words you typically encounter in scholarly and literary texts and in technical and business writing. It is language that helps to express complex ideas. Review the definitions of these academic vocabulary words.

appreciate (ə prē´ shē āt´) *v.* be aware of the value of something

argument (är´ gyo͞o mənt) *n.* discussion in which there is disagreement; dispute

articulate (är tik´ yo͞o lāt´) *v.* express clearly

compete (kəm pēt´) *v.* try to win against an opponent

competition (käm´ pə tish´ ən) *n.* contest or match; rivalry

controversy (kän´trə vʉr´sē) *n.* lengthy, often public discussion of a question in which opposing opinions clash

Gather Vocabulary Knowledge Additional words related to conflict are listed below. Categorize the words by deciding whether you know each one well, know it a little bit, or do not know it at all.

amicably	equity	mediate
antagonize	grievance	survival
cooperate	issue	war/battle
differences		

Once you have sorted the words, complete the following steps:

1. Write the definitions of the words you know.
2. Use a print or an online dictionary to confirm each word's meaning. If necessary, revise your original definitions.
3. Use the dictionary to look up the meanings of the words you do not know. Then, write the definitions.
4. If a word sounds familiar but you are not sure of its meaning, consult the dictionary. Then, record the word's meaning.
5. Use all of the words in a paragraph about the necessity of conflict.

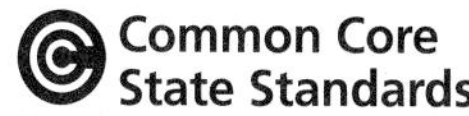

Speaking and Listening

1.b. Work with peers to set rules for collegial discussions and decision-making, clear goals and deadlines, and individual roles as needed.

Language

6. Acquire and use accurately general academic and domain-specific words and phrases, sufficient for reading, writing, speaking, and listening at the college and career readiness level; demonstrate independence in gathering vocabulary knowledge when considering a word or phrase important to comprehension or expression.

Close Reading Workshop

In this workshop, you will learn an approach to reading that will deepen your understanding of literature and will help you better appreciate the author's craft. The workshop includes models for the close reading, discussion, research, and writing activities you will complete as you study literature in this unit. After you have reviewed the strategies and models, practice your skills with the Independent Practice selection.

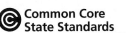

Common Core State Standards

RL.9-10.1, RL.9-10.2, RL.9-10.3, RL.9-10.4, RL.9-10.5; SL.9-10.1, SL.9-10.4; W.9-10.8, W.9-10.9, W.9-10.10

[For full standards wording, see the chart in the front of this book.]

CLOSE READING: **SHORT STORY**

In Part 2 of this unit, you will focus on reading various short stories. Use these strategies as you read the texts:

Comprehension: **Key Ideas and Details**

- Read first to unlock basic meaning.
- Use context clues to help you determine the meanings of unfamiliar words. Consult a dictionary, if necessary.
- Identify unfamiliar details that you might need to clarify through research.
- Distinguish between what is stated directly and what must be inferred.

Ask yourself questions such as these:

- Who are the main characters?
- When and where does the action take place?
- What problems do the characters face?

Text Analysis: **Craft and Structure**

- Think about the genre of the work and how the author presents ideas.
- Analyze the features that contribute to the author's voice and style. Notice the author's diction (word choice), syntax (arrangement of words in sentences), and tone (attitude toward the audience and subject).
- Take note of how the author uses language and literary elements to create memorable scenes or images.
- Consider the story's narrative structure, including flashbacks, foreshadowing, or multiple points of view.

Ask yourself questions such as these:

- How does the narrator's point of view affect my understanding of and feelings about the story?
- Why do the characters behave as they do? How do their actions advance the plot?
- What is the central conflict, or struggle, that characters face?

Connections: **Integration of Knowledge and Ideas**

- Look for relationships among key ideas. Identify causes and effects, and comparisons and contrasts.
- Look for important images or symbols and consider their deeper meanings. Then, connect ideas to determine the theme or central insight expressed by the author.
- Compare and contrast this work with other works you have read, either by the same author or different authors.

Ask yourself questions such as these:

- How has this work increased my knowledge of a subject, an author, or a literary movement?
- In what ways is this story special, unique, or worthy of reading?

Read

As you read this short story, take note of the annotations that model ways to closely read the text.

Reading Model

"Old Man at the Bridge" by Ernest Hemingway

An old man[1] with steel rimmed spectacles[2] and very dusty clothes sat by the side of the road. There was a pontoon bridge[3] across the river and carts, trucks, and men, women and children were crossing it. The mule-drawn carts staggered up the steep bank from the bridge with soldiers[3] helping push against the spokes of the wheels. The trucks ground up and away heading out of it all and the peasants plodded along in the ankle deep dust.[2] But the old man sat there without moving. He was too tired to go any farther.

It was my business[4] to cross the bridge, explore the bridgehead beyond and find out to what point the enemy had advanced. I did this and returned over the bridge. There were not so many carts now and very few people on foot, but the old man was still there.

"Where do you come from?" I asked him.

"From San Carlos," he said, and smiled.

That was his native town and so it gave him pleasure to mention it and he smiled.[5]

"I was taking care of animals," he explained.

"Oh," I said, not quite understanding.

"Yes," he said, "I stayed, you see, taking care of animals. I was the last one to leave the town of San Carlos."[5]

He did not look like a shepherd nor a herdsman and I looked at his black dusty clothes and his gray dusty face and his steel rimmed spectacles and said, "What animals were they?"

"Various animals," he said, and shook his head. "I had to leave them."

I was watching the bridge and the African looking country of the Ebro Delta and wondering how long now it would be before we would see the enemy, and listening all the while for the first noises that would signal that ever mysterious event called contact, and the old man still sat there.[6]

"What animals were they?" I asked.

"There were three animals altogether," he explained. "There were two goats and a cat and then there were four pairs of pigeons."

"And you had to leave them?" I asked.

"Yes. Because of the artillery. The captain told me to go because of the artillery."

Key Ideas and Details
1 The "old man" of the title is mentioned in the story's first sentence. The pronoun *an* suggests that the narrator does not know exactly who the old man is.

Craft and Structure
2 Hemingway's language is simple but poetic. The consonant sounds in the phrases *steel rimmed spectacles* and *peasants plodded along in the ankle deep dust* create strong rhythmic patterns and also convey vivid images.

Key Ideas and Details
3 You might consult a dictionary to determine that a *pontoon bridge* is a temporary floating bridge that is used by the military. The narrator also mentions *soldiers,* which may help you infer that the story takes place during wartime.

Craft and Structure
4 This phrase "It was my business" reveals that the narrator is telling the story in the first person. Further details in this sentence reveal the narrator's task.

Key Ideas and Details
5 The old man's smile and his words show that he was happy in San Carlos and did not want to leave. This fact might help you determine why he sits still while everyone around him is moving away.

Craft and Structure
6 This long sentence creates tension and reveals a conflict—the narrator expects that danger is approaching, but the old man will not move to safety.

"And you have no family?" I asked, watching the far end of the bridge where a few last carts were hurrying down the slope of the bank.

"No," he said, "only the animals I stated. The cat, of course, will be all right. A cat can look out for itself, but I cannot think what will become of the others."

"What politics have you?" I asked.

"I am without politics," he said.[7] "I am seventy-six years old. I have come twelve kilometers now and I think now I can go no further."

"This is not a good place to stop," I said. "If you can make it, there are trucks up the road where it forks for Tortosa."

"I will wait a while," he said, " and then I will go. Where do the trucks go?"

"Towards Barcelona," I told him.

"I know no one in that direction," he said, "but thank you very much. Thank you again very much."

He looked at me very blankly and tiredly, and then said, having to share his worry with someone, "The cat will be all right, I am sure. There is no need to be unquiet about the cat. But the others. Now what do you think about the others?"[8]

"Why they'll probably come through it all right."

"You think so?"

"Why not," I said, watching the far bank where now there were no carts.

"But what will they do under the artillery when I was told to leave because of the artillery?"

"Did you leave the dove cage unlocked?" I asked.[9]

"Yes."

"Then they'll fly."

"Yes, certainly they'll fly. But the others. It's better not to think about the others," he said.

"If you are rested I would go," I urged. "Get up and try to walk now."

"Thank you," he said and got to his feet, swayed from side to side and then sat down backwards in the dust.

"I was taking care of animals," he said dully, but no longer to me. "I was only taking care of animals."

There was nothing to do about him. It was Easter Sunday and the Fascists were advancing toward the Ebro. It was a gray overcast day with a low ceiling so their planes were not up. That and the fact that cats know how to look after themselves was all the good luck that old man would ever have.[10]

Integration of Knowledge and Ideas

7 The old man's statement that he is "without politics" develops the theme: War affects even those who do not take sides.

Key Ideas and Details

8 These details show that the old man is dazed and tired. His unwavering concern for his animals suggests that he either does not understand or does not care about his own well-being; he has given up.

Integration of Knowledge and Ideas

9 Earlier in the story, the birds were referred to as "pigeons,"but now the narrator calls them "doves." The fact that doves often symbolize peace underscores Hemingway's message about the effects of war on innocent civilians.

Craft and Structure

10 The narrator has done his best, but he realizes he cannot save the old man. He reports details about the time, place, and situation in a seemingly detached manner. The final sentence suggests that he holds little hope for the old man's survival, yet Hemingway leaves the story's conflict unresolved.

Discuss

Sharing your own ideas and listening to the ideas of others can deepen your understanding of a text and help you look at a topic in a whole new way. As you participate in collaborative discussions, work to have a genuine exchange in which classmates build upon one another's ideas. Support your points with evidence and ask meaningful questions.

Discussion Model

Student 1: It's interesting that Hemingway doesn't use a battle as the location of the story's conflict. No bombs fall, and no one is injured. Instead, he focuses on a more subtle conflict: What is to become of ordinary people caught up in a war?

Student 2: That's true. It's also important that the old man says he is "without politics." He seems to be an innocent bystander. But is it possible to really be "without politics"? In any case he seems to be suffering.

Student 3: I agree. People are usually aware of the dangers soldiers face but may not realize what happens to those who aren't actually fighting. Do you think Hemingway is talking about one war in particular or about war in general?

Research

Targeted research can clarify unfamiliar details and shed light on various aspects of a text. Consider questions that arise in your mind as you read, and use those questions as the basis for research.

Research Model

Questions: *Is this story set during a specific war? If so, which one, and how did Hemingway know about it?*

Key Words for Internet Search: Hemingway + War

Result: National Archives, Hemingway Collection

What I Learned: Hemingway was a journalist during the Spanish Civil War. He wrote an account of the war that appeared in *The New York Times* on April 19, 1938. His experience seems to have inspired "Old Man at the Bridge."

Write

Writing about a text will deepen your understanding of it and will also allow you to share your ideas more formally with others. The following model essay evaluates Hemingway's style and cites evidence to support the main ideas.

Writing Model: Argument

Hemingway's Approach to Character in "Old Man at the Bridge"

Ernest Hemingway is known for his tightly controlled, minimal style. In "Old Man at the Bridge," this style is evident. What is remarkable is how much this style helps the author achieve in such a brief story. In particular, Hemingway does a masterful job of developing his characters, drawing a rich portrait of two people, the narrator and the old man of the title, in just 762 words.

Strong critical writing presents and defends a writer's interpretation of a text. In this essay, the writer states a clear position in the first paragraph.

Readers know the narrator best because he is their eyes and ears. Everything about the story's setting and action is relayed through this first-person narrator. As we read, we begin to know the narrator through the details he shares. Also, as the narrator begins to understand something about the old man, readers do, too.

By defining the narrative structure of the story, the writer demonstrates understanding of the author's craft.

The first layer of details the narrator gives us describes the setting. The old man is at first part of the setting, seen sitting "with steel rimmed spectacles and very dusty clothes" by the side of a road. There is a lot of traffic and confusion, and the narrator reports that as well. Details such as, "The mule-drawn carts staggered up the steep bank from the bridge with soldiers helping push…" bring the urgent scene to life. However, the narrator takes note of the old man first.

The writer supports claims with specific details from the story.

The narrator has a job to do, which is to scout the enemy's position. As he says, "It was my business to cross the bridge, explore the bridgehead beyond and find out to what point the enemy had advanced." He does his job, but does not tell readers what he found. Instead, when he returns from scouting, he simply states, "the old man was still there." The narrator spends more time relaying details about the old man than he does about the war or even his own mission. He does not say it directly, but the narrator is clearly concerned about the old man.

This quality of not stating things directly fits the "iceberg theory"—a term Hemingway used to describe his style. In his memoir *A Moveable Feast,* Hemingway discusses how most of an iceberg sits below the water's surface. Only a small portion shows above. Hemingway felt that the meaning of a story should not be obvious. Instead, the writer should hint at it. In this story, he hints at but does not describe directly the old man's desperate situation.

Hemingway was a journalist as well as a fiction writer. His newspaper training taught him to work from facts and to observe. As he wrote in his memoir, "My aim is to put down on paper what I see and what I feel in the best and simplest way." He also would not turn away from difficult topics. Instead, he advised others to "write hard and clear about what hurts." That quality can be seen even in this very short story, which looks at an old man in a bad situation in a "hard and clear" way.

The writer seamlessly incorporates evidence from research to make an important connection.

As you read the following story, apply the close reading strategies you have learned. You may need to read the story multiple times.

The Jade Peony[1]

by Wayson Choy

Meet the Author

Award-winning novelist, memoirist, and short story writer **Wayson Choy** was born in 1939 in Vancouver, Canada. He spent his childhood in the city's Chinatown district, where he learned traditional Chinese myths and stories from his elders. These traditional tales inspired him to tell his own stories.

When Grandmama died at 83 our whole household held its breath. She had promised us a sign of her leaving, final proof that her present life had ended well. My parents knew that without any clear sign, our own family fortunes could be altered, threatened. My stepmother looked endlessly into the small cluttered room the ancient lady had occupied. Nothing was touched; nothing changed. My father, thinking that a sign should appear in Grandmama's garden, looked at the frost-killed shoots and cringed: *no, that could not be it.*

My two older teenage brothers and my sister, Liang, age 14, were embarrassed by my parents' behavior. What would all the white people in Vancouver[2] think of us? We were Canadians now, *Chinese-Canadians*, a hyphenated reality that my parents could never accept. So it seemed, for different reasons, we all held our breath waiting for *something*.

I was eight when she died. For days she had resisted going into the hospital . . . *a cold, just a cold* . . . and instead gave constant instruction to my stepmother and sister on the boiling of ginseng roots mixed with bitter extract. At night, between wracking coughs and deadly silences, Grandmama had her back and chest rubbed with heated camphor oil and sipped a bluish decoction of an herb called Peacock's Tail. When all these failed to abate her fever, she began to arrange the details of her will. This she did with my father, confessing finally: "I am too stubborn. The only cure for old age is to die."

My father wept to hear this. I stood beside her bed; she turned to me. Her round face looked darker, and the gentleness of her eyes, the thin, arching eyebrows, seemed weary. I brushed the few strands of gray, brittle hair from her face; she managed to smile at me. Being the youngest, I had spent nearly all my time with her and could not imagine that we would ever be parted. Yet when she spoke, and her voice hesitated, cracked, the somber shadows of her room chilled me. Her wrinkled brow grew wet with fever, and her small body seemed even more diminutive.

"I—I am going to the hospital, Grandson." Her hand reached out for mine. "You know, Little Son, whatever happens I will never leave you." Her palm felt plush and warm, the slender, old fingers boney and firm, so magically strong was her grip that I could not imagine how she could ever part from me. Ever.

Her hands *were* magical. My most vivid memories are of her hands: long, elegant fingers, with impeccable nails, a skein of fine, barely-seen veins,

CLOSE READING TOOL

Read and respond to this selection online using the **Close Reading Tool.**

1. **Jade Peony** (pē´ ə nē) jade is a hard, dense gemstone; a peony is a common garden flower, the Chinese variety of which produces large, single blossoms in early summer.
2. **Vancouver** (van ko͞o´ vər) large city in the province of British Columbia, Canada.

and wrinkled skin like light pine. Those hands were quick when she taught me, at six, simple tricks of juggling, learnt when she was a village girl in Southern Canton; a troupe of actors had stayed on her father's farm. One of them, "tall and pale as the whiteness of petals," fell in love with her, promising to return.

In her last years his image came back like a third being in our two lives. He had been magician, acrobat, juggler, and some of the things he taught her she had absorbed and passed on to me through her stories and games. But above all, without realizing it then, her hands conveyed to me the quality of their love.

Most marvelous for me was the quick-witted skill her hands revealed in making windchimes for our birthdays: windchimes in the likeness of her lost friend's only present to her, made of bits of string and scraps, in the center of which once hung a precious jade peony. This wondrous gift to her broke apart years ago, in China, but Grandmama kept the jade pendant in a tiny red silk envelope, and kept it always in her pocket, until her death.

These were not ordinary, carelessly made chimes, such as those you now find in our Chinatown stores, whose rattling noises drive you mad. But making her special ones caused **dissension** in our family, and some shame. Each one that she made was created from a treasure trove of glass fragments and castaway costume jewelry, in the same way that her first windchime had been made. The problem for the rest of the family was in the fact that Grandmama looked for these treasures wandering the back alleys of Keefer and Pender Streets, peering into our neighbors' garbage cans, chasing away hungry, nervous cats and shouting curses at them.

Vocabulary ▶
dissension (di sen´ shən) *n.* disagreement; difference of opinion

"All our friends are laughing at us!" Older Brother Jung said at last to my father, when Grandmama was away having tea at Mrs. Lim's.

"We are not poor," Oldest Brother Kiam declared, "Yet she and Sek-Lung poke through those awful things as if—" he shoved me in frustration and I stumbled against my sister, "—they were beggars!"

"She will make Little Brother crazy!" Sister Liang said. Without warning, she punched me sharply in the back; I jumped. "You see, look how *nervous* he is!"

I lifted my foot slightly, enough to swing it back and kick Liang in the shin. She yelled and pulled back her fist to punch me again. Jung made a menacing move towards me.

"Stop this, all of you!" My father shook his head in exasperation. How could he dare tell the Grand Old One, his aging mother, that what was somehow appropriate in a poor village in China, was an abomination here. How could he prevent me, his youngest, from accompanying her? If she went walking into those alleyways alone she could well be attacked by hoodlums. "She is not a beggar looking for food. She is searching for—for. . . ."

My stepmother attempted to speak, then fell silent. She, too, seemed perplexed and somewhat ashamed. They all loved Grandmama, but she was *inconvenient*, unsettling.

As for our neighbors, most understood Grandmama to be harmlessly crazy, others that she did indeed make lovely toys but for what purpose?

Why? they asked, and the stories she told me, of the juggler who smiled at her, flashed in my head.

Finally, by their cutting remarks, the family did exert enough pressure so that Grandmama and I no longer openly announced our expeditions. Instead, she took me with her on "shopping trips," ostensibly for clothes or groceries, while in fact we spent most of our time exploring stranger and more distant neighborhoods, searching for splendid junk: jangling pieces of a vase, cranberry glass fragments embossed with leaves, discarded glass beads from Woolworth[3] necklaces. . . . We would sneak them all home in brown rice sacks, folded into small parcels, and put them under her bed. During the day when the family was away at school or work, we brought them out and washed every item in a large black pot of boiling lye[4] and water, dried them quickly, carefully, and returned them, sparkling, under her bed.

Our greatest excitement occurred when a fire gutted the large Chinese Presbyterian Church, three blocks from our house. Over the still-smoking ruins the next day, Grandmama and I rushed precariously over the blackened beams to pick out the stained glass that glittered in the sunlight. Small figure bent over, wrapped against the autumn cold in a dark blue quilted coat, happily gathering each piece like gold, she became my spiritual playmate: "There's a good one! *There!*"

◀ **Vocabulary**
precariously (prē ker′ ē əs lē) *adv.* in a risky way; insecurely

Hours later, soot-covered and smelling of smoke, we came home with a carton full of delicate fragments, still early enough to steal them all into the house and put the small box under her bed. "These are special pieces," she said, giving the box a last push, "because they come from a sacred place." She slowly got up and I saw, for the first time, her hand begin to shake. But then, in her joy, she embraced me. Both of our hearts were racing, as if we were two dreamers. I buried my face in her blue quilt, and for a moment, the whole world seemed silent.

"My juggler," she said, "he never came back to me from Honan[5]. . . perhaps the famine. . . ." Her voice began to quake. "But I shall have my sacred windchime . . . I shall have it again."

◀ **Vocabulary**
famine (fam′ in) *n.* severe shortage of food

One evening, when the family was gathered in their usual places in the parlor, Grandmama gave me her secret nod: a slight wink of her eye and a flaring of her nostrils. There was *trouble* in the air. Supper had gone badly, school examinations were due, father had failed to meet an editorial deadline at the *Vancouver Chinese Times*. A huge sigh came from Sister Liang.

"But it is useless this Chinese they teach you!" she lamented, turning to Stepmother for support. Silence. Liang frowned, dejected, and went back to her Chinese book, bending the covers back.

"Father," Oldest Brother Kiam began, waving his bamboo brush in the air, "you must realize that this Mandarin only confuses us. We are Cantonese[6] speakers. . . ."

---

3. **Woolworth** variety store belonging to the chain founded by Frank Woolworth in 1879.
4. **lye** (lī) *n.* substance derived from wood ashes, commonly used in making soap or for washing.
5. **Honan** (hō′ nän′) province in east central China.
6. **Mandarin** (man′ də rin) **. . . Cantonese** (kan′ tə nēz′) Mandarin is the most commonly spoken form of Chinese; Cantonese is a variety of Chinese spoken in some parts of China, including the cities of Canton and Hong Kong, and by most Chinese emigrants.

"And you do not complain about Latin, French or German in your English school?" Father rattled his newspaper, a signal that his patience was ending.

"But, Father, those languages are *scientific*." Kiam jabbed his brush in the air. "We are now in a scientific, logical world."

Father was silent. We could all hear Grandmama's rocker.

"What about Sek-Lung?" Older Brother Jung pointed angrily at me. "He was sick last year, but this year he should have at least started Chinese school, instead of picking over garbage cans!"

"He starts next year," Father said, in a hard tone that immediately warned everyone to be silent. Liang slammed her book.

Grandmama went on rocking quietly in her chair. She complimented my mother on her knitting, made a remark about the "strong beauty" of Kiam's brushstrokes which, in spite of himself, immensely pleased him. All this babbling noise was her family torn and confused in a strange land: everything here was so very foreign and scientific.

The truth was, I was sorry not to have started school the year before. In my innocence I had imagined going to school meant certain privileges worthy of all my brothers' and sister's complaints. The fact that my lung infection in my fifth and sixth years, mistakenly diagnosed as TB,[7] earned me some reprieve, only made me long for school the more. Each member of the family took turns on Sunday, teaching me or annoying me. But it was the countless hours I spent with Grandmama that were my real education. Tapping me on my head she would say, "Come, Sek-Lung, we have *our* work," and we would walk up the stairs to her small crowded room. There, in the midst of her antique shawls, the old ancestral calligraphy and multi-colored embroidered hangings, beneath the mysterious shelves of sweet herbs and bitter potions, we would continue doing what we had started that morning: the elaborate windchime for her death.

Vocabulary ▶
reprieve (ri prēv′) *n.* temporary relief or escape

"I can't last forever," she declared, when she let me in on the secret of this one. "It will sing and dance and glitter," her long fingers stretched into the air, pantomiming the waving motion of her ghost chimes; "My spirit will hear its sounds and see its light and return to this house and say goodbye to you."

Deftly she reached into the carton she had placed on the chair beside me. She picked out a fish-shape amber piece, and with a long needle-like tool and a steel ruler, she scored[8] it. Pressing the blade of a cleaver against the line, with the fingers of her other hand, she lifted up the glass until it cleanly *snapped* into the exact shape she required. Her hand began to tremble, the tips of her fingers to shiver, like rippling water.

"You see that, Little One?" She held her hand up. "That is my body fighting with Death. He is in this room now."

My eyes darted in panic, but Grandmama remained calm, undisturbed, and went on with her work. Then I remembered the glue and uncorked the jar for her. Soon the graceful ritual movements of her hand returned

---

7. **TB** (tē′ bē′) *n.* abbreviation for *tuberculosis,* a contagious disease that begins in the lungs.
8. **scored** (skôrd) *v.* put a notch or groove in.

to her, and I became lost in the magic of her task: she dabbed a cabalistic[9] mixture of glue on one end and skillfully dropped the braided end of a silk thread into it. This part always amazed me: the braiding would slowly, *very* slowly, *unknot*, fanning out like a prized fishtail. In a few seconds the clear, homemade glue began to harden as I blew lightly over it, welding to itself each separate silk strand.

Each jam-sized pot of glue was precious; each large cork had been wrapped with a fragment of pink silk. I remember this part vividly, because each cork was treated to a special rite. First we went shopping in the best silk stores in Chinatown for the perfect square of silk she required. It had to be a deep pink, a shade of color blushing toward red. And the tone had to match—as closely as possible—her precious jade carving, the small peony of white and light-red jade, her most lucky possession. In the center of this semi-translucent carving, no more than an inch wide, was a pool of pink light, its veins swirling out into the petals of the flower.

"This color is the color of my spirit," she said, holding it up to the window so I could see the delicate pastel against the broad strokes of sunlight. She dropped her voice, and I held my breath at the wonder of the color. "This was given to me by the young actor who taught me how to juggle. He had four of them, and each one had a center of this rare color, the color of Good Fortune." The pendant seemed to pulse as she turned it: "Oh, Sek-Lung! He had white hair and white skin to *his toes!* It's *true,* I saw him bathing." She laughed and blushed, her eyes softened at the memory. The silk had to match the pink heart of her pendant: the color was magical for her, to hold the unraveling strands of her memory. . . .

It was just six months before she died that we really began to work on her last windchime. Three thin bamboo sticks were steamed and bent into circlets; 30 exact lengths of silk thread, the strongest kind, were cut and braided at both ends and glued to stained glass. Her hands worked on their own command, each hand racing with a life of its own: cutting, snapping, braiding, knotting. . . .

Sometimes she breathed heavily and her small body, growing thinner, sagged against me. *Death,* I thought, *He is in this room,* and I would work harder alongside her. For months Grandmama and I did this every other evening, a half dozen pieces each time. The shaking in her hand grew worse, but we said nothing. Finally, after discarding hundreds, she told me she had the necessary 30 pieces. But this time, because it was a sacred chime, I would not be permitted to help her tie it up or have the joy of raising it. "Once tied," she said, holding me against my disappointment, "not even I can raise it. Not a sound must it make until I have died."

"What will happen?"

"Your father will then take the center braided strand and raise it. He will hang it against my bedroom window so that my ghost may see it, and hear it, and return. I must say goodbye to this world properly or wander in this foreign land forever."

---

9. **cabalistic** (kab′ ə lis′ tik) *adj.* relating to a secret or mystical belief or practice.

"You can take the streetcar!" I blurted, suddenly shocked that she actually meant to leave me. I thought I could hear the clear-chromatic chimes, see the shimmering colors on the wall: I fell against her and cried, and there in my crying I knew that she would die. I can still remember the touch of her hand on my head, and the smell of her thick woolen sweater pressed against my face. "I will always be with you, Little Sek-Lung, but in a different way . . . you'll see."

Months went by, and nothing happened. Then one late September evening, when I had just come home from Chinese School, Grandmama was preparing supper when she looked out our kitchen window and saw a cat—a long, lean white cat—jump into our garbage pail and knock it over. She ran out to chase it away, shouting curses at it. She did not have her thick sweater on and when she came back into the house, a chill gripped her. She leaned against the door: "That was not a cat," she said, and the odd tone of her voice caused my father to look with alarm at her. "I can not take back my curses. It is too late." She took hold of my father's arm: "It was all white and had pink eyes like sacred fire."

My father started at this, and they both looked pale. My brothers and sister, clearing the table, froze in their gestures.

"The fog has confused you," Stepmother said. "It was just a cat."

But Grandmama shook her head, for she knew it was a sign. "I will not live forever," she said. "I am prepared."

The next morning she was confined to her bed with a severe cold. Sitting by her, playing with some of my toys, I asked her about the cat: "Why did father jump at the cat with the pink eyes? He didn't see it, you did."

"But he and your mother know what it means."

"What?"

"My friend, the juggler, the magician, was as pale as white jade, and he had pink eyes." I thought she would begin to tell me one of her stories, a tale of enchantment or of a wondrous adventure, but she only paused to swallow; her eyes glittered, lost in memory. She took my hand, gently opening and closing her fingers over it. "Sek-Lung," she sighed, "*he* has come back to me."

Then Grandmama sank back into her pillow and the embroidered flowers lifted to frame her wrinkled face. I saw her hand over my own, and my own began to tremble. I fell fitfully asleep by her side. When I woke up it was dark and her bed was empty. She had been taken to the hospital and I was not permitted to visit.

A few days after that she died of the complications of pneumonia. Immediately after her death my father came home and said nothing to us, but walked up the stairs to her room, pulled aside the drawn lace curtains of her window and lifted the windchimes to the sky.

I began to cry and quickly put my hand in my pocket for a handkerchief. Instead, caught between my fingers, was the small, round firmness of the jade peony. In my mind's eye I saw Grandmama smile and heard, softly, the pink center beat like a beautiful, cramped heart.

Close Reading Activities

Read

Comprehension: **Key Idea and Details**

1. **(a)** Citing details from the story, explain who gave the grandmother her first wind chime. **(b) Analyze Cause and Effect:** Using this information, explain why the making of wind chimes is so important to the grandmother in her later years.
2. **(a)** What is the main conflict between the grandmother and her family? **(b) Interpret:** How is this conflict resolved?
3. **(a) Compare and Contrast:** How do Sek-Lung's reactions to his grandmother's activities differ from those of other family members? **(b) Analyze:** How do you account for these differences? Cite details from the story to support your ideas.
4. **Summarize:** Write a brief, objective summary of the story. Describe the important characters, events, and details but do not state your opinion.

Text Analysis: **Craft and Structure**

5. **(a)** Who is the narrator of this story? **(b) Analyze:** How does the narrator's point of view shape what you, the reader, learn about the characters and events? Explain, citing specific passages from the story.
6. **(a) Describe:** How does the narrator describe the grandmother's physical appearance? Cite specific details. **(b) Interpret:** How does the physical description of the grandmother contribute to your understanding of her character?
7. **(a) Describe:** How does the narrator describe aspects of the setting, such as the grandmother's bedroom? Cite specific details. **(b) Interpret:** In what ways do details in the setting help to develop the characters?
8. **(a)** At what points in the story does the author introduce flashbacks? **(b) Distinguish:** Identify the mechanism—such as a memory or a dream—the author uses to introduce each flashback. **(c) Analyze:** What information does each flashback provide?

Connections: **Integration of Knowledge and Ideas**

Discuss

Conduct a **small-group discussion** about the use of symbols in this story. For example, consider the symbolic meanings of the jade peony or the white cat.

Research

Wayson Choy was influenced by the traditional Chinese tales he heard as a boy. Briefly research the types of stories Choy probably heard as he grew up. In particular, consider the following story elements:

a. attitudes toward elders and children

b. beliefs about death

c. presence of magical animals or objects

Take notes as you perform your research. Then, write a brief **explanation** of ways in which qualities typical of Chinese traditional tales are also found in "The Jade Peony."

Write

A good story will often express more than one theme. For example, one theme of "The Jade Peony" relates to mortality while another addresses the power of love. Write an **essay** in which you identify a key theme expressed in this story and explain how that theme is developed throughout the text. Cite details from the story to support your analysis.

THE BIG ?

Is conflict necessary?

Consider the conflict between cultures that is portrayed in "The Jade Peony." Does the narrator, Sek-Lung, grow from the challenges these conflicts present? Explain your answer.

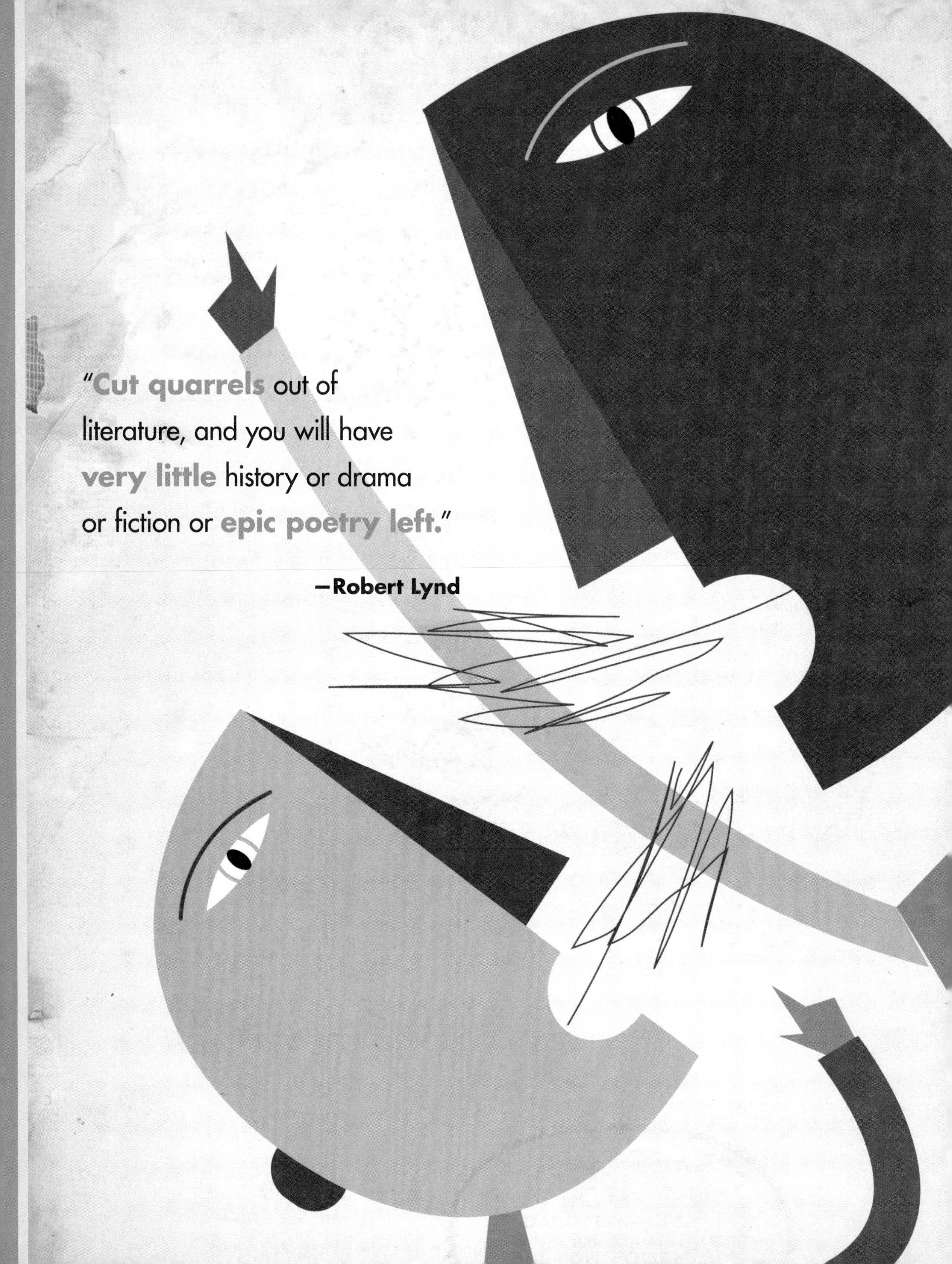
"Cut quarrels out of
literature, and you will have
very little history or drama
or fiction or epic poetry left."
—Robert Lynd

PART 2

TEXT ANALYSIS GUIDED EXPLORATION

FACING CONFLICT

Conflict is the fuel that starts the engine of a plot and keeps it going. In the selections that follow, some characters face life or death struggles, while others face subtler problems. The ways in which characters respond to conflicts reveal what they feel, think, want, and value. Those responses also suggest whether the character will learn and grow or remain the same. As you read, consider the conflicts these literary works explore and decide whether each one leads to characters' change or growth. In what ways do these selections answer the Big Question for this unit: **Is conflict necessary?**

◀ CRITICAL VIEWING What story could you tell to accompany this image? Is the illustration and the story it suggests more or less compelling because it depicts a quarrel? Explain.

READINGS IN PART 2

CLOSE READING TOOL

Use the **Close Reading Tool** to practice the strategies you learn in this unit.

Focus on Craft and Structure

Elements of a Short Story

In a short story, **characters**, **setting**, **plot**, and **conflict** combine to create a unified impression, or **main effect**.

Short stories are brief fictional narratives intended to be read in a single sitting. Because of a short story's length, the narration and character portrayals must be focused and compressed, adding a special energy and depth to the form. As a result, a good short story leaves the reader with a unified, strong impression—its **main effect.** Each element of a story can contribute to this effect.

Characters The **characters** are the people or animals who take part in the action of the story. Details in the story help readers understand characters' **traits,** or qualities, and **motives,** or reasons for acting. The main effect of a story often involves a change or revelation that a character experiences.

Setting The **setting** of a story is the time and place of its action. Often, a short story takes place in a single, unified setting. The setting often contributes to a story's **mood**—the general feeling the story conveys.

Plot The **plot** of a story is the sequence of events it tells. Plot often contributes to the unified effect of a story by building toward a **climax,** or turning point, in which a character reaches an insight or undergoes a change.

Conflict A plot is driven by a **conflict,** or struggle between two opposing forces. Short stories usually focus on one central conflict.

- An **internal conflict** takes place in the mind of a character. The character struggles to make a decision or overcome feelings.
- An **external conflict** takes place between a character and an outside force, such as another character or a force of nature.

Theme and Symbols As the elements of a story combine to create a unified effect, they also suggest a **theme,** or insight into life. Most often, readers come to understand the theme by making inferences from key elements, including symbols. A **symbol** is an object or a story element that stands for a larger meaning.

The elements of a short story are interrelated and contribute to a unified effect.

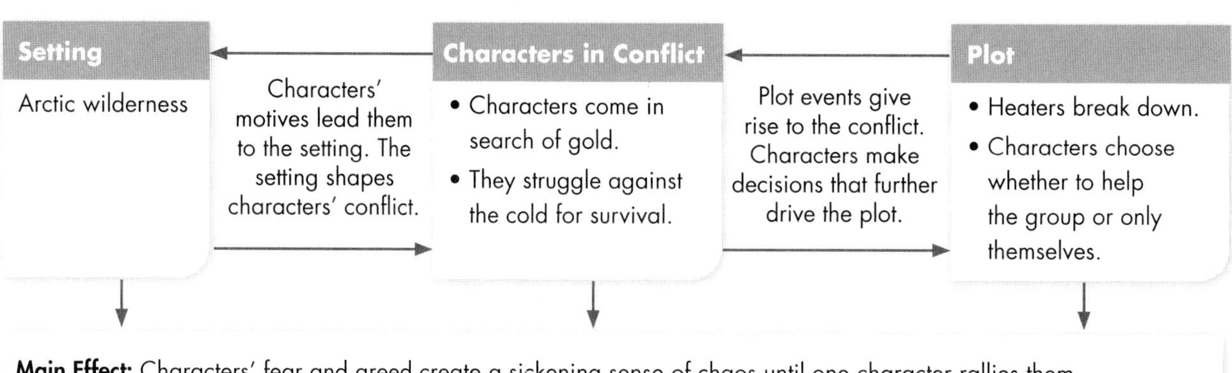
Setting
Arctic wilderness
Characters' motives lead them to the setting. The setting shapes characters' conflict.
Characters in Conflict
• Characters come in search of gold.
• They struggle against the cold for survival.
Plot events give rise to the conflict. Characters make decisions that further drive the plot.
Plot
• Heaters break down.
• Characters choose whether to help the group or only themselves.
Main Effect: Characters' fear and greed create a sickening sense of chaos until one character rallies them.

Plot Structure in a Short Story

Most stories share a basic plot structure. Understanding this structure can help you appreciate how a short story builds to a satisfying conclusion.

In the section of the plot called the **exposition,** the author introduces the setting and the characters. This section often includes an **inciting incident**—an event that establishes the **conflict,** or struggle between opposing forces, that drives the story. Types of conflicts include:

- a struggle between two characters;
- a struggle between a character and an outside force, such as nature;
- a struggle within the mind of a character, such as a battle with guilt.

The next part of a typical plot is the **rising action,** which includes events and complications that intensify the conflict. The rising action leads to the **climax,** which is the turning point in the story—the moment of highest tension or suspense. The climax is the part of the story that makes readers want to read on to find out what happens next.

The **falling action** sets up the story's ending. The intensity of the conflict lessens and events wind down, leading to the **resolution,** or **denouement,** which shows the outcome of the conflict. In some stories, the conflict is settled, meaning that the central problem is solved; in other stories, the conflict may be left unsettled. In still other stories, the ending may revisit the characters after time has passed to show how the situation changes after the conflict is resolved. Look at the example in the chart below.

Reading Literature

3. Analyze how complex characters develop over the course of a text, interact with other characters, and advance the plot or develop the theme.

5. Analyze how an author's choices concerning how to structure a text, order events within it, and manipulate time create such effects as mystery, tension, or surprise.

Example: Plot Structure

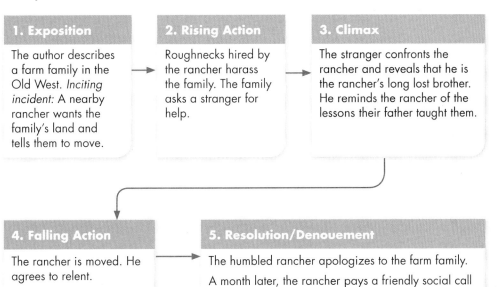

1. Exposition
The author describes a farm family in the Old West. *Inciting incident:* A nearby rancher wants the family's land and tells them to move.

2. Rising Action
Roughnecks hired by the rancher harass the family. The family asks a stranger for help.

3. Climax
The stranger confronts the rancher and reveals that he is the rancher's long lost brother. He reminds the rancher of the lessons their father taught them.

4. Falling Action
The rancher is moved. He agrees to relent.

5. Resolution/Denouement
The humbled rancher apologizes to the farm family.

A month later, the rancher pays a friendly social call on the farm family.

Analyzing Character, Structure, and Theme

An author develops **characters** in ways that advance a story's **plot** and **structures** a story in ways that create interest and help develop the **theme**.

Developing Complex Characters

In the best short stories, the main characters are interesting and **complex,** or well-rounded. Complex characters share these qualities:

- They show multiple or even contradictory **traits,** or qualities.
- They struggle with conflicting **motivations,** or reasons for acting as they do.
- They may change by the end of the story.

Example: Complex Character

Contradictory Traits Bob's ability to organize ideas leads the debate team to victory—but his room is a mess.

Conflicting Motives After high school, Bob wants to stay near his friends; he also wants to go to the best college he can.

Change After making a new friend on a trip, Bob decides he will move away for college.

Characterization To create and **develop** a character, a writer will use techniques of **characterization.**

- In **direct characterization,** the narrator makes direct statements about a character's personality: *Afshin focused on just one thing at a time, but the depth of his focus was remarkable. Before a race, his single-minded trance could only be broken by the sound of the starter's whistle.*
- In **indirect characterization**, readers learn what characters are like by analyzing what they say and do as well as how other characters respond to them: *Summer or winter, in sun, wind, or rain, Jess rose before dawn and jogged the two-mile loop around the reservoir. After a quick shower and two chocolate donuts, she always felt ready to face the day.*

How Characters Advance a Story

Characters Advance the Plot As characters interact with one another and struggle to overcome problems, their choices move the story along. A character's action—or decision *not* to take action—can lead to new plot developments and may intensify the conflict, heightening tension or suspense in the story.

Example: Intensified Conflict

Conflict Cindy is friendly with Matilda. Cindy's friends Staci and Ashley do not like Matilda and put pressure on Cindy to shun her.

Characters' Interactions Cindy decides that Staci and Ashley are being unfair and makes a point of attending a school game with Matilda.

Result: Intensified Conflict Staci and Ashley invite everyone to their party except Cindy.

Characters Develop Theme As in real life, a character's struggles with a situation can teach a general lesson. In this way, characters help develop a story's **theme**—the central insight that it conveys. As you read a short story, pay close attention to the ways that characters change and to the lessons that they learn. These details will point you toward the story's theme.

Example: Theme

Character's Experience After struggling to please her friends, Cindy realizes that they are shallow and decides to let them go.

Theme As people grow, they may outgrow their friendships with others.

Structuring a Text For Effect

The way in which an author structures or organizes information in a story can create effects like tension, mystery, and surprise.

Plot Structure Authors make decisions about the order in which to present information as well as the pacing of events.

- **Openings** The opening establishes the general feeling of a story.

Examples of Some Story Openings

Focus on Setting: *The hospital waiting room was empty at that hour of the night. It was so quiet I could hear the second hand on the large wall clock toll each passing second.*

Focus on Character: *I'll never forget my grandfather. He was the most charming man I ever met.*

in medias res (Latin for "in the middle of things"): *"Someone call for help!" shouted a man at the side of the road.*

- **Sequence** Narrators tell plot events mainly in **chronological order**—the order in which events occurred. However, they may break from chronological order for effect. **Flashbacks** are sections of a narrative that describe a time before the present time of the story. A flashback might give insight into a character's motivations. **Foreshadowing** gives readers hints about what will happen later in the story, as when a narrator says, "That would be the last time they spoke." Foreshadowing can create **suspense,** or a reader's feeling of anxious uncertainty about the outcome.
- **Pacing** refers to the "speed" with which a narrator relates events. For example, by describing a scene at length and giving many descriptive details, the narrator "slows down" the pace. This effect can be used to heighten suspense, as in the following example:

Example: Slow Pace

Beads of sweat stood out on Agent Vole's forehead. As he struggled with the ropes that bound him, he could hear each beat of his heart, rapid but distinct. Ba-dum, ba-dum. With each beat, the second hand on the timing device clicked one notch closer to catastrophe.

- A narrative can also create a sensation of "speed" and excitement by moving quickly from one idea to another in a scene that is loaded with tension.

Point of View The **point of view,** or narrative perspective, from which a story is told determines the information an author includes. There are three main points of view:

- **Third-person omniscient:** The narrator is outside the events of the story and tells the thoughts and feelings of all characters.
- **Third-person limited:** The narrator is outside the story but tells the thoughts and feelings of only one character.
- **First-person:** The narrator is a character in the story and uses the pronouns *I* and *me*.

Point of view can be used to achieve striking effects. For example, if the first-person narrator is naive, or unsophisticated, the reader may know more about what is going on than the narrator, creating an effect known as **dramatic irony.**

Building Knowledge

Meet the Author

Richard Connell (1893–1949) seemed destined to become a writer: he was a sports reporter at the age of ten! At sixteen, he was editing his father's newspaper, the *Poughkeepsie News-Press*, in upstate New York. Connell attended Harvard University, where he worked on the *Daily Crimson* and the *Lampoon*, an early version of the humor magazine *National Lampoon*. During World War I, Connell edited his army division's newspaper.

Common Core State Standards

Reading Literature

1. Cite strong and thorough textual evidence to support analysis of what the text says explicitly as well as inferences drawn from the text.

5. Analyze how an author's choices concerning how to structure a text, order events within it, and manipulate time create such effects as mystery, tension, or surprise.

Language

6. Acquire and use accurately grade-appropriate general academic and domain-specific words and phrases; gather vocabulary knowledge when considering a word or phrase important to comprehension or expression.

Is conflict necessary?

Explore the Big Question as you read "The Most Dangerous Game." Take notes on ways in which the story explores the nature of conflict.

CLOSE READING FOCUS

Key Ideas and Details: **Make Inferences**

Inferences are logical guesses a reader makes about information that is not directly stated in a text. When you make inferences, you use details from a text as clues to develop ideas about unstated information. To make inferences as you read a story, for example, you might ask questions such as the following:

- What does this detail suggest about the reasons for a character's thoughts, actions, or words?
- What does this detail suggest about the nature of the relationship between two characters?
- What does this passage say about the character's unstated feelings?

As you read this story, make inferences by paying attention to even small details and noting the larger ideas they suggest.

Craft and Structure: **Conflict**

Conflict is a struggle between opposing forces. It is the engine that drives the plot of all stories.

- **Internal conflict** occurs when a character grapples with his or her own opposing feelings, beliefs, needs, or desires.
- **External conflict** occurs when a character clashes with an outside force, such as another character, society, or nature.

In most stories, the ending of a conflict comes at the end in the section of the plot called the *resolution*.

Vocabulary

You will encounter the following words in this story. Decide whether you know each word well, know it a little bit, or do not know it at all. After you have read the selection, see how your knowledge of each word has increased.

palpable **indolently** **naive**
scruples **grotesque** **futile**

CLOSE READING MODEL

The passage below is from Richard Connell's short story "The Most Dangerous Game." The annotations to the right of the passage show ways in which you can use close reading skills to make inferences and analyze conflict.

from "The Most Dangerous Game"

"Off there to the right—somewhere—is a large island," said Whitney. "It's rather a mystery[1] —"

"What island is it?" Rainsford asked.

"The old charts call it 'Ship-Trap Island,'"[2] Whitney replied. "A suggestive name, isn't it? Sailors have a curious dread[1] of the place. I don't know why. Some superstition[1]—"

"Can't see it," remarked Rainsford, trying to peer through the dank tropical night[3] that was palpable as it pressed its thick warm blackness in upon the yacht.[3]

"You've good eyes," said Whitney, with a laugh, "and I've seen you pick off a moose moving in the brown fall bush[4] at four hundred yards, but even you can't see four miles or so through a moonless Caribbean night."

"Not four yards," admitted Rainsford. "Ugh! It's like moist black velvet."

"It will be light in Rio," promised Whitney. "We should make it in a few days. I hope the jaguar guns have come from Purdey's. We should have some good hunting up the Amazon. Great sport, hunting."

"The best sport in the world," agreed Rainsford.

Make Inferences

1 Whitney uses the words *mystery, curious dread,* and *superstition* to describe an island. You can infer from these word choices that the island has a dark, or sinister, history.

Conflict

2 The text reveals that the island is named "Ship-Trap Island," and that sailors dread the place. This information raises questions that may be related to the conflict: How did the island earn this name? Who or what trapped the ships?

Conflict

3 The setting is a yacht on a dank and dark tropical night. The men are having trouble seeing where they are going. These potentially dangerous conditions may lead to a larger conflict.

Make Inferences

4 Whitney has seen Rainsford "pick off a moose in the brown fall bush." Since a moose is brown, it would be very hard to see against brown foliage. This detail suggests that Rainsford is an excellent hunter.

The Most Dangerous Game

Richard Connell

"Off there to the right—

somewhere— is a large island," said Whitney. "It's rather a mystery —"

"What island is it?" Rainsford asked.

"The old charts call it 'Ship-Trap Island,'" Whitney replied. "A suggestive name, isn't it? Sailors have a curious dread of the place. I don't know why. Some superstition—"

"Can't see it," remarked Rainsford, trying to peer through the dank tropical night that was palpable as it pressed its thick warm blackness in upon the yacht.

"You've good eyes," said Whitney, with a laugh, "and I've seen you pick off a moose moving in the brown fall bush at four hundred yards, but even you can't see four miles or so through a moonless Caribbean[1] night."

"Not four yards," admitted Rainsford. "Ugh! It's like moist black velvet."

"It will be light in Rio," promised Whitney. "We should make it in a few days. I hope the jaguar guns have come from Purdey's. We should have some good hunting up the Amazon. Great sport, hunting."

"The best sport in the world," agreed Rainsford.

"For the hunter," amended Whitney. "Not for the jaguar."

"Don't talk rot, Whitney," said Rainsford. "You're a big-game hunter, not a philosopher. Who cares how a jaguar feels?"

◄ **Critical Viewing**
Based on the details in this image, what do you think this story will be about?

◄ **Vocabulary**
palpable (pal′ pə bəl) *adj.* able to be felt; easily perceived

Comprehension
What do Rainsford and Whitney see from the ship?

---

1. **Caribbean** (kar′ ə bē′ ən) the Caribbean Sea, a part of the Atlantic Ocean, bounded by the north coast of South America, Central America, and the West Indies.

Conflict
How does Rainsford's attitude about hunting differ from Whitney's?

Critical Viewing ▼
In what ways does this image differ from the Caribbean Sea as it is described in the story? In what ways is it similar?

"Perhaps the jaguar does," observed Whitney.

"Bah! They've no understanding."

"Even so, I rather think they understand one thing—fear. The fear of pain and the fear of death."

"Nonsense," laughed Rainsford. "This hot weather is making you soft, Whitney. Be a realist. The world is made up of two classes—the hunters and the huntees. Luckily, you and I are the hunters. Do you think we've passed that island yet?"

"I can't tell in the dark. I hope so."

"Why?" asked Rainsford.

"The place has a reputation—a bad one."

"Cannibals?" suggested Rainsford.

"Hardly. Even cannibals wouldn't live in such a God-forsaken place. But it's gotten into sailor lore, somehow. Didn't you notice that the crew's nerves seemed a bit jumpy today?"

"They were a bit strange, now you mention it. Even Captain Nielsen—"

"Yes, even that tough-minded old Swede, who'd go up to the devil himself and ask him for a light. Those fishy blue eyes held a look I never saw there before. All I could get out of him was: 'This place has an evil name among sea-faring men, sir.' Then he said to me, very gravely: 'Don't you feel anything?'—as if the air about us was actually poisonous. Now, you mustn't laugh when I tell you this—I did feel something like a sudden chill.

"There was no breeze. The sea was as flat as a plate-glass window. We were drawing near the island then. What I felt was a—a mental chill; a sort of sudden dread."

"Pure imagination," said Rainsford. "One superstitious sailor can taint the whole ship's company with his fear."

"Maybe. But sometimes I think sailors have an extra sense that tells them when they are in danger. Sometimes I think evil is a tangible thing—with wave lengths, just as sound and light have. An evil place can, so to speak, broadcast vibrations of evil. Anyhow, I'm glad we're getting out of this zone. Well, I think I'll turn in now, Rainsford."

"I'm not sleepy," said Rainsford. "I'm going to smoke another pipe on the afterdeck."

"Good night, then, Rainsford. See you at breakfast."

"Right. Good night, Whitney."

There was no sound in the night as Rainsford sat there, but the muffled throb of the engine that drove the yacht swiftly through the darkness, and the swish and ripple of the wash of the propeller.

Rainsford, reclining in a steamer chair, **indolently** puffed on his favorite brier. The sensuous drowsiness of the night was on him. "It's so dark," he thought, "that I could sleep without closing my eyes; the night would be my eyelids—"

◀ **Vocabulary**
indolently (in′ də lənt lē) *adv.* lazily; idly

An abrupt sound startled him. Off to the right he heard it, and his ears, expert in such matters, could not be mistaken. Again he heard the sound, and again. Somewhere, off in the blackness, someone had fired a gun three times.

Rainsford sprang up and moved quickly to the rail, mystified. He strained his eyes in the direction from which the reports had come, but it was like trying to see through a blanket. He leaped upon the rail and balanced himself there, to get greater elevation; his pipe, striking a rope, was knocked from his mouth. He lunged for it; a short, hoarse cry came from his lips as he realized he had reached too far and had lost his balance. The cry was pinched off short as the blood-warm waters of the Caribbean Sea closed over his head.

Comprehension
What "two classes" does Rainsford believe make up the world?

Conflict
With what external conflict is Rainsford suddenly confronted?

He struggled up to the surface and tried to cry out, but the wash from the speeding yacht slapped him in the face and the salt water in his open mouth made him gag and strangle. Desperately he struck out with strong strokes after the receding lights of the yacht, but he stopped before he had swum fifty feet. A certain cool-headedness had come to him; it was not the first time he had been in a tight place. There was a chance that his cries could be heard by someone aboard the yacht, but that chance was slender, and grew more slender as the yacht raced on. He wrestled himself out of his clothes, and shouted with all his power. The lights of the yacht became faint and ever-vanishing fireflies; then they were blotted out entirely by the night.

Rainsford remembered the shots. They had come from the right, and doggedly he swam in that direction, swimming with slow, deliberate strokes, conserving his strength. For a seemingly endless time he fought the sea. He began to count his strokes; he could do possibly a hundred more and then—

Rainsford heard a sound. It came out of the darkness, a high screaming sound, the sound of an animal in an extremity of anguish and terror.

He did not recognize the animal that made the sound; he did not try to; with fresh vitality he swam toward the sound. He heard it again; then it was cut short by another noise, crisp, staccato.

"Pistol shot," muttered Rainsford, swimming on.

Ten minutes of determined effort brought another sound to his ears—the most welcome he had ever heard—the muttering and growling of the sea breaking on a rocky shore. He was almost on the rocks before he saw them; on a night less calm he would have been shattered against them. With his remaining strength he dragged himself from the swirling waters. Jagged crags appeared to jut into the opaqueness, he forced himself upward, hand over hand. Gasping, his hands raw, he reached a flat place at the top. Dense jungle came down to the very edge of the cliffs. What perils that tangle of trees and underbrush might hold for him did not concern Rainsford just then. All he knew was that he was safe from his enemy, the sea, and that utter weariness was on him. He flung himself down at the jungle edge and tumbled headlong into the deepest sleep of his life.

When he opened his eyes he knew from the position of the sun that it was late in the afternoon. Sleep had given him new vigor; a sharp hunger was picking at him. He looked about him, almost cheerfully.

"Where there are pistol shots, there are men. Where there are men, there is food," he thought. But what kind of men, he

Critical Viewing ▶
What does the wildness of the island in the picture tell you about the island itself?

wondered, in so forbidding a place? An unbroken front of snarled and ragged jungle fringed the shore.

He saw no sign of a trail through the closely knit web of weeds and trees; it was easier to go along the shore, and Rainsford floundered along by the water. Not far from where he had landed, he stopped.

Some wounded thing, by the evidence a large animal, had thrashed about in the underbrush; the jungle weeds were crushed down and the moss was lacerated; one patch of weeds was stained crimson. A small, glittering object not far away caught Rainsford's eye and he picked it up. It was an empty cartridge.

"A twenty-two," he remarked. "That's odd. It must have been a fairly large animal too. The hunter had his nerve with him to tackle it with a light gun. It's clear that the brute put up a fight. I suppose the first three shots I heard was when the hunter flushed his quarry and wounded it. The last shot was when he trailed it here and finished it."

Make Inferences
What inferences does Rainsford make based on the evidence of pistol shots?

Comprehension
As Rainsford swims for shore, what sounds does he hear coming out of the darkness?

He examined the ground closely and found what he had hoped to find—the print of hunting boots. They pointed along the cliff in the direction he had been going. Eagerly he hurried along, now slipping on a rotten log or a loose stone, but making headway; night was beginning to settle down on the island.

Bleak darkness was blacking out the sea and jungle when Rainsford sighted the lights. He came upon them as he turned a crook in the coast line, and his first thought was that he had come upon a village, for there were many lights. But as he forged along he saw to his great astonishment that all the lights were in one enormous building—a lofty structure with pointed towers plunging upward into the gloom. His eyes made out the shadowy outlines of a palatial château;[2] it was set on a high bluff, and on three sides of it cliffs dived down to where the sea licked greedy lips in the shadows.

"Mirage," thought Rainsford. But it was no mirage, he found, when he opened the tall spiked iron gate. The stone steps were real enough; the massive door with a leering gargoyle[3] for a knocker was real enough; yet about it all hung an air of unreality.

He lifted the knocker, and it creaked up stiffly, as if it had never before been used. He let it fall, and it startled him with its booming loudness. He thought he heard steps within; the door remained closed. Again Rainsford lifted the heavy knocker, and let it fall. The door opened then, opened as suddenly as if it were on a spring, and Rainsford stood blinking in the river of glaring gold light that poured out. The first thing Rainsford's eyes discerned was the largest man Rainsford had ever seen—a gigantic creature, solidly made and black-bearded to the waist. In his hand the man held a long-barreled revolver, and he was pointing it straight at Rainsford's heart.

Out of the snarl of beard two small eyes regarded Rainsford.

"Don't be alarmed," said Rainsford, with a smile which he hoped was disarming. "I'm no robber. I fell off a yacht. My name is Sanger Rainsford of New York City."

The menacing look in the eyes did not change. The revolver pointed as rigidly as if the giant were a statue. He gave no sign that he understood Rainsford's words, or that he had even heard them. He was dressed in uniform, a black uniform trimmed with gray astrakhan.[4]

Make Inferences
Which details here lead you to infer that the two men Rainsford meets have a shared military past? Explain.

"I'm Sanger Rainsford of New York," Rainsford began again. "I fell off a yacht. I am hungry."

The man's only answer was to raise with his thumb the hammer of his revolver. Then Rainsford saw the man's free hand go to his forehead in a military salute, and he saw him click his heels together and stand at attention. Another man was coming down

---

2. **palatial** (pə lā´ shəl) **château** (sha tō´) a mansion as luxurious as a palace.
3. **gargoyle** (gär´ goil´) *n.* distorted animal sculpture projecting from a building.
4. **astrakhan** (as´ trə kən) *n.* loosely curled fur made from the skins of very young lambs.

the broad marble steps, an erect, slender man in evening clothes. He advanced to Rainsford and held out his hand.

In a cultivated voice marked by a slight accent that gave it added precision and deliberateness, he said: "It is a very great pleasure and honor to welcome Mr. Sanger Rainsford, the celebrated hunter, to my home."

Automatically Rainsford shook the man's hand.

"I've read your book about hunting snow leopards in Tibet, you see," explained the man. "I am General Zaroff."

Rainsford's first impression was that the man was singularly handsome; his second was that there was an original, almost bizarre quality about the general's face. He was a tall man past middle age, for his hair was a vivid white; but his thick eyebrows and pointed military mustache were as black as the night from which Rainsford had come. His eyes, too, were black and very bright. He had high cheek bones, a sharp-cut nose, a spare, dark face, the face of a man used to giving orders, the face of an aristocrat. Turning to the giant in uniform, the general made a sign. The giant put away his pistol, saluted, withdrew.

"Ivan is an incredibly strong fellow," remarked the general, "but he has the misfortune to be deaf and dumb. A simple fellow, but, I'm afraid, like all his race, a bit of a savage."

"Is he Russian?"

"He is a Cossack," said the general, and his smile showed red lips and pointed teeth. "So am I."

"Come," he said, "we shouldn't be chatting here. We can talk later. Now you want clothes, food, rest. You shall have them. This is a most restful spot."

Ivan had reappeared, and the general spoke to him with lips that moved but gave forth no sound.

"Follow Ivan, if you please, Mr. Rainsford," said the general. "I was about to have my dinner when you came. I'll wait for you. You'll find that my clothes will fit you, I think."

It was to a huge, beam-ceilinged bedroom with a canopied bed big enough for six men that Rainsford followed the silent giant. Ivan laid out an evening suit, and Rainsford, as he put it on, noticed that it came from a London tailor who ordinarily cut and sewed for none below the rank of duke.

The dining room to which Ivan conducted him was in many ways remarkable. There was a medieval magnificence about it; it suggested a baronial hall of feudal times with its oaken panels,

LITERATURE IN CONTEXT

History Connection

Cossacks

Ivan and Zaroff are Cossacks, members of a people from southern Russia who also made up a special Russian military unit. As a group, Cossacks were famous for their fierceness, and the soldiers enjoyed a privileged status. Because of their elite position, these soldiers were also fiercely independent. When the czar—the ruler of Russia—was overthrown in the Russian Revolution of 1917, Cossacks like Zaroff were executed or forced into exile. As a Cossack, Zaroff is unwilling to acknowledge that the rules of ordinary people apply to him.

Connect to the Literature

What traits does Zaroff exhibit that might be due, in part, to his having been a Cossack?

◀ **Czar Nicholas II,** overthrown in the Russian Revolution of 1917

Comprehension

What type of building does Rainsford encounter on the island he reaches?

its high ceiling, its vast refectory table where twoscore men could sit down to eat. About the hall were the mounted heads of many animals—lions, tigers, elephants, moose, bears; larger or more perfect specimens Rainsford had never seen. At the great table the general was sitting, alone.

"You'll have a cocktail, Mr. Rainsford," he suggested. The cocktail was surpassingly good; and, Rainsford noted, the table appointments were of the finest—the linen, the crystal, the silver, the china.

They were eating *borsch,* the rich, red soup with whipped cream so dear to Russian palates. Half apologetically General Zaroff said: "We do our best to preserve the amenities of civilization here. Please forgive any lapses. We are well off the beaten track, you know. Do you think the champagne has suffered from its long ocean trip?"

Conflict
Explain how Rainsford's discomfort in this passage is both an internal and an external conflict.

"Not in the least," declared Rainsford. He was finding the general a most thoughtful and affable host, a true cosmopolite.[5] But there was one small trait of the general's that made Rainsford uncomfortable. Whenever he looked up from his plate he found the general studying him, appraising him narrowly.

"Perhaps," said General Zaroff, "you were surprised that I recognized your name. You see, I read all books on hunting published in English, French, and Russian. I have but one passion in my life, Mr. Rainsford, and it is the hunt."

"You have some wonderful heads here," said Rainsford as he ate a particularly well cooked filet mignon. "That Cape buffalo is the largest I ever saw."

"Oh, that fellow. Yes, he was a monster."

"Did he charge you?"

"Hurled me against a tree," said the general. "Fractured my skull. But I got the brute."

"I've always thought," said Rainsford, "that the Cape buffalo is the most dangerous of all big game."

For a moment the general did not reply; he was smiling his curious red-lipped smile. Then he said slowly: "No. You are wrong, sir. The Cape buffalo is not the most dangerous big game." He sipped his wine. "Here in my preserve on this island," he said in the same slow tone, "I hunt more dangerous game."

Rainsford expressed his surprise. "Is there big game on this island?"

The general nodded. "The biggest."

"Really?"

"Oh, it isn't here naturally, of course. I have to stock the island."

"What have you imported, general?" Rainsford asked. "Tigers?"

---

5. **cosmopolite** (käz mäp´ ə līt´) *n.* person at home in all parts of the world.

The general smiled. "No," he said. "Hunting tigers ceased to interest me some years ago. I exhausted their possibilities, you see. No thrill left in tigers, no real danger. I live for danger, Mr. Rainsford."

The general took from his pocket a gold cigarette case and offered his guest a long black cigarette with a silver tip; it was perfumed and gave off a smell like incense.

"We will have some capital hunting, you and I," said the general. "I shall be most glad to have your society."

"But what game—" began Rainsford.

"I'll tell you," said the general. "You will be amused, I know. I think I may say, in all modesty, that I have done a rare thing. I have invented a new sensation. May I pour you another glass of port, Mr. Rainsford?"

"Thank you, general."

The general filled both glasses, and said: "God makes some men poets. Some He makes kings, some beggars. Me He made a hunter. My hand was made for the trigger, my father said. He was a very rich man with a quarter of a million acres in the Crimea,[6] and he was an ardent sportsman. When I was only five years old he gave me a little gun, specially made in Moscow for me, to shoot sparrows with. When I shot some of his prize turkeys with it, he did not punish me; he complimented me on my marksmanship. I killed my first bear in the Caucasus[7] when I was ten. My whole life has been one prolonged hunt. I went into the army—it was expected of noblemen's sons—and for a time commanded a division of Cossack cavalry, but my real interest was always the hunt. I have hunted every kind of game in every land. It would be impossible for me to tell you how many animals I have killed."

The general puffed at his cigarette.

"After the debacle[8] in Russia I left the country, for it was imprudent for an officer of the Czar to stay there. Many noble Russians lost everything. I, luckily, had invested heavily in American securities, so I shall never have to open a tea room in Monte Carlo or drive a taxi in Paris. Naturally, I continued to hunt—grizzlies in your Rockies, crocodiles in the Ganges, rhinoceroses in East Africa. It was in Africa that the Cape buffalo hit me and laid me up for six months. As soon as I recovered I started for the Amazon to hunt jaguars, for I had heard they were unusually cunning. They weren't." The Cossack sighed. "They were no match at all for a hunter with his wits about him, and a high-

"Here in my preserve on this island," he said in the same slow tone, "I hunt more dangerous game."

Make Inferences
How do the details about Zaroff's life support the inference that he feels neither guilt nor fear concerning hunting?

Comprehension
Why does Zaroff recognize Rainsford's name?

---

6. **Crimea** (krī mē′ ə) region in southwestern Ukraine extending into the Black Sea.
7. **Caucasus** (kô′ kə səs) mountain range between the Black and Caspian seas.
8. **debacle** (di bä′ kəl) *n.* bad defeat (Zaroff is referring to the Russian Revolution of 1917, a defeat for upper-class Russians like himself).

powered rifle. I was bitterly disappointed. I was lying in my tent with a splitting headache one night when a terrible thought pushed its way into my mind. Hunting was beginning to bore me! And hunting, remember, had been my life. I have heard that in America business men often go to pieces when they give up the business that has been their life."

"Yes, that's so," said Rainsford.

The general smiled. "I had no wish to go to pieces," he said. "I must do something. Now, mine is an analytical mind, Mr. Rainsford. Doubtless that is why I enjoy the problems of the chase."

"No doubt, General Zaroff."

"So," continued the general, "I asked myself why the hunt no longer fascinated me. You are much younger than I am, Mr. Rainsford, and have not hunted as much, but you perhaps can guess the answer."

"What was it?"

"Simply this: hunting had ceased to be what you call 'a sporting proposition.' It had become too easy. I always got my quarry. Always. There is no greater bore than perfection."

The general lit a fresh cigarette.

Conflict
How was the "tragic moment" Zaroff refers to the sign of an internal conflict?

"No animal had a chance with me any more. That is no boast; it is a mathematical certainty. The animal had nothing but his legs and his instinct. Instinct is no match for reason. When I thought of this it was a tragic moment for me, I can tell you."

Rainsford leaned across the table, absorbed in what his host was saying.

"It came to me as an inspiration what I must do," the general went on.

"And that was?"

The general smiled the quiet smile of one who has faced an obstacle and surmounted it with success. "I had to invent a new animal to hunt," he said.

"A new animal? You're joking."

"Not at all," said the general. "I never joke about hunting. I needed a new animal. I found one. So I bought this island, built this house, and here I do my hunting. The island is perfect for my purpose—there are jungles with a maze of trails in them, hills, swamps—"

"But the animal, General Zaroff?"

"Oh," said the general, "it supplies me with the most exciting hunting in the world. No other hunting compares with it for an instant. Every day I hunt, and I never grow bored now, for I have a quarry with which I can match my wits."

Rainsford's bewilderment showed in his face.

"I wanted the ideal animal to hunt," explained the general. "So I said: 'What are the attributes of an ideal quarry?' And the answer was, of course: 'It must have courage, cunning, and, above all, it must be able to reason.'"

"But no animal can reason," objected Rainsford.

"My dear fellow," said the general, "there is one that can."

"But you can't mean—" gasped Rainsford.

"And why not?"

"I can't believe you are serious, General Zaroff. This is a grisly joke."

"Why should I not be serious? I am speaking of hunting."

"Hunting? General Zaroff, what you speak of is murder."

The general laughed with entire good nature. He regarded Rainsford quizzically. "I refuse to believe that so modern and civilized a young man as you seem to be harbors romantic ideas about the value of human life. Surely your experiences in the war—"

"Did not make me condone cold-blooded murder," finished Rainsford stiffly.

Laughter shook the general. "How extraordinarily droll you are!" he said. "One does not expect nowadays to find a young man of the educated class, even in America, with such a naive, and, if I may say so, mid-Victorian point of view.[9] It's like finding a snuff-box in a limousine. Ah, well, doubtless you had Puritan ancestors. So many Americans appear to have had. I'll wager you'll forget your notions when you go hunting with me. You've a genuine new thrill in store for you, Mr. Rainsford."

"Thank you, I'm a hunter, not a murderer."

"Dear me," said the general, quite unruffled, "again that unpleasant word. But I think I can show you that your scruples are quite ill founded."

"Yes?"

"Life is for the strong, to be lived by the strong, and, if need be, taken by the strong. The weak of the world were put here to give the strong pleasure. I am strong. Why should I not use my gift? If I wish to hunt, why should I not? I hunt the scum of the earth—sailors from tramp ships—lascars,[10] blacks, Chinese, whites, mongrels—a thoroughbred horse or hound is worth more than a score of them."

"But they are men," said Rainsford hotly.

"Precisely," said the general. "That is why I use them. It gives me pleasure. They can reason, after a fashion. So they are dangerous."

"But where do you get them?"

The general's left eyelid fluttered down in a wink. "This island is called Ship-Trap," he answered. "Sometimes an angry god of the

Conflict
What does Rainsford suddenly understand about Zaroff?

◀ Vocabulary
naive (nä ēv′) *adj.* unsophisticated

scruples (skrōō′ pəlz) *n.* misgivings about something one feels is wrong

Comprehension
What does Zaroff do to ease his boredom with hunting?

---

9. **mid-Victorian point of view** a point of view emphasizing proper behavior and associated with the time of Queen Victoria of England (1819–1901).
10. **lascars** (las′ kərz) *n.* Indian or East Indian sailors, employed on European ships.

Make Inferences
Based on this description, what can you infer about the method Zaroff uses to lure his quarry to the island?

Conflict
Is Zaroff's statement that his captives do not have to participate in the hunt true? Explain.

high seas sends them to me. Sometimes, when Providence is not so kind, I help Providence a bit. Come to the window with me."

Rainsford went to the window and looked out toward the sea.

"Watch! Out there!" exclaimed the general, pointing into the night. Rainsford's eyes saw only blackness, and then, as the general pressed a button, far out to sea Rainsford saw the flash of lights.

The general chuckled. "They indicate a channel," he said, "where there's none: giant rocks with razor edges crouch like a sea monster with wide-open jaws. They can crush a ship as easily as I crush this nut." He dropped a walnut on the hardwood floor and brought his heel grinding down on it. "Oh, yes," he said, casually, as if in answer to a question, "I have electricity. We try to be civilized here."

"Civilized? And you shoot down men?"

A trace of anger was in the general's black eyes, but it was there for but a second, and he said, in his most pleasant manner: "Dear me, what a righteous young man you are! I assure you I do not do the thing you suggest. That would be barbarous. I treat these visitors with every consideration. They get plenty of good food and exercise. They get into splendid physical condition. You shall see for yourself tomorrow."

"What do you mean?"

"We'll visit my training school," smiled the general. "It's in the cellar. I have about a dozen pupils down there now. They're from the Spanish bark San Lucar that had the bad luck to go on the rocks out there. A very inferior lot, I regret to say. Poor specimens and more accustomed to the deck than to the jungle."

He raised his hand, and Ivan, who served as waiter, brought thick Turkish coffee. Rainsford, with an effort, held his tongue in check.

"It's a game, you see," pursued the general blandly. "I suggest to one of them that we go hunting. I give him a supply of food and an excellent hunting knife. I give him three hours' start. I am to follow, armed only with a pistol of the smallest caliber and range. If my quarry eludes me for three whole days, he wins the game. If I find him"—the general smiled—"he loses."

"Suppose he refuses to be hunted?"

"Oh," said the general, "I give him his option, of course. He need not play the game if he doesn't wish to. If he does not wish to hunt, I turn him over to Ivan. Ivan once had the honor of serving as official knouter[11] to the Great White Czar, and he has his own ideas of sport. Invariably, Mr. Rainsford, invariably they choose the hunt."

"And if they win?"

The smile on the general's face widened. "To date I have not lost," he said.

---

11. knouter (nout′ ər) *n.* someone who beats criminals with a leather whip, or knout.

Then he added, hastily: "I don't wish you to think me a braggart, Mr. Rainsford. Many of them afford only the most elementary sort of problem. Occasionally I strike a tartar.[12] One almost did win. I eventually had to use the dogs."

"The dogs?"

"This way, please. I'll show you."

The general steered Rainsford to a window. The lights from the windows sent a flickering illumination that made grotesque patterns on the courtyard below, and Rainsford could see moving about there a dozen or so huge black shapes; as they turned toward him, their eyes glittered greenly.

"A rather good lot, I think," observed the general. "They are let out at seven every night. If anyone should try to get into my house—or out of it—something extremely regrettable would occur to him." He hummed a snatch of song from the Folies Bergère.[13]

"And now," said the general, "I want to show you my new collection of heads. Will you come with me to the library?"

"I hope," said Rainsford, "that you will excuse me tonight, General Zaroff. I'm really not feeling at all well."

"Ah, indeed?" the general inquired solicitously. "Well, I suppose that's only natural, after your long swim. You need a good, restful night's sleep. Tomorrow you'll feel like a new man, I'll wager. Then we'll hunt, eh? I've one rather promising prospect—"

Rainsford was hurrying from the room.

"Sorry you can't go with me tonight," called the general. "I expect rather fair sport—a big, strong black. He looks resourceful—Well, good night, Mr. Rainsford; I hope you have a good night's rest."

The bed was good, and the pajamas of the softest silk, and he was tired in every fiber of his being, but nevertheless Rainsford could not quiet his brain with the opiate of sleep. He lay, eyes wide open. Once he thought he heard stealthy steps in the corridor outside his room. He sought to throw open the door; it would not

Critical Viewing ▼
Why might Zaroff have used dogs like these on his hunts?

◀ Vocabulary
grotesque (grō tesk′) *adj.* having a strange, bizarre design; shocking or offensive

Make Inferences
What kind of heads do you think Zaroff wants to show Rainsford? Explain.

Comprehension
Who are the "pupils" in Zaroff's cellar?

12. **tartar** (tärt′ ər) *n.* stubborn, violent person.
13. **Folies** (fô′ lē) **Bergère** (ber zher′) musical theater in Paris.

open. He went to the window and looked out. His room was high up in one of the towers. The lights of the château were out now, and it was dark and silent, but there was a fragment of sallow moon, and by its wan light he could see, dimly, the courtyard; there, weaving in and out in the pattern of shadow, were black, noiseless forms; the hounds heard him at the window and looked up, expectantly, with their green eyes. Rainsford went back to the bed and lay down. By many methods he tried to put himself to sleep. He had achieved a doze when, just as morning began to come, he heard, far off in the jungle, the faint report of a pistol.

General Zaroff did not appear until luncheon. He was dressed faultlessly in the tweeds of a country squire. He was solicitous about the state of Rainsford's health.

"As for me," sighed the general, "I do not feel so well. I am worried, Mr. Rainsford. Last night I detected traces of my old complaint."

To Rainsford's questioning glance the general said: "Ennui. Boredom."

Then, taking a second helping of crêpes suzette, the general explained: "The hunting was not good last night. The fellow lost his head. He made a straight trail that offered no problems at all. That's the trouble with these sailors; they have dull brains to begin with, and they do not know how to get about in the woods. They do excessively stupid and obvious things. It's most annoying. Will you have another glass of Chablis, Mr. Rainsford?"

"General," said Rainsford firmly, "I wish to leave this island at once."

Conflict
How does Rainsford's statement about wishing to leave make his internal conflict an external one?

The general raised his thickets of eyebrows; he seemed hurt. "But, my dear fellow," the general protested, "you've only just come. You've had no hunting—"

"I wish to go today," said Rainsford. He saw the dead black eyes of the general on him, studying him. General Zaroff's face suddenly brightened.

He filled Rainsford's glass with venerable Chablis from a dusty bottle.

"Tonight," said the general, "we will hunt—you and I."

Rainsford shook his head. "No, general," he said. "I will not hunt."

Make Inferences
What inference can you make about the hunting trip Zaroff is suggesting?

The general shrugged his shoulders and delicately ate a hothouse grape. "As you wish, my friend," he said. "The choice rests entirely with you. But may I not venture to suggest that you will find my idea of sport more diverting than Ivan's?"

He nodded toward the corner to where the giant stood, scowling, his thick arms crossed on his hogshead of chest.

"You don't mean—" cried Rainsford.

"My dear fellow," said the general, "have I not told you I always mean what I say about hunting? This is really an inspiration. I drink to a foeman worthy of my steel—at last."

The general raised his glass, but Rainsford sat staring at him.

"You'll find this game worth playing," the general said enthusiastically. "Your brain against mine. Your woodcraft against mine. Your strength and stamina against mine. Outdoor chess! And the stake is not without value, eh?"

"And if I win—" began Rainsford huskily.

"I'll cheerfully acknowledge myself defeated if I do not find you by midnight of the third day," said General Zaroff. "My sloop will place you on the mainland near a town."

The general read what Rainsford was thinking.

"Oh, you can trust me," said the Cossack. "I will give you my word as a gentleman and a sportsman. Of course you, in turn, must agree to say nothing of your visit here."

"I'll agree to nothing of the kind," said Rainsford.

"Oh," said the general, "in that case— But why discuss that now? Three days hence we can discuss it over a bottle of Veuve Cliquot, unless—"

The general sipped his wine.

Then a businesslike air animated him. "Ivan," he said to Rainsford, "will supply you with hunting clothes, food, a knife. I suggest you wear moccasins; they leave a poorer trail. I suggest too that you avoid the big swamp in the southeast corner of the island. We call it Death Swamp. There's quicksand there. One foolish fellow tried it. The deplorable part of it was that Lazarus followed him. You can imagine my feelings, Mr. Rainsford. I loved Lazarus; he was the finest hound in my pack. Well, I must beg you to excuse me now. I always take a siesta after lunch. You'll hardly have time for a nap, I fear. You'll want to start, no doubt. I shall not follow till dusk. Hunting at night is so much more exciting than by day, don't you think? Au revoir,[14] Mr. Rainsford, au revoir."

General Zaroff, with a deep, courtly bow, strolled from the room.

From another door came Ivan. Under one arm he carried khaki hunting clothes, a haversack of food, a leather sheath containing a long-bladed hunting knife; his right hand rested on a cocked revolver thrust in the crimson sash about his waist. . . .

Rainsford had fought his way through the bush for two hours. "I must keep my nerve. I must keep my nerve," he said through tight teeth.

"My dear fellow," said the general, "have I not told you I always mean what I say about hunting?"

Comprehension
What two suggestions does Zaroff give Rainsford before they begin the hunt?

---

14. **Au** (ō´) **revoir** (rə vwär´) French for "until we meet again."

He had not been entirely clear-headed when the château gates snapped shut behind him.

His whole idea at first was to put distance between himself and General Zaroff, and, to this end, he had plunged along, spurred on by the sharp rowels of something very like panic. Now he had got a grip on himself, had stopped, and was taking stock of himself and the situation.

Vocabulary ▶
futile (fyo͞ot´ 'l) *adj.* useless; hopeless

He saw that straight flight was futile; inevitably it would bring him face to face with the sea. He was in a picture with a frame of water, and his operations, clearly, must take place within that frame.

Critical Viewing ▼
How does this picture support Rainsford's thought that straight flight through the jungle is futile?

"I'll give him a trail to follow," muttered Rainsford, and he struck off from the rude paths he had been following into the trackless wilderness. He executed a series of intricate loops; he doubled on his trail again and again, recalling all the lore of the fox hunt, and all the dodges of the fox. Night found him leg-weary, with his hands

and face lashed by the branches, on a thickly wooded ridge. He knew it would be insane to blunder on through the dark, even if he had the strength. His need for rest was imperative and he thought: "I have played the fox, now I must play the cat of the fable." A big tree with a thick trunk and outspread branches was nearby, and, taking care to leave not the slightest mark, he climbed up into the crotch, and stretching out on one of the broad limbs, after a fashion, rested. Rest brought him new confidence and almost a feeling of security. Even so zealous a hunter as General Zaroff could not trace him there, he told himself; only the devil himself could follow that complicated trail through the jungle after dark. But, perhaps, the general was a devil—

Spiral Review
PACING The author shows Rainsford resting and waiting. How does the slower pace of this scene help to create tension in the story?

An apprehensive night crawled slowly by like a wounded snake, and sleep did not visit Rainsford, although the silence of a dead world was on the jungle. Toward morning when a dingy gray was varnishing the sky, the cry of some startled bird focused Rainsford's attention in that direction. Something was coming through the bush, coming slowly, carefully, coming by the same winding way Rainsford had come. He flattened himself down on the limb, and through a screen of leaves almost as thick as tapestry, he watched. The thing that was approaching was a man.

It was General Zaroff. He made his way along with his eyes fixed in utmost concentration on the ground before him. He paused, almost beneath the tree, dropped to his knees and studied the ground. Rainsford's impulse was to hurl himself down like a panther, but he saw the general's right hand held something metallic—a small automatic pistol.

The hunter shook his head several times, as if he were puzzled. Then he straightened up and took from his case one of his black cigarettes; its pungent incense-like smoke floated up to Rainsford's nostrils.

Make Inferences
Which details in the description of Zaroff's searching the tree suggest that he knows Rainsford is there?

Rainsford held his breath. The general's eyes had left the ground and were traveling inch by inch up the tree. Rainsford froze there, every muscle tensed for a spring. But the sharp eyes of the hunter stopped before they reached the limb where Rainsford lay; a smile spread over his brown face. Very deliberately he blew a smoke ring into the air; then he turned his back on the tree and walked carelessly away, back along the trail he had come. The swish of the underbrush against his hunting boots grew fainter and fainter.

Comprehension
On the first night of the hunt, where does Rainsford attempt to hide from Zaroff?

The pent-up air burst hotly from Rainsford's lungs. His first thought made him feel sick and numb. The general could follow a trail through the woods at night; he could follow an extremely difficult trail; he must have uncanny powers; only by the merest chance had the Cossack failed to see his quarry.

Rainsford's second thought was even more terrible. It sent a shudder of cold horror through his whole being. Why had the general smiled? Why had he turned back?

Rainsford did not want to believe what his reason told him was true, but the truth was as evident as the sun that had by now pushed through the morning mists. The general was playing with him! The general was saving him for another day's sport! The Cossack was the cat; he was the mouse. Then it was that Rainsford knew the full meaning of terror.

"I will not lose my nerve. I will not."

He slid down from the tree, and struck off again into the woods. His face was set and he forced the machinery of his mind to function. Three hundred yards from his hiding place he stopped where a huge dead tree leaned precariously on a smaller, living one. Throwing off his sack of food, Rainsford took his knife from its sheath and began to work with all his energy.

The job was finished at last, and he threw himself down behind a fallen log a hundred feet away. He did not have to wait long. The cat was coming again to play with the mouse.

Following the trail with the sureness of a bloodhound, came General Zaroff. Nothing escaped those searching black eyes, no crushed blade of grass, no bent twig, no mark, no matter how faint, in the moss. So intent was the Cossack on his stalking that he was upon the thing Rainsford had made before he saw it. His foot touched the protruding bough that was the trigger. Even as he touched it, the general sensed his danger and leaped back with the agility of an ape. But he was not quite quick enough; the dead tree, delicately adjusted to rest on the cut living one, crashed down and struck the general a glancing blow on the shoulder as it fell; but for his alertness, he must have been smashed beneath it. He staggered, but he did not fall; nor did he drop his revolver. He stood there, rubbing his injured shoulder, and Rainsford, with fear again gripping his heart, heard the general's mocking laugh ring through the jungle.

"Rainsford," called the general, "if you are within the sound of my voice, as I suppose you are, let me congratulate you. Not many men know how to make a Malay mancatcher. Luckily, for me, I too have hunted in Malacca. You are proving interesting, Mr. Rainsford. I am going now to have my wound dressed; it's only a slight one. But I shall be back. I shall be back."

Conflict
Who seems to be winning the conflict at this point in the story? Explain.

When the general, nursing his bruised shoulder, had gone, Rainsford took up his flight again. It was flight now, a desperate, hopeless flight, that carried him on for some hours. Dusk came, then darkness, and still he pressed on. The ground grew softer

LITERATURE IN CONTEXT

History Connection

World War I Trenches

When Rainsford digs himself in, he is drawing on his experiences as a soldier. During World War I (1914–1918), European armies on both sides dug hundreds of miles of deep, narrow ditches. The soldiers lived in these trenches, from where they would charge the enemy's trenches.

◀ Soldiers' equipment included masks to protect them from mustard gas and other chemical weapons.

LIFE IN THE TRENCHES

- Throughout the war, approximately seven thousand British soldiers were killed, wounded, or disabled every day while serving in the trenches.
- Soldiers living in trenches were plagued by lice, rats, beetles, and frogs.
- The trenches smelled terrible due to dead bodies, overflowing latrines, and unwashed men.

A single pair of trench rats could produce as many as 880 offspring in one year. ▼

Connect to the Literature

Rainsford says his time in the trenches was "placid" compared to his experience on the island. How does this information about trenches clarify his fear?

under his moccasins; the vegetation grew ranker, denser; insects bit him savagely. Then, as he stepped forward, his foot sank into the ooze. He tried to wrench it back, but the muck sucked viciously at his foot as if it were a giant leech. With a violent effort, he tore his foot loose. He knew where he was now. Death Swamp and its quicksand.

His hands were tight closed as if his nerve were something tangible that someone in the darkness was trying to tear from his grip. The softness of the earth had given him an idea. He stepped back from the quicksand a dozen feet or so, and, like some huge prehistoric beaver, he began to dig.

Rainsford had dug himself in in France when a second's delay meant death. That had been a placid pastime compared to his digging now. The pit grew deeper; when it was above his shoulders, he climbed out and from some hard saplings cut stakes and

Comprehension
What toll does Rainsford's trap take on Zaroff?

sharpened them to a fine point. These stakes he planted in the bottom of the pit with the points sticking up. With flying fingers he wove a rough carpet of weeds and branches and with it he covered the mouth of the pit. Then, wet with sweat and aching with tiredness, he crouched behind the stump of a lightning-charred tree.

He knew his pursuer was coming; he heard the padding sound of feet on the soft earth, and the night breeze brought him the perfume of the general's cigarette. It seemed to Rainsford that the general was coming with unusual swiftness; he was not feeling his way along, foot by foot. Rainsford, crouching there, could not see the general, nor could he see the pit. He lived a year in a minute. Then he felt an impulse to cry aloud with joy, for he heard the sharp crackle of the breaking branches as the cover of the pit gave way; he heard the sharp scream of pain as the pointed stakes found their mark. He leaped up from his place of concealment. Then he cowered back. Three feet from the pit a man was standing, with an electric torch in his hand.

"You've done well, Rainsford," the voice of the general called. "Your Burmese tiger pit has claimed one of my best dogs. Again you score. I think, Mr. Rainsford, I'll see what you can do against my whole pack. I'm going home for a rest now. Thank you for a most amusing evening."

At daybreak Rainsford, lying near the swamp, was awakened by a sound that made him know that he had new things to learn about fear. It was a distant sound, faint and wavering, but he knew it. It was the baying of a pack of hounds.

Rainsford knew he could do one of two things. He could stay where he was and wait. That was suicide. He could flee. That was postponing the inevitable. For a moment he stood there, thinking. An idea that held a wild chance came to him, and, tightening his belt, he headed away from the swamp.

The baying of the hounds drew nearer, then still nearer, nearer, ever nearer. On a ridge Rainsford climbed a tree. Down a watercourse, not a quarter of a mile away, he could see the bush moving. Straining his eyes, he saw the lean figure of General Zaroff; just ahead of him Rainsford made out another figure whose wide shoulders surged through the tall jungle weeds; it was the giant Ivan, and he seemed pulled forward by some unseen force; Rainsford knew that Ivan must be holding the pack in leash.

They would be on him any minute now. His mind worked frantically. He thought of a native trick he had learned in Uganda. He slid down the tree. He caught hold of a springy young sapling and to it he fastened his hunting knife, with the blade pointing down the trail; with a bit of wild grapevine he tied back the sapling. Then he ran for his life. The hounds raised their voices as they hit the fresh scent. Rainsford knew now how an animal at bay feels.

Conflict
What new internal conflict does the sound of the baying dogs create for Rainsford?

He had to stop to get his breath. The baying of the hounds stopped abruptly, and Rainsford's heart stopped too. They must have reached the knife.

He shinned excitedly up a tree and looked back. His pursuers had stopped. But the hope that was in Rainsford's brain when he climbed died, for he saw in the shallow valley that General Zaroff was still on his feet. But Ivan was not. The knife, driven by the recoil of the springing tree, had not wholly failed.

"Nerve, nerve, nerve!" he panted, as he dashed along. A blue gap showed between the trees dead ahead. Ever nearer drew the hounds. Rainsford forced himself on toward that gap. He reached it. It was the shore of the sea. Across a cove he could see the gloomy gray stone of the château. Twenty feet below him the sea rumbled and hissed. Rainsford hesitated. He heard the hounds. Then he leaped far out into the sea. . . .

When the general and his pack reached the place by the sea, the Cossack stopped. For some minutes he stood regarding the blue-green expanse of water. He shrugged his shoulders. Then he sat down, took a drink of brandy from a silver flask, lit a perfumed cigarette, and hummed a bit from *Madame Butterfly*.[15]

General Zaroff had an exceedingly good dinner in his great paneled dining hall that evening. With it he had a bottle of Pol Roger and half a bottle of Chambertin. Two slight annoyances kept him from perfect enjoyment. One was the thought that it would be difficult to replace Ivan; the other was that his quarry had escaped him; of course the American hadn't played the game—so thought the general as he tasted his after-dinner liqueur. In his library he

Comprehension
What does Rainsford do when he reaches the edge of the cliff?

15. ***Madame Butterfly*** an opera by Giacomo Puccini.

read, to soothe himself, from the works of Marcus Aurelius.[16] At ten he went up to his bedroom. He was deliciously tired, he said to himself, as he locked himself in. There was a little moonlight, so, before turning on his light, he went to the window and looked down at the courtyard. He could see the great hounds, and he called: "Better luck another time," to them. Then he switched on the light.

A man, who had been hiding in the curtain of the bed, was standing there.

"Rainsford!" screamed the general. "How in God's name did you get here?"

"Swam," said Rainsford. "I found it quicker than walking through the jungle."

The general sucked in his breath and smiled. "I congratulate you," he said. "You have won the game."

Rainsford did not smile. "I am still a beast at bay," he said, in a low, hoarse voice. "Get ready, General Zaroff."

The general made one of his deepest bows. "I see," he said. "Splendid! One of us is to furnish a repast for the hounds. The other will sleep in this very excellent bed. On guard, Rainsford. . . ."

He had never slept in a better bed, Rainsford decided.

---

16. Marcus Aurelius (ô rē´ lē əs) Roman emperor and philosopher (A.D. 121–180).

Language Study

Vocabulary The words listed below appear in "The Most Dangerous Game." Choose one word from the list to fill in the blank in each sentence. Then, identify the context clues in each sentence that helped you.

palpable **indolently** **naive** **scruples** **futile**

1. His cheating at the game demonstrated a lack of ___________.

2. At the wedding, the joy in the air seemed ___________.

3. She tried to climb, but her high heels made her efforts ___________.

4. The lazy sloth hung ___________ from the tree branch.

5. Only a very ___________ person would believe in the Tooth Fairy.

WORD STUDY

The **Latin suffix *-esque,*** means "in the style or manner of." In this story, Rainsford sees **grotesque** things that remind him of death. *Grotesque* is related to *grotto,* a word that once meant "burial vault."

Word Study

Part A Explain how the **Latin suffix *-esque*** contributes to the words *statuesque* and *Lincolnesque*. Consult a dictionary if necessary.

Part B Use the context of the sentences and your knowledge of the Latin suffix *-esque* to explain your answer to each question.

1. Why do people like to visit *picturesque* places?

2. If a film is called *Disneyesque*, whose movies does it resemble?

Close Reading Activities

Literary Analysis

Key Ideas and Details

1. **(a)** According to Zaroff, what is the most dangerous game? **(b) Define:** In Zaroff's point of view, what makes this creature so dangerous?
2. **Make Inferences (a)** Near the story's end, with what words does Zaroff congratulate Rainsford? **(b)** What action does Rainsford then take? Explain the details that support your inference.
3. **Make Inferences (a)** Describe two inferences you made about Whitney. **(b)** Based on your ideas, discuss how the story would be different if it had been Whitney rather than Rainsford on the island with Zaroff. Cite textual details to support your response.

Craft and Structure

4. **Conflict (a)** What is the central conflict in this story? Explain. **(b)** What is the ending, or resolution, to the story's central conflict?
5. **Conflict (a)** In addition to the central conflict, what external conflicts does Rainsford experience? **(b)** What internal conflicts does Rainsford experience? **(c)** Use a chart like the one shown to cite specific details from the story that support your answers.

Conflicts Rainsford Experiences

Supporting Textual Details

Integration of Knowledge and Ideas

6. Zaroff tells Rainsford that he tries to maintain the "amenities of civilization" on the island. **(a) Synthesize:** What other details in the description of Zaroff's appearance, home, and habits suggest his concern with living in a civilized manner? **(b) Make a Judgment:** Is Zaroff civilized? Explain your position.
7. **(a)** At the beginning of the story, what does Rainsford believe about the "two classes" that make up the world? **(b) Compare and Contrast:** Explain how Rainsford's initial beliefs compare to Zaroff's statement: "Life is for the strong, to be lived by the strong; and, if need be, taken by the strong."
8. **Analyze:** Does Rainsford's attitude toward the world's "two classes" change by the end of the story? Explain your position.

9. THE BIG ? **Is conflict necessary?** With a small group, discuss the following questions: **(a)** In what sense is conflict a "necessary" part of the hunting experience? **(b)** Does this story condemn Rainsford's original attitude toward hunting, or does it uphold some aspect of that position? **(c)** What relationship between civilization and conflict does this story suggest is appropriate?

ACADEMIC VOCABULARY

As you write and speak about "The Most Dangerous Game," use the words related to conflict that you explored on page 3.

Conventions: Parts of Speech

Part of speech is the term used to describe the category into which a word can be placed according to its function in a sentence. There are eight parts of speech in English: **nouns, pronouns, verbs, adjectives, adverbs, prepositions, conjunctions,** and **interjections.**

This sentence contains six parts of speech that are explained in the chart below: *Rainsford indolently puffed on his favorite brier.*

Word	Part of Speech	Function
brier	**Noun:** names a person, place, or thing	identifies an object
Rainsford	**Proper Noun:** names a specific person, place, or thing; begins with a capital letter	identifies a specific person who is the subject of the sentence
puffed	**Verb:** names an action	tells what Rainsford did
his	**Pronoun:** a word such as *I, our, he,* or *their,* that substitutes for a noun or another pronoun	substitutes for "Rainsford's"
favorite	**Adjective:** modifies a noun or pronoun	tells which "brier"
indolently	**Adverb:** modifies a verb, an adjective, or another adverb	tells how Rainsford "puffed"
on	**Preposition:** clarifies relationships of time, place, or direction between words	shows relationship of place between "puffed" and "brier"

Practice A

Identify the parts of speech in each sentence below. (Do not identify articles, such as "the" or "a.")

1. Rainsford discovers a remote island.
2. He struggles briefly in the jungle.
3. The magnificent castle rests atop a mountain.
4. Bravely, he traverses the difficult terrain.

Reading Application Select two sentences from "The Most Dangerous Game." Underline the nouns and pronouns and circle all the verbs.

Practice B

Label each underlined word as *adverb* or *adjective*.

1. Zaroff behaved evasively when asked about his mysterious past.
2. The island has an evil name among sea-faring men.
3. He gave a short cry as he suddenly lost balance.
4. As he lazily dozed, an abrupt sound startled him.

Writing Application Write a paragraph summarizing "The Most Dangerous Game." Use at least three adjectives and three adverbs.

Writing to Sources

Explanatory Text In "The Most Dangerous Game," three characters—Whitney, Rainsford, and Zaroff—present three different views of the relationship between people and nature. Write a **comparison-and-contrast essay** analyzing the characters' views. Consider the following questions:

- How do Whitney's views about hunting and animals differ from Rainsford's? What does Rainsford feel about Whitney's ideas?
- How are Rainsford's views of hunting both similar to and different from Zaroff's? Are Zaroff's views essentially the same as Rainsford's but taken to an extreme? Or are they fundamentally different?
- At the end of the story, what has Rainsford done? Do you think he has "become" Zaroff?

As you write, support your ideas with specific details from the text. Cite passages precisely and integrate them smoothly into your analysis.

Grammar Application As you write, use adjectives and adverbs to make your writing more interesting and precise.

Speaking and Listening

Presentation of Ideas In a group, research and prepare an **oral presentation** about two or three of the big game species mentioned in "The Most Dangerous Game." Use both print and non-print media sources. Include key facts about each species you research.

Follow these steps to research and write your presentation:

- Brainstorm for a list of questions to answer through research.
- Gather reliable data from varied sources. As you work, capture information you will later need to cite sources thoroughly and accurately.
- Organize the information and consider whether you have fully answered your list of questions. You may need to do additional research to supplement what you already have.
- Write an introduction that grabs the audience's attention and establishes your central idea. Write a conclusion that summarizes your central idea and supporting points in a memorable way.
- Gather images that illustrate your ideas and integrate them into the presentation so that they maintain audience interest, clarify points, and do not distract from the focus of the presentation.

Writing

2. Write explanatory texts to examine and convey complex ideas, concepts, and information clearly and accurately through the effective selection, organization, and analysis of content.

2.a. Introduce a topic; organize complex ideas, concepts, and information to make important connections and distinctions.

Speaking and Listening

4. Present information, findings, and supporting evidence clearly, concisely, and logically such that listeners can follow the line of reasoning and the organization, development, substance, and style are appropriate to purpose, audience, and task.

5. Make strategic use of digital media in presentations to enhance understanding of findings, reasoning, and evidence and to add interest.

Language

1. Demonstrate command of the conventions of standard English grammar and usage when writing or speaking.

Building Knowledge

Meet the Author

O. Henry (1862–1910) is the pen name of William Sydney Porter. In 1882, Porter left his home in North Carolina to seek his fortune in Texas. He worked on a ranch, at a bank, and then became a reporter, columnist, and cartoonist for the *Houston Post.* In 1896, Porter was jailed for his involvement in a bank scandal. While in prison, he began writing stories. After he was released, Porter moved to New York City, began publishing stories under the name O. Henry, and developed into one of America's most celebrated writers of short fiction.

Common Core State Standards

Reading Literature

1. Cite strong and thorough textual evidence to support analysis of what the text says explicitly as well as inferences drawn from the text.

5. Analyze how an author's choices concerning how to structure a text, order events within it, and manipulate time create such effects as mystery, tension, or surprise.

Is conflict necessary?

Explore the Big Question as you read "The Gift of the Magi." Take notes on ways in which the story explores the surprising nature of conflict.

CLOSE READING FOCUS

Key Ideas and Details: **Make Inferences**

An **inference** is a logical guess a reader makes based on details in a text. The author may state some information directly, but most of the ideas in a story are suggested through details.

- When reading short stories, notice important details in the text.
- Draw on your own knowledge by looking for ways in which the characters and situations resemble those you have read about, observed, or experienced.
- Apply your knowledge to the details in the text to make meaningful inferences.

Craft and Structure: **Situational Irony**

Irony is a contradiction between appearance and reality. **Situational irony** occurs when an action or event in a story contradicts the expectations of a character or the reader. For example, a runner who trains hard would be expected to do well in a race. It would be ironic if she trained so hard that she overslept and missed the race.

Surprise endings often present situational irony because they involve a sudden turn of events that contradicts what the reader has been led to expect. When such endings are effective, it is because the writer has built clues into the text that make the surprise logical. Ironies and surprise endings usually help convey a story's *theme*, or meaning.

As you read, look for clues in the text that set up your expectations about the story's outcome.

Vocabulary

The words below are critical to understanding the story that follows. Copy the words into your notebook. Which one is a synonym for *provokes?*

instigates	**depreciate**	**cascade**
faltered	**prudence**	**discreet**

CLOSE READING MODEL

The passage below is from O. Henry's short story "The Gift of the Magi." The annotations to the right of the passage show ways in which you can use close reading skills to make inferences and analyze irony.

from "The Gift of the Magi"

Now, there were two possessions of the James Dillingham Youngs in which they both took a mighty pride. One was Jim's gold watch that had been his father's and his grandfather's. The other was Della's hair. Had the queen of Sheba[1] lived in the flat across the airshaft, Della would have let her hair hang out the window some day to dry just to depreciate Her Majesty's jewels and gifts. Had King Solomon[1] been the janitor, with all his treasures piled up in the basement, Jim would have pulled out his watch every time he passed, just to see him pluck at his beard from envy.

So now Della's beautiful hair fell about her rippling and shining like a cascade of brown waters. It reached below her knee and made itself almost a garment for her.[2] And then she did it up again nervously[3] and quickly. Once she faltered[3] for a minute and stood still while a tear or two splashed on the worn red carpet.[3]

On went her old brown jacket; on went her old brown hat. With a whirl of skirts and with the brilliant sparkle still in her eyes,[3] she fluttered out the door and down the stairs to the street.

Situational Irony

1 The narrator mentions legendary figures—the queen of Sheba and King Solomon—rather than just any queen and king. These details tell you that Della's hair and Jim's watch are rare and splendid. They also hint that the characters' pride in those items matters more than anything else.

Situational Irony

2 The narrator describes Della's hair as though it is a river or waterfall—it is "rippling," "shining," and "like a cascade." These details reinforce the idea that Della's hair is dramatic and, like a force of nature, permanent.

Make Inferences

3 The words *nervously* and *faltered* suggest that Della is anxious and sad. She sheds "a tear or two." In the next paragraph her eyes have a "brilliant sparkle" and she leaves in "a whirl of skirts." You can infer that Della's mood has abruptly changed, as though she has made a decision and is taking action.

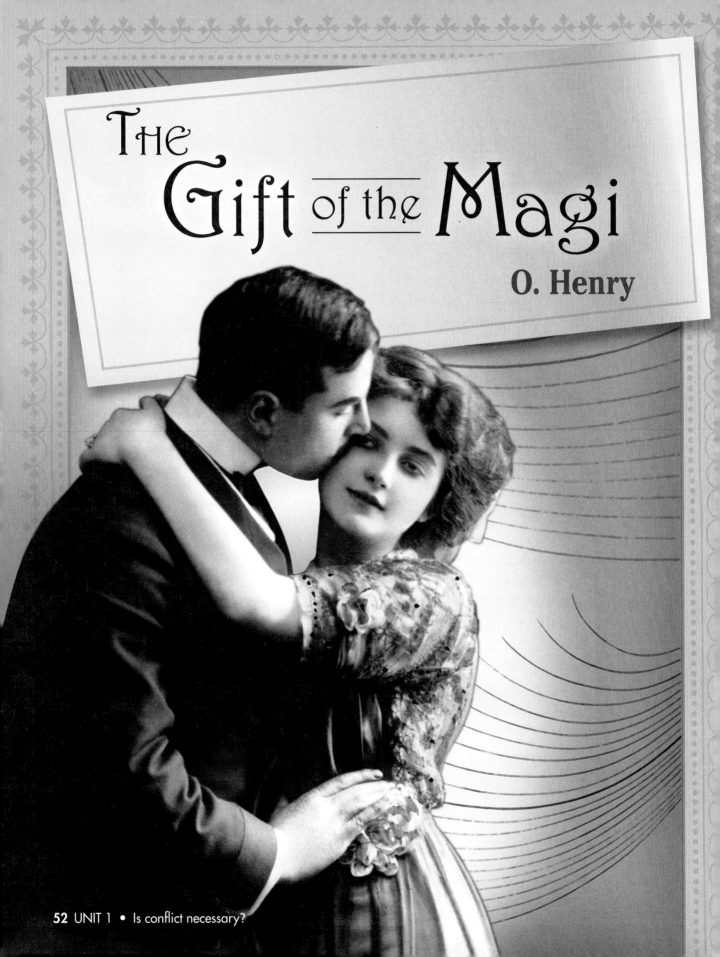

The Gift of the Magi

O. Henry

One dollar and eighty-seven cents. That was all. And sixty cents of it was in pennies. Pennies saved one and two at a time by bulldozing the grocer and the vegetable man and the butcher until one's cheeks burned with the silent imputation of parsimony[1] that such close dealing implied. Three times Della counted it. One dollar and eighty-seven cents. And the next day would be Christmas.

There was clearly nothing to do but flop down on the shabby little couch and howl. So Della did it. Which **instigates** the moral reflection that life is made up of sobs, sniffles, and smiles, with sniffles predominating.

◀ **Vocabulary**
instigates (in′ stə gātz′)
v. urges on; stirs up

While the mistress of the home is gradually subsiding from the first stage to the second, take a look at the home. A furnished flat at $8 per week. It did not exactly beggar description,[2] but it certainly had that word on the lookout for the mendicancy squad.[3]

In the vestibule below was a letter-box into which no letter would go, and an electric button from which no mortal finger could coax a ring. Also appertaining thereunto was a card bearing the name "Mr. James Dillingham Young."

The "Dillingham" had been flung to the breeze during a former period of prosperity when its possessor was being paid $30 per week. Now, when the income was shrunk to $20, the letters of "Dillingham" looked blurred, as though they were thinking seriously of contracting to a modest and unassuming D. But whenever Mr. James Dillingham Young came home and reached his flat above he was called "Jim" and greatly hugged by Mrs. James Dillingham Young, already introduced to you as Della. Which is all very good.

Make Inferences
Based on this paragraph, what can you infer about Jim and the kind of person he would like to be?

Della finished her cry and attended to her cheeks with the powder rag. She stood by the window and looked out dully at a gray cat walking a gray fence in a gray backyard. Tomorrow would be Christmas Day, and she had only $1.87 with which to buy

Comprehension
How much money does Della have to buy a present for Jim?

1. **imputation** (im′ pyōō tā′ shən) **of parsimony** (pär′ sə mō′ nē) accusation of stinginess.
2. **beggar description** make description seem inadequate or useless.
3. **it certainly . . . mendicancy** (men′ di kən′ sē) **squad** it would have been noticed by the police who arrest beggars.

▲ **Critical Viewing** How do you think Della felt in a street like this one as she approached Madame Sofronie's shop?

Jim a present. She had been saving every penny she could for months, with this result. Twenty dollars a week doesn't go far. Expenses had been greater than she had calculated. They always are. Only $1.87 to buy a present for Jim. Her Jim. Many a happy hour she had spent planning for something nice for him. Something fine and rare and sterling—something just a little bit near to being worthy of the honor of being owned by Jim.

There was a pier glass between the windows of the room. Perhaps you have seen a pier glass in an $8 flat. A very thin and very agile person may, by observing his reflection in a rapid sequence of longitudinal strips, obtain a fairly accurate conception of his looks. Della, being slender, had mastered the art.

Suddenly she whirled from the window and stood before the glass. Her eyes were shining brilliantly, but her face had lost its color within twenty seconds. Rapidly she pulled down her hair and let it fall to its full length.

Now, there were two possessions of the James Dillingham Youngs in which they both took a mighty pride. One was Jim's gold watch that had been his father's and his grandfather's. The other was Della's hair. Had the queen of Sheba lived in the flat across the airshaft, Della would have let her hair hang out the window some day to dry just to depreciate Her Majesty's jewels and gifts. Had King Solomon been the janitor, with all his treasures piled up in the basement, Jim would have pulled out his watch every time he passed, just to see him pluck at his beard from envy.

So now Della's beautiful hair fell about her rippling and shining like a cascade of brown waters. It reached below her knee and made itself almost a garment for her. And then she did it up again nervously and quickly. Once she faltered for a minute and stood still while a tear or two splashed on the worn red carpet.

On went her old brown jacket; on went her old brown hat. With a whirl of skirts and with the brilliant sparkle still in her eyes, she fluttered out the door and down the stairs to the street.

Where she stopped the sign read: "Mme. Sofronie. Hair Goods of All Kinds." One flight up Della ran, and collected herself, panting. Madame, large, too white, chilly, hardly looked the "Sofronie."

Vocabulary ▶

depreciate (dē prē´ shē āt´) *v.* reduce in value

cascade (kas kād´) *n.* small steep waterfall; anything suggesting such a waterfall

faltered (fôl´ tərd) *v.* acted hesitantly; showed uncertainty

"Will you buy my hair?" asked Della.

"I buy hair," said Madame. "Take yer hat off and let's have a sight at the looks of it."

Down rippled the brown cascade.

"Twenty dollars," said Madame, lifting the mass with a practiced hand.

"Give it to me quick," said Della.

Oh, and the next two hours tripped by on rosy wings. Forget the hashed metaphor. She was ransacking the stores for Jim's present.

She found it at last. It surely had been made for Jim and no one else. There was no other like it in any of the stores, and she had turned all of them inside out. It was a platinum fob chain simple and chaste in design, properly proclaiming its value by substance alone and not by meretricious ornamentation—as all good things should do. It was even worthy of The Watch. As soon as she saw it she knew that it must be Jim's. It was like him. Quietness and value—the description applied to both. Twenty-one dollars they took from her for it, and she hurried home with the 87 cents. With that chain on his watch Jim might be properly anxious about the time in any company. Grand as the watch was, he sometimes looked at it on the sly on account of the old leather strap that he used in place of a chain.

When Della reached home her intoxication gave way a little to prudence and reason. She got out her curling irons and lighted the gas and went to work repairing the ravages made by generosity added to love. Which is always a tremendous task, dear friends—a mammoth task.

Within forty minutes her head was covered with tiny, close-lying curls that made her look wonderfully like a truant schoolboy. She looked at her reflection in the mirror long, carefully, and critically.

LITERATURE IN CONTEXT

Cultural Connection

Watch Fob Chain

A fob chain is central to the plot of "The Gift of the Magi." The word *fob* probably entered the English language from the German dialect word *fuppe*, meaning "pocket." Before the wristwatch became common, a man would carry a pocket watch that fit in a special vest pocket. To keep the watch from falling or becoming lost, it was fastened to the vest by means of a strap or chain (sometimes with an ornament, or a fob, at the end) that was attached to a pin with a locking clasp, making it secure. Sometimes, as pictured here, a chain's finely detailed metalwork elevated the piece to a work of art.

Connect to the Literature

A pocket watch was often handed down from father to son, as was Jim Young's in O. Henry's story. Why might this fact alone make a fob chain and watch precious to its owner despite its modest cash value?

◀ **Vocabulary**
prudence (pro͞o´ dəns) *n.* sensible and careful attitude that makes you avoid some risks

Comprehension
What does Della sell for twenty dollars?

"If Jim doesn't kill me," she said to herself, "before he takes a second look at me, he'll say I look like a Coney Island[4] chorus girl. But what could I do—oh! what could I do with a dollar and eighty-seven cents?"

At 7 o'clock the coffee was made and the frying-pan was on the back of the stove hot and ready to cook the chops.

Jim was never late. Della doubled the fob chain in her hand and sat on the corner of the table near the door that he always entered. Then she heard his step on the stair away down on the first flight, and she turned white for just a moment. She had a habit of saying little silent prayers about the simplest everyday things, and now she whispered: "Please God, make him think I am still pretty."

"...I couldn't have lived through Christmas without giving you a present."

The door opened and Jim stepped in and closed it. He looked thin and very serious. Poor fellow, he was only twenty-two—and to be burdened with a family! He needed a new overcoat and he was without gloves.

Jim stopped inside the door, as immovable as a setter at the scent of quail. His eyes were fixed upon Della, and there was an expression in them that she could not read, and it terrified her. It was not anger, nor surprise, nor disapproval, nor horror, nor any of the sentiments that she had been prepared for. He simply stared at her fixedly with that peculiar expression on his face.

Della wriggled off the table and went for him.

"Jim, darling," she cried, "don't look at me that way. I had my hair cut off and sold it because I couldn't have lived through Christmas without giving you a present. It'll grow out again—you won't mind, will you? I just had to do it. My hair grows awfully fast. Say 'Merry Christmas!' Jim, and let's be happy. You don't know what a nice—what a beautiful, nice gift I've got for you."

"You've cut off your hair?" asked Jim, laboriously, as if he had not arrived at that patent fact yet even after the hardest mental labor.

"Cut it off and sold it," said Della. "Don't you like me just as well, anyhow? I'm me without my hair, ain't I?"

Jim looked about the room curiously.

"You say your hair is gone?" he said, with an air almost of idiocy.

---

4. **Coney** (kō′ nē) **Island** beach and amusement park in Brooklyn, New York.

"You needn't look for it," said Della. "It's sold, I tell you—sold and gone, too. It's Christmas Eve, boy. Be good to me, for it went for you. Maybe the hairs of my head were numbered," she went on with a sudden serious sweetness, "but nobody could ever count my love for you. Shall I put the chops on, Jim?"

Out of his trance Jim seemed quickly to wake. He enfolded his Della. For ten seconds let us regard with **discreet** scrutiny some inconsequential object in the other direction. Eight dollars a week or a million a year—what is the difference? A mathematician or a wit would give you the wrong answer. The Magi brought valuable gifts, but that was not among them. This dark assertion will be illuminated later on.

◀ **Vocabulary**
discreet (di skrēt′) *adj.* careful about what one says or does

Jim drew a package from his overcoat pocket and threw it upon the table.

"Don't make any mistake, Dell," he said, "about me. I don't think there's anything in the way of a haircut or a shave or a shampoo that could make me like my girl any less. But if you'll unwrap that package you may see why you had me going a while at first."

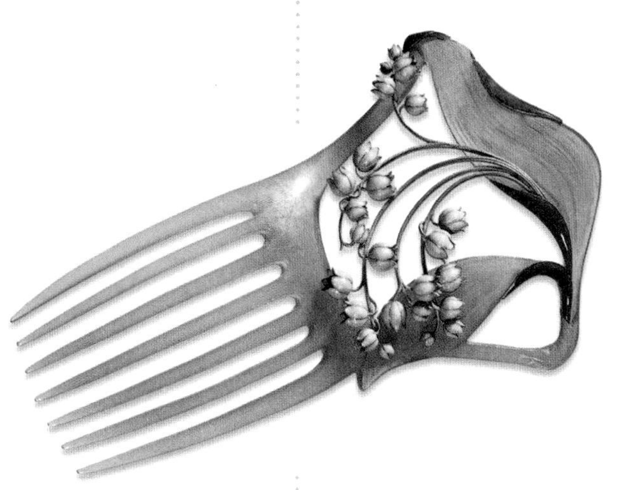

White fingers and nimble tore at the string and paper. And then an ecstatic scream of joy; and then, alas! a quick feminine change to hysterical tears and wails, necessitating the immediate employment of all the comforting powers of the lord of the flat.

For there lay The Combs—the set of combs, side and back, that Della had worshipped for long in a Broadway window. Beautiful combs, pure tortoise shell, with jeweled rims—just the shade to wear in the beautiful vanished hair. They were expensive combs, she knew, and her heart had simply craved and yearned over them without the least hope of possession. And now, they were hers, but the tresses that should have adorned the coveted adornments were gone.

Irony
In what way does Jim's gift to Della create an ironic situation?

But she hugged them to her bosom, and at length she was able to look up with dim eyes and a smile and say: "My hair grows so fast, Jim!"

And then Della leaped up like a little singed cat and cried, "Oh, oh!"

Jim had not yet seen his beautiful present. She held it out to him eagerly upon her open palm. The dull precious metal seemed to flash with a reflection of her bright and ardent spirit.

Comprehension
How does Jim react to Della's newly cut hair?

"Isn't it a dandy, Jim? I hunted all over town to find it. You'll have to look at the time a hundred times a day now. Give me your watch. I want to see how it looks on it."

Instead of obeying, Jim tumbled down on the couch and put his hands under the back of his head and smiled.

Surprise Ending
Explain why Jim's response to his gift is a surprise to both Della and the reader.

"Dell," said he, "let's put our Christmas presents away and keep 'em a while. They're too nice to use just at present. I sold the watch to get the money to buy your combs. And now suppose you put the chops on."

Spiral Review
NARRATOR Based on this final paragraph, how would you describe the narrator's attitude toward both the characters and the reader? Explain.

The magi, as you know, were wise men—wonderfully wise men—who brought gifts to the Babe in the manger. They invented the art of giving Christmas presents. Being wise, their gifts were no doubt wise ones, possibly bearing the privilege of exchange in case of duplication. And here I have lamely related to you the uneventful chronicle of two foolish children in a flat who most unwisely sacrificed for each other the greatest treasures of their house. But in a last word to the wise of these days let it be said that of all who give gifts these two were the wisest. Of all who give and receive gifts, such as they are wisest. Everywhere they are wisest. They are the magi.

Language Study

Vocabulary The words listed below appear in "The Gift of the Magi." Using your knowledge of these words, explain why each statement below is either usually true or usually false.

instigates **cascade** **faltered** **prudence** **discreet**

1. One who *instigates* conflict might be called a "problem solver."
2. Only a *discreet* person should be trusted with a secret.
3. It is a sign of *prudence* to drive a car before you have your license.
4. In a fireworks display, a shell might create a sparkling *cascade*.
5. The horse *faltered* in the home stretch and won as a result.

WORD STUDY
The **Latin prefix *de-*** has various meanings, including "down." In this story, Della's hair is said to **depreciate** a queen's treasures. Her hair is so lovely that, by comparison, it brings down the value of jewels.

Word Study

Part A Explain how the **Latin prefix *de-*** contributes to the meanings of *descend*, *decline*, and *depose*. Consult a dictionary if necessary.

Part B Use the context of the sentences and what you know about the Latin prefix *de-* to explain your answer to each question.

1. If you were to *depress* a friend, would he feel better?
2. What happens to food when people *devour* it?

Close Reading Activities

Literary Analysis

Key Ideas and Details

1. **Make Inferences (a)** What does Della do to get money for Jim's present? **(b)** What do Della's actions suggest about her character?
2. **(a)** After he arrives at home, how does Jim react when he first sees Della? **(b) Interpret:** Why does he react in this way? **(c) Connect:** Why does Della misunderstand Jim's reaction? Cite details from the story to support your responses.
3. **Make Inferences** What do you understand about Jim and Della's relationship based on Jim's final speech at the end of the story? Cite details to support your response.

Craft and Structure

4. **Situational Irony (a)** Use a chart like the one shown to examine irony in the story. In the top section, cite details that explain what the characters expect as they plan their gifts. In the bottom section, note what actually happens. **(b)** Which details earlier in the text make this surprise ending logical even though it is startling?
5. In the final paragraph, the narrator describes Jim and Della's story as "uneventful." **(a)** Identify other negative adjectives the narrator uses to describe the characters or their story. **(b)** Does the narrator really mean that Jim and Della's story is unimportant? Explain, citing story details.
6. **Connect:** Explain the relationship between the story's title, characters and events, and final paragraph.

Characters' Expectations
Actual Events

Integration of Knowledge and Ideas

7. **Draw Conclusions:** At the end of the story, the narrator says of Jim and Della that these "two foolish children" were "the wisest." How does the narrator define wisdom? Cite details from the story in your answer.
8. **Make a Judgment:** After Della and Jim exchange gifts, are they richer, poorer, or the same as they were at the beginning of the story? Use details from the text to support your answer.

9. THE BIG ? **Is conflict necessary? (a)** Citing details from the text, explain one internal conflict that Jim experiences and one that Della experiences. **(b)** Do you think each of these conflicts is necessary? Explain your position.

ACADEMIC VOCABULARY

As you write and speak about "The Gift of the Magi," use the words related to conflict that you explored on page 3 of this textbook.

Conventions: **Simple and Perfect Tenses**

A **verb** indicates an action or a state of being. Verbs have **tenses**, or different forms, that tell when something happens or exists.

In standard English, verbs have six tenses: present, past, future, present perfect, past perfect, and future perfect.

- **Present** indicates an action that happens regularly or states a general truth: *The Tigers <u>play</u> often.*
- **Past** indicates an action that has already happened: *Last week they <u>played</u> on Tuesday and Friday.*
- **Future** indicates an action that will happen: *They <u>will play</u> their final game next week.*
- **Present perfect** indicates an action that happened at some time in the past or an action that happened in the past and is still happening now: *We <u>have played</u> on this field for two years.*
- **Past perfect** indicates an action that was completed before another action in the past: *We <u>had played</u> on the old field until the new field was built.*
- **Future perfect** indicates an action that will have been completed before another: *We <u>will have played</u> twenty-six games before the season ends.*

Inconsistent verb tense occurs when a sentence begins in one tense and incorrectly switches to another.

Incorrect: Before we *played* in yesterday's game, the coach *gives* us a pep talk.

Correct: Before we *played* in yesterday's game, the coach *gave* us a pep talk.

Practice A

Identify the tense of each underlined verb.

1. Jim <u>had cleaned</u> his watch before he left.
2. Della <u>will have combed</u> her hair over a thousand times before she next has it cut.
3. Della <u>will cook</u> chops for dinner.
4. Della <u>selected</u> a beautiful watch fob for Jim.

Reading Application Choose three sentences from "The Gift of the Magi" that show different verb tenses. Identify the verb tense in each sentence.

Practice B

Revise each sentence, changing the verb tense to the one identified in parentheses.

1. O. Henry creates surprise endings. (past)
2. She has looked at the combs in the window. (future)
3. Jim will have purchased Della's gift by now. (past perfect)
4. Her hair will glow brighter than jewels. (present)

Writing Application Write four sentences about Jim and Della's gifts. Use four different verb tenses. Identify the tense in each sentence.

Writing to Sources

Narrative Write a **news report** about Jim and Della. Explain who they are, what they did, and how their actions resulted in irony.

- Reread the story, gathering facts by answering the questions *Who? What? Where? When? Why?* and *How?*
- Create a list of story events that follow a logical order.
- Write an opening paragraph that summarizes events and grabs the reader's interest. Add several more paragraphs that provide in-depth details.
- As you draft, follow the sequence of events from your original list. If necessary, revise the order to make sure the connections among events are clear. Write a strong conclusion in which you reflect on Jim and Della's story, sharing your insights and observations.
- Use quotations from the story to show characters' reactions. Choose logical points at which to integrate the quotations smoothly.

Grammar Application As you write, use verb tenses correctly to show the order of actions as they occur in time.

Speaking and Listening

Presentation of Ideas With a group of classmates, present a **debate** on whether sacrifice is the best expression of love. Use the characters and events from "The Gift of the Magi" as part of your supporting evidence. Follow these steps to complete the assignment:

- Take a clear position, one that can be stated in a single sentence.
- Sequence your ideas logically and choose strong evidence from the story to support each one.
- Conduct research to locate additional evidence, such as findings from scientific studies or quotations from experts. Make sure that the additional material logically supports your claim.
- Anticipate opposing arguments. Consider how the other side may counter your position. Be ready with a response and with supporting information.
- Use a serious speaking style and manner so that your audience is not distracted by language or gestures that are not on point.

After the debate, ask the audience to evaluate the presentation and decide which team's argument was more persuasive.

Common Core State Standards

Writing

3. Write narratives to develop real or imagined experiences or events using effective technique, well-chosen details, and well-structured event sequences.

3.c. Use a variety of techniques to sequence events so that they build on one another to create a coherent whole.

3.e. Provide a conclusion that follows from and reflects on what is experienced, observed, or resolved over the course of the narrative.

Speaking and Listening

4. Present information, findings, and supporting evidence clearly, concisely, and logically such that listeners can follow the line of reasoning and the organization, development, substance, and style are appropriate to purpose, audience, and task.

Language

1. Demonstrate command of the conventions of standard English grammar and usage when writing or speaking.

Building Knowledge

Meet the Author

Amy Tan (b. 1952) did not imagine that she would become a successful novelist. Her parents, who had emigrated from China, wanted her to become a doctor. Doubting her abilities in science, Tan instead majored in English in college. She went on to become a successful business writer. Then, in her mid-thirties, Tan began writing stories. While she was surprised by the pleasure of writing fiction, she was even more surprised by the content of her work. Tan had previously tried to play down her ethnicity but in her fiction, she found herself exploring the experiences of Chinese American women.

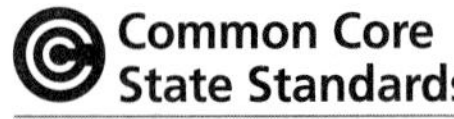

Common Core State Standards

Reading Literature

3. Analyze how complex characters develop over the course of a text, interact with other characters, and advance the plot or develop the theme.

Is conflict necessary?

Explore the Big Question as you read "Rules of the Game." Take notes on the story's portrayal of conflict between generations.

CLOSE READING FOCUS

Key Ideas and Details: **Analyze Cause and Effect**

A **cause** is an event, action, or feeling that produces a result. An **effect** is the result produced. A single cause may produce several effects. For example, a poor student starts to do well in school. Her success results in greater self-esteem. Effects, in turn, may become causes: the student's new confidence leads her to audition for a play. As you read the story, ask questions like these to analyze cause and effect:

- What happened? Why did it happen?
- What occurs as a result?
- Does that result cause something else to happen?

Craft and Structure: **Characterization**

A **character** is a person, animal, or even an object that participates in the action and experiences the events of a literary work. Writers develop a character's traits and personality through these **characterization** techniques:

- **Direct Characterization:** The writer (speaking through a narrator) simply tells readers about a character: "Seated across from me was an American man, about the same age as Lau Po, maybe fifty."
- **Indirect Characterization:** The writer suggests what a character is like through *dialogue*, or spoken words, and through descriptions of his or her actions, thoughts, and appearance. The writer may also show other characters' reactions: "I remember that his sweaty brow seemed to weep at my every move."

Vocabulary

The words below appear in the text that follows. Which is a synonym for *kindly?*

pungent	**benevolently**	**retort**
prodigy	**malodorous**	**concessions**

CLOSE READING MODEL

The passage below is from Amy Tan's short story "Rules of the Game." The annotations to the right of the passage show ways in which you can use close reading skills to analyze cause and effect and characterization.

from "Rules of the Game"

Vincent got the chess set, which would have been a very decent present to get at a church Christmas party except it was obviously used and, as we discovered later, it was missing a black pawn and a white knight.[1] My mother graciously thanked the unknown benefactor, saying, "Too good. Cost too much."[2] At which point, an old lady with fine white, wispy hair[3] nodded toward our family and said with a whistling whisper,[3] "Merry, merry Christmas."

When we got home, my mother told Vincent to throw the chess set away.[1] "She not want it. We not want it," she said, tossing her head stiffly to the side with a tight, proud smile.[2] My brothers had deaf ears. They were already lining up the chess pieces and reading from the dog-eared instruction book.[4]

I watched Vincent and Winston play during Christmas week. The chess board seemed to hold elaborate secrets waiting to be untangled. The chessmen were more powerful than Old Li's magic herbs that cured ancestral curses.

Cause and Effect

1 The chess set is missing two pieces and had been used, so its value as a gift is questionable. As a result, the mother is insulted and later tells Vincent to throw the set away.

Characterization

2 The author uses dialogue and description to show that the mother puts up a public face to hide her private feelings. She "graciously thanked" the gift-giver but later reveals with "a tight, proud smile" how she truly feels: "She not want it. We not want it."

Characterization

3 Details portray the old woman as pale and fragile. Her hair is "white, wispy" and she speaks "with a whistling whisper." The repetition of the *w* sound adds to the sense that the woman has a soft, breathy manner.

Cause and Effect

4 Vincent and Winston are kids and do not care about the game's condition. As a result, the boys ignore the mother's instructions.

Rules of the Game

from The Joy Luck Club

Amy Tan

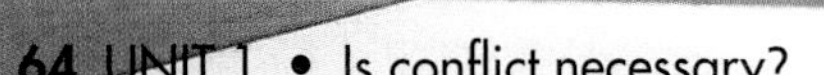

I was six when my mother taught me the art of invisible strength. It was a strategy for winning arguments, respect from others, and eventually, though neither of us knew it at the time, chess games.

"Bite back your tongue," scolded my mother when I cried loudly, yanking her hand toward the store that sold bags of salted plums. At home, she said, "Wise guy, he not go against wind. In Chinese we say, Come from South, blow with wind—poom!—North will follow. Strongest wind cannot be seen."

The next week I bit back my tongue as we entered the store with the forbidden candies. When my mother finished her shopping, she quietly plucked a small bag of plums from the rack and put it on the counter with the rest of the items.

My mother imparted her daily truths so she could help my older brothers and me rise above our circumstances. We lived in San Francisco's Chinatown. Like most of the other Chinese children who played in the back alleys of restaurants and curio shops, I didn't think we were poor. My bowl was always full, three five-course meals every day, beginning with a soup full of mysterious things I didn't want to know the names of.

We lived on Waverly Place, in a warm, clean, two-bedroom flat that sat above a small Chinese bakery specializing in steamed pastries and dim sum. In the early morning, when the alley was still quiet, I could smell fragrant red beans as they were cooked down to a pasty sweetness. By daybreak, our flat was heavy with the odor of fried sesame balls and sweet curried chicken crescents. From my bed, I would listen as my father got ready for work, then locked the door behind him, one-two-three clicks.

At the end of our two-block alley was a small sandlot playground with swings and slides well-shined down the middle with use. The play area was bordered by wood-slat benches where old-country people sat cracking roasted watermelon seeds with their golden teeth and scattering the husks to an impatient gathering of gurgling pigeons. The best playground, however, was the dark alley itself. It was crammed with daily mysteries and adventures. My brothers and I would peer into the medicinal herb shop, watching old Li dole out onto a stiff sheet of white paper the right amount of insect shells, saffron-colored seeds, and pungent leaves for his ailing customers. It was said that he once cured a woman dying of an ancestral curse that had eluded the best of American doctors. Next to the pharmacy was a printer who specialized in gold-embossed wedding invitations and festive red banners.

Vocabulary ▶
pungent (pun′ jənt) *adj.* producing a sharp smell

Spiral Review
SETTING What do details tell you about the cultural environment in which the narrator grew up?

Farther down the street was Ping Yuen Fish Market. The front window displayed a tank crowded with doomed fish and turtles struggling to gain footing on the slimy green-tiled sides. A hand-written sign informed tourists, "Within this store, is all for food, not for pet." Inside, the butchers with their bloodstained white smocks deftly gutted the fish while customers cried out their orders and shouted, "Give me your freshest," to which the butchers always protested, "All are freshest." On less crowded market days, we would inspect the crates of live frogs and crabs which we were warned not to poke, boxes of dried cuttlefish, and row upon row of iced prawns, squid, and slippery fish. The sanddabs made me shiver each time; their eyes lay on one flattened side and reminded me of my mother's story of a careless girl who ran into a crowded street and was crushed by a cab. "Was smash flat," reported my mother.

Characterization
What does this quotation reveal about the narrator's mother?

At the corner of the alley was Hong Sing's, a four-table cafe with a recessed stairwell in front that led to a door marked "Tradesmen." My brothers and I believed the bad people emerged from this door at night. Tourists never went to Hong Sing's, since the menu was printed only in Chinese. A Caucasian man with a big camera once posed me and my playmates in front of the restaurant. He had us move to the side of the picture window so the photo would capture the roasted duck with its head dangling from a juice-covered rope. After he took the picture, I told him he should go into Hong Sing's and eat dinner. When he smiled and asked me what they served, I shouted, "Guts and duck's feet and octopus gizzards!" Then I ran off with my friends, shrieking with laughter as we scampered across the alley and hid in the entryway grotto of the China Gem Company, my heart pounding with hope that he would chase us.

My mother named me after the street that we lived on: Waverly Place Jong, my official name for important American documents. But my family called me Meimei [mā́ mā́], "Little Sister." I was the youngest, the only daughter. Each morning before school, my mother would twist and yank on my thick black hair until she had formed two tightly wound pigtails. One day, as she struggled to weave a hard-toothed comb through my disobedient hair, I had a sly thought.

I asked her, "Ma, what is Chinese torture?" My mother shook her head. A bobby pin was wedged between her lips. She wetted her palm and smoothed the hair above my ear, then pushed the pin in so that it nicked sharply against my scalp.

"Who say this word?" she asked without a trace of knowing how wicked I was being. I shrugged my shoulders and said, "Some boy in my class said Chinese people do Chinese torture."

"Chinese people do many things," she said simply. "Chinese people do business, do medicine, do painting. Not lazy like American people. We do torture. Best torture."

Characterization
What does Mrs. Jong's response to the accusation that Chinese people do torture reveal about her personality?

My older brother Vincent was the one who actually got the chess set. We had gone to the annual Christmas party held at the First Chinese Baptist Church at the end of the alley. The missionary ladies had put together a Santa bag of gifts donated by members of another church. None of the gifts had names on them. There were separate sacks for boys and girls of different ages.

One of the Chinese parishioners had donned a Santa Claus costume and a stiff paper beard with cotton balls glued to it. I think the only children who thought he was the real thing were too young to know that Santa Claus was not Chinese. When my turn came up, the Santa man asked me how old I was. I thought it was a trick question; I was seven according to the American formula and eight by the Chinese calendar. I said I was born on March 17, 1951. That seemed to satisfy him. He then solemnly asked if I had been a very,

Comprehension
What gift does Vincent receive at the Christmas party?

very good girl this year and did I believe in Jesus Christ and obey my parents. I knew the only answer to that. I nodded back with equal solemnity.

Characterization
What does Waverly's thought process in this paragraph reveal indirectly about her character?

Having watched the other children opening their gifts, I already knew that the big gifts were not necessarily the nicest ones. One girl my age got a large coloring book of biblical characters, while a less greedy girl who selected a small box received a glass vial of lavender toilet water. The sound of the box was also important. A ten-year-old boy had chosen a box that jangled when he shook it. It was a tin globe of the world with a slit for inserting money. He must have thought it was full of dimes and nickels, because when he saw that it had just ten pennies, his face fell with such undisguised disappointment that his mother slapped the side of his head and led him out of the church hall, apologizing to the crowd for her son who had such bad manners he couldn't appreciate such a fine gift.

As I peered into the sack, I quickly fingered the remaining presents, testing their weight, imagining what they contained. I chose a heavy, compact one that was wrapped in shiny silver foil and a red satin ribbon. It was a twelve-pack of Life Savers and I spent the rest of the party arranging and rearranging the candy tubes in the order of my favorites. My brother Winston chose wisely as well. His present turned out to be a box of intricate plastic parts; the instructions on the box proclaimed that when they were properly assembled he would have an authentic miniature replica of a World War II submarine.

Vincent got the chess set, which would have been a very decent present to get at a church Christmas party except it was obviously used and, as we discovered later, it was missing a black pawn and a white knight. My mother graciously thanked the unknown benefactor, saying, "Too good. Cost too much." At which point, an old lady with fine white, wispy hair nodded toward our family and said with a whistling whisper, "Merry, merry Christmas."

Cause and Effect
What effect does the gift of the chess board have on Waverly?

When we got home, my mother told Vincent to throw the chess set away. "She not want it. We not want it," she said, tossing her head stiffly to the side with a tight, proud smile. My brothers had deaf ears. They were already lining up the chess pieces and reading from the dog-eared instruction book.

I watched Vincent and Winston play during Christmas week. The chess board seemed to hold elaborate secrets waiting to be untangled. The chessmen were more powerful than Old Li's magic herbs that cured ancestral curses. And my brothers wore such serious faces that I was sure something was at stake that was greater than avoiding the tradesmen's door to Hong Sing's.

"Let me! Let me!" I begged between games when one brother or the other would sit back with a deep sigh of relief and victory, the other annoyed, unable to let go of the outcome. Vincent at first refused to let me play, but when I offered my Life Savers as replacements for the buttons that filled in for the missing pieces, he relented. He chose the flavors: wild cherry for the black pawn and peppermint for the white knight. Winner could eat both. As our mother sprinkled flour and rolled out small doughy circles for the steamed dumplings that would be our dinner that night, Vincent explained the rules, pointing to each piece. "You have sixteen pieces and so do I. One king and queen, two bishops, two knights, two castles, and eight pawns. The pawns can only move forward one step, except on the first move. Then they can move two. But they can only take men by moving crossways like this, except in the beginning, when you can move ahead and take another pawn."

He chose the flavors: wild cherry for the black pawn and peppermint for the white knight.

"Why?" I asked as I moved my pawn. "Why can't they move more steps?"

"Because they're pawns," he said.

"But why do they go crossways to take other men? Why aren't there any women and children?"

"Why is the sky blue? Why must you always ask stupid questions?" asked Vincent. "This is a game. These are the rules. I didn't make them up. See. Here. In the book." He jabbed a page with a pawn in his hand. "Pawn. P-A-W-N. Pawn. Read it yourself."

Characterization What do you learn about Vincent based on this conversation?

My mother patted the flour off her hands. "Let me see book," she said quietly. She scanned the pages quickly, not reading the foreign English symbols, seeming to search deliberately for nothing in particular.

"This American rules," she concluded at last. "Every time people come out from foreign country, must know rules. You not know, judge say, Too bad, go back. They not telling you why so you can use their way go forward. They say, Don't know why, you find out yourself. But they knowing all the time. Better you take it, find out why yourself." She tossed her head back with a satisfied smile.

I found out about all the whys later. I read the rules and looked up all the big words in a dictionary. I borrowed books from the Chinatown library. I studied each chess piece, trying to absorb the power each contained.

Comprehension How does Waverly convince Vincent to let her play chess?

LITERATURE IN CONTEXT

Cultural Connection

Endgame

Endgame describes a tense period in a chess game when the end seems close at hand. With fewer pieces left, lines of attack and defense become clearer to both players. Mistakes are magnified in an endgame, when victory and defeat can be determined by a single ill-considered move. In this story, Waverly develops a keen awareness of the strategies needed to secure a victory in the endgame.

Connect to the Literature

Why might it be difficult for a young beginning chess player like Waverly to master the endgame?

I learned about opening moves and why it's important to control the center early on; the shortest distance between two points is straight down the middle. I learned about the middle game and why tactics between two adversaries are like clashing ideas; the one who plays better has the clearest plans for both attacking and getting out of traps. I learned why it is essential in the endgame to have foresight, a mathematical understanding of all possible moves, and patience; all weaknesses and advantages become evident to a strong adversary and are obscured to a tiring opponent. I discovered that for the whole game one must gather invisible strengths and see the endgame before the game begins.

I also found out why I should never reveal "why" to others. A little knowledge withheld is a great advantage one should store for future use. That is the power of chess. It is a game of secrets in which one must show and never tell.

I loved the secrets I found within the sixty-four black and white squares. I carefully drew a handmade chessboard and pinned it to the wall next to my bed, where at night I would stare for hours at imaginary battles. Soon I no longer lost any games or Life Savers, but I lost my adversaries. Winston and Vincent decided they were more interested in roaming the streets after school in their Hopalong Cassidy cowboy hats.

On a cold spring afternoon, while walking home from school, I detoured through the playground at the end of our alley. I saw a group of old men, two seated across a folding table playing a game of chess, others smoking pipes, eating peanuts, and watching. I ran home and grabbed Vincent's chess set, which was bound in a cardboard box with rubber bands. I also carefully selected two prized rolls of Life Savers. I came back to the park and approached a man who was observing the game.

"Want to play?" I asked him. His face widened with surprise and he grinned as he looked at the box under my arm.

"Little sister, been a long time since I play with dolls," he said, smiling **benevolently**. I quickly put the box down next to him on the bench and displayed my **retort**.

Lau Po, as he allowed me to call him, turned out to be a much better player than my brothers. I lost many games and many Life

Vocabulary ▶

benevolently (bə nev´ ə lənt lē) *adv.* in a well-meaning way

retort (ri tôrt´) *n.* sharp or clever reply

Savers. But over the weeks, with each diminishing roll of candies, I added new secrets. Lau Po gave me the names. The Double Attack from the East and West Shores. Throwing Stones on the Drowning Man. The Sudden Meeting of the Clan. The Surprise from the Sleeping Guard. The Humble Servant Who Kills the King. Sand in the Eyes of Advancing Forces. A Double Killing Without Blood.

There were also the fine points of chess etiquette. Keep captured men in neat rows, as well-tended prisoners. Never announce "Check" with vanity, lest someone with an unseen sword slit your throat. Never hurl pieces into the sandbox after you have lost a game, because then you must find them again, by yourself, after apologizing to all around you. By the end of the summer, Lau Po had taught me all he knew, and I had become a better chess player.

By the end of summer, Lau Po had taught me all he knew . . .

A small weekend crowd of Chinese people and tourists would gather as I played and defeated my opponents one by one. My mother would join the crowds during these outdoor exhibition games. She sat proudly on the bench, telling my admirers with proper Chinese humility, "Is luck."

A man who watched me play in the park suggested that my mother allow me to play in local chess tournaments. My mother smiled graciously, an answer that meant nothing. I desperately wanted to go, but I bit back my tongue. I knew she would not let me play among strangers. So as we walked home I said in a small voice that I didn't want to play in the local tournament. They would have American rules. If I lost, I would bring shame on my family.

Cause and Effect
What does Waverly anticipate would be the effect of her expressing her desire to play in local chess tournaments?

"Is shame you fall down nobody push you," said my mother.

During my first tournament, my mother sat with me in the front row as I waited for my turn. I frequently bounced my legs to unstick them from the cold metal seat of the folding chair. When my name was called, I leapt up. My mother unwrapped something in her lap. It was her *chang*, a small tablet of red jade which held the sun's fire. "Is luck," she whispered, and tucked it into my dress pocket. I turned to my opponent, a fifteen-year-old boy from Oakland. He looked at me, wrinkling his nose.

Comprehension
How does Waverly's mother respond to Waverly's admirers in the park?

As I began to play, the boy disappeared, the color ran out of the room, and I saw only my white pieces and his black ones waiting on the other side. A light wind began blowing past my ears. It whispered secrets only I could hear.

Cause and Effect How does Waverly's mindset affect the outcome of the match?

"Blow from the South," it murmured. "The wind leaves no trail." I saw a clear path, the traps to avoid. The crowd rustled. "Shhh! Shhh!" said the corners of the room. The wind blew stronger. "Throw sand from the East to distract him." The knight came forward ready for the sacrifice. The wind hissed, louder and louder. "Blow, blow, blow. He cannot see. He is blind now. Make him lean away from the wind so he is easier to knock down."

"Check," I said, as the wind roared with laughter. The wind died down to little puffs, my own breath.

My mother placed my first trophy next to a new plastic chess set that the neighborhood Tao society had given to me. As she wiped each piece with a soft cloth, she said, "Next time win more, lose less."

"Ma, it's not how many pieces you lose," I said. "Sometimes you need to lose pieces to get ahead."

"Better to lose less, see if you really need."

At the next tournament, I won again, but it was my mother who wore the triumphant grin.

Characterization What do Waverly's mother's comments here reveal indirectly about her ambitions for Waverly?

"Lost eight piece this time. Last time was eleven. What I tell you? Better off lose less!" I was annoyed, but I couldn't say anything.

I attended more tournaments, each one farther away from home. I won all games, in all divisions. The Chinese bakery downstairs from our flat displayed my growing collection of trophies in its window, amidst the dust-covered cakes that were never picked up. The day after I won an important regional tournament, the window encased a fresh sheet cake with whipped-cream frosting and red script saying, "Congratulations, Waverly Jong, Chinatown Chess Champion." Soon after that, a flower shop, headstone engraver, and funeral parlor offered to sponsor me in national tournaments. That's when my mother decided I no longer had to do the dishes. Winston and Vincent had to do my chores.

"Why does she get to play and we do all the work," complained Vincent.

"Is new American rules," said my mother. "Meimei play, squeeze all her brains out for win chess. You play, worth squeeze towel."

Vocabulary ▶ **prodigy** (präd´ ə jē) *n.* person, especially a child, of extraordinary talent or ability

By my ninth birthday, I was a national chess champion. I was still some 429 points away from grand-master status, but I was touted as the Great American Hope, a child **prodigy** and a girl to boot. They ran a photo of me in *Life* magazine next to a quote in which Bobby Fischer[1] said, "There will never be a woman grand master." "Your move, Bobby," said the caption.

The day they took the magazine picture I wore neatly plaited braids clipped with plastic barrettes trimmed with rhinestones. I was playing in a large high school auditorium that echoed with phlegmy coughs and the squeaky rubber knobs of chair legs sliding across freshly waxed wooden floors. Seated across from me was an American man, about the same age as Lau Po, maybe fifty. I remember that his sweaty brow seemed to weep at my every move. He wore a dark, malodorous suit. One of his pockets was stuffed with a great white kerchief on which he wiped his palm before sweeping his hand over the chosen chess piece with great flourish.

◀ **Vocabulary**
malodorous
(mal ō´ dər əs) *adj.*
having a bad smell

In my crisp pink-and-white dress with scratchy lace at the neck, one of two my mother had sewn for these special occasions, I would clasp my hands under my chin, the delicate points of my elbows poised lightly on the table in the manner my mother had shown me for posing for the press. I would swing my patent leather shoes back and forth like an impatient child riding on a school bus. Then I would pause, suck in my lips, twirl my chosen piece in midair as if undecided, and then firmly plant it in its new threatening place, with a triumphant smile thrown back at my opponent for good measure.

Comprehension
Why does Waverly no longer have to do her chores?

1. **Bobby Fischer** (1943–2008), this American chess prodigy attained the top rank of grandmaster in 1958.

I no longer played in the alley of Waverly Place. I never visited the playground where the pigeons and old men gathered. I went to school, then directly home to learn new chess secrets, cleverly concealed advantages, more escape routes.

But I found it difficult to concentrate at home. My mother had a habit of standing over me while I plotted out my games. I think she thought of herself as my protective ally. Her lips would be sealed tight, and after each move I made, a soft "Hmmmmph" would escape from her nose.

"Ma, I can't practice when you stand there like that," I said one day. She retreated to the kitchen and made loud noises with the pots and pans. When the crashing stopped, I could see out of the corner of my eye that she was standing in the doorway. "Hmmmmph!" Only this one came out of her tight throat.

Vocabulary ▶ concessions (kən sesh′ ənz) *n.* things given or granted as privileges

My parents made many concessions to allow me to practice. One time I complained that the bedroom I shared was so noisy that I couldn't think. Thereafter, my brothers slept in a bed in the living room facing the street. I said I couldn't finish my rice; my head didn't work right when my stomach was too full. I left the table with half-finished bowls and nobody complained. But there was one duty I couldn't avoid. I had to accompany my mother on Saturday market days when I had no tournament to play. My mother would proudly walk with me, visiting many shops, buying very little. "This my daughter Wave-ly Jong," she said to whoever looked her way.

Cause and Effect In what ways does Waverly's success at chess affect her family life? Explain.

One day, after we left a shop I said under my breath, "I wish you wouldn't do that, telling everybody I'm your daughter." My mother stopped walking. Crowds of people with heavy bags pushed past us on the sidewalk, bumping into first one shoulder, then another.

"Aiii-ya. So shame be with mother?" She grasped my hand even tighter as she glared at me.

I looked down. "It's not that, it's just so obvious. It's just so embarrassing."

"Embarrass you be my daughter?" Her voice was cracking with anger.

"That's not what I meant. That's not what I said."

"What you say?"

I knew it was a mistake to say anything more, but I heard my voice speaking. "Why do you have to use me to show off? If you want to show off, then why don't you learn to play chess."

My mother's eyes turned into dangerous black slits. She had no words for me, just sharp silence.

I felt the wind rushing around my hot ears. I jerked my hand out of my mother's tight grasp and spun around, knocking into an old woman. Her bag of groceries spilled to the ground.

"Aii-ya! Stupid girl!" my mother and the woman cried. Oranges and tin cans careened down the sidewalk. As my mother stooped to help the old woman pick up the escaping food, I took off.

I raced down the street, dashing between people, not looking back as my mother screamed shrilly, "Meimei! Meimei!" I fled down an alley, past dark curtained shops and merchants washing the grime off their windows. I sped into the sunlight, into a large street crowded with tourists examining trinkets and souvenirs. I ducked into another dark alley, down another street, up another alley. I ran until it hurt and I realized I had nowhere to go, that I was not running from anything. The alleys contained no escape routes.

My mother had a habit of standing over me while I plotted out my games.

My breath came out like angry smoke. It was cold. I sat down on an upturned plastic pail next to a stack of empty boxes, cupping my chin with my hands, thinking hard. I imagined my mother, first walking briskly down one street or another looking for me, then giving up and returning home to await my arrival. After two hours, I stood up on creaking legs and slowly walked home.

The alley was quiet and I could see the yellow lights shining from our flat like two tiger's eyes in the night. I climbed the sixteen steps to the door, advancing quietly up each so as not to make any warning sounds. I turned the knob; the door was locked. I heard a chair moving, quick steps, the locks turning—click! click! click!—and then the door opened.

"About time you got home," said Vincent. "Boy, are you in trouble."

He slid back to the dinner table. On a platter were the remains of a large fish, its fleshy head still connected to bones swimming upstream in vain escape. Standing there waiting for my punishment, I heard my mother speak in a dry voice.

"We not concerning this girl. This girl not have concerning for us."

Nobody looked at me. Bone chopsticks clinked against the insides of bowls being emptied into hungry mouths.

I walked into my room, closed the door, and lay down on my bed. The room was dark, the ceiling filled with shadows from the dinnertime lights of neighboring flats.

Comprehension
What do Waverly and her mother argue about at the market?

Cause and Effect Why do you think Waverly and her mother stop speaking to each other?

In my head, I saw a chessboard with sixty-four black and white squares. Opposite me was my opponent, two angry black slits. She wore a triumphant smile. "Strongest wind cannot be seen," she said.

Her black men advanced across the plane, slowly marching to each successive level as a single unit. My white pieces screamed as they scurried and fell off the board one by one. As her men drew closer to my edge, I felt myself growing light. I rose up into the air and flew out the window. Higher and higher, above the alley, over the tops of tiled roofs, where I was gathered up by the wind and pushed up toward the night sky until everything below me disappeared and I was alone.

I closed my eyes and pondered my next move.

Language Study

Vocabulary The words listed below appear in "Rules of the Game." Using your knowledge of these words, tell whether each sentence below makes sense. Use the meaning of the italicized vocabulary word to explain your answer.

pungent **retort** **prodigy** **malodorous** **concessions**

1. During play rehearsals, Mom made some *concessions* regarding my homework.
2. The *pungent* smell of chopped onions filled the kitchen.
3. He gave his wife a bottle of expensive, *malodorous* perfume.
4. The audience was bored by the comedian's brilliant *retort*.
5. With his average talent, the violin *prodigy* amazed no one.

WORD STUDY

The **Latin root *-bene-*** means "good or well." In this story, an elderly man smiles **benevolently** at Waverly. His smile shows that he wishes her well.

Word Study

Part A Explain how the **Latin root *-bene-*** contributes to the meanings of *beneficial*, *benediction*, and *beneficiary*. Consult a dictionary if necessary.

Part B Use the context of the sentences and what you know about the Latin root *-bene-* to explain your answer to each question.

1. Would you appreciate what a *benefactor* would do for you?
2. What are some of the *benefits* of exercise?

Close Reading Activities

Literary Analysis

Key Ideas and Details

1. **Analyze Cause and Effect (a)** Early in the story, what happens when Waverly cries to get a bag of salted plums? **(b)** What happens when she changes her behavior? **(c)** How does Waverly later apply that strategy to her desire to play chess competitively?
2. **Analyze Cause and Effect** Use a chart like the one shown to analyze cause and effect in this story. **(a)** Note two causes for Waverly's success with chess. **(b)** List three effects of her success.
3. **Analyze Cause and Effect (a)** Why does Mrs. Jong give Waverly special privileges? **(b)** How do these privileges affect Waverly and her relationship with her mother? Use details from the text in your response.

Causes of Waverly's Success
1.
2.
Effects of Waverly's Success
1.
2.
3.

Craft and Structure

4. **Characterization** Describe the character of Waverly. Support your response with examples of her actions, behavior, words, and thoughts, along with details about the effects she has on other people.
5. **Characterization (a)** Is the conversation in which Waverly, Vincent, and Mrs. Jong discuss the rules of chess an example of direct or indirect characterization? Explain your response. **(b)** What do you learn about Mrs. Jong's character from this exchange? Cite story details in your answer.
6. **Characterization (a)** What is Lau Po's reaction to Waverly's request to play chess? **(b)** How does the author reveal Lau Po's reaction? **(c)** Through the spring and summer, Lau Po teaches Waverly. What does this show the reader about his character? Explain.

Integration of Knowledge and Ideas

7. **Compare and Contrast: (a)** How would you describe Waverly's behavior at her first tournament? **(b)** How was her behavior different in later tournaments? **(c)** What do you think caused this change? Use text details to support your responses.
8. **Speculate:** Who do you think will "win" the game between Waverly and her mother? Use details from the text to explain your response.

9. THE BIG ? **Is conflict necessary? (a)** Is it necessary for Waverly to oppose her mother at the market? Explain. **(b)** How do their personal and cultural differences make it somehow necessary for Waverly to see her mother on the other side of the chessboard? Use details from the story to support your ideas.

ACADEMIC VOCABULARY

As you write and speak about "Rules of the Game," use the words related to conflict that you explored on page 3 of this book.

Conventions: Subjects and Predicates

The **simple subject** tells whom or what a sentence is about. The **complete subject** includes all the words that tell whom or what a sentence is about.

The **simple predicate** is the verb that tells what the subject of a sentence does or is. The **complete predicate** includes the verb and all the words that modify or complete it.

A complete sentence needs both a subject and a predicate. The chart below shows the complete subjects and the complete predicates of three example sentences. In each sentence, the simple subjects and predicates are underlined.

Complete Subject	Complete Predicate
Conflict between family members	is not unusual.
A group of old men	gathered in the park to play chess.
Waverly	argues dramatically with her mother in the market.

Practice A

Add a subject or predicate to complete each sentence. Identify the subject and predicate in each completed sentence.

1. ______ watched Vincent and Winston's chess games.
2. The book of rules ______.
3. Her interest in the game ______.
4. ______ soon made Waverly a skillful player.

Writing Application Write four new sentences by changing either the subject or the predicate of this example sentence: *Chess has been my favorite game for years.*

Practice B

Identify the complete subject and complete predicate in each sentence.

1. Waverly's family lives in San Francisco.
2. One of her brothers received a used chess set as a Christmas present.
3. Some pieces from the chess set were missing.
4. This did not stop Waverly from becoming an expert at the game.

Reading Application Choose two sentences from "Rules of the Game" that each contain just one complete subject and one complete verb. Identify the complete subject and predicate in each sentence.

Writing to Sources

Informative Text In "Rules of the Game," both Waverly and her mother learn a variety of lessons. Think about another lesson you could teach either character. Create a **written presentation** that details your ideas.

- Make notes about an issue that Waverly or Mrs. Jong faces. Use your notes to consider the lesson you might teach and how best to convey your ideas. Weave details from the text into your presentation to support your reasons for teaching this lesson.
- Consider your purpose, point of view as an outsider, and your audience of Waverly or Mrs. Jong. Use this information to choose the most effective genre, structure, and style for your presentation. For example, you might write a formal expository essay, an informal personal narrative, or a story with a moral.
- Check that your work is organized logically and your ideas are fully developed. Add transitions and vary your sentences for meaning, interest, and style.

As you write, support your ideas with details from the text. Cite passages precisely and integrate them smoothly into your analysis.

Grammar Application As you revise your sentences to add variety, check that they each contain a complete subject and a complete predicate.

Research and Technology

Build and Present Knowledge Although "Rules of the Game" is a short story, the author incorporates facts about the game of chess in order to clarify events and add authenticity. With a small group, create an **informational brochure** about the history, rules, and strategies of chess. Follow these steps to research and write your brochure:

- Collect information about chess from library and reliable Internet sources and take accurate notes. Develop clear questions to help you gather details from a variety of trustworthy sources.
- Organize the information logically into sections for a brochure.
- Decide whether to use illustrations to convey information. For example, you might include a diagram showing how chess pieces move.
- Design the brochure. As you do so, consider how you will be sharing it. For example, you may print it as a traditional paper brochure, or present it on a blog, Web site, or mobile device. Make sure the design will work in the format you choose.

Writing

4. Produce clear and coherent writing in which the development, organization, and style are appropriate to task, purpose, and audience.

Speaking and Listening

2. Integrate multiple sources of information presented in diverse media or formats evaluating the credibility and accuracy of each source.

Language

1. Demonstrate command of the conventions of standard English grammar and usage when writing or speaking.

Meet the Author

Edgar Allan Poe (1809–1849) is one of the first great American storytellers. He led a full but short and tragic life. Orphaned at the age of three, Poe was raised by foster parents, the Allans, from whom he took his middle name. The Allans gave Poe an education, but he left college when his foster father refused to pay Poe's gambling debts. Poe found happiness when he married Virginia Clemm, but he became increasingly withdrawn after her death from tuberculosis in 1847. In 1849, Poe was found delirious on a Baltimore street, and three days later he died.

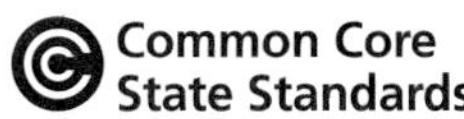

Common Core State Standards

Reading Literature

5. Analyze how an author's choices concerning how to structure a text, order events within it, and manipulate time create such effects as mystery, tension, or surprise.

Language

6. Acquire and use accurately general academic and domain-specific words and phrases; demonstrate independence in gathering vocabulary knowledge.

Is conflict necessary?

Explore the Big Question as you read "The Cask of Amontillado." Take notes about the story's portrayal of conflict and revenge.

CLOSE READING FOCUS

Key Ideas and Details: **Make Predictions**

A **prediction** is an idea you develop about what will happen later in a story. As you read, notice details that may hint at, or foreshadow, future events. Next, make predictions based on those details, and then read ahead to verify your predictions. If a prediction turns out to be wrong, evaluate your reasoning by asking yourself questions like these:

- Did I misread details?
- Did the author purposely create false expectations in order to surprise me later in the story?

Craft and Structure: **Plot**

Plot is the sequence of related events in a narrative. A plot is driven by a conflict, or problem, and follows a specific structure:

- **Exposition:** the characters and setting are introduced
- **Rising Action:** the central conflict begins and develops
- **Climax:** the high point of intensity in the conflict is reached
- **Falling Action:** the conflict's intensity lessens
- **Resolution:** the conflict concludes and loose ends are tied up

Writers use a variety of techniques, or *stylistic devices,* to keep readers interested in the plot. One of these devices, **foreshadowing,** is the use of clues to hint at later events. Foreshadowing also helps to create **suspense,** a feeling of tension that keeps readers wondering what will happen next. As you read, look for clues in the text that alert you to what might happen later.

Vocabulary

The words below are critical to understanding the text that follows. Copy the words into your notebook. Which are verbs? Explain how you know.

precluded	**afflicted**	**recoiling**
retribution	**explicit**	**subsided**

CLOSE READING MODEL

The passage below is from Edgar Allan Poe's short story "The Cask of Amontillado." The annotations to the right of the passage show ways in which you can use close reading skills to make predictions and analyze plot.

from "The Cask of Amontillado"

The thousand injuries of Fortunato I had borne as I best could, but when he ventured upon insult, I vowed revenge.[1] You, who so well know the nature of my soul, will not suppose, however, that I gave utterance to a threat. *At length* I would be avenged; this was a point definitely settled[2]—but the very definitiveness with which it was resolved, precluded the idea of risk. I must not only punish, but punish with impunity. A wrong is unredressed when retribution overtakes its redresser. It is equally unredressed when the avenger fails to make himself felt as such to him who has done the wrong.

It must be understood that neither by word nor deed had I given Fortunato cause to doubt my good will. I continued, as was my wont, to smile in his face, and he did not perceive that my smile *now* was at the thought of his immolation.[3]

Plot

1 The exposition introduces the characters and provides background information about their relationship: The narrator feels that Fortunato has insulted him and deserves punishment. This passage sets the conflict in motion.

Make Predictions

2 The narrator reveals that he is plotting against Fortunato, thus deepening the conflict. These sentences also show the narrator to be devious. Instead of acting rashly, he will take his revenge "at length." You may well predict that Fortunato is on a doomed path.

Plot

3 As the rising action continues, the narrator describes friendly behavior that masks evil intentions. He shows "good will" and "smile[s] in his [Fortunato's] face." However, the word *immolation* refers to death, which suggests the narrator's plans for Fortunato are quite grim.

The Cask of Amontillado[1]

Edgar Allan Poe

The thousand injuries of Fortunato I had borne as I best could, but when he ventured upon insult, I vowed revenge. You, who so well know the nature of my soul, will not suppose, however, that I gave utterance to a threat. *At length* I would be avenged; this was a point definitely settled—but the very definitiveness with which it was resolved, precluded the idea of risk. I must not only punish, but punish with impunity.[2] A wrong is unredressed when retribution overtakes its redresser. It is equally unredressed when the avenger fails to make himself felt as such to him who has done the wrong.

It must be understood that neither by word nor deed had I given Fortunato cause to doubt my good will. I continued, as was my wont, to smile in his face, and he did not perceive that my smile *now* was at the thought of his immolation.[3]

◀ Vocabulary
precluded (prē klo͞od′ id) *v.* prevented

retribution (re′ trə byo͞o′ shən) *n.* payback; punishment for a misdeed

Comprehension
Why does the narrator vow revenge on Fortunato?

1. **Amontillado** (ə män′ tə ya′ dō) *n.* a pale, dry sherry.
2. **impunity** (im pyo͞o′ nə tē′) *n.* freedom from consequences.
3. **immolation** (im′ ə lā′ shən) *n.* destruction.

Make Predictions
What role do you predict Fortunato's "weak point" will play in the narrator's revenge?

He had a weak point—this Fortunato—although in other regards he was a man to be respected and even feared. He prided himself on his connoisseurship[4] in wine. Few Italians have the true virtuoso[5] spirit. For the most part their enthusiasm is adopted to suit the time and opportunity, to practice imposture upon the British and Austrian *millionaires*. In painting and gemmary, Fortunato, like his countrymen, was a quack, but in the matter of old wines he was sincere. In this respect I did not differ from him materially; I was skillful in the Italian vintages myself, and bought largely whenever I could.

It was about dusk, one evening during the supreme madness of the carnival season, that I encountered my friend. He accosted me with excessive warmth, for he had been drinking much. The man wore motley.[6] He had on a tight-fitting parti-striped dress, and his head was surmounted by the conical cap and bells. I was so pleased to see him that I thought I should never have done wringing his hand.

I said to him, "My dear Fortunato, you are luckily met. How remarkably well you are looking today. But I have received a pipe[7] of what passes for Amontillado, and I have my doubts."

"How?" said he. "Amontillado? A pipe? Impossible! And in the middle of the carnival!"

"I have my doubts," I replied; "and I was silly enough to pay the full Amontillado price without consulting you in the matter. You were not to be found, and I was fearful of losing a bargain."

"Amontillado!"

"I have my doubts."

"Amontillado!"

"And I must satisfy them."

"Amontillado!"

"As you are engaged, I am on my way to Luchesi. If any one has a critical turn, it is he. He will tell me—"

"Luchesi cannot tell Amontillado from Sherry."

"And yet some fools will have it that his taste is a match for your own."

"Come, let us go."

---

4. **connoisseurship** (kän′ ə sʉr′ ship) *n.* expert judgment.
5. **virtuoso** (vʉr′ cho͞o ō′ sō) *adj.* masterly skill in a particular field.
6. **motley** (mät′ lē) *n.* a clown's multicolored costume.
7. **pipe** (pīp) *n.* large barrel, holding approximately 126 gallons.

"Whither?"

"To your vaults."

"My friend, no; I will not impose upon your good nature. I perceive you have an engagement. Luchesi—"

"I have no engagement—come."

"My friend, no. It is not the engagement, but the severe cold with which I perceive you are afflicted. The vaults are insufferably damp. They are encrusted with niter."

◀ **Vocabulary**
afflicted (ə flikt′ əd) *v.* suffering or sickened

"Let us go, nevertheless. The cold is merely nothing. Amontillado! You have been imposed upon. And as for Luchesi, he cannot distinguish Sherry from Amontillado."

Thus speaking, Fortunato possessed himself of my arm; and putting on a mask of black silk and drawing a *roquelaure*[8] closely about my person, I suffered him to hurry me to my palazzo.

There were no attendants at home; they had absconded to make merry in honor of the time. I had told them that I should not return until the morning, and had given them explicit orders not to stir from the house. These orders were sufficient, I well knew, to insure their immediate disappearance, one and all, as soon as my back was turned.

◀ **Vocabulary**
explicit (eks plis′ it) *adj.* clearly and directly stated

I took from their sconces two flambeaux, and giving one to Fortunato, bowed him through several suites of rooms to the archway that led into the vaults. I passed down a long and winding staircase, requesting him to be cautious as he followed. We came at length to the foot of the descent, and stood together upon the damp ground of the catacombs of the Montresors.

The gait of my friend was unsteady, and the bells upon his cap jingled as he strode.

"The pipe," he said.

"It is farther on," said I; "but observe the white web-work which gleams from these cavern walls."

He turned towards me, and looked into my eyes with two filmy orbs that distilled the rheum of intoxication.

"Niter?" he asked, at length.

"Niter," I replied. "How long have you had that cough?"

Comprehension
What common interest does the narrator share with Fortunato?

---

8. ***roquelaure*** (räk′ ə lôr) *n.* knee-length cloak.

Plot
What fate does this conversation foreshadow for Fortunato?

"Ugh! ugh! ugh!—ugh! ugh! ugh!—ugh! ugh! ugh!—ugh! ugh! ugh!—ugh! ugh! ugh!"

My poor friend found it impossible to reply for many minutes.

"It is nothing," he said, at last.

"Come," I said, with decision, "we will go back; your health is precious. You are rich, respected, admired, beloved; you are happy, as once I was. You are a man to be missed. For me it is no matter. We will go back; you will be ill, and I cannot be responsible. Besides, there is Luchesi—"

"Enough," he said; "the cough is a mere nothing; it will not kill me. I shall not die of a cough."

"True—true," I replied; "and, indeed, I had no intention of alarming you unnecessarily—but you should use all proper caution. A draft of this Médoc will defend us from the damps."

Here I knocked off the neck of a bottle which I drew from a long row of its fellows that lay upon the mold.

"Drink," I said, presenting him the wine.

He raised it to his lips with a leer. He paused and nodded to me familiarly, while his bells jingled.

"I drink," he said "to the buried that repose around us."

"And I to your long life."

He again took my arm, and we proceeded.

"These vaults," he said, "are extensive."

"The Montresors," I replied, "were a great and numerous family."

"I forget your arms."

"A huge human foot d'or, in a field azure; the foot crushes a serpent rampant whose fangs are imbedded in the heel."

"And the motto?"

"Nemo me impune lacessit."[9]

"Good!" he said.

The wine sparkled in his eyes and the bells jingled. My own fancy grew warm with the Médoc. We had passed through long walls of piled skeletons, with casks and puncheons[10] intermingling, into the inmost recesses of the catacombs. I paused again, and this time I made bold to seize Fortunato by an arm above the elbow.

---

9. ***Nemo me impune lacessit*** Latin for "No one attacks me with impunity."
10. **puncheons** (pun′ chənz) *n.* large barrels.

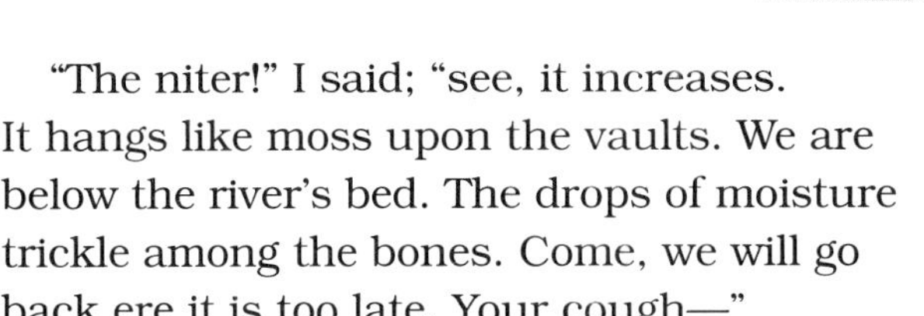

"The niter!" I said; "see, it increases. It hangs like moss upon the vaults. We are below the river's bed. The drops of moisture trickle among the bones. Come, we will go back ere it is too late. Your cough—"

"It is nothing," he said; "let us go on. But first, another draft of the Médoc."

I broke and reached him a flagon of De Grâve. He emptied it at a breath. His eyes flashed with a fierce light. He laughed and threw the bottle upwards with a gesticulation I did not understand.

I looked at him in surprise. He repeated the movement—a grotesque one.

"You do not comprehend?" he said.

"Not I," I replied.

"Then you are not of the brotherhood."

"How?"

"You are not of the masons."[11]

"Yes, yes," I said; "yes, yes."

"You? Impossible! A mason?"

"A mason," I replied.

"A sign," he said, "a sign."

"It is this," I answered, producing from beneath the folds of my *roquelaure* a trowel.

"You jest," he exclaimed, **recoiling** a few paces. "But let us proceed to the Amontillado."

"Be it so," I said, replacing the tool beneath the cloak and again offering him my arm. He leaned upon it heavily. We continued our route in search of the Amontillado. We passed through a range of low arches, descended, passed on, and descending again, arrived at a deep crypt, in which the foulness of the air caused our flambeaux rather to glow than flame.

At the most remote end of the crypt there appeared another less spacious. Its walls had been lined with human remains,

LITERATURE IN CONTEXT

Literature Connection

Poe and the Gothic Tradition
The literary genre known as gothic fiction emerged in England in the late 1700s in works like *Castle of Otranto* (1765) by Horace Walpole and *The Mysteries of Udolpho* (1794) by Ann Radcliffe. The word *gothic* was originally used to describe a style of building that was common in the late Middle Ages. To writers in the eighteenth century, the cold chambers and secret passages of such buildings suggested mystery and dark tales of vengeance and passion.

Edgar Allan Poe translated the imagery and atmosphere of British gothic fiction to an American landscape, pioneering an American gothic tradition. Contemporary writers like Stephen King and Anne Rice, as well as countless filmmakers, carry on that tradition today.

Connect to the Literature

What qualities of gothic fiction do you find in "The Cask of Amontillado"? Explain.

◀ **Vocabulary**
recoiling (ri koil′ iŋ) *v.* staggering back

Comprehension
Where does Montresor bring Fortunato?

---

11. masons *n.* the Freemasons, an international secret society.

piled to the vault overhead, in the fashion of the great catacombs of Paris. Three sides of this interior crypt were still ornamented in this manner. From the fourth side the bones had been thrown down, and lay promiscuously upon the earth, forming at one point a mound of some size. Within the wall thus exposed by the displacing of the bones, we perceived a still interior crypt or recess, in depth about four feet, in width three, in height six or seven. It seemed to have been constructed for no especial use within itself, but formed merely the *interval* between two of the colossal supports of the roof of the catacombs, and was backed by one of their circumscribing walls of solid granite.

It was in vain that Fortunato, uplifting his dull torch, endeavored to pry into the depth of the recess. Its termination the feeble light did not enable us to see.

▼ Critical Viewing
Explain how the context of this story might make masks like the one below seem sinister.

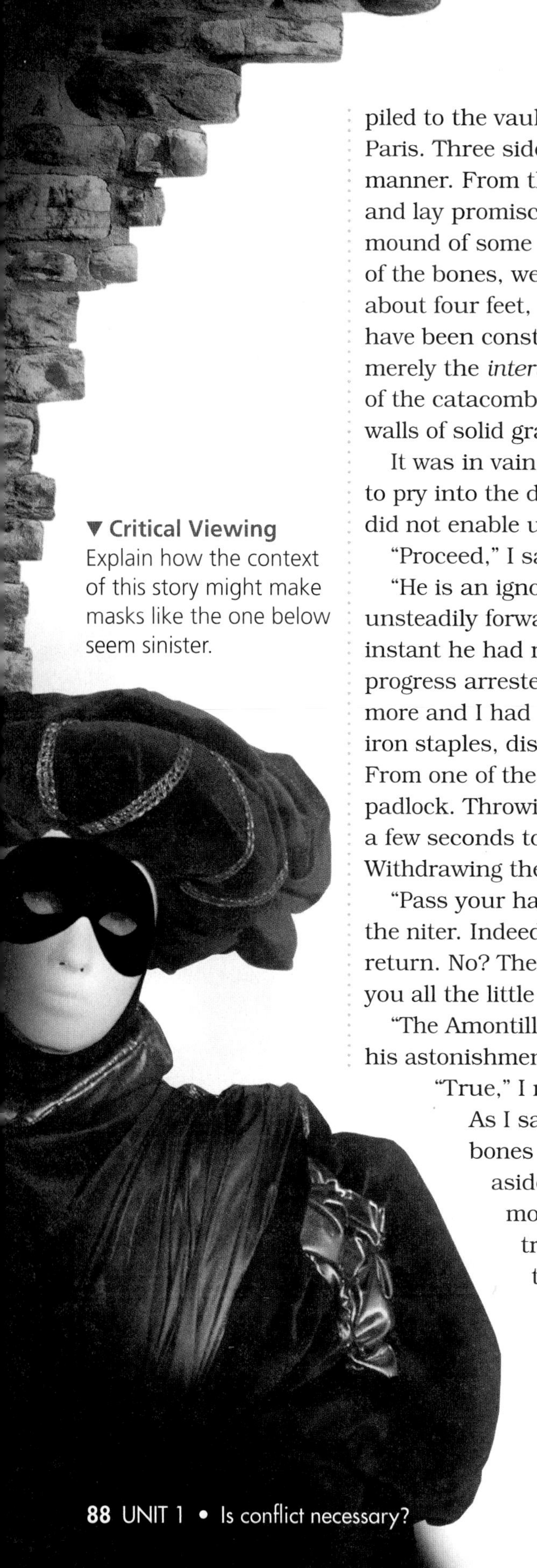

"Proceed," I said: "herein is the Amontillado. As for Luchesi—"

"He is an ignoramus," interrupted my friend, as he stepped unsteadily forward, while I followed immediately at his heels. In an instant he had reached the extremity of the niche, and finding his progress arrested by the rock, stood stupidly bewildered. A moment more and I had fettered him to the granite. In its surface were two iron staples, distant from each other about two feet, horizontally. From one of these depended a short chain, from the other a padlock. Throwing the links about his waist, it was but the work of a few seconds to secure it. He was too much astounded to resist. Withdrawing the key I stepped back from the recess.

"Pass your hand," I said, "over the wall; you cannot help feeling the niter. Indeed, it is very damp. Once more let me implore you to return. No? Then I must positively leave you. But I must first render you all the little attentions in my power."

"The Amontillado!" ejaculated my friend, not yet recovered from his astonishment.

"True," I replied; "the Amontillado."

As I said these words I busied myself among the pile of bones of which I have before spoken. Throwing them aside, I soon uncovered a quantity of building stone and mortar. With these materials and with the aid of my trowel, I began vigorously to wall up the entrance of the niche.

I had scarcely laid the first tier of the masonry when I discovered that the intoxication of Fortunato had in a great measure worn off. The earliest indication I had of this was a low moaning cry from the depth of the recess. It was not the cry of a drunken man. There was then a long and obstinate silence. I laid the second tier, and the third, and the fourth; and then I heard the furious vibrations of the chain. The noise lasted for several minutes, during which, that I might hearken to it with the more satisfaction, I ceased my labors and sat down upon the bones. When at last the clanking **subsided**, I resumed the trowel, and finished without interruption the fifth, the sixth, and the seventh tier. The wall was now nearly upon a level with my breast. I again paused, and holding the flambeaux over the masonwork, threw a few feeble rays upon the figure within.

A succession of loud and shrill screams, bursting suddenly from the throat of the chained form, seemed to thrust me violently back. For a brief moment I hesitated, I trembled. Unsheathing my rapier, I began to grope with it about the recess; but the thought of an instant reassured me. I placed my hand upon the solid fabric of the catacombs, and felt satisfied. I reapproached the wall; I replied to the yells of him who clamored. I reechoed, I aided, I surpassed them in volume and in strength. I did this, and the clamorer grew still.

It was now midnight, and my task was drawing to a close. I had completed the eighth, the ninth, and the tenth tier. I had finished a portion of the last and the eleventh; there remained but a single stone to be fitted and plastered in. I struggled with its weight; I placed it partially in its destined position. But now there came from out the niche a low laugh that erected the hairs upon my head. It was succeeded by a sad voice, which I had difficulty in recognizing as that of the noble Fortunato. The voice said—

"Ha! ha! ha!—he! he! he!—a very good joke, indeed—an excellent jest. We will have many a rich laugh about it at the palazzo—he! he! he!—over our wine—he! he! he!"

"The Amontillado!" I said.

"He! he! he!—he! he! he!—yes, the Amontillado. But is it not getting late? Will not they be awaiting us at the palazzo, the Lady Fortunato and the rest? Let us be gone."

"Yes," I said, "let us be gone."

"For the love of God, Montresor!"

◀ **Vocabulary**
subsided (səb sīd′ əd) *v.* settled down; became less active or intense

Make Predictions
Does this scene in which Montresor imprisons Fortunato verify your earlier predictions? Explain.

Comprehension
How does Fortunato become locked in the chains so easily?

"Yes," I said, "for the love of God!"

But to these words I hearkened in vain for a reply. I grew impatient. I called aloud—

"Fortunato!"

No answer. I called again—

"Fortunato!"

No answer still. I thrust a torch through the remaining aperture and let it fall within. There came forth in return only a jingling of the bells. My heart grew sick; it was the dampness of the catacombs that made it so. I hastened to make an end of my labor. I forced the last stone into its position; I plastered it up. Against the new masonry I reerected the old rampart of bones. For the half of a century no mortal has disturbed them. *In pace requiescat!*[12]

Spiral Review
THEME How many years have passed since Montresor took revenge on Fortunato? What insight into revenge does this detail suggest? Explain.

12. ***In pace requiescat!*** Latin for "May he rest in peace!"

Language Study

Vocabulary An **analogy** shows the relationship between pairs of words. The words printed in blue below appear in "The Cask of Amontillado." Choose a word from the list to complete each analogy. Your choice should create a word pair that matches the relationship between the first two words.

precluded **afflicted** **explicit** **recoiling** **subsided**

1. harmed : helped :: ____________ : allowed
2. delicious : food :: ____________ : instructions
3. graceful : awkward :: ____________ : increased
4. humor : laughing :: disgust : ____________
5. enormous : gigantic :: troubled : ____________

WORD STUDY
The **Latin suffix *-tion*** means "the act of." In this story, the narrator seeks **retribution**. A synonym for *revenge*, this word literally means "the act of retributing," or of paying someone back. Another, less formal synonym for *revenge* is *payback*.

Word Study

Part A The **Latin suffix *-tion*** often indicates that a word is a noun. For each of the following verbs, identify a related noun that uses the suffix *-tion*: *compensate, irritate, inflate, prevent.*

Part B Use the context of the sentences and what you know about the Latin suffix *-tion* to explain your answer to each question.

1. What is audience *participation?*
2. If you make a *contribution* to a cause, what have you done?

Close Reading Activities

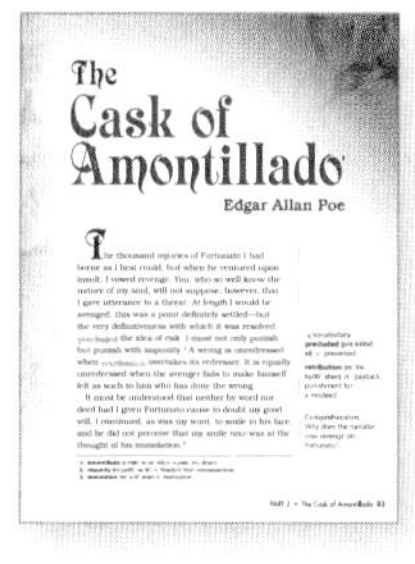

Literary Analysis

Key Ideas and Details

1. **(a)** How does Montresor describe Fortunato's strengths and weaknesses early in the story? **(b) Analyze:** Which of these character traits make Fortunato easy prey for Montresor? Explain.
2. **(a)** What steps does Montresor take to ensure that his plan works? Explain. **(b) Interpret:** Why do you think Montresor keeps urging Fortunato to turn back? Cite details from the story in your response.
3. **Make Predictions (a)** What prediction did you make after reading about Montresor's and Fortunato's shared interest in wine? **(b)** What details from the text helped you make your prediction? **(c)** Was your prediction verified? Explain, citing details from the story in your answer.

Craft and Structure

4. **Plot (a)** Identify a passage that foreshadows Fortunato's fate at the hands of Montresor. **(b)** In what ways does foreshadowing help create suspense in this story? Use details from the story to support your answer.
5. **Plot (a)** Fill out a plot diagram like the one shown. Identify two key events in the rising action of the story, the event that marks the climax, and one event that is part of the falling action. **(b)** Citing details from the text, explain the plot's resolution.

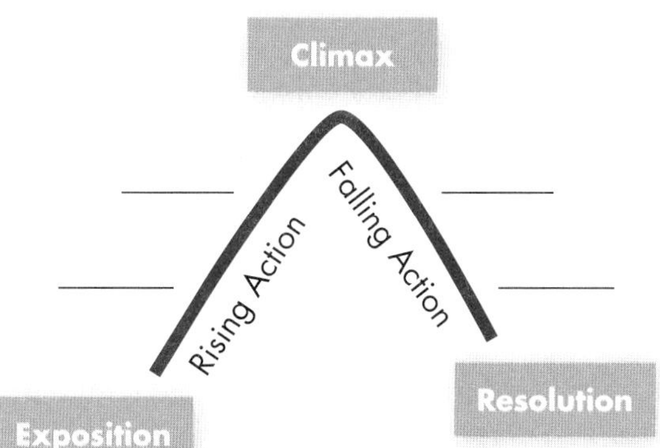

Integration of Knowledge and Ideas

6. **Draw Conclusions:** At the end of the story, Montresor describes the final moments of his act of revenge on Fortunato. How does Montresor feel about what he did? Cite details from the text to support your response.
7. **Make a Judgment:** Montresor acts as both victim and judge in the story. Do you think that Montresor sees the situation between himself and Fortunato accurately and then acts appropriately? Use details from the text to support your answer.

8. **Is conflict necessary? (a)** Does Montresor ever question whether the punishment he exacts on Fortunato is fair, just, or rational? Explain. **(b)** What view of human nature and the need for conflict does this story present? Explain, citing story details.

ACADEMIC VOCABULARY

As you write and speak about "The Cask of Amontillado," use the words related to conflict that you explored on page 3 of this book.

Conventions: Active and Passive Voice

A verb in the **active voice** expresses an action done *by* its subject.
A verb in the **passive voice** expresses an action done *to* its subject.

The "voice" of a verb tells whether the subject *performs* an action (active voice) or *receives* an action (passive voice).

Active Voice	Passive Voice
Poe has written stories about horrific events. (The subject, *Poe*, performs the action of the verb, *has written*.)	Stories about horrific events have been written by Poe. (The subject, *stories*, receives the action of the verb, *have been written*.)

Use the active voice to make your writing more lively and direct. Use the passive voice when the performer of the action is unknown or you wish to de-emphasize the performer. In order to change the passive voice to active voice, identify the noun that is performing the action and make it the subject of the sentence. Then, place the verb after the subject.

Passive voice: Fortunato was trapped by Montresor.

Active voice: Montresor trapped Fortunato.

Practice A

Identify the verb or verb phrase in each sentence. State whether the writer has used the active or the passive voice.

1. Fortunato has insulted Montresor.
2. Montresor plots against Fortunato.
3. The wine bottles were stacked in the crypt.
4. The trowel was used by Montresor to bury Fortunato.

Writing Application Rewrite the sentences in Practice A. If the verb is in the active voice, use the passive voice. If the verb is in the passive voice, use the active voice.

Practice B

Rewrite the following sentences using the active voice. You may need to add or change words to indicate who performed the action.

1. The detective story was invented by Edgar Allan Poe.
2. The servants were told not to leave the house.
3. Fortunato's cap was placed at a jaunty angle.
4. The stones and mortar had been covered with bones.

Speaking Application Write four sentences that describe Montresor's act of revenge against Fortunato, using the active voice twice and the passive voice twice. With a partner, discuss which sentences are more effective and why.

Writing to Sources

Argument In "The Cask of Amontillado," readers encounter a compelling, if disturbing, plot. Write a **critique** in which you analyze both the suspense of the story and the effectiveness of its ending. Present a clear claim, or position, and defend it with evidence from the text.

- Before you draft, list the qualities that you think a suspenseful story should have. Then, list the qualities that make an ending satisfactory.
- Use your lists to evaluate both the suspense and the ending of the story. Consider whether the author's use of foreshadowing adds to the suspense and makes the ending more or less effective. Note specific details from the story that demonstrate your ideas.
- Clearly state your claim early in the critique and develop at least three points that support it. Make sure to include details from the text as evidence to illustrate each point.

Grammar Application As you write, thoughtfully consider your use of active or passive voice. Use active voice when the subject performs the action. Use passive voice to express action done to the subject.

Speaking and Listening

Comprehension and Collaboration With a partner, **retell** "The Cask of Amontillado" from another point of view. You may choose to retell the story from Fortunato's point of view or from that of a hidden onlooker. Refresh your memory by rereading the selection. Then, follow these steps to complete the assignment.

- Identify your audience and the type of information they will need to understand the characters' backgrounds and motivations.
- Choose language that is appropriate for the audience and the story. Use words and expressions that are consistent with the character of the narrator you have chosen.
- As you speak, use facial expressions and body movements that help to convey the narrator's personality.
- Make eye contact with your audience to engage them in the story.
- Vary your intonation to reflect the emotions of the narrator.

After you and your partner have presented your work, invite questions from the audience about the choices you made in retelling the story. Answer with thoughtful, well-reasoned responses.

Common Core State Standards

Writing

1. Write arguments to support claims in an analysis of substantive topics or texts, using valid reasoning and relevant and sufficient evidence.

9. Draw evidence from literary or informational texts to support analysis, reflection, and research

9.a. Apply *grades 9–10 Reading standards* to literature.

Speaking and Listening

1. Initiate and participate effectively in a range of collaborative discussions with diverse partners, building on others' ideas and expressing their own clearly and persuasively.

1.a. Come to discussions prepared, having read and researched material under study; explicitly draw on that preparation by referring to evidence from texts and other research on the topic or issue to stimulate a thoughtful, well-reasoned exchange of ideas.

Language

5. Demonstrate understanding of figurative language, word relationships, and nuances in word meanings.

Is conflict necessary?

Explore the Big Question as you read these stories. Take notes on the ways in which each story portrays conflict. Then, compare and contrast the nature of the conflicts the two works explore.

READING TO COMPARE POINTS OF VIEW

Authors Cynthia Rylant and Ama Ata Aidoo use different points of view in these two stories. As you read each story, notice how the point of view controls what you are able to learn about the characters. Consider how this affects your understanding of their feelings, thoughts, and actions. After you have read both stories, compare the types of information a reader is able to learn through the use of first- and third-person points of view.

SHORT STORY

Checkouts
Cynthia Rylant

SHORT STORY

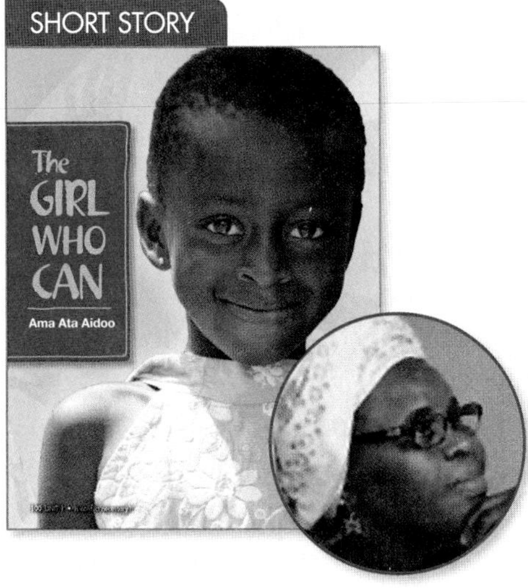
The GIRL WHO CAN
Ama Ata Aidoo

"Checkouts"

Cynthia Rylant (b.1945)
Cynthia Rylant spent four years as a child living with her grandparents in a small town in West Virginia. With no public library and little money to buy books, she started reading comic books. Once in college, she discovered great literature, but she did not consider becoming a writer until she took a job as a librarian and began reading children's books. To date, she has written many award-winning stories, poems, and novels.

"The Girl Who Can"

Ama Ata Aidoo (b. 1942)
Ama Ata Aidoo was born in Ghana, Africa, where her father was a village chief. Aidoo was educated in Ghana and in the United States, and later taught at universities in both countries. She has written plays, short stories, poetry, and novels. Her fiction, written in English, often explores the conflicts between Western and African cultures and the roles of women in modern society.

Comparing Points of View

Narrative point of view is the perspective from which a story is narrated, or told.

- **First-person point of view:** The narrator is a character who participates in the action and uses the first-person pronouns *I* and *me*.
- **Third-person point of view:** The narrator is not a character in the story but a voice outside it. The narrator uses the third-person pronouns *he, she, him, her, they,* and *them* to refer to all characters. There are two kinds of third-person point of view. In the **third-person omniscient point of view,** the narrator knows everything, including the thoughts of all the characters. In the **third-person limited point of view,** the narrator sees and reports things through one character's eyes.

These selections are written using different points of view. As you read, complete a Venn diagram like the one shown to compare and contrast how the point of view affects the way you understand the characters and the plot of each story.

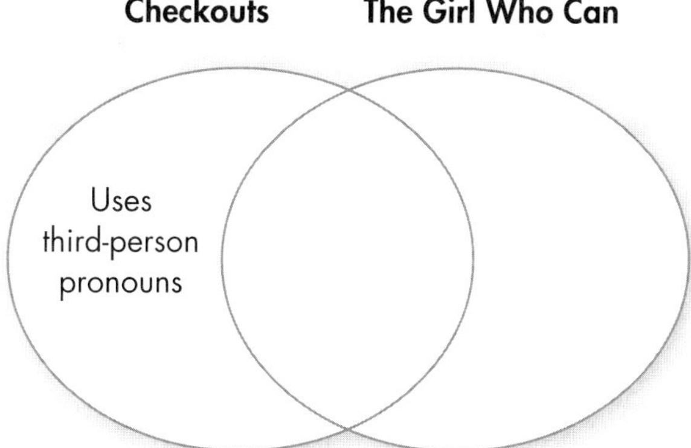

Cultural perspective is another aspect of many literary works. It is sometimes referred to as *cultural point of view* but should not be confused with narrative point of view as described above. The cultural perspective of a story refers to the customs, beliefs, and values of the place and time in which it is is set. For example, these two stories are set in different countries that observe very different customs and have different expectations for young women. As you read, notice how the two main characters' conflicts and insights reflect their culture's ideas and attitudes about the roles of women.

Common Core State Standards

Reading Literature

6. Analyze a particular point of view or cultural experience reflected in a work of literature from outside the United States, drawing on a wide reading of world literature.

Writing

2.a. Introduce a topic; organize complex ideas, concepts, and information to make important connections and distinctions; include formatting, graphics, and multimedia when useful to aiding comprehension.

Checkouts

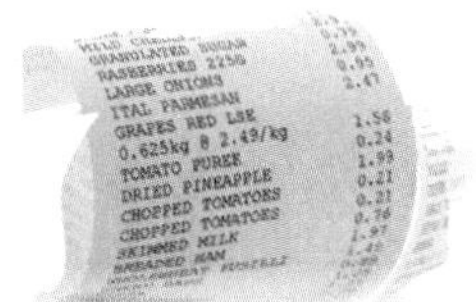

Cynthia Rylant

Her parents had moved her to Cincinnati, to a large house with beveled glass[1] windows and several porches and the *history* her mother liked to emphasize. You'll love the house, they said. You'll be lonely at first, they admitted, but you're so nice you'll make friends fast. And as an impulse tore at her to lie on the floor, to hold to their ankles and tell them she felt she was dying, to offer anything, anything at all, so they might allow her to finish growing up in the town of her childhood, they firmed their mouths and spoke from their chests and they said, It's decided.

They moved her to Cincinnati, where for a month she spent the greater part of every day in a room full of beveled glass windows, sifting through photographs of the life she'd lived and left behind. But it is difficult work, suffering, and in its own way a kind of art, and finally she didn't have the energy for it anymore, so she emerged from the beautiful house and fell in love with a bag boy at the supermarket. Of course, this didn't happen all at once, just like that, but in the sequence of things that's exactly the way it happened.

Point of View
How does the use of pronouns in this paragraph show that this story is being told from the third-person point of view?

She liked to grocery shop. She loved it in the way some people love to drive long country roads, because doing it she could think and relax and wander. Her parents wrote up the list and handed it to her and off she went without complaint to perform what they regarded as a great sacrifice of her time and a sign that she was indeed a very nice girl. She had never told them how much she loved grocery shopping, only that she was "willing" to do it. She had an intuition which told her that her parents were not safe for sharing such strong, important facts about herself. Let them think they knew her.

1. **beveled** (bev´ əld) **glass** *n.* glass having angled or slanted edges.

Once inside the supermarket, her hands firmly around the handle of the cart, she would lapse into a kind of reverie and wheel toward the produce. Like a Tibetan monk in solitary meditation, she calmed to a point of deep, deep happiness; this feeling came to her, reliably, if strangely, only in the supermarket.

◀ **Vocabulary**
reverie (rev′ ə rē)
n. dreamy thinking and imagining

Then one day the bag boy dropped her jar of mayonnaise and that is how she fell in love.

He was nervous—first day on the job—and along had come this fascinating girl, standing in the checkout line with the unfocused stare one often sees in young children, her face turned enough away that he might take several full looks at her as he packed sturdy bags full of food and the goods of modern life. She interested him because her hair was red and thick, and in it she had placed a huge orange bow, nearly the size of a small hat. That was enough to distract him, and when finally it was her groceries he was packing, she looked at him and smiled and he could respond only by busting her jar of mayonnaise on the floor, shards of glass and oozing cream decorating the area around his feet.

Point of View
Whose thoughts and feelings are expressed in this paragraph?

Comprehension
At first, why does the girl fascinate the boy?

She loved him at exactly that moment, and if he'd known this perhaps he wouldn't have fallen into the brown depression he fell into, which lasted the rest of his shift. He believed he must have looked the fool in her eyes, and he envied the sureness of everyone around him: the cocky cashier at the register, the grim and harried store manager, the bland butcher, and the brazen bag boys who smoked in the warehouse on their breaks. He wanted a second chance. Another chance to be confident and say witty things to her as he threw tin cans into her bags, persuading her to allow him to help her to her car so he might learn just a little about her, check out the floor of the

Then one day the bag boy dropped her jar of mayonnaise and that is how she fell in love.

Point of View
What does the narrator reveal about the boy's regrets?

Vocabulary ▶ dishevelment
(di shev´ əl ment) *n.* disorder; messiness

Point of View
Which details in this paragraph suggest the story is told from the omniscient point of view? Explain.

car for signs of hobbies or fetishes and the bumpers for clues as to beliefs and loyalties.

But he busted her jar of mayonnaise and nothing else worked out for the rest of the day.

Strange, how attractive clumsiness can be. She left the supermarket with stars in her eyes, for she had loved the way his long nervous fingers moved from the conveyor belt to the bags, how deftly (until the mayonnaise) they had picked up her items and placed them in her bags. She had loved the way the hair kept falling into his eyes as he leaned over to grab a box or a tin. And the tattered brown shoes he wore with no socks. And the left side of his collar turned in rather than out.

The bag boy seemed a wonderful contrast to the perfectly beautiful house she had been forced to accept as her home, to the *history* she hated, to the loneliness she had become used to, and she couldn't wait to come back for more of his awkwardness and **dishevelment**.

Incredibly, it was another four weeks before they saw each other again. As fate would have it, her visits to the supermarket never coincided with his schedule to bag. Each time she went to the store, her eyes scanned the checkouts at once, her heart in her mouth. And each hour he worked, the bag boy kept one eye on the door, watching for the red-haired girl with the big orange bow.

Yet in their disappointment these weeks there was a kind of ecstasy. It is reason enough to be alive, the hope you may see again some face which has meant something to you. The anticipation of meeting the bag boy eased the girl's painful transition into her new and jarring life in Cincinnati. It provided for her an anchor amid all that was impersonal and unfamiliar, and she spent less time on thoughts of what she had left behind as she concentrated on what might lie ahead. And for the boy, the long and often tedious hours at the supermarket which provided no challenge other than that of showing up the following workday . . . these hours became possibilities of mystery and romance for him as he watched the electric doors for the girl in the orange bow.

And when finally they did meet up again, neither offered a clue to the other that he, or she, had been the object of obsessive thought for weeks. She spotted him as soon as she came into the store, but she kept her eyes strictly in front of her as she pulled out a cart and wheeled it toward the produce. And he, too, knew the instant she came through the door—though the orange bow was gone, replaced by a small but bright yellow flower instead—and he never once turned his head in her direction but watched her from the corner of his vision as he tried to swallow back the fear in his throat.

It is odd how we sometimes deny ourselves the very pleasure we have longed for and which is finally within our reach. For some perverse reason she would not have been able to articulate, the girl did not bring her cart up to the bag boy's checkout when her shopping was done. And the bag boy let her leave the store, pretending no notice of her.

◀ **Vocabulary**
perverse (pər vʉrs′) *adj.* different from what is considered right or reasonable

This is often the way of children, when they truly want a thing, to pretend that they don't. And then they grow angry when no one tried harder to give them this thing they so casually rejected, and they soon find themselves in a rage simply because they cannot say yes when they mean yes. Humans are very complicated. (And perhaps cats, who have been known to react in the same way, though the resulting rage can only be guessed at.)

Point of View
Which details in this paragraph might be omitted if the story were told from the third-person limited point of view? Explain.

The girl hated herself for not checking out at the boy's line, and the boy hated himself for not catching her eye and saying hello, and they most sincerely hated each other without having ever exchanged even two minutes of conversation.

Eventually—in fact, within the week—a kind and intelligent boy who lived very near her beautiful house asked the girl to a movie and she gave up her fancy for the bag boy at the supermarket. And the bag boy himself grew so bored with his job that he made a desperate search for something better and ended up in a bookstore where scores of fascinating girls lingered like honeybees about a hive. Some months later the bag boy and the girl with the orange bow again crossed paths, standing in line with their dates at a movie theater, and, glancing toward the other, each smiled slightly, then looked away, as strangers on public buses often do, when one is moving off the bus and the other is moving on.

Critical Thinking

1. **Key Ideas and Details: (a)** What do the boy and girl think about while they are apart? **(b) Speculate:** How do you think the two characters feel when they see each other at the movie theater? Which story details support your answer?
2. **Key Ideas and Details:** Does the experience described in the story seem like a missed opportunity or a necessary outcome? Explain.
3. **Key Ideas and Details: (a)** Why do the boy and girl never act on their feelings? **(b) Make a Judgment:** Do you agree that "humans are very complicated"? Explain, using details from the story.
4. **Integration of Knowledge and Ideas: (a)** Is the situation described in this story a common conflict for American teenagers? Explain. **(b) Speculate:** How might the story be different if either the bag boy or the girl had handled the conflict differently? *[Connect to the Big Question: Is conflict necessary?]*

The GIRL WHO CAN

Ama Ata Aidoo

They say that I was born in Hasodzi; and it is a very big village in the central region of our country, Ghana. They also say that when all of Africa is not choking under a drought, Hasodzi lies in a very fertile lowland in a district known for its good soil. Maybe that is why any time I don't finish eating my food, Nana says, "You Adjoa, you don't know what life is about . . . you don't know what problems there are in this life . . ."

As far as I could see, there was only one problem. And it had nothing to do with what I knew Nana considered as "problems," or what Maami thinks of as "the problem." Maami is my mother. Nana is my mother's mother. And they say I am seven years old. And my problem is that at this seven years of age, there are things I can think in my head, but which, maybe, I do not have the proper language to speak them out with. And that, I think, is a very serious problem because it is always difficult to decide whether to keep quiet and not say any of the things that come into my head, or say them and get laughed at. Not that it is easy to get any grown-up to listen to you, even when you decide to take the risk and say something serious to them.

Take Nana. First, I have to struggle to catch her attention. Then I tell her something I had taken a long time to figure out. And then you know what always happens? She would at once stop whatever she is doing and, mouth open, stare at me for a very long time. Then, bending and turning her head slightly, so that one ear comes down towards me, she'll say in that voice: "Adjoa, you say what?" After I have repeated whatever I had said, she would either, still in that voice, ask me "never, never, but NEVER to repeat THAT," or she would immediately burst out laughing. She would laugh and laugh and laugh, until tears run down her cheeks and she would stop whatever she is doing and wipe away the tears with the hanging edges of her cloth. And she would continue laughing until she is completely tired. But then, as soon as another person comes by, just to make sure she doesn't forget whatever it was I had said, she would repeat it to her. And then, of course, there would be two old people laughing and screaming with tears running down their faces. Sometimes this show continues until there are three, four or even more of such laughing and screaming tear-faced grownups. And all that performance for whatever I'd said? I find something

◀ **Critical Viewing**
Describe the feelings the girl in the photograph expresses.

◀ **Vocabulary**
fertile (furt´ 'l) *adj.* rich in nutrients that promote growth

Point of View
Which pronouns in this paragraph show that this story is being told from the first-person point of view?

Comprehension
What does the narrator say is her problem?

quite confusing in all this. That is, no one ever explains to me why sometimes I shouldn't repeat some things I say; while at other times, some other things I say would not only be all right, but would be considered so funny they would be repeated so many times for so many people's enjoyment. You see how neither way of hearing me out can encourage me to express my thoughts too often?

Like all this business to do with my legs. I have always wanted to tell them not to worry. I mean Nana and my mother. It did not have to be an issue for my two favorite people to fight over. I didn't want to be told not to repeat it or for it to be considered so funny that anyone would laugh at me until they cried. After all, they were my legs . . . When I think back on it now, those two, Nana and my mother must have been discussing my legs from the day I was born. What I am sure of is that when I came out of the land of sweet, soft silence into the world of noise and **comprehension**, the first topic I met was my legs.

Vocabulary ▶
comprehension
(käm′ prē hen′ shen) *n.*
understanding

That discussion was repeated very regularly.

Nana: "Ah, ah, you know, Kaya, I thank my God that your very first child is female. But Kaya, I am not sure about her legs. Hm . . . hm . . . hm . . ."

And Nana would shake her head.

Maami: "Mother, why are you always complaining about Adjoa's legs? If you ask me . . ."

Nana: "They are too thin. And I am not asking you!"

Nana has many voices. There is a special one she uses to shut everyone up.

"Some people have no legs at all," my mother would try again with all her small courage.

"But Adjoa has legs," Nana would insist; "except that they are too thin. And also too long for a woman. Kaya, listen. Once in a while, but only once in a very long while, somebody decides —nature, a child's spirit mother, an accident happens, and somebody gets born without arms, or legs, or both sets of limbs. And then let me touch wood; it is a sad business. And you know, such things are not for talking about every day. But if any female child decides to come into this world with legs, then they might as well be legs."

"What kind of legs?" And always at that point, I knew from her voice that my mother was weeping

When I think back on it now, those two, Nana and my mother must have been discussing my legs from the day I was born.

inside. Nana never heard such inside weeping. Not that it would have stopped Nana even if she had heard it. Which always surprised me. Because, about almost everything else apart from my legs, Nana is such a good grown-up. In any case, what do I know about good grown-ups and bad grown-ups? How could Nana be a good grown-up when she carried on so about my legs? All I want to say is that I really liked Nana except for that.

Nana: "As I keep saying, if any woman decides to come into this world with her two legs, then she should select legs that have meat on them: with good calves. Because you are sure such legs would support solid hips. And a woman must have solid hips to be able to have children."

"Oh, Mother." That's how my mother would answer. Very, very quietly. And the discussion would end or they would move on to something else.

Sometimes, Nana would pull in something about my father:

How, "Looking at such a man, we have to be **humble** and admit that after all, God's children are many . . ."

How, "After one's only daughter had insisted on marrying a man like that, you still have to thank your God that the biggest problem you got later was having a granddaughter with spindly legs that are too long for a woman, and too thin to be of any use."

The way she always added that bit about my father under her breath, she probably thought I didn't hear it. But I always heard it. Plus, that is what always shut my mother up for good, so that even if I had not actually heard the words, once my mother looked like even her little courage was finished, I could always guess what Nana had added to the argument.

"Legs that have meat on them with good calves to support solid hips . . . to be able to have children."

So I wished that one day I would see, for myself, the legs of any woman who had had children. But in our village, that is not easy. The older women wear long wrap-arounds[1] all the time. Perhaps if they let me go bathe in the river in the evening, I could have checked. But I never had the chance. It took a lot of begging just to get my mother and Nana to let me go splash around in the shallow end of the river with my friends, who were other little girls like me. For proper baths, we used the small bathhouse behind our hut. Therefore, the only naked female legs I have ever really seen are those of other little girls like me, or older girls in the school. And those of my mother and Nana: two pairs of legs which must surely belong to the approved kind; because Nana gave birth to my mother

Point of View
What do we learn about the narrator's inner feelings from the words in this paragraph?

◀ Vocabulary
humble (hum′ bəl) *adj.* modest; having humility

Comprehension
According to the narrator, which topic makes the mother weep inside?

1. **wrap-arounds** (rap′ ə roundz′) *n.* a type of garment that is open down the side and is wrapped around the body.

and my mother gave birth to me. In my eyes, all my friends have got legs that look like legs, but whether the legs have got meat on them to support the kind of hips that . . . that I don't know.

According to the older boys and girls, the distance between our little village and the small town is about five kilometers. I don't know what five kilometers mean. They always complain about how long it is to walk to school and back. But to me, we live in our village, and walking those kilometers didn't matter. School is nice.

School is another thing Nana and my mother discussed often and appeared to have different ideas about. Nana thought it would be a waste of time. I never understood what she meant. My mother seemed to know—and disagreed. She kept telling Nana that she—that is, my mother—felt she was locked into some kind of darkness because she didn't go to school. So that if I, her daughter, could learn to write and read my own name and a little besides—perhaps be able to calculate some things on paper—that would be good. I could always marry later and maybe . . .

▼ Critical Viewing
How does your mental image of the narrator compare to the girls in this photograph?

Nana would just laugh. "Ah, maybe with legs like hers, she might as well go to school."

Running with our classmates on our small sports field and winning first place each time never seemed to me to be anything about which to tell anyone at home. This time it was different. I don't know how the teachers decided to let me run for the junior section of our school in the district games. But they did.

When I went home to tell my mother and Nana, they had not believed it at first. So Nana had taken it upon herself to go and "ask into it properly." She came home to tell my mother that it was really true. I was one of my school's runners.

"Is that so?" exclaimed my mother. I know her. Her mouth moved as though she was going to tell Nana, that, after all, there was a secret about me she couldn't be expected to share with anyone. But then Nana herself looked so pleased, out of surprise, my mother shut her mouth up. In any case, since the first time they heard the news, I have often caught Nana staring at my legs with a strange look on her face, but still pretending like she was not looking. All this week, she has been washing my school uniform herself. That is a big surprise. And she didn't stop at that,

LITERATURE IN CONTEXT

Social Studies Connection

Country Profile: Ghana

Location: southern coast of West Africa bordering the Atlantic Ocean

Climate: tropical; wet in the south and dry in the north

Terrain: low fertile plains and plateaus

Population: 25 million

Connect to the Literature

Adjoa says that she lives in a fertile lowland of central Ghana. What benefits and challenges might this region's climate and terrain present for a runner like Adjoa?

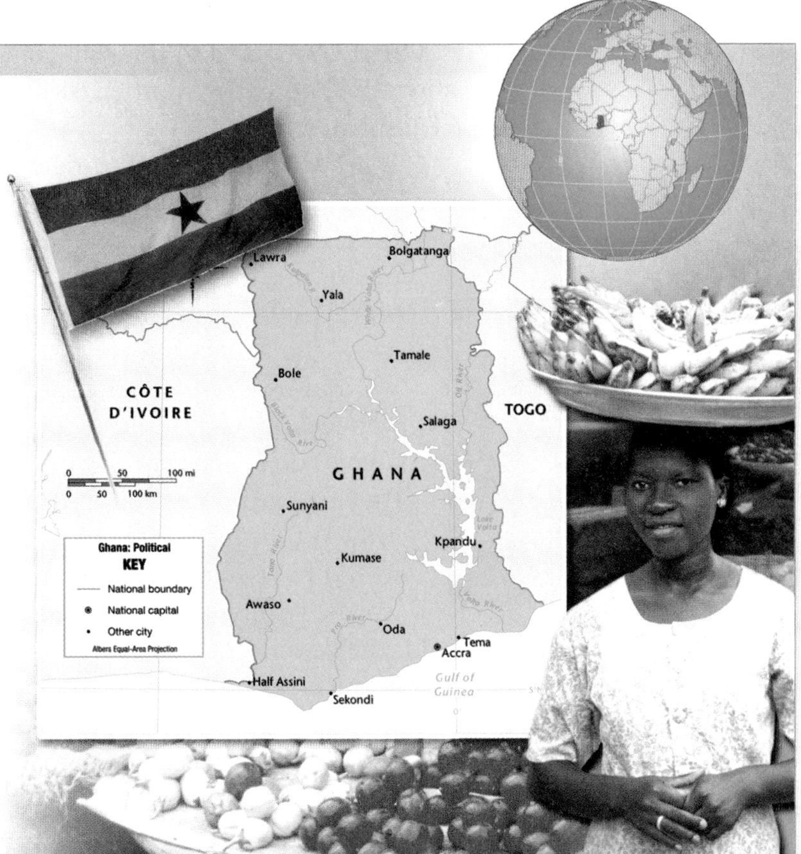

she even went to Mr. Mensah's house and borrowed his charcoal pressing iron. Each time she came back home with it and ironed and ironed and ironed the uniform, until, if I had been the uniform, I would have said aloud that I had had enough.

Wearing my school uniform this week has been very nice. At the parade, on the first afternoon, its sheen caught the rays of the sun and shone brighter than anybody else's uniform. I'm sure Nana saw that too, and must have liked it. Yes, she has been coming into town with us every afternoon of this district sports week. Each afternoon, she has pulled one set of fresh old cloth from the big brass bowl to wear. And those old clothes are always so stiffly starched, you can hear the cloth creak when she passes by. But she walks way behind us schoolchildren. As though she was on her own way to some place else.

Yes, I have won every race I ran for my school, and I have won the cup for the best all-round junior athlete. Yes, Nana said that she didn't care if such things are not done. She would do it. You know what she did? She carried the gleaming cup on her back. Like they do with babies, and other very precious things. And this time, not taking the trouble to walk by herself.

Spiral Review
THEME How does Nana's behavior toward Adjoa connect to a possible theme?

Comprehension
After learning about her running talent, what does Nana do with the narrator's uniform?

When we arrived in our village, she entered our compound to show the cup to my mother before going to give it back to the headmaster.

Oh, grown-ups are so strange. Nana is right now carrying me on her knee, and crying softly. Muttering, muttering, muttering that: "saa, thin legs can also be useful . . . thin legs can also be useful . . ." that "even though some legs don't have much meat on them, to carry hips . . . they can run. Thin legs can run . . . then who knows? . . ."

Oh, grown-ups are so strange.

I don't know too much about such things. But that's how I was feeling and thinking all along. That surely, one should be able to do other things with legs as well as have them because they can support hips that make babies. Except that I was afraid of saying that sort of thing aloud. Because someone would have told me never, never, but NEVER to repeat such words. Or else, they would have laughed so much at what I'd said, they would have cried.

It's much better this way. To have acted it out to show them, although I could not have planned it.

As for my mother, she has been speechless as usual.

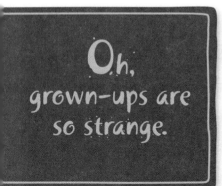

Critical Thinking

1. **Key Ideas and Details: (a)** Why does Nana criticize the narrator's legs? **(b) Draw Conclusions:** How does this criticism reveal Nana's fears for the narrator's future? Explain.
2. **Integration of Knowledge and Ideas: (a)** What are Nana's feelings about the narrator's going to school? **(b) Compare and Contrast:** How do the mother's feelings about school differ from Nana's? **(c) Generalize:** Based on these details, what kind of lives do you think many women in Ghana are expected to lead?
3. **Key Ideas and Details: (a)** After Adjoa is chosen for the district games, why does Nana keep staring at her legs? **(b) Draw Conclusions:** Why does Nana iron Adjoa's school uniform so carefully?
4. **Key Ideas and Details: (a)** At the end of the story, Adjoa says it was much better to "have acted it out to show them." What has she acted out? **(b) Evaluate:** Was it "better," as Adjoa says? Explain.
5. **Integration of Knowledge and Ideas:** What lesson does Adjoa's family learn as they face conflicts over her legs? Could they have learned those lessons without those conflicts? Use details from the story to support your answer. *[Connect to the Big Question: Is conflict necessary?]*

Comparing Points of View

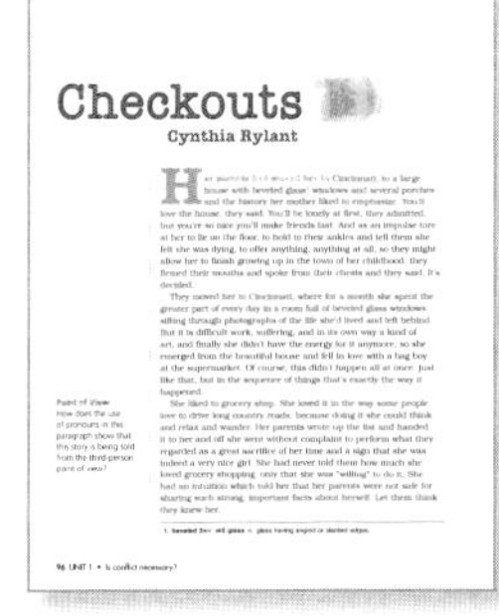

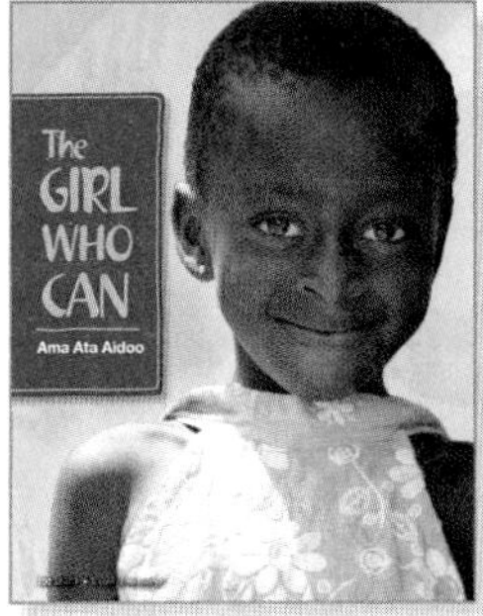

1. **Key Ideas and Details** Use a chart like the one shown to note the actions, thoughts, and feelings of the listed characters in both stories.

Checkouts	Actions	Thoughts	Feelings
Girl			
Boy			
The Girl Who Can	**Actions**	**Thoughts**	**Feelings**
Nana			
Adjoa			

2. **Craft and Structure (a)** Which details from your chart show that the **third-person omniscient point of view** in "Checkouts" gives readers insight into the inner lives of all the characters? Explain. **(b)** Which details show that the **first-person point of view** in "The Girl Who Can" lets the reader understand the narrator best of all? Explain.

Timed Writing

Explanatory Text: Essay

Compare and contrast the main character in "Checkouts" with the narrator in "The Girl Who Can." In an essay, analyze the way in which the development of each character is shaped by the narrative point of view. Also, consider the cultural perspectives that contribute to the portrayal of each character. **(30 minutes)**

5-Minute Planner

1. Read the prompt carefully and completely.
2. Organize your ideas to make important connections by answering these questions:
    - Who are the narrators in the two stories?
    - How do you know what each girl is thinking?
    - Do both narrators seem equally reliable? Why or why not?
    - How does each girl's culture influence her perspective?
3. Reread the prompt, and then draft your essay.

USE ACADEMIC VOCABULARY

As you write, use academic language, including the following words or their related forms:

character
context
differentiate
perspective

For more information about academic vocabulary, see page xlvi.

Language Study

Using a Dictionary and Thesaurus

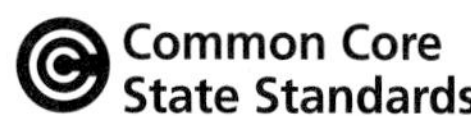

Common Core State Standards

Language

4.b. Identify and correctly use patterns of word changes that indicate different meanings or parts of speech.

4.c. Consult general and specialized reference materials, both print and digital, to find the pronunciation of a word or determine or clarify its precise meaning, its part of speech, or its etymology.

5.b. Analyze nuances in the meanings of words with similar denotations.

A **dictionary** is a resource that provides different kinds of information to help readers, writers, and speakers use words correctly. Consult a dictionary to find a word's pronunciation, its part of speech, and its history, or etymology. Look at this dictionary entry for the word *poet.*

Dictionary

poet (pō′ət) ***n.*** [ME < OFr. *poete* < L *poeta* < Gr *poietes*, one who makes, poet < *poiein*, to make: see POEM] **1.** a person who writes poems or verses **2.** a person who displays imaginative power and beauty of thought, language, etc. (— pō et′ik ***adj.*** — pō et′i kəl ***adj.*** — pō et′i kəl lē ***adv.***)

The pronunciation, set in parentheses right after the entry, uses letters, symbols, and accent marks to show how the word is pronounced. A key to these letters and symbols usually appears at the bottom of the dictionary page or in the front of the dictionary. The key includes a common word to show how the symbols are pronounced.

Many dictionaries also provide information about the related forms of words. Related forms are new words created by adding prefixes or suffixes to a base word. For example, the entry above shows that the adjectives *poetic* and *poetical,* and the adverb *poetically* can be formed from the noun *poet.*

A **thesaurus** is a book of synonyms. Use it to find the exact word to fit your meaning and to vary word selection to avoid repetition. A thesaurus can also help you locate words that share **denotations,** or dictionary definitions, but have different **connotations,** or shades of meaning.

Thesaurus

teaching ***n.*** teaching, education, schooling, instruction, tuition, coaching, tutoring ***v.*** teach, educate, instruct, give information, give lessons in, school, edify

Many types of dictionaries and thesauri can be found in the reference section of your library. You may also find them online and provided as mobile applications.

Practice A

Look up each word in a dictionary. Write the part of speech and the first definition for each word.

1. eminent
2. misconstrue
3. anecdote
4. illiterate
5. diversion
6. perceive

Practice B

Use a dictionary to answer questions 1 through 8.

1. Which syllable receives the heaviest accent in the word *integrity*?
2. Can *wane* be properly used as a noun? If so, what does it mean?
3. What word can be used to replace *agitate* in this sentence? "Jonathan began to *agitate* the fish tank."
4. What is the adverb form of the word *dire*? Which suffix is used to create the adverb form?
5. What part of speech is *expire*? Note two words that are related to *expire*. Define each one and identify its part of speech.
6. Does the vowel sound in *fray* sound like the vowel in *at*, *ate*, or *car*?
7. Which syllable of *upheaval* receives the heaviest accent?
8. **(a)** Note two words with similar denotations you might use to replace *melancholy* in this sentence. "At the end of her vacation, Alice felt melancholy." **(b)** For each word, explain how the connotations of the replacement words change the overall meaning of the sentence.

Activity Form a small group with classmates. Write a sentence about a story that you know. Then, pass your sentence to another student. That student should change the sentence that he or she receives by replacing one word with a synonym. See how long your group can keep passing the sentence on and coming up with new words while maintaining the meaning of the original sentence. Group members may refer to a thesaurus for help.

For Fortunato, the catacombs were a terrifying place to die.

For Fortunato, the catacombs were a frightening place to die.

For Fortunato, the catacombs were a frightening place to perish.

Comprehension and Collaboration

How do you pronounce these words: *feint, insignia, valise?* Look up each word in a dictionary, study the pronunciation, and practice saying it out loud. Then, compare your pronunciations of the words with those of three other students. If you disagree, review the pronunciation key and decide which of you is correct.

Evaluating a Speech

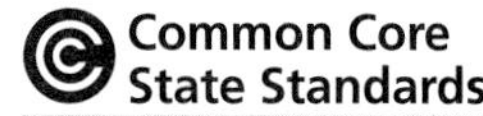

Speaking and Listening
3. Evaluate a speaker's point of view, reasoning, and use of evidence and rhetoric, identifying any fallacious reasoning or exaggerated or distorted evidence.

When you listen to any type of speech, strive to be active and attentive. Assess the credibility of the message and the effectiveness of the speaker's delivery. Learning how to evaluate a speech will make you a critical listener, allow you to judge the value of what you hear, and give you a solid basis for improving your own oral presentations.

Learn the Skills

Create a context. When listening to a speech or an informal talk, consider the following questions:

- What is the speaker's purpose?
- What knowledge of the subject does the speaker have?
- What traditional, cultural, or historical influences shape the message?
- As a listener, what prior knowledge do you bring to the topic?

Evaluate the development of arguments. A good speaker presents arguments that are clearly and logically stated and fully supported with evidence in the form of facts, statistics, anecdotes, and expert opinions. As you listen, ask yourself whether the speaker's information is accurate, complete, and relevant. Is important information deliberately or unintentionally excluded? Does the speaker have a point of view—the perspective from which he or she speaks—that might lead to bias, or a focus on only one side of an argument? Assess whether the speaker's use of facts is fair and thorough. Try to anticipate weaknesses in certain types of arguments.

Type of Argument	Potential Flaw
Analogy: compares one situation to another	Are the two situations really alike?
Authority: cites the opinion of an expert	Is the expert knowledge-able and unbiased?
Emotion: appeals to the audience's feelings	Is the full argument balanced between logic and emotion?
Causation: shows a cause-and-effect relationship	Does the speaker oversimplify his or her arguments?

Note the speaker's choice of language. Listen for the speaker's use of words and phrases with positive or negative connotations, or associations. Note repetition of key words or stress given to certain phrases. Be alert to the fact that some speakers, as a substitute for good evidence or logical argument, may rely on emotionally "loaded" language.

Note the speaker's technique. A speech is more than words. Use the following questions to analyze nonverbal elements:

- Is the speaker's tone of voice, word choice, and rate of speaking appropriate for the audience, subject, and occasion?
- What is the effect of the speaker's nonverbal signals, such as eye contact, facial expressions, and gestures?
- When and why does the speaker pause, speak more loudly or softly, or speak more rapidly or slowly?

Practice the Skills

Presentation of Knowledge and Ideas Use what you have learned in this workshop to perform the following task.

ACTIVITY: **Evaluate a Speech**

As a class, view a political speech or a televised editorial. As you watch the speech, use an evaluation checklist like the one shown below. Assess the content (including point of view, use of supporting details, and word choice), and the speaker's delivery technique (including tone, stresses, pauses, and gestures).

Comprehension and Collaboration After you have watched the delivery of the speech or editorial, form small groups and discuss your findings. State your opinion of the speech in general, and identify which aspects you thought were the strongest and which were the weakest. As you listen to classmates, take notes on one another's views. Then, referring to your completed checklist and your discussion notes, write a two-paragraph evaluation of the speech or editorial.

Evaluation Checklist

Rate the speaker's content on a scale of 1 (very poor) to 5 (excellent) for each of these items. Explain your ratings.

Speech Content	Rating
met the needs of the audience	1 2 3 4 5
achieved its purpose	1 2 3 4 5
was appropriate to the occasion	1 2 3 4 5
used effective main and supporting ideas	1 2 3 4 5
included convincing facts and expert opinions	1 2 3 4 5
demonstrated command of the conventions of standard written English	1 2 3 4 5

Rate the speaker's delivery on a scale of 1 (very poor) to 5 (excellent) for each of these items. Explain your ratings.

Speech Delivery	Rating
appropriate level of formality	1 2 3 4 5
eye contact	1 2 3 4 5
effective speaking rate	1 2 3 4 5
pauses for effect	1 2 3 4 5
appropriate volume	1 2 3 4 5
enunciation	1 2 3 4 5
appropriate gestures	1 2 3 4 5
conventions of language	1 2 3 4 5

Writing Process

Write an Argument

Response to Literature

Defining the Form A formal **response to literature** gives you an opportunity to present and defend your interpretation of a literary work. Like any argument, a response to literature requires you to develop a logical line of reasoning and to support your ideas with strong, persuasive evidence. You will use elements of argumentative writing in nearly every subject you study in school, as well as in many careers.

Assignment Write a response to a work of literature that engages you as a reader. Include these elements:

- ✓ an *analysis* of the work, including its content, organization, and style
- ✓ a *thesis statement* or precise *claim* that expresses your interpretation of the work
- ✓ inclusion of a *counterclaim*, or alternate interpretation, and a discussion of why it is less convincing than yours
- ✓ *textual evidence* that supports your interpretation
- ✓ a logical organization, including a *conclusion* that follows from and supports your claim
- ✓ a *formal style and objective tone* appropriate for an academic purpose and audience
- ✓ error-free grammar, including correct use of colons when introducing lists or quotations

To preview the criteria on which your response to literature may be judged, see the rubric on page 119.

FOCUS ON RESEARCH

When you write a response to literature, you might perform research to

- find other works by the same author to perform a comparison.
- find criticism written by the author to learn about his or her opinions on writing.
- locate critical writings about the author to gain additional insights.

Be sure to note all resources you use in your research, and credit those sources in your final drafts. See the Citing Sources pages in the Introductory Unit of this textbook for additional guidance.

Common Core State Standards

Writing

1. Write arguments to support claims in an analysis of substantive topics or texts, using valid reasoning and relevant and sufficient evidence.

4. Produce clear and coherent writing in which the development, organization, and style are appropriate to task, purpose, and audience.

9. Draw evidence from literary or informational texts to support analysis, reflection and research.

9.a. Apply grades 9-10 reading standards to literature.

10. Write routinely over extended time frames and shorter time frames for a range of tasks, purposes, and audiences.

READING-WRITING CONNECTION

To get a feel for responses to literature, read the excerpt from *Nothing to Fear: Lessons in Leadership from FDR* by Alan Axelrod on page 294.

Prewriting/Planning Strategies

Make a top-ten list. Think of stories, poems, or other works of literature that you found memorable. Create a top-ten list of these titles and authors. Next to each entry, briefly note your reactions to the work and ideas you might want to share about it. Review your list and choose one work as your topic.

Clarify your purpose and focus. Choose a focus for your response. For example, you may want to prove that your chosen text is the best work by its author or examine the choices made by a character in a short story. Write a statement of purpose for your essay. Use both the title and the author's name in your statement:

- **Example Statement of Purpose:** *In this essay, I will analyze the character of General Zaroff in Richard Connell's short story "The Most Dangerous Game." I will argue that his elegant manner serves to make his cruelty more rather than less evident.*

Identify types of details you will need. Your purpose and focus determine the kinds of details you need to include. Consider these tips:

- **To analyze,** support your ideas with evidence from the selection as well as other outside resources.
- **To refute,** identify other interpretations of a passage or the text as a whole. Gather details from the text that support your interpretation.
- **To explain a personal response,** show how the work connects to your own experiences, observations, and ideas.

Find supporting evidence. Return to the work you have selected to find passages that relate to your purpose and focus. Prepare a series of index cards, using one card for every piece of evidence that supports your claim. Write your main point or idea across the top of each card. Underneath, write your notes on the details you gathered from the text to support that point or idea. Use another set of cards to record details that support alternate interpretations.

Organizing your evidence in this way will help you present your ideas clearly. It will also help you defend your claim against other interpretations.

Identifying Supporting Evidence

Thesis: What I want to prove:
General Zaroff's civilized exterior conceals a ruthless, heartless murderer.

How I can prove it:
His elegant castle is also a prison.

Explain in detail:
Zaroff makes Rainsford comfortable in the castle in order to make him healthy and, therefore, the hunt more intriguing.

Drafting Strategies

State your thesis or claim. Your essay should have a clear thesis statement that you develop logically and support with strong evidence. Review your notes to draft a single sentence that combines the statement of purpose you wrote earlier with the ideas and evidence you gathered. This statement will direct the choices you make as you write.

> **Example Thesis Statement:** *In Richard Connell's short story "The Most Dangerous Game," the characterization of General Zaroff reveals a murderous mind that lurks behind an illusion of refinement.*

Organize your ideas. Fill out the details in an organizational chart like the one shown. Your introduction should include your thesis, and every body paragraph should provide its support.

Organize Your Ideas

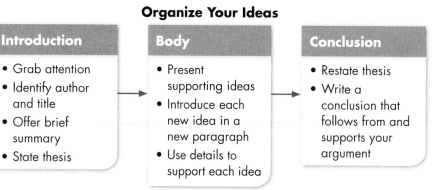

Introduction	→	Body	→	Conclusion
• Grab attention • Identify author and title • Offer brief summary • State thesis	→	• Present supporting ideas • Introduce each new idea in a new paragraph • Use details to support each idea	→	• Restate thesis • Write a conclusion that follows from and supports your argument

Consider your audience. Judge your audience's familiarity with the work and use that judgment to determine how much background information to include.

Address counterclaims. As you write, consider other ways to read the text that may conflict with your views but are not without merit. Introduce these alternate claims and refute them with logic and evidence.

> **Example Address of a Counterclaim:** *Some readers might say Zaroff is sophisticated because he is elegant and clever, but I disagree since elegance and cleverness are just surface traits.*

If your position changes as you work, be prepared to reflect this in your writing and even to modify your thesis statement.

Provide supporting details. Include evidence from the literary work for every claim you make in your essay. **Exact quotations** can illustrate a character's attitude, a writer's word choice, or an essayist's opinion. **Examples** of a character's actions or of a specific literary element can enhance your analysis. **Paraphrases,** or restatements in your own words, can help you clarify key ideas. Paraphrases must accurately reflect the original text.

Writing

1.a. Introduce precise claim(s), distinguish the claim(s) from alternate or opposing claims, and create an organization that establishes clear relationships among claim(s), counterclaims, reasons, and evidence.

1.b. Develop claim(s) and counterclaims fairly, supplying evidence for each while pointing out the strengths and limitations of both in a manner that anticipates the audience's knowledge level and concerns.

1.d. Establish and maintain a formal style and objective tone while attending to the norms and conventions of the discipline.

1.e. Provide a concluding statement or section that follows from and supports the argument presented.

5. Develop and strengthen writing as needed by planning, revising, editing, rewriting, or trying a new approach, focusing on addressing what is most significant for a specific purpose and audience.

Perfecting Your Word Choice

Word choice is the language a writer uses in order to create a specific impression. Finding exactly the right words can help you clarify your thinking as you write. If your word choice is strong and precise, it is likely that your thinking is, as well. The right words, carefully chosen, can transform an argument from weak to convincing.

Using Formal Language An essay written in response to a literary work should present ideas in a serious and thoughtful way. Review your draft to be sure the language you have chosen is appropriate to this purpose. Circle any words that are chatty or informal and replace them with more academic, precise language.

Informal: Rainsford does some cool things to trick Zaroff.

Formal: Rainsford employs many cunning tricks to fool Zaroff.

Choosing Specific Words As you write a first draft, you might use general words to simply get your ideas down. Go back through your draft, circling vague or dull word choices. Consider replacements that sharpen the point you are making and drive it home. Also, consider adding descriptors to enhance your argument. You can use a thesaurus to gather ideas for alternative word choices.

Vague	Specific
Zaroff is *evil.*	Zaroff is *calculating* and *devious.*
The castle is *fancy.*	The castle is *opulent* and *decadent.*
Zaroff *likes* hunting.	Zaroff *relishes* hunting.

Using Figurative Language Consider using similes and metaphors to clarify your ideas.

A **simile** is a comparison of two unlike things using *like* or as.

During the storm, the wind tore through the tree branches like a power saw.

A **metaphor** describes one thing in terms of another.

Tree trunks were matchsticks as they snapped in the wind.

Being Precise Choosing strong words does not mean using a lot of words or using a lot of long and complicated words. Rather, it means choosing words that say exactly what you mean.

Revising Strategies

Revise to eliminate unnecessary information. Reread your draft, looking for any words or phrases that are either not precise or not essential. Identify instances in which the details you provide do not support your main idea because they are either not relevant or you have not clearly explained the connections. To do so, follow these steps:

- Underline your thesis or claim and the main idea of each paragraph.
- Highlight sentences that do not support your thesis.
- Consider adding or revising details to make a tighter connection to your main idea.
- Eliminate any paragraphs or details that do not clearly contribute to your analysis.

Check words of praise or criticism. Review your response to literature, making sure your word choices are precise and that they accurately reflect your purpose, your audience, and your interpretation of the literary work.

Vague: This *factual* account of the author's life is *interesting*.

Precise: This *honest* account of the author's life *captures* the reader's attention.

In addition, pay close attention to the degree, or form, of the adjectives you use, especially when making comparisons. Use the degree that accurately reflects your meaning. The **comparative** degree, which is usually formed by adding *-er* to the adjective or by using the word *more,* is used to compare two items. The **superlative** degree, which is usually formed by adding *-est* to the adjective or by using the word *most,* is used to compare more than two items.

Comparative degree: Zaroff is a *more disagreeable* character than Rainsford. (*Compares two items*)

Superlative degree: Zaroff is the *most disagreeable* character in the story. (*Compares more than two items*)

Peer Review

Exchange drafts with a partner. Review each other's work, circling words that convey approval or criticism. Underline words that express degrees of comparison. Determine whether you have used these words correctly and whether they are precise or vague. Then, revise your draft, replacing vague, dull, or incorrect language with choices that pinpoint your meaning. As you revise, be sure to maintain a consistency in style and tone throughout your work.

Writing

1.c. Use words, phrases, and clauses to link major sections of the text, create cohesion, and clarify relationships between claim(s) and reasons, between reasons and evidence, and between claim(s) and counterclaims.

1.d. Establish and maintain a formal style and objective tone while attending to the norms and conventions of the discipline in which they are writing.

5. Develop and strengthen writing as needed by planning, revising, editing, rewriting, or trying a new approach, focusing on addressing what is most significant for a specific purpose and audience.

Language

2.b. Use a colon to introduce a list or quotation.

Using Quotations

Direct quotations are passages taken word for word from a work of literature. Indirect quotations are paraphrases, or restated passages, of the ideas in a text.

Setting and Punctuating Direct Quotations All direct quotations in the running text must be enclosed in quotation marks. A direct quotation is usually preceded by a comma and sometimes by a colon. It is followed by its corresponding page number enclosed in parentheses. Place the period or comma that is part of the quotation after the parenthesis. See the example below.

Example of Direct Quotations in Running Text:
Rainsford is horrified when he realizes the truth of his situation: "The Cossack was the cat; he was the mouse" (232).

When you quote a passage that is four lines or longer, set it apart from the paragraph and indent it by ten spaces. Do not use quotation marks. This type of quotation is often preceded by a colon. In addition, set the end punctuation for the quotation before the page number citation.

Example of Block Indented Quotations:
Huddled in the jungle, Rainsford breathes a sigh of relief when Zaroff leaves. Then, the horror of the situation hits him:

> *Rainsford did not want to believe what his reason told him was true, but the truth was as evident as the sun that had by now pushed through the morning mists. The general was playing with him! The general was saving him for another day's sport! (231)*

Zaroff's true character becomes apparent to Rainsford in this moment.

Punctuating Indirect Quotations Because indirect quotations are paraphrases of the text, you should not put them in quotation marks.

Example of Indirect Quotation in Running Text:
When Rainsford realizes that Zaroff is playing a game of cat and mouse, he is horrified.

Grammar in Your Writing

Scan your essay to identify any direct quotations. Make sure you have set quotation marks at the beginning and end of a direct quotation that you included in the running text of your paragraph. Make sure you have correctly set off and indented longer passages. Revise punctuation that is incorrect.

STUDENT MODEL: **Jeff Rutherford, Broken Arrow, OK**

Characterization of General Zaroff

What lies at the heart of a refined man? In Richard Connell's short story "The Most Dangerous Game," the deranged, yet cunning and elegant General Zaroff shares his taste for hunting with an unsuspecting visitor. Although he is civilized in his dress and habits, Zaroff's beliefs reveal a murderous mind behind the illusion of a charming, charismatic man.

The title indicates that the essay will focus on a single character.

Jeff uses vivid language to state his thesis clearly.

When we first encounter General Zaroff, our initial reaction is one of delight and admiration for his wealth and charm. Zaroff lives in a massive castle, feasts on the finest delicacies, and wears expensive clothes. His luxurious surroundings and lifestyle reflect a highly civilized, eloquent, and proper gentleman. As readers soon learn, however, there is more to Zaroff than food and elegance.

Beneath Zaroff's fine qualities lies an overwhelming attitude of arrogance. This attitude comes from his firm belief that his way of thinking is superior to that of the average person. Zaroff also fancies himself a phenomenal hunter: "My hand was made for the trigger," he claims. It is this deadly mixture of arrogance, superior hunting skills, and belief that it is natural for the strong to prevail over the weak that makes him disregard the value of human life.

Direct quotations provide evidence for this understanding of Zaroff.

Zaroff's extreme beliefs lead him to conclude that only the intelligent mind of a human being can provide him with the dangerous game he desires. Rationalizing that "the weak were created to please the strong," he chooses to hunt humans instead of animals. Unfortunately, Rainsford steps into this situation. The major conflicts in "The Most Dangerous Game" demonstrate what happens during such an inhumane hunt.

However, the general's arrogance and disregard for human life blind him to the fear and desperation of his prey. His attitude leads to his own demise at the hands of Rainsford, his prey. The characterization of Zaroff as a murderer hiding behind a mask of civility shows that beneath even the most beautiful rose can lie a sharp and deadly thorn.

Jeff concludes his response with an illuminating analogy that neatly summarizes his analysis.

Editing and Proofreading

Review your draft to correct errors in spelling, grammar, and punctuation.

Correcting Common Usage Problems *Among* and *between* are not interchangeable. *Among* always implies three or more elements, whereas *between* is generally used with only two elements. *Like, as, as if,* and *as though* are not interchangeable. *Like* is a preposition meaning "similar to" or "such as." It should not be used in place of *as, as if,* or *as though,* which are conjunctions that introduce clauses

Spiral Review
Earlier in this unit, you learned about **verb tenses** (p. 60). Check your response to literature to be sure you have used consistent verb tenses in your writing.

Publishing and Presenting

Consider one of the following ways to share your writing:

Deliver an oral presentation. Read your response to literature aloud. Have a copy of the literary work on hand in the event that your classmates wish to read or review it. Make sure your work is neatly presented and legible.

Publish a collection of responses to literature. Gather the essays of several of your classmates. Organize them in a binder and make the collection available in the school library.

Reflecting on Your Writing

Writer's Journal Jot down your answer to this question:
How did writing about the work help you to better understand it?

Self-Evaluation Rubric

Use the following criteria to evaluate the effectiveness of your response to literature.

Criteria	Rating Scale			
	not very	....		*very*
Purpose/Focus Introduces a precise claim and distinguishes the claim from opposing claims; provides a concluding section that follows from and supports the argument presented.	1	2	3	4
Organization Establishes a logical organization; uses words, phrases, and clauses to link the major sections of the text, create cohesion, and clarify relationships between ideas and evidence.	1	2	3	4
Development of Ideas/Elaboration Develops the claim and counterclaims fairly, supplying evidence for each while pointing out the strengths and limitations of both.	1	2	3	4
Language Establishes and maintains a formal style and objective tone.	1	2	3	4
Conventions Attends to the norms and conventions of the discipline.	1	2	3	4

SELECTED RESPONSE

RL.9-10.2, RL.9-10.3, RL.9-10.4, RL.9-10.5; W.9-10.10

[For full standards wording, see the chart in the front of this book.]

I. Reading Literature

Directions: *Read the excerpt from "The Golden Kite, the Silver Wind," a short story by Ray Bradbury. Then, answer each question that follows.*

Background: *Leaders of two neighboring towns have directed workers to rebuild their city walls in competing shapes.*

"Oh, Emperor," cried the messenger, "Kwan-Si has rebuilt their walls to resemble a mouth with which to drink all our lake!"

"Then," said the Emperor, standing very close to his silken screen, "build our walls like a needle to sew up that mouth!"

"Emperor!" screamed the messenger. "They make their walls like a sword to break your needle!"

The Emperor held, trembling, to the silken screen. "Then shift the stones to form a scabbard to sheathe that sword!"

"Mercy," wept the messenger the following morn, "they have worked all night and shaped their walls like lightning which will explode and destroy that sheath!"

Sickness spread in the city like a pack of evil dogs. Shops closed. The population, working now steadily for endless months upon the changing of the walls, resembled Death himself, clattering his white bones like musical instruments in the wind. Funerals began to appear in the streets, though it was the middle of summer, a time when all should be tending and harvesting. The Mandarin fell so ill that he had his bed drawn up by the silken screen and there he lay, miserably giving his architectural orders. The voice behind the screen was weak now, too, and faint, like the wind in the eaves.

"Kwan-Si is an eagle. Then our walls must be a net for that eagle. They are a sun to burn our net. Then we build a moon to eclipse their sun!"

Like a rusted machine, the city ground to a halt.

At last the whisper behind the screen cried out:

"In the name of the gods, send for Kwan-Si!"

Upon the last day of summer the Mandarin Kwan-Si, very ill and withered away, was carried into our Mandarin's courtroom by four starving footmen. The two mandarins were propped up, facing each other. Their breaths fluttered like winter winds in their mouths. A voice said:

"Let us put an end to this."

The old men nodded.

1. **Part A** What central **conflict** contributes to characters' actions in this excerpt?
   A. Two mandarins compete to build the more symbolically powerful city.
   B. The citizens of two towns fight over land.
   C. A population struggles to control a disease.
   D. The people of a town defy their leader.

   Part B Which detail from the excerpt best captures that conflict?
   A. "'Kwan-Si is an eagle. Then our walls must be a net for that eagle. They are a sun to burn our net. Then we build a moon to eclipse their sun!'"
   B. "Funerals began to appear in the streets..."
   C. "The population, working now steadily for endless months upon the changing of the walls, resembled Death himself..."
   D. "Like a rusted machine, the city ground to a halt."

2. **Part A** Which answer choice states the most probable **resolution** to the story?
   A. The mandarins begin a war between their towns.
   B. The mandarins do nothing and both towns die out.
   C. The people rebel and choose new leaders.
   D. The mandarins negotiate an agreement.

   Part B Which detail from the excerpt best supports this **prediction?**
   A. "Sickness spread in the city like a pack of evil dogs."
   B. "Their breaths fluttered like winter winds in their mouths."
   C. "'Let us put an end to this.' The old men nodded."
   D. "The Mandarin fell so ill that he had his bed drawn up by the silken screen..."

3. **Part A** How do the townspeople most likely feel about the Emperor's demands?
   A. They enjoy rebuilding the walls over and over.
   B. They find their situation funny.
   C. They are hostile and refuse to do the work.
   D. They are obedient and suffer in silence.

   Part B Which detail from the excerpt best supports that **inference?**
   A. "The population, working now steadily for endless months upon the changing walls, resembled Death himself..."
   B. "The Emperor held, trembling, to the silken screen."
   C. "The Mandarin fell so ill that he had his bed drawn up by the silken screen..."
   D. "Like a rusted machine, the city ground to a halt."

4. In the example below, which techniques does the author use to indirectly **characterize** the messenger?

   "Emperor!" screamed the messenger. "They make their walls like a sword to break your needle!"

   A. description of actions only
   B. dialogue and description of behavior
   C. dialogue and description of thoughts
   D. description of thoughts only

5. Which of the following answer choices best defines the literary concept of **situational irony?**
   A. a character's struggle to overcome a challenge
   B. a contradiction between appearance and reality
   C. a story outcome that contradicts expectations
   D. description of a character in a specific situation

6. What is the meaning of the underlined word *clattering* as it is used in the passage?
   A. breaking
   B. shimmering
   C. dissolving
   D. rattling

Timed Writing

7. Write a brief **cause-and-effect essay** in which you discuss the actions and reactions of the two mandarins in the excerpt. Explain how the chain of cause and effect moves the story forward.

GO ON

II. Reading Informational Text

Directions: *Read the passage. Then, answer each question that follows.*

Common Core State Standards

RI.9-10.1; L.9-10.1, L.9-10.2
[For full standards wording, see the chart in the front of this book.]

History of the Bicycle

The earliest known version of the bicycle was invented by Baron Karl Drais in 1817. This wooden, two-wheeled device lacked pedals or brakes and quickly faded from popularity. In 1819, British inventor Denis Johnson introduced a design that also lacked pedals but was easier to steer. The steps that then led from these early devices to today's sleek bicycles are shrouded in mystery.

The Nineteenth Century

The bicycles of the mid- to late-nineteenth century had iron frames and iron wheels. The front wheel was larger than the back wheel, which added to the bumpy ride. Hence, these models were nicknamed "boneshakers." Like their forerunners, these early bicycles lacked pedals. In the 1860s, inventors added pedals.

During the 1870s, bicycle design continued to improve. The British introduced the "ordinary," a bicycle with solid rubber tires, a large front wheel, and a small back wheel. The ordinary proved to be hazardous. When an ordinary struck ruts or had its brakes applied hard, riders ran the risk of "taking a header"—being pitched forward off the bicycle head-first. By 1885, the "safety," with wheels of equal size, was invented. Balanced wheels created a more stable ride. As a result, bicycling increased in popularity all over the world.

The Twentieth Century

In the early 1900s, the automobile was introduced and mass transit improved, giving the bicycle a second-class status. However, innovations in design, including the banana seat in the 1960s, led to a resurgence of the bicycle's popularity. Additional innovations, such as the 10-speed in the 1970s, and mountain bikes in the 1980s and 1990s, made bicycles even more popular.

Bicycling Today

Some of the most predominant styles today are the mountain bike, the racing bike, and the hybrid (a cross between the two). Bicycling has reached new heights of popularity.

1. Which of the following words best describes the "ordinary" bicycle?

A. boring
B. uncomfortable
C. dangerous
D. slow

2. Which answer choice best states the central idea of the passage?

A. Since the 1800s, the bicycle has evolved and increased in popularity.
B. Safer designs have made bicycling popular.
C. The full history of the bicycle is unknown.
D. Today, people enjoy mountain bikes, racing bikes, and hybrid bikes.

III. Writing and Language Conventions

Directions: *Read the passage. Then, answer each question that follows.*

(1) Jeff's face felt hot as the redness crawled up her cheeks. (2) Every time she introduced herself, she heard, "Isn't Jeff a boy's name?" (3) It was worse when she was little. (4) Everyone thought she is a boy. (5) Now it was just embarrassing. (6) As she struggled through the crowd in the cafeteria, she noticed that Joe, the attractive boy from her English class, was there. (7) She wanted to introduce herself to him. (8) Then, his friend had to ask the question she dreaded: What's your name? (9) Joe's friends chuckled, but he smiled kindly. (10) When lunch was over, Jeff walk away brokenhearted. (11) She would never talk to Joe again. (12) Suddenly, a tap was felt on her shoulder. (13) "Jeff is a great name. It makes you special," said Joe. (14) A smile spread across Jeff's face. (15) Maybe she needed to be proud of being different.

1. Which of the following revisions *best* corrects the inconsistent **verb tense** in sentence 4?

A. Change *is* to *were.*
B. Change *is* to *was.*
C. Change *is* to *will be.*
D. Leave as is.

2. Which words in the passage should be placed in **quotation marks?**

A. What's your name?
B. Then, his friend had to ask the question she dreaded
C. but he smiled kindly
D. Joe said

3. Which revision shows the *best* way to correct the use of **passive voice** in sentence 12?

A. Suddenly, she tapped on her shoulder.
B. Suddenly, on her shoulder a tap was felt by Jeff.
C. Suddenly, a tap is felt by Jeff on her shoulder.
D. Suddenly, she felt a tap on her shoulder.

4. Identify the complete subject and complete predicate in sentence 11.

A. *Complete subject:* She would *Complete predicate:* never talk to Joe again
B. *Complete subject:* She *Complete predicate:* would never talk
C. *Complete subject:* She *Complete predicate:* would never talk to Joe again
D. *Complete subject:* Joe *Complete predicate:* She would never talk to

5. Which of the following revisions is the *best* way to correct the **verb tense** shift in sentence 10?

A. Change *was* to *is.*
B. Change *walk* to *walks.*
C. Change *walk* to *walked.*
D. Change *walk* to *will walk.*

6. In sentence 9, which word is an adverb?

A. Joe's
B. chuckled
C. smiled
D. kindly

CONSTRUCTED RESPONSE

Directions: *Follow the instructions to complete the tasks below as required by your teacher.*

As you work on each task, incorporate both general academic vocabulary and literary terms you learned in Parts 1 and 2 of this unit.

RL.9-10.1, RL.9-10.3, RL.9-10.5; W.9-10.7, W.9-10.8, W.9-10.9.a; SL.9-10.1, SL.9-10.4; L.9-10.6
[For full standards wording, see the chart in the front of this book.]

Writing

TASK 1 Literature [RL.9-10.5; W.9-10.9.a]

Analyze Situational Irony

Analyze how an author's use of situational irony in a story from Part 2 of this unit creates surprise.

- State which story you chose and briefly summarize its plot.
- Explain what is ironic about the plot by describing what happens that contradicts the expectations of characters or the reader.
- Explain how the irony or surprise ending makes sense and fits with details or ideas from earlier in the work.
- Provide specific examples from the text to support your analysis.
- Use active rather than passive voice whenever possible.

TASK 2 Literature [RL.9-10.1; W.9-10.9.a]

Make and Support Inferences About a Main Character

Write an essay in which you explain how making inferences about a main character affected your understanding of a story from Part 2 of this unit.

- Introduce the story's characters, setting, and plot, and explain the main character's role in the story.
- Identify three inferences you made about the main character while reading this story. Cite specific details you used to make them.
- Show how making inferences led you to an understanding of the main character. For example, you might show how specific details suggest a character's personality traits, such as kindness, or help you predict the character's actions.

TASK 3 Literature [RL.9-10.5; W.9-10.9.a]

Analyze Plot Structure

Write an essay in which you analyze how events in a story from Part 2 of this unit are ordered by cause-and-effect relationships.

Part 1

- Review and evaluate a story from Part 2 of this unit in which cause-and-effect relationships play a key role.
- Summarize the story's plot.
- Answer the following question: How are causes and effects introduced and developed in the different stages of the plot—the exposition, rising action, climax, and resolution?

Part 2

- Write an essay in which you explain how one event causes or influences another and how events lead to the story's resolution or to a character's epiphany, or growth.
- Cite details and examples from the story that clearly support your ideas.

Speaking and Listening

TASK 4 **Literature [RL.9-10.3; SL.9-10.4]**

Analyze Techniques of Characterization

Deliver an oral presentation in which you analyze how an author develops a character in a story from Part 2 of this unit.

- Choose one character to describe. Explain his or her traits, focusing on three that are most distinctive.
- Cite specific passages from the story that reveal each of the three main traits you chose. For each passage, explain the technique the author uses to communicate those traits. Categorize each technique as either direct or indirect characterization.
- Make sure the literary terms you use are familiar to your audience. For example, define the two types of characterization.
- Present information clearly, concisely, and logically so that listeners can follow your reasoning.

TASK 5 **Literature [RL.9-10.5; SL.9-10.1; L.9-10.6]**

Analyze Conflicts

Deliver an oral presentation in which you compare the conflicts in two short stories from Part 2 of this unit.

- Identify two short stories from Part 2 that you feel have interesting conflicts.
- Outline the plot points of each story and explain whether the main conflicts are external, internal, or both.
- Draw meaningful comparisons and contrasts between the conflicts explored in the two stories. Explain how characters, dialogue, and settings contribute to the conflicts and to their resolutions.
- Use visual aids to help present your analysis to the class. For example, you might create plot diagrams on poster board to help your listeners follow your ideas.
- After your presentation, invite questions from the audience. Answer questions thoughtfully, using correct academic language and literary terms.

Research

TASK 6 **Literature [RL.9-10.5; W.9-10.7, W.9-10.8, W.9-10.9.a]**

Is conflict necessary?

In Part 2 of this unit, you have read literature that explores different kinds of conflicts. Now, conduct a short research project on a conflict that affects your peers, school, or community. Use both the literature you have read in Part 2 and your research to reflect on and write about this unit's Big Question. Review the following guidelines before you begin your research:

- Choose a conflict you feel comfortable exploring.
- Gather information from at least two reliable sources. Your sources may be print or digital.
- Represent all sides of the conflict evenly and fairly.
- Take notes as you investigate the conflict.
- Cite your sources.

When you have completed your research, write an essay in response to the Big Question. Discuss how your initial ideas have changed or been reinforced. Support your response with examples from both the literature you have read and the research you have conducted.

"One dog barks at something, and a hundred bark at the bark."
—Chinese Proverb

PART 3

TEXT SET DEVELOPING INSIGHT

CONFORMITY

Conflicts often arise because of differences, whether real or just perceived, among people. These differences may involve physical appearance, language, belief, culture, or some other quality. Are conflicts based on such differences inevitable—must they always happen? Conversely, is a world in which everyone conforms always conflict-free? The selections that follow explore the idea of conformity. As you read each one, decide what it suggests about the relationship between conformity and conflict. Then, think about the answer each text provides to the Big Question for this unit: **Is conflict necessary?**

CRITICAL VIEWING Is group behavior, whether that of dogs like these or of people, about conformity or is it about shared goals and leadership? Explain your position.

CLOSE READING TOOL

Use the **Close Reading Tool** to practice the strategies you learn in this unit.

READINGS IN PART 3

The Scarlet Ibis

James Hurst

It was in the clove of seasons, summer was dead but autumn had not yet been born, that the ibis lit in the bleeding tree. The flower garden was stained with rotting brown magnolia petals and ironweeds grew rank amid the purple phlox. The five o'clocks by the chimney still marked time, but the oriole nest in the elm was untenanted and rocked back and forth like an empty cradle. The last graveyard flowers were blooming, and their smell drifted across the cotton field and through every room of our house, speaking softly the names of our dead.

It's strange that all this is still so clear to me, now that the summer has long since fled and time has had its way. A grindstone stands where the bleeding tree stood, just outside the kitchen door, and now if an oriole sings in the elm, its song seems to die up in the leaves, a silvery dust. The flower garden is prim, the house a gleaming white, and the pale fence across the yard stands straight and spruce. But sometimes (like right now), as I sit in the cool, green-draped parlor, the grindstone begins to turn, and time with all its changes is ground away—and I remember Doodle.

Doodle was just about the craziest brother a boy ever had. Of course, he wasn't a crazy crazy like old Miss Leedie, who was in love with President Wilson and wrote him a letter every day, but was a nice crazy, like someone you meet in your dreams. He was born when I was six and was, from the outset, a disappointment. He seemed all head, with a tiny body which was red and shriveled like an old man's. Everybody thought he was going to die—everybody except Aunt Nicey, who had delivered him. She said he would live because he was born in a caul[1] and cauls were made from Jesus' nightgown. Daddy had Mr. Heath, the carpenter, build a little mahogany coffin for him. But he didn't die, and when he was three months old Mama and Daddy decided they might as well name him. They named him William Armstrong, which was like tying a big tail on a small kite. Such a name sounds good only on a tombstone.

I thought myself pretty smart at many things, like holding my breath, running, jumping, or climbing the vines in Old Woman Swamp, and I wanted more than anything else someone to race to Horsehead Landing, someone to box with, and someone to perch

---

1. **caul** (kôl) *n.* membrane enclosing a baby at birth.

with in the top fork of the great pine behind the barn, where across the fields and swamps you could see the sea. I wanted a brother. But Mama, crying, told me that even if William Armstrong lived, he would never do these things with me. He might not, she sobbed, even be "all there." He might, as long as he lived, lie on the rubber sheet in the center of the bed in the front bedroom where the white marquisette curtains billowed out in the afternoon sea breeze, rustling like palmetto fronds.[2]

It was bad enough having an invalid brother, but having one who possibly was not all there was unbearable, so I began to make plans to kill him by smothering him with a pillow. However, one afternoon as I watched him, my head poked between the iron posts of the foot of the bed, he looked straight at me and grinned. I skipped through the rooms, down the echoing halls, shouting, "Mama, he smiled. He's all there! He's all there!" and he was.

When he was two, if you laid him on his stomach, he began to try to move himself, straining terribly. The doctor said that with his weak heart this strain would probably kill him, but it didn't. Trembling, he'd push himself up, turning first red, then a soft purple, and finally collapse back onto the bed like an old worn-out doll. I can still see Mama watching him, her hand pressed tight across her mouth, her eyes wide and unblinking. But he learned to crawl (it was his third winter), and we brought him out of the front bedroom, putting him on the rug before the fireplace. For the first time he became one of us.

As long as he lay all the time in bed, we called him William Armstrong, even though it was formal and sounded as if we were referring to one of our ancestors, but with his creeping around on the deerskin rug and beginning to talk, something had to be done about his name. It was I who renamed him. When he crawled, he crawled backwards, as if he were in reverse and couldn't change gears. If you called him, he'd turn around as if he were going in the other direction, then he'd back right up to you to be picked up. Crawling backward made him look like a doodle-bug, so I began to call him Doodle, and in time even Mama and Daddy thought it was a better name than William Armstrong. Only Aunt Nicey disagreed. She said caul babies should be treated with special respect since they might turn out to be saints. Renaming my brother was perhaps the kindest thing I ever did for him, because nobody expects much from someone called Doodle.

Although Doodle learned to crawl, he showed no signs of walking, but he wasn't idle. He talked so much that we all quit listening to what he said. It was about this time that Daddy built him a go-cart

2. **palmetto** (pal met′ ō) **fronds** (frändz) *n.* palm leaves.

and I had to pull him around. At first I just paraded him up and down the piazza, but then he started crying to be taken out into the yard and it ended up by my having to lug him wherever I went. If I so much as picked up my cap, he'd start crying to go with me and Mama would call from wherever she was, "Take Doodle with you."

He was a burden in many ways. The doctor had said that he mustn't get too excited, too hot, too cold, or too tired and that he must always be treated gently. A long list of don'ts went with him, all of which I ignored once we got out of the house. To discourage his coming with me, I'd run with him across the ends of the cotton rows and careen him around corners on two wheels. Sometimes I accidentally turned him over, but he never told Mama. His skin was very sensitive, and he had to wear a big straw hat whenever he went out. When the going got rough and he had to cling to the sides of the go-cart, the hat slipped all the way down over his ears. He was a sight. Finally, I could see I was licked. Doodle was my brother and he was going to cling to me forever, no matter what I did, so I dragged him across the burning cotton field to share with him the only beauty I knew, Old Woman Swamp. I pulled the go-cart through the saw-tooth fern, down into the green dimness where the palmetto fronds whispered by the stream. I lifted him out and set him down in the soft rubber grass beside a tall pine. His eyes were round with wonder as he gazed about him, and his little hands began to stroke the rubber grass. Then he began to cry.

Although Doodle learned to crawl, he showed no signs of walking, but he wasn't idle.

"For heaven's sake, what's the matter?" I asked, annoyed.

"It's so pretty," he said. "So pretty, pretty, pretty."

After that day Doodle and I often went down into Old Woman Swamp. I would gather wildflowers, wild violets, honeysuckle, yellow jasmine, snakeflowers, and water lilies, and with wire grass we'd weave them into necklaces and crowns. We'd bedeck ourselves with our handiwork and loll about thus beautified, beyond the touch of the everyday world. Then when the slanted rays of the sun burned orange in the tops of the pines, we'd drop our jewels into the stream and watch them float away toward the sea.

There is within me (and with sadness I have watched it in others) a knot of cruelty borne by the stream of love, much as our blood sometimes bears the seed of our destruction, and at times I was mean to Doodle. One day I took him up to the barn loft and showed him his casket, telling him how we all had believed he would die. It was covered with a film of Paris green[3] sprinkled to kill the rats, and screech owls had built a nest inside it.

3. **Paris green** poisonous green powder used chiefly as an insecticide.

Doodle studied the mahogany box for a long time, then said, "It's not mine."

"It is," I said. "And before I'll help you down from the loft, you're going to have to touch it."

"I won't touch it," he said sullenly.

"Then I'll leave you here by yourself," I threatened, and made as if I were going down.

Doodle was frightened of being left. "Don't go leave me, Brother," he cried, and he leaned toward the coffin. His hand, trembling, reached out, and when he touched the casket he screamed. A screech owl flapped out of the box into our faces, scaring us and covering us with Paris green. Doodle was paralyzed, so I put him on my shoulder and carried him down the ladder, and even when we were outside in the bright sunshine, he clung to me, crying, "Don't leave me. Don't leave me."

When Doodle was five years old, I was embarrassed at having a brother of that age who couldn't walk, so I set out to teach him. We were down in Old Woman Swamp and it was spring and the sick-sweet smell of bay flowers hung everywhere like a mournful song. "I'm going to teach you to walk, Doodle," I said.

He was sitting comfortably on the soft grass, leaning back against the pine. "Why?" he asked.

I hadn't expected such an answer. "So I won't have to haul you around all the time."

"I can't walk, Brother," he said.

"Who says so?" I demanded.

"Mama, the doctor—everybody."

"Oh, you can walk," I said, and I took him by the arms and stood him up. He collapsed onto the grass like a half-empty flour sack. It was as if he had no bones in his little legs.

"Don't hurt me, Brother," he warned.

"Shut up. I'm not going to hurt you. I'm going to teach you to walk." I heaved him up again, and again he collapsed.

This time he did not lift his face up out of the rubber grass. "I just can't do it. Let's make honeysuckle wreaths."

"Oh yes you can, Doodle," I said. "All you got to do is try. Now come on," and I hauled him up once more.

It seemed so hopeless from the beginning that it's a miracle I didn't give up. But all of us must have something or someone to be proud of, and Doodle had become mine. I did not know then that pride is a wonderful, terrible thing, a seed that bears two vines, life and death. Every day that summer we went to the pine beside the stream of Old Woman Swamp, and I put him on his feet at least a hundred times each afternoon. Occasionally I too became discouraged because it didn't seem as if he was trying, and I would say, "Doodle, don't you want to learn to walk?"

He'd nod his head, and I'd say, "Well, if you don't keep trying, you'll never learn." Then I'd paint for him a picture of us as old men, white-haired, him with a long white beard and me still pulling him around in the go-cart. This never failed to make him try again.

Finally one day, after many weeks of practicing, he stood alone for a few seconds. When he fell, I grabbed him in my arms and hugged him, our laughter pealing through the swamp like a ringing bell. Now we knew it could be done. Hope no longer hid in the dark palmetto thicket but perched like a cardinal in the lacy toothbrush tree, brilliantly visible. "Yes, yes," I cried, and he cried it too, and the grass beneath us was soft and the smell of the swamp was sweet.

With success so **imminent**, we decided not to tell anyone until he could actually walk. Each day, barring rain, we sneaked into Old Woman Swamp, and by cotton-picking time Doodle was ready to show what he could do. He still wasn't able to walk far, but we could wait no longer. Keeping a nice secret is very hard to do, like holding your breath. We chose to reveal all on October eighth, Doodle's sixth birthday, and for weeks ahead we mooned around the house, promising everybody a most spectacular surprise. Aunt Nicey said that, after so much talk, if we produced anything less tremendous than the Resurrection,[4] she was going to be disappointed.

◀ **imminent** (im´ ə nənt) *adj.* likely to happen soon

At breakfast on our chosen day, when Mama, Daddy, and Aunt Nicey were in the dining room, I brought Doodle to the door in the go-cart just as usual and had them turn their backs, making them cross their hearts and hope to die if they peeked. I helped Doodle up, and when he was standing alone I let them look. There wasn't a sound as Doodle walked slowly across the room and sat down at his place at the table. Then Mama began to cry and ran over to him, hugging him and kissing him. Daddy hugged him too, so I went to Aunt Nicey, who was thanks praying in the doorway, and began to waltz her around. We danced together quite well until she came down on my big toe with her brogans, hurting me so badly I thought I was crippled for life.

Doodle told them it was I who had taught him to walk, so everyone wanted to hug me, and I began to cry.

"What are you crying for?" asked Daddy, but I couldn't answer. They did not know that I did it for myself; that pride, whose slave I was, spoke to me louder than all their voices, and that Doodle walked only because I was ashamed of having a crippled brother.

Within a few months Doodle had learned to walk well and his

---

4. **the Resurrection** (rez´ ə rek´ shən) the rising of Jesus Christ from the dead after his death and burial.

go-cart was put up in the barn loft (it's still there) beside his little mahogany coffin. Now, when we roamed off together, resting often, we never turned back until our destination had been reached, and to help pass the time, we took up lying. From the beginning Doodle was a terrible liar and he got me in the habit. Had anyone stopped to listen to us, we would have been sent off to Dix Hill.

My lies were scary, involved, and usually pointless, but Doodle's were twice as crazy. People in his stories all had wings and flew wherever they wanted to go. His favorite lie was about a boy named Peter who had a pet peacock with a ten-foot tail. Peter wore a golden robe that glittered so brightly that when he walked through the sunflowers they turned away from the sun to face him. When Peter was ready to go to sleep, the peacock spread his magnificent tail, enfolding the boy gently like a closing go-to-sleep flower, burying him in the gloriously iridescent, rustling vortex.[5] Yes, I must admit it. Doodle could beat me lying.

Doodle and I spent lots of time thinking about our future. We decided that when we were grown we'd live in Old Woman Swamp and pick dog-tongue for a living. Beside the stream, he planned, we'd build us a house of whispering leaves and the swamp birds would be our chickens. All day long (when we weren't gathering dog-tongue) we'd swing through the cypresses on the rope vines, and if it rained we'd huddle beneath an umbrella tree and play stickfrog. Mama and Daddy could come and live with us if they wanted to. He even came up with the idea that he could marry Mama and I could marry Daddy. Of course, I was old enough to know this wouldn't work out, but the picture he painted was so beautiful and serene that all I could do was whisper Yes, yes.

infallibility ▶ (in fal′ ə bil′ ə tē) *n.* condition of being unlikely to fail

Once I had succeeded in teaching Doodle to walk, I began to believe in my own **infallibility** and I prepared a terrific development program for him, unknown to Mama and Daddy, of course. I would teach him to run, to swim, to climb trees, and to fight. He, too, now believed in my infallibility, so we set the deadline for these accomplishments less than a year away, when, it had been decided, Doodle could start to school.

That winter we didn't make much progress, for I was in school and Doodle suffered from one bad cold after another. But when spring came, rich and warm, we raised our sights again. Success lay at the end of summer like a pot of gold, and our campaign got off to a good start. On hot days, Doodle and I went down to Horsehead Landing and I gave him swimming lessons or showed him how to row a boat. Sometimes we descended into the cool greenness of Old Woman

5. **vortex** (vôr′ teks′) *n.* rushing whirl, drawing in all that surrounds it.

Swamp and climbed the rope vines or boxed scientifically beneath the pine where he had learned to walk. Promise hung about us like the leaves, and wherever we looked, ferns unfurled and birds broke into song.

That summer, the summer of 1918, was blighted. In May and June there was no rain and the crops withered, curled up, then died under the thirsty sun. One morning in July a hurricane came out of the east, tipping over the oaks in the yard and splitting the limbs of the elm trees. That afternoon it roared back out of the west, blew the fallen oaks around, snapping their roots and tearing them out of the earth like a hawk at the entrails of a chicken. Cotton bolls were wrenched from the stalks and lay like green walnuts in the valleys between the rows, while the cornfield leaned over uniformly so that the tassels touched the ground. Doodle and I followed Daddy out into the cotton field, where he stood, shoulders sagging, surveying the ruin. When his chin sank down onto his chest, we were frightened, and Doodle slipped his hand into mine. Suddenly Daddy straightened his shoulders, raised a giant knuckly fist, and with a voice that seemed to rumble out of the earth itself began cursing heaven, hell, the weather, and the Republican Party. Doodle and I, prodding each other and giggling, went back to the house, knowing that everything would be all right.

Success lay at the end of summer like a pot of gold...

And during that summer, strange names were heard through the house: Chateau-Thierry, Amiens, Soissons, and in her blessing at the supper table, Mama once said, "And bless the Pearsons, whose boy Joe was lost at Belleau Wood."[6]

So we came to that clove of seasons. School was only a few weeks away, and Doodle was far behind schedule. He could barely clear the ground when climbing up the rope vines and his swimming was certainly not passable. We decided to double our efforts, to make that last drive and reach our pot of gold. I made him swim until he turned blue and row until he couldn't lift an oar. Wherever we went, I purposely walked fast, and although he kept up, his face turned red and his eyes became glazed. Once, he could go no further, so he collapsed on the ground and began to cry.

"Aw, come on, Doodle," I urged. "You can do it. Do you want to be different from everybody else when you start school?"

"Does it make any difference?"

"It certainly does," I said. "Now, come on," and I helped him up.

As we slipped through dog days, Doodle began to look feverish,

---

6. **Chateau-Thierry** (sha´ tō´ tē er´ ē), **Amiens** (á myan´), **Soissons** (swä sôn´), . . . **Belleau** (be lō´) **Wood** places in France where battles were fought during World War I.

and Mama felt his forehead, asking him if he felt ill. At night he didn't sleep well, and sometimes he had nightmares, crying out until I touched him and said, "Wake up, Doodle. Wake up."

It was Saturday noon, just a few days before school was to start. I should have already admitted defeat, but my pride wouldn't let me. The excitement of our program had now been gone for weeks, but still we kept on with a tired doggedness. It was too late to turn back, for we had both wandered too far into a net of expectations and had left no crumbs behind.

Daddy, Mama, Doodle, and I were seated at the dining-room table having lunch. It was a hot day, with all the windows and doors open in case a breeze should come. In the kitchen Aunt Nicey was humming softly. After a long silence, Daddy spoke. "It's so calm, I wouldn't be surprised if we had a storm this afternoon."

"I haven't heard a rain frog," said Mama, who believed in signs, as she served the bread around the table.

"I did," declared Doodle. "Down in the swamp."

"He didn't," I said contrarily.

"You did, eh?" said Daddy, ignoring my denial.

"I certainly did," Doodle reiterated, scowling at me over the top of his iced-tea glass, and we were quiet again.

Suddenly, from out in the yard, came a strange croaking noise. Doodle stopped eating, with a piece of bread poised ready for his mouth, his eyes popped round like two blue buttons. "What's that?" he whispered.

I jumped up, knocking over my chair, and had reached the door when Mama called, "Pick up the chair, sit down again, and say excuse me."

By the time I had done this, Doodle had excused himself and had slipped out into the yard. He was looking up into the bleeding tree. "It's a great big red bird!" he called.

The bird croaked loudly again, and Mama and Daddy came out into the yard. We shaded our eyes with our hands against the hazy glare of the sun and peered up through the still leaves. On the topmost branch a bird the size of a chicken, with scarlet feathers and long legs, was perched **precariously**. Its wings hung down loosely, and as we watched, a feather dropped away and floated slowly down through the green leaves.

precariously ▶ (pri ker´ ē əs lē) *adv.* insecurely

"It's not even frightened of us," Mama said.

"It looks tired," Daddy added. "Or maybe sick."

Doodle's hands were clasped at his throat, and I had never seen him stand still so long. "What is it?" he asked.

Daddy shook his head. "I don't know, maybe it's—"

At that moment the bird began to flutter, but the wings were uncoordinated, and amid much flapping and a spray of flying feathers, it tumbled down, bumping through the limbs of the bleeding tree and landing at our feet with a thud. Its long, graceful neck jerked twice into an S, then straightened out, and the bird was still. A white veil came over the eyes and the long white beak unhinged. Its legs were crossed and its clawlike feet were delicately curved at rest. Even death did not mar its grace, for it lay on the earth like a broken vase of red flowers, and we stood around it, awed by its exotic beauty.

"It's dead," Mama said.

"What is it?" Doodle repeated.

"Go bring me the bird book," said Daddy.

I ran into the house and brought back the bird book. As we watched, Daddy thumbed through its pages. "It's a scarlet ibis," he said, pointing to a picture. "It lives in the tropics—South America to Florida. A storm must have brought it here."

Sadly, we all looked back at the bird. A scarlet ibis! How many miles it had traveled to die like this, in our yard, beneath the bleeding tree.

"Let's finish lunch," Mama said, nudging us back toward the dining room.

"I'm not hungry," said Doodle, and he knelt down beside the ibis.

"We've got peach cobbler for dessert," Mama tempted from the doorway.

Doodle remained kneeling. "I'm going to bury him."

"Don't you dare touch him," Mama warned. "There's no telling what disease he might have had."

"All right," said Doodle. "I won't."

Daddy, Mama, and I went back to the dining-room table, but we watched Doodle through the open door. He took out a piece of string from his pocket and, without touching the ibis, looped one end around its neck. Slowly, while singing softly "Shall We Gather at the River," he carried the bird around to the front yard and dug a hole in the flower garden, next to the petunia bed. Now we were watching him through the front window, but he didn't know it. His awkwardness at digging the hole with a shovel whose handle was twice as long as he was made us laugh, and we covered our mouths with our hands so he wouldn't hear.

When Doodle came into the dining room, he found us seriously eating our cobbler. He was pale and lingered just inside the screen door. "Did you get the scarlet ibis buried?" asked Daddy.

Doodle didn't speak but nodded his head.

"Go wash your hands, and then you can have some peach cobbler," said Mama.

"I'm not hungry," he said.

"Dead birds is bad luck," said Aunt Nicey, poking her head from the kitchen door. "Specially red dead birds!"

As soon as I had finished eating, Doodle and I hurried off to Horsehead Landing. Time was short, and Doodle still had a long way to go if he was going to keep up with the other boys when he started school. The sun, gilded with the yellow cast of autumn, still burned fiercely, but the dark green woods through which we passed were shady and cool. When we reached the landing, Doodle said he was too tired to swim, so we got into a skiff and floated down the creek with the tide. Far off in the marsh a rail was scolding, and over on the beach locusts were singing in the myrtle trees. Doodle did not speak and kept his head turned away, letting one hand trail limply in the water.

After we had drifted a long way, I put the oars in place and made Doodle row back against the tide. Black clouds began to gather in the southwest, and he kept watching them, trying to pull the oars a little faster. When we reached Horsehead Landing, lightning was playing across half the sky and thunder roared out, hiding even the sound of the sea. The sun disappeared and darkness descended, almost like night. Flocks of marsh crows flew by, heading inland to their roosting trees, and two egrets, squawking, arose from the oyster-rock shallows and careened away.

Two Boys in a Punt, 1915–Cover Illustration, Popular Magazine, N.C. Wyeth (1882–1945), Private Collection, Photography courtesy of Brandywine River Museum.

Doodle was both tired and frightened, and when he stepped from the skiff he collapsed onto the mud, sending an armada of fiddler crabs rustling off into the marsh grass. I helped him up, and as he wiped the mud off his trousers, he smiled at me ashamedly. He had failed and we both knew it, so we started back home, racing the storm. We never spoke (What are the words that can solder cracked pride?), but I knew he was watching me, watching for a sign of mercy. The lightning was near now, and from fear he walked so close behind me he kept stepping on my heels. The faster I walked, the faster he walked, so I began to run. The rain was coming, roaring through the pines, and then, like a bursting Roman candle, a gum tree ahead of us was shattered by a bolt of lightning. When the deafening peal of thunder had died, and in the moment before the rain arrived, I heard Doodle, who had fallen behind, cry out, "Brother, Brother, don't leave me! Don't leave me!"

The knowledge that Doodle's and my plans had come to naught was bitter, and that streak of cruelty within me awakened. I ran as fast as I could, leaving him far behind with a wall of rain dividing us. The drops stung my face like nettles, and the wind flared the wet glistening leaves of the bordering trees. Soon I could hear his voice no more.

I hadn't run too far before I became tired, and the flood of childish spite evanesced as well. I stopped and waited for Doodle. The sound of rain was everywhere, but the wind had died and it fell straight down in parallel paths like ropes hanging from the sky. As I waited, I peered through the downpour, but no one came. Finally I went back and found him huddled beneath a red nightshade bush beside the road. He was sitting on the ground, his face buried in his arms, which were resting on his drawn-up knees. "Let's go, Doodle," I said.

He didn't answer, so I placed my hand on his forehead and lifted his head. Limply, he fell backwards onto the earth. He had been bleeding from the mouth, and his neck and the front of his shirt were stained a brilliant red.

"Doodle! Doodle!" I cried, shaking him, but there was no answer but the ropy rain. He lay very awkwardly, with his head thrown far back, making his vermilion neck appear unusually long and slim. His little legs, bent sharply at the knees, had never before seemed so fragile, so thin.

I began to weep, and the tear-blurred vision in red before me looked very familiar. "Doodle!" I screamed above the pounding storm and threw my body to the earth above his. For a long long time, it seemed forever, I lay there crying, sheltering my fallen scarlet ibis from the heresy[7] of rain.

---

7. **heresy** (her′ ə sē) *n.* idea opposed to the beliefs of a religion or philosophy.

ABOUT THE AUTHOR

James Hurst (b. 1922)

James Hurst grew up along the coast of North Carolina, a place of quiet landscapes and violent storms. After studying chemical engineering and opera and serving in the army during World War II, Hurst took a job at a New York bank. For thirty-four years, he worked as a banker and spent his evenings writing stories. "The Scarlet Ibis," published in 1960, is Hurst's best-known story.

Close Reading Activities

READ

Comprehension

Reread all or part of the text to help you answer the following questions.

1. What is different about Doodle?
2. What surprise do the brothers present to their parents?
3. What plan does the narrator make for Doodle's future?
4. What does Doodle find in the bleeding tree?
5. What happens to Doodle at the story's end?

Research: Clarify Details This story may include references that are unfamiliar to you. Choose at least one unfamiliar detail, and briefly research it. Then, explain how the information you learned from research sheds light on an aspect of the story.

Summarize Write an objective summary of the story. Remember that an objective summary is free from opinion and evaluation.

Language Study

Selection Vocabulary The following sentences appear in "The Scarlet Ibis." Define each boldface word, and use the word in a sentence of your own.

- With success so **imminent**, we decided not to tell anyone until he could actually walk.
- I began to believe in my own **infallibility** and I prepared a terrific development program for him, unknown to Mama and Daddy, of course.
- On the topmost branch a bird the size of a chicken, with scarlet feathers and long legs, was perched **precariously**.

Diction and Style Study the first sentence of the story, which appears below. Then, answer the questions that follow.

> It was in the clove of seasons, summer was dead but autumn had not yet been born, that the ibis lit in the bleeding tree.

1. **(a)** What does *clove* mean in this sentence? **(b)** What other meaning does *clove* have?
2. **(a)** What is the meaning of *lit*, as used in this sentence? **(b)** For what longer word does *lit* stand? **(c)** Why do you think the author chose to use the word *lit* instead of a synonym?

Conventions Read this passage from the story. Identify the tenses of the underlined verbs and verb phrases as present, past, or past perfect. Then, explain how the author's use of varied verb tenses clarifies the meaning of the passage.

> Within a few months Doodle had learned to walk well and his go-cart was put up in the barn loft (it's still there) beside his little mahagony coffin. Now, when we roamed off together, resting often, we never turned back until our destination had been reached, and to help pass the time, we took up lying.

Academic Vocabulary

The following words appear in blue in the instructions and questions on the facing page.

effective **detract** **pervade**

Categorize the words by deciding whether you know each one well, know it a little bit, or do not know it at all. Then, use a print or an online dictionary to look up the definitions of the words you are unsure of or do not know at all.

Literary Analysis

Reread the identified passages. Then, respond to the questions that follow.

Focus Passage 1 *(p. 129)*
Doodle was just about ... on a tombstone.

Key Ideas and Details

1. **(a) Interpret:** According to the narrator, what kind of "crazy" is Doodle? **(b) Analyze:** How does the reference to "dreams" hint at the role Doodle plays in the narrator's life? Explain.
2. **Infer:** What can you infer from the statement that "Mama and Daddy decided they might as well name him"? Explain.

Craft and Structure

3. **(a) Interpret:** Why is Doodle's official name, William Armstrong, "like tying a big tail on a small kite"? **(b) Connect:** What point does the narrator make with this simile? Explain.
4. **Analyze:** What clues to the story's ending are revealed with the use of the past tense and the comment about the tombstone? Explain.

Integration of Knowledge and Ideas

5. **(a) Compare and Contrast:** How does Aunt Nicey's opinion of Doodle differ from that of the rest of the family? **(b) Infer:** What does her comment about the caul suggest about Doodle's character?

Focus Passage 2 *(pp. 132–133)*
It seemed so hopeless ... swamp was sweet.

Key Ideas and Details

1. **Interpret:** What does the first sentence of this passage reveal about the narrator? Explain.
2. **(a) Distinguish:** What words does the narrator use to describe hope? **(b) Evaluate:** Do you find the description **effective**? Why or why not?

Craft and Structure

3. **Explain:** Explain the use of parallelism, or matching grammatical structures, in the third sentence. How does the use of this grammatical pattern affect the meaning?
4. **(a) Describe:** Describe the use of alliteration in the final sentence of the passage. **(b) Evaluate:** Does the use of this sound device add to or **detract** from the literal meaning of the sentence? Explain.

Integration of Knowledge and Ideas

5. **Analyze:** In what ways is the narrator's description of pride similar to the description of the season in the first two paragraphs of the story? Explain.

Symbolism

A **symbol** is anything—an object, person, animal, place, or image—that represents something else. A symbol has its own meaning, but it also stands for something more important, often an abstract idea. Reread the story, and take notes on ways in which the author uses symbolism.

1. **(a)** What qualities does the ibis exhibit? **(b)** In what ways does Doodle share those qualities? **(c)** Why do you think Hurst chose to title this work "The Scarlet Ibis"?
2. **(a)** What symbols of death **pervade** the text? **(b)** How do those symbols lend meaning to the story? Cite examples from the text in your response.
3. **Conformity:** What do you think Hurst is suggesting about conformity through the story elements of the ibis and Doodle? Explain, citing details and examples from the text.

Common Core State Standards

RL.9-10.1, RL.9-10.2, RL.9-10.3, RL.9-10.4, RL.9-10.5, RL.9-10.10; L.9-10.1, L.9-10.3, L.9-10.4.d, L.9-10.5, L.9-10.5.a, L.9-10.6

[For full standards wording, see the chart in the front of this book.]

DISCUSS

From Text to Topic **Group Discussion**

Discuss the following passage with a group of classmates. Take notes during the discussion. Contribute your own ideas, and support them with examples from the text.

> Once, he could go no further, so he collapsed on the ground and began to cry.
> "Aw, come on, Doodle," I urged. "You can do it. Do you want to be different from everybody else when you start school?"
> "Does it make any difference?"
> "It certainly does," I said.

QUESTIONS FOR DISCUSSION:

1. Why do you think the narrator wants to change Doodle?
2. Should Doodle try to be the same as other children? Why or why not?
3. What motivates Doodle to try to change?

WRITE

Writing to Sources **Informative Text**

Assignment
Write a **comparison-and-contrast essay** in which you analyze the two main characters in "The Scarlet Ibis"—the narrator and Doodle. In particular, consider each character's attitude toward fitting in.

Prewriting and Planning Reread the story, looking for details that describe each character's appearance and behavior as well as his thoughts, feelings, and motivations. Record your notes in a two-column chart or a Venn diagram.

Drafting Select an organizational structure. Most comparison-and-contrast writing follows either a block or point-by-point organization.

- **Block Method** Present all the details about one of your subjects, then all the details about the other subject.
- **Point-by-Point Method** Discuss one feature of both subjects, then another feature of both subjects. Continue this process until you have covered all the features.

In your draft, cite specific examples from the story to support your points.

Revising Reread your essay, making sure you have clearly explained comparisons and contrasts. Clarify your meaning by using transitional words or phrases, such as the ones shown below, to connect your ideas.

in contrast	*at the same time*	*by the same token*	*likewise*
in the same way	*on the contrary*	*on the other hand*	*nevertheless*

Editing and Proofreading Make sure the transitional expressions you have used clarify comparison and contrast relationships among your ideas. In addition, make sure you have correctly used semicolons to separate two independent clauses that are joined by a transitional word or phrase.

CONVENTIONS
An independent clause has a subject and verb and can stand alone as a sentence. When you join two such clauses with a transitional word or phrase, use a semicolon before the transition and a comma after it.

RESEARCH

Research **Investigate the Topic**

Cultural Attitudes Toward Conformity Most of Doodle's family members treat him gently because of his physical differences. His brother, however, treats him as if he is no different from anyone else. Attitudes toward physical or mental differences vary over time and across cultures. For example, in the United States, left-handedness was once considered to be a problem that needed correction. In some cultures, however, left-handedness is considered to be a sign of wisdom.

Assignment

Conduct research to find out how people born with physical or mental differences have been treated in various cultures or eras. Consult firsthand accounts, such as diaries and memoirs. Take clear notes and carefully identify your sources so that you can easily access the information later. Share your findings in an **informal speech or presentation** for the class.

PREPARATION FOR ESSAY

You may use the knowledge you gain during this research assignment to support your claims in an essay you will write at the end of this section.

Gather Sources Locate authoritative print and electronic sources. Primary sources, such as letters, journals, diaries, or memoirs, provide authentic firsthand information. These types of sources convey the writers' experiences and feelings in a direct and immediate way. You may also want to use secondary sources, such as news articles. Look for sources that feature expert authors and up-to-date information.

Take Notes Take notes on each source, either electronically or on note cards. Use an organized note-taking strategy.

- Label each note with its main idea. You may have several notes per main idea.
- You will probably want to quote directly from primary sources in order to capture the writers' attitudes. Remember to use quotation marks in those instances.
- Record source information to use in citations.

Synthesize Multiple Sources Assemble data from your sources and organize it into a cohesive presentation. If you mainly consulted primary sources, use what you learned from those particular writers to draw conclusions about how their cultures view physical and mental differences. Use your notes to construct an outline for your presentation. Create a Works Cited list to distribute at the end of your presentation. See the Citing Sources pages in the Introductory Unit of this textbook for additional guidance.

Organize and Present Ideas Review your outline and practice delivering your presentation. Be ready to take questions from your audience.

W.9-10.2.a–c, W.9-10.5, W.9-10.7, W.9-10.8, W.9-10.9.a, W.9-10.10; SL.9-10.1, SL.9-10.1.a–e
[For full standards wording, see the chart in the front of this book.]

Much Madness is divinest Sense—

Emily Dickinson

discerning ▶
(di surn′ iŋ) *adj.* having good judgment or understanding

prevail ▶
(prē vāl′) *v.* gain the advantage or mastery; be victorious; triumph

Much Madness is divinest Sense—
To a **discerning** Eye—
Much Sense—the starkest Madness—
'Tis the Majority
In this, as All, **prevail**—
Assent[1]—and you are sane—
Demur[2]—you're straightway dangerous—
And handled with a Chain—

1. **assent** (ə sent′) *v.* agree.
2. **demur** (dē mur′) *v.* hesitate because of doubts or objections.

ABOUT THE AUTHOR

Emily Dickinson (1830–1886)

Despite her quiet, outward behavior, Emily Dickinson's inner life overflowed with energy. She produced at least 1,775 poems. Dickinson looked deeply into simple subjects—a fly buzzing, a bird on a walk, the changing seasons. She also made profound explorations of love, death, and the relationship between the human and the divine. She remains unquestionably one of America's finest poets.

Close Reading Activities

READ • WRITE

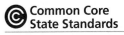

Common Core State Standards

RL.9-10.1, RL.9-10.2, RL.9-10.4, RL.9-10.10; W.9-10.1, W.9-10.4, W.9-10.9; L.9-10.4.b

[For full standards wording, see the chart in the front of this book.]

Comprehension

Reread the poem. Then, answer the following questions.

1. **(a)** According to the speaker, what is often incorrectly seen as "madness"? **(b)** What is often wrongly regarded as "sense"?
2. **(a)** According to the speaker, who determines what is sense and what is madness? **(b)** What happens to those who disagree with those viewpoints? Explain.

Language Study

Selection Vocabulary The following lines appear in the poem. For each boldface word, remove the suffix, add a suffix, or change the existing suffix to create a new, related word. Define each new word and identify its part of speech.

- Much Madness is divinest Sense— / To a **discerning** Eye—
- 'Tis the Majority / In this, as All, **prevail**—

Literary Analysis

Key Ideas and Details

1. **(a) Interpret:** What does the speaker mean by the statement, "'Tis the majority / In this, as All, prevail"? **(b) Analyze:** How do the poet's capitalization and punctuation choices emphasize this meaning? Explain.

Craft and Structure

2. **(a) Analyze:** How do the sounds of the words in the first three lines differ from those in the rest of the poem? **(b) Interpret:** In what ways do the sounds in the first three lines add to their meaning and effect?
3. **Analyze:** What is the effect of the poet's word choice in the seventh line? Be sure to discuss "demur" and "straightway" in your response.

Integration of Knowledge and Ideas

4. A paradox is a statement or idea that seems contradictory but actually expresses a truth. **(a) Synthesize:** What is the main paradox of this poem? **(b) Connect:** Is the poem's main paradox also its theme? Explain, citing details from the poem in your response.

ACADEMIC VOCABULARY

Academic terms appear in blue on these pages. If these words are not familiar to you, use a dictionary to find their definitions. Then, use them as you speak and write about the text.

Writing to Sources **Argument**

Write a brief **response** to the poem. Explain whether you agree or disagree with the speaker's central point. Cite details from the poem to support your ideas.

My English

Julia Alvarez

Mami and Papi used to speak it when they had a secret they wanted to keep from us children. We lived then in the Dominican Republic, and the family as a whole spoke only Spanish at home, until my sisters and I started attending the Carol Morgan School, and we became a **bilingual** family. Spanish had its many tongues as well. There was the castellano[1] of Padre[2] Joaquín from Spain, whose lisp we all loved to imitate. Then the educated español my parents' families spoke, aunts and uncles who were always correcting us children, for we spent most of the day with the maids and so had picked up their "bad Spanish." Campesinas,[3] they spoke a lilting, animated campuno,[4] *ss* swallowed, endings chopped off, funny turns of phrases. This campuno was my true mother tongue, not the Spanish of Calderón de la Barca or Cervantes or even Neruda,[5] but of Chucha and Iluminada and Gladys and Ursulina from Juncalito and Licey and Boca de Yuma and San Juan de la Maguana.[6] Those women yakked as they cooked, they storytold, they gossiped, they sang—boleros, merengues, canciones, salves.[7] Theirs were the voices that belonged to the rain and the wind and the teeny, teeny stars even a small child could blot out with her thumb.

◀ **bilingual** (bī liŋ´ gwəl) *adj.* using two languages

Besides all these versions of Spanish, every once in a while another strange tongue emerged from my papi's mouth or my mami's lips. What I first recognized was not a language, but a tone of voice, serious, urgent, something important and top secret being said, some uncle in trouble, someone divorcing, someone dead. *Say it in English so the children won't understand.* I would listen, straining

1. **castellano** (cä´ stā yä´ nō) Spanish for "Castilian," the most widely spoken dialect of the Spanish language.
2. **Padre** (pä´ drā) "Father" (Spanish), a form of address for a Roman Catholic priest.
3. **Campesinas** (cäm pā sē´ näs) simple rural women; peasant women (Spanish).
4. **campuno** (cäm po͞o´ nō) Spanish dialect spoken in rural areas of the Dominican Republic.
5. **Calderón de la Barca** (cäl de rôn´ dā lä bär´ cä) . . . **Cervantes** (ser vän´ tes) . . . **Neruda** (nā ro͞o´ dä) important literary figures.
6. **Juncalito** (ho͞oŋ cä lē´ tō) . . . **Licey** . . . **Boca de Yuma** (bō´ cä dā yo͞o´ mä) . . . **San Juan de la Maguana** (sän hwän´ dā lä mä gwä´ nä) small rural villages in the Dominican Republic.
7. **boleros** (bō ler´ ōs) . . . **merengues** (mə reŋ´ gās) . . . **canciones** (cän sē ō´ nes) . . . **salves** (säl´ ves) Spanish and Latin American songs and dances.

to understand, thinking that this was not a different language but just another and harder version of Spanish. *Say it in English so the children won't understand.* From the beginning, English was the sound of worry and secrets, the sound of being left out.

I could make no sense of this "harder Spanish," and so I tried by other means to find out what was going on. I knew my mother's face by heart. When the little lines on the corners of her eyes crinkled, she was amused. When her nostrils flared and she bit her lips, she was trying hard not to laugh. She held her head down, eyes glancing up, when she thought I was lying. Whenever she spoke that gibberish English, I translated the general content by watching the Spanish expressions on her face.

Soon, I began to learn more English, at the Carol Morgan School. That is, when I had stopped gawking. The teacher and some of the American children had the strangest coloration: light hair, light eyes, light skin, as if Ursulina had soaked them in bleach too long, to' deteñío.[8] I did have some blond cousins, but they had deeply tanned skin, and as they grew older, their hair darkened, so their earlier paleness seemed a phase of their acquiring normal color. Just as strange was the little girl in my reader who had a *cat* and a *dog*, that looked just like un gatito y un perrito. Her mami was *Mother* and her papi *Father*. Why have a whole new language for school and for books with a teacher who could speak it teaching you double the amount of words you really needed?

Butter, butter, butter, butter. All day, one English word that had particularly struck me would go round and round in my mouth and weave through all the Spanish in my head until by the end of the day, the word did sound like just another Spanish word. And so I would say, "Mami, please pass la mantequilla." She would scowl and say in English, "I'm sorry, I don't understand. But would you be needing some butter on your bread?"

Why my parents didn't first educate us in our native language by enrolling us in a Dominican school, I don't know. Part of it was that Mami's family had a tradition of sending the boys to the States to boarding school and college, and she had been one of the first girls to be allowed to join her brothers. At Abbot Academy,[9] whose school song was our lullaby as babies ("Although Columbus and Cabot[10] never heard of Abbot, it's quite the place for you and me"), she had

---

8. to' deteñío (tō dā tān yē´ ō) all washed out; completely colorless (Spanish).

9. Abbot Academy boarding school for girls in Andover, Massachusetts; merged in 1973 with the neighboring boys' school, Phillips Academy.

10. Cabot (kab´ ət) John Cabot (1450–1499), Italian explorer who sailed in the service of England and was the first European to discover the coast of North America in 1497.

become quite Americanized. It was very important, she kept saying, that we learn our English. She always used the possessive pronoun: *your* English, an inheritance we had come into and must wisely use. Unfortunately, my English became all mixed up with our Spanish.

Mix-up, or what's now called Spanglish, was the language we spoke for several years. There wasn't a sentence that wasn't colonized by an English word. At school, a Spanish word would suddenly slide into my English like someone butting into line. Teacher, whose face I was learning to read as minutely as my mother's, would scowl but no smile played on her lips. Her pale skin made her strange countenance hard to read, so that I often misjudged how much I could get away with. Whenever I made a mistake, Teacher would shake her head slowly, "In English, YU-LEE-AH, there's no such word as *columpio*. Do you mean a *swing?*"

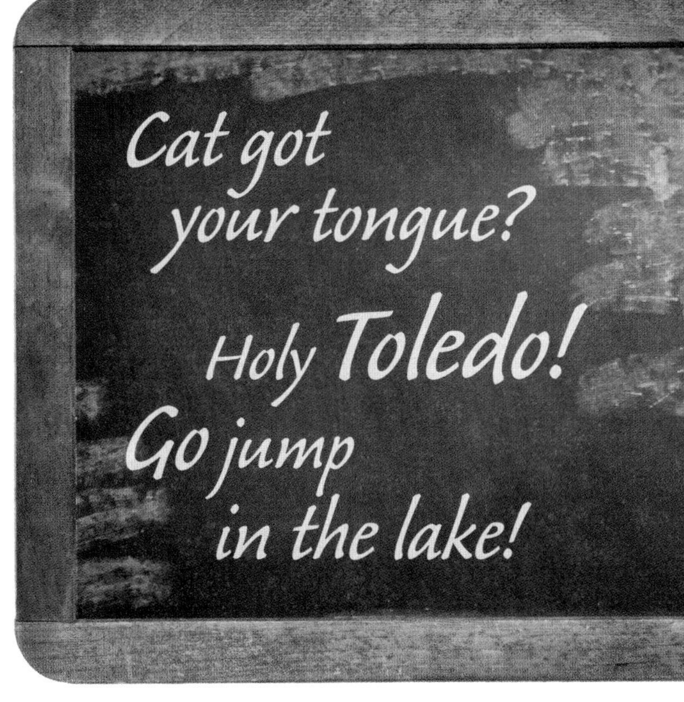

I would bow my head, humiliated by the smiles and snickers of the American children around me. I grew insecure about Spanish. My native tongue was not quite as good as English, as if words like *columpio* were illegal immigrants trying to cross a border into another language. But Teacher's discerning grammar-and-vocabulary-patrol ears could tell and send them back.

Soon, I was talking up an English storm. "Did you eat English parrot?" my grandfather asked one Sunday. I had just enlisted yet one more patient servant to listen to my rendition of "Peter Piper picked a peck of pickled peppers" at breakneck pace. "Huh?" I asked impolitely in English, putting him in his place. *Cat got your tongue? No big deal! So there! Take that! Holy Toledo!* (Our teacher's favorite "curse word.") *Go jump in the lake! Really dumb. Golly. Gosh.* Slang, clichés, sayings, hotshot language that our teacher called, ponderously, idiomatic expressions. Riddles, jokes, puns, conundrums. *What is yellow and goes click-click? Why did the chicken cross the road? See you later, alligator.* How wonderful to call someone an alligator and not be scolded for being disrespectful. In fact, they were supposed to say back, *In a while, crocodile.*

There was also a neat little trick I wanted to try on an English-speaking adult at home. I had learned it from Elizabeth, my smart-alecky friend in fourth grade, whom I alternately worshiped and resented. I'd ask her a question that required an explanation, and she'd answer, "Because . . ." "Elizabeth, how come you didn't go to Isabel's birthday party?" "Because . . ." "Why didn't you put your name in your reader?" "Because . . ." I thought that such a cool way to get around having to come up with answers. So, I practiced saying it under my breath, planning for the day I could use it on an unsuspecting English-speaking adult.

One Sunday at our extended family dinner, my grandfather sat down at the children's table to chat with us. He was famous, in fact, for the way he could carry on adult conversations with his grandchildren. He often spoke to us in English so that we could practice speaking it outside the classroom. He was a Cornell[11] man, a United Nations representative from our country. He gave speeches in English. Perfect English, my mother's phrase. That Sunday, he asked me a question. I can't even remember what it was because I wasn't really listening but lying in wait for my chance. "Because . . .," I answered him. Papito waited a second for the rest of my sentence and then gave me a thumbnail grammar lesson, "*Because* has to be followed by a clause."

"Why's that?" I asked, nonplussed.[12]

"Because," he winked. "Just because."

---

11. **Cornell** Cornell University in Ithaca, New York.
12. **nonplussed** (nän plüst′) *adj.* confused; baffled.

A beginning wordsmith, I had so much left to learn; sometimes it was disheartening. Once Tío[13] Gus, the family intellectual, put a speck of salt on my grandparents' big dining table during Sunday dinner. He said, "Imagine this whole table is the human brain. Then this teensy grain is all we ever use of our intelligence!" He enumerated geniuses who had perhaps used two grains, maybe three: Einstein, Michelangelo, da Vinci, Beethoven. We children believed him. It was the kind of impossible fact we thrived on, proving as it did that the world out there was not drastically different from the one we were making up in our heads.

enumerated (ē nōō′ mər āt id) *v.* named one by one; specified, as in a list

Later, at home, Mami said that you had to take what her younger brother said "with a grain of salt." I thought she was still referring to Tío Gus's demonstration, and I tried to puzzle out what she was saying. Finally, I asked what she meant. "Taking what someone says with a grain of salt is an idiomatic expression in English," she explained. It was pure voodoo is what it was—what later I learned poetry could also do: a grain of salt could symbolize both the human brain and a condiment for human nonsense. And it could be itself, too: a grain of salt to flavor a bland plate of American food.

When we arrived in New York, I was shocked. A country where everyone spoke English! These people must be smarter, I thought. Maids, waiters, taxi drivers, doormen, bums on the street, all spoke this difficult language. It took some time before I understood that Americans were not necessarily a smarter, superior race. It was as natural for them to learn their mother tongue as it was for a little Dominican baby to learn Spanish. It came with "mother's milk," my mother explained, and for a while I thought a mother tongue was a mother tongue because you got it from your mother's milk along with proteins and vitamins.

---

13. **Tío** (tē′ ō) "Uncle" (Spanish).

Soon it wasn't so strange that everyone was speaking in English instead of Spanish. I learned not to hear it as English, but as sense. I no longer strained to understand, I understood. I relaxed in this second language. Only when someone with a heavy southern or British accent spoke in a movie, or at church when the priest droned his sermon—only then did I experience that little catch of anxiety. I worried that I would not be able to understand, that I wouldn't be able to "keep up" with the voice speaking in this acquired language. I would be like those people from the Bible we had studied in religion class, whom I imagined standing at the foot of an enormous tower[14] that looked just like the skyscrapers around me. They had been punished for their pride by being made to speak different languages so that they didn't understand what anyone was saying.

I worried that I would not be able to understand, that I wouldn't be able to "keep up"...

But at the foot of those towering New York skyscrapers, I began to understand more and more—not less and less—English. In sixth grade, I had one of the first in a lucky line of great English teachers who began to nurture in me a love of language, a love that had been there since my childhood of listening closely to words. Sister Maria Generosa did not make our class interminably diagram sentences from a workbook or learn a catechism[15] of grammar rules. Instead, she asked us to write little stories imagining we were snowflakes, birds, pianos, a stone in the pavement, a star in the sky. What would it feel like to be a flower with roots in the ground? If the clouds could talk, what would they say? She had an expressive, dreamy look that was accentuated by the wimple[16] that framed her face.

accentuated ▶ (ak sen´ cho͞o āt id) *v.* emphasized; heightened the effect of

Supposing, just supposing . . . My mind would take off, soaring into possibilities, a flower with roots, a star in the sky, a cloud full of sad, sad tears, a piano crying out each time its back was tapped, music only to our ears.

Sister Maria stood at the chalkboard. Her chalk was always snapping in two because she wrote with such energy, her whole habit[17] shaking with the swing of her arm, her hand tap-tap-tapping on the board. "Here's a simple sentence: 'The snow fell.'" Sister

---

14. **enormous tower** a reference to the Tower of Babel in Genesis 11:1–9. According to Genesis, early Babylonians tried to build a tower to heaven, but they were thwarted when God caused them to speak many languages rather than one.
15. **catechism** (kat´ ə kiz´ əm) *n.* short book written in question-and-answer format.
16. **wimple** (wim´ pəl) *n.* cloth worn around the head, neck, and chin by some nuns.
17. **habit** (hab´ it) *n.* robe or dress worn by some nuns.

pointed with her chalk, her eyebrows lifted, her wimple poked up. Sometimes I could see wisps of gray hair that strayed from under her headdress. "But watch what happens if we put an adverb at the beginning and a prepositional phrase at the end: 'Gently, the snow fell on the bare hills.'"

I thought about the snow. I saw how it might fall on the hills, tapping lightly on the bare branches of trees. Softly, it would fall on the cold, bare fields. On toys children had left out in the yard, and on cars and on little birds and on people out late walking on the streets. Sister Marie filled the chalkboard with snowy print, on and on, handling and shaping and moving the language, scribbling all over the board until English, those verbal gadgets, those tricks and turns of phrases, those little fixed units and counters, became a charged, fluid mass that carried me in its great fluent waves, rolling and moving onward, to deposit me on the shores of my new homeland. I was no longer a foreigner with no ground to stand on. I had landed in the English language.

ABOUT THE AUTHOR

Julia Alvarez (b. 1950)

Julia Alvarez, the author of "My English," was born in New York but grew up in the Dominican Republic, a small Caribbean nation. An independent state since 1844, the Dominican Republic has often struggled with foreign conquest, political unrest, and dictatorship. Alvarez's family was forced to return to New York in 1960 because her father had participated in a movement against the brutal Dominican dictator Raphael Trujillo.

When her family fled the Dominican Republic and returned to New York, Julia Alvarez was ten years old, and Spanish was her primary language. Painfully aware of not fitting in, Julia took refuge in reading and making up stories. She says, "I landed, not in the United States, but in the English language. That became my new home."

Alvarez attended Middlebury College, where she won several poetry awards. She later earned a master's degree in creative writing from Syracuse University. Alvarez says that writing is "a way to understand yourself." Her writing has been praised for its humor, sensitivity, and insight.

Close Reading Activities

READ

Comprehension

Reread all or part of the text to help you answer the following questions.

1. What types of conversations did the author's parents have in English rather than Spanish?
2. At what point in her life does the author begin to understand English without difficulty?
3. How does Sister Maria Generosa change the author's attitude toward English?

Research: Clarify Details This essay may include references that are unfamiliar to you. Choose at least one unfamiliar detail, and briefly research it. Then, explain how the information you learned from research sheds light on an aspect of the essay.

Summarize Write an objective summary of the essay. Remember that an objective summary is free from opinion and evaluation.

Language Study

Selection Vocabulary The following passages appear in the essay. Identify the root of each boldface word. For each, explain what the root means and how that meaning is evident in the word.

- We lived then in the Dominican Republic, and the family as a whole spoke only Spanish at home, until my sisters and I started attending the Carol Morgan School, and we became a **bilingual** family.
- He **enumerated** geniuses who had perhaps used two grains...
- She had an expressive, dreamy look that was **accentuated** by the wimple that framed her face.

Literary Analysis

Reread the identified passage. Then, respond to the questions that follow.

Focus Passage *(p. 148)*

Soon I began ... on your bread?

Key Ideas and Details

1. **(a) Interpret:** What does *la mantequilla* mean in English? **(b) Draw Conclusions:** How does the author use this word to **illustrate** her early experiences learning English?

Craft and Structure

2. **Interpret:** In this passage, how does the author communicate her confusion between English and Spanish through visual aspects of the text, word choice, and sentence structure? Cite examples.

Integration of Knowledge and Ideas

3. **(a) Compare and Contrast:** How does the author's attitude toward English at the end of the essay compare to the one she describes in this passage? **(b) Support:** Cite examples from the text that show the author's changed feelings toward English.

Voice

Word choice, attitude, and syntax (sentence structure), contribute to an author's **voice**, his or her unique sound or personality. Reread the essay, and take notes on details that reveal Alvarez's voice.

1. **(a)** Identify one passage in the essay in which the word choice, attitude, and sentence structures seem especially **noteworthy**. **(b)** Using this example, describe Alvarez's voice.
2. **Conformity:** By making English part of both her life and voice as a writer, did Alvarez conform? Explain your position, citing details from the text.

DISCUSS • RESEARCH • WRITE

From Text to Topic **Partner Discussion**

Discuss the following passage with a partner. Take notes during the discussion. Contribute your own ideas, and support them with examples from the text.

> I would bow my head, humiliated by the smiles and snickers of the American children around me. I grew insecure about Spanish. My native tongue was not quite as good as English, as if words like *columpio* were illegal immigrants trying to cross a border into another language. But Teacher's discerning grammar-and-vocabulary-patrol ears could tell and send them back.

QUESTIONS FOR DISCUSSION

1. Why do you think Alvarez uses law-enforcement terms in this passage?
2. What does this passage say about the power of language to bring people together or to divide them?

Research **Investigate the Topic**

Learning English Some children who immigrate to the United States first learn English in school. Unlike Julia Alvarez, many of these children do not have the help of bilingual parents.

Assignment

Conduct research on the language **barrier** faced by some immigrants coming to the United States. Find memoirs, articles, or essays by people who immigrated as children and learned English once they arrived. Summarize your research in a **journal or blog entry** about individuality and conformity as it relates to the language one speaks.

PREPARATION FOR ESSAY

You may use the results of this research in an essay you will write at the end of this section.

Writing to Sources **Informative Text**

In "My English," Alvarez uses idioms to explain her growth as an English speaker. Idioms can be difficult for non-native speakers in any language.

Assignment

Write an **essay** in which you discuss Alvarez's understanding of idioms as she learned English and explain why English learners may struggle with these types of expressions. Include the following elements:

- a definition of idioms
- an explanation of Alvarez's feelings about idioms as she learned English
- conclusions about why idioms are often challenging for language learners

Use details from "My English" to support your ideas. In your conclusion, make connections between your analysis and Alvarez's experiences.

ACADEMIC VOCABULARY

Academic terms appear in blue on these pages. If these words are not familiar to you, use a dictionary to find their definitions. Then, use them as you speak and write about the text.

Common Core State Standards

RI.9-10.1, RI.9-10.3, RI.9-10.4, RI.9-10.5, RI.9-10.6; W.9-10.2, W.9-10.4, W.9-10.6, W.9-10.7, W.9-10.9; SL.9-10.1; L.9-10.4, L.9-10.5.a

[For full standards wording, see the chart in the front of this book.]

The Case for Fitting In

David Berreby

Americans have a prejudice in favor of lone wolves. Moral superiority, we like to think, belongs to the person who stands alone.

Until recently, social science went along with this idea. Lab-based research supposedly furnished slam-dunk evidence that, as the social psychologist Solomon Asch put it, "the social process is polluted" by "the dominance of conformity." That research, though, was rooted in its time and place: The United States in the aftermath of World War II, when psychologists and sociologists focused on the conformity that made millions give in to totalitarian regimes.[1]

Lately, however, some researchers have been dissenting from the textbook version. Where an earlier generation saw only a contemptible urge to go along, revisionists see normal people balancing their self-respect against their equally valuable respect for other people, and for human relationships. For evidence, revisionists say, look no further than those very experiments that supposedly proved the evils of conformity.

The psychologists Bert Hodges and Anne Geyer recently took a new look at a well-known experiment devised by Asch in the 1950s. Asch's subjects were asked to look at a line printed on a white card and then tell which of three similar lines was the same length. The answer was obvious, but the catch was that each volunteer was sitting in a small group whose other members were actually in on the experiment. Asch found that when those other people all agreed on the wrong answer, many of the subjects went along with the group, against the evidence of their own senses.

But the question (*Which of these lines matches the one on the card?*) was not posed just once. Each subject saw 18 sets of lines, and the group answer was wrong for 12 of them. Examining all the data, Hodges and Geyer found that many people were varying their answers, sometimes agreeing with the group, more often sticking up for their own view. (The average participant gave in to the group three times out of 12.)

◀ **prejudice** (prej´ə dis) *n.* strong opinion, often formed without good reason

1. **totalitarian regimes** forms of government based on total control of all aspects of public life.

solidarity▶ (säl′ə dar′ə tē) *n.* unity based on common interests or purpose

This means that the subjects in the most famous "people are sheep" experiment were not sheep at all—they were human beings who largely stuck to their guns, but now and then went along with the group. Why? Because in getting along with other people, most decent people know, as Hodges and Geyer put it, the "importance of cooperation, tact and social **solidarity** in situations that are tense or difficult."

The table below shows the results of the Asch conformity studies that are discussed in this article.

Majority Responses to Standard and Comparison Lines on Successive Trials*

Trial	Length of standard (in inches)	Length of standard (in inches)			Length of comparison lines (in inches)	Majority error (in inches)
a**	10	8 3/4	10	8	0	
b**	2	2	1	1 1/2	0	
1	3	**3 3/4**	4 1/4	3	+ 3/4	Moderate
2	5	5	**4**	6 1/2	– 1	Moderate
c**	4	3	5	4	0	
3	3	3 3/4	**4 1/4**	3	+ 1 1/4	Extreme
4	8	6 1/4	8	6 3/4	– 1 1/4	Moderate
5	5	5	4	6 1/2	+ 1 1/2	Extreme
6	8	**6 1/4**	8	6 3/4	– 1 3/4	Extreme
d**	10	**8 3/4**	10	8	0	
e**	2	**2**	1	1 1/2	0	
7	3	**3 3/4**	4 1/4	3	+ 3/4	Moderate
8	5	5	**4**	6 1/2	– 1	Moderate
f**	4	3	5	4	0	
9	3	3 3/4	**4 1/4**	3	+ 1 1/4	Extreme
10	8	6 1/4	8	6 3/4	– 1 1/4	Moderate
11	5	5	4	6 1/2	+ 1 1/2	Extreme
12	8	**6 1/4**	8	6 3/4	– 1 3/4	Extreme

* from *Studies of Independence and Conformity: A Minority of One Against a Unanimous Majority* by Solomon Asch

** Letters of the first column designate "neutral" trials, or trials to which the majority responded correctly.
The numbered trials were "critical," i.e., the majority responded incorrectly.
Bold face figures designate the incorrect majority responses.
Trials d to 12 are identical with trials a to 6; they followed each other without pause.

In a similar spirit, others have taken a new look at the famous experiments on "obedience to authority" conducted by Asch's student Stanley Milgram. Milgram's subjects, assuming they were part of a memory test, were asked to administer what they thought were increasingly strong electric shocks to another person (who was, in reality, another experimenter pretending to be pained). Encouraged only by an occasional "Please go on" and the like, every one went well beyond "Very Strong Shock," and the majority went to the 450-volt end of the scale, which was two notches above the one labeled "Danger: Severe Shock."

Horrifying, in most retellings. But, as the University of Chicago law professor Cass Sunstein has argued, Milgram's "subjects were not simply obeying a leader, but responding to someone whose credentials and good faith they thought they could trust." Without that kind of trust society would fall apart tomorrow, because most of what we know about the world comes to us from other people. Milgram's experiment, then, doesn't prove that people are inclined to obey any nut job in a white coat. It shows instead that in difficult situations, when they wrestle with the line between trust and skepticism, trust often wins. Much of the time, that's a good thing.

◀ **credentials** (kri den´shəlz) *n.* documents showing one's right to exercise power; qualifications

In other words, the interesting data in the Asch and Milgram studies have been distorted into a simple takeaway: "Call it like you see it"; never mind others' feelings, opinions, or traditions. Of course, no society should ask for knee-jerk obedience to any command. But, as the dissenters point out, there are dangers in a knee-jerk refusal to get in line. For example, in a version of the Milgram experiment in which the dupe is seated in a group of three, he will defy the "experimenter" and behave humanely—if the other two people refuse to inflict further shocks. That kind of conformity is, to put it mildly, desirable.

ABOUT THE AUTHOR

David Berreby (b. 1958)

David Berreby is a science journalist who often writes about human behavior. His articles have been published in numerous magazines, both print and electronic, including *Nature, The New York Times Magazine,* and *Slate.* He is the author of *Us and Them: The Science of Identity.*

Close Reading Activities

READ

Comprehension

Reread all or part of the text to help you answer the following questions.

1. Describe Solomon Asch's conformity experiment.
2. What did Hodges and Geyer find in their review of Asch's study?
3. How did Stanley Milgram test conformity?

Research: Clarify Details Choose an unfamiliar detail from this article and briefly research it. Then, explain how the information you learned sheds light on an aspect of the article.

Summarize Write an objective summary of the article, one that is free from opinion and evaluation.

Language Study

Selection Vocabulary The following passages appear in "The Case for Fitting In." Define each boldfaced word. Then, use the word in a new sentence.

- Americans have a **prejudice** in favor of lone wolves.
- Because in getting along with other people, most decent people know...the "importance of cooperation, tact and social **solidarity**...."
- Milgram's "subjects were not simply obeying a leader, but responding to someone whose **credentials** and good faith they thought they could trust."

Literary Analysis

Reread the identified passage. Then, respond to the questions that follow.

Focus Passage *(p. 159)*

In a similar spirit ... a good thing.

Key Ideas and Details

1. **(a)** What **distinction** between Milgram's researchers and other leaders does the quotation by Cass Sunstein point out? **(b) Analyze:** Why is this distinction so important?
2. **Interpret:** According to the author, is the reality of the Milgram study as "horrifying" as most people think? Explain, citing details from the text.

Craft and Structure

3. **(a)** What facts does the author present in the first paragraph? **(b) Connect:** How does the second paragraph relate to the first? Explain.
4. **(a) Distinguish:** Identify one example of slang and one sentence fragment in this passage.
   (b) Analyze: What tone, or attitude, do these choices help to create? Explain.

Integration of Knowledge and Ideas

5. **(a) Connect:** According to Berreby, why is trust in leaders so **critical** to the social fabric?
   (b) Evaluate: Do you agree with this idea? Explain why or why not.

Supporting Evidence

Supporting **evidence** is the proof used in an argument. It can include facts, examples, statistics, and expert testimony. Reread the article, and take notes on the author's use of evidence.

1. **(a)** Find two different kinds of evidence in the article. **(b)** What idea does each one support?
2. **Conformity:** Berreby includes a quote from Solomon Asch: "The social process is polluted by the dominance of conformity." Do you think Berreby's evidence proves his argument against Asch's views? Cite details from the article in your response.

DISCUSS • RESEARCH • WRITE

From Text to Topic **Partner Discussion**

Discuss the following passage with a partner. As you exchange ideas, support them with details from the text and take notes. Then, summarize your ideas and share them with the class as a whole.

> This means that the subjects in the most famous "people are sheep" experiment were not sheep at all—they were human beings who largely stuck to their guns, but now and then went along with the group. Why? Because in getting along with other people, most decent people know, as Hodges and Geyer put it, the "importance of cooperation, tact and social solidarity in situations that are tense or difficult."

QUESTIONS FOR DISCUSSION

1. Why do you think Berreby includes the expressions "people are sheep" and "stuck to their guns"?
2. Is following others for the purposes of cooperation or solidarity the same thing as conformity?

Research **Investigate the Topic**

Ethics Psychology studies, like the ones Berreby describes, must be ethical, or morally right. Any study that hurts people emotionally or physically is unethical.

Assignment

Conduct research on the ethical controversy surrounding Stanley Milgram's experiments and methods. **Consult** psychology journals and magazines to include the opinions of experts. Take careful notes and identify your sources. Share your findings in an **informal presentation.**

PREPARATION FOR ESSAY

You may use the results of this research in an essay you will write at the end of this section.

Writing to Sources **Argument**

In "The Case for Fitting In," David Berreby makes the following observation: "Americans have a prejudice in favor of lone wolves. Moral superiority, we like to think, belongs to the person who stands alone."

Assignment

Write an **argumentative essay** in which you take a position about Berreby's observation. Do you agree or disagree that Americans are biased in favor of "lone wolves," or those who refuse to conform? Follow these steps to draft your essay:

- Consider the types of people Americans admire. Identify politicians, military leaders, characters from movies and TV, and other types of heroes.
- Choose two to three of these figures and analyze the qualities they present that Americans admire. Do all of these figures stand alone?
- Organize your ideas logically and include strong supporting evidence for each main point. Clearly state whether you agree or disagree with Berreby's point and why.

ACADEMIC VOCABULARY

Academic terms appear in blue on these pages. If these words are not familiar to you, use a dictionary to find their definitions. Then, use them as you speak and write about the text.

RI.9-10.1, RI.9-10.2, RI.9-10.4, RI.9-10.5, RI.9-10.6, RI.9-10.8, RI.9-10.10; W.9-10.1, W.9-10.7, W.9-10.9; SL.9-10.1; L.9-10.3, L.9-10.4

[For full standards wording, see the chart in the front of this book.]

from

THE GEEKS SHALL INHERIT THE EARTH

Alexandra Robbins

In the decade I've spent examining various microcosms[1] of life in U.S. schools—from the multitude of students pressured to succeed in school and sports to the twenty-something products of this educational Rube Goldberg machine[2]—a disturbing pattern has emerged. Young people are trying frantically to force themselves into an unbending mold of expectations, convinced that they live in a two-tiered system in which they are either a resounding success or they have already failed. And the more they try to squeeze themselves into that shrinking, allegedly normative space, the faster the walls close in.

◀ **allegedly** (ə lej´id lē) *adv.* questionably true; supposed

The students outside these walls are the kids who typically are not considered part of the in crowd, the ones who are excluded, blatantly or subtly, from the premier table in the lunchroom. I refer to them as "cafeteria fringe." Whether alone or in groups, these geeks, loners, punks, floaters, nerds, freaks, dorks, gamers, bandies, art kids, theater geeks, choir kids, Goths, weirdos, indies, scenes, emos, skaters, and various types of racial and other minorities are often relegated to subordinate social status simply because they are, or seem to be, even the slightest bit different.

Students alone did not create these boundaries. The No Child Left Behind law, a disproportionate emphasis on SATs, APs, and other standardized tests, and a suffocating homogenization[3] of the U.S. education system have all contributed to a rabidly conformist atmosphere that stifles unique people, ideas, and expression. The methods that schools and government officials claimed would

1. **microcosms** (mī´krō kä´zəmz) *n.* small communities representative of a larger whole
2. **Rube Goldberg machine** a comical machine that makes a simple process needlessly complicated
3. **homogenization** (hə mäj´ə nīz ā´shun) *n.* blended into an even mixture

improve America's "progress" are the same methods that hold back the students who are most likely to further that progress.

In precisely the years that we should be embracing differences among students, urging them to pursue their divergent interests at full throttle, we're instead forcing them into a skyline of sameness, muffling their voices, grounding their dreams. The result? As a Midwestern senior told me for my book *The Overachievers*, high schoolers view life as "a conveyor belt," making **monotonous** scheduled stops at high school, college, graduate school, and a series of jobs until death. Middle schools in North America have been called "the Bermuda triangle of education." Only 22 percent of U.S. youth socialize with people of another race. U.S. students have some of the highest rates of emotional problems and the most negative views of peer culture among countries surveyed by the World Health Organization.

monotonous ▶ (mə nätʹ'n əs) *adj.* unvarying; dull and uniform

Too many students are losing hope because of exclusion or bullying that they believe they're doomed to experience for the rest of their lives. It is unacceptable that the system we rely on to develop children into well-adjusted, learned, cultured adults allows drones to dominate and increasingly devalues freethinkers. In 1957, theologian Paul Tillich told a graduating university class, "We hope for nonconformists among you, for your sake, for the sake of the nation, for the sake of humanity." More than half a century later, schools, students, and sometimes parents treat these nonconformists like second-class citizens, **squelching** that hope. There is too much pressure on children to conform to a narrowing in-crowd image, when we should be nurturing the outsiders who reject that image. In large part, those are the individuals who will turn out to be the kinds of interesting, admired, and inspiring adults who earn respect and attention for their impact on their community or the world.

squelching ▶ (skwelchʹ iŋ) *v.* suppressing; silencing

Or even the celebrisphere. ...

Musician Bruce Springsteen was so unpopular in high school that, "other people didn't even know I was there," he has said. He started a band because "I was on the outside looking in."

Television host Tim Gunn, who identified himself as "a classic nerd" in school, was "crazy about making things: I was addicted to my Lincoln Logs, Erector Set, and especially my Legos," he has said. "Between my stutter and my fetishizing of Lego textures, I was taunted and teased." Now Gunn is a fashion world icon precisely because of his eye toward "making things"—and his catchphrase, "Make it work," has become famous.

All of these people exemplify what I call **quirk theory**.

QUIRK THEORY:
Many of the differences that cause a student to be excluded in school are the same traits or real-world skills that others will value, love, respect, or find compelling about that person in adulthood and outside of the school setting.

Musician Bruce Springsteen was so unpopular in high school that, "other people didn't even know I was there," he has said. He started a band because "I was on the outside looking in."

To date, musician Bruce Springsteen (shown on the left in his 1967 high school senior yearbook photo and on the right in performance) has won a total of twenty Grammy Awards.

Quirk theory suggests that popularity in school is not a key to success and satisfaction in adulthood. Conventional notions of popularity are wrong. What if popularity is not the same thing as social success? What if students who are considered outsiders aren't really socially inadequate at all? Being an outsider doesn't necessarily indicate any sort of social failing. We do not view a tuba player as musically challenged if he cannot play the violin. He's just a different kind of musician. A sprinter is still considered an athlete even if she can't play basketball. She's a different kind of athlete. Rather than view the cafeteria fringe as less socially successful than the popular crowd, we could simply accept that they are a different kind of social.

ABOUT THE AUTHOR

Alexandra Robbins (b. 1976)

Best-selling author Alexandra Robbins has made a career out of writing about teenagers, college students, and recent graduates. After graduating from Yale University, she worked for *The New Yorker* magazine and wrote her first book. While researching her book about secret societies at Yale, Robbins found Yale graduate and former president George W. Bush's high school transcript and SAT scores. When published, the story made the young journalist famous. When not writing, Robbins speaks at schools about cliques, popularity, and bullying. In 2007, she won the Heartsongs Award for positive contributions to the mental health of children and young adults.

Close Reading Activities

READ

Comprehension

Reread all or part of the text to help you answer the following questions.

1. Name two factors that, according to Robbins, contribute to a conformist atmosphere in schools.
2. According to Robbins, what types of people are "freethinkers"?
3. What is "quirk theory"?

Research: Clarify Details Choose at least one unfamiliar detail from this essay and briefly research it. Then, explain how the information you learned sheds light on an aspect of the text.

Summarize Write an objective summary of the text. Remember that an objective summary is free from opinion and evaluation.

Language Study

Selection Vocabulary The following passages appear in the essay. Identify at least one synonym and one antonym for each boldfaced word. Then, use each word in a sentence of your own.

- And the more they try to squeeze themselves into that shrinking, **allegedly** normative space, the faster the walls close in.
- ...high schoolers view life as "a conveyor belt," making **monotonous** scheduled stops ...
- ...students, and sometimes parents treat these nonconformists like second-class citizens, **squelching** that hope.

Literary Analysis

Reread the identified passage. Then, respond to the questions that follow.

Focus Passage *(p. 164)*

Too many students ... community or the world.

Key Ideas and Details

1. **(a) Infer:** What is "the system" to which Robbins refers? **(b) Analyze:** What main problem does she see in this system?

Craft and Structure

2. **(a) Distinguish:** What words does the author use to identify or describe nonconformist students when they are young? **(b) Distinguish:** What words does she use to **characterize** those same students after they have become adults? **(c) Analyze:** How do these word choices help to emphasize the author's central ideas? Explain.

Integration of Knowledge and Ideas

3. **Draw Conclusions:** In Robbins's view, what is the cost of conformity for both individuals and society as a whole? Cite details from the passage in your answer.

Diction

Diction, or word choice, is a key part of a writer's style. Diction may be formal, informal, plain, ornate, technical, old-fashioned, or even slangy. Reread the essay and take notes on the author's diction.

1. **(a)** Identify two examples of slang in the essay. **(b)** What effect does the use of slang have?
2. **Conformity: (a)** Describe Robbins's overall diction in this essay. **(b)** How does this diction support her central idea about noncomformity?

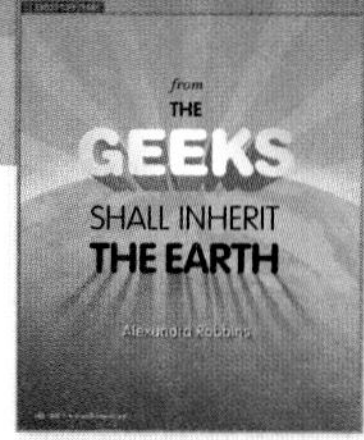

DISCUSS • RESEARCH • WRITE

From Text to Topic **Group Discussion**

Discuss the following passage with a group of classmates. Take notes during the discussion. Contribute your own ideas, and support them with examples from the text.

> The students outside ... slightest bit different. *(p. 163)*

QUESTIONS FOR DISCUSSION

1. What does the list of "cafeteria fringe" students suggest about the group?
2. Should the students on this list be encouraged to conform? Why or why not?

Research **Investigate the Topic**

Nonconformist Achievers Robbins claims nonconformists often become "interesting, admired, and inspired adults" and that young people who are different should be encouraged and allowed to flourish.

Assignment

Conduct research on a person who was considered unconventional in his or her youth but later made a great contribution to society. Consult encyclopedias and accounts from primary sources. Take notes and keep a list of all sources you use. Write a **short biography** of this person in which you **analyze** his or her contributions and consider how being different may have contributed to those achievements.

PREPARATION FOR ESSAY

You may use the results of this research in an essay you will write at the end of this section.

Writing to Sources **Argument**

In her essay, Robbins writes, "Conventional notions of popularity are wrong. What if popularity is not the same thing as social success?"

Assignment

Write a brief **position paper** in which you agree or disagree with Robbins's statement based on the **evidence** she presents in the essay. Follow these steps:

- Analyze Robbins's central idea in the essay.
- Evaluate her interpretation of popularity.
- Decide whether you agree with Robbins entirely, partially, or not at all. Clearly state your position.
- Use details from the text to support your claims.
- Provide a conclusion in which you make connections between your analysis of popularity and Robbins's interpretation.

ACADEMIC VOCABULARY

Academic terms appear in blue on these pages. Use a dictionary to find their definitions. Then, use them as you speak and write about the text.

Common Core State Standards

RI.9-10.1, RI.9-10.2, RI.9-10.4, RI.9-10.5, RI.9-10.6, RI.9-10.10; W.9-10.1, W.9-10.1.a-b, W.9-10.1.e, W.9-10.4, W.9-10.7, W.9-10.9, W.9-10.9.b; SL.9-10.1; L.9-10.1, L.9-10.4

[For full standards wording see the chart in the front of this book.]

from Blue Nines and Red Words

from Born on a Blue Day

Daniel Tammet

I was born on January 31, 1979—a Wednesday. I know it was a Wednesday, because the date is blue in my mind and Wednesdays are always blue, like the number 9 or the sound of loud voices arguing. I like my birth date, because of the way I'm able to visualize most of the numbers in it as smooth and round shapes, similar to pebbles on a beach. That's because they are prime numbers: 31, 19, 197, 97, 79, and 1979 are all divisible only by themselves and 1. I can recognize every prime up to 9,973 by their "pebble-like" quality. It's just the way my brain works.

I have a rare condition known as savant syndrome, little known before its portrayal by actor Dustin Hoffman in the Oscar-winning 1988 film *Rain Man*. Like Hoffman's character, Raymond Babbitt, I have an almost obsessive need for order and routine which affects virtually every aspect of my life. For example, I eat exactly 45 grams of porridge for breakfast each morning; I weigh the bowl with an electronic scale to make sure. Then I count the number of items of clothing I'm wearing before I leave my house. I get anxious if I can't drink my cups of tea at the same time each day. Whenever I become too stressed and I can't breathe properly, I close my eyes and count. Thinking of numbers helps me to become calm again.

Numbers are my friends, and they are always around me. Each one is unique and has its own personality. The number 11 is friendly and 5 is loud, whereas 4 is both shy and quiet—it's my favorite number, perhaps because it reminds me of myself. Some are big—23, 667, 1,179—while others are small: 6, 13, 581. Some are beautiful, like 333, and some are ugly, like 289. To me, every number is special.

No matter where I go or what I'm doing, numbers are never far from my thoughts. In an interview with talk show host David Letterman in New York, I told David he looked like the number 117—tall and lanky. Later outside, in the appropriately numerically named Times Square, I gazed up at the towering skyscrapers and felt surrounded by 9s—the number I most associate with feelings of immensity.

Scientists call my visual, emotional experience of numbers synesthesia, a rare neurological[1] mixing of the senses, which most commonly results in the ability to see alphabetical letters and/or numbers in color. Mine is an unusual and complex type, through which I see numbers as shapes, colors, textures and motions. The number 1, for example, is a brilliant and bright white, like someone shining a flashlight into my eyes. Five is a clap of thunder or the sound of waves crashing against rocks. Thirty-seven is lumpy like porridge, while 89 reminds me of falling snow.

No matter where I go or what I'm doing, numbers are never far from my thoughts.

Probably the most famous case of synesthesia was the one written up over a period of thirty years from the 1920s by the Russian psychologist A. R. Luria of a journalist called Shereshevsky with a prodigious memory. "S," as Luria called him in his notes for the book *The Mind of a Mnemonist*, had a highly visual memory which allowed him to "see" words and numbers as different shapes and colors. "S" was able to remember a matrix of 50 digits after studying it for three minutes, both immediately afterwards and many years later. Luria credited Shereshevsky's synesthetic experiences as the basis for his remarkable short- and long-term memory.

Using my own synesthetic experiences since early childhood, I have grown up with the ability to handle and calculate huge numbers in my head without any conscious effort, just like the Raymond Babbitt character. In fact, this is a talent common

1. **neurological** (no͝or′ə läj′i kəl) *adj.* occurring in the brain.

to several other real-life savants (sometimes referred to as "lightning calculators"). Dr. Darold Treffert, a Wisconsin physician and the leading researcher in the study of savant syndrome, gives one example, of a blind man with "a faculty of calculating to a degree little short of marvelous" in his book *Extraordinary People:*

> When he was asked how many grains of corn there would be in any one of 64 boxes, with 1 in the first, 2 in the second, 4 in the third, 8 in the fourth, and so on, he gave answers for the fourteenth (8,192), for the eighteenth (131,072) and the twenty-fourth (8,388,608) instantaneously, and he gave the figures for the forty-eighth box (140,737,488,355,328) in six seconds. He also gave the total in all 64 boxes correctly (18,446,744,073,709,551,616) in forty-five seconds.

◀ **calculating** (kal′ kyo͞o lāt′ iŋ) *v.* determining by using mathematics

My favorite kind of calculation is power multiplication, which means multiplying a number by itself a specified number of times. Multiplying a number by itself is called squaring; for example, the square of 72 is 72 × 72 = 5,184. Squares are always symmetrical shapes in my mind, which makes them especially beautiful to me. Multiplying the same number three times over is called cubing or "raising" to the third power. The cube, or third power, of 51 is equivalent to 51 × 51 × 51 = 132,651. I see each result of a power multiplication as a distinctive visual pattern in my head. As the sums and their results grow, so the mental shapes and colors I experience become increasingly more complex. I see 37's fifth power—37 × 37 × 37 × 37 × 37 = 69,343,957—as a large circle composed of smaller circles running clockwise from the top around.

◀ **symmetrical** (si me′ tri kəl) *adj.* capable of being divided into identical halves

When I divide one number by another, in my head I see a spiral rotating downwards in larger and larger loops, which seem to warp and curve. Different divisions produce different sizes of spirals with varying curves. From my mental imagery I'm able to calculate a sum like 13 ÷ 97 (0.1340206 . . .) to almost a hundred decimal places.

I never write anything down when I'm calculating, because I've always been able to do the sums in my head, and it's much easier for me to visualize the answer using my synesthetic shapes than to try to follow the "carry the one" techniques taught in the textbooks we are given at school. When multiplying, I see the two numbers as

distinct shapes. The image changes and a third shape emerges—the correct answer. The process takes a matter of seconds and happens spontaneously. It's like doing math without having to think.

In the illustration above I'm multiplying 53 by 131. I see both numbers as a unique shape and locate each spatially opposite the other. The space created between the two shapes creates a third, which I perceive as a new number: 6,943, the solution to the sum.

Different tasks involve different shapes, and I also have various sensations or emotions for certain numbers. Whenever I multiply with 11 I always experience a feeling of the digits tumbling downwards in my head. I find 6s hardest to remember of all the numbers, because I experience them as tiny black dots, without any distinctive shape or texture. I would describe them as like little gaps or holes. I have visual and sometimes emotional responses to every number up to 10,000, like having my own visual, numerical vocabulary. And just like a poet's choice of words, I find some combinations of numbers more beautiful than others: ones go well with darker numbers like 8s and 9s, but not so well with 6s. A telephone number with the sequence 189 is much more beautiful to me than one with a sequence like 116.

This aesthetic[2] dimension to my synesthesia is something that has its ups and downs. If I see a number I experience as particularly beautiful on a shop sign or a car license plate, there's a shiver of excitement and pleasure. On the other hand, if the numbers don't match my experience of them—if, for example, a shop sign's price has "99 pence" in red or green (instead of blue)—then I find that uncomfortable and irritating.

It is not known how many savants have synesthetic experiences to help them in the areas they excel in. One reason for this is that, like

2. aesthetic (es thet′ik) *adj.* pleasing in appearance; artistic.

Raymond Babbitt, many suffer profound disability, preventing them from explaining to others how they do the things that they do. I am fortunate not to suffer from any of the most severe impairments that often come with abilities such as mine.

Like most individuals with savant syndrome, I am also on the autistic spectrum. I have Asperger's syndrome, a relatively mild and high-functioning form of autism that affects around 1 in every 300 people in the United Kingdom. According to a 2001 study by the U.K.'s National Autistic Society, nearly half of all adults with Asperger's syndrome are not diagnosed until after the age of sixteen. I was finally diagnosed at age twenty-five following tests and an interview at the Autism Research Centre in Cambridge.

Autism, including Asperger's syndrome, is defined by the presence of impairments affecting social interaction, communication, and imagination (problems with abstract or flexible thought and empathy, for example). Diagnosis is not easy and cannot be made by a blood test or brain scan; doctors have to observe behavior and study the individual's developmental history from infancy.

And just like a poet's choice of words, I find some combinations of numbers more beautiful than others.

People with Asperger's often have good language skills and are able to lead relatively normal lives. Many have above-average IQs and excel in areas that involve logical or visual thinking. Like other forms of autism, Asperger's is a condition affecting many more men than women (around 80 percent of autistics and 90 percent of those diagnosed with Asperger's are men). Single-mindedness is a defining characteristic, as is a strong drive to analyze detail and identify rules and patterns in systems. Specialized skills involving memory, numbers, and mathematics are common. It is not known for certain what causes someone to have Asperger's, though it is something you are born with.

For as long as I can remember, I have experienced numbers in the visual, synesthetic way that I do. Numbers are my first language, one I often think and feel in. Emotions can be hard for me to understand or know how to react to, so I often use numbers to help me. If a friend says they feel sad or depressed, I picture myself sitting in the dark hollowness of number 6 to help me experience the same sort of feeling and understand it. If I read in an article that a person felt intimidated by something, I imagine myself standing next to the

number 9. Whenever someone describes visiting a beautiful place, I recall my numerical landscapes and how happy they make me feel inside. By doing this, numbers actually help me get closer to understanding other people.

Sometimes people I meet for the first time remind me of a particular number and this helps me to be comfortable around them. They might be very tall and remind me of the number 9, or round and remind me of the number 3. If I feel unhappy or anxious or in a situation I have no previous experience of (when I'm much more likely to feel stressed and uncomfortable), I count to myself. When I count, the numbers form pictures and patterns in my mind that are consistent and reassuring to me. Then I can relax and interact with whatever situation I'm in.

Tuesdays are a warm color, while Thursdays are fuzzy.

Thinking of calendars always makes me feel good, all those numbers and patterns in one place. Different days of the week elicit different colors and emotions in my head: Tuesdays are a warm color while Thursdays are fuzzy. Calendrical calculation—the ability to tell what day of the week a particular date fell or will fall on—is common to many savants. I think this is probably due to the fact that the numbers in calendars are predictable and form patterns between the different days and months. For example, the thirteenth day in a month is always two days before whatever day the first falls on, excepting leap years, while several of the months mimic the behavior of others, like January and October, September and December, and February and March (the first day of February is the same as the first day of March). So if the first of February is a fuzzy texture in my mind (Thursday) for a given year, the thirteenth of March will be a warm color (Tuesday).

In his book *The Man Who Mistook His Wife for a Hat*, writer and neurologist Oliver Sacks mentions the case of severely autistic twins John and Michael as an example of how far some savants are able to take calendrical calculations. Though unable to care for themselves (they had been in various institutions since the age of seven), the twins were capable of calculating the day of the week for any date over a 40,000-year span.

Sacks also describes John and Michael as playing a game that involved swapping **prime** numbers with each other for hours at a time. Like the twins, I have always been fascinated by prime numbers. I see each prime as a smooth-textured shape, distinct from composite numbers (non-primes) that are grittier and less distinctive.

prime ▶
(prīm) *adj.* referring to any number greater than 1 that is not evenly divisible by any number other than 1 and itself

Whenever I identify a number as prime, I get a rush of feeling in my head (in the front center) which is hard to put into words. It's a special feeling, like the sudden sensation of pins and needles.

Sometimes I close my eyes and imagine the first thirty, fifty, hundred numbers as I experience them spatially, synesthetically. Then I can see in my mind's eye just how beautiful and special the primes are by the way they stand out so sharply from the other number shapes. It's exactly for this reason that I look and look and look at them; each one is so different from the one before and the one after. Their loneliness among the other numbers makes them so conspicuous and interesting to me.

There are moments, as I'm falling into sleep at night, that my mind fills suddenly with bright light and all I can see are numbers—hundreds, thousands of them—swimming rapidly over my eyes. The experience is beautiful and soothing to me. Some nights, when I'm having difficulty falling asleep, I imagine myself walking around my numerical landscapes. Then I feel safe and happy. I never feel lost, because the prime number shapes act as signposts.

ABOUT THE AUTHOR

Daniel Tammet (b. 1979)

Daniel Tammet was raised in a suburb of London, England. He has a condition called savant syndrome, which gives him extraordinary mental abilities, especially in math. Since childhood, he has had a love of counting and has been able to visualize numbers. In 2004, he recited the number *pi* to 22,514 decimal places from memory. The feat took more than 5 hours and set a European record.

Tammet's first book, *Born on a Blue Day,* was a best seller in both the United States and Great Britain and has been translated into more than twenty languages. Tammet says he wrote the book "to show that such a journey is possible from profound isolation and sadness to achievement and happiness, to real happiness. Not just the happiness that comes from giving yourself up to the trends and expectations of others, but the real happiness that can only come from finding what it is that is unique about you and having the courage to live that out." Tammet has written two additional books, *Embracing the Wide Sky* and *Thinking in Numbers.* He lives in France.

Close Reading Activities

READ

Comprehension

Reread all or part of the text to help you answer the following questions.

1. What is synesthesia?
2. What characterizes Asperger's syndrome?
3. How do numbers help the author relate to other people and to stressful situations?

Research: Clarify Details Choose one unfamiliar detail from this text and briefly research it. Then, explain how the information helps you better understand an aspect of the text.

Summarize Write an objective summary of the text, one that is free from opinion and evaluation.

Language Study

Selection Vocabulary: Mathematics The following passages appear in the memoir. State the mathematical meaning of each boldfaced word. Then, identify at least one general meaning for each word. Use a dictionary as needed.

- I see each **prime** as a smooth-textured shape, distinct from composite numbers...
- Dr. Darold Treffert...gives one example, of a blind man with "a faculty of **calculating** to a degree little short of marvelous..."
- Squares are always **symmetrical** shapes in my mind, which makes them especially beautiful to me.

Literary Analysis

Reread the identified passage. Then, respond to the questions that follow.

Focus Passage *(pp. 173–174)*

For as long as I can remember ... situation I'm in.

Key Ideas and Details

1. **Interpret:** How does Tammet use numbers to understand other people's emotions? Cite textual details to support your answer.

Craft and Structure

2. **(a) Interpret:** How does Tammet see the number 6? **(b) Infer:** What can you infer about the visual images he sees for the numbers 9 and 3? Cite details from the text that support your inference.
3. **Analyze:** For most people, Tammet's image of the number 6 would be an example of figurative language. Is that true for Tammet? Explain.

Integration of Knowledge and Ideas

4. **(a) Analyze:** What does the author mean when he says numbers are his "first language"? **(b) Speculate:** What kinds of communication might be a second "language" for Tammet? Explain.

Description

Description is the use of sensory details to create a word picture for readers. Reread the excerpt and take notes on how Tammet uses description.

1. **(a)** Find two examples of description in the text. **(b)** How does Tammet's use of description help readers understand his unique perceptions?
2. **Conformity:** Do Tammet's descriptions emphasize his differences from or his similarities to other people? Explain.

DISCUSS • RESEARCH • WRITE

From Text to Topic **Group Discussion**

Discuss the following passage with a group of classmates. Listen carefully as your fellow students speak and build on one another's ideas. Support your contributions with details from the text.

> If I see a number I experience as particularly beautiful on a shop sign or a car license plate, there's a shiver of excitement and pleasure. On the other hand, if the numbers don't match my experience of them—if, for example, a shop sign's price has "99 pence" in red or green (instead of blue)—then I find that uncomfortable and irritating.

QUESTIONS FOR DISCUSSION

1. How is Tammet's life both similar to and different from that of most people?
2. Is Tammet's inability to conform a burden, a benefit, both, or neither?

Research **Investigate the Topic**

Prodigies Savants possess one type of exceptional intelligence, but there are also other types. For example, a prodigy is a person, who develops remarkable abilities at an unusually young age.

Assignment
Conduct research to find out what makes someone a prodigy and how being one can affect someone's life. Include at least two examples of famous prodigies. Take careful notes and identify your sources. Share your findings in an **informal speech or presentation.**

PREPARATION FOR ESSAY

You may use the results of this research in an essay you will write at the end of this section.

Writing to Sources **Narrative**

"Blue Nines and Red Words" focuses on Daniel Tammet's extraordinary way of seeing the world. While Tammet is unique, everyone's view of life is shaped by his or her particular traits and experiences.

Assignment
Write an **autobiographical narrative** in which you describe how a special trait of your own has either set you apart from others or helped you fit in. Follow these steps:

- Introduce a problem or conflict.
- Create a smooth progression of events that build on one another.
- Use description to convey a vivid picture of people, events, and ideas.
- Provide a conclusion in which you reflect on your story and make connections between your experience and Daniel Tammet's.

ACADEMIC VOCABULARY

Academic terms appear in blue on these pages. If these words are not familiar to you, use a dictionary to find their definitions. Then, use them as.you speak and write about the text.

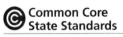

Common Core State Standards

RI.9-10.1, RI.9-10.2, RI.9-10.3, RI.9-10.4, RI.9-10.5, RI.9-10.6; W.9-10.3, W.9-10.3.a-e, W.9-10.4, W.9-10.7; SL.9-10.1; L.9-10.4
[For full standards wording, see the chart in the front of this book.]

from *The New Yorker*

"Sorry, we're all cat people. The dog people are in that boat over there."

Close Reading Activities

READ • DISCUSS • WRITE

Comprehension

Look at the cartoon again and reread the caption. Then, answer the questions that follow.

1. **(a)** What is the purpose of the boats with people in them? **(b)** Which details reveal that information?
2. **(a)** What is the person in the water hoping for? **(b)** What response does he get from the people in the boat?

Critical Analysis

Key Ideas and Details

1. **(a) Infer:** What inference can you make about what happened just prior to the scene shown in the cartoon? **(b) Support:** Which details in the drawing lead you to make that inference?
2. **(a)** What **literal** message is conveyed by the caption? **(b) Interpret:** What **implied** message is conveyed?

Craft and Structure

3. **Analyze:** The cartoon **depicts** a serious situation in an amusing way. What qualities in both the drawing and the caption make it lighthearted and funny rather than serious and scary? Explain.

Integration of Knowledge and Ideas

4. **Apply:** What does this cartoon suggest about the power of humor to deal with serious topics? Refer to details from the cartoon in your answer.

From Text to Topic **Class Discussion**

Discuss the cartoon with classmates. Use the following questions to focus your conversation.

1. If the man in the water were a "cat person" do you think he would be allowed to board the boat? Explain.
2. Could a scenario like the one in this cartoon ever come true?

Writing to Sources **Narrative**

Write a **short story** in which you describe the events that might have led up to the scene depicted in the cartoon. Establish a conflict and use dialogue and description to develop characters and events.

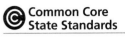

Common Core State Standards

RL.9-10.1, RL.9-10.2, RL.9-10.4; W.9-10.3, W.9-10.3.a, W.9-10.3.b; SL.9-10.1

[For full standards wording, see the chart in the front of this book.]

ACADEMIC VOCABULARY

Academic terms appear in blue on these pages. If these words are not familiar to you, use a dictionary to find their definitions. Then, use them as you speak and write about the text.

Assessment: Synthesis

Speaking and Listening: Group Discussion

Conformity and Conflict The texts in this section vary in genre, length, style, and perspective. However, all of them comment in some way on human difference and on whether people should conform to an accepted norm or should maximize their uniqueness. The issue of conformity, and the conflicts it creates for individuals and for society as a whole, is fundamentally related to the Big Question addressed in this unit: **Is conflict necessary?**

▲ Refer to the selections you read in Part 3 as you complete the activities on this assessment.

Assignment

Conduct discussions. With a small group of classmates, conduct a discussion about issues of conformity and conflict. Refer to the texts in this section, other texts you have read, and your personal experience and knowledge to support your ideas. Begin your discussion by addressing the following questions:

- Why do differences between people cause conflicts?
- Is conformity always negative?
- Do conflicts over conformity ever have positive results or benefits? If so, under what circumstances, and for whom?
- Are the conflicts caused by pressures to conform—or to avoid conforming—always necessary, sometimes necessary, or never necessary?

Summarize and present your ideas. After you have fully explored the topic, summarize your discussion and present your findings to the class as a whole.

Criteria for Success

✓ **Organizes the group effectively**
Appoint a group leader and a timekeeper. The group leader should present the discussion questions. The timekeeper should make sure the discussion takes no longer than 20 minutes.

✓ **Maintains focus of discussion**
As a group, stay on topic and avoid straying into other subject areas.

✓ **Involves all participants equally and fully**
No one person should monopolize the conversation. Rather, everyone should take turns speaking and contributing ideas.

✓ **Follows the rules for collegial discussion**
As each group member speaks, others should listen carefully. Build on one another's ideas and support viewpoints and opinions with sound reasoning and evidence. Express disagreement respectfully.

USE NEW VOCABULARY

As you speak and share ideas, work to use the vocabulary words you have learned in this unit. The more you use new words, the more you will "own" them.

Writing: **Narrative**

Conformity and Conflict Conflict is the engine that drives every story, whether it is a true-life adventure or an imagined tale. Likewise, all of us face conflicts in our own lives. Many of these conflicts relate to issues of individuality and conformity.

Assignment

Write an **autobiographical narrative,** or true story about your own life, in which you discuss a conflict you experienced that was driven either by the pressure to conform or to resist conforming. Note that an effective autobiographical narrative explores the significance of a related series of events in the writer's life. As you draft your narrative, make connections between your experiences, details in the texts you have read in this section, and the related research you have conducted. These connections will make your narrative richer.

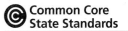

Common Core State Standards

SL.9–10.1.a–e; W.9–10.3.a–e

[For full standards wording, see the chart in the front of this book.]

Criteria for Success

Purpose/Focus

✓ **Connects specific incidents with larger ideas**
Make meaningful connections between your experiences and the texts you have read in this section.

✓ **Clearly conveys the significance of the story**
Provide a conclusion in which you reflect on what you experienced.

Organization

✓ **Sequences events logically**
Structure your narrative so that individual events build on one another to create a coherent whole.

Development of Ideas/Elaboration

✓ **Supports insights**
Include both personal examples and details from the texts you have read in this section.

✓ **Uses narrative techniques effectively**
Even though an autobiographical narrative is nonfiction, it may include storytelling elements like those found in fiction. Consider using dialogue to help readers "hear" how characters sound.

Language

✓ **Uses description effectively**
Use descriptive details to paint word pictures that help readers see settings and characters.

Conventions

✓ **Does not have errors**
Check your narrative to eliminate errors in grammar, spelling, and punctuation.

WRITE TO EXPLORE

Writing is a way to clarify what you feel and think. This means that you may change your mind or get new ideas as you work. Allowing for this will improve your final draft.

Writing to Sources: **Argument**

Conformity and Conflict The related readings in this section present a range of ideas about conformity and difference. They raise questions, such as the following, about the values of individuality and community:

- What does it mean to be an individual?
- How important is it to be like other people or part of a larger group?
- Is it the need to be an individual or the need to conform that most often leads to conflict? Why?
- Is conformity ever positive? If so, under what circumstances?

Focus on the question that intrigues you the most, and then complete the following assignment.

Assignment

Write an **argumentative essay** in which you state and defend a claim about the values of individuality or conformity. Build evidence for your claim by analyzing the presentation of individuality and conformity in two or more texts from this section. Clearly present, develop, and support your ideas with examples and details from the texts.

INCORPORATE RESEARCH

The research you have done in this section may provide support for your position. Review the notes you took and incorporate any relevant facts or details into your essay.

Prewriting and Planning

Choose texts. Review the texts in the section to determine which ones you will cite in your essay. Select at least two that will provide strong material to support your argument.

Gather details and craft a working thesis, or claim. Use a chart like the one shown to develop your claim. Though you may refine or change your ideas as you write, the working version will establish a clear direction.

Focus Question: How important is it to be like other people?

Text	Passage	Notes
"The Scarlet Ibis"	It was bad enough having an invalid brother, but [a mentally deficient one] was unbearable, so I began to make plans to kill him.	narrator places huge importance on conformity and shows a childish lack of compassion
from "Blue Nines and Red Words"	Thinking of calendars always makes me feel good, all those numbers and patterns in one place.	positive feelings come from author's differences
Example Claim: It takes more maturity to accept individuality than it does to demand conformity.		

Prepare counterarguments. For each point you intend to make to support your claim, note a possible objection to it. Plan to include the strongest of these counterclaims in your essay: introduce and supply evidence to refute them.

Drafting

Sequence your ideas and evidence. Present your ideas in a logical sequence. Use details from your chart to support each point you present. Make sure the evidence you select relates directly to the ideas you want to express.

Address counterclaims. Strong argumentation takes differing ideas into account and addresses them directly. As you order your ideas, build in sections in which you explain opposing opinions or differing interpretations. Then, write a thoughtful, well-supported response to those counterclaims.

Frame and connect ideas. Write an introduction that will grab the reader's attention. Consider beginning with a compelling quotation or a detail. Then, write a strong conclusion that ends your essay with a clear statement. Use transitional words and phrases to link the sections of your essay in a way that clarifies relationships among your ideas and evidence.

W.9-10.1.a–e; L.9-10.6
[For full standards wording, see the chart in the front of this book.]

Revising and Editing

Review content. Make sure that your claim is clearly stated and that you have supported it with convincing evidence from the texts. Underline main ideas in your essay and confirm that each one is supported. Add more proof as needed.

Review style. Revise to cut wordy language. Check that you have found the clearest, simplest way to communicate your ideas. Omit unnecessary words and replace vague words with better choices that clearly state what you mean.

CITE RESEARCH CORRECTLY

Follow accepted conventions to cite all sources you use in your essay. See the Citing Sources pages in the Introductory Unit for additional guidance.

Self-Evaluation Rubric

Use the following criteria to evaluate the effectiveness of your essay.

Criteria	Rating Scale
PURPOSE/FOCUS Introduces a precise claim and distinguishes the claim from (implied) alternate or opposing claims; provides a concluding section that follows from and supports the argument presented	*not very* .... *very* 1 2 3 4
ORGANIZATION Establishes a logical organization; uses words, phrases, and clauses to link the major sections of the text, create cohesion, and clarify relationships among claims, reasons, and evidence, and between claims and counterclaims	1 2 3 4
DEVELOPMENT OF IDEAS/ELABORATION Develops the claim and counterclaims fairly, supplying evidence for each while pointing out the strengths and limitations of both	1 2 3 4
LANGUAGE Establishes and maintains a formal style and an objective tone	1 2 3 4
CONVENTIONS Attends to the norms and conventions of the discipline	1 2 3 4

Independent Reading

Titles for Extended Reading

In this unit, you have read texts in a variety of genres. Continue to read on your own. Select works that you enjoy, but challenge yourself to explore new authors and works of increasing depth and complexity. The titles suggested below will help you get started.

INFORMATIONAL TEXTS

Literature of the Expanding Frontier

As pioneers spread across the Western frontier, they brought with them their passion for life and their hope for the future. This collection of **stories, poems, songs,** and **personal accounts** captures the spirits of everyone from Chinese immigrants building the nation's railroads to Native Americans dealing with the influx of new people as they all face the challenges of living together in the wilderness.

I Know Why The Caged Bird Sings
by Maya Angelou — EXEMPLAR TEXT

Maya Angelou's **memoir** of her Arkansas childhood is a classic of twentieth-century literature. This coming-of-age story reveals the author's strength and resilience in the face of racism, trauma, and poverty.

Biography and Autobiography

From Doris Kearns Goodwin's recollections of how television revolutionized her neighborhood to Stephen Hawking's story of how he overcame physical limitations, these **biographical** and **autobiographical narratives** give readers fresh perspectives on famous lives.

Black Like Me
by John Howard Griffin

In this fascinating **nonfiction** account, a white journalist passing as an African American man chronicles his experiences traveling by Greyhound bus through segregated states over a period of six weeks in 1959. This book provides an eye-opening window into strained race relations in America in the early years of the civil rights movement.

LITERATURE

The Tragedy of Macbeth
by William Shakespeare — EXEMPLAR TEXT

This spine-tingling **drama** is one of William Shakespeare's most popular plays. *The Tragedy of Macbeth* explores the dangers of unrestrained ambition as Macbeth and his scheming wife Lady Macbeth murder his competitors in a plot to seize the throne of Scotland.

Stories by O. Henry
by O. Henry — EXEMPLAR TEXT

O. Henry is considered one of America's greatest short story writers, famous for his colorful characters and surprise endings. This collection of **short stories** includes "The Gift of the Magi" and other famous tales.

The Joy Luck Club
by Amy Tan — EXEMPLAR TEXT

Amy Tan's best-selling **novel** explores the lives of Chinese American families who meet to play games and share meals. Told from the perspective of several female family members, the novel explores parent-child relationships and the dynamics of immigrant families.

ONLINE TEXT SET

POEM
All Watched Over by Machines of Loving Grace Richard Brautigan

SCIENCE ARTICLE
Careers in Robotics NASA Robotic Education Project

SCIENCE ARTICLE
Team Builds "Sociable" Robot
Elizabeth A. Thompson

Preparing to Read Complex Texts

Attentive Reading As you read literature on your own, bring your imagination and questions to the text. The questions shown below and others that you ask as you read will help you learn and enjoy literature even more.

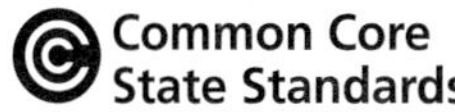

Reading Literature/ Informational Text
10. By the end of grade 9, read and comprehend literature, including stories, dramas, poems, and literary nonfiction in the grades 9–10 text complexity band proficiently, with scaffolding as needed at the high end of the range.

When reading narratives, ask yourself...

Comprehension: **Key Ideas and Details**

- Who is the story's main character? Who are the other characters and how do they relate to the main character?
- What problems do the characters face? How do they react to these problems?
- Which characters do I like or admire? Which do I dislike? How do my reactions to the characters make me feel about the work as a whole?
- Is the setting of the story—the place, time, and society—believable and interesting? Why or why not?
- What happens in the story? Why do these events happen?

Text Analysis: **Craft and Structure**

- Who is the narrator? Is this voice part of the story or is it an outside observer?
- Do I find the narrator's voice interesting and engaging? Why or why not?
- Is there anything different or unusual in the way the work is structured? Do I find that structure interesting or distracting?
- Are there any passages that I find especially strong or beautiful?
- Do I understand why characters act and feel as they do? Do their thoughts and actions seem real? Why or why not?

Connections: **Integration of Knowledge and Ideas**

- What does this story mean to me? Does it convey a theme or insight that I find important and true? Why or why not?
- Does the work remind me of others I have read? If so, how?
- Have I gained new knowledge from reading this story? If so, what have I learned?
- Would I recommend this work to others? If so, to whom?
- Would I like to read other fiction by this author? Why or why not?

UNIT 2

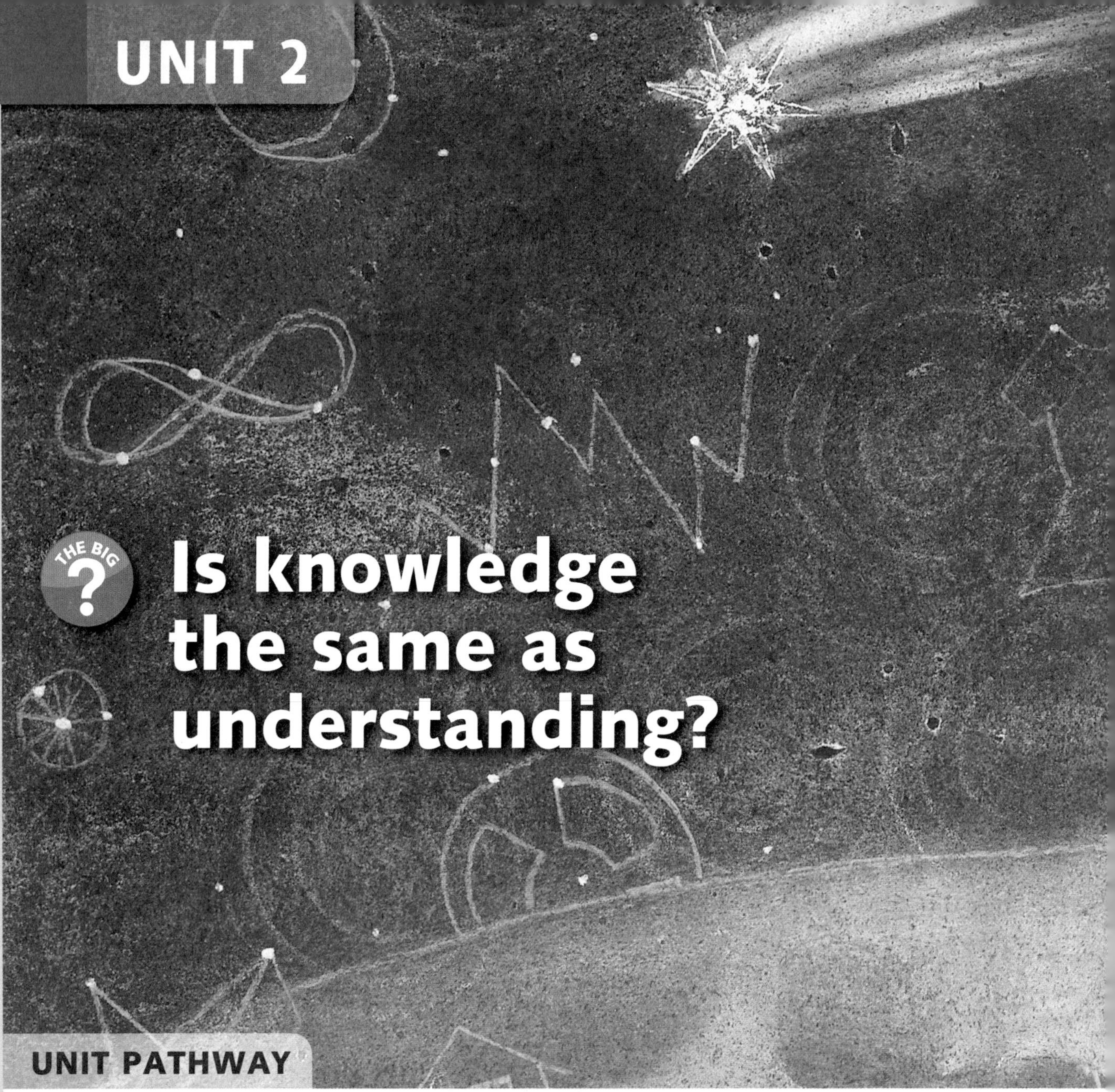

THE BIG ? Is knowledge the same as understanding?

UNIT PATHWAY

PART 1
SETTING EXPECTATIONS
- INTRODUCING THE BIG QUESTION
- CLOSE READING WORKSHOP

PART 2
TEXT ANALYSIS
GUIDED EXPLORATION
CHANGING PERSPECTIVES

PART 3
TEXT SET
DEVELOPING INSIGHT
THE GREAT DEPRESSION

PART 4
DEMONSTRATING INDEPENDENCE
- INDEPENDENT READING
- ONLINE TEXT SET

CLOSE READING TOOL

Use this tool to practice the close reading strategies you learn.

STUDENT eTEXT

Bring learning to life with audio, video, and interactive tools.

ONLINE WRITER'S NOTEBOOK

Easily capture notes and complete assignments online.

Find all Digital Resources at **pearsonrealize.com**

Introducing the Big Question

Is knowledge the same as understanding?

We are constantly working to learn more about the world. We find information in a variety of sources, and we struggle to comprehend the facts. We may study books, interpret charts, and conduct research. We may talk to others to gain insight. Through all these activities we gain knowledge, but does that mean we truly understand? For example, does knowing about relationships help us get along, or do we have to experience friendship to truly understand what it means? Is knowledge the same as understanding?

Exploring the Big Question

Collaboration: Group Discussion Begin thinking about the Big Question by analyzing what you know and how you know it. List topics that you have knowledge about and also understand. Describe an example from each of the following categories.

- a grandparent or an older adult you know well
- a concept you have learned in school
- a speech you have read over and over
- an argument you have had that still bothers you
- something you have read about but also experienced
- the memory of an important event in your life

Before you begin a formal discussion, share your list in a group. Talk about any differences you discover between your knowledge and your understanding of these topics. Then, set rules that will lead to a cooperative exchange. For example, consider any specific goals you want to achieve, whether to assign a mediator, and how you will handle disagreements. Capture the rules in a format everyone can use as the discussion takes place.

Connecting to the Literature Each reading in this unit will give you additional insight into the Big Question. After you read each selection, pause to consider ways in which you have gained knowledge or understanding.

Vocabulary

Acquire and Use Academic Vocabulary The term "academic vocabulary" refers to words you typically encounter in scholarly and literary texts and in technical and business writing. It is language that helps to express complex ideas. Review the definitions of these academic vocabulary words.

ambiguous (am big′ yo͞o əs) *adj.* having more than one meaning; able to be interpreted in different ways

clarify (klar′ə fī′) *v.* make something more clear or understandable

comprehend (käm′ prē hend′) *v.* understand

concept (kän′ sept′) *n.* idea; notion

interpret (in tʉr′ prət) *v.* understand or explain the meaning of a concept or an idea

Use these words as you complete Big Question activities that involve reading, writing, speaking, and listening.

Gather Vocabulary Knowledge Additional words related to knowledge and understanding are listed below. Categorize the words by deciding whether you know each one well, know it a little bit, or do not know it at all.

connection	insight	senses/sensory
fact	instinct	sources
feeling	research	statistics
information		

Then, complete the following steps:

1. Write the definitions of the words you know.
2. Consult a print or an online dictionary to confirm each word's meaning. Revise your original definitions if necessary.
3. Use the dictionary to look up the meanings of the words you do not know. Then, write the definitions.
4. If a word sounds familiar but you are not sure of its meaning, consult the dictionary. Then, record the meaning.
5. Use all of the words in a paragraph about knowledge and understanding. Choose words and phrases that convey your ideas precisely.

Speaking and Listening

1.b. Work with peers to set rules for collegial discussions and decision-making, clear goals and deadlines, and individual roles as needed.

Language

4.c. Consult general and specialized reference materials, both print and digital, to find the pronunciation of a word or determine or clarify its precise meaning, its part of speech, or its etymology.

4.d. Verify the preliminary determination of the meaning of a word or phrase.

6. Acquire and use accurately grade-appropriate general academic and domain-specific words and phrases, sufficient for reading, writing, speaking, and listening at the college and career readiness level; demonstrate independence in gathering vocabulary knowledge when considering a word or phrase important to comprehension or expression.

Close Reading Workshop

In this workshop, you will learn an approach to reading that will deepen your understanding of literature and will help you better appreciate the author's craft. The workshop includes models for the close reading, discussion, research, and writing activities you will complete as you study the texts in this unit. After you have reviewed the strategies and models, practice your skills with the Independent Practice selection.

RI.9-10.1, RI.9-10.2, RI.9-10.3, RI.9-10.5, RI.9-10.6; SL.9-10.1; W.9-10.2, W.9-10.7, W.9-10.9b, W.9-10.10

[For full standards wording, see the chart in the front of this book.]

CLOSE READING: **NONFICTION**

In Part 2 of this unit, you will focus on reading various nonfiction works. Use these strategies as you read the texts:

Comprehension: **Key Ideas and Details**

- Read first for comprehension.
- Determine the meanings of unfamiliar words. Consult a dictionary, if necessary.
- Briefly research unfamiliar details.
- Distinguish ideas that the author states directly from those he or she suggests through details.

Ask yourself questions such as these:

- What is the author's central idea, claim, or thesis?
- What is the author's point of view or opinion?
- What evidence does the author present to support or illustrate the central idea?

Text Analysis: **Craft and Structure**

- Consider how the genre of the work relates to the types of ideas the author presents.
- Analyze the structure of the work. Pay attention to connections among sentences, paragraphs, and sections.
- Take note of how the author uses figurative language or rhetorical devices.
- Consider the author's word choice. Notice whether the words are formal or informal, emotional or neutral. Determine what attitude toward the subject the words convey.

Ask yourself questions such as these:

- What is the author's purpose in writing this piece?
- What does the author's word choice reveal about his or her point of view or purpose?
- How does the author's point of view affect what he or she shares about the topic? How does it affect what I learn about the topic?

Connections: **Integration of Knowledge and Ideas**

- Look for relationships among key ideas. Identify problems and solutions, causes and effects, or comparisons and contrasts.
- Look for key passages and analyze how they fulfill the author's purpose or express a distinct point of view.
- Consider how this work relates to other works you have read on similar topics.

Ask yourself questions such as these:

- What have I learned from this work?
- In what way is this piece special, unique, or worthy of reading?

Read

As you read this speech, take note of the annotations that model ways to closely read the text.

Reading Model

"I Am An American Day" Address by Learned Hand[1]

We have gathered here to affirm a faith, a faith in a common purpose, a common conviction, a common devotion. Some of us have chosen America as the land of our adoption; the rest have come from those who did the same. For this reason we have some right to consider ourselves a picked group, a group of those who had the courage to break from the past and brave the dangers and the loneliness of a strange land. What was the object that nerved us, or those who went before us, to this choice?[2] We sought liberty; freedom from oppression, freedom from want, freedom to be ourselves. This we then sought; this we now believe that we are by way of winning. What do we mean when we say that first of all we seek liberty?[2] I often wonder whether we do not rest our hopes too much upon constitutions, upon laws and upon courts. These are false hopes; believe me, these are false hopes. Liberty lies in the hearts of men and women;[3] when it dies there, no constitution, no law, no court can save it; no constitution, no law, no court can even do much to help it. While it lies there it needs no constitution, no law, no court to save it. And what is this liberty which must lie in the hearts of men and women?[2] It is not the ruthless, the unbridled will; it is not freedom to do as one likes. That is the denial of liberty, and leads straight to its overthrow. A society in which men recognize no check upon their freedom soon becomes a society where freedom is the possession of only a savage few; as we have learned to our sorrow.

What then is the spirit of liberty? I cannot define it; I can only tell you my own faith. The spirit of liberty is the spirit which is not too sure that it is right; the spirit of liberty is the spirit which seeks to understand the minds of other men and women; the spirit of liberty is the spirit which weighs their interests alongside its own without bias;[4] the spirit of liberty remembers that not even a sparrow falls to earth unheeded; the spirit of liberty is the spirit of Him who, near two thousand years ago, taught mankind that lesson it has never learned, but has never quite forgotten; that there may be a kingdom where the least shall be heard and considered side by side with the greatest.[5] And now in that spirit, that spirit of an America which has never been, and which may never be; nay, which never will be except as the conscience and courage of Americans create it;[6] yet in the spirit of that America which lies hidden in some form in the aspirations of us all; in the spirit of that America for which our young men are at this moment fighting and dying; in that spirit of liberty and of America I ask you to rise and with me pledge our faith in the glorious destiny of our beloved country.

Key Ideas and Details

1 Brief research reveals that Learned Hand was a highly respected judge during the mid-twentieth century. He gave this speech in 1944, during World War II, before a ceremony in which people officially became American citizens.

Craft and Structure

2 Hand uses three questions to frame his argument: first, why people come to the U.S.; second, what it means to "seek liberty"; and, finally, what *liberty* means. This structure methodically walks the listener through Hand's ideas.

Key Ideas and Details

3 By dismissing the role of the law and placing liberty "in the hearts" of his listeners, Hand starts to present his central idea: Words promising liberty in the U.S. legal system are meaningless unless citizens dedicate themselves to that ideal.

Integration of Knowledge and Ideas

4 The repetition and parallelism in this sentence emphasize that each idea is equally important to Hand's definition of *liberty*.

Craft and Structure

5 Researching these phrases shows they are Biblical allusions. "Not even a sparrow falls" refers to Jesus's statement that every action is willed by God. "Him" is Jesus, who said that, in heaven, all people are equal.

Integration of Knowledge and Ideas

6 This parallel construction suggests *liberty* and *America* are synonymous, or the same. Hand sums up his argument: The perfect "spirit of liberty" does not exist, but it should remain an ideal for all Americans.

Discuss

Sharing your own ideas and listening to the ideas of others can deepen your understanding of a text and help you look at a topic in a whole new way. As you participate in collaborative discussions, work to have a genuine exchange in which classmates build upon one another's ideas. Support your points with evidence and ask meaningful questions.

Discussion Model

Student 1: Why would Hand, a federal judge, start his speech by saying people have too much faith in constitutions, laws, and courts? You'd think he would defend those things.

Student 2: I think Hand's position as a judge makes his argument stronger. As a part of the system that he is arguing against, Hand's opinion is worth a lot. He probably regularly saw people who thought it was up to the courts and the courts alone to defend liberty.

Student 3: I didn't think of that at first, but I agree. He is giving power to his audience, who are probably just ordinary people. He puts himself on an equal level with them, which, when you think about it, is a big part of democracy. I liked this speech a lot, and I thought it was powerful. But I wonder about the occasion of this speech—what was "I Am An American Day"?

Research

Targeted research can clarify unfamiliar details and shed light on various aspects of a text. Consider questions that arise in your mind as you read, and use those questions as the basis for research.

Research Model

Question: *What was "I Am An American Day"?*

Key Words for Internet Search: "I Am An American Day" and History

Result: Constitution Day and Citizenship Day site of the Library of Congress

What I Learned: "I Am An American Day" was created by a joint resolution of Congress in 1940. Originally celebrated in May, the day honored all new citizens of the United States. Then, in 1952, Congress passed a resolution to replace "I Am An American Day" with "Constitution Day." The same resolution called for the celebration to be moved to September 17th, the anniversary of the signing of the U.S. Constitution. In 2004, Congress renamed the day "Constitution Day and Citizenship Day."

Write

Writing about a text will deepen your understanding of it and will also allow you to share your ideas more formally with others. The following model essay explains Hand's use of rhetorical devices in his speech.

Writing Model: Explanatory Text

Rhetorical Devices in Learned Hand's "I Am An American Day" Address

Public speakers often use rhetorical devices to make their points more memorable. In his "I Am An American Day" speech, Learned Hand effectively uses repetition, parallelism, questions, and allusions to emphasize his central idea about liberty.

The writer makes a strong claim, or thesis statement, in the first paragraph. This reveals the focus of the essay to readers.

Hand structures the first part of his argument using three questions and his answers. He uses these questions to refine his definition and emphasize the previous point. These questions also anticipate questions that could come from the audience about his statements. Questions are an effective device because they cue the reader that it is time to pay attention: "What was the object that nerved us, or those who went before us, to this choice? We sought liberty; freedom from oppression, freedom from want, freedom to be ourselves." Hand's listeners may have had that same question, and he guided their thinking to his answer.

In explaining why Hand uses a specific structure, the writer demonstrates an understanding of rhetorical devices.

Through effective use of repetition and parallelism, Hand dismisses the possible counterclaim that liberty resides with the government, not with the citizens: "When it dies there, no constitution, no law, no court can save it; no constitution, no law, no court can even do much to help it. While it lies there it needs no constitution, no law, no court to save it." He repeats the phrase "no constitution, no law, no court" to emphasize his point and ensure listeners remember it. Hand later uses parallelism again to define what he calls the "spirit of liberty." His use of parallel structure in a long sentence reinforces the equal importance of each part of his definition.

The writer supports claims with evidence from the speech.

Hand also uses Biblical allusions to connect the idea that liberty is connected to faith: "The spirit of liberty remembers that not even a sparrow falls to earth unheeded." His other allusion reminds listeners of the idea of heaven, which encourages his audience to make comparisons between heaven and the United States. While every listener may not understand every allusion, these references are useful tools for clarifying ideas without wasting words.

At the time of Hand's speech, the country was involved in a deadly war in Europe and the Pacific. Americans at home during 1944 wanted patriotic messages that made them feel part of a noble cause. Hand's speech may have helped the nation really understand what they were fighting for. Hand has a clear answer: "the spirit of liberty."

The writer incorporates relevant information from research in order to support a claim more effectively.

INDEPENDENT PRACTICE

As you read the following essay, apply the close reading strategies you have learned. You may need to read the work multiple times to come to a full and deep understanding of the author's craft and the insights she expresses.

Meet the Author

When she was twenty-five, **Rebecca Walker** (b. 1969) was named by *Time* magazine as one of fifty influential American leaders under the age of forty. Her essays and articles have appeared in many magazines and publications. She has received awards for both her writing and her work as an advocate for young women.

Before Hip-Hop Was Hip-Hop

by Rebecca Walker

If you ask most kids today about hip-hop, they'll spit out the names of recording artists they see on TV: Eminem, P. Diddy, J. Lo, Beyoncé. They'll tell you about the songs they like and the clothes they want to buy. They'll tell you about the indisputable zones of hip-hop like "EO" (East Orange, New Jersey), the "ATL" (Atlanta, Georgia), and the "West Side" (Los Angeles, California), neighborhoods they feel they know because they've seen them in all the glossiest, "flossiest" music videos. Hip-hop is natural to these kids, like air or water, just there, a part of the digital landscape that streams through their lives.

I watch this cultural sea change with fascination. It astounds me that hip-hop has grown into a global industry, a force that dominates youth culture from Paris to Prague, Tokyo to Timbuktu. I can't believe that in small, all-white towns like Lincoln, Nebraska, high school boys wear their clothes in the latest "steelo": pants sagging off their waists, sports jerseys hanging to their knees, baseball hats cocked to one side. Even in the pueblos of Mexico, where mariachi bands and old school crooners still rule, it is hip-hop that sells cars, sodas, and children's toys on TV.

The vast empire of hip-hop amazes me because I knew hip-hop before it was hip-hop. I was there when it all began.

Way back then, in what today's ninth graders might call the ancient eighties, there was no MTV or VH-1. We found out about music by listening to the radio, flipping through the stacks at the record store, or buying "mix tapes" from local deejays at two dollars apiece. Back then, we carried combs in our back pockets and clipped long strands of feathers to the belt loops of our designer jeans. We wore our names in cursive gold letters around our necks or in big brass letters on our belt buckles. We picked up words and inverted them, calling something that we thought was really cool, "hot," and something that had a whole lot of life, "def."

CLOSE READING TOOL

Read and respond to this selection online using the **Close Reading Tool.**

We didn't know a whole new language was rolling off our tongues as we flipped English upside down and pulled some Spanish and even a few words from Africa into our parlance. We didn't know that young people for years to come would recycle our fashions and sample the bass lines from our favorite tracks. We thought we were just being kids and expressing ourselves, showing the grown-ups we were different from them in a way that was safe and fun. In fact we were at the epicenter[1] of one of America's most significant cultural revolutions, making it happen. Who knew?

Not me.

When I moved from Washington, D.C., to the Bronx the summer before seventh grade, I had one box of records, mostly albums I had ordered from the Columbia Record Club. In 1982, if you promised to buy a record a month for one whole year, the Club sent you eight records for a penny. I had Bruce Springsteen's "The River," REO Speedwagon's "The Letter," "Belladonna" by Stevie Nicks. I had "Stairway to Heaven," by Led Zeppelin and the soundtrack from the movie *Saturday Night Fever*, which I played so many times I thought my mother would go crazy from listening to me belt out the lyrics with those lanky, swanky Bee Gees.

Along with my albums I had loads of 45s, what today we would call singles, little records with just two songs on them, that I bought at the record store near my school for just a dollar a piece. I had Chaka Khan's "I'm Every Woman," and Luther Vandross's "Never Too Much," and Chuck Brown and Soul Searcher's big hit, "Bustin' Loose." I had Michael Jackson's "Rock with You" and even Aretha Franklin's cover of "You Make Me Feel Like a Natural Woman," which I sang along to in the mornings as I styled my hair.

If you had asked me then about rap music I would have shrugged my shoulders and looked at you like you were crazy. Rap music? What's that?

But then I started seventh grade and my whole world turned upside down. At Public School 141, I went to classes with kids from all over the Bronx. There were kids whose families came from Puerto Rico and the Dominican Republic, and kids whose families came from Russia and China. There were kids who were African-American and kids who were Irish-American, kids who were Italian-American and kids who were Greek-American. There were kids whose families were poor, kids whose families were well off, and kids whose families were somewhere in between. Some were Jewish, and others devout Catholics. Some were Muslim. Some of the Asian kids were even Buddhist.

---

1. **epicenter** (ep′ i sent′ ər) *n.* focal or central point.

Vocabulary ▶
entrenched (en trencht′) *adj.* securely established; unmovable

Vocabulary ▶
bravado (brə vä′ dō) *n.* pretended courage or defiant confidence

The charge created by so many different elements coming together was palpable.[2] The school crackled with energy, and as you can imagine, things weren't always smooth. There were some pretty entrenched cliques, and a few vicious fights in the schoolyard. But there was also so much "flavor." You could hear Spanish spoken with a thick "Nuyorican" accent to a kid wearing a "yamulke." A seemingly reserved Asian-American girl would get out of her parents' car, wait for them to drive off, and then unzip her coat to reveal a fire engine red Adidas sweatsuit. A guy in a preppy, button-down shirt would "sport" gold chains with pendants of every denomination: the Jewish Star of David, the Arabic lettering for Allah, and a shiny gold cross. He was everything, that was his "steelo," and everyone gave him "props" for it.

When I got to 141, I felt like a blank canvas. Nothing had prepared me for the dynamism, the screaming self-expression of the place and its students. For the first few weeks I secretly studied the habits of the seventh, eighth and ninth graders with whom I walked the halls and shared the cafeteria. I was transfixed by the way they infused their words with attitude and drama, moving their hands and heads as they spoke. I was captivated by the way many of them walked and ran and joked with each other with confidence and bravado. I noted what they wore and how they wore it: the razor sharp creases of their Jordache jeans, the spotless sneakers with the laces left loose and untied.

Slowly, I began to add some of what I saw into my "look." I convinced my grandmother to buy me a name chain to wear around my neck, and my stepmother to buy me dark dyed designer jeans. I bought my first pair of Nike sneakers, red, white and blue Air Cortez's, with money I saved from my allowance.

One by one, I started to make friends—Diane, Loida, James, Jesus, Maya. When James and Jesus weren't making fun of me for being so "square," they took me to parties on the Grand Concourse, the big boulevard lined with old apartment buildings and department stores that ran through the Bronx. The parties were incredible, filled with young people who didn't drink, smoke or fight, but who just wanted to dance and laugh and ooh and ahhh over the "scratching" sounds and funky beats the DJ's coaxed out of their turntables.

A lot of the kids at the parties were "breakers" or "poppers and lockers," which meant they could breakdance, a style of movement that blends the Brazilian martial art of Capoeira with a dance called the Robot, and incorporates classical dance moves as well. The "breakers" moved in "crews" that competed against each other.

---

2. **palpable** (pal′ pə bəl) *adj.* able to be touched, felt, or handled; tangible.

Standing in a circle we watched as members of the different groups "moonwalked" into the center, and then hurled themselves to the floor, spinning on their heads, kicking their legs into the air, and making elaborate hand gestures, each more intricate and acrobatic than the last. Everyone at the party who wasn't "breaking" was a judge by default, and we registered our scores by clapping and yelling.

When Loida and Diane weren't "capping on" or making fun of my clothes, they were "hipping" me to Kiss 98.7 and WBLS, the radio stations that had started to slip some of the songs we liked into their rotation. Songs like "Planet Rock" by Soul Sonic Force and "Take Me Home" by Lisa Lisa and the Cult Jam. After school and on the weekends, they took me to the street vendors that sold the accessories we all coveted: the big knockoff Porsche sunglasses everybody wanted but not everybody could afford, and the heavy gold chains people collected around their necks like so many pieces of string. Loida and Diane also took me around the city on the bus, familiarizing me with the routes of the M1 and M3 and M7, showing me all the different neighborhoods like Little Italy and Chinatown, Bed-Stuy and Harlem.

I remember looking out the big sliding glass windows of the bus at the lines drawn in concrete and glass and thinking that while the world outside seemed so divided, inside, in my circle, among my friends, those lines didn't seem to exist. Loida was Dominican and Diane was Puerto Rican. Our friend Mary was Irish-American, and Lisa was Italian-American. Maya's family was from Haiti. Julius was Russian-American. We were different ages, with different likes and dislikes, but we were united in our love of hip-hop. We loved the "dope"[3] beats, the ever changing and ever expanding lexicon, the outrageous dance moves, the cocky swagger, the feeling that we were part of something dynamic and "fresh"[4] that was bigger than any one of us. That world, that other realm that we created on the streets and in our minds, that streamed from the radio in the privacy of our bedrooms and coursed between us as we talked on the phone, that was where we lived.

That was where we felt free.

Looking back on it now, I can see that hip-hop was born of the diversity I found at 141. Unlike the hip-hop of today, it didn't come pre-packaged from a marketing department with millions of dollars to spend. Our hip-hop was the product of a bunch of kids from a bunch of different places trying to talk to each other, trying to create a common language that could cut through the many languages people spoke at home. Intuitively, kids were making a community where there was none; we were affirming our sameness in a

◀ **Vocabulary**
lexicon (lek′ si kän′) *n.* special vocabulary of a particular subject

3. **dope** (dōp) *adj.* slang term meaning "great; irresistible."
4. **fresh** (fresh) *adj.* slang term meaning "new."

world that seemed to only emphasize our difference. That desire to come together irrespective of superficial differences and sometimes in celebration of them, was what gave hip-hop authenticity, that was what kept it honest and as crucial to our well being as food. It's what kept it real.

I can't say much about hip-hop today, but I can say that old hip-hop, original hip-hop, changed my life forever. I only lived in the "Boogie Down Bronx" for a year, but those twelve months gave me so much. I learned that art could bring people together and make them forget their differences. I learned how good it could feel to move with a "posse," a group of friends who had my back no matter what. I learned that I could express myself and communicate with others through what I wore and how I walked and what music I liked. I learned that it doesn't take money or a special degree to transform the grit and drive and hardness of the city into something beautiful.

Loyalty. Community. Self-confidence. Creativity. Hip-hop taught me more about real life than anything I learned that year in class.

I hope when kids today look at shiny videos by their favorite hip-hop artists, they will see through the expensive cars and exotic locations, the women in skimpy outfits and the men trying to approximate a "gangsta" lean. I hope they will remember that hip-hop was born without a formula and without a lot of expensive props or violent undertones. I hope they will marvel at the fact that in the early days of hip-hop, young people were making it up as they went along, following their hearts, following what felt good. I hope they will think about what it takes to create culture that is unique and transcendent and honest, and I hope they begin to dream about creating a new world for themselves.

I hope hip-hop inspires them to make their own revolution.

Close Reading Activities

Read

Comprehension: **Key Ideas and Details**

1. According to Walker, why did Public School 141 "crackle" with energy?
2. **(a) Interpret:** Why was it so important for Walker and her friends to define themselves through clothing, language, dance, and music? **(b) Analyze:** What evidence does Walker use to support her assertions about early hip-hop culture?
3. **(a) Interpret:** What does Walker mean when she describes herself as a "blank canvas"? **(b) Infer:** In what ways did being a "blank canvas" allow Walker to fully experience her school's culture? Explain.
4. **Summarize:** Write a brief, objective summary of the essay. Cite details from the essay in your writing.

Text Analysis: **Craft and Structure**

5. **(a) Distinguish:** What structure, or organization, does Walker use to organize her essay? Explain. **(b) Evaluate:** What makes this structure effective? Cite details from the text to support your answer.
6. **Analyze:** What effect does Walker create through her use of repetition and parallelism at the end of the essay? Cite specific examples from the text in your response.
7. **(a) Infer:** Tone is the author's attitude toward the subject. What is the tone of Walker's essay? **(b) Defend:** Which details in the essay contribute to that tone?
8. **(a)** Identify two examples of Walker's use of slang. **(b) Infer:** Why might she have chosen to include slang in this essay? **(c) Interpret:** How does Walker's use of slang affect the tone of the essay? Explain.

Connections: **Integration of Knowledge and Ideas**

Discuss

Conduct a **small-group discussion** about Walker's purpose in writing "Before Hip-Hop Was Hip-Hop" and how she fulfills that purpose.

Research

Walker mentions that modern hip-hop "sample[s] the bass lines from our favorite tracks." Briefly research the practice of sampling in hip-hop and other pop music. In particular, consider the following:

a. early hip-hop songs that gained more fame later as samples
b. artists who have made careers out of sampling
c. the legal or copyright issues involved in sampling

Take notes as you perform your research. Then, write a brief **report** on the ways in which early hip-hop continues to influence people today, including musicians and writers like Walker.

Write

A good essayist uses strong evidence to support and develop a clear central idea. Write an **essay** in which you identify Walker's central idea and explain how she uses related ideas, facts, and other evidence to develop that idea. Cite details from Walker's essay to support your analysis.

Is knowledge the same as understanding?

What knowledge does Walker gain from learning about hip-hop at P.S. 141? How does that knowledge influence her understanding of her school, her culture, and her own identity? Explain your answer.

"It is a narrow mind
which cannot look
at a subject from
various points of view."
—George Eliot

PART 2

TEXT ANALYSIS GUIDED EXPLORATION

CHANGING PERSPECTIVES

Every author writes from a particular perspective, or unique way of seeing the world. The topics a writer chooses, the details he or she thinks are important, the connections that build meaning—all of these express that viewpoint. In turn, an author's perspective may change how readers see a topic, helping them to view a subject in a new way. As you read the texts in this section, consider the author's perspective. Think about what you learn by viewing the topic, however briefly, through the author's eyes. Then, consider how each selection provides a new perspective on the Big Question for this unit: **Is knowledge the same as understanding?**

◀ CRITICAL VIEWING From what point of view is this scene presented? From what other points of view could this subject be presented? What might be visible from those other points of view that is not visible in this image?

READINGS IN PART 2

CLOSE READING TOOL

Use the **Close Reading Tool** to practice the strategies you learn in this unit.

Elements of Essays, Articles, and Speeches

Essays, articles, and speeches organize factual information to present a picture of a topic—often from a particular **point of view**.

An essay can make you laugh. An article can make you cry. A speech can change your mind. Like all **nonfiction,** these forms of writing present facts or discuss real life.

- In an **essay,** an author supports a **thesis**—a central idea about a topic. In doing so, the author conveys his or her **point of view,** or perspective, on the topic.
- An **article** provides information about a topic. Articles are often divided into sections introduced by subheads. Each subhead names the central idea of the section it introduces. Many articles are written from an objective point of view—they give just the facts.
- A **speech** is a nonfiction text that a speaker delivers, or says, to an audience. Like the author of an essay, a speaker usually presents a thesis and expresses his or her point of view.

An author's approach to a topic depends on his or her **purpose,** or reason for writing. An author's purpose is related to the effect he or she wishes to have on readers. There are three main purposes for writing.

- **To inform,** or provide facts and explain how they relate to one another
- **To persuade,** or try to influence an audience's attitudes or actions
- **To entertain,** or engage and move the emotions of an audience

To achieve his or her purpose, a writer uses techniques such as these:

- **organizing information** in ways that make it clear (as when writing to inform) or dramatic (as when writing to persuade or to entertain)
- **choosing language** that makes ideas clear (as when writing to inform) or that creates **tone,** or conveys the writer's attitude (as when writing to persuade)

When you read nonfiction, analyze each element in the chart below.

Key Elements of Nonfiction

Element	Definition
Thesis or Central Idea	the main idea the author wants the audience to understand and remember
Purpose	the reason the author is writing about the topic
Organizational Structure	the order in which information and ideas are presented and the connections that are drawn between and among them
Tone	the author's attitude toward the topic and audience as conveyed in his or her word choices
Diction	the author's word choice, including the level of formality and difficulty; the use of **figurative language,** or language that is not meant to be taken literally; and **rhetoric,** or the patterning of words

Types of Essays and Articles

Most essays fit one of the following descriptions:

Types of Essays

- **Narrative essays** tell the story of actual experiences or events.
- **Expository essays** inform readers about a topic and explain the ideas it involves.
- **Persuasive,** or **argumentative, essays** attempt to convince audiences to accept an author's **claim,** or position on an issue, or to motivate audiences to take a particular course of action.
- **Descriptive essays** give vivid details about a person, place, or thing to help readers picture it.
- **Reflective essays** explore the meaning of an experience or offer the author's thoughts or feelings.

Authors may combine elements of different types of essays. For instance, in an argumentative essay persuading readers to adopt dogs from shelters, an author might include vivid descriptions of homeless dogs.

There are many types of articles. Two main types are news articles and feature articles.

Two Types of Articles

- **News articles** provide facts about current events. These articles usually answer the questions *Who? What? Where? When? Why?* and *How?* and are written from an objective, or neutral, point of view.
- **Feature articles** provide facts about current topics such as fashion or technology. These articles are often written in a friendly, conversational style.

Types of Speeches

What a writer says in a speech is shaped by its **occasion,** or the event at which the speech will be delivered, as well as by its **audience,** or the people to whom the speech will be addressed. Several examples of common types of speeches, along with a possible occasion and audience for each, appear below.

Three Types of Speeches

Speech of Public Advocacy: a formal, prepared speech intended to persuade an audience to take action

Example: an argumentative speech that describes a community problem and proposes a possible solution

Delivered by: a citizen

Occasion: a city council meeting

Audience: the city council; fellow citizens

Talk: an informal speech presented in a conversational style

Example: a report on a science fair

Delivered by: a student

Occasion: a science club meeting

Audience: student members of the club

Impromptu Speech: a speech presented with little or no preparation, often in a conversational style

Example: a speech of celebration

Delivered by: the subject's friend

Occasion: a birthday party

Audience: the person whose birthday is being celebrated, along with the guests

Common Core State Standards

Reading Informational Text

3. Analyze how the author unfolds an analysis or series of ideas or events, including the order in which the points are made, how they are introduced and developed, and the connections that are drawn between them.

4. Determine the meaning of words and phrases as they are used in a text, including figurative, connotative, and technical meanings; analyze the cumulative impact of specific word choices on meaning and tone.

5. Analyze in detail how an author's ideas or claims are developed and refined by particular sentences, paragraphs, or larger portions of a text.

6. Determine an author's point of view or purpose in a text and analyze how an author uses rhetoric to advance that point of view or purpose.

Analyzing the Development, Organization, and Communication of Ideas

Authors use varied methods to **introduce** and **develop** ideas logically. **Word choice and rhetoric** help writers achieve specific **purposes** and convey distinct **points of view**.

Introducing and Developing Ideas In a nonfiction work, the author will present ideas in a particular order and style. First, the author introduces the topic and key ideas. If these ideas are likely to be unfamiliar to readers, the author may introduce them with a familiar example or a simple comparison, as in this example:

Example: Sun Static

Although the sun is about 93 million miles away, solar activity can affect communications here on Earth. To understand why, picture water boiling in a pot. Bubbles on the surface burst and release steam. Similarly, solar flares on the surface of the sun can release particles that travel to our planet.

Then, the author **develops,** or elaborates on, ideas, explaining them and showing the connections from one idea to the next. Pieces of information that illustrate, expand on, or prove the author's ideas are called **supporting details.** Here are some types of supporting details:

- **Statements of fact,** or statements that can be proved true
- **Statistics,** or numbers used to compare members of a group of people or things
- **Examples,** or specific cases
- **Descriptions,** or details that tell what something looks like, tastes like, and so on
- **Reasons,** or claims that justify a belief
- **Expert opinions,** or the judgments of people with special knowledge of a subject

Overall Organizational Structures To develop ideas and show the connections among them, an author needs to present information in a clear order. An author's purpose for writing will guide his or her choice of an overall **structure,** or pattern of organization, as in these examples:

- A news report about a space shuttle launch written to inform might present events in **chronological order,** or the order in which they happened. This order will aid readers in following the series of events.
- A feature article comparing the space shuttle program with older programs might use **comparison-and-contrast organization,** grouping details according to their similarities and differences.
- An editorial about the space shuttle program written to persuade readers to support the program might have a **cause-and-effect organization.** By clearly showing how the program leads to important medical discoveries, for example, this organization could help convince readers.

Each part of a work plays its role in the development of ideas. For example, the author may organize the work into **sections,** or parts. In this case, each **paragraph** in a section would elaborate on the main idea of the section. In turn, each **sentence** within a paragraph would help develop the main idea of that paragraph. In this way, the various parts of a text work together to support the author's main idea, or thesis.

Author's Purpose and Word Choice

Whether an author's **purpose** is to inform, to persuade, or to entertain readers, the author will use words in ways designed to achieve his or her goal.

Diction An author's choice of words is called diction. By using simple diction—choosing familiar words—an author can make ideas clear. By using **technical language,** or language specific to a discipline, an author can be precise. By choosing words with strong **connotations,** or associations, an author can shape readers' views. For example, calling a situation *disastrous* creates one picture; calling it *challenging* creates a different picture.

Tone Word choice creates tone—the author's attitude toward the topic and audience. An author's tone may be formal or informal, solemn or playful, joyous or annoyed, and so on. For example, this sentence has a tone of outrage: *That scoundrel will disgrace our city!*

Figurative Language Authors also convey point of view using figurative language, or language not meant to be taken literally. Here are three common figures of speech:

- A **simile** is an indirect comparison of seemingly unlike things that contains the word *like* or *as: It was as tricky as skateboarding during an earthquake.*
- A **metaphor** describes one thing as if it were another, without using the words *like* or *as: Friendship is a warm place on a cold day.*
- **Personification** gives human traits—such as emotions, types of behavior, and even appearance—to a nonhuman subject: *The winter wind slapped my face with its icy hands.*

Rhetorical Devices and Purpose Rhetorical devices are patterns of words and ideas that writers use to emphasize points and to make them more memorable. If an author's purpose is to inform, he or she may use rhetorical devices to help readers remember key points. If an author's purpose is to persuade, he or she may use rhetorical devices that appeal to readers' emotions and stay in their minds. Rhetorical devices include the following forms.

Types of Rhetorical Devices

Repetition is the reuse of a key word, phrase, or idea:
He plays with skill. He plays with passion. He plays in a style all his own.

Parallel structure, or **parallelism,** is the use of similar grammatical structures to express related ideas:
The eagle soared above the treetops, into the heavens, and beyond reach.

Restatement is the expression of the same idea in different words to strengthen a point:
Aspire to greatness. (restatement 1:) *Aim high,* (restatement 2:) *and dream big.*

Rhetorical questions are inquiries that have obvious answers and that are asked for effect:
Is it really so much trouble to recycle? Isn't saving our planet worth your time?

Lorraine Hansberry (1930–1965) grew up on the South Side of Chicago, the daughter of a prosperous real-estate broker. With the 1959 production of her play *A Raisin in the Sun*, Hansberry became the first African American woman to have a drama produced on Broadway.

Is knowledge the same as understanding?

Explore the Big Question as you read "On Summer." Take notes about the details Hansberry uses to support her changing understanding of summer.

CLOSE READING FOCUS

Key Ideas and Details: **Main Idea**

The **main, or central, idea** is the key message, insight, or opinion expressed in a work of nonfiction. In some works, the author states his or her central idea directly. In other works the author suggests the central idea but does not state it explicitly. **Supporting details** help to develop the main idea by giving more information about it. These details may include facts, statistics, quotations, or anecdotes. Authors use supporting details to connect one idea to another, creating a continuous line of reasoning or thinking that supports and proves the main idea.

Craft and Structure: **Author's Style**

An **author's style** is his or her unique way of using language. Elements that contribute to an author's style include the following:

- **Diction:** the specific word choices the author makes
- **Syntax:** the arrangement of words in sentences

Individual words carry various shades of meaning, as well as different levels of formality and complexity. Because of these nuances, an author's diction and syntax are a key part of his or her unique style. These literary elements also contribute to the author's **tone,** or attitude toward the audience or subject. An author's tone may express any attitude—from playful to vicious—that a human being can feel.

Vocabulary

The words below are critical to understanding the text that follows. Copy the words into your notebook. Which word is a synonym for *prejudice*?

aloofness	**melancholy**	**bias**
duration	**pretentious**	**apex**

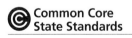

Common Core State Standards

Reading Informational Text

1. Cite strong and thorough textual evidence to support analysis of what the text says explicitly as well as inferences drawn from the text.

2. Determine a central idea of a text and analyze in detail its development, including how it is shaped and refined by specific details.

3. Analyze how the author unfolds an analysis or series of ideas or events, including the order in which the points are made, how they are introduced and developed, and the connections that are drawn between them.

4. Determine the meaning of words and phrases as they are used in a text; analyze the cumulative impact of specific word choices on meaning and tone.

CLOSE READING MODEL

The passage below is from Lorraine Hansberry's essay "On Summer." The annotations to the right of the passage show ways in which you can use close reading skills to identify the main idea and details and analyze the author's style.

from "On Summer"

It has taken me a good number of years to come to any measure of respect for summer.[1] I was, being May-born, literally an "infant of the spring" and, during the later childhood years, tended, for some reason or other, to rather worship the cold aloofness of winter. The adolescence, admittedly lingering still, brought the traditional passionate commitment to melancholy autumn—and all that.[2] For the longest kind of time I simply thought that *summer* was a mistake.

In fact, my earliest memory of anything at all is of waking up in a darkened room where I had been put to bed for a nap on a summer's afternoon, and feeling very, very hot. I acutely disliked the feeling then and retained the bias for years.[3] It had originally been a matter of the heat but, over the years, I came actively to associate displeasure with most of the usually celebrated natural features and social by-products of the season: the too-grainy texture of sand; the too-cold coldness of the various waters we constantly try to escape into, and the icky-perspiry feeling of bathing caps.[4]

Main Idea

1 Hansberry begins the essay with a direct statement: It took her "a good number of years" to find "any measure of respect" for summer. These details suggest that she will discuss her changing attitudes toward summer.

Author's Style

2 Some of the author's diction, including "May-born" and "rather worship," is old-fashioned and formal. However, the phrase "and all that" is modern slang. This mix of old-fashioned and modern, and formal and informal, creates a tone that is serious but not heavy or grave.

Main Idea

3 This anecdote further develops the author's main idea. *Bias* refers to an unfair prejudice. The author recognizes that her feelings about summer are, at this time in her life biased, or unfair.

Author's Style

4 Hansberry's adjectives—"too-grainy," "too-cold"—are distinctive. The repetition emphasizes how overwhelming the young Hansberry found the sensations of summer. The use of the childish word "icky" reinforces the idea that she is discussing her point of view as a little girl.

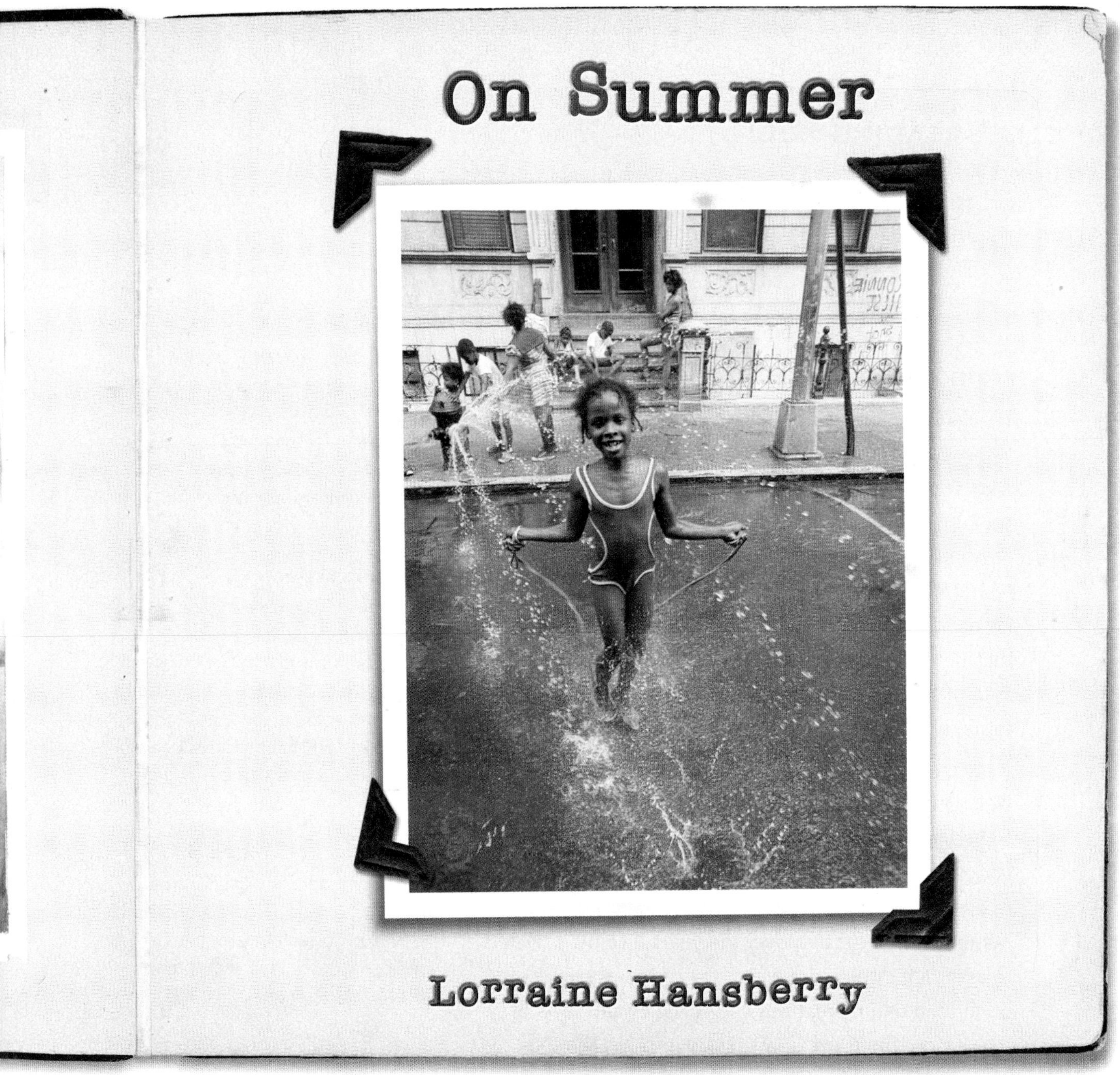

On Summer

Lorraine Hansberry

Vocabulary ▶
aloofness (ə lo͞of′ nəs) *n.* emotional distance

melancholy (mel′ ən käl′ ē) *adj.* sad; gloomy

It has taken me a good number of years to come to any measure of respect for summer. I was, being May-born, literally an "infant of the spring" and, during the later childhood years, tended, for some reason or other, to rather worship the cold aloofness of winter. The adolescence, admittedly lingering still, brought the traditional passionate commitment to melancholy autumn—and all that. For the longest kind of time I simply thought that *summer* was a mistake.

In fact, my earliest memory of anything at all is of waking up in a darkened room where I had been put to bed for a nap on a summer's afternoon, and feeling very, very hot. I acutely disliked the feeling then and retained the **bias** for years. It had originally been a matter of the heat but, over the years, I came actively to associate displeasure with most of the usually celebrated natural features and social by-products of the season: the too-grainy texture of sand; the too-cold coldness of the various waters we constantly try to escape into, and the icky-perspiry feeling of bathing caps.

It also seemed to me, esthetically[1] speaking, that nature had got inexcusably carried away on the summer question and let the whole thing get to be rather much. By **duration** alone, for instance, a summer's day seemed maddeningly excessive; an utter overstatement. Except for those few hours at either end of it, objects always appeared in too sharp a relief against backgrounds; shadows too pronounced and light too blinding. It always gave me the feeling of walking around in a motion picture which had been too artsily-craftsily exposed. Sound also had a way of coming to the ear without that muting influence, marvelously common to winter, across patios or beaches or through the woods. I suppose I found it too stark and yet too intimate a season.

My childhood Southside summers were the ordinary city kind, full of the street games which other rememberers have turned into fine ballets these days and rhymes that anticipated what some people insist on calling modern poetry:

Oh, Mary Mack, Mack, Mack
All dressed in black, black, black
With the silver buttons, buttons, buttons
All down her back, back, back
She asked her mother, mother, mother
For fifteen cents, cents, cents
To see the elephant, elephant, elephant
Jump the fence, fence, fence
Well, he jumped so high, high, high
'Til he touched the sky, sky, sky
And he didn't come back, back, back
'Til the Fourth of Ju-ly, ly, ly!

Evenings were spent mainly on the back porches where screen doors slammed in the darkness with those really very special summertime sounds. And, sometimes, when Chicago nights got too steamy, the whole family got into the car and went to the park and slept out in the

Author's Style
How would you describe Hansberry's tone as she explains her childhood feelings about summer?

◀ **Vocabulary**
bias (bī´ əs) *n.* mental leaning or inclination; partiality

duration (do͞o rā´ shən) *n.* time that a thing continues or lasts

Author's Style
What effect does the use of the made-up word "artsily-craftsily" create?

Comprehension
Identify one thing the author dislikes about summer.

1. **esthetically** (es thet´ ik lē) *adv.* artistically.

Author's Style
How does Hansberry's repeated use of the word *and* to begin sentences emphasize the flow and abundance of her memories?

Spiral Review
AUTHOR'S POINT OF VIEW Why do you think the author chose to relate this episode through her childhood perspective?

Main Idea
What do these anecdotes about her trips to Tennessee add to your understanding of the author's childhood summers?

open on blankets. Those were, of course, the best times of all because the grownups were invariably reminded of having been children in rural parts of the country and told the best stories then. And it was also cool and sweet to be on the grass and there was usually the scent of freshly cut lemons or melons in the air. And Daddy would lie on his back, as fathers must, and explain about how men thought the stars above us came to be and how far away they were. I never did learn to believe that anything could be as far away as *that*. Especially the stars.

My mother first took us south to visit her Tennessee birthplace one summer when I was seven or eight, I think. I woke up on the back seat of the car while we were still driving through some place called Kentucky and my mother was pointing out to the beautiful hills on both sides of the highway and telling my brothers and my sister about how her father had run away and hidden from his master in those very hills when he was a little boy. She said that his mother had wandered among the wooded slopes in the moonlight and left food for him in secret places. They were very beautiful hills and I looked out at them for miles and miles after that wondering who and what a *master* might be.

I remember being startled when I first saw my grandmother rocking away on her porch. All my life I had heard that she was a great beauty and no one had ever remarked that they meant a half century before. The woman that I met was as wrinkled as a prune and could hardly hear and barely see and always seemed to be thinking of other times. But she could still rock and talk and even make wonderful cupcakes which were like cornbread, only sweet. She was captivated by automobiles and, even though it was well into the Thirties,[2] I don't think she had ever been in one before we came down and took her driving. She was a little afraid of them and could not seem to negotiate the windows, but she loved driving. She died the next summer and that is all that I remember about her, except that she was born in slavery and had memories of it and they didn't sound anything like *Gone With the Wind*.[3]

Like everyone else, I have spent whole or bits of summers in many different kinds of places since then: camps and resorts in the Middle West and New York State; on an island; in a tiny Mexican village; Cape Cod, perched atop the Truro bluffs at Longnook Beach that Millay wrote about; or simply strolling the streets of Provincetown[4] before the hours when the parties begin.

And, lastly, I do not think that I will forget days spent, a few summers ago, at a beautiful lodge built right into the rocky cliffs

---

2. **Thirties** the 1930s.
3. ***Gone With the Wind*** novel set in the South during the Civil War period.
4. **Provincetown** resort town at the northern tip of Cape Cod, Massachusetts.

of a bay on the Maine coast. We met a woman there who had lived a purposeful and courageous life and who was then dying of cancer. She had, characteristically, just written a book and taken up painting. She had also been of radical viewpoint all her life; one of those people who energetically believe that the world *can* be changed for the better and spend their lives trying to do just that. And that was the way she thought of cancer; she absolutely refused to award it the stature of tragedy, a devastating instance of the brooding doom and inexplicability[5] of the absurdity of human destiny, etc., etc. The kind of characterization given, lately, as we all know, to far less formidable foes in life than cancer.

But for this remarkable woman it was a matter of nature in imperfection, implying, as always, work for man to do. It was an *enemy*, but a palpable one with shape and effect and source; and if it existed, it could be destroyed. She saluted it accordingly, without despondency, but with a lively, beautiful and delightfully ribald anger. There was one thing, she felt, which would prove equal to its relentless ravages and that was the genius of man. Not his mysticism, but man with tubes and slides and the stubborn human notion that the stars are very much within our reach.

Comprehension
Whom does Hansberry visit in Tennessee?

5. **inexplicability** (in eks′ pli kə bil′ ə tē) *n.* condition of being unexplainable.

Author's Style
What words has Hansberry used to convey her feelings about the woman in Maine?

Vocabulary ▶
pretentious (prē ten′ shəs) *adj.* grand in a showy way

apex (ā′ peks′) *n.* highest point; peak

The last time I saw her she was sitting surrounded by her paintings with her manuscript laid out for me to read, because, she said, she wanted to know what a *young person* would think of her thinking; one must always keep up with what *young people* thought about things because, after all, they were *change.*

Every now and then her jaw set in anger as we spoke of things people should be angry about. And then, for relief, she would look out at the lovely bay at a mellow sunset settling on the water. Her face softened with love of all that beauty and, watching her, I wished with all my power what I knew that she was wishing: that she might live to see at least one more *summer.* Through her eyes I finally gained the sense of what it might mean; more than the coming autumn with its **pretentious** melancholy; more than an austere and silent winter which must shut dying people in for precious months; more even than the frivolous spring, too full of too many false promises, would be the gift of another summer with its stark and intimate assertion of neither birth nor death but life at the **apex**; with the gentlest nights and, above all, the longest days.

I heard later that she did live to see another summer. And I have retained my respect for the noblest of the seasons.

Language Study

Vocabulary The italicized words in each sentence below appear in "On Summer." Determine whether each sentence is usually true or usually false. Use the meaning of the italicized word to explain your thinking.

1. Greeting a close friend with *aloofness* shows affection.
2. Cheerful songs might change someone's *melancholy* mood.
3. A *pretentious* politician is likely to be unpopular with many voters.
4. One must climb a mountain to reach its *apex*.
5. If a man has a *bias* toward cats, he feels neutral about them.

WORD STUDY

The **Latin root *-dur-*** means "to harden," "to hold out," or "to last." In this essay, the author describes the long **duration** of a summer day. She means that the day seems to last for a long time.

Word Study

Part A Explain how the **Latin root *-dur-*** contributes to the meanings of *obdurate, endure,* and *duress.* Consult a dictionary if necessary.

Part B Use the context of the sentences and what you know about the Latin root *-dur-* to explain your answer to each question.

1. If a manufacturer claims an item is *durable*, would you expect it to wear out quickly?
2. When a thief is caught *during* a robbery, has he or she been caught in the act?

Close Reading Activities

Literary Analysis

Key Ideas and Details

1. **(a)** When does Hansberry first visit her grandmother? **(b) Infer:** Why do you think she includes the section about her grandmother in her essay? Which details from the text support your inferences?
2. **Interpret:** What do the anecdotes about her trips to Tennessee add to your understanding of the author's childhood summers? Cite textual details to support your response.
3. **Main Idea (a)** State the main idea of "On Summer" in your own words. **(b)** List three supporting details that serve as evidence for the main idea. **(c)** Does the author adequately support her main idea with details? Explain.

Craft and Structure

4. **Author's Style** What one word might you use to describe the overall tone of "On Summer"? Explain your answer, citing details from the essay that help to convey that tone.
5. **Author's Style** Reread the last two paragraphs of "On Summer." Use a chart like the one shown to record examples of the diction Hansberry uses in describing her associations with summer. Identify the tone each example helps to create. Then, based on her diction and tone in these paragraphs, write three adjectives to describe Hansberry's style.

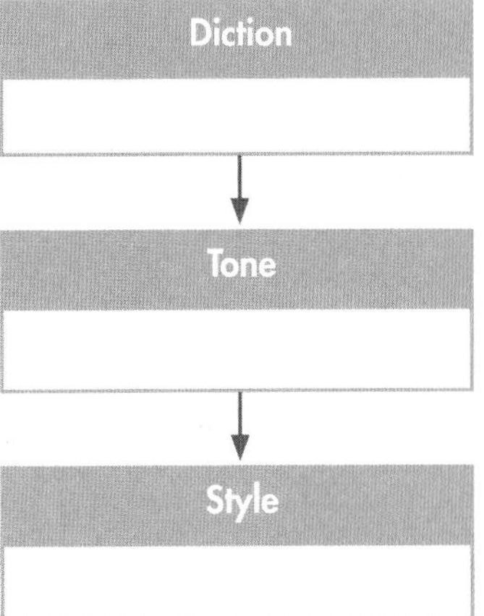

6. **Evaluate:** How clearly do you think Hansberry explains the way her feelings about summer change from childhood to adulthood? Explain your position, identifying evidence from the text to support your point of view.

Integration of Knowledge and Ideas

7. **(a) Interpret:** When does Hansberry's attitude toward summer begin to change? **(b) Support:** What experiences or insights account for this change? Explain.
8. **Define:** At the essay's end, Hansberry calls summer "the noblest of the seasons." What do you think she means by this phrase? Use evidence from the text in your explanation.

9. THE BIG ? **Is knowledge the same as understanding? (a)** In what ways does Hansberry's *knowledge* of summer stay the same from childhood to adulthood? **(b)** Does her *understanding* of summer change? Explain, citing details from the text to support your response.

ACADEMIC VOCABULARY

As you write and speak about "On Summer," use the words related to knowledge and understanding that you explored on page 189 of this book.

Conventions: Direct and Indirect Objects

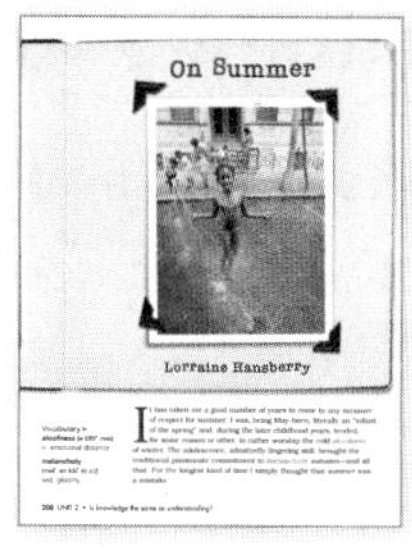

A **direct object** is a noun or pronoun that receives the action of an action verb. An **indirect object** appears with a direct object and names the person or thing that something is *given to* or *done for*.

You can determine whether a word is a direct object by asking *Whom?* or *What?* after an action verb. You can tell whether a word is an indirect object by asking *To* or *for whom?* or *To* or *for what?* An indirect object can only appear between a subject and a direct object.

Example	Explanation
I acutely disliked the **feeling**.	*Feeling* is a direct object; it answers the question *Disliked what?*
I remember being startled when I first saw my **grandmother**.	*Grandmother* is a direct object; it answers the question *Saw whom?*
The grownups told the **children stories**.	*Children* is an indirect object; it answers the question *Told to whom?* *Stories* is a direct object; it answers the question *Told what?*
My grandmother had left **me food**.	*Me* is an indirect object; it answers the question *Left for whom?* *Food* is a direct object; it answers the question *Left what?*

Practice A

Identify the direct and indirect objects in each sentence.

1. The author met a woman.
2. The woman showed her a manuscript.
3. The woman showed Lorraine Hansberry courage.
4. Hansberry gained a sense of meaning from the woman.

Reading Application Find two sentences in the essay that use direct objects.

Practice B

For each item, write an original sentence using the word or phrase as directed by the information in parentheses.

1. winter (as a direct object)
2. Maine coast (as a direct object in a question)
3. author (as an indirect object), manuscript (as a direct object)
4. grandmother (as an indirect object), gift (as a direct object)

Writing Application Use this sentence starter to write three sentences that each contain an indirect object (IO) and a direct object (DO): *I gave (IO) (DO).*

Writing to Sources

Explanatory Text In "On Summer," Hansberry presents a strong, personal view of a season. By exploring her feelings toward summer Hansberry shows how she changed over time and what she learned about life. Write an **analysis** of the text that identifies the qualities the author associates with summer at different points in her life.

- Write an outline that lists the order of events in Hansberry's life as presented in the selection.
- Choose details from the text that show how Hansberry feels about summer at each of the various points on your outline.
- Include an exploration of specific words Hansberry uses to support her perceptions of summer at the different stages of her life. For example, Hansberry comes to define summer as the "noblest" of seasons. In your essay, explain what *noble* means. Explain the details in Hansberry's essay that support her view of summer as a time of nobility.
- Conclude by discussing what Hansberry learns about herself and about life through her exploration of her attitudes toward summer.

Grammar Application After you finish your essay, review your draft to identify the direct and indirect objects you have used.

Speaking and Listening

Presentation of Ideas In a small group, hold a **panel discussion** on how the attitudes and opinions of others do or do not shape one's beliefs. Follow these steps to complete the assignment.

- To prepare, each panel member should review "On Summer," noting moments in which people's attitudes and opinions do not affect Hansberry's perceptions. Then, identify circumstances in which people and events do change Hansberry's view.
- Prepare notes to use during the discussion. These will help you keep on track and remind you about what you have planned to say.
- During the discussion, state your ideas clearly, and clarify them further if necessary. Help elaborate on the ideas of other panel members by adding useful supporting details.
- Use strong evidence from the text to support your points of view. You may also bring in other evidence, such as your own observations or any facts or data about the ways in which people influence one another.
- Consider recording your discussion and posting the video to a class or school Web site or blog. Then, invite other students to post responses.

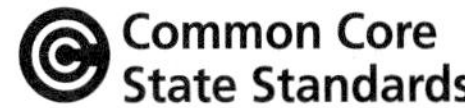

Common Core State Standards

Writing

2. Write informative/explanatory texts to examine and convey complex ideas, concepts, and information clearly and accurately through the effective selection, organization, and analysis of content.

2.a. Introduce a topic, organize complex ideas, concepts, and information to make important connections and distinctions.

2.b. Develop the topic with well-chosen, relevant, and sufficient facts, concrete details, or other information and examples.

2.d. Use precise language and domain-specific vocabulary to manage the complexity of the topic.

2.f. Provide a concluding statement or section that follows from and supports the information or explanation presented.

Speaking and Listening

1. Initiate and participate effectively in a range of collaborative discussions with diverse partners.

Language

1. Demonstrate command of the conventions of standard English grammar and usage when writing or speaking.

Building Knowledge

Meet the Author

Neil Postman (1931–2003) was a media critic and a revered professor of communications at New York University, where he taught for more than forty years. He called his field "media ecology," and his great concern was the effect of television on Americans. One of his most passionate arguments is set forth in *The Disappearance of Childhood* (1982), in which he asserts that television exposes children to adult concerns far too early in their lives.

Common Core State Standards

Reading Informational Text

1. Cite strong and thorough textual evidence to support analysis of what the text says explicitly as well as inferences drawn from the text.

2. Determine a central idea of a text and analyze its development over the course of the text; provide an objective summary of the text.

3. Analyze how the author unfolds an analysis or series of ideas or events.

5. Analyze in detail how an author's ideas or claims are developed and refined by particular sentences, paragraphs, or larger portions of a text.

Is knowledge the same as understanding?

Explore the Big Question as you read "The News." Take notes about how the author differentiates between information and understanding in TV news.

CLOSE READING FOCUS

Key Ideas and Details: **Main Idea**

The **main, or central, idea** is the key message, insight, or opinion expressed in a work of nonfiction. The author may state the central idea explicitly, or merely suggest it. **Supporting details** are the pieces of evidence a writer uses to prove his or her point. Reread to analyze the main idea in a text and to understand how it is introduced, developed with related ideas, and supported with evidence.

- Pay attention to the way in which the author introduces an idea and how he or she supports it with evidence. Identify the types of evidence the author uses.
- Notice how the author transitions from one idea to the next, and identify the ways in which ideas relate to those that precede and follow.

Craft and Structure: **Expository Essay**

An **expository essay** is a work of nonfiction that presents information, discusses ideas, or explains a process. An essay writer may use a variety of techniques to introduce and develop ideas and to draw connections among them.

- **Description:** use of imagery and figurative language, such as similes and metaphors, to help readers visualize ideas
- **Comparison and Contrast:** presentation of similarities and differences among ideas
- **Cause and Effect:** analysis of relationships between events or situations by showing how one can result from another

Vocabulary

The words below are critical to understanding the text that follows. Copy the words into your notebook and note which ones are nouns. Explain how you know.

compensation	temporal	medium
imposition	revered	daunting

CLOSE READING MODEL

The passage below is from Neil Postman's essay "The News." The annotations to the right of the passage show ways in which you can use close reading skills to determine the central idea and analyze how the author develops ideas.

from "The News"

While the form of a news broadcast emphasizes tidiness and control, its content can best be described as chaotic.[1] Because time is so precious on television, because the nature of the medium favors dynamic visual images, and because the pressures of a commercial structure require the news to hold its audience above all else, there is rarely any attempt to explain issues in depth or place events in their proper context.[2] The news moves nervously from a warehouse fire to a court decision, from a guerrilla war to a World Cup match,[3] the quality of the film often determining the length of the story. Certain stories show up only because they offer dramatic pictures. Bleachers collapse in South America: hundreds of people are crushed—a perfect television news story, for the cameras can record the face of disaster in all its anguish. Back in Washington, a new budget is approved by Congress. Here there is nothing to photograph because a budget is not a physical event; it is a document full of language and numbers.[4]

Main Idea

1 "Tidiness" often refers to little things being put away, whereas "chaotic" suggests powerful forces set loose. So, as Postman explicitly states one key idea he also implicitly suggests another: A newscast reduces important information into small, "tidy" but unrelated bits.

Expository Essay

2 Beginning three clauses with the word "because," the author briefly lists reasons TV news is shallow. The quick list is a reminder to readers about basic facts. It establishes a premise from which Postman can continue his analysis.

Main Idea

3 The author uses the word *nervously* to characterize a newscast. This is a form of figurative language called personification, in which an inanimate thing is described in human terms. This single word makes the newscast itself seem like an anxious person seeking attention.

Expository Essay

4 Postman makes a point about TV newscasts being driven by the need for "dramatic pictures." He then proves the point with the example of a "perfect" story that shows the "face of disaster."

The NEWS

Neil Postman

Vocabulary ▶
compensation
(käm´ pən sā´ shən) *n.* anything that makes up for a loss, damage, or debt

temporal
(tem´ pə rəl) *adj.* having to do with time

The whole problem with news on television comes down to this: all the words uttered in an hour of news coverage could be printed on one page of a newspaper. And the world cannot be understood in one page. Of course, there is a compensation: television offers pictures, and the pictures move. It is often said that moving pictures are a kind of language in themselves, and there is a good deal of truth in this. But the language of pictures differs radically from oral and written language, and the differences are crucial for understanding television news.

To begin with, the grammar of pictures is weak in communicating past-ness and present-ness. When terrorists want to prove to the world that their kidnap victims are still alive, they photograph them holding a copy of a recent newspaper. The dateline on the newspaper provides the proof that the photograph was taken on or after that date. Without the help of the written word, film and videotape cannot portray temporal dimensions with any precision. Consider a film clip showing an aircraft carrier at sea. One might be able to identify the ship as Soviet[1] or American, but there would be no way of telling where in the world the carrier was, where it was headed, or when the pictures were taken. It is only through language—words spoken over the pictures or reproduced in them—that the image of the aircraft carrier takes on meaning as a portrayal of a specific event.

1. **Soviet** (sō´ vē et´) *adj.* belonging to the Soviet Union, the formerly socialist nation in which the controlling state was Russia.

But the language of pictures differs radically from oral and written language, and the differences are crucial for understanding television news.

Still, it is possible to enjoy the image of the carrier for its own sake. One might find the hugeness of the vessel interesting; it signifies military power on the move. There is a certain drama in watching the planes come in at high speeds and skid to a stop on the deck. Suppose the ship were burning: that would be even more interesting. This leads to a second point about the language of pictures. The grammar of moving pictures favors images that change. That is why violence and destruction find their way onto television so often. When something is destroyed violently its constitution is altered in a highly visible way: hence the entrancing power of fire. Fire gives visual form to the ideas of consumption, disappearance, death—the thing which is burned is actually taken away by fire. It is at this very basic level that fires make a good subject for television news. Something was here, now it's gone, and the change is recorded on film.

Expository Essay
How do details about airplanes and fire support Postman's point that television favors change?

Earthquakes and typhoons have the same power: before the viewer's eyes the world is taken apart. If a television viewer has relatives in Mexico City and an earthquake occurs there, then she may take an interest in the images of destruction as a report from a specific place and time. That is, she may look to television news for information about an important event. But film of an earthquake can still be interesting if the viewer cares nothing about the event itself. Which is only to say that there is another way of participating in the news—as a spectator who desires to be entertained. Actually to see buildings topple is exciting, no matter where the buildings are. The world turns to dust before our eyes.

Comprehension
What does Postman mean by the "grammar" of pictures?

Vocabulary ▶
medium (mē´ dē əm)
n. a particular way of communicating information and news to people, such as a newspaper or a television broadcast

Those who produce television news in America know that their medium favors images that move. That is why they despise "talking heads," people who simply appear in front of a camera and speak. When talking heads appear on television, there is nothing to record or document, no change in process. In the cinema the situation is somewhat different. On a movie screen, close-ups of a good actor speaking dramatically can sometimes be interesting to watch. When Clint Eastwood narrows his eyes and challenges his rival to shoot first, the spectator sees the cool rage of the Eastwood character take visual form, and the narrowing of the eyes is dramatic. But much of the effect of this small movement depends on the size of the movie screen and the darkness of the theater, which make Eastwood and his every action "larger than life."

The television screen is smaller than life. It occupies about 15 percent of the viewer's visual field (compared to about 70 percent for the movie screen). It is not set in a darkened theater closed off from the world but in the viewer's ordinary living space. This means that visual changes must be more extreme and more dramatic to be interesting on television. A narrowing of the eyes will not do. A car crash, an earthquake, a burning factory are much better.

Expository Essay
What topic will Postman analyze more closely in this essay?

With these principles in mind, let us examine more closely the structure of a typical newscast. In America, almost all news shows begin with music, the tone of which suggests important events about to unfold. (Beethoven's Fifth Symphony would be entirely appropriate.) The music is very important, for it equates the news with various forms of drama and ritual—the opera, for example, or a wedding procession—in which musical themes underscore the meaning of the event. Music takes us immediately into the realm of the symbolic, a world that is not to be taken literally. After all, when events unfold in the real world, they do so without musical accompaniment. More symbolism follows. The sound of teletype machines can be heard in the studio, not because it is impossible to screen this noise out, but because the sound is a kind of music in itself. It tells us that data are pouring in from all corners of the globe, a sensation reinforced by the world map in the background (or clocks noting the time on different continents).

Already, then, before a single news item is introduced, a great deal has been communicated. We know that we are in the presence of a symbolic event, a form of theater in which the day's events are to be dramatized. This theater takes the entire globe as its subject, although it may look at the world from the perspective of a single nation. A certain tension is present, like the atmosphere in a theater just before the curtain goes up. The tension is represented by the music, the staccato beat of the teletype machines, and the sight of newsworkers scurrying around typing reports and answering phones. As a technical matter, it would be no problem to build a set in which the newsroom staff remained off camera, invisible to the viewer, but an important theatrical effect would be lost. By being busy on camera, the workers help communicate urgency about the events at hand, which it is suggested are changing so rapidly that constant revision of the news is necessary.

Main Idea
How do these descriptive details support Postman's idea that a newscast is a form of theater?

This theater takes the entire globe as its subject, although it may look at the world from the perspective of a single nation.

The staff in the background also helps signal the importance of the person in the center, the anchorman (or -woman) "in command" of both the staff and the news. The anchorman plays the role of host. He welcomes us to the newscast and welcomes us back from the different locations we visit during filmed reports. His voice, appearance, and manner establish the mood of the broadcast. It would be unthinkable for the anchor to be ugly, or a nervous sort who could not complete a sentence. Viewers must be able to believe in the anchor as a person of authority and skill, a person who would not panic in a crisis—someone to trust.

This belief is based not on knowledge of the anchorman's character or achievements as a journalist, but on his presentation of self while on the air. Does he look the part of a trusted man? Does he speak firmly and clearly? Does he have a warm smile? Does he project confidence without seeming arrogant? The value the anchor must communicate above all else is control. He must be in control of himself, his voice, his emotions. He must know what is coming next in the broadcast, and he must move smoothly and

Comprehension
What are "talking heads," and why do television producers despise them?

▲ Critical Viewing How does this image relate to the idea of people connecting to their world through the news?

confidently from segment to segment. Again, it would be unthinkable for the anchor to break down and weep over a story, or laugh uncontrollably on camera, no matter how "human" these responses may be.

Many other features of the newscast help the anchor to establish the impression of control. These are usually equated with professionalism in broadcasting. They include such things as graphics that tell the viewer what is being shown, or maps and charts that suddenly appear on the screen and disappear on cue, or the orderly progression from story to story, starting with the most important events first. They also include the absence of gaps or "deadtime" during the broadcast, even the simple fact that the news starts and ends at a certain hour. These common features are thought of as purely technical matters, which a professional crew handles as a matter of course. But they are also symbols of a dominant theme of television news: the **imposition** of an orderly world—called "the news"—upon the disorderly flow of events.

Vocabulary ▶ **imposition** (im′ pə zish′ ən) *n.* the introduction of something such as a rule, tax, or punishment

While the form of a news broadcast emphasizes tidiness and control, its content can best be described as chaotic. Because time is so precious on television, because the nature of the medium favors dynamic visual images, and because the pressures of a commercial structure require the news to hold its audience above all else, there is rarely any attempt to explain issues in depth or place events in their proper context. The news moves nervously from a warehouse fire to a court decision, from a guerrilla war to a World Cup match, the quality of the film often determining the length of the story. Certain stories show up only because they offer dramatic pictures. Bleachers collapse in South America: hundreds of people are crushed—a perfect television news story, for the cameras can record the face of disaster in all its anguish. Back in Washington, a new budget is approved by Congress. Here there is nothing to photograph because a budget is not a physical event; it is a document full of language and numbers. So the producers of the news will show a photo of the document itself, focusing on the cover where it says: "Budget of the United States of America." Or sometimes they will send a camera crew to the government printing plant where copies of the budget are produced. That evening, while the contents of the budget are summarized by a voice-over, the viewer sees stacks of documents being loaded into boxes at the government printing plant. Then a few of the budget's more important provisions will be flashed on the screen in written form, but this is such a time-consuming process—using television as a printed page—that the producers keep it to a minimum. In short, the budget is not televisable, and for that reason its time on the news must be brief. The bleacher collapse will get more minutes that evening.

With priorities of this sort, it is almost impossible for the news to offer an adequate account of important events. Indeed, it is the trivial event that is often best suited for television coverage. This is such a commonplace that no one even bothers to challenge it. Walter Cronkite, a revered figure in television and anchorman of the CBS Evening News for many years, has acknowledged several times that television cannot be relied on to inform the citizens of a democratic nation. Unless they also read newspapers and magazines, television viewers are helpless to understand their world, Cronkite has said. No one at CBS has ever disagreed with his conclusion, other than to say, "We do the best we can."

◀ **Vocabulary**
revered (ri vird′) *adj.* regarded with great respect and awe

Of course, it is a tendency of journalism in general to concentrate on the surface of events rather than underlying conditions; this is as true for the newspaper as it is for the newscast. But several features of television undermine whatever efforts journalists may make to give sense to the world. One is that a television broadcast is a series of events that occur in sequence, and the sequence is the same for all viewers. This is not true for a newspaper page, which displays many items simultaneously, allowing readers to choose the order in which they read them. If a newspaper reader wants only a summary of the latest tax bill, he can read the headline and the first paragraph of an article, and if he wants more, he can keep reading. In a sense, then, everyone reads a different newspaper, for no two readers will read (or ignore) the same items.

Expository Essay
According to Postman, how are newspaper and television journalism similar and different?

Comprehension
According to Postman, why must a news anchorperson convey *control* above all other values?

But all television viewers see the same broadcast. They have no choices. A report is either in the broadcast or out, which means that anything which is of narrow interest is unlikely to be included. As NBC News executive Reuven Frank once explained:

> A newspaper, for example, can easily afford to print an item of conceivable interest to only a fraction of its readers. A television news program must be put together with the assumption that each item will be of some interest to everyone that watches. Every time a newspaper includes a feature which will attract a specialized group it can assume it is adding at least a little bit to its circulation. To the degree a television news program includes an item of this sort . . . it must assume that its audience will diminish.

Vocabulary ▶
daunting (dônt′ iŋ) *adj.* intimidating

The need to "include everyone," an identifying feature of commercial television in all its forms, prevents journalists from offering lengthy or complex explanations, or from tracing the sequence of events leading up to today's headlines. One of the ironies of political life in modern democracies is that many problems which concern the "general welfare" are of interest only to specialized groups. Arms control, for example, is an issue that literally concerns everyone in the world, and yet the language of arms control and the complexity of the subject are so daunting that only a minority of people can actually follow the issue from week to week and month to month. If it wants to act responsibly, a newspaper can at least make available more information about arms control than most people want. But commercial television cannot afford to do so.

This illustrates an important point in the psychology of television's appeal. Many of the items in newspapers and magazines are not, in a strict sense, demanded by a majority of readers. They are there because some readers *might* be interested or because the editors think their readers *should* be interested. On commercial television, "might" and "should" are not the relevant words. The producers attempt to make sure that "each item will be of some interest to everyone that watches," as Reuven Frank put it. What this means is that a newspaper or magazine can challenge its audience in a way that television cannot. Print media have the luxury of suggesting or inviting interest, whereas television must always concern itself with conforming to existing interests. In a way, television is more strictly responsive to the demands of its huge audience. But there is one demand it cannot meet: the desire to be challenged, to be told "this is worth attending to," to be surprised by what one thought would not be of interest.

Another severe limitation on television is time. There is simply not enough of it. The evening news programs at CBS, NBC, and ABC all run for thirty minutes, eight of which are taken up by commercials. No one believes that twenty-two minutes for the day's news is adequate. For years news executives at ABC, NBC, and CBS have suggested that the news be expanded to one hour. But by tradition the half-hour after the national evening news is given over to the hundreds of local affiliate stations around the country to use as they see fit. They have found it a very profitable time to broadcast game shows or half-hour situation comedies, and they are reluctant to give up the income they derive from these programs.

Spiral Review
WORD CHOICE AND TONE Does the use of words and phrases such as *severe limitation, by tradition, affiliate stations,* and *situation comedies* contribute to an appropriate tone for the author's message? Explain.

The evening news produced by the three networks is profitable for both the networks and the local stations. The local stations are paid a fee by the network to broadcast the network news, and they profit from this fee since the news—produced by the network—costs them nothing. It is likely that they would also make money from a one-hour newscast, but not as much, they judge, as they do from the game shows and comedies they now schedule.

The result is that the evening news must try to do what cannot reasonably be done: give a decent account of the day's events in twenty-two minutes.

The result is that the evening news must try to do what cannot reasonably be done: give a decent account of the day's events in twenty-two minutes. What the viewer gets instead is a series of impressions, many of them purely visual, most of them unconnected to each other or to any sense of a history unfolding. Taken together, they suggest a world that is fundamentally ungovernable, where events do not arise out of historical conditions but rather explode from the heavens in a series of disasters that suggest a permanent state of crisis. It is this crisis—highly visual, ahistorical, and unsolvable—which the evening news presents as theater every evening.

Expository Essay
What sense of the world does television news cause?

The audience for this theater is offered a contradictory pair of responses. On the one hand, it is reassured by the smooth presentation of the news itself, especially the firm voice and steady gaze of the trusty anchorman. Newscasts frequently end with a "human-interest story," often with a sentimental or comic touch.

Comprehension
According to Postman, why are television news broadcasts so short?

Main Idea
What main idea does the anecdote about the little girl support?

Example: a little girl in Chicago writes Gorbachev a letter, and he answers her, saying that he and President Reagan are trying to work out their differences. This item reassures viewers that all is well, leaders are in command, we can still communicate with each other, and so on. But—and now we come to the other hand—the rest of the broadcast has told a different story. It has shown the audience a world that is out of control and incomprehensible, full of violence, disaster, and suffering. Whatever authority the anchorman may project through his steady manner is undermined by the terror inspired by the news itself.

This is where television news is at its most radical—not in giving publicity to radical causes, but in producing the impression of an ungovernable world. And it produces this impression not because the people who work in television are leftists or anarchists.[2] The anarchy in television news is a direct result of the commercial structure of broadcasting, which introduces into news judgments a single-mindedness more powerful than any ideology: the overwhelming need to keep people watching.

---

2. **leftists . . . anarchists** (an′ ər kists′) leftists desire to change the existing political order in the name of greater freedom for all; anarchists oppose any political authority.

Language Study

Vocabulary The words listed below appear in "The News." Using your knowledge of these words, identify the word in each numbered item that does not belong. Then, explain your response.

compensation **medium** **imposition** **revered** **daunting**

1. compensation, repayment, donation
2. revered, scorned, ridiculed
3. daunting, challenging, tempting
4. medium, magazine, memory
5. law, imposition, stamp

WORD STUDY
The **Latin root *-temp-*** means "time." In this essay, the author comments that film alone cannot accurately show the **temporal**, or time, aspects of events.

Word Study

Part A Explain how the **Latin root *-temp-*** contributes to the meanings of *temporize, extemporaneous,* and *contemporary*. Consult a dictionary if necessary.

Part B Use the context of the sentences and what you know about the Latin root *-temp-* to explain your answer to each question.

1. Is it essential for a musician to keep a reliable *tempo* while performing?
2. Should an employee plan to hold a *temporary* job for many years?

Close Reading Activities

Literary Analysis

Key Ideas and Details

1. **(a)** According to Postman, how long do TV news professionals feel the evening newscast should take to present information? **(b) Analyze Cause and Effect:** In Postman's view, what effects do time limits have on television news? Explain, citing details from the text.
2. **(a)** According to Postman, what role does the anchorperson play during a newscast? **(b) Connect:** How does the impression created by the anchor contrast with the "radical" nature of television? Explain.
3. **Main Idea** Restate the central idea of "The News" in your own words.
4. **Main Idea (a)** List three supporting details that serve as evidence for the points that Neil Postman makes. **(b)** Does the author adequately support his main idea with details? Explain.

Craft and Structure

5. **Expository Essay (a)** What quotations does Postman use to make his ideas clear to readers? **(b)** How does he use these quotations to develop and support ideas? Explain.
6. **Expository Essay (a)** Using a chart like the one shown, identify examples from the text in which Postman uses description, comparison and contrast, or cause and effect. Cite one example of each technique. **(b)** Explain how each example adds depth to the information and ideas Postman presents.

Example
Effect

Integration of Knowledge and Ideas

7. **(a)** According to Postman, what makes a newscast a form of theater? **(b) Interpret:** What problem does Postman see in the similarity between television news and theater? Explain.
8. **Evaluate:** Do you find Postman's argument valid and convincing? Explain your position, citing details from the essay to support your ideas.

9. THE BIG ? **Is knowledge the same as understanding? (a)** According to Postman, how does our knowledge of news events affect our understanding of the world? **(b)** Do TV and other broadcast forms of journalism provide knowledge, understanding, both, or neither? Explain, citing details from the essay.

ACADEMIC VOCABULARY

As you write and speak about "The News," use the words related to knowledge and understanding that you explored on page 189 of this book.

Conventions: **Predicate Nominatives and Predicate Adjectives**

A **predicate nominative** is a noun or a pronoun that renames the subject of the sentence.

The predicate nominative comes after a linking verb and *renames, identifies,* or *explains* the subject of the sentence. In a sentence with a predicate nominative, the linking verb acts as an equals sign between the subject and the predicate nominative.

A **predicate adjective** is an adjective that appears with a linking verb and *describes* the subject of the sentence.

	Example	Explanation
Predicate Nominative	The winner of the tournament is our *team.*	*Team* renames *winner.*
	That player was the *star.*	*Star* renames *player.*
Predicate Adjective	The swimmer was *fast.*	*Fast* describes *swimmer.*
	Josh is very *clever.*	*Clever* describes *Josh.*

Practice A

Identify the predicate nominatives and predicate adjectives in the following sentences.

1. Broadcast news is brief in its presentation of events.
2. Reuven Frank was an executive with NBC News.
3. She was the first reporter on the scene.
4. The film clip of the explosion was noisy.

Reading Application In "The News," find one sentence with a predicate nominative and one with a predicate adjective.

Practice B

Add a predicate nominative or a predicate adjective as indicated to complete the sentence.

1. The news anchor was ________. (predicate nominative)
2. News events can be ______. (predicate adjective)
3. That film was ______. (predicate adjective)
4. TV often is ______. (predicate adjective)

Writing Application Replace the underlined predicate adjective in this model sentence by writing two sentences with predicate nominatives and two with predicate adjectives: *Typical images in a TV newscast are vivid.*

Writing to Sources

Explanatory Text Neil Postman wrote this essay in 1992, before many recent developments in communications technology changed how people get news. Write an **expository essay** in which you update Neil Postman's examination of TV news by analyzing the pros and cons of a twenty-first century news source.

- Briefly conduct research to identify news sources developed after 1992 that are still important today.
- Choose one source and analyze its format, content, and style. (If you choose a form of social media or a Web site, get approval from your teacher beforehand.)
- Cite three criticisms Neil Postman makes about TV news in his essay. Analyze the new source in light of those criticisms.
- Identify other limitations or benefits in the type of information the news source provides. Consider how much time is devoted to each story, as well as the accuracy, thoroughness, and reliability of the coverage.
- Conclude your essay by speculating how Neil Postman might feel about the twenty-first century source.

Grammar Application Use predicate nominatives and predicate adjectives to add variety to your writing.

Research and Technology

Build and Present Knowledge Compare and contrast the ways in which two different forms of media cover a story about a famous person. Write a **journal entry** in which you explain your findings. Follow these steps:

- Choose a figure that has been the subject of significant news coverage.
- Locate at least one story about the figure from two different media forms. For example, you might choose a story from a weekly TV news magazine and another from a print news magazine.
- Make a list of questions to guide your analysis. Begin your list with these questions and add others: *Do the stories agree about facts? Do the stories emphasize different aspects of the subject's life?*
- Review each presentation and answer your list of questions.
- Write a summary of your findings, along with a list of details from each presentation that support your analysis.

Share your completed entry with the class.

Reading Informational Text

7. Analyze various accounts of a subject told in different mediums, determining which details are emphasized in each account.

Writing

2. Write informative/explanatory texts to examine and convey complex ideas, concepts, and information clearly and accurately through the effective selection, organization, and analysis of content.

2.b. Develop the topic with well-chosen, relevant, and sufficient facts, concrete details, or other information and examples appropriate to the audience's knowledge of the topic.

Speaking and Listening

4. Present information, findings, and supporting evidence clearly, concisely, and logically such that listeners can follow the line of reasoning and the organization, development, substance, and style are appropriate to purpose, audience, and task.

Language

1. Demonstrate command of the conventions of standard English grammar and usage when writing or speaking.

Meet the Author

Pete Hamill (b. 1935) has had two novels on *The New York Times* Bestseller List, but he is first and foremost a journalist. In 1960, Hamill went to work as a reporter for the *New York Post*. Although he would write for several other newspapers, Hamill loved his job at the *Post*. He wrote, "Nothing before (or since) could compare with walking into the *New York Post* at midnight, being sent into the dark scary city on assignment and coming back to write a story."

Common Core State Standards

Reading Informational Text

1. Cite strong and thorough textual evidence to support analysis of what the text says explicitly as well as inferences drawn from the text.

5. Analyze in detail how an author's ideas or claims are developed and refined by particular sentences, paragraphs, or larger portions of a text.

6. Determine the author's point of view or purpose in a text and analyze how an author uses rhetoric to advance the point of view or purpose.

8. Delineate and evaluate the argument and specific claims in a text, assessing whether the reasoning is valid and the evidence is relevant and sufficient; identify false statements and fallacious reasoning.

Is knowledge the same as understanding?

Explore the Big Question as you read "Libraries Face Sad Chapter." Take notes about the details that Hamill uses to encourage readers' understanding.

CLOSE READING FOCUS

Key Ideas and Details: **Evaluate Persuasion**

A persuasive argument is composed of a series of **claims,** or statements that express a position. To **analyze and evaluate an author's argument,** identify passages in which the author makes a claim. Then, reread those passages to test the author's reasoning and the quality of the supporting evidence. Ask yourself the following questions:

- Is the argument credible, or is it based on faulty reasoning?
- Is the evidence valid, relevant, and sufficient?
- Are any generalizations, or broad statements, supported by evidence?

In addition, look for **counterclaims,** or opposing opinions, that the author introduces and attempts to disprove.

Craft and Structure: **Persuasive Essay**

A **persuasive essay** is a short nonfiction work in which the author's purpose is to convince a reader to think or act in a certain way. To achieve that purpose, a writer may include varied types of persuasive appeals.

- **Appeals to Reason:** logical arguments based on verifiable evidence, such as facts, statistics, or expert testimony.
- **Appeals to Emotion:** statements intended to affect readers' feelings about a subject. These statements may include charged language—words with strong positive or negative associations.

As you read, think about the author's purpose, or intent. Ask, "Why does the writer include this information?"

Vocabulary

The following words are critical to understanding the essay. Decide whether you know each word well, know it a little bit, or do not know it at all. After you have read the selection, see how your knowledge of each word has increased.

volumes	**presumed**	**curtailed**
medium	**duration**	**emulate**

CLOSE READING MODEL

The passage below is from Pete Hamill's essay "Libraries Face Sad Chapter." The annotations to the right of the passage show ways in which you can use close reading skills to evaluate persuasive appeals and evidence in an essay.

from "Libraries Face Sad Chapter"

The library of my childhood is still there, since 1975 known as the Park Slope Branch of the Brooklyn Public Library. It was built with grant money from my favorite capitalist, Andrew Carnegie, in 1906. But once again, as happened in 1992, the teeming imaginative life of libraries[1] is in danger of being curtailed. Services might be cut. Hours trimmed. Staff reduced. The reason is the same: money, or the lack of it.[2]

Such reductions are absolutely understandable. As we all know, Mayor Bloomberg has more than a $4 billion shortfall that must be made up. Unlike the spend-more tax-less leaders of the federal government, the government of New York City can't print money to keep things going. In this season of post-September 11 austerities, something must give.[3] I hope it isn't the libraries.

The reason is simple: In hard times, libraries are more important than ever. Human beings need what books give them better than any other medium. Since those ancient nights around prehistoric campfires, we have needed myth. And heroes. And moral tales.[4] And information about the world beyond the nearest mountains or oceans.

Persuasive Essay

1 "Teeming, imaginative life" is an example of charged language. *Teeming* means "filled to overflowing" and suggests vitality and energy. This phrase appeals to readers' emotions by painting a portrait of a society rich in creativity and possibilities.

Persuasive Essay

2 These short, blunt sentences sound cold and unfeeling, and are similar to the language used in budget decisions. They contrast with the longer sentences Hamill uses to describe libraries and suggest a division between people making decisions and those affected by decisions.

Evaluate Persuasion

3 In acknowledging the realities of funding problems, Hamill addresses a counterclaim, or opposing opinion. He will then provide evidence against this counterclaim.

Evaluate Persuasion

4 "Prehistoric campfires," "myth," "heroes," and "moral tales," connect the present to the ancient past. These details imply that stories and culture are long-term investments whereas budgetary problems are temporary.

Libraries Face Sad Chapter

Pete Hamill

The library was four blocks from where we lived, on the corner of Ninth St. and Sixth Ave., and it was one of the treasure houses of our Brooklyn lives.

This was in the years before television, when we saw movies once a week at the Minerva or the Avon or the RKO Prospect, and fed our imaginations through radio and books. That is, it was in a time when *The Count of Monte Cristo* was as vivid in our minds, and talk, and dreams, as Jack Roosevelt Robinson. Dumas told the story of the count as vividly as Red Barber[1] recited the unfolding tale of No. 42.

We passed into that library between two mock-Corinthian columns that gave the building a majestic aura. For me, every visit was an astonishment. There was a children's room, first seen when I was 8, where I first read the wonderful Babar books, and then moved on to Howard Pyle's *Book of Pirates*, and all of Robert Louis Stevenson, with those rich, golden, mysterious illustrations by N.C. Wyeth.

There were bound volumes of a children's magazine called *St. Nicholas*, full of spidery drawings of animals that talked, and villains who didn't. There were picture books bursting with images of lost cities or the solar system. In that room, I learned that the world was larger than our neighborhood.

And then, at 10 or 11, I found my way into the adult stacks, to borrow books about the daily life of the Romans, the flight of Richard Hannay across Scotland, the conquests of Mexico and Peru, the cases of Sherlock Holmes. On a high shelf, presumed to be safe from the curious eyes of children, was a lavish (in memory) edition of *The Thousand and One Nights*.[2]

No teacher sent us to those leathery cliffs of books. Reading wasn't an assignment; it was a pleasure. We read for the combined thrills of villainy and heroism, along with knowledge of the vast world beyond the parish. Living in those other worlds, we could become other people: Jim Hawkins, or Edmund Dantes, or (most thrillingly) d'Artagnan, with his three musketeers.

We could live in the South Seas, or Paris, or the Rome of Caligula. It never occurred to us that we were inheriting our little share of civilization. But that's what was happening.

Persuasive Essay
Which words here suggest that the author appeals to positive feelings about childhood and imagination?

◀ Vocabulary
volumes (väl′ yo͞omz) *n.* books that are either part of a set or combined into one

presumed (prē zo͞omd′) *adj.* accepted as true; supposed

◀ Critical Viewing
How might the young Pete Hamill have regarded this empty library?

Comprehension
According to Hamill, why did he read so much?

---

1. ***The Count of Monte Cristo* . . . Red Barber** *The Count of Monte Cristo* is a nineteenth-century novel by Alexandre Dumas. Jackie Robinson was the first African American major league baseball player. He joined the Brooklyn Dodgers in 1947 and wore number 42. Dodgers games were broadcast on the radio, and the action was described by announcer Red Barber.
2. ***The Thousand and One Nights*** collection of ancient tales also known as *The Arabian Nights*. Although many of the tales, including "Aladdin," are now retold as children's stories, the original tellings are full of violence, bloodshed, poisonings, and betrayals.

Built by Carnegie

The library of my childhood is still there, since 1975 known as the Park Slope Branch of the Brooklyn Public Library. It was built with grant money from my favorite capitalist, Andrew Carnegie, in 1906. But once again, as happened in 1992, the teeming imaginative life of libraries is in danger of being curtailed. Services might be cut. Hours trimmed. Staff reduced. The reason is the same: money, or the lack of it.

Vocabulary ▶
curtailed (kər tāld′) *v.* cut short; reduced

Such reductions are absolutely understandable. As we all know, Mayor Bloomberg has more than a $4 billion shortfall[3] that must be made up. Unlike the spend-more tax-less leaders of the federal government, the government of New York City can't print money to keep things going. In this season of post-September 11 austerities,[4] something must give. I hope it isn't the libraries.

The reason is simple: In hard times, libraries are more important than ever. Human beings need what books give them better than any other medium. Since those ancient nights around prehistoric campfires, we have needed myth. And heroes. And moral tales. And information about the world beyond the nearest mountains or oceans.

Vocabulary ▶
medium (mē′ dē əm) *n.* means of communication

3. **shortfall** (shôrt′ fôl′) *n.* the difference between the amount you have and the amount you need or expect.
4. **austerities** (ô ster′ ə tēz) *n.* acts of self-discipline and self-denial.

▼ Critical Viewing
How does this photograph support Hamill's idea that a library is a "treasure house of the imagination"?

In hard times, libraries are more important than ever.

Today, with books and movies more expensive than ever, and television entertainment in free fall to the lowest levels of stupidity, freely circulating books are an absolute necessity. They are quite simply another kind of food. We imagine, and then we live.

Hard times are also an opportunity. Parents and teachers all moan about the refusal of the young to read. Here is the chance to revive the power of the printed page. The Harry Potter books show that the audience for young readers is potentially immense. A child who starts with Harry Potter can find his or her way to Dumas and Arthur Conan Doyle, to Mark Twain and Walt Whitman, and, yes, to Tolstoy and Joyce and Proust.

Immigrants' Appreciation

For those without money, the road to that treasure house of the imagination begins at the public library. When I was a boy, the rooms were crowded with immigrants and their children. That is, with people who came from places where there were no libraries for the poor. With their children, they built the New York in which we now live.

Today, the libraries of this city are still doing that work. The libraries of Brooklyn and Queens are jammed with the new immigrants and their astonishing children, the people who will build the New York of tomorrow. The older people want information about this new world, and how to get better jobs and green cards and citizenship. Their American children want to vanish into books their parents cannot afford, thus filling themselves with the endless possibilities of the future.

They are no different from the Irish, the Jews and the Italians of my childhood. My father only went to the eighth grade in Belfast. I remember my mother drilling him at our kitchen table for his citizenship test, and I know that he first read the Constitution in a book borrowed from the Prospect Branch of the Brooklyn Public Library. Lying in a darkened bed off that kitchen, I first heard the language of the Bill of Rights.

That process must go on in all the places where the poor now live. If it's impossible for the city to do it, then we must do it ourselves. Bloomberg can give us the hard numbers, explain the shortfall in the library budget and explain how much we need. Then we should try to make it up with the establishment of a private fund to maintain the libraries at full strength for the **duration** of the crisis.

LITERATURE IN CONTEXT

History Connection

Andrew Carnegie (1835–1919) was a Scottish immigrant who became enormously wealthy in the steel business. In 1889, Carnegie published an essay entitled "The Gospel of Wealth." In it, he argued that the rich should use their money for the public good. Under his plan, "the surplus wealth of the few will become, in the best sense, the property of the many." Unlike many other wealthy men of his time, Carnegie acted on his belief. His many charitable acts included the building of more than 2800 public libraries throughout the English-speaking world.

Connect to the Literature

How do you think Andrew Carnegie would react to the idea of cuts in library funding? Explain.

◀ **Vocabulary**
duration (do͞o rā′ shən) *n.* length of time something lasts

Vocabulary ▶
emulate (em´ yo͞o lāt´)
v. imitate (a person or thing admired)

Spiral Review
AUTHOR'S PURPOSE
What is the author's purpose for suggesting a voluntary library tax?

All of us whose lives have been affected by the treasures of public libraries could contribute. The rich could emulate Carnegie, who used his wealth to create more than 1,600 public libraries, including 65 in New York. But the middle class could also send in small amounts from $10 to $50.

This would be a kind of voluntary tax. On one level, it would be a powerful pledge to maintain the life of the mind among all classes in this city. That is obviously in our own interest. But above all, it would be a means of honoring the labor of those men and women who got us here, and who paid taxes to buy books for all New Yorkers, and first took us by the hand and walked us into the treasure houses. We who dreamed of Ebbets Field and the Chateau d'If on the same American nights owe debts to New York that we can never pay. This is one that must be honored.

Language Study

Vocabulary The words shown in blue appear in "Libraries Face Sad Chapter." Use one word from the list to complete each analogy that follows. In each, your choice should create a word pair that matches the relationship between the first words given.

volumes **curtailed** **medium** **duration** **emulate**

1. sugar : sweetness :: time : ____________
2. bucket : water :: ____________ : information
3. arrived : departed :: continued : ____________
4. people : groups :: pages : ____________
5. persuade : convince :: mimic : ____________

WORD STUDY

The **Latin root *-sum-*** means "to take." In this essay, the author describes a shelf that was presumed to be safe from children. The librarians took for granted that children could not reach the books placed there.

Word Study

Part A Explain how the **Latin root *-sum-*** contributes to the meanings of *assume, sumptuous,* and *consume*. Consult a dictionary if necessary.

Part B Use the context of the sentences and what you know about the Latin root *-sum-* to explain your answer to each question.

1. If you *resume* an activity, do you stop doing it?
2. Is it usually wise to make a *presumption* about someone else's wishes?

Close Reading Activities

Literary Analysis

Key Ideas and Details

1. **(a) Paraphrase:** In your own words, state the problem the author is addressing in this essay. **(b) Summarize:** What solution to the problem does the author propose? Explain.
2. **(a)** What books and magazines does Hamill remember from his early visits to the library? **(b) Infer:** What do these memories suggest about how Hamill felt about the library as a child? Explain.
3. **(a) Interpret:** For Hamill, how are New York's libraries intertwined with the idea of the United States as a land of opportunity made possible by hard work? **(b)** According to Hamill, in what ways are current New Yorkers in debt to generations past? Use textual details to support your answer.
4. **Evaluate Persuasion** Which passages in this essay are especially moving or convincing to you? Explain why.

Craft and Structure

5. **Persuasive Essay (a)** Using a chart like the one shown, identify three passages in which Hamill asserts his position on public libraries. Then, indicate whether each passage is an appeal to reason or to emotion. Explain your thinking. **(b)** Which kind of appeals does the author seem to favor in this essay—appeals to reason or appeals to emotion? Explain, citing details from the text.
6. **Persuasive Essay (a)** Identify one counterclaim that Hamill directly states and one that he implies. Explain your choices. **(b)** Explain the reasoning Hamill uses to defend his position against each opposing viewpoint. **(c)** Identify the evidence he uses as support.
7. **Persuasive Essay** Does Hamill present a strong, varied defense of his position? Explain your thinking, citing evidence from the essay.

Passage
1.
2.
3.
Reason or Emotion
1.
2.
3.

Integration of Knowledge and Ideas

8. **Take a Position:** Do you agree with Hamill's claims about the importance of free public libraries? Explain why or why not. Cite details from Hamill's essay in your explanation.

9. THE BIG ? **Is knowledge the same as understanding? (a)** What does Hamill want readers to know about the relationship between public libraries and the greater good of society? **(b)** Do the facts he presents make you understand enough to want to act? Explain your position, drawing on details from the essay.

ACADEMIC VOCABULARY

As you write and speak about "Libraries Face Sad Chapter," use the words related to knowledge and understanding that you explored on page 189 of this book.

Conventions: Colons, Semicolons, Ellipsis Points

Punctuation marks are symbols that clarify the meanings of sentences.

A **colon** (:) is used mainly to list items following an independent clause. A colon is also used to introduce a quotation after an independent clause.

A **semicolon** (;) is used to join independent clauses that are closely related in meaning. A semicolon may also be used to separate independent clauses or items in a series that already contain several commas.

Ellipsis points (...) show that text has been omitted or an idea has not been expressed. Ellipsis points usually indicate one of the following:

- words that have been left out of a quotation
- a series that continues beyond the items mentioned
- time passing or an action continuing in a narrative

Colon	Semicolon	Ellipsis Points
The flowers seemed human: nodding, bending, and dancing.	The teacher lifted the desk herself; the sight greatly impressed the students.	He struck out ... but the end of the game would surprise them all.

Practice A

Explain the use of the colon, semicolon, or ellipsis points in each passage.

1. Hamill writes, "Reading wasn't an assignment; it was a pleasure."
2. Living in those other worlds, we could become other people: Jim Hawkins, or Edmund Dantes, or (most thrillingly) d'Artagnan, with his three musketeers.
3. Hamill describes a time before TV, "when we saw movies once a week...and fed our imaginations through radio and books."
4. Pete Hamill believes that people could contribute money to support public libraries: "This would be a kind of voluntary tax."

Writing Application Write three sentences about the essay "Libraries Face Sad Chapter." Use a colon in one sentence, a semicolon in another, and ellipsis points in yet another.

Practice B

Copy these sentences, adding colons, semicolons, or ellipsis points where necessary.

1. Hamill's neighborhood was home to a diverse group of people the Irish, the Jews, and the Italians.
2. Pete looked around then he pulled up a chair so he could reach the copy of *The Thousand and One Nights* on the high shelf.
3. The federal government can print money a city government cannot.
4. Hamill convincingly describes his childhood reaction to going to the library "For me, every visit was an astonishment."

Writing Application Write three sentences about Hamill's arguments in "Libraries Face Sad Chapter." Use a colon in one, a semicolon in another, and ellipsis points in the third.

Writing to Sources

Informative Text Write an **abstract** of "Libraries Face Sad Chapter." An abstract is a summary of a work. Abstracts are often included in research databases and other reference sources. They provide a preview of the work so that researchers can determine if the entire work is relevant to their focus. As you work on your abstract, apply the following criteria:

- Include an introduction, body, and conclusion.
- Clearly state the main point of Hamill's essay.
- Briefly identify important supporting details in sequence.
- Use clear, concise language to make every word count.
- Do not include language verbatim from the original essay. Paraphrase, or restate the material in your own words.
- Reread your abstract to make sure your summary is thorough and that you have not expressed your own opinions.

Grammar Application As you write and revise your abstract, use colons and semicolons to help you sequence and condense information.

Research and Technology

Build and Present Knowledge Research the services offered by libraries today. Create a comparative chart that shows the variety of library services offered and the average numbers of people using them. Then, write a **persuasive speech** in which you convince your audience to use the library more. Use the chart as supporting evidence for your position. Follow these steps to research and write your speech:

- Gather and cite your source material thoroughly and accurately.
- Make your chart attractive and organize the information logically. If possible, use electronic media to design and present the information.
- Keep your audience in mind. Explain information listeners may not know and use strong, persuasive language.
- Organize your speech logically and include an introduction, body, and conclusion.
- Connect what you have learned from your research to points Hamill makes in his essay. In addition, note two details from the essay that are explained or supported by the facts you uncovered.
- Practice delivering your speech, modulating your voice and using appropriate gestures for emphasis.

Common Core State Standards

Writing

4. Produce clear and coherent writing in which the development, organization, and style are appropriate to task, purpose, and audience.

9.b. Apply grades 9–10 Reading standards to literary nonfiction.

Speaking and Listening

4. Present information, findings, and supporting evidence clearly, concisely, and logically such that listeners can follow the line of reasoning and the organization, development, substance, and style are appropriate to purpose, audience, and task.

5. Make strategic use of digital media in presentations to enhance understanding of findings, reasoning, and evidence and to add interest.

6. Adapt speech to a variety of contexts and tasks, demonstrating a command of formal English when indicated or appropriate.

Language

2. Demonstrate command of the conventions of standard English capitalization, punctuation, and spelling when writing.

2.a. Use a semicolon to link two or more closely related independent clauses.

2.b. Use a colon to introduce a list or a quotation.

Building Knowledge

Meet the Author

Dr. Martin Luther King, Jr., (1929–1968) was one of the most charismatic leaders of the civil rights movement. King first came to national attention in Montgomery, Alabama, in 1956 when he organized a boycott by African Americans of the city's segregated buses. He went on to lead other protests and to speak out against poverty and social injustice. He was assassinated on April, 4, 1968.

Common Core State Standards

Reading Informational Text

4. Determine the meaning of words and phrases; analyze the impact of specific word choices on meaning and tone.

5. Analyze how an author's ideas or claims are developed and refined by particular sentences, paragraphs, or larger portions of a text.

6. Determine an author's point of view or purpose; analyze how an author uses rhetoric.

8. Delineate and evaluate the argument and specific claims in a text; identify false statements and fallacious reasoning.

9. Analyze seminal U.S. documents of historical and literary significance.

Is knowledge the same as understanding?

Explore the Big Question as you read "I Have a Dream." Take notes on the language King uses to help listeners understand his dream of equality.

CLOSE READING FOCUS

Key Ideas and Details: **Evaluate Persuasion**

Persuasive techniques are the devices a writer or speaker uses to influence the audience in favor of his or her argument. To analyze and evaluate persuasive techniques as you read a speech, follow these steps:

- Read aloud to hear the emotional impact of certain words and the rhythm and momentum created by specific word patterns.
- Consider the effectiveness of the persuasive techniques the author uses and decide whether his or her ideas are supported with valid evidence.

Craft and Structure: **Persuasive Speech**

In a **persuasive speech,** a speaker tries to convince listeners to think or act in a certain way. Strong persuasive speakers present information and supporting evidence clearly and logically so listeners can follow the reasoning. Persuasive speakers may also use **emotional, or charged, language.** In addition, they often use **rhetorical devices,** patterns of words and ideas that create emphasis and emotion. These devices include the following forms:

- **Parallelism:** repeating a grammatical structure or an arrangement of words to create rhythm and momentum.
- **Restatement:** expressing the same idea in different words to clarify and stress key points.
- **Repetition:** using the same words frequently to reinforce concepts and unify the speech.
- **Analogy:** drawing a comparison that shows a similarity between two unlike things.

Vocabulary

The words below are critical to understanding the text that follows. Copy the words into your notebook. Which word is an antonym for *unimportant*?

momentous	**defaulted**	**hallowed**
degenerate	**creed**	**oppression**

CLOSE READING MODEL

The passage below is from Martin Luther King, Jr.'s famous "I Have a Dream" speech. The annotations to the right of the passage show ways in which you can use close reading skills to analyze a persuasive speech and the techniques the speaker uses.

from "I Have a Dream"

I have a dream that one day[1] this nation will rise up and live out the true meaning of its creed: "We hold these truths to be self-evident; that all men are created equal."[2]

I have a dream that one day[1] on the red hills of Georgia the sons of former slaves and the sons of former slaveowners will be able to sit down together at the table of brotherhood.

I have a dream that one day[1] even the state of Mississippi, a state sweltering with the heat of injustice, sweltering with the heat of oppression, will be transformed into an oasis of freedom and justice.[3]

I have a dream[1] that my four little children will one day live in a nation where they will not be judged by the color of their skin but by the content of their character.[4]

I have a dream today.[1]

Persuasive Speech

1 King repeats the phrase "I have a dream ..." five times in this section. This repetition structures this part of the speech, giving it rhythm and momentum. With each repetition, the speech gains power.

Evaluate Persuasion

2 King quotes the Declaration of Independence to support his point that all people should be treated equally. King's choice of this revered document lends weight to his argument because it suggests a promise that was made to all Americans but not kept.

Persuasive Speech

3 King transforms the physical heat of Mississippi into a vivid image of oppression. His use of parallelism ("sweltering with the heat of injustice, sweltering with the heat of oppression") intensifies the description.

Evaluate Persuasion

4 For most people, the idea that children are being treated unjustly has strong emotional impact. King's reference to his own "little" children makes his argument personal. In addition, his repetition of the hard "c" sound *(color; content; character)* makes this passage even more memorable.

"I HAVE A DREAM"

Martin Luther King, Jr.

BACKGROUND Because speeches are written to be spoken aloud, they are a more fluid form of literature than most other nonfiction. A strong speaker will react to unspoken signals from his or her listeners and adjust a speech accordingly. He or she might change words or add whole phrases. This is the case with Dr. Martin Luther King, Jr., one of the greatest speakers of the modern age. The text that appears here represents the speech exactly as it was delivered by Dr. King on the steps of the Lincoln Memorial.

Five score years ago, a great American, in whose symbolic shadow we stand today, signed the Emancipation Proclamation. This **momentous** decree came as a great beacon light of hope to millions of Negro slaves who had been seared in the flames of withering injustice. It came as a joyous daybreak to end the long night of their captivity.

But one hundred years later, the Negro still is not free. One hundred years later, the life of the Negro is still sadly crippled by the manacles of segregation and the chains of discrimination. One hundred years later, the Negro lives on a lonely island of poverty in the midst of a vast ocean of material prosperity. One hundred years later, the Negro is still languished in the corners of American society and finds himself an exile in his own land. So we've come here today to dramatize a shameful condition.

In a sense we've come to our nation's Capital to cash a check. When the architects of our republic wrote the magnificent words of the Constitution and the Declaration of Independence, they were signing a promissory note[1] to which every American was to fall heir. This note was a promise that all men, yes, black men as well as white men, would be guaranteed the unalienable rights of life, liberty, and the pursuit of happiness.

It is obvious today that America has **defaulted** on this promissory note insofar as her citizens of color are concerned. Instead of honoring this sacred obligation, America has given the Negro people a bad check; a check which has come back marked "insufficient funds." But we refuse to believe that the bank of justice is bankrupt. We refuse to believe that there are insufficient funds in the great vaults of opportunity of this nation. And so we've come to cash this check—a check that will give us upon demand the riches of freedom and the security of justice. We have also come to

◀ **Vocabulary**
momentous (mō men′ təs) *adj.* very important

defaulted (dē fôlt′ əd) *v.* failed to do something or be somewhere when required or expected; failed to make payment when due

Spiral Review
WORD CHOICE What ideas and images do King's words evoke in the paragraph beginning, "But one hundred years later..."?

Persuasive Speech
Explain King's analogy between a financial transaction and the idea of justice.

Comprehension
What injustices are King and his listeners protesting?

1. **promissory** (präm′ i sôr′ ē) **note** written promise to pay a specific amount.

◀ **Critical Viewing**
Which details in this photograph demonstrate the importance of the event at which King gave his speech?

Vocabulary ▶
hallowed (hal′ ōd)
adj. sacred

Persuasive Speech
What idea does King's repetition of the word "Now" help to emphasize?

▼ Critical Viewing
Describe King's expression as he delivers his speech.

this **hallowed** spot to remind America of the fierce urgency of *now*. This is no time to engage in the luxury of cooling off or to take the tranquilizing drug of gradualism.

Now is the time to make real the promises of Democracy.

Now is the time to rise from the dark and desolate valley of segregation to the sunlit path of racial justice.

Now is the time to lift our nation from the quicksands of racial injustice to the solid rock of brotherhood.

Now is the time to make justice a reality for all of God's children.

It would be fatal for the nation to overlook the urgency of the moment. This sweltering summer of the Negro's legitimate discontent will not pass until there is an invigorating autumn of freedom and equality. Nineteen sixty-three is not an end, but a beginning. Those who hope that the Negro needed to blow off steam and will now be content will have a rude awakening if the nation returns to business as usual. There will be neither rest nor tranquillity in America until the Negro is granted his citizenship rights. The whirlwinds of revolt will continue to shake the foundations of our nation until the bright day of justice emerges.

But there is something that I must say to my people who stand on the warm threshold which leads into the palace of justice. In the process of gaining our rightful place we must not be guilty of wrongful deeds. Let us not seek to satisfy our thirst for freedom

Now is the time to make justice a reality for all of God's children.

by drinking from the cup of bitterness and hatred. We must forever conduct our struggle on the high plane of dignity and discipline. We must not allow our creative protest to degenerate into physical violence. Again and again we must rise to the majestic heights of meeting physical force with soul force. The marvelous new militancy which has engulfed the Negro community must not lead us to a distrust of all white people, for many of our white brothers, as evidenced by their presence here today, have come to realize that their destiny is tied up with our destiny. And they have come to realize that their freedom is inextricably bound to our freedom. We cannot walk alone.

◀ **Vocabulary**
degenerate (dē jen′ ər āt′) *v.* grow worse

Persuasive Speech
What idea does King restate when he says, "We cannot walk alone"?

And as we walk, we must make the pledge that we shall always march ahead. We cannot turn back. There are those who are asking the devotees of civil rights, "When will you be satisfied?" We can never be satisfied as long as the Negro is the victim of the unspeakable horrors of police brutality. We can never be satisfied as long as our bodies, heavy with the fatigue of travel, cannot gain lodging in the motels of the highways and the hotels of the cities. We cannot be satisfied as long as the Negro's basic mobility is from a smaller ghetto to a larger one. We cannot be satisfied as long as a Negro in Mississippi cannot vote and a Negro in New York believes he has nothing for which to vote. No, no, we are not satisfied, and we will not be satisfied until justice rolls down like waters and righteousness like a mighty stream.

The Martin Luther King, Jr., Memorial in Washington, D.C.

I am not unmindful that some of you have come here out of great trials and tribulations. Some of you have come fresh from narrow jail cells. Some of you have come from areas where your quest for freedom left you battered by the storms of persecution and staggered by the winds of police brutality. You have been the veterans of creative suffering. Continue to work with the faith that unearned suffering is redemptive.

Go back to Mississippi, go back to Alabama, go back to South Carolina, go back to Georgia, go back to Louisiana, go back to the slums and ghettos of our northern cities, knowing that somehow this situation can and will be changed. Let us not wallow in the valley of despair.

I say to you today, my friends, so even though we face the difficulties of today and tomorrow, I still have a dream. It is a dream deeply rooted in the American dream.

Comprehension
According to King, how should his people react to physical force?

Vocabulary ▶
creed (krēd) *n.* statement of belief

oppression (ə presh′ ən) *n.* keeping others down by the unjust use of power

Persuasive Speech Identify the parallel clauses in this passage and explain how they emphasize King's ideas.

Persuasive Techniques What idea does King reinforce using the rhythm of repetition?

▶ Critical Viewing Based on this image, in what ways does King use body language to make his speech more effective?

I have a dream that one day this nation will rise up and live out the true meaning of its **creed**: "We hold these truths to be self-evident: that all men are created equal."

I have a dream that one day on the red hills of Georgia the sons of former slaves and the sons of former slaveowners will be able to sit down together at the table of brotherhood.

I have a dream that one day even the state of Mississippi, a state sweltering with the heat of injustice, sweltering with the heat of **oppression**, will be transformed into an oasis of freedom and justice.

I have a dream that my four little children will one day live in a nation where they will not be judged by the color of their skin but by the content of their character.

I have a dream today.

I have a dream that one day down in Alabama, with its vicious racists, with its governor having his lips dripping with the words of interposition and nullification;[2] one day right down in Alabama little black boys and black girls will be able to join hands with little white boys and white girls as sisters and brothers.

I have a dream today.

I have a dream that one day every valley shall be exalted, every hill and mountain shall be made low, the rough places will be made plains, and the crooked places will be made straight, and the glory of the Lord shall be revealed, and all flesh shall see it together.[3]

This is our hope. This is the faith that I go back to the South with. With this faith we will be able to hew out of the mountain of despair a stone of hope. With this faith we will be able to transform the jangling discords of our nation into a beautiful symphony of brotherhood. With this faith we will be able to work together, to pray together, to struggle together, to go to jail together, to stand up for freedom together, knowing that we will be free one day.

This will be the day, this will be the day, when all of God's children will be able to sing with new meaning:

My country, 'tis of thee,
Sweet land of liberty,
    Of thee I sing:
Land where my fathers died,
Land of the pilgrims' pride,
From every mountainside
    Let freedom ring.

---

2. **interposition** (in′ tər pə zish′ ən) **and nullification** (nul′ ə fi kā′ shən) disputed doctrine that a state can reject federal laws considered to be violations of its rights. Governor George C. Wallace of Alabama used this doctrine to reject federal civil rights legislation.
3. **every valley . . . all flesh shall see it together** reference to a Biblical passage (Isaiah 40:4–5). King is likening the struggle of African Americans to the struggle of the Israelites.

I HAVE A DREAM that one day this nation will rise up and live out the true meaning of its creed: "We hold these truths to be self-evident: that all men are created equal."

And if America is to be a great nation this must become true. So let freedom ring from the prodigious hilltops of New Hampshire. Let freedom ring from the mighty mountains of New York. Let freedom ring from the heightening Alleghenies of Pennsylvania!

From every mountainside, LET FREEDOM RING.

Let freedom ring from the snowcapped Rockies of Colorado!

Let freedom ring from the curvacious slopes of California!

But not only that; let freedom ring from Stone Mountain of Georgia!

Let freedom ring from Lookout Mountain of Tennessee!

Let freedom ring from every hill and molehill of Mississippi. From every mountainside, let freedom ring.

And when this happens, when we allow freedom to ring, when we let it ring from every village and every hamlet, from every state and every city, we will be able to speed up that day when all of God's children, black men and white men, Jews and Gentiles, Protestants and Catholics, will be able to join hands and sing in the words of the old Negro spiritual, "Free at last! free at last! thank God almighty, we are free at last!"

Language Study

Vocabulary The words listed below appear in "I Have a Dream." Use one word from the list to complete each analogy that follows. In each, your choice should create a word pair that matches the relationship between the first words given.

momentous **defaulted** **hallowed** **degenerate** **oppression**

1. stumble: glide :: ___________: improve

2. barren: desert :: ___________: church

3. dull: interesting :: trivial: ___________

4. supportive : harmful :: freedom : ___________

5. broken: promise :: ___________: agreement

WORD STUDY

The **Latin root *-cred-*** means "to trust; to believe." In this speech, King refers to America's **creed**, or statement of belief, that all people are created equal.

Word Study

Part A Explain how the **Latin root *-cred-*** contributes to the meanings of *credit, credential,* and *incredible*. Consult a dictionary if necessary.

Part B Use the context of the sentences and what you know about the Latin root *-cred-* to explain your answer to each question.

1. Should a judge in a criminal trial have *credibility*?

2. How would you feel if someone tried to *discredit* you?

Close Reading Activities

Literary Analysis

Key Ideas and Details

1. What central idea does King express in this speech—what does he want his audience to think or to do?
2. **(a)** Which words does King quote from the song "My Country 'Tis of Thee"? **(b) Interpret:** What message does King convey through these words? Explain.
3. **Evaluate Persuasion (a)** Which parts of the United States does King mention in his speech? **(b)** How does the mention of these places help to support King's central idea and purpose? Explain your reasoning.
4. **Evaluate Persuasion** What evidence in the speech supports the idea that African Americans were not treated equally in the United States? Cite specific examples from the text.

Craft and Structure

5. **Persuasive Speech (a)** Identify a passage in which King uses emotionally charged language. **(b)** How does this language contribute to the power of the speech? Explain.
6. **Persuasive Speech (a)** Use a chart like the one shown to list at least one example of each rhetorical device as King uses it in this speech. **(b)** Describe the effect of each device.

Example	Effect
Repetition:	
Restatement:	
Parallelism:	
Analogy:	

Integration of Knowledge and Ideas

7. **(a) Hypothesize:** Why do you think "I Have a Dream" has lived on as one of the best-known speeches in modern history? **(b) Make a Judgment:** Do you think it deserves this standing? Support your evaluation with evidence from the text.
8. **(a) Connect:** King begins this speech, "Five score years ago," and refers to a great American. To what famous document and great American is King alluding? **(b) Synthesize:** How does this reference suit both the location and the occasion of King's speech? Cite evidence from the text to support your answer.

9. THE BIG ? **Is knowledge the same as understanding? (a)** Cite facts and information from the speech that increase your understanding of America in the early 1960s. **(b)** How do the details King shares help you understand the importance of his dream? Explain.

ACADEMIC VOCABULARY

As you write and speak about "I Have a Dream," use the words related to knowledge and understanding that you explored on page 189 of this book.

Conventions: **Independent and Dependent Clauses**

A **clause** is a group of words that contains a subject and a verb. A clause can be an **independent clause** or a **dependent clause**.

An **independent clause** can stand by itself as a complete sentence. It may be used by itself, be connected to another independent clause, or be connected to a dependent clause. A **dependent clause** cannot stand by itself. It needs additional information to make sense. Dependent clauses usually begin with subordinating conjunctions, such as *when, if, after,* and *because*, or relative pronouns, such as *who, which,* and *that*. They can function as noun, adjective, or adverbial clauses. [Clauses can be combined in a variety of ways to make compound, complex, and compound-complex sentences. For more about sentence types and ways to punctuate them, see pages 238, 796, 826, 847, and R31.]

Independent Clause	Dependent Clause
Martin Luther King, Jr., dreamed	that all people would have equal rights.
The audience listened to the man	who stood before them.
They clapped loudly	when King finished speaking.

Practice A

Identify each of the following items as either an independent or a dependent clause. Then, add to each dependent clause to make it a complete sentence.

1. when King spoke
2. after King was finished
3. King spoke out about civil rights
4. he would not be satisfied until he got justice

Reading Application Find one example of an independent clause and one example of a dependent clause in Dr. King's speech.

Practice B

Combine each of the following pairs of sentences into one sentence by changing one independent clause into a dependent clause.

1. King wanted people to take action. He did not want them to be violent.
2. African Americans were not truly free. They did not have equal rights.
3. King spoke. Everyone listened.
4. King spoke to the people. The people were inspired.

Writing Application Write two sentences about Dr. King's speech that are made up of only independent clauses. Then, write two sentences that include at least one dependent clause.

Writing to Sources

Argument In his "I Have a Dream" speech, Dr. King uses persuasive techniques that inspire listeners. Write a **proposal** to a local, state, or national official or to a government agency about the idea of creating "I Have a Dream Day" to be celebrated on the day the speech was given.

- First, list reasons why you think "I Have a Dream Day" should be celebrated. Consider the positive effects it could have on your school, community, or the nation.
- Choose an official or specific government agency to address.
- Introduce your proposal with an attention-grabbing paragraph that clearly states your topic. Write with a formal, serious tone appropriate to your audience and purpose.
- Develop your argument with evidence and examples from King's speech. As you write, consider and address possible counterarguments—the reasons people might have for opposing your ideas.
- Use a variety of rhetorical devices, such as parallelism and repetition.
- End with a concluding statement or appeal that follows from the arguments you presented.

Make sure your argument is organized logically and that your use of rhetorical devices is effective. Revise to clarify relationships among your ideas.

Grammar Application As you draft, make sure that all dependent clauses are attached to independent clauses.

Speaking and Listening

Presentation of Ideas Compose a **radio news report** that provides on-the-spot coverage of the "I Have a Dream" speech. Include excerpts from the speech, a description of the crowd's reaction, and appropriate background information. If possible, watch a video of the speech before you begin. Follow these steps to complete the assignment:

- Analyze the rhetorical devices and features that make King's speech memorable.
- Consider how King's language and delivery affect the mood and tone of the speech, and imagine how the audience would respond. Quote examples from the speech.
- Add information about the civil rights movement for an audience who may not be familiar with the purpose of the speech.
- Deliver your report to the class. If possible, record it for later evaluation.

Common Core State Standards

Writing

1. Write arguments to support claims in an analysis of substantive topics or texts, using valid reasoning and relevant and sufficient evidence.

1.a. Introduce precise claim(s), distinguish the claim(s) from alternate or opposing claims.

1.b. Develop claim(s) and counterclaims fairly, supplying evidence for each in a manner that anticipates the audience's knowledge level and concerns.

1.c. Use words, phrases, and clauses to link major sections of the text, create cohesion, and clarify relationships between claim(s) and reasons, between reasons and evidence, and between claim(s) and counterclaims.

1.d. Establish and maintain a formal style and objective tone while attending to the norms and conventions of the discipline.

1.e. Provide a concluding statement or section that follows from and supports the argument presented.

Language

1.b. Use various types of clauses to convey specific meanings and add variety and interest to writing or presentations.

3. Apply knowledge of language to understand how language functions in different contexts, to make effective choices for meaning or style, and to comprehend more fully.

Comparing Texts

Is knowledge the same as understanding?

Explore the Big Question as you read these two selections. Take notes about the information that the two works present. Then, compare and contrast what each work suggests about the relationship between knowledge and true understanding.

READING TO COMPARE THEMES OR CENTRAL IDEAS

Authors Arthur C. Clarke and Rachel Carson use different genres to address similar topics. As you read each work, consider the message it conveys about humans' effect on our environment. After you have read both works, compare the central ideas they express.

SHORT STORY

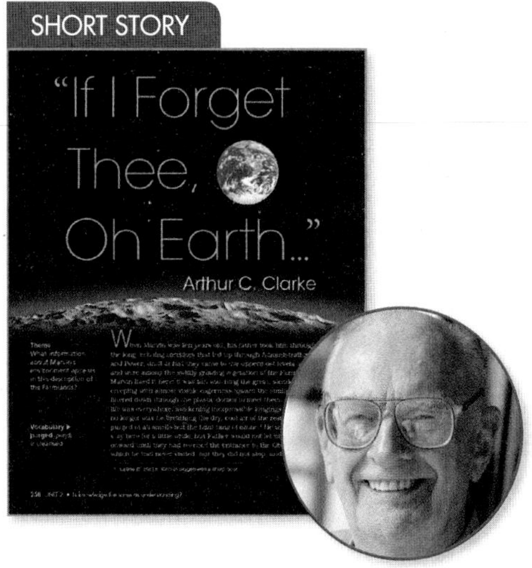

DESCRIPTIVE NONFICTION

"If I Forget Thee, Oh Earth..."

Arthur C. Clarke (1917–2008)
Born in England, Arthur C. Clarke was both a writer and a scientist. He wrote his first stories during his teens, and he later published more than fifty works of fiction and nonfiction. Although best known for his science fiction, Clarke was a serious scientist as well. In 1945, he published a technical article called "Extra-Terrestrial Relays" in which he established the principles of the satellite communications system we have today.

from *Silent Spring*

Rachel Carson (1907–1964)
Even as a child, Rachel Carson wanted to be a writer. Once in college, she renewed an interest in nature and majored in marine biology. She later earned a master's degree in zoology. Carson had long been worried about the overuse of pesticides and wanted to raise awareness about this problem. Her book, *Silent Spring,* became one of the most influential environmental texts ever written.

Comparing Themes

Theme is the message or insight about life that is conveyed in a short story, a play, or another literary work. Sometimes the theme is explicit, or stated directly. More often, it is implicit, or expressed indirectly, through the words and actions of the characters and the events of a story. The way in which a theme is developed depends in part on the **genre,** or form, of the work.

- **Informational Texts:** In works of persuasive or expository nonfiction, such as essays or articles, the meaning or insight is usually referred to as the **central idea.** The author generally states the central idea directly. A thesis statement expressing that idea may appear at the beginning of the work. Key ideas and supporting details presented throughout the work develop the central idea in a systematic way.
- **Literature:** In fiction, many nonfiction narratives, drama, and poetry, the theme is often implicit, or not directly stated. Readers figure it out by considering story events, the words and actions of characters, and patterns of related images and ideas. As readers make connections among various literary elements, the thematic message emerges.

Works of nonfiction and fiction can address the same subjects and express similar themes and central ideas. For example, the following selections share a similar basic topic: the effects of human behavior on the environment. However, "If I Forget Thee, Oh Earth . . ." is a short story, and the excerpt from *Silent Spring* is nonfiction. Because they represent two different genres, the two works develop meaning in different ways. As you read, use a Venn diagram like the one shown to analyze the insights the two works express and to compare the ways in which they convey those ideas.

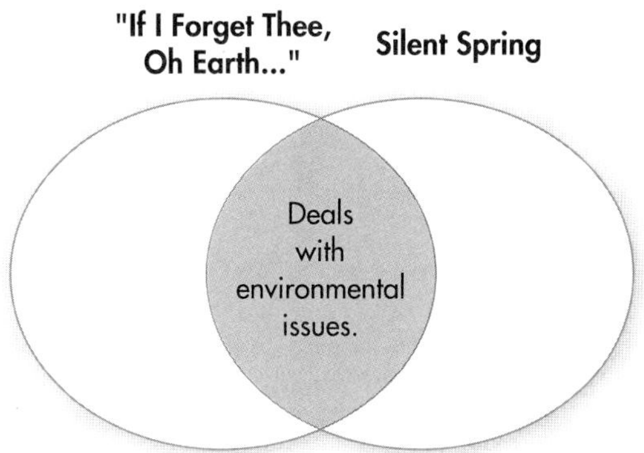

Common Core State Standards

Reading Literature/ Informational Text
1. Cite strong and thorough textual evidence to support analysis of what the text says explicitly as well as inferences drawn from the text.

Reading Literature/ Informational Text
2. Determine a theme or central idea of a text and analyze its development over the course of the text, including how it emerges and is shaped and refined by specific details; provide an objective summary of the text.

Writing
2. Write informative/explanatory texts to examine and convey complex ideas, concepts, and information clearly and accurately through the effective selection, organization, and analysis of content.
10. Write routinely over extended time frames and shorter time frames for a range of tasks, purposes, and audiences.

Language
6. Acquire and use accurately general academic and domain-specific words and phrases, sufficient for reading, writing, speaking, and listening at the college and career readiness level.

from Silent Spring

RACHEL CARSON

Central Idea
Which details in this paragraph paint a picture of the beauty and energy of nature? Explain.

There was once a town in the heart of America where all life seemed to live in harmony with its surroundings. The town lay in the midst of a checkerboard of prosperous farms, with fields of grain and hillsides of orchards where, in spring, white clouds of bloom drifted above the green fields. In autumn, oak and maple and birch set up a blaze of color that flamed and flickered across a backdrop of pines. Then foxes barked in the hills and deer silently crossed the fields, half hidden in the mists of the fall mornings.

Along the roads, laurel, viburnum and alder, great ferns and wildflowers delighted the traveler's eye through much of the year. Even in winter the roadsides were places of beauty, where countless birds came to feed on the berries and on the seed heads of the dried weeds rising above the snow. The countryside was, in fact, famous for the abundance and variety of its bird life, and when the flood of migrants was pouring through in spring and fall people traveled from great distances to observe them. Others came to fish the streams, which flowed clear and cold out of the hills and contained shady pools where trout lay. So it had been from the days many years ago when the first settlers raised their houses, sank their wells, and built their barns.

Then a strange **blight** crept over the area and everything began to change. Some evil spell had settled on the community: mysterious **maladies** swept the flocks of chickens; the cattle and sheep sickened and died. Everywhere was a shadow of death. The farmers spoke of much illness among their families. In the town the doctors had become more and more puzzled by new kinds of sickness appearing among their patients. There had been several sudden and unexplained deaths, not only among adults but even among children, who would be stricken suddenly while at play and die within a few hours.

◀ **Vocabulary**
blight (blīt) *n.* something that destroys or prevents growth

maladies (mal′ ə dēz) *n.* diseases

There was a strange stillness. The birds, for example—where had they gone? Many people spoke of them, puzzled and disturbed. The feeding stations in the backyards were deserted. The few birds seen anywhere were **moribund**; they trembled violently and could not fly. It was a spring without voices. On the mornings that had once throbbed with the dawn chorus of robins, catbirds, doves, jays, wrens, and scores of other bird voices there was now no sound; only silence lay over the fields and woods and marsh.

◀ **Vocabulary**
moribund (môr′ i bund′) *adj.* slowly dying

On the farms the hens brooded, but no chicks hatched. The farmers complained that they were unable to raise any pigs—the litters were small and the young survived only a few days. The apple trees were coming into bloom but no bees droned among the blossoms, so there was no pollination and there would be no fruit.

The roadsides, once so attractive, were now lined with browned and withered vegetation as though swept by fire. These, too, were silent, deserted by all living things. Even the streams were now lifeless. Anglers[1] no longer visited them, for all the fish had died.

Central Idea
How might your reaction to this sudden change suggest the author's message?

In the gutters under the eaves and between the shingles of the roofs, a white granular powder still showed a few patches; some

1. **anglers** (aŋ′ glərz) *n.* people who fish with a line and hook.

weeks before it had fallen like snow upon the roofs and the lawns, the fields and streams.

No witchcraft, no enemy action had silenced the rebirth of new life in this stricken world. The people had done it themselves.

This town does not actually exist, but it might easily have a thousand counterparts in America or elsewhere in the world. I know of no community that has experienced all the misfortunes I describe. Yet every one of these disasters has actually happened somewhere, and many real communities have already suffered a substantial number of them. A grim specter has crept upon us almost unnoticed, and this imagined tragedy may easily become a stark reality we all shall know.

Central Idea
Is the central idea stated directly here or is it implied? Explain.

◀ Critical Viewing
What details in this picture indicate that a "strange blight" may have affected this area?

Critical Thinking

1. **Key Ideas and Details: (a)** What is the condition of life at the beginning of this excerpt? **(b) Compare and Contrast:** How does the condition of life change as the narrative continues?
2. **Key Ideas and Details: (a)** What happens to the farm animals and the vegetation? **(b) Infer:** What causes this sudden change?
3. **Craft and Structure: (a)** What information about the town does Carson reveal at the end of the excerpt? **(b) Speculate:** Do you think her point would be more effective if the town was real? Explain, citing details from the text.
4. **Integration of Knowledge and Ideas: (a)** According to Carson, who caused the environmental problems? **(b) Speculate:** What suggestions do you think Carson would make to people today? Explain.
5. **Integration of Knowledge and Ideas:** Do you think most Americans' knowledge of environmental issues has changed since Carson first wrote *Silent Spring*? Has their understanding changed? Why or why not? ***[Connect to the Big Question: Is knowledge the same as understanding?]***

"If I Forget Thee, Oh Earth..."

Arthur C. Clarke

Theme
What information about Marvin's environment appears in this description of the Farmlands?

Vocabulary ▶
purged (purjd)
v. cleansed

When Marvin was ten years old, his father took him through the long, echoing corridors that led up through Administration and Power, until at last they came to the uppermost levels of all and were among the swiftly growing vegetation of the Farmlands. Marvin liked it here: it was fun watching the great, slender plants creeping with almost visible eagerness toward the sunlight as it filtered down through the plastic domes to meet them. The smell of life was everywhere, awakening inexpressible longings in his heart: no longer was he breathing the dry, cool air of the residential levels, purged of all smells but the faint tang of ozone.[1] He wished he could stay here for a little while, but Father would not let him. They went onward until they had reached the entrance to the Observatory, which he had never visited: but they did not stop, and Marvin knew

1. **ozone** (ō' zōn') *n.* form of oxygen with a sharp odor.

with a sense of rising excitement that there could be only one goal left. For the first time in his life, he was going Outside.

There were a dozen of the surface vehicles, with their wide balloon tires and pressurized cabins, in the great servicing chamber. His father must have been expected, for they were led at once to the little scout car waiting by the huge circular door of the airlock. Tense with expectancy, Marvin settled himself down in the cramped cabin while his father started the motor and checked the controls. The inner door of the lock slid open and then closed behind them: he heard the roar of the great air pumps fade slowly away as the pressure dropped to zero. Then the "Vacuum" sign flashed on, the outer door parted, and before Marvin lay the land which he had never yet entered.

He had seen it in photographs, of course: he had watched it imaged on television screens a hundred times. But now it was lying all around him, burning beneath the fierce sun that crawled so slowly across the jet-black sky. He stared into the west, away from the blinding splendor of the sun—and there were the stars, as he had been told but had never quite believed. He gazed at them for a long time, marveling that anything could be so bright and yet so tiny. They were intense unscintillating points, and suddenly he remembered a rhyme he had once read in one of his father's books:

Theme
What do the words "burning beneath the fierce sun" suggest about what Marvin is observing?

Twinkle, twinkle, little star,
How I wonder what you are.

Well, *he* knew what the stars were. Whoever asked that question must have been very stupid. And what did they mean by "twinkle"? You could see at a glance that all the stars shone with the same steady, unwavering light. He abandoned the puzzle and turned his attention to the landscape around him.

They were racing across a level plain at almost a hundred miles an hour, the great balloon tires sending up little spurts of dust behind them. There was no sign of the Colony: in the few minutes while he had been gazing at the stars, its domes and radio towers had fallen below the horizon. Yet there were other indications of man's presence, for about a mile ahead Marvin could see the curiously shaped structures clustering round the head of a mine. Now and then a puff of vapor would emerge from a squat smokestack and would instantly disperse.

They were past the mine in a moment: Father was driving with a reckless and exhilarating skill as if—it was a strange thought to come into a child's mind—he were trying to escape from something. In a few minutes they had reached the edge of the plateau on which the Colony had been built. The ground fell sharply away beneath them in a dizzying slope whose lower stretches were lost in shadow.

Comprehension
What astronomical bodies does Marvin see for the first time?

LITERATURE IN CONTEXT

Science Connection

International Space Station
In Arthur C. Clarke's story, a lunar colony is all that remains of humanity. At the time Clarke wrote the story, the idea of a space colony may have seemed implausible. However, today it is a reality in the form of the International Space Station (ISS), now orbiting more than 200 miles above Earth. Sixteen nations contributed scientific and technical resources to build the ISS, which began construction in 1998. The first astronaut crew arrived at the station in November of 2000. Since then, more than 200 people have lived and worked there, conducting experiments and research, and providing insight into the ways people can adjust to life in outer space.

Connect to the Literature

How do you think the astronauts' feelings about living in outer space compare to Marvin's feelings?

Ahead, as far as the eye could reach, was a jumbled wasteland of craters, mountain ranges, and ravines. The crests of the mountains, catching the low sun, burned like islands of fire in a sea of darkness: and above them the stars still shone as steadfastly as ever.

There could be no way forward—yet there was. Marvin clenched his fists as the car edged over the slope and started the long descent. Then he saw the barely visible track leading down the mountainside, and relaxed a little. Other men, it seemed, had gone this way before.

Night fell with a shocking abruptness as they crossed the shadow line and the sun dropped below the crest of the plateau. The twin searchlights sprang into life, casting blue-white bands on the rocks ahead, so that there was scarcely need to check their speed. For hours they drove through valleys and past the foot of mountains whose peaks seemed to comb the stars, and sometimes they emerged for a moment into the sunlight as they climbed over higher ground.

And now on the right was a wrinkled, dusty plain, and on the left, its ramparts and terraces rising mile after mile into the sky, was a wall of mountains that marched into the distance until its peaks sank from sight below the rim of the world. There was no sign that men had ever explored this land, but once they passed the skeleton of a crashed rocket, and beside it a stone cairn[2] surmounted by a metal cross.

It seemed to Marvin that the mountains stretched on forever: but at last, many hours later, the range ended in a towering, precipitous headland[3] that rose steeply from a cluster of little hills. They drove down into a shallow valley that curved in a great arc toward the far side of the mountains: and as they did so, Marvin slowly realized that something very strange was happening in the land ahead.

The sun was now low behind the hills on the right: the valley before them should be in total darkness. Yet it was awash with a cold white radiance that came spilling over the crags beneath which they were driving. Then, suddenly, they were out in the open plain, and the source of the light lay before them in all its glory.

---

2. **cairn** (kern) *n.* a cone-shaped pile of stones built as a monument.
3. **precipitous headland** (prē sip´ ə təs hed´ land´) *n.* steep cliff that juts out over water.

It was very quiet in the little cabin now that the motors had stopped. The only sound was the faint whisper of the oxygen feed and an occasional metallic crepitation as the outer walls of the vehicle radiated away their heat. For no warmth at all came from the great silver crescent that floated low above the far horizon and flooded all this land with pearly light. It was so brilliant that minutes passed before Marvin could accept its challenge and look steadfastly into its glare, but at last he could discern the outlines of continents, the hazy border of the atmosphere, and the white islands of cloud. And even at this distance, he could see the glitter of sunlight on the polar ice.

It was beautiful, and it called to his heart across the abyss of space. There in that shining crescent were all the wonders that he had never known—the hues of sunset skies, the moaning of the sea on pebbled shores, the patter of falling rain, the unhurried benison of snow. These and a thousand others should have been his rightful heritage, but he knew them only from the books and ancient records, and the thought filled him with the anguish of exile.

Theme
Which details in these paragraphs provide an insight into what Marvin and others in his colony have lost?

Why could they not return? It seemed so peaceful beneath those lines of marching cloud. Then Marvin, his eyes no longer blinded by the glare, saw that the portion of the disk that should have been in darkness was gleaming faintly with an evil phosphorescence[4] and he remembered. He was looking upon the funeral pyre of a world—upon the radioactive aftermath of Armageddon.[5] Across a quarter of a million miles of space, the glow of dying atoms was still visible, a perennial reminder of the ruinous past. It would be centuries yet before that deadly glow died from the rocks and life could return again to fill that silent, empty world.

◀ **Vocabulary**
perennial (pə ren´ ē əl) *adj.* happening over and over; perpetual

And now Father began to speak, telling Marvin the story which until this moment had meant no more to him than the fairy tales he had once been told. There were many things he could not understand: it was impossible for him to picture the glowing, multicolored pattern of life on the planet he had never seen. Nor could he comprehend the forces that had destroyed it in the end, leaving the Colony, preserved by its isolation, as the sole survivor. Yet he could share the agony of those final days, when the Colony had learned at last that never again would the supply ships come flaming down through the stars with gifts from home. One by one the radio stations had ceased to call: on the shadowed globe the lights of the cities had dimmed and died, and they were alone at last, as no men had ever been alone before, carrying in their hands the future of the race.

Comprehension
What does Marvin notice in a portion of the disk?

4. **phosphorescence** (fäs´ fə res´ əns) *n.* emission of light resulting from exposure to radiation.
5. **Armageddon** (är´ mə ged´ 'n) *n.* in the Bible, the place where the final battle between good and evil is to be fought.

Then had followed the years of despair, and the long-drawn battle for survival in their fierce and hostile world. That battle had been won, though barely: this little oasis of life was safe against the worst that Nature could do. But unless there was a goal, a future toward which it could work, the Colony would lose the will to live, and neither machines nor skill nor science could save it then.

So, at last, Marvin understood the purpose of this pilgrimage. He would never walk beside the rivers of that lost and legendary world, or listen to the thunder raging above its softly rounded hills. Yet one day—how far ahead?—his children's children would return to claim their heritage. The winds and the rains would scour the poisons from the burning lands and carry them to the sea, and in the depths of the sea they would waste their venom until they could harm no living things. Then the great ships that were still waiting here on the silent, dusty plains could lift once more into space, along the road that led to home.

Theme
What message about the future is conveyed through the details in this paragraph?

That was the dream: and one day, Marvin knew with a sudden flash of insight, he would pass it on to his own son, here at this same spot with the mountains behind him and the silver light from the sky streaming into his face.

He did not look back as they began the homeward journey. He could not bear to see the cold glory of the crescent Earth fade from the rocks around him, as he went to rejoin his people in their long exile.

Critical Thinking

1. **Key Ideas and Details: (a)** At the end of the story, what does Marvin realize? **(b) Draw Conclusions:** What was the purpose of Marvin's trip with his father?
2. **Craft and Structure: (a)** What evidence from the text indicates that the story is set on the moon? **(b) Analyze:** How does the choice of setting make the story more realistic? Explain, citing details from the text.
3. **Integration of Knowledge and Ideas: (a)** How did Earth come to be destroyed? **(b) Speculate:** What suggestions do you think Clarke might have offered today to prevent a situation like this from occurring in the future? Cite details from the story to support your response.
4. **Integration of Knowledge and Ideas:** How does Marvin's knowledge about Earth change after his trip with his father? Does he gain true understanding of what happened in the past? Explain, citing details from the story. *[Connect to the Big Question: Is knowledge the same as understanding?]*

Comparing Themes

1. **Key Ideas and Details** Use a chart like the one shown to analyze the theme expressed in "If I Forget Thee, Oh Earth . . ." and the central idea expressed in the excerpt from *Silent Spring.* First, list important details from each selection and what you think the details mean. Use this information to suggest the theme or central idea of the selection.

Details from "If I Forget Thee, Oh Earth..."	What They Mean	Theme
Details from *Silent Spring*	**What They Mean**	**Central Idea**

2. **Craft and Structure (a)** Using details from the chart, explain how the theme and central idea in the two selections are similar. **(b)** How is the meaning or insight expressed differently in each one?

Timed Writing

Explanatory Text: Essay

Write an essay in which you compare your reactions to "If I Forget Thee, Oh Earth . . ." and the excerpt from *Silent Spring*. In your response, explain how each work explores a theme and a central idea, and consider how the genre of each selection affects the reader's understanding and experience. **(25 minutes)**

5-Minute Planner

1. Read the prompt carefully and completely.
2. Jot down your answers to these questions to help organize your thoughts:
   - Do you feel more affected by the experiences of the character Marvin or by the words of Rachel Carson, the author of *Silent Spring?*
   - Which genre do you find more effective in shaping meaning and expressing ideas—fiction or nonfiction? Why?
   - Why do you think an author would choose one genre over another when conveying an important insight or idea?
3. Decide on a structure for your essay. Plan the points you will cover in each paragraph.
4. Reread the prompt and then draft your essay.

USE ACADEMIC VOCABULARY

As you write, use academic language, including the following words or their related forms:

argument
circumstance
determine
interpretation

For more information about academic vocabulary, see page xlvi.

Language Study

Etymology: **Word Origins and Modern Meanings**

The words that make up the English language come from a variety of sources. A word's **origin,** or source, is shown in its etymology. A word's **etymology** identifies the language in which the word first appeared and tells how its spelling and meaning have changed over time. The following excerpt from a dictionary entry shows the etymology of the word *make*.

Common Core State Standards

Language

4. Determine or clarify the meaning of unknown and multiple-meaning words and phrases based on grades 9–10 reading and content, choosing flexibly from a range of strategies.

4.c. Consult general and specialized reference materials, both print and digital, to find the pronunciation of a word or determine or clarify its precise meaning, its part of speech, or its etymology.

Sample Dictionary Entry

Middle English (Most dictionaries provide a separate key to abbreviations.)

The Middle English source word

make (māk) *vt.* [ME *maken* < OE *macian,* akin to Ger *machen* < IE base **mag-*, to knead, press, stretch > MASON, Gr *magis,* kneaded mass, paste, dough, *mageus,* kneader]

This symbol means "derived from."

Many English words are derived from Greek, Roman, and Norse mythology. Having some knowledge of myths from these cultures can help you to understand the origins and meanings of new words. This chart shows some examples.

Word	Definition	Origin
narcissistic	showing excessive self-love	reference to Narcissus, a young man in Greek mythology who falls in love with his own reflection
mercurial	lively and quick-witted	reference to Mercury, a god in Roman mythology who is swift and clever
Wednesday	the fourth day of the week	Old Norse word *Othinsdagr*, which means "Odin's day," a reference to the chief god in Norse mythology

Practice A

Look up each word in a print, digital, or online dictionary. Identify the original Greek, Latin, or Old Norse source word and its meaning.

1. skill

2. salute

3. antique

4. crisis

5. ship

6. north

Practice B

Find each underlined word, or its base form, in a print, digital, or online dictionary that provides word etymologies. Write the word's definition, and then use its etymology to explain how the original source word relates to the word's use in the sentence.

1. When the ambulance sounded its siren, cars moved out of its way.
2. She seemed to be in a hypnotic state.
3. A witness came forward and told what she saw.
4. When the mouse saw the cat, he made a quick escape.
5. The club's slogan is "Do your best!"
6. We had to pay a fee before entering the park.
7. I regret that I will be unable to attend the event.
8. The Sampsons have a robot that cleans the bottom of their pool.
9. He apologized for spilling the milk.

Activity Prepare a note card like the one shown for each of these words: *derive, choice, tantalize, window,* and *curfew*. Look up each word in a dictionary and record some details about the word's origin, including notes about how older words from other languages influenced its meaning. Then, write the word's modern meaning. Finally, write a sentence using the word.

Word:
Word's origin:
Modern word's meaning:
Sentence:

Comprehension and Collaboration

Work with two other classmates to research the figures from Greek and Roman mythology listed below. Then, use a dictionary to find an English word that is based on the figure's name. Finally, write a few sentences that explain how the word's meaning relates to the figure.

- **Mars**
- **Vulcan**
- **Jove**

Speaking and Listening

Delivering a Persuasive Speech

The ability to speak persuasively is a valuable life skill. The following speaking strategies can help you refine your persuasive speaking skills.

Learn the Skills

Organize your evidence. Once you have determined your position on an issue or idea, gather and arrange your evidence into an introduction, body, and conclusion. Decide which method of organization will lend power to your speech. For example, you may want to begin with less-important points and lead up to your strongest argument.

Know your audience. Understanding your audience will help you present your ideas effectively.

- Adjust **word choice, evidence,** and **rhetoric** to the interests, backgrounds, and knowledge levels of your listeners.
- **Anticipate questions** and **counterarguments.** You can often disarm skeptical listeners by discussing and refuting their ideas. Introduce opposing positions and demonstrate why their reasoning is faulty or they are otherwise not persuasive.
- **Respond to the interests of your listeners** by showing how they are affected by the issue and could benefit from your proposals.

Use varied appeals. Appeal to listeners' logic by constructing a reasoned argument. Appeal to their emotions by discussing the impact of your ideas on real people. Support your position by including an appeal to authority or evidence from an expert.

Use rhetorical devices. Strengthen your appeals to logic and emotion by using rhetorical devices.

- **Parallel structures**—the deliberate repetition of words, sentences, and phrases using the same grammatical forms—help to make your ideas clear and memorable.
- **Rhetorical questions**—questions with obvious answers that support your points—capture the attention of an audience.

Use your voice and gestures effectively. Demonstrate confidence in your ideas through your posture, bearing, and facial expression.

- Make eye contact with all your listeners, not just one or two people.
- Vary the volume, tone, and pacing of your voice to emphasize key points and to keep your audience engaged.
- Use hand gestures to support what you are saying.

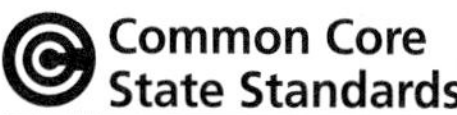

Common Core State Standards

Speaking and Listening

3. Evaluate a speaker's point of view, reasoning, and use of evidence and rhetoric, identifying any fallacious reasoning or exaggerated or distorted evidence.

4. Present information, findings, and supporting evidence clearly, concisely, and logically such that listeners can follow the line of reasoning and the organization, development, substance, and style are appropriate to purpose, audience, and task.

5. Make strategic use of digital media in presentations to enhance understanding of findings, reasoning, and evidence and to add interest.

6. Adapt speech to a variety of contexts and tasks, demonstrating command of formal English when indicated or appropriate.

INCORPORATE DIGITAL MEDIA

Consider enhancing your presentation by using digital media. Visuals, such as computer-generated charts or graphs, or audio and video clips can emphasize your points and add interest to your speech.

Practice the Skills

Presentation of Knowledge and Ideas Use what you have learned in this workshop to complete the following activity.

ACTIVITY: Deliver a Persuasive Speech

Develop a persuasive speech in which you take a stand on a current issue. Persuade your audience to agree with your views. Then, poll your classmates to see if your speech has altered their perspectives. Consider these questions as you prepare your speech.

- Which organization of ideas best serves my topic and argument?
- What facts and expert opinions support my claim?
- What counterarguments and questions should I anticipate and address?
- What is the knowledge level and background of my audience?
- What rhetorical devices will strengthen my appeals to logic and emotion?

Use a Presentation Checklist like the one shown below to help you evaluate your classmates' presentations.

Presentation Checklist

Persuasive Speech Content

Rate the speaker's content on a scale of 1(very poor) to 5 (very good) for each of these items. Explain your ratings.

- presented ideas clearly and in a logical order Rating: ___
- included well-chosen facts and expert opinions Rating: ___
- anticipated and addressed counterarguments and claims Rating: ___
- met the knowledge level and background of the audience Rating: ___
- used rhetorical devices effectively Rating: ___
- avoided fallacious or faulty reasoning Rating: ___

Persuasive Speech Delivery

Rate the speaker's delivery on a scale of 1 (very poor) to 5 (very good) for each of these items. Explain your ratings.

- appropriate language Rating: ___
- effective speaking rate Rating: ___
- enunciation Rating: ___
- conventions of language Rating: ___
- eye contact Rating: ___
- appropriate volume Rating: ___
- appropriate gestures Rating: ___

Comprehension and Collaboration With classmates, discuss how you evaluated each speaker. As a group, come to an agreement about the qualities that make a persuasive speech effective and why.

Write an Explanatory Text

Cause-and-Effect Essay

Defining the Form Whether the subject is human nature, historical trends, or weather patterns, cause-and-effect reasoning explains why things happen. A **cause-and-effect essay** examines the relationship between or among two or more events, explaining how one leads to another. You may use elements of this type of writing in many types of assignments, including science reports, history papers, and character studies.

Assignment Write a cause-and-effect essay to explain an event or a condition in a subject area that interests you, such as business, the arts, technology, history, sports, or music. Include these elements:

- ✓ a clear *identification of a cause-and-effect relationship*
- ✓ an *analysis of specific aspects of the cause or causes* that produce the effects
- ✓ *facts, details, examples, and reasons* that support your assertions and anticipate readers' questions
- ✓ a *logical organization* clarified by smooth transitions
- ✓ an appropriately *formal style* and *objective tone*
- ✓ error-free grammar, including correct *subject-verb agreement*

To preview the criteria on which your cause-and-effect essay may be judged, see the rubric on page 275.

Common Core State Standards

Writing

2. Write informative/explanatory texts to examine and convey complex ideas, concepts, and information clearly and accurately through the effective selection, organization, and analysis of content.

2.a. Introduce a topic; organize complex ideas, concepts, and information to make important connections and distinctions; include formatting, graphics, and multimedia when useful to aiding comprehension.

2.b. Develop the topic with well-chosen, relevant, and sufficient facts, extended definitions, concrete details, quotations, or other information and examples appropriate to the audience's knowledge of the topic.

5. Develop and strengthen writing as needed by planning, revising, editing, rewriting, or trying a new approach, focusing on addressing what is most significant for a specific purpose and audience.

FOCUS ON RESEARCH

When you write a cause-and-effect essay, you might perform research to

- find historical or scientific examples of similar cause-and-effect relationships.
- find data or statistics.
- locate expert testimony or quotations that relate to your topic.

Be sure to note all resources you use in your research, and credit those sources in your final drafts. See the Citing Sources pages in the Introductory Unit of this textbook for additional guidance.

READING-WRITING CONNECTION

To get a feel for cause-and-effect essays, read the excerpt from *Silent Spring* by Rachel Carson on page 254.

Prewriting/Planning Strategies

Examine current events. Scan newspapers or magazines for headlines that interest you. Use a three-column chart to speculate about possible causes and effects: In the middle column, write the event; in the left column, write the possible causes; in the right column, note possible effects. Notice how the event listed in the chart below (team wins championship) is an effect of the causes listed in the left column (practice, focus, and individual performance) as well as a cause of the effects listed in the right column (increased fan interest, harder to buy tickets, and revenue for city).

Causes
• practice, focus
• individual performance
Event
Team wins championship
Effects
• increased fan interest
• harder to buy tickets
• revenue for city

List and freewrite. Jot down any interesting events that come to mind from the worlds of business, science, technology, the arts, nature, politics, popular culture, or sports. Then, circle the item that most intrigues you. Freewrite for three minutes about that topic. As you write, note factors that contributed to the event (causes) and circumstances that happened as a result (effects). You can develop your topic from ideas you uncover in your freewriting.

Categorize to narrow your topic. You may find that your topic is too broad to manage in the scope of a single essay. If so, break your subject into smaller categories. For example, if your topic is a record-breaking sports event, you might create categories such as "key player," "great coach," and "new equipment." Choose a more focused topic that interests you from your list of categories.

Chart causes and effects. Using an index card or a self-sticking note, write the central event or circumstance that is your subject. Explore the causes that produced the event and the effects the event produced. Write those factors on separate cards or notes. Write key details related to each cause and effect on the cards or notes. Then, arrange the cards or notes in a logical sequence.

Drafting Strategies

Choose a structure. In your opening paragraph, introduce your topic and show why it is important. Here are two possibilities for organizing the body paragraphs of your essay:

- **Chronological order** is particularly valuable when describing a sequence of causes and effects. You can start with the cause and then continue by describing its effects. You can also start with the effect and then list its causes one at a time. Keep in mind, however, that a time-order relationship is not in itself proof of cause and effect.
- **Order of importance** organization can be structured in two ways. You can begin with your most important point and follow it with less important points—this approach grabs a reader's attention. Alternatively, you can begin with your least important point and build toward your most important point, which creates drama.

Use logical evidence and an objective tone. As you build support for your ideas, avoid opinions and trivial details. Rely instead on facts, statistics, and persuasive examples. Strengthen your ideas even more by using a formal writing style and an objective, serious tone.

- **Unsupported Assertion:** Members of the royal family probably liked the color purple more than any other color.
- **Convincing Support:** According to a primary-source historical document, members of the royal family believed the color purple symbolized power and prosperity.

Use the TRI method to develop paragraphs. Follow these steps:

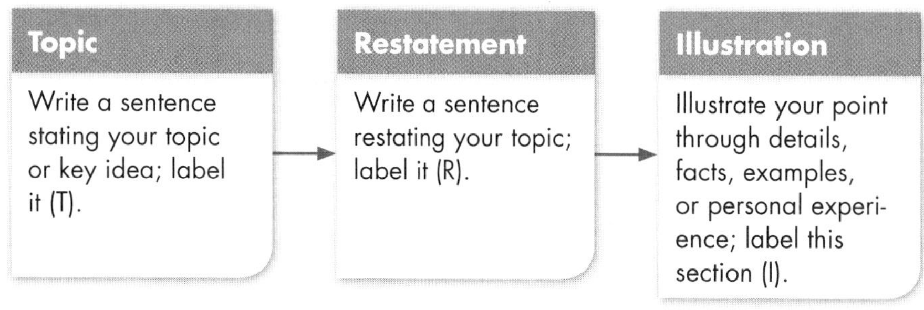

Topic
Write a sentence stating your topic or key idea; label it (T).
Restatement
Write a sentence restating your topic; label it (R).
Illustration
Illustrate your point through details, facts, examples, or personal experi-ence; label this section (I).

You can use the TRI pattern to shift the sequence to suit the information you present and add variety to your writing.

Example: Originally, the color purple was associated with royalty. **(T)** Only kings, queens, and members of the nobility wore purple-colored clothing. **(R)** In England, Queen Elizabeth I actually made a law prohibiting anyone except herself and her relatives from wearing purple. **(I)**

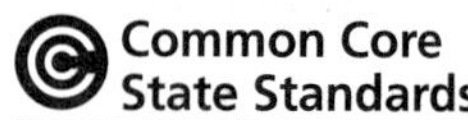

Writing

2.a. Introduce a topic; organize complex ideas, concepts, and information to make important connections and distinctions; include formatting, graphics, and multimedia when useful to aiding comprehension.

2.b. Develop the topic with well-chosen, relevant, and sufficient facts, extended definitions, concrete details, quotations, or other information and examples appropriate to the audience's knowledge of the topic.

2.d. Use precise language and domain-specific vocabulary to manage the complexity of the topic.

2.e. Establish and maintain a formal style and objective tone while attending to the norms and conventions of the discipline in which they are writing.

Setting Your Tone

A writer's **tone** is his or her attitude toward the audience or subject. In academic settings like school, the tone of an explanatory essay should be formal. Since the purpose of this kind of essay is to inform readers about a subject, it is important that the tone convey a sense of seriousness and authority.

Identifying Audience If you were explaining cause and effect to a close friend, you might use slang, abbreviations, and a loose structure. Your friend would pick up on the casual tone and likely respond in a similar manner. However, when you are writing an essay, your audience is not a personal friend. You are presenting ideas to a reader who is seeking information. Your tone needs to be appropriately thoughtful and calm. This does not mean you should sound stiff, false, or like someone you are not, but it does mean you should use a tone that reflects a serious purpose.

Maintaining Consistency Use these steps to create and maintain a formal tone:

- Avoid slang and contractions.
- Be aware of your word choices. Replace casual language with formal expressions.
- Generally, avoid the use of idioms, which tend to be less formal in tone.
- Refer to places, people, institutions, or formal concepts by their proper names.

These two passages explain the same information, but they are quite different in tone.

Casual Tone	Formal Tone
Did you see the game when the team won the championship? It was totally awesome! They must've practiced a lot. Now they're getting a massive trophy from the guv himself!	The high school basketball team won the state championship game on Friday night by a score of 87 to 64. The coach attributed the win to an increased practice schedule and greater focus by the players. Governor Talbot will present the championship trophy to the team at a ceremony on Monday that will be attended by local press.

Revising Strategies

Clarify cause-and-effect relationships. Review your entire draft, focusing on the causes and effects you have presented. With two highlighters, use one color to mark phrases that show causes and the other to mark effects. Add details to strengthen connections, insert transitional words to make links clear, and eliminate causes or effects that do not support your main point. Provide a clear concluding statement that follows logically from the information that preceded it and that supports your main idea.

Model: Revising to Clarify Cause and Effect

Our class scored in the top five percent on standardized tests.

, but, more often,

We took some practice tests~~. Mostly~~ ^ we focused on learning to

Because we could read well, we

read and to understand what we read. ~~We~~ ^ were able to do well on the test.

This writer adds transitional words and phrases to clarify the cause-and-effect relationships.

Combine short sentences. If you find too many short sentences, look for places to combine them. Try the following strategies:

- Use a semicolon to connect two short, related independent clauses.
- Use a coordinating conjunction *(and, but, or, nor, for, so, yet)* to combine ideas of equal importance.
- Use a subordinate clause—one that starts with a subordinating conjunction (for example, *after, although, despite, if,* or *whenever*) to show that one idea is dependent on the other.
- Use a semicolon and a conjunctive adverb (for example, *consequently, furthermore, otherwise,* or *therefore*) to show comparison or contrast between ideas. A comma always follows the conjunctive adverb.

Example Short Sentences: It was pouring rain. We ran to the house.

Combined Using a Semicolon: It was pouring rain; we ran to the house.

Combined Using a Coordinating Conjunction: It was pouring rain, so we ran to the house.

Combined Using a Subordinate Clause: It was pouring rain as we ran to the house.

Combined Using a Semicolon and Conjunctive Adverb: It was pouring rain; therefore, we ran to the house.

Peer Review

Ask a partner to read your draft and give you feedback about the clarity of the cause-and-effect relationships you present. If necessary, modify sentences, transitions, or paragraphs to improve the logical flow of your ideas.

Common Core State Standards

Writing

2.c. Use appropriate and varied transitions to link the major sections of the text, create cohesion, and clarify the relationships among complex ideas and concepts.

2.f. Provide a concluding statement or section that follows from and supports the information or explanation presented.

5. Develop and strengthen writing as needed by planning, revising, editing, rewriting, or trying a new approach, focusing on addressing what is most significant for a specific purpose and audience.

Language

2.a. Use a semicolon (and perhaps a conjunctive adverb) to link two or more closely related independent clauses.

Revising to Correct Faulty Subject-Verb Agreement

In order to be correct, a subject and verb must agree in number.

Identifying Errors in Subject-Verb Agreement Agreement errors often occur with compound subjects—subjects joined by *and, or,* or *nor*—and with indefinite pronouns as subjects. Below, subjects are underlined and verbs are italicized.

Compound Subject Joined by *And:*

The coach and the captain ~~is going~~ *are going* to attend.

Compound Subject Joined by *Or* or *Nor:*

Either Jason or his brother ~~are bringing~~ *is bringing* the snacks.

Indefinite Pronoun as Subject:

Everybody who supports our ideas ~~are helping~~ *is helping*.

If a plural subject is joined to a singular subject by *or* or *nor*, the verb should agree with the subject that is closer to it.

Correct: Either the coach or the co-captains *are going* to speak.

Correct: Either the co-captains or the coach *is going* to speak.

Fixing Errors To correct faulty subject-verb agreement, follow these steps:

1. **Identify whether the subject in a sentence is singular or plural.**
2. **Select the matching form of the verb:**
   - For compound subjects joined by *and,* use plural verb forms.
   - For singular subjects joined by *or* or *nor,* use singular verb forms.
   - When the subject is an indefinite pronoun, use the appropriate verb form. Use this chart for guidance.

Indefinite Pronouns	
Always Singular	anybody, anyone, anything, each, either, everybody, everyone, everything, neither, nobody, no one, nothing, somebody, someone, something
Always Plural	both, few, many, others, several
Singular or Plural	all, any, more, most, none, some

Grammar in Your Writing

Scan several paragraphs in your draft and underline all compound subjects and indefinite pronouns. In each case, make sure that the verb form you have used agrees with the subject.

STUDENT MODEL: **Glen Milner, Charlotte, NC**

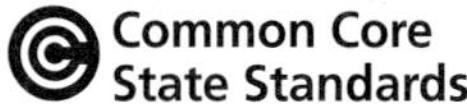

Language
2.c. Spell correctly.

Climate Effects of the North Atlantic Current

The oceans have been around since the beginning of time, yet we know relatively little about them. They are constantly moving and changing, turning up water that has been down in the depths for hundreds of years. One of these currents is the North Atlantic, also known as the Great Ocean Conveyor Belt.

Direct statements of fact form the basis of the essay.

The level of impact the current has on climate and the causes that change it are widely debated. The presumption held by most scientists is that we are currently experiencing global warming. Other theories state that global warming may influence the North Atlantic Current. This, consequently, may cause the exact opposite of warming—an ice age.

Glen builds interest by acknowledging that there are differing opinions on the topic.

The coordinating conjunction *consequently* is particularly useful in a cause-and-effect essay.

Models have shown that any change in speed or location of the current may well cause a rapid climate shift of great magnitude (Burroughs 17). This shift would be caused by two key changes: a decrease in salinity and an increase in the temperature of water in the North Atlantic Current. These factors would, in turn, cause the current to slow down or shut down, sending the Northern Hemisphere into an ice age.

The North Atlantic Current is a complicated system that runs for thousands of miles and combines water from all oceans. It moves heat from the tropics to the northern Atlantic. Robert Kunzig, the author of *The Restless Sea: Exploring the World Beneath the Waves,* said that oceanographers call this the "global journey" of the Thermohaline Circulation, which is run by heat and salt (268). It is called a conveyor belt because warm water moves north on surface currents and then back south in deep cold-water currents, folding over itself like a conveyor belt. The heat has a drastic effect on the climate for the Northern Hemisphere. Without it, the average temperature would be much lower.

The writer takes the knowledge level of his audience into account and provides explanations of scientific concepts. He supports his ideas with research.

The mechanisms by which the current works are very simple. As the water moves north, it cools down. In addition, its salinity rises because winds that blow east to west across the equator transport moisture from the Atlantic to the Pacific, leaving the Atlantic more saline. The water that feeds the Atlantic from the Mediterranean is also salty because it is nearly landlocked and moisture evaporates from the Mediterranean, leaving it saltier (Mayewski 105). As the temperature decreases and salinity increases, the water becomes denser, causing it to sink. As it sinks, it spreads out deep in the ocean basin where it is pulled back toward the equator, thus creating the conveyor-like characteristics....

Glen uses chronological order to explain the way the ocean currents work.

Editing and Proofreading

Check your draft for errors in spelling, grammar, and punctuation.

Focus on spelling. Double-check your spelling of words like *unnecessary* and *dissatisfied* in which a prefix is added to a base word that begins with a consonant. In most cases, the spelling of the base word does not change.

Focus on sentence clarity. Ensure that your sentences are clear by checking that the subjects agree with the verbs. In addition, read each sentence to be sure that each one expresses a complete thought.

Spiral Review
Earlier in this unit, you learned about **colons, semicolons, and ellipsis points** (p. 238) and **dependent and independent clauses** (p. 250). Check your essay to make sure you have used punctuation marks correctly and that all dependent clauses are linked to independent clauses.

Publishing and Presenting

Consider one of the following ways to share your work with others:

Present your essay. Use photographs, charts, and diagrams to help you explain the topic of your article. Include definitions of any challenging or specialized vocabulary your listeners will need to know in order to understand the information. Ask friends in the audience to provide feedback notes on your presentation.

Submit your essay for publication. If your essay focuses on a matter of local interest, send it to your school or community newspaper.

Reflecting on Your Writing

Writer's Journal Jot down your answer to this question:
How did writing about the topic help you better understand it?

Self-Assessment Rubric

Use the following criteria to evaluate the effectiveness of your essay.

Criteria	Rating Scale
PURPOSE/FOCUS Introduces a specific topic; provides a concluding section that follows from and supports the information or explanation presented	*not very* .... *very* 1 2 3 4
ORGANIZATION Organizes complex ideas, concepts, and information to make important connections and distinctions; uses appropriate and varied transitions to link the major sections, create cohesion, and clarify relationships among ideas	1 2 3 4
DEVELOPMENT OF IDEAS/ELABORATION Develops the topic with well-chosen, relevant and sufficient facts, extended definitions, concrete details, quotations, or other information and examples appropriate to the audience's knowledge of the topic	1 2 3 4
LANGUAGE Uses precise language and domain-specific vocabulary to manage the complexity of the topic; establishes and maintains a formal style and an objective tone	1 2 3 4
CONVENTIONS Attends to the norms and conventions of the discipline	1 2 3 4

SELECTED RESPONSE

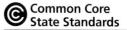

Common Core State Standards

RI.9-10.1, RI.9-10.2, RI.9-10.4, RI.9-10.5, RI.9-10.6, RI.9-10.8; W.9-10.10; L.9-10.4.a

[For full standards wording, see the chart in the front of this book.]

I. Reading Literature/Informational Text

Directions: *Read the excerpt from State of the Union Address (1941) by President Franklin D. Roosevelt. Then, answer each question that follows.*

For there is nothing mysterious about the foundations of a healthy and strong democracy. The basic things expected by our people of their political and economic systems are simple. They are:

Equality of opportunity for youth and for others.

Jobs for those who can work.

Security for those who need it.

The ending of special privilege for the few.

The preservation of civil liberties for all.

The enjoyment of the fruits of scientific progress in a wider and constantly rising standard of living.

These are the simple, basic things that must never be lost sight of in the turmoil and unbelievable complexity of our modern world. The inner and abiding strength of our economic and political systems is dependent upon the degree to which they fulfill these expectations.

Many subjects connected with our social economy call for immediate improvement. As examples:

We should bring more citizens under the coverage of old-age pensions and unemployment insurance.

We should widen the opportunities for adequate medical care.

We should plan a better system by which persons deserving or needing gainful employment may obtain it.

I have called for personal sacrifice. I am assured of the willingness of almost all Americans to respond to that call.

1. What is a **central idea** expressed in the excerpt?
   A. People's expectations of their political system must be lowered.
   B. Scientific progress is the most important factor in a strong democracy.
   C. Our modern world is too complex for simple, basic ideals.
   D. Some aspects of the social economy need immediate attention.

2. Which lines from the excerpt present the best example of **parallellism?**
   A. lines 1–3
   B. lines 11–14
   C. lines 4–10
   D. lines 15–16

3. **Part A** Which answer choice best indicates the general **purpose** of this speech?
   A. to persuade
   B. to reflect
   C. to entertain
   D. to describe

   Part B Which passage from the excerpt most clearly reflects the general purpose of the speech?
   A. "These are the simple, basic things..."
   B. "I am assured of the willingness of almost all Americans…"
   C. "For there is nothing mysterious…"
   D. "Many subjects connected with our social economy call for immediate improvement."

4. Which **rhetorical device** is used in lines 17–21?
   A. analogy
   B. repetition
   C. restatement
   D. rhetorical question

5. What is the meaning of the underlined word *democracy* as it is used in the passage?
   A. political party
   B. group of nations
   C. government by the people
   D. country of origin

6. Which passage from the excerpt is most clearly an **appeal to emotion?**
   A. "The basic things expected by our people of their political and economic systems are simple."
   B. "We should plan a better system…"
   C. "I have called for personal sacrifice."
   D. "Many subjects connected with our social economy call for immediate improvement."

7. Which word best describes the **tone** of this speech?
   A. lighthearted
   B. serious
   C. informal
   D. uncertain

Timed Writing

8. In an essay, describe President Roosevelt's **diction** and **syntax** as it appears in this excerpt. Explain how these elements of the **author's style** help to advance his purpose in this speech. Use textual evidence to support your ideas.

GO ON

II. Reading Informational Text

Directions: *Read the article. Then, answer each question that follows.*

Common Core State Standards

RI.9-10.2, RI.9-10.3, RI.9-10.5; L.9-10.2.a, L.9-10.3
[For full standards wording, see the chart in the front of this book.]

Dog Training: Dominance vs. Leadership

The traditional method for training dogs—dominance-based training—requires a human being to establish physical control over a dog in order to modify its behavior. The trainer handles the dog, rolling him or her over to force submission, and the dog is given few rewards. This method of training is based on the theory that dogs are similar to wolves, who establish dominance through physical confrontation.

Another approach—leadership training—employs gentler methods for teaching dogs acceptable behavior. One program of this type is called "Nothing In Life Is Free" (NILIF). The NILIF protocol requires a dog to perform a command before being rewarded with something he or she wants, such as food, attention, or a walk. For example, if a dog wants to go outside, he or she must first sit. The NILIF trainer waits until the dog performs the desired behavior, and only then provides rewards. The dog quickly learns to perform as commanded in order to get desirable things or experiences.

Traditional dominance-based training can result in a submissive dog, but can also create a relationship of fear between dog and human. Also, it can sometimes result in a more aggressive dog. With leadership training, no fear or aggression is involved. Thus, this method tends to create a stronger bond between pet and owner. Many trainers in the Association of Pet Dog Trainers prefer leadership-training methods.

1. Part A According to the article, what is one problem with dominance training?

A. Dominance training may result in a more aggressive dog.
B. Dominance training proved ineffective in taming wolves.
C. Dominance training takes too much time.
D. Dominance training involves too many rewards.

2. What organizational structure does the author use in the last paragraph of the article?

A. chronological order
B. comparison-and-contrast organization
C. cause-and-effect organization
D. spatial order

3. What is the best definition for the underlined word *protocol?*

A. network or grid
B. procedure or system
C. skill or talent
D. authority or control

III. Writing and Language Conventions

Directions: *Read the passage. Then, answer each question that follows.*

(1) Katrina wrote her cellular phone service provider a letter.
(2) Read her letter below.

(3) Dear Sir or Madam:

(4) I am writing to request a termination of the one-year cellular phone contract I signed three months ago. (5) The service has been sporadic. (6) I am unable to send or receive calls from my home or neighborhood. (7) In addition, when I make calls outside this area, the likelihood of the call being dropped is very high. (8) I am angry. (9) I am upset.

(10) I realize that there is normally a termination fee however, I was assured when the contract was signed that I would have no service problems in my area. (11) As a result of my difficulty, I would like the termination fee waived and want to receive a partial refund on the bills I have paid. (12) I need that cash! (13) Please notify me of your plan.

(14) Sincerely,
(15) *Katrina Vasquez*
(16) Katrina Vasquez

1. Which word in sentence 1 is a **direct object?**
   A. Katrina
   B. phone service
   C. provider
   D. letter

2. If Katrina decides to include a quotation from the contract in her letter, which introduction to her quotation uses the correct **punctuation mark?**
   A. The contract states the following,
   B. The contract states the following;
   C. The contract states the following:
   D. The contract states the following...

3. Which of the following structures is the result of combining sentences 8 and 9 below?

   I am angry and upset.

   A. a compound verb
   B. a compound object
   C. a compound predicate adjective
   D. a compound predicate nominative

4. Which sentence contains a **dependent clause?**
   A. sentence 1
   B. sentence 5
   C. sentence 6
   D. sentence 7

5. Which revision to the beginning of sentence 10 corrects the missing or incorrect **punctuation mark?**
   A. I realize that there is normally a termination fee: however,
   B. I realize that there is normally a termination fee; however,
   C. I realize that: there is normally a termination fee however
   D. I realize that there is normally a termination fee... however

CONSTRUCTED RESPONSE

RI.9-10.2, RI.9-10.4, RI.9-10.5, RI.9-10.6; W.9-10.2, W.9-10.7, W.9-10.9.b; SL.9-10.4
[For full standards wording, see the chart in the front of this book.]

Directions: *Follow the instructions to complete the tasks below as required by your teacher.*

As you work on each task, incorporate both general academic vocabulary and literary terms you learned in Parts 1 and 2 of this unit.

Writing

TASK 1 Informational Text [RI.9-10.4, RI.9-10.6]

Determine an Author's Purpose and Point of View

Write an essay in which you identify the author's purpose and point of view in a work from Part 2 of this unit.

- Identify the selection you will use as the focus for your essay. State the work's topic and explain the author's general and specific purposes for writing.
- Describe the author's point of view on the topic. Explain how that perspective influences his or her choices of supporting information and details.
- Evaluate the author's use of any rhetorical devices, such as parallel construction, repetition, and figurative language, to advance his or her point of view. Include examples from the text to support your evaluation.

TASK 2 Informational Text [RI.9-10.2; W.9-10.2]

Analyze the Development of Central Ideas

Write an essay in which you compare and contrast the development of the central ideas of two texts from Part 2 of this unit.

- Write a brief summary of each text. Clearly state the central idea each text expresses.
- Describe how each author introduces his or her central idea and explain the strategies he or she uses to develop that idea.
- Discuss specific details that contribute to the development of each central idea. Explain what each detail adds.
- Point out the similarities and differences in the techniques each author uses to develop his or her main idea. If possible, make connections between the techniques the author uses and the types of writing each text exemplifies.

TASK 3 Informational Text [RI.9-10.5; W.9-10.2]

Analyze Characteristics of Expository and Persuasive Texts

Write an essay in which you analyze in detail how expository and persuasive texts are alike and different.

Part A

- Select one expository text and one persuasive text from Part 2 of this unit.
- As you review each text, make notes about the author's purpose for writing. In addition, note key aspects of his or her style as well as the organizational structure he or she uses and the types of supporting details he or she includes.
- Answer the following questions: What is the most significant difference between the two texts? What qualities do the two texts share?

Part B

- Use your notes and answers to the questions in Part A to write an analytic essay in which you compare and contrast the two texts. Based on this analysis, draw conclusions about the ways in which expository and persuasive texts are both similar and different.
- Use examples from the texts you chose to illustrate and support your analysis and conclusions.

Speaking and Listening

TASK 4 Informational Text [RI.9-10.2; SL.9-10.4]

Determine the Central Idea

Write and deliver an oral report in which you determine the central idea in a nonfiction work from Part 2 of this unit.

- Identify the work you will discuss, explain who wrote it, and briefly summarize it.
- State your interpretation of the work's central idea.
- Show how you arrived at your interpretation by explaining how the author introduces and develops the key idea. Cite specific details from the work that support your interpretation.
- Present your information clearly, logically, and concisely. Aid your listeners' understanding by giving them an annotated copy of the work, a list of key supporting details you will discuss, or other helpful information.
- Use the conventions of standard English when presenting your report.

TASK 5 Informational Text [RI.9-10.4; SL.9-10.4]

Analyze Diction, Syntax, Meaning, and Tone

Write and deliver a visual presentation in which you analyze the impact of diction and syntax on the tone of a nonfiction work from Part 2 of this unit.

- Choose a work that exhibits interesting diction and syntax. Identify at least two examples of diction and two examples of syntax from that text.
- For each example of diction and syntax you chose, write a paragraph in which you analyze why the author chose to use that particular word, phrase, or arrangement of words. Explain how those choices affect the meaning and tone of the work as a whole.
- Find or create visuals, such as photographs, drawings, charts, or graphs, that illustrate your ideas.
- Organize your written materials and visuals into a presentation that sets out a clear line of reasoning.
- Share your presentation with the class, transitioning logically between reading from your text and showing the visuals.

Research

TASK 6 Informational Text [RI.9-10.2; W.9-10.7, W.9-10.9.b]

Is knowledge the same as understanding?

In Part 2 of this unit, you have read texts that explore different ways of knowing and understanding the world. Now you will conduct a short research project about the ways in which people learn or gain knowledge. Choose a topic that is focused enough for a short research project. For example, you might research how a particular musician learns a new piece, an athlete learns a new move, or a child learns a new word. Use both the texts you have read and the research you have conducted to reflect on and write about this unit's Big Question. Review the following guidelines before you begin your research:

- Use reliable print or digital sources.
- Take notes as you analyze the texts you find through research.
- Cite your sources accurately.

When you have completed your research, write an essay in response to the Big Question. Discuss how your initial ideas have changed or been reinforced. Support your response with examples from both a text you have read in Part 2 of this unit and those you discovered through research.

"**Brother**, can you spare a **dime**?"

—Yip Harburg and Jay Gorney

PART 3

TEXT SET DEVELOPING INSIGHT

THE GREAT DEPRESSION

The Great Depression was a dramatic and painful time in American history. The stock market crash, bank failures, massive unemployment, and devastating drought created a perfect storm of economic failure. The readings in this section provide different kinds of information about the era. Some focus on facts and data while others provide personal accounts of life during those years. As you read each selection, consider what it suggests about the Big Question for this unit: **Is knowledge the same as understanding?** Think about how each text adds to your knowledge of the Great Depression. By gaining this knowledge, do you also gain understanding of what it was like to live through that time in history?

◀ CRITICAL VIEWING This sentence comes from a famous song written during the Great Depression. How might this lyric connect to the experiences of the people in the photo?

READINGS IN PART 3

CLOSE READING TOOL

Use the **Close Reading Tool** to practice the strategies you learn in this unit.

First Inaugural Address

Franklin Delano Roosevelt

President Hoover, Mr. Chief Justice, my friends:

This is a day of national consecration,[1] and I am certain that my fellow-Americans expect that on my induction into the Presidency I will address them with a candor and a decision which the present situation of our nation impels.

◀ **candor** (kan′ dər) *n.* sharp honesty or frankness in expressing oneself

This is pre-eminently the time to speak the truth, the whole truth, frankly and boldly. Nor need we shrink from honestly facing conditions in our country today. This great nation will endure as it has endured, will revive and will prosper.

So first of all let me assert my firm belief that the only thing we have to fear is fear itself—nameless, unreasoning, unjustified terror which paralyzes needed efforts to convert retreat into advance.

In every dark hour of our national life a leadership of frankness and vigor has met with that understanding and support of the people themselves which is essential to victory. I am convinced that you will again give that support to leadership in these critical days.

In such a spirit on my part and on yours we face our common difficulties. They concern, thank God, only material things. Values have shrunken to fantastic levels; taxes have risen; our ability to pay has fallen, government of all kinds is faced by serious curtailment of income; the means of exchange are frozen in the currents of trade; the withered leaves of industrial enterprise lie on every side; farmers find no markets for their produce; the savings of many years in thousands of families are gone.

More important, a host of unemployed citizens face the grim problem of existence, and an equally great number toil with little return. Only a foolish optimist can deny the dark realities of the moment.

Yet our distress comes from no failure of substance. We are stricken by no plague of locusts.[2] Compared with the perils which our forefathers conquered because they believed and were not afraid, we have still much to be thankful for. Nature still offers her bounty and human efforts have multiplied it. Plenty is at our doorstep, but a generous use of it languishes in the very sight of the supply.

Primarily, this is because the rulers of the exchange of mankind's

1. **consecration** (kän′ si krā′ shən) *n.* dedication to something sacred.
2. **plague of locusts** According to Exodus 10:3–20, the plague of locusts was one of ten plagues inflicted by God on the Egyptians as punishment for enslaving the Israelites.

◀ President Frankin D. Roosevelt delivering his first inaugural address, 1933 goods have failed through their own stubbornness and their own incompetence, have admitted that failure and abdicated. Practices of the unscrupulous money changers stand indicted in the court of public opinion, rejected by the hearts and minds of men.

True, they have tried, but their efforts have been cast in the pattern of an outworn tradition. Faced by failure of credit, they have proposed only the lending of more money.

Stripped of the lure of profit by which to induce our people to follow their false leadership, they have resorted to exhortations, pleading tearfully for restored confidence. They know only the rules of a generation of self-seekers.

They have no vision, and when there is no vision the people perish.

The money changers have fled from their high seats in the temple[3] of our civilization. We may now restore that temple to the ancient truths.

The measure of the restoration lies in the extent to which we apply social values more noble than mere monetary profit.

Happiness lies not in the mere possession of money; it lies in the joy of achievement, in the thrill of creative effort.

The joy and moral stimulation of work no longer must be forgotten in the mad chase of evanescent profits. These dark days will be worth all they cost us if they teach us that our true destiny is not to be ministered unto but to minister to ourselves and to our fellow-men.

Recognition of the falsity of material wealth as the standard of success goes hand in hand with the abandonment of the false belief that public office and high political position are to be valued only by the standards of pride of place and personal profit; and there must be an end to a conduct in banking and in business which too often has given to a sacred trust the likeness of callous and selfish wrongdoing.

Small wonder that confidence languishes, for it thrives only on honesty, on honor, on the sacredness of obligations, on faithful protection, on unselfish performance. Without them it cannot live.

Restoration calls, however, not for changes in ethics alone. This nation asks for action, and action now.

Our greatest primary task is to put people to work. This is no unsolvable problem if we face it wisely and courageously. . . .

I favor as a practical policy the putting of first things first. I shall spare no effort to restore world trade by international economic readjustment, but the emergency at home cannot wait on that accomplishment.

---

3. **money changers . . . temple** allusion to Matthew 21:12–13, in which Jesus overturns the money changers' tables at the temple in Jerusalem. The president is comparing those ancient money changers to modern bankers who took great risks with depositors' money and who charged excessive interest rates for loans.

The basic thought that guides these specific means of national recovery is not narrowly nationalistic.

It is the insistence, as a first consideration, upon the interdependence of the various elements in, and parts of, the United States—a recognition of the old and permanently important manifestation of the American spirit of the pioneer.

It is the way to recovery. It is the immediate way. It is the strongest assurance that the recovery will endure.

In the field of world policy I would dedicate this nation to the policy of the good neighbor—the neighbor who resolutely respects himself and, because he does so, respects the rights of others—the neighbor who respects his obligations and respects the sanctity of his agreements in and with a world of neighbors.

If I read the temper of our people correctly, we now realize as we have never before, our interdependence on each other; that we cannot merely take, but we must give as well; that if we are to go forward we must move as a trained and loyal army willing to sacrifice for the good of a common discipline, because, without such discipline, no progress is made, no leadership becomes effective.

We are, I know, ready and willing to submit our lives and property to such discipline because it makes possible a leadership which aims at a larger good.

These dark days will be worth all they cost us if they teach us that our true destiny is not to be ministered unto but to minister to ourselves and to our fellow-men.

Bread line on a city street during the Depression

This I propose to offer, pledging that the larger purposes will bind upon us all as a sacred obligation with a unity of duty hitherto evoked only in time of armed strife.

With this pledge taken, I assume unhesitatingly the leadership of this great army of our people, dedicated to a disciplined attack upon our common problems.

feasible ▶ (fē´ zə bəl) *adj.* capable of being done or carried out; practicable; possible

Action in this image and to this end is feasible under the forms of government which we have inherited from our ancestors.

Our Constitution is so simple and practical that it is possible always to meet extraordinary needs by changes in emphasis and arrangement without loss of essential form.

That is why our constitutional system has proved itself the most superbly enduring political mechanism the modern world has produced. It has met every stress of vast expansion of territory, of foreign wars, of bitter internal strife, of world relations. . . .

I am prepared under my constitutional duty to recommend the measures that a stricken nation in the midst of a stricken world may require.

These measures, or such other measures as the Congress may build out of its experience and wisdom, I shall seek, within my constitutional authority, to bring to speedy adoption.

Presidential candidate Franklin Delano Roosevelt as his motorcade arrives in Atlanta,1932

But in the event that the Congress shall fail to take one of these two courses, and in the event that the national emergency is still critical, I shall not evade the clear course of duty that will then confront me.

I shall ask the Congress for the one remaining instrument to meet the crisis—broad executive power to wage a war against the emergency as great as the power that would be given me if we were in fact invaded by a foreign foe.

For the trust reposed in me I will return the courage and the devotion that befit the time. I can do no less.

We face the arduous days that lie before us in the warm courage of national unity; with the clear consciousness of seeking old and precious moral values; with the clean satisfaction that comes from the stern performance of duty by old and young alike.

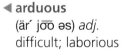

◀ **arduous** (är′ jo͞o əs) *adj.* difficult; laborious

We aim at the assurance of a rounded and permanent national life.

We do not distrust the future of essential democracy. The people of the United States have not failed. In their need they have registered a mandate that they want direct, vigorous action.

They have asked for discipline and direction under leadership. They have made me the present instrument of their wishes. In the spirit of the gift I take it.

In this dedication of a nation we humbly ask the blessing of God. May He protect each and every one of us. May He guide me in the days to come.

ABOUT THE AUTHOR

Franklin Delano Roosevelt

(1882–1945)

Franklin Delano Roosevelt had a relatively easy life until he was stricken with polio at age 39. Ironically, Roosevelt realized his potential as a leader only after falling victim to this illness. He was twice elected governor of New York; then, in 1932, he defeated President Herbert Hoover to become the nation's thirty-second president. Roosevelt won an unprecedented four terms as president.

On March 4, 1933, newly elected President Franklin Delano Roosevelt delivered his inaugural address to a nation close to despair. The Great Depression had weighed down American life for more than three years. Americans sat by their radios to hear the new president's address, a speech he had written himself.

Franklin Roosevelt led the nation through two great challenges: the Great Depression and World War II. The war was almost over when the president died in 1945.

Close Reading Activities

READ

Comprehension

Reread all or part of the text to help you answer the following questions.

1. What are the occasion and purpose of this speech?
2. According to Roosevelt, what are the "common difficulties" he and his audience face?
3. On whom does Roosevelt place the largest blame for the Great Depression?
4. What does Roosevelt say is the "greatest primary task" facing the nation?
5. According to Roosevelt, how should Congress respond to the crisis?

Research: Clarify Details This speech may include references that are unfamiliar to you. Choose at least one unfamiliar detail, and briefly research it. Then, explain how the information you learned from research sheds light on an aspect of the speech.

Summarize Write an objective summary of the speech. Remember that an objective summary is free from opinion and evaluation.

Language Study

Selection Vocabulary The following passages appear in "First Inaugural Address." Define each boldface word. Then, use the word in a sentence of your own.

- I am certain that my fellow-Americans expect that on my induction into the Presidency I will address them with a **candor** and a decision which the present situation of our nation impels.
- Action in this image and to this end is **feasible** under the forms of government which we have inherited from our ancestors.
- We face the **arduous** days that lie before us in the warm courage of national unity....

Diction and Style Study the excerpt from the speech that appears below. Then, answer the questions.

> Values have shrunken to fantastic levels; taxes have risen; our ability to pay has fallen, government of all kinds is faced by serious curtailment of income....

1. **(a)** What does *fantastic* mean in this passage? **(b)** How does this meaning relate to the idea of fantasy or imagination?
2. **(a)** Identify a synonym Roosevelt could have used in place of *fantastic*. **(b)** What aspects of America's economic problems does the word *fantastic* emphasize that the synonym does not?

Conventions Read this passage from the speech. Identify the predicate nominatives. Then, explain how the author's use of predicate nominatives helps create parallelism and strengthens the message of the text.

> It is the way to recovery. It is the immediate way. It is the strongest assurance that the recovery will endure.

Academic Vocabulary

The following words appear in blue in the instructions and questions on the facing page.

trace **signaled** **accentuate**

Categorize the words by deciding whether you know each one well, know it a little bit, or do not know it at all. Then, use a dictionary to look up the definitions of the words you are unsure of or do not know at all.

Literary Analysis

Reread the identified passages. Then, respond to the questions that follow.

Focus Passage 1 *(pp. 285–286)*
Yet our distress . . . the ancient truths.

Key Ideas and Details

1. According to Roosevelt, why should Americans be "thankful" even in the midst of their troubles?
2. **(a) Interpret:** Who are the "rulers of the exchange of mankind's goods"? **(b) Analyze:** According to Roosevelt, how have these people failed the country?

Craft and Structure

3. **(a) Trace** references to the "unscrupulous money changers" through the passage. **(b) Connect:** To what Biblical event do these references allude? **(c) Analyze:** What comparison is Roosevelt making through this allusion? Explain.
4. **(a) Interpret:** The president refers to the "temple" of civilization. What tone, or attitude toward his topic, is **signaled** by this term? **(b) Analyze:** Cite two other examples of Roosevelt's diction that contribute to that tone. Explain your choices.

Integration of Knowledge and Ideas

5. **Connect:** What does Roosevelt believe about the role of leaders in society? Explain, citing details from the text.

Focus Passage 2 *(p. 286)*
Happiness lies not . . . it cannot live.

Key Ideas and Details

1. **(a)** According to Roosevelt, what is the source of happiness? **(b) Interpret:** For Roosevelt, what lesson must Americans learn from the "dark days" of the Depression? Explain.

Craft and Structure

2. **(a) Distinguish:** Identify phrases in the passage in which *d, s, p,* or *b* sounds repeat at the beginnings of nearby words. **(b) Interpret:** In what ways might this use of alliteration affect how readers hear and remember the passage? Explain.
3. **(a)** Which words does Roosevelt repeat in the focus passage, either in whole or in a related form? **(b) Analyze:** What key ideas do these words **accentuate**? Explain.

Integration of Knowledge and Ideas

4. **(a) Summarize:** What is Roosevelt's message about the importance of wealth over other values? **(b) Analyze:** Why might such a message be particularly powerful at this point in history?

Persuasive Appeals

There are three types of **persuasive appeal:** *ethos,* or the appeal to the speaker's expertise and credibility; *logos,* or the appeal to reason and logic; and *pathos,* or the appeal to emotion.

1. **(a)** In the beginning of the speech, what does the president say about how he will speak to the people? **(b)** Explain how this is an appeal to ethos, or to the president's authority and trustworthiness.
2. **(a)** What information does Roosevelt provide about the "common difficulties" the nation faces? **(b)** Explain how this list of realities is an appeal to logos—to listeners' ability to think and reason.
3. **The Great Depression: (a)** Cite two examples of Roosevelt's use of pathos. **(b)** For each example, explain what the emotional message is and why it would appeal to audiences in the midst of the Great Depression.

Common Core State Standards

RI.9-10.1, RI.9-10.2, RI.9-10.3, RI.9-10.4, RI.9-10.5, RI.9-10.6, RI.9-10.8, RI.9-10.9, RI.9-10.10; L.9-10.4.a, L.9-10.4.c, L.9-10.4.d, L.9-10.5.b, L.9-10.6

[For full standards wording, see the chart in the front of this book.]

DISCUSS

From Text to Topic **Debate**

Debate the following passage with your classmates. Clearly state your ideas and support them with evidence from the text.

> But in the event that the Congress shall fail to take one of these two courses, and in the event that the national emergency is still critical, I shall not evade the clear course of duty that will then confront me.
>
> I shall ask the Congress for the one remaining instrument to meet the crisis—broad executive power to wage a war against the emergency as great as the power that would be given me if we were in fact invaded by a foreign foe.

QUESTIONS FOR DISCUSSION

1. What is Roosevelt's tone in this passage?
2. What image of a leader does Roosevelt project in this passage?
3. Do you think listeners at the time found the message of a "war" on the emergency to be comforting or disturbing? Explain.

WRITE

Writing to Sources **Argument**

Assignment

Write a **persuasive essay** in which you analyze and evaluate Roosevelt's use of charged, or emotionally loaded, language in this speech. Cite at least two examples of his use of charged words and discuss the appropriateness of such language given the occasion and purpose of the speech.

Prewriting and Planning Reread the speech, looking for passages in which Roosevelt uses words designed to stir listeners' emotions. Record your notes.

Drafting Select an organizational structure for your essay. Most persuasive writing follows order of importance organization. State your claim in a thesis statement, and then organize your ideas in the order that best supports that claim.

- **Most to Least Important** Present your most convincing support first to capture the audience's attention.
- **Least to Most Important** Begin with your least important point and build your argument, unleashing the most convincing support at the end.

In your draft, cite specific examples from the speech to support your points.

Revising Rearrange sentences or paragraphs as needed to strengthen the logical flow of your essay. Delete any sentences that do not contribute to your main idea. Also, be sure that you have included sufficient and convincing support in the form of evidence from the text.

Editing and Proofreading Check your spelling and punctuation as you prepare the final draft. In particular, use colons, semicolons, and ellipses correctly, especially when quoting from the text.

CONVENTIONS

A passage that supports your argument may include more information than is necessary to your purpose. Identify the relevant portions of the passage and use ellipsis points to indicate text you have eliminated.

RESEARCH

Research **Investigate the Topic**

Bankers and the Great Depression In his first inaugural address, Roosevelt names the actions of bankers, or in his words "money changers," as a primary cause of the Great Depression. He accuses the entire banking industry of unscrupulous behavior, incompetence, greed, and a focus on profits that ignored all other values.

Assignment

Conduct research to determine the role that the banking industry played in causing the Great Depression. Consult historical documents, such as newspaper articles covering the stock market crash of 1929, as well as modern analyses of the banks' role in that event. Take clear notes and carefully identify your sources for citation. Share your findings in an **oral presentation.**

PREPARATION FOR ESSAY

You may use the knowledge you gain during this research assignment to support your claims in an essay you will write at the end of this section.

Gather Sources Locate authoritative sources. Secondary sources, such as history books and modern analyses, provide insight into the cause-and-effect relationship of events. You may also use primary sources, such as interviews with bankers of the era or historical documents from Wall Street. Look for reliable sources that feature credible authors and sound information.

Take Notes Use an organized note-taking strategy for each source your consult.

- If you takes notes electronically, use the copy and paste functions of your word-processing program to capture Web addresses and publication information from online sources. Doing so will help you avoid errors.
- When you copy direct quotations from print sources, be sure to record the page number on which you found the quotation. You will need it for your in-text citation.
- Save time by writing down only the basics. Make quick notes about the most pertinent ideas and then revisit sources to check the details.

Synthesize Multiple Sources Use your notes to organize your research into a cohesive presentation. Use what you learned from primary and secondary sources to draw conclusions about the role the banking industry played in the Great Depression. Construct a thorough outline for your presentation and include a Works Cited list. See the Citing Sources pages in the Introductory Unit of this textbook for additional guidance.

Organize and Present Ideas Practice delivering your presentation, maintaining eye contact with your audience, and pacing your speech. Anticipate questions your audience might have and prepare answers, with reliable citations, to address them.

Common Core State Standards

W.9-10.1, W.9-10.1.a, W.9-10.4, W.9-10.5, W.9-10.7, W.9-10.8, W.9-10.9, W.9-10.9.b; SL.9-10.4; L.9-10.1, L.9-10.2, L.9-10.2.b–c, L.9-10.3.a, L.9-10.6

[For full standards wording, see the chart in the front of this book.]

President Franklin Delano Roosevelt at his desk in the Oval Office

from

Nothing to Fear: Lessons in Leadership from FDR

Alan Axelrod

"This great nation will endure as it has endured, will revive and will prosper. So, first of all, let me assert my firm belief that the only thing we have to fear is fear itself—nameless, unreasoning, unjustified terror which paralyzes needed efforts to convert retreat into advance."

— Franklin Delano Roosevelt; First Inaugural Address, March 4, 1933

In *Defending Your Life*, a charmingly provocative 1991 movie written and directed by its star, Albert Brooks, we discover that the only truly unforgivable sin in life is fear. Killed in a head-on crash with a bus, yuppie Brooks finds himself transported to Judgment City, where he must "defend his life" before a pair of judges who will decide whether he is to be returned to Earth for another crack at life or be permitted to progress to the next plane of existence. His attorney (for the benevolent managers of the universe provide defense assistance) explains to him the nature of fear, which is, he says, a "fog" that obscures everything and that makes intelligent, productive action impossible.

provocative ▶ (prə väk′ə tiv) *adj.* exciting; stimulating

obscures ▶ (əb skyoorz′) *v.* conceals; hides

It is a stimulating thought—that fear is not so much the sensation accompanying the realization of danger, but a fog, an obscurer of truth, an interference with how we may productively engage reality. Certainly this is the way FDR saw it. In 1921 polio threatened first to kill him and then paralyzed him, subjected him to a life of relentless pain, and nearly ended his career in public service. He could then and there have given in to the fog of fear, but he chose not to. He chose instead to understand polio, to see clearly the extent of his disability, and then to assess—also clearly—his options for overcoming that disability. He did not blink at the odds. He looked at them, contemplated them, assessed them, and then acted on them.

Now, more than a decade later, assuming the office of president of the United States, he began by asking the American people to sweep aside the fog of fear, "nameless, unreasoning, unjustified terror which paralyzes needed efforts to convert retreat into advance." He didn't ask them to stop being afraid, but to stop letting fear obscure their vision of reality. He asked the people to confront what they feared, so that they could see clearly what needed to be done and thereby overcome (and the word is significant) the terror that *paralyzes.*

In the second paragraph of his inaugural speech, FDR lifted the fog of fear. What did he reveal to his audience, the American people?

> Values have shrunken to fantastic levels; taxes have risen; our ability to pay has fallen; government of all kinds is faced by serious curtailment of income; the means of exchange are frozen in the currents of trade; the withered leaves of industrial enterprise lie on every side; farmers find no markets for their produce; the savings of many years in thousands of families are gone.

There is no sugarcoating of reality here! The fog has lifted, the scene is sharply etched and downright frightening: "a host of unemployed citizens face the grim problem of existence, and an equally great number toil with little return. Only a foolish optimist can deny the dark realities of the moment."

FDR did not blink at reality and he did not allow his audience to do so either. He embarked on this catalog of economic disasters by defining them as "our common difficulties," which "concern, thank God, only material things."

The fog was lifted and the president's listeners could see the reality they already knew, a reality of poverty and despair, to be sure; yet with the fog of fear lifted, they could see it in a new light: Our common difficulties "concern, thank God, only material things."

Not one to blink at disaster, FDR also saw a way out of it:

> Yet our distress comes from no failure of substance. We are stricken by no plague of locusts. Compared with the perils which our forefathers conquered because they believed and were not afraid, we have still much to be thankful for. Nature still offers her bounty and human efforts have multiplied it. Plenty is at our doorstep. . .

Lift the fog of fear and you could see that the Great Depression was not of natural, supernatural, or **inevitable** origin. It was not a plague of biblical proportion. Our kind has conquered worse in the past.

◂ **inevitable**
(in ev′i tə bəl) *adj.* certain to happen; incapable of being avoided

Close Reading Activities

READ

Comprehension

Reread all or part of the text to help you answer the following questions.

1. What event in FDR's life does Axelrod use as an example of the president's facing down fear?
2. According to the author, how does FDR's first inaugural address ease people's fears?
3. In Axelrod's view, what does the easing of fear allow FDR's listeners to perceive?

Research: Clarify Details This essay may include references that are unfamiliar to you. Choose at least one unfamiliar detail and briefly research it. Then, explain how the information you learned from research sheds light on an aspect of the essay.

Summarize Write an objective summary of the essay. Remember that an objective summary is free from opinion and evaluation.

Language Study

Selection Vocabulary The following passages appear in the essay. Define each boldfaced word. Then, use all three terms in a paragraph.

- His attorney...explains to him the nature of fear, which is...a "fog" that **obscures** everything...
- In *Defending Your Life*, a charmingly **provocative** 1991 movie...
- Lift the fog of fear and you could see that the Great Depression was not of natural, supernatural, or **inevitable** origin.

Literary Analysis

Reread the identified passage. Then, respond to the questions that follow.

Focus Passage *(p. 294)*
It is a stimulating thought...acted on them.

Key Ideas and Details

1. **Interpret:** According to Axelrod, what relationship exists between fear and truth? Explain.

Craft and Structure

2. **(a) Distinguish:** What words and phrases does Axelrod use to describe fear? **(b) Interpret:** How does this description support the author's idea that fear is not a "sensation" but a natural force?
3. **(a) Distinguish:** Which words in the passage relate to the idea of seeing or clear judgment? **(b) Analyze:** How do these context clues clarify the meaning of the idiom "to blink at"?

Integration of Knowledge and Ideas

4. In the last sentence of the focus passage, Axelrod lists steps in FDR's reaction to illness. How do these steps support Axelrod's point about FDR's leadership during the Depression? Explain.

Metaphor

A **metaphor** is a comparison between two unlike things. Nonfiction authors may use metaphors to make abstract ideas more real and understandable for readers. Reread the essay, and take notes on the author's use of metaphors.

1. What metaphor does Axelrod repeat to characterize fear and its effects on people?
2. How does this metaphor connect to Axelrod's discussion of FDR's ability to confront "reality"?
3. **The Great Depression:** In what ways does Axelrod's use of metaphor support his judgment that FDR was a **visionary** leader? Explain.

DISCUSS • RESEARCH • WRITE

From Text to Topic **Group Discussion**

Discuss the following passage with a group of classmates. Take notes during the discussion. Contribute your own ideas, and support them with examples from the text.

> He didn't ask them to stop being afraid, but to stop letting fear obscure their vision of reality. He asked the people to confront what they feared, so that they could see clearly what needed to be done and thereby overcome (and the word is significant) the terror that *paralyzes.*

QUESTIONS FOR DISCUSSION

1. What does Axelrod find remarkable about FDR's leadership?
2. Why would attitude adjustments like those Axelrod describes be important in a time of national crisis?

Research **Investigate the Topic**

Action During a Crisis At the end of this essay, Alan Axelrod **asserts** that President Roosevelt saw a way to lead the nation out of the Great Depression.

Assignment

Conduct research to learn about the steps President Roosevelt took to address the causes of economic failure and to provide relief to a suffering nation. Consult a variety of sources, including Web sites run by reliable news organizations. Record your notes carefully, making sure to identify all source information for citation. Share your findings in a **research report.**

PREPARATION FOR ESSAY

You may use the results of this research project in an essay you will write at the end of this section.

Writing to Sources **Argument**

In the excerpt from *Nothing to Fear,* Alan Axelrod analyzes and provides an interpretation of part of FDR's first inaugural address.

Assignment

Write an **argumentative essay** in which you evaluate Axelrod's interpretation of FDR's speech. Follow these steps:

- Make notes about Axelrod's claims and the evidence he uses to support them. Consider whether each piece of evidence is relevant and whether the evidence as a whole provides sufficient support for his position.
- Use your notes to help you sum up your **critique** in a thesis statement. Structure your essay around this statement.
- Review and evaluate your argument, adding and changing support in areas where you feel your position is not sufficiently defended.
- Review your writing for errors in grammar, usage, and mechanics. Eliminate any sentences that do not directly relate to your argument.

ACADEMIC VOCABULARY

Academic terms appear in blue on these pages. If these words are not familiar to you, use a dictionary to find their definitions. Then, use them as you speak and write about the text.

Common Core State Standards

RI.9-10.1, RI.9-10.2, RI.9-10.3, RI.9-10.4, RI.9-10.5, RI.9-10.6, RI.9-10.8; SL.9-10.1; W.9-10.1, W.9-10.4, W.9-10.7; L.9-10.4, L.9-10.5, L.9-10.6

[For full standards wording, see the chart in the front of this book.]

from AMERICANS IN THE GREAT DEPRESSION

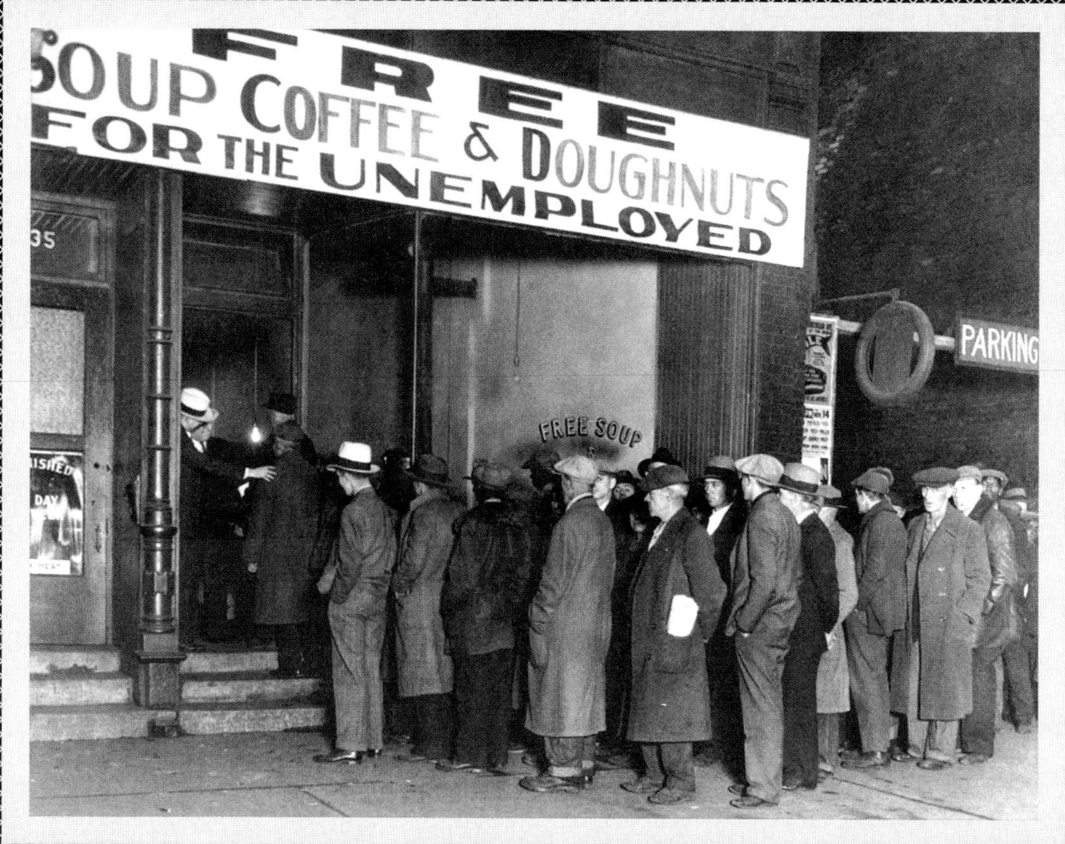

Unemployed men line up at a soup kitchen opened by notorious gangster Al Capone in Chicago (1931).

from *The Great Depression and the New Deal: A Very Short Introduction*

Eric Rauchway

The United States endured depressions before the 1930s, but the Great Depression, in its breadth and duration, and in the immediacy of its chronicling, produced also a great compression.

The newly interconnected country (Americans in their twenties could remember when there were still western territories, rather than fully fledged states) now had radio and newsreels throughout its towns to show itself how its people suffered. As the Depression lasted, it put the middle class more and more into the circumstances of the poor and encouraged empathy across class lines. . . .

Americans in need asked for help reluctantly, and when circumstances forced them to seek help, they went to those closest to them. But in the Depression, each of their customary sources of support failed them, one by one. As a New York City official explained in 1932, "when the breadwinner is out of a job he usually exhausts his savings if he has any. . . . He borrows from his friends and from relatives until they can stand the burden no longer. He gets credit from the corner grocery store and the butcher shop, and the landlord forgoes collecting the rent until interest and taxes have to be paid and something has to be done. All of these resources are finally exhausted over a period of time, and it becomes necessary for these people, who have never before been in want, to ask for assistance."

Historically, American cities had through their own treasuries provided relief to their poor, but soon even cities could not help their citizens. In 1932, a Detroit official put it this way:

> Many essential public services have been reduced beyond the minimum point absolutely essential to the health and safety of the city. . . . The salaries of city employees have been twice reduced . . . and hundreds of faithful employees . . . have been furloughed. Thus has the city borrowed from its own future welfare to keep its unemployed on the barest subsistence levels. . . . A wage work plan which had supported 11,000 families collapsed last month because the city was unable to find funds to pay these unemployed—men who wished to earn their own support. For the coming year, Detroit can see no possibility of preventing wide-spread hunger and slow starvation through its own unaided resources.

Sometimes municipal funds might find their way to the needy through nontraditional routes: in New York, where the Health Department found that one in five of the city's schoolchildren suffered from malnutrition, public school teachers, threatened with pay cuts, paid into a fund from their own pockets for the relief of their pupils. As civic organizations and governments crumbled under the weight, often so did families. "A man is not a man without work," one of the unemployed told an interviewer. Those men who felt differently—who made for themselves a place in the world outside the workplace, who as husbands and fathers and friends and hobbyists knew what was worthwhile to strive for—shouldered the burden of crisis more easily. But they were in the minority. As one sociologist wrote, "The average American has the feeling that work . . . is the only dignified way of life. . . . While theoretically, economic activities are supposed to be the means to the good life, as a matter of fact it is not the end, but the means themselves, that have the greater prestige."

"A man is not a man without work," one of the unemployed told an interviewer.

More often than not, men took this sense of duty to heart. They knew how closely their children watched them, how much hung on their ability to get even a little work, how much joy it could bring to a house, or at least how much sorrow it could hold off. As one man who had been a boy during the Depression remembered,

> A lot of fathers—mine, among them—had a habit of taking off. They'd go to . . . look for work. . . . This left the family at home, waiting and hoping that the old man would find something. And there was always the Saturday night ordeal as to whether or not the old man would get home with his paycheck. . . . Heaven would break out once in a while, and the old man would get a week's work . . . that smell of fresh sawdust on the carpenter's overalls, and the fact that Dad was home, and there was a week's wages. . . . That's the good you remember. And then there was always the bad part. That's when you'd see your father coming home with the toolbox on his shoulder. Or carrying it. That meant the job was over.

Sometimes men who left to look for work never came back, finding homes in doorways or subways or the communities of shacks on the edges of cities or landfills that, soon enough, Americans learned to call "Hoovervilles[1]." Children who were old enough and independent

1. **Hoovervilles** named after President Herbert Hoover, shantytowns of temporary shelters that impoverished people built during the Great Depression.

might themselves leave, foraging on the road instead of relying on overburdened parents. Usually such tramps were young men prepared to fend for themselves, racing to catch boxcars and steal rides. Sometimes the railroad detectives turned a blind eye to their unscheduled human cargo, sometimes not. Sometimes other travelers helped, sometimes they did not. In all, maybe two million Americans made their homes on the road in the years after the Crash.

When employers advertised jobs, they had their pick of workers and could indulge their preferences, or prejudices. Increasingly, they hired or kept on white men with work experience, leaving the young and old, the women, and the African Americans **disproportionately** represented among the unemployed. Before the Crash, as women first entered the workforce in significant numbers, Americans

◀ **disproportionately** (dis′prə pôr′shə nət lē) *adv.* in a way that is out of proportion or unfair

A "Hoover Village" built in the old Central Park reservoir (New York City, 1937)

already found it easy to believe that if a woman worked, she was doing it for frivolous spending money—that properly, women would rely on men who, as heads of households, would supply their wives and children with a living. In the labor glut of the Depression, employers—sometimes by policy, sometimes simply by habit—hired fewer married women and more readily dismissed those they already had on the rolls. Yet women increasingly sought work, mainly to keep families afloat, though sometimes to maintain a middle-class life in the face of the Depression. Women faced a harder market than their fathers, husbands, brothers, or sons. And if they had to leave their families, life on the road presented an even greater threat of physical exploitation than it posed to their male relations. Accounts of women out of work and without family tell of them establishing communities to protect themselves, sharing meager resources and small rooms, scheduling shifts for the use of beds and clothes. One politician remarked that the woman worker in America was "the first orphan in the storm."

If so, the black worker followed close behind her into the rough weather. In the cities of the United States, African Americans lost their jobs more quickly than their white counterparts. In part they suffered a misfortune of historical timing: black Americans, long a rural population, had on average moved to cities less recently and had less opportunity to develop careers as skilled laborers than white Americans. But a comparative lack of skills accounted only partially for the high levels of African American unemployment. Black workers noticed that they were "last hired, first fired," and that employers deliberately laid off black workers to replace them with white ones. "So general is this practice that one is warranted in suspecting that it has been adopted as a method of relieving unemployment of whites without regard to the consequences upon Negroes," a National Urban League study concluded in 1931.

These inequities in the job market ensured the Depression-era working class actually in work, or nearest to it, looked much more white, much more male, and overall much more uniform than the working classes of earlier eras. The laborers who held jobs had much visibly in common with one another, and the issues of cultural conflict that so consumed Americans of earlier eras diminished. The object of Americans' **solicitude** became the imperiled white, male head-of-household, whose hardship they could understand as the nation's concern.

solicitude ▶ (sə lis′i to͞od′) *n.* state of being concerned; anxiety

These nationwide hardships crossed the lines between urban and rural populations to an unprecedented degree. Unemployment, as a cyclical problem, had plagued cities as long as there had been cities,

A family preparing to leave Florida during the Great Depression

and Americans had a folk tradition of returning to the countryside when the cities went into a slump. Farm jobs traditionally enjoyed a resistance to the problems that plagued cities, and in the Depression many Americans did seek out the security of a subsistence farm[2]—in 1932 the farm population rose to the highest point it would reach between the two world wars. But a series of unfortunate events made sure that the countryside suffered the Great Depression as the cities did.

Farm incomes reached their peak around World War I, when the dangers of shipping and general scarcity drove up the price of

---

2. **subsistence farm** farm that produces very little profit; almost all crops are used to feed those who work the land.

agricultural produce. High prices inspired farmers to put more land under the plow. Newly available tractors let them do it quickly. Then in the postwar depression, farm prices fell sharply; even after they rose again in the middle 1920s, the prices of the goods farmers had to buy rose higher still. The fresh **prevalence** of farm machines made it cheaper to produce more agricultural goods on a large scale, and as tractors appeared, mules and men went away. "Tractored out" hands left the countryside to seek opportunity elsewhere. Even the new city prosperity hurt farmers: as urban Americans improved their circumstances, they chose their diets based on taste, rather than need. Once, a wider waistband had signaled health and success, but now thin was fashionable, and food producers' income declined. Further, farmers, like other Americans, took on considerable debt in their expansion and mechanization, rendering them vulnerable to shock.

prevalence ▶ (prev′ ə ləns) *n.* state of being prevalent or happening often

"We made a crop that year, the owner takin' all the crop. This horrible way of livin' with almost nothin'."

When the Crash shook this system, the fragile supports for farmers collapsed. Farm income tumbled downward. Creditors forced farmers to sell their property to cover delinquent debt payments. Often, and increasingly, farmers and their neighbors tried to thwart attempts to dispossess them. They might band together and buy property at a delinquency auction, then return it for free to the owner, or they might threaten lawmen who sought forcibly to sell property.

The weather conspired with the man-made calamity. Beginning in 1931, rainfall on the Great Plains lessened until it dropped below the level necessary to sustain crops. Soon the earth would dry and crack so that it could no longer hold itself together, and great winds would simply blow it way.

The South suffered from its continuing peculiarity. Since slavery, its people depended on poorly paid farm jobs to get by. Containing only about a quarter of the nation's population, the South accounted for more than 40 percent of America's farmworkers, and they were the worst-paid hands in the country. Often they were tenant farmers who owed their landlords a share of the crop they produced and had little control over their livelihoods. "In 1929, me and my husband were sharecroppers,"[3] one woman recalled. "We made a crop that year, the owner takin' all the crop. This horrible way of livin' with almost nothin'."

3. **sharecroppers** farmers who work land owned by another and are given credit for seeds, tools, and housing in return for an agreed upon share of the crop.

As both progress and disaster pushed people off the farms, they left, as able people throughout history have done, seeking better chances. As they did before the Depression, many migrants went West, to California, where the job market might be, and the weather generally was, better. Luckier ones came by car: in 1931, more than 800,000 automobiles entered the Golden State. Less fortunate travelers came by train: in a single month of 1932, the Southern Pacific Railroad company, whose lines ran into and along the length of California, figured it had evicted 80,000 freight-hoppers from the cars it carried. Many of both kinds of migrants wound up encamped throughout California's long valleys, living in tents or small cabins, picking crops for what passed for a living, surviving—or failing to—on beans and rice. Observers figured more than a quarter of the children in such camps suffered from malnutrition, and some of them died of it.

The image of Americans living with almost nothing, driven by drought and storm from their homes, bent under hardship and persevering by will, soon seared itself into the minds of people all over the country. In later years, in reporters' stories and in tales survivors told, in enduring photographs by Walker Evans and Dorothea Lange, and accounts by James Agee and Lorena Hickok, these pictures of poverty in the land of dreamed plenty came to represent the Depression.

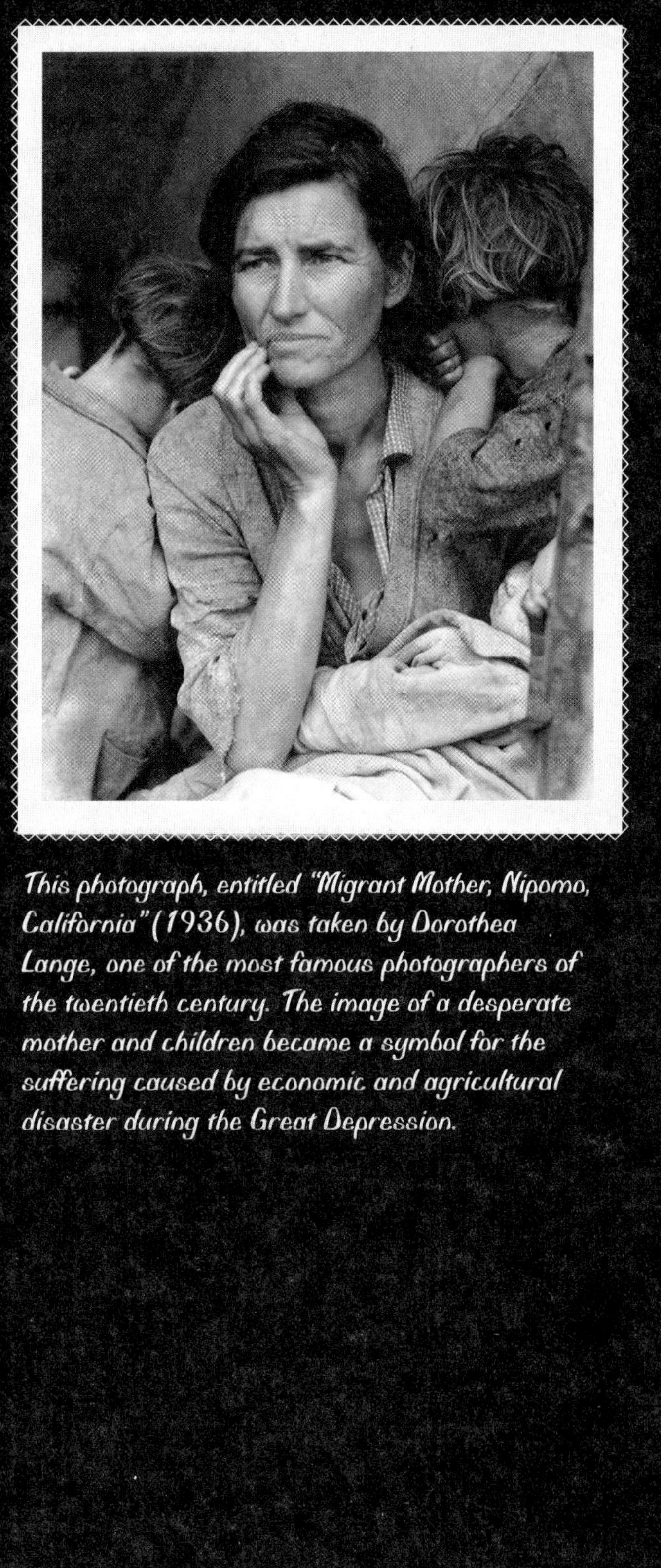

This photograph, entitled "Migrant Mother, Nipomo, California" (1936), was taken by Dorothea Lange, one of the most famous photographers of the twentieth century. The image of a desperate mother and children became a symbol for the suffering caused by economic and agricultural disaster during the Great Depression.

Close Reading Activities

READ

Comprehension

Reread all or part of the text to help you answer the following questions.

1. According to Rauchway, what connection did many Depression-era Americans see between work and personal dignity?
2. How did the profile of the American workforce change during the Depression?
3. What happened in 1931 that caused farms throughout the Great Plains to fail?

Research: Clarify Details This text may include references that are unfamiliar to you. Choose at least one unfamiliar detail, and briefly research it. Then, explain how the information you learned from research sheds light on an aspect of the text.

Summarize Write an objective summary of the text. Remember that an objective summary is free from opinion and evaluation.

Language Study

Selection Vocabulary The phrases at right appear in the text. Define each boldface word. Then, use the word in a sentence of your own.

- **disproportionately** represented
- object of Americans' **solicitude**
- The fresh **prevalence** of farm machines

Literary Analysis

Reread the identified passage. Then, respond to the questions that follow.

Focus Passage *(p. 304–305)*
The South suffered . . . some of them died of it.

Key Ideas and Details

1. **(a)** What are sharecroppers? **(b) Interpret:** How are the "continuing peculiarity" of the South—slavery—and sharecroppers related?
2. **Summarize:** Why did many people leave the farms and head West?

Craft and Structure

3. **Connect:** What ideas does the quotation from the sharecropper **illuminate**?
4. **(a)** Identify the statistics used throughout the passage. **(b) Connect:** Explain what idea the data supports. **(c) Analyze:** How does this use of data add to the scholarly tone of the writing?

Integration of Knowledge and Ideas

5. **Synthesize:** Which details in the focus passage add to the reader's understanding of the "breadth" of the Depression? Explain.

Author's Perspective

An **author's perspective** is the way he or she sees a topic. An author's knowledge, attitudes, and beliefs help to shape his or her perspective on a given subject.

1. **(a)** What types of people does Rauchway primarily discuss in this text? **(b)** What other groups of people might Rauchway have discussed but did not? **(c)** How do these choices **establish** the author's perspective? Explain.
2. **The Great Depression:** In what ways does Rauchway's perspective shape what readers learn about the Depression from this text?

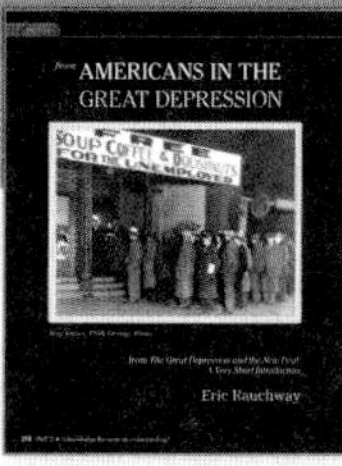

DISCUSS • RESEARCH • WRITE

From Text to Topic **Partner Discussion**

Discuss the following passage with a partner. Take notes during the discussion. Then, summarize your key ideas and share them with the class as a whole.

> As one sociologist wrote, "The average American has the feeling that work... is the only dignified way of life.... While theoretically, economic activities are supposed to be the means to the good life, as a matter of fact it is not the end, but the means themselves, that have the greater prestige."

QUESTIONS FOR DISCUSSION

1. How did circumstances during the Great Depression make this a particularly difficult—even damaging—attitude?
2. Do you think most Americans still hold this attitude today? Explain.

Research **Investigate the Topic**

The Dust Bowl The drought of the 1930s, along with the "Great Plow-Up" at the end of the previous decade, contributed even further to the economic catastrophes of the Great Depression.

Assignment

Conduct research to discover how the drought in the Great Plains, which resulted in the Dust Bowl, contributed to the economic **devastation** of the Great Depression. Consider looking at historical almanacs to note the weather differences from year to year during that era. Take clear notes and carefully identify your sources so that you can cite information correctly in your writing. Share your findings in a **short essay.**

PREPARATION FOR ESSAY

You may use the results of this research in an essay you will write at the end of this section.

Writing to Sources **Narrative**

Rauchway describes how different groups of people were affected by the Great Depression, including men, women, African Americans, city dwellers, and farmers.

Assignment

Write a **fictional narrative** in which you tell a story of the Great Depression from the point of view of someone in one of the groups Rauchway discusses. Follow these steps:

- Choose a main character and review the text for details about how a person from this group was affected by the Depression.
- Craft a first-person narrative based on your ideas about the character as well as the factual details Rauchway includes.
- Include dialogue and description. Read your story aloud so you can "hear" the dialogue and make it sound realistic and natural.
- Check your use of capitalization, commas, and quotation marks throughout your narrative, especially with respect to dialogue.

ACADEMIC VOCABULARY

Academic terms appear in blue on these pages. If these words are not familiar to you, use a dictionary to find their definitions. Then, use them as you speak and write about the text.

Common Core State Standards

RI.9-10.1, RI.9-10.2, RI.9-10.4, RI.9-10.5, RI.9-10.6; SL.9-10.1; W.9-10.3, W.9-10.3.b, W.9-10.4, W.9-10.7; L.9-10.4, L.9-10.6

[For full standards wording, see the chart in the front of this book.]

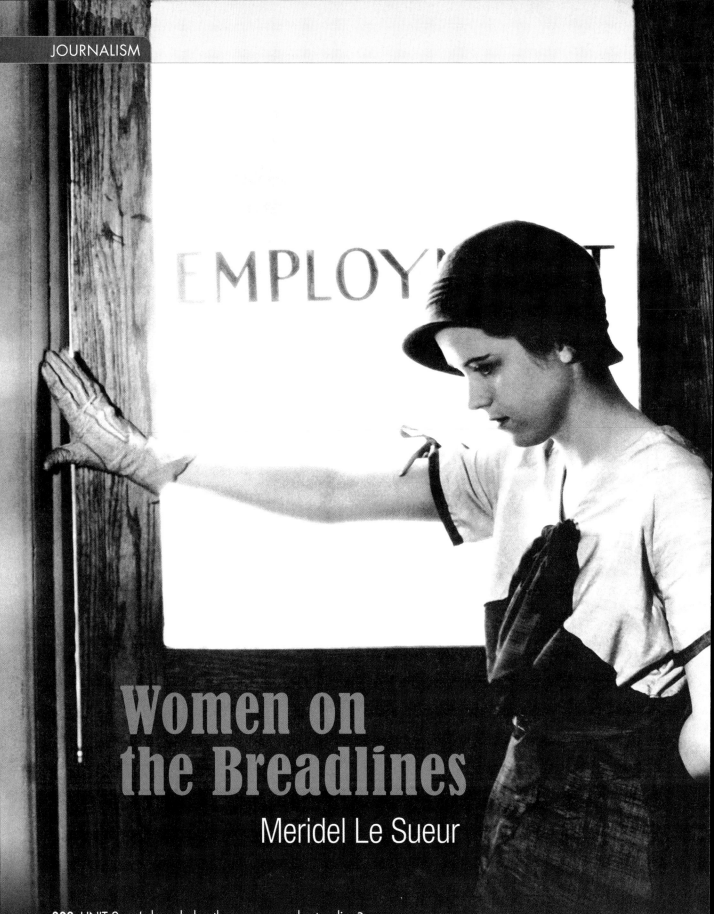

Women on the Breadlines

Meridel Le Sueur

I am sitting in the city free employment bureau. It's the women's section. We have been sitting here now for four hours. We sit here every day, waiting for a job. There are no jobs. Most of us have had no breakfast. Some have had scant rations for over a year. Hunger makes a human being lapse into a state of lethargy, especially city hunger. Is there any place else in the world where a human being is supposed to go hungry amidst plenty without an outcry, without protest, where only the boldest steal or kill for bread, and the timid crawl the streets, hunger like the beak of a terrible bird at the vitals?

We sit looking at the floor. No one dares think of the coming winter. There are only a few more days of summer. Everyone is anxious to get work to lay up something for that long siege of bitter cold. But there is no work. Sitting in the room we all know it. That is why we don't talk much. We look at the floor dreading to see that knowledge in each other's eyes. There is a kind of humiliation in it. We look away from each other. We look at the floor. It's too terrible to see this animal terror in each other's eyes.

So we sit hour after hour, day after day, waiting for a job to come in. There are many women for a single job. A thin sharp woman sits inside a wire cage looking at a book. For four hours we have watched her looking at that book. She has a hard little eye. In the small bare room there are half a dozen women sitting on the benches waiting. Many come and go. Our faces are all familiar to each other, for we wait here every day.

This is a domestic employment bureau. Most of the women who come here are middle-aged, some have families, some have raised their families and are now alone, some have men who are out of work. Hard times and the man leaves to hunt for work. He doesn't find it. He drifts on. The woman probably doesn't hear from him for a long time. She expects it. She isn't surprised. She struggles alone to feed the many mouths. Sometimes she gets help from the charities. If she's clever she can get herself a good living from the charities, if she's naturally a lick spittle,[1] naturally a little docile and cunning. If she's proud then she starves silently, leaving her children to find work, coming home after a day's searching to wrestle with her house, her children.

---

1. **lick spittle** (likʹ spitʹ əl) fawning flatterer that inspires contempt.

Some such story is written on the faces of all these women. There are young girls too, fresh from the country. Some are made brazen too soon by the city. There is a great **exodus** of girls from the farms into the city now. Thousands of farms have been vacated completely in Minnesota. The girls are trying to get work. The prettier ones can get jobs in the stores when there are any, or waiting on tables, but these jobs are only for the attractive and the adroit. The others, the real peasants, have a more difficult time.

exodus ▶ (eks′ ə dəs) *n.* departure from an area in large numbers

Bernice sits next to me. She is a Polish woman of thirty-five. She has been working in people's kitchens for fifteen years or more. She is large, her great body in mounds, her face brightly scrubbed. She has a peasant mind and finds it hard even yet to understand the maze of the city where trickery is worth more than brawn. Her blue eyes are not clever but slow and trusting. She suffers from loneliness and lack of talk. When you speak to her, her face lifts and brightens as if you had spoken through a great darkness, and she talks magically of little things as if the weather were magic, or tells some crazy tale of her adventures on the city streets, embellishing them in bright colors until they hang heavy and thick like embroidery. She loves the city anyhow. It's exciting to her, like a bazaar. She loves to go shopping and get a bargain, hunting out the places where stale bread and cakes can be had for a few cents. She likes walking the streets looking for men to take her to a picture show. Sometimes she goes to five picture shows in one day, or she sits through one the entire day until she knows all the dialogue by heart.

She hadn't had work for eight months. "You've got to give me something," she kept saying.

She came to the city a young girl from a Wisconsin farm. The first thing that happened to her, a charlatan dentist took out all her good shining teeth and the fifty dollars she had saved working in a canning factory. After that she met men in the park who told her how to look out for herself, corrupting her peasant mind, teaching her to mistrust everyone. Sometimes now she forgets to mistrust everyone and gets taken in. They taught her to get what she could for nothing, to count her change, to go back if she found herself cheated, to demand her rights.

She lives alone in little rooms. She bought seven dollars' worth of second-hand furniture eight years ago. She rents a room for perhaps three dollars a month in an attic, sometimes in a cold house. Once the house where she stayed was condemned and everyone else moved out and she lived there all winter alone on the top floor. She spent only twenty-five dollars all winter.

She wants to get married but she sees what happens to her married friends, left with children to support, worn out before their time. So she stays single. She is virtuous. She is slightly deaf from hanging out clothes in winter. She had done people's washing and cooking for fifteen years and in that time saved thirty dollars. Now she hasn't worked steady for a year and she has spent the thirty dollars. She had dreamed of having a little house or a houseboat perhaps with a spot of ground for a few chickens. This dream she will never realize.

She has lost all her furniture now along with the dream. A married friend whose husband is gone gives her a bed for which she pays by doing a great deal of work for the woman. She comes here every day now sitting bewildered, her pudgy hands folded in her lap. She is hungry. Her great flesh has begun to hang in folds. She has been living on crackers. Sometimes a box of crackers lasts a week. She has a friend who's a baker and he sometimes steals the stale loaves and brings them to her.

A girl we have seen every day all summer went crazy yesterday at the YW. She went into hysterics, stamping her feet and screaming.

She hadn't had work for eight months. "You've got to give me something," she kept saying. The woman in charge flew into a rage that probably came from days and days of suffering on her part, because she is unable to give jobs, having none. She flew into a rage at the girl and there they were facing each other in a rage both helpless, helpless. This woman told me once that she could hardly bear the suffering she saw, hardly hear it, that she couldn't eat sometimes and had nightmares at night.

So they stood there, the two women, in a rage, the girl weeping and the woman shouting at her. In the eight months of unemployment she had gotten ragged, and the woman was shouting that she would not send her out like that. "Why don't you shine your shoes?" she kept scolding the girl, and the girl kept sobbing and sobbing because she was starving.

"We can't recommend you like that," the harassed YWCA woman said, knowing she was starving, unable to do anything. And the girls and the women sat docilely, their eyes on the ground, ashamed to look at each other, ashamed of something.

Sitting here waiting for a job, the women have been talking in low voices about the girl Ellen. They talk in low voices with not too much pity for her, unable to see through the mist of their own torment. "What happened to Ellen?" one of them asks. She knows the answer already. We all know it.

A young girl who went around with Ellen tells about seeing her last evening back of a cafe downtown, outside the kitchen door, kicking, showing her legs so that the cook came out and gave her some food and some men gathered in the alley and threw small coin on the ground for a look at her legs. And the girl says enviously that Ellen had a swell breakfast and treated her to one too, that cost two dollars.

A scrub woman whose hips are bent forward from stooping with hands gnarled like watersoaked branches clicks her tongue in disgust. No one saves their money, she says, a little money and these foolish young things buy a hat, a dollar for breakfast, a bright scarf. And they do. If you've ever been without money, or food, something very strange happens when you get a bit of money, a kind of madness. You don't care. You can't remember that you had no money before, that the money will be gone. You can remember nothing but that there is the money for which you have been suffering. Now here it is. A lust takes hold of you. You see food in the windows. In imagination you eat hugely; you taste a thousand meals. You look in windows. Colors are brighter; you buy something to dress up in. An excitement takes hold of you. You know it is suicide but you can't help it. You must have food, dainty, splendid food, and a bright hat so once again you feel blithe, rid of that ratty gnawing shame.

"I guess she'll go on the street now," a thin woman says faintly, and no one takes the trouble to comment further. Like every commodity now the body is difficult to sell and the girls say you're lucky if you get fifty cents.

It's very difficult and humiliating to sell one's body.

Perhaps it would make it clear if one were to imagine having to go out on the street to sell, say, one's overcoat. Suppose you have to sell your coat so you can have breakfast and a place to sleep, say, for fifty cents. You decide to sell your only coat. You take it off and put it on your arm. The street, that has before been just a street, now becomes a mart, something entirely different. You must approach someone now and admit you are destitute and are now selling your clothes, your most intimate possessions. Everyone will watch you talking to the stranger showing him your overcoat, what a good coat it is. People will stop and watch curiously. You will be quite naked on the street. It is even harder to try to sell one's self, more humiliating. It is even humiliating to try to sell one's labor. When there is no buyer.

The thin woman opens the wire cage. There's a job for a nursemaid, she says. The old gnarled women, like old horses, know that no one will have them walk the streets with the young so they don't move. Ellen's friend gets up and goes to the window. She is unbelievably jaunty. I know she hasn't had work since last January. But she has a flare of life in her that glows like a tiny red flame and some tenacious thing, perhaps only youth, keeps it burning bright.

Her legs are thin but the runs in her old stockings are neatly mended clear down her flat shank. Two bright spots of rouge conceal her pallor. A narrow belt is drawn tightly around her thin waist, her long shoulders stoop and the blades show. She runs wild as a colt hunting pleasure, hunting sustenance.

It's one of the great mysteries of the city where women go when they are out of work and hungry. There are not many women in the bread line. There are no flop houses for women as there are for men, where a bed can be had for a quarter or less. You don't see women lying on the floor at the mission in the free flops. They obviously don't sleep in the jungle or under newspapers in the park. There is no law I suppose against their being in these places but the fact is they rarely are.

Yet there must be as many women out of jobs in cities and suffering extreme poverty as there are men. What happens to them? Where do they go? Try to get into the YW without any money or looking down at heel.[2] Charities take care of very few and only those that are called "deserving." The lone girl is under suspicion by the women who dispense charity.

I've lived in cities for many months broke, without help, too timid to get in bread lines. I've known many women to live like this until they simply faint on the street from **privations**, without saying a word to anyone. A woman will shut herself up in a room until it is taken away from her, and eat a cracker a day and be as quiet as a mouse so there are no social statistics concerning her.

◀ **privations** (prī vā′shənz) *n.* state of being deprived of what is needed to survive

I don't know why it is, but a woman will do this unless she has dependents, will go for weeks verging on starvation, crawling in some hole, going through the streets ashamed, sitting in libraries, parks, going for days without speaking to a living soul like some exiled beast, keeping the runs mended in her stockings, shut up in terror in her own misery, until she becomes too super-sensitive and timid to even ask for a job.

Bernice says even strange men she has met in the park have sometimes, that is in better days, given her a loan to pay her room rent. She has always paid them back.

In the afternoon the young girls, to forget the hunger and the deathly torture and fear of being jobless, try to pick up a man to take them to a ten-cent show. They never go to more expensive ones, but they can always find a man willing to spend a dime to have the company of a girl for the afternoon.

Sometimes a girl facing the night without shelter will approach a man for lodging. A woman always asks a man for help. Rarely

---

2. **down at heel** shabby or poor.

another woman. I have known girls to sleep in men's rooms for the night on a pallet without molestation and be given breakfast in the morning.

It's no wonder these young girls refuse to marry, refuse to rear children. They are like certain savage tribes, who, when they have been conquered, refuse to breed.

Not one of them but looks forward to starvation for the coming winter. We are in a jungle and know it. We are beaten, entrapped. There is no way out. Even if there were a job, even if that thin acrid woman came and gave everyone in the room a job for a few days, a few hours, at thirty cents an hour, this would all be repeated tomorrow, the next day and the next.

We cannot meet her eyes. When she looks at any of us we look away.

Not one of these women but knows that despite years of labor there is only starvation, humiliation in front of them.

Mrs. Gray, sitting across from me, is a living spokesman for the futility of labor. She is a warning. Her hands are scarred with labor. Her body is a great puckered scar. She has given birth to six children, buried three, supported them all alive and dead, bearing them, burying them, feeding them. Bred in hunger they have been spare, susceptible to disease. For seven years she tried to save her boy's arm from amputation, diseased from tuberculosis of the bone. It is almost too suffocating to think of that long close horror of years of child-bearing, child-feeding, rearing, with the bare suffering of providing a meal and shelter.

futility ▶ (fyo͞o tilʹə tē) *n.* quality of having no result or effect; uselessness

Now she is fifty. Her children, economically insecure, are drifters. She never hears of them. She doesn't know if they are alive. She doesn't know if she is alive. Such subtleties of suffering are not for her. For her the brutality of hunger and cold. Not until these are done away with can those subtle feelings that make a human being be indulged.

She is lucky to have five dollars ahead of her. That is her security. She has a tumor that she will die of. She is thin as a worn dime with her tumor sticking out of her side. She is brittle and bitter. Her face is not the face of a human being. She has borne more than it is possible for a human being to bear. She is reduced to the least possible denominator of human feelings.

It is terrible to see her little bloodshot eyes like a beaten hound's, fearful in terror.

We cannot meet her eyes. When she looks at any of us we look away. She is like a woman drowning and we turn away. We must ignore those eyes that are surely the eyes of a person drowning, doomed. She doesn't cry out. She goes down decently. And we all look away.

The young ones know though. I don't want to marry. I don't want any children. So they all say. No children. No marriage. They arm themselves alone, keep up alone. The man is helpless now. He cannot provide. If he propagates he cannot take care of his young. The means are not in his hands. So they live alone. Get what fun they can. The life risk is too horrible now. Defeat is too clearly written on it.

So we sit in this room like cattle, waiting for a nonexistent job, willing to work to the farthest atom of energy, unable to work, unable to get food and lodging, unable to bear children—here we must sit in this shame looking at the floor, worse than beasts at a slaughter.

It is appalling to think that these women sitting so listless in the room may work as hard as it is possible for a human being to work, may labor night and day, like Mrs. Gray wash streetcars from midnight to dawn and offices in the early evening, scrub for fourteen and fifteen hours a day, sleep only five hours or so, do this their whole lives, and never earn one day of security, having always before them the pit of the future. The endless labor, the bending back, the water-soaked hands, earning never more than a week's wages, never having in their hands more life than that.

It's not the suffering of birth, death, love that the young reject, but the suffering of endless labor without dream, eating the spare bread in bitterness, being a slave without the security of a slave.

ABOUT THE AUTHOR

Meridel Le Sueur (1900–1996)

Poet, novelist, children's book author, and journalist Meridel Le Sueur was born in Iowa and lived in a variety of Midwestern states during her childhood. In both her life and work, Le Sueur championed the poor in general and women in particular, bringing to light realities that had, for the most part, remained hidden. Her work opened doors for later generations of writers who also focused their attention on less visible members of society. Le Sueur died at the age of 96 in Wisconsin.

Close Reading Activities

READ

Comprehension

Reread all or part of the text to help you answer the following questions.

1. Where is the writer as she shares her observations?
2. Why is the time of year important to Le Sueur and the women she describes?
3. According to the text, what do men and women do differently when they are out of work and hungry?

Research: Clarify Details This selection may include references that are unfamiliar to you. Choose at least one unfamiliar detail and briefly research it. Then, explain how the information you learned from research sheds light on an aspect of the text.

Summarize Write an objective summary of the text. Remember that an objective summary is free from opinion and evaluation.

Language Study

Selection Vocabulary The following passages appear in "Women on the Breadlines." Create a chart in which you identify the part of speech, one synonym, and one antonym for each boldfaced word.

- There is a great **exodus** of girls from the farms…
- I've known many women to live like this until they simply faint on the street from **privations**…
- Mrs. Gray, sitting across from me, is a living spokesman for the **futility** of labor.

Literary Analysis

Reread the identified passage. Then, respond to the questions that follow.

Focus Passage *(p. 311)*

A girl we…ashamed of something.

Key Ideas and Details

1. **(a) Summarize:** What is the fight in this passage about? **(b) Analyze:** What central idea does the author express by portraying this **interaction**?
2. **Analyze Cause and Effect:** What vicious cycle is captured in the description of the girl's appearance and her jobless situation? Explain.

Craft and Structure

3. **(a)** Identify three words or phrases the author repeats in this passage. **(b) Analyze:** Explain how Le Sueur's use of repetition helps to portray the intensity of the women's experience.

Integration of Knowledge and Ideas

4. **Synthesize:** How does the specific incident described in this passage capture the more general problems women faced during the Depression?

Reportage

Reportage is a type of journalism in which the writer includes him- or herself in the story. Today, this sort of reporting is called **subjective** or new journalism.

1. **(a)** What narrative point of view does Le Sueur use? **(b)** How does the point of view qualify this text as a subjective, rather than an objective, report?
2. What details is Le Sueur able to include as a subjective journalist that she might not include as an objective journalist? Explain.
3. **The Great Depression:** How does Le Sueur's subjective account capture both factual information and the atmosphere of the Depression?

DISCUSS • RESEARCH • WRITE

From Text to Topic **Group Discussion**

Discuss the following passage with a small group. Take notes during the discussion. Contribute your own ideas, and support them with examples from the text.

> Hunger makes a human being lapse into a state of lethargy, especially city hunger. Is there any place else in the world where a human being is supposed to go hungry amidst plenty without an outcry, without protest, where only the boldest steal or kill for bread, and the timid crawl the streets, hunger like the beak of a terrible bird at the vitals?

QUESTIONS FOR DISCUSSION

1. Do you agree that being hungry in a city is, somehow, worse than being hungry in the country?
2. What does Le Sueur's distinction between the "boldest" and the "timid" suggest about human nature in times of crisis?

Research **Investigate the Topic**

The Value of Money In "Women on the Breadlines," Le Sueur names specific dollar amounts for certain items.

Assignment

Conduct research to learn about the value of a dollar during the Depression. Explore what poverty and wealth meant in dollar amounts during that era. In addition to secondary sources, consult historical documents that list prices or salaries. To clarify your understanding, compare the value of a dollar during the Depression to its value today. Use spreadsheet software to organize your notes and citation information. Share your findings in an **informational chart** that combines figures and examples with explanatory text.

PREPARATION FOR ESSAY

You may use the results of this research in an essay you will write at the end of this section.

Writing to Sources **Explanatory Text**

Meridel Le Sueur reports on the challenges many urban women faced during the Great Depression.

Assignment

Write an **explanatory essay** in which you describe and summarize the plight of urban women during the Depression. Follow these steps:

- Review Le Sueur's text and gather evidence that explains the difficulties many women living in cities faced during the Depression.
- Clearly **articulate** the hardships women endured that, according to Le Sueur, men generally did not. Cite evidence from your notes on the text.
- Review your writing and eliminate extraneous details to strengthen the focus of your work.

ACADEMIC VOCABULARY

Academic terms appear in blue on these pages. If these words are not familiar to you, use a dictionary to find their definitions. Then, use them as you speak and write about the text.

Common Core State Standards

RI.9-10.1, RI.9-10.2, RI.9-10.3, RI.9-10.4, RI.9-10.5; SL.9-10.1; W.9-10.1, W.9-10.4, W.9-10.5, W.9-10.7; L.9-10.4, L.9-10.5, L.9-10.6

[For full standards wording, see the chart in the front of this book.]

Bread Line, New York City, 1932

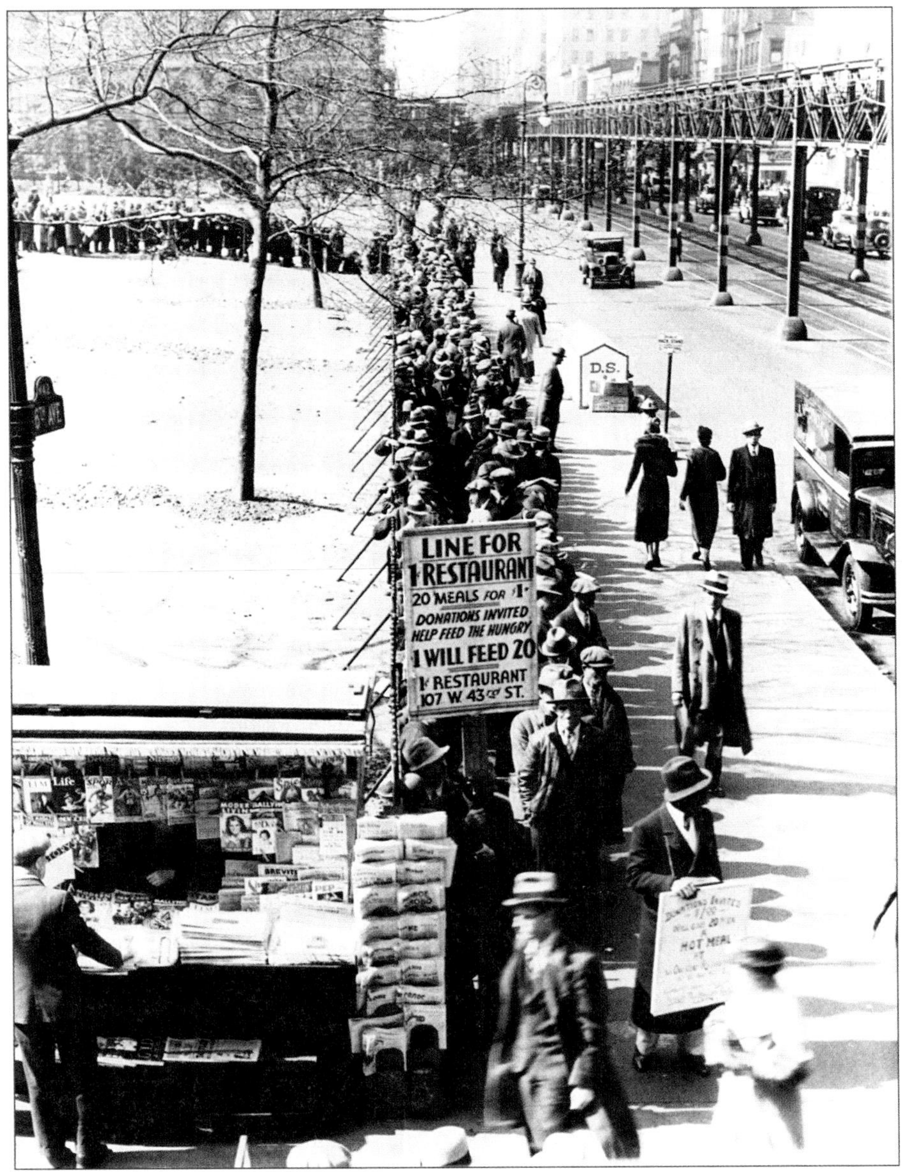

H.W. Fechner (b. circa 1897–?)

Harold W. Fechner was the staff photographer of the New York Central Railroad from the 1920s through the early 1950s. He also worked for R.I. Nesmith and Associates, a commercial photography firm active during the mid-twentieth century. Fechner shot this image of a bread line at the intersection of Sixth Avenue and 42nd Street in New York City in 1932.

Close Reading Activities

READ • DISCUSS • WRITE

Critical Analysis

Look at the photograph carefully. Notice details about the event it depicts as well as the **composition** to help you answer the following questions.

Key Ideas and Details

1. **(a) Infer:** At what time of year was this photograph taken? **(b) Support:** Which details in the image support your answer? **(c) Connect:** How might the season affect people living through financial crisis?

Craft and Structure

2. **Analyze:** How does the photographer's **elevated** perspective affect both the visual organization of the image and the message it conveys?
3. **Interpret:** Why do you think the photographer chose to frame the shot with the sign figuring so prominently in the foreground?
4. **Analyze: (a)** How do passersby in the photo seem to be reacting to the people in the line? **(b) Infer:** What do their reactions suggest about their attitudes toward the situation captured in the scene?

Integration of Knowledge and Ideas

5. **Evaluate:** Is this photograph making a statement or simply presenting a scene in an **objective** way? Explain your position.

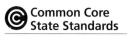

Common Core State Standards

RI.9-10.7; W.9-10.2, W.9-10.4; SL.9-10.1, SL.9-10.2

[For full standards wording, see the chart in the front of this book.]

ACADEMIC VOCABULARY

Academic terms appear in blue on these pages. If these words are not familiar to you, use a dictionary to find their definitions. Then, use them as you speak and write about the text.

From Text to Topic **Class Discussion**

Discuss the photograph and its message with classmates. Use the following questions to focus your conversation.

1. Based on the information in the sign, what can you infer about the restaurant owners?
2. How does this photograph relate to the other texts you have read about the Great Depression in this section? Explain, citing details from the photograph and examples from the verbal texts.

Writing to Sources **Informative Text**

The Great Depression Write an **explanatory caption** that could accompany this photograph in an exhibit of images from the Great Depression. Explain how this photograph documents one of the major issues people faced during the Depression—hunger. Provide useful background information that will help viewers appreciate the photograph and make clear connections to details in the image itself.

Assessment: Synthesis

Speaking and Listening: Group Discussion

The Great Depression and Knowledge The texts in this section focus on the Great Depression. They provide facts and details that may increase readers' knowledge, as well insights that may help readers understand what it was like to live during that era. This contrast highlights the Big Question addressed in this unit: **Is knowledge the same as understanding?**

Assignment

Conduct discussions. With a small group, conduct a discussion about the Great Depression. Refer to the texts in this section, other texts you have read, and research you have conducted to support your ideas. Begin your discussion by addressing the following questions:

- What facts and details do these texts offer about the Great Depression, including its causes and effects?
- How did ordinary people deal with the stresses caused by the Depression?
- How were the experiences of different groups of people similar and different during the Great Depression?
- Does knowledge about the Depression lead to an understanding of the era?
- Which texts in this section best convey an understanding of what life was like during the Depression? Why?

Summarize and present your ideas. After you have fully explored the topic, summarize your discussion and present your findings to the class as a whole.

▲ Refer to the selections you read in Part 3 as you complete the activities on this assessment.

Criteria for Success

✓ **Organizes the group effectively**
Appoint a group leader to present the discussion questions and keep the conversation moving. Elect a timekeeper to make sure the discussion is completed within the allotted time.

✓ **Conducts a thorough, informed discussion**
Cite evidence from selections you have read. Take time to explore all facets of the discussion issues.

✓ **Involves all participants in lively discussion**
Make sure all group members have an opportunity to contribute to the discussion and invite everyone to respond to ideas and conclusions.

✓ **Adheres to the rules of academic discussion**
Take turns sharing ideas and avoid interrupting one another. In cases of disagreement, clarify the points of each position and come to a consensus, if only to agree to disagree.

USE NEW VOCABULARY

As you speak and share ideas, work to use the vocabulary words you have learned in this unit. The more you use new words, the more you will "own" them.

Writing: **Narrative**

The Great Depression and Understanding The ability to understand allows us both to know facts and to internalize what those facts mean. We may know that many people were out of work during the Great Depression, but understanding how they felt and behaved as a result is key to building a deeper connection to history.

Assignment

Write a **reflective essay** in which you discuss a hardship you have either experienced, read about, or observed in today's world. As you draft your essay, refer back to the texts you have read in this section and the research you performed. Make connections between the historical experiences described in the texts and more recent situations you have experienced, read about, or witnessed.

Common Core State Standards

W.9-10.3, W.9-10.3.a–e, W.9-10.4, W.9-10.9; SL.9-10.1, SL.9-10.1.a–d, SL.9-10.4, SL.9-10.6; L.9-10.6

[For full standards wording, see the chart in the front of this book.]

Criteria for Success

Purpose/Focus

✓ **Makes connections between experiences and larger ideas**
Consider how the experiences you discuss are similar to and different from those described in the texts you have read in this section.

✓ **Demonstrates clear perspective**
Show how your understanding of more immediate experiences helps you better understand the historical events you read about and researched.

Organization

✓ **Sequences events logically**
Interweave your descriptions of events with discussion of your thought process and insights. Include an ending in which you reflect on those insights.

Development of Ideas/Elaboration

✓ **Includes vivid details**
Include precise information that will engage readers and enhance their understanding.

✓ **Uses structure effectively**
Establish a clear focus for each section of your essay and use transitional words and phrases to guide readers through your ideas.

Language

✓ **Uses language effectively**
Use focused, direct language to describe complex ideas.

Conventions

✓ **Does not have errors**
Check your narrative to eliminate errors in grammar, spelling, and punctuation.

WRITE TO EXPLORE

Writing about your experiences may lead you to new realizations. Be aware of these and incorporate them into your essay. Including new discoveries will make your writing more compelling.

Writing to Sources: **Explanatory Text**

The Great Depression The readings in this section present a wealth of knowledge about the Great Depression and enhance readers' understanding of the experiences of the people who lived during that time. They raise questions, such as the following, about the ways in which we as individuals and as a nation deal with hard times:

- How do circumstances such as the Depression affect people's perspective of life?
- What personal qualities are key to coping well with hard times?
- What does an individual's response to difficulties say about his or her character?
- How did our nation's response to the Great Depression help to define our national character?

Focus on the question that intrigues you the most, and then complete the following assignment.

Assignment

Write an **expository essay** in which you convey information and ideas about the Great Depression and the experiences of people who lived during that time. Develop your topic by analyzing the understanding you gained from two or more readings in this section. Clearly present, develop, and support your ideas with details from the texts.

INCORPORATE RESEARCH

Strengthen your analysis by including facts, quotations, and data you gathered while conducting research related to the readings in this section. Make sure to cite your sources correctly.

Prewriting and Planning

Select sources. Review the texts in the section, paying attention to the ones that contributed the most to your understanding of the era. Select at least two that will provide strong material to support your analysis.

Gather information and develop your central idea. Use a chart like the one shown to gather your observations and generate a central idea to explore in your essay.

Focus Question: How did our nation's response to the Great Depression help to define our national character?

Response	Evidence	Notes
Unwilling to give up self-reliance	Americans turned to family and local businesses before seeking help from government. (will cite "Americans in the Great Depression")	Americans have a strong do-it-yourself spirit.
Tried hard to seek employment	Women returned to employment offices on a daily basis in the hopes of getting work. (will cite "Women on the Breadlines")	Americans are very determined.
Example Central Idea: Despite the harsh circumstances of the Depression, Americans were resilient, determined, and self-reliant.		

Drafting

Focus your ideas. Present your ideas in a logical sequence. Use details from your chart to support each point you present. Decide which evidence best supports each idea and which ideas are most strongly supported with evidence. Eliminate weaker ideas and less robust evidence.

Develop your topic. Include facts, concrete details, quotations, or other information and examples to support your analysis. Use textual support and include information from the research you conducted throughout this section, if applicable. Cite all sources thoroughly and accurately.

Make connections among ideas. State your central idea in your introduction. Then, present your ideas in a logical sequence. Use transitions to connect paragraphs and to unify your thoughts. End with a strong conclusion that restates your central idea and summarizes your evidence.

W.9-10.2a–f, W.9-10.4, W.9-10.5, W.9-10.9; L.9-10.3.a
[For full standards wording, see the chart in the front of this book.]

CITE RESEARCH CORRECTLY

Use a style guide from a reliable source, such as the one provided by the MLA (Modern Language Association), to check the formatting of your citations.

Revising and Editing

Evaluate content. Review your draft to ensure that your ideas are logically organized so that readers can follow their progression from the beginning to the end of your essay.

Review language. Examine your draft to make sure you have expressed yourself in a lively yet precise way. Replace vague wording with more specific choices.

Self-Evaluation Rubric

Use the following criteria to evaluate the effectiveness of your essay.

Criteria	Rating Scale
PURPOSE/FOCUS Introduces a specific topic; provides a concluding section that follows from and supports the information or explanation presented	*not very* .... *very* 1 2 3 4
ORGANIZATION Organizes complex ideas, concepts, and information to make important connections and distinctions; uses appropriate and varied transitions to link the major sections, create cohesion, and clarify relationships among ideas	1 2 3 4
DEVELOPMENT OF IDEAS/ELABORATION Develops the topic with well-chosen, relevant, and sufficient facts, extended definitions, concrete details, quotations, or other information and examples appropriate to the audience's knowledge of the topic	1 2 3 4
LANGUAGE Uses precise language and domain-specific vocabulary to manage the complexity of the topic; establishes and maintains a formal style and an objective tone	1 2 3 4
CONVENTIONS Attends to the norms and conventions of the discipline	1 2 3 4

Independent Reading

Titles for Extended Reading

In this unit, you have read texts in a variety of genres. Continue to read on your own. Select works that you enjoy, but challenge yourself to explore new topics, new authors, and works of increasing depth and complexity. The titles suggested below will help you get started.

INFORMATIONAL TEXT

Why We Can't Wait
by Martin Luther King, Jr.
Signet, 2000 — **EXEMPLAR TEXT**

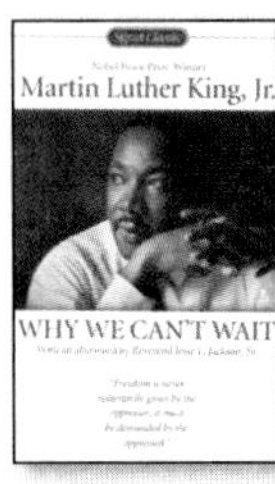

In the 1950s and 60s, Dr. King captured the mind and conscience of the country with his principled stand for justice. This **nonfiction book** is both a description of the Civil Rights movement and a poetic testament to the wisdom and courage of its author.

Abraham Lincoln—DK Biography
by Tanya Lee Stone
Dorling Kindersley Publishing, 2005

During the perilous days of the Civil War, Abraham Lincoln found himself at the center of events that would transform America as a nation. This biography traces Lincoln's life from his boyhood in rural Illinois to the stormy days of his presidency.

Life by the Numbers
by Keith Devlin
John Wiley & Sons, 1998 — **EXEMPLAR TEXT**

This **nonfiction book** shows readers how math applies to everything: the shape of flowers, the realization of virtual reality, and the physics of sports. The author also provides interesting information about some careers in the field of mathematics.

Cod: A Biography of the Fish That Changed the World
by Mark Kurlansky

This **nonfiction book** shows how the cod, a simple fish, fed whole villages, caused several wars, and spurred European transatlantic exploration. On a darker note, Kurlansky describes the dramatic decline of this important species as a result of overfishing.

LITERATURE

The Killer Angels
by Michael Shaara
Ballantine Books, 1974 — **EXEMPLAR TEXT**

This Pulitzer Prize–winning **novel** tells the story of the Battle of Gettysburg, three of the most crucial days of the Civil War. Several points of view are used to draw a complete picture of the moments before and during the battle.

Words Under the Words: Selected Poems
by Naomi Shihab Nye
Far Corner, 1995

This rich collection of **poetry** reveals how short poems can make big statements about life. Nye explores everything from her Palestinian heritage to the mysterious donor of a music box in poems that burst with imagery and questions and insights about life.

Fahrenheit 451
by Ray Bradbury — **EXEMPLAR TEXT**

In a desolate future, firemen no longer put out fires—they start them, using books as fuel. This **science-fiction novel** critiques thoughtless conformity, the media, and what the author saw as the abuses of technology.

ONLINE TEXT SET

SPEECH
***from* State of the Union Address** Franklin Delano Roosevelt

SHORT STORY
The Golden Kite, the Silver Wind Ray Bradbury

BIOGRAPHY
***from* A Lincoln Preface** Carl Sandburg

Preparing to Read Complex Texts

Attentive Reading As you read literature on your own, bring your imagination and questions to the text. The questions shown below and others that you ask as you read will help you learn and enjoy literature even more.

Reading Literature/ Informational Text

10. By the end of grade 9, read and comprehend literature, including stories, dramas, poems, and literary nonfiction in the grades 9–10 text complexity band proficiently, with scaffolding as needed at the high end of the range.

When reading literary nonfiction, ask yourself…

Comprehension: **Key Ideas and Details**

- Who is the author? Why did he or she write the work?
- What does the author state about the topic? What information is left unstated?
- Does any one idea strike me as being the most important? Why?
- What is the author's point of view on the topic?
- What details or evidence support the author's ideas?
- What can I learn from this text?

Text Analysis: **Craft and Structure**

- Does the author order ideas so that I can follow them? If not, what is wrong with the way the text is ordered?
- Does the author capture my interest right from the beginning, or do I have to work to get into the text? Why do I think that is?
- Does the author give me a new way of looking at a topic? If so, how? If not, why?
- Is the author an expert on the topic? How do I know?
- How does the author's use of language create meaning or tone?
- Does the author use strong evidence? Do I find any of the evidence unconvincing? If so, why?

Connections: **Integration of Knowledge and Ideas**

- Does the work seem authentic and true? Does any aspect of the work seem exaggerated, false, or unsupported?
- Do I agree or disagree with the author's basic premise? Why?
- Have I read other works about this or a related topic? What does this work add to my knowledge of the topic?
- How would I write about a similar topic? Would I follow a similar approach as the author's, or would I handle the topic differently?

UNIT 3

THE BIG ?

How does communication change us?

UNIT PATHWAY

PART 1
SETTING EXPECTATIONS

- INTRODUCING THE BIG QUESTION
- CLOSE READING WORKSHOP

PART 2
TEXT ANALYSIS
GUIDED EXPLORATION

THE RIGHT WORDS

PART 3
TEXT SET
DEVELOPING INSIGHT

THE KENNEDY ASSASSINATION

PART 4
DEMONSTRATING INDEPENDENCE

- INDEPENDENT READING
- ONLINE TEXT SET 

CLOSE READING TOOL

Use this tool to practice the close reading strategies you learn.

STUDENT eTEXT

Bring learning to life with audio, video, and interactive tools.

ONLINE WRITER'S NOTEBOOK

Easily capture notes and complete assignments online.

Find all Digital Resources at **pearsonrealize.com**

Introducing the Big Question

How does communication change us?

Communication involves an exchange of ideas between people. It takes place when you discuss an issue with a friend or respond to a piece of writing. Communication is the understanding you get when you read a poem. It is the empathy you feel for others after listening to an interview with victims of a natural disaster. All of this communication may change us, but how? Does it make us smarter, wiser, kinder, angrier? Does it make us better people—or just more experienced?

Exploring the Big Question

Collaboration: Group Discussion Begin thinking about the Big Question by listing examples of the many ways in which you communicate. Describe an example from each of the following categories:

- a discussion with a friend or parent
- a movie that moved you emotionally
- a speech or dramatic presentation you gave or heard
- a poem or story you will always remember
- an important conversation you have had
- a commercial or news story that moved you to take action
- a photograph, painting, or song that touched you deeply

Share your list with a small group. Talk about how these significant communications led to change.

Before you begin the discussion, establish rules that will help you communicate effectively as a group. For example, you might set time limits or requirements for each person's participation. Then, as you conduct your discussion, use the words related to communication listed on the page at right.

Connecting to the Literature Each reading in this unit will give you additional insight into the Big Question. After you read each selection, pause to consider the ideas it communicates.

Vocabulary

Acquire and Use Academic Vocabulary The term "academic vocabulary" refers to words you typically encounter in scholarly and literary texts and in technical and business writing. It is language that helps to express complex ideas. Review the definitions of these academic vocabulary words.

comprehension (käm′ prē hen′ shən) *n.* understanding; ability to understand something

discuss (di skus′) *v.* talk about with others; consider a topic in writing or in conversation

illuminate (i lo͞o′ mən āt) *v.* make clear; explain

informed (in fôrmd′) *v.* gave someone information; *adj.* having much knowledge, information, or education

interpretation (in tʉr′ prə tā′ shən) *n.* explanation of the meaning of a concept or an idea

Use these words as you complete Big Question activities that involve reading, writing, speaking, and listening.

Gather Vocabulary Knowledge Additional words related to communication are listed below. Categorize the words by deciding whether you know each one well, know it a little bit, or do not know it at all.

aware	meaning	resolution
communication	react	respond
empathy	relationship	understanding
exchange		

Then, complete the following steps:

1. Write the definitions of the words you know.
2. Consult a dictionary to confirm the word's meaning. Revise your definition if necessary.
3. Use all of the words in a paragraph about how communication changes people. Write in complete sentences, avoiding fragments and run-ons.

Common Core State Standards

Speaking and Listening

1. Initiate and participate effectively in a range of collaborative discussions with diverse partners, building on others' ideas and expressing their own clearly and persuasively.

1.b. Work with peers to set rules for collegial discussions and decision-making, clear goals and deadlines, and individual roles as needed.

Language

4.c. Consult general and specialized reference materials, both print and digital, to find the pronunciation of a word or determine or clarify its precise meaning, its part of speech, or its etymology.

4.d. Verify the preliminary determination of the meaning of a word or phrase.

6. Acquire and use accurately general academic and domain-specific words and phrases, sufficient for reading, writing, speaking, and listening at the college and career readiness level; demonstrate independence in gathering vocabulary knowledge when considering a word or phrase important to comprehension or expression.

Close Reading Workshop

In this workshop, you will learn an approach to reading that will deepen your understanding of literature and will help you better appreciate the author's craft. The workshop includes models for the close reading, discussion, research, and writing activities you will complete as you study literature in this unit. After you have reviewed the strategies and models, practice your skills with the Independent Practice selection.

RL.9-10.1, RL.9-10.2, RL.9-10.4, RL.9-10.5, RL.9-10.10; W.9-10.1, W.9-10.2, W.9-10.7, W.9-10.9.a; SL.9-10.1

[For full standards wording, see the chart in the front of this book.]

CLOSE READING: **POETRY**

In Part 2 of this unit, you will focus on reading various poems. Use these strategies as you read the texts:

Comprehension: **Key Ideas and Details**

- Read first to grasp the poem's basic meaning.
- Use a dictionary or draw inferences from context clues to define unfamiliar words.
- Notice unfamiliar details that you might wish to research further.
- Appreciate the beauty or power of images and figurative language.

Ask yourself questions such as these:

- Who is the speaker in the poem?
- What inferences can I draw from the poem?
- How does the poet's word choice express specific ideas and emotions?

Text Analysis: **Craft and Structure**

- Consider the poem's form, including how it gives structure to the described events or experiences.
- Analyze the features that add meaning or emotional qualities to the poem. Notice imagery (word pictures that appeal to the senses), sound devices (such as alliteration and repetition), rhyme, and meter.
- Take note of the poet's use of figurative language, such as similes, metaphors, and personification, to capture ideas and express shades of meaning.

Ask yourself questions such as these:

- Are related or repeated images clues to a poem's deeper meaning?
- How do sound devices and figurative language emphasize meaning or appeal to readers' emotions?
- In what way does the poem's structure relate to its meaning?

Connections: **Integration of Knowledge and Ideas**

- Look for important imagery or patterns of images that seem connected, and then analyze possible deeper meanings. Consider how these images suggest a theme or central insight.
- Compare and contrast this poem with other poems you have read, either by the same poet or different poets.

Ask yourself questions such as these:

- How has this work increased my knowledge of a subject, poet, poetic form, or poetry itself?
- In what ways is this poem special, unique, or worthy of reading?

Read

As you read this poem, take note of the annotations that model ways to closely read the text.

Reading Model

"Barter"[1] by Sara Teasdale

Life has loveliness to sell,[2]
    All beautiful and splendid things,
Blue waves whitened on a cliff,
    Soaring fire that sways and sings,[3]
And children's faces looking up
Holding wonder like a cup.

Life has loveliness to sell, [2]
    Music like a curve of gold,[4]
Scent of pine trees in the rain,
    Eyes that love you, arms that hold,[4]
And for your spirit's still delight,[4]
Holy thoughts that star the night.[4]

Spend all you have for loveliness,[5]
    Buy it and never count the cost;[5]
For one white singing hour of peace
    Count many a year of strife well lost,[5]
And for a breath of ecstasy
Give all you have been, or could be.

Key Ideas and Details

1 To *barter* is to trade items without using money. The title suggests that the poem will be about exchanges that have value unrelated to finances.

Craft and Structure

2 The speaker repeats the line "Life has loveliness to sell" at the beginning of the first two stanzas. This repetition acts like a song's chorus, giving meaning to the varied details in both stanzas—all are examples of life's "loveliness."

Craft and Structure

3 Here, the fire does not just leap or crackle—it "sings." This is an example of personification, a type of figurative language in which nonhuman things are given human qualities. Through personification, the fire becomes a living being.

Craft and Structure

4 End rhymes help create a strong, songlike rhythm. This lends the poem an atmosphere of joy, which fits its subject matter.

Integration of Knowledge and Ideas

5 The phrases "Spend all you have," "Buy it," and "never count the cost" use monetary language to describe nonfinancial exchanges. These phrases connect to the title. They also contribute to the theme that life's joys—the rewards of a "white singing hour of peace"—are worth the payments of sorrow and "strife."

Discuss

Sharing your own ideas and listening to the ideas of others can deepen your understanding of a text and help you look at a topic in a whole new way. As you participate in collaborative discussions, work to have a genuine exchange in which classmates build upon one another's ideas. Support your points with evidence and ask meaningful questions.

Discussion Model

Student 1: I think the speaker repeats the phrase "Life has loveliness to sell" to emphasize the idea of "selling" and to connect it to the title, "Barter." The reader thinks: If life is selling "loveliness," what does it want in return? Plus this repetition helps Teasdale present the idea in a musical way.

Student 2: Well, the speaker "count[s]" lost years of "strife," which answers the question about what "life" charges for loveliness. The answer is that you have to have bad times, or "strife"—that's the payment—in order to get good times.

Student 3: I agree. Rhyme also helps make that answer clear. Each stanza has the same rhyme pattern. End rhyme pairs include "gold" and "hold" and "cost" and "lost." The words "gold" and "cost" relate to things of value. The rhymes create a song-like effect. Do you think this musical effect was common in Teasdale's work?

Research

Targeted research can clarify unfamiliar details and shed light on various aspects of a text. Consider questions that arise in your mind as you read, and use those questions as the basis for research.

Research Model

Question: *Do Teasdale's other poems display similar musical qualities?*

Key Words for Internet Search: Sara Teasdale and lyric poetry

Result: Sara Teasdale, Poetry Foundation; Modern Lyric Poet, St. Louis Public Library

What I Learned: Sara Teasdale wrote lyric poems featuring the themes of love, death, beauty, and nature. She was active during the early twentieth century, and her work was very popular during her lifetime. Critics praised Teasdale's use of musical language. In fact, some of her poems were later set to music.

Write

Writing about a text will deepen your understanding of it and will also allow you to share your ideas more formally with others. The following model essay evaluates Teasdale's style and cites evidence to support the main ideas.

Writing Model: Argument

Teasdale's Approach to Theme in "Barter"

Sara Teasdale is known for her musical style. Her poem "Barter" contains musical language, rhyme, and comparisons that express the speaker's beliefs and emotions. Teasdale effectively conveys the theme of hope and optimism through sound devices and figurative language.

The writer states the main claim in the first paragraph. This is an effective strategy for a short response to literature.

Sound devices create musical effects and help develop meaning and tone. In "Barter," the same rhyme scheme appears in each stanza. This rhyme pattern gives the poem a structure and emphasizes connections among the lines. For example, this rhyme in the second stanza, "And for your spirit's still delight, / Holy thoughts that star the night," shows the relationship between spiritual happiness and faith. The line, "Life has loveliness to sell," repeats in the first two stanzas, with the word "loveliness" reappearing in the first line of the third stanza. The repetition adds to the importance of this message: Life's positive experiences come with a cost. The repeated "l" sound of this line also has a musical feeling.

The writer demonstrates clear understanding of form and other literary elements often used in poetry.

Teasdale's "Barter" does not just use music in its structure but also in its content. Figurative language connects unrelated images in new ways. The fire "sings" is one example of Teasdale's use of figurative language. Another example appears in the second stanza with the simile "Music like a curve of gold." This comparison allows readers to "see" music as something physical. Teasdale convinces her readers that years of strife will lead to "one white singing hour of peace," or happier times. The loveliness of life cannot be enjoyed without experiencing bad times too.

Specific details from the poem clearly support the writer's interpretations.

This musical quality is present in much of Teasdale's poetry. One critic during her lifetime wrote: "Miss Teasdale is first, last, and always a singer." One could easily sing "Barter" thanks to the even meter and clear rhyme scheme. Teasdale's poetry offers different perspectives, but her lyrical, musical style remains consistent and compelling.

Information gained from research provides a larger context for the discussion of a single poem and provides a strong conclusion to the essay.

INDEPENDENT PRACTICE

As you read the following poems, apply the close reading strategies you have learned. You may need to read the poems multiple times.

Meet the Author

Bilingual and bicultural Mexican American poet **Pat Mora** was born in 1942. She stresses the importance of family and cultural heritage in her poems, often by including Spanish words and phrases. Her poetry is spare yet rich in imagery and feeling.

CLOSE READING TOOL

Read and respond to this selection online using the **Close Reading Tool.**

Uncoiling

by Pat Mora

With thorns, she scratches
on my window, tosses her hair dark with rain,
snares lightning, cholla,[1] hawks, butterfly
swarms in the tangles.

She sighs clouds,
head thrown back, eyes closed, roars
and rivers leap,
boulders retreat like crabs
into themselves.

She spews gusts and thunder,
spooks pale women who scurry to
lock doors, windows
when her tumbleweed skirt starts its spin.

They sing lace lullabies
so their children won't hear
her uncoiling
through her lips, howling
leaves off trees, flesh
off bones, until she becomes

sound, spins herself
to sleep, sand stinging her ankles,
whirring into her raw skin like stars.

---

1. **cholla** (chô′ yä) *n.* spiny cactus found in the southwestern United States and Mexico.

A Voice
by Pat Mora

Even the lights on the stage unrelenting
as the desert sun couldn't hide the other
students, their eyes also unrelenting,
students who spoke English every night

as they ate their meat, potatoes, gravy.
Not you. In your house that smelled like
rose powder, you spoke Spanish formal
as your father, the judge without a courtroom

in the country he floated to in the dark
on a flatbed truck. He walked slow
as a hot river down the narrow hall
of your house. You never dared to race past him

to say, "Please move," in the language
you learned effortlessly, as you learned to run,
the language forbidden at home, though your mother
said you learned it to fight with the neighbors.

You like winning with words. You liked
writing speeches about patriotism and democracy.
You liked all the faces looking at you, all those eyes.
"How did I do it?" you ask me now. "How did I do it

when my parents didn't understand?"
The family story says your voice is the voice
of an aunt in Mexico, spunky[1] as a peacock.
Family stories sing of what lives in the blood.

---

1. **spunky** (spuŋ´ kē) *adj.* courageous; spirited.

You told me only once about the time you went
to the state capitol, your family proud as if
you'd been named governor. But when you looked
around, the only Mexican in the auditorium,

you wanted to hide from those strange faces.
Their eyes were pinpricks, and you faked
hoarseness. You, who are never at a loss
for words, felt your breath stick in your throat

like an ice cube. "I can't," you whispered.
"I can't." Yet you did. Not that day but years later.
You taught the four of us to speak up.
This is America, Mom. The undoable is done

in the next generation. Your breath moves
through the family like the wind
moves through the trees.

Close Reading Activities

Read

Comprehension: **Key Ideas and Details**

1. **(a) Infer:** What kind of storm does the speaker describe in "Uncoiling?" Cite details from the poem to support your inference. **(b) Interpret:** Identify three actions that the storm takes. **(c) Analyze:** How do these actions show the storm's violence?
2. **(a)** In "A Voice," what is the speaker's mother's attitude toward speaking English? **(b) Support:** What specific language does the speaker use to strengthen this viewpoint? Explain.
3. **(a)** Citing details from "A Voice," explain what happens to the speaker's mother at the state capitol. **(b) Analyze:** According to the speaker, how does the mother turn the pain of that experience into triumph later in life?
4. **Summarize:** Write a brief, objective summary of each poem. Cite textual details in your summary.

Text Analysis: **Craft and Structure**

5. **(a)** In "Uncoiling," what words and phrases, including examples of figurative language, does Mora use to describe the storm? **(b) Interpret:** What is the effect of these choices? Explain.
6. In "Uncoiling," how do the sounds used in the lines "sound, spins herself / to sleep, sand stinging her ankles" emphasize the actions described?
7. **(a)** Identify one simile and one metaphor in "A Voice." **(b) Interpret:** What action does each example describe?
8. **Interpret:** In "A Voice," the speaker describes the mother's voice as being "spunky as a peacock." What meaning does this comparison suggest?

Connections: **Integration of Knowledge and Ideas**

Discuss

Conduct a **small-group discussion** about the use of imagery in Mora's poems. For example, compare and contrast the image of the wind in the last stanza of "A Voice" with the image of the wind in "Uncoiling." Explain differences in both tone and meaning.

Research

Pat Mora is influenced by the two cultures of her family—American and Mexican. Briefly research Mora's life and literary career as a Mexican American author. Consider the following types of sources:

a. biographies that comment on Mora's writing
b. critical writing that discusses how Mexican culture, language, and settings appear in Mora's work

Take notes as you perform your research. Then, write an **explanation** of the ways in which "Uncoiling" and "A Voice" express Mora's cultural influences.

Write

Poets choose words with great care, considering each word's connotations, or shades of meaning. Pat Mora, for example, uses active verbs and vivid adjectives to describe the land and people of the Southwest United States. Write an **essay** in which you examine the effects of specific word choices in Mora's poetry. Cite details from both poems to support your analysis.

How does communication change us?

Consider how language, listening, and speaking are portrayed in "A Voice." How do the choices the mother makes regarding language affect her children? What does the speaker suggest about the power of one's voice to achieve the "undoable"? Use details from the poem to explain your answer.

"The difference between the almost right word and the **right word** is really a large matter—'tis the difference between the **lightning bug** and the **lightning**."

—**Mark Twain**

PART 2

TEXT ANALYSIS GUIDED EXPLORATION

THE RIGHT WORDS

Literature is the art of language. Functional texts require the use of precise words, but literature requires even more precision—the right words that convey meaning, express emotion, awaken the senses, and lift off the page into the reader's imagination. As you read the texts in this section, notice words that stand out as being exactly "right" and think about why that is. Then, consider how these finely crafted works relate to the Big Question for this unit: **How does communication change us?**

◀ CRITICAL VIEWING In what ways are lightning bugs appropriate to this scene in a way that lightning would not be?

READINGS IN PART 2

CLOSE READING TOOL

Use the **Close Reading Tool** to practice the strategies you learn in this unit.

Focus on Craft and Structure

Elements of Poetry

Poetry is **imaginative literature** that uses **precise, musical,** and **emotionally charged language.**

Poetry is a literary form that combines the precise meanings of words with their emotional associations and musical qualities, such as rhythm and sounds. There are three main types of poetry:

- **Lyric:** a short poem that expresses the thoughts and feelings of a single speaker
- **Narrative:** a poem that tells a story
- **Dramatic:** a poem that presents the speech of one or more speakers in a dramatic situation

Poems of all types are made up of certain elements. When you read poetry, consider the poem's "voice," structure, and sound.

Speaker The speaker in a poem serves the same function as the narrator in a story: to "tell" the poem. In some poems, the speaker is an imagined character. For example, in the poem "The Raven" (page 382), the speaker is not Edgar Allan Poe, the poet, but a character who describes a mysterious bird. Even in poems that are based on the poet's life, the speaker is not the poet. Instead, the speaker is a constructed, imagined voice.

Lines and Stanzas Most poetry is arranged in lines and **stanzas,** or groupings of lines. Stanzas are named after the number of lines they contain. For example, a couplet consists of two lines, a tercet consists of three lines, and a quatrain consists of four lines.

Example: Quatrain

Sweetest love, I do not go,
        For weariness of thee,
Nor in hope the world can show
        A fitter love for me
(from "Song" by John Donne)

In the quatrain, notice that each line *breaks,* or ends, before a complete thought is expressed.

Rhythm and Meter Language has its own natural rhythms, created by the stressed and unstressed syllables of words. Poets make use of this innate property of language to create **meter,** or rhythmic patterns.

Readers identify the kind of meter used in a poem by counting the number and types of stresses in each line. Stressed syllables are marked with an accent symbol (´), and unstressed syllables are marked with a horseshoe symbol (˘). The stressed and unstressed syllables are then divided into units called **feet.** In the following stanza from "The Eagle" by Alfred, Lord Tennyson, the vertical lines (|) divide each line into four feet.

Example: Meter

Thĕ wrín|klĕd seá|ben̆eáth|him̆ cráwls,
Hĕ wátch|ĕs fróm|his̆ moúnt|ain̆ wálls,
An̆d liké|ă thún|dĕrbólt|hĕ fálls.

Each foot is made up of one unstressed syllable and one stressed syllable. This type of foot, called an **iamb,** mimics the rise and fall of the "wrinkled sea" described in the poem. Other types of metrical feet are as follows:

- **Trochee:** a stressed syllable followed by an unstressed syllable, as in the word *twinkle.*
- **Spondee:** two stressed syllables in a row, as in the word *schoolyard*
- **Dactyl:** a stressed syllable followed by two unstressed syllables, as in the word *beautiful*
- **Anapest:** two unstressed syllables followed by a stressed syllable, as in the word *comprehend*

Rhyme In addition to meter, poets use other **sound devices,** or techniques that create musical effects. Rhyme is a sound device commonly associated with poetry, although many poems do not rhyme. Types of rhyme include the following:

- **Exact, or true, rhyme:** words that end in both the same vowel and the same consonant sounds
  Example: *sun* and *run*
- **Slant rhyme:** words that end in similar but not exact sounds
  Example: *prove* and *love*
- **End rhyme:** rhyming words that fall at the ends of two or more lines
  Example: *crawls, walls,* and *falls* in the passage from "The Eagle"
- **Internal rhyme:** rhyming words placed within a line
  Example: The mouse in the house woke the cat.

Rhyme Scheme A set pattern of rhyme is called a **rhyme scheme.** The rhyme scheme of a poem is identified by assigning a different letter of the alphabet to each rhyme. Notice the rhyme scheme of the following stanza from the poem "I Wandered Lonely as a Cloud" by William Wordsworth.

Example: Rhyme Scheme

For oft, when on my couch I lie	a
In vacant or in pensive mood,	b
They flash upon that inward eye	a
Which is the bliss of solitude;	b
And then my heart with pleasure fills,	c
And dances with the daffodils.	c

Rhyme scheme helps shape the structure of a stanza and clarifies the relationships among the lines. In the example, the *abab* pattern creates a close connection among the first four lines, which describe the speaker's habit of daydreaming about the daffodils. The *cc* rhyme creates a close connection between the last two lines, which sum up the speaker's feelings during those daydreams.

Other Sound Devices A poet may use a variety of other sound devices to create musical effects. The box below explains sound devices that are often used in poetry.

Types of Sound Devices

Repetition is the use of any language element more than once.

Example: *Above the town, above the lake, and high above the trees.*

Alliteration is the repetition of consonant sounds at the beginning of words.

Example: *The snake sneaked past the snail.*

Assonance is the repetition of vowel sounds followed by different consonants in two or more stressed syllables.

Example: *The green leaves fluttered in the breeze.*

Consonance is the repetition of final consonant sounds in stressed syllables with different vowel sounds.

Example: *The king sang a song.*

Onomatopoeia is the use of words to imitate sounds.

Example: *The bees buzzed, and the brook gurgled.*

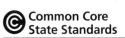

Common Core State Standards

Reading Literature

4. Determine the meaning of words and phrases as they are used in the text, including figurative and connotative meanings; analyze the cumulative impact of specific word choices on meaning and tone.

5. Analyze how an author's choices concerning how to structure a text, order events within it, and manipulate time create such effects as mystery, tension, or surprise.

Analyzing Poetic Language

Poets use the **connotations** of words and **figurative language** to express ideas precisely and imaginatively.

Poetry relies not only on the sounds and rhythms of language but also on the precise meanings of words. Poets choose each word carefully, considering both its **denotation,** or literal definition, and its **connotation,** or emotional associations.

Denotative and Connotative Meanings

Consider the words *thrifty* and *penny-pinching.* Though both words literally mean "careful in the spending of money," their connotative meanings are quite different. *Thrifty* is associated with admirable qualities, such as economy, and therefore conveys a positive attitude. *Penny-pinching* is associated with undesirable qualities, such as stinginess, and therefore conveys a negative attitude. These types of nuances help poets express precise meaning, emotion, and attitudes.

Meaning and Tone The connotative meanings of words are especially instrumental in conveying a poem's **tone**—the poet's emotional attitude toward his or her subject. The tone of a poem can be formal, informal, lighthearted, solemn, or anything in between.

As you read the following lines from "I Hear America Singing" (page 406), try to identify the tone that the words create.

Example: Tone

I hear America singing, the varied
    carols I hear, . . .
at night the party of young fellows,
    robust, friendly,
Singing with open mouths their strong
    melodious songs.

The positive connotations of the words *singing, carols, robust, friendly, strong,* and *melodious* create a tone that might be described as joyous or cheerful.

Imagery Poetic language is also often rich with imagery, or descriptive language that creates word pictures. Through the use of details that appeal to the senses of sight, touch, sound, taste, and smell, poets re-create sensory experiences and emotions in words.

Notice the imagery in the following poem, and analyze the overall impression it creates.

Example: Imagery

On that long summer day,
    each breath was a labor.
The air was wet wool,
    Heavy and warm.

A thick, yellow haze
    hung over the city,
blocking out buildings,
    blinding the sun.

Not a sound could be heard.
    All was sullen and silent,
save for the whir of
    electric fans.

In the first stanza, the description of the heavy, warm air appeals to the sense of touch. In the second stanza, the description of the yellow haze appeals to the sense of sight. In the third stanza, the onomatopoeic word *whir* appeals to the sense of sound. The overall impression is one of exhaustion and heat.

Figurative Language Poetry also often features figurative language, or language that is not meant to be interpreted literally. Most figurative language points out a striking and significant similarity between dissimilar things. Through unexpected comparisons, poets help readers see feelings, experiences, and familiar, everyday objects in a fresh new light.

Types of Figurative Language

A **simile** compares two apparently unlike things using the word *like* or *as*: *Her visit was as welcome as a flower in winter.*

A **metaphor** compares two apparently unlike things without the use of a connecting word: *Her visit was a flower in winter.*

Personification gives human qualities or abilities to nonhuman things: *The alarm clock nagged me to get out of bed.*

As you read the following poem, look for examples of each type of figurative language described above.

Example: Figurative Language

Tall, strong, and silent,
the stalks of corn
guarded the garden
like sentries.

All ears, they listened
for the caws of the crows.
The birds approached,
a hungry, invading force.

In the simile "guarded the garden / like sentries," the cornstalks are compared to watchful soldiers. In a playful example of personification, the ears on the stalks of corn listen for crows. In the metaphor "The birds approached, / a hungry, invading force," the crows flying to the garden are compared to an enemy force.

Free and Formal Verse The example poem on this page is **free verse**—a type of poetry that exhibits poetic language but does not follow fixed patterns. Free verse may use rhyme, sound devices, varied types of stanzas, and meter but will not do so in a set structure.

By contrast, **formal verse** follows fixed, established patterns. A pattern may require a specific rhyme scheme, meter, line structure, stanza structure, or other element. Throughout history, poets have invented lyric forms. Eventually, some of these forms, including those defined in the chart below, became part of literary tradition.

Types of Formal Poetry

Ballad	a songlike narrative poem, usually written in rhymed stanzas of four to six lines that feature repetition and strong meter
Haiku	an unrhymed three-line lyric poem, usually focused on images from nature, in which lines 1 and 3 have five syllables and line 2 has seven syllables
English Sonnet	a fourteen-line lyric poem consisting of three quatrains and a couplet, usually rhymed *abab cdcd efef gg*
Ode	a lyric poem on a serious subject, usually written in a precise structure
Concrete Poem	a poem with a shape that suggests its subject; the poet arranges letters, words, punctuation, and lines to create a picture

The process of formal invention in poetry is ongoing. Today, some poets experiment with forms based on mathematical equations, while others write hypertext poetry—poems that use electronic links online and are different for every reader.

How does communication change us?

Explore the Big Question as you read these poems. Take notes about the way in which a poem communicates and how that message affects the reader.

CLOSE READING FOCUS

Key Ideas and Details: **Read Fluently**

Reading fluently means reading continuously while also understanding the text and appreciating the writer's artistry. Many poems have line breaks—the ending points of lines—that are not guided by punctuation. Line breaks are key parts of a poem's structure and contribute to its meaning. However, when reading poetry, it can help to first read in sentences, following the punctuation rather than line breaks. After you acquire a basic understanding of the poem, reread it fluently, following the line breaks as the poet intended.

Craft and Structure: **Figurative Language**

Figurative language is language used imaginatively rather than literally. Figures of speech, literary devices that make unexpected comparisons or play with word meanings, are a form of figurative language. The following are specific types of figures of speech:

- **Simile:** a comparison of two apparently unlike things using *like, as, than,* or *resembles:* "The morning sun is like a red rubber ball."
- **Metaphor:** a description of one thing as if it were another: "The morning sun is a red rubber ball."
- **Personification:** assignment of human characteristics to a non-human subject: "The sea was angry that day, my friends."
- **Paradox:** a statement, an idea, or a situation that seems contradictory but actually expresses a truth: "The more things change, the more they stay the same."

Imagery, or language that appeals to the senses, often appears in figures of speech (as in the first two examples above).

Common Core State Standards

Reading Literature
4. Determine the meaning of words and phrases as they are used in the text, including figurative and connotative meanings; analyze the cumulative impact of specific word choices on meaning and tone.

Language
5. Demonstrate understanding of figurative language, word relationships, and nuances in meanings.

Vocabulary

The words below are critical to understanding the text that follows. Copy the words into your notebook. Which word is an antonym for *fertile*?

deferred **barren** **abash**
fester **paradoxical**

CLOSE READING MODEL

The passages below are from Langston Hughes's poem "Dream Deferred" and Jean de Sponde's poem "Sonnet on Love XIII." The annotations to the right of the passages show ways in which you can use close reading skills to read fluently and analyze figurative language.

from "Dream Deferred"

What happens to a dream deferred?

Does it dry up
like a raisin in the sun?[1]
Or fester like a sore—
And then run?[2]

Figurative Language

1 The speaker compares a dream that has been deferred, or delayed, to a raisin—a grape that has shriveled in the sun. Using this simile, the speaker wonders if dreams that are neglected or ignored lose their power.

Figurative Language

2 In another simile, the speaker compares an unfulfilled dream to a sore, or wound. The vivid verb *fester* creates an unpleasant image of rot and infection. Using this simile, the speaker wonders if dreams that are delayed become a kind of illness.

from "Sonnet on Love XIII"

What could be more immovable or stronger?
What becomes more and more secure, the longer
it is battered by inconstancy and the stress

we find in our lives?[3] Here is that fine fixed point
from which to move a world that is out of joint,
as he could have done, had he known a love like this.

Read Fluently

3 A single sentence stretches over three lines and two stanzas. In order to read according to punctuation, you would read through the line and stanza breaks, coming to a full stop at the question mark.

Meet the Poets

"Dream Deferred" • "Dreams"

Langston Hughes (1902–1967)

Born in Joplin, Missouri, Langston Hughes was the first African American to earn a living as a poet and writer. As a young man, he held a variety of jobs—teacher, ranch hand, and farmer, among others. He drew on all of these experiences, but primarily on his perspective as an African American, to create his great body of work.

"Sonnet on Love XIII"

Jean de Sponde (1557–1595)

The French poet Jean de Sponde was a true Renaissance man who served in the court of King Henry IV, dabbled in chemistry, and published scholarly editions of ancient Greek texts. "Sonnet on Love XIII" is part of his finest work, *Sonnets of Love and Death*.

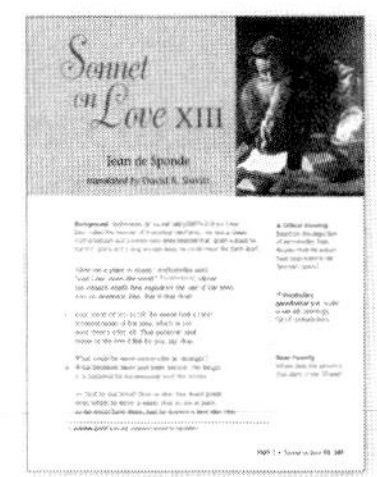

"Meciendo/Rocking"

Gabriela Mistral (1889–1957)

Born in Chile as Lucila Godoy y Alcayaga, this writer formed her pen name from the names of her two favorite poets, the Italian Gabriele D'Annunzio and the French Frederic Mistral. Gabriela Mistral wrote many moving poems about children and motherhood. She was awarded the Nobel Prize in Literature in 1945.

"'Hope' is the thing with feathers—"

Emily Dickinson (1830–1886)

Despite her quiet outward behavior, Emily Dickinson's inner life overflowed with energy. She produced more than 1,700 poems. Dickinson looked deeply into simple subjects—a fly buzzing, a bird on a walk, the changing seasons. She also made profound explorations of love, death, and the relationship between the human and the divine. She remains unquestionably one of America's finest poets.

Street Shadows, 1959, Jacob Lawrence, © ARS, NY/ Photo courtesy of: The Jacob and Gwendolyn Lawrence Foundation / Art Resource, NY

Dream Deferred

Langston Hughes

Harlem

What happens to a dream deferred?

Does it dry up
like a raisin in the sun?
Or fester like a sore—
And then run?
Does it stink like rotten meat?
Or crust and sugar over—
like a syrupy sweet?

Maybe it just sags
like a heavy load.

Or does it explode?

▲ **Critical Viewing**
Does the context of this poem make the image above seem hopeless or hopeful? Explain.

◀ **Vocabulary**
deferred (dē fʉrd′) *adj.* put off until a future time

fester (fes′ tər) *v.* become infected; form pus

DREAMS

Langston Hughes

Read Fluently
How many sentences are in the first stanza?

Vocabulary ▶
barren (bar´ ən) *adj.* empty; having little or no vegetation

Hold fast to dreams
For if dreams die
Life is a broken-winged bird
That cannot fly.

Hold fast to dreams
For when dreams go
Life is a barren field
Frozen with snow.

Sonnet on Love XIII

Jean de Sponde

translated by David R. Slavitt

Background Archimedes (är′ kə mē′ dēz′) (287?–212 B.C.) has been called the founder of theoretical mechanics. He was a Greek mathematician and inventor who once boasted that, given a place to stand in space and a long enough lever, he could move the Earth itself.

▲ **Critical Viewing**
Based on this depiction of Archimedes, how do you think he would have responded to de Sponde's poem?

"Give me a place to stand," Archimedes said,
"and I can move the world." Paradoxical, clever,
his remark which first explained the use of the lever
was an academic joke. But if that dead

sage could return to life, he would find a clear
demonstration of his idea, which is not
pure theory after all. That putative[1] spot
exists in the love I feel for you, my dear.

What could be more immovable or stronger?
What becomes more and more secure, the longer
it is battered by inconstancy and the stress

we find in our lives? Here is that fine fixed point
from which to move a world that is out of joint,
as he could have done, had he known a love like this.

◀ **Vocabulary**
paradoxical (par′ ə däk′ si kəl) *adj.* seemingly full of contradictions

Read Fluently
Where does the sentence that starts in line 10 end?

1. **putative** (pyo͞ot′ ə tiv) *adj.* supposed; known by reputation.

Meciendo (Rocking)

Gabriela Mistral

▲ **Critical Viewing**
How well does this photograph illustrate the "loving sea" described in the poem? Explain.

El mar sus millares de olas
mece, divino.
Oyendo a los mares amantes,
mezo a mi niño.

El viento errabundo en la noche
mece a los trigos.
Oyendo a los vientos amantes,
mezo a mi niño.

Dios Padre sus miles de mundos
mece sin ruido.
Sintiendo su mano en la sombra,
mezo a mi niño.

Rocking (Meciendo)

Gabriela Mistral

translated by Doris Dana

The sea rocks her thousands of waves.
The sea is divine.
Hearing the loving sea
I rock my son.

The wind wandering by night
rocks the wheat.
Hearing the loving wind
I rock my son.

God, the Father, soundlessly rocks
His thousands of worlds.
Feeling His hand in the shadow
I rock my son.

Figurative Language
What human traits does the wind show in the second stanza?

"Hope" is the thing with feathers—

Emily Dickinson

Read Fluently
Where in the second stanza could you replace a dash with a period to signify the end of a sentence?

Vocabulary ▶
abash (ə bash′)
v. embarrass

"Hope" is the thing with feathers—
That perches in the soul—
And sings the tune without the words—
And never stops—at all—

And sweetest—in the Gale[1]—is heard—
And sore must be the storm—
That could abash the little Bird
That kept so many warm—

I've heard it in the chillest land—
And on the strangest Sea—
Yet, never, in Extremity,
It asked a crumb—of Me.

1. **Gale** (gāl) *n.* strong wind.

Language Study

Vocabulary Analogies show the relationships between pairs of words. The words listed below appear in the poems from Poetry Collection 1. Use a word from the list to complete each analogy, creating a second word pair that matches the relationship between the first two given words.

fester **barren** **paradoxical** **abash**

1. rainy : weather :: ___________ : statement
2. empty : full :: ___________ : fruitful
3. blaze : burn :: ___________ : rot
4. praise : confidence :: ___________ : shame

WORD STUDY
The **Latin root *-fer-*** means "bring" or "carry." Hughes's poem "Dream Deferred" is about a dream that has been **deferred**—the dream has been carried away, or put off until a future time.

Word Study

Part A Explain how the **Latin root *-fer-*** contributes to the meanings of *infer, referral,* and *fertile*. Consult a dictionary if necessary.

Part B Use the context of the sentences and what you know about the Latin root *-fer-* to explain your answer to each question.

1. If you *transfer* something, do you keep it in one place?
2. Does a *conference* bring people together?

Close Reading Activities

Literary Analysis

Key Ideas and Details

1. **Contrast:** In "Dream Deferred," how does the last question differ from the ones the speaker asks earlier? Explain your response.
2. **(a)** To what two things does the speaker in "Dreams" compare life? **(b) Interpret:** Restate in your own words the advice that the speaker in "Dreams" offers.
3. **Interpret:** In "Sonnet on Love XIII," how does the speaker express the power of his love? Explain.
4. **(a)** In "'Hope' is the thing with feathers—," at what times does hope sing sweetest? **(b) Interpret:** What is the speaker saying about adversity? Explain.
5. **(a)** In "Meciendo/Rocking," what natural elements does the speaker describe? **(b) Generalize:** How does the speaker see herself in relation to nature? Use details from the poem to support your answer.
6. **Read Fluently (a)** Using a graphic organizer like the one shown, rewrite one stanza from Poetry Collection 1 as a prose paragraph. **(b)** Read the stanza and paragraph aloud. Explain how reading in sentences and following the punctuation aids your understanding.

Stanza
Paragraph

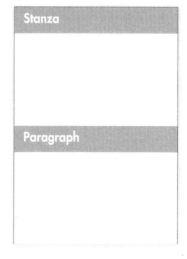

Craft and Structure

7. **Figurative Language (a)** Identify one simile in "Dream Deferred" and one metaphor in "Dreams." **(b)** Explain what each figure of speech adds to the meaning of the poem in which it appears.
8. **Figurative Language (a)** Identify an example of personification in "'Hope is the thing with feathers—." **(b)** How does this use of figurative language contribute to the poem's meaning?
9. **Figurative Language** Identify and explain the paradox "Sonnet on Love XIII" expresses.

Integration of Knowledge and Ideas

10. **Analyze:** In what ways does each poem create images that help the reader visualize an abstract concept or feeling, such as beauty, hope, love, and longing? Explain, citing details from the poems in your response.

11. THE BIG ? **How does communication change us?** Do the poems in Poetry Collection 1 communicate thoughts, feelings, and ideas in ways that change or challenge readers' usual perceptions? Cite specific details from the poems to support your answer.

ACADEMIC VOCABULARY

As you write and speak about these poems, use the words related to communication that you explored on page 329 of this book.

Conventions: **Prepositions and Prepositional Phrases**

A **preposition** is a word, such as *in, out, on, with, through, about,* or *at,* that relates a noun or pronoun that appears with it to another word in the sentence. A **prepositional phrase** is a group of words beginning with a preposition and ending with a noun or pronoun, called the object of the preposition.

A prepositional phrase may function as either an adjective or an adverb, depending on the word it modifies. An adjective phrase modifies a noun or a pronoun by telling *what kind* or *which one*. An adverb phrase modifies a verb, an adjective, or an adverb by pointing out *where, when, in what way,* or *to what extent*.

Adjective phrase: The players <u>on their team</u> are more experienced. (modifies the noun *players*)

Adjective phrase: The flowers <u>with yellow petals</u> are my favorites. (modifies the noun *flowers*)

Adverb phrase: They played <u>with more skill</u>. (modifies the verb *played*)

Adverb phrase: My parents walked <u>through the door</u> <u>at that moment.</u> (both phrases modify the verb *walked*)

Practice A

Identify the prepositional phrase in each sentence, and tell whether it functions as an adjective or an adverb.

1. Hughes's poem asks questions about dreams.
2. Archimedes stood on a precise spot.
3. The wind blew through the wheat.
4. Mistral's poem about her son is affectionate.
5. Dickinson wrote poetry in solitude.

Reading Application In Poetry Collection 1, find one prepositional phrase that functions as an adjective and one that functions as an adverb.

Practice B

Following the instructions in parentheses, use each prepositional phrase in a sentence of your own.

1. of joyful singing (adjective phrase)
2. in the woods (adverb phrase)
3. under the bridge (adverb phrase)
4. through the hoop (adverb phrase)
5. about the sea (adjective phrase)

Writing Application Following these two model sentences, write four new sentences. Identify which prepositional phrases are used as adjectives and which are used as adverbs.

Do not run with a knife.

This book contains animal illustrations of many kinds.

Writing to Sources

Informative Text Using one of the scenes described in Poetry Collection 1 as a model, write a **description of a scene** in nature. Use the figurative language techniques of the poet you are emulating to develop your own descriptive word picture in a few paragraphs or a poem.

- Choose a scene that you know firsthand or from photographs.
- List details to include in the scene that appeal to one or more of the senses.
- Refer to your list of details and to the poem you chose as a model as you draft your description.
- Finally, write an introductory statement in which you identify the poem you used as a model and explain the reasons for your choice. Note specific elements in the poem that you found effective and explain how you incorporated similar qualities into your writing.

Grammar Application Make sure you use prepositions and prepositional phrases to add descriptive detail.

Speaking and Listening

Presentation of Ideas Write a **speech** in which you explain your interpretation of one of the poems in Poetry Collection 1.

- Write an outline for your speech. Begin by jotting down the central point you want to convey and two to three points that support that main idea.
- Engage your audience by choosing interesting details that are appropriate to the purpose of your speech and support your interpretation of the poem.
- Make your ideas memorable by using figurative language.
- Use a variety of sentence types, including long and short sentences and simple and complex sentences.
- As you deliver your speech, make eye contact with your audience and use gestures to emphasize ideas.
- Create a rubric so that classmates can assess your speech. Invite your listeners to give you feedback about your performance.

After you deliver the speech, evaluate the feedback you receive and make notes about how you can improve your delivery of future speeches.

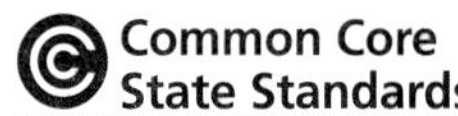

Common Core State Standards

Writing

3.d. Use precise words and phrases, telling details, and sensory language to convey a vivid picture of the experiences, events, setting, and/or characters.

Speaking and Listening

4. Present information, findings, and supporting evidence clearly, concisely, and logically such that listeners can follow the line of reasoning and the organization, development, substance, and style are appropriate to purpose, audience, and task.

Language

1. Demonstrate command of the conventions of standard English grammar and usage when writing or speaking.

1.b. Use various types of phrases and clauses to convey specific meanings and add variety and interest to writing or presentations.

How does communication change us?

Explore the Big Question as you read Poetry Collection 2. Note how each poem adds to or changes your understanding of a topic.

CLOSE READING FOCUS

Key Ideas and Details: **Read Fluently**

Reading fluently means reading smoothly and continuously while also comprehending the text. Because poetry is a condensed literary form that employs figurative language, you may need to read poems several times to fully unlock their layers of meaning. Your focus might change for each reading, as follows:

- First Reading: Read for basic meaning.
- Second Reading: Read to unlock deeper meanings.
- Third Reading: Read to recognize and appreciate the poet's craft.

Craft and Structure: **Sound Devices**

Poets use **sound devices** to emphasize the sound relationships among words. Sound devices, such as those listed below, also contribute to the meaning and tone of a poem and help bring it to life for readers.

- **Alliteration:** the repetition of initial consonant sounds in stressed syllables: *"The fair breeze blew, the white foam flew..."*
- **Consonance:** the repetition of final consonant sounds in stressed syllables with different vowel sounds, as in *sit* and *cat*
- **Assonance:** the repetition of similar vowel sounds in stressed syllables that end with different consonants, as in *seal* and *meet*
- **Onomatopoeia:** the use of a word whose sound imitates its meaning, such as *pop* or *hiss*

All of these sound devices work to engage the reader's senses and create musical and emotional effects.

Vocabulary

The words below are critical to understanding the text that follows. Copy the words into your notebook. Which word is a synonym for *spiritual*?

voluminously **endeavor** **palpitating** **monotone**
disgrace **metaphysical** **jibed**

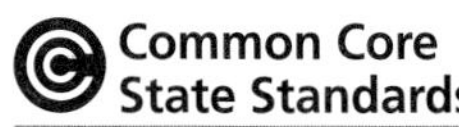

Common Core State Standards

Reading Literature
4. Determine the meaning of words and phrases as they are used in the text, including figurative and connotative meanings; analyze the cumulative impact of specific word choices on meaning and tone.

Language
5. Demonstrate understanding of figurative language, word relationships, and nuances in word meanings.

CLOSE READING MODEL

The passages below are from the poems "Slam, Dunk, & Hook" and "Jabberwocky." The annotations to the right of the passages show ways in which you can use close reading skills to read fluently and analyze sound devices.

from "Slam, Dunk, & Hook"

When Sonny Boy's mama died
He played nonstop all day, so hard
Our backboard splintered.[1]
Glistening with sweat, we jibed
& rolled the ball off our
Fingertips. Trouble
Was there slapping a blackjack
Against an open palm.
Dribble, drive[2] to the inside, feint,
& glide like a sparrow hawk.

Read Fluently

1 With a first reading, you might understand the basic meaning: Sonny Boy's mom died, and he is using basketball to deal with his grief. Another reading might lead you to appreciate the poet's choice of the word *splintered*, which brings to life the intensity of Sonny Boy's pain.

Sound Devices

2 The poet uses alliteration with the words *dribble* and *drive*. The choppy sound of *dr* helps contribute to the hurried, anxious tone of this section of the poem.

from "Jabberwocky"

He took his vorpal sword in hand;
    Long time the manxome[3] foe he sought—
So rested he by the Tumtum tree,
    And stood awhile in thought.

And, as in uffish[3] thought he stood,
    The Jabberwock, with eyes of flame,
Came whiffling through the tulgey wood,
    And burbled as it came![4]

Read Fluently

3 The poet's use of invented language makes fluency challenging. You may need to reread these lines several times in order to grasp their basic meaning.

Sound Devices

4 The words *whiffling* and *burbled* are examples of onomatopoeia. They imbue the scene with sound, which helps the reader imagine the chaos of the Jabberwock's arrival.

Meet the Poets

"The Bells"

Edgar Allan Poe (1809–1849)

As poems like "The Bells" illustrate, Edgar Allan Poe was a master at using rhythm and sound devices to powerful effect. Many scholars believe that the idea for "The Bells" was suggested to Poe by Marie Louise Shew, a woman with medical training who treated Poe when his health began to fail.

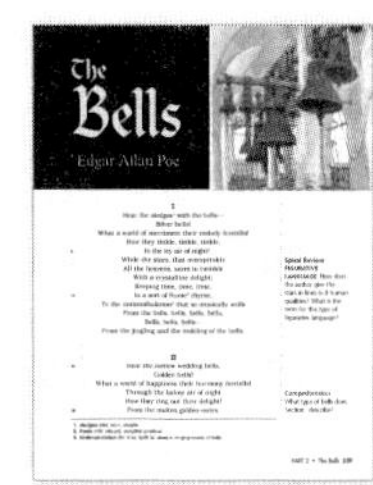

"Analysis of Baseball"

May Swenson (1919–1989)

May Swenson has been called "one of the surest poets, clear-eyed and absolute." She was born in Logan, Utah, and attended Utah State University. After working for a while as a newspaper reporter, she moved to New York City, where she worked as an editor and as a college lecturer. Her poems were published in such magazines as *The New Yorker, Harper's,* and *The Nation*. Swenson also served as Chancellor of The Academy of American Poets from 1980 to 1989.

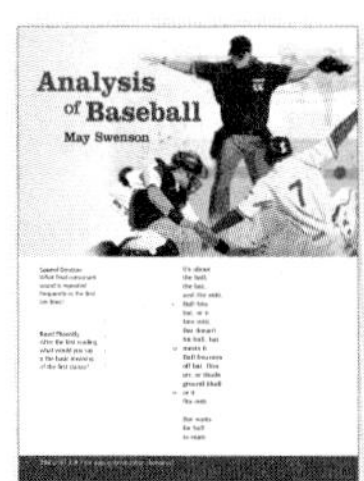

"Slam, Dunk, & Hook"

Yusef Komunyakaa (b. 1947)

Yusef Komunyakaa grew up in Bogalusa, Louisiana. During the mid-1960s, he served in Vietnam as a reporter and an editor for the military newspaper *The Southern Cross*. Komunyakaa later turned his attention to poetry, winning a Pulitzer Prize for his book *Neon Vernacular: New and Selected Poems* (1993). Komunyakaa has said that he likes "connecting the abstract to the concrete."

"Jabberwocky"

Lewis Carroll (1832–1898)

Charles Lutwidge Dodgson was a professor of mathematics and a talented early photographer. Today, he is best remembered for two children's books he wrote under the pen name Lewis Carroll: *Alice's Adventures in Wonderland* (1865) and its sequel, *Through the Looking Glass* (1871). Huge bestsellers almost from the moment they appeared, the Alice books have been the basis of numerous stage plays and films.

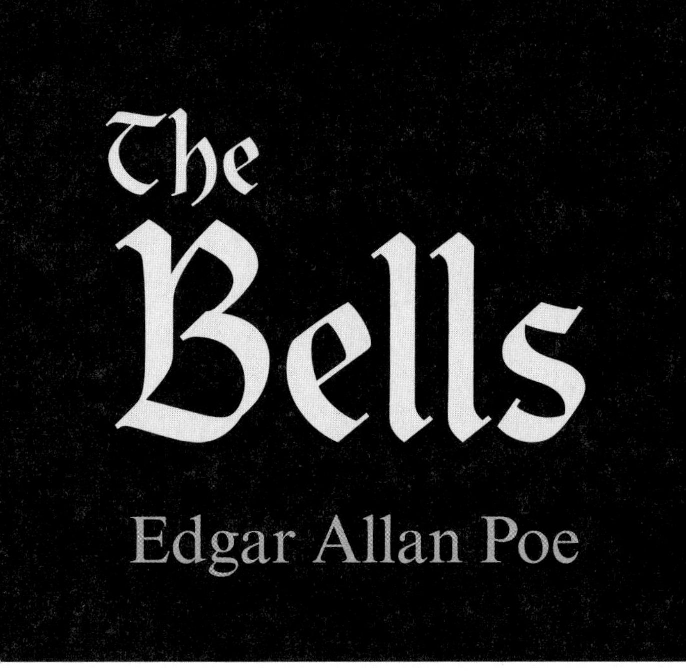

I

Hear the sledges[1] with the bells—
Silver bells!
What a world of merriment their melody foretells!
How they tinkle, tinkle, tinkle,
In the icy air of night!
While the stars, that oversprinkle
All the heavens, seem to twinkle
With a crystalline delight;
Keeping time, time, time,
In a sort of Runic[2] rhyme,
To the tintinnabulation[3] that so musically wells
From the bells, bells, bells, bells,
Bells, bells, bells—
From the jingling and the tinkling of the bells.

II

Hear the mellow wedding bells,
Golden bells!
What a world of happiness their harmony foretells!
Through the balmy air of night
How they ring out their delight!
From the molten golden-notes,

Spiral Review
FIGURATIVE LANGUAGE How does the author give the stars in lines 6–8 human qualities? What is the term for this type of figurative language?

Comprehension
What type of bells does Section I describe?

1. **sledges** (slej´ əz) *n.* sleighs.
2. **Runic** (ro͞o´ nik) *adj.* songlike; poetical.
3. **tintinnabulation** (tin´ ti na´ byo͞o la´ shən) *n.* ringing sound of bells.

And all in tune,
What a liquid ditty[4] floats
To the turtle-dove[5] that listens, while she gloats
On the moon!
Oh, from out the sounding cells,
What a gush of euphony[6] voluminously wells!
How it swells!
How it dwells
On the future! how it tells
Of the rapture that impels
To the swinging and the ringing
Of the bells, bells, bells,
Of the bells, bells, bells, bells
Bells, bells, bells—
To the rhyming and the chiming of the bells!

Vocabulary ▶ voluminously (və lo͞om′ ə nəs lē) *adv.* fully; in great volume

III

Sound Devices What quality of alarm bells might the alliteration of the *t* sound in line 38 imitate?

Hear the loud alarum[7] bells!
Brazen[8] bells!
What a tale of terror now their turbulency tells!
In the startled ear of night
How they scream out their affright!
Too much horrified to speak,
They can only shriek, shriek,
Out of tune,
In a clamorous appealing to the mercy of the fire,
In a mad expostulation[9] with the deaf and frantic fire
Leaping higher, higher, higher,
With a desperate desire,
And a resolute endeavor
Now—now to sit or never,
By the side of the pale-faced moon.
Oh, the bells, bells, bells!
What a tale their terror tells
Of Despair!
How they clang, and clash, and roar!
What a horror they outpour
On the bosom of the palpitating air!

Vocabulary ▶ endeavor (en dev′ ər) *n.* earnest attempt or effort

palpitating (pal′ pə tāt′ iŋ) *v.* beating rapidly; throbbing

4. **ditty** (dit′ ē) *n.* short, simple song.
5. **turtle-dove** (turt′ 'l duv′) The turtle dove is traditionally associated with love.
6. **euphony** (yo͞o′ fə nē) *n.* pleasing sound.
7. **alarum** (ə ler′ əm) *n. used as adj.* sudden call to arms; alarm.
8. **Brazen** (brā′ zən) *adj.* made of brass; having the ringing sound of brass.
9. **expostulation** (ek späs′ chə lā′ shən) *n.* objection; complaint.

Yet the ear it fully knows,
By the twanging
And the clanging,
How the danger ebbs and flows;
Yet the ear distinctly tells,
In the jangling,
And the wrangling,
How the danger sinks and swells,
By the sinking or the swelling in the anger of the bells—
Of the bells—
Of the bells, bells, bells, bells,
Bells, bells, bells—
In the clamor and the clangor of the bells!

Sound Devices
What is the effect of the repetition in lines 67–68?

IV

Hear the tolling of the bells—
Iron bells!
What a world of solemn thought their monody[10] compels!

Comprehension
What kind of story do the alarm bells tell?

10. **monody** (mä´ nə dē) *n.* poem of mourning; a steady sound; music in which one instrument or voice is dominant.

In the silence of the night,
How we shiver with affright
At the melancholy menace of their tone!
For every sound that floats
From the rust within their throats
Is a groan.
And the people—ah, the people—
They that dwell up in the steeple,
All alone,
And who tolling, tolling, tolling,
In that muffled monotone,
Feel a glory in so rolling
On the human heart a stone—
They are neither man nor woman—
They are neither brute nor human—
They are Ghouls:[11]
And their king it is who tolls;
And he rolls, rolls, rolls,
Rolls
A pæan from the bells!
And his merry bosom swells
With the pæan of the bells!
And he dances and he yells;
Keeping time, time, time,
In a sort of Runic rhyme,
To the pæan of the bells—
Of the bells:
Keeping time, time, time,
In a sort of Runic rhyme,
To the throbbing of the bells—
Of the bells, bells, bells—
To the sobbing of the bells;
Keeping time, time, time,
As he knells, knells, knells,
In a happy Runic rhyme,
To the rolling of the bells—
Of the bells, bells, bells—
To the tolling of the bells,
Of the bells, bells, bells, bells,
Bells, bells, bells—
To the moaning and the groaning of the bells.

Sound Devices
What alliteration appears in lines 83–85?

◀ **Vocabulary**
monotone (män′ ə tōn′) *n.* uninterrupted repetition of the same tone; utterance of successive syllables or words without change of pitch or key

Read Fluently
Which repeated words in this stanza might sound like the repetitive tolling of bells?

◀ **Critical Viewing**
Which kind of bells do you think this painting best illustrates? Why?

---

11. Ghouls (go͞olz) *n.* evil spirits that rob graves.

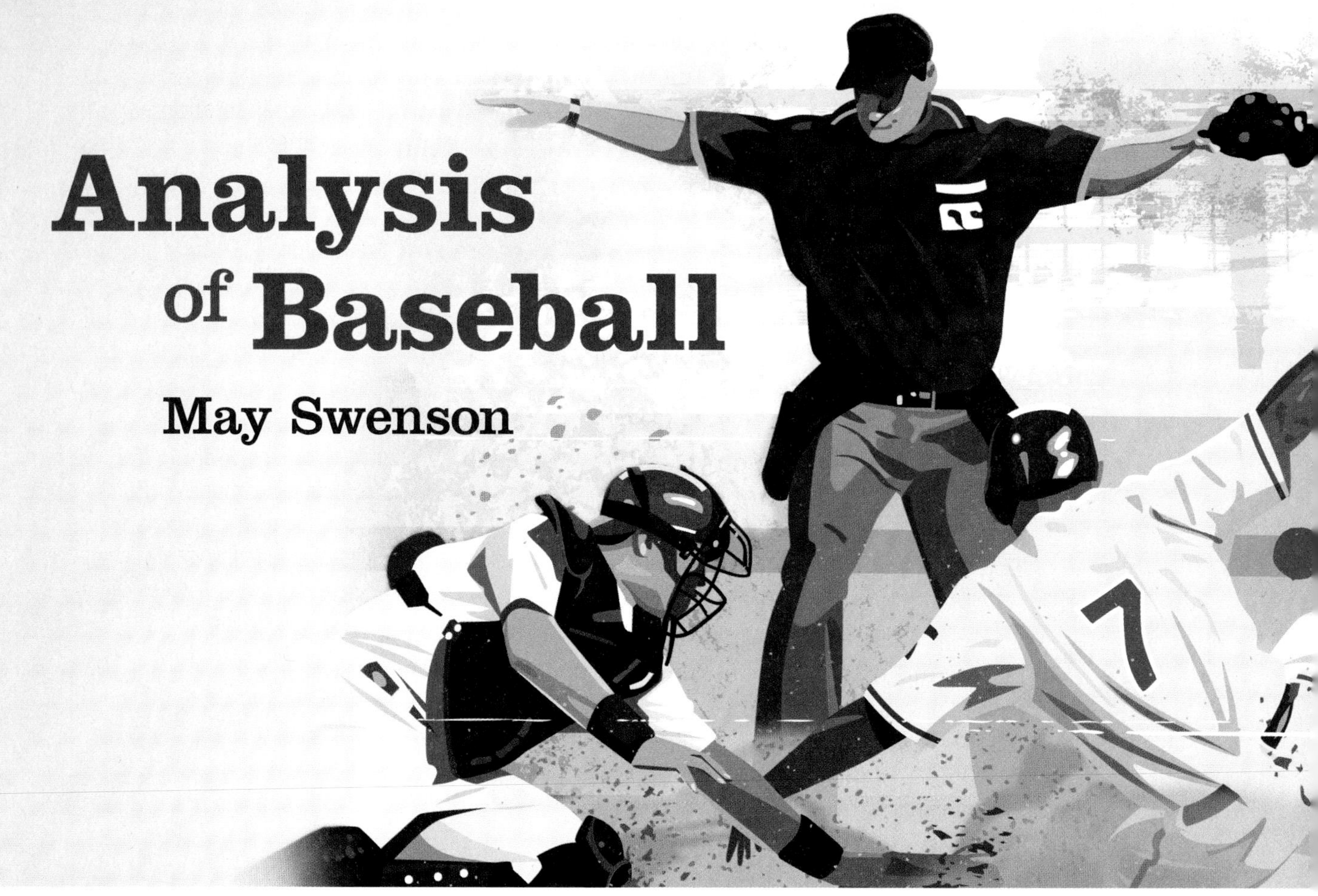

Analysis of Baseball

May Swenson

Sound Devices
What final consonant sound is repeated frequently in the first ten lines?

Read Fluently
After the first reading, what would you say is the basic meaning of the first stanza?

It's about
the ball,
the bat,
and the mitt.
Ball hits
bat, or it
hits mitt.
Bat doesn't
hit ball, bat
meets it.
Ball bounces
off bat, flies
air, or thuds
ground (dud)
or it
fits mitt.

Bat waits
for ball
to mate.

Ball hates
to take bat's
bait. Ball
flirts, bat's
late, don't
keep the date.
Ball goes in
(thwack) to mitt,
and goes out
(thwack) back
to mitt.

Ball fits
mitt, but
not all
the time.
Sometimes
ball gets hit
(pow) when bat
meets it,
and sails
to a place
where mitt
has to quit
in disgrace.
That's about
the bases
loaded,
about 40,000
fans exploded.

It's about
the ball,
the bat,
the mitt,
the bases
and the fans.
It's done
on a diamond,
and for fun.
It's about
home, and it's
about run.

Spiral Review
FIGURATIVE LANGUAGE
What examples of personification can you find in the stanza that runs from lines 17 to 30?

◀ **Vocabulary**
disgrace (dis grās′) *n.* loss of respect, honor, or esteem; shame

Slam, Dunk, & Hook

Yusef Komunyakaa

Fast breaks. Lay ups. With Mercury's[1]
Insignia[2] on our sneakers,
We outmaneuvered the footwork
Of bad angels. Nothing but a hot
Swish of strings like silk
Ten feet out. In the roundhouse[3]
Labyrinth[4] our bodies
Created, we could almost
Last forever, poised in midair
Like storybook sea monsters.
A high note hung there
A long second. Off
The rim. We'd corkscrew
Up & dunk balls that exploded
The skullcap of hope & good
Intention. Bug-eyed, lanky,
All hands & feet . . . sprung rhythm.
We were **metaphysical** when girls
Cheered on the sidelines.
Tangled up in a falling,
Muscles were a bright motor
Double-flashing to the metal hoop
Nailed to our oak.
When Sonny Boy's mama died
He played nonstop all day, so hard
Our backboard splintered.
Glistening with sweat, we **jibed**
& rolled the ball off our
Fingertips. Trouble
Was there slapping a blackjack
Against an open palm.
Dribble, drive to the inside, feint,
& glide like a sparrow hawk.
Lay ups. Fast breaks.
We had moves we didn't know
We had. Our bodies spun
On swivels of bone & faith,
Through a lyric slipknot
Of joy, & we knew we were
Beautiful & dangerous.

1. **Mercury's** Mercury was the Roman god of travel, usually depicted with wings on his feet.
2. **Insignia** (in sig′ nē ə) *n.* emblems or badges; logos.
3. **roundhouse** (round′ hous′) *n.* area on the court beneath the basket.
4. **Labyrinth** (lab′ ə rinth′) *n.* maze.

◀ Critical Viewing
Which details in this painting relate to lines in "Slam, Dunk, & Hook"?

◀ Vocabulary
metaphysical (met′ ə fiz′ i kəl) *adj.* spiritual; beyond the physical

jibed (jībd) *v.* changed direction

Sound Devices
What sound does the poet emphasize with the use of assonance in lines 30 and 31?

Jabberwocky

Lewis Carroll

'Twas brillig, and the slithy toves
Did gyre and gimble in the wabe;
All mimsy were the borogoves,
And the mome raths outgrabe.

"Beware the Jabberwock, my son
The jaws that bite, the claws that catch!
Beware the Jubjub bird, and shun
The frumious Bandersnatch!"

He took his vorpal sword in hand;
Long time the manxome foe he sought—
So rested he by the Tumtum tree,
And stood awhile in thought.

And, as in uffish thought he stood,
The Jabberwock, with eyes of flame,
Came whiffling through the tulgey wood,
And burbled as it came!

◄▼ **Critical Viewing**
Which aspects of these illustrations convey the fantastical quality of "Jabberwocky"?

Sound Devices
What sound or noise does the onomatopoeia *burbled* reflect?

LITERATURE IN CONTEXT

Language Connection

Carroll's Invented Language In the first chapter of *Through the Looking-Glass,* Alice encounters a creature called a Jabberwock. She cannot understand it, so Humpty Dumpty explains some of the words it uses, including these:

brillig: four o'clock in the afternoon, the time when you begin broiling things for dinner

toves: creatures that are something like badgers, something like lizards, and something like corkscrews

gyre: go round and round like a gyroscope

gimble: make holes like a gimlet (a hand tool that bores holes)

wabe: grass plot around a sundial

mome: having lost the way home

raths: something like green pigs

Connect to the Literature

What challenges do you think Carroll faced in writing a poem with invented language?

One, two! One, two! And through and through
  The vorpal blade went snicker-snack!
He left it dead, and with its head
  He went galumphing back.

"And hast thou slain the Jabberwock?
  Come to my arms, my beamish boy!
O frabjous day! Callooh! Callay!"
  He chortled in his joy.

'Twas brillig, and the slithy toves
  Did gyre and gimble in the wabe;
All mimsy were the borogoves,
  And the mome raths outgrabe.

Language Study

Vocabulary The words printed in blue appear in Poetry Collection 2. Using your knowledge of these words, identify the word in each group that does not belong. Then, explain your response.

1. **metaphysical,** transcendent, bodily

2. **jibed,** turn, straight

3. **voluminously,** tiny, huge

4. **palpitating,** pulse, hum

5. **endeavor,** avoid, attempt

6. **disgrace,** pride, honor

WORD STUDY

The **Greek prefix *mono-*** means "one." In "The Bells," the speaker describes the "muffled **monotone**" of certain bells. This describes a kind of ringing that has only one tone, or pitch, and repeats without changing.

Word Study

Part A Explain how the **Greek prefix *mono-*** contributes to the meanings of *monologue, monarch,* and *monopoly*. Consult a dictionary if necessary.

Part B Use the context of the sentences and what you know about the Greek prefix *mono-* to explain your answer to each question.

1. If a painting is *monochromatic*, does it have one color or many?

2. If Joe is *monolingual*, how many languages does he speak?

Close Reading Activities

Literary Analysis

Key Ideas and Details

1. **(a) Interpret:** Identify the different types of bells the speaker describes in each section of "The Bells." Cite details from each section that support your answer. **(b) Distinguish:** How does the final section of the poem differ from the preceding ones? Explain.
2. **Evaluate:** Does the speaker in "Analysis of Baseball" actually analyze the game? Explain, citing details from the poem to support your response.
3. **(a)** In lines 4–5 of "Slam, Dunk, & Hook," what sound does the speaker describe? **(b) Infer:** What action causes this sound? Explain.
4. **(a)** In "Jabberwocky," what does the hero do after being warned about the Jabberwock? **(b) Evaluate:** Do you think the poem mocks typical portrayals of heroes and heroism? Explain, citing details from the text in your response.
5. **Reading Fluently** Explain how your understanding of each poem changed as you read it multiple times. Provide specific examples of details you understood or saw differently with each successive reading.

Craft and Structure

6. **Sound Devices (a)** For each poem in Poetry Collection 2, use a chart like the one shown to identify one example of each sound device listed. **(b)** How does each example add to both the musical quality of the poem and its meaning?

Example	Effect
Alliteration:	
Assonance:	
Consonance:	

7. **Sound Devices (a)** Identify an example of onomatopoeia in "The Bells." **(b)** What sound does the word imitate? **(c)** How does this imitation contribute to the poem's effect? Explain your answer, citing textual details.

Integration of Knowledge and Ideas

8. **Take a Position:** The poet T. S. Eliot once said that poetry must be enjoyed before it is understood. Could any of the poems in this collection be used as evidence to support this idea? Explain, citing details from the texts.

9. THE BIG ? **How does communication change us? (a)** Which, if any, of the poems in this collection challenge the reader's usual way of thinking about a subject? Explain. **(b)** When we think differently about a topic, does that change us in some essential way? Cite details from the poems to support your response.

ACADEMIC VOCABULARY

As you write and speak about Poetry Collection 2, use the words related to communication that you explored on page 329 of this textbook.

Conventions: **Participles and Participial Phrases; Gerunds and Gerund Phrases**

A **participle** is a verb form that is used as an adjective. A **gerund** is a verb form that acts as a noun.

A **present participle** ends in *-ing*. The **past participle** of a regular verb ends in *-ed*. A **participial phrase** is a participle and any modifiers, object, or complement; the entire phrase acts as an adjective.

Present Participle	Past Participle	Participial Phrase
growing child	*troubled* child	*Focusing intently,* the driver stopped in time.

A gerund ends in *-ing*. It can function as a subject, an object of a verb or preposition, or a predicate noun. A **gerund phrase** is a gerund and any modifiers, object, or complement; the entire phrase acts as a noun.

Subject	*Remodeling* the building's style was a good idea.
Direct Object	Michael enjoys *painting*.
Predicate Noun	His favorite sport is *fishing*.
Object of a Preposition	Lucille never gets tired of *singing*.
Gerund Phrase	*The loud, shrill howling* continued all morning.

Practice A

Identify the participle or gerund in each sentence.

1. The friends enjoyed playing basketball.
2. The doomed Jabberwock stepped out of the woods.
3. Loud ringing spread throughout the town.
4. Smiling, he swung the bat.

Reading Application In Poetry Collection 2, find one line that uses a participle or participial phrase and one that uses a gerund or gerund phrase.

Practice B

Change one of the verbs in each sentence to a participle or a gerund. Then, use that word or phrase to combine the two sentences.

1. He wanted to hear the bells. It was his only thought.
2. The boy felt great sorrow. He played basketball.
3. The man thought of baseball. It was his greatest joy.
4. He wanted to kill the Jabberwock. He walked into the clearing.

Writing Application Write two sentences in which you use a gerund or gerund phrase and two in which you use a participle or participial phrase.

Writing to Sources

Argument An **editorial** is a brief nonfiction work that presents and defends the writer's opinion on an issue. Write an editorial related to one of the poems you read in Poetry Collection 2. For example, a reading of "Slam, Dunk, & Hook" might inspire you to write about the importance of maintaining funding for community sports facilities.

- State the issue and your position clearly.
- Anticipate questions from those who might disagree with you.
- As you build your argument, return to the poem to identify specific ideas or details that support your position.
- Cite words, phrases, or larger sections of the poem to support your reasoning. Smoothly integrate these citations into your argument.

Ask several people to respond to your editorial, including someone who disagrees with you. Revise your work, making sure to refute opposing arguments.

Grammar Application Make sure to use participial and gerund phrases to create variety in your writing.

Speaking and Listening

Comprehension and Collaboration In a group, create an **illustrated presentation** of one of the poems you read. Find or create photographs or artwork and, with the group, debate the merits of each choice. Negotiate to reach an agreement about which images best capture the content and mood of the poem. Then, choose one member of the group to present a dramatic reading of the poem. Have the speaker rehearse in front of the group, and have the group use the following questions to assess the speaker's performance:

- Does the speaker maintain eye contact with the audience?
- Does the speaker use gestures that fit the poem and are appropriate for the occasion?
- Does the speaker articulate clearly and modulate his or her voice to capture the audience's attention?
- Does the speaker's delivery convey the mood and tone of the poem and match the mood depicted in the images the group selected?

Once you have organized your images and rehearsed the reading, present your work to your class. Use visual aids or electronic media to display the images and enhance your presentation.

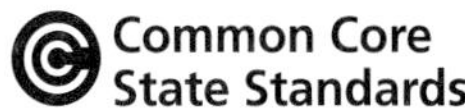

Writing

1. Write arguments to support claims in an analysis of substantive topics or texts, using valid reasoning and relevant and sufficient evidence.

1.b. Develop claim(s) and counterclaims fairly, supplying evidence for each while pointing out the strengths and limitations of both in a manner that anticipates the audience's knowledge level and concerns.

Speaking and Listening

1. Initiate and participate effectively in a range of collaborative discussions with diverse partners on grades 9–10 topics, texts, and issues, building on others' ideas and expressing their own clearly and persuasively.

5. Make strategic use of digital media in presentations to enhance understanding of findings, reasoning, and evidence and to add interest.

Language

1. Demonstrate command of the conventions of standard English grammar and usage when writing or speaking.

1.b. Use various types of phrases and clauses to convey specific meanings and add variety and interest to writing or presentations.

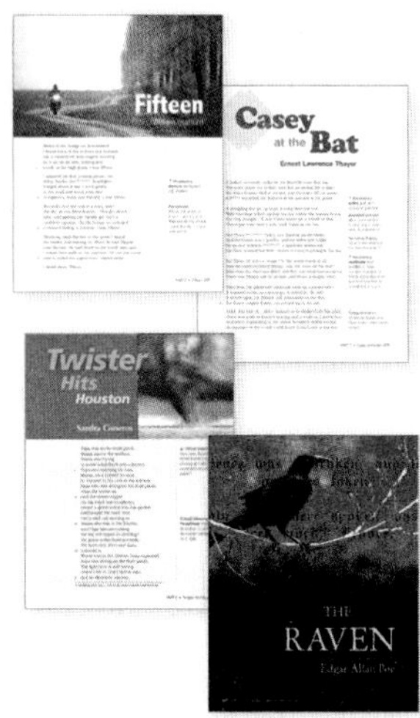

How does communication change us?

Explore the Big Question as you read the poems. Think about how the characters in these poems communicate and what they learn as a result.

CLOSE READING FOCUS

Key Ideas and Details: **Paraphrase**

Paraphrasing is restating in your own words what someone else has written or said. A paraphrase retains the meaning of the original but is simpler. Paraphrasing is especially useful in understanding poems that contain **figurative language**—words used imaginatively rather than literally. To paraphrase a narrative poem, picture the action.

- Pay attention to figurative language.
- Use those details to form a mental image of the setting and characters and the characters' actions.
- Be certain you understand what the figurative language suggests about the characters and their behavior.
- Describe your mental images.

Craft and Structure: **Narrative Poetry**

Narrative poetry tells a story. It includes the same elements as narrative prose: conflict; plot; specific settings; a narrator, or speaker; and characters.

Like short stories, narrative poems convey a **mood,** or **atmosphere**—an overall feeling built by the setting, plot, word choices, and images. For example, a fast-paced plot may create an exciting mood.

The speaker's persona, or point of view and character traits, also adds to the meaning, tone, and mood of a narrative poem. For example, the grieving persona of the speaker in "The Raven" is an important ingredient in that poem's effect.

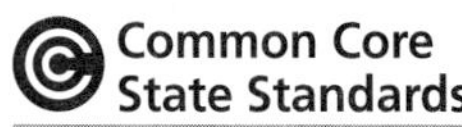

Common Core State Standards

Reading Literature

4. Determine the meaning of words and phrases as they are used in the text, including figurative and connotative meanings; analyze the cumulative impact of specific word choices on meaning and tone.

5. Analyze how an author's choices concerning how to structure a text, order events within it, and manipulate time create such effects as mystery, tension, or surprise.

Language

5.a. Interpret figures of speech in context and analyze their role in the text.

Vocabulary

The following words are critical to understanding the poems that follow. Copy the words into your notebook, and note which ones are nouns. Explain how you know.

pallor	preceded	multitude
writhing	defiance	demure
pondered	beguiling	respite

CLOSE READING MODEL

The passages below are from the poems "Fifteen" and "The Raven." The annotations to the right of the passages show ways in which you can use close reading skills to paraphrase and analyze a narrative poem.

from "Fifteen"

South of the bridge on Seventeenth
I found back of the willows one summer
day a motorcycle with engine running
as it lay on its side, ticking over
slowly in the high grass. I was fifteen.[1]

Narrative Poem

1 The first-person speaker describes the setting and tells us he or she is fifteen years old. The "ticking" motorcycle is an unstable element, a hint of danger introduced into an ordinary day. The story this poem will tell will center on this motorcycle and what it means to the speaker.

from "The Raven"

Once upon a midnight dreary, while I pondered, weak and weary,
Over many a quaint and curious volume of forgotten lore,[2]
While I nodded, nearly napping, suddenly there came a tapping,
As of someone gently rapping, rapping at my chamber door.
"Tis some visitor," I muttered, "tapping at my chamber door—
Only this, and nothing more."[3]

Narrative Poem

2 A first-person speaker introduces the setting and situation of this famous work. It is the middle of a "dreary" night, and the speaker, who is "weak and weary," has stayed up late reading old books. These details establish a mood of darkness, oppression, and depression that will characterize the entire poem.

Paraphrase

3 A reader might paraphrase these lines as follows: *While I sat there, almost asleep, I heard a tapping at the door. I thought a late-night visitor was making the noise, and I ignored it.*

Meet the Poets

"Fifteen"

William Stafford (1914–1993)

William Stafford was raised in Kansas. He did not publish his first book, *West of Your City,* until he was 46. However, he made up for lost time after that, publishing many collections, including *Traveling Through the Dark*. Fellow poet Robert Bly has said that Stafford's poems are "spoken like a friend over coffee."

"Casey at the Bat"

Ernest Lawrence Thayer (1863–1940)

It is not surprising that "Casey at the Bat" reads like a sports story in verse. The poet, Ernest Lawrence Thayer, worked for many years as a sports reporter on the staff of newspapers in New York and California. "Casey at the Bat," which first appeared in the *San Francisco Examiner* in 1888, is one of the most popular narrative poems in American literature. Thayer actually wrote three different versions of the poem; the one that begins on page 379 is his second version.

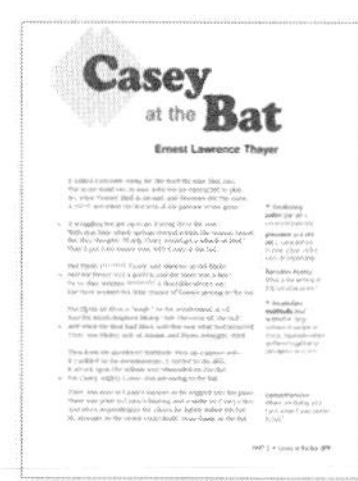

"Twister Hits Houston"

Sandra Cisneros (b. 1954)

Sandra Cisneros was born in Chicago, but her family moved frequently between Chicago and Mexico City. She began her first novel, *The House on Mango Street*, while she was still a college student. Cisneros has worked with high-school students, serving as poet-in-residence in several schools. She has received many awards for her writing.

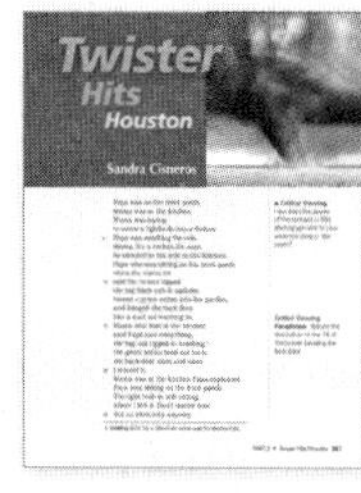

"The Raven"

Edgar Allan Poe (1809–1849)

One of the first great American storytellers, Edgar Allan Poe explored dark and bizarre events in his stories and poems. His inspiration may have come from his own life, which was often filled with sadness. Poe found some happiness in his marriage to Virginia Clemm, but after her death, he became depressed and antisocial. Many of his poems and stories focus on an ideal love that is lost.

Fifteen

William Stafford

South of the bridge on Seventeenth
I found back of the willows one summer
day a motorcycle with engine running
as it lay on its side, ticking over
slowly in the high grass. I was fifteen.

I admired all that pulsing gleam, the
shiny flanks, the **demure** headlights
fringed where it lay; I led it gently
to the road and stood with that
companion, ready and friendly. I was fifteen.

We could find the end of a road, meet
the sky on out Seventeenth. I thought about
hills, and patting the handle got back a
confident opinion. On the bridge we indulged
a forward feeling, a tremble. I was fifteen.

Thinking, back farther in the grass I found
the owner, just coming to, where he had flipped
over the rail. He had blood on his hand, was pale—
I helped him walk to his machine. He ran his hand
over it, called me a good man, roared away.

I stood there, fifteen.

◀ **Vocabulary**
demure (di myoor′)
adj. modest

Paraphrase
Picture the action in lines 11 and 12, and then restate the phrase "meet the sky" in your own words.

▲ Critical Viewing
Compare and contrast the stance and attitude of the batter in this painting with Casey's stance and attitude in the poem.

Casey at the Bat

Ernest Lawrence Thayer

It looked extremely rocky for the Mudville nine that day;
The score stood two to four, with but an inning left to play.
So, when Cooney died at second, and Burrows did the same,
A pallor wreathed the features of the patrons of the game.

A straggling few got up to go, leaving there the rest,
With that hope which springs eternal within the human breast.
For they thought: "If only Casey would get a whack at that,"
They'd put even money now, with Casey at the bat.

But Flynn preceded Casey, and likewise so did Blake,
And the former was a pudd'n, and the latter was a fake.
So on that stricken multitude a deathlike silence sat;
For there seemed but little chance of Casey's getting to the bat.

But Flynn let drive a "single," to the wonderment of all.
And the much-despised Blakey "tore the cover off the ball."
And when the dust had lifted, and they saw what had occurred,
There was Blakey safe at second, and Flynn a-huggin' third.

Then from the gladdened multitude went up a joyous yell—
It rumbled in the mountaintops, it rattled in the dell;
It struck upon the hillside and rebounded on the flat;
For Casey, mighty Casey, was advancing to the bat.

There was ease in Casey's manner as he stepped into his place,
There was pride in Casey's bearing and a smile on Casey's face;
And when responding to the cheers he lightly doffed his hat,
No stranger in the crowd could doubt 'twas Casey at the bat.

◀ **Vocabulary**
pallor (pal′ ər) *n.* unnatural paleness

preceded (prē sēd′ əd) *v.* came before in time, place, order, rank, or importance

Narrative Poetry
What is the setting of this narrative poem?

◀ **Vocabulary**
multitude (mul′ tə to͞od′) *n.* large number of people or things, especially when gathered together or considered as a unit

Comprehension
Where are Blakey and Flynn when Casey comes to bat?

Vocabulary ▶
writhing (rīth´ iŋ) *adj.* twisting; turning

defiance (dē fī´ əns) *n.* open, bold resistance to authority

Ten thousand eyes were on him as he rubbed his hands with dirt,
Five thousand tongues applauded when he wiped them on his shirt;
Then when the **writhing** pitcher ground the ball into his hip,
Defiance glanced in Casey's eye, a sneer curled Casey's lip.

And now the leather-covered sphere came hurtling through the air,
And Casey stood a-watching it in haughty grandeur there.
Close by the sturdy batsman the ball unheeded sped;
"That ain't my style," said Casey. "Strike one," the umpire said.

Spiral Review
DICTION AND SYNTAX How does word choice and word arrangement in this stanza help convey the feelings of the crowd?

From the benches, black with people, there went up a muffled roar,
Like the beating of the storm waves on the stern and distant shore.
"Kill him! Kill the umpire!" shouted someone on the stand;
And it's likely they'd have killed him had not Casey raised his hand.

With a smile of Christian charity great Casey's visage shone;
He stilled the rising tumult, he made the game go on;
He signaled to the pitcher, and once more the spheroid flew;
But Casey still ignored it, and the umpire said, "Strike two."

"Fraud!" cried the maddened thousands, and the echo answered "Fraud!"
But one scornful look from Casey and the audience was awed;
They saw his face grow stern and cold, they saw his muscles strain,
And they knew that Casey wouldn't let the ball go by again.

Narrative Poetry
In what way does the poem's mood change in this stanza?

The sneer is gone from Casey's lips, his teeth are clenched in hate,
He pounds with cruel vengeance his bat upon the plate:
And now the pitcher holds the ball, and now he lets it go,
And now the air is shattered by the force of Casey's blow.

Oh, somewhere in this favored land the sun is shining bright,
The band is playing somewhere, and somewhere hearts are light:
And somewhere men are laughing, and somewhere children shout,
But there is no joy in Mudville: Mighty Casey has struck out.

Twister Hits Houston

Sandra Cisneros

Papa was on the front porch.
Mama was in the kitchen.
Mama was trying
to screw a lightbulb into a fixture.
Papa was watching the rain.
Mama, it's a cyclone for sure,
he shouted to his wife in the kitchen.
Papa who was sitting on his front porch
when the storm hit
said the twister ripped
the big black oak to splinter,
tossed a green sedan into his garden,
and banged the back door
like a mad cat wanting in.
Mama who was in the kitchen
said Papa saw everything,
the big oak ripped to kindling,[1]
the green sedan land out back,
the back door slam and slam.
I missed it.
Mama was in the kitchen Papa explained.
Papa was sitting on the front porch.
The light bulb is still sitting
where I left it. Don't matter now.
Got no electricity anyway.

▲ Critical Viewing
How does the power of the tornado in this photograph add to your understanding of the poem?

Critical Viewing
Paraphrase Restate the description in line 14 of the twister banging the back door.

---

1. **kindling** (kind′ liŋ) *n.* bits of dry wood used for starting fires.

THE RAVEN

Edgar Allan Poe

Once upon a midnight dreary, while I pondered, weak and weary,
Over many a quaint and curious volume of forgotten lore,
While I nodded, nearly napping, suddenly there came a tapping,
As of someone gently rapping, rapping at my chamber door.
"Tis some visitor," I muttered, "tapping at my chamber door—
Only this, and nothing more."

Ah, distinctly I remember it was in the bleak December,
And each separate dying ember wrought its ghost upon the floor.
Eagerly I wished the morrow—vainly I had tried to borrow
From my books surcease[1] of sorrow—sorrow for the lost Lenore—
For the rare and radiant maiden whom the angels name Lenore—
Nameless *here* for evermore.

And the silken, sad, uncertain rustling of each purple curtain
Thrilled me—filled me with fantastic terrors never felt before;
So that now, to still the beating of my heart, I stood repeating
"'Tis some visitor entreating entrance at my chamber door—
Some late visitor entreating entrance at my chamber door—
This it is and nothing more."

Presently my soul grew stronger; hesitating then no longer,
"Sir," said I, "or Madam, truly your forgiveness I implore;
But the fact is I was napping, and so gently you came rapping,
And so faintly you came tapping, tapping at my chamber door,
That I scarce was sure I heard you"—here I opened wide the door—
Darkness there, and nothing more.

Deep into that darkness peering, long I stood there wondering, fearing,
Doubting, dreaming dreams no mortal ever dared to dream before;
But the silence was unbroken, and the darkness gave no token,
And the only word there spoken was the whispered word, "Lenore!"
This I whispered, and an echo murmured back the word, "Lenore!"
Merely this, and nothing more.

Then into the chamber turning, all my soul within me burning,
Soon I heard again a tapping somewhat louder than before.
"Surely," said I, "surely that is something at my window lattice;
Let me see, then, what thereat[2] is, and this mystery explore—

◀ **Vocabulary**
pondered (pän′ dərd) *v.* thought deeply about

Narrative Poetry
Which details provide information about the setting and the speaker?

Paraphrase
Picture the action the speaker describes, and paraphrase this stanza.

Narrative Poetry
How has the speaker's emotional state changed since the first stanza?

Comprehension
What sorrow is the speaker hoping to ease by reading?

---

1. **surcease** (sʉr sēs′) *n.* end.
2. **thereat** (*th*er at′) *adv.* there.

Paraphrase
In your own words, describe how the raven behaved as it entered the chamber.

Vocabulary ▶
beguiling (bē gīl′ iŋ)
v. tricking; charming

Spiral Review
DICTION AND SYNTAX Which words in lines 43–48 help create a dark and gloomy tone?

Let my heart be still a moment and this mystery explore—
'Tis the wind, and nothing more!"

Open here I flung the shutter, when, with many a flirt[3] and flutter,
In there stepped a stately raven of the saintly days of yore;
Not the least obeisance[4] made he; not an instant stopped or stayed he;
But, with mien[5] of lord or lady, perched above my chamber door—
Perched upon a bust of Pallas just above my chamber door—
Perched, and sat, and nothing more.

Then this ebony bird **beguiling** my sad fancy[6] into smiling,
By the grave and stern decorum of the countenance[7] it wore,
"Though thy crest be shorn and shaven, thou," I said, "art sure no craven,[8]
Ghastly grim and ancient raven wandering from the Nightly shore—
Tell me what thy lordly name is on the Night's Plutonian[9] shore!"
Quoth[10] the raven, "Nevermore."

Much I marveled this ungainly fowl to hear discourse so plainly,
Though its answer little meaning—little relevancy bore;
For we cannot help agreeing that no sublunary[11] being
Ever yet was blessed with seeing bird above his chamber door—
Bird or beast upon the sculptured bust above his chamber door,
With such name as "Nevermore."

But the raven, sitting lonely on the placid bust, spoke only
That one word, as if his soul in that one word he did outpour.
Nothing further then he uttered—not a feather then he fluttered—
Till I scarcely more than muttered, "Other friends have flown before—
On the morrow *he* will leave me, as my hopes have flown before."
Quoth the raven, "Nevermore."

Wondering at the stillness broken by reply so aptly spoken,
"Doubtless," said I, "what it utters is its only stock and store,

---

3. **flirt** (flʉrt) *n.* quick, uneven movement.
4. **obeisance** (ō bā′ səns) *n.* bow or another sign of respect.
5. **mien** (mēn) *n.* manner.
6. **fancy** (fan′ sē) *n.* imagination.
7. **countenance** (kount′ 'n əns) *n.* facial appearance.
8. **craven** (krā′ vən) *n.* coward (usually an adjective).
9. **Plutonian** (plo͞o tō′ nē ən) *adj.* like the underworld, ruled by the ancient Roman god Pluto.
10. **Quoth** (kwōth) *v.* said.
11. **sublunary** (sub lo͞on′ ər ē) *adj.* earthly.

Caught from some unhappy master whom unmerciful Disaster
Followed fast and followed faster—so, when Hope he would
adjure,[12]
Stern Despair returned, instead of the sweet Hope he dared
adjure—
That sad answer, 'Nevermore.'"

But the raven still beguiling all my sad soul into smiling,
Straight I wheeled a cushioned seat in front of bird, and
bust, and door;
Then upon the velvet sinking, I betook myself to linking
Fancy unto fancy, thinking what this ominous bird of yore—
What this grim, ungainly, ghastly, gaunt, and ominous bird
of yore
Meant in croaking "Nevermore."

This I sat engaged in guessing, but no syllable expressing
To the fowl whose fiery eyes now burned into my bosom's core;
This and more I sat divining,[13] with my head at ease reclining
On the cushion's velvet lining that the lamplight gloated o'er,
But whose velvet violet lining with the lamplight gloating o'er,
She shall press, ah, nevermore!

Narrative Poetry What two conflicts or problems does the speaker face in this stanza?

Then, methought, the air grew denser, perfumed from
an unseen censer[14]
Swung by angels whose faint footfalls tinkled on the tufted floor.
"Wretch," I cried, "thy God hath lent thee—by these angels
he hath sent thee
Respite—respite and Nepenthe[15] from thy memories of Lenore!
Let me quaff this kind Nepenthe and forget this lost Lenore!"
Quoth the raven, "Nevermore."

◀ **Vocabulary**
respite (res´ pit)
n. rest; relief

"Prophet!" said I, "thing of evil!—prophet still, if bird or devil!—
Whether Tempter sent, or whether tempest tossed thee here
ashore,
Desolate, yet all undaunted, on this desert land enchanted—
On this home by Horror haunted—tell me truly, I
implore—
Is there—is there balm in Gilead?[16]—tell me—tell me, I
implore!"
Quoth the raven, "Nevermore."

Comprehension What one word does the raven repeat?

---

12. **adjure** (ə jo͝or´) *v.* appeal to; ask earnestly.
13. **divining** (də vīn´ iŋ) *v.* guessing.
14. **censer** (sen´ sər) *n.* container for burning incense.
15. **Nepenthe** (nē pen´ thē) *n.* drug believed by the ancient Greeks to cause forgetfulness of sorrow.
16. **balm** (bäm) **in Gilead** (gil´ ē əd) cure for suffering; the Bible refers to a medicinal ointment, or balm, made in a region called Gilead.

"Prophet!" said I, "thing of evil!—prophet still, if bird or devil!
By that Heaven that bends above us—by that God we both adore—
Tell this soul with sorrow laden if, within the distant Aidenn,[17]
It shall clasp a sainted maiden whom the angels name Lenore—
Clasp a rare and radiant maiden whom the angels name Lenore."
Quoth the raven, "Nevermore."

"Be that word our sign of parting, bird or fiend!" I shrieked, upstarting—
"Get thee back into the tempest and the Night's Plutonian shore!
Leave no black plume as a token of that lie thy soul hath spoken!
Leave my loneliness unbroken!—quit the bust above my door!
Take thy beak from out my heart, and take thy form from off my door!"
Quoth the raven, "Nevermore."

Narrative Poetry
How does the mood here compare with the mood at the beginning of the poem? Explain.

And the raven, never flitting, still is sitting, *still* is sitting
On the pallid bust of Pallas just above my chamber door;
And his eyes have all the seeming of a demon that is dreaming,
And the lamplight o'er him streaming throws his shadow on the floor;
And my soul from out that shadow that lies floating on the floor
Shall be lifted—nevermore!

17. **Aidenn** name meant to suggest Eden, or paradise.

Language Study

Vocabulary The words printed in blue below appear in Poetry Collection 3. Use one word from the list to complete each analogy. Your choice should create a word pair that matches the relationship between the first words given.

pallor	**pondered**	**multitude**	**beguiling**
writhing	**respite**	**defiance**	**demure**

1. flapping : bird :: ______ : snake
2. blush : red :: ______ : white
3. boastful : proud :: ______ : humble
4. approval : happy :: ______ : angry
5. club : member :: ______ : individual
6. kicked : foot :: ______ : mind
7. teaching : professor :: ______ : trickster
8. exertion : labor :: ______ : relief

WORD STUDY
The **Latin prefix *pre-*** means "before." In "Casey at the Bat," the speaker says that Flynn **preceded** Casey, meaning that Flynn went before Casey.

Word Study

Part A Explain how the **Latin prefix *pre-*** contributes to the meanings of *predict, preview,* and *preface*. Consult a dictionary if necessary.

Part B Use the context of the sentences and what you know about the Latin prefix *pre-* to explain your answer to each question.

1. To *prevent* a fire, when should you take action against it?
2. Are there any records of *prehistoric* events?

Close Reading Activities

Literary Analysis

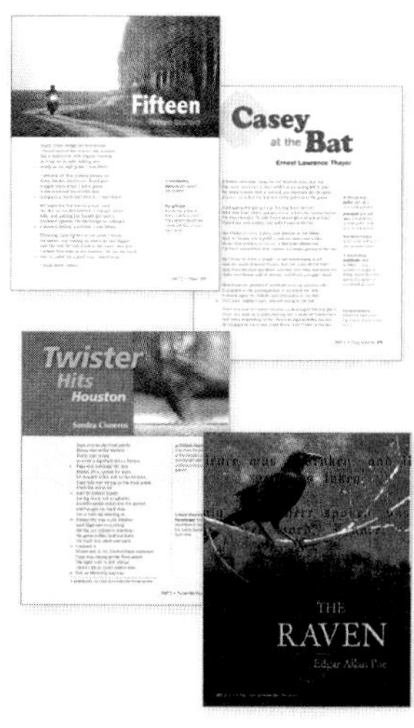

Key Ideas and Details

1. **(a)** In the third stanza of "Fifteen," what does the speaker imagine doing with the motorcycle? **(b) Interpret:** What does the motorcycle represent to the speaker? Cite details from the poem in your answer.
2. **(a) Distinguish:** Which details in "Casey at the Bat" show Casey has the following traits: strength, confidence, and showmanship? Cite at least two details for each trait and explain each choice. **(b) Interpret:** Which details suggest that both Casey and the crowd believe in his inability to fail? **(c) Connect:** How does Casey's larger-than-life persona lead to the surprise and humor of the poem's ending? Explain.
3. **(a)** In the first line of "The Raven," how does the speaker describe his state of mind? **(b) Deduce:** What is the speaker's state of mind at the poem's end? **(c) Analyze Cause and Effect:** What has caused the speaker to change? Cite textual details to support your response.
4. **Paraphrase (a)** Paraphrase lines 8–14 and lines 15–19 of "Twister Hits Houston." **(b)** Based on your paraphrase, explain differences and similarities between Papa and Mama's accounts of the twister.
5. **Paraphrase (a)** Paraphrase lines 37 through 39 of "The Raven." **(b)** Explain how picturing the action helps you restate those lines.

Craft and Structure

6. **Narrative Poetry (a)** Using a chart like the one shown, identify the story elements in each poem from Poetry Collection 3. **(b)** Explain why you think each poet chose to tell his or her story in verse.
7. **Narrative Poetry** Identify three phrases in "Fifteen" that contribute to the poem's mood, or atmosphere, of longing. Explain each choice.

"Fifteen"
Setting
Characters
Plot
"Casey..."
Setting
Characters
Plot
"Twister ..."
Setting
Characters
Plot
"The Raven"
Setting
Characters
Plot

Integration of Knowledge and Ideas

8. **Evaluate:** Is a poem an effective way to tell a story? Use evidence from at least two of the poems in this collection to support your response.

9. THE BIG ? **How does communication change us?** In a small group, discuss the types of communication that occur between characters in these poems. As a result of those communications, which characters gain new insights and which become lost or confused? Support your interpretations with details from the poems.

ACADEMIC VOCABULARY

As you write and speak about Poetry Collection 3 use the words related to communication that you explored on page 329 of this book.

Conventions: Appositive and Absolute Phrases

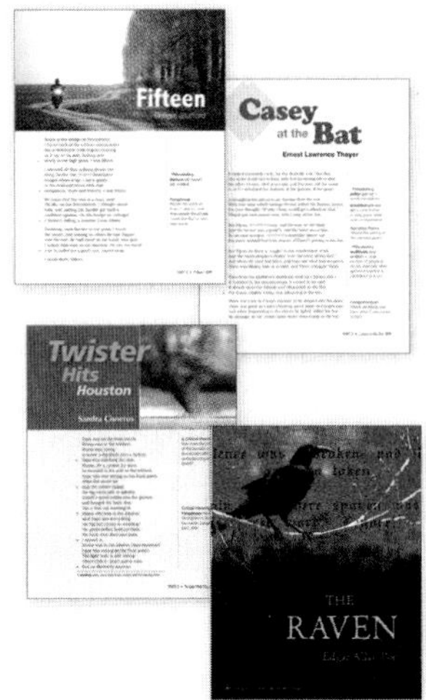

An **appositive phrase** is a noun or pronoun with modifiers that identifies, renames, or explains a noun or pronoun right next to it. An **absolute phrase** adds information to an entire sentence, and consists of a noun or a pronoun followed by a participle and its object, complement, and/or modifiers.

An appositive phrase is usually set off with commas. An absolute phrase is set off with commas or dashes.

Using appositive and absolute phrases is a good way to make your writing more concise and to add variety to your sentences.

Less Concise	Revision With Phrases
"The Raven" is a poem by Edgar Allan Poe. "The Raven" tells the story of an unwelcome midnight visitor.	"The Raven," *a poem by Edgar Allan Poe,* tells the story of an unwelcome visitor. (using appositive phrase)
In "Twister Hits Houston," a couple tell about surviving a tornado. Their voices rise in excitement as they talk.	In "Twister Hits Houston," a couple, *their voices rising in excitement,* tell about surviving a tornado. (using absolute phrase)

Practice A

Identify the appositive or absolute phrase in each sentence.

1. "Casey at the Bat" takes place in Mudville, a fictional town.
2. The narrator of "The Raven"—his heart pounding—opens the door.
3. Its hope defeated, the crowd watched the mighty Casey drop his bat.
4. Houston, the largest city in Texas, is the setting for Cisneros's poem.

Reading Application Rewrite lines 9 and 10 of "Casey at the Bat" as two sentences. Use an appositive phrase in each sentence.

Practice B

For each item, combine the two sentences using an appositive or absolute phrase.

1. The raven perches on a bust of Pallas. Pallas was an ancient Greek goddess.
2. Casey wags his bat confidently. Casey sneers at the pitcher.
3. The rider of the motorcycle reaches for the handlebars. His hand is bloodied.
4. In "Fifteen," the narrator finds a motorcycle lying in the grass. He is fifteen years old.

Writing Application Write two sentences about the effects of the twister described in "Twister Hits Houston." Use an absolute phrase in each one.

Writing to Sources

Informative Text Imagine you have been hired by a movie studio to make a short film based on one of the poems in Poetry Collection 3. Write a **description of the scene** that could be used to develop a script.

- Choose a section of the poem that features particularly interesting figurative language and imagery so the scene will have a strong visual appeal. Explain why you chose this scene, citing specific ways in which the poet uses language.
- Jot down details about the characters, setting, and action of the poem that you will portray on film.
- Explain the mood you want to set, and note how details about characters, setting, and action can evoke this mood.
- Consider the filmmaking techniques that might bring the scene to life. Suggest camera angles, lighting, sound effects, special effects, and music.

Share the poem and your proposed scene with the class, describing the cinematic techniques you would use to bring it to life. Ask for feedback to determine whether your description accurately reflects the story, characters, setting, and mood of the poem.

Grammar Application Use appositive and absolute phrases to make your writing more concise.

Speaking and Listening

Presentation of Ideas With a partner, write and present a **dialogue** between the speaker and the motorcyclist in "Fifteen" or Papa and Mama in "Twister Hits Houston."

- Decide who will play each character.
- Before writing, review the poem and identify details your dialogue should either adapt or include precisely.
- Analyze the situation in the poem to determine each character's concerns or interests.
- Use speaking styles that are suitable for each character. You may include humor, idioms, slang, formal language, or poetic images.
- When performing, choose appropriate gestures and posture. Likewise, use appropriate eye contact while both speaking and listening.

As you present your dialogue, listen carefully to what the other character says, interpreting and evaluating his or her intent.

Writing

4. Produce clear and coherent writing in which the development, organization, and style are appropriate to task, purpose, and audience.

Speaking and Listening

1.a. Come to discussions prepared, having read and researched material under study; explicitly draw on that preparation by referring to evidence from texts and other research on the topic or issue to stimulate a thoughtful, well-reasoned exchange of ideas.

Language

1.b. Use various types of phrases and clauses to convey specific meanings and add variety and interest to writing or presentations.

3. Apply knowledge of language to understand how language functions in different contexts, to make effective choices for meaning or style, and to comprehend more fully when reading or listening.

Building Knowledge

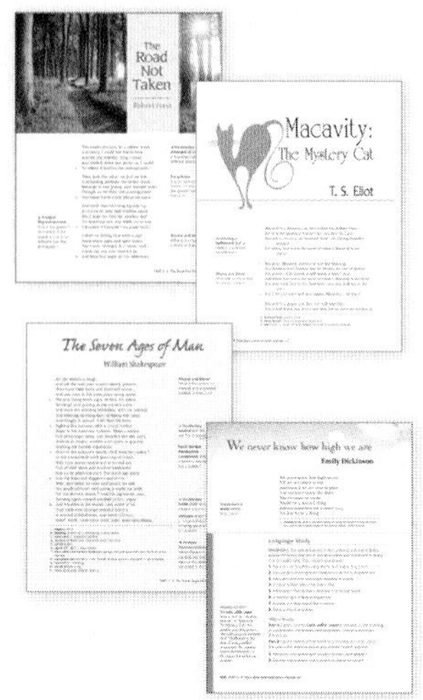

How does communication change us?

Explore the Big Question as you read the poems in Poetry Collection 4. Take notes on which seem to communicate messages for the private self and which seem to communicate ideas for public entertainment.

CLOSE READING FOCUS

Key Ideas and Details: **Paraphrase**

Paraphrasing is restating in your own words what someone else has written or said. A paraphrase should retain the essential meaning and central ideas of the original but should be simpler to read and to understand. One way to simplify the text that you are paraphrasing is to **break down long sentences.** To do so, follow these steps:

- Divide long sentences into parts and paraphrase those parts.
- If a sentence contains multiple subjects or verbs, see if it can be separated into smaller sentences that contain one subject and one verb.
- If a sentence contains colons, semicolons, or dashes, create separate sentences by treating those punctuation marks as periods.

Poets often write sentences that span several lines to give their poems fluidity. By breaking down long sentences and paraphrasing them, you can better understand how the poet gradually develops his or her central idea.

Common Core State Standards

Reading Literature

1. Cite strong and thorough textual evidence to support analysis of what the text says explicitly as well as inferences drawn from the text.

2. Determine a theme or central idea of a text.

4. Determine the meaning of words and phrases, including figurative and connotative meanings; analyze the cumulative impact of specific word choices.

7. Analyze the representation of a subject or a key scene in two different artistic mediums.

Vocabulary

The words below are critical to understanding the text that follows. Copy the words into your notebook. Which word is an antonym for *concealed*?

diverged	**bafflement**	**depravity**
rifled	**disclosed**	**woeful**
treble	**oblivion**	**warp**

Craft and Structure: **Rhyme and Meter**

Rhyme and meter are two literary devices often used in poetry. **Rhyme** is the repetition of sounds at the ends of words. There are several types of rhyme:

- **Exact Rhyme:** the repetition of words that end with the same vowel and consonant sounds, as in *love* and *dove*
- **Slant Rhyme:** the repetition of words that end with similar sounds but do not rhyme perfectly, as in *prove* and *glove*
- **End Rhyme:** the rhyming of words at the ends of lines
- **Internal Rhyme:** the rhyming of words within a line

A **rhyme scheme** is a regular pattern of end rhymes in a poem or stanza, in which a letter is assigned to each set of rhyming sounds. For example, in "Ring Out, Wild Bells," Alfred, Lord Tennyson uses the rhyme scheme *abba:*

Ring out, wild bells, to the wild sky, a
The flying cloud, the frosty light: b
The year is dying in the night; b
Ring out, wild bells, and let him die. a

Lewis Carroll opens "Jabberwocky" with the rhyme scheme *abab*:

'Twas brillig, and the slithy toves a
Did gyre and gimble in the wabe; b
All mimsy were the borogroves, a
And the mome raths outgrabe. b

Meter is the rhythmical pattern in a line of poetry that results from the arrangement of stressed (´) and unstressed (˘) syllables. The stress goes on the syllable that is accented in natural speech. Reading the line aloud reveals the steady rhythmic pulse of the stressed syllables:

T̆he flȳiňg clóud, t̆he fróstў liğht
Hálf ă leăgue, hálf ă leăgue, / Hálf ă leăgue oňwărd

Each meter is named based on its length and rhythmical pattern. A common pattern uses *iambs*, beats in which the stress is on the second syllable, such as hĕlló or ălóud. In *iambic pentameter*, each line of a poem contains five iambs.

Nŏr friénds nŏr fóes, tŏ mé wĕlcóme yŏu áre:
Thiňgs pást rĕdréss ăre nów wiťh mé păst cáre.

Craft and Structure: **Rhyme and Meter** *(continued)*

An *iambic dimeter* would consist of two iambs, a *trimeter* would consist of three iambs, a *tetrameter* would consist of four iambs, and so on. See the chart below for examples of these metric groupings.

Iambic Meter	Example
Dimeter (2 beats per line)	Ăňd fór / rĕdréss Ŏf áll / m̆y páin,
Trimeter (3 beats per line)	W̆e romṕed / ŭnt́il / thĕ pańs Slíd frŏm / th̆e kítch / eň shélf;
Tetrameter (4 beats per line)	Ĭ thínk / th̆at Í / shăll ńe / vĕr sée ă pó / ĕm lóve / Ĭy aś / ă trée.

Not all poems include rhyme, a rhyme scheme, or a regular meter. Nonmetrical poetry, or poems that do not contain a regular pattern of meter, are known as **free verse.**

"Uncoiling" by Pat Mora is written as free verse:

With thorns she scratches
        on my window, tosses her hair dark with rain,
            snares lightning, cholla, hawks, butterfly
                swarms in the tangles.

Poems that do not rhyme but consist of iambic pentameter are known as **blank verse.** William Shakespeare wrote many of his plays in blank verse as in this line from *The Tragedy of Romeo and Juliet*:

Bŭt sóft! / Wȟat liǵht / thrŏugh yón / dĕr wín / dŏw bréaks?
Ĭt ís / tȟe eást, / ănd Júl / iĕt ís / tȟe sún!

Poets often use one or more rhyming techniques to create musical effects and achieve a sense of unity in their poems.

As you read the poems in this collection, notice their uses of rhyme and meter and the effects these poetic elements create.

- Look for examples of different types of rhyme.
- Determine whether the lines follow a rhyme scheme.
- Notice whether or not the lines follow a regular meter.

CLOSE READING MODEL

The passage below is from Robert Frost's poem "The Road Not Taken." The annotations to the right of the passage show ways in which you can use close reading skills to paraphrase poetry and analyze rhyme and meter.

from "The Road Not Taken"

And both that morning equally lay
In leaves no step had trodden black.[1]
Oh, I kept the first for another day!
Yet knowing how way leads on to way,
I doubted if I should ever come back.[2]

I shall be telling this with a sigh[3]
Somewhere ages and ages hence:
Two roads diverged in a wood, and I—[3]
I took the one less traveled by,[3]
And that has made all the difference.[3]

Rhyme and Meter

1 If you read the first two lines aloud, you can hear the meter. The first stress falls on the word *both*. After that, the stresses fall on every other syllable. That tells you Frost used iambs. You can then count the number of iambs to find four in each line. That means this poem is written in iambic tetrameter, a meter Frost often used.

Paraphrase

2 The clause "how way leads on to way" is a lyrical and concise way of saying that once one starts down a path one tends to continue. A paraphrase of both lines might read, "Once I took a particular path, I knew I would not start over."

Rhyme and Meter

3 In this stanza, Frost uses an *abaab* rhyme scheme. The ends of the first, third, and fourth lines rhyme, and the ends of the third and fifth lines rhyme. In this stanza, all the rhymes are exact.

Meet the Poets

"The Road Not Taken"

Robert Frost (1874–1963)

In January 1961, when John. F. Kennedy became president of the United States, he called on fellow New Englander Robert Frost to recite two poems at the inauguration. At the time, Frost was America's most famous living poet. He became famous when *A Boy's Will* (1913) and *North of Boston* (1914) won wide praise in both the United Kingdom and the United States.

"Macavity: The Mystery Cat"

T. S. Eliot (1888–1965)

A whimsical poem like "Macavity: The Mystery Cat" was a rarity in the writing of Thomas Stearns Eliot. He was better known for serious, philosophical poems. Born in the United States, Eliot settled in the United Kingdom. He became a highly influential poet and won the Nobel Prize in 1948.

"The Seven Ages of Man"

William Shakespeare (1564–1616)

William Shakespeare forged a perfect blend of high drama and exalted language. He wrote more than three dozen plays, and because of the timelessness of his themes and the beauty of his language, lines from his plays are quoted more often than those of any other writer. "The Seven Ages of Man," from the play *As You Like It*, is considered one of the best monologues ever written.

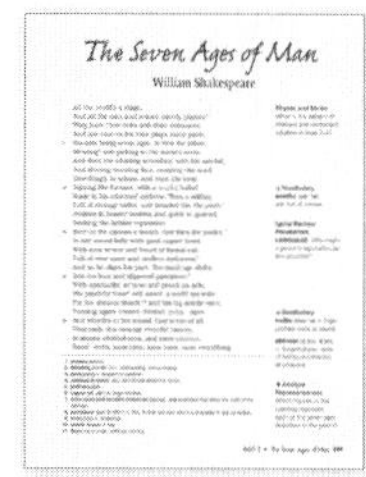

"We never know how high we are"

Emily Dickinson (1830–1886)

Emily Dickinson's life in Amherst, Massachusetts, seemed to be quiet and uneventful. Yet, the emotional power of her poems shows extraordinary energy and imagination. She found profound meanings in simple subjects, and her poems still delight readers.

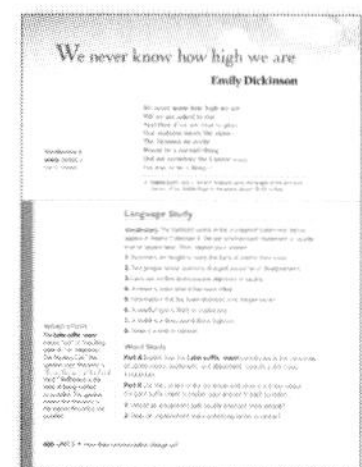

The Road Not Taken

Robert Frost

Two roads diverged in a yellow wood,
And sorry I could not travel both
And be one traveler, long I stood
And looked down one as far as I could
To where it bent in the undergrowth;

Then took the other, as just as fair,
And having perhaps the better claim,
Because it was grassy and wanted wear;
Though as for that, the passing there
Had worn them really about the same,

And both that morning equally lay
In leaves no step had trodden black.
Oh, I kept the first for another day!
Yet knowing how way leads on to way,
I doubted if I should ever come back.

I shall be telling this with a sigh
Somewhere ages and ages hence:
Two roads diverged in a wood, and I—
I took the one less traveled by,
And that has made all the difference.

◀ **Vocabulary**
diverged (dī vʉrjd′)
v. branched out in different directions

Paraphrase
In your own words, restate the decision the speaker makes in lines 6–8.

▲ **Analyze Representations**
How is the speaker's description of the woods similar to or different from this photograph?

Rhyme and Meter
What is the rhyme scheme of stanza four?

Macavity: The Mystery Cat

T. S. Eliot

Vocabulary ▶
bafflement (baf′ əl mənt) *n.* puzzlement; bewilderment

Rhyme and Meter
What type of rhyme does this stanza contain?

Macavity's a Mystery Cat: he's called the Hidden Paw—
For he's the master criminal who can defy the Law.
He's the bafflement of Scotland Yard,[1] the Flying Squad's[2] despair:
For when they reach the scene of crime—*Macavity's not there!*

Macavity, Macavity, there's no one like Macavity,
He's broken every human law, he breaks the law of gravity.
His powers of levitation would make a fakir[3] stare,
And when you reach the scene of crime—*Macavity's not there!*
You may seek him in the basement, you may look up in the air—
But I tell you once and once again, *Macavity's not there!*

Macavity's a ginger cat, he's very tall and thin;
You would know him if you saw him, for his eyes are sunken in.

1. **Scotland Yard** London police.
2. **Flying Squad** criminal-investigation department.
3. **fakir** (fə kir′) *n.* Muslim or Hindu beggar who claims to perform miracles.

His brow is deeply lined with thought, his head is highly domed;
His coat is dusty from neglect, his whiskers are uncombed.
He sways his head from side to side, with movements like a snake;
And when you think he's half asleep, he's always wide awake.

Macavity, Macavity, there's no one like Macavity,
For he's a fiend in feline shape, a monster of **depravity**.
You may meet him in a by-street, you may see him in the square—
But when a crime's discovered, then *Macavity's not there!*

He's outwardly respectable. (They say he cheats at cards.)
And his footprints are not found in any file of Scotland Yard's.
And when the larder's looted, or the jewel-case is **rifled**,
Or when the milk is missing, or another Peke's[4] been stifled,
Or the greenhouse glass is broken, and the trellis past repair—
Ay, there's the wonder of the thing! *Macavity's not there!*

And when the Foreign Office find a Treaty's gone astray,
Or the Admiralty lose some plans and drawings by the way,
There may be a scrap of paper in the hall or on the stair—
But it's useless to investigate—*Macavity's not there!*
And when the loss has been **disclosed**, the Secret Service say:
'It *must* have been Macavity!'—but he's a mile away.
You'll be sure to find him resting, or a-licking of his thumbs,
Or engaged in doing complicated long division sums.

Macavity, Macavity, there's no one like Macavity,
There never was a Cat of such deceitfulness and suavity.
He always has an alibi, and one or two to spare:
At whatever time the deed took place—MACAVITY WASN'T THERE!
And they say that all the Cats whose wicked deeds are widely known
(I might mention Mungojerrie, I might mention Griddlebone)
Are nothing more than agents for the Cat who all the time
Just controls their operations: the Napoleon of Crime![5]

◀ **Vocabulary**
depravity (dē prav´ ə tē) *n.* crookedness; corruption

rifled (rī´ fəld) *v.* ransacked and robbed; searched quickly through a cupboard or drawer

◀ **Vocabulary**
disclosed (dis klōzd´) *v.* revealed; made known

Paraphrase
Break down the sentence in lines 37–38 into three smaller sentences. Restate each sentence in your own words.

4. **Peke** short for Pekingese, a small dog with long, silky hair and a pug nose.
5. **the Napoleon of Crime** criminal mastermind; emperor of crime—just as Napoleon Bonaparte (1769–1821) was a masterful military strategist who had himself crowned emperor.

The Seven Ages of Man

William Shakespeare

All the world's a stage,
And all the men and women merely players:[1]
They have their exits and their entrances;
And one man in his time plays many parts,
His acts being seven ages. At first the infant,
Mewling[2] and puking in the nurse's arms.
And then the whining schoolboy, with his satchel,
And shining morning face, creeping like snail
Unwillingly to school. And then the lover,
Sighing like furnace, with a woeful ballad
Made to his mistress' eyebrow. Then a soldier,
Full of strange oaths, and bearded like the pard,[3]
Jealous in honor,[4] sudden and quick in quarrel,
Seeking the bubble reputation
Even in the cannon's mouth. And then the justice,[5]
In fair round belly with good capon[6] lined,
With eyes severe and beard of formal cut,
Full of wise saws and modern instances;[7]
And so he plays his part. The sixth age shifts
Into the lean and slippered pantaloon,[8]
With spectacles on nose and pouch on side,
His youthful hose[9] well saved, a world too wide
For his shrunk shank;[10] and his big manly voice,
Turning again toward childish treble, pipes
And whistles in his sound. Last scene of all,
That ends this strange eventful history,
Is second childishness, and mere oblivion,
Sans[11] teeth, sans eyes, sans taste, sans everything.

Rhyme and Meter What is the pattern of stressed and unstressed syllables in lines 2–4?

◀ **Vocabulary**
woeful (wō´ fəl) *adj.* full of sorrow

Spiral Review
FIGURATIVE LANGUAGE Why might a person's reputation be like a bubble?

◀ **Vocabulary**
treble (treb´ əl) *n.* high-pitched voice or sound

oblivion (ə bliv´ ē ən) *n.* forgetfulness; state of being unconscious or unaware

◀ **Analyze Representations**
Which figures in this painting represent each of the seven ages described in the poem?

---

1. **players** actors.
2. **Mewling** (myo͞ol´ iŋ) *v.* whimpering; crying weakly.
3. **pard** (pärd) *n.* leopard or panther.
4. **Jealous in honor** very concerned about his honor.
5. **justice** judge.
6. **capon** (kā´ pän´) *n.* large chicken.
7. **wise saws and modern instances** sayings, and examples that show the truth of the sayings.
8. **pantaloon** (pan´ tə lo͞on´) *n.* thin, foolish old man who is a character in old comedies.
9. **hose** (hōz) *n.* stockings.
10. **shank** (shaŋk) *n.* leg.
11. **Sans** (sanz) *prep.* without; lacking.

We never know how high we are

Emily Dickinson

We never know how high we are
Till we are asked to rise
And then if we are true to plan
Our statures touch the skies—
The Heroism we recite
Would be a normal thing
Did not ourselves the Cubits[1] warp
For fear to be a King—

Vocabulary ▶
warp (wôrp) *v.* twist; distort

1. **Cubits** (kyo͞o´ bitz) *n.* ancient measure using the length of the arm from the end of the middle finger to the elbow (about 18–22 inches).

Language Study

Vocabulary The italicized words in the numbered statements below appear in Poetry Collection 4. Decide whether each statement is usually true or usually false. Then, explain your answer.

1. Reporters are taught to *warp* the facts of events they cover.
2. Two people whose opinions *diverged* would be in disagreement.
3. Laws are written to encourage *depravity* in society.
4. A closet is tidier after it has been *rifled*.
5. Information that has been *disclosed* is no longer secret.
6. A *woeful* sight is likely to inspire pity.
7. A *treble* is a deep sound like a foghorn.
8. Sleep is a kind of *oblivion*.

WORD STUDY

The **Latin suffix *-ment*** means "act" or "resulting state of." In "Macavity: The Mystery Cat," the speaker says Macavity is "the **bafflement** of Scotland Yard." Bafflement is the state of being baffled, or puzzled. The speaker means that Macavity is the reason the police are puzzled.

Word Study

Part A Explain how the **Latin suffix *-ment*** contributes to the meanings of *contentment, excitement,* and *abasement*. Consult a dictionary if necessary.

Part B Use the context of the sentences and what you know about the Latin suffix *-ment* to explain your answer to each question.

1. Would an *amusement* park usually entertain most people?
2. Does an *improvement* make something better or worse?

Close Reading Activities

Literary Analysis

Key Ideas and Details

1. **(a)** In "The Road Not Taken," what does the traveler do when faced with a fork in the road? **(b) Interpret:** Is the speaker happy with this decision? Explain, citing details from the poem.
2. **Interpret:** What circumstances or experiences in life do the diverging roads in "The Road Not Taken" symbolize? Explain.
3. **Analyze:** In "The Seven Ages of Man," what are the seven ages of a human life and what qualities distinguish each age? Use details from the poem in your answer.
4. **Interpret:** In "Macavity: The Mystery Cat," what is Macavity's great talent? Use details from the poem to support your answer.
5. **(a) Interpret:** According to the speaker of "We never know how high we are," what happens when people are challenged? **(b) Analyze:** In the speaker's view, why is "Heroism" not a "normal thing"? Explain.
6. **Paraphrase (a)** Write a paraphrase of the first stanza of "The Road Not Taken." **(b)** In what ways does breaking down long sentences help you to write a paraphrase that accurately expresses the poem's meaning?

Craft and Structure

7. **Rhyme and Meter** Identify two lines in "The Road Not Taken" that illustrate both **exact rhyme** and **end rhyme**. Explain your choices.
8. **Rhyme and Meter** Which two words in line 17 of "The Seven Ages of Man" illustrate both **slant rhyme** and **internal rhyme?**
9. **Rhyme and Meter (a)** Use letters to identify the rhyme scheme in "We never know how high we are." **(b)** In what way does the shift in rhyme scheme midway through the poem signal a turning point in the poem's message? Explain.

Integration of Knowledge and Ideas

10. **Interpret:** Explain how Eliot's use of repetition and description add to the mood and humor of "Macavity: The Mystery Cat." Cite examples from the poem in your response.

11. THE BIG ? **How does communication change us?** In what ways do the poems by Frost, Shakespeare, and Dickinson explore ideas about the roles people play and the ways we communicate, both with one another and with ourselves. Are the roles we play throughout our lives true reflections of who we are? Discuss these questions with a small group, using details and examples from the poems.

ACADEMIC VOCABULARY

As you write and speak about Poetry Collection 4, use the words related to communication that you explored on page 329 of this book.

Conventions: **Infinitives and Infinitive Phrases**

An **infinitive** is a verb form that generally appears with the word *to* and acts as a noun, an adjective, or an adverb.

An **infinitive phrase** is an infinitive with any modifiers, object, or complement, all acting together as a single part of speech. Like infinitives, infinitive phrases can function as nouns, adjectives, or adverbs.

Infinitive	Infinitive Phrase
Used as a Noun *To write* requires dedication.	**Used as a Noun** *To win a Pulitzer Prize* is an honor.
Used as an Adjective Emily Dickinson is a good poet *to study*.	**Used as an Adjective** Dickinson had a desire *to write deceptively simple poetry*.
Used as an Adverb When Shakespeare sat down *to work,* he used a quill dipped in ink.	**Used as an Adverb** Shakespeare wrote his plays *to be performed on a stage.*

Infinitives include *to* and a verb, as in *to hear.* These are not to be confused with prepositional phrases that include the preposition *to* and a noun or pronoun, as in *to the house*.

Practice A

Identify the infinitive or infinitive phrase and its function in each sentence.

1. She remained at home to write poetry.
2. A hero has the confidence to be a leader.
3. The speaker of "The Road Not Taken" chooses to take the more difficult, less trodden path.
4. Although they try, the police never manage to catch Macavity.

Reading Application Find two infinitives or infinitive phrases in "Macavity: The Mystery Cat" and identify each one's function.

Practice B

Identify the infinitive or infinitive phrase in each sentence. Then, rewrite the sentence using a different infinitive or infinitive phrase.

1. We all have a chance to rise.
2. Frost uses roads to represent choices.
3. To pass through seven ages is everyone's destiny.
4. "The Seven Ages of Man" is not the only speech to be quoted by other writers.

Writing Application Write two sentences about a favorite picture or place. Use an infinitive or an infinitive phrase in each one.

Writing to Sources

Poetry Write a **poem** using the same rhyme scheme, meter, and format as one of the poems from Poetry Collection 4.

- Choose a poem and identify its rhyme scheme, using the *ab* letter system.
- Decide on a topic, an event, an experience, or an emotion to use as the subject of your poem.
- Brainstorm for a list of images, precise details, phrases, and vivid words related to your topic.
- Draft your poem, adding rhyme only after you have expressed your ideas and feelings.
- Read your poem aloud to check that your rhyme scheme matches the rhyme scheme of the poem you selected.

Write a brief explanation of why you chose the poem you did as a model, and how your poem reflects that influence. Then, share your poem with a classmate. Ask your classmate to identify the rhyme scheme you have used and discuss how it contributes to the mood of the poem.

Grammar Application When using infinitive phrases, be sure that the verb directly follows the word *to.*

Speaking and Listening

Presentation of Ideas With classmates, hold a **panel discussion** about possible interpretations of a poem by Robert Frost. To prepare, conduct research about the poet's extensive works. Identify both primary and secondary sources about Frost's poetry, and assemble an electronic database of texts by and about Frost, the topics and themes Frost often addresses, the style he most frequently uses, and what critics have written about his work. Write concise notes for use during the discussion. When you are ready to hold your discussion, follow these steps:

- Begin by stating the purpose of the discussion.
- As fellow panelists speak, listen closely. Check your interpretation of their ideas by summarizing their comments before contributing your own.
- Look for connections among the ideas all the panel members present. Use these connections to come to an agreement about Frost's work.

Common Core State Standards

Writing

4. Produce clear and coherent writing in which the development, organization, and style are appropriate to the task, purpose, and audience.

Speaking and Listening

1.a. Come to discussions prepared; draw on that preparation to stimulate a thoughtful, well-reasoned exchange of ideas.

1.c. Propel conversations by posing and responding to questions; incorporate others into the discussion; clarify, verify, or challenge ideas and conclusions.

1.d. Respond thoughtfully to diverse perspectives, summarize points of agreement and disagreement and, when warranted, qualify or justify their own views and understanding, and make new connections.

Language

1.b. Use various types of phrases and clauses to convey specific meanings and add variety and interest to writing or presentations.

Comparing Texts

How does communication change us?

Explore the Big Question as you read these poems. Take notes on the insight each poem conveys. Then, compare and contrast how that insight affects you as a reader.

READING TO COMPARE POETIC FORMS

The poets in this collection express ideas, attitudes, and emotions in different types of lyric poems. As you read, consider how the form of each poem affects its meaning and message.

"I Hear America Singing"
Walt Whitman (1819–1892)
American poet Walt Whitman celebrated individual freedom. His first volume of poetry, *Leaves of Grass,* is regarded as one of the most important works in all of American literature.

Three Haiku
Bashō (1644–1694); **Chiyojo** (1703–1775)
Bashō (pictured at left) raised the haiku from a comic form to a high art. Chiyojo was the wife of a samurai's servant. After her husband died, she became a nun and wrote acclaimed poems.

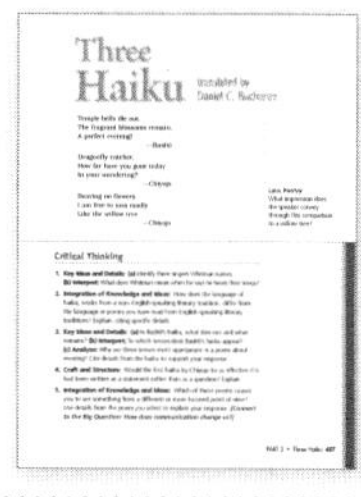

"Women"
Alice Walker (b. 1944)
From the age of eight, Alice Walker kept a journal and wrote poems. Her many works include the novel *The Color Purple,* which was made into a movie and a Broadway show.

Sonnet 30
William Shakespeare (1564–1616)
English poet and playwright William Shakespeare is one of the most beloved writers of all time. His many plays are still performed around the world.

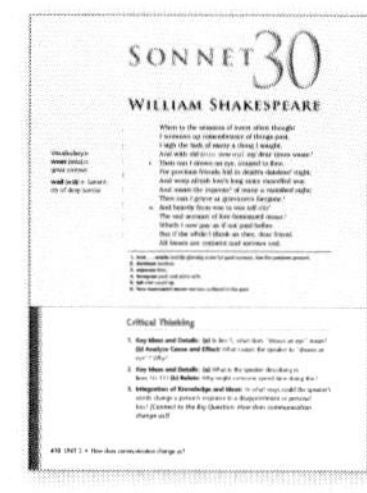

Comparing Forms of Lyric Poetry

Lyric poetry has a musical quality that expresses the thoughts and feelings of a speaker. It does not tell a complete story, but it does describe an emotion or a mood, often by using vivid imagery. A lyric poem is relatively short and produces a single effect. Poets can use a variety of **lyric forms** or structures to explore topics and themes, and to create different effects.

- A **sonnet** is a fourteen-line poem that is usually written in iambic pentameter and often rhymes. Two common sonnet types are the Italian, or Petrarchan, and the English, or Shakespearean.
- A **haiku** is a classical Japanese form of poetry. Haiku is an unrhymed verse form arranged into three lines of five, seven, and five syllables. The author of a haiku often uses a striking image from nature to convey a strong emotion.
- A **free verse** poem does not follow a regular pattern of rhythm or rhyme. The poet may use sound and rhythmic devices and even rhyme—but not in a regular pattern.

Each of the following poems depicts one speaker's thoughts. As you read, consider how the poet's choice of a particular lyric form adds to the poem's meaning. Use a chart like the one shown and the other information on this page to analyze how each poem's structure enhances its message.

Shakespearean Sonnet Structure	
Formatting: English sonnets are usually presented with no spaces between the stanzas, which are unified by their distinct ideas and rhyme schemes.	**Three Quatrains (four-line stanzas):** Each quatrain explores a different aspect of the poem's theme.
Final Couplet: The two lines at the end of an English sonnet rhyme and present a concluding comment or twist on the poem's central idea.	**Rhyme Scheme:** The lines in each quatrain follow a regular pattern of rhyme: *abab cdcd efef gg.*

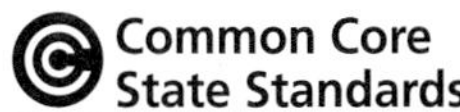

Common Core State Standards

Reading Literature
5. Analyze how an author's choices concerning how to structure a text, order events within it, and manipulate time create such effects as mystery, tension, or surprise.

Writing
2.a. Introduce a topic; organize complex ideas, concepts, and information to make important connections and distinctions; include formatting, graphics, and multimedia when useful to aiding comprehension.
10. Write routinely over extended time frames and shorter time frames for a range of tasks, purposes, and audiences.

I Hear America Singing

Walt Whitman

Lyric Poetry
Which word in the opening line helps identify this as a lyric poem?

Vocabulary ▶
intermission (in´ tər mish´ ən) *n.* any kind of break; more specifically, a break during a performance

I hear America singing, the varied carols I hear,
Those of mechanics, each one singing his as it should be blithe and strong,
The carpenter singing his as he measures his plank or beam,
The mason singing his as he makes ready for work, or leaves off work,
The boatman singing what belongs to him in his boat, the deckhand singing on the steamboat deck,
The shoemaker singing as he sits on his bench, the hatter singing as he stands,
The wood-cutter's song, the ploughboy's on his way in the morning, or at noon intermission or at sundown,
The delicious singing of the mother, or of the young wife at work, or of the girl sewing or washing,
Each singing what belongs to him or her and to none else,
The day what belongs to the day—at night the party of young fellows, robust, friendly,
Singing with open mouths their strong melodious songs.

Three Haiku

translated by
Daniel C. Buchanan

Temple bells die out.
The fragrant blossoms remain.
A perfect evening!
—Bashō

Dragonfly catcher,
How far have you gone today
In your wandering?
—Chiyojo

Bearing no flowers,
I am free to toss madly
Like the willow tree.
—Chiyojo

Lyric Poetry
What impression does the speaker convey through this comparison to a willow tree?

Critical Thinking

1. **Key Ideas and Details: (a)** Identify three singers Whitman names. **(b) Interpret:** What does Whitman mean when he says he hears their songs?
2. **Integration of Knowledge and Ideas:** How does the language of haiku, works from a non–English-speaking literary tradition, differ from the language in poems you have read from English-speaking literary traditions? Explain, citing specific details.
3. **Key Ideas and Details: (a)** In Bashō's haiku, what dies out and what remains? **(b) Interpret:** To which senses does Bashō's haiku appeal? **(c) Analyze:** Why are these senses most appropriate in a poem about evening? Cite details from the haiku to support your response.
4. **Craft and Structure:** Would the first haiku by Chiyojo be as effective if it had been written as a statement rather than as a question? Explain.
5. **Integration of Knowledge and Ideas:** Which of these poems causes you to see something from a different or more focused point of view? Use details from the poem you select to explain your response. *[Connect to the Big Question: How does communication change us?]*

Women

Alice Walker

Background In "Women," the speaker praises African American women who fought for public school desegregation in the American South. Until the 1950s, African American students and white students attended separate schools in the South. In 1954, the U.S. Supreme Court ruled that segregated public schooling was unconstitutional.

They were women then
My mama's generation
Husky of voice—**Stout** of
Step
With fists as well as
Hands
How they battered down
Doors
And ironed
Starched white
Shirts
How they led
Armies
Headragged Generals
Across mined
Fields
Booby-trapped
Ditches
To discover books
Desks
A place for us
How they knew what we
Must know
Without knowing a page
Of it
Themselves.

◀ **Vocabulary**
stout (stout) *adj.* sturdy

Lyric Poetry
What emotion or feeling does the phrase "Headragged Generals" evoke?

◀ **Critical Viewing**
Is the photographer's attitude toward these women similar to the one expressed by the speaker?

Critical Thinking

1. **Craft and Structure: (a)** List three images in the poem that convey the women's determination to help their children. **(b) Assess:** Which image did you find the most powerful? Why?
2. **Key Ideas and Details: (a)** What do the women want to "discover" and for whom? **(b) Interpret:** In lines 22–26, why is the women's knowledge so remarkable? Explain your response.
3. **Integration of Knowledge and Ideas: (a)** What message about education do the women communicate with their actions? Use details to support your answer. **(b)** What impact do you think this message had on their children? Explain your answer. ***[Connect to the Big Question: How does communication change us?]***

SONNET 30

WILLIAM SHAKESPEARE

Vocabulary ▶
woes (wōz) *n.* great sorrows

wail (wāl)) *n.* lament; cry of deep sorrow

When to the sessions of sweet silent thought
I summon up remembrance of things past,
I sigh the lack of many a thing I sought,
And with old woes new wail my dear times waste:[1]
Then can I drown an eye, unused to flow,
For precious friends hid in death's dateless[2] night,
And weep afresh love's long since cancelled woe,
And moan the expense[3] of many a vanished sight:
Then can I grieve at grievances foregone,[4]
And heavily from woe to woe tell o'er[5]
The sad account of fore-bemoanèd moan,[6]
Which I new pay as if not paid before.
But if the while I think on thee, dear friend,
All losses are restored and sorrows end.

1. **And . . . waste** and by grieving anew for past sorrows, ruin the precious present.
2. **dateless** endless.
3. **expense** loss.
4. **foregone** past and done with.
5. **tell o'er** count up.
6. **fore-bemoanèd moan** sorrows suffered in the past.

Critical Thinking

1. **Key Ideas and Details: (a)** In line 5, what does "drown an eye" mean? **(b) Analyze Cause and Effect:** What causes the speaker to "drown an eye"? Why?
2. **Key Ideas and Details: (a)** What is the speaker describing in lines 10–12? **(b) Relate:** Why might someone spend time doing this?
3. **Integration of Knowledge and Ideas:** In what ways could the speaker's words change a person's response to a disappointment or personal loss? *[Connect to the Big Question: How does communication change us?]*

Writing to Sources

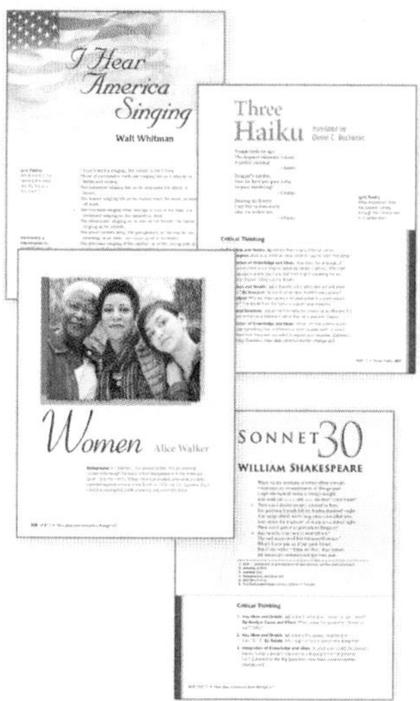

Comparing Forms of Lyric Poetry

1. **Craft and Structure** Both "I Hear America Singing" and "Women" are free verse, with a form imposed by the poet. **(a)** Compare the ideas and emotions conveyed in these poems. **(b)** Which poem follows more of a pattern? Explain.
2. **Craft and Structure** Compare and contrast the subjects and structure of the three **haiku** to the three poems from English-speaking traditions.
3. **Craft and Structure** In his sonnet, Shakespeare presents an idea or a question in the first quatrain (four lines), explores the idea in the next two quatrains, and reaches a conclusion in the final couplet. Use a chart like the one shown to analyze the content of Sonnet 30.

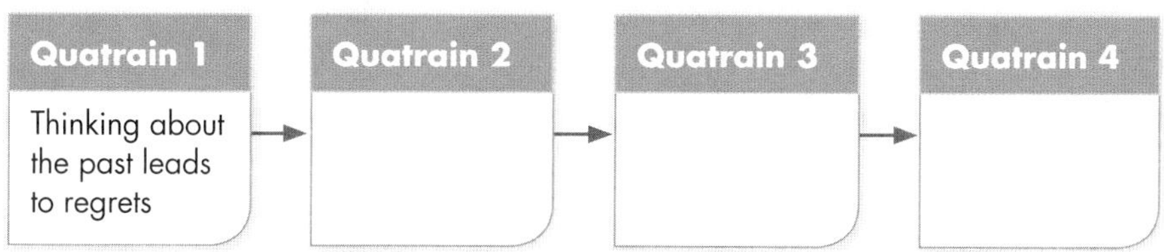

Timed Writing

Explanatory Text: Essay

In an essay, compare the ways the structures of the different lyric forms affect the meanings of these poems. Choose two poems and structures to discuss. Cite textual evidence to support your response. **(30 minutes)**

5-Minute Planner

1. Read the prompt carefully and completely.
2. Gather your ideas by jotting down answers to these questions:
   - How does the free verse structure of Whitman's and Walker's poems contribute to the message of each poem?
   - How does the strict form of the haiku help to capture the feeling of a brief moment in time?
   - How would the meaning of Sonnet 30 be different without the final two lines?
3. Reread the prompt. Then, refer to your notes as you draft your essay.

USE ACADEMIC VOCABULARY

As you write, use academic language, including the following words or their related forms:

articulate
concept
interpretation
unique

For more information about academic vocabulary, see page xlvi.

Language Study

Words With Multiple Meanings

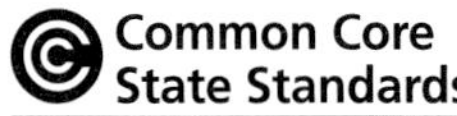

Language
4. Determine or clarify the meaning of unknown and multiple-meaning words or phrases based on grades 9–10 reading and content, choosing flexibly from a range of strategies.
4.a. Use context as a clue to the meaning of a word or phrase.
4.d. Verify the preliminary determination of the meaning of a word or phrase.

Many words in English have **multiple meanings,** or definitions that vary greatly. Consider the varied meanings of the word *mine* as it is used in the following sentences.

- This book is *mine*, but you are welcome to borrow it. (possessive pronoun)
- The coal *mine* has been in operation for many years. (noun describing a place where coal is dug)
- You can *mine* that report for many good ideas. (verb meaning "take from")

When it is not clear how a multiple-meaning word is being used in a sentence, look for **context clues.** Context clues are other words and phrases that appear in the text. These can be used to help you determine the meaning of a word as it is used in a particular way. You may also refer to a dictionary to find the definition that fits the context. Notice the context clues in this sentence:

The three people made a compact to meet again in a year's time.

"Three people" is a context clue that tells you a small group worked together and "made" the compact. "Meet again" is another context clue that tells you the group planned to do something together in the future.

By checking a dictionary, you will find that *compact* has many different meanings. It can be an adjective that means "packed closely together" or a verb that means "compress." *Compact* can also be a noun that means "an agreement." Based on the context clues, you can determine that the relevant definition for the word *compact* in the example sentence is "an agreement between two or more individuals."

Practice A

Write the meaning of each italicized word in the sentences below. If necessary, consult a dictionary.

1. **(a)** Spinach is a good source of *iron*.
   (b) When using an *iron*, make sure that it is not too hot for the fabric.
2. **(a)** The truck moved slowly up the steep *grade*.
   (b) My teacher had to stay up most of the night to *grade* the essays.
3. **(a)** The hikers were able to find a *pass* through the mountain.
   (b) Were you able to *pass* the entrance exam for the university?
4. **(a)** Cook the sauce over *medium* heat until it begins to boil.
   (b) The artist's favorite *medium* is pastels.

Practice B

Using context clues, write a definition for the underlined word in each sentence. With a partner, discuss which context clues helped you to determine the meaning of the word. Then, look up the word in a dictionary and confirm or correct your definition.

1. A deeply rounded back gave the violin a rich tone.
2. The stern of the boat swung around, and we floated backward down the stream.
3. George was uncomfortable about taking the money, so he skirted the issue.
4. The kids came thundering down the stairs when they were called for dinner.
5. Which branch of the bank is located nearest to your house?
6. My sister got a ticket for peddling cosmetics door to door without a license.
7. It is important for cooks to keep their cupboards full of the staples they use every day.
8. I wouldn't hire Sue because she has base motives for wanting this job.
9. The child scrambled up the bluff through thorn bushes in pursuit of his runaway cat.
10. The movie does not warrant all the rave reviews it has been getting.

Activity Choose five of the underlined words in Practice B. Look in a dictionary to find the multiple meanings of these words. Write each word on a separate note card like the one shown. Fill in the center column of the note card according to one of the word's meanings. Fill in the right column according to another of the word's meanings. Then, trade note cards with a partner, and discuss the different meanings and uses of the words that each of you found.

Word	First Meaning	Second Meaning

Comprehension and Collaboration

Working with a partner, look up each of these words in a dictionary and talk about their multiple meanings: *scale, review, charge*. Then, write sentences using context clues that clearly show three distinct meanings for each word.

Oral Interpretation of Literature

Common Core State Standards

Speaking and Listening
6. Adapt speech to a variety of contexts and tasks, demonstrating command of formal English when indicated or appropriate.

An oral interpretation of literature can be fun: Sharing stories, poems, or plays aloud is an activity that people of all ages enjoy. An oral interpretation of literature is also challenging: In order to present one well, you must understand the work's structure and meaning. As you prepare your interpretation and engage with the work in a detailed, specific way, you will learn more about it. You can then share what you learned with others. The following strategies can help you prepare and deliver an oral interpretation.

Learn the Skills

Understand the literature. Your interpretation should demonstrate an accurate understanding of the literary work's content and meaning. Make sure you are thoroughly familiar with your selection.

Rehearse the interpretation. Make a copy of the literary work to mark performance notes as you practice. Plan and practice appropriate gestures, facial expressions, intonations, and timing until they feel natural. If certain words or phrases become stumbling points, memorize them to assure confidence and poise. Always practice aloud. Use the checklist shown here to help you prepare.

Consider your audience. Provide context to help your audience better understand the literary work you are presenting. Write an introduction to help your readers visualize the situation and characters. You may also include information about the author, including his or her style and the circumstances in which he or she wrote the selection.

Your familiarity with the selection should give you the freedom to maintain eye contact with your audience as you read.

Practice reading poetry. Use the poem's punctuation, not the ends of lines, as cues to pause when reading. Avoid lapsing into sing-song rhythms; instead, maintain a flow that sounds like natural speech. Vary your volume and pace to create emphasis.

Practice reading stories and plays. When expressing a character's quoted words, use a change in intonation to distinguish speech from narration. Modulate your vocal inflections, facial expressions, and posture to indicate whether a speaker is male or female, adult or child.

Oral Interpretation Tips

- Read the text multiple times.
- Mark performance notes and cues on your reading copy.
- Choose appropriate gestures, costumes, and props to suggest characters or situations.
- Vary your pace and tone of voice to create emphasis.

Practice the Skills

Presentation of Knowledge and Ideas Use what you have learned in this workshop to complete the following activity.

ACTIVITY: **Prepare and Deliver an Oral Presentation**

Choose a favorite poem, story, or dramatic speech and prepare an oral interpretation using the strategies outlined in this workshop. Remember that your interpretation should enhance the literature's meaning for your audience. Consider these questions as you prepare and rehearse your presentation:

- What is the knowledge level and cultural perspective of my audience? What context best sets up my presentation?
- How will I organize and present ideas in my introduction?
- What props or costume will best enhance my presentation?
- What gestures are most appropriate for this work of literature?
- What pace and tone of voice best enhance this particular piece?

Use the Presentation Checklist below to analyze your classmates' presentations.

Presentation Checklist

Presentation Content

Determine whether or not the speaker provided support for the audience's understanding.

❑ considered audience and provided context
❑ provided organized and informative introduction
❑ included props and costumes effectively

Presentation Delivery

Determine whether or not the speaker engaged with the audience.

❑ made appropriate eye contact
❑ used an effective speaking rate and volume
❑ used an effective tone of voice
❑ made appropriate gestures

Comments on most effective elements of presentation:________________________________

Comprehension and Collaboration With your classmates, discuss how you evaluated each presenter. As a group, discuss what makes an oral presentation effective and why.

Write an Argument

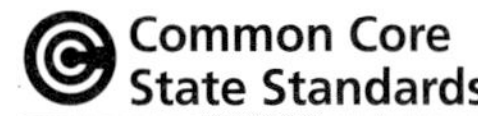
Common Core State Standards

Writing
1. Write arguments to support claims in an analysis of substantive topics or texts, using valid reasoning and relevant and sufficient evidence.
1.a. Introduce precise claim(s), distinguish the claim(s) from alternate or opposing claims, and create an organization that establishes clear relationships among claim(s), counterclaims, reasons, and evidence.
1.b. Develop claim(s) and counterclaims fairly, supplying evidence for each while pointing out the strengths and limitations of both in a manner that anticipates the audience's knowledge level and concerns.
1.d. Establish and maintain a formal style and objective tone while attending to the norms and conventions of the discipline in which they are writing.
5. Develop and strengthen writing as needed by planning, revising, editing, rewriting, or trying a new approach, focusing on addressing what is most significant for a specific purpose and audience.

Problem-and-Solution Essay

Some forms of writing engage us in the struggles and resolutions of our daily lives. In a **problem-and-solution essay,** an author identifies a problem and then argues for a possible solution. You might use this type of writing in letters, memos, proposals, or editorials.

Assignment Write a problem-and-solution essay about an issue that confronts your school or community. Your essay should feature the following elements:

✓ a statement of the *problem* and a suggested *solution*
✓ *valid reasoning* and *evidence,* such as *facts* and *expert opinions,* that show the problem's scope and support an effective solution
✓ consideration of *counterclaims,* or opposing positions, and a discussion of their strengths and weaknesses
✓ formal and objective *language* appropriate to your audience and purpose
✓ logical *organization* and a *concluding statement* or section that supports your argument
✓ *error-free grammar,* including correct use of pronouns

To preview the criteria by which your problem-and-solution essay may be evaluated, see page 423.

FOCUS ON RESEARCH

When you write a problem-and-solution essay, you might perform research to

- learn about past attempts to solve the problem in your community and the results of those efforts.
- determine the resources that might be available to help solve the problem.
- locate information about how similar problems were solved in other communities.

Be sure to note all resources you use in your research, and credit those sources in your final draft. See the Citing Sources pages in the Introductory Unit of this textbook for additional guidance.

READING-WRITING CONNECTION

To get a feel for the use of problem-and-solution structure in a speech, read "First Inaugural Address" by Franklin Delano Roosevelt on page 284.

Prewriting/Planning Strategies

Choose a topic. To select a topic for your problem-and-solution essay, use one of the following strategies:

- **Media Scan** Review local newspapers and television news programs for items about issues and problems in your community. List problems for which you can imagine practical solutions, and select one as your topic.
- **Sentence Starters** Complete the following sentence starters and jot down any associated ideas that come to mind. Then, choose one of the issues generated by the sentence starters as your topic.

  One issue that needs to be addressed is _____.
  The biggest problem people my age face is _____.
  Life would be better in my community if _____.
  The world would be a much better place if _____.

Create a problem profile. Once you have chosen a topic, create a profile like the one shown to help you focus your essay on a specific aspect of the problem. Include a list of possible solutions and consider their effectiveness. Be realistic about the costs and benefits of each, and evaluate whether the benefits outweigh the costs. Also, consider how those with differing opinions may feel about your solutions.

Problem Profile
Problem: Litter is creating an unsafe and unsightly environment.
Who is affected? Everyone on Earth
What causes the problem? Lack of: • responsibility • environmental education • sense of ownership
What are some possible solutions? Stiffer fines, more policing, more environmental education, volunteer trash pickup
What are possible objections to these solutions? costs of more policing; other community priorities

Consider your audience. Once you have clearly defined the problem, collect the details and information you will need to start your draft. Assess all possible solutions and weed out the less practical ones. Then, determine whom you want to reach with your essay and which aspects of the problem affect them most. For example, if you are trying to reach community leaders, you may shape your message differently than if you are trying to reach a peer group. As you narrow your focus, identify the ideas that will have the strongest impact on your target audience.

Drafting Strategies

Engage your audience immediately. To make the problem real to your audience, consider one of these strategies for starting your essay:

- **Personal Example:** Describe an experience you have had that your audience may also have experienced.
- **Anecdote:** Give a factual account of how the problem has already affected your community.
- **Scenario:** Present a hypothetical but realistic picture of future consequences if the problem is not addressed.

Outline the problem clearly. Clearly introduce your analysis of the problem and support it with evidence. Use an organizer like the one shown to display aspects of the central problem, their causes, and their direct effects on people's lives. Then, select and develop those details that will make the problem clear, significant, and urgent to your audience.

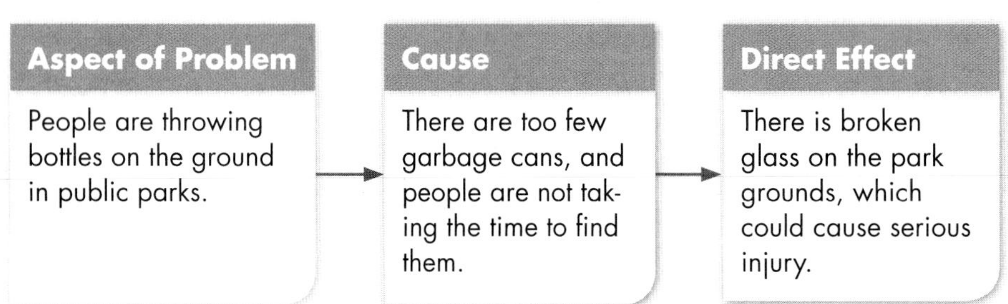

Aspect of Problem
People are throwing bottles on the ground in public parks.
Cause
There are too few garbage cans, and people are not taking the time to find them.
Direct Effect
There is broken glass on the park grounds, which could cause serious injury.

Select convincing details. You cannot "prove" your solution in advance, but you can persuade the audience that your proposal is likely to work by using the following types of evidence.

- **Statistics:** Provide relevant numerical data.
- **Expert Opinions:** Include the advice of those who have training or experience related to your topic problem. Integrate quotations and citations from experts to support the evidence.
- **Comparable Situations:** Describe other real-life difficulties that were resolved by actions similar to the ones you propose.

Use primary and secondary sources that are appropriate to your purpose and audience. To maintain the flow of ideas, explain the value of each quotation you include, and make sure that you establish clear connections among the various types of evidence you use.

Address readers' concerns. You have already anticipated the types of arguments that you might get from people with differing opinions. Weave that understanding into your draft. For example, you might include one or two skeptical questions to show you know both sides of the issue. Then, provide well-supported answers and a concluding statement that supports your argument.

Writing

1.a. Introduce precise claim(s), distinguish the claim(s) from alternate or opposing claims, and create an organization that establishes clear relationships among claim(s), counterclaims, reasons, and evidence.

1.b. Develop claim(s) and counterclaims fairly, supplying evidence for each while pointing out the strengths and limitations of both in a manner that anticipates the audience's knowledge level and concerns.

1.c. Use words, phrases, and clauses to link major sections of the text, create cohesion, and clarify relationships between claim(s) and reasons, between reasons and evidence, and between claim(s) and counterclaims.

1.e. Provide a concluding statement or section that follows from and supports the argument presented.

Expressing Your Ideas

Ideas are the basis for any form of writing. To persuade people to accept a solution to a problem, you must express your ideas clearly and organize them logically. In a problem-and-solution essay, your ideas about both the problem and the solution must be equally strong.

Inform your audience. Even if your audience is somewhat aware of the problem you hope to solve, it is likely they do not know everything about it. Outline the basic facts of the problem: what it is, who it affects, where it occurs, when it began, why it occurs, and why it must be solved. Use a logical progression of ideas and strong supporting evidence to convince your audience of the reality of the problem and the importance of solving it.

Present solutions. Once you have convinced your audience that the problem is real and deserving of attention, propose solutions. Consider the following two ways to organize your ideas:

- **Best Solution First** Present your most powerful, thorough solution first. In a paragraph, describe this idea and outline its merits and costs. Conclude with a strong persuasive statement about why this is the best option. You can then use another paragraph to address other solutions collectively and explain why they would be less effective than your choice.
- **Order of Ease** Present your ideas for solutions in the order that reflects how easily and quickly they could be implemented. Devote a paragraph to each one, including a discussion of both its benefits and drawbacks.

Whichever structure you choose, make sure it advances your position and presents your ideas clearly and thoroughly.

Address and refute counterclaims. As you lay out your claims and evidence, continue to address opposing ideas directly. Provide evidence that shows why other solutions will not be as effective as yours.

Use visual aids. Visuals, such as photographs, illustrations, charts, and graphs, can help you explain your ideas. For example, if you are making a case that litter is a problem in your community, you may wish to use photographs of polluted local sites. If one of your solutions is to add more trash and recycling bins, you may wish to show photos of those alternatives. Likewise, you may wish to display statistical data or other information graphically to clarify your ideas.

Evaluate your ideas. Go back to your essay and make sure you have presented your ideas thoroughly, in a logical order, and with strong supporting evidence.

Revising Strategies

Support your generalizations. Look at each paragraph in your essay to be certain that every detail supports or explains the main idea that you expressed in the topic sentence. Use the following strategy to check and, if necessary, revise your paragraphs.

1. Highlight your topic sentence, the general statement in which you present the main idea of the paragraph.
2. Underline the sentences that develop and support this idea.
3. Eliminate any sentences that do not support the main idea or do not provide convincing and important evidence.

Model: Revising to Support Generalizations

Litter can be dangerous, as well as unsightly. <u>When glass bottles are left on the ground, they eventually break into tiny, sharp pieces. These pieces of glass are hard to see and could easily cut someone walking barefoot or diving for a soccer ball.</u> ~~Also, broken bottles are more difficult to recycle.~~

Clarify connections. Add transitions to clarify the relationships between ideas and evidence within each paragraph and between paragraphs or sections of your essay. For example, introduce supporting details with transitional expressions such as *for example,* or *to illustrate this point.*

Evaluate your vocabulary. Review your draft as if you were a member of your target audience. Find specialized or technical terms that need to be defined. Look for vocabulary that seems too difficult or too easy. Then, adjust your language so that it is appropriate for your readers. Use resources and reference materials to select more effective and precise language. Even if you simplify your language to address the needs of your audience, make sure to maintain an academic style and objective tone.

General Audience	Target Audience of Experts
Another way to lower your blood sugar is to exercise.	Another way to reduce high blood glucose is to exercise.

Peer Review

Exchange drafts with a partner. Review each other's work, circling words that are either too specialized and technical or too simple and basic for your target audience. Use reference materials such as a dictionary or thesaurus to suggest more effective and precise language. Review your concluding section, and make sure it sums up your argument and supports the evidence you presented. Discuss your decisions with your partner, and make the revisions you think will improve your writing.

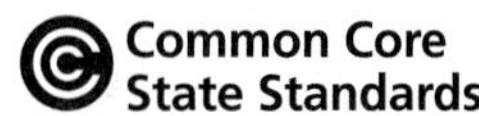

Writing

1.c. Use words, phrases, and clauses to link the major sections of the text, create cohesion, and clarify the relationships between claim(s) and reasons, between reasons and evidence, and between claim(s) and counterclaims.

1.d. Establish and maintain a formal style and objective tone while attending to the norms and conventions of the discipline in which they are writing.

Language

6. Acquire and use accurately general academic and domain-specific words and phrases, sufficient for reading, writing, speaking, and listening at the college and career readiness level; demonstrate independence in gathering vocabulary knowledge when considering a word or phrase important to comprehension or expression.

Revising to Combine Choppy Sentences

Revising to Combine Choppy Sentences Avoid choppy, disconnected sentences by combining two or more related ideas into a single sentence.

Methods of Sentence Combining **Compound verbs**—more than one verb linked to a single subject—can be used to combine two short sentences:

Choppy: I *disconnected* my phone. I *brought* it in for service.

Compound Verb: I *disconnected* my phone and *brought* it in for service.

Compound Subjects—more than one subject performing the action of the same verb—can also be used to combined sentences.

Choppy: Simone bought a scanner. Asher bought a scanner.

Compound Subject: Simone and Asher bought a scanner.

Compound objects—more than one object linked to a single verb—can help combine sentences.

Choppy: I purchased a *scanner*. I purchased *a fax machine*.

Compound Object: I purchased *a scanner and a fax machine*.

A third option is the use of **compound predicate nominatives** or **predicate adjectives.**

Choppy: My newest device *is a printer.* It is also a *scanner*. It is also *a fax machine.*

Compound Predicative Nominative: My newest device *is a printer, scanner, and fax machine.*

Choppy: The fax is *automated*. It is *fast*.

Compound Predicative Adjective: The fax is *automated and fast.*

Fixing Choppy Sentences Scan your draft for sentence variety.

1. **Read your draft aloud.** Listen for overuse of short sentences.
2. **Identify sentences that can be combined.** Look for sentences that share a common subject or a common predicate element.
3. **Use a variety of sentence combining techniques.** Use compound verbs, compound direct objects, or compound predicate nominatives or predicate adjectives to create a wider variety of flowing sentences.

Grammar in Your Writing

Review the body paragraphs in your essay, highlighting central ideas or images. Use various types of phrases and clauses to convey specific meanings and to add interest. Be sure to use punctuation to separate items in a series.

STUDENT MODEL: **Naomi Barrowclough, Maplewood, NJ**

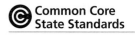

Common Core State Standards

Language
2.c. Spell correctly.

Environmental Un-Consciousness

During a recent Earth Day cleanup, I became disgusted by the amount of trash I picked up within a two-hour period. People had thrown little papers, bits of plastic, and candy wrappers until the mess formed a multicolored carpet over the green grass. Those who litter may not realize that litter creates serious environmental problems.

In the opening paragraph, Naomi provides a general statement of the problem.

We've all been told not to litter, but it does not seem to sink in. One person may think his or her contribution is only a microscopic addition when viewed against the whole. But if every person shared this sense of irresponsibility, Earth would soon be overwhelmed by pollution.

Here, the author provides greater detail to explain the problem more fully.

Litter is harmful for many reasons. For one, roadside litter eventually washes into waterways and oceans—water we use for drinking and recreation. Also, animals might entangle themselves or mistake trash for food and swallow it. In our public spaces, children spend a great deal of time in areas where they could be physically harmed by the pollution caused by litter.

There is no simple solution to the problem of litter, only an array of possible solutions with one strategy in common: Create a feeling of ownership over public spaces. Some of the most popular sites for litter are beaches and parks because people feel no sense of ownership over these places. These same people would never litter in their own homes.

Naomi introduces a general solution here.

To create a feeling of ownership, it is necessary to educate children early about the environmental consequences of littering. According to research done by Keep America Beautiful, a non-profit organization, most people do not feel responsible for public spaces. They think "someone else" will clean up. To change this attitude, schools could lead field trips to local beaches or parks where students pick up trash and test water quality. If kids have to fish two shopping carts from the side of a stream, as I did, they might think twice about throwing something else on the ground. If they see that contaminated water is harmful to both humans and wildlife, they might stop someone they see littering.

In this paragraph, specific strategies for achieving the solution are introduced.

There is no easy way to stop littering. Fines and policing alone will not do the trick because people will just look before they litter. Until people understand that littering is irresponsible and has devastating environmental consequences, they will continue to litter. The solution lies in education and creating a sense of ownership about our public spaces.

In the final paragraph, Naomi addresses a potential concern and then restates her solution.

Editing and Proofreading

Check your draft for errors in spelling, grammar, and punctuation.

Focus on spelling. As you proofread, circle any words that you are not sure how to spell, frequently misspell, or seldom use. Then, use reference resources, such as a dictionary or a thesaurus, to confirm the correct spelling. Follow these steps to find spellings in a dictionary:

- **Check the first letters of a word.** Think of homophones for that sound.
- **Check the other letters.** Once you spell the first sound correctly, try sounding out the rest of the word. Look for likely spellings in the dictionary. If you do not find your word, look for more unusual spellings of the sound.

Spiral Review
Earlier in this unit, you learned about **appositive and absolute phrases** (p. 388) and **infinitives and infinitive phrases** (p. 402). Consider using these types of phrases to add variety to your sentences in this essay.

Publishing and Presenting

To make the best use of your problem-and-solution essay, share it with people who can help you make a difference.

Send a letter. Send your essay to the appropriate government official, agency, or organization. Make sure it is neatly presented and legible. When you receive a response, share it with your classmates in a presentation. Save both the essay and response in your portfolio.

Make a speech. Deliver your essay as a speech to a group that shares your concerns about the problem. Then, lead a question-and-answer session. Be sure to restate your answers if the audience seems confused. Report any consequences of your speech to your classmates.

Reflecting on Your Writing

Writer's Journal Jot down your answer to this question:
How did writing about the problem help you to better understand it?

Self-Evaluation Rubric

Use the following criteria to evaluate the effectiveness of your essay.

Criteria	Rating Scale
PURPOSE/FOCUS Introduces a precise claim and distinguishes the claim from opposing claims; provides a concluding section that follows from and supports the argument presented	*not very* .... *very* 1 2 3 4
ORGANIZATION Establishes a logical organization; uses words, phrases, and clauses to link the major sections of the text, create cohesion, and clarify relationships between ideas and evidence	1 2 3 4
DEVELOPMENT OF IDEAS/ELABORATION Develops the claim and counterclaims fairly, supplying evidence for each while pointing out the strengths and limitations of both	1 2 3 4
LANGUAGE Establishes and maintains a formal style and an objective tone	1 2 3 4
CONVENTIONS Attends to the norms and conventions of the discipline	1 2 3 4

Assessment: Skills

SELECTED RESPONSE

Common Core State Standards

RL.9-10.4, RL.9-10.5; W.9-10.10; L.9-10.5, L.9-10.6
[For full standards wording, see the chart in the front of this book.]

I. Reading Literature

Directions: *Read "The Writer" by Richard Wilbur. Then, answer each question that follows.*

In her room at the prow[1] of the house
Where light breaks, and the windows are tossed
with linden,[2]
My daughter is writing a story.

I pause in the stairwell, hearing
From her shut door a commotion of typewriter-keys
Like a chain hauled over a gunwale.[3]

Young as she is, the stuff
Of her life is a great cargo, and some of it heavy:
I wish her a lucky passage.

But now it is she who pauses,
As if to reject my thought and its easy figure.
A stillness greatens, in which

The whole house seems to be thinking,
And then she is at it again with a bunched <u>clamor</u>
Of strokes, and again is silent.

I remember the dazed starling[4]
Which was trapped in that very room, two years ago;
How we stole in, lifted a sash

And retreated, not to affright it;
And how for a helpless hour, through the crack of
the door,
We watched the sleek, wild, dark

And iridescent[5] creature
Batter against the brilliance, drop like a glove
To the hard floor, or the desk-top,

And wait then, humped and bloody,
For the wits to try it again; and how our spirits
Rose when, suddenly sure,

It lifted off from a chair-back,
Beating a smooth course for the right window
And clearing the sill of the world.

It is always a matter, my darling,
Of life or death, as I had forgotten. I wish
What I wished you before, but harder.

---

1. **prow** (prou) *n.* front part of a ship or boat.
2. **linden** (lin´ dən) *n.* type of tree.
3. **gunwale** (gun´ əl) *n.* upper edge of the side of a ship or boat.
4. **starling** (stär´ liŋ) *n.* bird with black feathers that shine in a greenish or purplish way.
5. **iridescent** (ir´ i des´ ənt) *adj.* rainbow-like; having or showing changes in colors when seen from different angles

1. Which of the following passages from the poem contains a **simile?**
   A. "...a commotion of typewriter-keys
   Like a chain hauled over a gunwale."
   B. "And then she is at it again with a bunched clamor"
   C. "I remember the dazed starling
   Which was trapped in that very room..."
   D. "Beating a smooth course for the right window"

2. **Part A** "The Writer" is most clearly an example of which general type of **poem**?
   A. dramatic poem
   B. narrative poem
   C. concrete poem
   D. lyric poem

   Part B Which qualities of "The Writer" most clearly reflect this category of poetry?
   A. It has a songlike rhythm and uses repetition.
   B. It has the same number of lines in each stanza.
   C. It expresses the thoughts of a single speaker in a moment of time.
   D. It tells a complete story.

3. Which passage from the poem provides the best example of **assonance?**
   A. "prow of the house"
   B. "lucky passage"
   C. "My daughter is writing a story."
   D. "Young as she is"

4. Which of the following passages from the poem contains a **metaphor?**
   A. "My daughter is writing a story."
   B. "Young as she is, the stuff
   Of her life is a great cargo..."
   C. "Batter against the brilliance, drop like a glove"
   D. "How we stole in, lifted a sash
   And retreated, not to affright it"

5. Which phrase from the poem provides the best example of **alliteration?**
   A. "sleek, wild, dark"
   B. "suddenly sure"
   C. "drop like a glove"
   D. "life or death"

6. **Part A** What is the meaning of the underlined word *clamor* as it is used in the poem?
   A. pulsing, rhythmic sound; drumbeat
   B. loud, sustained noise; commotion
   C. musical interlude; melody
   D. crackling, snapping sound

   Part B Which context clues in the poem support your understanding of the meaning of *clamor?*
   A. "prow of the house"; "windows tossed with linden"
   B. "I wish her a lucky passage"; "reject my thought and its easy figure"
   C. "I remember the dazed starling"; "not to affright it"
   D. "commotion of typewriter-keys"; "A stillness greatens...And then she is at it again"

Timed Writing

7. Identify one example of **figurative language** and one example of a **sound device** in this poem. In a short essay, analyze how the examples you chose contribute to the meaning and tone of the poem.

II. Reading Informational Text

Directions: *Read the passage. Then, answer each question that follows.*

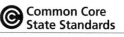

Common Core State Standards

RI.9-10.1, RI.9-10.3; L.9-10.1, L.9-10.1.b, L.9-10.3, L.9-10.4.a
[For full standards wording, see the chart in the front of this book.]

MP3 Mania!

The new wave in technology is the MP3 format for music files. Long gone are the days of vinyl records, cassettes, and even CDs. What was once considered new technology is now overshadowed by MP3 files. Who needs to carry around bulky CDs when your whole music collection can be stored on a palm-sized MP3 player? With this <u>revolutionary</u>, new technology, you can not only carry around your entire CD collection, but you can also purchase files on the Internet, totally bypassing the need for storage space outside of the computer and player. MP3s provide hours of entertainment without the hassles of bulky players and the need for excess storage.

Simple Instructions for MP3 Players

MP3 files have brought music into the computer age. With this technology, you can carry your entire music library in a tiny player. All you need is a computer, an MP3 player, and a USB cord. Follow these directions to start rocking.

Step 1. Download the music from your CDs onto your computer. Your computer should come equipped with a program to store and access music. Insert the CD, choose Download, and let the computer do the work.

Step 2. Connect your MP3 player to your computer with the USB cord. Your computer will update your MP3 player, loading all your music onto it.

Step 3. Allow the battery of your MP3 player to charge as it is connected to the computer. Your player will alert you when the battery is charged.

Step 4. Disconnect your MP3 player and follow the manual to play your music.

1. What is the best definition for the underlined word *revolutionary*?

A. causing a change
B. more affordable
C. upsetting
D. without consequences

2. To convert to MP3 format, you must first

A. allow your MP3 player battery to charge.
B. use the USB cord to connect your MP3 player.
C. download your CDs onto your computer.
D. disconnect your MP3 player from the computer.

3. Part A According to the passage, why is the MP3 format better than other formats?

A. It is inexpensive.
B. It is convenient.
C. It is complex.
D. It involves computers.

Part B Which detail from the passage best supports the answer to Part A?

A. "Long gone are the days of vinyl records"
B. "without the hassles of bulky players and the need for excess storage"
C. "once considered new technology"
D. "brought music into the computer age"

III. Writing and Language Conventions

Directions: *Read the passage. Then, answer each question that follows.*

(1) The smell of turkey filled my room, and before my eyes even opened, my mouth widened to a smile. (2) This was Thanksgiving, my favorite holiday. (3) All the members of my huge family were arriving at my house. (4) I heard the soft murmur of voices bubbling up from the kitchen. (5) I ran downstairs to greet my aunts, uncles, and cousins. (6) Within three hours, dinner was ready. (7) I loved the steaming turkey. (8) I loved the seasoned stuffing. (9) I loved the conversation, my favorite part of Thanksgiving. (10) Year after year, my family has amazed me with the stories they tell. (11) This year, my cousin Ana talked about her surfing lessons in Florida. (12) My uncle Charlie, a resident of New Orleans, told a funny story about his jazz band. (13) My grandpa Joe explained how he dug himself out of his house when three feet of snow fell on his home in Buffalo. (14) When my family described their lives all over the country, I felt like I got to visit each place without leaving my home. (15) My favorite activity is hiking. (16) I told my family about my hiking adventures in the nearby forest, so they learned a little bit about living in my part of the country, too.

1. Which of these sentences contains an **infinitive phrase?**

A. sentence 1
B. sentence 5
C. sentence 9
D. sentence 11

2. Which of the following choices is the **appositive phrase** in sentence 12?

A. My uncle Charlie
B. a resident of New Orleans
C. told a funny story
D. about his jazz band

3. What sort of phrase is *at my house* in sentence 3?

A. an appositive phrase
B. a participial phrase
C. a gerund phrase
D. a prepositional phrase

4. How does the **gerund** *hiking* function in sentence 15?

A. as a predicate nominative
B. as the subject
C. as the object of a preposition
D. as a gerund phrase

5. Which sentence contains a **past participle** serving as an adjective?

A. sentence 8
B. sentence 7
C. sentence 10
D. sentence 1

6. How should choppy sentences 7 and 8 be combined?

A. I loved turkey and stuffing I loved, too.
B. I loved the turkey, steaming, and I loved the stuffing, seasoned.
C. I loved the steaming turkey and the seasoned stuffing.
D. The steaming turkey, seasoned stuffing were both loved.

STOP

CONSTRUCTED RESPONSE

Directions: *Follow the instructions to complete the tasks below as required by your teacher.*

As you work on each task, incorporate both general academic vocabulary and literary terms you learned in Parts 1 and 2 of this unit.

RL.9-10.4, RL.9-10.5; W.9-10.2.b, W.9-10.7, W.9-10.8, W.9-10.9.a; SL.9-10.2, SL.9-10.4
[For full standards wording, see the chart in the front of this book.]

Writing

TASK 1 Literature [RL.9-10.4; W.9-10.9.a]

Analyze Figurative Language in a Poem

Write an essay in which you analyze the figurative language in a poem from Part 2 of this unit.

- State which poem you chose, and explain why you chose it.
- Identify a key metaphor, simile, or other example of figurative language in the poem. Explain why this example is important to the poem's meaning.
- Analyze the meaning of the example you chose. Explain your analysis clearly.
- Explain how your chosen example contributes to the tone of the poem. For example, explain how the poet's word choices build or maintain a sense of formality or informality. Cite details to support your ideas.
- Edit your essay for correct punctuation and spelling.

TASK 2 Literature [RL.9-10.5; W.9-10.9.a]

Analyze the Structure in a Narrative Poem

Analyze how a poet uses structure to present events in a narrative poem from Part 2 of this unit. Consider how the order of events creates an effect, such as mystery or suspense.

- Give a brief summary of the plot.
- Describe how the poem is structured, or arranged in lines and stanzas.
- Explain how the poet uses the structure to organize information and tell the story. For example, consider how the poet uses the structure to introduce characters, describe the setting, or show action.
- Explain how other structural elements, such as rhyme scheme, add to the poem's effect.
- Consider whether the poet uses any devices to manipulate time. For example, explain whether the poet uses a flashback or alters the pacing. Explain the effects of these choices.
- Cite specific details from the poem to support your analysis.

TASK 3 Literature [RL.9-10.5; W.9-10.2.b]

Compare Forms of Lyric Poetry

Compare two different forms of lyric poetry from Part 2 of this unit, and show how the form of each helps to express the speaker's thoughts and feelings.

Part 1

- Review the different forms of lyric poetry from Part 2 of this unit—sonnet, haiku, and free verse. Choose two poems, each with a different structure, as the basis for your comparison.
- Analyze each poem, taking notes on its form.
- Answer the following question: How does each poem's structure aid the speaker in conveying important thoughts and feelings? Provide specific examples from each poem.

Part 2

- Compare and contrast the structures of the two poems. Explain how the patterns of rhythm and rhyme in a formally structured poem or the absence of a set pattern in a free verse poem affect the overall mood and feeling each expresses.
- Finally, write an essay in which you critique each poem, and explain which one conveys the speaker's ideas most effectively. Use text evidence to support your judgments.

Speaking and Listening

TASK 4 **Literature [RL.9-10.4; SL.9-10.4]**

Analyze How Sound Devices Affect the Tone of a Poem

Write and deliver an oral presentation in which you analyze how a poet's use of sound devices affects the tone of a poem from Part 2 of this unit.

- Introduce the poem and briefly summarize it. If the poem is short, read it aloud.
- Describe the tone of the poem. Cite specific examples of sound devices that help to develop this tone. Explain how a variety of different sound devices combine to create an overall effect.
- Organize your findings and supporting evidence logically so your audience can follow your reasoning.
- Provide a concluding statement that follows from and supports the information you presented earlier.
- As you speak, maintain consistency in your style and tone.

TASK 5 **Literature [RL.9-10.4; W.9-10.7; SL.9-10.2]**

Deliver a Multimedia Presentation on a Poem's Rhyme and Meter

Deliver a multimedia presentation in which you explain the rhyme and meter of a poem from Part 2 of this unit.

- Choose a poem from Part 2 in which rhyme and meter are especially interesting or important. Conduct research to find video or audio clips of the poem being read aloud, or record your own audio or video. Likewise, locate graphics and other images that will help you explain your ideas.
- Introduce the poem you chose and clearly describe its rhyme and meter. Incorporate visual elements to highlight key ideas in your description.
- Explain how the rhyme and meter of the poem contribute to its overall effect and meaning.
- End with a conclusion that clearly follows from the information you presented.

Research

TASK 6 **Literature [RL.9-10.5; W.9-10.7, W.9-10.8; W.9-10.9.a]**

How does communication change us?

In Part 2 of this unit, you have read poetry that explores different aspects of communication. Now you will conduct a short research project on one of the poets whose work you have read. Explain how the poet's life experiences and beliefs about poetry are reflected in his or her work. Use both the poems you have read and the research you have conducted to reflect on and write about this unit's Big Question. Review the following guidelines before you begin your research:

- Focus your research on one poet.
- Gather information from at least two reliable sources. Your sources may be print or digital.
- Take notes as you research the poet's life and work.
- Cite your sources.

When you have finished your research, write an essay in response to the Big Question. Discuss how your initial ideas have changed or been reinforced. Support your response with examples from both the poems you have read and the research you have completed.

"**Why** *then*? Why *there*?
Why *thus, we cry,* **did he die**?
The Heavens are silent."

—W.H. Auden

PART 3

TEXT SET DEVELOPING INSIGHT

THE KENNEDY ASSASSINATION

The assassination of President John F. Kennedy on November 22, 1963, shocked the nation and the world. In the immediate hours and days after the shooting, Americans of every walk of life expressed their grief. At the same time, leaders took steps to ensure that the government would remain stable and the country would move on. The readings in this section reflect varied responses to the tragic events of that day. Each piece communicates the sorrow, dismay, and understanding that in a single violent moment, America had changed.

◀ CRITICAL VIEWING This photograph was taken shortly after President Kennedy's assassination. What does this image reveal about Americans' reactions to the event?

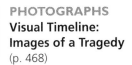

CLOSE READING TOOL

Use the **Close Reading Tool** to practice the strategies you learn in this unit.

READINGS IN PART 3

THE ASSASSINATION OF John F. Kennedy

GWENDOLYN BROOKS

. . . this Good, this Decent, this Kindly man . . .
—SENATOR MANSFIELD[1]

I hear things crying in the world.
A nightmare congress of obscure
Delirium uttering overbreath
The tilt and jangle of this death.

Who had a sense of world and man,
Who had an apt and antic grace
Lies lenient, lapsed and large beneath
The tilt and jangle of this death.

The world goes on with what it has.
Its reasoned, right and only code.
Coaxing, with military faith,
The tilt and jangle of this death.

◀ **delirium**
(di lir′ē əm) *n.* mental disturbance marked by confusion, disturbed speech, and hallucinations

◀ **antic**
(an′tik) *adj.* wildly playful

1. **Senator Mansfield** (1903–2001) Senate majority leader at the time of Kennedy's death.

ABOUT THE POET

GWENDOLYN BROOKS (1917–2000)

Gwendolyn Brooks spent most of her life in Chicago. She published her first poem at age 13 and wrote a poetry column for the *Chicago Defender* newspaper as a teenager. During a prolific, storied career, she published many books of poetry, one novel, and a two-part autobiography. Among her many honors, Brooks became the first African American woman to win a Pulitzer Prize, was named poet laureate of Illinois, and, in 1985, became the poetry consultant to the Library of Congress—the first African American woman to serve in that role.

INSTEAD OF AN ELEGY

G. S. FRASER

Bullets blot out the Life-Time-smile,
Apollo of the picture-page,
Blunt-faced young lion
        Caught by vile
Death in an everlasting cage:

And, no more young men in the world,
The old men troop to honor him.
The drums beat glum,
        Slight snow is swirled
In dazzling sun, pale **requiem**.

requiem ▶
(rek′ wē əm) *n.*
musical service in
honor of the dead

And pale dark-veiled Persephone,
A golden child in either hand,
Stands by white pillars;
        Silently,
It seems she might for ever stand.

In bright grey sun, processionals
Of pomp and honor, and of grief,
Crown that dead head
        With coronals.
Some stony hearts feel some relief:

But not your heart, America,
Beating so slow and sure and strong,
Stricken in his
        Triumphal car,
Guard Caesar's bitter laurels long

With soldiers' music, rites of war:
He had proved bravely when put on!
The soldiers shoot.
        Rage echoes far
Above the grave at Arlington.[1]

---

1. **Arlington** U.S. national burial ground for soldiers killed in war and civilians who have given special service to the nation.

ABOUT THE POET

G. S. FRASER (1915–1980)

George Sutherland Fraser, a Scottish poet and literary critic, served in the British army during World War II. After the war, he worked as a freelance journalist. In addition to his own poetry, Fraser wrote several books of poetry criticism. Fraser taught English for many years at the University of Leicester in England.

Close Reading Activities

READ

Comprehension

Reread the poems. Then, answer the following questions.

1. What sounds does the speaker describe in the first stanza of "The Assassination of John F. Kennedy"?
2. What phrases does the speaker use to describe Kennedy in the second stanza of "The Assassination . . ."?
3. What event does "Instead of an Elegy" describe?
4. In "Instead of an Elegy," what mythical figures does the speaker use to refer to the President and First Lady?

Research: Clarify Details These poems may include references that are unfamiliar to you. Choose at least one unfamiliar detail, and briefly research it. Then, explain how the information you learned from research sheds light on an aspect of the poems.

Summarize Write an objective summary of each poem. Remember that in an objective summary you avoid making statements of opinion or evaluation.

Language Study

Selection Vocabulary The following passages appear in the two poems. Research the etymology (history) of each boldface word. Then, explain each word's modern English meaning.

- A nightmare congress of obscure / **Delirium** uttering overbreath
- Who had an apt and **antic** grace
- Slight snow is swirled / In dazzling sun, pale **requiem**.

Diction and Style Study the lines from the poem by Gwendolyn Brooks that appear below. Then, answer the questions that follow.

A nightmare congress of obscure
Delirium uttering overbreath
The tilt and jangle of this death.

1. **(a)** What does *congress* mean in this line? **(b)** What does the word *Congress* mean when the *c* is capitalized? **(c)** How is the second meaning appropriate in a poem about a fallen American leader?
2. **(a)** What do *tilt* and *jangle* mean in the last line? **(b)** Why do you think Brooks chose to repeat these words in each stanza? Explain, citing evidence from the text.

Conventions Read this passage from the poem by G. S. Fraser. Identify two prepositional phrases, and determine which word each phrase modifies. Then, explain how the poet's use of these phrases helps to both clarify meaning and communicate the speaker's feelings about the subject.

Bullets blot out the Life-Time-smile,
Apollo of the picture-page,
Blunt-faced young lion
Caught by vile
Death in an everlasting cage:

Academic Vocabulary

The following words appear in blue in the instructions and questions on the facing page.

resolution **counteract** **implicit**

Copy the words into your notebook. For each word, find another word that comes from the same root.

Literary Analysis

Reread the identified passages. Then, respond to the questions that follow.

Focus Passage 1 *(p. 433)*
I hear . . . faith / The tilt and jangle of this death.

Key Ideas and Details

1. **Infer:** In the first stanza, what "things" are "crying" in the world? Explain.
2. **(a) Interpret:** What is the focus of the second stanza? **(b) Analyze:** Which words express a sense of admiration for this figure?

Craft and Structure

3. **(a) Describe:** Describe the poem's structure—the length of each stanza and the use of both exact and slant rhyme. **(b) Interpret:** In what ways does the formality of the poem's structure contrast with its topic? Explain, citing textual details.
4. **(a) Interpret:** Which words in the poem relate to a sense of order and which to disorder? **(b) Analyze:** How does this diction add to the poem's meaning? Explain.

Integration of Knowledge and Ideas

5. **(a) Interpret:** Which words or phrases convey a sense of **resolution** or acceptance in the final stanza? **(b) Analyze:** How does the repetition of "tilt and jangle of this death" **counteract** that air of acceptance? Explain.

Focus Passage 2 *(pp. 434–435)*
And, no more young men . . . for ever stand.

Key Ideas and Details

1. **Infer:** How might the events the poem describes contribute to the idea that there are "no more young men" in the world? Explain.
2. **(a) Distinguish:** What words or phrases does the poet use to describe Persephone and her family? **(b) Interpret:** In the context of the poem, who is Persephone?

Craft and Structure

3. **(a) Connect:** Who is Persephone in Greek mythology? **(b) Interpret:** How does this allusion add to the speaker's characterization of this figure in these lines? Explain.
4. **(a) Distinguish:** In line three of the focus passage, which words create internal rhyme? **(b) Interpret:** How does that sound device echo the occasion the poem describes and add to the mood of these lines? Explain.

Integration of Knowledge and Ideas

5. **(a) Distinguish:** Identify four references in the poem as a whole to ancient Greek or Roman myth and culture. **(b) Interpret:** What **implicit** message do these details help to convey? Explain.

Alliteration

Alliteration is the repetition of consonant sounds at the beginnings of nearby words. Reread the two poems aloud, and take notes on ways in which the poets use alliteration.

1. **(a)** In the poem by Brooks, what quality does the alliteration in "Lies lenient, lapsed and large" add to the line? **(b)** What does the sound sense communicate about the person being described?
2. **(a)** In the poem by Fraser, what sound does the alliteration of the phrase "Slight snow is swirled / In dazzling sun" suggest? **(b)** How does the alliteration add to the vividness of the scene?
3. **The Kennedy Assassination:** Based on your answers, explain how each poet uses alliteration to enrich his or her presentation of the world's reaction to the assassination.

Common Core State Standards

RL.9-10.1, RL.9-10.2, RL.9-10.4, RL.9-10.5, RL.9-10.9, RL.9-10.10; L.9-10.1, L.9-10.3, L.9-10.4, L.9-10.5, L.9-10.6

[For full standards wording, see the chart in the front of this textbook.]

DISCUSS

From Text to Topic **Group Discussion**

Discuss the following passage from "Instead of an Elegy" with a group of classmates. Take notes during the discussion. Contribute your own ideas, and support them with examples from the text.

> Bullets blot out the Life-Time-smile, / Apollo of the picture-page, / Blunt-faced young lion / Caught by vile / Death in an everlasting cage:

QUESTIONS FOR DISCUSSION

1. What literary techniques does the poet use in this stanza? Are they effective? Why or why not?
2. What overall impression of Kennedy does the speaker communicate?

WRITE

Writing to Sources **Explanatory Text**

Assignment

Write an **expository essay** in which you explain how the two poets communicate a sense of grief for Kennedy, both as a private person and as a public figure. Support your thesis with details from the text, including a discussion of literary techniques, word choice, and poetic structure.

Prewriting and Planning Reread the poems, looking for details that describe Kennedy's personal qualities and those that describe him in his role as a public figure. Record your observations.

Drafting Follow an organizational structure consisting of an opening paragraph, a body, and a conclusion. In your opening paragraph, state your thesis. In the body of your essay, expand on your thesis and develop your ideas. End with a conclusion that restates your thesis.

Revising Reread your essay, making sure you have used sufficient quotations from the poems and have woven them smoothly into your text. The following are some methods for incorporating quoted material:

Introductory phrase followed by a quotation:

Example: *Brooks begins with a description of widespread grief. The speaker says, "I hear things crying in the world."*

Sentence followed by a colon and a quotation:

Example: *The speaker describes widespread grief: "I hear things crying in the world."*

Quoted phrase integrated with an assertion:

Example: *The speaker describes widespread grief as "things crying in the world."*

CONVENTIONS

When including short quotations from poetry within a paragraph, add a slash mark to indicate a line break: "A nightmare congress of obscure / Delirium."

Editing and Proofreading Be sure that you have accurately transcribed all quotations, including correct punctuation and capitalization.

RESEARCH

Research **Investigate the Topic**

Not Just a Nation, but a World In the aftermath of the assassination of President Kennedy, writers, artists, the general public, and leaders from all over the world expressed sorrow and shock. Research the world's reactions to the tragic events of that day.

Assignment

Conduct research to learn how people all over the world reacted to the assassination of President Kennedy. Consult magazine and newspaper articles, TV and radio broadcasts, and government documents. Carefully organize your notes and gather thorough source information for citation. Share your findings in an **oral research report.**

PREPARATION FOR ESSAY

You may use the knowledge you gain during this research assignment to support your claims in an essay you will write at the end of this section.

Gather Sources Consult reliable and authoritative print and electronic sources. Consider using primary sources, such as newspaper accounts, magazine articles, letters, speeches, and government documents from the era. You may also use secondary sources, such as later writings by historians or encyclopedia articles. If possible, also view media sources, such as documentaries.

Take Notes Use notecards or spreadsheet software to record information from each source carefully and thoughtfully. Apply an organized strategy in which you identify important ideas from your sources, capture information you will need in order to cite sources correctly, and start to make connections among details.

- Label each note with the key idea it supports. You should have several notes for each one of your key ideas.
- Identify the source information for every idea or example you plan to use.
- Quote directly from primary sources in order to capture people's attitudes and quality of expression. Use quotation marks to indicate that your wording is exact.
- Paraphrase ideas that are important but that you do not plan to quote verbatim. Make sure to capture source information for paraphrases as you will need to cite any ideas that are not your own regardless of the wording.

Synthesize Multiple Sources Assemble information from your sources and organize it for presentation. Use your notes to construct a logical outline, noting points at which to integrate quoted material. Make sure to cite all quotations or paraphrased ideas accurately. Create a Works Cited list to distribute as a hand-out to your audience. See the Citing Sources pages in the Introductory Unit of this textbook for additional guidance.

Organize and Present Present your report. After you have finished speaking, invite questions from your listeners.

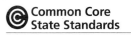

Common Core State Standards

W.9-10.2, W.9-10.2.a–b, W.9-10.2.f, W.9-10.4, W.9-10.5, W.9-10.7, W.9-10.8, W.9-10.9.a, W.9-10.10; SL.9-10.1, SL.9-10.2, SL.9-10.4; L.9-10.2.b

[For full standards wording, see the chart in the front of this book.]

from A White House Diary

Lady Bird Johnson

Dallas, Friday, November 22, 1963

It all began so beautifully. After a drizzle in the morning, the sun came out bright and clear. We were driving into Dallas. In the lead car were President and Mrs. Kennedy, John and Nellie Connally,[1] a Secret Service[2] car full of men, and then our car with Lyndon and me and Senator Ralph Yarborough.

The streets were lined with people—lots and lots of people—the children all smiling, placards, confetti, people waving from windows. One last happy moment I had was looking up and seeing Mary Griffith leaning out of a window waving at me. (Mary for many years had been in charge of altering the clothes which I purchased at Neiman-Marcus.)

Then, almost at the edge of town, on our way to the Trade Mart for the Presidential luncheon, we were rounding a curve, going down a hill, and suddenly there was a sharp, loud report. It sounded like a shot. The sound seemed to me to come from a building on the right above my shoulder. A moment passed, and then two more shots rang out in rapid succession. There had been such a gala air about the day that I thought the noise must come from firecrackers—part of the celebration. Then the Secret Service men were suddenly down in the lead car. Over the car radio system, I heard "Let's get out of here!" and our Secret Service man, Rufus Youngblood, vaulted over the front seat on top of Lyndon, threw him to the floor, and said, "Get down."

Senator Yarborough and I ducked our heads. The car accelerated terrifically—faster and faster. Then, suddenly, the brakes were put on so hard that I wondered if we were going to make it as we wheeled left and went around the corner. We pulled up to a building. I looked up and saw a sign, "HOSPITAL." Only then did I believe that this

1. **John and Nellie Connally** John Connally, then governor of Texas, and his wife, Nellie.
2. **Secret Service** division of the U.S. Treasury Department, responsible for protecting the president.

might be what it was. Senator Yarborough kept saying in an excited voice, "Have they shot the President? Have they shot the President?" I said something like, "No, it can't be."

As we ground to a halt—we were still the third car—Secret Service men began to pull, lead, guide, and hustle us out. I cast one last look over my shoulder and saw in the President's car a bundle of pink, just like a drift of blossoms, lying on the back seat. It was Mrs. Kennedy lying over the President's body.

The Secret Service men rushed us to the right, then to the left, and then onward into a quiet room in the hospital—a very small room. It was lined with white sheets, I believe.

People came and went—Kenny O'Donnell, the President's top aide, Congressman Homer Thornberry, Congressman Jack Brooks. Always there was Rufe right there and other Secret Service agents—Emory Roberts, Jerry Kivett, Lem Johns, and Woody Taylor. People spoke of how widespread this might be. There was talk about where we would go—to the plane, to our house, back to Washington.

Through it all Lyndon was remarkably calm and quiet. He suggested that the Presidential plane ought to be moved to another part of the field. He spoke of going back out to the plane in unmarked black cars. Every face that came in, you searched for the answer. I think the face I kept seeing the answer on was the face of Kenny O'Donnell, who loved President Kennedy so much.

It was Lyndon who spoke of it first, although I knew I would not leave without doing it. He said, "You had better try to see Jackie and Nellie." We didn't know what had happened to John.

I asked the Secret Service if I could be taken to them. They began to lead me up one corridor and down another. Suddenly I found myself face to face with Jackie in a small hallway. I believe it was right outside the operating room. You always think of someone like her as being insulated, protected. She was quite alone. I don't think I ever saw anyone so much alone in my life. I went up to her, put my arms around her, and said something to her. I'm sure it was something like "God, help us all," because my feelings for her were too tumultuous to put into words.

And then I went to see Nellie. There it was different, because Nellie and I have gone through so many things together since 1938. I hugged her tight and we both cried and I said, "Nellie, John's going to be all right." And Nellie said, "Yes, John's going to be all right." Among her many other fine qualities, she is also strong.

I turned and went back to the small white room where Lyndon was. Mac Kilduff, the President's press man on this trip, and Kenny

Senator Yarborough kept saying in an excited voice, "Have they shot the President? Have they shot the President?" I said something like, "No, it can't be."

O'Donnell were coming and going. I think it was from Kenny's face that I first knew the truth and from Kenny's voice that I first heard the words "The President is dead." Mr. Kilduff entered and said to Lyndon, "Mr. President."

It was decided that we would go immediately to the airport. Hurried plans were made about how we should get to the cars and who was to ride in which car. Our departure from the hospital and approach to the cars was one of the swiftest walks I have ever made.

We got in. Lyndon told the agents to stop the sirens. We drove along as fast as we could. I looked up at a building and there, already, was a flag at half-mast. I think that was when the enormity of what had happened first struck me.

When we got to the field, we entered *Air Force One*[3] for the first time. There was a TV set on and the commentator was saying, "Lyndon B. Johnson, now President of the United States." The news commentator was saying the President had been shot with a 30-30 rifle. The police had a suspect. They were not sure he was the assassin.

On the plane, all the shades were lowered. We heard that we were going to wait for Mrs. Kennedy and the coffin. There was a telephone call to Washington—I believe to the Attorney General.[4]

---

3. ***Air Force One*** name of the airplane officially assigned to transport the president of the United States.
4. **Attorney General** chief law officer of the nation, head of the U.S. Department of Justice; at the time, the position was held by Robert Kennedy, JFK's brother.

It was decided that Lyndon should be sworn in here as quickly as possible, because of national and world implications, and because we did not know how widespread this was as to intended victims. Judge Sarah Hughes, a Federal Judge in Dallas—and I am glad it was she—was called and asked to come in a hurry to administer the oath.

confines ▶ (kän´ fīnz) *n.* regions within a border; limits

Mrs. Kennedy had arrived by this time, as had the coffin. There, in the very narrow **confines** of the plane—with Jackie standing by Lyndon, her hair falling in her face but very composed, with me beside him, Judge Hughes in front of him, and a cluster of Secret Service people, staff, and Congressmen we had known for a long time around him—Lyndon took the oath of office.

It's odd the little things that come to your mind at times of utmost stress, the flashes of deep compassion you feel for people who are really not at the center of the tragedy. I heard a Secret Service man say in the most desolate voice—and I hurt for him: "We never lost a President in the Service." Then, Police Chief Curry of Dallas came on the plane and said, "Mrs. Kennedy, believe me, we did everything we possibly could." That must have been an agonizing moment for him.

We all sat around the plane. The casket was in the corridor. I went in the small private room to see Mrs. Kennedy, and though it was a very hard thing to do, she made it as easy as possible. She said things like, "Oh, Lady Bird, we've liked you two so much. . . . Oh, what if I had not been there. I'm so glad I was there."

I looked at her. Mrs. Kennedy's dress was stained with blood. One leg was almost entirely covered with it and her right glove was caked,

On the day of the assassination, Mrs. Johnson accompanies her husband, the newly sworn-in President Johnson, on his way to address the nation.

it was caked with blood—her husband's blood. Somehow that was one of the most poignant sights—that immaculate woman exquisitely dressed, and caked in blood.

◀ **poignant** (poin´ yənt) *adj.* emotionally touching

◀ **immaculate** (i mak´ yə lit) *adj.* perfectly correct; without a flaw, fault, or error

I asked her if I couldn't get someone in to help her change and she said, "Oh, no. Perhaps later I'll ask Mary Gallagher but not right now." And then with almost an element of fierceness—if a person that gentle, that dignified, can be said to have such a quality—she said, "I want them to see what they have done to Jack."

I tried to express how we felt. I said, "Oh, Mrs. Kennedy, you know we never even wanted to be Vice President and now, dear God, it's come to this." I would have done anything to help her, but there was nothing I could do, so rather quickly I left and went back to the main part of the airplane where everyone was seated.

The flight to Washington was silent, each sitting with his own thoughts. One of mine was a recollection of what I had said about Lyndon a long time ago—he's a good man in a tight spot. I remembered one little thing he had said in that hospital room—"Tell the children to get a Secret Service man with them."

Finally we got to Washington, with a cluster of people waiting and many bright lights. The casket went off first, then Mrs. Kennedy, and then we followed. The family had come to join her. Lyndon made a very simple, very brief, and, I think, strong statement to the people there. Only about four sentences. We got in helicopters, dropped him off at the White House, and I came home in a car with Liz Carpenter.[5]

5. **Liz Carpenter** Mrs. Johnson's press secretary.

ABOUT THE AUTHOR

Lady Bird Johnson (1912–2007)

Texas-born Claudia Alta Taylor received her nickname when a nurse said the two-year-old was "as pretty as a lady bird." A graduate of the University of Texas, Lady Bird met and married Lyndon Johnson, then a young congressional aide, in 1934. Even though she was a shy woman, Lady Bird was a valued advisor and an effective campaigner for her husband, who said that voters "would happily have elected her over me."

When President Kennedy was assassinated, Vice President Lyndon Johnson became President, and Lady Bird became First Lady of the United States. In this role, she made many contributions to her husband's agenda, including the launch of Head Start, a project that makes early childhood education available to all children.

Close Reading Activities

READ

Comprehension

Reread all or part of the text to help you answer the following questions.

1. What does Mrs. Johnson see that makes her realize "the enormity of what had happened"?
2. When and where does Lyndon Johnson take the oath of office?
3. Why does Mrs. Kennedy refuse Mrs. Johnson's offer of help to change her clothes?

Research: Clarify Details Choose at least one unfamiliar detail from this memoir, and briefly research it. Then, explain how the information you learned from research sheds light on an aspect of the text.

Summarize Write an objective summary of the memoir, one that is free of statements of opinion or evaluation.

Language Study

Selection Vocabulary The passages at right appear in *A White House Diary*. Define each boldface word. Then, explain why each word is a strong choice to express the author's meaning.

- There, in the very narrow **confines** of the plane
- that was one of the most **poignant** sights
- that **immaculate** woman exquisitely dressed

Literary Analysis

Reread the identified passage. Then, respond to the questions that follow.

Focus Passage *(pp. 444–445)*

It's odd the little things . . . caked in blood.

Key Ideas and Details

1. **(a)** What descriptive details does Mrs. Johnson use to describe Mrs. Kennedy? **(b) Interpret:** What overall impression of Mrs. Kennedy do these details convey?

Craft and Structure

2. **(a) Distinguish:** Which words does Mrs. Johnson repeat in the third paragraph? **(b) Analyze:** What is the effect of that repetition? Explain.
3. **(a) Interpret:** What punctuation marks create pauses in the passage? **(b) Evaluate:** How do these pauses contribute to both the meaning and tone of the passage? Explain.

Integration of Knowledge and Ideas

4. **Draw Conclusions:** What overall idea is Mrs. Johnson communicating by describing the pain and grief of "people who are really not at the center of the tragedy"? Explain.

Memoir

A **memoir** is an autobiography that focuses on a specific period or experience in the writer's life. Reread the text as a whole, and note how Mrs. Johnson offers an **intimate**, or private, view of a public tragedy.

1. **(a)** On what aspects of the events does Mrs. Johnson focus? **(b)** How is her perspective on the assassination unique? Explain.
2. **The Kennedy Assassination:** The surviving members of the presidential party were aware that their private **conduct** would have public impact. Cite specific details that show how President and Mrs. Johnson and Mrs. Kennedy behave as a result of that awareness. Explain your choices.

DISCUSS • RESEARCH • WRITE

From Text to Topic Partner Discussion

Discuss the following passage with a partner. Take notes during the discussion. Contribute your own ideas, and support them with examples from the text.

> The flight to Washington was silent, each sitting with his own thoughts. One of mine was a recollection of what I had said about Lyndon a long time ago—he's a good man in a tight spot. I remembered one little thing he had said in that hospital room—"Tell the children to get a Secret Service man with them."

QUESTIONS FOR DISCUSSION

1. What does it mean to be "in a tight spot"? How do President Johnson's actions demonstrate that he is "a good man" in such a situation?
2. What does this recollection suggest about Mrs. Johnson's role and conduct as a political wife?

Research Investigate the Topic

First Ladies Lady Bird Johnson and First Ladies before and after her have used their public position to **advocate** for important causes.

Assignment
Conduct research about the causes either Jacqueline Kennedy or Lady Bird Johnson supported during and after her husband's presidency. Discuss how the First Lady's involvement affected that cause. Share your findings in an **annotated outline**—list your ideas in a logical sequence, and note the evidence, including source information, you will use for each one.

PREPARATION FOR ESSAY

You may use the results of this research project in an essay you will write at the end of this section.

Writing to Sources Argument

In her memoir, Mrs. Johnson indirectly reveals a great deal about herself. Although this is a work of nonfiction, in a sense Mrs. Johnson becomes a character in her own story.

Assignment
Write a **character analysis** of Lady Bird Johnson based on the actions, reactions, observations, and statements she presents in this memoir. Follow these steps:

- Analyze the memoir, taking notes about the details that reveal Mrs. Johnson's character.
- Develop a central claim about Mrs. Johnson and the sort of person you believe that she was.
- Use your notes to provide specific details to support your claim. Be sure to use some direct quotations to illustrate your argument.

ACADEMIC VOCABULARY

Academic terms appear in blue on these pages. If these words are not familiar to you, use a dictionary to find their definitions. Then, use them as you speak and write about the text.

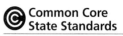

Common Core State Standards

RI.9-10.1, RI.9-10.2, RI.9-10.3, RI.9-10.4, RI.9-10.5; W.9-10.1, W.9-10.1.a, W.9-10.4, W.9-10.7, W.9-10.9.b; SL.9-10.1; L.9-10.4, L.9-10.4.a, L.9-10.6
[For full standards wording, see the chart in the front of this book.]

SHORT STORY

American History

Judith Ortiz Cofer

I once read in a "Ripley's Believe It or Not" column that Paterson, New Jersey, is the place where the Straight and Narrow (streets) intersect. The Puerto Rican tenement known as *El Building* was one block up from Straight. It was, in fact, the corner of Straight and Market; not "at" the corner, but *the* corner. At almost any hour of the day, El Building was like a monstrous jukebox, blasting out *salsas*[1] from open windows as the residents, mostly new immigrants just up from the island, tried to drown out whatever they were currently enduring with loud music. But the day President Kennedy was shot there was a profound silence in El Building; even the abusive tongues of *viragoes*,[2] the cursing of the unemployed, and the screeching of small children had been somehow muted. President Kennedy was a saint to these people. In fact, soon his photograph would be hung alongside the Sacred Heart and over the spiritist altars that many women kept in their apartments. He would become part of the hierarchy of martyrs they prayed to for favors that only one who had died for a cause would understand.

◀ **profound** (prō found′) *adj.* deep; intense

On the day that President Kennedy was shot, my ninth grade class had been out in the fenced playground of Public School Number 13. We had been given "free" exercise time and had been ordered by our P.E. teacher, Mr. DePalma, to "keep moving." That meant that the girls should jump rope and the boys toss basketballs through a hoop at the far end of the yard. He in the meantime would "keep an eye" on us from just inside the building.

It was a cold gray day in Paterson. The kind that warns of early snow. I was miserable, since I had forgotten my gloves, and my knuckles were turning red and raw from the jump rope. I was also taking a lot of abuse from the black girls for not turning the rope hard and fast enough for them.

---

1. ***salsas*** (säl′ səs) songs written in a particular Latin American musical style.
2. ***viragoes*** (vi rä′ gōz) fierce, irritable women who often shout.

"Hey, Skinny Bones, pump it, girl. Ain't you got no energy today?" Gail, the biggest of the black girls who had the other end of the rope, yelled, "Didn't you eat your rice and beans and pork chops for breakfast today?"

The other girls picked up the "pork chops" and made it into a refrain: "pork chop, pork chop, did you eat your pork chop?" They entered the double ropes in pairs and exited without tripping or missing a beat. I felt a burning on my cheeks and then my glasses fogged up so that I could not manage to coordinate the jump rope with Gail. The chill was doing to me what it always did, entering my bones, making me cry, humiliating me. I hated the city, especially in winter. I hated Public School Number 13. I hated my skinny flat-chested body, and I envied the black girls who could jump rope so fast that their legs became a blur. They always seemed to be warm while I froze.

There was only one source of beauty and light for me that school year. The only thing I had anticipated at the start of the semester. That was seeing Eugene. In August, Eugene and his family had moved into the only house on the block that had a yard and trees. I could see his place from my window in El Building. In fact, if I sat on the fire escape I was literally suspended above Eugene's backyard. It was my favorite spot to read my library books in the summer. Until that August the house had been occupied by an old Jewish couple. Over the years I had become part of their family, without their knowing it, of course. I had a view of their kitchen and their backyard, and though I could not hear what they said, I knew when they were arguing, when one of them was sick, and many other things. I knew all this by watching them at mealtimes. I could see their kitchen table, the sink, and the stove. During good times, he sat at the table and read his newspapers while she fixed the meals. If they argued, he would leave and the old woman would sit and stare at nothing for a long time. When one of them was sick, the other would come and get things from the kitchen and carry them out on a tray. The old man had died in June. The last week of school I had not seen him at the table at all. Then one day I saw that there was a crowd in the kitchen. The old woman had finally emerged from the house on the arm of a stocky, middle-aged woman, whom I had seen there a few times before, maybe her daughter. Then a man had carried out suitcases. The house had stood empty for weeks. I had had to resist the temptation to climb down into the yard and water the flowers the old lady had taken such good care of.

By the time Eugene's family moved in, the yard was a tangled mass of weeds. The father had spent several days mowing, and when he finished, from where I sat, I didn't see the red, yellow, and purple clusters that meant flowers to me. I didn't see this family sit down at the kitchen table together. It was just the mother, a red-headed tall woman who wore a white uniform—a nurse's, I guessed it was; the father was gone before I got up in the morning and was never there at dinner time. I only saw him on weekends when they sometimes sat on lawn chairs under the oak tree, each hidden behind a section of the newspaper; and there was Eugene. He was tall and blond, and he wore glasses. I liked him right away because he sat at the kitchen table and read books for hours. That summer, before we had even spoken one word to each other, I kept him company on my fire escape.

There was only one source of beauty and light for me that school year.

Once school started I looked for him in all my classes, but P.S. 13 was a huge, overpopulated place and it took me days and many discreet questions to discover that Eugene was in honors classes for all his subjects; classes that were not open to me because English was not my first language, though I was a straight A student. After much maneuvering, I managed "to run into him" in the hallway where his locker was—on the other side of the building from mine—and in study hall at the library, where he first seemed to notice me but did not speak; and finally, on the way home after school one day when I decided to approach him directly, though my stomach was doing somersaults.

I was ready for rejection, snobbery, the worst. But when I came up to him, practically panting in my nervousness, and blurted out: "You're Eugene. Right?" he smiled, pushed his glasses up on his nose, and nodded. I saw then that he was blushing deeply. Eugene liked me, but he was shy. I did most of the talking that day. He nodded and smiled a lot. In the weeks that followed, we walked home together. He would linger at the corner of El Building for a few minutes then walk down to his two-story house. It was not until

Eugene moved into that house that I noticed that El Building blocked most of the sun, and that the only spot that got a little sunlight during the day was the tiny square of earth the old woman had planted with flowers.

I did not tell Eugene that I could see inside his kitchen from my bedroom. I felt dishonest, but I liked my secret sharing of his evenings, especially now that I knew what he was reading since we chose our books together at the school library.

vigilant ▶ (vij′ ə lənt) *adj.* watchful and alert

One day my mother came into my room as I was sitting on the windowsill staring out. In her abrupt way she said: "Elena, you are acting 'moony.'" *Enamorada*[3] was what she really said, that is—like a girl stupidly infatuated. Since I had turned fourteen . . . my mother had been more vigilant than ever. She acted as if I was going to go crazy or explode or something if she didn't watch me and nag me all the time about being a *señorita*[4] now. She kept talking about virtue, morality, and other subjects that did not interest me in the least. My mother was unhappy in Paterson, but my father had a good job at the blue jeans factory in Passaic and soon, he kept assuring us, we would be moving to our own house there. Every Sunday we drove out to the suburbs of Paterson, Clifton, and Passaic, out to where people mowed grass on Sundays in the summer, and where children made snowmen in the winter from pure white snow, not like the gray slush of Paterson which seemed to fall from the sky in that hue. I had learned to listen to my parents' dreams, which were spoken in Spanish, as fairy tales, like the stories about life in the island paradise of Puerto Rico before I was born. I had been to the island once as a little girl, to grandmother's funeral, and all I remembered was wailing women in black, my mother becoming hysterical and being given a pill that made her sleep two days, and me feeling lost in a crowd of strangers all claiming to be my aunts, uncles, and cousins. I had actually been glad to return to the city. We had not been back there since then, though my parents talked constantly about buying a house on the beach someday, retiring on the island—that was a common topic among the residents of El Building. As for me, I was going to go to college and become a teacher.

But after meeting Eugene I began to think of the present more than of the future. What I wanted now was to enter that house I had watched for so many years. I wanted to see the other rooms where the old people had lived, and where the boy spent his time.

---

3. ***Enamorada*** (ā nä′ mō rä′ dä) Spanish for "enamored; lovesick."
4. ***señorita*** (se′ nyô rē′ tä) *n.* Spanish for "young lady."

Most of all, I wanted to sit at the kitchen table with Eugene like two adults, like the old man and his wife had done, maybe drink some coffee and talk about books. I had started reading *Gone with the Wind*. I was enthralled by it, with the daring and the passion of the beautiful girl living in a mansion, and with her devoted parents and the slaves who did everything for them. I didn't believe such a world had ever really existed, and I wanted to ask Eugene some questions since he and his parents, he had told me, had come up from Georgia, the same place where the novel was set. His father worked for a company that had transferred him to Paterson. His mother was very unhappy, Eugene said, in his beautiful voice that rose and fell over words in a strange, lilting way. The kids at school called him "the hick" and made fun of the way he talked. I knew I was his only friend so far, and I liked that, though I felt sad for him sometimes. "Skinny Bones" and the "Hick" was what they called us at school when we were seen together.

I did not tell Eugene that I could see inside his kitchen from my bedroom.

The day Mr. DePalma came out into the cold and asked us to line up in front of him was the day that President Kennedy was shot. Mr. DePalma, a short, muscular man with slicked-down black hair, was the science teacher, P.E. coach, and disciplinarian at P.S. 13. He was the teacher to whose homeroom you got assigned if you were a troublemaker, and the man called out to break up playground fights, and to escort violently angry teenagers to the office. And Mr. DePalma was the man who called your parents in for "a conference."

That day, he stood in front of two rows of mostly black and Puerto Rican kids, brittle from their efforts to "keep moving" on a November day that was turning bitter cold. Mr. DePalma, to our complete shock, was crying. Not just silent adult tears, but really sobbing. There were a few titters from the back of the line where I stood shivering.

"Listen," Mr. DePalma raised his arms over his head as if he were about to conduct an orchestra. His voice broke, and he covered his face with his hands. His barrel chest was heaving. Someone giggled behind me.

"Listen," he repeated, "something awful has happened." A strange gurgling came from his throat, and he turned around and spat on the cement behind him.

"Gross," someone said, and there was a lot of laughter.

"The president is dead, you idiots. I should have known that wouldn't mean anything to a bunch of losers like you kids. Go home." He was shrieking now. No one moved for a minute or two, but then a big girl let out a "Yeah!" and ran to get her books piled up with the others against the brick wall of the school building. The others followed in a mad scramble to get to their things before somebody caught on. It was still an hour to the dismissal bell.

A little scared, I headed for El Building. There was an eerie feeling on the streets. I looked into Mario's drugstore, a favorite hangout for the high school crowd, but there were only a couple of old Jewish men at the soda bar talking with the short order cook in tones that sounded almost angry, but they were keeping their voices low. Even the traffic on one of the busiest intersections in Paterson—Straight Street and Park Avenue—seemed to be moving slower. There were no horns blasting that day. At El Building, the usual little group of unemployed men were not hanging out on the front stoop making it difficult for women to enter the front door. No music spilled out from open doors in the hallway. When I walked into our apartment, I found my mother sitting in front of the grainy picture of the television set.

She looked up at me with a tear-streaked face and just said: "*Dios mío*,"[5] turning back to the set as if it were pulling at her eyes. I went into my room.

Though I wanted to feel the right thing about President Kennedy's death, I could not fight the feeling of elation that stirred in my chest. Today was the day I was to visit Eugene in his house. He had asked me to come over after school to study for an American history test with him. We had also planned to walk to the public library together. I looked down into his yard. The oak tree was bare of leaves and the ground looked gray with ice. The light through the large kitchen window of his house told me that El Building blocked the sun to such an extent that they had to turn lights on in the middle of the day. I felt ashamed about it. But the white kitchen table with the lamp hanging just above it looked cozy and inviting. I would soon sit there, across from Eugene, and I would tell him about my perch just above his house. Maybe I should.

---

5. ***Dios mío*** (dē´ ōs mē´ ō) Spanish for "My God!"

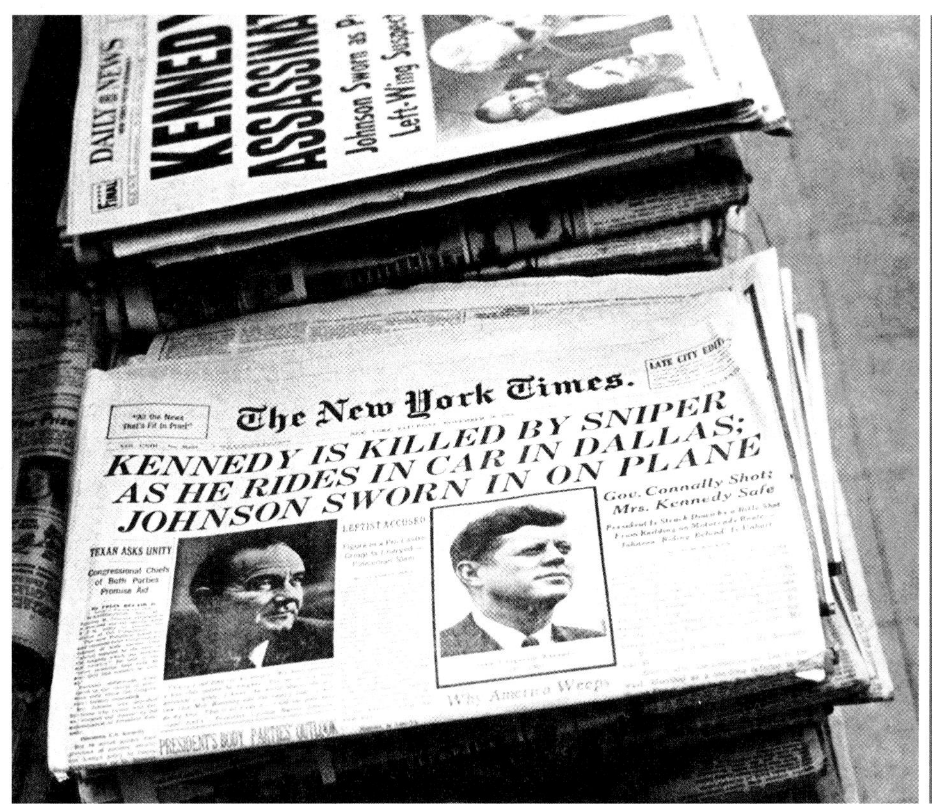

"*Hija*, the president has been killed. We must show respect. He was a great man."

In the next thirty minutes I changed clothes, put on a little pink lipstick, and got my books together. Then I went in to tell my mother that I was going to a friend's house to study. I did not expect her reaction.

"You are going out *today?* " The way she said "today" sounded as if a storm warning had been issued. It was said in utter disbelief. Before I could answer, she came toward me and held my elbows as I clutched my books.

"*Hija*,[6] the president has been killed. We must show respect. He was a great man. Come to church with me tonight."

She tried to embrace me, but my books were in the way. My first impulse was to comfort her, she seemed so distraught, but I had to meet Eugene in fifteen minutes.

"I have a test to study for, Mama. I will be home by eight."

"You are forgetting who you are, *Niña*.[7] I have seen you staring down at that boy's house. You are heading for humiliation and pain." My mother said this in Spanish and in a resigned tone that surprised me, as if she had no intention of stopping me from "heading for

---

6. ***Hija*** (ē´ hä) Spanish for "daughter."
7. ***Niña*** (nē´ nyä) Spanish for "child."

humiliation and pain." I started for the door. She sat in front of the TV holding a white handkerchief to her face.

I walked out to the street and around the chain-link fence that separated El Building from Eugene's house. The yard was neatly edged around the little walk that led to the door. It always amazed me how Paterson, the inner core of the city, had no apparent logic to its architecture. Small, neat, single residences like this one could be found right next to huge, **dilapidated** apartment buildings like El Building. My guess was that the little houses had been there first, then the immigrants had come in droves, and the monstrosities had been raised for them—the Italians, the Irish, the Jews, and now us, the Puerto Ricans and the blacks. The door was painted a deep green: *verde*, the color of hope, I had heard my mother say it: *Verde-Esperanza.*[8]

dilapidated ▶ (də lap´ ə dāt´ əd) *adj.* broken down

I knocked softly. A few suspenseful moments later the door opened just a crack. The red, swollen face of a woman appeared. She had a halo of red hair floating over a delicate ivory face—the face of a doll—with freckles on the nose. Her smudged eye make-up made her look unreal to me, like a mannequin seen through a warped store window.

"What do you want?" Her voice was tiny and sweet-sounding, like a little girl's, but her tone was not friendly.

"I'm Eugene's friend. He asked me over. To study." I thrust out my books, a silly gesture that embarrassed me almost immediately.

"You live there?" She pointed up to El Building, which looked particularly ugly, like a gray prison with its many dirty windows and rusty fire escapes. The woman had stepped halfway out and I could see that she wore a white nurse's uniform with "St. Joseph's Hospital" on the name tag.

"Yes. I do."

She looked intently at me for a couple of heartbeats, then said as if to herself, "I don't know how you people do it." Then directly to me: "Listen. Honey. Eugene doesn't want to study with you. He is a smart boy. Doesn't need help. You understand me. I am truly sorry if he told you you could come over. He cannot study with you. It's nothing personal. You understand? We won't be in this place much longer, no need for him to get close to people—it'll just make it harder for him later. Run back home now."

I couldn't move. I just stood there in shock at hearing these things said to me in such a honey-drenched voice. I had never heard an accent like hers, except for Eugene's softer version. It was as if she were singing me a little song.

---

8. ***Verde-Esperanza*** (ver´ dā es pā rän´ zä) Spanish for "green-hope."

"What's wrong? Didn't you hear what I said?" She seemed very angry, and I finally snapped out of my trance. I turned away from the green door, and heard her close it gently.

Our apartment was empty when I got home. My mother was in someone else's kitchen, seeking the solace she needed. Father would come in from his late shift at midnight. I would hear them talking softly in the kitchen for hours that night. They would not discuss their dreams for the future, or life in Puerto Rico, as they often did; that night they would talk sadly about the young widow and her two children, as if they were family. For the next few days, we would observe *luto*[9] in our apartment; that is, we would practice restraint and silence—no loud music or laughter. Some of the women of El Building would wear black for weeks.

That night, I lay in my bed trying to feel the right thing for our dead president. But the tears that came up from a deep source inside me were strictly for me. When my mother came to the door, I pretended to be sleeping. Sometime during the night, I saw from my bed the streetlight come on. It had a pink halo around it. I went to my window and pressed my face to the cool glass. Looking up at the light I could see the white snow falling like a lace veil over its face. I did not look down to see it turning gray as it touched the ground below.

---

9. *luto* (lo͞o´ tō) Spanish for "mourning."

ABOUT THE AUTHOR

Judith Ortiz Cofer (b. 1952)

Judith Ortiz Cofer spent her childhood in two different cultures. Born in Puerto Rico, she moved with her parents to Paterson, New Jersey, when she was four years old. She grew up mostly in Paterson, but she also spent time in Puerto Rico with her *abuela* (grandmother).

It was from her grandmother that Ortiz Cofer learned the art of storytelling. "When my *abuela* sat us down to tell a story," she says, "we learned something from it, even though we always laughed. That was her way of teaching." In her own work, Ortiz Cofer teaches readers about the richness and difficulty of coming of age in two cultures at once.

Close Reading Activities

READ

Comprehension

Reread all or part of the story to help you answer the following questions.

1. Who is Eugene and how does Elena first become aware of him?
2. How does Mr. DePalma's reaction to news of the assassination differ from the students' reactions?
3. What reason does Eugene's mother give Elena for sending her away?

Research: Clarify Details This story may include references that are unfamiliar to you. Choose at least one unfamiliar detail, and briefly research it. Then, explain how the information you learned from research sheds light on an aspect of the story.

Summarize Write an objective summary of the story. Remember that an objective summary does not include statements of opinion or evaluation.

Language Study

Selection Vocabulary The following passages appear in "American History." Define each boldface word. Then, use the word in a sentence of your own.

- there was a **profound** silence in El Building
- my mother had been more **vigilant** than ever.
- residences like this one could be found right next to huge, **dilapidated** apartment buildings

Literary Analysis

Reread the identified passage. Then, respond to the questions that follow.

Focus Passage *(p. 454)*

A little scared . . . I went into my room.

Key Ideas and Details

1. **(a) Contrast:** How does Elena's neighborhood differ from its usual state? **(b) Interpret:** What does this passage suggest about the mood of the nation as a whole? Explain.

Craft and Structure

2. **(a) Analyze:** Cite details the author uses to elaborate on Elena's observation that there was "an eerie feeling on the streets." **(b) Analyze:** What quality is common to all of these details?
3. **(a)** How does Elena describe her mother's reaction to the TV set? **(b) Interpret:** How does this simile clarify the effect the news is having on Elena's mother? **(c) Analyze:** In what ways does the simile contribute to the picture the author is painting of the world's reaction to the assassination?

Integration of Knowledge and Ideas

4. **Connect:** Based on this passage and what you know about the rest of the story, explain the significance of the story's title.

Historical Context

The **historical context** of a work is the collection of events, beliefs, technologies, and customs common to people in the time and place of a story's setting. Reread the story, and take notes on ways in which the historical context shapes the plot.

1. Explain how these story elements reflect social issues facing America in the 1960s: **a.** The description of Elena's neighborhood; **b.** Eugene's mother's reaction to Elena.
2. **The Kennedy Assassination:** How does the assassination both add to and minimize the importance of Elena's tale? Explain.

DISCUSS • RESEARCH • WRITE

From Text to Topic **One-on-One Discussion**

Discuss the following passage with a partner. **Pose** and respond to one another's questions about the passage, and connect your comments to broader ideas about the story and its setting. Cite examples from the text as support.

> I would hear them talking softly in the kitchen for hours that night. They would not discuss their dreams for the future, or life in Puerto Rico, as they often did; that night they would talk sadly about the young widow and her two children, as if they were family. For the next few days, we would observe *luto* in our apartment; that is, we would practice restraint and silence—no loud music or laughter. Some of the women of El Building would wear black for weeks.

QUESTIONS FOR DISCUSSION

1. What does this passage reveal about the effect of the president's death on Elena's community?
2. Based on this passage, what can you infer about the reactions most Americans had to the assassination?

Research **Investigate the Topic**

Media and the Kennedy Assassination In "American History," the narrator describes how news of President Kennedy's assassination spreads quickly through her community. She refers to specific forms of media, including television, that people access to get information.

Assignment

Research the role the media played in **disseminating** information about the Kennedy assassination and providing a **forum** for national mourning. Consult archival materials, such as footage of TV newscasts and copies of newspapers. Share your findings in a **research report**.

PREPARATION FOR ESSAY

You may use the results of this research project in an essay you will write at the end of this section.

ACADEMIC VOCABULARY

Academic terms appear in blue on these pages. If these words are not familiar to you, use a dictionary to find their definitions. Then, use them as you speak and write about the text.

Writing to Sources **Informative Text**

In "American History," Elena develops an emotional connection to the people who live in the house next door. She also describes how members of her community identify with the Kennedy family.

Assignment

Write an **analytical essay** in which you compare and contrast Elena's feelings of connection to the people in the house next door with those that her family and neighbors feel for the presidential family. Follow these steps:

- Review the story and take notes about Elena's feelings for her neighbors and her community's feelings for the presidential family.
- Clearly state your thesis and cite examples from the story, including direct quotations, to develop and support your ideas.

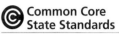

Common Core State Standards

RL.9-10.1, RL.9-10.2, RL.9-10.3, RL.9-10.4; W.9-10.2, W.9-10.4, W.9-10.7, W.9-10.9; SL.9-10.1, SL.9-10.1.c, SL.9-10.2; L.9-10.4, L.9-10.5.a

[For full standards wording, see the chart in the front of this book.]

Address Before a Joint Session of the Congress

NOVEMBER 27, 1963

Lyndon Baines Johnson

Mr. Speaker, Mr. President, Members of the House, Members of the Senate, my fellow Americans:

All I have I would have given gladly not to be standing here today.

The greatest leader of our time has been struck down by the foulest deed of our time. Today John Fitzgerald Kennedy lives on in the immortal words and works that he left behind. He lives on in the mind and memories of mankind. He lives on in the hearts of his countrymen.

No words are sad enough to express our sense of loss. No words are strong enough to express our determination to continue the forward thrust of America that he began.

The dream of conquering the vastness of space—the dream of partnership across the Atlantic—and across the Pacific as well—the dream of a Peace Corps[1] in less developed nations—the dream of education for all of our children—the dream of jobs for all who seek them and need them—the dream of care for our elderly—the dream of an all-out attack on mental illness—and above all, the dream of equal rights for all Americans, whatever their race or color—these and other American dreams have been vitalized by his drive and by his dedication.

And now the ideas and the ideals which he so nobly represented must and will be translated into effective action.

Under John Kennedy's leadership, this Nation has demonstrated that it has the courage to seek peace, and it has the fortitude to risk war. We have proved that we are a good and reliable friend to those who seek peace and freedom. We have shown that we can also be a formidable foe to those who reject the path of peace and those who seek to impose upon us or our allies the yoke of tyranny.

This Nation will keep its commitments from South Viet-Nam to West Berlin. We will be unceasing in the search for peace; resourceful in our pursuit of areas of agreement even with those with whom we differ; and generous and loyal to those who join with us in common cause.

◀ **fortitude** (fôrt´ə to͞od´) *n.* strength of mind that lets one encounter danger or bear pain or adversity with courage

◀ **formidable** (fôr´mə də bəl) *adj.* causing fear or dread

1. **Peace Corps** (pēs kôr) a government agency of volunteers established to assist other countries in development efforts.

In this age when there can be no losers in peace and no victors in war, we must recognize the obligation to match national strength with national restraint. We must be prepared at one and the same time for both the confrontation of power and the limitation of power. We must be ready to defend the national interest and to negotiate the common interest. This is the path that we shall continue to pursue. Those who test our courage will find it strong, and those who seek our friendship will find it honorable. We will demonstrate anew that the strong can be just in the use of strength; and the just can be strong in the defense of justice.

And let all know we will extend no special privilege and impose no persecution. We will carry on the fight against poverty and misery, and disease and ignorance, in other lands and in our own.

We will serve all the Nation, not one section or one sector, or one group, but all Americans. These are the United States—a united people with a united purpose.

Our American unity does not depend upon unanimity. We have differences; but now, as in the past, we can derive from those differences strength, not weakness, wisdom, not despair. Both as a people and a government, we can unite upon a program, a program which is wise and just, enlightened and constructive.

For 32 years Capitol Hill has been my home. I have shared many moments of pride with you, pride in the ability of the Congress of the United States to act, to meet any crisis, to distill from our differences strong programs of national action.

An assassin's bullet has thrust upon me the awesome burden of the Presidency. I am here today to say I need your help; I cannot bear this burden alone. I need the help of all Americans, and all America. This Nation has experienced a profound shock, and in this critical moment, it is our duty, yours and mine, as the Government of the United States, to do away with uncertainty and doubt and delay, and to show that we are capable of decisive action; that from the brutal loss of our leader we will derive not weakness, but strength; that we can and will act and act now.

From this chamber of representative government, let all the world know and none misunderstand that I rededicate this Government to the unswerving support of the United Nations, to the honorable and determined execution of our commitments to our allies, to the maintenance of military strength second to none, to the defense of the strength and the stability of the dollar, to the expansion of our foreign trade, to the reinforcement of our programs of mutual assistance and cooperation in Asia and Africa, and to our Alliance for Progress[2] in this hemisphere.

---

2. **Alliance for Progress** an economic partnership between the U.S. and twenty-two Latin American countries.

▲ President Johnson addresses both houses of Congress five days after President Kennedy's assassination.

On the 20th day of January, in 1961, John F. Kennedy told his countrymen that our national work would not be finished "in the first thousand days, nor in the life of this administration, nor even perhaps in our lifetime on this planet. But," he said, "let us begin."

Today, in this moment of new resolve, I would say to all my fellow Americans, let us continue.

This is our challenge—not to hesitate, not to pause, not to turn about and linger over this evil moment, but to continue on our course so that we may fulfill the destiny that history has set for us. Our most immediate tasks are here on this Hill.

First, no memorial oration or eulogy could more eloquently honor President Kennedy's memory than the earliest possible passage of the civil rights bill for which he fought so long. We have talked long enough in this country about equal rights. We have talked for one hundred years or more. It is time now to write the next chapter, and to write it in the books of law.

◀ **eulogy** (yo͞o′lə jē) *n.* speech in honor of someone who has died

I urge you again, as I did in 1957 and again in 1960, to enact a civil rights law so that we can move forward to eliminate from this Nation every trace of discrimination and oppression that is based upon race or color. There could be no greater source of strength to this Nation both at home and abroad.

And second, no act of ours could more fittingly continue the work of President Kennedy than the early passage of the tax bill for which he fought all this long year. This is a bill designed to increase our national income and Federal revenues, and to provide insurance against recession. That bill, if passed without delay, means more security for those now working, more jobs for those now without them, and more incentive for our economy.

In short, this is no time for delay. It is a time for action—strong, forward-looking action on the pending education bills to help bring the light of learning to every home and hamlet[3] in America—strong, forward-looking action on youth employment opportunities; strong, forward-looking action on the pending foreign aid bill, making clear that we are not forfeiting our responsibilities to this hemisphere or to the world, nor erasing Executive flexibility in the conduct of our foreign affairs—and strong, prompt, and forward-looking action on the remaining appropriation bills.

We meet in grief, but let us also meet in renewed dedication and renewed vigor.

In this new spirit of action, the Congress can expect the full cooperation and support of the executive branch. And in particular, I pledge that the expenditures of your Government will be administered with the utmost thrift and frugality. I will insist that the Government get a dollar's value for a dollar spent. The Government will set an example of prudence and economy. This does not mean that we will not meet our unfilled needs or that we will not honor our commitments. We will do both.

As one who has long served in both Houses of the Congress, I firmly believe in the independence and the integrity of the legislative branch. And I promise you that I shall always respect this. It is deep in the marrow of my bones. With equal firmness, I believe in the capacity and I believe in the ability of the Congress, despite the divisions of opinions which characterize our Nation, to act—to act wisely, to act vigorously, to act speedily when the need arises.

The need is here. The need is now. I ask your help.

We meet in grief, but let us also meet in renewed dedication and renewed vigor. Let us meet in action, in tolerance, and in mutual understanding. John Kennedy's death commands what his life conveyed—that America must move forward. The time has come for Americans of all races and creeds and political beliefs to

3. **hamlet** (ham′lit) a small village.

understand and to respect one another. So let us put an end to the teaching and the preaching of hate and evil and violence. Let us turn away from the fanatics of the far left and the far right, from the apostles of bitterness and bigotry, from those defiant of law, and those who pour venom into our Nation's bloodstream.

I profoundly hope that the tragedy and the torment of these terrible days will bind us together in new fellowship, making us one people in our hour of sorrow. So let us here highly resolve that John Fitzgerald Kennedy did not live—or die—in vain. And on this Thanksgiving eve, as we gather together to ask the Lord's blessing, and give Him our thanks, let us unite in those familiar and cherished words:

America, America,
God shed His grace on thee,
And crown thy good
With brotherhood
From sea to shining sea.

ABOUT THE AUTHOR

Lyndon Baines Johnson

(1908-1973)

Lyndon Baines Johnson was the 36th president of the United States (1963–1969). Johnson started his political career in the U.S. House of Representatives in 1937 and became a U.S. Senator in 1949. While in Congress, Johnson earned a reputation for negotiating and brokering compromises.

Johnson was elected John F. Kennedy's vice president in 1960 and became president in 1963 when President Kennedy was assassinated. On November 27, 1963, five days after the assassination, Johnson gave a speech to Congress to urge them to pass Kennedy's legislative agenda, especially a civil rights bill that had been stalled in committee. The following February, the House passed a stronger version of the bill than even Kennedy himself had proposed. The Civil Rights Act of 1964, the most comprehensive civil rights legislation in the twentieth century, passed the Senate in June and Johnson signed it into law. Johnson's presidency is also known for a series of programs, collectively called the Great Society, which were aimed at fighting poverty and injustice. These programs include the Job Corps, Head Start, Medicare, Medicaid, and the Voting Rights Act of 1965. Johnson lost popularity due to his escalation of American military involvement in the Vietnam war and did not seek a second full term in office.

Close Reading Activities

READ

Comprehension

Reread all or part of the text to help you answer the following questions.

1. What "ideas and ideals" does Johnson believe President Kennedy represented?
2. What does Johnson identify as "our challenge"?
3. On what issue does the president say it is "time now to write the next chapter"?

Research: Clarify Details This speech may include references that are unfamiliar to you. Choose at least one unfamiliar detail, and briefly research it. Then, explain how the information you learned from research sheds light on an aspect of the speech.

Summarize Write an objective summary of the speech. Remember that an objective summary is free from opinion and evaluation.

Language Study

Selection Vocabulary The phrases at right appear in the speech. Identify a synonym for each boldface word. Then, use the word in a sentence of your own.

- **fortitude** to risk war
- be a **formidable** foe
- memorial oration or **eulogy**

Literary Analysis

Reread the identified passage. Then, respond to the questions that follow.

Focus Passage *(p. 461)*

The dream of conquering . . . the yoke of tyranny.

Key Ideas and Details

1. **(a)** Whose dreams does Johnson describe? **(b) Interpret:** What does Johnson want to do with these dreams?

Craft and Structure

2. **(a) Classify:** Cite at least two examples of charged, or emotional, language in the passage. **(b) Evaluate:** For each choice, explain which emotions the word most likely **stirs** in listeners.
3. **(a) Analyze:** In the third paragraph, identify two examples of antithesis, or opposing ideas placed side by side. **(b) Evaluate:** How does this device add to the power of Johnson's ideas?

Integration of Knowledge and Ideas

4. **Interpret:** How does this passage lay a foundation for the central message President Johnson wants to share with the nation and the world?

Parallelism

Parallelism is a rhetorical device in which related ideas are repeated using the same grammatical pattern. Reread the speech, and take notes on Johnson's use of parallelism.

1. **(a)** Cite two examples of parallelism in the speech. **(b)** For each, explain the grammatical pattern that is repeated. **(c)** What ideas and emotions does each example emphasize? Explain.
2. **The Kennedy Assassination:** In the fourth paragraph, how does Johnson use parallelism to convey Kennedy's vision for America in a **concise** and powerful way? Explain.

DISCUSS • RESEARCH • WRITE

From Text to Topic **Partner Discussion**

Discuss the passage below with a partner. Take notes, contribute your own ideas, and support them with textual details.

> John Kennedy's death commands what his life conveyed—that America must move forward. The time has come for Americans of all races and creeds and political beliefs to understand and to respect one another. So let us put an end to the teaching and the preaching of hate and evil and violence.

QUESTIONS FOR DISCUSSION

1. What lesson does Johnson take from Kennedy's death?
2. Is President Johnson's response to the Kennedy assassination appropriate? Why or why not?

Research **Investigate the Topic**

Presidential Speeches Speeches are a key means of communication between presidents and the American people.

Assignment
Conduct research to locate another speech by President Johnson or one by President Kennedy, and find out how it was received by audiences at the time. Write an outline of your findings, and share your work in a **group discussion** with classmates.

PREPARATION FOR ESSAY

You may use the results of this research project in an essay you will write at the end of this section.

Writing to Sources **Narrative**

In his speech to Congress, President Johnson makes it clear to the American people that, despite the tragic loss of their president, the country would pursue the vision Kennedy had **articulated**.

Assignment
Write a **historical narrative** in which your main character responds to hearing President Johnson's speech to Congress. Follow these steps:

- Know your character. Decide his or her age, appearance, occupation, and personality traits. Describe how he or she was affected by Kennedy's death.
- Write in the voice of your character, which may be different from your own.
- Choose a conflict that drives the plot of your story. Weave in details related to the Kennedy assassination and Johnson's speech.
- Use precise words and phrases, telling details, and sensory language to convey a vivid picture of the characters, events, and settings.

ACADEMIC VOCABULARY

Academic terms appear in blue on these pages. If these words are not familiar to you, use a dictionary to find their definitions. Then, use them as you speak and write about the text.

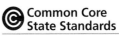

Common Core State Standards

RI.9-10.1, RI.9-10.2, RI.9-10.4, RI.9-10.5, RI.9-10.6, RI.9-10.9; W.9-10.3, W.9-10.3.a–b, W.9-10.3.d, W.9-10.4, W.9-10.7; SL.9-10.1, SL.9-10.3, SL.9-10.4; L.9-10.4

[For full standards wording, see the chart in the front of this book.]

Visual Timeline

Images of a Tragedy

President and Mrs. Kennedy's visit to Dallas, Texas, on November 22, 1963, was a highly photographed event that turned unexpectedly tragic. Follow these images that depict the events of that day to gain a new perspective on the Kennedy assassination.

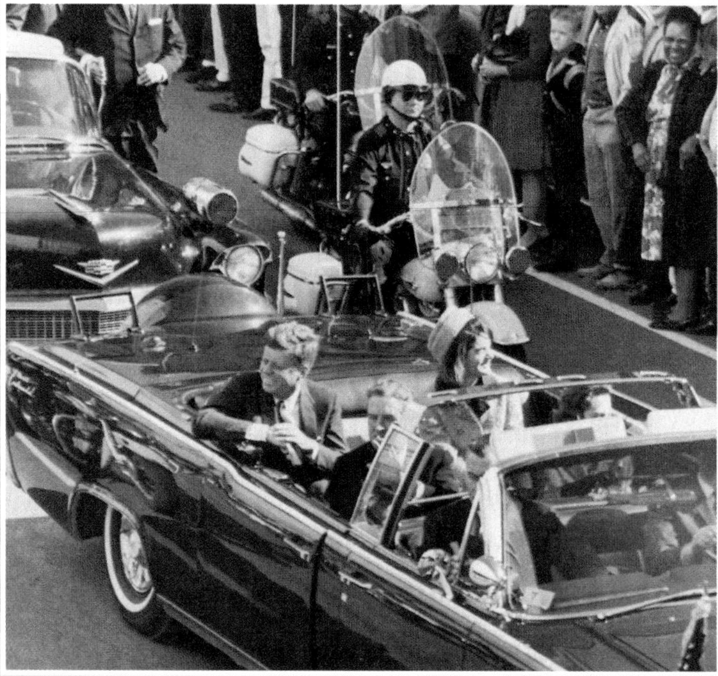

November 22, 1963 ▶

The president and first lady arrive in Dallas, Texas, for a strategic political visit.

President and Mrs. Kennedy in the presidential motorcade en route to Dealey Plaza; they ride with John and Nellie Connally, the governor and first lady of Texas.

Moments after shots are fired, spectators drop to the ground.

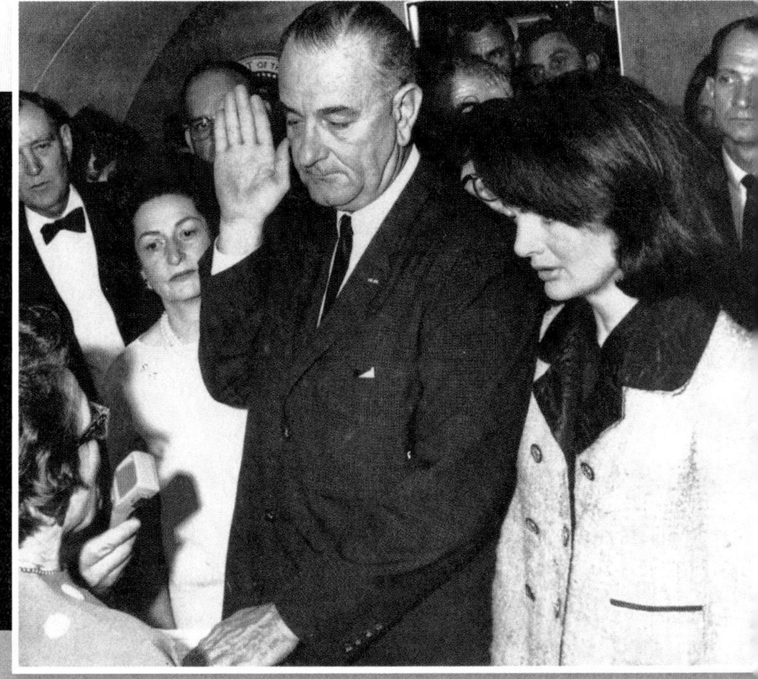

On the day of the shooting, Lyndon Johnson is sworn in as president. Lady Bird Johnson is on his right and Mrs. Kennedy is on his left.

November 25, 1963

Upon arrival in Washington, D.C., President Kennedy's coffin is removed from Air Force One.

Edward (left) and Robert Kennedy (right), the president's brothers, stand with Jacqueline and the two Kennedy children, Caroline and John, during the state funeral in Washington, D.C. John, Jr., salutes his father's coffin as it passes.

READ • RESEARCH • WRITE

Critical Analysis

Look closely at the photographs both individually and in sequence. Then, answer the following questions.

Key Ideas and Details

1. **(a)** What is the mood of the first photograph? **(b)** Which details create that mood?
2. **(a) Connect:** Based on your reading of Lady Bird Johnson's memoir, where was the photograph of Lyndon Johnson taking the oath of office shot? **(b) Distinguish:** What other details in this photo connect to texts you have read in this section? Explain.
3. **Connect:** Which line or lines from "Instead of an Elegy" by G. S. Fraser would be a good **caption** for the image from November 25th? Explain.

Craft and Structure

4. **Draw Conclusions:** **Consider** the image of John F. Kennedy, Jr., saluting during his father's funeral procession. Which details in that image make it so powerful and poignant? Explain.

Integration of Knowledge and Ideas

5. **(a) Compare and Contrast:** How does Mrs. Kennedy's appearance change from photograph to photograph? **(b) Analyze:** In what ways do these changes capture the enormity of the events she is experiencing? Explain, citing details from the photographs in your response.

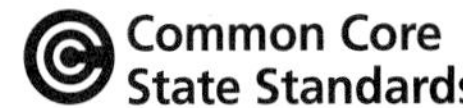
Common Core State Standards

RI.9-10.7; W.9-10.2, W.9-10.2.b, W.9-10.4, W.9-10.7
[For full standards wording, see the chart in the front of this book.]

ACADEMIC VOCABULARY

Academic terms appear in blue on this page. If these words are not familiar to you, use a dictionary to find their definitions. Then, use them as you speak and write about the text.

Research **Investigate the Topic**

Most people who were alive when President Kennedy was shot remember precisely where they were and what they were doing when they heard the news. Conduct interviews with people in your family or community who remember the assassination and record their recollections, or locate archival interviews with people recounting their experiences. Prepare an **oral history** and share it with the class.

PREPARATION FOR ESSAY

You may use the results of this research project in an essay you will write at the end of this section.

Writing to Sources **Informative Text**

Pictures like those in this sequence may help **crystallize** the details of events. Write a **magazine article** that could be illustrated by the pictures from the timeline. Keep your audience in mind, and structure your article so that it is informative to a reader who does not know about these events.

Assessment: Synthesis

Speaking and Listening: Group Discussion

The Kennedy Assassination and Communication The texts in this section vary in genre, length, style, and perspective. All of them, however, transform grief over a national tragedy into powerful messages of honor, history, and aspiration. In doing so, they raise questions about the transformative power of communication and relate directly to the Big Question addressed in this unit: **How does communication change us?**

▲ Refer to the selections you read in Part 3 as you complete the activities on this assessment.

Assignment

Conduct discussions. With a small group of classmates, conduct a discussion about the Kennedy Assassination and communication. Refer to the texts in this section, other texts you have read, research you have done, and your personal experience and knowledge to support your ideas. Begin your discussion by addressing the following questions:

- What forms of communication did people use to learn of the Kennedy assassination?
- Can communication in the wake of such a tragedy be negative?
- What are the benefits of communication after tragic events?
- Are those who communicate information after a tragedy affected differently from those who receive the information?

Summarize and present your ideas. After you have fully explored the topic, summarize your discussion and present your findings to the class as a whole.

Criteria for Success

✓ **Sets goals and boundaries**
As a group, determine how each member should prepare for the discussion by reading, viewing, or organizing notes. Then, decide upon the main goals of the discussion and set a time frame—a half hour or less—for reaching those goals. Appoint a leader to keep the discussion organized.

✓ **Conducts a focused discussion**
All group members should focus exclusively on the questions at hand. If other topics come up, agree to return to them at another time.

✓ **Involves all participants**
After making a point, invite others to contribute, especially those who have not already spoken. Respond to one another's thoughts with respect.

✓ **Follows the rules for collegial discussion**
Listen carefully and thoughtfully to one another's opinions. Build ideas from others' viewpoints, and support opinions with sound reasoning and evidence.

USE NEW VOCABULARY

As you speak and share ideas, work to use the vocabulary words you have learned in this unit. The more you use new words, the more you will "own" them.

Writing: **Narrative**

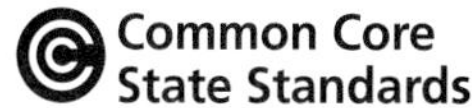

W.9-10.3.a–e; SL.9-10.1.a–d
[For full standards wording, see the chart in the front of this book.]

The Kennedy Assassination and Communication The selections in this section show varying responses to the same terrible event. In the wake of a national tragedy, we are all affected, but perhaps in different ways.

> **Assignment**
> Write a **memoir** about a newsworthy event that occurred in your community or elsewhere in the country and affected you. Include details about how you learned about the event, how you and others responded, how you felt at the time, and how you view those experiences in hindsight. Draw parallels between your reactions and those of others to the texts you have read in this section and the research you have conducted.

Criteria for Success

Purpose/Focus

✓ **Develops connections among texts, experiences, and larger ideas**
Relate your ideas to larger concepts by making connections between your experience and one or more of the texts in this section.

✓ **Expresses insights**
Reflect on the event and the ways in which your communications and those of others contributed to your experience.

Organization

✓ **Structures ideas logically**
Introduce the event and briefly explain it. Then, describe your perceptions of it.

✓ **Sequence events logically**
Describe events in an order that will help readers understand both what happened and how people reacted.

Development of Ideas/Elaboration

✓ **Supports insights**
Include sensory details, factual information, and textual details that clarify your ideas and explain your insights.

✓ **Engages audience**
Use dialogue, description, and carefully chosen language to maintain your audience's interest.

Language

✓ **Uses literary devices effectively**
Use figurative language, imagery, and rhetorical devices to express ideas and convey emotion.

Conventions

✓ **Contains no errors**
Check your work to eliminate errors in grammar, spelling, and punctuation.

WRITE TO EXPLORE

Writing is a way to explore thoughts, feelings, and opinions. As you examine your subject, new ideas may occur to you. Including these and explaining how you arrived at them will improve your writing.

Writing to Sources: **Argument**

The Kennedy Assassination and Communication The texts in this section present a range of perspectives on a single subject: the assassination of President Kennedy. All relate to the ways in which different people responded to the tragedy. They raise questions, such as the following, about the role of communications—particularly those that occur in the media—in a national conversation about tragedy:

- In what ways can media coverage of a national tragedy be helpful?
- Are there negative aspects to media coverage of national tragedies?
- What types of information should the media focus on after a national tragedy? What, if anything, should be avoided?
- How does media coverage of a tragic event affect the perceptions of generations that follow?

Focus on the question that intrigues you the most, and then complete the following assignment.

Assignment

Write an **argumentative essay** in which you state and defend a claim about media coverage of a national tragedy such as the Kennedy assassination. Build evidence for your claim by using details from at least two of the selections as well as from research you have conducted in this section.

Prewriting and Planning

Find support. Examine the texts in the section to determine which ones provide strong support for your ideas about media coverage during a national tragedy.

Gather evidence. Review the selections and take notes about details that relate to your topic. Use a chart like the one shown to organize your materials. Then, use these notes to frame your argument and identify key supporting details.

Focus Question: In what ways can media coverage of a national tragedy be helpful?

Selection	Evidence	Conclusions
Visual Timeline	Photographs provided real-time evidence of the events.	The photos allowed people all over the world to have a common understanding of the events.
Address Before a Joint Session of the Congress	Johnson spoke of honoring President Kennedy's memory through action.	Broadcast over TV, the speech gave people a united, common purpose.
Example Claim: Media coverage can help people understand events and mourn as a community.		

INCORPORATE RESEARCH

The research you have done in this section may provide support for your position. Review the notes you took, and incorporate any relevant facts or details into your essay.

Drafting

Sequence your ideas and evidence. Introduce your main claim or thesis early in your essay, and then explain your supporting ideas in a logical order. Restate your main idea in your conclusion.

Support your claims. Choose relevant and sufficient facts that pertain to your argument. Use textual details, quotations, and other information and examples to develop your claim. Include support from the research you have conducted in this section.

Anticipate counterclaims. Your argument will be more effective if you demonstrate that you have carefully considered a wide range of viewpoints. As you draft your essay, introduce opposing claims and consider the evidence that supports them. Then, answer those opposing views by showing how your position is stronger. For example, you might prove that your claim is more thorough, more accurate, or more useful in explaining contradictions.

Create a cohesive structure. Set out your claim in your introduction. Then, lead readers through a logical progression of ideas. End with a strong conclusion that restates your claim.

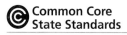

W.9–10.1.a–e, W.9-10.4, W.9-10.5, W.9-10.9

[For full standards wording, see the chart in the front of this book.]

CITE RESEARCH CORRECTLY

Even if you do not use their exact words, it is important to credit authors when using their ideas. Mention the author's name in connection with your paraphrase. Then, include the source in your Works Cited list.

Revising and Editing

Evaluate ideas. If your ideas seem unclear or disjointed, reexamine your claim. You should be able to express a strong claim simply and clearly.

Evaluate style. Check that you have expressed ideas accurately, concisely, and with appropriate style and tone.

Self-Evaluation Rubric

Use the following criteria to evaluate the effectiveness of your essay.

Criteria	Rating Scale
PURPOSE/FOCUS Introduces a precise claim and distinguishes the claim from opposing claims; provides a concluding section that follows from and supports the argument presented	*not very .... very* 1 2 3 4
ORGANIZATION Establishes a logical organization; uses words, phrases, and clauses to link the major sections of the text, create cohesion, and clarify relationships between ideas and evidence	1 2 3 4
DEVELOPMENT OF IDEAS/ELABORATION Develops the claim and counterclaims fairly, supplying evidence for each while pointing out the strengths and limitations of both	1 2 3 4
LANGUAGE Establishes and maintains a formal style and an objective tone	1 2 3 4
CONVENTIONS Attends to the norms and conventions of the discipline	1 2 3 4

Independent Reading

Titles for Extended Reading

In this unit, you have read texts in a variety of genres. Continue to read on your own. Select works that you enjoy, but challenge yourself to explore new authors and works of increasing depth and complexity. The titles suggested below will help you get started.

INFORMATIONAL TEXT

House of Houses
by Pat Mora
Beacon Press, 1997

In this **memoir,** five generations of Pat Mora's Mexican American family come alive to retell their stories and weave in and out of one another's lives. In the retelling, history is shared and their understanding of one another is changed.

The Hot Zone: A Terrifying True Story
by Richard Preston **EXEMPLAR TEXT**

This **nonfiction thriller** dramatizes a real-life outbreak of the Ebola virus in an animal laboratory located in a Washington, D.C., suburb. Known for its chilling suspense, this "bio-thriller" was a bestseller when it first appeared and has fascinated readers ever since.

Rosa Parks: My Story
by Rosa Parks with Jim Haskins

In this **autobiography,** Rosa Parks tells the story of how her refusal to give up a bus seat to a white man in 1955 inspired a year of boycotts, lawsuits, and, ultimately, a new future for civil rights in America.

How to Read a Poem and Fall in Love with Poetry
by Edward Hirsch

In this collection of **essays,** celebrated poet Hirsch explores the elements that make poetry so powerful. He offers examples of many different types of poetry from a variety of times and places. With passion, clarity, and verve, he shows why poetry is really not so difficult and how it can be nothing short of magical.

LITERATURE

The Collected Poems of Emily Dickinson **EXEMPLAR TEXT**

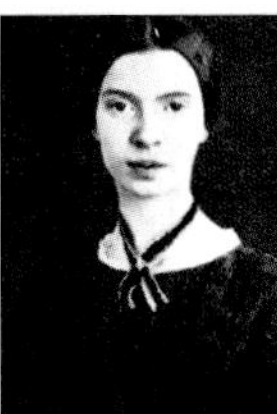

In contrast to her current reputation as an important poet, Emily Dickinson was little known during her lifetime. Shy, Dickinson spent most of her time at home, reading and writing. In one of the best-known **poems** in this collection, the now-famous recluse wrote: "I'm nobody! Who are you?"

Trouble the Water: 250 Years of African-American Poetry
Edited by Jerry W. Ward, Jr. **EXEMPLAR TEXT**

African American heritage comes alive in this collection of **poems** covering 300 years. From the spirituals sung in the days of slavery to vibrant poems from the 1990s, this volume spans many aspects of the African American experience. This collection contains poems by Countee Cullen and Alice Walker.

The Book Thief
by Markus Zusak **EXEMPLAR TEXT**

Death is the narrator of this **novel** about a nine-year-old girl who goes to live in a tough German neighborhood in the late 1930s. The fast-paced action of this book complements the poetic language.

ONLINE TEXT SET

POETRY
The Writer Richard Wilbur

SHORT STORY
***from* I Stand Here Ironing** Tillie Olsen

PERSUASIVE ESSAY
Carry Your Own Skis Lian Dolan

Preparing to Read Complex Texts

Attentive Reading As you read literature on your own, bring your imagination and questions to the text. The questions shown below and others that you ask as you read will help you learn and enjoy literature even more.

Reading Literature/ Informational Text

10. By the end of grade 9, read and comprehend literature, including stories, dramas, poems, and literary nonfiction in the grades 9–10 text complexity band proficiently, with scaffolding as needed at the high end of the range.

When reading poetry, ask yourself...

Comprehension: **Key Ideas and Details**

- What do I understand about the poem from its title?
- Who is the speaker of the poem? What is the speaker telling me?
- What subject matter does the poem address?
- Is the poem telling a story? If so, who are the characters, and what are they doing?
- Is the poem exploring a moment in time? If so, what are the circumstances of that moment?

Text Analysis: **Craft and Structure**

- How does the poem's structure and appearance affect the way I read it?
- What do I notice about the length of stanzas and the look of the poem on the page? Is the poem an example of a particular form? If so, how does the form affect what I understand and feel about the poem?
- Is the poem an example of free verse? If so, does it have any formal elements?
- Does the poet use repetition, rhyme, or other sound devices? If so, what effect do these devices create?
- Does the poem use symbols, figurative language, or imagery? If so, how do these devices add to the poem's deeper meaning?

Connections: **Integration of Ideas**

- What theme or insight does the poem express? Does any one line or section simply state that theme? If so, which one? If not, which details help me understand the poem's deeper meaning?
- Has the poem helped me see something in a new way? If so, how?
- In what ways is this poem similar to others I have read? In what ways is it different from others I have read?
- Would I like to read more poems by this poet? Why or why not?
- Could this poem serve as an inspiration to other writers, artists, or musicians? Why or why not?

Do our differences define us?

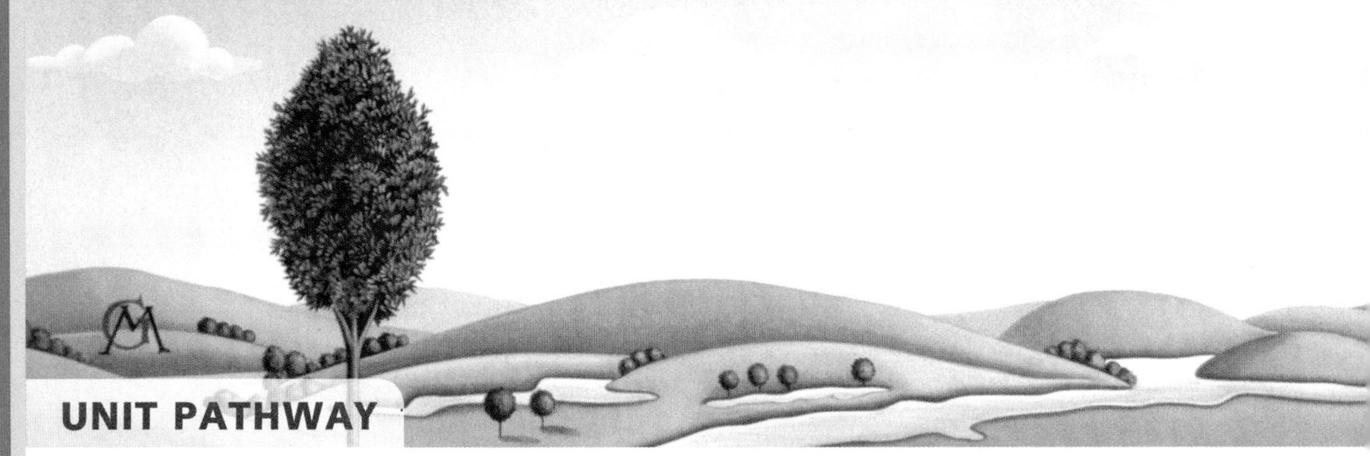

UNIT PATHWAY

PART 1
SETTING EXPECTATIONS
- INTRODUCING THE BIG QUESTION
- CLOSE READING WORKSHOP

PART 2
TEXT ANALYSIS
GUIDED EXPLORATION

TRAGIC ROMANCES

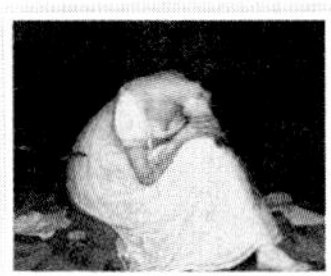

PART 3
TEXT SET
DEVELOPING INSIGHT

ASPIRATION

PART 4
DEMONSTRATING INDEPENDENCE
- INDEPENDENT READING
- ONLINE TEXT SET 

CLOSE READING TOOL

Use this tool to practice the close reading strategies you learn.

STUDENT eTEXT

Bring learning to life with audio, video, and interactive tools.

ONLINE WRITER'S NOTEBOOK

Easily capture notes and complete assignments online.

Find all Digital Resources at **pearsonrealize.com**

Introducing the Big Question

Do our differences define us?

Some differences between people are obvious—we recognize them on first meeting. These include physical attributes, such as our hair color and height. Other visible but more complex differences relate to the persona, or image, we project. For example, one person loves to wear bright colors while another wears only black; one person always has the latest tech gadgets, while another sticks to pen and paper. Even more complex and subtle differences become apparent only when we get to know each other well. These differences might show up in our values and in the traditions that are rooted in our individual cultures. While differences make us unique, they may also put us at odds with each other. Are the qualities that divide us more significant than those that unite us? Do our differences define who we are?

Exploring the Big Question

Collaboration: One-on-One Discussion Start thinking about the Big Question by listing examples of ways in which people may differ. List differences that you have observed or read about among people. Describe one specific example of each of these differences:

- physical appearance
- culture or family traditions
- personal style, such as the way people dress and talk
- values
- personal opinions
- personality traits
- interests, sports, or hobbies

Share your list with a partner. Talk about whether these differences help to define the people around us or whether people are more than just the sum of their individual attributes and interests.

Before you begin the conversation, work out an agreement about how you will share ideas and observations. For example, you might agree to exchange one another's lists of differences, read them separately, and then discuss them. As you conduct your discussion, use the words related to differences listed on the page at right.

Connecting to the Literature Each reading in this unit will give you additional insight into the Big Question. After you read each selection, pause to consider what it suggests about the ways in which perceptions of difference affect individuals, families, and communities.

Vocabulary

Acquire and Use Academic Vocabulary The term "academic vocabulary" refers to words you typically encounter in scholarly and literary texts and in technical and business writing. It is language that helps to express complex ideas. Review the definitions of these academic vocabulary words.

defend (dē fend′) *v.* protect against attack; support, maintain, or justify

determine (dē tŭr′ mən) *v.* cause something to happen in a certain way; control

differentiate (dif ər en′ shē āt′) *v.* distinguish between items or ideas

discriminate (di skrim′ i nāt′) *v.* recognize differences; show partiality (in favor of) or prejudice (against)

unique (yo͞o nēk′) *adj.* one of a kind

Use these words as you complete Big Question activities in this unit that involve reading, writing, speaking, and listening.

Gather Vocabulary Knowledge Additional words related to differences are listed below. Categorize the words by deciding whether you know each one well, know it a little bit, or do not know it at all.

accept	assimilated	background
conformity	culture	differences
individuality	similarity	understanding
values		

Then, complete the following steps:

1. Write the definitions of the words you know.
2. Using either a print or an online dictionary, confirm the meanings of the words you defined. Revise your definitions if necessary.
3. Then, use the dictionary to look up the meanings of the words you are unsure of or do not know at all. Write definitions for those words.
4. Use all of the words in several paragraphs about how strongly our differences define us.

Common Core State Standards

Speaking and Listening

1. Initiate and participate effectively in a range of collaborative discussions (one-on-one, in groups, and teacher-led) with diverse partners, building on others' ideas and expressing their own clearly and persuasively.

1.b. Work with peers to set rules for collegial discussions and decision-making, clear goals and deadlines, and individual roles as needed.

Language

4.c. Consult general and specialized reference materials, both print and digital, to find the pronunciation of a word or determine or clarify its precise meaning, its part of speech, or its etymology.

4.d. Verify the preliminary determination of the meaning of a word or phrase.

6. Acquire and use accurately grade-appropriate general academic and domain-specific words and phrases, sufficient for reading, writing, speaking, and listening at the college and career readiness level; demonstrate independence in gathering vocabulary knowledge when considering a word or phrase important to comprehension or expression.

Close Reading Workshop

In this workshop, you will learn an approach to reading that will deepen your understanding of literature and will help you better appreciate the author's craft. The workshop includes models for the close reading, discussion, research, and writing activities you will complete as you study literature in this unit. After you have reviewed the strategies and models, practice your skills with the Independent Practice selection.

Common Core State Standards

RL.9-10.1, RL.9-10.2, RL.9-10.3, RL.9-10.6; W.9-10.2, W.9-10.7, W.9-10.9, W.9-10.9.a; SL.9-10.1

[For full standards wording, see the chart in the front of this book.]

CLOSE READING: **DRAMA**

In Part 2 of this unit, you will focus on reading various dramas. Use these strategies as you read the texts:

Comprehension: **Key Ideas and Details**

- Read first to identify the main characters and events.
- Use textual aids, such as footnotes and glosses, to learn the meanings of unfamiliar words.
- Identify unfamiliar details that you might need to clarify through research.
- Distinguish between what characters state directly and what readers must infer.

Ask yourself questions such as these:

- Who are the main characters?
- What are the characters' relationships?
- What conflicts do the characters face?

Text Analysis: **Craft and Structure**

- Consider whether the play is a comedy or a tragedy and note how the genre contributes to the portrayal of characters and events.
- Analyze specific words and phrases that the playwright uses to convey information.
- Notice how the playwright uses dialogue and stage directions to develop the characters and advance the plot.

Ask yourself questions such as these:

- What do the characters say and do? What do their statements and actions reveal about their motivations and emotions?
- How do the characters' words and actions advance the plot?
- What is the overall mood of the piece? Does the mood change? What techniques does the playwright use to create specific moods?

Connections: **Integration of Knowledge and Ideas**

- Look for relationships among key ideas and events. Identify causes and effects, and comparisons and contrasts.
- Identify specific details that show character development. Use these details, along with background knowledge, to synthesize your own ideas about the work's deeper meaning.
- Compare and contrast this work with other works you have read, either by the same author or different authors.

Ask yourself questions such as these:

- How has this work increased my knowledge of a subject, an author, or drama in general?
- What larger messages or themes does the work suggest?

Read

As you read this scene from Tennessee Williams's *The Glass Menagerie,* take note of the annotations that model ways to closely read the text.

The Glass Menagerie tells the story of the struggling Wingfield family: Amanda, a fading Southern belle, and her two children, Tom and Laura. Tom, who works at a warehouse, wants to be a poet instead of a businessman. Laura is so shy that she can barely leave the house. In the following scene, Tom and Amanda discuss a friend from Tom's workplace whom Tom has invited home for dinner.

Reading Model

from *The Glass Menagerie* by Tennessee Williams

Tom: What are you doing?

Amanda: I'm brushing that cowlick down! (*She attacks his hair with the brush*)[1] What is this young man's position at the warehouse?

Tom: (*submitting grimly to the brush and the interrogation*)[1] This young man's position is that of a shipping clerk, Mother.

Amanda: Sounds to me like a fairly responsible job, the sort of a job *you* would be in if you just had more *get-up*. What is his salary? Have you any idea?

Tom: I would judge it to be approximately eighty-five dollars a month.

Amanda: Well—not princely, but—

Tom: Twenty more than I make.

Amanda: Yes, how well I know![2] But for a family man, eighty-five dollars a month is not much more than you can just get by on...

Tom: Yes, but Mr. O'Connor is not a family man.

Amanda: He might be, mightn't he? Some time in the future?[3]

Tom: I see. Plans and provisions.

Amanda: You are the only young man that I know of who ignores the fact that the future becomes the present, the present the past, and the past turns into everlasting regret if you don't plan for it!

Tom: I will think that over and see what I can make of it.[4]

Craft and Structure

1 The stage directions reveal the characters' strained relationship. The word "attack" provides a clue to Amanda's anger toward Tom. The words "submitting," "grimly," and "interrogation" suggest Tom's reluctance to interact with his mother.

Craft and Structure

2 In this dialogue, Amanda reveals the source of her irritation toward Tom—she believes her son lacks ambition. The dialogue's quick pace creates tension and suggests that the characters have discussed this topic repeatedly.

Key Ideas and Details

3 Tom states directly that Mr. O'Connor does not have a family. Amanda's response indicates that she is thinking about the young man's potential. You might infer from this exchange that she is concerned about her family's future and thinks the young man might be able to help.

Craft and Structure

4 Here, the conflict between Tom and Amanda escalates. Amanda's words show her concern for the future and regret about the past. Tom's response suggests that he does not share his mother's viewpoint.

AMANDA: Don't be supercilious[5] with your mother! Tell me some more about this—what do you call him?

TOM: James D. O'Connor. The D. is for Delaney.

AMANDA: Irish on *both* sides! *Gracious!* And doesn't drink?

TOM: Shall I call him up and ask him right this minute?

AMANDA: The only way to find out about those things is to make discreet inquiries at the proper moment. When I was a girl in Blue Mountain and it was suspected that a young man drank, the girl whose attentions he had been receiving, if any girl *was*, would sometimes speak to the minister of his church, or rather her father would if her father was living, and sort of feel him out on the young man's character.[6] That is the way such things are discreetly handled to keep a young woman from making a tragic mistake!

TOM: Then how did you happen to make a tragic mistake?

AMANDA: That innocent look of your father's had everyone fooled! He *smiled*—the world was *enchanted!*[7] No girl can do worse than put herself at the mercy of a handsome appearance! I hope that Mr. O'Connor is not too good-looking.[8]

Key Ideas and Details

5 You might consult a dictionary to learn that *supercilious* means "disdainful, or condescending." Amanda's use of this word indicates that she feels defensive about her son's comment.

Key Ideas and Details

6 These descriptive details suggest that Amanda's memories of her girlhood are romantic and idealized. Based on Amanda's views of the past, you might infer that she also has an unrealistic view of the present.

Craft and Structure

7 The use of exclamation points and italics conveys Amanda's strong emotions and vivid memories of her long-vanished husband.

Integration of Knowledge and Ideas

8 Amanda's reference to being "at the mercy" of a handsome man and her hope "that Mr. O'Connor is not too good-looking" underscore the themes of regret for the past and anxiety for the future.

Discuss

Sharing your own ideas and listening to the ideas of others can deepen your understanding of a text and help you look at a topic in a whole new way. As you participate in collaborative discussions, work to have a genuine exchange in which classmates build upon one another's ideas. Support your points with evidence and ask meaningful questions.

Discussion Model

Student 1: One thing that really struck me is how strongly Amanda's memories seem to affect her. She gets angry with Tom for ignoring "the fact that...the past turns into everlasting regret if you don't plan for it." Regret is a very painful feeling and if it is "everlasting" that's even more extreme. Amanda seems extremely bitter about her past.

Student 2: I noticed that, too. I wonder if her regret has to do with worries about money. She seems very interested in knowing what Mr. O'Connor's salary is, and thinks that Tom doesn't make enough money at the warehouse. Later, she asks Tom if Mr. O'Connor drinks, so maybe she has bad memories about someone's drinking problem.

Student 3: A lot of Amanda's memories do seem to be negative. But when she talks about being a girl in Blue Mountain it sounds like a dream. It almost doesn't sound real. Tom and Amanda are very vivid characters and it seems Williams really understood them. Do you think the play is based on his life?

Research

Targeted research can clarify unfamiliar details and shed light on various aspects of a text. Consider questions that arise in your mind as you read, and use those questions as the basis for research.

Research Model

Question: *Did Tennessee Williams base any parts of* The Glass Menagerie *on his own life?*

Key Words for Internet Search: The Glass Menagerie AND Memory

Result: *The Glass Menagerie*, Southeastern Louisiana University

What I Learned: *The Glass Menagerie* is a "memory play," and there are many similarities between parts of the play and Williams's own life. The playwright's real name was Tom, and he once worked in a shoe factory. Williams's mother was a former Southern belle who fell on hard times, just like the character of Amanda. Laura, Tom's sister in the play, is painfully shy and spends most of her time with her collection of glass animals. Williams's sister, too, was an emotionally delicate young woman.

Write

Writing about a text will deepen your understanding of it and will also allow you to share your ideas more formally with others. The following model essay analyzes Williams's use of memory to develop the character of Amanda in a scene from *The Glass Menagerie*.

Writing Model: Explanatory Text

Memory and Characterization in *The Glass Menagerie*

Memory plays an important role in Tennessee Williams's *The Glass Menagerie*. In this scene, Williams uses memory to develop the character of Amanda. Amanda's memories seem to be the driving force behind her aggressive actions and her obsession with planning for a secure future.

The writer states the main claim of the essay in the first paragraph. This is an effective strategy for a short response.

As the scene opens, Williams conveys information about Amanda's personality through stage directions and dialogue. The stage directions say that she "attacks" her son's hair with a brush, and also refer to her "interrogation" of Tom about another young man's position at the warehouse. She tells her son that he could have more responsibility at work if he "just had more get-up," and then asks about the other young man's salary, which is not "princely," in her opinion, but is still better than her son's pay. These details reveal Amanda's forceful personality as well as her admiration of ambition and desire for a comfortable lifestyle.

Specific details from the play provide support for the writer's claims.

Williams then uses dialogue to illustrate how Amanda's memories have shaped her personality. She scolds Tom for ignoring that "the future becomes the present, the present the past, and the past turns into everlasting regret if you don't plan for it!" Amanda's use of the phrase "everlasting regret" indicates that she is extremely bitter about the past. Perhaps this is why she is so forceful with Tom and so concerned about the future.

By narrowing in on particular details from the play—just two key words—the writer draws a broad conclusion about Amanda's character.

Amanda then recalls how questions about a young man's character were handled when she was a girl. Her description of "discreet inquiries at the proper moment" is romantic and idealized. The reader soon learns, however, that these "discreet inquiries" did not prevent her from making "a tragic mistake." Amanda claims that "everyone" was "fooled" by her husband's innocent good looks, and wants desperately to keep that from happening again. Elsewhere in the play we learn that she is deeply concerned about the future of her daughter Laura, who is painfully shy and spends most of her time with her collection of glass animals. Laura does not appear in this scene, but Amanda's fears for her daughter lie at the heart of her anxiety.

The writer incorporates evidence from further reading and research to draw a reasonable conclusion.

In this scene, the playwright effectively shows how Amanda's memories of the past influence her present actions and motivations. *The Glass Menagerie* is known as a memory play, and Williams's own memories clearly influenced this work. For example, the characters of Amanda and Laura in *The Glass Menagerie* are based on his real-life mother and sister.

The writer concludes by incorporating additional evidence from research to support a deeper connection of ideas.

As you read the following one-act play, apply the close reading strategies you have learned. You may need to read the play multiple times to fully understand the relationships among events, the characters' interactions, and the importance of specific details to the larger meaning.

The Inspector-General
by Anton Chekhov

The curtain goes up to reveal falling snow and a cart facing away from us. Enter the STORYTELLER, *who begins to read the story. Meanwhile, the* TRAVELER *enters. He is a middle-aged man of urban appearance, wearing dark glasses and a long overcoat with its collar turned up. He is carrying a small traveling bag. He climbs into the cart and sits facing us.*

STORYTELLER. The Inspector-General. In deepest incognito, first by express train, then along back roads, Pyotr Pavlovich Posudin[1] was hastening toward the little town of N, to which he had been summoned by an anonymous letter. "I'll take them by surprise," he thought to himself. "I'll come down on them like a thunderbolt out of the blue. I can just imagine their faces when they hear who I am . . ." [*Enter the* DRIVER, *a peasant, who climbs onto the cart, so that he is sitting with his back to us, and the cart begins to trundle slowly away from us.*] And when he'd thought to himself for long enough, he fell into conversation with the driver of the cart. What did he talk about? About himself, of course. [*Exit the* STORYTELLER.]

TRAVELER. I gather you've got a new Inspector-General in these parts.

DRIVER. True enough.

TRAVELER. Know anything about him? [*The driver turns and looks at the* TRAVELER, *who turns his coat collar up a little higher.*]

1. **Pyotr Pavlovich Posudin** (pyō´ tər päv lō´ vich pō syo͞o´ dən)

Meet the Author

An acclaimed playwright, **Anton Chekhov** (1860–1904) grew up in a small Russian coastal town. Chekhov also wrote many short stories and is considered a master of that literary form.

Vocabulary

incognito (in´ käg nēt´ ō) *adj.* with true identity unrevealed or disguised; under an assumed name

anonymous (ə nän´ ə məs) *adj.* without a known or an acknowledged name

trundle (trun´ dəl) *v.* roll along

CLOSE READING TOOL

Read and respond to this selection online using the **Close Reading Tool.**

DRIVER. Know anything about him? Of course we do! We know everything about all of them up there! Every last little clerk—we know the color of his hair and the size of his boots! [*He turns back to the front, and the* TRAVELER *permits himself a slight smile.*]

TRAVELER. So, what do you reckon? Any good, is he? [*The* DRIVER *turns around.*]

DRIVER. Oh, yes, he's a good one, this one.

TRAVELER. Really?

DRIVER. Did one good thing straight off.

TRAVELER. What was that?

DRIVER. He got rid of the last one. Holy terror he was! Hear him coming five miles off! Say he's going to this little town. Somewhere like we're going, say. He'd let all the world know about it a month before. So now he's on his way, say, and it's like thunder and lightning coming down the road. And when he gets where he's going he has a good sleep, he has a good eat and drink—and then he starts. Stamps his feet, shouts his head off. Then he has another good sleep, and off he goes.

TRAVELER. But the new one's not like that?

DRIVER. Oh, no, the new one goes everywhere on the quiet, like. Creeps around like a cat. Don't want no one to see him, don't want no one to know who he is. Say he's going to this town down the road here. Someone there sent him a letter on the sly, let's say. "Things going on here you should know about." Something of that kind. Well, now, he creeps out of his office, so none of them up there see him go. He hops on a train just like anyone else, just like you or me. Then when he gets off he don't go jumping into a cab or nothing fancy. Oh, no. He wraps himself up from head to toe so you can't see his face, and he wheezes away like an old dog so no one can recognize his voice.

TRAVELER. Wheezes? That's not wheezing! That's the way he talks! So I gather.

DRIVER. Oh, is it? But the tales they tell about him. You'd laugh till you burst your tripes![2]

TRAVELER. [*sourly*]. I'm sure I would.

DRIVER. He drinks, mind!

TRAVELER. [*startled*]. Drinks?

DRIVER. Oh, like a hole in the ground. Famous for it.

TRAVELER. He's never touched a drop! I mean, from what I've heard.

---

2. **tripes** (trīps) *n.* parts of the stomach, usually of an ox or a sheep, when used as food.

DRIVER. Oh, not in public, no. Goes to some great ball—"No thank you, not for me." Oh, no, he puts it away at home! Wakes up in the morning, rubs his eyes, and the first thing he does, he shouts, "Vodka!" So in runs his valet with a glass. Fixed himself up a tube behind his desk, he has. Leans down, takes a pull on it, no one the wiser.

TRAVELER. [*offended*]. How do you know all this, may I ask?

DRIVER. Can't hide it from the servants, can you? The valet and the coachman have got tongues in their heads. Then again, he's on the road, say, going about his business, and he keeps the bottle in his little bag. [*The* TRAVELER *discreetly pushes the traveling bag out of the* DRIVER'S *sight.*] And his housekeeper . . .

◀ **Vocabulary**
discreetly (di skrēt′ lē) *adv.* without drawing attention.

TRAVELER. What about her?

DRIVER. Runs circles around him, she does, like a fox round his tail. She's the one who wears the trousers.[3] The people aren't half so frightened of him as they are of her.

TRAVELER. But at least he's good at his job, you say?

DRIVER. Oh, he's a blessing from heaven, I'll grant him that.

TRAVELER. Very cunning—you were saying.

◀ **Vocabulary**
cunning (kun′ iŋ) *adj.* skilled in deception

DRIVER. Oh, he creeps around all right.

TRAVELER. And then he pounces, yes? I should think some people must get the surprise of their life, mustn't they?

DRIVER. No, no—let's be fair, now. Give him his due. He don't make no trouble.

TRAVELER. No, I mean, if no one knows he's coming . . .

DRIVER. Oh, that's what *he* thinks, but *we* all know.

TRAVELER. You know?

DRIVER. Oh, some gentleman gets off the train at the station back there with his greatcoat up to his eyebrows and says, "No, I don't want a cab, thank you, just an ordinary horse and cart for me"—well, we'd put two and two together, wouldn't we! Say it was you, now, creeping along down the road here. The lads would be down there in a cab by now! By the time you got there the whole town would be as regular as clockwork! And you'd think to yourself, "Oh, look at that! As clean as a whistle! And they didn't know I was coming!" No, that's why he's such a blessing after the other one. This one believes it!

---

3. **wears the trousers** has the greatest authority; is really in charge.

TRAVELER. Oh, I see.

DRIVER. What, you thought we wouldn't know him? Why, we've got the electric telegraph these days! Take today, now. I'm going past the station back there this morning, and the fellow who runs the buffet comes out like a bolt of lightning. Arms full of baskets and bottles. "Where are you off to?" I say. "Doing drinks and refreshments for the Inspector-General!" he says, and he jumps into a carriage and goes flying off down the road here. So there's the old Inspector-General, all muffled up like a roll of carpet, going secretly along in a cart somewhere—and when he gets there, nothing to be seen but vodka and cold salmon!

Vocabulary ▶
telegraph (tel′ ə graf′) *n.* apparatus or system that converts a coded message into electric impulses and sends it to a distant receiver

TRAVELER. [*shouts*]. Right—turn around, then . . . !

DRIVER. [*to the horse*]. Whoa, boy! Whoa! [*To the* TRAVELER.] Oh, so what's this, then? Don't want to go running into the Inspector-General, is that it? [*The* TRAVELER *gestures impatiently for the* DRIVER *to turn the cart around.* DRIVER *to the horse.*] Back we go, then, boy. Home we go. [*He turns the cart around, and the* TRAVELER *takes a swig from his traveling bag.*] Though if I know the old devil, he's like as not turned around and gone home again himself. [*Blackout.*]

Close Reading Activities

Read

Comprehension: **Key Ideas and Details**

1. **(a)** What does the Traveler do after the Driver states, "we know the color of his hair and the size of his boots!"? **(b) Draw Conclusions:** What conclusion about the Traveler can you draw from this action?
2. **(a)** What does the Traveler do when the Driver mentions that the Inspector-General travels with a flask of vodka? **(b) Infer:** What does this action tell you about the Traveler? Explain.
3. **(a)** According to the Driver, what preparations does the town make for the Inspector-General's arrival? **(b) Interpret:** Why does the Driver's account prompt the Traveler's demand to turn around?
4. **Summarize:** Write a brief, objective summary of the play. Cite specific details from the play in your writing.

Text Analysis: **Craft and Structure**

5. **(a)** How does the playwright convey information about the Inspector-General's thoughts at the beginning of the play? **(b) Infer:** How does this information help you understand the character?
6. **(a) Distinguish:** Identify an example of dialogue between the Driver and the Traveler that highlights the situation's dramatic irony (circumstance in which the audience knows more than the characters). **(b) Analyze:** How does this example create humor? Explain.
7. **(a)** What does the Driver do when the Traveler asks, "Know anything about him?" **(b) Infer:** Why might the playwright have chosen to include this detail in the stage direction?
8. **(a)** What words and phrases does the Driver use to describe the former Inspector-General? **(b) Compare and Contrast:** According to the Driver, how does the new Inspector-General compare to the old one? **(c) Interpret:** How does the Driver's description of the new Inspector-General contribute to the play's humor?

Connections: **Integration of Knowledge and Ideas**

Discuss

Conduct a **small-group discussion** about the portrayal of government authority in this play. Consider how the relationship between government and the community is depicted in this comic work and how it might be portrayed differently in a tragic work.

Research

Anton Chekhov's "The Inspector-General" is a comedy, a form of drama that often, but not always, features humor. Briefly research comedy as a genre, focusing on the following elements:

a. the formal definition of comedy

b. depictions of ordinary people in everyday life

c. explorations of common human weaknesses

Using your research, write a brief **explanation** of how "The Inspector-General" represents comedy as a dramatic form.

Write

Anton Chekhov is known for his realistic portrayal of characters and their motivations. Write an **essay** in which you describe a specific behavior of either the Traveler or the Driver and analyze what might have motivated the character to act as he does. Cite details from the play to support your analysis.

THE BIG ? Do our differences define us?

Think about the differences between the Traveler and the Driver in "The Inspector-General." What do these differences reveal about each character? Explain your answer.

"For never was a
story of more **woe**
than this of
Juliet and her Romeo."
—William Shakespeare

PART 2

TEXT ANALYSIS GUIDED EXPLORATION

TRAGIC ROMANCES

A feud is a state of continuing mutual hostility between families or communities. In William Shakespeare's tale of doomed love, *The Tragedy of Romeo and Juliet,* the title characters come from feuding families. When the two meet and fall in love, family differences rise to the fore. Shakespeare borrowed this story from much older texts, which suggests that the concept of the feud is extremely long-lived. As you read this play, think about how it frames the Big Question for this unit: **Do our differences define us?** Through this tale of tragic romance, what is Shakespeare suggesting about the power of anger and hostility? Do our differences define us, even when love gives us other options?

◀ CRITICAL VIEWING What ideas about romance, love, and heartbreak does this painting suggest? How do details in the setting, the woman's posture, and her clothing contribute to the portrayal of those ideas?

READINGS IN PART 2

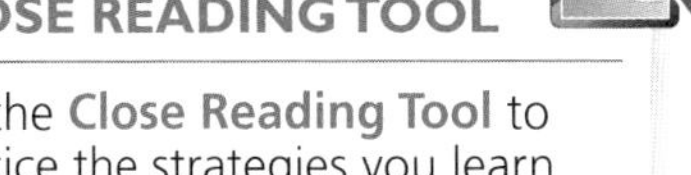

CLOSE READING TOOL

Use the **Close Reading Tool** to practice the strategies you learn in this unit.

Focus on Craft and Structure

Elements of Drama

Drama is **narrative**, or storytelling, written for **performance**.

A **drama** is a play, a story written to be performed by actors on a stage or in a film. Sometimes, people use the word *drama* to refer to a work about a serious subject. However, the broad genre of drama includes every type of performed narrative work, whether lighthearted or serious.

Like other works of narrative literature, dramatic works feature **characters,** or personalities who take part in the action of the story. The main characters face a **conflict,** a struggle or problem that propels the sequence of events called the **plot.** The highest point of interest in the plot, the **climax,** occurs during the point of greatest tension between characters. As the story winds down, the **resolution** of the conflict leads to the conclusion of the play.

Acts are the basic units of organization in a drama. Acts are often further divided into **scenes.** A scene may move the action to a new setting or time of day, it may introduce new characters, or it may shift a play's mood. For example, an evening scene may follow a daytime scene, or a comic scene may lighten the mood of a serious play.

The author of a play, called a **playwright** or **dramatist,** writes the **script,** or text of the story. The script contains **dialogue,** or the characters' spoken words. It also contains **stage directions,** which are instructions about how the play should be performed. In some plays, the playwright gives detailed stage directions, while in others he or she provides few or none at all.

All the elements of drama combine in performance to produce an illusion of reality known as **dramatic effect.** Dramatic effect allows viewers to believe in the events of the story, even though they know the play is artificial. Through this effect, the dramatist explores a **theme**—a deeper meaning or insight about life.

The Elements of Drama	
Acts and Scenes	Acts and scenes are the basic sections of drama. A drama may consist of one or more acts, each of which may contain any number of scenes.
Stage Directions	Stage directions are the playwright's instructions about how a play should be performed. They are usually set in italics and/or set off by brackets. They may include the following information: • Background about the setting or characters • Abbreviations for where actors should move or say their lines—for example, *D.S.* means downstage, or closer to the audience, while *U.S.* means upstage, or farther from the audience • Details about physical elements of the performance, such as sets, lighting, and costumes
Sets	Sets are constructions that define the area in which the play's action occurs. Sets may be realistic and look like actual places. They may also be abstract or minimalist and merely suggest real places.
Props	Props are movable objects, like swords or pens, that actors use on stage.

Forms of Drama

The ancient Greeks, who developed drama as an organized literary form, created two basic types of plays. We still use these two categories to define dramatic forms.

- A **tragedy** traces the downfall of the main character, often called the **tragic hero.** In classical drama, the tragic hero is always an important person, such as a general or a king. The hero is admirable but is defeated by a **tragic flaw**—a mistake or a character defect.
- A **comedy** has a happy ending. Comedies usually feature a series of events in which the order or balance of the world is disrupted. A comic ending restores order and harmony.

Comedies are often funny, but humor is not their defining trait. The main distinction between tragedy and comedy is how the story ends: Tragedies end in death, defeat, or exile, while comedies end in weddings, births, reunions, or other positive, joyful events.

Dramatic Structures Classical dramas, such as most works written by the ancient Greeks and by Shakespeare, take place in five acts and are called **five-act plays.** The acts follow the structure of most narrative works: **Act 1** = introduction/exposition; **Act 2** = rising action; **Act 3** = climax; **Act 4** = falling action; **Act 5** = resolution.

In some dramatic works, the five segments of plot are compressed into fewer acts. For example, many **screenplays,** or scripts written for films, occur in three acts. Act 1 introduces the main characters and the basic situation. Act 2 sets up a problem. Act 3 provides the resolution.

One-act plays are dramatic works that are organized in a single act. The one act may still contain multiple scenes.

Types of Dramatic Speeches

In most dramatic works, dialogue is the playwright's main tool for developing characters and furthering the plot. Ancient Greek playwrights also used the convention of the **chorus,** a group of observers who were part of the play but not part of the story. The chorus provided background information and reacted to the events that unfolded on stage.

In some modern dramas, a **narrator** replaces the chorus. The narrator is a personality or voice that comments on but does not participate in the story.

Playwrights use other types of dramatic speeches to supplement dialogue and reveal the thoughts, feelings, and motivations of the characters. The main types of dramatic speeches are explained in the chart below.

Common Core State Standards

Reading Literature

3. Analyze how complex characters develop over the course of a text, interact with other characters, and advance the plot or develop the theme.

4. Determine the meaning of words and phrases as they are used in the text, including figurative and connotative meanings; analyze the cumulative impact of specific word choices on meaning and tone.

5. Analyze how an author's choices concerning how to structure a text, order events within it, and manipulate time create such effects as mystery, tension, or surprise.

Type of Speech	Definition	Examples from *The Tragedy of Romeo and Juliet*
Monologue	A long, uninterrupted speech delivered by a character to other characters on stage	Romeo speaks about love to Benvolio. *(p. 515, lines 167–179)*
Soliloquy	A speech in which a character, alone on stage, reveals private thoughts that the audience is allowed to overhear	Juliet reveals her private thoughts. *(pp. 572–573, lines 1–31)*
Aside	A brief remark a character makes to the audience rather than to other characters	Juliet tells the audience that Romeo is no villain. *(p. 587, line 83)*

Analyzing Character Development

Characters' reactions to conflict propel the plot and point to **thematic meanings.**

Characters and Conflict

In both tragedies and comedies, characters face **conflicts,** or struggles between opposing forces. There are two main types of conflict: external and internal.

- **External Conflict:** a struggle against an outside force, such as an enemy, nature, or the pressures of society

Example: External Conflict

Romeo and Juliet struggle against pressures from their feuding families.

- **Internal Conflict:** a struggle posed by a character's own beliefs, thoughts, or feelings

Example: Internal Conflict

As she enacts the plan that will allow her to join Romeo, Juliet struggles with her fears.

The most interesting dramatic works feature important conflicts that engage the audience. For tragic characters, the conflict is often literally life threatening. In a tragedy, the resolution to the conflict involves the main character's destruction or downfall. For comic characters, the conflict is often symbolically life threatening. For example, the hero in a romantic comedy may not win the woman of his dreams. The quality of his life, if not its substance, is at risk. In a comedy, the resolution to the conflict involves the main character's restoration to health or happiness.

Protagonist and Antagonist Most plays focus on a single main character—the **protagonist.** The character who opposes the main character and either creates or adds to the conflict is called the **antagonist.**

Complex Characters Great dramas present interesting characters, both protagonists and antagonists, whose stories are compelling to audiences. Such characters are complex, which means they have strengths and weaknesses and experience mixed emotions. Complex characters have multiple motivations, or a variety of reasons for feeling and behaving as they do. In literary terms, complex characters are round, rather than flat, and dynamic, rather than static.

Character Types

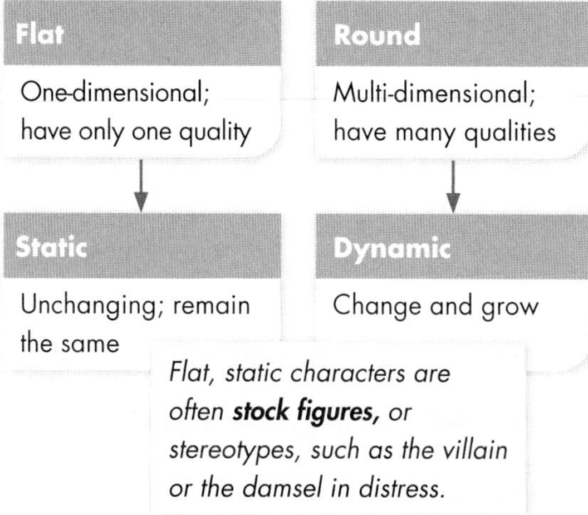

Flat
One-dimensional; have only one quality
Round
Multi-dimensional; have many qualities
Static
Unchanging; remain the same
Dynamic
Change and grow
Flat, static characters are often stock figures, or stereotypes, such as the villain or the damsel in distress.

A play is, in part, an exploration of a round, dynamic character's journey from one state of being to another. By dramatizing that journey, a playwright also explores insights into the human condition, or thematic meaning.

Character Development

In any work of literature, a writer uses the tools of character development, or **characterization,** to show what characters are like. There are two general approaches available to a writer: direct and indirect characterization.

In **direct characterization,** a writer simply tells the audience about a character. In dramatic works, direct characterization may appear in stage directions. Alternatively, the chorus, a narrator, or another character might tell the audience what a character is like. For example, in Shakespeare's *The Tragedy of Julius Caesar,* Caesar describes the suspicious character of Cassius:

He is a great observer, and he looks
Quite through the deeds of men.

In **indirect characterization,** the writer shows the audience what a character is like in any of the following ways:

- Descriptions of a character's physical appearance
- The character's own words
- The character's actions and behavior
- Other characters' reactions to the character

An actor brings a character to life on the stage or in a movie by using his or her voice, facial expressions, gestures, and body language, as well as the pitch and phrasing of his or her speech. Costumes and sets then help to emphasize elements of a character's personality. However, when you read a drama, you must use textual clues to understand characters' motivations, feelings, actions, and thoughts.

Clues to Characterization When Reading Drama Playwrights help readers understand complex characters by using dialogue, stage directions, punctuation, and word choice to show emotions, relationships, and differences in characters' status, education, and environment. As you read drama, look for these clues to complex characters.

Example: Characterization in Drama

Punctuation Showing Emotion: That's unbelievable! You mean—the bank will give us the loan?

Stage Directions Showing Attitude: *[Stanley runs to Anna, arms outstretched.]*

Dialogue Suggesting Social Class: Really, Madam. I don't see why we can't just enjoy our tea!

Word Choice Showing Relationships: You're fantastic, sweet pea! You rustled up my favorite meal!

Dramatic Speeches The different types of dramatic speeches, described on page 495, also provide critical clues to characters' motivations and actions. For example, in a monologue or soliloquy, a character can explain what he or she thinks and feels. The audience learns about the character's conflicts and even his or her secrets. Such speeches help propel the plot because they explain why characters do what they do. Often, these types of speeches also express ideas that are key to the play's theme.

Characters and Theme There are many ways in which characters provide clues to a play's theme. To determine and analyze the theme of a drama, pay attention to characters' words, motivations, actions, and reactions. Ask yourself questions such as the following:

- How do the characters respond to conflicts?
- What are their reasons for responding as they do?
- What change or growth do characters undergo as a result of their experiences?
- What central ideas are emphasized throughout the drama through the words and actions of the characters?
- What insights about life or the human condition do these ideas convey?

Preparing to Read
The Tragedy of Romeo and Juliet

The works of William Shakespeare are among the greatest achievements of the Renaissance.

▲ Elizabeth ruled from 1558 to 1603, but her reign was so successful that the entire Renaissance in England is often called the Elizabethan Age.

Historical Background: Elizabethan England

The Rebirth of Learning Sometime around the year 1350, at the end of the Middle Ages, Italian city-states, such as Venice and Genoa, began to trade extensively with the East. With trade came more knowledge and growing curiosity about the world. Soon, Italy was leading the way in a flowering of European learning known as the Renaissance (**ren′ ə sans′**). Commerce, science, and the arts blossomed as people shifted their focus to the interests and pursuits of human life here on earth. The astronomers Copernicus and Galileo questioned long-held beliefs to prove that the world was round and that it circled the sun, not vice versa. Navigators, including Christopher Columbus and Ferdinand Magellan, braved the seas in tiny boats to explore new lands and seek new trade routes. Religious thinkers, such as Martin Luther and John Calvin, challenged the authority of the Roman Catholic Church and spurred the Protestant Reformation. Artists, including Michelangelo and Leonardo da Vinci, painted and sculpted lifelike human beings. Writers, such as Miguel de Cervantes and William Shakespeare, wrote insightfully about complex human personalities in fiction and drama.

The Renaissance in England The Renaissance was slow to come to England. The delay was caused mainly by civil war between two great families, or houses, claiming the English throne—the House of York and the House of Lancaster. The conflict ended in 1485 when Henry Tudor of the House of Lancaster took the throne as King Henry VII. After a successful rule in which English commerce expanded, he was succeeded by his son Henry VIII, whose reign was filled with turmoil. Henry sought a divorce from the Spanish princess Catherine of Aragon so that he could remarry and possibly have a son. He was convinced that only a male would be strong enough to hold the throne. When the Pope refused to grant the divorce, Henry renounced the Roman Catholic Church and made England a Protestant nation. Ironically, his remarriage, to a woman named Anne Boleyn, produced not a son but a daughter, Elizabeth. Even more ironically, when Elizabeth took the throne, she proved to be one of the strongest monarchs that England has ever known.

The symbol of the House of York was a white rose, while the symbol of the House of Lancaster was a red rose. For that reason, the civil wars fought between the two houses were called the Wars of the Roses. Shakespeare wrote several plays about English monarchs involved in these conflicts.

The Elizabethan World The reign of Elizabeth I is often seen as a golden age in English history. Treading a moderate and frugal path, Elizabeth brought economic and political stability to the nation, thus allowing commerce and culture to thrive. Advances in mapmaking helped English explorers sail the Old World and claim lands in the New. Practical inventions improved transportation at home. Craft workers created lovely wares for the homes of the wealthy. Musicians composed fine works for the royal court, and literature thrived, peaking with the plays of William Shakespeare.

London became a bustling capital on the busy River Thames (**temz**), where ships from all over the world sailed into port. The city attracted newcomers from the countryside and immigrants from foreign lands. Streets were narrow, dirty, and crowded, but they were also lined with shops where vendors sold merchandise from near and far. English women enjoyed more freedoms than did women elsewhere in Europe, and the class system was more fluid as well. To be sure, those of different ranks led very different lives. Yet even the lowborn were able to attend one of the city's most popular new amusements: the theater.

Elizabeth I and the Spanish Armada

In 1588, King Phillip of Spain sent an armada, or fleet of military ships, to invade England. At the time, Spain was the most powerful nation on earth. Nevertheless, the English soundly defeated the invading forces. The victory cemented Elizabeth's popularity with her people. Prior to the battle, the Queen visited her troops to inspire them to fight. Here is a portion of the speech she delivered:

> *. . . And therefore I am come amongst you at this time, not as for my recreation or sport, but being resolved, in the midst and heat of the battle, to live or die amongst you all; to lay down, for my God, and for my kingdom, and for my people, my honor and my blood, even the dust. I know I have but the body of a weak and feeble woman; but I have the heart of a king, and of a king of England too. . . .*

▼ In 1796, more than 200 years after the defeat of the Spanish Armada, English artist Philippe-Jacques de Loutherbourg painted this image of those dramatic events.

Theater in Elizabethan England

Elizabethan audiences included all levels of society, from the "groundlings," who paid a penny entrance fee, to the nobility.

During the Middle Ages, simple religious plays were performed at inns, in castle halls, and on large wagons at pageants. In early Elizabethan times, acting companies still traveled the countryside to perform their plays. However, the best companies acquired noble patrons, or sponsors, who then invited the troupes to perform in their homes. At the same time, Elizabethan dramatists began to use the tragedies and comedies of ancient Greece and Rome as models for their plays. By the end of the sixteenth century, many talented playwrights had emerged, including Christopher Marlowe, Ben Jonson, and, of course, William Shakespeare.

England's First Theater England's first successful public theater opened in 1576. Known simply as the Theatre, it was built by an actor named James Burbage. Since officials had banned the performance of plays in London, Burbage built his theater in an area called Shoreditch, just outside the London city walls. Some of Shakespeare's earliest plays were first performed here, including *The Tragedy of Romeo and Juliet,* which probably starred James Burbage's son, Richard, as Romeo.

When the lease on the Theatre expired, Richard Burbage, in charge of the company after his father died, decided to move the company to Southwark (su*th*′ ərk), just across the River Thames from London proper. The Shoreditch landlord had been causing problems, and Southwark was emerging as a popular theater district. Using timbers from the old theater building, Burbage had a new theater built, bigger and better than the one before. It opened in 1599 and was called the Globe. Under that name it would become the most famous theater in the history of the English stage, for many more of Shakespeare's plays were first performed there.

Audience members ate and drank while they watched the plays and apparently made a lot of noise. In 1990, archaeologists found the remains of the foundation of the original Globe Theatre. They also found the discarded shells of the many hazelnuts audiences munched on while watching performances.

During Shakespeare's day, acting companies were entirely male. Women did not perform because it was considered improper. The roles of women were usually played by boys of about eleven or twelve—that is, before their voices changed.

◄ This photograph of the reconstructed Globe Theatre was made with a special lens. It shows the pit, where the groundlings stood to watch the show, as well as the sheltered galleries.

Theater Layout No floor plans of the Theatre or the Globe survive, but people's descriptions and sketches of similar buildings suggest what they were like. They were either round or octagonal, with a central stage open to the sky. This stage stretched out into an area called the pit, where theatergoers called groundlings paid just a penny to stand and watch the play. The enclosure surrounding this open area consisted of two or three galleries, or tiers. The galleries accommodated audience members who paid more to watch the play while under shelter from the elements, and with some distance from the groundlings. The galleries probably also included a few elegant box seats where members of the nobility could both watch the play and be seen by the masses.

Staging the Play The enclosure directly behind the stage was used not for seating but for staging the play. Actors entered and left the stage from doors at stage level. The stage also had a trap door through which mysterious characters, such as ghosts or witches, could disappear suddenly. Some space above the backstage area was used for storage or dressing rooms. The first gallery, however, was visible to the audience and used as a second stage. It would have been on a second stage like this that the famous balcony scene in *Romeo and Juliet* was performed.

These open-air theaters did not use artificial light. Instead, performances took place in the afternoon, when it was still light outside. There was also no scenery in the theaters of Shakespeare's day. Instead, the setting for each scene was communicated through dialogue. With no need for set changes, scenes could follow one another in rapid succession. Special effects were simple—smoke might billow at the disappearance of a ghost, for example. By contrast, costumes were often elaborate. The result was a fast-paced, colorful production that lasted about two hours.

The Blackfriars In 1609, Shakespeare's acting company began staging plays in the Blackfriars Theatre as well as the Globe. Located in London proper, the Blackfriars was different from the earlier theaters in which Shakespeare's plays were performed. It was an indoor space with no open area for groundlings. Instead, it relied entirely on a wealthier clientele. It was also one of the first English theaters to use artificial lighting, an innovation that allowed for nighttime performances.

The Globe Theatre

The three-story structure, open to the air, could house as many as 3,000 people in the pit and surrounding galleries.

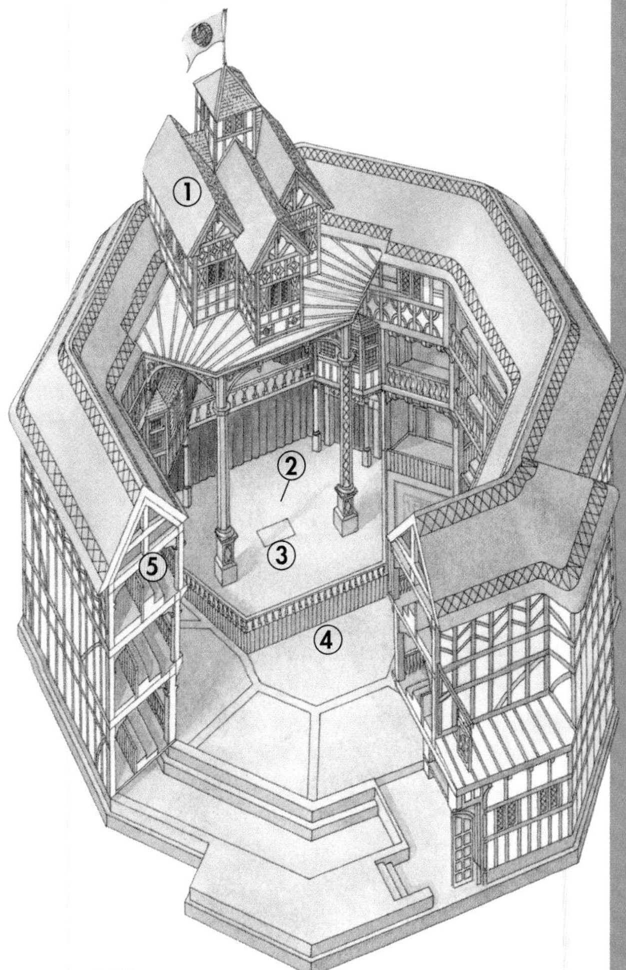

KEY

1. The hut, housing machinery used to lower characters and props to the stage
2. The stage trap, often used for the entrances and exits of special characters, such as ghosts or witches
3. The stage
4. The pit, where groundlings stood to watch the show
5. The galleries

Meet the Author

William Shakespeare (1564–1616)

Shakespeare's plays and poetry are regarded as the finest works ever written in English.

William Shakespeare is revered as England's greatest writer. Four centuries after his death, his plays are still read and performed every single day. Who was this remarkable author of so many masterpieces? In actual fact, we know very little about him.

From Stratford to London Shakespeare grew up in Stratford-upon-Avon, a busy market town on the Avon River about seventy-five miles northwest of London. Church and town records indicate that his mother, Mary Arden, was the daughter of a wealthy farmer who owned the land on which Shakespeare's grandfather lived. Shakespeare's father, John, was a prosperous merchant who also served for a time as Stratford's mayor. Shakespeare most likely went to the local grammar school, where he would have studied Latin and Greek as well as English and world history. He would eventually put all those lessons to use in plays about historical figures, such as Julius Caesar and King Henry IV.

In 1582, when he was eighteen, Shakespeare married a woman named Anne Hathaway and had three children with her, including a set of twins. The next decade of his life is shrouded in mystery, but by 1592 he had moved to London, where he gravitated to the theater. Starting off as an actor, he soon began writing plays as well. By 1594, he had become the principal playwright of the Lord Chamberlain's Men, the Burbages' acting company. Some of the early plays Shakespeare wrote at this time include the romantic comedy *The Taming of the Shrew* and the romantic tragedy *The Tragedy of Romeo and Juliet.*

Shakespeare was not just a performer and a playwright, however; he was also part owner of the theater company. This meant that he earned money in three ways—from fees for his plays, from his acting salary, and from his share of the company's profits. Those profits rose substantially after the Lord Chamberlain's Men moved to the Globe Theatre, where as many as 3,000 people might attend a single performance. It was at the Globe that many of Shakespeare's later masterpieces premiered, probably beginning with *The Tragedy of Julius Caesar* in 1599.

The King's Players In 1603 Queen Elizabeth I died, and her Scottish cousin took the throne as James I. Partial to the theater, James was particularly supportive of the Lord Chamberlain's Men, which had emerged as one of the two best acting companies in the land. Not only did it have a brilliant playwright in William Shakespeare, but it also had a fine actor in Richard Burbage, who starred in most of Shakespeare's plays. In 1606, flattered by the king's patronage, the company changed its name to the King's Men. It is believed that Shakespeare wrote his great Scottish play, *The Tragedy of Macbeth,* to appeal particularly to James I.

Three years later, the King's Men began performing at the Blackfriars Theatre, using the Globe only in summer months. By utilizing this indoor theater in winter, the King's Men further increased profits. The company did so well that Shakespeare was soon able to retire. In 1610, he moved back to Stratford-upon-Avon, buying one of the finest homes in town. He died of unknown causes in 1616.

Shakespeare Says...

Shakespeare's impact on the English language has been enormous. Not only did he coin new words and new meanings for old words, but he also used many expressions that have become part of our everyday speech. Here are just a few examples:

Expression and Source	Meaning
Eat out of house and home *(Henry VI, Part II)*	Eat so much that it makes the provider poor
For ever and a day *(The Taming of the Shrew)*	Indefinitely; with no end in sight
Give the devil his due *(Henry IV, Part I)*	Recognize an opponent's achievement
Greek to me *(Julius Caesar)*	Completely unintelligible to me
Green-eyed monster *(Othello)*	Jealousy
In a pickle *(The Tempest)*	In trouble
In stitches *(Twelfth Night)*	Laughing so hard it hurts
Lay it on with a trowel *(As You Like It)*	Flatter excessively
Makes your hair stand on end *(Hamlet)*	Really frightens you
The milk of human kindness *(Macbeth)*	Compassion
A plague on both your houses *(Romeo and Juliet)*	I'm fed up with both sides (in an argument)
Salad days *(Anthony and Cleopatra)*	Green, or naïve, youth
Star-crossed lovers *(Romeo and Juliet)*	Ill-fated lovers
Wear your heart upon your sleeve *(Othello)*	Show your love to all
Won't budge an inch *(The Taming of the Shrew)*	Will not give in; stands firm

Background for the Play

STAR-CROSSED LOVERS

Written in 1594 or 1595, when Shakespeare was still a fairly young man, *The Tragedy of Romeo and Juliet* is a play about young love. The basic plot is simple: Two teenagers from feuding families fall in love and marry against their families' wishes, with tragic results. The story is set in Verona, Italy, and is based on an Italian legend that was fairly well known in England at the time.

Shakespeare's Sources Elizabethan writers deeply respected Italy as the birthplace of the Renaissance and often drew on Italian sources for inspiration. In 1562, an English poet named Arthur Brooke wrote *The Tragicall History of Romeus and Juliet,* a long narrative poem based on the Romeo and Juliet legend. Three years later, a prose version of the legend also appeared in England. Scholars believe, however, that Brooke's poem was Shakespeare's chief source.

That poem contains a great deal of moralizing, stressing the disobedience of the young lovers, along with fate, as the cause of their doom. Shakespeare's portrayal of the young lovers is more sympathetic, but he does stress the strong role that fate plays in their tragedy. In fact, at the very start of the play, the Chorus describes Romeo and Juliet as "star-crossed lovers," indicating that their tragic ending is written in the stars, or fated by forces beyond their control.

The Play Through the Centuries Of all the love stories ever written, *The Tragedy of Romeo and Juliet* may well be the most famous. Acting celebrities down through the centuries have played the leading roles—Edwin Booth and Ellen Terry in the nineteenth century, for example, and John Gielgud and Judi Dench in the twentieth. There have been dozens of film versions of the play, numerous works of art depicting its scenes, over twenty operatic versions, a famous ballet version by Prokofiev, and an equally famous musical overture by Tchaikovsky. The play is often adapted to reflect the concerns of different eras: *West Side Story,* for example, adapts the story as a musical set amid the ethnic rivalries of 1950s New York City; *Romanoff and Juliet* is a comedy of the Cold War set during the 1960s. One of the most recent popular adaptations was the 1996 film *Romeo + Juliet* starring Leonardo di Caprio and Claire Danes, which sets the play in the fictional location of Verona Beach, California.

Elizabethan Language

English has changed a great deal since Shakespeare's time. Some of the words he uses are now archaic, or outdated. For instance, Shakespeare uses *anon* for "soon" and *haply* for "perhaps." He also uses outdated grammatical forms, such as the pronouns *thou, thee, thy,* and *thine* instead of *you, your,* and *yours.* In addition, Shakespeare's verbs often have archaic endings: *cometh* for "come," for example, and *dost* for "do." Word order, too, is sometimes different from modern English, especially in questions. For instance, instead of "What do you say?" Shakespeare writes, "What say you?" The numbered marginal notes, or glosses, that accompany the text of the play will help you with the unfamiliar language.

Do our differences define us?

Explore the Big Question as you read Act I of *The Tragedy of Romeo and Juliet*. Take notes on how Shakespeare introduces the conflict between the Capulets and the Montagues.

CLOSE READING FOCUS

Key Ideas and Details: **Summarize**

Summarizing is briefly and objectively stating the main ideas in a piece of writing. Pausing to summarize as you read helps you check your comprehension before you read further. To be sure that you understand Shakespeare's language before you summarize, use the glosses—the numbered explanations that appear next to the text.

Craft and Structure: **Dialogue and Stage Directions**

Dialogue is conversation between characters. In prose, dialogue is usually set off with quotation marks. In drama, dialogue generally follows the name of the speaker:

> **BENVOLIO.** My noble uncle, do you know the cause?
>
> **MONTAGUE.** I neither know it nor can learn of him.

Dialogue reveals characters' personalities and relationships, advances the action, and captures the language of the times in which a play is set.

Stage directions are notes in a play that describe how the work should be performed, or staged. They describe scenes, lighting, sound effects, and characters' actions. Stage directions are usually set in italics and are sometimes set off in brackets or parentheses.

> *Scene iii.* FRIAR LAWRENCE'S cell.
>
> [*Enter* FRIAR LAWRENCE *alone, with a basket.*]

As you read, notice how the dialogue and stage directions help you "hear" and "see" the play in your mind.

Vocabulary

The words below are critical to understanding the text that follows. Copy the words into your notebook. Which is an antonym for *friend*?

pernicious	adversary	augmenting
grievance	oppression	transgression

Common Core State Standards

Reading Literature

1. Cite strong and thorough textual evidence to support analysis of what the text says explicitly as well as inferences drawn from the text.

2. Determine a theme or central idea of a text and analyze in detail its development over the course of the text, including how it emerges and is shaped and refined by specific details; provide an objective summary of the text.

3. Analyze how complex characters develop over the course of a text, interact with other characters, and advance the plot or develop the theme.

5. Analyze how an author's choices concerning how to structure a text, order events within it, and manipulate time create such effects as mystery, tension, or surprise.

CLOSE READING MODEL

The passage below is from Act I of Shakespeare's *The Tragedy of Romeo and Juliet*. The annotations to the right of the passage show ways in which you can use close reading skills to summarize and analyze dialogue and stage directions.

from *The Tragedy of Romeo and Juliet,* Act I

TYBALT. What, art thou drawn among these heartless hinds?

Turn thee, Benvolio; look upon thy death.

BENVOLIO. I do but keep the peace. Put up thy sword,

Or manage it to part these men with me.[1]

TYBALT. What, drawn, and talk of peace? I hate the word

As I hate hell, all Montagues, and thee.[2]

Have at thee, coward! [*They fight.*]

[*Enter an OFFICER, and three or four* CITIZENS *with clubs or partisans.*][3]

OFFICER. Clubs, bills, and partisans! Strike! Beat them down!

Down with the Capulets! Down with the Montagues!

[*Enter old CAPULET in his gown, and his WIFE.*]

CAPULET. What noise is this? Give me my long sword, ho!

LADY CAPULET. A crutch, a crutch! Why call you for a sword?

CAPULET. My sword, I say! Old Montague is come

And flourishes his blade in spite of me.[4]

Summarize

1 A summary of this passage might read as follows: *Tybalt approaches Benvolio and challenges him to a fight. Benvolio asks him to keep the peace.*

Dialogue and Stage Directions

2 Tybalt's dialogue reveals that he is hot-headed and quick to anger. It also reveals the nature of his relationship with Benvolio: Benvolio is a Montague and Tybalt, a Capulet, hates all Montagues.

Dialogue and Stage Directions

3 The stage direction explains the actions of the officer and citizens, who enter the scene brandishing weapons.

Summarize

4 A summary of this section might read as follows: *The Capulets arrive and see the fighting. The old man calls for his sword and tries to engage in the fight. Lady Capulet mocks her elderly husband, saying it would be better if he had a crutch.*

The Tragedy of ROMEO *and* JULIET

William Shakespeare

Characters

Chorus
Escalus, Prince of Verona
Paris, a young count, kinsman to the Prince
Montague
Capulet
An Old Man, of the Capulet family
Romeo, son to Montague
Mercutio, kinsman to the Prince and friend to Romeo
Benvolio, nephew to Montague and friend to Romeo
Tybalt, nephew to Lady Capulet
Friar Lawrence, Franciscan
Friar John, Franciscan
Balthasar, servant to Romeo
Sampson, servant to Capulet
Gregory, servant to Capulet
Peter, servant to Juliet's nurse
Abram, servant to Montague
An Apothecary
Three Musicians
An Officer
Lady Montague, wife to Montague
Lady Capulet, wife to Capulet
Juliet, daughter to Capulet
Nurse to Juliet
Citizens of Verona, Gentlemen and Gentlewomen of both houses, Maskers, Torchbearers, Pages, Guards, Watchmen, Servants, and Attendants

Scene: Verona; Mantua

[Enter Chorus.*]*

Chorus. Two households, both alike in dignity,[1]
In fair Verona, where we lay our scene,
From ancient grudge break to new mutiny.[2]
Where civil blood makes civil hands unclean.[3]
From forth the fatal loins of these two foes
A pair of star-crossed[4] lovers take their life;
Whose misadventured piteous overthrows[5]
Doth with their death bury their parents' strife.
The fearful passage of their death-marked love,
And the continuance of their parents' rage,
Which, but[6] their children's end, naught could remove,
Is now the two hours' traffic[7] of our stage;
The which if you with patient ears attend,
What here shall miss, our toil shall strive to mend.[8] *[Exit.]*

1. **dignity** high social rank.
2. **mutiny** violence.
3. **Where . . . unclean** in which the blood of citizens stains citizens' hands.
4. **star-crossed** ill-fated by the unfavorable positions of the stars.
5. **Whose . . . overthrows** whose unfortunate, sorrowful destruction.
6. **but** except.
7. **two hours' traffic** two hours' business.
8. **What . . . mend** What is not clear in this prologue we actors shall try to clarify in the course of the play.

Scene i. Verona. A public place.

[*Enter* Sampson *and* Gregory, *with swords and bucklers,*[1] *of the house of Capulet.*]

1. **bucklers** small shields.
2. **carry coals** endure insults.
3. **colliers** sellers of coal.
4. **an . . . draw** If we are angered, we'll draw our swords.
5. **collar** hangman's noose.

Sampson. Gregory, on my word, we'll not carry coals.[2]

Gregory. No, for then we should be colliers.[3]

Sampson. I mean, an we be in choler, we'll draw.[4]

Gregory. Ay, while you live, draw your neck out of collar.[5]

Sampson. I strike quickly, being moved.

Gregory. But thou art not quickly moved to strike.

Sampson. A dog of the house of Montague moves me.

Gregory. To move is to stir, and to be valiant is to stand. Therefore, if thou art moved, thou run'st away.

Sampson. A dog of that house shall move me to stand. I will take the wall[6] of any man or maid of Montague's.

6. **take the wall** assert superiority by walking nearer the houses and therefore farther from the gutter.

Gregory. That shows thee a weak slave; for the weakest goes to the wall.

Sampson. 'Tis true; and therefore women, being the weaker vessels, are ever thrust to the wall. Therefore I will push Montague's men from the wall and thrust his maids to the wall.

Gregory. The quarrel is between our masters and us their men.

Dialogue and Stage Directions
What does this conversation among servants reveal about the Montagues?

Sampson. Tis all one. I will show myself a tyrant. When I have fought with the men, I will be civil with the maids—I will cut off their heads.

Gregory. The heads of the maids?

Sampson. Ay, the heads of the maids or their maidenheads. Take it in what sense thou wilt.

Gregory. They must take it in sense that feel it.

Sampson. Me they shall feel while I am able to stand; and 'tis known I am a pretty piece of flesh.

Gregory. Tis well thou art not fish; if thou hadst, thou hadst been Poor John. Draw thy tool![7] Here comes two of the house of Montagues.

[*Enter two other Servingmen,* Abram *and* Balthasar.]

Sampson. My naked weapon is out. Quarrel! I will back thee.

Gregory. How? Turn thy back and run?

Sampson. Fear me not.

Gregory. No, marry. I fear thee!

Sampson. Let us take the law of our sides;[8] let them begin.

Gregory. I will frown as I pass by, and let them take it as they list.[9]

Sampson. Nay, as they dare. I will bite my thumb[10] at them, which is disgrace to them if they bear it.

Abram. Do you bite your thumb at us, sir?

Sampson. I do bite my thumb, sir.

Abram. Do you bite your thumb at us, sir?

Sampson. [*Aside to* Gregory] Is the law of our side if I say ay?

Gregory. [*Aside to* Sampson] No.

Sampson. No, sir, I do not bite my thumb at you, sir; but I bite my thumb, sir.

Gregory. Do you quarrel, sir?

Abram. Quarrel, sir? No, sir.

Sampson. But if you do, sir, I am for you. I serve as good a man as you.

Abram. No better.

Sampson. Well, sir.

[*Enter* Benvolio.]

Gregory. [*Aside to* Sampson.] Say "better." Here comes one of my master's kinsmen.

Sampson. Yes, better, sir.

Abram. You lie.

7. **tool** weapon.

Summarize
How does gloss 8 help you understand Sampson's logic in line 36?

8. **take . . . sides** make sure the law is on our side.
9. **list** please.
10. **bite . . . thumb** make an insulting gesture.

Dialogue and Stage Directions
Which words in the stage directions in line 44 clarify that Sampson is not speaking to Abram?

Comprehension
With which family are the quarreling servants affiliated?

11. **swashing** hard downward swordstroke.

12. **heartless hinds** cowardly servants. *Hind* also means "a female deer."

13. **partisans** spearlike weapons with broad blades.

14. **bills** weapons consisting of hook-shaped blades with long handles.

15. **spite** defiance.

SAMPSON. Draw, if you be men. Gregory, remember thy
swashing[11] blow. [*They fight.*]

BENVOLIO. Part, fools!
Put up your swords. You know not what you do.

[*Enter* TYBALT.]

TYBALT. What, art thou drawn among these heartless hinds?[12]
Turn thee, Benvolio; look upon thy death.

BENVOLIO. I do but keep the peace. Put up thy sword,
Or manage it to part these men with me.

TYBALT. What, drawn, and talk of peace? I hate the word
As I hate hell, all Montagues, and thee.
Have at thee, coward! [*They fight.*]

[*Enter an* OFFICER, *and three or four* CITIZENS *with clubs or partisans.*[13]]

OFFICER. Clubs, bills,[14] and partisans! Strike! Beat them down!
Down with the Capulets! Down with the Montagues!

[*Enter old* CAPULET *in his gown, and his* WIFE.]

CAPULET. What noise is this? Give me my long sword, ho!

LADY CAPULET. A crutch, a crutch! Why call you for a sword?

CAPULET. My sword, I say! Old Montague is come
And flourishes his blade in spite[15] of me.

[*Enter old* MONTAGUE *and his* WIFE.]

LITERATURE IN CONTEXT

History Connection

Prince of Verona

When Prince Escalus intervenes in the fight between the Capulets and the Montagues, he does so under his authority as the podesta, or "chief magistrate," of Verona. The powers and duties of the podesta combined those of a modern mayor, chief of police, and head of the local militia. Scholars believe that Shakespeare based the character of Prince Escalus on Bartolomeo della Scala, who ruled the northern Italian city of Verona during the early fourteenth century.

Connect to the Literature

Which part of his authority is Prince Escalus exercising in this scene—mayor, police chief, or head of the army? Explain.

Montague. Thou villain Capulet!—Hold me not; let me go.

Lady Montague. Thou shalt not stir one foot to seek a foe.

[*Enter* Prince Escalus, *with his Train.*[16]]

Prince. Rebellious subjects, enemies to peace,
Profaners[17] of this neighbor-stainèd steel—
Will they not hear? What, ho! You men, you beasts,
That quench the fire of your pernicious rage
With purple fountains issuing from your veins!
On pain of torture, from those bloody hands
Throw your mistempered[18] weapons to the ground
And hear the sentence of your moved prince.
Three civil brawls, bred of an airy word
By thee, old Capulet, and Montague,
Have thrice disturbed the quiet of our streets
And made Verona's ancient citizens
Cast by their grave beseeming ornaments[19]
To wield old partisans, in hands as old,
Cank'red with peace, to part your cank'red hate.[20]
If ever you disturb our streets again,
Your lives shall pay the forfeit of the peace.
For this time all the rest depart away.
You, Capulet, shall go along with me;
And, Montague, come you this afternoon,
To know our farther pleasure in this case,
To old Freetown, our common judgment place.
Once more, on pain of death, all men depart.

[*Exit all but* Montague, *his* Wife, *and* Benvolio.]

Montague. Who set this ancient quarrel new abroach?[21]
Speak, nephew, were you by when it began?

Benvolio. Here were the servants of your adversary
And yours, close fighting ere I did approach.
I drew to part them. In the instant came
The fiery Tybalt, with his sword prepared;
Which, as he breathed defiance to my ears,
He swung about his head and cut the winds,
Who, nothing hurt withal, hissed him in scorn.
While we were interchanging thrusts and blows,
Came more and more, and fought on part and part,[22]
Till the Prince came, who parted either part.

Lady Montague. O, where is Romeo? Saw you him today?
Right glad I am he was not at this fray.

16. **Train** attendants.
17. **Profaners** those who show disrespect or contempt.

◀ **Vocabulary**
pernicious (pər nish´ əs) *adj.* causing great injury or ruin

18. **mistempered** hardened for a wrong purpose; bad-tempered.
19. **Cast . . . ornaments** put aside their dignified and appropriate clothing.
20. **Cank'red . . . hate** rusted from lack of use, to put an end to your malignant feuding.

Summarize
Summarize the warning that the Prince issues to the Montagues and Capulets in this speech.

21. **Who . . . abroach?** Who reopened this old fight?

◀ **Vocabulary**
adversary (ad´ vər ser´ ē) *n.* person who opposes or fights against another

22. **on . . . part** on one side and the other.

Comprehension
Who stops the brawl between the Montagues and the Capulets?

Benvolio. Madam, an hour before the worshiped sun
Peered forth the golden window of the East,
A troubled mind drave me to walk abroad:
Where, underneath the grove of sycamore
That westward rooteth from this city side,
So early walking did I see your son.
Towards him I made, but he was ware[23] of me
And stole into the covert[24] of the wood.
I, measuring his affections[25] by my own,
Which then most sought where most might not be found,[26]
Being one too many by my weary self,
Pursued my humor not pursuing his,[27]
And gladly shunned who gladly fled from me.

Montague. Many a morning hath he there been seen,
With tears augmenting the fresh morning's dew,
Adding to clouds more clouds with his deep sighs;
But all so soon as the all-cheering sun
Should in the farthest East begin to draw
The shady curtains from Aurora's bed,
Away from light steals home my heavy[28] son
And private in his chamber pens himself,
Shuts up his windows, locks fair daylight out,
And makes himself an artificial night.
Black and portentous[29] must this humor prove
Unless good counsel may the cause remove.

Benvolio. My noble uncle, do you know the cause?

Montague. I neither know it nor can learn of him.

Benvolio. Have you importuned[30] him by any means?

Montague. Both by myself and many other friends;
But he, his own affections' counselor,
Is to himself—I will not say how true—
But to himself so secret and so close,
So far from sounding[31] and discovery,
As is the bud bit with an envious worm
Ere he can spread his sweet leaves to the air
Or dedicate his beauty to the sun.
Could we but learn from whence his sorrows grow,
We would as willingly give cure as know.

[*Enter* Romeo.]

23. ware aware; wary.
24. covert hidden place.
25. measuring . . . affections judging his feelings.
26. Which . . . found which wanted to be where there was no one else.
27. Pursued . . . his followed my own mind by not following after Romeo.

Vocabulary ▶
augmenting (ôg ment′ iŋ) *v.* increasing; enlarging

28. heavy sad; moody.

29. portentous promising bad fortune.

30. importuned questioned deeply.

31. sounding understanding.

Benvolio. See, where he comes. So please you step aside;
I'll know his grievance, or be much denied.

Montague. I would thou wert so happy by thy stay
To hear true shrift.[32] Come, madam, let's away.

[*Exit* Montague *and* Wife.]

Benvolio. Good morrow, cousin.

Romeo. Is the day so young?

Benvolio. But new struck nine.

Romeo. Ay me! Sad hours seem long.
Was that my father that went hence so fast?

Benvolio. It was. What sadness lengthens Romeo's hours?

Romeo. Not having that which having makes them short.

Benvolio. In love?

Romeo. Out—

Benvolio. Of love?

Romeo. Out of her favor where I am in love.

Benvolio. Alas that love, so gentle in his view,[33]
Should be so tyrannous and rough in proof![34]

Romeo. Alas that love, whose view is muffled still,[35]
Should without eyes see pathways to his will!
Where shall we dine? O me! What fray was here?
Yet tell me not, for I have heard it all.
Here's much to do with hate, but more with love.[36]
Why then, O brawling love, O loving hate,
O anything, of nothing first created!
O heavy lightness, serious vanity,
Misshapen chaos of well-seeming forms,
Feather of lead, bright smoke, cold fire, sick health,
Still-waking sleep, that is not what it is!
This love feel I, that feel no love in this.
Dost thou not laugh?

Benvolio. No, coz,[37] I rather weep.

Romeo. Good heart, at what?

Benvolio. At thy good heart's oppression.

Romeo. Why, such is love's transgression.
Griefs of mine own lie heavy in my breast,

◀ **Vocabulary**
grievance (grēv´ əns) *n.* injustice; complaint

32. **I . . . shrift** I hope you are lucky enough to hear him confess the truth.

Dialogue
What does this conversation reveal about Romeo's state of mind?

33. **view** appearance.
34. **in proof** when experienced.
35. **whose . . . still** Cupid is traditionally represented as blindfolded.
36. **but . . . love** loyalty to family and love of fighting. In the following lines, Romeo speaks of love as a series of contradictions—a union of opposites.
37. **coz** cousin.

◀ **Vocabulary**
oppression (ə presh´ ən) *n.* feeling of being weighed down with worries or problems

transgression (trans gresh´ ən) *n.* wrongdoing; sin

Comprehension
What reason for his sadness does Romeo give to Benvolio?

38. **Which . . . thine** which griefs you will increase by adding your own sorrow to them.

39. **discreet** intelligently sensitive.

40. **gall** a bitter liquid.

41. **Soft!** Wait!

42. **in sadness** seriously.

43. **Dian's wit** the mind of Diana, goddess of chastity.

44. **proof** armor.

45. **stay** endure; put up with.

46. **That . . . store** in that her beauty will die with her if she does not marry and have children.

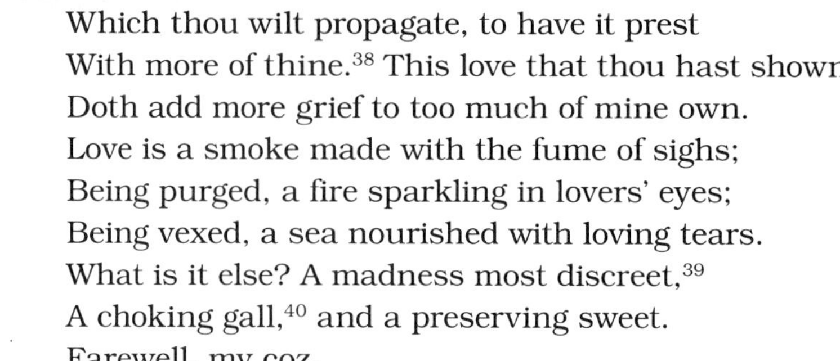

Which thou wilt propagate, to have it prest
With more of thine.[38] This love that thou hast shown
Doth add more grief to too much of mine own.
Love is a smoke made with the fume of sighs;
Being purged, a fire sparkling in lovers' eyes;
Being vexed, a sea nourished with loving tears.
What is it else? A madness most discreet,[39]
A choking gall,[40] and a preserving sweet.
Farewell, my coz.

Benvolio. Soft![41] I will go along.
And if you leave me so, you do me wrong.

Romeo. Tut! I have lost myself; I am not here;
This is not Romeo, he's some other where.

Benvolio. Tell me in sadness,[42] who is that you love?

Romeo. What, shall I groan and tell thee?

Benvolio. Groan? Why, no;
But sadly tell me who.

Romeo. Bid a sick man in sadness make his will.
Ah, word ill urged to one that is so ill!
In sadness, cousin, I do love a woman.

Benvolio. I aimed so near when I supposed you loved.

Romeo. A right good markman. And she's fair I love.

Benvolio. A right fair mark, fair coz, is soonest hit.

Romeo. Well, in that hit you miss. She'll not be hit
With Cupid's arrow. She hath Dian's wit,[43]
And, in strong proof[44] of chastity well armed,
From Love's weak childish bow she lives uncharmed.
She will not stay[45] the siege of loving terms,
Nor bide th' encounter of assailing eyes,
Nor ope her lap to saint-seducing gold.
O, she is rich in beauty; only poor
That, when she dies, with beauty dies her store.[46]

Benvolio. Then she hath sworn that she will still live chaste?

Romeo. She hath, and in that sparing make huge waste;
For beauty, starved with her severity,

◀ Critical Viewing
What does this photograph reveal about Romeo's feelings?

Cuts beauty off from all posterity.[47]
She is too fair, too wise, wisely too fair
To merit bliss by making me despair.[48]
She hath forsworn to[49] love, and in that vow
Do I live dead that live to tell it now.

Benvolio. Be ruled by me; forget to think of her.

Romeo. O, teach me how I should forget to think!

Benvolio. By giving liberty unto thine eyes.
Examine other beauties.

Romeo. 'Tis the way
To call hers, exquisite, in question more.[50]
These happy masks that kiss fair ladies' brows,
Being black puts us in mind they hide the fair.
He that is strucken blind cannot forget
The precious treasure of his eyesight lost.
Show me a mistress that is passing fair:
What doth her beauty serve but as a note
Where I may read who passed that passing fair?[51]
Farewell. Thou canst not teach me to forget.

Benvolio. I'll pay that doctrine, or else die in debt.[52] [*Exit all.*]

47. **in . . . posterity** By denying herself love and marriage, she wastes her beauty, which will not live on in future generations.
48. **She . . . despair** She is being too good—she will earn happiness in heaven by dooming me to live without her love.
49. **forsworn to** sworn not to.
50. **'Tis . . . more** That way will only make her beauty more strongly present in my mind.
51. **who . . . fair** who surpassed in beauty that very beautiful woman.
52. **I'll . . . debt** I will teach you to forget, or else die trying.

Scene ii. A street.

[*Enter* Capulet, County Paris, *and the* Clown, *Capulet's servant.*]

Capulet. But Montague is bound as well as I,
In penalty alike; and 'tis not hard, I think,
For men so old as we to keep the peace.

Paris. Of honorable reckoning[1] are you both,
And pity 'tis you lived at odds so long.
But now, my lord, what say you to my suit?

Capulet. But saying o'er what I have said before:
My child is yet a stranger in the world,
She hath not seen the change of fourteen years;
Let two more summers wither in their pride
Ere we may think her ripe to be a bride.

Paris. Younger than she are happy mothers made.

Capulet. And too soon marred are those so early made.
Earth hath swallowed all my hopes[2] but she;
She is the hopeful lady of my earth.[3]
But woo her, gentle Paris, get her heart;
My will to her consent is but a part.

1. **reckoning** reputation.
2. **hopes** children.
3. **She . . . earth** My hopes for the future rest in her; she will inherit all that is mine.

Comprehension
What advice does Benvolio give to Romeo about the woman he loves?

4. **An . . . voice** If she agrees, I will consent to and agree with her choice.

5. **Earth-treading stars** young ladies.

6. **Which . . . none** If you look at all the young girls, you may see her as merely one among many, and not worth special admiration.
7. **stay** await.

Summarize
Use gloss 8 to help you summarize the servant's remarks here.

8. **shoemaker . . . nets** The servant is confusing workers and their tools. He intends to say that people should stick with what they know.
9. **In good time!** Just in time! The servant has seen Benvolio and Romeo, who can read.

10. **Turn . . . turning** If you are dizzy from turning one way, turn the other way.
11. **plantain leaf** leaf used to stop bleeding.

An she agree, within her scope of choice
Lies my consent and fair according voice,[4]
This night I hold an old accustomed feast,
Whereto I have invited many a guest,
Such as I love; and you among the store,
One more, most welcome, makes my number more.
At my poor house look to behold this night
Earth-treading stars[5] that make dark heaven light.
Such comfort as do lusty young men feel
When well-appareled April on the heel
Of limping Winter treads, even such delight
Among fresh fennel buds shall you this night
Inherit at my house. Hear all, all see,
And like her most whose merit most shall be;
Which, on more view of many, mine, being one,
May stand in number, though in reck'ning none.[6]
Come, go with me. [*To* SERVANT, *giving him a paper*]
Go, sirrah, trudge about
Through fair Verona; find those persons out
Whose names are written there, and to them say
My house and welcome on their pleasure stay.[7]

[*Exit with* PARIS.]

SERVANT. Find them out whose names are written here? It is written that the shoemaker should meddle with his yard and the tailor with his last, the fisher with his pencil and the painter with his nets;[8] but I am sent to find those persons whose names are here writ, and can never find what names the writing person hath here writ. I must to the learned. In good time![9]

[*Enter* BENVOLIO *and* ROMEO.]

BENVOLIO. Tut, man, one fire burns out another's burning;
One pain is less'ned by another's anguish;
Turn giddy, and be holp by backward turning;[10]
One desperate grief cures with another's languish.
Take thou some new infection to thy eye,
And the rank poison of the old will die.

ROMEO. Your plantain leaf[11] is excellent for that.

BENVOLIO. For what, I pray thee?

ROMEO. For your broken shin.

BENVOLIO. Why, Romeo, art thou mad?

ROMEO. Not mad, but bound more than a madman is;
Shut up in prison, kept without my food,
Whipped and tormented and—God-den,[12] good fellow.

SERVANT. God gi' go-den. I pray, sir, can you read?

ROMEO. Ay, mine own fortune in my misery.

SERVANT. Perhaps you have learned it without book.
But, I pray, can you read anything you see?

ROMEO. Ay, if I know the letters and the language.

SERVANT. Ye say honestly. Rest you merry.[13]

ROMEO. Stay, fellow; I can read. [*He reads the letter.*]
"Signior Martino and his wife and daughters;
County Anselm and his beauteous sisters;
The lady widow of Vitruvio;
Signior Placentio and his lovely nieces;
Mercutio and his brother Valentine;
Mine uncle Capulet, his wife and daughters;
My fair niece Rosaline; Livia;
Signior Valentio and his cousin Tybalt;
Lucio and the lively Helena."
A fair assembly. Whither should they come?

SERVANT. Up.

ROMEO. Whither? To supper?

SERVANT. To our house.

ROMEO. Whose house?

SERVANT. My master's.

ROMEO. Indeed I should have asked you that before.

SERVANT. Now I'll tell you without asking. My master is the great rich Capulet; and if you be not of the house of Montagues, I pray come and crush a cup of wine. Rest you merry. [*Exit.*]

BENVOLIO. At this same ancient[14] feast of Capulet's
Sups the fair Rosaline whom thou so loves;
With all the admirèd beauties of Verona.
Go thither, and with unattainted[15] eye
Compare her face with some that I shall show,
And I will make thee think thy swan a crow.

ROMEO. When the devout religion of mine eye
Maintains such falsehood, then turn tears to fires:

12. **God-den** good afternoon; good evening.

13. **Rest you merry** May God keep you happy—a way of saying farewell.

Dialogue and Stage Directions
What important information in the stage directions clarifies Romeo's speech here?

14. **ancient** long-established; traditional.
15. **unattainted** unprejudiced.

Comprehension
Why does Capulet's servant talk to Romeo and Benvolio?

And these, who, often drowned, could never die,
Transparent heretics, be burnt for liars![16]
One fairer than my love? The all-seeing sun
Ne'er saw her match since first the world begun.

Benvolio. Tut! you saw her fair, none else being by,
Herself poised with herself in either eye;[17]
But in that crystal scales[18] let there be weighed
Your lady's love against some other maid
That I will show you shining at this feast,
And she shall scant show well that now seems best.

Romeo. I'll go along, no such sight to be shown,
But to rejoice in splendor of mine own.[19] [*Exit all.*]

16. **When . . . liars!** When I see Rosaline as just a plain-looking girl, may my tears turn to fire and burn my eyes out!
17. **Herself . . . eye** Rosaline compared with no one else.
18. **crystal scales** your eyes.
19. **mine own** my own love, Rosaline.

Scene iii. A room in Capulet's house.

[*Enter* Capulet's Wife, *and* Nurse.]

Lady Capulet. Nurse, where's my daughter? Call her forth to me.

Nurse. Now, by my maidenhead at twelve year old,
I bade her come. What, lamb! What, ladybird!
God forbid, where's this girl? What, Juliet!

[*Enter* Juliet.]

Juliet. How now? Who calls?

Nurse. Your mother.

Juliet. Madam, I am here.
What is your will?

Lady Capulet. This is the matter—Nurse, give leave[1] awhile;
We must talk in secret. Nurse, come back again.
I have rememb'red me; thou's hear our counsel.[2]
Thou knowest my daughter's of a pretty age.

1. **give leave** Leave us alone.
2. **thou's . . . counsel** You shall hear our conference.

Nurse. Faith, I can tell her age unto an hour.

Lady Capulet. She's not fourteen.

Nurse. I'll lay fourteen of my teeth—
And yet, to my teen[3] be it spoken, I have but four—
She's not fourteen. How long is it now
To Lammastide?[4]

Lady Capulet. A fortnight and odd days.[5]

Nurse. Even or odd, of all days in the year,
Come Lammas Eve at night shall she be fourteen.

3. **teen** sorrow.
4. **Lammastide** August 1, a holiday celebrating the summer harvest.
5. **A fortnight and odd days** two weeks plus a few days.

Susan and she (God rest all Christian souls!)
Were of an age.[6] Well, Susan is with God;
She was too good for me. But, as I said,
On Lammas Eve at night shall she be fourteen;
That shall she, marry; I remember it well.
'Tis since the earthquake now eleven years.
And she was weaned (I never shall forget it),
Of all the days of the year, upon that day;
For I had then laid wormwood to my dug,
Sitting in the sun under the dovehouse wall.
My lord and you were then at Mantua.
Nay, I do bear a brain. But, as I said,
When it did taste the wormwood on the nipple
Of my dug and felt it bitter, pretty fool,
To see it tetchy and fall out with the dug!
Shake, quoth the dovehouse! 'Twas no need, I trow,
To bid me trudge.
And since that time it is eleven years,
For then she could stand high-lone; nay, by th' rood,
She could have run and waddled all about;
For even the day before, she broke her brow;
And then my husband (God be with his soul!
'A was a merry man) took up the child.
"Yea," quoth he, "dost thou fall upon thy face?
Thou wilt fall backward when thou hast more wit;
Wilt thou not, Jule?" and, by my holidam,
The pretty wretch left crying and said, "Ay."
To see now how a jest shall come about!
I warrant, and I should live a thousand years,
I never should forget it. "Wilt thou not, Jule?" quoth he,
And, pretty fool, it stinted and said, "Ay."

Lady Capulet. Enough of this. I pray thee hold thy peace.

Nurse. Yes, madam. Yet I cannot choose but laugh
To think it should leave crying and say, "Ay."
And yet, I warrant, it had upon it brow
A bump as big as a young cock'rel's stone;
A perilous knock; and it cried bitterly.
"Yea," quoth my husband, "fall'st upon thy face?
Thou wilt fall backward when thou comest to age,
Wilt thou not, Jule?" It stinted and said, "Ay."

Juliet. And stint thou too, I pray thee, nurse, say I.

Nurse. Peace, I have done. God mark thee to His grace!

6. **Susan . . . age** Susan, the Nurse's child, and Juliet were the same age.

Dialogue and Stage Directions
What do the Nurse's words here reveal about her devotion to Juliet?

Dialogue and Stage Directions
What does this conversation reveal about the Nurse's personality?

Comprehension
How old is Juliet?

Thou wast the prettiest babe that e'er I nursed.
And I might live to see thee married once,
I have my wish.

Lady Capulet. Marry, that "marry" is the very theme
I came to talk of. Tell me, daughter Juliet,
How stands your dispositions to be married?

Juliet. It is an honor that I dream not of.

Nurse. An honor? Were not I thine only nurse,
I would say thou hadst sucked wisdom from thy teat.

Lady Capulet. Well, think of marriage now. Younger than you,
Here in Verona, ladies of esteem,
Are made already mothers. By my count,
I was your mother much upon these years
That you are now a maid.[7] Thus then in brief;
The valiant Paris seeks you for his love.

Nurse. A man, young lady! Lady, such a man
As all the world—Why, he's a man of wax.[8]

Lady Capulet. Verona's summer hath not such a flower.

Nurse. Nay, he's a flower, in faith—a very flower.

Lady Capulet. What say you? Can you love the gentleman?
This night you shall behold him at our feast.
Read o'er the volume of young Paris' face,
And find delight writ there with beauty's pen;
Examine every married lineament,
And see how one another lends content;[9]
And what obscured in this fair volume lies
Find written in the margent[10] of his eyes.
This precious book of love, this unbound lover,
To beautify him only lacks a cover.[11]
The fish lives in the sea, and 'tis much pride
For fair without the fair within to hide.
That book in many's eyes doth share the glory,
That in gold clasps locks in the golden story;
So shall you share all that he doth possess,
By having him making yourself no less.

Nurse. No less? Nay, bigger! Women grow by men.

Lady Capulet. Speak briefly, can you like of Paris' love?

Juliet. I'll look to like, if looking liking move;[12]
But no more deep will I endart mine eye

7. **I . . . maid** I was your mother when I was as old as you are now.
8. **he's . . . wax** He's a model of a man.

Summarize
Use the information in gloss 8 and the dialogue to help you summarize the Nurse's opinion of Paris.

9. **Examine . . . content** Examine every harmonious feature of his face, and see how each one enhances every other. Throughout this speech, Lady Capulet compares Paris to a book.
10. **margent** margin. Paris's eyes are compared to the margin of a book, where whatever is not clear in the text (the rest of his face) can be explained by notes.
11. **cover** metaphor for wife.
12. **I'll . . . move** If looking favorably at someone leads to liking him, I will look at Paris in a way that will lead to liking him.

Than your consent gives strength to make it fly.[13]

[*Enter* SERVINGMAN.]

SERVINGMAN. Madam, the guests are come, supper served up, you called, my young lady asked for, the nurse cursed in the pantry, and everything in extremity. I must hence to wait. I beseech you follow straight. [*Exit.*]

LADY CAPULET. We follow thee. Juliet, the County stays.[14]

NURSE. Go, girl, seek happy nights to happy days. [*Exit all.*]

Dialogue and Stage Directions
What does the dialogue reveal about Juliet's attitude toward marriage and Paris?

13. **But . . . fly** But I will not look harder than you want me to.
14. **the County stays** The Count, Paris, is waiting.

Scene iv. A street.

[*Enter* ROMEO, MERCUTIO, BENVOLIO, *with five or six other* MASKERS; TORCHBEARERS.]

ROMEO. What, shall this speech[1] be spoke for our excuse?
Or shall we on without apology?

BENVOLIO. The date is out of such prolixity.[2]
We'll have no Cupid hoodwinked with a scarf,
Bearing a Tartar's painted bow of lath,
Scaring the ladies like a crowkeeper,
Nor no without-book prologue, faintly spoke
After the prompter, for our entrance;
But, let them measure us by what they will,
We'll measure them a measure and be gone.

ROMEO. Give me a torch. I am not for this ambling.
Being but heavy,[3] I will bear the light.

MERCUTIO. Nay, gentle Romeo, we must have you dance.

ROMEO. Not I, believe me. You have dancing shoes
With nimble soles; I have a soul of lead
So stakes me to the ground I cannot move.

MERCUTIO. You are a lover. Borrow Cupid's wings
And soar with them above a common bound.

ROMEO. I am too sore enpiercèd with his shaft
To soar with his light feathers; and so bound
I cannot bound a pitch above dull woe.
Under love's heavy burden do I sink.

MERCUTIO. And, to sink in it, should you burden love—
Too great oppression for a tender thing.

1. **this speech** Romeo asks whether he and his companions, being uninvited guests, should follow custom by announcing their arrival in a speech.
2. **The . . . prolixity** Such wordiness is outdated. In the following lines, Benvolio says, in sum, "Let us forget about announcing our entrance with a show. The other guests can look over as they see fit. We will dance a while, then leave."
3. **heavy** weighed down with sadness.

Comprehension
Why has Lady Capulet come to talk to Juliet?

ROMEO. Is love a tender thing? It is too rough,
Too rude, too boist'rous, and it pricks like thorn.

MERCUTIO. If love be rough with you, be rough with love.
Prick love for pricking, and you beat love down.
Give me a case to put my visage[4] in.
A visor for a visor![5] What care I
What curious eye doth quote deformities?[6]
Here are the beetle brows shall blush for me.

BENVOLIO. Come, knock and enter; and no sooner in
But every man betake him to his legs.[7]

ROMEO. A torch for me! Let wantons light of heart
Tickle the senseless rushes[8] with their heels;
For I am proverbed with a grandsire phrase,[9]
I'll be a candleholder and look on;
The game was ne'er so fair, and I am done.[10]

MERCUTIO. Tut! Dun's the mouse, the constable's own word![11]
If thou art Dun,[12] we'll draw thee from the mire
Of this sir-reverence love, wherein thou stickest
Up to the ears. Come, we burn daylight, ho!

ROMEO. Nay, that's not so.

MERCUTIO. I mean, sir, in delay
We waste our lights in vain, like lights by day.
Take our good meaning, for our judgment sits
Five times in that ere once in our five wits.[13]

ROMEO. And we mean well in going to this masque,
But ' tis no wit to go.

MERCUTIO. Why, may one ask?

ROMEO. I dreamt a dream tonight.

MERCUTIO. And so did I.

ROMEO. Well, what was yours?

MERCUTIO. That dreamers often lie.

ROMEO. In bed asleep, while they do dream things true.

MERCUTIO. O, then I see Queen Mab[14] hath been with you.
She is the fairies' midwife, and she comes
In shape no bigger than an agate stone
On the forefinger of an alderman,
Drawn with a team of little atomies[15]
Over men's noses as they lie asleep;

4. **visage** mask.
5. **A visor . . . visor!** A mask for a mask—which is what my real face is like!
6. **quote deformities** notice my ugly features.
7. **betake . . . legs** start dancing.
8. **Let . . . rushes** Let fun-loving people dance on the floor coverings.
9. **proverbed . . . phrase** directed by an old saying.
10. **The game . . . done** No matter how much enjoyment may be had, I will not have any.
11. **Dun's . . . word!** Lie low like a mouse—that is what a constable waiting to make an arrest might say.
12. **Dun** proverbial name for a horse.

Dialogue and Stage Directions

What contrast between Mercutio and Romeo does the dialogue reveal?

13. **Take . . . wits** Understand my intended meaning. That shows more intelligence than merely following what your senses perceive.
14. **Queen Mab** the queen of fairyland.
15. **atomies** creatures.

Her wagon spokes made of long spinners'[16] legs,
The cover, of the wings of grasshoppers;
Her traces, of the smallest spider web;
Her collars, of the moonshine's wat'ry beams;
Her whip, of cricket's bone; the lash, of film;[17]
Her wagoner, a small gray-coated gnat,
Not half so big as a round little worm
Pricked from the lazy finger of a maid;
Her chariot is an empty hazelnut,
Made by the joiner squirrel or old grub,[18]
Time out o' mind the fairies' coachmakers.
And in this state she gallops night by night
Through lovers' brains, and then they dream of love;
On courtiers' knees, that dream on curtsies straight;
O'er lawyers' fingers, who straight dream on fees;
O'er ladies' lips, who straight on kisses dream,
Which oft the angry Mab with blisters plagues,
Because their breath with sweetmeats[19] tainted are.
Sometimes she gallops o'er a courtier's nose,
And then dreams he of smelling out a suit;[20]
And sometime comes she with a tithe pig's[21] tail
Tickling a parson's nose as 'a lies asleep,
Then he dreams of another benefice.[22]
Sometime she driveth o'er a soldier's neck,
And then dream he of cutting foreign throats,
Of breaches, ambuscadoes,[23] Spanish blades,
Of healths[24] five fathom deep; and then anon

16. **spinners** spiders.
17. **film** spider's thread.
18. **old grub** insect that bores holes in nuts.
19. **sweetmeats** candy.
20. **smelling . . . suit** finding someone who has a petition (suit) for the king and who will pay the courtier to gain the king's favor for the petition.
21. **tithe pig** pig donated to a parson.
22. **benefice** church appointment that included a guaranteed income.
23. **ambuscadoes** ambushes.
24. **healths** toasts ("To your health!").

Comprehension
How does Romeo feel about going to the Capulets' feast?

Drums in his ear, at which he starts and wakes,
And being thus frighted, swears a prayer or two
And sleeps again. This is that very Mab
That plats[25] the manes of horses in the night
And bakes the elflocks[26] in foul sluttish hairs,
Which once untangled much misfortune bodes.
This is the hag, when maids lie on their backs,
That presses them and learns them first to bear,
Making them women of good carriage.[27]
This is she—

25. plats tangles.
26. elflocks tangled hair.
27. carriage posture.

ROMEO. Peace, peace, Mercutio, peace!
Thou talk'st of nothing.

Summarize
Review Mercutio's speech and summarize his ideas about Queen Mab.

MERCUTIO. True, I talk of dreams;
Which are the children of an idle brain,
Begot of nothing but vain fantasy;
Which is as thin of substance as the air,
And more inconstant than the wind, who woos
Even now the frozen bosom of the North
And, being angered, puffs away from thence,
Turning his side to the dew-dropping South.

Dialogue and Stage Directions
What do Mercutio's comments about dreams reveal about his character?

BENVOLIO. This wind you talk of blows us from ourselves.
Supper is done, and we shall come too late.

Summarize
Use gloss 28 to help you summarize Romeo's response to Benvolio.

ROMEO. I fear, too early; for my mind misgives
Some consequence yet hanging in the stars
Shall bitterly begin his fearful date
With this night's revels and expire the term
Of a despisèd life, closed in my breast,
By some vile forfeit of untimely death.[28]
But he that hath the steerage of my course
Direct my sail! On, lusty gentlemen!

28. my mind . . . death My mind is fearful that some future event, fated by the stars, shall start to run its course tonight and cut my life short.

BENVOLIO. Strike, drum.

[*They march about the stage, and retire to one side.*]

Scene v. A hall in Capulet's house.

[SERVINGMEN *come forth with napkins.*]

FIRST SERVINGMAN. Where's Potpan, that he helps not to take away? He shift a trencher![1] He scrape a trencher!

1. trencher wooden platter.

SECOND SERVINGMAN. When good manners shall lie all in one or two men's hands, and they unwashed too, 'tis a foul thing.

First Servingman. Away with the joint-stools, remove the court cupboard, look to the plate. Good thou, save me a piece of marchpane,[2] and, as thou loves me, let the porter let in Susan Grindstone and Nell. Anthony and Potpan!

Second Servingman. Ay, boy, ready.

First Servingman. You are looked for and called for, asked for and sought for, in the great chamber.

Third Servingman. We cannot be here and there too. Cheerly, boys! Be brisk awhile, and the longest liver take all. [*Exit.*]

[*Enter* Capulet, *his* Wife, Juliet, Tybalt, Nurse, *and all the* Guests *and* Gentlewomen *to the* Maskers.]

Capulet. Welcome, gentlemen! Ladies that have their toes
Unplagued with corns will walk a bout[3] with you.
Ah, my mistresses, which of you all
Will now deny to dance? She that makes dainty,[4]
She I'll swear hath corns. Am I come near ye now?
Welcome, gentlemen! I have seen the day
That I have worn a visor and could tell
A whispering tale in a fair lady's ear,
Such as would please. 'Tis gone, 'tis gone, 'tis gone.
You are welcome, gentlemen! Come, musicians,
play.
[*Music plays, and they dance.*]
A hall,[5] a hall! Give room! And foot it, girls.
More light, you knaves, and turn the tables up,
And quench the fire; the room is grown too hot.
Ah, sirrah, this unlooked-for sport comes well.
Nay, sit; nay, sit, good cousin Capulet;
For you and I are past our dancing days.
How long is't now since last yourself and I
Were in a mask?

Second Capulet. By'r Lady, thirty years.

Capulet. What, man? 'Tis not so much, 'tis not so
much;
'Tis since the nuptial of Lucentio,
Come Pentecost as quickly as it will,
Some five-and-twenty years, and then we masked.

Second Capulet. 'Tis more, 'tis more. His son is elder, sir;
His son is thirty.

2. **marchpane** marzipan, a confection made of sugar and almonds.

3. **walk a bout** dance a turn.

4. **makes dainty** hesitates; acts shy.

5. **A hall** clear the floor, make room for dancing.

Spiral Review
CHARACTER What do lines 15 through 32 reveal about Capulet?

Comprehension
What does Romeo fear might happen in the near future?

▲ ▶ **Critical Viewing**
What can you tell about Romeo and Juliet's feelings for each other at this point from these images?

Dialogue and Stage Directions
What do the stage direction in line 40 and the dialogue that follows reveal about Romeo?

CAPULET. Will you tell me that?
His son was but a ward[6] two years ago.

ROMEO. [*To a* SERVINGMAN] What lady's that which doth enrich the hand
Of yonder knight?

SERVINGMAN. I know not, sir.

ROMEO. O, she doth teach the torches to burn bright!
It seems she hangs upon the cheek of night
As a rich jewel in an Ethiop's ear—
Beauty too rich for use, for earth too dear!
So shows a snowy dove trooping with crows
As yonder lady o'er her fellows shows.
The measure done, I'll watch her place of stand
And, touching hers, make blessèd my rude hand.
Did my heart love till now? Forswear[7] it, sight!
For I ne'er saw true beauty till this night.

TYBALT. This, by his voice, should be a Montague.
Fetch me my rapier, boy. What! Dares the slave
Come hither, covered with an antic face,[8]
To fleer[9] and scorn at our solemnity?
Now, by the stock and honor of my kin,
To strike him dead I hold it not a sin.

CAPULET. Why, how now, kinsman? Wherefore storm you so?

TYBALT. Uncle, this is a Montague, our foe,
A villain, that is hither come in spite

6. **ward** minor.
7. **Forswear** deny.
8. **antic face** strange, fantastic mask.
9. **fleer** mock.

To scorn at our solemnity this night.

Capulet. Young Romeo is it?

Tybalt. 'Tis he, that villain Romeo.

Capulet. Content thee, gentle coz,[10] let him alone.
'A bears him like a portly gentleman,[11]
And, to say truth, Verona brags of him
To be a virtuous and well-governed youth.
I would not for the wealth of all this town
Here in my house do him disparagement.[12]
Therefore be patient; take no note of him.
It is my will, the which if thou respect,
Show a fair presence and put off these frowns,
An ill-beseeming semblance[13] for a feast.

Tybalt. It fits when such a villain is a guest.
I'll not endure him.

Capulet. He shall be endured.
What, goodman[14] boy! I say he shall. Go to![15]
Am I the master here, or you? Go to!
You'll not endure him, God shall mend my soul![16]
You'll make a mutiny among my guests!
You will set cock-a-hoop.[17] You'll be the man!

Tybalt. Why, uncle, 'tis a shame.

Capulet. Go to, go to!
You are a saucy boy. Is't so, indeed?
This trick may chance to scathe you.[18] I know what.
You must contrary me! Marry, 'tis time—
Well said, my hearts!—You are a princox[19]—go!
Be quiet, or—more light, more light!—For shame!
I'll make you quiet. What!—Cheerly, my hearts!

10. **coz** Here, "coz" is used as a term of address for a relative.
11. **'A . . . gentleman** He behaves like a dignified gentleman.
12. **disparagement** insult.
13. **ill-beseeming semblance** inappropriate appearance.
14. **goodman** term of address for someone below the rank of gentleman.
15. **Go to!** expression of angry impatience.
16. **God . . . soul!** expression of impatience, equivalent to "God save me!"
17. **You will set cock-a-hoop** You want to swagger like a barnyard rooster.

Dialogue

What does the dialogue between Capulet and Tybalt show about their relationship?

18. **This . . . you** This trait of yours may turn out to hurt you.
19. **princox** rude youngster; wise guy.

Comprehension

How does Capulet respond when Tybalt says he will not tolerate Romeo's presence at the party?

Tybalt. Patience perforce with willful choler meeting[20]
Makes my flesh tremble in their different greeting.
I will withdraw; but this intrusion shall,
Now seeming sweet, convert to bitt'rest gall. [*Exit.*]

Romeo. If I profane with my unworthiest hand
This holy shrine,[21] the gentle sin is this:
My lips, two blushing pilgrims, ready stand
To smooth that rough touch with a tender kiss.

Juliet. Good pilgrim, you do wrong your hand too much,
Which mannerly devotion shows in this;
For saints have hands that pilgrims' hands do touch
And palm to palm is holy palmers'[22] kiss.

Romeo. Have not saints lips, and holy palmers too?

Juliet. Ay, pilgrim, lips that they must use in prayer.

Romeo. O, then, dear saint, let lips do what hands do!
They pray; grant thou, lest faith turn to despair.

Juliet. Saints do not move,[23] though grant for prayers' sake.

Romeo. Then move not while my prayer's effect I take.
Thus from my lips, by thine my sin is purged. [*Kisses her.*]

Juliet. Then have my lips the sin that they have took.

Romeo. Sin from my lips? O trespass sweetly urged![24]
Give me my sin again. [*Kisses her.*]

Juliet. You kiss by th' book.[25]

Nurse. Madam, your mother craves a word with you.

Romeo. What is her mother?

Nurse. Marry, bachelor,
Her mother is the lady of the house,
And a good lady, and a wise and virtuous.
I nursed her daughter that you talked withal.
I tell you, he that can lay hold of her
Shall have the chinks.[26]

Romeo. Is she a Capulet?
O dear account! My life is my foe's debt.[27]

Benvolio. Away, be gone; the sport is at the best.

Romeo. Ay, so I fear; the more is my unrest.

20. **Patience . . . meeting** enforced self-control mixing with strong anger.

21. **shrine** Juliet's hand.

22. **palmers** pilgrims who at one time carried palm branches from the Holy Land.

23. **move** initiate involvement in earthly affairs.

Dialogue and Stage Directions

What do the dialogue and stage directions in this passage reveal about Romeo's and Juliet's feelings?

24. **O . . . urged!** Romeo is saying, in substance, that he is happy. Juliet calls his kiss a sin, for now he can take it back—by another kiss.

25. **by th' book** as if you were following a manual of courtly love.

26. **chinks** cash.

27. **My life . . . debt** Since Juliet is a Capulet, Romeo's life is at the mercy of the enemies of his family.

CAPULET. Nay, gentlemen, prepare not to be gone;
We have a trifling foolish banquet towards.[28]
Is it e'en so?[29] Why then, I thank you all.
I thank you, honest gentlemen. Good night.
More torches here! Come on then; let's to bed.
Ah, sirrah, by my fay,[30] it waxes late;
I'll to my rest. *[Exit all but* JULIET *and* NURSE.*]*

JULIET. Come hither, nurse. What is yond gentleman?

NURSE. The son and heir of old Tiberio.

JULIET. What's he that now is going out of door?

NURSE. Marry, that, I think, be young Petruchio.

JULIET. What's he that follows here, that would not dance?

NURSE. I know not.

JULIET. Go ask his name—If he is married,

28. towards being prepared.
29. Is . . . so? Is it the case that you really must leave?
30. fay faith.

Dialogue and Stage Directions
How can you tell that the dialogue that follows line 126 is a private conversation?

Comprehension
How does Romeo get Juliet to kiss him?

My grave is like to be my wedding bed.

Nurse. His name is Romeo, and a Montague,
The only son of your great enemy.

Juliet. My only love, sprung from my only hate!
Too early seen unknown, and known too late!
Prodigious[31] birth of love it is to me
That I must love a loathèd enemy.

Nurse. What's this? What's this?

Juliet. A rhyme I learnt even now.
Of one I danced withal. [*One calls within,* "Juliet."]

Nurse. Anon, anon!
Come, let's away; the strangers all are gone. [*Exit all.*]

31. Prodigious monstrous; foretelling misfortune.

Language Study

Vocabulary An **oxymoron** is a figure of speech that combines contradictory or opposing ideas for poetic effect. Review the words shown in blue below, all of which come from *Romeo and Juliet,* Act I. Then, explain the meaning of each numbered phrase and tell why it is an oxymoron.

pernicious **adversary** **augmenting** **grievance** **oppression**

1. pernicious blessing
2. augmenting scarcity
3. flattering grievance
4. cooperative adversary
5. cheerful oppression

Word Study

Part A Explain how the **Latin prefix *trans-*** contributes to the meanings of *transport, translucent,* and *transition*. Consult a dictionary if necessary.

Part B Use the context of the sentences and what you know about the Latin prefix *trans-* to explain your answer to each question.

1. Can you *transfer* information from the Internet to a computer?
2. If the operation of a government office is *transparent*, will people know what is going on? Explain.

WORD STUDY

The **Latin prefix *trans-*** means "across," "over," or "through." In the play, Romeo describes his friend's sympathy for him as love's **transgression**. The word suggests that love has crossed a boundary and unfairly involved his friend.

Close Reading Activities

Literary Analysis

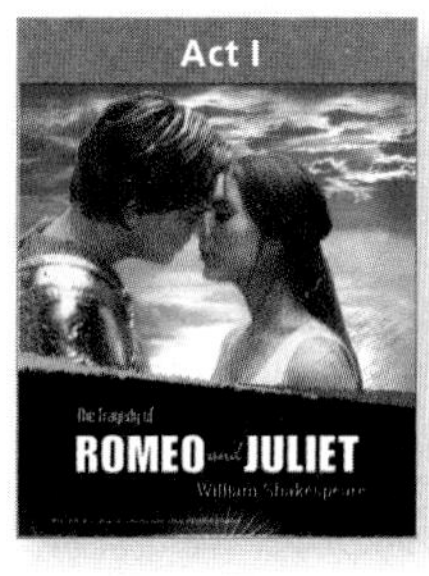

Key Ideas and Details

1. **(a)** What do you know about Romeo's and Juliet's lives at this point in the play? Explain, citing details from the play that support your answer. **(b) Compare and Contrast:** How are their circumstances both similar and different? Explain.
2. **Analyze:** What threats to Romeo and Juliet's love are evident in Act I? Support your answer with details from the play.
3. **(a)** What information about the two feuding households is presented in the Prologue? **(b) Connect:** How does Juliet's comment in Act I, Scene v, lines 137–138, echo the Prologue? Explain your response.
4. **Summarize** Refer to the glosses to clarify details. Then, summarize Capulet's scolding of Tybalt in Act I, Scene v, lines 77–87.
5. **Summarize** **(a)** Explain Juliet's play on words in her speech from Act I, Scene v, lines 96–99. **(b)** Write a summary of her speech.

Craft and Structure

6. **Dialogue and Stage Directions** Cite two examples of dialogue in Act I, Scene i, that show Benvolio's peacemaking personality.
7. **Dialogue and Stage Directions** Using a chart like the one shown, explain what the dialogue between the Nurse, Juliet, and Lady Capulet in Scene iii reveals about the three characters.
8. **Dialogue and Stage Directions** **(a)** Identify three examples of stage directions from the text that do more than simply dictate characters' movements on and off stage. **(b)** Explain what each direction shows about the characters and the action.

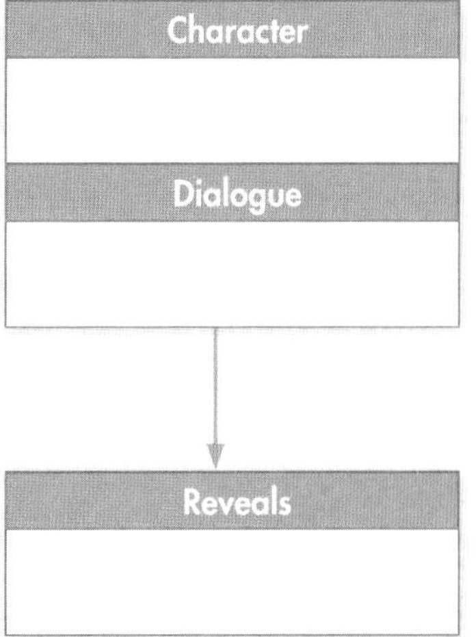

Integration of Knowledge and Ideas

9. **Evaluate:** Judging from Romeo's behavior in Act I, do you think Shakespeare accurately portrays a teenager in love? Cite details from the text to support your answer.

10. THE BIG ? **Do our differences define us?** Which most defines the relationship between Romeo and Juliet at this point in the play—their similarities or their differences? Support your response with examples from Act I.

ACADEMIC VOCABULARY

As you write and speak about *The Tragedy of Romeo and Juliet,* Act 1, use the words related to differences that you explored on page 481 of this book.

Do our differences define us?

Explore the Big Question as you read Act II of *The Tragedy of Romeo and Juliet*. Take notes on how characters handle differences they perceive between the two feuding families.

CLOSE READING FOCUS

Key Ideas and Details: **Read in Sentences**

Shakespeare's plays often include long passages of poetry. When you encounter such a long passage, **read in sentences** and pause according to the punctuation instead of at the end of each line. Doing so will clarify the meaning of each sentence, thus allowing you to better understand the passage and the action of the play as a whole.

Craft and Structure: **Blank Verse**

Blank verse is unrhymed poetry written in a meter call iambic pentameter. A line of iambic pentameter has five stressed syllables, each preceded by an unstressed syllable, as in this example:

> Bŭt sóft! Wȟat liğht thrŏugh yóndĕr wíndŏw bréaks?
> Ĭt ís tȟe eást, aňd Júliĕt ís tȟe sún!

In all of Shakespeare's plays, including *The Tragedy of Romeo and Juliet,* high-ranking, aristocratic characters speak in blank verse. By contrast, comic characters or those of low rank usually speak in prose, which is writing that is not divided into poetic lines and does not follow a specific meter. These two distinct styles clarify characters' social status and contribute to the tone and mood of their interactions.

Vocabulary

The words below are critical to understanding the text that follows. Copy the words into your notebook. Which word contains a prefix meaning "between"? Explain how this prefix contributes to the word's meaning.

procure	**intercession**	**lamentable**
predominant	**sallow**	**unwieldy**

Common Core State Standards

Reading Literature

2. Determine a theme or central idea of a text; provide an objective summary of the text.

5. Analyze how an author's choices concerning how to structure a text, order events within it, and manipulate time create such effects as mystery, tension, or surprise.

Language

6. Acquire and use accurately grade-appropriate general academic and domain-specific words and phrases, gather vocabulary knowledge when considering a word or phrase important to comprehension or expression.

CLOSE READING MODEL

The passage below is from Act II of William Shakespeare's *The Tragedy of Romeo and Juliet*. The annotations to the right of the passage show ways in which you can read in sentences and analyze blank verse.

from *The Tragedy of Romeo and Juliet*, Act II

Romeo. She speaks.
O, speak again, bright angel, for thou art
As glorious to this night, being o'er my head,
As is a wingèd messenger of heaven[1]
Unto the white-upturnèd wond'ring eyes
Of mortals that fall back to gaze on him
When he bestrides the lazy puffing clouds
And sails upon the bosom of the air.
Juliet. O Romeo, Romeo! Wherefore art thou Romeo?
Deny thy father and refuse thy name;
Or, if thou wilt not, be but sworn my love,
And I'll no longer be a Capulet.[2]
Romeo. *[Aside]* Shall I hear more, or shall I speak at this?
Juliet. Tis but thy name that is my enemy.
Thou art thyself, though not a Montague.
What's Montague? It is nor hand, nor foot,
Nor arm, nor face, nor any other part
Belonging to a man. O, be some other name!
What's in a name? That which we call a rose
By any other name would smell as sweet.
So Romeo would, were he not Romeo called,
Retain that dear perfection which he owes
Without that title.[3] Romeo, doff thy name;
And for thy name, which is no part of thee,
Take all myself.

Blank Verse

1 The first highlighted line is perfect iambic pentameter. However, in the second highlighted line, Shakespeare breaks the perfect meter slightly. This variation creates a subtle emphasis on the words *glorious* and *o'er* (or "over" in modern English).

Blank Verse

2 Both Romeo and Juliet speak in blank verse because they are aristocratic characters. This famous speech in which Juliet wishes Romeo were not a Montague deviates only slightly from perfect iambic pentameter.

Read in Sentences

3 To better understand Juliet's reasoning, do not pause at the ends of lines but follow the punctuation. She is saying that the name of Montague is not essential to Romeo in the same way as are his hands, feet, arms, and face. Even if he had a different name, he would still be the same person.

Review and Anticipate

Act I reveals a bitter, long-standing feud between the Montagues and the Capulets. It also introduces the play's title characters, who meet at a feast and immediately fall in love, only to discover that they come from opposing sides of the feud.

Based on what you have learned about the personalities of Romeo and Juliet, how do you expect them to respond to their love for each other and to the problems it poses? How do you think their families will react?

Prologue

[*Enter* CHORUS.]

CHORUS. Now old desire[1] doth in his deathbed lie,
And young affection gapes to be his heir;[2]
That fair[3] for which love groaned for and would die,
With tender Juliet matched, is now not fair.
Now Romeo is beloved and loves again,
Alike bewitchèd[4] by the charm of looks;
But to his foe supposed he must complain,[5]
And she steal love's sweet bait from fearful hooks.

1. **old desire** Romeo's love for Rosaline.
2. **young . . . heir** Romeo's new love for Juliet is eager to replace his love for Rosaline.
3. **fair** beautiful woman (Rosaline).
4. **Alike bewitchèd** Both Romeo and Juliet are enchanted.
5. **complain** address his words of love.

Being held a foe, he may not have access
To breathe such vows as lovers use to swear,
And she as much in love, her means much less
To meet her new belovèd anywhere;
But passion lends them power, time means to meet,
Temp'ring extremities with extreme sweet.[6]
[*Exit.*]

6. **Temp'ring . . . sweet** easing their difficulties with great delights.

Scene i. Near Capulet's orchard.

[*Enter* Romeo *alone.*]

Romeo. Can I go forward when my heart is here?
Turn back, dull earth,[1] and find thy center[2] out.

1. **dull earth** lifeless body.
2. **center** heart, or possibly soul (Juliet).

[*Enter* Benvolio *with* Mercutio. Romeo *retires.*]

Benvolio. Romeo! My cousin Romeo! Romeo!

Mercutio. He is wise.
And, on my life, hath stol'n him home to bed.

Benvolio. He ran this way and leapt this orchard wall.
Call, good Mercutio.

Mercutio. Nay, I'll conjure[3] too.
Romeo! Humors! Madman! Passion! Lover!
Appear thou in the likeness of a sigh;
Speak but one rhyme, and I am satisfied!
Cry but "Ay me!" Pronounce but "love" and "dove";
Speak to my gossip[4] Venus one fair word,
One nickname for her purblind son and heir,
Young Abraham Cupid, he that shot so true
When King Cophetua loved the beggar maid!
He heareth not, he stirreth not, he moveth not;
The ape is dead,[5] and I must conjure him.
I conjure thee by Rosaline's bright eyes,
By her high forehead and her scarlet lip,
By her fine foot, straight leg, and quivering thigh,
And the demesnes that there adjacent lie,
That in thy likeness thou appear to us!

3. **conjure** recite a spell to make Romeo appear.
4. **gossip** merry old lady.
5. **The ape is dead** Romeo, like a trained monkey, seems to be playing.

Blank Verse
Based on the meter of this speech, how can you tell that Mercutio is an aristocratic character?

Benvolio. And if he hear thee, thou wilt anger him.

Mercutio. This cannot anger him. 'Twould anger him
To raise a spirit in his mistress' circle
Of some strange nature, letting it there stand
Till she had laid it and conjured it down.

That were some spite; my invocation
Is fair and honest; in his mistress' name,
I conjure only but to raise up him.

Benvolio. Come, he hath hid himself among these trees
To be consorted[6] with the humorous[7] night.
Blind is his love and best befits the dark.

Mercutio. If love be blind, love cannot hit the mark.
Now will he sit under a medlar[8] tree
And wish his mistress were that kind of fruit
As maids call medlars when they laugh alone.
O, Romeo, that she were, O that she were
An open *et cetera*, thou a pop'rin pear!
Romeo, good night. I'll to my truckle bed;[9]
This field bed is too cold for me to sleep.
Come, shall we go?

Benvolio. Go then, for 'tis in vain
To seek him here that means not to be found.
[*Exit with others.*]

6. **consorted** associated.
7. **humorous** humid; moody, like a lover.

8. **medlar** applelike fruit.

9. **truckle bed** trundlebed, placed under a larger bed when not in use.

Scene ii. Capulet's orchard.

Romeo. [*Coming forward*] He jests at scars that never felt a wound.

[*Enter* Juliet *at a window.*]

But soft! What light through yonder window breaks?
It is the East, and Juliet is the sun!
Arise, fair sun, and kill the envious moon,
Who is already sick and pale with grief
That thou her maid art far more fair than she.
Be not her maid, since she is envious.
Her vestal livery[1] is but sick and green,
And none but fools do wear it. Cast it off.
It is my lady! O, it is my love!
O, that she knew she were!
She speaks, yet she says nothing. What of that?
Her eye discourses; I will answer it.
I am too bold; 'tis not to me she speaks.
Two of the fairest stars in all the heaven,
Having some business, do entreat her eyes
To twinkle in their spheres[2] till they return.
What if her eyes were there, they in her head?

Blank Verse
Which line in Romeo's speech breaks the pattern of five stressed syllables per line?

1. **livery** clothing or costume worn by a servant.

2. **spheres** orbits.

Comprehension
Whom does Romeo see at the window?

The brightness of her cheek would shame those stars
As daylight doth a lamp; her eyes in heaven
Would through the airy region stream so bright
That birds would sing and think it were not night.
See how she leans her cheek upon that hand,
O, that I were a glove upon that hand,
That I might touch that cheek!

Juliet. Ay me!

Romeo. She speaks.
O, speak again, bright angel, for thou art
As glorious to this night, being o'er my head,
As is a wingèd messenger of heaven
Unto the white-upturnèd wond'ring eyes
Of mortals that fall back to gaze on him
When he bestrides the lazy puffing clouds
And sails upon the bosom of the air.

Juliet. O Romeo, Romeo! Wherefore art thou Romeo?[3]
Deny thy father and refuse thy name;
Or, if thou wilt not, be but sworn my love,
And I'll no longer be a Capulet.

▼ Critical Viewing
Which line of dialogue in this scene might this photograph capture?

3. **Wherefore . . . Romeo?** Why are you Romeo—a Montague?

Romeo. [*Aside*] Shall I hear more, or shall I speak at this?

Juliet. Tis but thy name that is my enemy.
Thou art thyself, though not[4] a Montague.
What's Montague? It is nor hand, nor foot,
Nor arm, nor face, nor any other part
Belonging to a man. O, be some other name!
What's in a name? That which we call a rose
By any other name would smell as sweet.
So Romeo would, were he not Romeo called,
Retain that dear perfection which he owes[5]
Without that title. Romeo, doff[6] thy name;
And for thy name, which is no part of thee,
Take all myself.

Romeo. I take thee at thy word.
Call me but love, and I'll be new baptized;
Henceforth I never will be Romeo.

Juliet. What man art thou, thus bescreened in night,
So stumblest on my counsel?[7]

Romeo. By a name
I know not how to tell thee who I am.
My name, dear saint, is hateful to myself
Because it is an enemy to thee.
Had I it written, I would tear the word.

Juliet. My ears have yet not drunk a hundred words
Of thy tongue's uttering, yet I know the sound.
Art thou not Romeo, and a Montague?

Romeo. Neither, fair maid, if either thee dislike.

Juliet. How camest thou hither, tell me, and wherefore?
The orchard walls are high and hard to climb,
And the place death, considering who thou art,
If any of my kinsmen find thee here.

Romeo. With love's light wings did I o'erperch[8] these walls;
For stony limits cannot hold love out,
And what love can do, that dares love attempt.
Therefore thy kinsmen are no stop to me.

Juliet. If they do see thee, they will murder thee.

Romeo. Alack, there lies more peril in thine eye
Than twenty of their swords! Look thou but sweet,
And I am proof[9] against their enmity.

4. **though not** even if you were not.

Read in Sentences
Read in sentences to summarize Juliet's speech about Romeo's name.

5. **owes** owns; ossesses.
6. **doff** remove.

7. **counsel** secret thoughts.

Blank Verse
How do the stressed syllables in line 57 reinforce Romeo's meaning?

8. **o'erperch** fly over.

9. **proof** protected, as by armor.

Comprehension
Why does Romeo say his name is hateful to him?

JULIET. I would not for the world they saw thee here.

ROMEO. I have night's cloak to hide me from their eyes;
And but[10] thou love me, let them find me here.
My life were better ended by their hate
Than death proroguèd,[11] wanting of thy love.

JULIET. By whose direction found'st thou out this place?

ROMEO. By love, that first did prompt me to inquire.
He lent me counsel, and I lent him eyes.
I am no pilot; yet, wert thou as far
As that vast shore washed with the farthest sea,
I should adventure[12] for such merchandise.

JULIET. Thou knowest the mask of night is on my face;
Else would a maiden blush bepaint my cheek
For that which thou hast heard me speak tonight.
Fain would I dwell on form[13]—fain, fain deny
What I have spoke; but farewell compliment![14]
Dost thou love me? I know thou wilt say "Ay";
And I will take thy word. Yet, if thou swear'st,
Thou mayst prove false. At lovers' perjuries,
They say Jove laughs. O gentle Romeo,
If thou dost love, pronounce it faithfully.
Or if thou thinkest I am too quickly won,
I'll frown and be perverse[15] and say thee nay,
So thou wilt woo; but else, not for the world.
In truth, fair Montague, I am too fond,[16]
And therefore thou mayst think my havior light;[17]
But trust me, gentleman, I'll prove more true
Than those that have more cunning to be strange.[18]
I should have been more strange, I must confess,
But that thou overheard'st, ere I was ware,
My true-love passion. Therefore pardon me,
And not impute this yielding to light love,
Which the dark night hath so discoverèd.[19]

ROMEO. Lady, by yonder blessèd moon I vow,
That tips with silver all these fruit-tree tops—

JULIET. O, swear not by the moon, th' inconstant moon,
That monthly changes in her circle orb,
Lest that thy love prove likewise variable.

10. **And but** unless.

11. **proroguèd** postponed.

12. **adventure** risk a long journey, like a sea adventurer.

13. **Fain . . . form** eagerly would I follow convention (by acting reserved).

14. **compliment** conventional behavior.

15. **be perverse** act contrary to my true feelings.

16. **fond** affectionate.

17. **my havior light** my behavior immodest or unserious.

18. **strange** distant and cold.

19. **discoverèd** revealed.

Romeo. What shall I swear by?

Juliet. Do not swear at all;
Or if thou wilt, swear by thy gracious self,
Which is the god of my idolatry,
And I'll believe thee.

Romeo. If my heart's dear love—

Juliet. Well, do not swear. Although I joy in thee,
I have no joy of this contract[20] tonight.
It is too rash, too unadvised, too sudden;
Too like the lightning, which doth cease to be
Ere one can say it lightens. Sweet, good night!
This bud of love, by summer's ripening breath,
May prove a beauteous flow'r when next we meet.
Good night, good night! As sweet repose and rest
Come to thy heart as that within my breast!

Romeo. O, wilt thou leave me so unsatisfied?

Juliet. What satisfaction canst thou have tonight?

Romeo. Th'exchange of thy love's faithful vow for mine.

Blank Verse
The five stressed syllables of lines 112 and 115 are split between the two speakers. What does this weaving together of dialogue suggest about the speakers' relationship?

20. contract betrothal.

Comprehension
Why does Juliet tell Romeo not to swear his love by the moon?

21. **frank** generous.

22. **bounty** what I have to give.

Juliet. I gave thee mine before thou didst request it;
And yet I would it were to give again.

Romeo. Wouldst thou withdraw it? For what purpose, love?

Juliet. But to be frank[21] and give it thee again.
And yet I wish but for the thing I have.
My bounty[22] is as boundless as the sea,
My love as deep; the more I give to thee,
The more I have, for both are infinite.

[Nurse *calls within.*]

I hear some noise within. Dear love, adieu!
Anon, good nurse! Sweet Montague, be true.
Stay but a little, I will come again. [*Exit.*]

LITERATURE IN CONTEXT

Culture Connection

Falconry

When Juliet longs for "a falc'ners voice," she is referring to someone who practices falconry, the sport of hunting with falcons. Falcons are swift, hawk-like birds of prey. The falconer trains the bird to respond to a combination of physical and vocal commands.

During Shakespeare's time, one's rank in society determined the kind of bird one could own:

Rank	Type of Bird
King	Gyr falcon
Prince	Peregrine falcon (male)
Knight	Saker falcon
Squire	Lanner falcon
Lady	Merlin (female)
Yeoman (landowner)	Goshawk
Servants, children	Kestrel

◀ Falconry began as a way to obtain food but gradually evolved into the "sport of kings."

Thick leather gloves protected the falconer from the bird's talons. ▶

Connect to the Literature

Why do you think Juliet wishes Romeo would respond to her voice as a falcon does to the falconer's commands?

Romeo. O blessèd, blessèd night! I am afeard,
Being in night, all this is but a dream,
Too flattering-sweet to be substantial.[23]

[*Enter* Juliet *again.*]

Juliet. Three words, dear Romeo, and good night indeed.
If that thy bent[24] of love be honorable,
Thy purpose marriage, send me word tomorrow,
By one that I'll procure to come to thee,
Where and what time thou wilt perform the rite;
And all my fortunes at thy foot I'll lay
And follow thee my lord throughout the world.

Nurse. [*Within*] Madam!

Juliet. I come anon.—But if thou meanest not well,
I do beseech thee—

Nurse. [*Within*] Madam!

Juliet. By and by[25] I come.—
To cease thy strife[26] and leave me to my grief.
Tomorrow will I send.

Romeo. So thrive my soul—

Juliet. A thousand times good night! [*Exit.*]

Romeo. A thousand times the worse, to want thy light!
Love goes toward love as schoolboys from their books;
But love from love, toward school with heavy looks.

[*Enter* Juliet *again.*]

Juliet. Hist! Romeo, hist! O for a falc'ner's voice
To lure this tassel gentle[27] back again!
Bondage is hoarse[28] and may not speak aloud,
Else would I tear the cave where Echo[29] lies
And make her airy tongue more hoarse than mine
With repetition of "My Romeo!"

Romeo. It is my soul that calls upon my name.
How silver-sweet sound lovers' tongues by night,
Like softest music to attending ears!

Juliet. Romeo!

Romeo. My sweet?

Juliet. What o'clock tomorrow
Shall I send to thee?

23. **substantial** real.

24. **bent** purpose; intention.

◀ **Vocabulary**
procure (prō kyo͝or′)
v. get; obtain

25. **By and by** at once.
26. **strife** efforts.

Blank Verse
Based on the fact that Romeo and Juliet speak in blank verse, what can you conclude about their character rank?

27. **tassel gentle** male falcon.
28. **Bondage is hoarse** Being bound in by my family restricts my speech.
29. **Echo** In classical mythology, the nymph Echo, unable to win the love of Narcissus, wasted away in a cave until nothing was left of her but her voice.

Comprehension
Why must Juliet speak quietly to Romeo?

Romeo. By the hour of nine.

Juliet. I will not fail. 'Tis twenty year till then.
I have forgot why I did call thee back.

Romeo. Let me stand here till thou remember it.

Juliet. I shall forget, to have thee still stand there,
Rememb'ring how I love thy company.

Romeo. And I'll stay, to have thee still forget,
Forgetting any other home but this.

Juliet. 'Tis almost morning. I would have thee gone—
And yet no farther than a wanton's[30] bird,
That lets it hop a little from his hand,
Like a poor prisoner in his twisted gyves,[31]
And with a silken thread plucks it back again,
So loving-jealous of his liberty.

Romeo. I would I were thy bird.

Juliet. Sweet, so would I.
Yet I should kill thee with much cherishing.
Good night, good night! Parting is such sweet sorrow
That I shall say good night till it be morrow. [*Exit.*]

Romeo. Sleep dwell upon thine eyes, peace in thy breast!
Would I were sleep and peace, so sweet to rest!
Hence will I to my ghostly friar's[32] close cell,[33]
His help to crave and my dear hap[34] to tell. [*Exit.*]

30. wanton's spoiled, playful child's.
31. gyves (jīvz) chains.

32. ghostly friar's spiritual father's.
33. close cell small room.
34. dear hap good fortune.

Scene iii. Friar Lawrence's cell.

[*Enter* Friar Lawrence *alone, with a basket.*]

Friar. The gray-eyed morn smiles on the frowning night,
Check'ring the eastern clouds with streaks of light;
And fleckèd[1] darkness like a drunkard reels
From forth day's path and Titan's burning wheels.[2]
Now, ere the sun advance his burning eye
The day to cheer and night's dank dew to dry,
I must upfill this osier cage[3] of ours
With baleful[4] weeds and precious-juicèd flowers.
The earth that's nature's mother is her tomb.
What is her burying grave, that is her womb;
And from her womb children of divers kind[5]
We sucking on her natural bosom find,
Many for many virtues excellent,

Read in Sentences
Read the sentences in the Friar's speech. State the main points in lines 1–30.

1. **fleckèd** spotted.
2. **Titan's burning wheels** wheels of the sun god's chariot.
3. **osier cage** willow basket.
4. **baleful** poisonous.
5. **divers kind** different kinds.

None but for some, and yet all different.
O, mickle[6] is the powerful grace[7] that lies
In plants, herbs, stones, and their true qualities;
For naught so vile that on the earth doth live
But to the earth some special good doth give;
Nor aught so good but, strained[8] from that fair use,
Revolts from true birth,[9] stumbling on abuse.
Virtue itself turns vice, being misapplied,
And vice sometime by action dignified.

[*Enter* ROMEO.]

Within the infant rind[10] of this weak flower
Poison hath residence and medicine power;[11]
For this, being smelt, with that part cheers each part;[12]
Being tasted, stays all senses with the heart.[13]
Two such opposèd kings encamp them still[14]
In man as well as herbs—grace and rude will;
And where the worser is predominant,
Full soon the canker[15] death eats up that plant.

ROMEO. Good morrow, father.

FRIAR. *Benedicite!*[16]
What early tongue so sweet saluteth me?
Young son, it argues a distemperèd head[17]
So soon to bid good morrow to thy bed.
Care keeps his watch in every old man's eye,
And where care lodges, sleep will never lie;
But where unbruisèd youth with unstuffed[18] brain
Doth couch his limbs, there golden sleep doth reign,
Therefore thy earliness doth me assure
Thou art uproused with some distemp'rature;[19]
Or if not so, then here I hit it right—
Our Romeo hath not been in bed tonight.

ROMEO. That last is true. The sweeter rest was mine.

FRIAR. God pardon sin! Wast thou with Rosaline?

ROMEO. With Rosaline, my ghostly father? No.
I have forgot that name and that name's woe.

FRIAR. That's my good son! But where hast thou been then?

ROMEO. I'll tell thee ere thou ask it me again.
I have been feasting with mine enemy,
Where on a sudden one hath wounded me
That's by me wounded. Both our remedies

6. **mickle** great.
7. **grace** divine power.
8. **strained** turned away.
9. **Revolts . . . birth** conflicts with its real purpose.
10. **infant rind** tender skin.
11. **and medicine power** and medicinal quality has power.
12. **with . . . part** with that quality—odor—revives each part of the body.
13. **stays . . . heart** kills (stops the working of the five senses along with the heart).
14. **still** always.
15. **canker** destructive caterpillar.

◀ **Vocabulary**
predominant (prē däm′ ə nənt) *adj.* having greater frequency, strength, or influence

16. ***Benedicite!*** God bless you!
17. **distemperèd head** troubled mind.

18. **unstuffed** not filled with cares.
19. **distemp'rature** illness.

Blank Verse
What sets the Friar's lines apart from normal blank verse?

Comprehension
What plan do Romeo and Juliet make for the following day?

Vocabulary ▶
intercession (in′ tər sesh′ ən) *n.* the act of pleading on another's behalf

20. **physic** (fiz′ ik) medicine.
21. **My . . . foe** my plea also helps my enemy (Juliet, a Capulet).
22. **and . . . drift** and simple in your speech.
23. **Riddling . . . shrift** A confusing confession will get you uncertain forgiveness. The Friar means that unless Romeo speaks clearly, he will not get clear and direct advice.
24. **And . . . save** and we are united in every way, except for (save).
25. **brine** salt water (tears).

Vocabulary ▶
sallow (sal′ ō) *adj.* of a sickly, pale-yellowish hue

26. **fall** be weak or inconstant.
27. **strength** constancy; stability.
28. **doting** being infatuated.
29. **badst** urged.

30. **grace** favor.
31. **allow** give.
32. **Thy . . . spell** your love recited words from memory with no understanding of them.

Within thy help and holy physic[20] lies.
I bear no hatred, blessèd man, for, lo,
My **intercession** likewise steads my foe.[21]

Friar. Be plain, good son, and homely in thy drift.[22]
Riddling confession finds but riddling shrift.[23]

Romeo. Then plainly know my heart's dear love is set
On the fair daughter of rich Capulet;
As mine on hers, so hers is set on mine,
And all combined, save[24] what thou must combine
By holy marriage. When and where and how
We met, we wooed, and made exchange of vow,
I'll tell thee as we pass; but this I pray,
That thou consent to marry us today.

Friar. Holy Saint Francis! What a change is here!
Is Rosaline, that thou didst love so dear,
So soon forsaken? Young men's love then lies
Not truly in their hearts, but in their eyes.
Jesu Maria! What a deal of brine[25]
Hath washed thy **sallow** cheeks for Rosaline!
How much salt water thrown away in waste
To season love, that of it doth not taste!
The sun not yet thy sighs from heaven clears,
Thy old groans ring yet in mine ancient ears.
Lo, here upon thy cheek the stain doth sit
Of an old tear that is not washed off yet.
If e'er thou wast thyself, and these woes thine,
Thou and these woes were all for Rosaline.
And art thou changed? Pronounce this sentence then:
Women may fall[26] when there's no strength[27] in men.

Romeo. Thou chidst me oft for loving Rosaline.

Friar. For doting,[28] not for loving, pupil mine.

Romeo. And badst[29] me bury love.

Friar. Not in a grave
To lay one in, another out to have.

Romeo. I pray thee chide me not. Her I love now
Doth grace[30] for grace and love for love allow.[31]
The other did not so.

Friar. O, she knew well
Thy love did read by rote, that could not spell.[32]

But come, young waverer, come go with me.
In one respect I'll thy assistant be;
For this alliance may so happy prove
To turn your households' rancor[33] to pure love.

Romeo. O, let us hence! I stand on[34] sudden haste.

Friar. Wisely and slow. They stumble that run fast. [*Exit all.*]

33. **rancor** hatred.
34. **stand on** insist on.

Scene iv. A street.

[*Enter* Benvolio *and* Mercutio.]

Mercutio. Where the devil should this Romeo be? Came he not home tonight?

Benvolio. Not to his father's. I spoke with his man.

Mercutio. Why, that same pale hardhearted wench, that Rosaline,
torments him so that he will sure run mad.

Benvolio. Tybalt, the kinsman to old Capulet,
Hath sent a letter to his father's house.

Mercutio. A challenge, on my life.

Benvolio. Romeo will answer it.

Mercutio. Any man that can write may answer a letter.

Benvolio. Nay, he will answer the letter's master, how he dares, being dared.

Mercutio. Alas, poor Romeo, he is already dead: stabbed with a white wench's black eye; run through the ear with a love song; the very pin of his heart cleft with the blind bow-boy's butt-shaft;[1] and is he a man to encounter Tybalt?

Benvolio. Why, what is Tybalt?

Mercutio. More than Prince of Cats.[2] O, he's the courageous captain of compliments.[3] He fights as you sing pricksong[4]—keeps time, distance, and proportion; he rests his minim rests,[5] one, two, and the third in your bosom! The very butcher of a silk button,[6] a duelist, a duelist! A gentleman of the very first house,[7] of the first and second cause.[8] Ah, the immortal *passado*! The *punto reverso*! The hay![9]

Benvolio. The what?

Mercutio. The pox of such antic, lisping, affecting

Blank Verse
In what way is Mercutio's and Benvolio's speech in this scene different from what it was earlier in Act II?

1. **blind bow-boy's butt-shaft** Cupid's blunt arrow.
2. **Prince of Cats** Tybalt, or a variation of it, is the name of the cat in medieval stories of Reynard the Fox.
3. **captain of compliments** master of formal behavior.
4. **as you sing pricksong** with attention to precision.
5. **rests . . . rests** observes all formalities.
6. **button** exact spot on his opponent's shirt.
7. **first house** finest school of fencing.
8. **the first and second cause** reasons that would cause a gentleman to challenge another to a duel.
9. ***passado! . . . punto reverso! . . . hay!*** lunge . . . backhanded stroke . . . home thrust.

Comprehension
What does the Friar think Romeo and Juliet's love will do for the Capulets and Montagues?

10. **The pox . . . accent** May the plague strike these absurd characters with their phony manners.

Vocabulary ▶
lamentable (lam´ ən tə bəl) *adj.* distressing; sad

fantasticoes—these new tuners of accent![10] "By Jesu, a very good blade! A very tall man! A very good whore!" Why, is not this a **lamentable** thing, grandsir, that we should be thus afflicted with these strange flies, these fashionmongers, these pardon-me's,[11] who stand so much on the new form that they cannot sit at ease on the old bench? O, their bones, their bones!

[*Enter* ROMEO.]

11. **these pardon-me's** these men who are always saying "Pardon me."
12. **Without . . . herring** worn out.
13. **numbers** verses of love poems.

BENVOLIO. Here comes Romeo! Here comes Romeo!

MERCUTIO. Without his roe, like a dried herring.[12] O flesh, flesh, how art thou fishified! Now is he for the numbers[13] that Petrarch flowed in. Laura, to his lady, was a kitchen wench (marry, she had a better love to berhyme her), Dido a dowdy, Cleopatra a gypsy, Helen and Hero hildings and harlots, Thisbe a gray eye or so, but not to the purpose. Signior Romeo, *bonjour*! There's a French salutation to your French slop. You gave us the counterfeit fairly last night.

ROMEO. Good morrow to you both. What counterfeit did I give you?

14. **slip** escape. Slip is also a term for a counterfeit coin.

MERCUTIO. The slip,[14] sir, the slip. Can you not conceive?

LITERATURE IN CONTEXT

History Connection

Mercutio's Allusions

The women Mercutio names as he taunts Romeo are famous figures in European literature and history. Laura was the name of a woman to whom the Italian poet Petrarch addressed much of his love poetry. Dido, according to Roman mythology, was the queen of Carthage and love interest of Aeneas, the founder of Rome. Cleopatra was the famed Egyptian queen with whom Julius Caesar and later Mark Antony fell in love. Helen, Hero, and Thisbe are all legendary beauties in Greek mythology. Mercutio mocks Romeo by saying that Romeo thinks none of them compare with Rosaline.

Connect to the Literature

Why is Mercutio's use of grand references and exaggerated language a fitting way to tease Romeo?

Romeo. Pardon, good Mercutio. My business was great, and in such a case as mine a man may strain courtesy.

Mercutio. That's as much as to say, such a case as yours constrains a man to bow in the hams.[15]

Romeo. Meaning, to curtsy.

Mercutio. Thou hast most kindly hit it.

Romeo. A most courteous exposition.

Mercutio. Nay, I am the very pink of courtesy.

Romeo. Pink for flower.

Mercutio. Right.

Romeo. Why, then is my pump[16] well-flowered.

Mercutio. Sure wit, follow me this jest now till thou hast worn out thy pump, that, when the single sole of it is worn, the jest may remain, after the wearing, solely singular.[17]

Romeo. O single-soled jest, solely singular for the singleness![18]

Mercutio. Come between us, good Benvolio! My wits faints.

Romeo. Swits and spurs, swits and spurs; or I'll cry a match.[19]

Mercutio. Nay, if our wits run the wild-goose chase, I am done; for thou hast more of the wild goose in one of thy wits than, I am sure, I have in my whole five. Was I with you there for the goose?

Romeo. Thou wast never with me for anything when thou wast not there for the goose.

Mercutio. I will bite thee by the ear for that jest.

Romeo. Nay, good goose, bite not!

Mercutio. Thy wit is a very bitter sweeting;[20] it is a most sharp sauce.

Romeo. And is it not, then, well served in to a sweet goose?

Mercutio. O, here's a wit of cheveril,[21] that stretches from an inch narrow to an ell broad!

Romeo. I stretch it out for that word "broad," which added to the goose, proves thee far and wide a broad goose.

15. **hams** hips.

16. **pump** shoe.

17. **when . . . singular** the jest will outwear the shoe and will then be all alone.

18. **O . . . singleness!** O thin joke, unique for only one thing—weakness!

19. **Swits . . . match** Drive your wit harder to beat me or else I will claim victory in this match of word play.

Blank Verse

Why do you think Romeo does not speak in blank verse in this conversation with his friends?

20. **sweeting** kind of apple.

21. **cheveril** easily stretched kid leather.

Comprehension

How does Romeo respond when Mercutio says that Romeo gave his friends "the slip" the night before?

MERCUTIO. Why, is not this better now than groaning for love? Now art thou sociable, now art thou Romeo; now art thou what thou art, by art as well as by nature. For this driveling love is like a great natural[22] that runs lolling[23] up and down to hide his bauble[24] in a hole.

22. **natural** idiot.
23. **lolling** with tongue hanging out.
24. **bauble** toy.
25. **the hair** natural inclination.

BENVOLIO. Stop there, stop there!

MERCUTIO. Thou desirest me to stop in my tale against the hair.[25]

BENVOLIO. Thou wouldst else have made thy tale large.

MERCUTIO. O, thou art deceived! I would have made it short; for I was come to the whole depth of my tale, and meant indeed to occupy the argument[26] no longer.

ROMEO. Here's goodly gear![27]

26. **occupy the argument** talk about the matter.
27. **goodly gear** good stuff for joking (Romeo sees Nurse approaching).
28. **A shirt and a smock** a man and a woman.

[*Enter* NURSE *and her Man,* PETER.]

A sail, a sail!

MERCUTIO. Two, two! A shirt and a smock.[28]

NURSE. Peter!

PETER. Anon.

NURSE. My fan, Peter.

MERCUTIO. Good Peter, to hide her face; for her fan's the fairer face.

NURSE. God ye good morrow, gentlemen.

MERCUTIO. God ye good-den, fair gentlewoman.

NURSE. Is it good-den?

Blank Verse
How does Shakespeare reveal Romeo and Mercutio's intelligence even when they are not speaking in blank verse?

MERCUTIO. 'Tis no less, I tell ye; for the bawdy hand of the dial is now upon the prick of noon.

NURSE. Out upon you! What a man are you!

ROMEO. One, gentlewoman, that God hath made, himself to mar.

NURSE. By my troth, it is well said. "For himself to mar," quoth 'a? Gentlemen, can any of you tell me where I may find the young Romeo?

ROMEO. I can tell you; but young Romeo will be older when you have found him than he was when you sought him. I am the youngest of that name, for fault[29] of a worse.

29. **fault** lack.

Nurse. You say well.

Mercutio. Yea, is the worst well? Very well took,[30] i' faith! Wisely, wisely.

Nurse. If you be he, sir, I desire some confidence[31] with you.

Benvolio. She will endite him to some supper.

Mercutio. A bawd, a bawd, a bawd! So ho!

Romeo. What hast thou found?

Mercutio. No hare, sir; unless a hare, sir, in a lenten pie, that is something stale and hoar ere it be spent.

[*He walks by them and sings.*]

An old hare hoar,
And an old hare hoar,
Is very good meat in Lent;
But a hare that is hoar
Is too much for a score
When it hoars ere it be spent.

30. **took** understood.

31. **confidence** Nurse means "conference."

Comprehension
Who interrupts Romeo and his friends to ask about Romeo?

Romeo, will you come to your father's? We'll to dinner thither.

Romeo. I will follow you.

Mercutio. Farewell, ancient lady. Farewell, [*singing*] "Lady, lady, lady."[32] [*Exit* Mercutio, Benvolio.]

32. **"Lady . . . lady"** line from an old ballad, "Chaste Susanna."

33. **ropery** Nurse means "roguery," the talk and conduct of a rascal.

Nurse. I pray you, sir, what saucy merchant was this that was so full of his ropery?[33]

Romeo. A gentleman, nurse, that loves to hear himself talk and will speak more in a minute than he will stand to in a month.

34. **'a** he.

Nurse. And 'a[34] speak anything against me, I'll take him down, and 'a were lustier than he is, and twenty such Jacks; and if I cannot, I'll find those that shall. Scurvy knave! I am none of his flirt-gills;[35] I am none of his skainsmates.[36] And thou must stand by too, and suffer every knave to use me at his pleasure!

35. **flirt-gills** common girls.

36. **skainsmates** criminals; cutthroats.

Peter. I saw no man use you at his pleasure. If I had, my weapon should quickly have been out, I warrant you. I dare draw as soon as another man, if I see occasion in a good quarrel, and the law on my side.

Spiral Review

CHARACTER What do Nurse's comments to Romeo reveal about her feelings for Juliet?

Nurse. Now, afore God, I am so vexed that every part about me quivers. Scurvy knave! Pray you, sir, a word; and, as I told you, my young lady bid me inquire you out. What she bid me say, I will keep to myself; but first let me tell ye, if ye should lead her in a fool's paradise, as they say, it were a very gross kind of behavior, as they say; for the gentlewoman is young; and therefore, if you should deal double with her, truly it were an ill thing to be off'red to any gentlewoman, and very weak[37] dealing.

37. **weak** unmanly.

38. **commend** convey my respect and best wishes.

Romeo. Nurse, commend[38] me to thy lady and mistress. I protest unto thee—

Nurse. Good heart, and i' faith I will tell her as much. Lord, Lord, she will be a joyful woman.

Romeo. What wilt thou tell her, nurse? Thou dost not mark me.

Nurse. I will tell her, sir, that you do protest, which, as I take it, is a gentlemanlike offer.

ROMEO. Bid her devise
Some means to come to shrift[39] this afternoon;
And there she shall at Friar Lawrence' cell
Be shrived and married. Here is for thy pains.

NURSE. No, truly, sir; not a penny.

ROMEO. Go to! I say you shall.

NURSE. This afternoon, sir? Well, she shall be there.

ROMEO. And stay, good nurse, behind the abbey wall.
Within this hour my man shall be with thee
And bring thee cords made like a tackled stair.[40]
Which to the high topgallant[41] of my joy
Must be my convoy[42] in the secret night.
Farewell. Be trusty, and I'll quit[43] thy pains.
Farewell. Commend me to thy mistress.

NURSE. Now God in heaven bless thee! Hark you, sir.

ROMEO. What say'st thou, my dear nurse?

NURSE. Is your man secret? Did you ne'er hear say,
Two may keep counsel, putting one away?[44]

ROMEO. Warrant thee my man's as true as steel.

NURSE. Well, sir, my mistress is the sweetest lady. Lord, Lord! When 'twas a little prating[45] thing—O, there is a nobleman in town, one Paris, that would fain lay knife aboard;[46] but she, good soul, had as lieve[47] see a toad, a very toad, as see him. I anger her sometimes, and tell her that Paris is the properer man; but I'll warrant you, when I say so, she looks as pale as any clout[48] in the versal world.[49] Doth not rosemary and Romeo begin both with a letter?

ROMEO. Ay, nurse; what of that? Both with an R.

NURSE. Ah, mocker! That's the dog's name.[50] R is for the— No; I know it begins with some other letter; and she hath the prettiest sententious[51] of it, of you and rosemary, that it would do you good to hear it.

ROMEO. Commend me to thy lady.

NURSE. Ay, a thousand times. [*Exit* ROMEO.] Peter!

PETER. Anon.

NURSE. Before, and apace.[52] [*Exit, after* PETER.]

---

39. shrift confession.

Read in Sentences
Read in sentences to summarize Romeo's instructions to the Nurse in lines 175–181.

40. tackled stair rope ladder.
41. topgallant summit.
42. convoy conveyance.
43. quit reward; pay you back for.

44. Two . . . away Two can keep a secret if one is ignorant, or out of the way.
45. prating babbling.
46. fain . . . aboard eagerly seize Juliet for himself.
47. had as lieve would as willingly.
48. clout cloth.
49. versal world universe.
50. dog's name *R* sounds like a growl.
51. sententious Nurse means "sentences"—clever, wise sayings.
52. Before, and apace Go ahead of me, and quickly.

Blank Verse
What is the effect of hearing Romeo's blank verse after long passages of prose?

Comprehension
What does Romeo ask the Nurse to tell Juliet?

Scene v. Capulet's orchard.

[*Enter* JULIET.]

JULIET. The clock struck nine when I did send the nurse;
In half an hour she promised to return.
Perchance she cannot meet him. That's not so.
O, she is lame! Love's heralds should be thoughts,
Which ten times faster glides than the sun's beams
Driving back shadows over low'ring[1] hills.
Therefore do nimble-pinioned doves draw Love,[2]
And therefore hath the wind-swift Cupid wings.
Now is the sun upon the highmost hill
Of this day's journey, and from nine till twelve
Is three long hours; yet she is not come.
Had she affections and warm youthful blood,
She would be as swift in motion as a ball;
My words would bandy her[3] to my sweet love,
And his to me.
But old folks, many feign[4] as they were dead—
Unwieldy, slow, heavy and pale as lead.

1. **low'ring** darkening.
2. **Therefore . . . Love** therefore, doves with quick wings pull the chariot of Venus, goddess of love.
3. **bandy her** send her rapidly.

Vocabulary ▶
unwieldy (un wēl′ dē) *adj.* awkward; clumsy

4. **feign** act.

[*Enter* NURSE *and* PETER.]

O God, she comes! O honey nurse, what news?
Hast thou met with him? Send thy man away.

NURSE. Peter, stay at the gate. [*Exit* PETER.]

JULIET. Now, good sweet nurse—O Lord, why lookest thou sad?
Though news be sad, yet tell them merrily;
If good, thou shamest the music of sweet news
By playing it to me with so sour a face.

NURSE. I am aweary, give me leave[5] awhile.
Fie, how my bones ache! What a jaunce[6] have I!

5. **give me leave** excuse me; give me a moment's rest.
6. **jaunce** rough trip.

JULIET. I would thou hadst my bones, and I thy news.
Nay, come, I pray thee speak. Good, good nurse, speak.

NURSE. Jesu, what haste? Can you not stay a while?
Do you not see that I am out of breath?

JULIET. How art thou out of breath when thou hast breath
To say to me that thou art out of breath?
The excuse that thou dost make in this delay
Is longer than the tale thou dost excuse.
Is thy news good or bad? Answer to that.

Say either, and I'll stay the circumstance.[7]
Let me be satisfied, is't good or bad?

Nurse. Well, you have made a simple[8] choice; you know not how to choose a man. Romeo? No, not he. Though his face be better than any man's, yet his leg excels all men's; and for a hand and a foot, and a body, though they be not to be talked on, yet they are past compare. He is not the flower of courtesy, but, I'll warrant him, as gentle as a lamb. Go thy ways, wench; serve God. What, have you dined at home?

Juliet. No, no. But all this I did know before.
What says he of our marriage? What of that?

Nurse. Lord, how my head aches! What a head have I!
It beats as it would fall in twenty pieces.
My back a[9] t'other side—ah, my back, my back!
Beshrew[10] your heart for sending me about
To catch my death with jauncing up and down!

Juliet. I' faith, I am sorry that thou art not well.
Sweet, sweet, sweet nurse, tell me, what says my love?

Nurse. Your love says, like an honest gentleman, and a courteous, and a kind, and a handsome, and, I warrant, a virtuous—Where is your mother?

Juliet. Where is my mother? Why, she is within.
Where should she be? How oddly thou repliest!
"Your love says, like an honest gentleman,
'Where is your mother?'"

Nurse. O God's Lady dear!
Are you so hot?[11] Marry come up, I trow.[12]
Is this the poultice[13] for my aching bones?
Henceforward do your messages yourself.

Juliet. Here's such a coil![14] Come, what says Romeo?

Nurse. Have you got leave to go to shrift today?

Juliet. I have.

Nurse. Then hie you hence to Friar Lawrence' cell;
There stays a husband to make you a wife.
Now comes the wanton[15] blood up in your cheeks:
They'll be in scarlet straight at any news.
Hie you to church: I must another way,

7. **stay the circumstance** wait for the details.
8. **simple** foolish; simpleminded.
9. **a** on.
10. **Beshrew** shame on.

Blank Verse
What might Shakespeare be indicating about the Nurse's character by having her switch between prose and blank verse?

11. **hot** impatient; hot-tempered.
12. **Marry . . . trow** Indeed, cool down, I say.
13. **poultice** remedy.
14. **coil** disturbance.
15. **wanton** excited.

Comprehension
How does the Nurse describe Romeo?

Blank Verse
What effect is created by making Juliet's last line rhyme with the Nurse's last line?

To fetch a ladder, by the which your love
Must climb a bird's nest soon when it is dark.
I am the drudge, and toil in your delight:
But you shall bear the burden soon at night.
Go; I'll to dinner; hie you to the cell.

Juliet. Hie to high fortune! Honest nurse, farewell.

[*Exit all.*]

Scene vi. Friar Lawrence's cell.

[*Enter* Friar Lawrence *and* Romeo.]

Friar. So smile the heavens upon this holy act
That afterhours with sorrow chide us not![1]

Romeo. Amen, amen! But come what sorrow can,
It cannot countervail[2] the exchange of joy
That one short minute gives me in her sight.
Do thou but close our hands with holy words,
Then love-devouring death do what he dare—
It is enough I may but call her mine.

Friar. These violent delights have violent ends
And in their triumph die, like fire and powder,[3]
Which, as they kiss, consume. The sweetest honey

1. **That . . . not!** that the future does not punish us with sorrow.
2. **countervail** equal.
3. **powder** gunpowder.

▶ Critical Viewing
Which details in this picture reflect the feelings Romeo and Juliet have for each other?

Is loathsome in his own deliciousness
And in the taste confounds[4] the appetite.
Therefore love moderately: long love doth so;
Too swift arrives as tardy as too slow.

[*Enter* JULIET.]

Here comes the lady. O, so light a foot
Will ne'er wear out the everlasting flint.[5]
A lover may bestride the gossamers[6]
That idles in the wanton summer air,
And yet not fall; so light is vanity.[7]

JULIET. Good even to my ghostly confessor.

FRIAR. Romeo shall thank thee, daughter, for us both.

4. **confounds** destroys.

5. **flint** stone.
6. **gossamers** spider webs.
7. **vanity** foolish things that cannot last.

Juliet. As much to him,[8] else is his thanks too much.

Romeo. Ah, Juliet, if the measure of thy joy
Be heaped like mine, and that thy skill be more
To blazon it,[9] then sweeten with thy breath
This neighbor air, and let rich music's tongue
Unfold the imagined happiness that both
Receive in either by this dear encounter.

Juliet. Conceit, more rich in matter than in words,
Brags of his substance, not of ornament.[10]
They are but beggars that can count their worth;
But my true love is grown to such excess
I cannot sum up sum of half my wealth.

Friar. Come, come with me, and we will make short work,
For, by your leaves, you shall not stay alone
Till Holy Church incorporate two in one. [*Exit all.*]

8. **As . . . him** the same greeting to him.
9. **and . . . it** and if you are better able to proclaim it.
10. **Conceit . . . ornament** Understanding does not need to be dressed up in words.

Language Study

Vocabulary The words listed below appear in Act II of *The Tragedy of Romeo and Juliet.* Answer each question that follows. Then, explain your answer.

predominant **intercession** **sallow** **lamentable** **unwieldy**

1. What is the *predominant* feeling at a celebration?
2. How many people are needed for an *intercession* to occur?
3. Is a *sallow* complexion a sign of good health?
4. If a situation is *lamentable*, are people likely to be happy about it?
5. Is an *unwieldy* package something you would want to carry far?

WORD STUDY

The **Latin suffix *-able*** means "like" or "capable of being." In Act II, Mercutio mocks fashionable people, saying their presence is **lamentable,** or something that is capable of being lamented or mourned.

Word Study

Part A Explain how the **Latin suffix *-able*** contributes to the meanings of the words *adorable, achievable,* and *arguable.* Consult a dictionary if necessary.

Part B Use the context of the sentences and what you know about the Latin suffix *-able* to explain your answer to each question.

1. Which is *perishable,* an oak tree or a diamond?
2. Are ancient scripts, such as hieroglyphics, *decipherable* by most modern readers?

Close Reading Activities

Literary Analysis

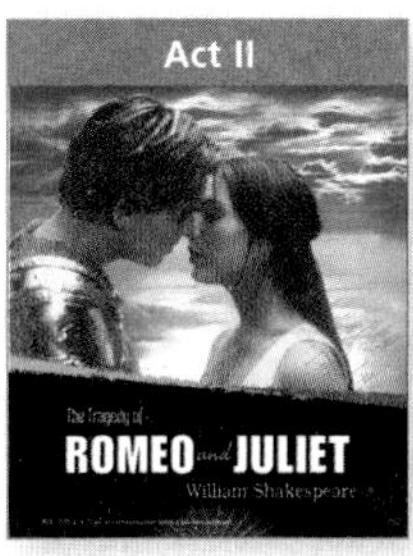

Key Ideas and Details

1. **(a)** Where do Romeo and Juliet first mutually declare their love? **(b) Interpret:** What roles do darkness and light play in the scene? Support your answer with details from the text.
2. **(a)** What weakness in Romeo does the Friar point out before agreeing to help? **(b) Compare and Contrast:** How do the Friar's motives differ from the couple's motives? Explain your answer based on details from the text.
3. **(a)** For whom does Juliet wait in Act II, Scene v? **(b) Analyze:** What are her feelings as she waits? Explain your answer.
4. **Read in Sentences (a)** How many sentences are in lines 1–8 of Act II, Scene v? **(b)** Write a summary of these lines.

Craft and Structure

5. **Blank Verse** Using a chart like the one shown, rewrite the following two lines and indicate the pattern of accented (´) and unaccented (˘) syllables in each line. Then, identify the key words stressed in each line, and explain what meaning is conveyed: **(a) ROMEO.** Can I go forward when my heart is here? **(b) JULIET.** But my true love is grown to such excess.
6. **Blank Verse (a)** Identify the aristocratic and common characters in Act II based on whether they speak in blank verse. **(b)** Why might Shakespeare have chosen blank verse for the dialogue spoken by aristocrats? Support your answer with textual evidence.

Blank Verse Pattern
Key Words
Significance

Integration of Knowledge and Ideas

7. **(a) Evaluate:** Based on conclusions you draw about the text, why do you think the love scene in Capulet's garden is one of the most famous dramatic scenes in all literature? Explain and support your answer with details from the scene.

8. THE BIG ? **Do our differences define us?** Have the differences between Romeo and Juliet become more or less defined as their story continues? Do those differences affect their relationship? Use details from the text to support your response.

ACADEMIC VOCABULARY

As you write and speak about *The Tragedy of Romeo and Juliet,* use the words related to differences that you explored on page 481 of this book.

Do our differences define us?

Explore the Big Question as you read Act III of *The Tragedy of Romeo and Juliet.* Take notes on how dramatic speeches reveal characters' differences.

CLOSE READING FOCUS

Key Ideas and Details: **Paraphrase**

Paraphrasing means restating the meaning of a passage in your own words. When you read Shakespearean drama, paraphrasing can help you better understand unfamiliar sentence structures and word choices, thereby clarifying the meaning of an entire passage or scene.

Original: This gentleman, the Prince's near ally, / My very friend, hath got his mortal hurt/In my behalf . . .

Paraphrase: My good friend, a close relative of the prince, has been killed in defending me.

Craft and Structure: **Dialogue and Dramatic Speeches**

In most plays, the dramatic action takes place through **dialogue**—the conversations between characters. Some playwrights, however, use specialized dialogue in the form of these types of **dramatic speeches:**

- **Soliloquy:** a lengthy speech in which a character—usually alone on stage—expresses his or her true thoughts or feelings.
- **Aside:** a brief remark, often addressed to the audience and unheard by other characters.
- **Monologue:** a lengthy speech by one character. Unlike a soliloquy or an aside, a monologue is addressed to other characters.

Dialogue and dramatic speeches reveal characters' personalities and desires. Characters' actions also reveal who they are and what they want. A character who provides a strong contrast to a main character is called a **foil.** For example, if the main character is rebellious, the foil is obedient. As you read, look for foils that show strong contrasts to the main characters.

Vocabulary

The following words are critical to understanding the play. Copy the words into your notebook. Which is an antonym for *peace*?

gallant	**fray**	**martial**
exile	**eloquence**	**fickle**

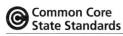

Common Core State Standards

Reading Literature

1. Cite strong and thorough textual evidence to support analysis of what the text says explicitly as well as inferences drawn from the text.

2. Determine a theme or central idea of a text and analyze in detail its development over the course of the text, including how it emerges and is shaped and refined by specific details; provide an objective summary of the text.

5. Analyze how an author's choices concerning how to structure a text, order events within it, and manipulate time create such effects as mystery, tension, or surprise.

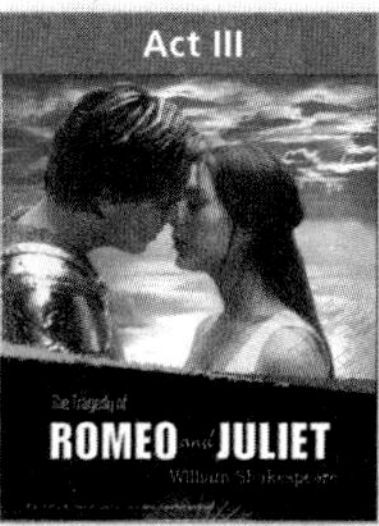

CLOSE READING MODEL

The passage below is from Act III of Shakespeare's *The Tragedy of Romeo and Juliet.* The annotations to the right of the passage show ways in which you can use close reading skills to paraphrase and analyze dialogue and dramatic speeches.

from *The Tragedy of Romeo and Juliet,* Act III

ROMEO. It was the lark, the herald of the morn;
No nightingale. Look, love, what envious streaks
Do lace the severing clouds in yonder East.
Night's candles are burnt out, and jocund day
Stands tiptoe on the misty mountaintops.
I must be gone and live, or stay and die.[1]

JULIET. Yond light is not daylight; I know it, I.
It is some meteor that the sun exhales
To be to thee this night a torchbearer
And light thee on thy way to Mantua.
Therefore stay yet; thou need'st not be gone.[2]

ROMEO. Let me be ta'en, let me be put to death.
I am content, so thou wilt have it so.
I'll say yon gray is not the morning's eye,
'Tis but the pale reflex of Cynthia's brow;
Nor that is not the lark whose notes do beat
The vaulty heaven so high above our heads.
I have more care to stay than will to go.
Come, death, and welcome! Juliet wills it so.[3]
How is't, my soul? Let's talk; it is not day.

JULIET. It is, it is! Hie hence, be gone away!
It is the lark that sings so out of tune,
Straining harsh discords and unpleasuring sharps.[4]

Paraphrase

1 Here, Romeo responds to Juliet's claim that it is still dark. A paraphrase of this passage might read as follows: *That was the lark that sings at dawn, not the nightingale that sings at night. Look, see the sunrise. Night is over and I must leave or die.*

Dialogue and Dramatic Speeches

2 In this scene, Shakespeare uses dialogue between the young lovers, instead of a monologue or soliloquy, to emphasize their closeness. In these lines, Juliet is revealing her true feelings to Romeo.

Paraphrase

3 This is a paraphrase of Romeo's lines: *I can say that is not the sun rising, but the moon; and the lark is not singing in the sky. I would rather die than go since Juliet wants me to stay.*

Dialogue and Dramatic Speeches

4 Juliet's urgent words show her feelings have changed. Fearing for Romeo's life, she now frantically insists that he leave.

Review and Anticipate

In Act II, Romeo and Juliet express their mutual love and enlist the aid of Juliet's nurse and Friar Lawrence to arrange a secret marriage ceremony. As the act closes, the young couple is about to be married. Before performing the ceremony, the Friar warns, "These violent delights have violent ends. . . ." How might this statement hint at events that will occur in Act III or later in the play?

Scene i. A public place.

[*Enter* Mercutio, Benvolio, *and* Men.]

Benvolio. I pray thee, good Mercutio, let's retire.
The day is hot, the Capulets abroad,
And, if we meet, we shall not 'scape a brawl,
For now, these hot days, is the mad blood stirring.

Mercutio. Thou art like one of these fellows that, when he enters the confines of a tavern, claps me his sword upon the table and says, "God send me no need of thee!" and by the operation of the second cup draws him on the drawer,[1] when indeed there is no need.

Benvolio. Am I like such a fellow?

Mercutio. Come, come, thou art as hot a Jack in thy mood as any in Italy; and as soon moved to be moody, and as soon moody to be moved.[2]

1. **and . . . drawer** and by the effect of the second drink, draws his sword against the waiter.
2. **and . . . moved** and as quickly stirred to anger as you are eager to be so stirred.

Comprehension
Why does Benvolio want to get off the street?

Dramatic Speeches
Which details of Mercutio's speech indicate that it is a monologue and not a soliloquy?

3. **addle** scrambled; crazy.

4. **doublet** jacket.
5. **riband** ribbon.
6. **tutor . . . quarreling** instruct me not to quarrel.
7. **fee simple** complete possession.
8. **an hour and a quarter** length of time that a man with Mercutio's fondness for quarreling may be expected to live.
9. **O simple!** O stupid!

Paraphrase
How would you paraphrase the exchange between Tybalt and Mercutio?

10. **occasion** cause; reason.
11. **consortest** associate with.
12. **Consort** associate with; "consort" also meant a group of musicians.
13. **discords** harsh sounds.
14. **Zounds** exclamation of surprise or anger ("By God's wounds").

Dramatic Speeches
How does the dialogue here set Mercutio and Benvolio as foils?

Benvolio. And what to?

Mercutio. Nay, and there were two such, we should have none shortly, for one would kill the other. Thou! Why, thou wilt quarrel with a man that hath a hair more or a hair less in his beard than thou hast. Thou wilt quarrel with a man for cracking nuts, having no other reason but because thou hast hazel eyes. What eye but such an eye would spy out such a quarrel? Thy head is as full of quarrels as an egg is full of meat; and yet thy head hath been beaten as addle[3] as an egg for quarreling. Thou hast quarreled with a man for coughing in the street, because he hath wakened thy dog that hath lain asleep in the sun. Didst thou not fall out with a tailor for wearing his new doublet[4] before Easter? With another for tying his new shoes with old riband?[5] And yet thou wilt tutor me from quarreling![6]

Benvolio. And I were so apt to quarrel as thou art, any man should buy the fee simple[7] of my life for an hour and a quarter.[8]

Mercutio. The fee simple? O simple![9]

[*Enter* Tybalt, Petruchio, *and* Others.]

Benvolio. By my head, here comes the Capulets.

Mercutio. By my heel, I care not.

Tybalt. Follow me close, for I will speak to them.
Gentlemen, good-den. A word with one of you.

Mercutio. And but one word with one of us? Couple it with something; make it a word and a blow.

Tybalt. You shall find me apt enough to that, sir, and you will give me occasion.[10]

Mercutio. Could you not take some occasion without giving?

Tybalt. Mercutio, thou consortest[11] with Romeo.

Mercutio. Consort?[12] What, dost thou make us minstrels? And thou make minstrels of us, look to hear nothing but discords.[13] Here's my fiddlestick; here's that shall make you dance. Zounds,[14] consort!

Benvolio. We talk here in the public haunt of men.
Either withdraw unto some private place,
Or reason coldly of your grievances,
Or else depart. Here all eyes gaze on us.

MERCUTIO. Men's eyes were made to look, and let them gaze.
I will not budge for no man's pleasure, I.

[*Enter* ROMEO.]

TYBALT. Well, peace be with you, sir. Here comes my man.[15]

MERCUTIO. But I'll be hanged, sir, if he wear your livery.[16]
Marry, go before to field,[17] he'll be your follower!
Your worship in that sense may call him man.

TYBALT. Romeo, the love I bear thee can afford
No better term than this: thou art a villain.[18]

ROMEO. Tybalt, the reason that I have to love thee
Doth much excuse the appertaining[19] rage
To such a greeting. Villain am I none.
Therefore farewell. I see thou knowest me not.

15. **man** man I am looking for; "man" also meant "manservant."
16. **livery** servant's uniform.
17. **field** dueling place.
18. **villain** low, vulgar person.
19. **appertaining** appropriate.

Comprehension
What are Mercutio and Benvolio arguing about?

Tybalt. Boy, this shall not excuse the injuries
That thou hast done me; therefore turn and draw.

Romeo. I do protest I never injured thee,
But love thee better than thou canst devise[20]
Till thou shalt know the reason of my love;
And so, good Capulet, which name I tender[21]
As dearly as mine own, be satisfied.

Mercutio. O calm, dishonorable, vile submission!
Alla stoccata[22] carries it away. [*Draws.*]
Tybalt, you ratcatcher, will you walk?

Tybalt. What wouldst thou have with me?

Mercutio. Good King of Cats, nothing but one of your nine lives. That I mean to make bold withal,[23] and, as you shall use me here-after, dry-beat[24] the rest of the eight. Will you pluck your sword out of his pilcher[25] by the ears? Make haste, lest mine be about your ears ere it be out.

Tybalt. I am for you. [*Draws.*]

Romeo. Gentle Mercutio, put thy rapier up.

Mercutio. Come, sir, your passado! [*They fight.*]

Romeo. Draw, Benvolio; beat down their weapons.
Gentlemen, for shame! Forbear this outrage!
Tybalt, Mercutio, the Prince expressly hath

20. **devise** understand; imagine.
21. **tender** value.

22. ***Alla stoccata*** at the thrust—an Italian fencing term that Mercutio uses as a nickname for Tybalt.

23. **make bold withal** make bold with; take.
24. **dry-beat** thrash.
25. **pilcher** scabbard.

▼▶ Critical Viewing
Which details in these photographs suggest that a duel is about to take place?

Forbid this bandying in Verona streets.
Hold, Tybalt! Good Mercutio!

[TYBALT *under* ROMEO'S *arm thrusts* MERCUTIO *in, and flies.*]

MERCUTIO. I am hurt.
A plague a[26] both your houses! I am sped.[27]
Is he gone and hath nothing?

BENVOLIO. What, art thou hurt?

MERCUTIO. Ay, ay, a scratch, a scratch. Marry, 'tis enough.
Where is my page? Go, villain, fetch a surgeon. [*Exit* PAGE.]

ROMEO. Courage, man. The hurt cannot be much.

MERCUTIO. No, 'tis not so deep as a well, nor so wide as a church door; but 'tis enough, 'twill serve. Ask for me tomorrow, and you shall find me a grave man. I am peppered,[28] I warrant, for this world. A plague a both your houses! Zounds, a dog, a rat, a mouse, a

26. **a** on.
27. **sped** wounded; done for.

28. **peppered** finished off.

Comprehension
What is the outcome of the duel between Tybalt and Mercutio?

29. **by . . . arithmetic** by formal rules.

Paraphrase
Paraphrase Mercutio's line "A plague a both your houses!" and summarize his reasons for uttering this curse.

30. **I have it** I have got my deathblow.
31. **ally** relative.

Vocabulary ▶
gallant (gal´ ənt) *adj.* brave and noble

32. **aspired** climbed to.
33. **moe** more.
34. **depend** hang over.

35. **respective lenity** thoughtful mercy.
36. **conduct** guide.

cat, to scratch a man to death! A braggart, a rogue,
a villain, that fights by the book of arithmetic![29] Why
the devil came you between us? I was hurt under
your arm.

Romeo. I thought all for the best.

Mercutio. Help me into some house, Benvolio,
Or I shall faint. A plague a both your houses!
They have made worms' meat of me. I have it,[30]
And soundly too. Your houses! [*Exit* Mercutio *and* Benvolio.]

Romeo. This gentleman, the Prince's near ally,[31]
My very friend, hath got his mortal hurt
In my behalf—my reputation stained
With Tybalt's slander—Tybalt, that an hour
Hath been my cousin. O sweet Juliet,
Thy beauty hath made me effeminate
And in my temper soft'ned valor's steel!

[*Enter* Benvolio.]

Benvolio. O Romeo, Romeo, brave Mercutio is dead!
That gallant spirit hath aspired[32] the clouds,
Which too untimely here did scorn the earth.

Romeo. This day's black fate on moe[33] days doth depend;[34]
This but begins the woe others must end.

[*Enter* Tybalt.]

Benvolio. Here comes the furious Tybalt back again.

Romeo. Alive in triumph, and Mercutio slain?
Away to heaven respective lenity,[35]
And fire-eyed fury be my conduct[36] now!
Now, Tybalt, take the "villain" back again
That late thou gavest me; for Mercutio's soul
Is but a little way above our heads,
Staying for thine to keep him company.
Either thou or I, or both, must go with him.

Tybalt. Thou, wretched boy, that didst consort him here,
Shalt with him hence.

Romeo. This shall determine that.
[*They fight.* Tybalt *falls.*]

Benvolio. Romeo, away, be gone!

The citizens are up, and Tybalt slain.
Stand not amazed. The Prince will doom thee death
If thou art taken. Hence, be gone, away!

Romeo. O, I am fortune's fool![37]

Benvolio. Why dost thou stay?

[*Exit* Romeo.]

[*Enter* citizens.]

Citizen. Which way ran he that killed Mercutio?
Tybalt, that murderer, which way ran he?

Benvolio. There lies that Tybalt.

Citizen. Up, sir, go with me.
I charge thee in the Prince's name obey.

[*Enter* Prince, Old Montague, Capulet, *their* Wives, *and all.*]

Prince. Where are the vile beginners of this fray?

Benvolio. O noble Prince, I can discover[38] all
The unlucky manage[39] of this fatal brawl.
There lies the man, slain by young Romeo,
That slew thy kinsman, brave Mercutio.

Lady Capulet. Tybalt, my cousin! O my brother's child!
O Prince! O cousin! Husband! O, the blood is spilled
Of my dear kinsman! Prince, as thou art true,
For blood of ours shed blood of Montague.
O cousin, cousin!

Prince. Benvolio, who began this bloody fray?

Benvolio. Tybalt, here slain, whom Romeo's hand did slay.
Romeo, that spoke him fair, bid him bethink
How nice[40] the quarrel was, and urged withal
Your high displeasure. All this—utterèd
With gentle breath, calm look, knees humbly bowed—
Could not take truce with the unruly spleen[41]
Of Tybalt deaf to peace, but that he tilts[42]
With piercing steel at bold Mercutio's breast;
Who, all as hot, turns deadly point to point,
And, with a martial scorn, with one hand beats
Cold death aside and with the other sends
It back to Tybalt, whose dexterity
Retorts it. Romeo he cries aloud,
"Hold, friends! Friends, part!" and swifter than his tongue,
His agile arm beats down their fatal points,

37. **fool** plaything.

◀ **Vocabulary**
fray (frā) *n.* noisy fight

38. **discover** reveal.
39. **manage** course.

40. **nice** trivial.

41. **spleen** angry nature.
42. **tilts** thrusts.

◀ **Vocabulary**
martial (mär′ shəl) *adj.* military; warlike

Comprehension
Who does Benvolio say started the brawl?

Dramatic Speeches Which details of Benvolio's speech suggest that he is trying to portray Romeo favorably?

43. **envious** full of hatred.
44. **entertained** considered.

And 'twixt them rushes; underneath whose arm
An envious[43] thrust from Tybalt hit the life
Of stout Mercutio, and then Tybalt fled;
But by and by comes back to Romeo,
Who had but newly entertained[44] revenge,
And to't they go like lightning; for, ere I
Could draw to part them, was stout Tybalt slain;
And, as he fell, did Romeo turn and fly.
This is the truth, or let Benvolio die.

Lady Capulet. He is a kinsman to the Montague;
Affection makes him false, he speaks not true.
Some twenty of them fought in this black strife,
And all those twenty could but kill one life.
I beg for justice, which thou, Prince, must give.
Romeo slew Tybalt; Romeo must not live.

Prince. Romeo slew him; he slew Mercutio.
Who now the price of his dear blood doth owe?

Montague. Not Romeo, Prince; he was Mercutio's friend;
His fault concludes but what the law should end,
The life of Tybalt.[45]

45. **His fault . . . Tybalt** by killing Tybalt, he did what the law would have done.

Prince. And for that offense
Immediately we do exile him hence.
I have an interest in your hate's proceeding.
My blood[46] for your rude brawls doth lie a-bleeding;
But I'll amerce[47] you with so strong a fine
That you shall all repent the loss of mine.
I will be deaf to pleading and excuses;
Nor tears nor prayers shall purchase out abuses.
Therefore use none. Let Romeo hence in haste,
Else, when he is found, that hour is his last.
Bear hence this body and attend our will.[48]
Mercy but murders, pardoning those that kill.

[*Exit with others.*]

Vocabulary ▶ **exile** (eks′ īl′) *v.* banish

46. **My blood** Mercutio was related to the Prince.
47. **amerce** punish.
48. **attend our will** await my decision.

Scene ii. Capulet's orchard.

[*Enter* Juliet *alone.*]

Juliet. Gallop apace, you fiery-footed steeds,[1]
Towards Phoebus' lodging![2] Such a wagoner
As Phaëton[3] would whip you to the west
And bring in cloudy night immediately.

1. **fiery-footed steeds** horses of the sun god, Phoebus.
2. **Phoebus' lodging** below the horizon.
3. **Phaëton** Phoebus' son, who tried to drive his father's horses but was unable to control them.

Spread thy close curtain, love-performing night,
That runaways' eyes may wink,[4] and Romeo
Leap to these arms untalked of and unseen.
Lovers can see to do their amorous rites,
And by their own beauties; or, if love be blind,
It best agrees with night. Come, civil night,
Thou sober-suited matron all in black,
And learn me how to lose a winning match,
Played for a pair of stainless maidenhoods.
Hood my unmanned blood, bating in my cheeks,[5]
With thy black mantle till strange[6] love grow bold,
Think true love acted simple modesty,
Come, night; come, Romeo; come, thou day in night;
For thou wilt lie upon the wings of night
Whiter than new snow upon a raven's back.
Come, gentle night; come, loving, black-browed night;
Give me my Romeo; and when I shall die,
Take him and cut him out in little stars,
And he will make the face of heaven so fine
That all the world will be in love with night
And pay no worship to the garish sun.
O, I have bought the mansion of a love,
But not possessed it; and though I am sold,
Not yet enjoyed. So tedious is this day
As is the night before some festival
To an impatient child that hath new robes
And may not wear them. O, here comes my nurse,

Dramatic Speeches
How can you tell that Juliet's speech is a soliloquy?

4. **That runaways' eyes may wink** so that the eyes of busybodies may not see.
5. **Hood . . . cheeks** hide the untamed blood that makes me blush.
6. **strange** unfamiliar.

Spiral Review
CHARACTER What does Juliet reveal about herself in this soliloquy?

[*Enter* NURSE, *with cords.*]

And she brings news; and every tongue that speaks
But Romeo's name speaks heavenly eloquence.
Now, nurse, what news? What hast thou there, the cords
That Romeo bid thee fetch?

NURSE. Ay, ay, the cords.

JULIET. Ay me! What news? Why dost thou wring thy hands?

NURSE. Ah, weraday![7] He's dead, he's dead, he's dead!
We are undone, lady, we are undone!
Alack the day! He's gone, he's killed, he's dead!

JULIET. Can heaven be so envious?

NURSE. Romeo can,
Though heaven cannot. O Romeo, Romeo!
Who ever would have thought it? Romeo!

◀ **Vocabulary**
eloquence (el´ ə kwəns) *n.* speech or writing that is graceful and persuasive

7. **Ah, weraday!** alas!

Comprehension
What punishment does the Prince order for Romeo?

LITERATURE IN CONTEXT

History Connection

Cockatrice

In a play on words, Juliet links "Ay" with the dangerous "eye" of a cockatrice (Act III, scene ii, line 47). The cockatrice is a serpent that, according to myth, could kill with a look or transform people into stone. The creature resembles a snake with the head and yellow feathers of a rooster. It feared the song of the rooster and its own reflection in a mirror.

Connect to the Literature

How does Juliet's allusion to a cockatrice reinforce the nature of her conversation with the Nurse?

Juliet. What devil art thou that dost torment me thus?
This torture should be roared in dismal hell.
Hath Romeo slain himself? Say thou but "Ay,"
And that bare vowel "I" shall poison more
Than the death-darting eye of cockatrice.
I am not I, if there be such an "Ay,"[8]
Or those eyes' shot[9] that makes thee answer "Ay."
If he be slain, say "Ay"; or if not, "No."
Brief sounds determine of my weal or woe.

Nurse. I saw the wound, I saw it with mine eyes,
(God save the mark![10]) here on his manly breast.
A piteous corse,[11] a bloody piteous corse;
Pale, pale as ashes, all bedaubed in blood,
All in gore-blood. I swounded[12] at the sight.

Juliet. O, break, my heart! Poor bankrout,[13] break at once!
To prison, eyes; ne'er look on liberty!
Vile earth, to earth resign;[14] end motion here,
And thou and Romeo press one heavy bier![15]

Nurse. O Tybalt, Tybalt, the best friend I had!
O courteous Tybalt! Honest gentleman!
That ever I should live to see thee dead!

Juliet. What storm is this that blows so contrary?[16]
Is Romeo slaught'red, and is Tybalt dead?
My dearest cousin, and my dearer lord?
Then, dreadful trumpet, sound the general doom![17]

8. **"Ay"** yes.
9. **eyes' shot** the Nurse's glance.
10. **God save the mark!** May God save us from evil!
11. **corse** corpse.
12. **swounded** swooned; fainted.
13. **bankrout** bankrupt.
14. **Vile . . . resign** let my body return to the earth.
15. **bier** platform on which a corpse is displayed before burial.
16. **contrary** in opposite directions.
17. **dreadful . . . doom** let the trumpet that announces doomsday be sounded.

For who is living, if those two are gone?

Nurse. Tybalt is gone, and Romeo banishèd;
Romeo that killed him, he is banishèd.

Juliet. O God! Did Romeo's hand shed Tybalt's blood?

Nurse. It did, it did! Alas the day, it did!

Juliet. O serpent heart, hid with a flow'ring face!
Did ever dragon keep so fair a cave?
Beautiful tyrant! Fiend angelical!
Dove-feathered raven! Wolvish-ravening lamb!
Despisèd substance of divinest show!
Just opposite to what thou justly seem'st—
A damnèd saint, an honorable villain!
O nature, what hadst thou to do in hell
When thou didst bower the spirit of a fiend
In mortal paradise of such sweet flesh?
Was ever book containing such vile matter
So fairly bound? O, that deceit should dwell
In such a gorgeous palace!

Paraphrase
Use your own words to summarize Juliet's remarks about Romeo in lines 73–84.

Nurse. There's no trust,
No faith, no honesty in men; all perjured,
All forsworn,[18] all naught, all dissemblers.[19]
Ah, where's my man? Give me some aqua vitae.[20]
These griefs, these woes, these sorrows make me old.
Shame come to Romeo!

18. **forsworn** are liars.
19. **dissemblers** hypocrites.
20. **aqua vitae** brandy.

Juliet. Blistered be thy tongue
For such a wish! He was not born to shame.
Upon his brow shame is ashamed to sit;
For 'tis a throne where honor may be crowned
Sole monarch of the universal earth.
O, what a beast was I to chide at him!

Nurse. Will you speak well of him that killed your cousin?

Juliet. Shall I speak ill of him that is my husband?
Ah, poor my lord, what tongue shall smooth thy name
When I, thy three-hours wife, have mangled it?
But wherefore, villain, didst thou kill my cousin?
That villain cousin would have killed my husband.
Back, foolish tears, back to your native spring!
Your tributary[21] drops belong to woe,
Which you, mistaking, offer up to joy.
My husband lives, that Tybalt would have slain;

21. **tributary** contributing; also honoring.

Comprehension
What is Juliet's initial reaction to Romeo's involvement in Tybalt's death?

Dramatic Speeches What makes this speech a monologue but not a soliloquy?

And Tybalt's dead, that would have slain my husband.
All this is comfort; wherefore weep I then?
Some word there was, worser than Tybalt's death,
That murd'red me. I would forget it fain;
But O, it presses to my memory
Like damnèd guilty deeds to sinners' minds!
"Tybalt is dead, and Romeo—banishèd."
That "banishèd," that one word "banishèd,"
Hath slain ten thousand Tybalts. Tybalt's death
Was woe enough, if it had ended there;
Or, if sour woe delights in fellowship
And needly will be ranked with[22] other griefs,
Why followed not, when she said "Tybalt's dead,"
Thy father, or thy mother, nay, or both,
Which modern[23] lamentation might have moved?
But with a rearward[24] following Tybalt's death,
"Romeo is banishèd"—to speak that word
Is father, mother, Tybalt, Romeo, Juliet,
All slain, all dead. "Romeo is banishèd"—
There is no end, no limit, measure, bound,
In that word's death; no words can that woe sound.
Where is my father and my mother, nurse?

Nurse. Weeping and wailing over Tybalt's corse.
Will you go to them? I will bring you thither.

Juliet. Wash they his wounds with tears? Mine shall be spent,
When theirs are dry, for Romeo's banishment.
Take up those cords. Poor ropes, you are beguiled,
Both you and I, for Romeo is exiled.
He made you for a highway to my bed;
But I, a maid, die maiden-widowèd.
Come, cords; come, nurse. I'll to my wedding bed;
And death, not Romeo, take my maidenhead!

Nurse. Hie to your chamber. I'll find Romeo
To comfort you. I wot[25] well where he is.
Hark ye, your Romeo will be here at night.
I'll to him; he is hid at Lawrence' cell.

Juliet. O, find him! Give this ring to my true knight
And bid him come to take his last farewell. [*Exit with* Nurse]

22. **needly . . . with** must be accompanied by.

23. **modern** ordinary.

24. **rearward** follow up; literally, a rear guard.

25. **wot** know.

Scene iii. Friar Lawrence's cell.
[*Enter* FRIAR LAWRENCE.]

FRIAR. Romeo, come forth; come forth, thou fearful man.
Affliction is enamored of thy parts,[1]
And thou art wedded to calamity.

[*Enter* ROMEO.]

ROMEO. Father, what news? What is the Prince's doom?[2]
What sorrow craves acquaintance at my hand
That I yet know not?

FRIAR. Too familiar
Is my dear son with such sour company.
I bring thee tidings of the Prince's doom.

ROMEO. What less than doomsday[3] is the Prince's doom?

FRIAR. A gentler judgment vanished[4] from his lips—
Not body's death, but body's banishment.

ROMEO. Ha, banishment? Be merciful, say "death";
For exile hath more terror in his look,
Much more than death. Do not say "banishment."

FRIAR. Here from Verona art thou banishèd.
Be patient, for the world is broad and wide.

ROMEO. There is no world without[5] Verona walls,
But purgatory, torture, hell itself.
Hence banishèd is banished from the world,
And world's exile is death. Then "banishèd"
Is death mistermed. Calling death "banishèd,"
Thou cut'st my head off with a golden ax
And smilest upon the stroke that murders me.

FRIAR. O deadly sin! O rude unthankfulness!
Thy fault our law calls death;[6] but the kind Prince,
Taking thy part, hath rushed[7] aside the law,
And turned that black word "death" to "banishment."
This is dear mercy, and thou seest it not.

ROMEO. 'Tis torture, and not mercy. Heaven is here,
Where Juliet lives; and every cat and dog
And little mouse, every unworthy thing,
Live here in heaven and may look on her;
But Romeo may not. More validity,[8]
More honorable state, more courtship lives
In carrion flies than Romeo. They may seize

1. **Affliction . . . parts** misery is in love with your attractive qualities.
2. **doom** final decision.
3. **doomsday** my death.
4. **vanished** escaped; came forth.
5. **without** outside.
6. **Thy fault . . . death** for what you did our law demands the death penalty.
7. **rushed** pushed.
8. **validity** value.

Paraphrase
Paraphrase Romeo's complaint in lines 29–33, and then summarize his reaction to his banishment.

Comprehension
What punishment does the Friar say Romeo could have received for his crime?

On the white wonder of dear Juliet's hand
And steal immortal blessing from her lips,
Who, even in pure and vestal modesty,
Still blush, as thinking their own kisses sin;
But Romeo may not, he is banishèd.
Flies may do this but I from this must fly;
They are freemen, but I am banishèd.
And sayest thou yet that exile is not death?
Hadst thou no poison mixed, no sharp-ground knife,
No sudden mean[9] of death, though ne'er so mean,[10]
But "banishèd" to kill me—"banishèd"?
O friar, the damnèd use that word in hell;
Howling attends it! How hast thou the heart,
Being a divine, a ghostly confessor,
A sin-absolver, and my friend professed,
To mangle me with that word "banishèd"?

Friar. Thou fond mad man, hear me a little speak.

Romeo. O, thou wilt speak again of banishment.

Friar. I'll give thee armor to keep off that word;
Adversity's sweet milk, philosophy,
To comfort thee, though thou art banishèd.

9. **mean** method.
10. **mean** humiliating.

Romeo and Juliet Through the Years

These illustrations and images from various productions of *Romeo and Juliet* mark the timelessness of Shakespeare's most dramatized piece. The core qualities of the play, including its theme and language, have moved forward into the present with updated costumes and props, diverse casts, and new technology.

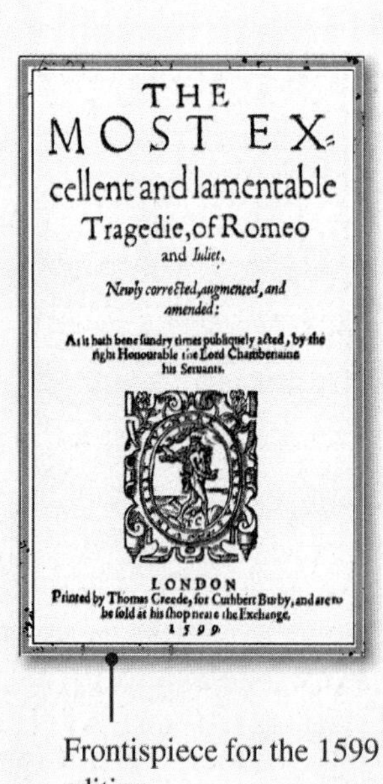

THE MOST EXcellent and lamentable Tragedie, of Romeo and Juliet.

Newly corrected, augmented, and amended:

As it hath bene sundry times publiquely acted, by the right Honourable the Lord Chamberlaine his Seruants.

LONDON
Printed by Thomas Creede, for Cuthbert Burby, and are to be sold at his shop neare the Exchange.
1599.

Frontispiece for the 1599 edition

Movie – 1916 Romeo and Juliet

Book illustration – 1905

Romeo. Yet "banishèd"? Hang up philosophy!
Unless philosophy can make a Juliet,
Displant a town, reverse a prince's doom,
It helps not, it prevails not. Talk no more.

Friar. O, then I see that madmen have no ears.

Romeo. How should they, when that wise men have no eyes?

Friar. Let me dispute[11] with thee of thy estate.[12]

Romeo. Thou canst not speak of that thou dost not feel.
Wert thou as young as I, Juliet thy love,
An hour but married, Tybalt murderèd,
Doting like me, and like me banishèd,
Then mightst thou speak, then mightst thou tear thy hair,
And fall upon the ground, as I do now,
Taking the measure of an unmade grave.

[*Knock.*]

Friar. Arise, one knocks. Good Romeo, hide thyself.

Romeo. Not I; unless the breath of heartsick groans
Mistlike infold me from the search of eyes. [*Knock.*]

Paraphrase
In your own words, summarize Romeo's ideas in lines 57–60. What do they suggest about his state of mind?

11. dispute discuss.
12. estate condition; situation.

Comprehension
How does Romeo view his banishment?

Movie – 1936
Poster and balcony scene
(Director: George Cukor
Actors: Norma Shearer and Leslie Howard)

Movie – 1968
Balcony scene
(Director: Franco Zeffirelli
Actors: Leonard Whiting and Olivia Hussey)

Friar. Hark, how they knock! Who's there? Romeo, arise;
Thou wilt be taken.—Stay awhile!—Stand up; [Knock.]
Run to my study.—By and by![13]—God's will,
What simpleness[14] is this.—I come, I come! [Knock.]
Who knocks so hard? Whence come you? What's your will?

13. **By and by!** In a minute! (said to the person knocking).
14. **simpleness** silly behavior (Romeo does not move).

[*Enter* NURSE.]

Nurse. Let me come in, and you shall know my errand.
I come from Lady Juliet.

Friar. Welcome then.

Nurse. O holy friar, O, tell me, holy friar,
Where is my lady's lord, where's Romeo?

Friar. There on the ground, with his own tears made drunk.

Dramatic Speeches
What does this brief speech by the Nurse reveal about her relationship with Romeo?

Nurse. O, he is even in my mistress' case,
Just in her case! O woeful sympathy!
Piteous predicament! Even so lies she,
Blubb'ring and weeping, weeping and blubb'ring.
Stand up, stand up! Stand, and you be a man.
For Juliet's sake, for her sake, rise and stand!
Why should you fall into so deep an O?[15]

15. **O** cry of grief.

Stage production – 1990s
Royal Shakespeare Company

Stage production – 2004
Royal Shakespeare Company
Friar and Juliet

Ballet – 2001
Kirov Ballet of St. Petersburg, Russia

Romeo. [*Rises.*] Nurse—

Nurse. Ah sir, ah sir! Death's the end of all.

Romeo. Spakest thou of Juliet? How is it with her?
Doth not she think me an old murderer,
Now I have stained the childhood of our joy
With blood removed but little from her own?
Where is she? And how doth she? And what says
My concealed lady[16] to our canceled love?

Nurse. O, she says nothing, sir, but weeps and weeps;
And now falls on her bed, and then starts up,
And Tybalt calls; and then on Romeo cries,
And then down falls again.

Romeo. As if that name,
Shot from the deadly level[17] of a gun,
Did murder her; as that name's cursèd hand
Murdered her kinsman. O, tell me, friar, tell me,
In what vile part of this anatomy
Doth my name lodge? Tell me, that I may sack[18]
The hateful mansion.

[*He offers to stab himself, and* Nurse *snatches the dagger away.*]

16. **concealed lady** secret bride.

17. **level** aim.

18. **sack** plunder.

Comprehension
What does Romeo nearly do before the Nurse stops him?

Stage production – 2004
Royal Shakespeare Company
Fight scene

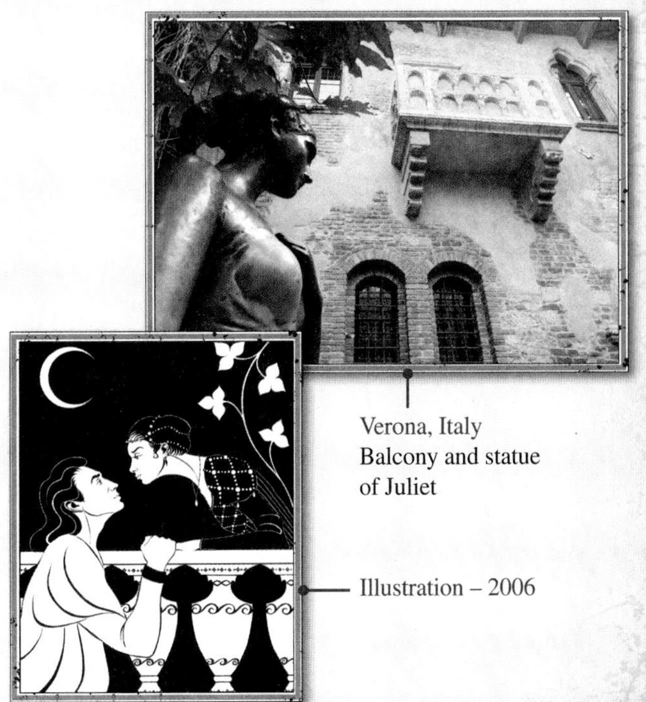

Verona, Italy
Balcony and statue of Juliet

Illustration – 2006

Friar. Hold thy desperate hand.
Art thou a man? Thy form cries out thou art;
Thy tears are womanish, thy wild acts denote
The unreasonable fury of a beast.
Unseemly[19] woman in a seeming man!
And ill-beseeming beast in seeming both![20]
Thou hast amazed me. By my holy order,
I thought thy disposition better tempered.
Hast thou slain Tybalt? Wilt thou slay thyself?
And slay thy lady that in thy life lives,
By doing damnèd hate upon thyself?
Why railest thou on thy birth, the heaven, and earth?
Since birth and heaven and earth, all three do meet
In thee at once; which thou at once wouldst lose.
Fie, fie, thou shamest thy shape, thy love, thy wit,[21]
Which, like a usurer,[22] abound'st in all,
And usest none in that true use indeed
Which should bedeck[23] thy shape, thy love, thy wit.
Thy noble shape is but a form of wax,
Digressing from the valor of a man;
Thy dear love sworn but hollow perjury,
Killing that love which thou hast vowed to cherish;
Thy wit, that ornament to shape and love,
Misshapen in the conduct[24] of them both,
Like powder in a skilless soldier's flask,[25]
Is set afire by thine own ignorance,
And thou dismemb'red with thine own defense.[26]
What, rouse thee, man! Thy Juliet is alive,
For whose dear sake thou wast but lately dead.[27]
There art thou happy.[28] Tybalt would kill thee,
But thou slewest Tybalt. There art thou happy.
The law, that threat'ned death, becomes thy friend
And turns it to exile. There art thou happy.
A pack of blessings light upon thy back;
Happiness courts thee in her best array;
But, like a misbehaved and sullen wench,[29]
Thou puts up[30] thy fortune and thy love.
Take heed, take heed, for such die miserable.
Go get thee to thy love, as was decreed,
Ascend her chamber, hence and comfort her.
But look thou stay not till the watch be set,[31]
For then thou canst not pass to Mantua,
Where thou shalt live till we can find a time
To blaze[32] your marriage, reconcile your friends,

19. **Unseemly** inappropriate (because unnatural).
20. **And . . . both!** Romeo has inappropriately lost his human nature because he seems like a man and woman combined.
21. **wit** mind; intellect.
22. **Which, like a usurer** who, like a rich money-lender.
23. **bedeck** do honor to.
24. **conduct** management.
25. **flask** powder flask.
26. **And thou . . . defense** the friar is saying that Romeo's mind, which is now irrational, is destroying rather than aiding him.
27. **but lately dead** only recently declaring yourself dead.
28. **happy** fortunate.
29. **wench** low, common girl.
30. **puts up** pouts over.
31. **watch be set** watchmen go on duty.
32. **blaze** announce publicly.

Beg pardon of the Prince, and call thee back
With twenty hundred thousand times more joy
Than thou went'st forth in lamentation.
Go before, nurse. Commend me to thy lady,
And bid her hasten all the house to bed,
Which heavy sorrow makes them apt unto.[33]
Romeo is coming.

Paraphrase
Restate the main points of the Friar's speech to Romeo in your own words.

NURSE. O Lord, I could have stayed here all the night
To hear good counsel. O, what learning is!
My lord, I'll tell my lady you will come.

33. **apt unto** likely to do.

ROMEO. Do so, and bid my sweet prepare to chide.[34]
[NURSE *offers to go in and turns again.*]

34. **chide** rebuke me (for slaying Tybalt).

NURSE. Here, sir, a ring she bid me give you, sir.
Hie you, make haste, for it grows very late. [*Exit.*]

ROMEO. How well my comfort is revived by this!

FRIAR. Go hence; good night; and here stands all your state:[35]
Either be gone before the watch be set,
Or by the break of day disguised from hence.
Sojourn[36] in Mantua. I'll find out your man,
And he shall signify[37] from time to time
Every good hap to you that chances here.
Give me thy hand. 'Tis late. Farewell; good night.

35. **here . . . state** this is your situation.

36. **Sojourn** remain.

37. **signify** let you know.

ROMEO. But that a joy past joy calls out on me,
It were a grief so brief to part with thee.
Farewell. [*Exit all.*]

Scene iv. A room in Capulet's house.

[*Enter old* CAPULET, *his* WIFE, *and* PARIS.]

CAPULET. Things have fall'n out, sir, so unluckily
That we have had no time to move[1] our daughter.
Look you, she loved her kinsman Tybalt dearly,
And so did I. Well, we were born to die.
'Tis very late; she'll not come down tonight.
I promise you, but for your company,
I would have been abed an hour ago.

1. **move** discuss your proposal with.

2. **mewed . . . heaviness** locked up with her sorrow.

PARIS. These times of woe afford no times to woo.
Madam, good night. Commend me to your daughter.

LADY. I will, and know her mind early tomorrow;
Tonight she's mewed up to her heaviness.[2]

Comprehension
What reason do the Capulets give Paris to explain why Juliet cannot see him?

3. **desperate tender** risky offer.

4. **son** son-in-law.

CAPULET. Sir, Paris, I will make a desperate tender[3]
Of my child's love. I think she will be ruled
In all respects by me; nay more, I doubt it not.
Wife, go you to her ere you go to bed;
Acquaint her here of my son[4] Paris' love
And bid her (mark you me?) on Wednesday next—
But soft! What day is this?

PARIS. Monday, my lord.

5. **A** on.

6. **We'll . . . ado** We will not make a great fuss.

7. **held him carelessly** did not respect him enough.

CAPULET. Monday! Ha, ha! Well, Wednesday is too soon.
A[5] Thursday let it be—a Thursday, tell her,
She shall be married to this noble earl.
Will you be ready? Do you like this haste?
We'll keep no great ado[6]—a friend or two;
For hark you, Tybalt being slain so late,
It may be thought we held him carelessly,[7]
Being our kinsman, if we revel much.
Therefore we'll have some half a dozen friends,
And there an end. But what say you to Thursday?

Paraphrase
Paraphrase Lord Capulet's remarks about the timing of Juliet's marriage to Paris.

PARIS. My lord, I would that Thursday were tomorrow.

8. **against** for.

9. **Afore me** indeed (a mild oath).

CAPULET. Well, get you gone. A Thursday be it then.
Go you to Juliet ere you go to bed;
Prepare her, wife, against[8] this wedding day.
Farewell, my lord.—Light to my chamber, ho!
Afore me,[9] it is so very late
That we may call it early by and by.
Good night. [*Exit all.*]

Scene v. Capulet's orchard.
[*Enter* ROMEO *and* JULIET *aloft.*]

JULIET. Wilt thou be gone? It is not yet near day.
It was the nightingale, and not the lark,
That pierced the fearful hollow of thine ear.
Nightly she sings on yond pomegranate tree.
Believe me, love, it was the nightingale.

1. **severing** parting.

2. **Night's candles** stars.

ROMEO. It was the lark, the herald of the morn;
No nightingale. Look, love, what envious streaks
Do lace the severing[1] clouds in yonder East.
Night's candles[2] are burnt out, and jocund day
Stands tiptoe on the misty mountaintops.
I must be gone and live, or stay and die.

LITERATURE IN CONTEXT

Literature Connection

The Nightingale and the Lark

The nightingale and the lark are two birds that appear frequently in literature, particularly in poetry. Both birds are admired for their beautiful singing, and they also have symbolic associations. The nightingale and its song are traditionally associated with night; the lark and its song with dawn. Shakespeare draws on these associations in this exchange between Romeo and Juliet.

Lark

Connect to the Literature

Why do Romeo and Juliet have negative associations with the lark at this point in the play?

Juliet. Yond light is not daylight; I know it, I.
It is some meteor that the sun exhales[3]
To be to thee this night a torchbearer
And light thee on thy way to Mantua.
Therefore stay yet; thou need'st not to be gone.

Romeo. Let me be ta'en, let me be put to death.
I am content, so thou wilt have it so.
I'll say yon gray is not the morning's eye,
'Tis but the pale reflex of Cynthia's brow;[4]
Nor that is not the lark whose notes do beat
The vaulty heaven so high above our heads.
I have more care to stay than will to go.
Come, death, and welcome! Juliet wills it so.
How is't, my soul? Let's talk; it is not day.

Juliet. It is, it is! Hie hence, be gone, away!
It is the lark that sings so out of tune,
Straining harsh discords and unpleasing sharps.[5]
Some say the lark makes sweet division;[6]
This doth not so, for she divideth us.
Some say the lark and loathèd toad change eyes;[7]
O, now I would they had changed voices too,
Since arm from arm that voice doth us affray,[8]
Hunting thee hence with hunt's-up[9] to the day.
O, now be gone! More light and light it grows.

Romeo. More light and light—more dark and dark our woes.

3. **exhales** sends out.

4. **reflex . . . brow** reflection of the moon (Cynthia was a name for the moon goddess).

5. **sharps** shrill high notes.
6. **division** melody.
7. **change eyes** exchange eyes (because the lark has a beautiful body with ugly eyes and the toad has an ugly body with beautiful eyes).
8. **affray** frighten.
9. **hunt's-up** morning song for hunters.

Comprehension
What do the Capulets plan for Juliet on Thursday?

[*Enter* NURSE.]

NURSE. Madam!

JULIET. Nurse?

NURSE. Your lady mother is coming to your chamber.
The day is broke; be wary, look about. [*Exit.*]

JULIET. Then, window, let day in, and let life out.

ROMEO. Farewell, farewell! One kiss, and I'll descend.
[*He goeth down.*]

Paraphrase
Restate the key points of the farewell conversation between Romeo and Juliet in your own words.

JULIET. Art thou gone so, love-lord, ay husband-friend?
I must hear from thee every day in the hour,
For in a minute there are many days.
O, by this count I shall be much in years[10]
Ere I again behold my Romeo!

10. much in years much older.

ROMEO. Farewell!
I will omit no opportunity
That may convey my greetings, love, to thee.

JULIET. O, think'st thou we shall ever meet again?

ROMEO. I doubt it not; and all these woes shall serve
For sweet discourses[11] in our times to come.

11. discourses conversations.

12. ill-divining predicting evil.

JULIET. O God, I have an ill-divining[12] soul!
Methinks I see thee, now thou art so low,
As one dead in the bottom of a tomb.
Either my eyesight fails, or thou lookest pale.

ROMEO. And trust me, love, in my eye so do you.
Dry sorrow drinks our blood.[13] Adieu, adieu! [*Exit.*]

13. Dry sorrow . . . blood It was once believed that sorrow drained away the blood.

14. dost thou do you have to do.

JULIET. O Fortune, Fortune! All men call thee **fickle**.
If thou art fickle, what dost thou[14] with him
That is renowned for faith? Be fickle, Fortune,
For then I hope thou wilt not keep him long
But send him back.

Vocabulary ▶
fickle (fik´ əl) *adj.* changeable

[*Enter* MOTHER.]

LADY CAPULET. Ho, daughter! Are you up?

JULIET. Who is't that calls? It is my lady mother.
Is she not down so late,[15] or up so early?
What unaccustomed cause procures her hither?[16]

15. Is she . . . late Has she stayed up so late?

16. What . . . hither? What unusual reason brings her here?

LADY CAPULET. Why, how now, Juliet?

Juliet. Madam, I am not well.

Lady Capulet. Evermore weeping for your cousin's death?
What, wilt thou wash him from his grave with tears?
An if thou couldst, thou couldst not make him live.
Therefore have done. Some grief shows much of love;
But much of grief shows still some want of wit.

Juliet. Yet let me weep for such a feeling[17] loss.

Lady Capulet. So shall you feel the loss, but not the friend
Which you weep for.

Juliet. Feeling so the loss,
I cannot choose but ever weep the friend.

Lady Capulet. Well, girl, thou weep'st not so much for his death
As that the villain lives which slaughtered him.

Juliet. What villain, madam?

Lady Capulet. That same villain Romeo.

Juliet. [*Aside*] Villain and he be many miles asunder.[18]—
God pardon him! I do, with all my heart;
And yet no man like he doth grieve my heart.

Lady Capulet. That is because the traitor murderer lives.

Juliet. Ay, madam, from the reach of these my hands.
Would none but I might venge my cousin's death!

Lady Capulet. We will have vengeance for it, fear thou not.
Then weep no more. I'll send to one in Mantua,
Where that same banished runagate[19] doth live,
Shall give him such an unaccustomed dram[20]
That he shall soon keep Tybalt company;
And then I hope thou wilt be satisfied.

Juliet. Indeed I never shall be satisfied
With Romeo till I behold him—dead[21]—
Is my poor heart so for a kinsman vexed.
Madam, if you could find out but a man
To bear a poison, I would temper[22] it,
That Romeo should, upon receipt thereof,
Soon sleep in quiet. O, how my heart abhors
To hear him named and cannot come to him,
To wreak[23] the love I bore my cousin
Upon his body that hath slaughtered him!

17. **feeling** deeply felt.

18. **asunder** apart.

Dramatic Speeches
What qualities of an aside do you find in line 82?

19. **runagate** renegade; runaway.
20. **unaccustomed dram** unexpected dose of poison.

21. **dead** Juliet is deliberately ambiguous here. Her mother thinks dead refers to Romeo. But Juliet is using the word with the following line, in reference to her heart.
22. **temper** mix; weaken.

23. **wreak** (rēk) avenge; express.

Comprehension
What are Lady Capulet's plans for Romeo?

Lady Capulet. Find thou the means, and I'll find such a man.
But now I'll tell thee joyful tidings, girl.

Juliet. And joy comes well in such a needy time.
What are they, I beseech your ladyship?

24. **careful** considerate.

25. **sorted out** selected.

Lady Capulet. Well, well, thou hast a careful[24] father, child;
One who, to put thee from thy heaviness,
Hath sorted out[25] a sudden day of joy
That thou expects not nor I looked not for.

26. **in happy time** just in time.

Juliet. Madam, in happy time![26] What day is that?

Dramatic Speeches
How does Lady Capulet's dialogue here show Paris as a foil to Romeo?

Lady Capulet. Marry, my child, early next Thursday morn
The gallant, young, and noble gentleman,
The County Paris, at Saint Peter's Church,
Shall happily make thee there a joyful bride.

Juliet. Now by Saint Peter's Church, and Peter too,
He shall not make me there a joyful bride!
I wonder at this haste, that I must wed
Ere he that should be husband comes to woo.
I pray you tell my lord and father, madam,
I will not marry yet; and when I do, I swear
It shall be Romeo, whom you know I hate,
Rather than Paris. These are news indeed!

Lady Capulet. Here comes your father. Tell him so yourself,
And see how he will take it at your hands.

[*Enter* Capulet *and* Nurse.]

Capulet. When the sun sets the earth doth drizzle dew,
But for the sunset of my brother's son
It rains downright.
How now? A conduit,[27] girl? What, still in tears?
Evermore show'ring? In one little body
Thou counterfeits a bark,[28] a sea, a wind:
For still thy eyes, which I may call the sea,
Do ebb and flow with tears; the bark thy body is,
Sailing in this salt flood; the winds, thy sighs,
Who, raging with thy tears and they with them,
Without a sudden calm will overset
Thy tempest-tossèd body. How now, wife?
Have you delivered to her our decree?

27. **conduit** water pipe.

28. **bark** boat.

Summarize
Summarize the comparison Lord Capulet makes in lines 130–138.

Lady Capulet. Ay, sir; but she will none, she gives you thanks.[29]
I would the fool were married to her grave!

29. **she will none . . . thanks** she will have nothing to do with it, thank you.

CAPULET. Soft! Take me with you,[30] take me with you, wife.
How? Will she none? Doth she not give us thanks?
Is she not proud?[31] Doth she not count her blest,
Unworthy as she is, that we have wrought[32]
So worthy a gentleman to be her bride?

JULIET. Not proud you have, but thankful that you have.
Proud can I never be of what I hate,
But thankful even for hate that is meant love.

CAPULET. How, how, how, how, chopped-logic?[33] What is this?
"Proud"—and "I thank you"—and "I thank you not"—
And yet "not proud"? Mistress minion[34] you,
Thank me no thankings, nor proud me no prouds,
But fettle[35] your fine joints 'gainst Thursday next
To go with Paris to Saint Peter's Church,
Or I will drag thee on a hurdle[36] thither.
Out, you greensickness carrion![37] Out, you baggage![38]
You tallow-face![39]

LADY CAPULET. Fie, fie! What, are you mad?

JULIET. Good father, I beseech you on my knees,
Hear me with patience but to speak a word.

CAPULET. Hang thee, young baggage! Disobedient wretch!
I tell thee what—get thee to church a Thursday
Or never after look me in the face.
Speak not, reply not, do not answer me!
My fingers itch. Wife, we scarce thought us blest
That God had lent us but this only child;
But now I see this one is one too much,
And that we have a curse in having her.
Out on her, hilding![40]

NURSE. God in heaven bless her!
You are to blame, my lord, to rate[41] her so.

CAPULET. And why, my Lady Wisdom? Hold your tongue,
Good Prudence. Smatter with your gossips, go![42]

NURSE. I speak no treason.

CAPULET. O, God-i-god-en!

NURSE. May not one speak?

CAPULET. Peace, you mumbling fool!
Utter your gravity[43] o'er a gossip's bowl,
For here we need it not.

30. **Soft! Take . . . you** Wait a minute. Let me understand you.
31. **proud** pleased.
32. **wrought** arranged.
33. **chopped-logic** contradictory, unsound thought and speech.
34. **Mistress minion** Miss Uppity; overly proud.
35. **fettle** prepare.
36. **hurdle** sled on which prisoners were taken to their execution.
37. **greensickness carrion** anemic lump of flesh.
38. **baggage** naughty girl.
39. **tallow-face** wax-pale face.

Dramatic Speeches

What feelings and personality traits does Lord Capulet reveal in this brief speech?

40. **hilding** worthless person.
41. **rate** scold; berate.
42. **Smatter . . . go!** Go chatter with the other old women.
43. **gravity** wisdom.

Comprehension

Rather than Paris, whom does Juliet threaten to marry?

Lady Capulet. You are too hot.

Capulet. God's bread![44] It makes me mad.
Day, night; hour, tide, time; work, play;
Alone, in company; still my care hath been
To have her matched; and having now provided
A gentleman of noble parentage,
Of fair demesnes,[45] youthful, and nobly trained,
Stuffed, as they say, with honorable parts,[46]
Proportioned as one's thought would wish a man—
And then to have a wretched puling[47] fool,
A whining mammet,[48] in her fortune's tender,[49]
To answer "I'll not wed, I cannot love;
I am too young, I pray you pardon me"!
But, and you will not wed, I'll pardon you!
Graze where you will, you shall not house with me.
Look to't, think on't; I do not use to jest.
Thursday is near; lay hand on heart, advise:[50]
And you be mine, I'll give you to my friend;
And you be not, hang, beg, starve, die in the streets,
For, by my soul, I'll ne'er acknowledge thee,
Nor what is mine shall never do thee good.
Trust to't. Bethink you. I'll not be forsworn.[51] [*Exit.*]

Juliet. Is there no pity sitting in the clouds
That sees into the bottom of my grief?
O sweet my mother, cast me not away!
Delay this marriage for a month, a week;
Or if you do not, make the bridal bed
In that dim monument where Tybalt lies.

Lady Capulet. Talk not to me, for I'll not speak a word.
Do as thou wilt, for I have done with thee. [*Exit.*]

Juliet. O God!—O nurse, how shall this be prevented?
My husband is on earth, my faith in heaven.[52]
How shall that faith return again to earth
Unless that husband send it me from heaven
By leaving earth?[53] Comfort me, counsel me.

44. God's bread! By the holy Eucharist!

45. demesnes property.

46. parts qualities.

47. puling whining.

48. mammet doll.

49. in . . . tender when good fortune is offered her.

50. advise consider.

Paraphrase

Paraphrase the threat that Lord Capulet makes to Juliet in this monologue.

51. forsworn made to violate my promise.

52. my faith in heaven my marriage vow is recorded in heaven.

53. leaving earth dying.

Alack, alack, that heaven should practice stratagems[54]
Upon so soft a subject as myself!
What say'st thou? Hast thou not a word of joy?
Some comfort, nurse.

Nurse. Faith, here it is.
Romeo is banished; and all the world to nothing[55]
That he dares ne'er come back to challenge[56] you;
Or if he do, it needs must be by stealth.
Then, since the case so stands as now it doth,
I think it best you married with the County.
O, he's a lovely gentleman!
Romeo's a dishclout to him.[57] An eagle, madam,
Hath not so green, so quick, so fair an eye
As Paris hath. Beshrew my very heart,
I think you are happy in this second match,
For it excels your first; or if it did not,
Your first is dead—or 'twere as good he were
As living here and you no use of him.

Juliet. Speak'st thou from thy heart?

Nurse. And from my soul too; else beshrew them both.

Juliet. Amen!

54. **stratagems** tricks; plots.

55. **all . . . nothing** the odds are overwhelming.

56. **challenge** claim.

57. **a dishclout to him** a dishcloth compared with him.

Comprehension
How do the Capulets respond to the Nurse's attempts to defend Juliet?

▶ Critical Viewing
In what ways does this picture suggest Juliet's vulnerability? Explain.

NURSE. What?

JULIET. Well, thou hast comforted me marvelous much.
Go in; and tell my lady I am gone,
Having displeased my father, to Lawrence' cell,
To make confession and to be absolved.[58]

NURSE. Marry, I will; and this is wisely done. [*Exit.*]

JULIET. Ancient damnation![59] O most wicked fiend!
Is it more sin to wish me thus forsworn,
Or to dispraise my lord with that same tongue
Which she hath praised him with above compare
So many thousand times? Go, counselor!
Thou and my bosom henceforth shall be twain.[60]
I'll to the friar to know his remedy.
If all else fail, myself have power to die. [*Exit.*]

58. **absolved** receive forgiveness for my sins.
59. **Ancient damnation!** Old devil!
60. **Thou . . . twain** You will from now on be separated from my trust.

Dramatic Speeches What feelings toward her Nurse does Juliet reveal in this soliloquy?

Language Study

Vocabulary The words printed in blue appear in Act III of *The Tragedy of Romeo and Juliet.* Identify which two words in each group are synonyms and which one is an antonym of the other two. Explain your responses.

1. **gallant**, courageous, cowardly
2. **fray**, truce, brawl
3. **exile**, banishment, welcome
4. **martial**, peaceful, warlike
5. **fickle**, unpredictable, constant

WORD STUDY

The **Latin root *-loque-*** means "talk," "speak," or "say." In Act III, Juliet says that everyone who speaks Romeo's name speaks **eloquence**. She means that the name itself is a graceful, vivid expression.

Word Study

Part A Explain how the **Latin root *-loque-*** contributes to the meanings of the words *ventriloquist, soliloquy,* and *loquacious*. Consult a dictionary if necessary.

Part B Use the context of the sentences and what you know about the Latin root *-loque-* to explain your answer to each question.

1. Would a *colloquialism* be out of place when used among friends?
2. What would you expect to happen at a *colloquium* on William Shakespeare?

Close Reading Activities

Literary Analysis

Key Ideas and Details

1. **(a)** How and why does Romeo kill Tybalt? **(b) Interpret:** What does Romeo mean when he says, after killing Tybalt, "I am fortune's fool?"
2. **(a) Analyze:** Describe the clashing emotions Juliet feels when the Nurse reports Tybalt's death and Romeo's punishment. **(b) Compare and Contrast:** In what ways are Romeo's and Juliet's reactions to Romeo's banishment similar and different? Explain.
3. **Paraphrase (a)** Paraphrase lines 29–51 in Act III, Scene iii. **(b)** Write several sentences that summarize Romeo's feelings in that speech. **(c)** Summarize the events of Act III.

Craft and Structure

4. **Dialogue and Dramatic Speeches (a)** What thoughts and feelings does Juliet express in the soliloquy that opens Scene ii of Act III? **(b)** When Juliet makes an allusion to Phoebus and Phaëton, what is she hoping will happen? Explain.
5. **Dialogue and Dramatic Speeches** What criticisms of Romeo does the Friar express in his Scene iii monologue beginning, "Hold thy desperate hand"? Cite details from the monologue in your response.
6. **Dialogue and Dramatic Speeches** In Act III, Scene v, when her mother refers to Romeo as a villain, Juliet utters the aside, "Villain and he be many miles asunder." What has happened? Why does Juliet speak only to the audience? Explain.
7. **(a) Analyze:** How would you describe the personality of each of the following characters: Romeo, Tybalt, Benvolio, Mercutio? **(b) Distinguish:** Which of these men are foils to one another? Explain.

Integration of Knowledge and Ideas

8. Complete a chart like the one shown. **(a)** In the first row, write the remark regarding the Montagues and the Capulets that Mercutio makes three times as he is dying. **(b) Infer:** In the second row, explain what Mercutio means by this exclamation. **(c) Interpret:** In the third row, explain how his remark reinforces ideas set forth in the play's Prologue.

Mercutio's Dialogue
Meaning
Explanation

9. THE BIG ? **Do our differences define us?** How have the differences between Romeo and Juliet returned to threaten their future together? Explain how Shakespeare develops this concept.

ACADEMIC VOCABULARY

As you write and speak about *The Tragedy of Romeo and Juliet,* use the words related to differences that you explored on page 481 of this textbook.

Do our differences define us?

Explore the Big Question as you read Act IV of *The Tragedy of Romeo and Juliet*. Consider how the feud between the Montagues and the Capulets continues to drive the young lovers apart.

CLOSE READING FOCUS

Key Ideas and Details: **Break Down Long Sentences**

To better understand complex or extended passages of Shakespearean dialogue, **break down long sentences** into shorter units of meaning.

- If a sentence contains multiple subjects or verbs, separate it into smaller sentences with one subject and one verb.
- If a sentence contains colons, semicolons, or dashes, treat these marks as periods in order to make shorter sentences.

After you have broken down the sentences into smaller units of meaning, reconstruct the ideas into a short summary.

Craft and Structure: **Dramatic Irony**

Dramatic irony is a contradiction between what a character thinks and what the audience knows to be true. Dramatic irony engages the audience emotionally; tension and suspense build as the audience waits for the truth to be revealed to the characters. In Shakespearean drama, that tension and suspense is sometimes broken, at least temporarily, by the use of comic elements. These include the following devices:

- **Comic Relief:** the introduction of a humorous character or situation into an otherwise tragic sequence of events
- **Pun:** a play on words involving either one word that has two different meanings or two words that sound alike but have different meanings; For example, the dying Mercutio makes a pun using the word *grave:* "Ask for me tomorrow, and you shall find me a grave man."

As you read, notice how Shakespeare uses dramatic irony, comic relief, and puns to balance strong emotion with humor and wit.

Vocabulary

The following words are key to understanding the text that follows. Which of these words have negative connotations?

pensive	**vial**	**enjoined**
wayward	**dismal**	**loathsome**

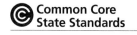

Common Core State Standards

Reading Literature

1. Cite strong and thorough textual evidence to support analysis of what the text says explicitly as well as inferences drawn from the text.

2. Determine a theme or central idea of a text and analyze in detail its development over the course of the text, including how it emerges and is shaped and refined by specific details; provide an objective summary of the text.

5. Analyze how an author's choices concerning how to structure a text, order events within it, and manipulate time create such effects as mystery, tension, or surprise.

Language

5.a. Interpret figures of speech in context and analyze their role in the text.

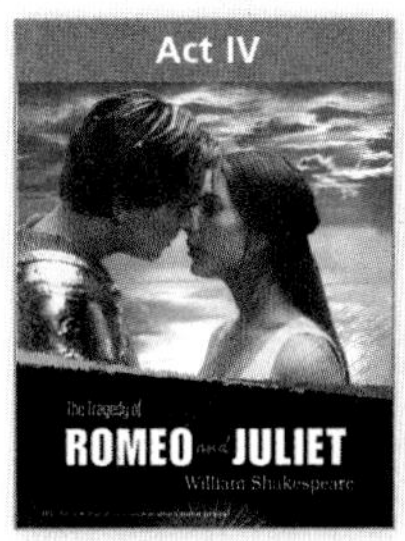

CLOSE READING MODEL

The passage below is from Act IV of *The Tragedy of Romeo and Juliet.* The annotations to the right of the passage show ways in which you can use close reading skills to break down long sentences and analyze dramatic irony.

from *The Tragedy of Romeo and Juliet,* Act IV

CAPULET. Ha! Let me see her. Out alas! She's cold,
Her blood is settled, and her joints are stiff;
Life and these lips have long been separated.
Death lies on her like an untimely frost
Upon the sweetest flower of all the field.[1]

NURSE. O lamentable day!

LADY CAPULET. O woeful time!

CAPULET. Death, that hath ta'en her hence to make me wail,
Ties up my tongue and will not let me speak.
[*Enter* FRIAR LAWRENCE *and the* COUNTY PARIS, *with* MUSICIANS.]

FRIAR. Come, is the bride ready to go to church?

CAPULET. Ready to go, but never to return.
O son, the night before thy wedding day[2]
Hath Death lain with thy wife. There she lies,
Flower as she was, deflowerèd by him.
Death is my son-in-law, Death is my heir;
My daughter he hath wedded. I will die
And leave him all. Life, living, all is Death's.[3]

PARIS. Have I thought, love, to see this morning's face,
And doth it give me such a sight as this?

Dramatic Irony

1 Convinced of his daughter's death, Capulet is distraught. However, the reader is aware that Juliet drank a potion that simulates death.

Dramatic Irony

2 Capulet tells Paris that his bride has died before their wedding day. The reader is aware that Juliet is neither unmarried nor dead. This creates tension for the audience as we wonder when Capulet and Paris will learn the truth.

Summarize

3 By breaking down longer sentences into shorter ideas, it becomes clear that Capulet is personifying death as the only heir to his name and fortune.

Review and Anticipate

Romeo and Juliet are married for only a few hours when disaster strikes. In Act III, Juliet's cousin Tybalt kills Mercutio, and then Romeo kills Tybalt. This leads to Romeo's banishment from Verona. To make matters worse, Juliet's parents are determined to marry her to Paris. Will Romeo and Juliet ever be able to live together as husband and wife? What, if anything, can the lovers now do to preserve their relationship?

Scene i. Friar Lawrence's cell.

[*Enter* Friar Lawrence *and* County Paris.]

Friar. On Thursday, sir? The time is very short.

Paris. My father[1] Capulet will have it so,
And I am nothing slow to slack his haste.[2]

Friar. You say you do not know the lady's mind.
Uneven is the course;[3] I like it not.

Paris. Immoderately she weeps for Tybalt's death,
And therefore have I little talked of love;
For Venus smiles not in a house of tears.
Now, sir, her father counts it dangerous

1. **father** future father-in-law.
2. **I . . . haste** I will not slow him down by being slow myself.
3. **Uneven . . . course** irregular is the plan.

Comprehension
What is the Friar's complaint to Paris about the impending wedding?

4. **inundation** flood.
5. **minded** thought about.

Dramatic Irony
In what way does Paris' comment show that he does not understand the real reason that Juliet is crying?

That she do give her sorrow so much sway,
And in his wisdom hastes our marriage
To stop the inundation[4] of her tears,
Which, too much minded[5] by herself alone,
May be put from her by society.
Now do you know the reason of this haste.

FRIAR. [*Aside*] I would I knew not why it should be slowed.—
Look, sir, here comes the lady toward my cell.

[*Enter* JULIET.]

PARIS. Happily met, my lady and my wife!

JULIET. That may be, sir, when I may be a wife.

PARIS. That "may be" must be, love, on Thursday next.

JULIET. What must be shall be.

FRIAR. That's a certain text.[6]

6. **That's . . . text** That is a certain truth.

PARIS. Come you to make confession to this father?

JULIET. To answer that, I should confess to you.

PARIS. Do not deny to him that you love me.

JULIET. I will confess to you that I love him.

PARIS. So will ye, I am sure, that you love me.

JULIET. If I do so, it will be of more price,[7]
Being spoke behind your back, than to your face.

7. **price** value.

PARIS. Poor soul, thy face is much abused with tears.

JULIET. The tears have got small victory by that,
For it was bad enough before their spite.[8]

8. **before their spite** before the harm that the tears did.

PARIS. Thou wrong'st it more than tears with that report.

JULIET. That is no slander, sir, which is a truth;
And what I spake, I spake it to my face.

PARIS. Thy face is mine, and thou hast sland'red it.

JULIET. It may be so, for it is not mine own.
Are you at leisure, holy father, now,
Or shall I come to you at evening mass?

FRIAR. My leisure serves me, pensive daughter, now.
My lord, we must entreat the time alone.[9]

Vocabulary ▶
pensive (pen´ siv) *adj.* deeply thoughtful

9. **entreat . . . alone** ask to have this time to ourselves.

Paris. God shield[10] I should disturb devotion!
Juliet, on Thursday early will I rouse ye.
Till then, adieu, and keep this holy kiss. [*Exit.*]

Juliet. O, shut the door, and when thou hast done so,
Come weep with me—past hope, past care, past help!

Friar. O Juliet, I already know thy grief;
It strains me past the compass of my wits.[11]
I hear thou must, and nothing may prorogue[12] it,
On Thursday next be married to this County.

Juliet. Tell me not, friar, that thou hearest of this,
Unless thou tell me how I may prevent it.
If in thy wisdom thou canst give no help,
Do thou but call my resolution wise
And with this knife I'll help it presently.[13]
God joined my heart and Romeo's, thou our hands;
And ere this hand, by thee to Romeo's sealed,
Shall be the label to another deed,[14]
Or my true heart with treacherous revolt
Turn to another, this shall slay them both.
Therefore, out of thy long-experienced time,
Give me some present counsel; or, behold,
'Twixt my extremes and me[15] this bloody knife
Shall play the umpire, arbitrating[16] that
Which the commission of thy years and art
Could to no issue of true honor bring.[17]
Be not so long to speak. I long to die
If what thou speak'st speak not of remedy.

Friar. Hold, daughter. I do spy a kind of hope,
Which craves[18] as desperate an execution
As that is desperate which we would prevent.
If, rather than to marry County Paris,
Thou hast the strength of will to slay thyself,
Then is it likely thou wilt undertake
A thing like death to chide away this shame,
That cop'st with death himself to scape from it;[19]
And, if thou darest, I'll give thee remedy.

Juliet. O, bid me leap, rather than marry Paris,
From off the battlements of any tower,
Or walk in thievish ways,[20] or bid me lurk

10. **shield** forbid.

11. **past . . . wits** beyond the ability of my mind to find a remedy.

12. **prorogue** delay.

13. **presently** at once.

14. **Shall . . . deed** shall give the seal of approval to another marriage contract.

15. **'Twixt . . me** between my misfortunes and me.

16. **arbitrating** deciding.

17. **Which . . . bring** which the authority that derives from your age and ability could not solve honorably.

Dramatic Irony
Which two meanings of the word "long" does Juliet use to make a pun in line 66?

18. **craves** requires.

19. **That cop'st . . .** it that bargains with death itself to escape from it.

20. **thievish ways** roads where criminals lurk.

Comprehension
What does Juliet threaten to do to avoid marrying Paris?

21. **charnel house** vault for bones removed from graves to be reused.
22. **reeky** foul-smelling.
23. **chapless** jawless.

Where serpents are; chain me with roaring bears,
Or hide me nightly in a charnel house,[21]
O'ercovered quite with dead men's rattling bones,
With reeky[22] shanks and yellow chapless[23] skulls;
Or bid me go into a new-made grave
And hide me with a dead man in his shroud—
Things that, to hear them told, have made me tremble—
And I will do it without fear or doubt,
To live an unstained wife to my sweet love.

Friar. Hold, then. Go home, be merry, give consent
To marry Paris. Wednesday is tomorrow.
Tomorrow night look that thou lie alone;
Let not the nurse lie with thee in thy chamber.
Take thou this vial, being then in bed,
And this distilling liquor drink thou off;
When presently through all thy veins shall run
A cold and drowsy humor;[24] for no pulse
Shall keep his native[25] progress, but surcease;[26]
No warmth, no breath, shall testify thou livest;
The roses in thy lips and cheeks shall fade
To wanny ashes,[27] thy eyes' windows[28] fall
Like death when he shuts up the day of life;
Each part, deprived of supple government,[29]
Shall, stiff and stark and cold, appear like death;
And in this borrowed likeness of shrunk death
Thou shalt continue two-and-forty hours,
And then awake as from a pleasant sleep.
Now, when the bridegroom in the morning comes
To rouse thee from thy bed, there art thou dead.
Then, as the manner of our country is,
In thy best robes uncovered on the bier[30]
Thou shalt be borne to that same ancient vault
Where all the kindred of the Capulets lie.
In the meantime, against[31] thou shalt awake,
Shall Romeo by my letters know our drift;[32]
And hither shall he come; and he and I

Vocabulary ▶
vial (vī´ əl) *n.* small bottle containing medicine or other liquids

24. **humor** fluid; liquid.
25. **native** natural.
26. **surcease** stop.
27. **wanny ashes** to the color of pale ashes.
28. **eyes' windows** eyelids.
29. **supple government** ability for maintaining motion.

30. **uncovered on the bier** displayed on the funeral platform.
31. **against** before.
32. **drift** purpose; plan.

Will watch thy waking, and that very night
Shall Romeo bear thee hence to Mantua.
And this shall free thee from this present shame,
If no inconstant toy[33] nor womanish fear
Abate thy valor[34] in the acting it.

33. **inconstant toy** passing whim.
34. **Abate thy valor** Lessen your courage.

Dramatic Irony
What information does Juliet now have that Romeo does not?

JULIET. Give me, give me! O, tell not me of fear!

FRIAR. Hold! Get you gone, be strong and prosperous
In this resolve. I'll send a friar with speed
To Mantua, with my letters to thy lord.

JULIET. Love give me strength, and strength shall help afford.
Farewell, dear father. [*Exit with* FRIAR.]

Scene ii. Hall in Capulet's house.

[*Enter* FATHER CAPULET, MOTHER, NURSE, *and* SERVINGMEN, *two or three.*]

CAPULET. So many guests invite as here are writ.
[*Exit a* SERVINGMAN.]
Sirrah, go hire me twenty cunning[1] cooks.

SERVINGMAN. You shall have none ill, sir; for I'll try[2] if they can lick their fingers.

CAPULET. How canst thou try them so?

SERVINGMAN. Marry, sir, 'tis an ill cook that cannot lick his own fingers.[3] Therefore he that cannot lick his fingers goes not with me.

1. **cunning** skillful.
2. **try** test.
3. **'tis . . . fingers** It is a bad cook who will not taste his own cooking.

CAPULET. Go, begone.
[*Exit* SERVINGMAN.]
We shall be much unfurnished[4] for this time.
What, is my daughter gone to Friar Lawrence?

NURSE. Ay, forsooth.[5]

CAPULET. Well, he may chance to do some good on her.
A peevish self-willed harlotry it is.[6]

4. **unfurnished** unprepared.
5. **forsooth** in truth.
6. **A peevish . . . it is** It is the ill-tempered, selfish behavior of a woman without good breeding.

[*Enter* JULIET.]

NURSE. See where she comes from shrift with merry look.

CAPULET. How now, my headstrong? Where have you been gadding?

Comprehension
According to the Friar, how will Romeo learn of Juliet's plan to meet him?

Vocabulary ▶
enjoined (en jɔind′)
v. directed or ordered to do something

Juliet. Where I have learnt me to repent the sin
Of disobedient opposition
To you and your behests,[7] and am enjoined
By holy Lawrence to fall prostrate[8] here
To beg your pardon. Pardon, I beseech you!
Henceforward I am ever ruled by you.

7. **behests** requests.
8. **fall prostrate** lie face down in humble submission.

Capulet. Send for the County. Go tell him of this.
I'll have this knot knit up tomorrow morning.

Juliet. I met the youthful lord at Lawrence' cell
And gave him what becomèd[9] love I might,
Not stepping o'er the bounds of modesty.

9. **becomèd** suitable; proper.

Capulet. Why, I am glad on't. This is well. Stand up.
This is as't should be. Let me see the County.
Ay, marry, go, I say, and fetch him hither.
Now, afore God, this reverend holy friar,
All our whole city is much bound[10] to him.

Dramatic Irony
What is ironic about Lord Capulet's relief in this scene?

Juliet. Nurse, will you go with me into my closet[11]
To help me sort such needful ornaments[12]
As you think fit to furnish me tomorrow?

10. **bound** indebted.
11. **closet** private room.
12. **ornaments** clothes.

Lady Capulet. No, not till Thursday. There is time enough.

Capulet. Go, nurse, go with her. We'll to church tomorrow.
[*Exit* Juliet *and* Nurse.]

Lady Capulet. We shall be short in our provision.[13]
'Tis now near night.

13. **short . . . provision** lacking time for preparation.

Capulet. Tush, I will stir about,
And all things shall be well, I warrant thee, wife.
Go thou to Juliet, help to deck up her.[14]
I'll not to bed tonight; let me alone.
I'll play the housewife for this once. What, ho![15]
They are all forth; well, I will walk myself
To County Paris, to prepare up him
Against tomorrow. My heart is wondrous light,
Since this same wayward girl is so reclaimed.
[*Exit with* Mother.]

14. **deck up her** dress her; get her ready.
15. **What, ho!** Capulet is calling for his servants.

Vocabulary ▶
wayward (wā′ wərd)
adj. headstrong

Scene iii. Juliet's chamber.

[*Enter* JULIET *and* NURSE.]

JULIET. Ay, those attires are best; but, gentle nurse,
I pray thee leave me to myself tonight;
For I have need of many orisons[1]
To move the heavens to smile upon my state,[2]
Which, well thou knowest, is cross[3] and full of sin.

[*Enter* LADY CAPULET.]

LADY CAPULET. What, are you busy, ho? Need you my help?

JULIET. No, madam; we have culled[4] such necessaries
As are behoveful[5] for our state tomorrow.
So please you, let me now be left alone,
And let the nurse this night sit up with you:
For I am sure you have your hands full all
In this so sudden business.

LADY CAPULET. Good night.
Get thee to bed, and rest: for thou hast need.

[*Exit* LADY CAPULET *and* NURSE.]

JULIET. Farewell! God knows when we shall meet again.
I have a faint cold fear thrills through my veins
That almost freezes up the heat of life.
I'll call them back again to comfort me.
Nurse!—What should she do here?
My dismal scene I needs must act alone.
Come, vial.
What if this mixture do not work at all?
Shall I be married then tomorrow morning?
No, no! This shall forbid it. Lie thou there.

[*Lays down a dagger.*]

What if it be a poison which the friar
Subtly hath minist'red[6] to have me dead,
Lest in this marriage he should be dishonored
Because he married me before to Romeo?
I fear it is; and yet methinks it should not,
For he hath still been tried[7] a holy man.
How if, when I am laid into the tomb,
I wake before the time that Romeo
Come to redeem me? There's a fearful point!

Spiral Review
CHARACTER What is Juliet's motivation for deceiving the Nurse?

1. **orisons** prayers.
2. **state** condition.
3. **cross** selfish; disobedient.

Break Down Long Sentences
Break down the long sentences in Juliet's lines. State the reasons she gives her Nurse and Lady Capulet for why she should be alone.

4. **culled** chosen.
5. **behoveful** desirable; appropriate.

◄ Vocabulary
dismal (diz′ məl) *adj.* causing gloom or misery

6. **minist'red** given me.

7. **tried** proved.

Comprehension
How does Juliet regain her parents' favor?

Shall I not then be stifled in the vault,
To whose foul mouth no healthsome air breathes in,
And there die strangled ere my Romeo comes?
Or, if I live, is it not very like
The horrible conceit[8] of death and night,
Together with the terror of the place—
As in a vault, an ancient receptacle
Where for this many hundred years the bones
Of all my buried ancestors are packed;
Where bloody Tybalt, yet but green in earth,[9]
Lies fest'ring in his shroud; where, as they say,
At some hours in the night spirits resort—
Alack, alack, is it not like[10] that I,
So early waking—what with **loathsome** smells,
And shrieks like mandrakes[11] torn out of the earth,
That living mortals, hearing them, run mad—
O, if I wake, shall I not be distraught,[12]
Environèd[13] with all these hideous fears,
And madly play with my forefathers' joints,
And pluck the mangled Tybalt from his shroud,
And, in this rage, with some great kinsman's bone
As with a club dash out my desp'rate brains?
O, look! Methinks I see my cousin's ghost
Seeking out Romeo, that did spit his body
Upon a rapier's point. Stay, Tybalt, stay!
Romeo, Romeo, Romeo, I drink to thee.

[*She falls upon her bed within the curtains.*]

8. **conceit** idea; thought.
9. **green in earth** newly entombed.
10. **like** likely.

◀ **Vocabulary**
loathsome (lōth′ səm) *adj.* disgusting; detestable

11. **mandrakes** plants with forked roots that resemble human legs. The mandrake was believed to shriek when uprooted and cause the hearer to go mad.
12. **distraught** insane.
13. **Environèd** surrounded.

Break Down Long Sentences
Break down the long sentences in Juliet's soliloquoy to summarize the fears she expresses.

Comprehension
What does Juliet do after her mother and the Nurse leave her chambers?

◀ **Critical Viewing**
In what way do the colors in this photograph enhance the mood of the scene?

Scene iv. Hall in Capulet's house.

[*Enter* Lady of the House *and* Nurse.]

Lady Capulet. Hold, take these keys and fetch more spices, nurse.

Nurse. They call for dates and quinces[1] in the pastry.[2]

[*Enter old* Capulet.]

Capulet. Come, stir, stir, stir! The second cock hath crowed,
The curfew bell hath rung, 'tis three o'clock.
Look to the baked meats, good Angelica;[3]
Spare not for cost.

Nurse. Go, you cotquean,[4] go,
Get you to bed! Faith, you'll be sick tomorrow
For this night's watching.[5]

Capulet. No, not a whit. What, I have watched ere now
All night for lesser cause, and ne'er been sick.

Lady Capulet. Ay, you have been a mouse hunt[6] in your time;
But I will watch you from such watching now.

[*Exit* Lady *and* Nurse.]

Capulet. A jealous hood,[7] a jealous hood!

[*Enter three or four* Fellows *with spits and logs and baskets.*]

Now, fellow,
What is there?

First Fellow. Things for the cook, sir; but I know not what.

Capulet. Make haste, make haste. [*Exit* First Fellow.] Sirrah, fetch drier logs.
Call Peter; he will show thee where they are.

Second Fellow. I have a head, sir, that will find out logs
And never trouble Peter for the matter.

Capulet. Mass,[8] and well said; a merry whoreson, ha!
Thou shalt be loggerhead.[9]

[*Exit* Second Fellow, *with the others.*]

Good faith, 'tis day.
The County will be here with music straight,
For so he said he would. [*Play music.*]
I hear him near.
Nurse! Wife! What, ho! What, nurse, I say!

1. **quinces** golden, apple-shaped fruits.
2. **pastry** baking room.
3. **Angelica** This is probably the Nurse's name.
4. **cotquean** (kat′ kwēn′) man who does housework.
5. **watching** staying awake.
6. **mouse hunt** woman chaser.
7. **jealous hood** jealousy.
8. **Mass** by the Mass (an oath).
9. **loggerhead** blockhead.

Dramatic Irony
Reread lines 16–21. In what way does Capulet's pun in line 21 contribute to the mood of Scene iv?

[*Enter* NURSE.]

Go waken Juliet; go and trim her up.
I'll go and chat with Paris. Hie, make haste,
Make haste! The bridegroom he is come already:
Make haste, I say. [*Exit.*]

Scene v. Juliet's chamber.

NURSE. Mistress! What, mistress! Juliet! Fast,[1] I warrant her, she.
Why, lamb! Why, lady! Fie, you slugabed.[2]
Why, love, I say! Madam; Sweetheart! Why, bride!
What, not a word? You take your pennyworths now;
Sleep for a week; for the next night, I warrant,
The County Paris hath set up his rest
That you shall rest but little. God forgive me!
Marry, and amen. How sound is she asleep!
I needs must wake her. Madam, madam, madam!
Ay, let the County take you in your bed;
He'll fright you up, i' faith. Will it not be?
[*Draws aside the curtains.*]
What, dressed, and in your clothes, and down again?[3]
I must needs wake you. Lady! Lady! Lady!
Alas, alas! Help, help! My lady's dead!
O weraday that ever I was born!
Some aqua vitae, ho! My lord! My lady!

1. **Fast** fast asleep.
2. **slugabed** sleepyhead.

Dramatic Irony
In what way does the Nurse's carefree chatter add to the irony of the scene?

3. **down again** back in bed.

[*Enter* LADY CAPULET.]

LADY CAPULET. What noise is here?

NURSE. O lamentable day!

LADY CAPULET. What is the matter?

NURSE. Look, look! O heavy day!

LADY CAPULET. O me, O me! My child, my only life!
Revive, look up, or I will die with thee!
Help, help! Call help.

[*Enter* CAPULET.]

CAPULET. For shame, bring Juliet forth; her lord is come.

NURSE. She's dead, deceased; she's dead, alack the day!

LADY CAPULET. Alack the day, she's dead, she's dead, she's dead!

Comprehension
What does the Nurse find when she draws aside the curtains in Juliet's chamber?

Capulet. Ha! Let me see her. Out alas! She's cold,
Her blood is settled, and her joints are stiff;
Life and these lips have long been separated.
Death lies on her like an untimely frost
Upon the sweetest flower of all the field.

Nurse. O lamentable day!

Lady Capulet. O woeful time!

Capulet. Death, that hath ta'en her hence to make me wail,
Ties up my tongue and will not let me speak.

[*Enter* Friar Lawrence *and the* County Paris, *with* Musicians.]

Dramatic Irony
In what way does the Friar's question add to the dramatic irony of the scene?

Friar. Come, is the bride ready to go to church?

Capulet. Ready to go, but never to return.
O son, the night before thy wedding day
Hath Death lain with thy wife. There she lies,
Flower as she was, deflowerèd by him.
Death is my son-in-law, Death is my heir;
My daughter he hath wedded. I will die
And leave him all. Life, living, all is Death's.

Paris. Have I thought, love, to see this morning's face,
And doth it give me such a sight as this?

Lady Capulet. Accursed, unhappy, wretched, hateful day!
Most miserable hour that e'er time saw
In lasting labor of his pilgrimage!
But one, poor one, one poor and loving child,
But one thing to rejoice and solace[4] in,
And cruel Death hath catched it from my sight.

Nurse. O woe! O woeful, woeful, woeful day!
Most lamentable day, most woeful day
That ever ever I did yet behold!
O day, O day, O day! O hateful day!
Never was seen so black a day as this.
O woeful day! O woeful day!

Paris. Beguiled,[5] divorcèd, wrongèd, spited, slain!
Most detestable Death, by thee beguiled,
By cruel, cruel thee quite overthrown.
O love! O life!—not life, but love in death!

Capulet. Despised, distressèd, hated, martyred, killed!
Uncomfortable[6] time, why cam'st thou now
To murder, murder our solemnity?[7]

4. **solace** find comfort.

5. **Beguiled** cheated.

6. **Uncomfortable** painful, upsetting.

7. **solemnity** solemn rites.

LITERATURE IN CONTEXT

Culture Connection

Rosemary

When the Capulets discover Juliet apparently dead, the Friar advises, "Dry up your tears and stick your rosemary / On this fair corse." Rosemary is an evergreen herb that traditionally signifies remembrance, loyalty, and love. Shakespeare often included references to herbs in his plays for symbolic purposes, and rosemary is one herb that turned up often in his works. *Hamlet, King Lear, The Winter's Tale,* and *Pericles* all include references to rosemary as a symbol of remembrance.

Connect to the Literature

Why do you think the Friar tells the Capulets to lay a sprig of rosemary on Juliet's body?

O child, O child! My soul, and not my child!
Dead art thou—alack, my child is dead,
And with my child my joys are burièd!

Friar. Peace, ho, for shame! Confusion's cure lives not
In these confusions.[8] Heaven and yourself
Had part in this fair maid—now heaven hath all,
And all the better is it for the maid.
Your part in her you could not keep from death,
But heaven keeps his part in eternal life.
The most you sought was her promotion,
For 'twas your heaven she should be advanced;
And weep ye now, seeing she is advanced
Above the clouds, as high as heaven itself?
O, in this love, you love your child so ill
That you run mad, seeing that she is well.[9]
She's not well married that lives married long,
But she's best married that dies married young.
Dry up your tears and stick your rosemary[10]
On this fair corse, and, as the custom is,
And in her best array bear her to church:
For though fond nature[11] bids us all lament,
Yet nature's tears are reason's merriment.[12]

8. **Confusion's . . . confusions** The remedy for this calamity is not to be found in these outcries.
9. **well** blessed in heaven.
10. **rosemary** evergreen herb signifying love and remembrance.
11. **fond nature** mistake-prone human nature.
12. **Yet . . . merriment** While human nature causes us to weep for Juliet, reason should cause us to be happy (since she is in heaven).

Comprehension
What does the Friar recommend that the Capulets do when they discover Juliet and believe she is dead?

13. **ordainèd festival** planned to be part of a celebration.

14. **dirges** funeral hymns.

Dramatic Irony
In what way does the dramatic irony of the Friar's words heighten the play's suspense?

15. **low'r** frown.

16. **case** situation; instrument case.

17. **dump** sad tune.

18. **gleek** scornful speech.
19. **give you** call you.
20. **minstrel** a contemptuous term (as opposed to "musician").

CAPULET. All things that we ordainèd festival[13]
Turn from their office to black funeral—
Our instruments to melancholy bells,
Our wedding cheer to a sad burial feast;
Our solemn hymns to sullen dirges[14] change;
Our bridal flowers serve for a buried corse;
And all things change them to the contrary.

FRIAR. Sir, go you in; and, madam, go with him;
And go, Sir Paris. Everyone prepare
To follow this fair corse unto her grave.
The heavens do low'r[15] upon you for some ill;
Move them no more by crossing their high will.

[*Exit, casting rosemary on her and shutting the curtains. The* NURSE *and* MUSICIANS *remain.*]

FIRST MUSICIAN. Faith, we may put up our pipes and be gone.

NURSE. Honest good fellows, ah, put up, put up!
For well you know this is a pitiful case.[16] [*Exit.*]

FIRST MUSICIAN. Ay, by my troth, the case may be amended.

[*Enter* PETER.]

PETER. Musicians, O, musicians, "Heart's ease," "Heart's ease"!
O, and you will have me live, play "Heart's ease."

FIRST MUSICIAN. Why "Heart's ease"?

PETER. O, musicians, because my heart itself plays "My heart is full."
O, play me some merry dump[17] to comfort me.

FIRST MUSICIAN. Not a dump we! 'Tis no time to play now.

PETER. You will not then?

FIRST MUSICIAN. No.

PETER. I will then give it you soundly.

FIRST MUSICIAN. What will you give us?

PETER. No money, on my faith, but the gleek.[18] I will give you[19] the minstrel.[20]

First Musician. Then will I give you the serving-creature.

Peter. Then will I lay the serving-creature's dagger on your pate.
I will carry no crotchets.[21] I'll *re* you, I'll *fa* you. Do you note me?

First Musician. And you re us and fa us, you note us.

Second Musician. Pray you put up your dagger, and put out your wit.

Peter. Then have at you with my wit! I will dry-beat you with an iron wit, and put up my iron dagger. Answer me like men.
"When griping grief the heart doth wound,
And doleful dumps the mind oppress,
Then music with her silver sound"—
Why "silver sound"? Why "music with her silver sound"?
What say you, Simon Catling?

First Musician. Marry, sir, because silver hath a sweet sound.

Peter. Pretty! What say you, Hugh Rebeck?

21. **crotchets** whims; quarter notes.

Dramatic Irony
What kind of mood does the pun in line 126 help to create in this scene?

22. cry you mercy beg your pardon.

Second Musician. I say "silver sound" because musicians sound for silver.

Peter. Pretty too! What say you, James Soundpost?

Third Musician. Faith, I know not what to say.

Peter. O, I cry you mercy,[22] you are the singer. I will say for you. It is "music with her silver sound" because musicians have no gold for sounding.
"Then music with her silver sound
With speedy help doth lend redress." [*Exit.*]

First Musician. What a pestilent knave is this same!

Second Musician. Hang him, Jack! Come, we'll in here, tarry for the mourners, and stay dinner. [*Exit with others.*]

Language Study

Vocabulary The words printed in blue in the statements below appear in Act IV of *The Tragedy of Romeo and Juliet*. Read each statement and indicate whether it is usually true or usually false. Revise the statements that are false to make them true.

1. Clowns make children laugh by appearing **pensive**.
2. A **wayward** person would probably dislike orders.
3. If you were in a **dismal** mood, you would be good company.
4. A **loathsome** meal is not likely to be eaten quickly.
5. A **vial** would be a good container for a cough syrup.

WORD STUDY
The **Latin prefix *en-*** means "in," "into," or "within." In Act IV, Juliet says she is **enjoined** by Friar Lawrence to be ruled by her father. She means that Friar Lawrence wants her to join in with him and obey her father's wishes.

Word Study

Part A Explain how the **Latin prefix *en-*** contributes to the meanings of the words *encage, entrap,* and *engrave*. Consult a dictionary if necessary.

Part B Use the context of the sentences and what you know about the Latin prefix *en-* to explain your answer to each question.

1. Would a terrible insult *enrage* you?
2. What happens when someone *enlists* in the armed forces?

Close Reading Activities

Literary Analysis

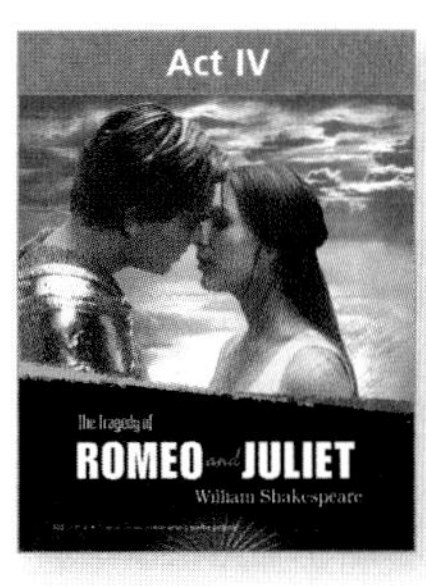

Key Ideas and Details

1. **(a)** What is Friar Lawrence's plan for Juliet? **(b) Analyze:** Why do you think Juliet trusts the Friar? Explain using details from the text.
2. **(a)** What three fears does Juliet reveal in her Act IV, Scene iii, soliloquy? **(b) Interpret:** What does the soliloquy reveal about her personality? Explain your response and support it with references to the text.
3. **Break Down Long Sentences (a)** Summarize lines 50–59 of Juliet's monologue to Friar Lawrence in Act IV, Scene i. **(b)** Then, summarize the events that take place in Act IV. Break long sentences into smaller ones as necessary to clarify speakers' thoughts.

Craft and Structure

4. **Dramatic Irony** In what way is Juliet's encounter with Paris in Friar Lawrence's cell an instance of dramatic irony? Explain.
5. **Dramatic Irony (a)** Complete a chart like the one shown to demonstrate why Capulet's statement in Act IV, Scene iv, line 25, is an example of dramatic irony. **(b)** Explain the key role dramatic irony plays in Act IV, Scene v, lines 1–95.

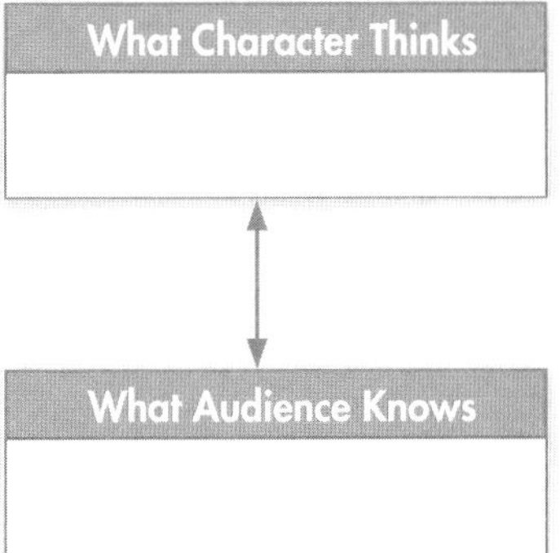

6. **Interpret:** Explain how Capulet's encounter with the fellows in Act IV, Scene iv, lines 13–21, represents a moment of comic relief.
7. **(a) Interpret:** Explain the pun in the Nurse's exchange with the First Musician in Act IV, Scene v, lines 97–98. **(b) Analyze:** How is the conversation that follows among the musicians and Peter an instance of comic relief? Explain.

Integration of Knowledge and Ideas

8. **(a) Evaluate:** Do you think Juliet's drinking of the potion is a brave act or a foolish act? Explain. **(b) Draw Conclusions:** How has Juliet changed in the course of the play? Give specific details to explain your perceptions.

9. THE BIG ? **Do our differences define us? (a)** In what ways do Juliet's ideas about love differ from her parents' ideas? Cite specific examples from the text. **(b)** What do Juliet's rebellious actions reveal about her character? Explain.

ACADEMIC VOCABULARY

As you write and speak about *The Tragedy of Romeo and Juliet,* use the words related to differences that you explored on page 481 of this book.

Do our differences define us?

Explore the Big Question as you read Act V of *The Tragedy of Romeo and Juliet*. Note how differences among the characters in this drama lead to a tragic end. Then, decide if the events of the play are inevitable.

CLOSE READING FOCUS

Key Ideas and Details: **Analyze Cause and Effect**

When reading a work—such as a Shakespearean tragedy—that has many dimensions, it is useful to **analyze causes and effects.**

- A *cause* is an event, action, or emotion that produces a result.
- An *effect* is the result produced by the cause.

Tragedies often involve a chain of causes and effects that lead to the tragic outcome. Recognizing the sequence will help you better understand the characters and their actions.

Craft and Structure: **Tragedy and Motive**

A **tragedy** is a drama in which the main character, who is of noble stature, meets with great misfortune. In Shakespearean tragedies, the hero's doom is the result of fate, a tragic flaw, or a combination of both.

- **Fate** is a pre-planned destiny over which the hero has little or no control. In some Shakespearean tragedies, errors, the poor judgment of others, or accidents can be interpreted as the workings of fate.
- A **tragic flaw** is a personality defect, such as jealousy, that contributes to the hero's choices and, thus, to the tragic downfall.

A character's **motives** direct his or her thoughts and actions. Often, the hero's motives are good but misguided, and the hero suffers a tragic fate that may seem undeserved. Although tragedies are sad, they also show the nobility of the human spirit.

Vocabulary

Read each word and its definition. Decide whether you know the word well, know it a little bit, or do not know it at all. After you read, see how your knowledge of each word has increased.

remnants	**penury**	**disperse**
haughty	**ambiguities**	**scourge**

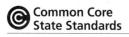

Common Core State Standards

Reading Literature

1. Cite strong and thorough textual evidence to support analysis of what the text says explicitly as well as inferences drawn from the text.

2. Determine a theme or central idea of a text and analyze in detail its development over the course of the text, including how it emerges and is shaped and refined by specific details; provide an objective summary of the text.

3. Analyze how complex characters develop over the course of a text, interact with other characters, and advance the plot or develop the theme.

CLOSE READING MODEL

The passage below is from Act V of *The Tragedy of Romeo and Juliet.* The annotations to the right of the passage show how you can use close reading skills to analyze both cause and effect and the ways in which the hero's motives and flaws lead to tragedy.

from *The Tragedy of Romeo and Juliet,* Act V

[*Enter* ROMEO'S MAN, BALTHASAR, *booted.*]

Romeo. News from Verona! How now, Balthasar?
Dost thou not bring me letters from the friar?
How doth my lady? Is my father well?
For nothing can be ill if she be well.

Man. Then she is well, and nothing can be ill.
Her body sleeps in Capels' monument,
And her immortal part with angels lives.
I saw her laid low in her kindred's vault
And presently took post to tell it you.[1]
O, pardon me for bringing these ill news,
Since you did leave it for my office, sir.

Romeo. Is it e'en so? Then I defy you, stars.
Thou knowest my lodging. Get me ink and paper
And hire post horses. I will hence tonight.[2]

Man. I do beseech you, sir, have patience.
Your looks are pale and wild and do import
Some misadventure.[3]

Romeo. Tush, thou art deceived.
Leave me and do the thing I bid thee do.
Hast thou no letters to me from the friar?

Analyze Cause and Effect

1 Believing Juliet is dead, Balthasar has sought out Romeo to relate the news. His actions start a chain of events that propel the play toward its tragic conclusion.

Analyze Cause and Effect

2 Balthasar's words cause Romeo to decide to go to Juliet immediately. Romeo's hasty decision advances the chain of events that Balthasar's news set in motion.

Tragedy and Motive

3 Balthasar warns Romeo to have patience, but Romeo disregards his advice. This highlights Romeo's impulsiveness. His hasty, unthinking behavior may be Romeo's tragic flaw.

Review and Anticipate

To prevent her marriage to Paris, Juliet has taken the Friar's potion and, as Act V begins, is in a temporary deathlike sleep. Her unsuspecting family plans her funeral. Meanwhile, the Friar has sent a messenger to Mantua to tell Romeo of the ruse, so that he may return and rescue Juliet from her family tomb. What do you think might go wrong with the Friar's plan?

Scene i. Mantua. A Street.

[*Enter* ROMEO.]

ROMEO. If I may trust the flattering truth of sleep,[1]
My dreams presage[2] some joyful news at hand.
My bosom's lord[3] sits lightly in his throne,
And all this day an unaccustomed spirit
Lifts me above the ground with cheerful thoughts.
I dreamt my lady came and found me dead
(Strange dream that gives a dead man leave to think!)
And breathed such life with kisses in my lips
That I revived and was an emperor.
Ah me! How sweet is love itself possessed,
When but love's shadows[4] are so rich in joy!

[*Enter* ROMEO'S MAN, BALTHASAR, *booted.*]
News from Verona! How now, Balthasar?

1. **flattering . . . sleep** pleasing illusions of dreams.
2. **presage** foretell.
3. **bosom's lord** heart.
4. **shadows** dreams; unreal images.

Comprehension
Why is Romeo in a good mood?

5. **Capels' monument** the Capulets' burial vault.
6. **presently took post** immediately set out on horseback.
7. **office** duty.

Tragedy and Motive
In what way does Romeo's remark in line 24 reinforce fate's role in the tragedy?

Dost thou not bring me letters from the friar?
How doth my lady? Is my father well?
How fares my Juliet? That I ask again,
For nothing can be ill if she be well.

Man. Then she is well, and nothing can be ill.
Her body sleeps in Capels' monument,[5]
And her immortal part with angels lives.
I saw her laid low in her kindred's vault
And presently took post[6] to tell it you.
O, pardon me for bringing these ill news,
Since you did leave it for my office,[7] sir.

Romeo. Is it e'en so? Then I defy you, stars!
Thou knowest my lodging. Get me ink and paper
And hire post horses. I will hence tonight.

MAN. I do beseech you, sir, have patience.
Your looks are pale and wild and do import
Some misadventure.[8]

ROMEO. Tush, thou art deceived.
Leave me and do the thing I bid thee do.
Hast thou no letters to me from the friar?

MAN. No, my good lord.

ROMEO. No matter. Get thee gone.
And hire those horses. I'll be with thee straight.

[*Exit* BALTHASAR.]

Well, Juliet, I will lie with thee tonight.
Let's see for means. O mischief, thou art swift
To enter in the thoughts of desperate men!
I do remember an apothecary,[9]
And hereabouts 'a dwells, which late I noted
In tatt'red weeds, with overwhelming brows,
Culling of simples.[10] Meager were his looks,
Sharp misery had worn him to the bones;
And in his needy shop a tortoise hung,
An alligator stuffed, and other skins
Of ill-shaped fishes; and about his shelves
A beggarly account[11] of empty boxes,
Green earthen pots, bladders, and musty seeds,
Remnants of packthread, and old cakes of roses[12]
Were thinly scatterèd, to make up a show.
Noting this penury to myself I said,

8. **import / Some misadventure** suggest some misfortune.

9. **apothecary** one who prepares and sells drugs and medicines.

10. **In tatt'red . . . simples** in torn clothing, with overhanging eyebrows, sorting out herbs.

11. **beggarly account** small number.

12. **cakes of roses** pressed rose petals (used for perfume).

◀ **Vocabulary**

remnants (rem´ nənts) *n.* what is left over; remainders

penury (pen´ yo͞o rē) *n.* extreme poverty

Comprehension

What does Romeo learn from Balthasar?

13. **caitiff** miserable.

"And if a man did need a poison now
Whose sale is present death in Mantua,
Here lives a caitiff[13] wretch would sell it him."
O, this same thought did but forerun my need,
And this same needy man must sell it me.
As I remember, this should be the house.
Being holiday, the beggar's shop is shut.
What, ho! Apothecary!

[*Enter* APOTHECARY.]

APOTHECARY. Who calls so loud?

14. **ducats** (duk ´əts) gold coins.
15. **soon-speeding gear** fast-working stuff.

ROMEO. Come hither, man. I see that thou art poor.
Hold, there is forty ducats.[14] Let me have
A dram of poison, such soon-speeding gear[15]
As will **disperse** itself through all the veins
That the life-weary taker may fall dead,
And that the trunk[16] may be discharged of breath
As violently as hasty powder fired
Doth hurry from the fatal cannon's womb.

Vocabulary ▶
disperse (di spurs´) *v.* break up and scatter in all directions; spread about; distribute widely

APOTHECARY. Such mortal drugs I have; but Mantua's law
Is death to any he that utters[17] them.

16. **trunk** body.
17. **utters** sells.

LITERATURE IN CONTEXT

History Connection

Plague Searchers

The Black Plague, or Black Death, was a disease that swept through Europe, Asia, and the Middle East during the 1300s, with outbreaks continuing until 1400. It is thought that as much as a third of Europe's population died of the disease between 1347 and 1351. During an outbreak of plague, officials would appoint plague searchers to quarantine people infected with the disease and dispose of victims' remains. In *Romeo and Juliet*, Friar John is quarantined by plague searchers who fear he has been infected. As a result, he is unable to deliver Friar Lawrence's letter to Romeo.

Connect to the Literature

In what way does the Black Death contribute to the tragedy in *Romeo and Juliet?*

Romeo. Art thou so bare and full of wretchedness
And fearest to die? Famine is in thy cheeks,
Need and oppression starveth in thy eyes,
Contempt and beggary hangs upon thy back:
The world is not thy friend, nor the world's law;
The world affords no law to make thee rich;
Then be not poor, but break it and take this.

Apothecary. My poverty but not my will consents.

Romeo. I pay thy poverty and not thy will.

Apothecary. Put this in any liquid thing you will
And drink it off, and if you had the strength
Of twenty men, it would dispatch you straight.

Romeo. There is thy gold—worse poison to men's souls,
Doing more murder in this loathsome world,
Than these poor compounds[18] that thou mayst not sell.
I sell thee poison; thou hast sold me none.
Farewell. Buy food and get thyself in flesh.
Come, cordial[19] and not poison, go with me
To Juliet's grave; for there must I use thee. [*Exit all.*]

Spiral Review
CONFLICT What conflicting motivations does the Apothecary face?

Tragedy and Motive
What is the apothecary's motive for selling Romeo the poison?

18. compounds mixtures.

19. cordial health-giving drink.

Scene ii. Friar Lawrence's cell.

[*Enter* Friar John, *calling* Friar Lawrence.]

John. Holy Franciscan friar, brother, ho!

[*Enter* Friar Lawrence.]

Lawrence. This same should be the voice of Friar John.
Welcome from Mantua. What says Romeo?
Or, if his mind be writ, give me his letter.

John. Going to find a barefoot brother out,
One of our order, to associate[1] me
Here in this city visiting the sick,
And finding him, the searchers of the town,
Suspecting that we both were in a house
Where the infectious pestilence did reign,
Sealed up the doors, and would not let us forth,
So that my speed to Mantua there was stayed.

Lawrence. Who bare my letter, then, to Romeo?

John. I could not send it—here it is again—
Nor get a messenger to bring it thee,
So fearful were they of infection.

Analyze Cause and Effect
Briefly state the causes and effects of Friar John's failure to deliver Friar Lawrence's letter.

1. associate accompany.

Comprehension
What does Romeo plan to do with the apothecary's help?

Tragedy and Motive What motivates Friar Lawrence's decision to go to the monument?

2. **nice** trivial.
3. **full of charge, / Of dear import** urgent and important.

4. **beshrew** blame.
5. **accidents** happenings.

LAWRENCE. Unhappy fortune! By my brotherhood,
The letter was not nice,[2] but full of charge,
Of dear import;[3] and the neglecting it
May do much danger. Friar John, go hence,
Get me an iron crow and bring it straight
Unto my cell.

JOHN. Brother, I'll go and bring it thee. [*Exit.*]

LAWRENCE. Now must I to the monument alone.
Within this three hours will fair Juliet wake.
She will beshrew[4] me much that Romeo
Hath had no notice of these accidents;[5]
But I will write again to Mantua,
And keep her at my cell till Romeo come—
Poor living corse, closed in a dead man's tomb! [*Exit.*]

Scene iii. A churchyard; in it a monument belonging to the Capulets.

[*Enter* PARIS *and his* PAGE *with flowers and sweet water.*]

1. **aloof** apart.

2. **lay . . . along** lie down flat.

PARIS. Give me thy torch, boy. Hence, and stand aloof.[1]
Yet put it out, for I would not be seen.
Under yond yew trees lay thee all along,[2]
Holding thy ear close to the hollow ground.
So shall no foot upon the churchyard tread
(Being loose, unfirm, with digging up of graves)
But thou shalt hear it. Whistle then to me,
As signal that thou hearest something approach.
Give me those flowers. Do as I bid thee, go.

3. **adventure** chance it.

PAGE. [*Aside*] I am almost afraid to stand alone
Here in the churchyard; yet I will adventure.[3] [*Retires.*]

4. **sweet** perfumed.

5. **obsequies** memorial ceremonies.

6. **cross** interrupt.

PARIS. Sweet flower, with flowers thy bridal bed I strew
(O woe! thy canopy is dust and stones)
Which with sweet[4] water nightly I will dew;
Or, wanting that, with tears distilled by moans.
The obsequies[5] that I for thee will keep
Nightly shall be to strew thy grave and weep. [**BOY** *whistles.*]
The boy gives warning something doth approach.
What cursèd foot wanders this way tonight
To cross[6] my obsequies and true love's rite?
What, with a torch? Muffle me, night, awhile. [*Retires.*]

[*Enter* ROMEO, *and* BALTHASAR *with a torch, a mattock, and a crow of iron.*]

Romeo. Give me that mattock and the wrenching iron.
Hold, take this letter. Early in the morning
See thou deliver it to my lord and father.
Give me the light. Upon thy life I charge thee,
Whate'er thou hearest or seest, stand all aloof
And do not interrupt me in my course.
Why I descend into this bed of death
Is partly to behold my lady's face,
But chiefly to take thence from her dead finger
A precious ring—a ring that I must use
In dear employment.[7] Therefore hence, be gone.
But if thou, jealous,[8] dost return to pry
In what I farther shall intend to do,
By heaven, I will tear thee joint by joint
And strew this hungry churchyard with thy limbs.
The time and my intents are savage-wild,
More fierce and more inexorable[9] far
Than empty[10] tigers or the roaring sea.

Balthasar. I will be gone, sir, and not trouble ye.

Romeo. So shalt thou show me friendship. Take thou that.
Live, and be prosperous; and farewell, good fellow.

Balthasar. [*Aside*] For all this same, I'll hide me hereabout.
His looks I fear, and his intents I doubt. [*Retires.*]

Romeo. Thou detestable maw,[11] thou womb of death,
Gorged with the dearest morsel of the earth,
Thus I enforce thy rotten jaws to open,
And in despite[12] I'll cram thee with more food.

[Romeo *opens the tomb.*]

Paris. This is that banished haughty Montague
That murd'red my love's cousin—with which grief
It is supposed the fair creature died—
And here is come to do some villainous shame
To the dead bodies. I will apprehend[13] him.
Stop thy unhallowèd toil, vile Montague!
Can vengeance be pursued further than death?
Condemnèd villain, I do apprehend thee.
Obey, and go with me; for thou must die.

Romeo. I must indeed; and therefore came I hither.
Good gentle youth, tempt not a desp'rate man.

Tragedy and Motive
What different motives do Paris and Romeo have for visiting Juliet's tomb?

7. **dear employment** important business.
8. **jealous** curious.

9. **inexorable** uncontrollable.
10. **empty** hungry.

11. **maw** stomach.

12. **despite** scorn.

◀ **Vocabulary**
haughty (hôt´ ē)
adj. arrogant

13. **apprehend** seize; arrest.

Comprehension
How does Paris react to seeing Romeo at Juliet's tomb?

Analyze Cause and Effect
Summarize the causes that you think will produce a tragic effect in the confrontation between Romeo and Paris.

Fly hence and leave me. Think upon these gone;
Let them affright thee. I beseech thee, youth,
Put not another sin upon my head
By urging me to fury. O, be gone!
By heaven, I love thee better than myself,
For I come hither armed against myself.
Stay not, be gone. Live, and hereafter say
A madman's mercy bid thee run away.

14. conjurations solemn appeals.
15. felon criminal.

PARIS. I do defy thy conjurations.[14]
And apprehend thee for a felon[15] here.

ROMEO. Wilt thou provoke me? Then have at thee, boy!
[*They fight.*]

PAGE. O Lord, they fight! I will go call the watch.

[*Exit.* PARIS *falls.*]

PARIS. O, I am slain! If thou be merciful,
Open the tomb, lay me with Juliet. [*Dies.*]

16. peruse look over.

ROMEO. In faith, I will. Let me peruse[16] this face.
Mercutio's kinsman, noble County Paris!
What said my man when my betossèd[17] soul
Did not attend[18] him as we rode? I think
He told me Paris should have married Juliet.
Said he not so, or did I dream it so?
Or am I mad, hearing him talk of Juliet,
To think it was so? O, give me thy hand,
One writ with me in sour misfortune's book!
I'll bury thee in a triumphant grave.
A grave? O, no, a lanthorn,[19] slaught'red youth,
For here lies Juliet, and her beauty makes
This vault a feasting presence[20] full of light.
Death, lie thou there, by a dead man interred.

17. betossèd upset.
18. attend give attention to.

19. lanthorn windowed structure on top of a room to admit light; also, a lantern.
20. feasting presence chamber fit for celebration.

[*Lays him in the tomb.*]

How oft when men are at the point of death
Have they been merry! Which their keepers[21] call
A lightning before death. O, how may I
Call this a lightning? O my love, my wife!
Death, that hath sucked the honey of thy breath,
Hath had no power yet upon thy beauty.
Thou art not conquered. Beauty's ensign[22] yet
Is crimson in thy lips and in thy cheeks,
And death's pale flag is not advancèd there.

21. keepers jailers.
22. ensign banner.

Tragedy and Motive
What tragic mistake does Romeo make regarding Juliet's appearance?

Tybalt, liest thou there in thy bloody sheet?
O, what more favor can I do to thee
Than with that hand that cut thy youth in twain
To sunder[23] his that was thine enemy?
Forgive me, cousin! Ah, dear Juliet,
Why art thou yet so fair? Shall I believe
That unsubstantial Death is amorous,[24]
And that the lean abhorrèd monster keeps
Thee here in dark to be his paramour?
For fear of that I still will stay with thee
And never from this pallet[25] of dim night
Depart again. Here, here will I remain
With worms that are thy chambermaids. O, here
Will I set up my everlasting rest
And shake the yoke of inauspicious[26] stars
From this world-wearied flesh. Eyes, look your last!

23. sunder cut off.

24. amorous full of love.

25. pallet bed.

26. inauspicious promising misfortune.

Comprehension
What happens to Paris at Juliet's tomb?

27. **dateless** eternal.
28. **engrossing** all-encompassing.
29. **conduct** guide (poison).
30. **pilot** captain (Romeo himself).

Arms, take your last embrace! And, lips, O you
The doors of breath, seal with a righteous kiss
A dateless[27] bargain to engrossing[28] death!
Come, bitter conduct;[29] come, unsavory guide!
Thou desperate pilot,[30] now at once run on
The dashing rocks thy seasick weary bark!
Here's to my love! [*Drinks.*] O true apothecary!
Thy drugs are quick. Thus with a kiss I die. [*Falls.*]

[*Enter* FRIAR LAWRENCE, *with lanthorn, crow, and spade.*]

31. **speed** help.
32. **stumbled** stumbling was thought to be a bad omen.
33. **grubs** worms.

FRIAR. Saint Francis be my speed![31] How oft tonight
Have my old feet stumbled[32] at graves! Who's there?

BALTHASAR. Here's one, a friend, and one that knows you well.

FRIAR. Bliss be upon you! Tell me, good my friend,
What torch is yond that vainly lends his light
To grubs[33] and eyeless skulls? As I discern,
It burneth in the Capels' monument.

BALTHASAR. It doth so, holy sir; and there's my master,
One that you love.

FRIAR. Who is it?

▼ **Critical Viewing**
What feelings in the scene does this image convey?

Balthasar. Romeo.

Friar. How long hath he been there?

Balthasar. Full half an hour.

Friar. Go with me to the vault.

Balthasar. I dare not, sir.
My master knows not but I am gone hence,
And fearfully did menace me with death
If I did stay to look on his intents.

Friar. Stay then; I'll go alone. Fear comes upon me.
O, much I fear some ill unthrifty[34] thing.

Balthasar. As I did sleep under this yew tree here,
I dreamt my master and another fought,
And that my master slew him.

Friar. Romeo!
Alack, alack, what blood is this which stains
The stony entrance of this sepulcher?
What mean these masterless[35] and gory swords
To lie discolored by this place of peace? [*Enters the tomb.*]
Romeo! O, pale! Who else? What, Paris too?
And steeped in blood? Ah, what an unkind[36] hour
Is guilty of this lamentable chance!
The lady stirs. [Juliet *rises.*]

Juliet. O comfortable[37] friar! Where is my lord?
I do remember well where I should be,
And there I am. Where is my Romeo?

Friar. I hear some noise. Lady, come from that nest
Of death, contagion, and unnatural sleep.
A greater power than we can contradict
Hath thwarted our intents. Come, come away.
Thy husband in thy bosom there lies dead;
And Paris too. Come, I'll dispose of thee
Among a sisterhood of holy nuns.
Stay not to question, for the watch is coming.
Come, go, good Juliet. I dare no longer stay.

Juliet. Go, get thee hence, for I will not away. [*Exit* Friar.]
What's here? A cup, closed in my truelove's hand?
Poison, I see, hath been his timeless[38] end.
O churl![39] Drunk all, and left no friendly drop
To help me after? I will kiss thy lips.

Tragedy and Motive
In what way is Friar Lawrence's late arrival another example of chance contributing to this tragedy?

34. **unthrifty** unlucky.

35. **masterless** discarded (without masters).

36. **unkind** unnatural.

37. **comfortable** comforting.

Tragedy and Motive
Why do you think Friar Lawrence wants to "dispose of Juliet" in a sisterhood of nuns?

38. **timeless** untimely; too soon.

39. **churl** rude fellow.

Comprehension
How does Juliet react when she wakes up?

40. **restorative** medicine.

41. **happy** convenient; opportune.

42. **attach** arrest.

43. **ground** cause.

44. **without circumstance descry** see clearly without details.

Haply some poison yet doth hang on them
To make me die with a restorative.[40] [*Kisses him.*]
Thy lips are warm!

Chief Watchman. [*Within*] Lead, boy. Which way?

Juliet. Yea, noise? Then I'll be brief. O happy[41] dagger!
[*Snatches* Romeo's *dagger.*]
This is thy sheath; there rust, and let me die.
[*She stabs herself and falls.*]

[*Enter* Paris' Boy *and* Watch.]

Boy. This is the place. There, where the torch doth burn.

Chief Watchman. The ground is bloody. Search about the churchyard.
Go, some of you; whoe'er you find attach.[42]
[*Exit some of the* Watch.]
Pitiful sight! Here lies the County slain;
And Juliet bleeding, warm, and newly dead,
Who here hath lain this two days burièd.
Go, tell the Prince; run to the Capulets;
Raise up the Montagues; some others search.
[*Exit others of the* Watch.]
We see the ground whereon these woes do lie,
But the true ground[43] of all these piteous woes
We cannot without circumstance descry.[44]

[*Enter some of the* Watch, *with* Romeo's Man, Balthasar.]

Second Watchman. Here's Romeo's man. We found him in the churchyard.

Chief Watchman. Hold him in safety till the Prince come hither.

[*Enter* Friar Lawrence *and another* Watchman.]

Third Watchman. Here is a friar that trembles, sighs and weeps.
We took this mattock and this spade from him
As he was coming from this churchyard's side.

Chief Watchman. A great suspicion! Stay the friar too.

[*Enter the* Prince *and* Attendants.]

Tragedy and Motive
How might the tragic ending have been averted if Paris, Romeo, and the Friar had come to Juliet's tomb in a different order?

Prince. What misadventure is so early up,
That calls our person from our morning rest?

[*Enter* Capulet *and his* Wife *with others.*]

Capulet. What should it be, that is so shrieked abroad?

Lady Capulet. O, the people in the street cry "Romeo,"
Some "Juliet," and some "Paris"; and all run
With open outcry toward our monument.

Prince. What fear is this which startles in your ears?

Chief Watchman. Sovereign, here lies the County Paris slain;
And Romeo dead; and Juliet, dead before,
Warm and new killed.

Prince. Search, seek, and know how this foul murder comes.

Chief Watchman. Here is a friar, and slaughtered Romeo's man,
With instruments upon them fit to open
These dead men's tombs.

Capulet. O heavens! O wife, look how our daughter bleeds!
This dagger hath mista'en, for, lo, his house[45]
Is empty on the back of Montague,
And it missheathèd in my daughter's bosom!

Lady Capulet. O me, this sight of death is as a bell
That warns my old age to a sepulcher.

[*Enter* Montague *and others.*]

Prince. Come, Montague; for thou art early up
To see thy son and heir more early down.

Montague. Alas, my liege,[46] my wife is dead tonight!
Grief of my son's exile hath stopped her breath.
What further woe conspires against mine age?

Prince. Look, and thou shalt see.

Montague. O thou untaught! What manners is in this,
To press before thy father to a grave?

Prince. Seal up the mouth of outrage[47] for a while,
Till we can clear these ambiguities
And know their spring, their head, their true descent;
And then will I be general of your woes[48]
And lead you even to death. Meantime forbear,
And let mischance be slave to patience.[49]
Bring forth the parties of suspicion.

Analyze Cause and Effect
Summarize the losses that the families have experienced that were caused by Romeo and Juliet's relationship.

45. house sheath.
46. liege (lēj) lord.
47. mouth of outrage violent cries.
48. general . . . woes leader in your sorrow.
49. let . . . patience be patient in the face of misfortune.

◀ Vocabulary
ambiguities (am′ bə gyo͞o′ ə tēz) *n.* statements or events whose meanings are unclear

Comprehension
What effect did Romeo's exile have on his mother?

50. **direful** terrible.

51. **impeach and purge** accuse and declare blameless.

52. **date of breath** term of life.

Tragedy and Motive
What examples of fate or character flaws do you find in the tragic events that the Friar recounts?

53. **as** on.

54. **closely** hidden; secretly.

FRIAR. I am the greatest, able to do least,
Yet most suspected, as the time and place
Doth make against me, of this direful[50] murder;
And here I stand, both to impeach and purge[51]
Myself condemnèd and myself excused.

PRINCE. Then say at once what thou dost know in this.

FRIAR. I will be brief, for my short date of breath[52]
Is not so long as is a tedious tale.
Romeo, there dead, was husband to that Juliet;
And she, there dead, that's Romeo's faithful wife.
I married them; and their stol'n marriage day
Was Tybalt's doomsday, whose untimely death
Banished the new-made bridegroom from this city;
For whom, and not for Tybalt, Juliet pined.
You, to remove that siege of grief from her,
Betrothed and would have married her perforce
To County Paris. Then comes she to me
And with wild looks bid me devise some mean
To rid her from this second marriage,
Or in my cell there would she kill herself.
Then gave I her (so tutored by my art)
A sleeping potion; which so took effect
As I intended, for it wrought on her
The form of death. Meantime I writ to Romeo
That he should hither come as[53] this dire night
To help to take her from her borrowed grave,
Being the time the potion's force should cease,
But he which bore my letter, Friar John,
Was stayed by accident, and yesternight
Returned my letter back. Then all alone
At the prefixèd hour of her waking
Came I to take her from her kindred's vault;
Meaning to keep her closely[54] at my cell
Till I conveniently could send to Romeo.
But when I came, some minute ere the time
Of her awakening, here untimely lay
The noble Paris and true Romeo dead.
She wakes; and I entreated her come forth
And bear this work of heaven with patience;
But then a noise did scare me from the tomb,
And she, too desperate, would not go with me,
But, as it seems, did violence on herself.
All this I know, and to the marriage

Her nurse is privy;[55] and if aught in this
Miscarried by my fault, let my old life
Be sacrificed some hour before his time
Unto the rigor[56] of severest law.

Prince. We still have known thee for a holy man.
Where's Romeo's man? What can he say to this?

Balthasar. I brought my master news of Juliet's death;
And then in post he came from Mantua
To this same place, to this same monument.
This letter he early bid me give his father,
And threat'ned me with death, going in the vault,
If I departed not and left him there.

Prince. Give me the letter. I will look on it.
Where is the County's page that raised the watch?
Sirrah, what made your master[57] in this place?

Boy. He came with flowers to strew his lady's grave;
And bid me stand aloof, and so I did.
Anon comes one with light to ope the tomb;
And by and by my master drew on him;
And then I ran away to call the watch.

Prince. This letter doth make good the friar's words,
Their course of love, the tidings of her death;
And here he writes that he did buy a poison
Of a poor 'pothecary and therewithal
Came to this vault to die and lie with Juliet.
Where be these enemies? Capulet, Montague,
See what a scourge is laid upon your hate,
That heaven finds means to kill your joys with love.
And I, for winking at[58] your discords too,
Have lost a brace[59] of kinsmen. All are punished.

Capulet. O brother Montague, give me thy hand.
This is my daughter's jointure,[60] for no more
Can I demand.

Montague. But I can give thee more;
For I will raise her statue in pure gold,
That whiles Verona by that name is known,
There shall no figure at such rate[61] be set
As that of true and faithful Juliet.

Capulet. As rich shall Romeo's by his lady's lie—
Poor sacrifices of our enmity![62]

55. **privy** secretly informed about.

56. **rigor** strictness.

57. **made your master** was your master doing.

◀ **Vocabulary**
scourge (skurj) *n.* instrument for inflicting punishment

58. **winking at** closing my eyes to.
59. **brace** pair (Mercutio and Paris).
60. **jointure** wedding gift; marriage settlement.
61. **rate** value.
62. **enmity** hostility.

Comprehension
How does the Friar explain his role in the fate of Romeo and Juliet?

63. **glooming** cloudy; gloomy.

Tragedy and Motive
What might be Lord Montague's motive for the promise he makes to Lord Capulet?

PRINCE. A glooming[63] peace this morning with it brings.
The sun for sorrow will not show his head.
Go hence, to have more talk of these sad things;
Some shall be pardoned, and some punishèd;
For never was a story of more woe
Than this of Juliet and her Romeo. [*Exit all.*]

Language Study

Vocabulary The words printed in blue in each numbered item below appear in Act V of *The Tragedy of Romeo and Juliet*. Identify the word in each group that does not belong with the others. Explain your responses.

1. **remnants,** future, past
2. **penury,** poverty, wealthy
3. **haughty,** proud, insecure
4. **scourge,** pleasure, happiness
5. **disperse,** scatter, collect

WORD STUDY

The **Latin prefix *ambi-*** (a variant of *amphi-*) means "both." In Act V of *The Tragedy of Romeo and Juliet*, the Prince says he wants to clear up **ambiguities** and learn the truth. He means that the facts are uncertain and can be understood from two or more points of view.

Word Study

Part A Explain how the **Latin prefix *ambi-*** (or *amphi-*) contributes to the meanings of the words *ambivalent, ambient,* and *amphibian.* Consult a dictionary if necessary.

Part B Use the context of the sentences and what you know about the Latin prefix *ambi-* to explain your answer to each question.

1. Would you be absolutely certain of how to respond if someone asked an *ambiguous* question?
2. If a person is *ambidextrous,* what can he or she do?

Close Reading Activities

Literary Analysis

Key Ideas and Details

1. **(a) Interpret:** In Act V, Scene I, why does Romeo exclaim, "Then I defy you, stars"? **(b) Analyze:** In what way are Romeo's words consistent with what you know of his character? Explain.
2. **Analyze Cause and Effect (a)** Identify at least three events that cause the Friar's scheme to fail. **(b) Analyze:** Why is it not surprising that the scheme fails? Cite text evidence to support your analysis.
3. **Analyze Cause and Effect (a)** What events cause Romeo and Paris to arrive at Juliet's tomb at the same time? **(b)** What is the effect of this circumstance? Explain your answer.
4. **Analyze Cause and Effect (a)** Analyze the chain of causes and effects that leads to the tragic ending. **(b)** Summarize the events that occur at the tomb.

Craft and Structure

5. **Tragedy and Motive (a)** Use a chart like the one shown to identify details of the elements that contribute to the tragedy in the play. Consider aspects of Romeo and Juliet's personalities, details related to fate or chance, and other elements you observe in the text. **(b)** Explain which element you think is most responsible for the story's tragic outcome. Support your answer with the specific details you gathered.

Romeo and Juliet's Personalities
Fate or Chance
Other Causes

6. **Tragedy and Motive (a)** What is the Friar's motive for helping Romeo and Juliet? **(b)** To what extent is he responsible for their tragedy? Cite text evidence to support your answer.
7. **Tragedy and Motive** What theme or message does Shakespeare convey through the tragic events in the play? Explain and support your answer with details from the play.

Integration of Knowledge and Ideas

8. **(a) Analyze:** How does the relationship between the feuding families change at the end of the play? **(b) Draw Conclusions:** Were the deaths of Romeo and Juliet necessary for this change to occur? Explain. **(c) Make a Judgment:** Is the end of long-term hostility between the Capulets and the Montagues a fair exchange for the deaths of Romeo and Juliet? Cite evidence from the play to support your answer.

9. THE BIG ? **Do our differences define us?** Did Romeo and Juliet have any control over the differences that separated them and led to their tragic end? Support your answer with specific details from the play.

ACADEMIC VOCABULARY

As you write and speak about *The Tragedy of Romeo and Juliet,* use the words related to differences that you explored on page 481 of this textbook.

Conventions: Parallelism

Parallelism is the use of similar grammatical forms or patterns to express similar ideas. Effective use of parallelism adds rhythm and balance to your writing and strengthens connections among your ideas.

When writing lacks parallelism, it presents equal ideas in an unnecessary mix of grammatical forms. This produces awkward, distracting shifts for readers. By contrast, parallel constructions place equal ideas in words, phrases, or clauses of similar types.

Nonparallel: Dress codes are less restrictive, less costly, and are not a controversial system.

Parallel: Dress codes are less restrictive, less costly, and less controversial.

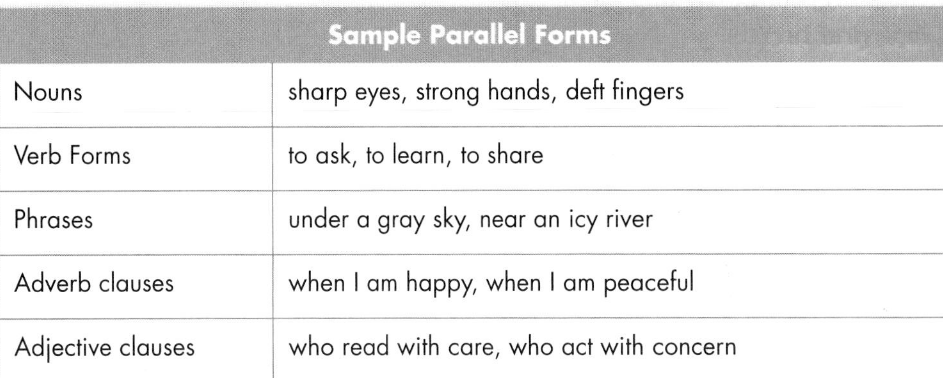

Sample Parallel Forms	
Nouns	sharp eyes, strong hands, deft fingers
Verb Forms	to ask, to learn, to share
Phrases	under a gray sky, near an icy river
Adverb clauses	when I am happy, when I am peaceful
Adjective clauses	who read with care, who act with concern

Practice A

State whether each sentence has a parallel structure. If it does not, rewrite it correctly.

1. Capulet and Montague joined hands, made up, and promised to build statues.
2. Romeo is rash, has a romantic streak, and unfortunate.
3. Romeo asked about Juliet, about his father, and then about Juliet again.
4. Tonight, Romeo will get horses, write a letter, and be riding to Juliet's tomb.

Reading Application Choose one sentence from Act V of *The Tragedy of Romeo and Juliet* that has a parallel structure. Rewrite the sentence and underline the parallel parts.

Practice B

Choose the boldface word or words that will give each sentence a parallel structure.

1. Paris grieved for Juliet and **asked/is asking** to be buried with her.
2. Tragic heroes are often jealous, proud, or **they are impulsive/impulsive.**
3. Romeo thinks the apothecary will help him because he is poor, he is hungry, and **needs money/he needs money.**
4. Romeo was rash and **he would/was bound to** meet with misfortune.

Writing Application Write three sentences about *The Tragedy of Romeo and Juliet* in which you use parallel structure correctly.

Writing to Sources

Argument Imagine that you are the editor of a newspaper in Verona at the time of the play. Write an **editorial** expressing the Prince's response to the deaths of Tybalt and Mercutio.

- Reread the Prince's dialogue in Act III, Scene i.
- Decide whether Romeo's sentence was appropriate. Explain whether you agree or disagree with the Prince's order.
- Write the editorial, supporting your ideas with details from Act III, Scenes i–iii.

Share your editorial with classmates, and encourage them to write letters to the editor to support or oppose your position.

Argument As Friar Lawrence, write a **persuasive letter** to both Lord Capulet and Lord Montague. Urge them to end their feud.

- List factual evidence and emotional pleas that support your argument. Consider appealing to the families' sense of logic and ethical beliefs.
- Begin your draft by explaining the benefits of marriage and the benefits of becoming allies rather than enemies.
- Use persuasive techniques, such as powerful word choice, repetition, and rhetorical questions, to strengthen your argument.

Argument Imagine that your school is putting on a play and the students are responsible for deciding which play to perform. Write a **persuasive speech** to your fellow students urging them to select *The Tragedy of Romeo and Juliet.*

- Begin by drafting three to five reasons why you think the student body should choose *The Tragedy of Romeo and Juliet.*
- Provide convincing support. All evidence should be relevant and sufficient to support your claims.
- Revise to address readers' concerns, create parallelism, and incorporate powerful language.
- Present your finished speech to the class. Use proper eye contact, body language and gestures to maintain your audience's interest.

Grammar Application Make sure to use parallelism for both clarity and stylistic effect in your editorial, persuasive letter, and persuasive speech.

Common Core State Standards

Writing

1. Write arguments to support claims in an analysis of substantive topics or texts, using valid reasoning and relevant and sufficient evidence.

1.a. Introduce precise claim(s), distinguish the claim(s) from alternate or opposing claims, and create an organization that establishes clear relationships among claim(s), counterclaims, reasons, and evidence.

1.b. Develop claim(s) and counterclaims fairly, supplying evidence for each while pointing out the strengths and limitations of both in a manner that anticipates the audience's knowledge level and concerns.

1.c. Use words, phrases, and clauses to link the major sections of the text, create cohesion, and clarify the relationships between claim(s) and reasons, between reasons and evidence, and between claim(s) and counterclaims.

4. Produce clear and coherent writing in which the development, organization, and style are appropriate to task, purpose, and audience.

Speaking and Listening

4. Present information, findings, and supporting evidence clearly, concisely, and logically such that listeners can follow the line of reasoning and the organization, development, substance, and style are appropriate to purpose, audience, and task.

Language

1.a. Use parallel structure.

Speaking and Listening

Comprehension and Collaboration Select a scene from *The Tragedy of Romeo and Juliet* and plan a **staged performance** with classmates. Choose a scene with at least three characters. Then, plan and rehearse the scene. Follow these steps:

- Decide who will play each role.
- As you rehearse, use appropriate gestures, body movements, and eye contact that convey the qualities of your character. Adjust your tone of voice and speed of delivery to dramatize the performance.
- Pause periodically during your rehearsal to assess the group's work. Take turns critiquing the performance. Express your thoughts clearly and convey your criticism in a respectful way. As others present criticism, listen carefully and ask questions to clarify comments. Discuss ways to respond to comments and to improve the performance.

When you are ready, perform the scene for the class, and invite comments and feedback from the audience on whether the staged performance has influenced their view of any aspect of *The Tragedy of Romeo and Juliet*

Comprehension and Collaboration As a class, conduct a **mock trial** to investigate the causes of the tragedy in *The Tragedy of Romeo and Juliet*. Follow these steps:

- Assign roles for the main characters of the play, the lawyers, and the judge. The rest of the class should serve as the jury.
- Take depositions, or statements in which each character tells the story from his or her perspective. After witnesses give their testimony, lawyers should ask follow-up questions to clarify information.
- All participants should use appropriate gestures, eye contact, and a speaking voice that projects the correct tone and mood. Consult the text as necessary.
- Choose language—formal, informal, slang, or jargon—that fits the social, cultural, and professional status of each character. Consult the text as necessary.

Jury members should listen carefully to distinguish between valid claims and biased or distorted arguments. Listeners should also evaluate the clarity, quality, effectiveness, and coherence of each speaker's arguments, evidence, and delivery.

When the trial is completed, the jury members should present their verdict, explaining which characters bear the most blame for the tragedy.

Research and Technology

Presentation of Ideas Conduct research to create an **annotated flowchart** that accurately displays and explains the structure of the nobility in sixteenth-century Verona. Your flowchart should show the relative positions of the Prince, Count Paris, the Montagues, and the Capulets.

- Use both primary and secondary sources as you learn more about the time period in which the story unfolds.
- Evaluate the validity and reliability of the information you research and the sources you use.
- Organize your text and images logically.
- Remember to document sources for both ideas and images, using standard citation style.

Present your flowchart to the class, and explain whether Shakespeare's representation of sixteenth-century Verona is accurate. Include your information sources in your presentation.

Presentation of Ideas With a small group, view a filmed version of *Romeo and Juliet,* and then write a **film review.** It might be a movie version, a filmed stage production, or a filmed version of the ballet. Take notes as you view, using the following questions to guide your note taking:

- What specific effects contribute to the beauty or artistry of the film?
- How do the movements of the actors or dancers communicate the play's ideas?
- How does the film use music, sets, and camerawork to convey mood?
- How do key scenes in the film compare to those in the written version? If scenes are changed or omitted in the filmed version, how does the change affect meaning?

After viewing, use your notes to draft your review. Be sure to highlight the key differences between the filmed version and the written version, and explain which version you thought was more effective. Finally, present your review to the class.

Presentation of Ideas With a partner, create a **multimedia presentation** on Renaissance music. Use library or Internet resources to collect examples of music that would have been played by the musicians in Act IV, Scene v. Find pictures of instruments from the period as well. Record accurate bibliographic information about your sources, using correct citation style.

Present your findings in class using available props, visual aids, and electronic media. Then, lead a discussion about the music and whether it influences readers' perception of *The Tragedy of Romeo and Juliet*.

Common Core State Standards

Reading Literature

7. Analyze the representation of a subject or a key scene in two different artistic mediums, including what is emphasized or absent in each treatment.

Writing

7. Conduct short as well as more sustained research projects to answer a question or solve a problem; narrow or broaden the inquiry when appropriate; synthesize multiple sources on the subject, demonstrating understanding of the subject under investigation.

8. Gather relevant information from multiple authoritative print and digital sources, using advanced searches effectively; assess the usefulness of each source in answering the research question; integrate information into the text selectively to maintain the flow of ideas, avoiding plagiarism and following a standard format for citation.

Speaking and Listening

1. Initiate and participate effectively in a range of collaborative discussions.

3. Evaluate a speaker's point of view, reasoning, and use of evidence and rhetoric, identifying any fallacious reasoning or exaggerated or distorted evidence.

4. Present information, findings, and supporting evidence clearly, concisely, and logically such that listeners can follow the line of reasoning.

Do our differences define us?

Explore the Big Question as you read this tale and excerpt from a play. Take notes on the differences among the characters in each narrative. Then, compare and contrast what those differences say about human nature in general.

READING TO COMPARE ARCHETYPAL THEMES

Ovid's tales are part of the foundations of Western literature. They express universal, or archetypal, ideas. Shakespeare borrowed characters, plots, and themes from Ovid, transforming them for his own era and purposes. As you read these selections, compare them to one another and to similar ideas expressed in *The Tragedy of Romeo and Juliet*.

SHORT STORY

"Pyramus and Thisbe"

Ovid (43 B.C.–A.D. 17)
Educated in Rome, Ovid began his career writing poems about love and became both popular and successful. For an unknown reason, he fell out of favor with the Emperor Augustus who banished the poet from Rome. Even though Ovid spent the rest of his life in a remote fishing village, his influence only grew after his death and continues to this day.

DRAMA

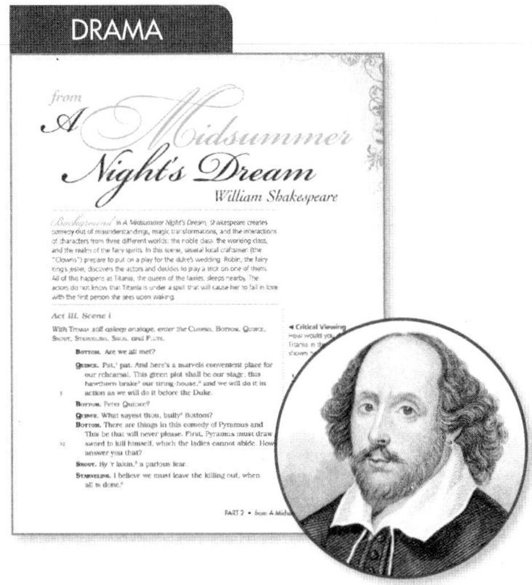

from *A Midsummer Night's Dream*

William Shakespeare (1564–1616)
Perhaps the greatest of all playwrights, William Shakespeare gained his success in the flourishing theatrical world of Elizabethan London. Shakespeare's thirty-seven plays are populated with a wide range of characters who embody the depth and variety of human experience. No other writer has played a more significant role in shaping the English language and its literature.

Comparing Archetypal Themes

An **archetype** is a plot, character, image, or setting that appears in literature, mythology, and folklore from around the world and throughout history. Archetypes represent universal themes and truths about life and are said to mirror the working of the human mind. The following are some common archetypes:

- **Archetypal Characters:** the hero; the outcast; the fool
- **Archetypal Plot Types:** the quest, or search; the task
- **Archetypal Symbols:** water as a symbol of life; fire as a symbol of power
- **Archetypal Story Patterns:** patterns of threes, sevens, and twelves (three wishes, seven brothers, twelve princesses, etc.)

Archetypal stories can be thought of as original models on which other stories are based.

The **theme** of a literary work is the central idea, message, or insight about life that it expresses. **Archetypal themes** develop or explore fundamental or universal ideas. Ill-fated love is one archetypal idea that appears in literature from all over the world. A complex character's fall from grace is another archetypal concept. Works of literature can differ for a variety of reasons in their presentations of the same archetypal theme. The values of the work's era, the author's purpose, and the author's culture and language may affect how a writer presents a universal theme.

As you read Ovid's "Pyramus and Thisbe," a classic tale from ancient Rome, make comparisons to Shakespeare's treatment of a similar tale in two of his works: *The Tragedy of Romeo and Juliet* and the comedy *A Midsummer Night's Dream*. Consider how Shakespeare draws on the original source to develop his story and theme in both the full-length tragedy and the subplot of the comedy. Use a chart like the one shown to organize your observations.

	Similarities	Differences
Characters		
Events		

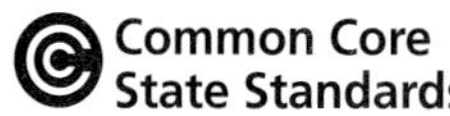

Reading Literature

2. Determine a theme or central idea of a text and analyze in detail its development over the course of the text, including how it emerges and is shaped and refined by specific details; provide an objective summary of the text.

3. Analyze how complex characters develop over the course of a text, interact with other characters, and advance the plot or develop the theme.

9. Analyze how an author draws on and transforms source material in a specific work (e.g., how Shakespeare treats a theme or topic from Ovid or the Bible or how a later author draws on a play by Shakespeare).

Writing

2. Write informative/explanatory texts to examine and convey complex ideas, concepts, and information clearly and accurately through the effective selection, organization, and analysis of content.

9.a. Apply grades 9–10 Reading standards to literature.

10. Write routinely over extended time frames and shorter time frames for a range of tasks, purposes, and audiences.

Pyramus and Thisbe

Ovid

retold by **Edith Hamilton**

Background The tale of Pyramus and Thisbe appears in Book IV of *Metamorphoses,* Ovid's greatest achievement. A poem of nearly 12,000 lines, it tells a series of stories beginning with the creation of the world and ending with the death of Julius Caesar. In each story, someone or something undergoes a change. Divided into fifteen books, the stories are linked by clever transitions, so that the entire work reads as one long, uninterrupted tale.

Once upon a time the deep red berries of the mulberry tree[1] were white as snow. The change in color came about strangely and sadly. The death of two young lovers was the cause.

Pyramus and Thisbe, he the most beautiful youth and she the loveliest maiden of all the East, lived in Babylon, the city of Queen Semiramis, in houses so close together that one wall was common to both. Growing up thus side by side they learned to love each other. They longed to marry, but their parents forbade. Love, however, cannot be forbidden. The more that flame is covered up, the hotter it burns. Also love can always find a way. It was impossible that these two whose hearts were on fire should be kept apart.

In the wall both houses shared there was a little chink.[2] No one before had noticed it, but there is nothing a lover does not notice. Our two young people discovered it and through it they were able to whisper sweetly back and forth. Thisbe on one side, Pyramus on the other. The hateful wall that separated them had become their means of reaching each other. "But for you we could touch, kiss," they would say. "But at least you let us speak together. You give a passage for loving words to reach loving ears. We are not ungrateful." So they would talk, and as night came on and they must part, each would press on the wall kisses that could not go through to the lips on the other side.

Every morning when the dawn had put out the stars, and the sun's rays had dried the hoarfrost on the grass, they would steal to the crack and, standing there, now utter words of burning love and now lament their hard fate, but always in softest whispers. Finally a day came when they could endure no longer. They decided that that very night they would try to slip away and steal out through the city into the open country where at last they could be together in freedom. They agreed to meet at a well-known place, the Tomb of Ninus, under a tree there, a tall mulberry full of snow-white berries, near which a cool spring bubbled up. The plan pleased them and it seemed to them the day would never end.

◄ Critical Viewing What do you think Thisbe is feeling as she listens through the crack in the wall?

Archetypal Theme What is the main obstacle the lovers face?

◄ Vocabulary
lament (lə ment′) *v.* express deep sorrow; mourn

Comprehension How do Pyramus and Thisbe communicate with each other?

1. **mulberry** (mul′ ber′ rē) **tree** *n.* tree with an edible, purplish-red fruit.
2. **chink** (chiŋk) *n.* narrow opening; crack.

Archetypal Theme What does Thisbe's "bold" behavior suggest about the power of love?

Vocabulary ▶
inevitable (in ev′ i tə bəl) *adj.* certain to happen; incapable of being avoided

At last the sun sank into the sea and night arose. In the darkness Thisbe crept out and made her way in all secrecy to the tomb. Pyramus had not come; still she waited for him, her love making her bold. But of a sudden she saw by the light of the moon a lioness. The fierce beast had made a kill; her jaws were bloody and she was coming to slake her thirst in the spring. She was still far enough away for Thisbe to escape, but as she fled she dropped her cloak. The lioness came upon it on her way back to her lair and she mouthed it and tore it before disappearing into the woods. That is what Pyramus saw when he appeared a few minutes later. Before him lay the bloodstained shreds of the cloak and clear in the dust were the tracks of the lioness. The conclusion was **inevitable**. He never doubted that he knew all. Thisbe was dead. He had let his love, a tender maiden, come alone to a place full of danger, and not been there first to protect her. "It is I who killed you," he said. He lifted up from the trampled dust what was left of the cloak and kissing it again and again carried it to the mulberry tree. "Now," he said, "you shall drink my blood too." He drew his sword and plunged it into his side. The blood spurted up over the berries and dyed them a dark red.

Thisbe, although terrified of the lioness, was still more afraid to fail her lover. She ventured to go back to the tree of the tryst, the mulberry with the shining white fruit. She could not find it. A tree was there, but not one gleam of white was on the branches. As she stared at it, something moved on the ground beneath. She started back shuddering. But in a moment, peering through the shadows, she

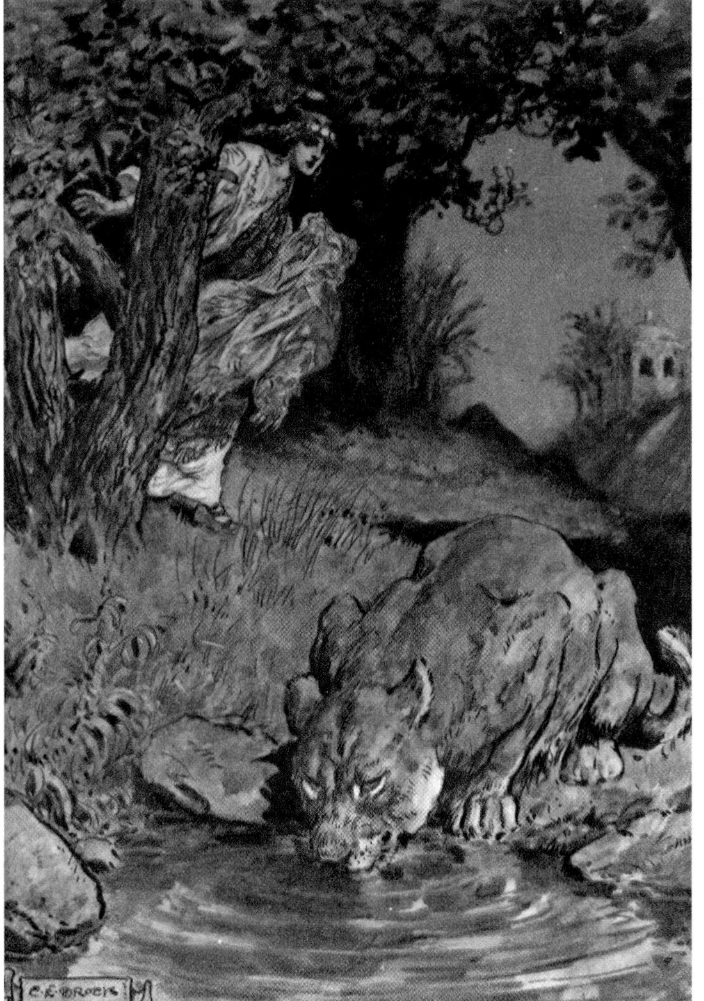

◀ Critical Viewing
Explain the similarities and differences between this lioness and the one Thisbe sees.

saw what was there. It was Pyramus, bathed in blood and dying. She flew to him and threw her arms around him. She kissed his cold lips and begged him to look at her, to speak to her. "It is I, your Thisbe, your dearest," she cried to him. At the sound of her name he opened his heavy eyes for one look. Then death closed them.

She saw his sword fallen from his hand and beside it her cloak stained and torn. She understood all. "Your own hand killed you," she said, "and your love for me. I too can be brave. I too can love. Only death would have had the power to separate us. It shall not have that power now." She plunged into her heart the sword that was still wet with his life's blood.

The gods were pitiful at the end, and the lovers' parents too. The deep red fruit of the mulberry is the everlasting memorial of these true lovers, and one urn holds the ashes of the two whom not even death could part.

Archetypal Theme
In deciding to return to the tree, is Thisbe guided more by love or by reason? Explain.

Critical Thinking

1. **Key Ideas and Details: (a)** How do their parents feel about the romance between Pyramus and Thisbe? **(b) Analyze Cause and Effect:** What actions do Pyramus and Thisbe take as a result of their parents' feelings? **(c) Make a Judgment:** Do you think Pyramus and Thisbe or their parents are more responsible for the story's tragic outcome?
2. **Key Ideas and Details: (a)** What does the chink in the wall enable the couple to do? **(b) Speculate:** How might the story be different if the chink did not exist?
3. **Integration of Knowledge and Ideas: (a)** What does the mulberry tree symbolize in this story? Explain. **(b) Analyze:** In what way does this symbol reinforce the story's theme? Explain, citing details from the story in your response.
4. **Integration of Knowledge and Ideas:** Do you think this story will continue to appeal to readers in the future? Why or why not?
5. **Integration of Knowledge and Ideas: (a)** How do Pyramus and Thisbe's wishes differ from those of their families? **(b)** In what way do those differences lead to tragedy? *[Connect to the Big Question: Do our differences define us?]*

from

A Midsummer Night's Dream

William Shakespeare

Background In *A Midsummer Night's Dream,* Shakespeare creates comedy out of misunderstandings, magic transformations, and the interactions of characters from three different worlds: the noble class, the working class, and the realm of the fairy spirits. In this scene, several local craftsmen (the "Clowns") prepare to put on a play for the duke's wedding. Robin, the fairy king's jester, discovers the actors and decides to play a trick on one of them. All of this happens as Titania, the queen of the fairies, sleeps nearby. The actors do not know that Titania is under a spell that will cause her to fall in love with the first person she sees upon waking.

Act III, Scene i

With Titania *still asleep onstage, enter the* Clowns, Bottom, Quince, Snout, Starveling, Snug, *and* Flute.

Bottom. Are we all met?

Quince. Pat,[1] pat. And here's a marvelous convenient place for our rehearsal. This green plot shall be our stage, this hawthorn brake[2] our tiring-house,[3] and we will do it in action as we will do it before the Duke.

Bottom. Peter Quince?

Quince. What sayest thou, bully[4] Bottom?

Bottom. There are things in this comedy of Pyramus and Thisbe that will never please. First, Pyramus must draw a sword to kill himself, which the ladies cannot abide. How answer you that?

Snout. By 'r lakin,[5] a parlous fear.

Starveling. I believe we must leave the killing out, when all is done.[6]

◀ **Critical Viewing**
How would you describe Titania in the image shown here?

1. **pat** exactly; right on time.
2. **brake** thicket.
3. **tiring house** room used for dressing, or attiring.
4. **bully** jolly fellow.
5. **By 'r lakin** shortened version of "By your ladykin (little lady)."
6. **when all is done** after all.

Comprehension
Who is asleep onstage when the Clowns enter?

Bottom. Not a whit! I have a device to make all well. Write me a prologue, and let the prologue seem to say we will do no harm with our swords, and that Pyramus is not killed indeed. And, for the more better assurance, tell them that I, Pyramus, am not Pyramus, but Bottom the weaver. This will put them out of fear.

Quince. Well, we will have such a prologue, and it shall be written in eight and six.[7]

7. **eight and six** ballad meter containing alternating eight- and six-syllable lines.

Bottom. No, make it two more. Let it be written in eight and eight.

Snout. Will not the ladies be afeard of the lion?

Starveling. I fear it, I promise you.

Archetypal Theme
How do the Clowns plan to soften their presentation of the lion?

Bottom. Masters, you ought to consider with yourselves, to bring in God shield us! a lion among ladies is a most dreadful thing. For there is not a more fearful wildfowl than your lion living, and we ought to look to it.

Snout. Therefore another prologue must tell he is not a lion.

Bottom. Nay, you must name his name, and half his face must be seen through the lion's neck, and he himself must speak through, saying thus, or to the same defect: "Ladies," or "Fair ladies, I would wish you," or "I would request you," or "I would entreat you not to fear, not to tremble! My life for yours. If you think I come hither as a lion, it were pity of my life.[8] No, I am no such thing. I am a man as other men are." And there indeed let him name his name and tell them plainly he is Snug the joiner.

8. **it were . . . my life** risky for me.

LITERATURE IN CONTEXT

Science Connection

Almanacs

When Bottom calls for an almanac, he is referring to a type of book that was very popular in Elizabethan times. The almanac was essentially a calendar, but it also provided lists of upcoming natural events, such as tides, full moons, and eclipses. The book was especially useful to farmers because it included gardening tips and weather predictions. Almanacs of various kinds are still published and consulted today.

Connect to the Literature

Do you think the "Clowns" are wise to rely on the accuracy of the almanac with regard to moonlight? Why or why not?

Quince. Well, it shall be so. But there is two hard things: that is, to bring the moonlight into a chamber, for you know Pyramus and Thisbe meet by moonlight.

Snout. Doth the moon shine that night we play our play?

Bottom. A calendar, a calendar! Look in the almanac. Find out moonshine, find out moonshine.

Quince *takes out a book.*

Quince. Yes, it doth shine that night.

Bottom. Why, then, may you leave a casement of the great chamber window, where we play, open, and the moon may shine in at the casement.

Quince. Ay, or else one must come in with a bush of thorns[9] and a lantern and say he comes to disfigure[10] or to present the person of Moonshine. Then there is another thing: we must have a wall in the great chamber, for Pyramus and Thisbe, says the story, did talk through the chink of a wall.

Snout. You can never bring in a wall. What say you, Bottom?

Bottom. Some man or other must present Wall. And let him have some plaster, or some loam, or some roughcast[11] about him to signify wall, or let him hold his fingers thus, and through that cranny shall Pyramus and Thisbe whisper.

Quince. If that may be, then all is well. Come, sit down, every mother's son, and rehearse your parts. Pyramus, you begin. When you have spoken your speech, enter into that brake, and so every one according to his cue.

Enter Robin *invisible to those onstage.*

Robin. *(aside)*
What hempen homespuns[12] have we swaggring
here
So near the cradle[13] of the Fairy Queen?
What, a play toward?[14] I'll be an auditor—
An actor too perhaps, if I see cause.

Quince. Speak, Pyramus.—Thisbe, stand forth.

Bottom. *(as Pyramus)*
Thisbe, the flowers of odious savors sweet—

Quince. Odors, odors!

Bottom. *(as Pyramus)*
. . . odors savors sweet.
So hath thy breath, my dearest Thisbe dear—

9. **a bush of thorns** according to legend, the man in the moon collected firewood on Sundays and was thus banished to the sky.

10. **disfigure** Quince means figure, as in "symbolize" or "stand for."

11. **plaster . . . roughcast** three different blended materials, each used for plastering walls.

12. **hempen homespuns** characters wearing clothing homemade from hemp, probably from the country.

13. **cradle** bower where Titania sleeps.

14. **toward** being rehearsed.

Comprehension
How do the Clowns plan to present the wall that separates Pyramus and Thisbe?

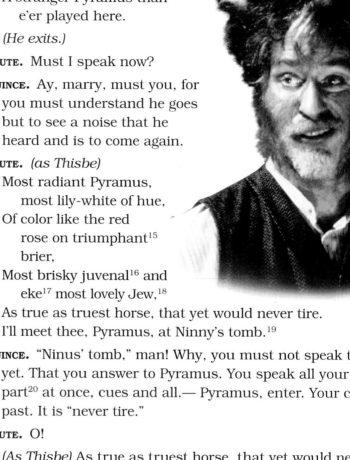

But hark, a voice! Stay thou
but here awhile.
And by and by I will to thee
appear. *(He exits.)*

Robin. *(aside)*
A stranger Pyramus than
e'er played here.

(He exits.)

▶ **Critical Viewing**
How would Bottom feel if he knew how he looked to others?

Flute. Must I speak now?

Quince. Ay, marry, must you, for you must understand he goes but to see a noise that he heard and is to come again.

Flute. *(as Thisbe)*
Most radiant Pyramus,
most lily-white of hue,
Of color like the red
rose on triumphant[15]
brier,
Most brisky juvenal[16] and
eke[17] most lovely Jew,[18]
As true as truest horse, that yet would never tire.
I'll meet thee, Pyramus, at Ninny's tomb.[19]

Quince. "Ninus' tomb," man! Why, you must not speak that yet. That you answer to Pyramus. You speak all your part[20] at once, cues and all.— Pyramus, enter. Your cue is past. It is "never tire."

Flute. O!

(As Thisbe) As true as truest horse, that yet would never
tire.

Enter Robin, *and* Bottom *as Pyramus with the ass-head.*[21]

Bottom. *(as Pyramus)*
If I were fair, fair Thisbe, I were[22] only thine.

Quince. O monstrous! O strange! We are haunted. Pray, masters, fly, masters! Help!

Quince, Snout, Snug, *and* Starveling *exit.*

Robin. I'll follow you. I'll lead you about a round,[23]
Through bog, through bush, through brake, through
brier.
Sometime a horse I'll be, sometime a hound,
A hog, a headless bear, sometime a fire.[24]

15. **triumphant** splendid; magnificent.
16. **juvenal** juvenile; a young person.
17. **eke** also.
18. **Jew** shortening of "jewel" to complete the rhyme.
19. **Ninny's tomb** refers to Ninus, legendary founder of biblical city of Nineveh.
20. **part** script containing stage cues, which Flute is accused of missing or misreading.
21. **with the ass-head** wearing an ass-head.
22. **were** would be.
23. **about a round** in a roundabout, like a circle dance.
24. **fire** will-o'-the-wisp.

And neigh, and bark, and grunt, and roar, and burn,
Like horse, hound, hog, bear, fire, at every turn.
(He exits.)

Bottom. Why do they run away? This is a knavery of them to make me afeard.

Enter Snout.

Snout. O Bottom, thou art changed! What do I see on thee?

Bottom. What do you see? You see an ass-head of your own, do you? *(*Snout *exits.)*

Enter Quince.

Quince. Bless thee, Bottom, bless thee! Thou art translated![25] *(He exits.)*

Bottom. I see their knavery. This is to make an ass of me, to fright me, if they could. But I will not stir from this place, do what they can. I will walk up and down here, and I will sing, that they shall hear I am not afraid.
(He sings.) The ouzel cock,[26] *so black of hue,*
With orange-tawny bill,
The throstle[27] *with his note so true,*
The wren with little quill—[28]

Titania. *(waking up)*
What angel wakes me from my flow'ry bed?

Bottom. *(sings)*
The finch, the sparrow, and the lark,
The plainsong cuckoo[29] *gray,*
Whose note full many a man doth mark
And dares not answer "nay"—[30]
for, indeed, who would set his wit to so foolish a bird? Who would give a bird the lie[31] though he cry "cuckoo" never so?[32]

Titania.
I pray thee, gentle mortal, sing again.
Mine ear is much enamored of thy note,
So is mine eye enthralled to thy shape,
And thy fair virtue's force perforce doth move me[33]
On the first view to say, to swear, I love thee.

Bottom. Methinks, mistress, you should have little reason for that. And yet, to say the truth, reason and love keep little company together nowadays. The more the pity that some

Archetypal Theme
How does Bottom's transformation make fun of the character of Pyramus?

25. **translated** changed; transformed.
26. **ouzel cock** male blackbird.
27. **throstle** thrush; a bird.
28. **quill** literally, a small reed pipe, but here meaning a tiny piping song.
29. **plainsong cuckoo** bird whose song is likened to church music called plainsong.
30. **Whose . . . "nay"** whose song married men listen to as a sign that their wlves may be unfaithful, and who cannot deny that this may be so.
31. **Who would . . .the lie** who would use his intelligence to answer a foolish bird, yet who would dare to contradict the cuckoo's taunt?
32. **never so** over and over; ever so much.
33. **thy . . . move me** your beauty is so powerful it moves me whether I want it to or not.

◀ **Vocabulary**
enamored (en am′ ərd) *v.* filled with love and desire; charmed

enthralled (en thrôld′) *v.* held as in a spell; captivated

Comprehension
What physical change happens to Bottom?

▲ Critical Viewing How do Titania and Bottom seem to feel about each other in this image?

honest neighbors will not make them friends. Nay, I can gleek[34] upon occasion.

TITANIA.
Thou art as wise as thou art beautiful.

BOTTOM. Not so neither; but if I had wit enough to get out of this wood, I have enough to serve mine own turn.

TITANIA.
Out of this wood do not desire to go.
Thou shalt remain here whether thou wilt or no.
I am a spirit of no common rate.[35]
The summer still doth tend[36] upon my state,
And I do love thee. Therefore go with me.
I'll give thee fairies to attend on thee,
And they shall fetch thee jewels from the deep
And sing while thou on pressed flowers dost sleep.

34. gleek jest; joke.
35. rate value; rank.
36. still doth tend still serves.

And I will purge thy mortal grossness[37] so
That thou shalt like an airy spirit go.—
Peaseblossom, Cobweb, Mote,[38] and Mustardseed!

Enter four Fairies: PEASEBLOSSOM, COBWEB, MOTE, *and* MUSTARDSEED.

PEASEBLOSSOM. Ready.

COBWEB. And I.

MOTE. And I.

MUSTARDSEED. And I.

ALL. Where shall we go?

TITANIA.
Be kind and courteous to this gentleman.
Hop in his walks and gambol in his eyes;
Feed him with apricocks and dewberries,[39]
With purple grapes, green figs, and mulberries;
The honey-bags steal from the humble-bees,
And for night-tapers crop their waxen thighs
And light them at the fiery glowworms' eyes
To have my love to bed and to arise;
And pluck the wings from painted butterflies
To fan the moonbeams from his sleeping eyes.
Nod to him, elves, and do him courtesies.

PEASEBLOSSOM. Hail, mortal!

COBWEB. Hail!

MOTE. Hail!

MUSTARDSEED. Hail!

BOTTOM. I cry your Worships mercy,[40] heartily.—I beseech your Worship's name.

COBWEB. Cobweb.

BOTTOM. I shall desire you of more acquaintance, good Master Cobweb. If I cut my finger, I shall make bold with you.[41]—Your name, honest gentleman?

PEASEBLOSSOM. Peaseblossom.

BOTTOM. I pray you, commend me to Mistress Squash,[42] your mother, and to Master Peascod,[43] your father. Good Master Peaseblossom, I shall desire you of more acquaintance, too.—Your name, I beseech you, sir?

MUSTARDSEED. Mustardseed.

37. **mortal grossness** the physical, mortal state of human beings.
38. **Mote** a speck, but also moth, as this word was pronounced similarly.
39. **apricocks and dewberries** apricots and blackberries.

Archetypal Theme
How do Titania's commands emphasize the absurdity of her feelings toward Bottom?

40. **cry. . . mercy** beg your pardon.
41. **Master . . . you** cobwebs were used to stop bleeding.
42. **squash** an unripe pea pod.
43. **peascod** a ripe pea pod.

Comprehension
How does Titania want the fairies to treat Bottom?

44. **your patience** your story; your experience.

45. **enforcèd chastity** violation; requirement.

BOTTOM. Good Master Mustardseed, I know your patience[44] well. That same cowardly, giantlike ox-beef hath devoured many a gentleman of your house. I promise you, your kindred hath made my eyes water ere now. I desire you of more acquaintance, good Master Mustardseed.

TITANIA. Come, wait upon him. Lead him to my bower.
The moon, methinks, looks with a watery eye,
And when she weeps, weeps every little flower,
Lamenting some enforcèd chastity.[45]
Tie up my lover's tongue. Bring him silently.

They exit.

Critical Thinking

1. **Key Ideas and Details: (a)** What are the Clowns trying to accomplish in this scene? **(b) Analyze Cause and Effect:** What events prevent their success? Explain.
2. **Key Ideas and Details: (a)** How is Bottom transformed? **(b) Infer:** Is Bottom aware of his transformation? Explain. **(c) Analyze:** Does the transformation alter Bottom's personality as well as his appearance? Why or why not?
3. **Key Ideas and Details: (a)** Who is Titania? **(b) Analyze:** In what ways does the match between Titania and Bottom mock typical portrayals of romantic love? Explain.
4. **Integration of Knowledge and Ideas:** Does Bottom's transformation actually reveal a truth about his character? Explain.
5. **Key Ideas and Details:** What alterations to script and costumes do the Clowns plan in order to minimize the frightening aspects of their play? **(b) Speculate:** Do you think the Clowns' eventual audience will enjoy their production of "Pyramus and Thisbe"? Explain.
6. **Integration of Knowledge and Ideas: (a)** What are the major differences between Titania and Bottom? **(b)** What similarities help them overcome their differences? **(c)** Do you think their differences or their similarities will matter more in the end? Explain. *[Connect to the Big Question: Do our differences define us?]*

Writing to Sources

Comparing Archetypal Themes

1. **Key Ideas and Details** Use a chart like the one shown to identify the characters, obstacles, and main events depicted in the scene Bottom and his friends rehearse in *A Midsummer Night's Dream,* the full version of *The Tragedy of Romeo and Juliet,* and Ovid's "Pyramus and Thisbe."

Selection	Characters	Obstacles	Main Events
A Midsummer Night's Dream			
The Tragedy of Romeo and Juliet			
Pyramus and Thisbe			

2. **Craft and Structure (a)** Using your chart, explain how Shakespeare draws on and transforms Ovid's story in both *A Midsummer Night's Dream* and *Romeo and Juliet.* **(b)** What are the differences in the ways the three selections present the idea of ill-fated love?
3. **Integration of Knowledge and Ideas (a)** Why is Titania and Bottom's love ill-fated? **(b)** How do these reasons compare to the obstacles faced by Romeo and Juliet or Pyramus and Thisbe?

Timed Writing

Explanatory Text: Essay

In an essay, compare the way Shakespeare uses the characters and events from "Pyramus and Thisbe" in *The Tragedy of Romeo and Juliet* with the way he uses them in *A Midsummer Night's Dream.* Discuss why Shakespeare might explore the same story in both a tragedy and a comedy. **(40 minutes)**

5-Minute Planner

1. Read the prompt carefully and completely.
2. Gather your ideas by jotting down answers to these questions:
   - How do the different settings and characters in each of Shakespeare's plays affect the two presentations of the archetypal theme?
   - How do you think Shakespeare wanted audiences to feel about the ill-fated love in each play?
3. Reread the prompt, and then draft your essay.

USE ACADEMIC VOCABULARY

As you write, use academic language, including the following words or their related forms:

articulate
character
illuminate
standard

For more information about academic vocabulary, see page xlvi.

Language Study

Connotation and Denotation

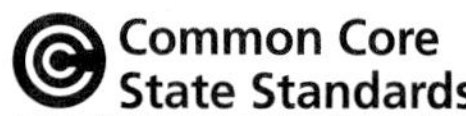

Language
3. Apply knowledge of language to understand how language functions in different contexts, to make effective choices for meaning and style, and to comprehend more fully when reading or listening.
5.b. Analyze nuances in the meaning of words with similar denotations.

The **denotation** of a word is its direct, dictionary meaning. Its **connotations** include the ideas, images, and feelings that are associated with the word.

Consider the words *fragrance, smell,* and *stench*. These words are synonyms, which means they share a similar denotation—having a scent or odor. However, their connotations are very different.

The connotation of *smell* is nearly the same as its denotation. It has a neutral connotation and can be defined as "the quality that you recognize by using your nose." The connotation of *fragrance* is positive, suggesting a pleasant, sweet smell or scent. *Stench* has negative connotations, suggesting a foul, unpleasant odor.

Connotative meaning becomes more intricate for words that relate to abstract concepts, ideas, and emotions. For example, the denotations of the words *love, affection,* and *admiration* are similar. However, their connotations are extremely different. The following graphic shows the positive, neutral, and negative connotations of some synonyms.

Positive →	Neutral →	Negative
fragrance	smell	stench
modest	shy	mousy
inquisitive	curious	nosy
home	house	shack

Practice A

Choose the word that has the more neutral connotation.

1. On Friday, the Bridgeport Wolves (defeated, crushed) the North Point Beacons.
2. Helen was embarrassed by her (sloppy, untidy) appearance.
3. Julian remained (silent, sullen) as I told him the news.
4. Because of the weekend-long festival, the street was (filthy, dirty).
5. The (tyrant, leader) signed the new legislation into law.
6. She seemed (surprised, staggered) by the question.

Practice B

Rewrite each sentence, replacing the italicized word with a word that has a more positive connotation. Use a dictionary or thesaurus if necessary.

1. Adrian is too *cheap* to spend money on a ticket to the play.
2. I've been around Elena long enough to appreciate her *cunning*.
3. Jevon's *arrogance* makes him a natural leader.
4. When I told him the joke, Marcus *cackled* uncontrollably.
5. Michelle was *lazy* and spent the day reading.
6. The boy and his *cronies* are playing ball.
7. I would never forgive him for his *treachery*.
8. Ana was *stubborn* and kept practicing to make the team.
9. Janine was *disgusted* when her friend moved out of town.
10. The *old* man walked slowly across the street.

Activity In this activity, you will explore the connotative meanings of the following words: *argue, fashionable, rumpled,* and *chuckle*. For each word, prepare a note card with the headings shown in the sample card below. Then, on each card, write a sentence in which you use the word correctly. Using a dictionary and thesaurus, find four synonyms for each word and write them down. Circle the synonym with the connotation that best matches the meaning of the word as you used it in your sentence. Exchange cards with a partner and compare your work. Discuss differences you found in the connotations of the four words and their synonyms.

Word:
Sentence:
Synonyms:

Comprehension and Collaboration

For each of the following pairs of words, write sentences that show how their connotations of differ:

visionary/dreamer

investigate/snoop

clumsy/awkward

Use a dictionary and thesaurus if necessary. After you have written your sentences, meet with a small group and compare your work, discussing the connotations of the words.

Multimedia Presentation of a Research Report

Modern classrooms offer students several ways to add sound and images to an oral research report. Students may choose from an array of equipment to make multimedia presentations. The following strategies will help you develop and deliver a multimedia presentation of a research report.

Learn the Skills

Organizing Content Your choice of media depends on the equipment and software available to you, your topic, and your target audience. Use the following tips:

- Use a two-column format for your outline. Arrange the content of your report in the left column; plan media elements in the right column. Use this same pattern in your final script: Run your speaking text in the left column and your media cues in the right.
- Use media strategically. Incorporate audio, video, and graphic elements where they will be the most effective. Media should enhance your audience's understanding of material in a presentation.
- Choose media appropriate to your content. Dry recitation of statistics can be replaced with colorful graphs and charts to enhance the appeal and accuracy of your presentation. If your report is historical, incorporate music from the time period. Photographs or video images may clarify complex procedures.
- Use reliable sources to locate audio or video files. Then, evaluate any audio or visual files you choose to make sure they are credible and accurate.
- Distribute audio, video, and still images evenly throughout your report to make it easier for you to manage the equipment and to maintain audience interest.

Preparing the Presentation An effective multimedia presentation is the result of planning and practice. Use these tips to prepare to deliver your presentation to the class:

- If possible, rehearse your presentation in the room where it will take place. Check sight lines to make sure that your graphic materials will be visible to the entire audience. Do a sound check as well.
- Make sure that words on your slides are legible. Do not put too much content on any one slide.
- Practice shifting from spoken content to media elements. Plan what you will do and say if any piece of equipment fails.

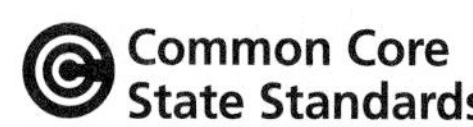

Speaking and Listening

1.d. Respond thoughtfully to diverse perspectives, summarize points of agreement and disagreement, and, when warranted, qualify or justify their own views and understanding and make new connections in light of the evidence and reasoning presented.

2. Integrate multiple sources of information presented in diverse media or formats evaluating the credibility and accuracy of each source.

5. Make strategic use of digital media in presentations to enhance understanding of findings, reasoning, and evidence and to add interest.

Writing

6. Use technology, including the Internet, to produce, publish, and update individual or shared writing products, taking advantage of technology's capacity to link to other information and to display information flexibly and dynamically.

Practice the Skills

Presentation of Knowledge and Ideas Use what you have learned in this workshop to perform the following task.

ACTIVITY: **Give a Multimedia Presentation**

Use a research report from your portfolio as the basis for a multimedia presentation. Plan and practice your presentation using the guidelines from page 656. Remember the following important points:

- Write a script based on your research report that includes media elements.
- Choose media from credible sources and make sure it relates directly to your content.
- Use media evenly throughout your report.
- Use media to enhance your key points.

As your classmates deliver their presentations, use the Presentation Checklist below to assess their work. Your classmates will also use the checklist to analyze your presentation. After you have delivered your presentations, share the feedback you gathered in the checklists.

Presentation Checklist

Presentation Content

Does the presentation meet the requirements of the activity? Check all that apply.

- ❑ The media related to the content.
- ❑ Media was used evenly throughout the report.
- ❑ Media helped listeners to understand key points.

Presentation Delivery

Did the speaker use the media successfully?

- ❑ Equipment functioned properly.
- ❑ Media was visible and audible.
- ❑ Transitions between media uses were smooth.

Comprehension and Collaboration With a small group, discuss the presentations you have viewed. Consider the ways in which media added to your understanding of information in each presentation. Ask what group members learned from multimedia presentations that they might not have learned from reading the research reports. In addition, discuss which of the student presentations used media most effectively, and why. If students express differing opinions, work to summarize points of agreement and disagreement.

Write an Explanatory Text

Comparison-and-Contrast Essay

Defining the Form A **comparison-and-contrast essay** is a written exploration of the similarities and differences between or among two or more things. You may use elements of this type of writing in essays on historical figures and events, consumer reports, or essays on works of art, literature, or music.

Assignment Write a comparison-and-contrast essay about two events, ideas, or historical leaders. Include these elements:

- ✓ an *analysis* and *discussion* of the similarities and differences between two things, people, places, or ideas
- ✓ *accurate, well-chosen factual details* about each subject
- ✓ a *purpose* for comparing and contrasting
- ✓ a *balanced presentation* of each subject using either *subject-by-subject* or *point-by-point organization*
- ✓ clear *transitions* that clarify comparison and contrasts
- ✓ a *conclusion* that summarizes the comparisons and contrasts presented throughout the essay
- ✓ error-free grammar, including *varied sentence structure and length*

To preview the criteria on which your comparison-and-contrast essay may be judged, see the rubric on page 665.

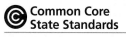

Writing

2. Write informative/explanatory texts to examine and convey complex ideas, concepts, and information clearly and accurately through the effective selection, organization, and analysis of content.

2.a. Introduce a topic, organize complex ideas, concepts, and information to make important connections and distinctions.

5. Develop and strengthen writing as needed by planning, revising, editing, rewriting, or trying a new approach, focusing on addressing what is most significant for a specific purpose and audience.

FOCUS ON RESEARCH

When you write a comparison-and-contrast essay, you might perform research to

- learn about the history of the topics you are comparing to see if they have always had the same relationship to one another.
- find critical texts or articles to see how others have discussed these topics.
- discover other comparisons that are similar to the relationship your items share.

Be sure to note all resources you use in your research, and credit those sources in your final drafts. See the Citing Sources pages in the Introductory Unit of this textbook for additional guidance.

READING-WRITING CONNECTION

To get a feel for comparison-and-contrast writing, read "The News" by Neil Postman on page 218.

Prewriting/Planning Strategies

Explore categories. Working with a group, make a list of categories that your intended audience would find interesting, such as famous athletes, artists, historical figures, authors, or activities. Then, choose one category and discuss it in greater depth. Identify specific topics within the category that present clear similarities and differences.

Find related pairs. Explore topics in terms of clear opposites, clear similarities, or close relationships. Start with names of people, places, objects, or ideas. Note related subjects that come to mind, as well as relationships that interest you. Choose one of these idea pairs to develop.

Specify your purpose. To identify a purpose for your essay, consider the following possibilities:

- To persuade—You may want readers to accept your opinion that one subject is preferable to another.
- To explain—You may want readers to understand something special about the subjects.
- To describe—You may want readers to understand the basic similarities and differences between your subjects.

Use specific criteria. When you compare and contrast, you should examine specific criteria as a basis for your writing. Use a three-column chart like the one shown to identify criteria and the similarities and differences between subjects.

Criteria	Playing Chess	Swimming
Requirements	Partner, chess set, knowledge of the rules of the game, practice	Access to a body of water, knowledge of how to swim, practice
Benefits	Excellent mental challenge, sense of satisfaction in winning, can be done competitively for awards, can be done any time	Excellent physical challenge, keeps body healthy, can be done competitively for awards, can be done alone
Drawbacks	Cannot be done alone, can take a long time to complete a game, mastering skills can be difficult	Can be difficult to find a place to swim, especially in cold weather, can be tiring

Drafting Strategies

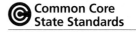

Prepare to compare. Use the details from your Criteria chart to fill in a Venn diagram, listing similarities and differences between your two topics. Record similarities in the space where the circles overlap, and note differences in the outer sections of the circles. Doing so will help you organize your essay.

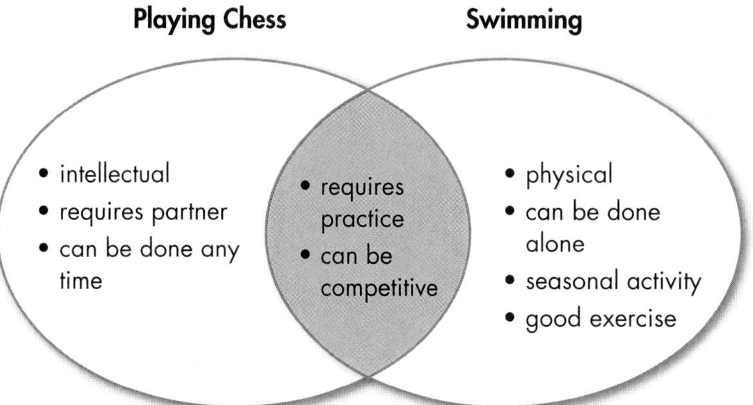

Choose the best evidence. After you have evaluated your subjects, you will likely have more information than will fit into your essay. Consider which information is most important and meaningful.

- **Importance:** Choose the most important facts about each subject. You may wish to examine a particular play in chess or stroke in swimming, but the broad overall qualities of each activity may provide the best points of comparison.
- **Values:** The two subjects you choose may represent different values or perspectives about what is important in life. For example, in comparing and contrasting swimming and chess, you might discuss the value of physical fitness versus the value of mental challenges.
- **Relevance:** While you may use your personal experiences with the topics as supporting examples or evidence, your discussion should take into account a broader understanding. For example, you may wish to compare playing chess and swimming based on the length of time each activity takes, but remember that this may vary from person to person.

Add transitions. As you draft your essay, use transitional words and phrases to connect your ideas. To make comparisons, use words such as *similarly, in comparison,* or *likewise*. If you are contrasting ideas, use transitions such as *on the other hand, in contrast,* or *however*.

Support generalizations with specifics. Whether your purpose in comparing and contrasting two subjects is to describe, to persuade, or to explain, provide enough detail to fully develop your points. Support your statements about similarities and differences with a sufficient number of facts, examples, and other forms of evidence that clearly relate to your ideas and are well suited to your audience.

Writing

2.a. Organize complex ideas, concepts, and information to make important connections and distinctions.

2.b. Develop the topic with well-chosen, relevant, and sufficient facts.

2.c. Use appropriate and varied transitions to link the major sections of the text, create cohesion, and clarify the relationships among complex ideas and concepts.

2.e. Establish and maintain a formal style and objective tone while attending to the norms and conventions of the discipline in which they are writing.

2.f. Provide a concluding statement or section that follows from and supports the information or explanation presented.

Getting Organized

The **organization** of an essay is the order in which information is assembled. Organization is especially important in a comparison-and-contrast essay because the reader must learn about two subjects at once. A solid organizational structure can help you to unfold a clear analysis and keep your reader on track. There are two common ways to organize a comparison-and-contrast essay:

- **point-by-point organization,** in which you move between your subjects as you discuss points of comparison and contrast.
- **subject-by-subject organization,** in which you compare and contrast your subjects as complete units.

Point-by-Point Organization This method allows you to discuss both subjects together, thereby keeping both subjects in your audience's mind at the same time. To use this method of organization, compare and contrast one aspect, or criterion, of both subjects. Then, compare and contrast the next aspect, and so on. Continue this process until you have covered all the criteria you are using to compare and contrast your topics. This method allows you to sharpen points of similarity and difference.

Subject-by-Subject Organization This method allows you to discuss each subject in great detail on its own. To use this method, discuss all the features of one subject, and then discuss all the features of the other. This format allows your audience to get an in-depth view of each subject. The comparisons and contrasts will, then, become more obvious.

Choosing an Organizational Structure The organizational structure you use will depend upon the comparisons you are exploring. The structure you choose should help you present your ideas; it should not fight against them. As you draft, review your notes and lay them out as shown on the cards at right. This visual display will help you choose a structure that works best for your topic.

Concluding Regardless of the organizational structure you choose, conclude with a paragraph that summarizes your analysis. Restate your purpose for analyzing the two topics and remind readers of the main similarities and differences you discussed.

Point-by-Point Plan

Point 1
- Subject A
- Subject B

Point 2
- Subject A
- Subject B

Subject-by-Subject Plan

Subject A
- Point 1
- Point 2

Subject B
- Point 1
- Point 2

Revising Strategies

Revise to make comparisons and contrasts clear. Using two different colors, mark your draft to distinguish between the two subjects you discuss. Whether you have used point-by-point or subject-by-subject organization, this color coding will clearly reveal if you have organized a balanced presentation of both subjects. If necessary, you can expand or reduce coverage of one of your subjects to achieve balance. Next, evaluate the places where the two colors—and subjects—meet. Add transitional words to make the shifts clear.

Model: Revising for Clarity

Playing chess and swimming are two of my favorite pastimes.

^Playing chess is an excellent way to exercise my brain and challenge myself to think differently. Swimming is challenging in other ways, most of them physical.

Both
^~~P~~laying chess and swimming can be competitive activities.

However,
^~~P~~laying chess is something I can do only if I have a partner.

The author uses the transitions "both" and "however" to move more fluidly from one idea to the next.

Revise to add specifics. To achieve your purpose and to help your readers understand the comparisons you make, add enough detail to explain the differences and similarities you see. Look for places where you can add related information that strengthens your description or analysis, such as well-chosen facts, quotations, definitions, or examples.

Peer Review

Exchange drafts with a partner. As you read each other's essays, circle any vague language that you find, and suggest more precise alternatives. Then, discuss with your reader specific details that would make your comparisons more vivid. Incorporate these details into your draft.

Vague: In contrast to playing chess, swimming provides many health benefits.

Specific: In contrast to playing chess, which challenges the mind, swimming provides many health benefits. Swimming improves coordination and balance and provides a great cardiovascular workout. It does all this without placing undue pressure on joints or other parts of the body that are easily injured.

As you review your partner's work, be sensitive to its style and tone. Suggest revisions that would help maintain an appropriately formal style and an objective, or neutral, tone.

Common Core State Standards

Writing

2.c. Use appropriate and varied transitions to link the major sections of the text, create cohesion, and clarify the relationships among complex ideas and concepts.

2.d. Use precise language and domain-specific vocabulary to manage the complexity of the topic.

2.e. Establish and maintain a formal style and objective tone while attending to the norms and conventions of the discipline in which they are writing.

Language

1.b. Use various types of phrases and clauses to convey specific meanings and add variety and interest to writing or presentations.

Revising to Combine Sentences With Phrases

To avoid a series of too many simple sentences, combine some sentences by converting the idea in one sentence into a modifying phrase in another.

Identifying Modifying Phrases An **appositive phrase** is a group of words that clarifies the meaning of a noun or pronoun. The following sentences can be combined using an appositive phrase.

Original: Sophia is a talented actress. She has appeared in more than twenty productions.

Combined: Sophia, *a talented actress*, has appeared in more than twenty productions.

Verbal phrases, which use verbs as nouns, adjectives, or adverbs, can also be used to combine sentences. Verbal phrases may be classified as participial, gerund, or infinitive, depending on their function.

Participial	Gerund	Infinitive
Finding himself alone onstage, Aaron paced nervously.	*Meeting with new people* is difficult for some people.	The director's advice was *to focus first on learning the lines.*
Adjective modifies *Aaron*	Noun acts as subject of sentence	Noun acts as complement of verb *was*

When adding a modifying phrase to a sentence, place the phrase close to the word it modifies. A misplaced modifier can confuse readers.

Misplaced: *Hanging from a silken thread,* Jeremy noticed a spider. (Participial phrase seems to modify *Jeremy*.)

Correct: Jeremy noticed a spider *hanging from a silken thread*.

Combining With Phrases Follow these steps to revise a series of short sentences by using phrases to combine them.

1. Express the information from one sentence as an appositive or a verbal phrase.
2. Insert the phrase in the other sentence, revising it if needed.
3. Make sure that any modifying phrase is placed near the word it modifies and that the revised sentence is punctuated correctly.

Grammar in Your Writing

Review your draft, looking for short sentences that might be combined using appositive, participial, gerund, or infinitive phrases. Consider combining these sentences.

STUDENT MODEL: **Lauren De Loach, Bernice, LA**

Ambivalence

When I consider my conflicting feelings about my hometown, I see that there are things that I love and hate about living in Bernice, Louisiana, a nineties version of Mayberry. I love the security of a small town, and I hate it. I love the way that my town is not clouded by the smog of a city, and I hate it too. I love it and I hate that I love it.

Lauren's essay will compare two feelings: what she loves and what she hates about her hometown.

I love and hate the security in my town for a number of reasons. I love it because I know that it is my dog scratching at my door at 5:30 in the morning and not some dangerous stranger. In my town, a fifteen-car traffic jam is front-page news. On the other hand, I hate that it gets a little boring sometimes. I don't want criminals at my door, but a little excitement would be nice.

Using a point-by-point organization, Lauren addresses the first contrast in her attitudes about her town: She feels ambivalence about its security.

I am fond of the size of Bernice and I detest it, too. I'm glad that only fifteen cars is a major traffic jam. But I hate that I have to drive sixteen miles to the nearest major store. I love and hate that my town is so small that I know everybody's first, middle, and last names. I like it because I have a "tab" at the grocery store and the drug store, so that eliminates the necessity of carrying money. I hate that everybody knows me because that means that everybody finds out about whom I'm dating, whom I once dated, my height, weight, and age. I also hate that we all know each other so well that the most entertaining news we can come up with to put in the *Bernice Banner* is that Peggy Jane and her brother JC visited their Aunt Goosey Lou in the nursing home. But by knowing everyone so well, I've made friends who are trustworthy because we know all of one another's deepest secrets.

These facts support Lauren's ideas and opinions.

Even though I say that I detest some things, home wouldn't be home without these silly quirks. I love that my parents and their friends are known as the "elite group" because they have traveled beyond Texas, Arkansas, and Mississippi. I love saying that I have read the *Iliad* to people who think I would not read such a book. I know that it sounds like I love the provincialism that small towns can impose, but the smells of fresh-cut grass and the gardenia bush outside my door are what make my home my home.

This is what I love and what I hate, but I don't really. The overall feeling I get from living in Bernice is ambivalence. I love it and I hate that I love such goofy things. But the parts of home that seem so trivial are the ones that make you who you are. That makes a place your home.

Lauren's comparison allows her to be funny, but it also helps her reflect on her ideas.

Editing and Proofreading

Check your draft to correct errors in spelling, grammar, and punctuation.

Focus on compound sentences. Comparison-and-contrast essays often contain compound sentences—those with two independent clauses joined by a semicolon or a coordinating conjunction, such as *or, and,* or *but*. Check that you have correctly punctuated these sentences.

Conjunction: I liked the chili, but it was spicy.

Semicolon: I rushed out; I was late for the bus.

Spiral Review
Earlier in this unit, you learned about **parallelism** (p. 634). Make sure you have used parallelism effectively in your essay.

Publishing and Presenting

Consider one of the following ways to share your writing:

Deliver an oral presentation. Read your comparison-and-contrast essay aloud to an audience of your classmates. If possible, include props or visuals to enhance the reading.

Make a poster. Present your comparison-and-contrast findings visually in a poster. Use a graphic organizer, such as a Venn diagram, to show the similarities and differences of your subjects. If possible, add photographs and illustrations to show the distinctive elements of your subjects. Make sure your poster is attractively designed and legible.

Reflecting on Your Writing

Writer's Journal Jot down your answer to this question:
How did writing about the topics help you better understand them?

Self-Evaluation Rubric

Use the following criteria to evaluate the effectiveness of your essay.

Criteria	Rating Scale			
	not very	....		*very*
PURPOSE/FOCUS Introduces a specific topic; provides a concluding section that follows from and supports the information or explanation presented	1	2	3	4
ORGANIZATION Organizes complex ideas, concepts, and information to make important connections and distinctions; uses appropriate and varied transitions to link the major sections, create cohesion, and clarify relationships among ideas	1	2	3	4
DEVELOPMENT OF IDEAS/ELABORATION Develops the topic with well-chosen, relevant and sufficient facts, extended definitions, concrete details, quotations or other information and examples appropriate to the audience's knowledge of the topic	1	2	3	4
LANGUAGE Uses precise language and domain-specific vocabulary to manage the complexity of the topic; establishes and maintains a formal style and an objective tone	1	2	3	4
CONVENTIONS Attends to the norms and conventions of the discipline	1	2	3	4

SELECTED RESPONSE

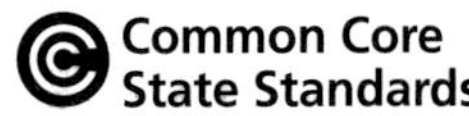

RL.9-10.3, RL.9-10.4; W.9-10.3.b, W.9-10.10; L.9-10.4.a

[For full standards wording, see the chart in the front of this book.]

I. Reading Literature

Directions: *Read the excerpt from Act I, Scene 2 of* A Midsummer Night's Dream *by William Shakespeare. Then, answer each question that follows.*

Background *A group of local tradesmen—Quince, Flute, Bottom, Starveling, Snug, and Snout—are rehearsing a play they plan to perform at the duke's wedding. The play is a retelling of the tragic love story of Pyramus and Thisbe. Quince is assigning parts and has already given Bottom the role of Pyramus.*

Quince. Flute, you must take Thisby on you.
Flute. What is Thisby? A wandering knight?
Quince. It is the lady that Pyramus must love.
Flute. Nay, faith, let me not play a woman; I have a beard coming.
Quince. That's all one: you shall play it in a mask, and you may speak as small as you will.
Bottom. An I may hide my face, let me play Thisby too, I'll speak in a monstrous little voice. "Thisne, Thisne;" "Ah, Pyramus, lover dear! thy Thisby dear, and lady dear!"
Quince. No, no; you must play Pyramus: and, Flute, you Thisby.
Bottom. Well, proceed.
Quince. Robin Starveling, the tailor.
Starveling. Here, Peter Quince.
Quince. Robin Starveling, you must play Thisby's mother. Tom Snout, the tinker.
Snout. Here, Peter Quince.
Quince. You, Pyramus' father: myself, Thisby's father: Snug, the joiner; you, the lion's part: and, I hope, here is a play fitted.
Snug. Have you the lion's part written? Pray you, if it be, give it me, for I am slow of study.
Quince. You may do it extempore, for it is nothing but roaring.
Bottom. Let me play the lion too: I will roar, that I will do any man's heart good to hear me; I will roar, that I will make the duke say "Let him roar again, let him roar again."

1. What is **blank verse?**
   A. unrhymed iambic pentameter
   B. rhyming iambic pentameter
   C. poetry that does not have a specific meter
   D. poetry that contains dialogue

2. How does the **dialogue** in this excerpt show that the characters are commoners rather than aristocrats?
   A. The characters speak in asides and monologues.
   B. The characters speak in rhyming couplets.
   C. The characters speak in blank verse rather than in prose.
   D. The characters speak in prose rather than in blank verse.

3. In drama, how does a **tragedy** differ from a **comedy?**
   A. In a comedy, the main character is usually a commoner, whereas in a tragedy the main character is of noble birth.
   B. A tragedy always includes comedic scenes but a comedy never includes tragic scenes.
   C. A tragedy ends sorrowfully with the destruction of the hero, whereas a comedy ends happily with the restoration of order.
   D. A comedy ends in destruction, whereas a tragedy ends in harmony.

4. **Part A** A humorous scene that is part of a tragedy is called
   A. comic relief.
   B. comedy.
   C. pun.
   D. aside.

   Part B What main purpose does such a humorous scene serve in a tragedy?
   A. It summarizes events in a funny way so the audience can better understand them.
   B. It provides insight into the motivations of the tragic hero.
   C. It provides a break from the tension of the tragic events.
   D. It allows the actors to show their versatility.

5. In the excerpt, Bottom represents the **archetypal character** of a clown. Which detail in the scene does *not* show this quality?
   A. his volunteering to play all the parts
   B. his following of Quince's directions
   C. his boasting of his ability to roar
   D. his portrayal of Thisby

6. What information is provided by the following **stage direction?**

   [Enter QUINCE, SNUG, BOTTOM, FLUTE, SNOUT, and STARVELING]

   A. the act number
   B. the setting
   C. the characters who appear in the scene
   D. details about the stage setup

7. The following lines are an example of which dramatic element?

   Quince. Robin Starveling, the tailor.
   Starveling. Here, Peter Quince.

   A. a scene
   B. dialogue
   C. dramatic irony
   D. conflict

8. What is the meaning of the underlined word *extempore* as it is used in the excerpt?
   A. loudly
   B. after much practice
   C. poorly
   D. without preparation

9. Write a **monologue** that continues Bottom's last speech in the excerpt. Make sure your work reflects Bottom's character as it is portrayed in this scene. The monologue should be at least eight lines long.

GO ON

II. Reading Informational Text

Directions: *Read the article. Then, answer each question that follows.*

RI.9-10.1; W.9-10.5; L.9-10.1.a, L.9-10.3, L.9-10.4.a
[For full standards wording, see the chart in the front of this book.]

Planet Protection: The EPA

Although it may seem that climate change has only recently become a major news item, scientists and policy makers have been concerned about the environment for decades. One government organization devoted to environmental issues is the Environmental Protection Agency (EPA).

The EPA was founded in 1970 to limit pollution, monitor pesticide use, and ensure clean air and water for all. Since that time, the EPA has been involved in everything from cleaning up oil spills to enforcing laws that ensure the safety of the public water supply.

The EPA has recently established the U.S. Climate Change site in order to provide balanced information to the public about climate change. According to the EPA, we know that the earth's temperature has increased over 1 degree in the last century. EPA sources suggest that planetary temperatures will continue to rise. However, scientists do not know the rate of this increase. Scientists are currently working to prove theories about climate change, thus allowing them to make more accurate predictions about events to come.

The EPA Web site states, "Climate change may be a big problem, but there are many little things we can do to make a difference." The site suggests a variety of ways that people, old and young, can make small changes to reduce their environmental impacts. Although improving the environment may seem to be a daunting task that is too much for one person, these tips can guide people to small daily changes that can make a real difference.

1. Part A What does the underlined word *daunting* mean as it is used in the article?

A. extremely responsible
B. somewhat important
C. kindly attentive
D. incredibly difficult

Part B Which phrase from the article best helps the reader understand the meaning of *daunting*?

A. "take better care of the environment"
B. "changes that do make a difference"
C. "too much for one person"
D. "old and young"

2. Which answer choice best summarizes scientists' current knowledge about climate change as presented in the article?

A. They know planetary temperature has risen and will keep rising, but do not know how fast this will happen.
B. They do not know how much the planet has warmed.
C. At this point, they have few questions about climate change.
D. They are not focused on climate change.

3. According to the article, how will accurate theories about climate change help matters?

A. They will help scientists limit pollution, monitor pesticide use, and ensure clean air and water.
B. They will help scientists make better predictions.
C. They will disprove old theories.
D. They will help scientists establish a U.S. Climate Change site.

III. Writing and Language Conventions

Directions: *Read the passage. Then, answer each question that follows.*

(1) A well-trained dog is a pleasure to own and people like encountering well-trained dogs, too. (2) One of the easiest and most basic commands to teach your dog is *Sit.* (3) With a little practice, the right technique, and by training your dog with treats, you will have a dog that knows how to sit on command. (4) The dog will pick it up within a few brief training sessions. (5) Use the following procedure:

(6) • First, gather small training treats.
(7) • Next, stand in front of your dog.
(8) • Then, hold the treat in your hand. (9) Place your hand in front of the dog's nose. (10) Then, move the treat over its head toward the tail as you say your dog's name and "Sit." (11) The dog's head and nose should follow the treat and the rear end should hit the ground. (12) Be sure not to hold the treat too high or the dog will jump up to get it.
(13) • When the dog's hindquarters hit the ground, say "Good sit" and immediately give the dog the treat. (14) Do not give the dog the treat if it doesn't sit.
(15) • Start over again.
(16) • Repeat the process until your dog has learned how to sit.

1. How can sentences 15 and 16 best be combined using a **verbal phrase?**

A. Start over again, repeating the process until your dog has learned how to sit.
B. Start over again, and repeat the process until your dog starts sitting.
C. You should then start over again and you should repeat the process until your dog has learned to sit.
D. Start over again until your dog has learned how to sit.

2. How can sentences 8 and 9 best be combined using a **verbal phrase?**

A. Before you hold your hand in front of the dog's nose, hold the treat there.
B. When holding the treat with your hand.
C. Then, holding the treat in your hand, place it in front of the dog's nose.
D. Then, hold the treat in your hand.

3. How can sentence 3 be revised for **parallelism?**

A. With a little practice and the right technique and with dog training with treats...
B. With a little practice, the right technique, and a few treats...
C. With practice, technique, and by training with treats...
D. With practice, using the right technique and a few treats...

4. How can sentence 1 be revised for **parallelism?**

A. A well-trained dog is a pleasure for everyone.
B. Owners find pleasure in encountering a well-trained dog.
C. A dog is a pleasure to own and others appreciate well-trained dogs.
D. A well-trained dog is a pleasure to own and a pleasure to encounter.

CONSTRUCTED RESPONSE

Directions: *Follow the instructions to complete the tasks below as required by your teacher.*

As you work on each task, incorporate both general academic vocabulary and literary terms you learned in Parts 1 and 2 of this unit.

RL.9-10.2, RL.9-10.3, RL.9-10.5; W.9-10.2, W.9-10.7, W.9-10.8, W.9-10.9.a; SL.9-10.1, SL.9-10.4

[For the complete wording of the standards, see the standards chart in the front of your textbook.]

Writing

TASK 1 Literature [RL.9-10.9; W.9-10.2, W.9-10.9.a]

Analyze Theme in Related Works

Write an essay in which you analyze how Shakespeare draws on the work of Ovid to convey a theme.

- Explain that you will discuss similarities and differences between Ovid's "Pyramus and Thisbe" and Shakespeare's *Romeo and Juliet.*
- Identify specific ways in which the story and the play are similar and different. Consider main characters, minor characters, settings, and events. For each work, describe the reasons that characters act as they do. Finally, explain the themes each work expresses.
- Choose an organizational style that allows you to express ideas clearly and logically. Use a variety of transitional words and phrases to clarify the relationships among ideas.
- Include a clear thesis statement, explaining what you believe to be the theme of both works. Use well-chosen details and quotations to support your interpretation.
- Provide a clear and concise conclusion that summarizes your analysis.

TASK 2 Literature [RL.9-10.3; W.9-10.9.a]

Analyze an Archetypal Character

Write an essay in which you analyze an archetypal character in a literary work from Part 2 of this unit.

- Explain which work and character you will discuss. Summarize the plot and describe which archetype the character represents.
- Present a well-reasoned analysis of the character's actions and motivations. Explain whether the character has multiple or conflicting motivations.
- Explain how the character interacts with other characters. Discuss whether the character changes over the course of the work, and describe the nature of any changes.
- Explain specific ways in which the character's behavior, thoughts, statements, and actions make him or her an archetypal character.
- Cite specific details and use quotations from the work to support your ideas.

TASK 3 Literature [RL.9-10.5; W.9-10.2]

Analyze Structural Choices

Write an essay in which you analyze the role of one dramatic speech or a section of dialogue from The Tragedy of Romeo and Juliet.

Part 1

- Identify the soliloquy, monologue, or section of dialogue you will discuss.
- Reread the soliloquy, monologue, or section of dialogue. Take notes as you review.
- Using your notes, write a summary of the circumstances in which the speech or dialogue is delivered. Then, answer this question: Why do you think the playwright chose to include this speech or dialogue at this point in the play?

Part 2

- In an essay, explain your interpretation of the message conveyed in the speech or dialogue. Consider both explicit and implicit meanings.
- Cite specific details to support your ideas.

Speaking and Listening

TASK 4 **Literature [RL.9-10.3; SL.9-10.4]**

Present a Tragic Character

Deliver a speech in which you discuss how a complex character from a literary work in Part 2 of this unit qualifies as a tragic figure.

- Begin your speech by presenting background for the work—its setting and plot. Then, introduce and describe the character in detail, including his or her role in the plot.
- Consider your audience, purpose, and task as you compose and deliver your presentation. Include information your audience needs in order to understand the general concept of a tragic figure as well as details about your character's choices, motivations, thoughts, and feelings.
- Present your information and supporting evidence clearly, concisely, and logically so that your audience can understand your ideas. Use relevant examples and quotations from the work to support your analysis.
- End with a memorable conclusion that restates the key elements of your analysis.

TASK 5 **Literature [RL.9-10.2; SL.9-10.1]**

Analyze the Development of a Theme

Participate in a small-group discussion about the theme expressed in a literary work from Part 2 of this unit.

- Conduct your own analysis of the text and take notes on your interpretation of the theme. Cite details from the beginning, middle, and end of the work that support your point of view.
- Write down three questions you have about the theme and its development throughout the play.
- Share your ideas with the group. Take turns asking questions and responding to those of others to propel the discussion. Actively incorporate all members of the group into the conversation.
- As you continue the discussion, respond thoughtfully to group members' ideas. Work with your group to arrive at a shared understanding of the theme.

Research

TASK 6 **Literature [RL.9-10.5; W.9-10.7, W.9-10.8; W.9-10.9.a]**

Do our differences define us?

In Part 2 of this unit, you have read literature in which characters' differences lead to devastating consequences. Now you will conduct a short research project about a real-life situation, whether a historic event or a current one, driven by differences between people. Research one situation in which people resolved their differences for a positive result and one in which they failed to do so. Then, use both the literature you have read and your research to reflect on and write about this unit's Big Question. Review the following guidelines before you begin your research:

- Focus your research on two news stories.
- Gather information from reliable sources. Your sources may be print or digital.
- Take notes as you investigate the news stories.
- Cite your sources thoroughly and accurately.

When you have completed your research, write an essay in response to the Big Question. Discuss how your initial ideas have changed or been reinforced. Support your response with examples from the literature you have read and the research you have conducted.

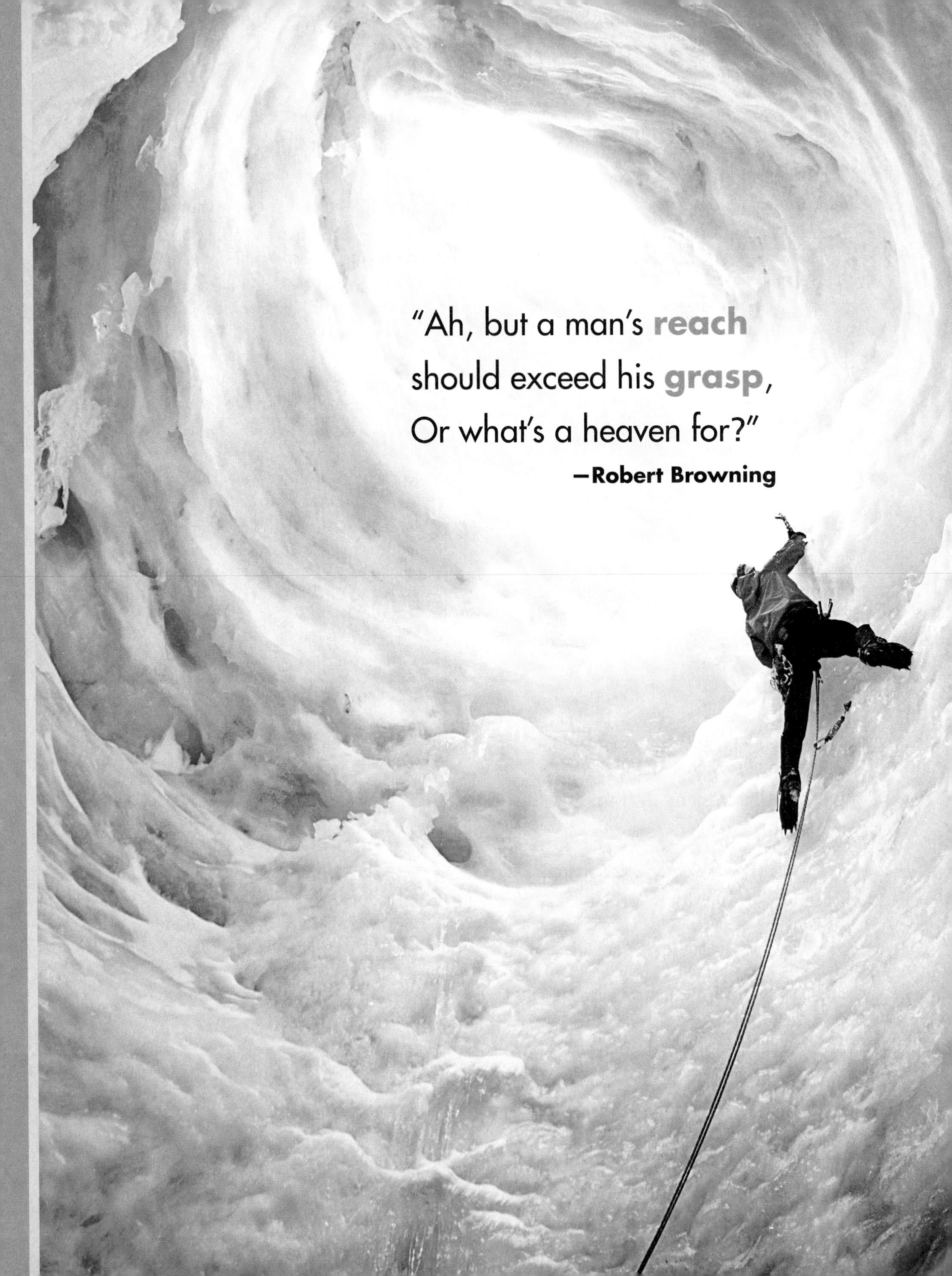
"Ah, but a man's reach
should exceed his grasp,
Or what's a heaven for?"
—Robert Browning

PART 3

TEXT SET DEVELOPING INSIGHT

ASPIRATION

Aspiration is the desire to achieve a success, own a prized possession, or rise in life in some way. An individual's aspirations are deeply connected to his or her sense of identity. They involve the perception that who we are is not who we want to or should be. In some cases, aspiration involves surface values, such as the desire to own luxury items or have status. In other cases, aspiration comes from deeper values, such as a wish for a more stable, secure life. All the readings in this section focus on the concept of aspiration. As you read each text, consider the nature of the aspiration it describes. Then, think about how these ideas relate to the Big Question for this unit: **Do our differences define us?**

◀ CRITICAL VIEWING How do the image and the quotation present aspiration as both a tangible, physical experience and as a symbolic or emotional one?

CLOSE READING TOOL

Use the **Close Reading Tool** to practice the strategies you learn in this unit.

READINGS IN PART 3

from

The Importance of Being Earnest

Oscar Wilde

The following excerpt is from Act I of *The Importance of Being Earnest.* The play takes place in England in the 1890s, during the reign of Queen Victoria. In this scene, John Worthing, nicknamed Jack, visits the London apartment of his friend Algernon. Jack loves Algernon's cousin, Gwendolen. In order to maintain his spotless reputation at his home in the country, Jack takes on a different identity when he is in the city. When he is out in the country, he pretends to have a brother named Ernest, and when he visits London, Jack pretends to be Ernest. Gwendolen knows nothing about Jack's real name or his double identity.

CHARACTERS

John Worthing, JP
Lady Bracknell
Hon. Gwendolen Fairfax
Algernon

LADY BRACKNELL *and* ALGERNON *go into the music room,* GWENDOLEN *remains behind.*

JACK. Charming day it has been, Miss Fairfax.

GWENDOLEN. Pray don't talk to me about the weather, Mr Worthing. Whenever people talk to me about the weather, I always feel quite certain that they mean something else. And that makes me so nervous.

JACK. I do mean something else.

GWENDOLEN. I thought so. In fact, I am never wrong.

JACK. And I would like to be allowed to take advantage of Lady Bracknell's temporary absence. . . .

GWENDOLEN. I would certainly advise you to do so. Mamma has a way of coming back suddenly into a room that I have often had to speak to her about.

JACK. *(nervously)* Miss Fairfax, ever since I met you I have admired you more than any girl . . . I have ever met since . . . I met you.

GWENDOLEN. Yes, I am quite aware of the fact. And I often wish that in public, at any rate, you had been more demonstrative. For me you have always had an irresistible fascination. Even before I met you I was far from indifferent to you. *(Jack looks at her in amazement)* We live, as I hope you know, Mr Worthing, in an age of ideals. The fact is constantly mentioned in the more expensive monthly magazines, and has reached the provincial pulpits I am told; and my ideal has always been to love someone of the name of Ernest. There is something in that name that inspires absolute confidence. The moment Algernon first mentioned to me that he had a friend called Ernest, I knew I was destined to love you.

◂ **demonstrative** (di män´strə tiv) *adj.* showing feelings openly

Jack. You really love me, Gwendolen?

Gwendolen. Passionately!

Jack. Darling! You don't know how happy you've made me.

Gwendolen. My own Ernest!

Jack. But you don't really mean to say that you couldn't love me if my name wasn't Ernest?

Gwendolen. But your name is Ernest.

Jack. Yes, I know it is. But supposing it was something else? Do you mean to say you couldn't love me then?

Gwendolen. *(glibly)* Ah! that is clearly a metaphysical speculation, and like most metaphysical speculations has very little reference at all to the actual facts of real life, as we know them.

Jack. Personally, darling, to speak quite candidly, I don't much care about the name Ernest. . . . I don't think the name suits me at all.

Gwendolen. It suits you perfectly. It is a divine name. It has music of its own. It produces vibrations.

Jack. Well, really, Gwendolen, I must say that I think there are lots of other much nicer names. I think Jack, for instance, a charming name.

Gwendolen. Jack? . . . No, there is very little music in the name Jack, if any at all, indeed. It does not thrill. It produces absolutely no vibrations. . . . I have known several Jacks, and they all, without exception, were more than usually plain. Besides, Jack is a notorious domesticity for John! And I pity any woman who is married to a man called John. She would probably never be allowed to know the entrancing pleasure of a single moment's solitude. The only really safe name is Ernest.

Jack. Gwendolen, I must get christened at once—I mean we must get married at once. There is no time to be lost.

Gwendolen. Married, Mr Worthing?

Jack. *(astounded)* Well . . . surely. You know that I love you, and you led me to believe, Miss Fairfax, that you were not absolutely indifferent to me.

Gwendolen. I adore you. But you haven't proposed to me yet. Nothing has been said at all about marriage. The subject has not even been touched on.

Jack. Well . . . may I propose to you now?

Gwendolen. I think it would be an admirable opportunity. And to spare you any possible disappointment, Mr Worthing, I think it only fair to tell you quite frankly beforehand that I am fully determined to accept you.

Jack. Gwendolen!

Gwendolen. Yes, Mr Worthing, what have you got to say to me?

Jack. You know what I have got to say to you.

Gwendolen. Yes, but you don't say it.

Jack. Gwendolen, will you marry me? *(Goes on his knees)*

Gwendolen. Of course I will, darling. How long you have been about it! I am afraid you have had very little experience in how to propose.

Jack. My own one, I have never loved anyone in the world but you.

Gwendolen. Yes, but men often propose for practice. I know my brother Gerald does. All my girlfriends tell me so. What wonderfully blue eyes you have, Ernest! They are quite, quite blue. I hope you will always look at me just like that, especially when there are other people present.

(Enter Lady Bracknell*)*

Lady Bracknell. Mr Worthing! Rise, sir, from this semi-recumbent posture. It is most indecorous.

Gwendolen. Mamma! *(He tries to rise; she restrains him)* I must beg you to retire. This is no place for you. Besides, Mr Worthing has not quite finished yet.

Lady Bracknell. Finished what, may I ask?

Gwendolen. I am engaged to Mr Worthing, Mamma.

(They rise together)

Lady Bracknell. Pardon me, you are not engaged to anyone. When you do become engaged to someone, I, or your father, should his health permit him, will inform you of the fact. An engagement should come on a young girl as a surprise, pleasant or unpleasant, as the case may be. It is hardly a matter that she could be allowed to arrange for herself. . . . And now I have a few questions to put to you, Mr Worthing. While I am making these inquiries, you, Gwendolen, will wait for me below in the carriage.

Gwendolen. *(reproachfully)* Mamma!

Lady Bracknell. In the carriage, Gwendolen!

Gwendolen goes to the door. She and Jack blow kisses to each other behind Lady Bracknell's back. Lady Bracknell looks vaguely about as if she could not understand what the noise was. Finally turns round

Gwendolen, the carriage!

Gwendolen. Yes, mamma.

Goes out, looking back at Jack

Lady Bracknell. *(sitting down)* You can take a seat, Mr Worthing. *(Looks in her pocket for note-book and pencil)*

Jack. Thank you, Lady Bracknell, I prefer standing.

Lady Bracknell. *(pencil and note-book in hand)* I feel bound to tell you that you are not down on my list of eligible young men, although I have the same list as the dear Duchess of Bolton has. We work together, in fact. However, I am quite ready to enter your name, should your answers be what a really affectionate mother requires. How old are you?

Jack. Twenty-nine.

Lady Bracknell. A very good age to be married at. I have always been of opinion that a man who desires to get married should know either everything or nothing. Which do you know?

Jack. *(after some hesitation)* I know nothing, Lady Bracknell.

ignorance ▶ (igˊ nə rəns) *n.* lack of knowledge

Lady Bracknell. I am pleased to hear it. I do not approve of anything that tampers with natural ignorance. Ignorance is like a delicate exotic fruit; touch it and the bloom is gone. The whole theory of modern education is radically unsound. Fortunately in England, at any rate, education produces no effect whatsoever. If it did, it would prove a serious danger to the upper classes, and probably lead to acts of violence in Grosvenor Square. What is your income?

Jack. Between seven and eight thousand a year.

Lady Bracknell. *(makes a note in her book)* In land, or in investments?

Jack. In investments, chiefly.

Lady Bracknell. That is satisfactory. What between the duties expected of one during one's lifetime, and the duties exacted from one after one's death, land has ceased to be either a profit or a pleasure. It gives one position, and prevents one from keeping it up. That's all that can be said about land.

Jack. I have a country house with some land, of course, attached to it, about fifteen hundred acres, I believe; but I don't depend on that for my real income. In fact, as far as I can make out, the poachers are the only people who make anything out of it.

Lady Bracknell. A country house! How many bedrooms? Well, that point can be cleared up afterwards. You have a town house, I hope? A girl with a simple, unspoiled nature, like Gwendolen, could hardly be expected to reside in the country.

Jack. Well, I own a house in Belgrave Square, but it is let by the year to Lady Bloxham. Of course, I can get it back whenever I like, at six months' notice.

Lady Bracknell. Lady Bloxham? I don't know her.

Jack. Oh, she goes about very little. She is a lady considerably advanced in years.

Lady Bracknell. Ah, nowadays that is no guarantee of respectability of character. What number in Belgrave Square?

Jack. 149.

Lady Bracknell. *(shaking her head)* The unfashionable side. I thought there was something. However, that could easily be altered.

Jack. Do you mean the fashion, or the side?

Lady Bracknell. *(sternly)* Both, if necessary, I presume. What are your politics?

Jack. Well, I am afraid I really have none. I am a Liberal Unionist.

Lady Bracknell. Oh, they count as Tories. They dine with us. Or come in the evening, at any rate. Now to minor matters. Are your parents living?

Jack. I have lost both my parents.

Lady Bracknell. Both? . . . That seems like carelessness. Who was your father? He was evidently a man of some wealth. Was he born in what the Radical papers call the purple of commerce, or did he rise from the ranks of the aristocracy?

Jack. I am afraid I really don't know. The fact is, Lady Bracknell, I said I had lost my parents. It would be nearer the truth to say that my parents seem to have lost me. . . . I don't actually know who I am by birth. I was . . . well, I was found.

Lady Bracknell. Found!

Jack. The late Mr Thomas Cardew, an old gentleman of a very charitable and kindly disposition, found me, and gave me the name of Worthing, because he happened to have a first-class ticket for Worthing in his pocket at the time. Worthing is a place in Sussex. It is a seaside resort.

Lady Bracknell. Where did the charitable gentleman who had a first-class ticket for this seaside resort find you?

Jack. *(gravely)* In a hand-bag.

Lady Bracknell. A hand-bag?

Jack. *(very seriously)* Yes, Lady Bracknell. I was in a hand-bag—a somewhat large, black leather handbag, with handles to it—an ordinary hand-bag in fact.

Lady Bracknell. In what locality did this Mr James, or Thomas, Cardew come across this ordinary hand-bag?

Jack. In the cloak-room at Victoria Station. It was given to him in mistake for his own.

Lady Bracknell. The cloak-room at Victoria Station?

Jack. Yes. The Brighton line.

Lady Bracknell. The line is immaterial. Mr Worthing, I confess I feel somewhat bewildered by what you have just told me. To be born, or at any rate bred, in a hand-bag, whether it had handles or not, seems to me to display a contempt for the ordinary decencies of family life that reminds one of the worst excesses of the French Revolution. And I presume you know what that unfortunate movement led to? As for the particular locality in which the hand-bag was found, a cloak-room at a railway station might serve to conceal a social **indiscretion**—has

indiscretion ▶ (in′di skresh′ən) *n.* action or remark that shows bad judgment and may offend someone probably, indeed, been used for that purpose before now—but it could hardly be regarded as an assured basis for a recognized position in good society.

Jack. May I ask you then what you would advise me to do? I need hardly say I would do anything in the world to ensure Gwendolen's happiness.

Lady Bracknell. I would strongly advise you, Mr Worthing, to try and acquire some relations as soon as possible, and to make a definite effort to produce at any rate one parent, of either sex, before the season is quite over.

Jack. Well, I don't see how I could possibly manage to do that. I can produce the hand-bag at any moment. It is in my dressing-room at home. I really think that should satisfy you, Lady Bracknell.

Lady Bracknell. Me, sir! What has it to do with me? You can hardly imagine that I and Lord Bracknell would dream of allowing our only daughter—a girl brought up with the utmost care—to marry into a cloak-room, and form an alliance with a parcel? Good morning, Mr Worthing!

Lady Bracknell sweeps out in majestic indignation

Jack. Good morning! (Algernon, *from the other room, strikes up the Wedding March.* Jack *looks perfectly furious, and goes to the door)* For goodness' sake don't play that ghastly tune, Algy! How idiotic you are!

ABOUT THE AUTHOR

Oscar Wilde (1854–1900)

Oscar Wilde was born in Ireland in 1854. The child of successful Dublin intellectuals, he was educated both in Dublin and at Oxford University. After university, he moved to London and became a part of the fashionable social circles that would later become the subject of much of his work. Throughout the 1890s, Wilde became notorious for his sharp, satiric wit. While he wrote poems and celebrated works of fiction—including the novel *The Picture of Dorian Gray*—it was in his plays that Wilde's genius found its voice. His masterpiece is *The Importance of Being Earnest,* a drama about Victorian values that still entertains audiences today.

Close Reading Activities

READ

Comprehension

Reread all or part of the text to help you answer the following questions.

1. Why does Gwendolen love Jack?
2. Which details indicate that Jack is a very wealthy man?
3. According to Lady Bracknell, how should a young girl learn that she is engaged?
4. What is Lady Bracknell's opinion of Jack's house in Belgrave Square?
5. What does Lady Bracknell advise Jack to do "before the season is quite over"?

Research: Clarify Details This scene from the play may include references that are unfamiliar to you. Choose at least one unfamiliar detail, and briefly research it. Then, explain how the information you learned from research helps you better understand an aspect of the scene.

Summarize Write an objective summary of this scene. Remember that an objective summary is free from opinion and evaluation.

Language Study

Selection Vocabulary The following passages appear in the scene from *The Importance of Being Earnest.* Define each boldface word. Then, write a paragraph that uses all three boldface words correctly.

- And I often wish that in public, at any rate, you had been more **demonstrative.**
- **Ignorance** is like a delicate exotic fruit; touch it and the bloom is gone.
- As for the particular locality in which the hand-bag was found, a cloak-room at a railway station might serve to conceal a social **indiscretion**...

Diction and Style Study the line from the play that appears below. Then, answer the questions that follow.

> **LADY BRACKNELL.** Mr Worthing! Rise, sir, from this semi-recumbent posture. It is most indecorous.

1. **(a)** What does "semi-recumbent posture" mean? **(b)** What does this choice of phrase, rather than plainer language, suggest about Lady Bracknell?
2. **(a)** What is one synonym for *indecorous*? **(b)** How do the connotations of *indecorous* differ from those of the synonym? **(c)** How does this word choice add to Lady Bracknell's portrayal?

Conventions Read this passage from the play and identify the elements that make Gwendolen's speech parallel. Then, explain how the author's use of parallelism adds meaning and helps to develop Gwendolen's character.

> **JACK.** ...I don't much care about the name Ernest....I don't think the name suits me at all.
> **GWENDOLEN.** It suits you perfectly. It is a divine name. It has music of its own. It produces vibrations.

Academic Vocabulary

The following words appear in blue in the instructions and questions on the facing page.

ideals **status** **ancestry**

Categorize the words by deciding whether you know each one well, know it a little bit, or do not know it at all. Then, use a print or online dictionary to look up the definitions of the words you are unsure of or do not know at all.

Literary Analysis

Reread the identified passages. Then, respond to the questions that follow.

Focus Passage 1 *(pp. 675–676)*

GWENDOLEN. Yes, I am quite...safe name is Ernest.

Key Ideas and Details

1. **Analyze:** According to Gwendolen, how did she feel about Jack even before she met him?
2. **Compare and Contrast:** What qualities does Gwendolen think people named Ernest have that people named Jack do not? Explain.

Craft and Structure

3. **(a)** How does Gwendolen know that she and Jack "live in an age of **ideals**"? **(b) Infer:** What do these details suggest about how Gwendolen gets information and forms her opinions? Explain.
4. **Analyze:** Gwendolen refers to "ideals" and "metaphysical speculation." Does she understand what those concepts mean? Explain, citing details from the passage.

Integration of Knowledge and Ideas

5. **(a) Define:** What does the word *earnest* mean? **(b) Analyze:** Why is it ironic that Jack has assumed the name of Ernest? Explain, citing details from the text.

Focus Passage 2 *(pp. 680–681)*

JACK. I am afraid...in good society.

Key Ideas and Details

1. Where was Jack found as a baby?
2. **(a)** What name did Mr. Cardew give Jack and why? **(b) Infer:** What else can the reader infer Mr. Cardew gave to Jack? Cite details from the text that support your inference.

Craft and Structure

3. **(a)** In Lady Bracknell's view, how did the infant Jack "display a contempt" for Victorian family values? **(b) Analyze:** Why is it funny that Lady Bracknell feels the presence or absence of handles on the hand-bag is even worth mentioning? Explain.
4. **(a) Interpret:** How is Lady Bracknell's reaction to Jack's story highly exaggerated? **(b) Analyze:** How does Wilde's use of hyperbole make her character both funny and ridiculous? Explain.

Integration of Knowledge and Ideas

5. **(a) Generalize:** What Victorian values about personal **status,** reputation, and wealth does this play reflect? **(b) Compare and Contrast:** Do all three characters in this scene view those values with equal seriousness and respect? Explain.

Satire

A **satire** is a literary work that ridicules the foolishness and faults of individuals, an institution, or human nature in general. Reread the scene, and take notes about Wilde's use of satire.

1. In what ways does Lady Bracknell's interview with Jack satirize the following aspects of Victorian society: **(a)** the educational system; **(b)** courtship and marriage rituals; **(c)** the notion that girls are "simple and unspoiled"; **(d)** the importance of family and **ancestry.**
2. **Aspiration: (a)** What does Lady Bracknell mean by the term "good society"? **(b)** What view of marriage is suggested by her shock at the idea of an "alliance" with a parcel? Explain.

Common Core State Standards

RL.9-10.1, RL.9-10.2, RL.9-10.3, RL.9-10.4, RL.9-10.6, RL.9-10.10; L.9-10.4, L.9-10.4.d, L.9-10.5, L.9-10.6

[For full standards wording, see the chart in the front of this book.]

DISCUSS

From Text to Topic **Group Discussion**

Discuss the following passage with a group of classmates. Take notes during the discussion. Contribute your own ideas, and support them with examples from the text.

> I would strongly advise you, Mr Worthing, to try and acquire some relations as soon as possible, and to make a definite effort to produce at any rate one parent, of either sex, before the season is quite over.

QUESTIONS FOR DISCUSSION:

1. How would acquiring "some relations" help Jack?
2. What does Lady Bracknell's advice to Jack tell you about a key ingredient of social status in Victorian England?
3. Do you think Oscar Wilde agrees with Lady Bracknell? Explain.

WRITE

Writing to Sources **Informative Text**

Assignment

Write a **character analysis** of one character from the scene. Explain how dialogue and other details reveal the character's personality and values. Then, make a connection between the character and Wilde's satiric criticism of Victorian society.

Prewriting and Planning Reread the scene, taking note of how both dialogue and descriptions in the stage directions portray the character's personality, values, insights, and behavior. Record your notes in a two-column chart. Use the first column to note details and examples from the scene and the second to note what those lines suggest.

Drafting Use an outline to organize your writing. Begin with a thesis statement that summarizes your analysis of the character. Use bullet points to note the examples from the text you will use to make your point. End with a concluding statement that explains what Wilde is saying about Victorian society through this character. As you write, expand on each of the points in your outline.

Revising Reread your essay, making sure you have varied your sentence structures. If you have multiple simple sentences, consider combining them using phrases.

- **Simple Sentences:** Gwendolen is a silly character. She likes the name Ernest. She wants to marry Jack. This is because she thinks his name is Ernest.
- **Combined Sentence:** Gwendolen, a silly character, likes the name Ernest. She wants to marry Jack because she thinks his name is Ernest.

Editing and Proofreading Make sure every example you cite explains an aspect of the character and that all of your assertions are supported with evidence from the text. Eliminate any unnecessary sentences. Review your draft for correct spelling, punctuation, and grammar.

CONVENTIONS

If you are quoting dialogue between two characters, use a block quotation. Start the quotation on a new line. Begin with the character's name in capital letters, followed by a period. Indent all but the first line by 5 letter spaces. When the next character speaks, start a new line.

RESEARCH

Research **Investigate the Topic**

Victorian Society In this scene from the play, we learn that Lady Bracknell considers Jack an unsuitable match for her daughter because he lacks family of any social standing. While Wilde's take on this situation is humorous, class structure and family connections were important parts of Victorian society.

Assignment

Conduct research about class structure in Victorian England. Consult history books, encyclopedias, and scholarly articles. Keep your notes from each source separate, so that you will be able to identify information for citation. Share your findings in an **annotated bibliography**—a list of sources that include brief annotations, or paragraphs, that inform readers about the content and quality of each source.

PREPARATION FOR ESSAY

You may use the knowledge you gain during this research assignment to support your claims in an essay you will write at the end of this section.

Gather Sources Locate print and electronic sources you might want to recommend to other researchers. History books will provide insight into the hierarchy of the class structure and the qualities that define each category. Primary sources, such as letters or diaries, may show you how people felt about their positions in society. Use a variety of sources to ensure that you present your readers with a strong list of choices.

Take Notes Take notes on each source. Label each page or set of notes with the title and author of the source. As you record information, be sure to note the page or location where you found it so that you will be able to retrace your steps as needed.

Synthesize Multiple Sources Assemble data about each source, organize it into bibliography form, and write the annotations. Use either MLA (Modern Language Association) or APA (American Psychological Association) citation format—your teacher may tell you which one. Refer to the MLA or APA style guides to construct citations correctly. Provide objective information, including the type of source and the scope of its content. Then, write your evaluation, including your observations about the usefulness, quality, and thoroughness of each text.

Organize and Present Ideas Share your bibliography with a small group and discuss what you learned about Victorian class structures as you gathered the source information.

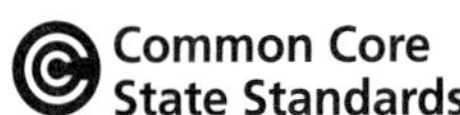

Common Core State Standards

RL.9-10.1; W.9-10.2.a–c, W.9-10.2.f, W.9-10.5, W.9-10.7, W.9-10.8, W.9-10.9.a, W.9-10.10; SL.9-10.1, SL.9-10.4; L.9-10.1, L.9-10.2, L.9-10.2.c, L.9-10.3.a

[For full standards wording, see the chart in the front of this book.]

The Necklace

Guy de Maupassant

She was one of those pretty, charming young women who are born, as if by an error of Fate, into a petty official's family. She had no dowry,[1] no hopes, not the slightest chance of being appreciated, understood, loved, and married by a rich and distinguished man; so she slipped into marriage with a minor civil servant at the Ministry of Education.

Unable to afford jewelry, she dressed simply: but she was as wretched as a déclassée, for women have neither caste nor breeding—in them beauty, grace, and charm replace pride of birth. Innate refinement, instinctive elegance, and suppleness of wit give them their place on the only scale that counts, and these qualities make humble girls the peers of the grandest ladies.

She suffered constantly, feeling that all the attributes of a gracious life, every luxury, should rightly have been hers. The poverty of her rooms—the shabby walls, the worn furniture, the ugly upholstery—caused her pain. All these things that another woman of her class would not even have noticed, tormented her and made her angry. The very sight of the little Breton girl who cleaned for her awoke rueful thoughts and the wildest dreams in her mind. She dreamt of thick-carpeted reception rooms with Oriental hangings, lighted by tall, bronze torches, and with two huge footmen in knee breeches,

1. **dowry** (dou´ rē) *n.* wealth or property given by a woman's family to her husband upon their marriage.

made drowsy by the heat from the stove, asleep in the wide armchairs. She dreamt of great drawing rooms upholstered in old silks, with fragile little tables holding priceless knick-knacks, and of enchanting little sitting rooms redolent of perfume, designed for tea-time chats with intimate friends—famous, sought-after men whose attentions all women longed for.

When she sat down to dinner at her round table with its three-day-old cloth, and watched her husband opposite her lift the lid of the soup tureen and exclaim, delighted: "Ah, a good homemade beef stew! There's nothing better . . ." she would visualize elegant dinners with gleaming silver amid tapestried walls peopled by knights and ladies and exotic birds in a fairy forest; she would think of exquisite dishes served on gorgeous china, and of gallantries whispered and received with sphinx-like smiles while eating the pink flesh of trout or wings of grouse.

She had no proper wardrobe, no jewels, nothing. And those were the only things that she loved—she felt she was made for them. She would have so loved to charm, to be envied, to be admired and sought after.

She had a rich friend, a schoolmate from the convent she had attended, but she didn't like to visit her because it always made her so miserable when she got home again. She would weep for whole days at a time from sorrow, regret, despair, and distress.

Then one evening her husband arrived home looking triumphant and waving a large envelope.

"There," he said, "there's something for you."

She tore it open eagerly and took out a printed card which said:

"The Minister of Education and Madame Georges Ramponneau [ma dam′ zhôrzh ram pə nō′] request the pleasure of the company of M. and Mme. Loisel [lwa zel′] at an evening reception at the Ministry on Monday, January 18th."

Instead of being delighted, as her husband had hoped, she tossed the invitation on the table and muttered, annoyed:

"What do you expect me to do with that?"

"Why, I thought you'd be pleased, dear. You never go out and this would be an occasion for you, a great one! I had a lot of trouble getting it. Everyone wants an invitation; they're in great demand and there are only a few reserved for the employees. All the officials will be there."

She looked at him, irritated, and said impatiently:

"I haven't a thing to wear. How could I go?"

It had never even occurred to him. He stammered:

"But what about the dress you wear to the theater? I think it's lovely. . . ."

He fell silent, amazed and bewildered to see that his wife was crying. Two big tears escaped from the corners of her eyes and rolled slowly toward the corners of her mouth. He mumbled:

"What is it? What is it?"

But, with great effort, she had overcome her misery; and now she answered him calmly, wiping her tear-damp cheeks:

"It's nothing. It's just that I have no evening dress and so I can't go to the party. Give the invitation to one of your colleagues whose wife will be better dressed than I would be."

He was overcome. He said:

"Listen, Mathilde [ma tēld′], how much would an evening dress cost—a suitable one that you could wear again on other occasions, something very simple?"

She thought for several seconds, making her calculations and at the same time estimating how much she could ask for without eliciting an immediate refusal and an exclamation of horror from this economical government clerk.

At last, not too sure of herself, she said:

"It's hard to say exactly but I think I could manage with four hundred francs."

He went a little pale, for that was exactly the amount he had put aside to buy a rifle so that he could go hunting the following summer near Nanterre, with a few friends who went shooting larks around there on Sundays.

However, he said:

"Well, all right, then. I'll give you four hundred francs. But try to get something really nice."

As the day of the ball drew closer, Madame Loisel seemed depressed, disturbed, worried—despite the fact that her dress was ready. One evening her husband said:

"What's the matter? You've really been very strange these last few days."

And she answered:

"I hate not having a single jewel, not one stone, to wear. I shall look so dowdy.[2] I'd almost rather not go to the party."

He suggested:

"You can wear some fresh flowers. It's considered very chic[3] at this time of year. For ten francs you can get two or three beautiful roses."

That didn't satisfy her at all.

"No . . . there's nothing more humiliating than to look

---

2. **dowdy** (dou′dē) *adj.* shabby.
3. **chic** (shēk) *adj.* fashionable.

poverty-stricken among a lot of rich women."

Then her husband exclaimed:

"Wait—you silly thing! Why don't you go and see Madame Forestier [fôr əs tyā'] and ask her to lend you some jewelry. You certainly know her well enough for that, don't you think?"

She let out a joyful cry.

"You're right. It never occurred to me."

The next day she went to see her friend and related her tale of woe.

Madame Forestier went to her mirrored wardrobe, took out a big jewel case, brought it to Madame Loisel, opened it, and said:

"Take your pick, my dear."

Her eyes wandered from some bracelets to a pearl necklace, then to a gold Venetian cross set with stones, of very fine workmanship. She tried on the jewelry before the mirror, hesitating, unable to bring herself to take them off, to give them back. And she kept asking:

"Do you have anything else, by chance?"

"Why yes. Here, look for yourself. I don't know which ones you'll like."

All at once, in a box lined with black satin, she came upon a superb diamond necklace, and her heart started beating with overwhelming desire. Her hands trembled as she picked it up. She fastened it around her neck over her high-necked dress and stood there gazing at herself ecstatically.

Hesitantly, filled with terrible anguish, she asked:

"Could you lend me this one—just this and nothing else?"

"Yes, of course."

She threw her arms around her friend's neck, kissed her ardently, and fled with her treasure.

The day of the party arrived. Madame Loisel was a great success. She was the prettiest woman there—resplendent, graceful, beaming, and deliriously happy. All the men looked at her, asked who she was, tried to get themselves introduced to her. All the minister's aides wanted to waltz with her. The minister himself noticed her.

She danced enraptured—carried away, intoxicated with pleasure, forgetting everything in this triumph of her beauty and the glory of her success, floating in a cloud of happiness formed by all this homage, all this admiration, all the desires she had stirred up—by this victory so complete and so sweet to the heart of a woman.

When she left the party, it was almost four in the morning. Her husband had been sleeping since midnight in a small, deserted sitting room, with three other gentlemen whose wives were having a wonderful time.

He brought her wraps so that they could leave and put them around her shoulders—the plain wraps from her everyday life whose

> *"I hate not having a single jewel, not one stone, to wear. I shall look so dowdy."*

shabbiness jarred with the elegance of her evening dress. She felt this and wanted to escape quickly so that the other women, who were enveloping themselves in their rich furs, wouldn't see her.

Loisel held her back.

"Wait a minute. You'll catch cold out there. I'm going to call a cab."

But she wouldn't listen to him and went hastily downstairs. Outside in the street, there was no cab to be found; they set out to look for one, calling to the drivers they saw passing in the distance.

They walked toward the Seine,[4] shivering and miserable. Finally, on the embankment, they found one of those ancient nocturnal broughams[5] which are only to be seen in Paris at night, as if they were ashamed to show their shabbiness in daylight.

It took them to their door in the Rue des Martyrs, and they went sadly upstairs to their apartment. For her, it was all over. And he was thinking that he had to be at the Ministry by ten.

She took off her wraps before the mirror so that she could see herself in all her glory once more. Then she cried out. The necklace was gone; there was nothing around her neck.

Her husband, already half undressed, asked:

"What's the matter?"

She turned toward him in a frenzy:

"The . . . the . . . necklace—it's gone."

He got up, thunderstruck.

"What did you say? . . . What! . . . Impossible!"

And they searched the folds of her dress, the folds of her wrap, the pockets, everywhere. They didn't find it.

He asked:

"Are you sure you still had it when we left the ball?"

"Yes. I remember touching it in the hallway of the Ministry."

"But if you had lost it in the street, we would have heard it fall. It must be in the cab."

"Yes, most likely. Do you remember the number?"

"No. What about you—did you notice it?"

"No."

dejection ▶ (di jek′ shən) *n.* lowness of spirits; depression

They looked at each other in utter dejection. Finally Loisel got dressed again.

"I'm going to retrace the whole distance we covered on foot," he said, "and see if I can't find it."

And he left the house. She remained in her evening dress, too weak to go to bed, sitting crushed on a chair, lifeless and blank.

Her husband returned at about seven o'clock. He had found nothing.

---

4. **Seine** (sān) river flowing through Paris.
5. **broughams** (bro͞omz) *n.* horse-drawn carriages.

He went to the police station, to the newspapers to offer a reward, to the offices of the cab companies—in a word, wherever there seemed to be the slightest hope of tracing it.

She spent the whole day waiting, in a state of utter hopelessness before such an appalling catastrophe.

Loisel returned in the evening, his face lined and pale; he had learned nothing.

"You must write to your friend," he said, "and tell her that you've broken the clasp of the necklace and that you're getting it mended. That'll give us time to decide what to do."

She wrote the letter at his dictation.

By the end of the week, they had lost all hope.

Loisel, who had aged five years, declared:

"We'll have to replace the necklace."

The next day they took the case in which it had been kept and went to the jeweler whose name appeared inside it. He looked through his ledgers:

"I didn't sell this necklace, madame. I only supplied the case."

Then they went from one jeweler to the next, trying to find a necklace like the other, racking their memories, both of them sick with worry and distress.

In a fashionable shop near the Palais Royal, they found a diamond necklace which they decided was exactly like the other. It was worth 40,000 francs. They could have it for 36,000 francs.

They asked the jeweler to hold it for them for three days, and they stipulated that he should take it back for 34,000 francs if the other necklace was found before the end of February.

Loisel possessed 18,000 francs left him by his father. He would borrow the rest.

He borrowed, asking a thousand francs from one man, five hundred from another, a hundred here, fifty there. He signed promissory notes,[6] borrowed at exorbitant rates, dealt with usurers and the entire race of moneylenders. He compromised his whole career, gave his signature even when he wasn't sure he would be able to honor it, and horrified by the anxieties with which his future would be filled, by the black misery about to descend upon him, by the prospect of physical privation and moral suffering, went to get the new necklace, placing on the jeweler's counter 36,000 francs.

When Madame Loisel went to return the necklace, Madame Forestier said in a faintly waspish tone:

"You could have brought it back a little sooner! I might have needed it."

She didn't open the case as her friend had feared she might. If she

6. **promissory** (präm´ i sôr´ ē) **notes** written promises to pay back borrowed money.

had noticed the substitution, what would she have thought? What would she have said? Mightn't she have taken Madame Loisel for a thief?

Madame Loisel came to know the awful life of the poverty-stricken. However, she resigned herself to it with unexpected fortitude. The crushing debt had to be paid. She would pay it. They dismissed the maid; they moved into an attic under the roof.

She came to know all the heavy household chores, the loathsome work of the kitchen. She washed the dishes, wearing down her pink nails on greasy casseroles and the bottoms of saucepans. She did the laundry, washing shirts and dishcloths which she hung on a line to dry; she took the garbage down to the street every morning, and carried water upstairs, stopping at every floor to get her breath. Dressed like a working-class woman, she went to the fruit store, the grocer, and the butcher with her basket on her arm, bargaining, outraged, contesting each sou[7] of her pitiful funds.

Every month some notes had to be honored and more time requested on others.

Her husband worked in the evenings, putting a shopkeeper's ledgers in order, and often at night as well, doing copying at twenty-five centimes a page.

And it went on like that for ten years.

After ten years, they had made good on everything, including the usurious rates and the compound interest.

disheveled ▶
(di shev′ əld) *adj.* untidy

Madame Loisel looked old now. She had become the sort of strong woman, hard and coarse, that one finds in poor families. **Disheveled**, her skirts askew, with reddened hands, she spoke in a loud voice, slopping water over the floors as she washed them. But sometimes, when her husband was at the office, she would sit down by the window and muse over that party long ago when she had been so beautiful, the belle of the ball.

How would things have turned out if she hadn't lost that necklace? Who could tell? How strange and fickle life is! How little it takes to make or break you!

Then one Sunday when she was strolling along the Champs Elysées[8] to forget the week's chores for a while, she suddenly caught sight of a woman taking a child for a walk. It was Madame Forestier, still young, still beautiful, still charming.

Madame Loisel started to tremble. Should she speak to her? Yes, certainly she should. And now that she had paid everything back, why shouldn't she tell her the whole story?

She went up to her.

---

7. **sou** (so͞o) *n.* former French coin, worth very little; the centime (sän′ tēm′), mentioned later, was also of little value.
8. **Champs Elysées** (shän zā lē zā′) fashionable street in Paris.

"Hello, Jeanne."

The other didn't recognize her and was surprised that this plainly dressed woman should speak to her so familiarly. She murmured:

"But . . . madame! . . . I'm sure . . . You must be mistaken."

"No, I'm not. I am Mathilde Loisel."

Her friend gave a little cry.

"Oh! Oh, my poor Mathilde, how you've changed!"

"Yes, I've been through some pretty hard times since I last saw you and I've had plenty of trouble—and all because of you!"

"Because of me? What do you mean?"

"You remember the diamond necklace you lent me to wear to the party at the Ministry?"

"Yes. What about it?"

"Well, I lost it."

"What are you talking about? You returned it to me."

"What I gave back to you was another one just like it. And it took us ten years to pay for it. You can imagine it wasn't easy for us, since we were quite poor. . . . Anyway, I'm glad it's over and done with."

Madame Forestier stopped short.

"You say you bought a diamond necklace to replace that other one?"

"Yes. You didn't even notice then? They really were exactly alike."

And she smiled, full of a proud, simple joy.

Madame Forestier, profoundly moved, took Mathilde's hands in her own.

profoundly (prō fʊund′ lē) *adv.* deeply

"Oh, my poor, poor Mathilde! Mine was false. It was worth five hundred francs at the most!"

ABOUT THE AUTHOR

Guy de Maupassant (1850–1893)

One of the best-known short-story writers in the world, Guy de Maupassant (gē′ də mō pä sän′) wrote tales that are realistic and pessimistic, and often offer surprise endings.

Following his army service, Maupassant settled in Paris, where he began to develop his skills as a writer, guided by the famous French author Gustave Flaubert. Maupassant also joined a circle of writers led by French novelist Emile Zola. With Zola's encouragement, Maupassant published his first short story, "Ball of Fat," in 1880. The story earned him immediate fame and freed him to write full time. "The Necklace" is his most widely read story.

Close Reading Activities

READ

Comprehension

Reread all or part of the text to help you answer the following questions.

1. From whom does Mathilde borrow the necklace?
2. Why does Mathilde rush off after the party?
3. How long does it take the Loisels to pay their debts?
4. What does Mathilde learn from her friend at the end of the story?

Research: Clarify Details This short story may include references that are unfamiliar to you. Choose at least one unfamiliar detail, and briefly research it. Then, explain how the information you learned from research sheds light on an aspect of the story.

Summarize Write an objective summary of the story. Remember that an objective summary is free from opinion and evaluation.

Language Study

Selection Vocabulary The passages at right appear in "The Necklace." Define each boldface word. Then, for each word, remove the suffix or change the existing suffix to create a new, related word. Identify the new word's part of speech and use it in a sentence.

- They looked at each other in utter **dejection.**
- **Disheveled,** her skirts askew, with reddened hands, she spoke in a loud voice...
- Madame Forestier, **profoundly** moved...

Literary Analysis

Reread the identified passage. Then, respond to the questions that follow.

Focus Passage *(p. 687)*
When she sat down...despair, and distress.

Key Ideas and Details

1. **(a) Interpret:** How do visits to her rich friend affect Mathilde? **(b) Analyze Cause and Effect:** Why does Mathilde react in this way? Explain.

Craft and Structure

2. Mathilde dreams of "knights and ladies...in a fairy forest." **(a) Connect:** What types of stories do these details sound like? **(b) Analyze:** What do these details suggest about the reasons Mathilde is so disappointed by her life? Explain.
3. **Infer:** Mathilde does not think she has a "proper" wardrobe. What would a "proper" wardrobe be, in her **estimation**? Cite details to support your answer.

Integration of Knowledge and Ideas

4. **Make a Judgment:** What contributes more to Mathilde's misery—her circumstances or her desires? Cite story details to support your interpretation.

Situational Irony

In **situational irony,** something happens that directly contradicts the expectations of the characters, the readers, or the audience. Reread the story, and note how it presents situational irony.

1. How do Mathilde's emotions contribute to the loss of the necklace? Explain.
2. How might Mathilde's life have been different if she had told Madame Forestier the truth in the first place? Explain.
3. **Aspiration:** How is the irony of the necklace symbolic of a larger irony in Mathilde's life? Explain, citing examples from the story.

DISCUSS • RESEARCH • WRITE

From Text to Topic **Partner Discussion**

Discuss the following passage with a partner. Listen closely and build on one another's ideas, supporting them with examples from the text.

> Madame Loisel looked old now. She had become the sort of strong woman, hard and coarse, that one finds in poor families. Disheveled, her skirts askew, with reddened hands, she spoke in a loud voice, slopping water over the floors as she washed them. But sometimes, when her husband was at the office, she would sit down by the window and muse over that party long ago when she had been so beautiful, the belle of the ball.

QUESTIONS FOR DISCUSSION

1. How does the life Mathilde aspired to compare with the one she creates?
2. When she muses about the party, do you think her memories are happy? Explain.
3. Does this story teach a lesson? If so, what is it?

Research **Investigate the Topic**

Aspiration in 19th Century France During the nineteenth century—the time setting of "The Necklace"—the old social order in Europe was changing as the Industrial Revolution created a new middle **class** called the *bourgeoisie*. Unlike the nobility or the peasants of the old order, this new class was not clearly defined and included many who aspired to greater wealth and higher status.

Assignment

Conduct research to explore the changing social order of France in the nineteenth century. Consult history books, encyclopedias, and articles about the period. Take clear notes and organize information into categories that reflect each social class. Share your findings in an **infographic** that combines data, images, and text.

PREPARATION FOR ESSAY

You may use the results of this research project in an essay you will write at the end of this section.

ACADEMIC VOCABULARY

Academic terms appear in blue on these pages. If these words are not familiar to you, use a dictionary to find their definitions. Then, use them as you speak and write about the text.

Writing to Sources **Explanatory Text**

In "The Necklace," a borrowed necklace shapes the lives of Mathilde and her husband in a profound way. From the delight it gives Mathilde at the party, to the hardship it causes when lost, to the ironic twist at the end, the necklace is the story's central symbol.

Assignment

Write an **expository essay** in which you analyze and explain the symbolic meaning of the necklace in this story. Follow these steps:

- Write a thesis statement based on your analysis of the necklace as a symbol.
- Create an outline that lays out the points of your analysis.
- **Elaborate** on your analysis with details from the story. Use direct quotations when appropriate to illustrate your ideas.
- End your essay with a conclusion that deepens your thesis statement.

Common Core State Standards

RL.9-10.1, RL.9-10.2, RL.9-10.3, RL.9-10.4, RL.9-10.5, RL.9-10.6, RL.9-10.10; W.9-10.2, W.9-10.2.a–b, W.9-10.2.f, W.9-10.4, W.9-10.7; SL.9-10.1, SL.9-10.4; L.9-10.4, L.9-10.4.b–c

[For full standards wording, see the chart in the front of this book.]

New Directions

Maya Angelou

In 1903 the late Mrs. Annie Johnson of Arkansas found herself with two toddling sons, very little money, a slight ability to read and add simple numbers. To this picture add a disastrous marriage and the burdensome fact that Mrs. Johnson was a Negro.

When she told her husband, Mr. William Johnson, of her dissatisfaction with their marriage, he conceded that he too found it to be less than he expected, and had been secretly hoping to leave and study religion. He added that he thought God was calling him not only to preach but to do so in Enid, Oklahoma. He did not tell her that he knew a minister in Enid with whom he could study and who had a friendly, unmarried daughter. They parted amicably, Annie keeping the one-room house and William taking most of the cash to carry himself to Oklahoma.

◀ **amicably** (am´ i kə blē) *adv.* in a friendly manner

Annie, over six feet tall, big-boned, decided that she would not go to work as a domestic and leave her "precious babes" to anyone else's care. There was no possibility of being hired at the town's cotton gin or lumber mill, but maybe there was a way to make the two factories work for her. In her words, "I looked up the road I was going and back the way I come, and since I wasn't satisfied, I decided to step off the road and cut me a new path." She told herself that she wasn't a fancy cook but that she could "mix groceries well enough to scare hungry away and from starving a man."

She made her plans meticulously and in secret. One early evening to see if she was ready, she placed stones in two five-gallon pails and carried them three miles to the cotton gin. She rested a little, and then, discarding some rocks, she walked in the darkness to the saw mill five miles farther along the dirt road. On her way back to her little house and her babies, she dumped the remaining rocks along the path.

That same night she worked into the early hours boiling chicken and frying ham. She made dough and filled the rolled-out pastry with meat. At last she went to sleep.

The next morning she left her house carrying the meat pies, lard, an iron brazier,[1] and coals for a fire. Just before lunch she appeared in an empty lot behind the cotton gin. As the dinner noon bell rang, she dropped the savors into boiling fat and the aroma rose and floated over to the workers who spilled out of the gin, covered with white lint, looking like specters.

Most workers had brought their lunches of pinto beans and biscuits or crackers, onions and cans of sardines, but they were tempted by the hot meat pies which Annie ladled out of the fat. She wrapped them in newspapers, which soaked up the grease, and offered them for sale at a nickel each. Although business was slow, those first days Annie was determined. She balanced her appearances between the two hours of activity.

So, on Monday if she offered hot fresh pies at the cotton gin and sold the remaining cooled-down pies at the lumber mill for three cents, then on Tuesday she went first to the lumber mill presenting fresh, just-cooked pies as the lumbermen covered in sawdust emerged from the mill.

balmy ▶
(bäm´ ē) *adj.* having the qualities of balm; soothing, mild, pleasant

For the next few years, on balmy spring days, blistering summer noons, and cold, wet, and wintry middays, Annie never disappointed her customers, who could count on seeing the tall, brown-skin woman bent over her brazier, carefully turning the meat pies. When she felt certain that the workers had become dependent on her, she

1. **brazier** (brā´ zhər) *n.* a pan or bowl that holds burning coals or charcoal as a heat source for cooking. In some braziers, food is placed on a grill directly over the flames. Johnson uses hers to heat a pot of boiling fat so that she can deep-fry her pies.

built a stall between the two hives of industry and let the men run to her for their lunchtime provisions.

She had indeed stepped from the road which seemed to have been chosen for her and cut herself a brand-new path. In years that stall became a store where customers could buy cheese, meal, syrup, cookies, candy, writing tablets, pickles, canned goods, fresh fruit, soft drinks, coal, oil, and leather soles for worn-out shoes.

Each of us has the right and the responsibility to assess the roads which lie ahead, and those over which we have traveled, and if the future road looms ominous or unpromising, and the roads back uninviting, then we need to gather our resolve and, carrying only the necessary baggage, step off that road into another direction. If the new choice is also unpalatable, without embarrassment, we must be ready to change that as well.

◀ **ominous** (äm´ ə nəs) *adj.* threatening

ABOUT THE AUTHOR

Maya Angelou (1928–2014)

Maya Angelou's life is a story of overcoming hardships and achieving success. She was born Marguerite Johnson in St. Louis, Missouri, and raised in a rural, segregated section of Arkansas. Growing up, she faced racial discrimination, but also learned strong family values. In 1940, having won a scholarship to study dance and drama, she moved with her mother to San Francisco. Later, as a single mother, Angelou worked as a waitress and a cook. During the 1950s, she toured as a dancer, performing in many important productions.

In 1958, Angelou moved to New York, where she discovered her talents as a writer. She went on to become a poet, a playwright, an editor, an actress, a director, and a teacher. She also became an important leader in the civil rights movement, speaking out for racial and gender equality. Her many literary honors include a nomination for a Pulitzer Prize. In January 1993, she read her poem "On the Pulse of the Morning" at President Bill Clinton's inauguration.

Close Reading Activities

READ

Comprehension

Reread all or part of the text to help you answer the following questions.

1. Why does Annie Johnson have to find a source of income?
2. Why does she decide against a job as a domestic?
3. What does Annie Johnson do once the workers became dependent on her small business?
4. What happens to Annie's business in later years?

Research: Clarify Details This selection may include references that are unfamiliar to you. Choose at least one unfamiliar detail, and briefly research it. Then, explain how the information you learned from research sheds light on an aspect of the text.

Summarize Write an objective summary of the text. Remember that an objective summary is free from opinion and evaluation.

Language Study

Selection Vocabulary The following passages appear in "New Directions." Define each boldface word. Then, use the word in a sentence of your own.

- They parted **amicably,** Annie keeping the one-room house and William taking most of the cash to carry himself to Oklahoma.
- For the next few years, on **balmy** spring days, blistering summer noons, and cold, wet, and wintry middays, Annie never disappointed her customers…
- …and if the future road looms **ominous** or unpromising, and the roads back uninviting, then we need to gather our resolve…

Literary Analysis

Reread the identified passage. Then, respond to the questions that follow.

Focus Passage *(p. 698)*
She made her…looking like specters.

Key Ideas and Details

1. **(a)** What did Annie do to "see if she was ready"? **(b) Infer:** What was her experiment designed to test? Cite details that support your inference.

Craft and Structure

2. **(a) Infer:** Which details suggest the effort it took for Annie to fulfill her plans? Explain. **(b) Distinguish:** Which detail shows how Annie makes her presence known to the cotton gin workers? **(c) Connect:** How do both types of details support the idea that Annie worked out her business **strategy** "meticulously and in secret"?

Integration of Knowledge and Ideas

3. **Interpret:** Explain how the title of this text relates to the story of Annie Johnson's achievement. Cite details from the text to support your explanation.

Anecdote

An **anecdote** is a brief story told to entertain or to make a point. Reread the selection and take notes on ways in which the author uses anecdote.

1. **(a)** What challenges does Annie face? **(b)** Which aspects of those challenges does she accept and which does she reject? Explain.
2. **Aspiration: (a)** What larger lesson about life and its promise does the author believe Annie's example teaches? Explain. **(b)** Do you agree with this position? Support your opinion with sound evidence.

New Directions
Maya Angelou

DISCUSS • RESEARCH • WRITE

From Text to Topic **Panel Discussion**

Conduct a panel discussion about the following passage. Prepare for the discussion by reading the passage closely and taking notes. During the discussion, contribute your ideas, and support them with examples.

> Each of us has the right and the responsibility to assess the roads which lie ahead, and those over which we have traveled, and if the future road looms ominous or unpromising, and the roads back uninviting, then we need to gather our resolve and, carrying only the necessary baggage, step off that road into another direction. If the new choice is also unpalatable, without embarrassment, we must be ready to change that as well.

QUESTIONS FOR DISCUSSION

1. What might be the "necessary baggage?" one would carry on a new path?
2. In what ways is it the individual's right to assess his or her choices in life? In what ways is it a responsibility to chart one's way?

Research **Investigate the Topic**

Aspiration and Social Change Movements When Annie Johnson chose to chart her own path few options were open to her as an African American woman. The women's and civil rights movements would eventually change the possibilities open to both women and African Americans.

Assignment
Conduct research to learn about major events in either the civil or women's rights movements in the United States. Consult history books, encyclopedias, and oral histories. Take clear notes and carefully identify the years in which key events occurred. Share your findings in an annotated **timeline.**

PREPARATION FOR ESSAY

You may use the results of this research in an essay you will write at the end of this section.

Writing to Sources **Argument**

"New Directions" tells the story of a woman who can be considered a "trailblazer"—someone who refused to accept limited choices and, instead, created her own opportunities.

Assignment
Write an **advice column** in which you explain the qualities that make someone a trailblazer and suggest how others can **emulate** those traits. Follow these steps:

- Explain the criteria you will use to define a trailblazer.
- Use Annie Johnson as a model and cite textual details that explain what she did and how she **exemplifies** a trailblazer.
- Use transitional words and phrases to make sure readers can follow the logic of your ideas.

ACADEMIC VOCABULARY

Academic terms appear in blue on these pages. If these words are not familiar to you, use a dictionary to find their definitions. Then, use them as you speak and write about the text.

Common Core State Standards

RI.9-10.1, RI.9-10.2, RI.9-10.4, RI.9-10.5, RI.9-10.6; W.9-10.1, W.9-10.1.c, W.9-10.4, W.9-10.7; SL.9-10.1, SL.9-10.1.a, SL.9-10.4; L.9-10.4
[For full standards wording, see the chart in the front of this book.]

from FRAGILE SELF-WORTH

from The High Price of Materialism

Tim Kasser

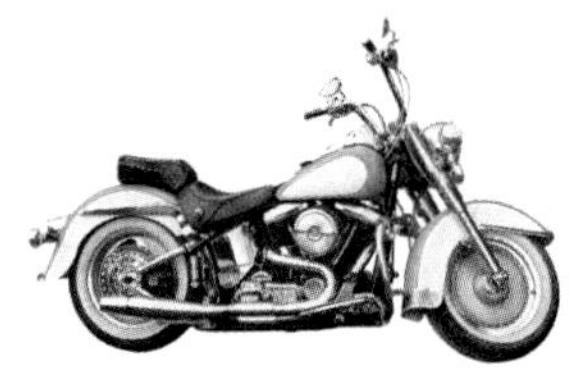

Consider an individual whose goal is to make a million dollars. This is what she conceives of as ideal, having been exposed throughout her life to countless messages claiming that wealth is the primary sign of success, and that the purchase of particular goods and services will make her life meaningful and happy. At the moment, she is worth only about $100,000 and, instead of living in the lap of luxury, she works long hours at a job she does not particularly like, commuting forty-five minutes each way in her six-year-old sedan to and from her comfortable but far from opulent single-family dwelling in the suburbs. Clearly this woman has a discrepancy in her life and, to the extent that her materialistic ideals are central, she is probably dissatisfied. This dissatisfaction motivates her to pursue her materialistic ideals even more strongly, which perpetuates her value system and her unhappiness.

◀ **discrepancy** (di skrep´ən sē) *n.* difference; being in disagreement

Although no single study, to my knowledge, has yet simultaneously verified all the links in this cycle, empirical research does exist that supports each individual link. And as I will show, this vicious cycle can operate even when people's ideals are less immoderate than extreme wealth.

◀ **empirical** (em pir´i kəl) *adj.* based on observations and experiments rather than theory

To begin, materialistic individuals seem to have overly inflated, unrealistic ideas about the worth of wealth and possessions. For example, Shivani Kharina and I asked United States students about qualities that characterize wealthy individuals. Respondents with strong materialistic values were likely to believe that a significant majority of rich people were "smart," "cultured," and "successful in everything." Such inflated ideals about what it means to be wealthy likely set up discrepancies for materialists, most of whom will feel they fall short when they assess these qualities in themselves.

One of the main reasons materialistic individuals have unrealistic ideals about wealth and possessions is that they frequently view such images in the media. In searching out messages that reinforce their value system, they spend many hours watching one primary agent of this value system: television. Research studies using different materialism scales and conducted with individuals in Australia, Denmark, Finland, Hong Kong, India, and the United States have shown that materialistic individuals watch a great deal of television. Although this fact is interesting in some other regards, the main point here is that the minds of materialistic people become saturated with shows and ads exhibiting levels of attractiveness and wealth well above the norm, and thus beyond the level of attainment of the average viewer.

In particular, advertisements on television (and elsewhere) are specifically designed to present idealized images of people who own or use a particular product, in the hope that by pairing these images with the product, viewers will be convinced to purchase the product. We see that a newly improved laundry detergent has better chemicals that our older, dull detergent lacks, and that the woman who uses this detergent has a family pleased with their crisp, clean clothes; whereas, our family never has a word to say about their washed clothes, except to complain. We see that this year's new cars have many improved features compared with our automobile—although it is only two years old—and that people who drive these new cars live in nice neighborhoods, travel to fun places, and have happy spouses. Put in terms of discrepancy theory, ads create an image (being like the person in the ad who has the product and a great life) that is different from our actual state (being ourself, sans product, with an average life). Marketers and businesspeople are banking that advertisement-induced discrepancies will convince us to buy the new improved detergent or take out a lease on the new car, so that our discrepancies can be reduced, and so their bank accounts can be enlarged.

The consequences of believing that the wealthy have wonderful lives and of frequently viewing idealized ads are that people become frustrated with their current state and thus less happy. In a series of studies, Joseph Sirgy, H. Lee Meadow, and Don Rahtz[1] have explored the interrelations of materialism, television, discrepancies, and life satisfaction. In some of this early work, conducted with large samples of elderly Americans, people who watched a lot of television reported low satisfaction with their lives and low overall morale, and also compared themselves unfavorably with other "people in your position." Watching television presumably made viewers feel that they measured up less favorably than other people because they could not live up to what they saw on television; thus, they experienced increased discrepancies and low overall life satisfaction.

In another project, Sirgy, Meadow, Rahtz and their colleagues surveyed over 1,200 adults from the United States, Canada, Australia, China, and Turkey about life satisfaction, their levels of

1. **Joseph Sirgy, H. Lee Meadow, and Don Rahtz** Sirgy and Meadow are professors of marketing at Virginia Tech University; Rahtz is a professor of marketing at the College of William and Mary.

materialism (using the Richins and Dawson scale), and the extent to which they watched television. Participants also reported how favorably they felt in comparison with people they saw on television by responding to statements such as, "I am more well off financially than most people shown on television commercials," and "I consider

Marketing professors Marsha Richins and Scott Dawson developed this scale as part of their 1992 study on materialism. It has since become a key tool for researchers.

Sample items from Richins and Dawson's (1992) materialism scale.

Success

- I admire people who own expensive homes, cars and clothes.
- Some of the most important achievements in life include acquiring material possessions.
- I don't place much emphasis on the amount of material objects a person owns as a sign of succsses.*
- The things I own say a lot about how well I'm doing in life.
- I like to own things that impress people.
- I don't pay much attention to the material objects other people own.*

Centrality

- I usually buy only the things I need.*
- I try to keep my life simple, as far as possessions are concerned.*
- The things I own aren't all that important to me.*
- I enjoy spending money on things that aren't practical.
- Buying things gives me a lot of pleasure.
- I like a lot of luxury in my life.
- I put less emphasis on material things than most people I know.*

Happiness

- I have all the things I really need to enjoy life.*
- My life would be better if I owned certain things I don't have.
- I wouldn't be any happier if I owned nicer things.*
- I'd be happier if I could afford to buy more things.
- It sometimes bothers me quite a bit that I can't afford to buy all the things I'd like.

Participants are presented with these statments and asked how strongly they agree or disagree with them. Items with a * are scored so that disagreement indicates more materialism.

my family to be lower class compared to the typical family they show on television." Finally, participants expressed how satisfied they were in general and with their standard of living or income on the whole.

People with a strong materialistic orientation were likely to watch a lot of television, compare themselves unfavorably with people they saw on television, be dissatisfied with their standard of living, and have low life satisfaction. Using a statistical technique called structural equation modeling, the investigators showed that by watching a great deal of television, materialistic individuals are exposed to images of wealth and beauty that make them dissatisfied with their current economic state. This dissatisfaction with the material realm of their lives "spills over" into their overall sense of satisfaction with their entire life. Of note, most of the support for these results came from the United States sample....

realm ▶ (relm) *n.* area; region

We have seen thus far that materialistic individuals are likely to over-idealize wealth and possessions, and as a result, they are likely to be dissatisfied with aspects of their life, as their actual state cannot measure up to their ideals. The next step in the cycle occurs when this discrepancy drives people to engage in further materialistic behavior. Evidence for this comes from a set of experiments in which Ottmar Braun and Robert Wicklund[2] tested whether people lay claim to materialistic status symbols when they feel that their identity is incomplete (their actual state is below their ideal). In one study, first-year United States college students were more likely to report owning articles displaying the name of their university than were fourth-year students. Similarly, inexperienced German adult tennis players were more likely to prefer certain brands of tennis clothing than were experienced tennis players. In both cases, less experienced individuals were likely to feel that they had not yet reached their ideals (graduation, proficiency in tennis); as a result, they compensated by possessing material symbols to bolster their identity.

In two experiments Braun and Wicklund actually made people feel incomplete in their identities. In one experiment, German law students were randomly assigned to answer questions that made it clear that they had not yet successfully reached their goals; that is, to become lawyers. For example, they were asked about their years of experience, how many conventions they had attended, how many papers they had published, and so on. Participants in the control group were asked about more routine matters unlikely to heighten

2. **Ottmar Braun and Robert Wicklund** Braun is a professor of psychology at the University of Koblenz in Germany; Wicklund is a professor of psychology at the University of Bergen in Norway.

awareness of the discrepancy between their ideal and actual states. Next, all subjects reported where they were going on vacation the coming summer and rated how prestigious and "in fashion" their vacation spot was. Students who felt committed to becoming lawyers (really wanted the goal) and who had been made aware of the discrepancy between their actual and ideal states were especially likely to report that their vacation spot was prestigious and in fashion. This was not the case for students who were uncommitted to becoming lawyers or who were not made more aware of the discrepancy. This study was conceptually replicated by a similar experiment with German business students.

What these results show is that when people realize that they have not reached an ideal they hold, they desire material means of conspicuously demonstrating that they are in fact high-status, worthy individuals. This is compatible with the argument about the ways people who feel insecure sometimes compensate by pursuing materialistic aims. Furthermore, it provides the final piece of evidence for the vicious cycle outlined above: materialistic people over-idealize wealth and possessions and therefore experience discrepancies that cause them to feel dissatisfied and to want further materialistic means of feeling good about themselves. But the satisfactions from this compensation only temporarily improve their sense of worth, and soon they return to another cycle of dissatisfaction.

People with a strong materialistic orientation were likely to watch a lot of television…

ABOUT THE AUTHOR

Tim Kasser (b.1966)

Tim Kasser is a psychologist and a professor of psychology at Knox College in Galesburg, Illinois. He has written numerous books and articles on materialism and aspiration. He has also served as an associate editor for the *Journal of Personality and Social Psychology*. Discussing his work, Kasser says, "My primary interest concerns people's values and goals, and how they relate to quality of life." On the subject of materialism, Kasser comments, "My colleagues and I have found that when people believe materialistic values are important, they report less happiness and more distress, have poorer interpersonal relationships, contribute less to the community, and engage in more ecologically damaging behaviors."

Close Reading Activities

READ

Comprehension

Reread all or part of the text to help you answer the following questions.

1. What is "discrepancy theory"?
2. According to Kasser, how do marketers use discrepancy theory to their advantage?
3. In the author's viewpoint, how do materialistic people perceive what it means to be wealthy?

Research: Clarify Details This essay may include references that are unfamiliar to you. Choose at least one unfamiliar detail, and briefly research it. Then, explain how the information you learned from research sheds light on an aspect of the essay.

Summarize Write an objective summary of the essay. Remember that an objective summary is free from opinion and evaluation.

Language Study

Selection Vocabulary The passages at right appear in the text. Define each boldface word. Then, use each word in a paragraph of your own.

- this woman has a **discrepancy** in her life
- **empirical** research does exist
- the material **realm** of their lives

Literary Analysis

Reread the identified passage. Then, respond to the questions that follow.

Focus Passage *(p. 706)*
People with a strong...bolster their identity.

Key Ideas and Details

1. **(a)** According to Kasser, are materialistic people more or less likely to watch a lot of television? **(b)** In what three ways do TV messages affect materialistic individuals? Explain.

Craft and Structure

2. **(a)** Which statement in the focus passage summarizes ideas stated earlier in the essay? **(b) Connect:** How do the ideas that follow the summary statement relate to those that precede it? Explain. **(c) Analyze:** What purpose does the summary statement serve? Explain.
3. **Analyze:** How does the author support the idea that "incomplete" identity leads to an interest in status symbols? Explain.

Integration of Knowledge and Ideas

4. **Connect:** How does discrepancy theory account for the choices many people make in their purchasing and behavior? Explain.

Evidence

Evidence is the proof an author uses to support an argument. Reread the essay, and take notes on the author's use of evidence.

1. **(a)** Cite one example of each of the following types of evidence in the essay: anecdote; findings from a study; descriptive examples; and, data from experiments. **(b)** For each example you chose, explain the idea or ideas it helps to support.
2. **Aspiration:** Judging from this essay, what are the possible negative effects of certain types of aspiration? Explain.

DISCUSS • RESEARCH • WRITE

From Text to Topic **Group Discussion**

Discuss the following passage with a small group. Build on one another's ideas and support them with details from the text. Summarize your discussion to share with the class as a whole.

> ...materialistic people over-idealize wealth and possessions and therefore experience discrepancies that cause them to feel dissatisfied and to want further materialistic means of feeling good about themselves. But the satisfactions from this **compensation** only temporarily improve their sense of worth, and soon they return to another cycle of dissatisfaction.

QUESTIONS FOR DISCUSSION

1. What does it mean to over-idealize wealth and possessions?
2. Do your observations of both real life and television support Kasser's claims?
3. What is the difference between striving for a better life and being materialistic?

Research **Investigate the Topic**

Social Media Kasser makes a number of claims about television and its role in increasing people's sense of materialism and dissatisfaction. In recent years, television advertising has had to compete with Internet-based media.

Assignment

Conduct research to determine the impact of social media, including its presentation of advertising, on people's materialism and feelings of satisfaction. Consult magazine articles, credible Web sites, and professional publications. Take clear notes and carefully record your sources. Write an **outline** of your findings and share them in a small group discussion.

PREPARATION FOR ESSAY

You may use the results of this research project in an essay you will write at the end of this section.

Writing to Sources **Argument**

This essay makes some strong **assertions** about the level of materialism in Western culture. Which aspects of Tim Kasser's argument do you find most and least **compelling**?

Assignment

Write a **critical response** in which you evaluate Tim Kasser's argument. Follow these steps:

- Write an outline that sets up your argument in your opening paragraph, develops and supports your ideas with evidence in the body, and restates and deepens your claim in the conclusion.
- Cite specific details from the text to support your analysis. Use direct quotations and cite your sources correctly.

ACADEMIC VOCABULARY

Academic terms appear in blue on these pages. If these words are not familiar to you, use a dictionary to find their definitions. Then, use them as you speak and write about the text.

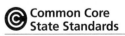

Common Core State Standards

RI.9-10.1, RI.9-10.2, RI.9-10.4, RI.9-10.5, RI.9-10.8; W.9-10.1, W.9-10.1.a, W.9-10.1.e, W.9-10.7; SL.9-10.1, SL.9-10.2; L.9-10.4

[For full standards wording, see the chart in the front of this textbook.]

MAGAZINE ARTICLE

My Possessions Myself

Russell W. Belk

Burglary victims often say that they feel they have been personally polluted.... Since they never had any personal contact with the burglar, what has been violated is the sense of self that exists in their jewelry, clothing, photographs and other personal possessions.

The feeling of violation goes even deeper since the burglar has also wounded the family's sense of identity by penetrating its protective skin, the family home. Clearly, the sense of self is not only individual. Heirlooms, for example, can represent and extend a family's sense of identity, while public buildings, monuments and parks help us develop regional and national identities. Although we Americans think of ourselves as highly individualistic, aggregate, identity is important to us, as the willingness to preserve and restore symbols such as the Statue of Liberty shows.

◀ **aggregate** (ag′rə git) *adj.* gathered together into a whole; taken as one

What we possess is, in a very real way, part of ourselves. Our thoughts and our bodies are normally the most central part of our self-concept. But next in importance are what we do—our occupations and skills—and what we have—our unique set of possessions. The fact that jewelry, weapons and domestic utensils are found in prehistoric burial sites is evidence that we have long considered possessions as part of the person, even after death.

◀ **domestic** (dō mes′ tik) *adj.* having to do with the home, house, or family

We find the same identification of people with possessions in examples as diverse as the reverence religions pay to relics of saints and prophets, the intensity of autograph hounds, the emphasis auctioneers place on the previous ownership of objects up for bid and the difficulty secondhand stores have in selling ... garments worn close to the body. In each case a sense of the prior owners is thought to remain in the things that touched their lives.

We generally include four types of possessions in our personal sense of self: body and body parts, objects, places and time periods, persons and pets. Body parts are normally so well integrated into our identities that we think of them as "me" rather than merely "mine." But several studies have shown that body parts vary widely in their importance to us.

Recently, doctoral student Mark Austin and I gave 248 adults a group of cards, each of which listed a single item in one of the four categories: body parts such as kidneys, hearts and knees; objects such as a favorite dessert or the contents (other than money) of your wallet: places and times such as a favorite city or time of life; and particular people or pets.

We asked people to put the 96 cards in two piles, things they considered self and nonself. They then sorted each of these into two piles representing a little or a lot of self or nonself. We then gave each pile a "self" score (1, 2, 3, 4) and calculated average scores for each card. This gave us a rating of how central each item was to the sense of identity....

Objects were somewhat less central than body parts to the sense of self. Not surprisingly, the most important material possessions were dwellings, automobiles and favorite clothes—each a kind of second skin that embellishes the self we present to others. Automobiles were particularly important to the identities of the men.

embellishes ▶ (em bel´ish əz) *v.* improves; adds decoration

For both houses and cars, the more recently they had been acquired and the better their condition, the more important they were to someone's sense of self; and the more important they were, the better care they got—dusting, painting and remodeling in the case of houses; washing, waxing and oil changing for the cars. The similarities stopped when it came to the possession's age. Here, older houses and newer cars were considered more important parts of the self. It may be that houses are looked on as heirlooms, for which age is a virtue, while new cars run and look better.

Other objects important to a sense of self included favorite rooms, artwork, jewelry and clothing—all meaningful attachments to the body and the home. We found that academics were especially likely to cite books as favorite possessions, perhaps because they represent the knowledge on which their work is based. For other people, sporting goods represent what they can or could do, while the contents of wallets or purses were important because they indicated central characteristics such as age, sex and organizational memberships, as well as personal power to spend (credit cards) and travel (driver's license).

For some, collections were a significant part of their extended selves—possessions that had been acquired through considerable personal effort. For others, heirlooms were vital parts of family self, providing a sense of the past and of continuity with prior generations.

The third category of possessions important to the extended self is the less tangible one of time and place. To most of the people in our study, and others we interviewed, childhood was an especially important time of life. They tended to cherish memories, accurate or otherwise, of this period. We found that older people were most likely to name nearby cities, states and countries as important to their sense of self, while younger ones generally named places farther away.

Our interviews showed that people can be as acquisitive of places they visit as they are of objects they collect. We even found a sedentary form of place acquisition. An Amish[1] man whose religion forbids him to drive a motorized vehicle collected the hometowns of people who visited his community. While speaking to us, he reeled off a list of their states and countries much as other people mention the places they have visited personally.

There were few surprises in the final major category of possessions—people and pets—that individuals used to define themselves. The most important people were generally parents, spouses, siblings, children and favorite friend of the same sex. Prominent political figures and favorite stars of movies and television were usually at the opposite end of the "selfness" continuum, unrelated to the sense of identity.

The common idea that some people consider their pets part of the family (and therefore of themselves) was supported by a series of interviews with people who owned dogs, cats, ferrets, birds and various other animals. While not all owners identified strongly with their pets, some felt closer to them than to their immediate families.

Is the fact that we are what we possess desirable or undesirable? There is no simple answer, but certain advantages and disadvantages seem evident. Among the advantages is that possessions provide a sense of the past. Many studies have shown that the loss of possessions that follows natural disasters or that occurs when elderly people are put in institutions is often traumatic. What people feel in these circumstances is, quite literally, a loss of self. Possessions also help children develop self-esteem, and learning to share possessions may be important in the growth of both individual and aggregate senses of self.

Incorporating possessions deeply into the sense of self can also have undesirable consequences. Too much attachment to pets can reflect an unhealthy drive to dominate and possess power and result in less devotion to family and friends. Investing too much of the self in collections and other possessions may displace love from people to things. Regarding other people as parts of our self can lead to jealousy and excessive possessiveness. Or by identifying too strongly with a spouse or child, we may end up living vicariously, instead of developing our own potential. As Erich Fromm[2] asked in his book *To Have or To Be*, "If I am what I have and if what I have is lost, who then am I?"

---

1. **Amish** (äm´ish) belonging to a Christian group whose members favor plain lives free of modern conveniences.
2. **Erich Fromm** (1900–1980) philosopher who studied the connections between psychology and society.

Close Reading Activities

READ

Comprehension

Reread all or part of the text to help you answer the following questions.

1. According to Belk, what four types of possessions define our identities?
2. Which type of possession is most central to our sense of self?
3. What have studies shown about how the loss of possessions affects people?

Research: Clarify Details This article may include references that are unfamiliar to you. Choose at least one unfamiliar detail, and briefly research it. Then, explain how the information you learned from research sheds light on an aspect of the article.

Summarize Write an objective summary of the article. Remember that an objective summary is free from opinion and evaluation.

Language Study

Selection Vocabulary The phrases at right appear in the article. Define each boldface word. Then, explain why each is a strong choice to express the author's ideas.

- ...jewelry, weapons and **domestic** utensils...
- ...**aggregate** identity is important to us...
- ...a kind of second skin that **embellishes** the self we present to others...

Literary Analysis

Reread the identified passage. Then, respond to the questions that follow.

Focus Passage *(p. 711)*

The feeling of violation...touched their lives.

Key Ideas and Details

1. What evidence shows that possessions have long been part of people's identities? Explain.

Craft and Structure

2. Answer the following questions about the second paragraph of the focus passage: **(a) Distinguish:** Which sentence states the main idea? **(b) Paraphrase:** How might that idea be restated? **(c) Connect:** What evidence supports that idea? **(d) Analyze:** How does the paragraph's structure help readers follow the evidence to the author's conclusion? Explain.

Integration of Knowledge and Ideas

3. **Extend:** Explain how memories are a type of possession. Cite textual details in your response.

Connotations

Denotation is the literal meaning of a word. **Connotations** are the emotional connections a word carries. Synonyms share denotations but often differ widely in their connotations. Reread the article, and take notes on the connotations of key words.

1. **(a)** What are the connotations of *polluted*? **(b)** How does that word add to Belk's discussion of burglary victims' feelings? Explain.
2. **(a)** What are the connotations of *cherish*? **(b)** How does that word help convey people's attitudes towards childhood memories?

DISCUSS • RESEARCH • WRITE

From Text to Topic **Partner Discussion**

Discuss the following passage with a partner. Take notes during the discussion. Contribute your own ideas, and support them with examples from the text.

> ...possessions provide a sense of the past. Many studies have shown that the loss of possessions that follows natural disasters or that occurs when elderly people are put in institutions is often traumatic. What people feel in these circumstances is, quite literally, a loss of self.

QUESTIONS FOR DISCUSSION

1. This passage suggests that a sense of the past is important to a strong sense of identity. Do you agree?
2. How might cultural differences add to or minimize this strong identification with possessions?

Research **Investigate the Topic**

Grave Goods Belk cites the objects that have been found in ancient burial grounds as evidence that people have always considered possessions important to their identities. For archeologists, these "grave goods" provide valuable insights into how early peoples lived, what they valued, and how their societies were structured.

Assignment

Conduct research on an ancient culture and what grave goods reveal about the society. Consult books and articles, especially on the topics of archaeology, anthropology, and art history. Take clear notes and organize them into a brief outline, carefully recording your sources. Write up your findings in a **research report.**

PREPARATION FOR ESSAY

You may use the results of this research in an essay you will write at the end of this section.

Writing to Sources **Argument**

In "My Possessions Myself," Russell Belk asks, "Is the fact that we are what we possess desirable or undesirable?" Although he cites evidence for both answers, he does not arrive at a final determination on the question.

Assignment

Write a **persuasive essay** in which you take and defend a position on the question Belk poses, citing evidence from both the text and your own experience. Follow these steps:

- Restate Belk's question and express a clear position for one answer or the other.
- Organize your reasoning logically and support your ideas with relevant evidence from Belk's article and from your own observations.
- Use rhetorical devices such as parallelism to give rhythm and balance to your writing and lend strength to your position.

ACADEMIC VOCABULARY

Academic terms appear in blue on these pages. If these words are not familiar to you, use a dictionary to find their definitions. Then, use them as you speak and write about the text.

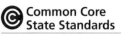

Common Core State Standards

RI.9-10.1, RI.9-10.2, RI.9-10.4, RI.9-10.5, RI.9-10.6; W.9-10.1, W.9-10.1a, W.9-10.7; SL.9-10.1; L.9-10.1.a, L.9-10.4, L.9-10.5, L.9-10.5.a

[For full standards wording, see the chart in the front of this book.]

from *The New Yorker*

"Have you ever tried buying lots of stuff?"

Close Reading Activities

READ • DISCUSS • WRITE

Comprehension

Look at the cartoon again and reread the caption to help you answer the following questions.

1. What is the setting and who are the two characters in this cartoon? Explain how you know.
2. **(a)** Which character is asking the question in the caption? **(b)** Which details reveal that information?

Common Core State Standards

RL.9-10.7; W.9-10.3, W.9-10.3.a, W.9-10.3.b; SL.9-10.1, SL.9-10.1.a
[For full standards wording, see the chart in the front of this book.]

Critical Analysis

Key Ideas and Details

1. **Infer:** What inferences can you make about the nature of the conversation that has preceded the question stated in the caption? Explain your thinking.
2. **(a)** What suggestion is the woman making to the man? **(b) Evaluate:** Is that the kind of suggestion you would expect in this setting? Why or why not?

Craft and Structure

3. **Interpret:** Which details in the drawing of the man suggest his feelings or state of mind? Explain.
4. **Analyze:** How does the **incongruity** between the man's situation and the woman's response create humor? Explain.

Integration of Knowledge and Ideas

5. **Connect:** How does the problem and proposed solution suggested by this cartoon connect to the texts you have read in this section? Explain.

ACADEMIC VOCABULARY

Academic terms appear in blue on these pages. If these words are not familiar to you, use a dictionary to find their definitions. Then, use them as you speak and write about the cartoon.

From Text to Topic **Group Discussion**

Discuss the cartoon and its message with classmates. Use the following questions to focus your conversation.

1. What advice might Lady Bracknell give to the man in this cartoon?
2. What advice might Annie Johnson give?
3. What advice might Tim Kasser give?

Writing to Sources **Narrative**

Write a brief **short story** in which you describe the events that might have led up to the scene **depicted** in the cartoon. Be sure to establish a conflict or problem and use dialogue and description to portray characters and events.

Assessment: Synthesis

Speaking and Listening: Group Discussion

Aspiration and Difference The texts in this section vary in genre, length, style, and perspective. However, all of them address the idea of aspiration. To a great extent, our aspirations reflect our perceptions of difference. After all, we can only aspire to become something if we see it as different from who or what we already are. This topic is, thus, fundamentally related to the Big Question addressed in this unit: **Do our differences define us?**

Assignment

Conduct discussions. With a small group of classmates, conduct a discussion about issues of aspiration and difference. Refer to the texts in this section, other texts you have read, the research you have conducted and your personal experience and knowledge to support your ideas. Begin your discussion by addressing the following questions:

- Why do people often want what they do not have?
- Which kinds of aspirations can be positive and which can be negative?
- How can our aspirations make us feel part of a group?
- How can our aspirations separate or divide us?
- Should we value the opinions of others when we make decisions about what we want for ourselves?

Summarize and present your ideas. After you have fully explored the topic, summarize your discussion and present your findings to the class as a whole.

▲ Refer to the selections you read in Part 3 as you complete the activities on this assessment.

Criteria for Success

✓ **Organizes the group effectively**
Agree upon your goals for the discussion and rules for achieving those goals. Choose a timekeeper to make sure the discussion takes no longer than twenty minutes. Have another volunteer present the questions.

✓ **Focuses discussion on the central issues**
As a group, keep the discussion on point and avoid straying into unrelated topics.

✓ **Allows for all viewpoints**
Structure the discussion so that each person presents his or her initial reactions. Then, open the floor to comments.

✓ **Settles disagreements fairly**
If disagreement occurs, invite those expressing opposing viewpoints to summarize their positions. Then, work to arrive at a consensus on the disputed issue. Respect all opinions, regardless of the group decision.

USE NEW VOCABULARY

As you speak and share ideas, work to use the vocabulary words you have learned in this unit. The more you use new words, the more you will "own" them.

Writing: **Narrative**

Aspiration and Differences What we want and the ways in which we are unique—our aspirations and our differences—help us build our personal identities.

Assignment

Write a **personal narrative,** or true story about your own life, in which you discuss a quality, experience, or trait that sets you apart. Describe how you have embraced that difference or how you have struggled against it. Explain how the difference has affected your aspirations. Relate your experiences to one or more of the texts you have read in this section as well as the research you have conducted.

Common Core State Standards

W.9-10.3, W.9-10.3.a–e; SL.9-10.1, SL.9-10.1.a–d; L.9-10.6

[For full standards wording, see the chart in the front of this book.]

Criteria for Success

Purpose/Focus

✓ **Connects specific incidents with larger ideas**
Make meaningful connections between your experiences and the texts you have read in this section.

✓ **Clearly conveys the significance of the story**
Describe meaningful insights you have gained through your personal observations and through your reading and research.

Organization

✓ **Creates a smooth progression of events**
Avoid stringing together a series of unrelated events. Instead, construct a narrative in which one event leads logically to the next and builds to a meaningful whole.

Development of Ideas/Elaboration

✓ **Includes well-chosen details**
Choose relevant details from your readings and research and pertinent observations from your life.

✓ **Uses narrative techniques effectively**
Consider using plot devices, such as flashback or foreshadowing, as well as imagery and sensory language to bring your narrative to life.

Language

✓ **Uses precise language**
Convey observations and insights with vivid, accurate language.

Conventions

✓ **Eliminates errors**
Check your narrative to eliminate errors in grammar, spelling, and punctuation.

WRITE TO EXPLORE

Writing can help you appreciate your own experiences and learn more about an issue. As you write, you may have insights you did not expect. If these insights are relevant to the topic, include them in your draft.

Writing to Sources: **Explanatory Text**

Aspiration and Differences The related readings in this section present a range of ideas about identity and aspiration. They raise questions, such as the following, about how we define ourselves, how we choose what we want, and how we change the roles we play role in the world:

- What is the relationship between our identities, our perceptions, and our aspirations?
- In what ways, if any, do the things we own define who we are?
- Are aspiration and materialism related? If so, how?
- Is dissatisfaction with one's lot healthy or unhealthy, positive or negative?

Focus on the question that intrigues you the most, and then complete the following assignment.

Assignment

Write an **essay** in which you examine connections between aspiration and identity. Support your ideas with textual evidence from two or more of the texts in this section as well as from the related research you have conducted.

Prewriting and Planning

Organize evidence and generate ideas. Use a chart like the one shown to gather textual details and develop your central and supporting ideas. Modify the chart as your ideas change or as you draw on new information.

Focus Question: Are aspiration and materialism related? If so, in what ways?

Text	Passage	Notes
"The Necklace"	She suffered constantly, feeling that all the attributes of a gracious life, every luxury, should rightly have been hers.	Mathilde's identity and her desires are completely connected to material things.
"Fragile Self-Worth"	This dissatisfaction motivates her to pursue her materialistic ideals even more strongly, which perpetuates her value system and her unhappiness.	People whose aspirations center on material goals often remain unhappy.
Example Central Idea: Certain types of aspiration are driven by materialism and insecurity, while others are not.		

Establish a clear organization. Write an informal outline in which you state your central and supporting ideas, show how one leads to the next, and identify strong and relevant supporting evidence for each idea. Use this outline to create a structured, well-organized essay.

INCORPORATE RESEARCH

As you write an informal outline, refer to the notes you made while doing research in this section. You may find details that will support your central idea.

Drafting

Sequence your ideas. Present your ideas in a logical sequence, either building up to your strongest point or beginning with it. Choose details from your chart to support each point. Be sure that every idea is supported with strong, relevant evidence.

Frame and connect ideas. Introduce your topic and central idea. Then, organize your supporting ideas into paragraphs and connect them with appropriate transitional words. If relationships between your ideas are unclear, consider why you chose to connect those ideas and revise to clarify the relationships.

Vary your presentation of ideas. Consider using special formatting such as bulleted lists or graphics to present information concisely.

Revising and Editing

Evaluate support. Make sure that your central idea is clearly stated, that your supporting ideas follow logically, and that evidence is relevant and accurate. Look for ideas that are inadequately developed or supported and consider adding details to strengthen them.

Review word choice. Use vocabulary specific to the topic. Make sure your word choices accurately convey your ideas.

W.9-10.2, W.9-10.2.a–f, W.9-10.5, W.9-10.9; L.9-10.3

[For full standards wording, see the chart in the front of this book.]

CITE RESEARCH CORRECTLY

You may use either parenthetical references or footnotes to cite sources. Parenthetical citations are more immediate, but footnotes allow you to minimize interruptions to your essay.

Self-Evaluation Rubric

Use the following criteria to evaluate the effectiveness of your essay.

Criteria	Rating Scale			
	not very .... *very*			
PURPOSE/FOCUS Introduces a specific topic; provides a concluding section that follows from and supports the information or explanation presented	1	2	3	4
ORGANIZATION Organizes complex ideas, concepts, and information to make important connections and distinctions; uses appropriate and varied transitions to link the major sections, create cohesion, and clarify relationships among ideas	1	2	3	4
DEVELOPMENT OF IDEAS/ELABORATION Develops the topic with well-chosen, relevant, and sufficient facts, extended definitions, concrete details, quotations, or other information and examples appropriate to the audience's knowledge of the topic	1	2	3	4
LANGUAGE Uses precise language and domain-specific vocabulary to manage the complexity of the topic; establishes and maintains a formal style and an objective tone	1	2	3	4
CONVENTIONS Attends to the norms and conventions of the discipline	1	2	3	4

Independent Reading

Titles for Extended Reading

In this unit, you have read texts in a variety of genres. Continue to read on your own. Select works that you enjoy, but challenge yourself to explore new authors and works of increasing depth and complexity. The titles suggested below will help you get started.

INFORMATIONAL TEXT

American Speeches: Political Oratory from the Revolution to the Civil War EXEMPLAR TEXT
Edited by Ted Widmer
Library of America, 2006

This collection of famous American **speeches** features works from some of the country's most memorable speakers, including Martin Luther King, Jr., and Patrick Henry.

Reaching Out
by Francisco Jiménez

In this award-winning **autobiography,** the son of Mexican immigrants shares his experiences as the first member of his family to attend university. As Jiménez adjusts to university life, his family's traditions of hard work and determination help him overcome the challenges of poverty and prejudice.

Up Close: Rachel Carson
by Ellen Levine

With a love of nature and a passion for science, Rachel Carson revolutionized the world's thinking about the environment. This **biography** tells the story of her struggle to protect the beauty of nature for us all.

Narrative of Sojourner Truth
by Mark Kurlansky

Born a slave in New York State, Sojourner Truth became a symbol of freedom and justice for both African Americans and women. Her **autobiographical narrative,** dictated by Truth to a neighbor, reveals the transformation of an illiterate slave into a provocative, passionate speaker who paved the way for African American civil rights and feminism.

LITERATURE

Our Town
by Thornton Wilder
Harper Collins, 2003

This Pulitzer Prize–winning **drama** explores the daily lives of the citizens of Grover's Corners, a typical American small town. Through everyday events and conversations, the play's characters reveal the impermanence of life and the desperate need to value every moment, no matter how ordinary.

The Glass Menagerie
by Tennessee Williams EXEMPLAR TEXT

In his first major **drama,** Williams shows what happens when the lid is lifted off lives of quiet desperation. The situation appears simple. Tom Wingfield, a man frustrated with his dead-end life, invites a friend to meet his sister Laura. However, when Tom's fragile sister and overprotective mother meet his friend, the consequences prove complicated—and devastating.

Twentieth-Century American Drama EXEMPLAR TEXT

The **plays** in this volume speak powerfully about the American mind and spirit during the twentieth century. Through these pages, get acquainted with some giants of the American theater—Lorraine Hansberry, Arthur Miller, Thornton Wilder, and Tennessee Williams.

ONLINE TEXT SET

POEM
The Horses Edwin Muir

REFLECTIVE ESSAY
A Celebration of Grandfathers
Rudolfo Anaya

REFLECTIVE ESSAY
Desiderata Elizabeth McCracken

Preparing to Read Complex Texts

Attentive Reading As you read literature on your own, bring your imagination and questions to the text. The questions shown below and others that you ask as you read will help you learn and enjoy literature even more.

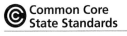

Reading Literature/ Informational Text

10. By the end of grade 9, read and comprehend literature, including stories, dramas, poems, and literary nonfiction in the grades 9–10 text complexity band proficiently, with scaffolding as needed at the high end of the range.

When reading drama, ask yourself...

Comprehension: **Key Ideas and Details**

- Who is the main character? What struggles does this character face?
- What other characters are important? How do these characters relate to the main character?
- Is there more than one conflict? If so, how do they connect?
- What is the setting of the play? Does the setting cause conflicts or affect the characters' actions? Why or why not?
- Is there more than one setting? If so, do the settings create different moods or conflicts?
- Are the characters, setting, and events believable? Why or why not?

Text Analysis: **Craft and Structure**

- How is the play structured? How many acts does it have? What events unfold in each act?
- Are there multiple plots—a main plot and a subplot? If so, how do the different plots relate to each other?
- Does the dialogue sound authentic and believable? Why or why not?
- What do the stage directions tell me about the characters and situations? In what other ways do I learn about the characters?
- At what point in the play do I feel the most concern for the characters? Why?

Connections: **Integration of Knowledge and Ideas**

- What theme or insight do I think the play conveys? Is that theme or insight important and true?
- What do I find most interesting, unusual, or powerful about this play?
- In what ways is the play similar to or different from others I have read or seen?
- What actors would I choose to play the roles in this play?
- If I were directing this play, how might I stage it?
- After reading this play, do I want to read others by this playwright? Why or why not?

UNIT 5

THE BIG ?

Do heroes have responsibilities?

UNIT PATHWAY

PART 1
SETTING EXPECTATIONS

- INTRODUCING THE BIG QUESTION
- CLOSE READING WORKSHOP

PART 2
TEXT ANALYSIS
GUIDED EXPLORATION

PERILOUS JOURNEYS

PART 3
TEXT SET
DEVELOPING INSIGHT

DEFINING HEROISM

PART 4
DEMONSTRATING INDEPENDENCE

- INDEPENDENT READING
- ONLINE TEXT SET

CLOSE READING TOOL

Use this tool to practice the close reading strategies you learn.

STUDENT eTEXT

Bring learning to life with audio, video, and interactive tools.

ONLINE WRITER'S NOTEBOOK

Easily capture notes and complete assignments online.

Find all Digital Resources at **pearsonrealize.com**

Introducing the Big Question

Do heroes have responsibilities?

Heroes are all around us. We find them in literature, film and TV, and in the real world. Some heroes show great strength of character or unusual depth of wisdom and knowledge. They may make selfless choices, serving others and fighting for justice. Often, they exhibit courage, honesty, and leadership. However, some heroes display none of these qualities—or not in obvious ways. They may be ordinary people who, in a moment of crisis, stand up when no one else does. Think about the qualities or circumstances that spur a hero to action. Is it simply a question of character? Is it a sense of responsibility?

Exploring the Big Question

Collaboration: One-on-One Discussion Start thinking about the Big Question by listing heroes you have encountered in media or in real life. They might be people you know personally, have read about in works of nonfiction, have watched on TV shows or in movies, or have discovered in works of fiction. Describe a hero from each of these categories:

- a person whose courageous act saves or protects those who are in danger
- someone who chooses honesty or integrity over self-interest
- a leader who guides others to success
- a person who sacrifices himself or herself to help others
- someone who acts to help others without a desire for reward or recognition

After you have completed your list, share it with a partner. As you describe each person on your list, provide details that show why he or she is a hero. As your partner reads from his or her list, listen carefully and ask questions to clarify details. Then, use the vocabulary listed on the page at right as you discuss whether a sense of responsibility motivated the heroes on your lists. Work to clarify, challenge, and enrich each other's ideas. Finally, come to an agreement on the qualities that make a hero. Select one or two examples to share with the class.

Connecting to the Literature Each reading in this unit will give you additional insight into the Big Question. After reading each selection, pause to consider the heroic qualities of the characters.

Vocabulary

Acquire and Use Academic Vocabulary The term "academic vocabulary" refers to words you typically encounter in scholarly and literary texts and in technical and business writing. It is language that helps to express complex ideas. Review the definitions of these academic vocabulary words.

choices (choi´ səz) *n.* alternatives, a variety of possibilities from which a person can make a selection

hero (hir´ o) *n.* person who is admired for brave or noble actions

identify (ī den´ tə fī´) *v.* recognize as being a particular person or thing

intentions (in ten´ shənz) *n.* aims, ends, or purposes of someone's actions or behavior

serve (surv) *v.* perform duties or take on responsibilities for the benefit of others or for a higher purpose

Use these words as you complete Big Question activities in this unit that involve reading, writing, speaking, and listening.

Gather Vocabulary Knowledge Additional words related to heroes and responsibility are listed below. Categorize the words by deciding whether you know each one well, know it a little bit, or do not know it at all.

character	justice	standard
honesty	morality	wisdom
imitate	obligation	
involvement	responsibility	

Then, complete the following steps:

1. Work with a partner to write each word on one side of an index card and its definition on the other side.
2. Verify each definition by looking the word up in a print or an online dictionary. Revise your definitions as needed.
3. Place the cards with the words facing up in a pile.
4. Take turns drawing a word card, pronouncing the word, and making a true or false statement that uses the word and is related to ideas of heroism and responsibility. Here is an example: *Thoughtlessness is typical of a heroic character.* Invite your partner to determine whether the statement is usually true or usually false.

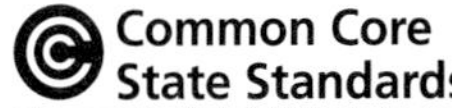

Common Core State Standards

Speaking and Listening

1. Initiate and participate effectively in a range of collaborative discussions with diverse partners on *grades 9–10 topics, texts, and issues,* building on others' ideas and expressing their own clearly and persuasively.

1.c. Propel conversations by posing and responding to questions that relate to broader themes or larger ideas; actively incorporate others into the discussion; and clarify, verify, or challenge ideas and conclusions.

Language

4.c. Consult general and specialized reference materials, both print and digital, to find the pronunciation of a word or determine or clarify its precise meaning, its part of speech, or its etymology.

4.d. Verify the preliminary determination of the meaning of a word or phrase.

6. Acquire and use accurately general academic and domain-specific words and phrases, sufficient for reading, writing, speaking, and listening at the college and career readiness level; demonstrate independence in gathering vocabulary knowledge when considering a word or phrase important to comprehension or expression.

Close Reading Workshop

In this workshop, you will learn an approach to reading that will deepen your understanding of literature and will help you better appreciate the author's craft. The workshop includes models for the close reading, discussion, research, and writing activities you will complete as you study literature in this unit. After you have reviewed the strategies and models, practice your skills with the Independent Practice selection.

Common Core State Standards

RL.9-10.1, RL.9-10.2, RL.9-10.3, RL.9-10.4, RL.9-10.5; W.9-10.2, W.9-10.7, W.9-10.9.a; SL.9-10.1

[For full standards wording, see the chart in the front of this book.]

CLOSE READING: **THE ORAL TRADITION**

In Part 2 of this unit, you will focus on reading various types of literature influenced by the oral tradition. Use these strategies as you read the texts:

Comprehension: **Key Ideas and Details**

- Read first for basic meaning.
- Use context clues to help you determine the meanings of unfamiliar words.
- Identify unfamiliar details, such as place names or cultural references, that you might need to clarify through research.
- Distinguish between information a narrator or characters state directly and ideas readers must infer.

Ask yourself questions such as these:

- Who are the main characters, and what are their relationships to one another?
- When and where does the action take place?
- What conflicts do characters face, and how do they respond to those conflicts?

Text Analysis: **Craft and Structure**

- Think about the relationship between the genre, or type of work, and the story it tells.
- Analyze the features that contribute to the style of the work. Notice the use of regional speech or cultural content.
- Note the presence of unusual figures of speech and other literary elements that create memorable characters and situations.
- Consider the story's narrative structure, including the use of flashbacks and foreshadowing.

Ask yourself questions such as these:

- How does the story's setting (both time and place) contribute to the conflict?
- Are characters realistic or exaggerated? Do they have a single dominant trait, or do they display complex qualities? Do they remain the same, or do they change?
- Why do the characters behave as they do? How do their actions advance the plot?

Connections: **Integration of Knowledge and Ideas**

- Look for connections among ideas. Identify causes and effects, and comparisons and contrasts.
- Look for symbols and archetypes, and evaluate their effect on the meaning of the story.
- Compare this work with similar works you have read.

Ask yourself questions such as these:

- How has this work increased my knowledge of a subject, culture, or type of traditional tale?
- In what ways is this work unique or worthy of reading?

Read

As you read this tall tale, take note of the annotations that model ways to closely read the text.

Reading Model

"Sally Ann Thunder Ann Whirlwind Crockett"
Retold by Caron Lee Cohen

Sally Ann Thunder Ann Whirlwind Crockett lived long ago near the Mississippi River. Her husband was Davy Crockett.[1] Now that lady was made of thunder with a little dash of whirlwind. She wore a beehive for a bonnet and a bearskin for a dress. Her toothpick was a bowie knife. She could stomp a litter of wildcats and smash a band of starving wolves. She could outscream an eagle and outclaw a mountain lion. She could skin a bear faster than an alligator swallows a fish. She walked like an ox and ran like a fox. She could wade the wide Mississippi without getting wet. And she could jump over the Grand Canyon with both eyes shut. She could do just about anything. And nothing on earth scared her. Nothing! But she never bragged. And she never fought a man, woman, or critter for no good reason.[2]

Now Mike Fink lived along the Mississippi, too. He was a bad man, always looking for a fight. He could beat any man except his enemy Davy Crockett. Their fights ended in a draw. And when Mike Fink wasn't fighting, he was bragging!

One day, Mike walked into a tavern. He jumped on a table and roared, "Half of me is wild horse and half is alligator. And the rest is crooked nails and red-hot snapping turtles. I can outrun, outshoot, outfight any man! If any man says that's not true, let him step up and fight."[3]

No man dared to fight bad man Mike Fink. But Davy Crockett was in that tavern. And he was sick of hearing Mike Fink brag. "You don't scare me," Davy said. "And you couldn't even scare my sweet little wife, Sally Ann Thunder Ann Whirlwind Crockett."[4] Mike roared, "I'll bet you a dozen wildcats I can SCARE HER TEETH LOOSE!" And the bet was made.

So one evening, by the river, Mike found an alligator. He skinned it and crept inside the skin. Then he crawled along the river. And there was Sally Ann Thunder Ann Whirlwind Crockett out for her nightly walk. Mike crawled toward Sally Ann. He poked the alligator's head here and there. He opened its jaws big and wide. He let out a horrible cry. He nearly scared himself out of the alligator's skin. But Sally Ann wasn't scared. Not one little bit. She just stepped aside as if that alligator were a dead stump.

Key Ideas and Details

1 Although the Mississippi River is a real place, the fictional character of Sally Ann lived in the nonspecific time of "long ago." In stories, she is married to Davy Crockett, a real-life American frontiersman whose adventures became the basis for dozens of tales.

Craft and Structure

2 Sally Ann has all the qualities of a classic American tall tale hero. She is a fearless force of nature who can vanquish fierce animals and tame the wilderness. She also happens to be female—a trait less common in tall tale heroes.

Integration of Knowledge and Ideas

3 Bad bragging Mike Fink is a stock (or common) character type in folk literature. This character type may be strong or smart, but never equals the hero. Mike's challenge introduces a classic story pattern that gives the hero—whom the reader knows cannot be defeated—another chance to shine.

Craft and Structure

4 Sally Ann is many things, but "sweet" and "little" she is not. This play on gender stereotypes shows that the Crocketts know how to manipulate Mike Fink. The verbal irony also adds humor.

So Mike crawled closer and stood up on his hind legs. Then he threw his front paws around Sally Ann. Sally Ann Thunder Ann Whirlwind Crockett didn't let just any critter hug her. Her rage rose higher than a Mississippi flood. Her eyes flashed lightning. The night sky lit up like day.[5] Mike was scareder[6] than a raccoon looking down a rifle barrel. But he thought of his bet with Davy Crockett. He kept circling Sally Ann and wagging his tail.

"That's enough, you worm!" said Sally Ann Thunder Ann Whirlwind Crockett. And she pulled out her toothpick. With one swing, she cut off the head of that alligator. It flew fifty feet into the Mississippi River. Then she could see it was just bad man Mike Fink playing a trick.

"You lowly skunk!" she said. "Trying to scare a lady out on her nightly walk.[7] Now stand up and fight like a man." She threw down her toothpick and rolled up her sleeves. She battered poor Mike till he fainted. She was still in a rage, but she wouldn't touch a man who was down. So she just walked off.

Mike didn't wake up till the next day. He couldn't tell his friends he had been beaten by a woman. Instead he bragged! "I got swallowed by an alligator. But I was chock full of fight and cut my way out. And here I am." Still a bet was a bet. So he caught a dozen wildcats and gave them to Davy Crockett.

But that wasn't the end of it. One night by the river, Sally Ann Thunder Ann Whirlwind Crockett met bad man Mike Fink. Her rage rose higher than a Mississippi flood. She lit the sky with lightning from her eye. And this time it scared Mike Fink's teeth loose. From then on bad man Mike Fink had a mouth full of loose teeth. And every time he bragged, those teeth rattled![8]

Craft and Structure

5 Sally Ann's reactions to the fake alligator are examples of understatement (deliberate minimizing of something) and hyperbole (deliberate exaggeration). These literary elements often appear in tall tales. They help to portray characters and situations and add humor.

Craft and Structure

6 *Scareder* for "more scared" is an example of dialect, or regional speech (*critter,* earlier in the passage, is another example). This type of diction lends authenticity to the characters and vividness to the tale.

Key Ideas and Details

7 Sally Ann's absurd description of herself extends Davy Crockett's earlier joke: his reference to "my sweet little wife."

Integration of Knowledge and Ideas

8 In this tall tale, as in most, characters do not really change. At the end of this story, Sally Ann is still the strongest and angriest person alive and Mike Fink will never stop bragging.

Discuss

Sharing your own ideas and listening to the ideas of others can deepen your understanding of a text and help you look at a topic in a whole new way. As you participate in collaborative discussions, work to have a genuine exchange in which classmates build upon one another's ideas. Support your points with evidence and ask meaningful questions.

Discussion Model

Student 1: Sally Ann is a different sort of hero in some ways. Even though she is tougher than everyone else, she still insists on being treated politely. She won't "let just any critter hug her." She gets furious when Mike Fink interrupts "a lady out on her nightly walk."

Student 2: I agree that Sally Ann is interesting. She has the same exaggerated physical and emotional traits as a traditional tall tale hero, but she's female. The story plays with that, especially in those references to Sally Ann's being sweet and little and a lady. The story is funny partly for that reason.

Student 3: I wonder about Sally Ann's husband, too. Sally Ann may be fictional, but I know Davy Crockett was a real person. He served in Congress and died in Texas at the battle of the Alamo. Why did the Americans of his time turn this real man into a tall-tale hero?

Research

Targeted research can clarify unfamiliar details and shed light on various aspects of a text. Consider questions that arise in your mind as you read, and use those questions as the basis for research.

Research Model

Question: *How did the historical David Crockett become Davy Crockett, the legendary hero?*

Key Words for Internet Search: David Crockett AND Texas

Result: Handbook of Texas Online, "David Crockett"

What I Learned: The real David Crockett gained a widespread reputation as a sharpshooter, hunter, and storyteller. As a result, playwright James Kirke Paulding used him as a model for a frontier hero in an 1831 play entitled *The Lion of the West.* After that, the fictional Davy Crockett became a featured character in many other works, including "almanacs" of outrageous tall tales.

Write

Writing about a text will deepen your understanding of it and will also allow you to share your ideas more formally with others. The following model essay draws conclusions about frontier values from tall tales and cites text evidence to support these claims.

Writing Model: Argument

Frontier Values in "Sally Ann Thunder Ann Whirlwind Crockett"

A society's heroes display the values of its people. For example, American tall-tale heroes display the values of pioneers struggling to create a life for themselves in the wilderness. "Sally Ann Thunder Ann Whirlwind Crockett" celebrates strength, courage, hunting skill, big talk, rough humor—and even good manners.

Many effective essays state the claim in the first paragraph, which is a good strategy for a short response.

Building a town or homestead in unfamiliar territory takes purpose and nerve. Tall-tale heroes often represented this determination. They are described as being similar to forces of nature, such as storms or floods. Sally Ann Thunder Ann Whirlwind Crockett "was made of thunder with a little dash of whirlwind." When she got mad, "her rage rose higher than a Mississippi flood." Along with strength, American pioneers needed a lot of courage. Sally Ann was certainly brave—"nothing on earth scared her."

The writer supports claims with specific details from the story.

Americans who lived on the frontier used wild animals as sources of both food and clothing. Surviving in the wilderness required pioneers to be skilled hunters. Real-life frontiersman David Crockett gained a national reputation in the United States of the 1820s as a sharpshooter. In tall-tale America, Davy Crockett's wife Sally Ann wore "a bearskin for a dress. Her toothpick was a bowie knife." Sally Ann could "skin a bear faster than an alligator swallows a fish."

The writer incorporates research to provide context for a point.

Some Americans who told tall tales must have loved big talk and rough humor. Such tastes would be natural for people who provided their own entertainment. Mike Fink's brag in the tavern that he is half-horse and half-alligator is crude stand-up comedy. Finding good manners in a tall tale, however, might seem more of a stretch. Yet Sally Ann, who "didn't let just any critter hug her," clearly values politeness.

By focusing on the tellers of the tales, the writer shows an understanding of the author's craft.

The writer anticipates that the reader might question a claim and directly addresses it.

The Americans who told and retold tall tales needed strength, courage, and a sense of humor to survive in the wilderness. So they made up larger-than-life characters who "could wade the wide Mississippi without getting wet." The exaggerated feats of tall-tale heroes helped pioneers face the huge challenges of making the frontier into a home.

As you read the following tall tale, apply the close reading strategies you have learned. You may need to read the tale multiple times to fully appreciate its characters, events, and humor.

Pecos Bill: The Cyclone

by Harold W. Felton

One of Bill's greatest feats, if not the greatest feat of all time, occurred unexpectedly one Fourth of July. He had invented the Fourth of July some years before. It was a great day for the cowpunchers.[1] They had taken to it right off like the real Americans they were. But the celebration had always ended on a dismal note. Somehow it seemed to be spoiled by a cyclone.

Bill had never minded the cyclone much. The truth is he rather liked it. But the other celebrants ran into caves for safety. He invented cyclone cellars for them. He even named the cellars. He called them "'fraid holes." Pecos wouldn't even say the word "afraid." The cyclone was something like he was. It was big and strong too. He always stood by musing pleasantly as he watched it.

The cyclone caused Bill some trouble, though. Usually it would destroy a few hundred miles of fence by blowing the postholes away. But it wasn't much trouble for him to fix it. All he had to do was to go and get the postholes and then take them back and put the fence posts in them. The holes were rarely ever blown more than twenty or thirty miles.

In one respect Bill even welcomed the cyclone, for it blew so hard it blew the earth away from his wells. The first time this happened, he thought the wells would be a total loss. There they were, sticking up several hundred feet out of the ground. As wells they were useless. But he found he could cut them up into lengths and sell them for postholes to farmers in Iowa and Nebraska. It was very profitable, especially after he invented a special posthole saw to cut them with. He didn't use that type of posthole himself.

1. **cowpunchers** (kou′ pun′ chərz) *n.* cowboys.

Meet the Author

Harold W. Felton (1902–1991) practiced law and worked for the Internal Revenue Service, but over the years he became interested in the legends and folklore of the United States. In particular, he collected and retold stories about folk heroes and cowboys of the West.

CLOSE READING TOOL

Read and respond to this selection online using the **Close Reading Tool.**

He got the prairie dogs to dig his for him. He simply caught a few gross[2] of prairie dogs and set them down at proper intervals. The prairie dog would dig a hole. Then Bill would put a post in it. The prairie dog would get disgusted and go down the row ahead of the others and dig another hole. Bill fenced all of Texas and parts of New Mexico and Arizona in this manner. He took a few contracts and fenced most of the Southern Pacific right of way too. That's the reason it is so crooked. He had trouble getting the prairie dogs to run a straight fence.

As for his wells, the badgers dug them. The system was the same as with the prairie dogs. The labor was cheap so it didn't make much difference if the cyclone did spoil some of the wells. The badgers were digging all of the time anyway. They didn't seem to care whether they dug wells or just badger holes.

One year he tried shipping the prairie dog holes up north, too, for postholes. It was not successful. They didn't keep in storage and they couldn't stand the handling in shipping. After they were installed they seemed to wear out quickly. Bill always thought the difference in climate had something to do with it.

It should be said that in those days there was only one cyclone. It was the first and original cyclone, bigger and more terrible by far than the small cyclones of today. It usually stayed by itself up north around Kansas and Oklahoma and didn't bother anyone much. But it was attracted by the noise of the Fourth of July celebration and without fail managed to put in an appearance before the close of the day.

On this particular Fourth of July, the celebration had gone off fine. The speeches were loud and long. The contests and games were hard fought. The high point of the day was Bill's exhibition with Widow Maker, which came right after he showed off Scat and Rat.[3] People seemed never to tire of seeing them in action. The mountain lion was almost useless as a work animal after his accident, and the snake had grown old and somewhat infirm, and was troubled with rheumatism in his rattles. But they too enjoyed the Fourth of July and liked to make a public appearance. They relived the old days.

Widow Maker had put on a good show, bucking as no ordinary horse could ever buck. Then Bill undertook to show the gaits[4] he had taught the palomino.[5] Other mustangs at that time had only two gaits. Walking and running. Only Widow Maker could pace. But now Bill had developed and taught him other gaits. Twenty-seven in all. Twenty-three forward and three reverse. He was very proud of the achievement. He showed off the slow gaits and the crowd was eager for more.

---

2. **gross** (grōs) *n.* twelve dozen.
3. **Widow Maker . . . Scat and Rat.** Widow Maker is a mustang, a type of wild horse. Scat is Bill's mountain lion, and Rat is Bill's pet rattlesnake.
4. **gaits** (gāts) *n.* foot movements of a horse.
5. **palomino** (pal′ ə mē′ nō) *n.* golden-tan or cream-colored horse that has a white, silver, or ivory tail and, often, white spots on the face and legs.

He showed the walk, trot, canter, lope, jog, slow rack, fast rack, single foot, pace, stepping pace, fox trot, running walk and the others now known. Both men and horses confuse the various gaits nowadays. Some of the gaits are now thought to be the same, such as the rack and the single foot. But with Widow Maker and Pecos Bill, each one was different. Each was precise and to be distinguished from the others. No one had ever imagined such a thing.

Then the cyclone came! All of the people except Bill ran into the 'fraid holes. Bill was annoyed. He stopped the performance. The remaining gaits were not shown. From that day to this horses have used no more than the gaits Widow Maker exhibited that day. It is unfortunate that the really fast gaits were not shown. If they were, horses might be much faster today than they are.

Bill glanced up at the cyclone and the quiet smile on his face faded into a frown. He saw the cyclone was angry. Very, very angry indeed.

The cyclone had always been the center of attention. Everywhere it went people would look up in wonder, fear and amazement. It had been the undisputed master of the country. It had observed Bill's rapid climb to fame and had seen the Fourth of July celebration grow. It had been keeping an eye on things all right.

In the beginning, the Fourth of July crowd had aroused its curiosity. It liked nothing more than to show its superiority and power by breaking the crowd up sometime during the day. But every year the crowd was larger. This preyed on the cyclone's mind. This year it did not come to watch. It deliberately came to spoil the celebration. Jealous of Bill and of his success, it resolved to do away with the whole institution of the Fourth of July once and for all. So much havoc and destruction would be wrought that there would never be another Independence Day Celebration. On that day, in future years, it would circle around the horizon leering and gloating. At least, so it thought.

The cyclone was resolved, also, to do away with this bold fellow who did not hold it in awe and run for the 'fraid hole at its approach. For untold years it had been the most powerful thing in the land. And now, here was a mere man who threatened its position. More! Who had **usurped** its position!

◀ **Vocabulary**
usurped (yo͞o sʉrpt′) *v.* took power without right

When Bill looked at the horizon and saw the cyclone coming, he recognized the anger and rage. While a cyclone does not often smile, Bill had felt from the beginning that it was just a grouchy fellow who never had a pleasant word for anyone. But now, instead of merely an unpleasant character, Bill saw all the viciousness of which an angry cyclone is capable. He had no way of knowing that the cyclone saw its kingship tottering and was determined to stop this man who threatened its supremacy.

But Bill understood the violence of the onslaught even as the monster came into view. He knew he must meet it. The center of the cyclone was larger than ever before. The fact is, the cyclone had been training for this fight all winter and spring. It was in best form and at top weight. It headed straight for Bill intent on his destruction. In an instant it was upon him. Bill had sat quietly and silently on the great pacing mustang. But his mind was working rapidly. In the split second between his first sight of the monster and the time for action he had made his plans. Pecos Bill was ready! Ready and waiting!

Green clouds were dripping from the cyclone's jaws. Lightning flashed from its eyes as it swept down upon him. Its plan was to envelop Bill in one mighty grasp. Just as it was upon him, Bill turned Widow Maker to its left. This was a clever move for the cyclone was right-handed, and while it had been training hard to get its left in shape, that was not its best side. Bill gave rein to his mount. Widow Maker wheeled and turned on a dime which Pecos had, with great foresight and accuracy, thrown to the ground to mark the exact spot for this maneuver. It was the first time that anyone had thought of turning on a dime. Then he urged the great horse forward. The cyclone, filled with surprise, lost its balance and rushed forward at an increased speed. It went so fast that it met itself coming back. This confused the cyclone, but it did not confuse Pecos Bill. He had expected that to happen. Widow Maker went into his twenty-first gait and edged up close to the whirlwind. Soon they were running neck and neck.

At the proper instant Bill grabbed the cyclone's ears, kicked himself free of the stirrups and pulled himself lightly on its back. Bill never used spurs on Widow Maker. Sometimes he wore them for show and because he liked the jingling sound they made. They made a nice accompaniment for his cowboy songs. But he had not been singing, so he had no spurs. He did not have his rattlesnake for a quirt.[6] Of course there was no bridle. It was man against monster! There he was! Pecos Bill astride a raging cyclone, slick heeled and without a saddle!

The cyclone was taken by surprise at this sudden turn of events. But it was undaunted. It was sure of itself. Months of training had given it a conviction that it was invincible. With a mighty heave, it twisted to its full height. Then it fell back suddenly, twisting and turning violently, so that before it came back to earth, it had turned around a thousand times. Surely no rider could ever withstand such an attack. No rider ever had. Little wonder. No one had ever ridden a cyclone before. But Pecos Bill did! He fanned the tornado's ears with his hat and dug his heels into the demon's flanks and yelled, "Yipee-ee!"

---

6. **quirt** (kwurt) *n.* riding whip with a braided lash and a short handle.

The people who had run for shelter began to come out. The audience further enraged the cyclone. It was bad enough to be disgraced by having a man astride it. It was unbearable not to have thrown him. To have all the people see the failure was too much! It got down flat on the ground and rolled over and over. Bill retained his seat throughout this ruse. Evidence of this desperate but futile stratagem[7] remains today. The great Staked Plains, or as the Mexicans call it, *Llano Estacado*, is the result. Its small, rugged mountains were covered with trees at the time. The rolling of the cyclone destroyed the mountains, the trees, and almost everything else in the area. The destruction was so complete, that part of the country is flat and treeless to this day. When the settlers came, there were no landmarks to guide them across the vast unmarked space, so they drove stakes in the ground to mark the trails. That is the reason it is called "Staked Plains." Here is an example of the proof of the events of history by careful and painstaking research. It is also an example of how seemingly inexplicable geographical facts can be explained.

It was far more dangerous for the rider when the cyclone shot straight up to the sky. Once there, the twister tried the same thing it had tried on the ground. It rolled on the sky. It was no use. Bill could not be unseated. He kept his place, and he didn't have a sky hook with him either.

As for Bill, he was having the time of his life, shouting at the top of his voice, kicking his opponent in the ribs and jabbing his thumb in its flanks. It responded and went on a wild bucking rampage over the entire West. It used all the bucking tricks known to the wildest broncos as well as those known only to cyclones. The wind howled furiously and beat against the fearless rider. The rain poured. The lightning flashed around his ears. The fight went on and on. Bill enjoyed himself immensely. In spite of the elements he easily kept his place. . . .

The raging cyclone saw this out of the corner of its eye. It knew then who the victor was. It was twisting far above the Rocky Mountains when the awful truth came to it. In a horrible heave it disintegrated! Small pieces of cyclone flew in all directions. Bill still kept his seat on the main central portion until that rained out from under him. Then he jumped to a nearby streak of lightning and slid down it toward earth. But it was raining so hard that the rain put out the lightning. When it fizzled out from under him, Bill dropped the rest of the way. He lit in what is now called Death Valley. He hit quite hard, as is apparent from the fact that he so compressed the place that it is still two hundred and seventy-six feet below sea level. The Grand

---

7. **futile** (fyo͞ot′'l) **stratagem** (strat′ ə jəm) useless or hopeless plan.

Canyon was washed out by the rain, though it must be understood that this happened after Paul Bunyan had given it a good start by carelessly dragging his ax behind him when he went west a short time before.

The cyclones and the hurricanes and the tornadoes nowadays are the small pieces that broke off of the big cyclone Pecos Bill rode. In fact, the rainstorms of the present day came into being in the same way. There are always skeptics, but even they will recognize the logic of the proof of this event. They will recall that even now it almost always rains on the Fourth of July. That is because the rainstorms of today still retain some of the characteristics of the giant cyclone that met its comeuppance at the hands of Pecos Bill.

Vocabulary ▶
skeptics (skep´ tiks) *n.* people who doubt accepted ideas

Bill lay where he landed and looked up at the sky, but he could see no sign of the cyclone. Then he laughed softly as he felt the warm sand of Death Valley on his back. . . .

It was a rough ride though, and Bill had resisted unusual tensions and pressures. When he got on the cyclone he had a twenty-dollar gold piece and a bowie knife in his pocket. The tremendous force of the cyclone was such that when he finished the ride he found that his pocket contained a plugged nickel[8] and a little pearl-handled penknife. His two giant six-shooters were compressed and transformed into a small water pistol and a popgun.

It is a strange circumstance that lesser men have monuments raised in their honor. Death Valley is Bill's monument. Sort of a monument in reverse. Sunk in his honor, you might say. Perhaps that is as it should be. After all, Bill was different. He made his own monument. He made it with his hips, as is evident from the great depth of the valley. That is the hard way.

---

8. **plugged nickel** fake nickel.

Close Reading Activities

Read

Comprehension: **Key Ideas and Details**

1. **(a)** What term does Pecos Bill use to refer to the cyclone cellars? **(b) Interpret:** What does this term show about Bill's character?
2. **(a) Analyze:** Identify three human emotions that the cyclone displays. **(b)** What other human qualities does the cyclone display? Explain. **(c) Compare:** In what ways are Bill and the cyclone similar? Explain, citing details from the tale.
3. **(a)** What happens to the cyclone after Bill defeats it? **(b) Connect:** In what ways does the cyclone's behavior after its defeat both express the character's human-like traits and match the pattern of an actual storm?
4. **Summarize:** Write a brief, objective summary of the story. Cite story details in your writing. Explain.

Text Analysis: **Craft and Structure**

5. **(a)** What word is Bill unwilling to say out loud? **(b) Draw Conclusions:** How does Bill's resolve never to say this word explain, in part, why he is a hero? Explain.
6. **Contrast:** How does the narrator distinguish Bill's cyclone from today's cyclones? Cite specific details from the text that support this distinction.
7. **(a) Analyze Cause and Effect:** How does the narrator support the claim that modern rainstorms are pieces of the original cyclone? **(b) Evaluate:** How does this detail represent the author's tone? Explain.
8. **(a)** What does the author identify as Bill's "monument"? **(b) Contrast:** In what ways is Bill's monument different from those of "lesser men"?

Connections: **Integration of Knowledge and Ideas**

Discuss

Literature from the oral tradition often explains the origins of natural phenomena or cultural practices. With a small group, conduct a **discussion** about the ways in which "Pecos Bill: The Cyclone" fits the definition of an origin story.

Research

Tall tales often include *archetypes,* or elements common to stories from all cultures. Briefly research archetypal characters, settings, and events and assess their possible influence on this tall tale. In particular, consider the following:

a. Bill's horse, Widow Maker

b. Bill's combat with the cyclone

c. Bill's "monument"

Take notes as you perform your research. Then, write a brief **explanation** of the archetypal elements you find in this tall tale.

Write

Nearly all tall tale heroes and their counterparts in epics, myths, and legends display superhuman abilities. Modern forms of entertainment, such as comic books and action movies, also feature heroes with superpowers. In an **essay,** discuss how Pecos Bill's abilities are similar to or different from those of another heroic character with which you are familiar. Cite details from the tale to support your ideas.

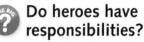

Do heroes have responsibilities?

In what ways does Pecos Bill show responsibility to his community? Do you think Bill has an obligation to use his abilities to serve his community, or can he, in good conscience, choose not to do so? Explain.

"It is good to have an
end to journey toward,
but it is the journey that
matters in the end."
—Ursula K. Le Guin

PART 2

TEXT ANALYSIS GUIDED EXPLORATION

PERILOUS JOURNEYS

The texts in this section tell the story of Odysseus, the ancient Greek hero whose adventures make up one of the first perilous journeys in literature. In fact, the word *odyssey* means a long journey, full of dangers, surprises, twists, and turns. As you read the texts in this section, think about the obstacles that Odysseus confronts, how he overcomes them, and what his responses say about his character. Then, think about how these texts speak to the Big Question for this unit: **Do heroes have responsibilities?** Consider what type of hero Odysseus is and how he views his responsibilities toward his men, the gods, characters he meets, and his family.

◀ CRITICAL VIEWING Which details in the painting suggest the ship is in the midst of a dangerous journey?

READINGS IN PART 2

EPIC EXEMPLAR TEXT

***from the* Odyssey, Part 1: The Adventures of Odysseus**

Homer (p. 756)

- Sailing from Troy
- The Lotus-Eaters
- The Cyclops
- The Land of the Dead
- The Sirens
- Scylla and Charybdis
- The Cattle of the Sun God

EPIC EXEMPLAR TEXT

***from the* Odyssey, Part 2: The Return of Odysseus**

Homer (p. 800)

- Argus
- The Suitors
- Penelope
- The Challenge
- Odysseus' Revenge
- Penelope's Test

CLOSE READING TOOL

Use the **Close Reading Tool** to practice the strategies you learn in this unit.

Focus on Craft and Structure

Theme and the Oral Tradition

Stories from the oral tradition teach a culture's central **values** and **beliefs**. They also convey **universal themes**.

Oral Tradition Storytellers and poets of long ago did not write down the tales they told. Instead, they learned the stories and poems of their culture from others and recited them from memory. The term **oral tradition** refers to the literature they passed down through the ages by word of mouth. Eventually, these spoken stories and poems were retold in writing.

The tales of love, ambition, and friendship in the oral tradition do more than entertain. They record the history, customs, beliefs, and values of the cultures from which they sprang. The **points of view,** or perspectives on life, expressed in this literature reflect the **cultural experiences** of the tellers—the basic experiences that shaped life in their society. For example, the stories of a warrior culture tell of battle and adventure, heroism and sacrifice. Experiences of war along with the emphasis placed on bravery and loyalty form the **social and cultural context** for such tales—the values, beliefs, and experiences the tales reflect and affirm.

Themes Like much literature, works in the oral tradition convey **themes**—deeper meanings or insights. A **universal theme** is an insight into life and human nature that appears in the literature of many different times and cultures. Universal themes concern fundamental ideas such as the importance of heroism, the strength of loyalty, the power of love, the responsibilities of leadership, the struggle between good and evil, and the dangers of greed.

Storytellers in the oral tradition often explore universal themes, and they frequently do so using archetypes. An **archetype** is an element that recurs throughout the literature of different cultures. Character types, plot patterns, images, and symbols all may be archetypes, as in the examples shown below.

Examples: Archetypes

- The **trickster** is a clever person or animal that can fool others but often gets into trouble through curiosity.
- In the **hero's quest,** a clever or brave person undergoes a series of tests or trials while on a search for something of great importance.
- The character of the hero is often called the **protagonist,** and the **antagonist** is the character or force that stands in opposition. Often, the opposing force is a **monster,** a nonhuman or semi-human figure that menaces society and must be destroyed by the hero.

The **hero's quest** follows an archetypal plot pattern similar to the one shown here.

The Quest Begins	→	Series of Tests or Trials	→	The Quest Ends
The conflict between the protagonist and antagonist is introduced.	→	During an extended journey, the protagonist reveals the traits of a true hero by overcoming hardships and performing difficult tasks.	→	The hero achieves the goal, usually after a final confrontation with the antagonist.

Forms From the Oral Tradition

Across cultures, storytellers in the oral tradition developed specific narrative forms. Among these forms are myths, folk tales, legends, and epics. Narratives in each of these forms express the values, ideals, and behaviors held important by the culture from which they came. They also reflect the oral nature of the tradition. For example, epics may feature *epithets,* or descriptive phrases that are repeated when a character is named. These epithets may have helped storytellers memorize the story. They might also have helped listeners recognize and remember the characters.

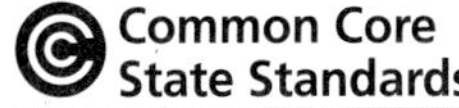

Common Core State Standards

Reading Literature

2. Determine a theme or central idea of a text and analyze in detail its development over the course of the text, including how it emerges and is shaped and refined by specific details; provide an objective summary of the text.

6. Analyze a particular point of view or cultural experience reflected in a work of literature from outside the United States, drawing on a wide reading of world literature.

Literary Forms in the Oral Tradition

Form	Characteristics	Example
Myth	• describes the actions of gods or heroes or explains the origins of elements of nature • is present in the literature of every culture (Ancient Greek and Roman myths are known as **classical mythology.**)	Prometheus, son of the Greek god Zeus, defies his father and the other gods by giving fire to humanity.
Folk Tale	• follows a simple formula • deals with heroics, adventure, magic, or romance • frequently features animal characters with human traits, such as the trickster Coyote • includes fables and fairy tales	A poor fisherman catches a golden fish. The fish and the man strike a deal: In exchange for its freedom, the fish will grant the man a wish. The man agrees, but he and his wife become greedy and demand more wishes. The fish vanishes, leaving the fisherman in poverty once more.
Legend	• recounts the adventures of a hero from the past • often relates events that are based on historical truth • includes tall tales, which feature exaggeration	Stories of Davy Crockett portray this real-life man as a superhero who frees the sun, uses lightning to fly, and defeats the entire British navy single-handedly.
Epic	• is a long narrative poem • combines features of myths and legends • depicts a larger-than-life hero who usually goes on a dangerous journey; the hero is helped or hindered by supernatural creatures or gods • gives a detailed portrait of a culture	The ancient Mesopotamian king Gilgamesh, who is part human and part god, displays wisdom and strength as he struggles against the gods, nature, and his own human weaknesses.

Analyzing Theme and Cultural Experience

A literary work conveys a **theme**—an insight about life. Authors' **cultural backgrounds** influence their **points of view** and the themes they express.

The **theme,** or central insight or message of a literary work, may be stated directly. For example, a fable ends with a statement of the moral of the story, such as "He who hesitates is lost." Frequently, however, the theme of a work is **implied,** or suggested, by story details. Readers can determine an implied theme by analyzing the way storytellers pattern details.

Development of Themes To introduce and develop a theme, writers create patterns of events and actions or of contrasts between characters and their fates. As the story unfolds, new events may reinforce these patterns or alter them, suggesting new ideas to readers.

By identifying such patterns as you read, you will gain clues to the implied theme. Restating the patterns in general terms will help you reach a conclusion about an implied theme, as shown in the following example:

Title	"Midas and the Golden Touch"
Pattern	Everything King Midas touches turns to gold, including his beloved daughter.
Generalized Restatement	Driven by greed, a person destroys what he loves.
Theme	Greed can destroy all that is good in a person's life.

Determining Universal Themes In the oral tradition, universal themes—themes found in the literature of many cultures—are often conveyed through the use of **archetypes,** or recurring elements common to many stories.

Your ability to recognize these archetypes as the story develops and to interpret their meanings can help you determine a story's universal themes, as in the following example:

Story	**The Tortoise and the Hare** A tortoise and a hare compete in a race. The hare assumes he will win and stops for a nap. The tortoise keeps going and wins.
Archetypes	• Overconfident, boastful character (hare) • Quiet, confident character (tortoise) • Plot pattern: Competition in which a weaker character succeeds because of the pride of a stronger character
Universal Themes	• Slow and steady wins the race. • Too much pride can have bad results.

Culturally Specific Themes Not all themes in the oral tradition are universal. Some are specific to the time and the culture in which the story originated. These themes reflect the specific social or cultural concerns of their tellers and do not apply more generally to people in modern cultures. Still, they provide an interesting window into the values, beliefs, and customs of bygone eras.

Point of View An author's **point of view,** or perspective, consists of his or her attitudes toward, and beliefs about, a subject. Point of view determines how the writer approaches a subject. An author's point of view is influenced in part by his or her cultural experiences—the basic experiences, beliefs, and values that shape life in his or her society.

Literature in the oral tradition usually expresses a cultural—rather than an individual—point of view. By contrast, works of modern literature usually express an author's unique and individual point of view. This point of view may even be critical of the author's own culture. In both cases, it is important for readers to recognize the point of view and cultural experiences that shape a literary text.

Cultural Point of View

The history, beliefs, ideals, and behaviors shared or valued by an entire society or group

↓

Individual Author's Point of View

The author's subjective, or personal, attitudes, feelings, values, and ideas; his or her distinct view of the world

Cultural Experience and Purpose The author's **purpose** is his or her main reason for writing. Writers usually write **to entertain, to inform or explain,** or **to persuade.** Although entertainment was a means for getting the attention of listeners, storytellers in the oral tradition also felt responsible for preserving the identity of their cultures. Through stories and poems, they reminded people of their history; they communicated values to younger members of their group; and they shared religious beliefs. Storytellers were more than just entertainers; they served as historians, teachers, and advisors.

Modern writers may also create literature with more than one purpose in mind. For example, an author might write a story that includes information about a serious problem in the world and at the same time provide readers with a satisfying narrative that entertains.

Changing Points of View As stories were passed among generations and cultures, details changed to reflect different values and attitudes. Consider this example of a story that has been retold in numerous cultures:

Example: Cinderella

After Cinderella's mother dies, her father remarries and leaves Cinderella with his new wife and her two daughters. Cinderella is enslaved by the unreasonable demands of her cruel stepmother and stepsisters. She attends the King's ball and meets the Prince. Eventually, Cinderella and the Prince marry and live happily ever after.

Culture/ Version	Cultural Viewpoint	Specific Details
German tale retold by the Brothers Grimm in 1812	Medieval view: Cruelty and violence are part of the world.	At the end, birds peck out the eyes of the stepsisters.
American version, based on a retelling by the French writer Charles Perrault in 1697	Modern view: Violence and cruelty should be hidden from children's view.	At the end, Cinderella forgives her stepsisters and invites them to live in the castle.

Preparing to Read the *Odyssey*

Homer's epic poems celebrate the legendary heroes and heritage of a great culture.

Historical Background: Ancient Greece

The world of ancient Greece included the Greek mainland, dipping down from continental Europe, and western Asia Minor, the Asian part of present-day Turkey. It also included hundreds of islands in the Aegean (ē jē´ ən) Sea, the arm of the Mediterranean Sea between mainland Greece and Asia Minor, and in the Ionian (ī ō´ nē ən) Sea, the arm of the Mediterranean to the west of mainland Greece. Odysseus, the legendary hero of Homer's *Odyssey*, was said to be the ruler of Ithaca, one of the western islands.

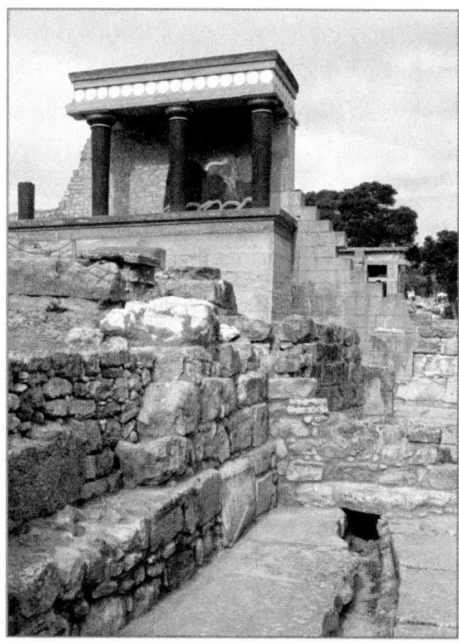

▲ The photograph above shows a reconstruction of one wall of The Palace of Minos at Knossos, Crete.

Sir Arthur Evans, the British archaeologist who worked extensively on Crete, named Minoan civilization for King Minos (mī´ näs), a ruler of Crete in Greek mythology.

The Minoans and Mycenaeans Nearly a thousand years before Odysseus would have lived, Greek civilization rose to greatness on Crete, another island south of the mainland. By about 2000 B.C., a sophisticated society called the Minoan (mi nō´ ən) civilization had developed on Crete. Judging by the archaeological evidence, the Minoans produced elegant stone palaces and fine carvings and metalwork. They also developed a writing system, preserved on a few hundred of the clay tablets on which they wrote. Scholars call that writing system Linear A and have yet to decipher it.

For several centuries, Minoan civilization dominated the Greek world. Then, in about 1450 B.C., it collapsed rather suddenly, perhaps due to earthquakes and invasion. With the weakening of Minoan culture, the Mycenaeans (mī´sə nē´ ənz) became the dominant force in the Greek world. Originating on mainland Greece, the Mycenaeans had swept south and into Crete. Strongly influenced by Minoan civilization, the Mycenaeans too had a palace culture, an economy based on trade, and a writing system that mostly used clay tablets. Evidence of their writing is found in Knossos and Chania on Crete as well as in Mycenae, Pylos, and Thebes, three of their mainland strongholds. Because the Mycenaeans spoke an archaic, or older, form of Greek, scholars have been able to decipher their writing, known as Linear B. It was used primarily to keep palace records.

▶ The photo on the right shows a fresco, or wall painting, from the palace's interior.

◀ Ancient Greece included mainland territories and hundreds of islands clustered in the the Aegean and Ionian Seas. Odysseus' kingdom of Ithaca is a small island in the Ionian Sea.

Legendary Conflicts The writing and archaeological remains suggest early cities with large central palaces and thick protective walls, each ruled by a wanax, or king. Others in society included priests, slaves, workers in trades or crafts, administrative officials, and a warrior class. The Mycenaens wore armor in battle, in which they engaged with apparent frequency. Their warfare with Troy, on the northwest coast of Asia Minor, has become one of the most famous military ventures of all time—the Trojan War. If there really was a King Odysseus, he would have been a key player in that conflict.

Scholars date the Trojan War to somewhere around 1200 B.C. Shortly thereafter, Mycenaean civilization collapsed as the Greek world fell into chaos and confusion. For some three hundred years, writing seems to have disappeared in what is often called the Greek Dark Ages. Then, in about 850 B.C., Greece began emerging from this darkness, spurred by flourishing trade throughout the Mediterranean region. Along with the economic boom came a resurgence of the arts and learning that peaked with the epic poems of Homer. These poems—the *Iliad* and the *Odyssey*—chronicle the Trojan War and the subsequent adventures of the hero Odysseus.

The Rise of City-States After Homer's time, Greek civilization grew more organized and sophisticated. Smaller communities organized as city-states—cities that functioned independently, as countries do. Among them were Sparta, known for its military prowess, and Athens, the birthplace of democracy. Though rivalries sometimes led to warfare among city-states, the Greeks still recognized their common heritage as Hellenes, as they usually called themselves by that time. They coordinated efforts to fight common enemies, such as the Persians. They participated in the Olympic games, which records indicate began in 776 B.C. Together, too, they saw the works of Homer as pillars of their heritage, two great epics that celebrated their common past and its heroes.

The Greek word for "city-state" is *polis,* the origin of our words *metropolis* and *politics*.

Greek Mythology and Customs

All aspects of Greek culture reflected belief in the Olympian gods.

Ancient Greek religion was based on a belief in many gods. Zeus was king of the gods; Hera, his beautiful and powerful wife. Other gods and goddesses were associated with different aspects of nature or human behavior. The most important ones were said to dwell on Mount Olympus, the tallest mountain in Greece, where Zeus sat on a throne of gold. These Olympians, however, were not the first gods.

The Titans Are Overthrown The early poet Hesiod **(hē′ sē əd)** wrote a mythic account of the origin of the gods in *Theogony,* a work the Greeks revered almost as much as Homer's epics. According to that origin myth, first there was Chaos, a dark, empty void. Out of Chaos came the Earth, personified as the goddess Gaea. The Earth generated the skies, personified as the god Uranus, who with Gaea produced the giant gods known as Titans. Cronus, the chief Titan, ruled the universe until he was displaced by his three sons, who split the universe among them. Zeus, the most powerful of these sons, became ruler of the heavens. His brother Poseidon became ruler of the seas. The third brother, Hades, became ruler of the underworld, a dark region also called Hades, which was inhabited by shades of the dead.

The Greek gods were powerful, but they were not all-powerful: even Zeus had to bow to fate. The gods displayed many human qualities and were often vengeful and quarrelsome. They were also quick to punish human beings guilty of hubris **(hyo͞o′ or ho͞o′ bris)**, or excessive pride. To appease the gods, human beings performed sacrifices, which often involved the killing of animals. In the *Odyssey*, Odysseus makes several sacrifices to plead for divine aid on his journey home.

Celebrating the Gods The Greeks worshipped the gods in temples dedicated to many gods or just one. The Parthenon in Athens, for instance, was a temple dedicated to the goddess Athena. The Greeks also celebrated their gods at great festivals such as the Olympic games, which were dedicated to Zeus.

The Greeks believed in prophecy, which they associated with the god Apollo. In the *Odyssey*, Odysseus journeys all the way to the underworld to consult the blind prophet Tiresias **(tī rē′ sē əs)**, who continues to have the gift of prophecy even though he has died. The Greeks also believed in myths, stories about gods and heroes that they used to explain the world around them. The *Iliad* and the *Odyssey* drew on these myths; however, for future generations of ancient Greeks, Homer's two epics—like Hesiod's *Theogony*—took on the aura of myths themselves.

▼ Apollo, the god of light and music (among many other things), is often shown with a lyre, the stringed instrument from which the English word *lyric* derives.

Gods in Greek Mythology

You may be more familiar with the Roman names for the Greek gods. The ancient Romans accepted Greek mythology, but they had their own names for its gods and heroes. For example, they called Odysseus *Ulysses*. For each Greek god listed below, the Roman equivalent is also given.

Zeus (zo͞os) king of the gods and ruler of the heavens; Roman *Jupiter,* sometimes called *Jove*
Hera (her′ ə) wife of Zeus and goddess of married women; Roman *Juno*
Poseidon (pō sī′dən) god of the seas; Roman *Neptune*
Hades (hā′dēz) god of the underworld; Roman *Pluto*
Aphrodite (af′ rə dīt̄ē) goddess of love and beauty; Roman *Venus*
Ares (er′ ēz) god of war; Roman *Mars*
Apollo (əp ol′ ō) god of prophecy and music; also called Phoebus (fē′ bəs); Roman *Apollo*
Artemis (är′ tə mis) goddess of the hunt and the moon; Roman *Diana*
Athena (ə thē′ nə) goddess of wisdom, skills, and war; Roman *Minerva*
Hephaestus (hē fes′ təs) god of fire and metalwork; Roman *Vulcan*
Hermes (hʉr′ mēz) god of commerce and cunning; messenger of the gods; Roman *Mercury*
Demeter (di mē′ tər) goddess of the harvest; Roman *Ceres* (sir′ ēz)
Dionysus (dī′ ən ī′səs) god of wine and revelry, also called Bacchus (bak′ əs); Roman *Dionysus* or *Bacchus*
Hestia (hes′ tē ə) goddess of home and hearth; Roman *Vesta*
Helios (hē′ lē os′) sun god; Roman *Sol*
Uranus (yo͞o rə′ nəs) sky god supplanted by his son Cronus; Roman *Uranus*
Gaea (jē′ ə) earth goddess and mother of the Titans and Cyclopes; Roman *Tellus* or *Terra*
Cronus (krō′ nəs) Titan who ruled the universe before his son Zeus dethroned him; Roman *Saturn*
Rhea (rē′ ə) wife of Cronus and mother of Zeus; Roman *Cybele* (sib′ ə lē)
Cyclops (sī′ klops) any one of three Titans who forged thunderbolts for Zeus; plural, Cyclopes (sī′ klō pēs)
The Fates three goddesses who wove the threads of each person's life: Clotho (klō′ thō) spun the thread; Lachesis (lak′ i sis) measured out the amount of thread; Atropos (a′ trə pis) snipped the thread
The Muses (myo͞o′ ziz) nine goddesses who presided over the arts and sciences, including Calliope (kə lī′ ə pē′), the Muse of epic poetry

▼ Poseidon, god of the sea, was also the god of earthquakes and horses. His symbols include the trident, a three-pronged spear.

Meet the Author

Homer EPIC POET

The poems attributed to Homer still influence literature and culture today.

Homer is the legendary poet credited with writing the *Iliad* and the *Odyssey*. These epics, known for their sweeping scope, gripping stories, and vivid style, have captured readers' imaginations for almost 3,000 years.

Was there really a Homer? No one can prove his existence with any certainty, for no authentic record of Homer's life exists. Tradition has it that he was born in Ionia in western Asia Minor, perhaps on the island of Chios, and that he was blind. The location is not unreasonable, for Ionia was a center of poetry and learning, where eastern and western cultures met and new intellectual currents were born. Descriptions of Asia Minor in the *Iliad* show in-depth knowledge of the landscape; moreover, both the *Iliad* and the *Odyssey* contain plot elements found in the world's first known epic, *Gilgamesh*, which by Homer's era had traveled from Mesopotamia (present-day Iraq) to become familiar in Asia Minor. For example, the hero Gilgamesh visits the underworld, just like the hero of the *Odyssey*; he also has a very good friend who is killed, just like Achilles has in the *Iliad*.

Most efforts to date Homer's life place him somewhere between 850 and 750 B.C. As a Greek oral poet, it is unlikely he lived much later, for by then writing had been reintroduced to Greek culture. The details in Homer's epics make clear that the poems were orally composed and that the *Iliad* was written first and probably some years before the *Odyssey*. The two epics differ in style: the *Iliad* is a single long, highly dramatic narrative, while the *Odyssey* is episodic and reads more like an adventure novel than a drama. For these reasons, some scholars even speculate that the epics were composed by two different poets.

Inspiring Poems Whatever the truth about Homer may be, no one disputes the quality of the two epics with which he is credited. The ancient Greeks revered the *Iliad* and the *Odyssey*. They recited the poems at religious festivals and had children memorize them in school. All the Greek writers and philosophers who came after Homer drew on the two epics. Their influence spread to Rome and beyond, and they became foundational works of western literature. Even in modern times, great works from James Joyce's *Ulysses* to Derek Walcott's *Omeros* have been directly inspired by Homer's verse.

The Epic Form

An **epic** is a long narrative poem that relates important events in the history or folklore of the culture that produced it. Its central character, or **epic hero,** is a larger-than-life figure who embodies traits that the culture values. Typical among those characteristics are physical strength, bravery, high birth, fame, and effective skills as a leader and in battle.

The *Iliad* and the *Odyssey* influenced virtually all the great western epics that followed them. From the *Aeneid*, the great epic of ancient Rome, to *Beowulf*, the foundational epic of Old English; from *The Divine Comedy*, the masterful epic by the Italian poet Dante, to *Paradise Lost,* the brilliant epic by Britain's John Milton—all had Homer's epics as models. Literary devices in Homer's epics are often imitated in these later works, even though many of the later epics were not orally composed. Influential literary devices found in Homer's epics include the following:

- **Opening invocation to the Muse:** The speaker of the poem asks the Muse for inspiration.
- **Starting the story in medias res,** or "in the middle of things": Beginning (after the invocation) with action instead of background information helps capture audience attention.
- **Lofty style:** Elegant language stresses the nobility of the subject.
- **Objective tone:** By keeping an emotional distance, the poet focuses attention on the story.
- **Meter,** or a fixed rhythmic pattern: A strong meter helps the oral poet remember the lines. In the original Greek, the *Odyssey* uses hexameter, or six beats to a line, which helps create a fast pace.
- **Epithet,** a characterizing phrase for a person, place, or thing: Recurring epithets are easy to remember and can help fill out the meter. Some examples of Homer's epithets include "rosy-fingered dawn" and "son of Laertes" for Odysseus.
- **Epic simile,** a long comparison over many lines: Such similes were another way to fill out the meter and aid the poet's memory.

Ionia, Homer's possible birthplace, was on the west coast of Asia Minor. The Ionian Sea, where Odysseus' island of Ithaca lies, is off the west coast of Greece. The duplicated names are likely no coincidence; Greek speakers from Ionia probably migrated to the west of Greece and brought the name with them (just as British settlers often brought British place names to America).

▼ The island of Ionia, Homer's possible birthplace, as it appears today

Background for the Story

The Trojan War

In the *Iliad*, Homer focuses on the final year of the Trojan War; in the *Odyssey*, he tells what happened to one of the key warriors afterward.

It Begins With Strife According to legend, the Trojan War began when Eris, goddess of strife, brought among the gods a golden apple inscribed "To the fairest." Hera, Athena, and Aphrodite all wanted that apple. They asked Paris, son of the king of Troy, to decide which of them deserved it. Each tried to bribe him: Hera offered power; Athena, wisdom; and Aphrodite, the world's most beautiful woman. The famous Judgment of Paris was that Aphrodite was the fairest. Soon, on a diplomatic mission to Sparta, Paris met Helen, the world's most beautiful woman and Sparta's queen. With Aphrodite's help, the two fell in love and eloped. When Menelaus (men′ ə lā′ əs), king of Sparta, could not persuade the Trojans to send his wife, Helen, back, he went to his brother Agamemnon (ag′ ə mem′ nän), king of Mycenae and the most powerful Greek leader. Agamemnon called on all the Greek rulers to honor a pact and go to Troy to fight to bring Helen home. The Greeks agreed and sailed to Troy. They laid siege to the city, but for ten long years could not breach its impregnable walls.

"Trojan" is the adjective form of the ancient city of Troy. It is also the name for a person from Troy.

War Crimes and Punishment Agamemnon might have been a more powerful king and Achilles (ə kil′ ēz) a superior warrior, but Odysseus, king of Ithaca, was cleverest of them all. He devised a scheme in which the Greeks left a great wooden horse outside the walls of Troy and tricked the Trojans into taking it inside. That night, the Greeks hiding inside the horse—Odysseus among them—slipped out, unlocked the gates of the city, and allowed their fellow warriors to come swarming in to defeat the Trojans and sack the city. The fighting was brutal and destructive. King Priam (prī′ əm), Paris' father, for example, was killed while he was praying. The Greeks' behavior angered many of the gods, who made their voyages home very difficult.

Named for Odysseus, the *Odyssey* gave rise to our English word *odyssey*, meaning "an extended journey."

Odysseus was no exception. Following the Greek victory, he set sail for Ithaca but encountered a series of perilous misadventures that made his journey last ten years. It is this difficult, adventure-filled journey that Homer's *Odyssey* recounts.

Do heroes have responsibilities?

Explore the Big Question as you read the *Odyssey*, Part 1. Consider whether the hero, Odysseus, demonstrates a sense of responsibility toward his men.

CLOSE READING FOCUS

Key Ideas and Details: **Historical and Cultural Context**

The **historical and cultural context** of a work is the collection of details that reflect the time and place in which it is set or written. When you read a work from another culture, apply knowledge you gain from reading biographies, footnotes, and other sources to analyze how the cultural context influences the characters, conflicts, and themes.

Craft and Structure: **Epic Hero**

An **epic hero** is the larger-than-life character in an **epic**—a long narrative poem that is central to a culture's national identity. The epic hero possesses traits that his society values most highly. Here, Odysseus speaks about his own courage and leadership:

> Now, by the gods, I drove my big hand spike
> deep in the embers, charring it again,
> and cheered my men along with battle talk
> to keep their courage up: no quitting now.

Traditional epics like the *Odyssey* use certain plot devices, or structures, that both provide information and allow the story to unfold in an exciting way. For example, many epics begin *in medias res* ("in the middle of things"), meaning that major events occurred before the action of the poem begins. The audience is, thus, thrust into the middle of the story. In addition, the hero's adventures are often recounted in a **flashback,** a scene that interrupts a narrative to relate earlier events.

Vocabulary

The words below are critical to understanding the text that follows. Decide whether you know the word well, know it a little bit, or do not know it at all. After you read, see how your knowledge of each word has increased.

plundered	**dispatched**	**assuage**
bereft	**ardor**	**insidious**

Common Core State Standards

Reading Literature

1. Cite strong and thorough textual evidence to support analysis of what the text says explicitly as well as inferences drawn from the text.

3. Analyze how complex characters develop over the course of a text, interact with other characters, and advance the plot or develop the theme.

5. Analyze how an author's choices concerning how to structure a text, order events within it, and manipulate time create such effects as mystery, tension, or surprise.

6. Analyze a particular point of view or cultural experience reflected in a work of literature from outside the United States, drawing on a wide reading of world literature.

CLOSE READING MODEL

The passages below are from the *Odyssey*, Part 1. The annotations to the right of the passages show ways in which you can use close reading skills to analyze the cultural context and the qualities of an epic hero.

from the *Odyssey*, Part I

...We served under Agamemnon, son of Atreus—
the whole world knows what city
he laid waste, what armies he destroyed.[1]
It was our luck to come here; here we stand,
beholden for your help, or any gifts
you give—as custom is to honor strangers.
We would entreat you, great Sir, have a care
for the gods' courtesy; Zeus will avenge
the unoffending guest.[2]

....

The storms continued.
So one day[3] I withdrew to the interior
to pray the gods in solitude, for hope
that one might show me some way of salvation.
Slipping away, I struck across the island
to a sheltered spot, out of the driving gale.
I washed my hands there, and made supplication
to the gods who own Olympus, all the gods—
but they, for answer, only closed my eyes
under slow drops of sleep.[4]

Epic Hero

1 Odysseus, who is telling his own story, refers to Agamemnon, the leader of the Greek forces during the Trojan War. Odysseus was one of the great heroes of that war. His success as a warrior is part of what makes him an epic hero.

Historical and Cultural Context

2 Use your background knowledge to recall that Zeus is king of the gods in Greek mythology. This statement also alludes to a cultural code of conduct that includes the rule: Honor strangers and do not offend a guest.

Epic Hero

3 These words are a reminder that the story Odysseus is telling is a memory, or flashback.

Historical and Cultural Context

4 The epic reflects the Greek belief in many gods who participate actively in the lives of mortals, sometimes for good and sometimes for ill. Here, Odysseus blames the gods for letting him fall asleep.

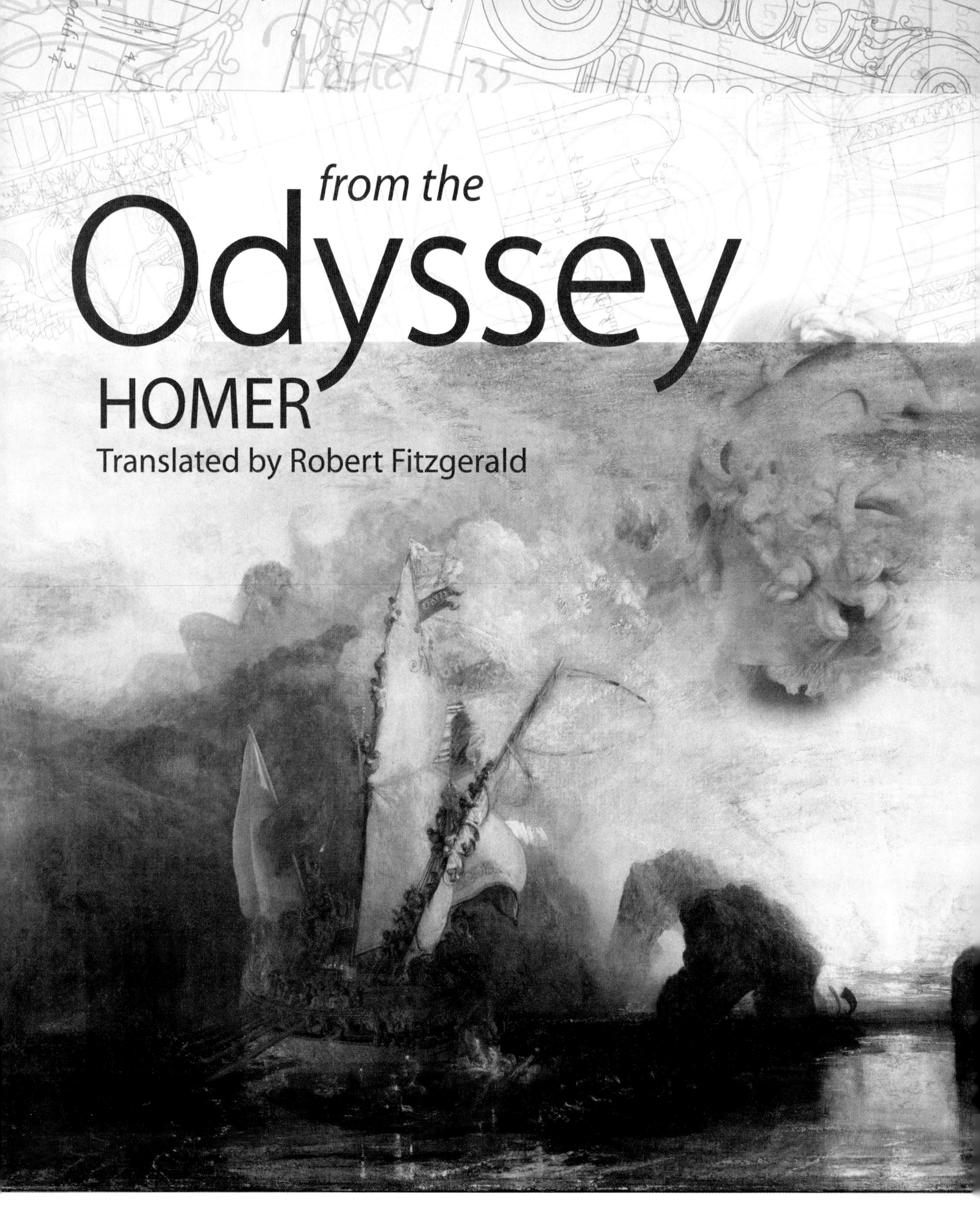

from the

Odyssey

HOMER

Translated by Robert Fitzgerald

Part 1
THE ADVENTURES OF ODYSSEUS

In the opening verses, Homer addresses the muse of epic poetry. He asks her help in telling the tale of Odysseus.

Sing in me, Muse,[1] and through me tell the story
of that man skilled in all ways of contending,
the wanderer, harried for years on end,
after he plundered the stronghold
on the proud height of Troy.[2]
He saw the townlands
and learned the minds of many distant men,
and weathered many bitter nights and days
in his deep heart at sea, while he fought only
to save his life, to bring his shipmates home.
But not by will nor valor could he save them,
for their own recklessness destroyed them all—
children and fools, they killed and feasted on
the cattle of Lord Helios,[3] the Sun,
and he who moves all day through heaven
took from their eyes the dawn of their return.
Of these adventures, Muse, daughter of Zeus,[4]
tell us in our time, lift the great song again.

1. **Muse** (myo͞oz) any one of the nine goddesses of the arts, literature, and sciences; the spirit that is thought to inspire a poet or other artist.
2. **Troy** (troi) city in northwest Asia Minor; site of the Trojan War.

◀ **Vocabulary**
plundered (plun′ dərd) *v.* took goods by force; looted

3. **Helios** (hē′ lē äs′) sun god.
4. **Zeus** (zo͞os) king of the gods.

Note: In translating the *Odyssey*, Fitzgerald spelled Greek names to suggest the sound of the original Greek. In these excerpts, more familiar spellings have been used. For example, Fitzgerald's "Kirkê," "Kyklops," and "Seirênês" are spelled here as "Circe," "Cyclops," and "Sirens."

CHARACTERS

Alcinous (al sin´ ō əs)—king of the Phaeacians, to whom Odysseus tells his story
Odysseus (ō dis´ ē əs)—king of Ithaca
Calypso (kə lip´ sō)—sea goddess who loved Odysseus
Circe (sʉr´ sē)—enchantress who helped Odysseus
Zeus (zo͞os)—king of the gods
Apollo (ə päl´ ō)—god of music, poetry, prophecy, and medicine
Agamemnon (ag´ ə mem´ nän´)—king and leader of Greek forces
Poseidon (pō sī´ dən)—god of sea, earthquakes, horses, and storms at sea
Athena (ə thē´ nə)—goddess of wisdom, skills, and warfare
Polyphemus (päl´ i fē´ məs)—the Cyclops who imprisoned Odysseus
Laertes (lā ʉr´ tēz´)—Odysseus' father
Cronus (krō´ nəs)—Titan ruler of the universe; father of Zeus
Perimedes (per´ ə mē´ dēz)—member of Odysseus' crew
Eurylochus (yo͞o ril´ ə kəs)—another member of the crew
Tiresias (tī rē´ sē əs)—blind prophet who advised Odysseus
Persephone (pər sef´ ə nē)—wife of Hades
Telemachus (tə lem´ ə kəs)—Odysseus and Penelope's son
Sirens sī´ rənz)—creatures whose songs lure sailors to their deaths
Scylla (sil´ ə)—sea monster of gray rock
Charybdis (kə rib´ dis)—enormous and dangerous whirlpool
Lampetia (lam pē´ shə)—nymph
Hermes (hʉr´ mēz´)—herald and messenger of the gods
Eumaeus (yo͞o mē´ əs)—old swineherd and friend of Odysseus
Antinous (an tin´ ō əs)—leader among the suitors
Eurynome (yo͞o rin´ ə mē)—housekeeper for Penelope
Penelope (pə nel´ ə pē)—Odysseus' wife
Eurymachus (yo͞o ri´ mə kəs)—suitor
Amphinomus (am fin´ ə məs)—suitor

SAILING FROM TROY

Ten years after the Trojan War, Odysseus departs from the goddess Calypso's island. He arrives in Phaeacia, ruled by Alcinous. Alcinous offers a ship to Odysseus and asks him to tell of his adventures.

"I am Laertes'[5] son, Odysseus.
Men hold me
formidable for guile[6] in peace and war:
this fame has gone abroad to the sky's rim.

My home is on the peaked sea-mark of Ithaca[7]
under Mount Neion's wind-blown robe of leaves,
in sight of other islands—Dulichium,
Same, wooded Zacynthus—Ithaca
being most lofty in that coastal sea,
and northwest, while the rest lie east and south.
A rocky isle, but good for a boy's training;
I shall not see on earth a place more dear,
though I have been detained long by Calypso,[8]
loveliest among goddesses, who held me
in her smooth caves, to be her heart's delight,
as Circe of Aeaea,[9] the enchantress,
desired me, and detained me in her hall.
But in my heart I never gave consent.
Where shall a man find sweetness to surpass
his own home and his parents? In far lands
he shall not, though he find a house of gold.

What of my sailing, then, from Troy?
What of those years
of rough adventure, weathered under Zeus?
The wind that carried west from Ilium[10]
brought me to Ismarus, on the far shore,
a strongpoint on the coast of Cicones.[11]
I stormed that place and killed the men who fought.
Plunder we took, and we enslaved the women,
to make division, equal shares to all—
but on the spot I told them: 'Back, and quickly!
Out to sea again!' My men were mutinous,[12]
fools, on stores of wine. Sheep after sheep

5. **Laertes** (lā ʉr´ tēz´)
6. **guile** (gīl) *n.* craftiness; cunning.
7. **Ithaca** (*ith*´ ə kə) island off the west coast of Greece.

Epic Hero
For what quality does Odysseus say he is famous?

8. **Calypso** (kə lip´ sō) sea goddess who loved Odysseus.

9. **Circe** (sʉr´ sē) **of Aeaea** (ē´ ē ə)

10. **Ilium** (il´ ē əm) Troy.

11. **Cicones** (si kō´ nēz)
12. **mutinous** (myo͞ot´'n əs) *adj.* rebellious.

Comprehension
Who has asked Odysseus to tell his tale?

they butchered by the surf, and shambling cattle,
feasting,—while fugitives went inland, running
to call to arms the main force of Cicones.
This was an army, trained to fight on horseback
or, where the ground required, on foot. They came
with dawn over that terrain like the leaves
and blades of spring. So doom appeared to us,
dark word of Zeus for us, our evil days.
My men stood up and made a fight of it—
backed on the ships, with lances kept in play,
from bright morning through the blaze of noon
holding our beach, although so far outnumbered;
but when the sun passed toward unyoking time,
then the Achaeans,[13] one by one, gave way.
Six benches were left empty in every ship
that evening when we pulled away from death.
And this new grief we bore with us to sea:
our precious lives we had, but not our friends.
No ship made sail next day until some shipmate
had raised a cry, three times, for each poor ghost
unfleshed by the Cicones on that field.

13. **Achaeans** (ə kē´ ənz) *n.* Greeks; here, Odysseus' men.

Historical and Cultural Context
What beliefs and values are reflected in lines 65–69?

The Lotus-Eaters

Now Zeus the lord of cloud roused in the north
a storm against the ships, and driving veils
of squall moved down like night on land and sea.
The bows went plunging at the gust; sails
cracked and lashed out strips in the big wind.
We saw death in that fury, dropped the yards,
unshipped the oars, and pulled for the nearest lee:[14]
then two long days and nights we lay offshore
worn out and sick at heart, tasting our grief,
until a third Dawn came with ringlets shining.
Then we put up our masts, hauled sail, and rested,
letting the steersmen and the breeze take over.

I might have made it safely home, that time,
but as I came round Malea the current
took me out to sea, and from the north
a fresh gale drove me on, past Cythera.
Nine days I drifted on the teeming sea
before dangerous high winds. Upon the tenth

14. **lee** (lē) *n.* area sheltered from the wind.

Epic Hero
What words in line 82 remind you that this part is a flashback?

we came to the coastline of the Lotus-Eaters,
who live upon that flower. We landed there
to take on water. All ships' companies
mustered alongside for the mid-day meal.
Then I sent out two picked men and a runner
to learn what race of men that land sustained.
They fell in, soon enough, with Lotus-Eaters,
who showed no will to do us harm, only
offering the sweet Lotus to our friends—
but those who ate this honeyed plant, the Lotus,
never cared to report, nor to return:
they longed to stay forever, browsing on
that native bloom, forgetful of their homeland.
I drove them, all three wailing, to the ships,
tied them down under their rowing benches,
and called the rest: 'All hands aboard;
come, clear the beach and no one taste
the Lotus, or you lose your hope of home.'
Filing in to their places by the rowlocks
my oarsmen dipped their long oars in the surf,
and we moved out again on our sea faring.

Epic Hero
Which characteristics of an epic hero does Odysseus show in this episode?

Critical Thinking

1. **Key Ideas and Details: (a)** While on Ismarus, in what ways do Odysseus' men disobey orders? **(b) Analyze Cause and Effect:** What is the result of this disobedience? **(c) Speculate:** What lesson might Odysseus take away from this experience? Explain your answer and cite details from the text to support your speculation.
2. **Key Ideas and Details: (a)** What happens to the men who eat the Lotus? **(b) Infer:** What does this episode suggest about the main problem that Odysseus has with his men? **(c) Evaluate:** Do you think Odysseus responds appropriately to the three men who long to stay with the Lotus-Eaters? Why or why not?
3. **Integration of Knowledge and Ideas: (a)** Note two points at which Odysseus mentions a longing for home. **(b) Infer:** What significant role might his longing for home play in Odysseus' epic journey? **(c) Connect:** What does this aspect of the story suggest about ancient Greek values? Explain.
4. **Integration of Knowledge and Ideas: (a)** In this episode, does Odysseus prove himself to be a hero? **(b)** What responsibilities does he demonstrate, if any? *[Connect to the Big Question: Do heroes have responsibilities?]*

The Cyclops

15. **Cyclopes** (sī klō′ pēz′) *n.* plural form of Cyclops (sī′ kläps′), race of giants with one eye in the middle of the forehead.

In the next land we found were Cyclopes,[15]
giants, louts, without a law to bless them.
In ignorance leaving the fruitage of the earth in mystery
to the immortal gods, they neither plow
nor sow by hand, nor till the ground, though grain—
wild wheat and barley—grows untended, and
wine-grapes, in clusters, ripen in heaven's rains.
Cyclopes have no muster and no meeting,
no consultation or old tribal ways,
but each one dwells in his own mountain cave
dealing out rough justice to wife and child,
indifferent to what the others do. . . .

Historical and Cultural Context
Based on Odysseus' criticism of the Cyclopes, what kind of society do you think the Greeks valued?

As we rowed on, and nearer to the mainland,
at one end of the bay, we saw a cavern
yawning above the water, screened with laurel,
and many rams and goats about the place
inside a sheepfold—made from slabs of stone
earthfast between tall trunks of pine and rugged
towering oak trees.
A prodigious[16] man
slept in this cave alone, and took his flocks
to graze afield—remote from all companions,
knowing none but savage ways, a brute
so huge, he seemed no man at all of those
who eat good wheaten bread; but he seemed rather
a shaggy mountain reared in solitude.
We beached there, and I told the crew
to stand by and keep watch over the ship:
as for myself I took my twelve best fighters
and went ahead. I had a goatskin full
of that sweet liquor that Euanthes' son,
Maron, had given me. He kept Apollo's[17]
holy grove at Ismarus; for kindness
we showed him there, and showed his wife and child,
he gave me seven shining golden talents[18]
perfectly formed, a solid silver winebowl,
and then this liquor—twelve two-handled jars
of brandy, pure and fiery. Not a slave
in Maron's household knew this drink; only
he, his wife and the storeroom mistress knew;

16. **prodigious** (prō dij′ əs) *adj.* enormous.

Historical and Cultural Context
What does this passage reveal about ancient Greek attitudes toward the importance of community?

17. **Apollo** (ə päl′ ō) god of music, poetry, prophecy, and medicine.

18. **talents** units of money in ancient Greece.

and they would put one cupful—ruby-colored,
honey-smooth—in twenty more of water,
but still the sweet scent hovered like a fume
over the winebowl. No man turned away
when cups of this came round.
A wineskin full
I brought along, and victuals[19] in a bag,
for in my bones I knew some towering brute
would be upon us soon—all outward power,
a wild man, ignorant of civility.

19. **victuals** (vit′ əlz) *n.* food or other provisions.

We climbed, then, briskly to the cave. But Cyclops
had gone afield, to pasture his fat sheep,
so we looked round at everything inside:
a drying rack that sagged with cheeses, pens
crowded with lambs and kids,[20] each in its class:
firstlings apart from middlings, and the 'dewdrops,'
or newborn lambkins, penned apart from both.
And vessels full of whey[21] were brimming there—
bowls of earthenware and pails for milking.
My men came pressing round me, pleading:
'Why not
take these cheeses, get them stowed, come back,
throw open all the pens, and make a run for it?
We'll drive the kids and lambs aboard. We say
put out again on good salt water!'

20. **kids** young goats.

21. **whey** (hwā) *n.* thin, watery part of milk separated from the thicker curds.

Ah,
how sound that was! Yet I refused. I wished
to see the cave man, what he had to offer—
no pretty sight, it turned out, for my friends.
We lit a fire, burnt an offering,
and took some cheese to eat; then sat in silence
around the embers, waiting. When he came
he had a load of dry boughs[22] on his shoulder
to stoke his fire at suppertime. He dumped it
with a great crash into that hollow cave,
and we all scattered fast to the far wall.
Then over the broad cavern floor he ushered
the ewes he meant to milk. He left his rams
and he-goats in the yard outside, and swung
high overhead a slab of solid rock

Epic Hero
What character flaw does the hero Odysseus reveal by refusing to leave the cave?

22. **boughs** (bouz) *n.* tree branches.

Comprehension
Where is Cyclops when Odysseus and his men enter the cave?

to close the cave. Two dozen four-wheeled wagons,
with heaving wagon teams, could not have stirred
the tonnage of that rock from where he wedged it
over the doorsill. Next he took his seat
and milked his bleating ewes. A practiced job
he made of it, giving each ewe her suckling;
thickened his milk, then, into curds and whey,
sieved out the curds to drip in withy[23] baskets,
and poured the whey to stand in bowls
cooling until he drank it for his supper.
When all these chores were done, he poked the fire,
heaping on brushwood. In the glare he saw us.

'Strangers,' he said, 'who are you? And where from?
What brings you here by seaways—a fair traffic?
Or are you wandering rogues, who cast your lives
like dice, and ravage other folk by sea?'

We felt a pressure on our hearts, in dread
of that deep rumble and that mighty man.
But all the same I spoke up in reply:
'We are from Troy, Achaeans, blown off course
by shifting gales on the Great South Sea;
homeward bound, but taking routes and ways
uncommon; so the will of Zeus would have it.
We served under Agamemnon,[24] son of Atreus—
the whole world knows what city
he laid waste, what armies he destroyed.
It was our luck to come here; here we stand,
beholden for your help, or any gifts
you give—as custom is to honor strangers.
We would entreat you, great Sir, have a care
for the gods' courtesy; Zeus will avenge
the unoffending guest.'

He answered this

from his brute chest, unmoved:

'You are a ninny,

or else you come from the other end of nowhere,
telling me, mind the gods! We Cyclopes
care not a whistle for your thundering Zeus
or all the gods in bliss; we have more force by far.

23. withy (with´ ē) *adj.* made from tough, flexible twigs.

24. Agamemnon (ag´ ə mem´ nän´) king who led the Greek army during the Trojan War.

Historical and Cultural Context
What ancient Greek beliefs regarding the gods, military might, and respect for strangers does Odysseus express in his words to the Cyclops?

I would not let you go for fear of Zeus—
you or your friends—unless I had a whim[25] to.
Tell me, where was it, now, you left your ship—
around the point, or down the shore, I wonder?'

He thought he'd find out, but I saw through this,
and answered with a ready lie:

'My ship?
Poseidon[26] Lord, who sets the earth a-tremble,
broke it up on the rocks at your land's end.
A wind from seaward served him, drove us there.
We are survivors, these good men and I.'

Neither reply nor pity came from him,
but in one stride he clutched at my companions
and caught two in his hands like squirming puppies
to beat their brains out, spattering the floor.
Then he dismembered them and made his meal,
gaping and crunching like a mountain lion—
everything: innards, flesh, and marrow bones.
We cried aloud, lifting our hands to Zeus,
powerless, looking on at this, appalled;
but Cyclops went on filling up his belly
with manflesh and great gulps of whey,
then lay down like a mast among his sheep.
My heart beat high now at the chance of action,
and drawing the sharp sword from my hip I went
along his flank to stab him where the midriff
holds the liver. I had touched the spot
when sudden fear stayed me: if I killed him
we perished there as well, for we could never
move his ponderous doorway slab aside.
So we were left to groan and wait for morning.

When the young Dawn with fingertips of rose
lit up the world, the Cyclops built a fire
and milked his handsome ewes, all in due order,
putting the sucklings to the mothers. Then,
his chores being all **dispatched**, he caught
another brace[27] of men to make his breakfast,
and whisked away his great door slab

25. **whim** (hwim) *n.* sudden thought or wish to do something.

26. **Poseidon** (pō sī´ dən) god of the sea, earthquakes, horses, and storms at sea.

Epic Hero
In what way does Odysseus' response show that he is "formidable for guile"?

Epic Hero
How do lines 244–250 show Odysseus' ability to think ahead?

◀ **Vocabulary**
dispatched (di spacht´)
v. finished quickly

27. **brace** (brās) *n.* pair.

Comprehension
What does Odysseus tell the Cyclops happened to his ship?

28. **cap a quiver** (kwiv´ ər) close a case holding arrows.
29. **din** (din) *n.* loud, continuous noise; uproar.
30. **Athena** (ə thē´ nə) goddess of wisdom, skills, and warfare.
31. **felled green and left to season** chopped down and exposed to the weather to age the wood.
32. **lugger** (lug´ ər) *n.* small sailing vessel.

Epic Hero
What heroic qualities does Odysseus reveal as he plots against the Cyclops?

to let his sheep go through—but he, behind,
reset the stone as one would cap a quiver.[28]
There was a din[29] of whistling as the Cyclops
rounded his flock to higher ground, then stillness.
And now I pondered how to hurt him worst,
if but Athena[30] granted what I prayed for.
Here are the means I thought would serve my turn:

a club, or staff, lay there along the fold—
an olive tree, felled green and left to season[31]
for Cyclops' hand. And it was like a mast
a lugger[32] of twenty oars, broad in the beam—
a deep-sea-going craft—might carry:
so long, so big around, it seemed. Now I
chopped out a six foot section of this pole
and set it down before my men, who scraped it;
and when they had it smooth, I hewed again
to make a stake with pointed end. I held this
in the fire's heart and turned it, toughening it,
then hid it, well back in the cavern, under
one of the dung piles in profusion there.
Now came the time to toss for it: who ventured
along with me? whose hand could bear to thrust
and grind that spike in Cyclops' eye, when mild
sleep had mastered him? As luck would have it,
the men I would have chosen won the toss—
four strong men, and I made five as captain.

At evening came the shepherd with his flock,
his woolly flock. The rams as well, this time,
entered the cave: by some sheepherding whim—
or a god's bidding—none were left outside.
He hefted his great boulder into place
and sat him down to milk the bleating ewes
in proper order, put the lambs to suck,
and swiftly ran through all his evening chores.
Then he caught two more men and feasted on them.
My moment was at hand, and I went forward
holding an ivy bowl of my dark drink,
looking up, saying:
'Cyclops, try some wine.
Here's liquor to wash down your scraps of men.
Taste it, and see the kind of drink we carried

Epic Hero
What plan do you think Odysseus has in mind by offering the Cyclops the wine?

under our planks. I meant it for an offering
if you would help us home. But you are mad,
unbearable, a bloody monster! After this,
will any other traveler come to see you?'

He seized and drained the bowl, and it went down
so fiery and smooth he called for more:

'Give me another, thank you kindly. Tell me,
how are you called? I'll make a gift will please you.
Even Cyclopes know the wine grapes grow
out of grassland and loam in heaven's rain,
but here's a bit of nectar and ambrosia!'[33]

Three bowls I brought him, and he poured them down.
I saw the fuddle and flush come over him,
then I sang out in cordial tones:

▲ Critical Viewing
What traits does this image of the Cyclops illustrate?

33. nectar (nek´ tər) **and ambrosia** (am brō´ zhə) drink and food of the gods.

Comprehension
What does Odysseus plan to do with the stake that he and his men make?

'Cyclops,
you ask my honorable name? Remember
the gift you promised me, and I shall tell you.
My name is Nohbdy: mother, father, and friends,
everyone calls me Nohbdy.'
And he said:
'Nohbdy's my meat, then, after I eat his friends.
Others come first. There's a noble gift, now.'

Even as he spoke, he reeled and tumbled backward,
his great head lolling to one side; and sleep
took him like any creature. Drunk, hiccuping,
he dribbled streams of liquor and bits of men.

Historical and Cultural Context
What cultural values are represented in Odysseus' reference to "the gods" in line 323?

Now, by the gods, I drove my big hand spike
deep in the embers, charring it again,
and cheered my men along with battle talk
to keep their courage up: no quitting now.
The pike of olive, green though it had been,
reddened and glowed as if about to catch.
I drew it from the coals and my four fellows
gave me a hand, lugging it near the Cyclops
as more than natural force nerved them; straight
forward they sprinted, lifted it, and rammed it
deep in his crater eye, and leaned on it
turning it as a shipwright turns a drill
in planking, having men below to swing
the two-handled strap that spins it in the groove.
So with our brand we bored[34] that great eye socket
while blood ran out around the red-hot bar.
Eyelid and lash were seared; the pierced ball
hissed broiling, and the roots popped.

34. bored (bôrd) *v.* made a hole in.

In a smithy
one sees a white-hot axehead or an adze
plunged and wrung in a cold tub, screeching steam—
the way they make soft iron hale and hard—:
just so that eyeball hissed around the spike.
The Cyclops bellowed and the rock roared round him,
and we fell back in fear. Clawing his face
he tugged the bloody spike out of his eye,
threw it away, and his wild hands went groping;

then he set up a howl for Cyclopes
who lived in caves on windy peaks nearby.
Some heard him; and they came by divers[35] ways
to clump around outside and call:
'What ails you,
Polyphemus?[36] Why do you cry so sore
in the starry night? You will not let us sleep.
Sure no man's driving off your flock? No man
has tricked you, ruined you?'
Out of the cave
the mammoth Polyphemus roared in answer:

'Nohbdy, Nohbdy's tricked me, Nohbdy's ruined me!'

To this rough shout they made a sage[37] reply:

'Ah well, if nobody has played you foul
there in your lonely bed, we are no use in pain
given by great Zeus. Let it be your father,
Poseidon Lord, to whom you pray.'

So saying
they trailed away. And I was filled with laughter
to see how like a charm the name deceived them.
Now Cyclops, wheezing as the pain came on him,
fumbled to wrench away the great doorstone
and squatted in the breach with arms thrown wide
for any silly beast or man who bolted—
hoping somehow I might be such a fool.
But I kept thinking how to win the game:
death sat there huge; how could we slip away?
I drew on all my wits, and ran through tactics,
reasoning as a man will for dear life,
until a trick came—and it pleased me well.
The Cyclops' rams were handsome, fat, with heavy
fleeces, a dark violet.
Three abreast
I tied them silently together, twining
cords of willow from the ogre's bed;
then slung a man under each middle one
to ride there safely, shielded left and right.

35. divers (dī′ vərz) *adj.* several; various.

36. Polyphemus (päl′ i fē′ məs)

37. sage (sāj) *adj.* wise.

Epic Hero
What does Odysseus' gleeful response to his successful trick reveal about his character?

Comprehension
What do the other Cyclopes think Polyphemus is saying when he says, "Nohbdy's tricked me"?

So three sheep could convey each man. I took
the woolliest ram, the choicest of the flock,
and hung myself under his kinky belly,
pulled up tight, with fingers twisted deep
in sheepskin ringlets for an iron grip.
So, breathing hard, we waited until morning.

When Dawn spread out her fingertips of rose
the rams began to stir, moving for pasture,
and peals of bleating echoed round the pens
where dams with udders full called for a milking.
Blinded, and sick with pain from his head wound,
the master stroked each ram, then let it pass,
but my men riding on the pectoral[38] fleece
the giant's blind hands blundering never found.
Last of them all my ram, the leader, came,
weighted by wool and me with my meditations.
The Cyclops patted him, and then he said:

'Sweet cousin ram, why lag behind the rest
in the night cave? You never linger so,
but graze before them all, and go afar
to crop sweet grass, and take your stately way
leading along the streams, until at evening
you run to be the first one in the fold.
Why, now, so far behind? Can you be grieving
over your Master's eye? That carrion rogue[39]
and his accurst companions burnt it out
when he had conquered all my wits with wine.
Nohbdy will not get out alive, I swear.
Oh, had you brain and voice to tell
where he may be now, dodging all my fury!
Bashed by this hand and bashed on this rock wall
his brains would strew the floor, and I should have
rest from the outrage Nohbdy worked upon me.'

He sent us into the open, then. Close by,
I dropped and rolled clear of the ram's belly,
going this way and that to untie the men.
With many glances back, we rounded up
his fat, stiff-legged sheep to take aboard,
and drove them down to where the good ship lay.

38. pectoral (pek´ tə rəl) *adj.* located in or on the chest.

Epic Hero
What details of this speech show that Polyphemus is far less clever than Odysseus?

39. carrion (kar´ ē ən) **rogue** (rōg) repulsive scoundrel.

◀ Critical Viewing
How does this image compare with your mental picture of the Cyclops?

Comprehension
How do the men escape from the Cyclops' cave?

▶ Critical Viewing
Odysseus and his surviving men escape in their ship as the blinded Cyclops hurls boulders and curses. How does this illustration compare to your mental image of the scene?

Spiral Review
UNIVERSAL THEME
What universal theme does the fight between Odysseus and the Cyclops suggest?

Epic Hero
Despite his heroism, what human weaknesses does Odysseus reveal as he sails away?

We saw, as we came near, our fellows' faces
shining; then we saw them turn to grief
tallying those who had not fled from death.
I hushed them, jerking head and eyebrows up,
and in a low voice told them: 'Load this herd;
move fast, and put the ship's head toward the breakers.'
They all pitched in at loading, then embarked
and struck their oars into the sea. Far out,
as far off shore as shouted words would carry,
I sent a few back to the adversary:
'O Cyclops! Would you feast on my companions?
Puny, am I, in a cave man's hands?
How do you like the beating that we gave you,
you damned cannibal? Eater of guests
under your roof! Zeus and the gods have paid you!'

The blind thing in his doubled fury broke
a hilltop in his hands and heaved it after us.
Ahead of our black prow it struck and sank
whelmed in a spuming geyser, a giant wave
that washed the ship stern foremost back to shore.
I got the longest boathook out and stood
fending us off, with furious nods to all
to put their backs into a racing stroke—
row, row, or perish. So the long oars bent
kicking the foam sternward, making head
until we drew away, and twice as far.
Now when I cupped my hands I heard the crew
in low voices protesting:

'Godsake, Captain!
Why bait the beast again? Let him alone!'

'That tidal wave he made on the first throw
all but beached us.'

'All but stove us in!'
'Give him our bearing with your trumpeting,
he'll get the range and lob a boulder.'

'Aye
He'll smash our timbers and our heads together!'
I would not heed them in my glorying spirit,

Polyphemus, The Cyclops from Homer's ***The Odyssey***, N.C. Wyeth, Brandywine River Museum.

but let my anger flare and yelled:
'Cyclops,
if ever mortal man inquire
how you were put to shame and blinded, tell him
Odysseus, raider of cities, took your eye:
Laertes' son, whose home's on Ithaca!'

At this he gave a mighty sob and rumbled:
'Now comes the weird[40] upon me, spoken of old.
A wizard, grand and wondrous, lived here—Telemus,[41]
a son of Eurymus;[42] great length of days
he had in wizardry among the Cyclopes,
and these things he foretold for time to come:
my great eye lost, and at Odysseus' hands.
Always I had in mind some giant, armed
in giant force, would come against me here.
But this, but you—small, pitiful and twiggy—
you put me down with wine, you blinded me.
Come back, Odysseus, and I'll treat you well,
praying the god of earthquake[43] to befriend you—
his son I am, for he by his avowal
fathered me, and, if he will, he may
heal me of this black wound—he and no other
of all the happy gods or mortal men.'

Few words I shouted in reply to him:

'If I could take your life I would and take
your time away, and hurl you down to hell!
The god of earthquake could not heal you there!'

At this he stretched his hands out in his darkness
toward the sky of stars, and prayed Poseidon:

'O hear me, lord, blue girdler of the islands,
if I am thine indeed, and thou art father:
grant that Odysseus, raider of cities, never
see his home: Laertes' son, I mean,
who kept his hall on Ithaca. Should destiny
intend that he shall see his roof again
among his family in his father land,
far be that day, and dark the years between.

40. weird (wird) *n.* fate or destiny.
41. Telemus (tel e´ məs)
42. Eurymus (yo͞o rim´ əs)

43. god of earthquake Poseidon.

Historical and Cultural Context
What do lines 472–493 suggest about ancient Greek beliefs about the gods' involvement in the mortal world?

Let him lose all companions, and return
under strange sail to bitter days at home.'
In these words he prayed, and the god heard him.
Now he laid hands upon a bigger stone
and wheeled around, titanic for the cast,
to let it fly in the black-prowed vessel's track.
But it fell short, just aft the steering oar,
and whelming seas rose giant above the stone
to bear us onward toward the island.

There
as we ran in we saw the squadron waiting,
the trim ships drawn up side by side, and all
our troubled friends who waited, looking seaward.
We beached her, grinding keel in the soft sand,
and waded in, ourselves, on the sandy beach.
Then we unloaded all the Cyclops' flock
to make division, share and share alike,
only my fighters voted that my ram,
the prize of all, should go to me. I slew him
by the seaside and burnt his long thighbones
to Zeus beyond the stormcloud, Cronus'[44] son,
who rules the world. But Zeus disdained my offering;
destruction for my ships he had in store
and death for those who sailed them, my companions.
Now all day long until the sun went down
we made our feast on mutton and sweet wine,
till after sunset in the gathering dark
we went to sleep above the wash of ripples.

When the young Dawn with fingertips of rose
touched the world, I roused the men, gave orders
to man the ships, cast off the mooring lines;
and filing in to sit beside the rowlocks
oarsmen in line dipped oars in the gray sea.
So we moved out, sad in the vast offing,[45]
having our precious lives, but not our friends.

Epic Hero
What admirable quality does Odysseus show by dividing the sheep among his men?

44. Cronus (krō´ nəs) Titan who was ruler of the universe until he was overthrown by his son Zeus.

45. offing (ôf´ iŋ) *n.* distant part of the sea visible from the shore.

Comprehension
What does the Cyclops ask for in his prayer to Poseidon?

The Land of the Dead

Odysseus and his men sail to Aeolia, where Aeolus,[46] *king of the winds, sends Odysseus on his way with a gift: a sack containing all the winds except the favorable west wind. When they are near home, Odysseus' men open the sack, letting loose a storm that drives them back to Aeolia. Aeolus casts them out, having decided that they are detested by the gods. They sail for seven days and arrive in the land of the Laestrygonians,*[47] *a race of cannibals. These creatures destroy all of Odysseus' ships except the one he is sailing in. Odysseus and his reduced crew escape and reach Aeaea, the island ruled by the sorceress-goddess Circe. She transforms half of the men into swine. Protected by a magic herb, Odysseus demands that Circe change his men back into human form. Before Odysseus departs from the island a year later, Circe informs him that in order to reach home he must journey to the land of the dead, Hades, and consult the blind prophet Tiresias.*

46. **Aeolia** (ē ō′ lē ə) . . . **Aeolus** (ē′ ə ləs)

47. **Laestrygonians** (les tri gō′ nē ənz)

We bore down on the ship at the sea's edge
and launched her on the salt immortal sea,
stepping our mast and spar in the black ship;
embarked the ram and ewe and went aboard
in tears, with bitter and sore dread upon us.
But now a breeze came up for us astern—
a canvas-bellying landbreeze, hale shipmate
sent by the singing nymph with sunbright hair;[48]
so we made fast the braces, took our thwarts,
and let the wind and steersman work the ship
with full sail spread all day above our coursing,
till the sun dipped, and all the ways grew dark
upon the fathomless unresting sea.

By night
our ship ran onward toward the Ocean's bourne,
the realm and region of the Men of Winter,
hidden in mist and cloud. Never the flaming
eye of Helios lights on those men
at morning, when he climbs the sky of stars,
nor in descending earthward out of heaven;
ruinous night being rove over those wretches.
We made the land, put ram and ewe ashore,

48. **singing nymph . . . hair** Circe.

Historical and Cultural Context
What details here suggest that the source of wind was mysterious to ancient Greeks?

and took our way along the Ocean stream
to find the place foretold for us by Circe.
There Perimedes and Eurylochus[49]
pinioned[50] the sacred beasts. With my drawn blade
I spaded up the votive[51] pit, and poured
libations[52] round it to the unnumbered dead:
sweet milk and honey, then sweet wine, and last
clear water; and I scattered barley down.
Then I addressed the blurred and breathless dead,
vowing to slaughter my best heifer for them
before she calved, at home in Ithaca,
and burn the choice bits on the altar fire;
as for Tiresias,[53] I swore to sacrifice
a black lamb, handsomest of all our flock.
Thus to assuage the nations of the dead
I pledged these rites, then slashed the lamb and ewe,
letting their black blood stream into the wellpit.
Now the souls gathered, stirring out of Erebus,[54]
brides and young men, and men grown old in pain,
and tender girls whose hearts were new to grief;
many were there, too, torn by brazen lanceheads,
battle-slain, bearing still their bloody gear.
From every side they came and sought the pit
with rustling cries; and I grew sick with fear.
But presently I gave command to my officers
to flay those sheep the bronze cut down, and make
burnt offerings of flesh to the gods below—
to sovereign Death, to pale Persephone.[55]
Meanwhile I crouched with my drawn sword to keep
the surging phantoms from the bloody pit
till I should know the presence of Tiresias.

One shade came first—Elpenor, of our company,
who lay unburied still on the wide earth
as we had left him—dead in Circe's hall,
untouched, unmourned, when other cares compelled us.
Now when I saw him there I wept for pity
and called out to him:
'How is this, Elpenor,
how could you journey to the western gloom
swifter afoot than I in the black lugger?'
He sighed, and answered:

49. Perimedes (per´ ə mē´ dēz) **and Eurylochus** (yo͞o ril´ ə kəs)

50. pinioned (pin´ yənd) *v.* confined or shackled.

51. votive (vōt´ iv) *adj.* done to fulfill a vow or express thanks.

52. libations (lī bā´ shənz) *n.* wine or other liquids poured upon the ground as a sacrifice or offering.

53. Tiresias (tī rē´ sē əs)

◀ Vocabulary
assuage (ə swāj´)
v. calm; pacify

54. Erebus (er´ ə bəs) dark region under the earth through which the dead pass before entering the realm of Hades.

55. Persephone (pər sef´ ə nē) wife of Hades.

Comprehension
What does Circe say that Odysseus must do in order to reach home?

Odysseus in the Land of the Dead from Homer's ***The Odyssey,*** N.C. Wyeth, Brandywine River Museum

'Son of great Laertes,
Odysseus, master mariner and soldier,
bad luck shadowed me, and no kindly power;
ignoble death I drank with so much wine.
I slept on Circe's roof, then could not see
the long steep backward ladder, coming down,
and fell that height. My neckbone, buckled under,
snapped, and my spirit found this well of dark.
Now hear the grace I pray for, in the name
of those back in the world, not here—your wife
and father, he who gave you bread in childhood,
and your own child, your only son, Telemachus,[56]
long ago left at home.
When you make sail
and put these lodgings of dim Death behind,
you will moor ship, I know, upon Aeaea Island;
there, O my lord, remember me, I pray,
do not abandon me unwept, unburied,
to tempt the gods' wrath, while you sail for home;
but fire my corpse, and all the gear I had,
and build a cairn[57] for me above the breakers—
an unknown sailor's mark for men to come.
Heap up the mound there, and implant upon it
the oar I pulled in life with my companions.'

He ceased, and I replied:

'Unhappy spirit,
I promise you the barrow and the burial.'

So we conversed, and grimly, at a distance,
with my long sword between, guarding the blood,
while the faint image of the lad spoke on.
Now came the soul of Anticlea, dead,
my mother, daughter of Autolycus,[58]
dead now, though living still when I took ship
for holy Troy. Seeing this ghost I grieved,
but held her off, through pang on pang of tears,
till I should know the presence of Tiresias.
Soon from the dark that prince of Thebes[59] came forward
bearing a golden staff; and he addressed me:

◀ Critical Viewing
What can you infer about ancient Greek beliefs concerning death and the afterlife from lines 555–577 on page 777 and from this illustration?

56. Telemachus (tə lem′ ə kəs)

57. cairn (kern) *n.* conical heap of stones built as a monument.

Historical and Cultural Context
What ancient Greek values and beliefs are suggested by Elpenor's requests?

58. Autolycus (ô täl′ i kəs)

59. Thebes (thēbz)

Comprehension
What does Elpenor's spirit ask of Odysseus?

'Son of Laertes and the gods of old,
Odysseus, master of landways and seaways,
why leave the blazing sun, O man of woe,
to see the cold dead and the joyless region?
Stand clear, put up your sword;
let me but taste of blood, I shall speak true.'

At this I stepped aside, and in the scabbard
let my long sword ring home to the pommel silver,
as he bent down to the somber blood. Then spoke
the prince of those with gift of speech:
'Great captain,
a fair wind and the honey lights of home
are all you seek. But anguish lies ahead;
the god who thunders on the land prepares it,
not to be shaken from your track, implacable,
in rancor for the son whose eye you blinded.
One narrow strait may take you through his blows:
denial of yourself, restraint of shipmates.
When you make landfall on Thrinacia first
and quit the violet sea, dark on the land
you'll find the grazing herds of Helios
by whom all things are seen, all speech is known.
Avoid those kine,[60] hold fast to your intent,
and hard seafaring brings you all to Ithaca.
But if you raid the beeves, I see destruction
for ship and crew. Though you survive alone,
bereft of all companions, lost for years,
under strange sail shall you come home, to find
your own house filled with trouble: insolent men
eating your livestock as they court your lady.
Aye, you shall make those men atone in blood!
But after you have dealt out death—in open
combat or by stealth—to all the suitors,
go overland on foot, and take an oar,
until one day you come where men have lived
with meat unsalted, never known the sea,
nor seen seagoing ships, with crimson bows
and oars that fledge light hulls for dipping flight.
The spot will soon be plain to you, and I
can tell you how: some passerby will say,

Historical and Cultural Context
What ancient Greek value is reflected in the "narrow strait" that Tiresias describes (lines 637–638)?

60. kine (kīn) *n.* cattle.

Vocabulary ▶
bereft (bē reft′) *adj.* deprived

"What winnowing fan is that upon your shoulder?"
Halt, and implant your smooth oar in the turf
and make fair sacrifice to Lord Poseidon:
a ram, a bull, a great buck boar; turn back,
and carry out pure hecatombs[61] at home
to all wide heaven's lords, the undying gods,
to each in order. Then a seaborne death
soft as this hand of mist will come upon you
when you are wearied out with rich old age,
your country folk in blessed peace around you.
And all this shall be just as I foretell.'

61. **hecatombs** (hek´ ə tōmz´) *n.* large-scale sacrifices to the gods in ancient Greece; often, the slaughter of 100 cattle at one time.

Critical Thinking

1. **Key Ideas and Details: (a)** Before the meeting with the Cyclops, what had Odysseus received from Maron at Ismarus? **(b) Generalize:** What does the encounter with Maron reveal about ancient Greek attitudes regarding hospitality? Explain.
2. **Key Ideas and Details: (a)** How do Odysseus and his companions expect to be treated by the Cyclops? **(b) Infer:** What "laws" of behavior and attitude does Polyphemus violate? Explain.
3. **Key Ideas and Details: (a)** How do Odysseus and his crew escape from the Cyclops? **(b) Evaluate:** What positive and negative character traits does Odysseus demonstrate in his adventure with the Cyclops? Explain, citing specific examples from the text.
4. **Key Ideas and Details: (a)** What difficulty does Tiresias predict for the journey to come? **(b) Speculate:** Why would Odysseus continue, despite Tiresias' grim prophecies? Explain, citing details from the text to support your answer.
5. **Integration of Knowledge and Ideas:** Judging from Tiresias' prediction, which heroic qualities will Odysseus need to rely upon as he continues his journey? Explain.
6. **Integration of Knowledge and Ideas: (a)** What are Odysseus' responsibilities as he reaches the land of the Cyclopes? **(b)** How well does he fulfill these responsibilities? Support your answer with details from the epic. ***[Connect to the Big Question: Do heroes have responsibilities?]***

Circe Meanwhile Had Gone Her Ways . . ., 1924, William Russell Flint Collection of the New York Public Library, Special Collections/ Art Resources

The Sirens

Odysseus returns to Circe's island. The goddess reveals his course to him and gives advice on how to avoid the dangers he will face: the Sirens, who lure sailors to their destruction; the Wandering Rocks, sea rocks that destroy even birds in flight; the perils of the sea monster Scylla and, nearby, the whirlpool Charybdis;[62] and the cattle of the sun god, which Tiresias has warned Odysseus not to harm.

62. **Charybdis** (kə rib′ dis)

As Circe spoke, Dawn mounted her golden throne,
and on the first rays Circe left me, taking
her way like a great goddess up the island.
I made straight for the ship, roused up the men
to get aboard and cast off at the stern.
They scrambled to their places by the rowlocks
and all in line dipped oars in the gray sea.
But soon an offshore breeze blew to our liking—
a canvas-bellying breeze, a lusty shipmate
sent by the singing nymph with sunbright hair.
So we made fast the braces, and we rested,
letting the wind and steersman work the ship.
The crew being now silent before me, I
addressed them, sore at heart:

'Dear friends,
more than one man, or two, should know those things
Circe foresaw for us and shared with me,
so let me tell her forecast: then we die
with our eyes open, if we are going to die,
or know what death we baffle if we can. Sirens
weaving a haunting song over the sea
we are to shun, she said, and their green shore
all sweet with clover; yet she urged that I
alone should listen to their song. Therefore
you are to tie me up, tight as a splint,
erect along the mast, lashed to the mast,
and if I shout and beg to be untied,
take more turns of the rope to muffle me.'

I rather dwelt on this part of the forecast,
while our good ship made time, bound outward down
the wind for the strange island of Sirens.

◀ Critical Viewing
The sorceress Circe both helps and hinders Odysseus on his journey home. What can you tell about Circe from this illustration?

Epic Hero
What does Odysseus reveal about his character by sharing information with his men?

Comprehension
What instructions does Odysseus give his shipmates as they prepare to deal with the Sirens?

Then all at once the wind fell, and a calm
came over all the sea, as though some power
lulled the swell.
The crew were on their feet
briskly, to furl the sail, and stow it; then,
each in place, they poised the smooth oar blades
and sent the white foam scudding by. I carved
a massive cake of beeswax into bits
and rolled them in my hands until they softened—
no long task, for a burning heat came down
from Helios, lord of high noon. Going forward
I carried wax along the line, and laid it
thick on their ears. They tied me up, then, plumb
amidships, back to the mast, lashed to the mast,
and took themselves again to rowing. Soon,
as we came smartly within hailing distance,
the two Sirens, noting our fast ship
off their point, made ready, and they sang:

Historical and Cultural Context What does Odysseus' mention of Helios reveal about ancient Greek beliefs regarding astronomical events?

This way, oh turn your bows,
Achaea's glory,
As all the world allows—
Moor and be merry.

Sweet coupled airs we sing.
No lonely seafarer
Holds clear of entering
Our green mirror.

Pleased by each purling note
Like honey twining
From her throat and my throat,
Who lies a-pining?

Epic Hero Which details in the Sirens' song are designed to flatter the epic hero?

Sea rovers here take joy
Voyaging onward,
As from our song of Troy
Graybeard and rower-boy
Goeth more learnèd.

All feats on that great field
In the long warfare,
Dark days the bright gods willed,
Wounds you bore there,

Argos' old soldiery[63]
On Troy beach teeming,
Charmed out of time we see.
No life on earth can be
Hid from our dreaming.

The lovely voices in ardor appealing over the water
made me crave to listen, and I tried to say
'Untie me!' to the crew, jerking my brows;
but they bent steady to the oars. Then Perimedes
got to his feet, he and Eurylochus,
and passed more line about, to hold me still.
So all rowed on, until the Sirens
dropped under the sea rim, and their singing
dwindled away.
My faithful company
rested on their oars now, peeling off
the wax that I had laid thick on their ears;
then set me free.

63. **Argos' old soldiery** soldiers from Argos, a city in ancient Greece.

◀ **Vocabulary**
ardor (är′ dər) *n.* passion; enthusiasm

Spiral Review
Universal Theme
What details in this scene suggest the importance of having loyal friends and companions?

Scylla and Charybdis

But scarcely had that island
faded in blue air than I saw smoke
and white water, with sound of waves in tumult—
a sound the men heard, and it terrified them.
Oars flew from their hands; the blades went knocking
wild alongside till the ship lost way,
with no oar blades to drive her through the water.
Well, I walked up and down from bow to stern,
trying to put heart into them, standing over
every oarsman, saying gently,

'Friends,
have we never been in danger before this?
More fearsome, is it now, than when the Cyclops
penned us in his cave? What power he had!
Did I not keep my nerve, and use my wits
to find a way out for us?

Comprehension
How does Odysseus keep his shipmates from hearing the Sirens sing?

Epic Hero
What parts of Odysseus' speech demonstrate his strength as a leader?

Now I say
by hook or crook this peril too shall be
something that we remember.
Heads up, lads!
We must obey the orders as I give them.
Get the oar shafts in your hands, and lay back
hard on your benches; hit these breaking seas.
Zeus help us pull away before we founder.
You at the tiller, listen, and take in
all that I say—the rudders are your duty;
keep her out of the combers and the smoke;[64]
steer for that headland; watch the drift, or we
fetch up in the smother, and you drown us.'

That was all, and it brought them round to action.
But as I sent them on toward Scylla,[65] I
told them nothing, as they could do nothing.
They would have dropped their oars again, in panic,
to roll for cover under the decking. Circe's
bidding against arms had slipped my mind,
so I tied on my cuirass[66] and took up
two heavy spears, then made my way along
to the foredeck—thinking to see her first from there,
the monster of the gray rock, harboring
torment for my friends. I strained my eyes
upon the cliffside veiled in cloud, but nowhere
could I catch sight of her.
And all this time,
in travail,[67] sobbing, gaining on the current,
we rowed into the strait—Scylla to port
and on our starboard beam Charybdis, dire
gorge[68] of the salt seatide. By heaven! when she
vomited, all the sea was like a cauldron
seething over intense fire, when the mixture
suddenly heaves and rises.
The shot spume
soared to the landside heights, and fell like rain.
But when she swallowed the sea water down
we saw the funnel of the maelstrom,[69] heard
the rock bellowing all around, and dark
sand raged on the bottom far below.
My men all blanched against the gloom, our eyes

64. **the combers** (kōm′ ərs) **and the smoke** the large waves that break on the beach and the ocean spray.

65. **Scylla** (sil′ ə)

66. **cuirass** (kwi ras′) *n.* armor for the upper body.

67. **travail** (trə vāl′) *n.* very hard work.

68. **gorge** (gôrj) *n.* throat or gullet.

69. **maelstrom** (māl′ strəm) *n.* large, violent whirlpool.

were fixed upon that yawning mouth in fear
of being devoured.
                    Then Scylla made her strike,
whisking six of my best men from the ship.
I happened to glance aft at ship and oarsmen
and caught sight of their arms and legs, dangling
high overhead. Voices came down to me
in anguish, calling my name for the last time.

A man surfcasting on a point of rock
for bass or mackerel, whipping his long rod
to drop the sinker and the bait far out,

◀ Critical Viewing
How does this image compare with the description of Scylla in the scene?

Comprehension
What demand does Odysseus make of his men as they approach the rough waters?

will hook a fish and rip it from the surface
to dangle wriggling through the air:
so these
were borne aloft in spasms toward the cliff.

Epic Hero
What quality of heroic leadership does Odysseus show in lines 823–825?

She ate them as they shrieked there, in her den,
in the dire grapple, reaching still for me—
and deathly pity ran me through
at that sight—far the worst I ever suffered,
questing the passes of the strange sea.
We rowed on.
The Rocks were now behind; Charybdis, too,
and Scylla dropped astern.

The Cattle of the Sun God

Historical and Cultural Context
Which details here suggest that ancient Greeks believed the gods controlled the weather?

In the small hours of the third watch, when stars
that shone out in the first dusk of evening
had gone down to their setting, a giant wind
blew from heaven, and clouds driven by Zeus
shrouded land and sea in a night of storm;
so, just as Dawn with fingertips of rose
touched the windy world, we dragged our ship
to cover in a grotto, a sea cave
where nymphs had chairs of rock and sanded floors.
I mustered all the crew and said:

'Old shipmates,
our stores are in the ship's hold, food and drink;
the cattle here are not for our provision,
or we pay dearly for it.
Fierce the god is
who cherishes these heifers and these sheep:
Helios; and no man avoids his eye.'

Historical and Cultural Context
How does this passage show that ancient Greeks believed their gods had human-like emotions?

To this my fighters nodded. Yes. But now
we had a month of onshore gales, blowing
day in, day out—south winds, or south by east.
As long as bread and good red wine remained
to keep the men up, and appease their craving,
they would not touch the cattle. But in the end,
when all the barley in the ship was gone,

hunger drove them to scour the wild shore
with angling hooks, for fishes and sea fowl,
whatever fell into their hands; and lean days
wore their bellies thin.
                                        The storms continued.
So one day I withdrew to the interior
to pray the gods in solitude, for hope
that one might show me some way of salvation.
Slipping away, I struck across the island
to a sheltered spot, out of the driving gale.
I washed my hands there, and made supplication
to the gods who own Olympus,[70] all the gods—
but they, for answer, only closed my eyes
under slow drops of sleep.
                                        Now on the shore Eurylochus
made his **insidious** plea:
                                        'Comrades,' he said,
'You've gone through everything; listen to what I say.
All deaths are hateful to us, mortal wretches,
but famine is the most pitiful, the worst
end that a man can come to.
                                        Will you fight it?
Come, we'll cut out the noblest of these cattle
for sacrifice to the gods who own the sky;
and once at home, in the old country of Ithaca,
if ever that day comes—
we'll build a costly temple and adorn it
with every beauty for the Lord of Noon.[71]
But if he flares up over his heifers lost,
wishing our ship destroyed, and if the gods
make cause with him, why, then I say: Better
open your lungs to a big sea once for all
than waste to skin and bones on a lonely island!'

Thus Eurylochus; and they murmured 'Aye!'
trooping away at once to round up heifers.
Now, that day tranquil cattle with broad brows
were grazing near, and soon the men drew up
around their chosen beasts in ceremony.
They plucked the leaves that shone on a tall oak—
having no barley meal—to strew the victims,
performed the prayers and ritual, knifed the kine

70. Olympus (ō lim′ pəs) Mount Olympus, home of the gods.

◀ **Vocabulary**
insidious (in sid′ ē əs) *adj.* characterized by craftiness and betrayal

71. Lord of Noon Helios.

Epic Hero
How are the values of Eurylochus different from those of Odysseus?

Comprehension
Who owns the heifers and sheep on the island?

LITERATURE IN CONTEXT

Geography Connection

Real Places and Imaginary Events in the *Odyssey*

Odysseus' journey carries him to real places, including Troy, Sparta, and the Strait of Gibraltar. However, in the story, many of these real places are populated by imaginary creatures, such as the Cyclops and the Sirens. The combination of real places and fantastic events is part of the story's appeal.

Connect to the Literature How does the inclusion of real places make the story's imaginary events more believable?

and flayed each carcass, cutting thighbones free
to wrap in double folds of fat. These offerings,
with strips of meat, were laid upon the fire.
Then, as they had no wine, they made libation
with clear spring water, broiling the entrails first;
and when the bones were burnt and tripes shared,
they spitted the carved meat.
Just then my slumber
left me in a rush, my eyes opened,
and I went down the seaward path. No sooner
had I caught sight of our black hull, than savory
odors of burnt fat eddied around me;
grief took hold of me, and I cried aloud:

'O Father Zeus and gods in bliss forever,
you made me sleep away this day of mischief!
O cruel drowsing, in the evil hour!
Here they sat, and a great work they contrived.'[72]

72. **contrived** (kən trīvd′) *v.* thought up; devised.

Lampetia[73] in her long gown meanwhile
had borne swift word to the Overlord of Noon:
'They have killed your kine.'
And the Lord Helios
burst into angry speech amid the immortals:

'O Father Zeus and gods in bliss forever,
punish Odysseus' men! So overweening,
now they have killed my peaceful kine, my joy
at morning when I climbed the sky of stars,
and evening, when I bore westward from heaven.
Restitution or penalty they shall pay—
and pay in full—or I go down forever
to light the dead men in the underworld.'

Then Zeus who drives the stormcloud made reply:
'Peace, Helios: shine on among the gods,
shine over mortals in the fields of grain.
Let me throw down one white-hot bolt, and make
splinters of their ship in the winedark sea.'

—Calypso later told me of this exchange,
as she declared that Hermes[74] had told her.
Well, when I reached the sea cave and the ship,
I faced each man, and had it out; but where
could any remedy be found? There was none.
The silken beeves[75] of Helios were dead.
The gods, moreover, made queer signs appear:
cowhides began to crawl, and beef, both raw
and roasted, lowed like kine upon the spits.

Now six full days my gallant crew could feast
upon the prime beef they had marked for slaughter
from Helios' herd; and Zeus, the son of Cronus,
added one fine morning.
All the gales
had ceased, blown out, and with an offshore breeze
we launched again, stepping the mast and sail,
to make for the open sea. Astern of us
the island coastline faded, and no land
showed anywhere, but only sea and heaven,
when Zeus Cronion piled a thunderhead
above the ship, while gloom spread on the ocean.

73. Lampetia (lam pē´ shə) a nymph.

74. Hermes (hʉr´ mēz´) *n.* god who serves as herald and messenger of the other gods.

75. beeves (bēvz) *n.* alternate plural form of "beef."

Epic Hero
What details in lines 920–921 clarify the flashback presented here?

Comprehension
What do Odysseus' shipmates do while he is sleeping?

La Nef de Telemachus (The Ship of Telemachus), New York Public Library Picture Collection

We held our course, but briefly. Then the squall
struck whining from the west, with gale force, breaking
both forestays, and the mast came toppling aft
along the ship's length, so the running rigging
showered into the bilge.
On the afterdeck
the mast had hit the steersman a slant blow
bashing the skull in, knocking him overside,
as the brave soul fled the body, like a diver.
With crack on crack of thunder, Zeus let fly
a bolt against the ship, a direct hit,
so that she bucked, in reeking fumes of sulphur,
and all the men were flung into the sea.
They came up 'round the wreck, bobbing awhile
like petrels[76] on the waves.
No more seafaring
homeward for these, no sweet day of return;
the god had turned his face from them.
I clambered
fore and aft my hulk until a comber
split her, keel from ribs, and the big timber
floated free; the mast, too, broke away.
A backstay floated dangling from it, stout
rawhide rope, and I used this for lashing
mast and keel together. These I straddled,
riding the frightful storm.

Nor had I yet
seen the worst of it: for now the west wind
dropped, and a southeast gale came on—one more
twist of the knife—taking me north again,
straight for Charybdis. All that night I drifted,
and in the sunrise, sure enough, I lay
off Scylla mountain and Charybdis deep.
There, as the whirlpool drank the tide, a billow
tossed me, and I sprang for the great fig tree,
catching on like a bat under a bough.
Nowhere had I to stand, no way of climbing,
the root and bole[77] being far below, and far
above my head the branches and their leaves,
massed, overshadowing Charybdis pool.
But I clung grimly, thinking my mast and keel
would come back to the surface when she spouted.

◀ Critical Viewing
In the *Odyssey*, Odysseus' son Telemachus searches for his father in a ship like this one. From what you observe in the painting, how does this ship compare with modern ships?

76. petrels (pe´ trəlz) *n.* small, dark sea birds.

Epic Hero
Which of Odysseus' heroic qualities does he demonstrate in this passage?

77. bole (bōl) *n.* tree trunk.

Comprehension
How is Odysseus' ship destroyed?

And ah! how long, with what desire, I waited!
till, at the twilight hour, when one who hears
and judges pleas in the marketplace all day
between contentious men, goes home to supper,
the long poles at last reared from the sea.

Now I let go with hands and feet, plunging
straight into the foam beside the timbers,
pulled astride, and rowed hard with my hands
to pass by Scylla. Never could I have passed her
had not the Father of gods and men,[78] this time,
kept me from her eyes. Once through the strait,
nine days I drifted in the open sea
before I made shore, buoyed up by the gods,
upon Ogygia[79] Isle. The dangerous nymph
Calypso lives and sings there, in her beauty,
and she received me, loved me.

But why tell

the same tale that I told last night in hall
to you and to your lady? Those adventures
made a long evening, and I do not hold
with tiresome repetition of a story."

78. Father . . . men Zeus.

79. Ogygia (o jij′ ī ə)

Epic Hero
In what way do lines 994–997 remind you that Odysseus is telling his story to an audience?

Language Study

Vocabulary The italicized words in each numbered item appear in the *Odyssey*, Part 1. Using your knowledge of these words, identify the word in each group that does not belong. Then, explain your response.

1. *plundered,* robbed, donated

2. *dispatched,* hesitated, completed

3. *assuage,* soothe, increase

4. *ardor,* spirit, fear

5. *insidious,* traitorous, friendly

Word Study

Part A Explain how the **Old English prefix *be-*** contributes to the meanings of *bemuse, belittle,* and *befriend*. Consult a dictionary if necessary.

Part B Use the context of the sentences and what you know about the Old English prefix *be-* to explain your answer to each question.

1. If people *begrudge* your success, are they happy for you?

2. What happens if a sailing ship is *becalmed*?

WORD STUDY
The **Old English prefix *be-*** means "around," "make," or "covered with." In this selection, Tiresias warns Odysseus that he will be **bereft** of his companions. Tiresias means that Odysseus will lose his companions. *Bereft* is a form of *bereave,* which means "made to suffer a loss."

Close Reading Activities

Literary Analysis

Key Ideas and Details

1. **(a)** In the episode of the Lotus-Eaters, how does Odysseus handle the men who eat the lotus? **(b) Interpret:** What does Odysseus understand that his men do not? **(c) Infer:** What does this episode suggest about the main problem that Odysseus has with his men?
2. **(a)** In the episode of the Cattle of the Sun God, why does the crew kill the cattle? **(b) Interpret:** How does Odysseus react to this action? **(c) Analyze:** What does Odysseus' reaction show about his attitudes toward the gods? Explain.
3. **Historical and Cultural Context** Consider the historical and cultural context of Homer's *Odyssey*. What role do ancient Greek religious beliefs play in the epic? Cite specific examples from the epic in your answer.

Craft and Structure

4. **Epic Hero (a)** Using a chart like the one shown, identify three other actions that Odysseus performs. **(b)** For each action, identify the character trait that it reveals. **(c)** Using the results of your analysis, explain which character traits the ancient Greeks admired most.

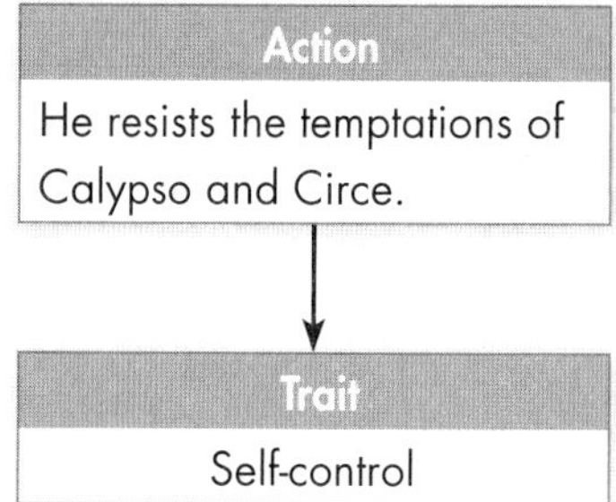

5. **Epic Hero** Odysseus recounts most of the action in Part 1 in the form of a flashback. List the events of Part 1 in chronological sequence, beginning with the end of the Trojan War.
6. **Epic Hero** In this epic, the hero Odysseus recounts his own adventures. In what way does this affect your reaction to the events he describes? Cite an example from the text to support your response.

Integration of Knowledge and Ideas

7. **(a) Compare and Contrast:** Compare and contrast Odysseus' reactions to the three ghosts he meets in the Land of the Dead—Elpenor, Anticlea, and Tiresias. **(b) Analyze:** What character trait does Odysseus display in the Land of the Dead that he did not reveal earlier? **(c) Connect:** Does he show similar traits during any other episode in Part 1? Explain, supporting your answer with details from the text.

8. **Do heroes have responsibilities? (a)** Is Odysseus' sense of responsibility for his men unlimited, or are there boundaries? Answer this question by explaining how Odysseus sees and executes his responsibilities during three of the events described in Part 1. **(b)** On the island of Helios, could Odysseus have prevented his men from eating the cattle and so saved their lives? Explain.

ACADEMIC VOCABULARY

As you write and speak about the *Odyssey*, use the words related to heroism and responsibility that you explored on page 727 of this textbook.

Conventions: **Simple and Compound Sentences**

A **simple sentence** consists of a single independent clause.

Although a simple sentence is just one independent clause with one subject and one verb, the subject, verb, or both may be compound.

A **compound sentence** consists of two or more independent clauses.

The clauses can be joined by a comma and a coordinating conjunction or by a semicolon. The coordinating conjunctions are *and, but, or, nor, for, yet,* and *so.*

Simple Sentence	He remembered an old story.
Simple Sentence with Compound Subject	He and she remembered an old story.
Compound Sentence (joined with a comma and a coordinating conjunction)	They laughed together, and they remembered an old story.
Compound Sentence (joined by a semicolon)	They laughed together for hours that day; their friendship was never stronger.

Practice A

Identify each of the following sentences as simple or compound. For compound sentences, identify the coordinating conjunction, if there is one.

1. Odysseus led his ship through the perils of Scylla and Charybdis.
2. The Cyclops captured the Greeks, and he ate some of them.
3. The men were starving, but Odysseus commanded them not to eat Helios' cattle.
4. Calypso and Circe both helped and hindered Odysseus.

Reading Application In the *Odyssey*, find one simple sentence and one compound sentence.

Practice B

Combine each pair of simple sentences to form a compound sentence. Use a comma and coordinating conjunction or a semicolon to separate the independent clauses.

1. Odysseus yelled insults at Polyphemus. The Cyclops hurled a rock at the ship.
2. The Sirens sang. The ship sailed on.
3. Scylla swooped down on the ship. She grabbed six men.
4. The men screamed for help. Odysseus stood by helplessly.

Writing Application Write four sentences about your response to the *Odyssey*. Use two simple sentences and two compound sentences.

Writing to Sources

Narrative Write a **retelling** of the *Odyssey* set in modern times.

- Before drafting, look through the poem and make a list of characters, monsters, and actions by the gods that interfere with Odysseus' journey. Decide how you will represent these ancient ideas using modern-day equivalents.
- Outline the plot of your retelling, adding points in the action where you can demonstrate your hero's traits, such as generosity and bravery.
- Decide how your modern-day Odysseus will travel.
- Review the *Odyssey* for examples of figurative language. Use these as models for figurative language you will incorporate into your retelling.
- Reveal the emotions of your characters through dialogue.

Grammar Application Make sure to use both simple and compound sentences as you draft your retelling.

Speaking and Listening

Presentation of Ideas With two classmates, write and deliver a **conversation** among ordinary Greeks discussing Odysseus' exploits. Each character's statements should reflect ancient Greek values shown in the *Odyssey*.

- Decide each character's position toward Odysseus. For example, one character may be a fan while another may be a cynic. One may know Odysseus well while another may have barely heard of him.
- Plan your conversation for an audience of contemporaries—imagine that they, like your characters, also live in Greece during the time the *Odyssey* takes place.
- As a group, agree on an overall plan for the conversation, but leave room for improvisation.
- As you speak, use verbal techniques—such as varied tone, volume, and pace—to convey different emotions and add realism.
- In addition, use nonverbal techniques—such as gestures, facial expressions, and eye contact—to help convey your ideas.

Practice your conversation, including both the verbal and nonverbal techniques. Then, present the conversation to your class, using the techniques you rehearsed with your group.

Common Core State Standards

Writing

3. Write narratives to develop real or imagined experiences or events using effective technique, well-chosen details, and well-structured event sequences.

3.a Engage and orient the reader by setting out a problem, situation, or observation, establishing one or multiple point(s) of view, and introducing a narrator and/or characters.

3.b Use narrative techniques, such as dialogue, pacing, description, reflection, and multiple plot lines.

3.c Use a variety of techniques to sequence events so that they build on one another to create a coherent whole.

Speaking and Listening

1. Initiate and participate effectively in a range of collaborative discussions with diverse partners on grades 9–10 topics, texts, and issues, building on others' ideas and expressing their own clearly and persuasively.

1.a. Come to discussions prepared, having read and researched material under study.

1.b. Work with peers to set individual roles as needed.

Language

1. Demonstrate command of the conventions of standard English grammar and usage when writing or speaking.

 Do heroes have responsibilities?

Explore the Big Question as you read this epic poem. Note whether the hero's decisions reflect a sense of responsibility.

CLOSE READING FOCUS

Key Ideas and Details: **Historical and Cultural Context**

The **historical and cultural context** of a work is the time and place in which it is set or was written. Details in a work reflect the beliefs and customs of that time and place. When you read, keep your own beliefs and customs in mind, and notice how your reactions to ideas and situations in the work differ from those of the characters. These differences will help you better understand the values and attitudes that are part of the work's historical and cultural context.

Craft and Structure: **Epic Simile**

An **epic simile** is an elaborate comparison that may extend for several lines and that may use the words *like, as, just as,* or *so*. Unlike a regular simile, which draws a relatively limited comparison and creates a single image, an epic simile might recall an entire place or story. In Part 1, lines 268–271, Odysseus uses an epic simile to describe the size of the tree from which he creates a weapon.

> And it was like a mast / a lugger of twenty oars, broad in the beam— / a deep-sea-going craft—might carry: / so long, so big around, it seemed.

As you read, notice how Homer uses epic similes—sometimes called Homeric similes—to bring descriptions to life.

Vocabulary

The words below are critical to understanding the text that follows. Copy the words into your notebook. Which words share the same suffix? What part of speech is created by using this suffix?

dissemble	**bemusing**	**maudlin**
incredulity	**equity**	**contempt**

Common Core State Standards

Reading Literature

4. Determine the meaning of words and phrases as they are used in a text, including figurative and connotative meanings; analyze the cumulative impact of specific word choices on meaning and tone.

6. Analyze a particular point of view or cultural experience reflected in a work of literature from outside the United States, drawing on a wide reading of world literature.

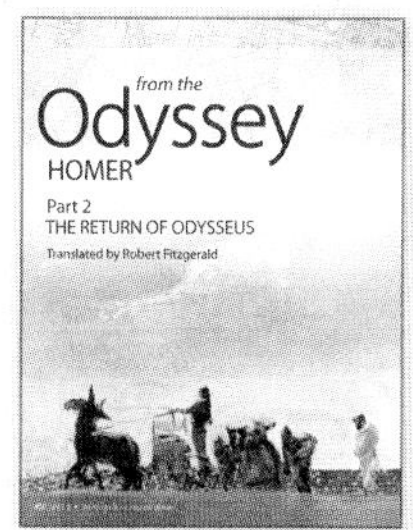

CLOSE READING MODEL

The passages below are from Homer's *Odyssey*. The annotations to the right of the passages show ways in which you can use close reading skills to understand the historical and cultural context and to analyze epic similes.

from the *Odyssey*, Part 2

Then Lord Odysseus
reappeared—and his son was thunderstruck.
Fear in his eyes, he looked down and away
as though it were a god, and whispered:
"Stranger,
you are no longer what you were just now!
Your cloak is new; even your skin! You are
one of the gods who rule the sweep of heaven![1]
Be kind to us, we'll make you fair oblation
and gifts of hammered gold. Have mercy on us!"
The noble and enduring man replied:
"No god. Why take me for a god? No, no.
I am that father whom your boyhood lacked
and suffered pain for lack of. I am he."
Held back too long, the tears ran down his cheeks
as he embraced his son.[2]

....

But the man skilled in all ways of contending,
satisfied by the great bow's look and heft,[3]
like a musician, like a harper, when
with quiet hand upon his instrument
he draws between his thumb and forefinger
a sweet new string upon a peg: so effortlessly
Odysseus in one motion strung the bow.[4]

Historical and Cultural Context
1 The cultural context of the poem includes belief in a group of gods, who often disguise themselves to interact with mortals on Earth. Odysseus' son assumes the altered man before him is a god. This response accurately reflects the poem's context.

Historical and Cultural Context
2 Odysseus is overcome with emotion when he reveals his identity to his son. A modern reunion between a long-lost father and child might look much the same. This suggests that the ancient Greeks shared some of the values—specifically, attitudes toward parents and children—that we hold in the modern world.

Epic Simile
3 This text contains the first part of an epic simile. The man, Odysseus, and the bow are the subject of the simile.

Epic Simile
4 This text contains the second part of the simile, which is introduced with the word *like*. The simile suggests that Odysseus strings the heavy weapon with the same ease that a master musician strings a harp.

from the

Odyssey

HOMER

Part 2
THE RETURN OF ODYSSEUS

Translated by Robert Fitzgerald

"Twenty years gone, and I am back again . . ."

Odysseus has finished telling his story to the Phaeacians. The next day, young Phaeacian noblemen conduct him home by ship. He arrives in Ithaca after an absence of twenty years. The goddess Athena appears and informs him of the situation at home. Numerous suitors, believing Odysseus to be dead, have been continually seeking the hand of his wife, Penelope, in marriage, while overrunning Odysseus' palace and enjoying themselves at Penelope's expense. Moreover, they are plotting to murder Odysseus' son, Telemachus, before he can inherit his father's lands. Telemachus, who, like Penelope, still hopes for his father's return, has journeyed to Pylos and Sparta to learn what he can about his father's fate. Athena disguises Odysseus as a beggar and directs him to the hut of Eumaeus,[1] his old and faithful swineherd. While Odysseus and Eumaeus are eating breakfast, Telemachus arrives. Athena then appears to Odysseus.

. . . From the air
she walked, taking the form of a tall woman,
handsome and clever at her craft, and stood
beyond the gate in plain sight of Odysseus,
unseen, though, by Telemachus, unguessed,
for not to everyone will gods appear.
Odysseus noticed her; so did the dogs,
who cowered whimpering away from her. She only
nodded, signing to him with her brows,
a sign he recognized. Crossing the yard,
he passed out through the gate in the stockade
to face the goddess. There she said to him:
"Son of Laertes and the gods of old,
Odysseus, master of landways and seaways,
dissemble to your son no longer now.
The time has come: tell him how you together
will bring doom on the suitors in the town.
I shall not be far distant then, for I
myself desire battle."
Saying no more,
she tipped her golden wand upon the man,
making his cloak pure white, and the knit tunic
fresh around him. Lithe and young she made him,
ruddy with sun, his jawline clean, the beard

1. **Eumaeus** (yo͞o mē′ əs)

◀ **Critical Viewing**
Which details in this image suggest that Odysseus, the figure at the far right, is returning home from a long journey?

◀ **Vocabulary**
dissemble (di sem′ bəl) *v.* conceal under a false appearance; disguise

Historical and Cultural Context What do lines 1021–1029 suggest about ancient Greek attitudes toward the gods?

no longer gray upon his chin. And she
withdrew when she had done.
Then Lord Odysseus
reappeared—and his son was thunderstruck.
Fear in his eyes, he looked down and away
as though it were a god, and whispered:

"Stranger,
you are no longer what you were just now!
Your cloak is new; even your skin! You are
one of the gods who rule the sweep of heaven!
Be kind to us, we'll make you fair oblation[2]
and gifts of hammered gold. Have mercy on us!"

The noble and enduring man replied:

"No god. Why take me for a god? No, no.
I am that father whom your boyhood lacked
and suffered pain for lack of. I am he."

Held back too long, the tears ran down his cheeks
as he embraced his son.
Only Telemachus,
uncomprehending, wild
with incredulity, cried out:
"You cannot
be my father Odysseus! Meddling spirits
conceived this trick to twist the knife in me!
No man of woman born could work these wonders
by his own craft, unless a god came into it
with ease to turn him young or old at will.
I swear you were in rags and old,
and here you stand like one of the immortals!"

Odysseus brought his ranging mind to bear
and said:
"This is not princely, to be swept
away by wonder at your father's presence.
No other Odysseus will ever come,
for he and I are one, the same; his bitter
fortune and his wanderings are mine.
Twenty years gone, and I am back again
on my own island.

2. **oblation** (äb lā′ shən) *n.* offering to a god.

Spiral Review
ARCHETYPES Is the encounter described in lines 1034–1035 an example of an archetype? Why or why not?

Vocabulary ▶
incredulity (in′ krə do͞o′ lə tē) *n.* unwillingness or inability to believe

As for my change of skin,
that is a charm Athena, Hope of Soldiers,
uses as she will; she has the knack
to make me seem a beggar man sometimes
and sometimes young, with finer clothes about me.
It is no hard thing for the gods of heaven
to glorify a man or bring him low."

When he had spoken, down he sat.
Then, throwing
his arms around this marvel of a father
Telemachus began to weep. Salt tears
rose from the wells of longing in both men,
and cries burst from both as keen and fluttering
as those of the great taloned hawk,
whose nestlings farmers take before they fly.
So helplessly they cried, pouring out tears,
and might have gone on weeping so till sundown,
had not Telemachus said:

"Dear father! Tell me
what kind of vessel put you here ashore
on Ithaca? Your sailors, who were they?
I doubt you made it, walking on the sea!"

Then said Odysseus, who had borne the barren sea:

"Only plain truth shall I tell you, child.
Great seafarers, the Phaeacians, gave me passage
as they give other wanderers. By night
over the open ocean, while I slept,
they brought me in their cutter,[3] set me down
on Ithaca, with gifts of bronze and gold
and stores of woven things. By the gods' will
these lie all hidden in a cave. I came
to this wild place, directed by Athena,
so that we might lay plans to kill our enemies.
Count up the suitors for me, let me know
what men at arms are there, how many men.
I must put all my mind to it, to see
if we two by ourselves can take them on
or if we should look round for help."

Epic Simile
To what are Odysseus' and Telemachus' cries compared in the epic simile in lines 1063–1065?

3. **cutter** (kut´ər) *n.* small, swift ship or boat carried aboard a large ship to transport personnel or supplies.

Comprehension
Why is Telemachus initially doubtful that the man before him is Odysseus, his father?

Telemachus
replied:
"O Father, all my life your fame
as a fighting man has echoed in my ears—
your skill with weapons and the tricks of war—
but what you speak of is a staggering thing,
beyond imagining, for me. How can two men
do battle with a houseful in their prime?[4]
For I must tell you this is no affair
of ten or even twice ten men, but scores,
throngs of them. You shall see, here and now.
The number from Dulichium alone
is fifty-two picked men, with armorers,
a half dozen; twenty-four came from Same,
twenty from Zacynthus; our own island
accounts for twelve, high-ranked, and their retainers,
Medon the crier, and the Master Harper,
besides a pair of handymen at feasts.
If we go in against all these
I fear we pay in salt blood for your vengeance.
You must think hard if you would conjure up
the fighting strength to take us through."
Odysseus
who had endured the long war and the sea
answered:
"I'll tell you now.
Suppose Athena's arm is over us, and Zeus
her father's, must I rack my brains for more?"

Clearheaded Telemachus looked hard and said:

"Those two are great defenders, no one doubts it,
but throned in the serene clouds overhead;
other affairs of men and gods they have
to rule over."

And the hero answered:
"Before long they will stand to right and left of us
in combat, in the shouting, when the test comes—
our nerve against the suitors' in my hall.
Here is your part: at break of day tomorrow
home with you, go mingle with our princes.
The swineherd later on will take me down

4. **in their prime** in the best or most vigorous stage of their lives.

Historical and Cultural Context
What does Odysseus' statement in lines 1109–1111 suggest about ancient Greek beliefs about the gods' interest in human affairs?

the port-side trail—a beggar, by my looks,
hangdog and old. If they make fun of me
in my own courtyard, let your ribs cage up
your springing heart, no matter what I suffer,
no matter if they pull me by the heels
or practice shots at me, to drive me out.
Look on, hold down your anger. You may even
plead with them, by heaven! in gentle terms
to quit their horseplay—not that they will heed you,
rash as they are, facing their day of wrath.
Now fix the next step in your mind.

Athena,
counseling me, will give me word, and I
shall signal to you, nodding: at that point
round up all armor, lances, gear of war
left in our hall, and stow the lot away
back in the vaulted storeroom. When the suitors
miss those arms and question you, be soft
in what you say: answer:

'I thought I'd move them
out of the smoke. They seemed no longer those
bright arms Odysseus left us years ago
when he went off to Troy. Here where the fire's
hot breath came, they had grown black and drear.
One better reason, too, I had from Zeus:
suppose a brawl starts up when you are drunk,
you might be crazed and bloody one another,
and that would stain your feast, your courtship.
Tempered
iron can magnetize a man.'

Say that.
But put aside two broadswords and two spears
for our own use, two oxhide shields nearby
when we go into action. Pallas Athena
and Zeus All-Provident will see you through,
bemusing our young friends.

Now one thing more.
If son of mine you are and blood of mine,
let no one hear Odysseus is about.
Neither Laertes, nor the swineherd here,
nor any slave, nor even Penelope.

LITERATURE IN CONTEXT

Cultural Connection

Athena

Athena was the goddess of wisdom, skills, and warfare. When she helps Odysseus in this epic, it is not the first time that she offers assistance to a Greek hero. In Homer's *Iliad,* Athena helps the Greek hero Achilles defeat the Trojan warrior Hector. Athena favored Achilles for his unmatched skill in battle, but Odysseus was her favorite among the Greeks. He displayed not only skill in warfare, but also ingenuity and cunning.

Connect to the Literature

Which of Odysseus' deeds in the *Odyssey* might have helped him to earn Athena's favor? Explain.

◀ **Vocabulary**
bemusing (bē myo͞oz´ iŋ) *v.* stupefying; muddling

Comprehension
How does Odysseus tell his son to respond if the suitors "practice shots" on Odysseus?

But you and I alone must learn how far
the women are corrupted; we should know
how to locate good men among our hands,
the loyal and respectful, and the shirkers[5]
who take you lightly, as alone and young."

5. **shirkers** (shurk′ ərz) *n.* people who get out of doing what needs to be done.

Argus

Odysseus heads for town with Eumaeus. Outside the palace, Odysseus' old dog, Argus, is lying at rest as his long-absent master approaches.

While he spoke
an old hound, lying near, pricked up his ears
and lifted up his muzzle. This was Argus,
trained as a puppy by Odysseus,
but never taken on a hunt before
his master sailed for Troy. The young men, afterward,
hunted wild goats with him, and hare, and deer,
but he had grown old in his master's absence.
Treated as rubbish now, he lay at last
upon a mass of dung before the gates—
manure of mules and cows, piled there until
fieldhands could spread it on the king's estate.
Abandoned there, and half destroyed with flies,
old Argus lay.
But when he knew he heard
Odysseus' voice nearby, he did his best
to wag his tail, nose down, with flattened ears,
having no strength to move nearer his master.
And the man looked away,
wiping a salt tear from his cheek; but he
hid this from Eumaeus. Then he said:

"I marvel that they leave this hound to lie
here on the dung pile;
he would have been a fine dog, from the look of him,
though I can't say as to his power and speed
when he was young. You find the same good build
in house dogs, table dogs landowners keep
all for style."

▼ Critical Viewing
What can you infer about the ancient Greeks based on the fact that they depicted their gods on everyday objects like this urn?

And you replied, Eumaeus:

"A hunter owned him—but the man is dead
in some far place. If this old hound could show
the form he had when Lord Odysseus left him,
going to Troy, you'd see him swift and strong.
He never shrank from any savage thing
he'd brought to bay in the deep woods; on the scent
no other dog kept up with him. Now misery
has him in leash. His owner died abroad,
and here the women slaves will take no care of him.
You know how servants are: without a master
they have no will to labor, or excel.
For Zeus who views the wide world takes away
half the manhood of a man, that day
he goes into captivity and slavery."

Historical and Cultural Context
How do Eumaeus' beliefs about servitude and slavery compare with those of your own culture?

Eumaeus crossed the court and went straight forward
into the megaron[6] among the suitors:
but death and darkness in that instant closed
the eyes of Argus, who had seen his master,
Odysseus, after twenty years.

6. **megaron** (meg′ ə rön) *n.* great, central hall of the house, usually containing a center hearth.

The Suitors

Still disguised as a beggar, Odysseus enters his home. He is confronted by the haughty[7] suitor Antinous.[8]

7. **haughty** (hôt′ ē) *adj.* arrogant.
8. **Antinous** (an tin′ ō əs)

But here Antinous broke in, shouting:

"God!
What evil wind blew in this pest?
Get over,
stand in the passage! Nudge my table, will you?
Egyptian whips are sweet
to what you'll come to here, you nosing rat,
making your pitch to everyone!
These men have bread to throw away on you
because it is not theirs. Who cares? Who spares
another's food, when he has more than plenty?"

Comprehension
How does Antinous react to Odysseus, who is disguised as a beggar?

With guile Odysseus drew away, then said:

"A pity that you have more looks than heart.
You'd grudge a pinch of salt from your own larder
to your own handyman. You sit here, fat
on others' meat, and cannot bring yourself
to rummage out a crust of bread for me!"

Historical and Cultural Context
What conflicting values does this exchange between Antinous and Odysseus reveal?

Then anger made Antinous' heart beat hard,
and, glowering under his brows, he answered:
"Now!
You think you'll shuffle off and get away
after that impudence?[9] Oh, no you don't!"

9. impudence (im′ pyo͞o dəns) *n.* quality of being shamelessly bold; disrespectful.

The stool he let fly hit the man's right shoulder
on the packed muscle under the shoulder blade—
like solid rock, for all the effect one saw.
Odysseus only shook his head, containing
thoughts of bloody work, as he walked on,
then sat, and dropped his loaded bag again
upon the door sill. Facing the whole crowd
he said, and eyed them all:

Historical and Cultural Context
What values regarding the use of physical force are evident in this speech?

"One word only,
my lords, and suitors of the famous queen.
One thing I have to say.
There is no pain, no burden for the heart
when blows come to a man, and he defending
his own cattle—his own cows and lambs.
Here it was otherwise. Antinous
hit me for being driven on by hunger—
how many bitter seas men cross for hunger!
If beggars interest the gods, if there are Furies[10]
pent in the dark to avenge a poor man's wrong, then may
Antinous meet his death before his wedding day!"

10. Furies (fyo͝or′ ēz) *n.* three terrible female spirits who punish the doers of unavenged crimes.

Then said Eupeithes' son, Antinous:

"Enough.
Eat and be quiet where you are, or shamble elsewhere,
unless you want these lads to stop your mouth
pulling you by the heels, or hands and feet,
over the whole floor, till your back is peeled!"

But now the rest were mortified, and someone
spoke from the crowd of young bucks to rebuke him:

"A poor show, that—hitting this famished tramp—
bad business, if he happened to be a god.
You know they go in foreign guise, the gods do,
looking like strangers, turning up
in towns and settlements to keep an eye
on manners, good or bad."
But at this notion
Antinous only shrugged.
Telemachus,
after the blow his father bore, sat still
without a tear, though his heart felt the blow.
Slowly he shook his head from side to side,
containing murderous thoughts.
Penelope
on the higher level of her room had heard
the blow, and knew who gave it. Now she murmured:

"Would god you could be hit yourself, Antinous—
hit by Apollo's bowshot!"

Historical and Cultural Context
What ancient Greek belief is conveyed in this suitor's speech?

Comprehension
How does Penelope regard Antinous?

11. Eurynome (yo͞o rin′ əm ē)

And Eurynome[11]
her housekeeper, put in:

"He and no other?
If all we pray for came to pass, not one
would live till dawn!"

Her gentle mistress said:

"Oh, Nan, they are a bad lot; they intend
ruin for all of us; but Antinous
appears a blacker-hearted hound than any.
Here is a poor man come, a wanderer,
driven by want to beg his bread, and everyone
in hall gave bits, to cram his bag—only
Antinous threw a stool, and banged his shoulder!"

Spiral Review
ARCHETYPE Odysseus hides his true identity from Penelope. How does this behavior suggest the trickster archetype?

So she described it, sitting in her chamber
among her maids—while her true lord was eating.
Then she called in the forester and said:

"Go to that man on my behalf, Eumaeus,
and send him here, so I can greet and question him.
Abroad in the great world, he may have heard
rumors about Odysseus—may have known him!"

Penelope

In the evening, Penelope interrogates the old beggar.

"Friend, let me ask you first of all:
who are you, where do you come from, of what nation
and parents were you born?"

And he replied:
"My lady, never a man in the wide world
should have a fault to find with you. Your name
has gone out under heaven like the sweet
honor of some god-fearing king, who rules
in equity over the strong: his black lands bear
both wheat and barley, fruit trees laden bright,
new lambs at lambing time—and the deep sea
gives great hauls of fish by his good strategy,
so that his folk fare well.

Vocabulary ▶
equity (ek′ wit ē) *n.* fairness; justice

O my dear lady,
this being so, let it suffice to ask me
of other matters—not my blood, my homeland.
Do not enforce me to recall my pain.
My heart is sore; but I must not be found
sitting in tears here, in another's house:
it is not well forever to be grieving.
One of the maids might say—or you might think—
I had got **maudlin** over cups of wine."

◀ **Vocabulary**
maudlin (môd′ lin)
adj. tearfully and foolishly sentimental

And Penelope replied:

"Stranger, my looks,
my face, my carriage,[12] were soon lost or faded
when the Achaeans crossed the sea to Troy,
Odysseus my lord among the rest.
If he returned, if he were here to care for me,
I might be happily renowned!
But grief instead heaven sent me—years of pain.
Sons of the noblest families on the islands,
Dulichium, Same, wooded Zacynthus,[13]
with native Ithacans, are here to court me,
against my wish; and they consume this house.
Can I give proper heed to guest or suppliant
or herald on the realm's affairs?
How could I?
wasted with longing for Odysseus, while here
they press for marriage.
Ruses[14] served my turn
to draw the time out—first a close-grained web
I had the happy thought to set up weaving
on my big loom in hall. I said, that day:
'Young men—my suitors, now my lord is dead,
let me finish my weaving before I marry,
or else my thread will have been spun in vain.
It is a shroud I weave for Lord Laertes
when cold Death comes to lay him on his bier.
The country wives would hold me in dishonor
if he, with all his fortune, lay unshrouded.'
I reached their hearts that way, and they agreed.
So every day I wove on the great loom,
but every night by torchlight I unwove it;
and so for three years I deceived the Achaeans.

12. **carriage** (kar′ ij) *n.* posture.

13. **Zacynthus** (za sin′ *th*us)

14. **Ruses** (ro͞oz′ iz) *n.* tricks.

Historical and Cultural Context
How do the ancient Greek ideas in Penelope's speech about honoring the dead compare to modern ideas?

Comprehension
How was Penelope able to delay marriage for three years?

The Trial of the Bow from Homer's ***The Odyssey***, N.C. Wyeth, Brandywine River Museum.

But when the seasons brought a fourth year on,
as long months waned, and the long days were spent,
through impudent folly in the slinking maids
they caught me—clamored up to me at night;
I had no choice then but to finish it.
And now, as matters stand at last,
I have no strength left to evade a marriage,
cannot find any further way; my parents
urge it upon me, and my son
will not stand by while they eat up his property.
He comprehends it, being a man full-grown,
able to oversee the kind of house
Zeus would endow with honor.
                                        But you too
confide in me, tell me your ancestry.
You were not born of mythic oak or stone."

Penelope again asks the beggar to tell about himself. He makes up a tale in which Odysseus is mentioned and declares that Penelope's husband will soon be home.

"You see, then, he is alive and well, and headed
homeward now, no more to be abroad
far from his island, his dear wife and son.
Here is my sworn word for it. Witness this,
god of the zenith, noblest of the gods,[15]
and Lord Odysseus' hearthfire, now before me:
I swear these things shall turn out as I say.
Between this present dark and one day's ebb,
after the wane, before the crescent moon,
Odysseus will come."

The Challenge

Pressed by the suitors to choose a husband from among them, Penelope says she will marry the man who can string Odysseus' bow and shoot an arrow through twelve ax handle sockets. The suitors try and fail. Still in disguise, Odysseus asks for a turn and gets it.

                                        And Odysseus took his time,
turning the bow, tapping it, every inch,
for borings that termites might have made

◀ Critical Viewing
The winner of the archery contest will win Penelope's hand in marriage. What details or artistic techniques capture the tension in this scene?

15. god of the zenith, noblest of the gods Zeus.

Comprehension
What means does Penelope decide she will use to choose a husband?

while the master of the weapon was abroad.
The suitors were now watching him, and some
jested among themselves:

"A bow lover!"

"Dealer in old bows!"

"Maybe he has one like it
at home!"

"Or has an itch to make one for himself."

"See how he handles it, the sly old buzzard!"

And one disdainful suitor added this:
"May his fortune grow an inch for every inch he bends it!"

▲ **Critical Viewing**
Does the hunter pictured here show the same grace as does Odysseus in lines 1370–1392? Explain.

But the man skilled in all ways of contending,
satisfied by the great bow's look and heft,
like a musician, like a harper, when
with quiet hand upon his instrument
he draws between his thumb and forefinger
a sweet new string upon a peg: so effortlessly
Odysseus in one motion strung the bow.
Then slid his right hand down the cord and plucked it,
so the taut gut vibrating hummed and sang
a swallow's note.

In the hushed hall it smote the suitors
and all their faces changed. Then Zeus thundered
overhead, one loud crack for a sign.
And Odysseus laughed within him that the son
of crooked-minded Cronus had flung that omen down.
He picked one ready arrow from his table
where it lay bare: the rest were waiting still
in the quiver for the young men's turn to come.
He nocked[16] it, let it rest across the handgrip,
and drew the string and grooved butt of the arrow,
aiming from where he sat upon the stool.

16. **nocked** (näkt) set an arrow into the bowstring.

Now flashed
arrow from twanging bow clean as a whistle
through every socket ring; and grazed not one,
to thud with heavy brazen head beyond.
Then quietly
Odysseus said:

"Telemachus, the stranger
you welcomed in your hall has not disgraced you.
I did not miss, neither did I take all day
stringing the bow. My hand and eye are sound,
not so contemptible as the young men say.
The hour has come to cook their lordships' mutton—
supper by daylight. Other amusements later,
with song and harping that adorn a feast."

He dropped his eyes and nodded, and the prince
Telemachus, true son of King Odysseus,
belted his sword on, clapped hand to his spear,
and with a clink and glitter of keen bronze
stood by his chair, in the forefront near his father.

Critical Thinking

1. **Key Ideas and Details: (a)** Who does Telemachus think Odysseus is when they first reunite? **(b) Compare and Contrast:** Compare Odysseus' emotions with those of Telemachus at their reunion.
2. **Key Ideas and Details: (a)** Describe Antinous' treatment of Odysseus. **(b) Analyze Cause and Effect:** Why do you think Antinous treats Odysseus as he does?
3. **Integration of Knowledge and Ideas: (a)** What does Odysseus tell Penelope about himself? **(b) Infer:** Why do you think Odysseus chooses not to reveal his identity to his wife? **(c) Take a Position:** Is it wrong for Odysseus to deceive Penelope? Explain your response.
4. **Integration of Knowledge and Ideas: (a)** Which of Odysseus' responsibilities are revealed in this section? **(b)** Do you think he manages them heroically? Explain your response. ***[Connect to the Big Question: Do heroes have responsibilities?]***

M.J.R

Odysseus' Revenge

Now shrugging off his rags the wiliest[17] fighter of the islands
leapt and stood on the broad doorsill, his own bow in his hand.
He poured out at his feet a rain of arrows from the quiver
and spoke to the crowd:

"So much for that. Your clean-cut game is over.
Now watch me hit a target that no man has hit before,
if I can make this shot. Help me, Apollo."

He drew to his fist the cruel head of an arrow for Antinous
just as the young man leaned to lift his beautiful drinking cup,
embossed, two-handled, golden: the cup was in his fingers:
the wine was even at his lips: and did he dream of death?
How could he? In that revelry[18] amid his throng of friends
who would imagine a single foe—though a strong foe indeed—
could dare to bring death's pain on him and darkness on his eyes?
Odysseus' arrow hit him under the chin
and punched up to the feathers through his throat.

Backward and down he went, letting the winecup fall
from his shocked hand. Like pipes his nostrils jetted
crimson runnels, a river of mortal red,
and one last kick upset his table
knocking the bread and meat to soak in dusty blood.
Now as they craned to see their champion where he lay
the suitors jostled in uproar down the hall,
everyone on his feet. Wildly they turned and scanned
the walls in the long room for arms; but not a shield,
not a good ashen spear was there for a man to take and throw.
All they could do was yell in outrage at Odysseus:

"Foul! to shoot at a man! That was your last shot!"
"Your own throat will be slit for this!"
"Our finest lad is down!
You killed the best on Ithaca."
"Buzzards will tear your eyes out!"

17. **wiliest** (wīl′ ē əst) *adj.* craftiest; slyest.

◀ Critical Viewing
Do you think this illustration presents the slaughter of the suitors accurately? Explain.

18. **revelry** (rev′ əl rē) *n.* noisy festivity.

Historical and Cultural Context
Does the manner in which Odysseus kills Antinous agree with your idea of a "fair fight"? Explain.

Comprehension
Whom does Odysseus kill first?

Historical and Cultural Context
What cultural values are revealed by Odysseus' explanation for his anger in lines 1439–1444?

Vocabulary ▶
contempt (kən tempt′)
n. disdain; scorn

For they imagined as they wished—that it was a wild shot,
an unintended killing—fools, not to comprehend
they were already in the grip of death.
But glaring under his brows Odysseus answered:

"You yellow dogs, you thought I'd never make it
home from the land of Troy. You took my house to
plunder. . .
You dared bid for my wife while I was still alive.
Contempt was all you had for the gods who rule wide
heaven,
contempt for what men say of you hereafter.
Your last hour has comc. You dic in blood."

As they all took this in, sickly green fear
pulled at their entrails, and their eyes flickered
looking for some hatch or hideaway from death.
Eurymachus[19] alone could speak. He said:

"If you are Odysseus of Ithaca come back,
all that you say these men have done is true.
Rash actions, many here, more in the countryside.
But here he lies, the man who caused them all.
Antinous was the ringleader, he whipped us on
to do these things. He cared less for a marriage
than for the power Cronion has denied him
as king of Ithaca. For that
he tried to trap your son and would have killed him.
He is dead now and has his portion. Spare
your own people. As for ourselves, we'll make
restitution of wine and meat consumed,
and add, each one, a tithe of twenty oxen
with gifts of bronze and gold to warm your heart.
Meanwhile we cannot blame you for your anger."

Odysseus glowered under his black brows
and said:
"Not for the whole treasure of your fathers,
all you enjoy, lands, flocks, or any gold
put up by others, would I hold my hand.
There will be killing till the score is paid.
You forced yourselves upon this house. Fight your way out,
or run for it, if you think you'll escape death.

19. **Eurymachus** (yo͞o ri′ mə kəs)

I doubt one man of you skins by."

They felt their knees fail, and their hearts—but heard
Eurymachus for the last time rallying them.
"Friends," he said, "the man is implacable.
Now that he's got his hands on bow and quiver
he'll shoot from the big doorstone there
until he kills us to the last man.
Fight, I say,
let's remember the joy of it. Swords out!
Hold up your tables to deflect his arrows.
After me, everyone: rush him where he stands.
If we can budge him from the door, if we can pass
into the town, we'll call out men to chase him.
This fellow with his bow will shoot no more."

He drew his own sword as he spoke, a broadsword of fine bronze,
honed like a razor on either edge. Then crying hoarse and loud
he hurled himself at Odysseus. But the kingly man let fly
an arrow at that instant, and the quivering feathered butt
sprang to the nipple of his breast as the barb stuck in his liver.
The bright broadsword clanged down. He lurched and fell aside,
pitching across his table. His cup, his bread and meat,
were spilt and scattered far and wide, and his head slammed on the ground.
Revulsion, anguish in his heart, with both feet kicking out,
he downed his chair, while the shrouding wave of mist closed on his eyes.

Amphinomus now came running at Odysseus,
broadsword naked in his hand. He thought to make
the great soldier give way at the door.
But with a spear throw from behind Telemachus hit him
between the shoulders, and the lancehead drove
clear through his chest. He left his feet and fell
forward, thudding, forehead against the ground.
Telemachus swerved around him, leaving the long dark spear
planted in Amphinomus. If he paused to yank it out

Epic Simile
Why is the comparison of Eurymachus' sharp sword to a razor only a simile and not an epic simile?

Comprehension
What does Eurymachus offer Odysseus to try to calm his anger?

someone might jump him from behind or cut him down with
a sword
at the moment he bent over. So he ran—ran from the tables
to his father's side and halted, panting, saying:

"Father let me bring you a shield and spear,
a pair of spears, a helmet.
I can arm on the run myself; I'll give
outfits to Eumaeus and this cowherd.
Better to have equipment."

Said Odysseus:
"Run then, while I hold them off with arrows
as long as the arrows last. When all are gone
if I'm alone they can dislodge me."

Quick
upon his father's word Telemachus
ran to the room where spears and armor lay.
He caught up four light shields, four pairs of spears,
four helms of war high-plumed with flowing manes,
and ran back, loaded down, to his father's side.
He was the first to pull a helmet on
and slide his bare arm in a buckler strap.
The servants armed themselves, and all three took their
stand
beside the master of battle.

While he had arrows
he aimed and shot, and every shot brought down
one of his huddling enemies.
But when all barbs had flown from the bowman's fist,
he leaned his bow in the bright entryway
beside the door, and armed: a four-ply shield
hard on his shoulder, and a crested helm,
horsetailed, nodding stormy upon his head,
then took his tough and bronze-shod spears. . . .

Historical and Cultural Context
What cultural values are reflected in Telemachus' behavior toward his father?

Aided by Athena, Odysseus, Telemachus, Eumaeus, and other faithful herdsmen kill all the suitors.

And Odysseus looked around him, narrow-eyed,
for any others who had lain hidden
while death's black fury passed.

In blood and dust
he saw that crowd all fallen, many and many slain.

Think of a catch that fishermen haul in to a half-moon bay
in a fine-meshed net from the whitecaps of the sea:
how all are poured out on the sand, in throes for the salt sea,
twitching their cold lives away in Helios' fiery air:
so lay the suitors heaped on one another.

Epic Simile
Which aspects of the slain suitors' appearance does the epic simile in lines 1535–1539 emphasize?

Penelope's Test

Penelope tests Odysseus to prove he really is her husband.

Greathearted Odysseus, home at last,
was being bathed now by Eurynome
and rubbed with golden oil, and clothed again
in a fresh tunic and a cloak. Athena
lent him beauty, head to foot. She made him
taller, and massive, too, with crisping hair
in curls like petals of wild hyacinth
but all red-golden. Think of gold infused
on silver by a craftsman, whose fine art
Hephaestus[20] taught him, or Athena: one
whose work moves to delight: just so she lavished
beauty over Odysseus' head and shoulders.
He sat then in the same chair by the pillar,
facing his silent wife, and said:

"Strange woman,
the immortals of Olympus made you hard,
harder than any. Who else in the world
would keep aloof as you do from her husband
if he returned to her from years of trouble,
cast on his own land in the twentieth year?

Nurse, make up a bed for me to sleep on.
Her heart is iron in her breast."

Penelope
spoke to Odysseus now. She said:

"Strange man,
if man you are . . . This is no pride on my part

Epic Simile
Which details in the epic simile in lines 1547–1551 compare Odysseus' hair to a work of art?

20. **Hephaestus** (hē fes´ təs) god of fire and metalworking.

Comprehension
Who helps Odysseus defeat the suitors?

nor scorn for you—not even wonder, merely.
I know so well how you—how he—appeared
boarding the ship for Troy. But all the same . . .

Make up his bed for him, Eurycleia.
Place it outside the bedchamber my lord
built with his own hands. Pile the big bed
with fleeces, rugs, and sheets of purest linen."

With this she tried him to the breaking point,
and he turned on her in a flash raging:

"Woman, by heaven you've stung me now!
Who dared to move my bed?
No builder had the skill for that—unless
a god came down to turn the trick. No mortal
in his best days could budge it with a crowbar.
There is our pact and pledge, our secret sign,
built into that bed—my handiwork
and no one else's!

An old trunk of olive
grew like a pillar on the building plot,
and I laid out our bedroom round that tree,
lined up the stone walls, built the walls and roof,
gave it a doorway and smooth-fitting doors.
Then I lopped off the silvery leaves and branches,
hewed and shaped that stump from the roots up
into a bedpost, drilled it, let it serve
as model for the rest. I planed them all,
inlaid them all with silver, gold and ivory,
and stretched a bed between—a pliant web
of oxhide thongs dyed crimson.

There's our sign!
I know no more. Could someone else's hand
have sawn that trunk and dragged the frame away?"

Epic Simile
Explain why the simile comparing the olive trunk to a pillar is not an epic simile.

Their secret! as she heard it told, her knees
grew tremulous and weak, her heart failed her.
With eyes brimming tears she ran to him,
throwing her arms around his neck, and kissed him,
murmuring:

"Do not rage at me, Odysseus!

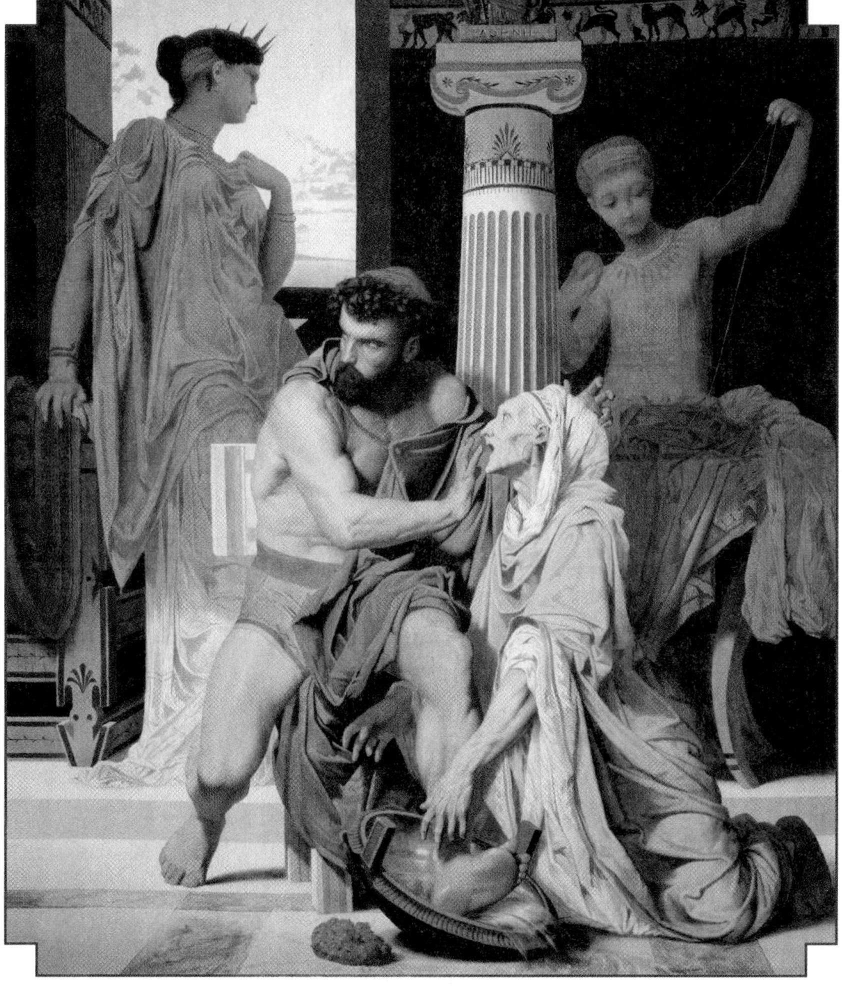

◀ Critical Viewing Which aspects of the scene shown in this painting are similar to those Homer describes in Odysseus' return home?

No one ever matched your caution! Think
what difficulty the gods gave: they denied us
life together in our prime and flowering years,
kept us from crossing into age together.
Forgive me, don't be angry. I could not
welcome you with love on sight! I armed myself
long ago against the frauds of men,
impostors who might come—and all those many
whose underhanded ways bring evil on! . . .
But here and now, what sign could be so clear
as this of our own bed?
No other man has ever laid eyes on it—
only my own slave, Actoris, that my father
sent with me as a gift—she kept our door.
You make my stiff heart know that I am yours."

Comprehension How does Odysseus react to Penelope's attitude toward him?

Epic Simile
In what way does this epic simile recall the dangers Odysseus faced on his journey home?

Now from his breast into his eyes the ache
of longing mounted, and he wept at last,
his dear wife, clear and faithful, in his arms,
longed for as the sunwarmed earth is longed for by a swimmer
spent in rough water where his ship went down
under Poseidon's blows, gale winds and tons of sea.
Few men can keep alive through a big surf
to crawl, clotted with brine, on kindly beaches
in joy, in joy, knowing the abyss[21] behind:
and so she too rejoiced, her gaze upon her husband,
her white arms round him pressed as though forever.

21. **abyss** (ə bis′) *n.* ocean depths.

The Ending

Odysseus is reunited with his father. Athena commands that peace prevail between Odysseus and the relatives of the slain suitors. Odysseus has regained his family and his kingdom.

Language Study

Vocabulary The italicized word in each sentence appears in the excerpt from the *Odyssey*, Part 2. Indicate whether each statement is usually true or usually false. Explain your answers. Then, revise false sentences to make them true.

1. An event that is common and predictable evokes *incredulity*.
2. If road signs are *bemusing* drivers, the signs are working perfectly.
3. A good judge is one with a strong sense of *equity*.
4. A marching band should play *maudlin* songs if it wants to excite fans.
5. Successful salespeople always show *contempt* for customers.

WORD STUDY
The **Latin prefix *dis-*** means "away," "apart," or "not." In this selection, the goddess Athena tells Odysseus not to **dissemble**, or disguise himself, before his son Telemachus.

Word Study

Part A Explain how the **Latin prefix *dis-*** contributes to the meanings of *dispute*, *dishevel*, and *disembark*. Consult a dictionary if necessary.

Part B Use the context of the sentences and what you know about the Latin prefix *dis-* to explain your answer to each question.

1. If a reporter *discloses* the source of information, does she tell where she got the story?
2. If you are *disheartened* by some news, do you feel happy?

Close Reading Activities

Literary Analysis

Key Ideas and Details

1. **(a)** When Odysseus returns to his home, who helps him? **(b) Interpret:** What does the varying social status of Odysseus' helpers suggest about his character? Explain.
2. **(a)** What reasons does Odysseus give for his taking revenge on the suitors? **(b) Analyze Cause and Effect:** Why do you think Odysseus reacts so intensely? Support your answer with details from the epic.
3. **(a)** What is Penelope's test, and how does Odysseus pass it? **(b) Infer:** Why does Penelope feel the need to test Odysseus even though he has abandoned his disguise? **(c) Interpret:** Is the mood after the test altogether happy? Cite details from the epic in your answers.
4. **Historical and Cultural Context (a)** What attitudes and values are reflected in Odysseus' actions toward the suitors? Explain. **(b)** What do his actions suggest about the attitudes and values of ancient Greeks? Use details from the text to support your response.
5. **Historical and Cultural Context (a)** Name one of Odysseus' cultural beliefs, attitudes, or practices that is similar to an idea or a tradition in your own culture. Explain the similarities. **(b)** Name one that is significantly different. Explain the contrasts. Cite details from the epic in your responses.

Craft and Structure

6. **Epic Simile (a)** Reread the epic simile in lines 1535–1539. Identify the two things being compared. **(b)** Explain how Homer uses this simile to bring the descriptions to life.
7. **Epic Simile (a)** Using a chart like the one shown, analyze the epic simile in lines 1613–1624. **(b)** How does this simile connect to other episodes in the story to make it a powerful and fitting image for the conclusion of the *Odyssey*? Explain.

Things Being Compared
Details of Epic Simile
Purpose

Integration of Knowledge and Ideas

8. **Connect:** Are Odysseus' actions in dealing with the suitors consistent with his actions in earlier episodes of the epic? Explain, supporting your response with examples from the text.

9. THE BIG ? **Do heroes have responsibilities? (a)** Do you think Odysseus kills the suitors to fulfill his responsibilities? Explain. **(b)** In the historical and cultural context of ancient Greece, is Odysseus' revenge justified? Why or why not?

ACADEMIC VOCABULARY

As you write and speak about the *Odyssey*, use the words related to heroism and responsibility that you explored on page 727 of this book.

Close Reading Activities Continued

Conventions: Complex and Compound-Complex Sentences

Sentences can be classified by the number of dependent and independent clauses they contain. An *independent clause* contains a subject and a verb and can stand alone as a sentence. A *dependent clause* contains a subject and a verb but cannot stand alone as a sentence. A dependent clause begins with a subordinating conjunction such as *when, although, because, before, since,* or *while*, or a relative pronoun, such as *who, whom, whose, which,* and *that*.

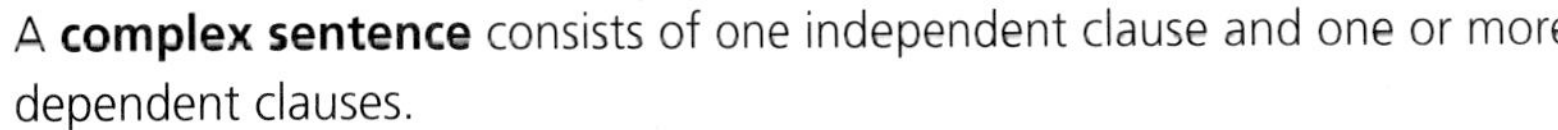

A **complex sentence** consists of one independent clause and one or more dependent clauses.
A **compound-complex sentence** consists of two or more independent clauses and one or more dependent clauses.

Independent clauses in both compound and compound-complex sentences are connected by a comma and a coordinating conjunction.

Complex Sentence	Compound-Complex Sentence
When the lights came on, he saw the audience.	When the lights came on, he saw the audience, and he waved to his parents.

Practice A

State whether each sentence below is complex or compound-complex. Then, identify the independent clauses and the dependent clauses.

1. Because Odysseus was disguised, Penelope did not recognize her husband.
2. When Odysseus strung the bow, the suitors were amazed, and they stopped laughing.
3. Telemachus grabbed a sword, and he stood by his father while they fought.
4. Although there were many suitors, Odysseus killed every one of them.

Reading Application In the *Odyssey*, find one complex sentence and one compound-complex sentence.

Practice B

Combine the simple sentences below to form one new sentence of the type indicated in parentheses.

1. Argus recognized Odysseus. He died. (complex)
2. Odysseus strung the bow. Telemachus looked on. (complex)
3. Odysseus tested the bow. The suitors mocked him. They called him names. (compound-complex)
4. He shot the arrow. It passed through each ring. The suitors were awed. (compound-complex)

Writing Application Write six simple sentences about the *Odyssey*. Choose from among these sentences to build two complex and two compound-complex sentences.

Writing to Sources

Informative Text Write a short **biography** of Odysseus based on details presented in the *Odyssey*. Include the basic facts of the hero's life and adventures, including his important relationships, and hold your reader's attention by describing dramatic situations in detail.

- List events from the *Odyssey* that are suitable for your biography. Focus on events that reveal the character of Odysseus.
- Include quotations from the epic to add detail and depth.
- Share your biography with classmates, and compare the events you each chose to include. In your discussion, consider what makes some events more significant than others.
- Based on your discussion with classmates, consider whether your version of Odysseus' life is complete, accurate, and interesting to readers. Revise your work as needed.

Grammar Application As you write your biography, use a variety of sentence types, including complex and compound-complex sentences.

Speaking and Listening

Comprehension and Collaboration Conduct a **debate** to decide whether Odysseus should be prosecuted for the murders of Penelope's suitors. Follow these steps to effectively practice the art of persuasion and debate:

- Within a small group, divide into two opposing teams. One team should argue the affirmative—that Odysseus should be prosecuted—and the other should argue the negative.
- Both affirmative and negative teams should prepare a rational argument expressing its position. Each team should also prepare an argument against the opposing team's position. Be sure to identify evidence from the *Odyssey* to support all arguments.
- Plan an introduction to your remarks, a body that includes your arguments, and a conclusion that summarizes your position.
- Use presentation techniques to enhance your arguments. Speak clearly and make eye contact with listeners.
- During the debate, listen carefully and evaluate the opposing team's facts and reasoning so you can respond effectively.

Conduct the debate for the class, and ask your audience to judge which team was more persuasive.

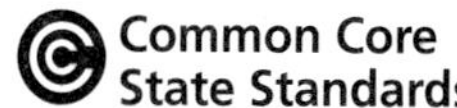

Writing

4. Produce clear and coherent writing in which the development, organization, and style are appropriate to task, purpose, and audience.

Speaking and Listening

1. Initiate and participate effectively in a range of collaborative discussions with diverse partners, building on others' ideas and expressing their own clearly and persuasively.

3. Evaluate a speaker's point of view, reasoning, and use of evidence and rhetoric, identifying any fallacious reasoning or exaggerated or distorted evidence.

Language

1. Demonstrate command of the conventions of standard English grammar and usage when writing or speaking.

1.b. Use various types of phrases and clauses to convey specific meanings and add variety and interest to writing or presentations.

Do heroes have responsibilities?

Explore the Big Question as you read these poems. Take notes about the heroic characters, both obvious and less so, and consider the attitudes they express toward duty and responsibility.

READING TO COMPARE CONTEMPORARY INTERPRETATIONS

All the poems in this section are retellings of segments of the *Odyssey*. As you read each poem, consider how it both reflects and transforms the original characters and story.

"An Ancient Gesture"

Edna St. Vincent Millay (1892–1950)
American poet Edna St. Vincent Millay lived a bohemian, unconventional life and wrote experimental, often passionate poems. Her poetry collection *The Harp Weaver and Other Poems* (1923) earned her a Pulitzer Prize.

"Siren Song"

Margaret Atwood (b. 1930)
Novelist and poet Margaret Atwood has received extensive critical acclaim, literary honors, and popular success—a feat few writers achieve. Her work has been translated into numerous languages and published in more than twenty-five countries.

from The Odyssey

Derek Walcott (b. 1930)
Derek Walcott was born in St. Lucia, West Indies, and his work reflects his Caribbean heritage. A master poet, he has won numerous awards for his work, including the 1992 Nobel Prize in Literature.

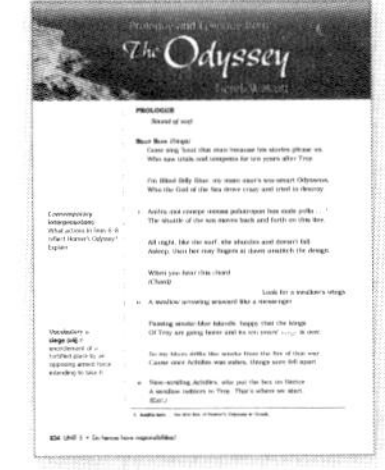

"Ithaca"

Constantine Cavafy (1860–1933)
Constantine Cavafy was born to Greek parents in Alexandria, Egypt. He is considered by many to be the most influential and important Greek poet of the twentieth century.

Comparing Contemporary Interpretations

A **contemporary interpretation** of a literary work is a new piece of writing that a modern-day author bases on an older text. Even when they are based on the same text, contemporary interpretations can differ widely in purpose and theme. Each writer's cultural and historical background, attitudes, and beliefs profoundly affect his or her perceptions of the older work and influence the creation of the new work.

Writers draw from classical, traditional, or simply well-known source material for a variety of reasons, such as the following:

- The work presents timeless or universal themes that are relevant to modern-day life.
- The work offers recognizable characters that the writer recasts in a modern setting.
- The work, or some part of it, bears similarities to a modern-day conflict. The original work functions as a metaphor for the modern conflict the author wishes to explore.
- The writer wants to bring to the forefront characters who might have played minor or supporting roles in the original text.
- The work simply provides a rich basis for additional interpretations and new layers of meaning.

The characters and events of Homer's *Odyssey* are timeless and universal in their appeal. They have inspired many contemporary interpretations, including the poems you are about to read. By reinventing and transforming Homer's tales, modern-day writers shed new light on Homer's ancient words.

Contemporary interpretations of literature from ages past can be viewed as extended allusions to the ancient or traditional texts. An **allusion** is a reference to a well-known person, place, event, or work of literature or art. As you read, use a chart like the one shown to note the extended allusion each poet makes to Homer's *Odyssey*. Then, think about the ways in which the allusion helps each poet express a new, modern meaning.

Poem	Allusion to the *Odyssey*	Meaning

Common Core State Standards

Reading Literature

6. Analyze a particular point of view or cultural experience reflected in a work of literature from outside the United States, drawing on a wide reading of world literature.

7. Analyze the representation of a subject or a key scene in two different artistic mediums.

9. Analyze how an author draws on and transforms source material in a specific work.

Writing

2. Write informative/explanatory texts to examine and convey complex ideas, concepts, and information clearly and accurately through the effective selection, organization, and analysis of content.

2.a. Introduce a topic; organize complex ideas, concepts, and information to make important connections and distinctions.

9. Draw evidence from literary or informational texts to support analysis, reflection, and research.

9.a. Apply *grades 9–10 Reading standards* to literature (e.g., "Analyze how an author draws on and transforms source material in a specific work.").

10. Write routinely over extended time frames and shorter time frames for a range of tasks, purposes, and audiences.

An Ancient Gesture

Edna St. Vincent Millay

I thought, as I wiped my eyes on the corner of my apron:
Penelope did this too.
And more than once: you can't keep weaving all day
And undoing it all through the night;
Your arms get tired, and the back of your neck gets tight;
And along towards morning, when you think it will never
  be light,
And your husband has been gone, and you don't know
  where, for years,
Suddenly you burst into tears;
There is simply nothing else to do.

And I thought, as I wiped my eyes on the corner of my apron:
This is an ancient gesture, authentic, antique,
In the very best tradition, classic, Greek;
Ulysses[1] did this too.
But only as a gesture,—a gesture which implied
To the assembled throng that he was much too moved
  to speak.
He learned it from Penelope . . .
Penelope, who really cried.

Contemporary Interpretations
What connection does the speaker make between herself and Penelope?

◀ **Vocabulary**
authentic (ô then′ tik) *adj.* genuine

◀ **Analyze Representations**
How does the representation of Penelope in this painting compare to her portrayal in the poem?

1. **Ulysses** Latin name for Odysseus.

Critical Thinking

1. **Key Ideas and Details: (a)** What is the "ancient gesture"? **(b) Summarize:** According to the speaker, what caused Penelope to employ this gesture? **(c) Infer:** Why might the speaker have made a similar gesture? Explain.
2. **Key Ideas and Details: (a)** According to the speaker, in addition to Penelope who else made this ancient gesture? **(b) Compare and Contrast:** How did this other gesture differ from Penelope's? **(c) Analyze:** What do the different qualities of their gestures show about these characters? Use details from the poem to support your answer.
3. **Integration of Knowledge and Ideas: (a)** What questions about the speaker are left unanswered? Explain. **(b) Analyze Cause and Effect:** What effect do these unanswered questions create? Explain.
4. **Integration of Knowledge and Ideas: (a)** According to this interpretation, does Odysseus live up to his responsibility as a husband? Explain. **(b)** Who do you think the poet feels is the hero of the *Odyssey*—Penelope or Odysseus? ***[Connect to the Big Question: Do heroes have responsibilities?]***

SIREN SONG

Margaret Atwood

Contemporary Interpretations What allusion do lines 4–9 make to the *Odyssey?*

This is the one song everyone
would like to learn: the song
that is irresistible:

the song that forces men
to leap overboard in squadrons
even though they see the beached skulls

the song nobody knows
because anyone who has heard it
is dead, and the others can't remember.

Shall I tell you the secret
and if I do, will you get me
out of this bird suit?[1]

1. **bird suit** Sirens are usually represented as half bird and half woman.

I don't enjoy it here
squatting on this island
looking picturesque and mythical

with these two feathery maniacs,
I don't enjoy singing
this trio, fatal and valuable.

I will tell the secret to you,
to you, only to you.
Come closer. This song

is a cry for help: Help me!
Only you, only you can,
you are unique

at last. Alas
it is a boring song
but it works every time.

◀ **Vocabulary**
picturesque (pik′ chər esk′) *adj.* attractive and interesting

Contemporary Interpretations
What does the contemporary Siren say to flatter and lure the listener?

Critical Thinking

1. **Key Ideas and Details: (a)** In the first stanza, what song does the speaker say everyone wants to learn? **(b) Analyze Cause and Effect:** What does this song have the power to do?
2. **Key Ideas and Details: (a)** What does the speaker want in exchange for revealing the song's secret? **(b) Interpret:** Why does the speaker want to make this deal? Explain.
3. **Integration of Knowledge and Ideas: (a)** Why do you think the speaker's compliment in lines 23 and 24 is so effective? **(b) Make Generalizations:** What might the speaker be saying about the relationships between men and women? Cite details from the poem in your answer.
4. **Key Ideas and Details: (a)** How does the speaker feel about her song and its secret? **(b) Support:** Which details in the poem support your answer?
5. **Integration of Knowledge and Ideas: (a)** How does the Siren affect heroes? Explain. **(b)** Do you think the Siren should be held responsible for her effect on heroes? Why or why not? ***[Connect to the Big Question: Do heroes have responsibilities?]***

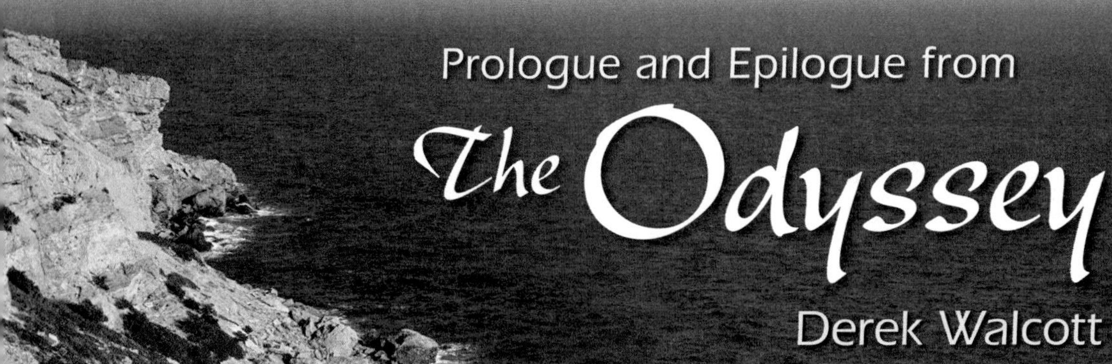

Prologue and Epilogue from *The Odyssey*

Derek Walcott

PROLOGUE

Sound of surf.

Billy Blue *(Sings)*

Gone sing 'bout that man because his stories please us,
Who saw trials and tempests for ten years after Troy.

I'm Blind Billy Blue, my main man's sea-smart Odysseus,
Who the God of the Sea drove crazy and tried to destroy.

Andra moi ennepe mousa polutropon hos mala polla . . .[1]
The shuttle of the sea moves back and forth on this line,

All night, like the surf, she shuttles and doesn't fall
Asleep, then her rosy fingers at dawn unstitch the design.

When you hear this chord
(Chord)
Look for a swallow's wings
A swallow arrowing seaward like a messenger

Passing smoke-blue islands, happy that the kings
Of Troy are going home and its ten years' siege is over.

So my blues drifts like smoke from the fire of that war,
Cause once Achilles was ashes, things sure fell apart.

Slow-striding Achilles, who put the hex on Hector
A swallow twitters in Troy. That's where we start.
(Exit.)

Contemporary Interpretations
What actions in lines 6–8 reflect Homer's *Odyssey*? Explain.

Vocabulary ▶
siege (sēj) *n.* encirclement of a fortified place by an opposing armed force intending to take it

1. **Andra moi. . .** the first line of Homer's *Odyssey* in Greek.

EPILOGUE

Billy Blue *(Sings)*

I sang of that man against whom the sea still rages,
Who escaped its terrors, that despair could not destroy,

Since that first blind singer, others will sing down the ages
Of the heart in its harbour, then long years after Troy,
after Troy.

And a house, happy for good, from a swallow's omen,
Let the trees clap their hands, and the surf whisper amen.

For a rock, a rock, a rock, a rock-steady woman
Let the waves clap their hands and the surf whisper amen.

For that peace which, in their mercy, the gods allow men.
(Fade. Sound of surf.)

Contemporary Interpretations Which words suggest that the story of Homer's *Odyssey* will always be meaningful?

Spiral Review CULTURAL CONTEXT What aspect of Derek Walcott's Caribbean background might these lines suggest?

Critical Thinking

1. **Key Ideas and Details: (a)** Who is the speaker's "main man"? **(b) Interpret:** What is the speaker's attitude toward this "main man"?
2. **Key Ideas and Details: (a)** What type of music does the speaker sing? **(b) Analyze:** Considering the loneliness, death, and defeat that occur in Homer's *Odyssey*, why is the speaker's musical style appropriate? Explain.
3. **Key Ideas and Details: (a)** How is Penelope described in the Epilogue? **(b) Infer:** What seems to be the speaker's attitude toward Penelope?
4. **Integration of Knowledge and Ideas:** Overall, which elements from Homer's *Odyssey* seem most interesting to Walcott? Use details from the poem in your answer.
5. **Integration of Knowledge and Ideas: (a)** Which details suggest that the poet felt a responsibility to show respect for Homer's *Odyssey*? **(b)** Do you think Billy Blue feels responsible for sharing Odysseus' story? Why or why not? *[Connect to the Big Question: Do heroes have responsibilities?]*

Ithaca

Constantine Cavafy

When you start on your journey to Ithaca,
then pray that the road is long,
full of adventure, full of knowledge.
Do not fear the Lestrygonians[1]
and the Cyclopes and the angry Poseidon.
You will never meet such as these on your path,
if your thoughts remain lofty, if a fine
emotion touches your body and your spirit.
You will never meet the Lestrygonians,
the Cyclopes and the fierce Poseidon,
if you do not carry them within your soul,
if your soul does not raise them up before you.

Then pray that the road is long.
That the summer mornings are many,
that you will enter ports seen for the first time
with such pleasure, with such joy!
Stop at Phoenician markets,
and purchase fine merchandise,
mother-of-pearl and corals, amber and ebony,
and pleasurable perfumes of all kinds,
buy as many pleasurable perfumes as you can;
visit hosts of Egyptian cities,
to learn and learn from those who have knowledge.

◀ Critical Viewing Which aspects of this image relate to Odysseus' journey?

◀ Vocabulary
lofty (lôf′ tē) *adj.* very high; noble

Comprehension What advice does the speaker give about meeting the Lestrygonians?

1. **Lestrygonians** (les tri gō′ nē ənz) *n.* cannibals who destroy all of Odysseus' ships except his own and kill the crews.

Always keep Ithaca fixed in your mind.
To arrive there is your ultimate goal.
But do not hurry the voyage at all.
It is better to let it last for long years;
and even to anchor at the isle when you are old,
rich with all that you have gained on the way,
not expecting that Ithaca will offer you riches.

Ithaca has given you the beautiful voyage.
Without her you would never have taken the road.
But she has nothing more to give you.

And if you find her poor, Ithaca has not defrauded you.
With the great wisdom you have gained, with so much experience,
You must surely have understood by then what Ithaca means.

Contemporary Interpretations
How does Odysseus' desire for an end to his journey differ from the speaker's attitude toward the journey?

Vocabulary ▶
defrauded (dē frôd′ əd) *v.* cheated

Critical Thinking

1. **Key Ideas and Details: (a)** According to the speaker, how can you avoid meeting the Lestrygonians, the Cyclopes, and Poseidon? **(b) Infer:** Why might a person carry such terrors as these in his or her own soul? Explain.
2. **Key Ideas and Details: (a)** What three things does the speaker say you should pray for on the journey to Ithaca? **(b) Connect:** What activities and pleasures are linked to these prayers?
3. **Key Ideas and Details: (a)** According to the speaker, why is Ithaca important? **(b) Interpret:** What might Ithaca symbolize in this poem?
4. **Integration of Knowledge and Ideas: (a) Interpret:** What message is conveyed in the last three lines of the poem? **(b) Assess:** Do you agree with this message? Explain.
5. **Integration of Knowledge and Ideas: (a)** What advice might the speaker have given to Odysseus during his long journey? **(b) Take a Position:** Do you agree with this advice? Explain.
6. **Integration of Knowledge and Ideas: (a)** What does the "journey to Ithaca" symbolize? **(b)** Do you think people have a responsibility to take a "journey to Ithaca" in their own lives? Why or why not? *[Connect to the Big Question: Do heroes have responsibilities?]*

Writing to Sources

Comparing Contemporary Interpretations

1. **Craft and Structure** The author of each contemporary interpretation in this section uses Homer's work as inspiration for new ideas. Use a chart like the one shown to explain how each poem is like and unlike Homer's *Odyssey*.

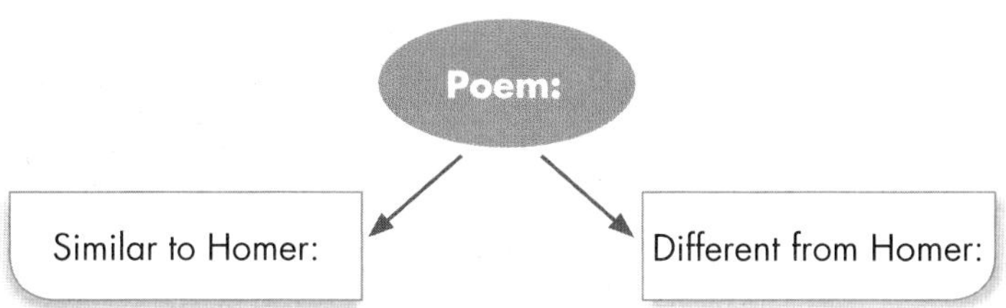

2. **Key Ideas and Details** Select one poem in this section, and identify the comment the poet is making about modern life. Support your explanation with details from your completed chart.
3. **Craft and Structure (a)** Identify an allusion in at least two of the poems. **(b)** Explain what the reference adds to the meaning of the poem. **(c)** Tell which allusion you think is more (or most) effective, and why.

Timed Writing

Explanatory Text: Essay

Each writer in this section draws on Homer's epic to communicate a message suited to today's world. In an essay, compare how each poet uses classical allusions in combination with his or her own perspective. Support your ideas with evidence from the texts. **(40 minutes)**

5-Minute Planner

1. Read the prompt carefully and completely.
2. Think about these questions, and jot down ideas for your essay:
   - What is each poet's main message?
   - What makes each poet's allusion appropriate for his or her message?
   - In what ways does each poem shed new light on the events or characters of Homer's *Odyssey*?
3. Choose and plan an organizational strategy for your essay.
4. Reread the prompt. Then, refer to your notes as you draft your essay.

USE ACADEMIC VOCABULARY

As you write, use academic language, including the following words or their related forms:

circumstance
discuss
interpret
perspective

For more information about academic vocabulary, see page xlvi.

Language Study

Idioms, Technical Terms, and Jargon

Common Core State Standards

Language
3. Apply knowledge of language to understand how language functions in different contexts, to make effective choices for meaning or style, and to comprehend more fully when reading or listening.
4.c. Consult general and specialized reference materials, both print and digital, to find the pronunciation of a word or determine or clarify its precise meaning, its part of speech, or its etymology.
5.a. Interpret figures of speech in context and analyze their role in the text.

An **idiom** is an expression that is characteristic of a language, region, community, or class of people. It cannot be understood literally. For example, *throw in the towel* has nothing to do with a towel; instead, it refers to a boxer's act of forfeiting a match. Now, the phrase has reached past sports to become an idiom that means "give up." Often, dictionaries list idioms at the end of the entry for the main word in the idiom.

Many fields of study, work, and play have **technical terms.** These are words that may be familiar in general use but also have specialized meanings in a particular field. Examples from the field of computers include *software, hard drive, the Web,* and *USB port.* Technical terms help people who share knowledge of the field communicate more effectively.

Like technical language, **jargon** refers to the specialized words and phrases used in a specific field. Jargon is useful and practical for those working in a particular profession because it makes communications efficient and precise. However, jargon can also make simple things sound complex or mask what a speaker really means.

Jargon	Meaning
The vehicle's internal combustion engine became depleted of its distilled mixture of hydrocarbons.	The car ran out of gas.
This cleansing bar is hot off the shelf.	This soap is brand new.
Stakeholders in our educational setting need new informational resources.	Students in our school need new textbooks.

Practice A

Match the definition in the box with the underlined technical term or jargon in each sentence. Use context clues to figure out the meanings.

screen	clarinet	new sidewalks
car-washer	black eye	

1. When the ball hit me in the face, I ended up with a periorbital hematoma.
2. On the large monitor, I can see more of the document at once.
3. The jazz musician put his licorice stick to his lips and played.
4. The vehicle appearance operative washed and dried the car.
5. Public infrastructure upgrades are needed so people can walk safely.

Practice B

Identify the idiom in each sentence. Then, write a definition for each one. If you are unsure of the meaning of the word or phrase, check your definition in a print or online dictionary.

1. She let us down by not showing up for the game.
2. I am up to my ears in homework.
3. Marvin, please cool it and sit down over there.
4. It's been a long day, so I'm going to turn in.
5. Jurors must try to keep an open mind during the trial.
6. Let's just nip this problem in the bud.
7. What are you driving at?
8. Your question has put the salesperson on the spot.
9. If you cheat in that game, I will blow the whistle on you.
10. I'm going to whip this team into shape.

Activity Prepare five notecards like the one shown below for each of the following words: *mouse, spare, snake, key,* and *single*. Write the word on a card. Look the word up in a dictionary, and write down its main meaning. Then, identify the field or profession in which the word is used technically, and write the technical meaning on the card.

Word:
Common Definition:
Field:
Technical Definition:

Comprehension and Collaboration

Education is a specialized field. Work with several classmates to create a glossary of technical terms that apply to a school setting. You might begin with words like *computer lab, activity, bus,* and *hall pass.* Discuss how these terms may not be familiar to people outside of a school environment.

Comparing Media Coverage

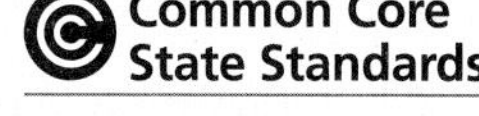

Common Core State Standards

Reading Informational Text
7. Analyze various accounts of a subject told in different mediums, determining which details are emphasized in each account.

Most forms of news media, including TV, newspapers, magazines, and documentaries use combinations of verbal, visual, and even audio texts to convey information. It is important to understand how media makers shape readers' and viewers' understanding of events through the presentation choices they make.

Learn the Skills

Analyze and then compare and contrast the ways in which different types of media convey similar news stories.

Comparing and Contrasting Presentations As you look at different types of media coverage, compare and contrast the ways in which text, graphics, video, audio, and photographs portray people and events.

- *When examining verbal texts, ask:* In what order are the events described? What event, if any, is identified as most important? What words or phrases indicate that importance? How much context for a story is provided? How much detail is included?
- *When viewing visual images, ask:* Why was this image chosen? What attitude toward the story does the image reveal?

Comparing and Contrasting Communication Once you have analyzed the presentation of events, compare and contrast the ways in which information is communicated. Ask these questions:

- How is the information in the verbal text and in the visual images similar and different?
- Are any statements or images unflattering or negative? If so, how?
- Which treatment, the verbal text or the visual image, gives more detailed information or is more powerful? Why?

Twin Pandas Reach Critical Milestone

Veterinarians at the Beijing Zoo have announced that twin pandas born in September are now expected to survive. Their mother, Yong Yong, was unable to nurse them from birth. The zoo staff quickly intervened, but the future of the young pandas was uncertain. Now that the pandas have survived their first seven weeks, veterinarians are optimistic that the pandas will survive.

When asked how long the pandas will require care

▲ **1.** This article describes an event. Compare and contrast how this article and the photograph present the same event.

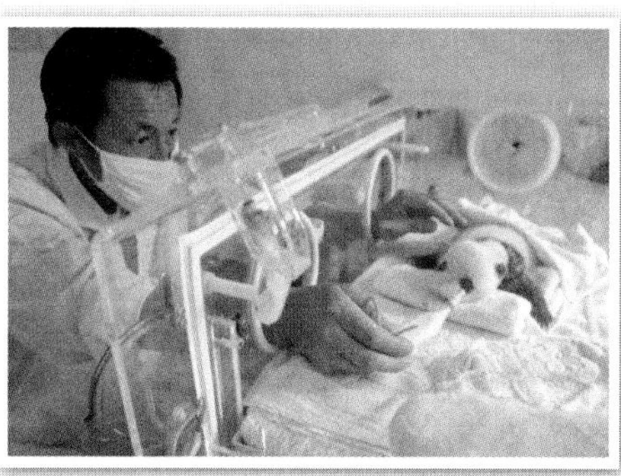

▲ **2.** This photograph shows a scene that is part of the event the text describes. Compare and contrast how the photograph and the text communicate information.

Practice the Skills

Apply what you have learned and use the discussion guide below to complete the activity.

ACTIVITY: Compare and Contrast Text and Visuals

With a partner, analyze two pairings of image and text that report on the same subject. Use the encyclopedia entry shown below as your first pairing. Then, research print and online sources to locate another example of text and images that address the same subject. Take notes on both pairings as you analyze how the visual and the verbal texts present events and communicate information. Use the discussion guide below to organize your observations about similarities and differences between the verbal texts and the visuals. Then, write and present a summary of your findings to your class.

San Francisco Earthquake

Damage from the San Francisco Earthquake

The San Francisco earthquake of 1906 had its epicenter near San Francisco, but the effects of the quake reached from southern Oregon to Los Angeles. Those who experienced the quake described it as about a minute of forceful shaking and powerful shocks.

The conditions of the earthquake challenged the views of contemporary scientists and resulted in extensive studies by scientists of the time. The insights that resulted from their research are the basis for

Use a **discussion guide** like this to compare and contrast how events are presented and information is communicated in visual and non-visual texts.

1. **Compare:** What event is depicted in both the visual and verbal texts?
2. **Contrast:** What aspect of the event does the verbal text describe that the visual does not? What aspect of the event does the visual bring to life that the verbal text does not?
3. **Compare and contrast:** What overall information, or main idea, is communicated by the visual text alone? What overall information is communicated by the verbal text alone?
4. **Evaluate:** Would the encyclopedia entry be as effective if it contained words only? Would your second example be as effective as verbal text only? Why or why not?
5. **Generalize:** What generalizations might you make about the kinds of information that are best conveyed with visual texts and the kinds of information that seem better suited to verbal text?

Writing Process

Write a Narrative

Autobiographical Narrative

Defining the Form An **autobiographical narrative** describes real events in the writer's life and shares the lessons or wisdom the writer gained from the experiences. You might use elements of autobiographical narration in letters, journals, reflective essays, or persuasive essays.

Assignment Write an autobiographical narrative about an event that taught you a valuable lesson. Include the following elements:

- ✓ a *sequence of events* involving you, the writer
- ✓ a *problem, or conflict,* and a lesson you learned from it
- ✓ *precise sensory language* and *informative details* that convey a vivid picture of events and characters
- ✓ effective story elements such as *dialogue, pacing, description, reflection,* and *multiple plot lines*
- ✓ a structure that *introduces* an event and point of view, has a *smooth progression* of events, and a *strong, reflective conclusion*
- ✓ your thoughts, feelings, or views about the *significance* of events
- ✓ error-free grammar, including *varied sentence structure*

To preview the criteria on which your autobiographical narrative may be judged, see the rubric on page 851.

Common Core State Standards

Writing

3. Write narratives to develop real or imagined experiences or events using effective technique, well-chosen details, and well-structured event sequences.

3.a. Engage and orient the reader by setting out a problem, situation, or observation, establishing one or multiple point(s) of view, and introducing a narrator and/or characters; create a smooth progression of experiences or events.

3.c. Use a variety of techniques to sequence events so that they build on one another to create a coherent whole.

3.d. Use precise words and phrases, telling details, and sensory language to convey a vivid picture of the experiences, events, setting, and/or characters.

5. Develop and strengthen writing as needed by planning, revising, editing, rewriting, or trying a new approach, focusing on addressing what is most significant for a specific purpose and audience.

FOCUS ON RESEARCH

When you write narrative texts, you might perform research to

- gather authentic details about the setting of your story.
- find out how others who participated in the events perceived or were affected by them.
- gather background information, such as historical data, that provides a context for the events you describe.

Incorporate direct quotes from others smoothly into your story, noting who spoke and under what circumstances. If you use quotations from other writers, cite them accurately.

READING-WRITING CONNECTION

To get a feel for autobiographical narratives, read "My English" by Julia Alvarez on page 146.

Prewriting/Planning Strategies

Choose an event to explore. Your purpose for writing is to relate a meaningful experience and to share your insights with readers. It may be an experience in which you learned something about yourself, solved a problem, or understood a situation in a new way. To find a topic, try either of these strategies:

- **Consider the moment.** Make a chart with the following column headings: *Funny, Exciting, Interesting, Puzzling*. Then, recall moments in your life that fit each of these categories. Choose one of those moments as the basis for your narrative.
- **Make a map.** Draw the map or floor plan of a place that is important to you. Label the areas and draw in details. Then, list words, phrases, activities, and people that you associate with this place. Review your ideas and choose one on which to focus your narrative.

Structure the sequence. Create a detailed record of events by making a timeline like the one shown. Write down the first incident related to your subject, and record subsequent incidents in the order and place in which they occurred. Take into account that different events in your story might happen at or around the same time. Weave these multiple aspects of your plot into your timeline. Note the significance of each event so that you will be able to communicate it to your audience in your narrative.

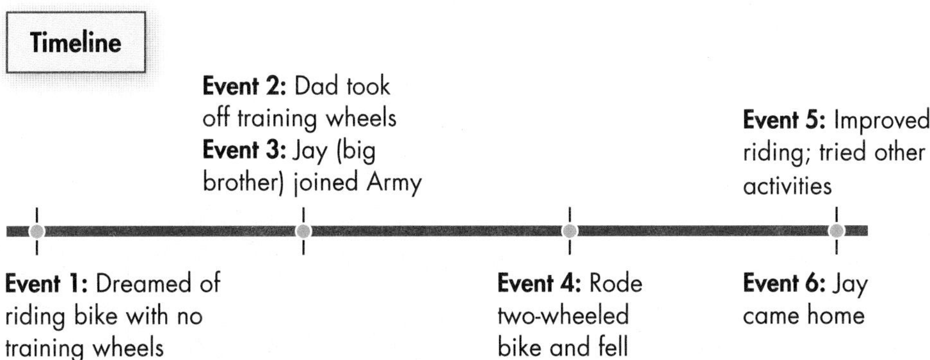
Timeline
Event 1: Dreamed of riding bike with no training wheels
Event 2: Dad took off training wheels
Event 3: Jay (big brother) joined Army
Event 4: Rode two-wheeled bike and fell
Event 5: Improved riding; tried other activities
Event 6: Jay came home

Create a details bank. Before you draft, gather details about your characters and settings that will bring them to life for readers. Quickly jot down words and phrases that describe how different characters look, speak, and behave. Likewise, note sensory details—words that appeal to the senses of sight, smell, taste, touch, and hearing—about key places in your story. As you draft, draw on these details to add interest and precision to your writing.

Drafting Strategies

Writing
3.b. Use narrative techniques, such as dialogue, pacing, description, reflection, and multiple plot lines, to develop experiences, events, and/or characters.
3.e. Provide a conclusion that follows from and reflects on what is experienced, observed, or resolved over the course of the narrative.

Language
1.b. Use various types of phrases and clauses to convey specific meanings and add variety and interest to writing or presentations.

Identify your main point. As you draft, think about why this experience matters to you. To convey that importance to readers, clearly state the main problem you faced and what you learned from it. Then, organize your details to highlight the significance of that main point.

Show, don't tell. Use descriptions, dialogue, movements, gestures, and characters' thoughts to make events vivid for your readers. For example, do not simply report that a street was noisy—provide details that help readers hear the commotion. Additionally, add sensory details from the details bank you made earlier. Appeal to as many senses as possible to bring scenes to life for readers.

Pace the action. Details and description add substance to your essay, but too much can slow the pace, or flow, of the story. Be sure that every detail you include has a clear purpose and keeps the reader engaged.

- Emphasize the central conflict that sets the story in motion.
- Create suspense by withholding some details until later in the narrative.
- Conclude by reflecting on the experience and telling what you learned from it.

Use a flow chart like the one shown below to help you decide which details to include in your narrative and the most effective time to reveal them.

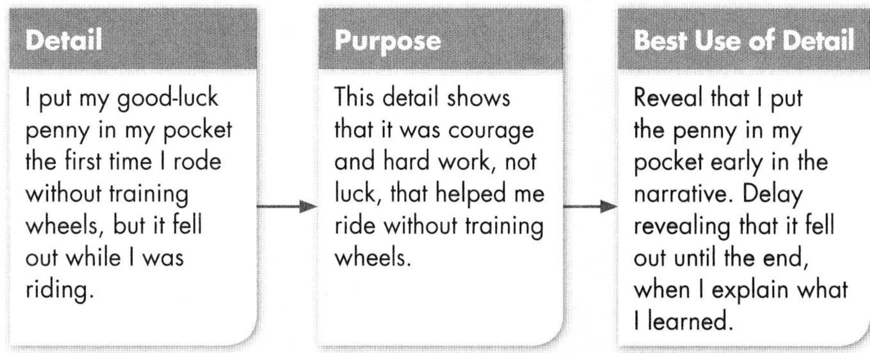

Detail
I put my good-luck penny in my pocket the first time I rode without training wheels, but it fell out while I was riding.
Purpose
This detail shows that it was courage and hard work, not luck, that helped me ride without training wheels.
Best Use of Detail
Reveal that I put the penny in my pocket early in the narrative. Delay revealing that it fell out until the end, when I explain what I learned.

Create realistic dialogue. Dialogue can help move your story along, reveal what your characters are like, and break up long passages of prose. Work to write dialogue that sounds authentic rather than stiff or unnatural. As you write, pause occasionally to read the dialogue aloud. Listen to make sure the dialogue sounds as if real people are speaking to one another.

Revising to Combine Sentences Using Adverb Clauses

Adverb clauses can be used to combine information from two sentences into one sentence. Often, the revised sentence will make the intended meaning more obvious.

Two sentences: I joined the panel. Jay is the leader.

Combined: I joined the panel because Jay is the leader.

Identifying Adverb Clauses A clause is any group of words with a subject and a verb. An *independent* clause can stand by itself as a complete sentence; a *dependent,* or *subordinate,* clause cannot. An *adverb clause* is a dependent clause that modifies a verb, an adjective, or another adverb. It begins with a subordinating conjunction such as *when* or *because* and tells *where, when, in what way, to what extent, under what condition,* or *why.*

When: *After I read the report,* I agreed with the mayor.

Condition: Dan will ask for a refund *if you will go with him.*

In what way: The bulldog yawned *as if he were utterly bored.*

Why: I drew a map *so that they would not get lost.*

Combining Sentences When combining two short sentences using adverb clauses, follow these steps:

1. Look for a relationship between the ideas of the two clauses.
2. Select the appropriate subordinating conjunction to show that relationship. Place the adverb clause at the beginning or end of the combined sentence—wherever it conveys your intent more clearly.
3. Use a comma to separate a subordinate clause when it begins a sentence.

Common Subordinating Conjunctions			
after	because	since	when
although	before	so that	whenever
as	even though	unless	whether
as soon as	if	until	while

Grammar in Your Writing

Review several paragraphs of your narrative and highlight any consecutive short sentences that you find. Look for a possible adverbial relationship (*where, when, in what way,* and so on) in two of the sentences. Following the steps outlined here, combine the sentences using an appropriate subordinating conjunction.

Revising Strategies

Maintain an effective sequence of events. In planning your narrative, you created a timeline to sequence the events. Revisit that timeline and compare it to your draft. Consider any differences between your plan and your execution, and make sure those changes are warranted. In addition, identify any passages that interrupt the flow of your story or stray off point. Consider modifying or deleting those passages to strengthen your overall narrative.

Explode a moment. Reread your draft and identify the most important moments, such as passages that capture the conflict or show a realization. For each moment, answer *who, what, when, where, why,* and *how* questions, and jot down any new details your answers reveal. Consider whether additional details will help make the moment more precise and memorable. If so, incorporate them into your draft.

Choose vivid words. Your narrative will be more interesting for your reader if you use precise words and phrases that supply appealing details and engage the audience's senses. Doing so will create a vivid picture of the people, places, and experiences you describe.

Vague: Mia *sat* on the porch as her brother *drove* away.

Vivid: Mia *slumped* on the porch as her brother *sped* away.

If necessary, consult a thesaurus to find vivid word choices like the examples in this chart.

Vague	Vivid
Walk	Pace, trudge, scramble, shuffle
Like	Be fond of, enjoy, appreciate, adore
Nice	Pleasant, kind, gentle, thoughtful
Boring	Uninteresting, tedious, dreary, dull, mind-numbing

Peer Review

Exchange drafts with a partner. Review each other's work, highlighting weak words that could be replaced by stronger ones. Then, revise your draft, replacing vague language with vivid words that will capture your reader's interest. After you have made your revisions, exchange drafts with your partner again. Discuss whether the new word choices are more effective.

Writing

3.c. Use a variety of techniques to sequence events so that they build on one another to create a coherent whole.

3.d. Use precise words and phrases, telling details, and sensory language to convey a vivid picture of the experiences, events, setting, and/or characters.

5. Develop and strengthen writing as needed by planning, revising, editing, rewriting, or trying a new approach, focusing on addressing what is most significant for a specific purpose and audience.

Language

1.b. Use various types of phrases and clauses to convey specific meanings and add variety and interest to writing or presentations.

Varying Sentence Structure and Length

A sequence of sentences of the same length and structural pattern can have a tedious effect on readers. You can make your paragraphs more interesting and readable by varying sentence length, introducing new sentence beginnings, and inverting subject-verb order.

Vary Sentence Length If you find an unbroken series of long sentences, look for an opportunity to include a short sentence. Since the short sentence will draw the reader's attention, use it to emphasize an important detail or idea. Be sure that it is a complete thought and not a fragment.

Original: Memories of long hours of practice, the brutal weather, the aches and bruises of an endless season were erased by the single fact that we had won the championship.

Revised: Memories of long hours of practice, the brutal weather, the aches and bruises of an endless season were erased by a single fact. We had won the championship.

Vary Sentence Beginnings If you have written a series of sentences beginning with a noun or pronoun, look for opportunities to start sentences with different parts of speech. Look at these techniques:

Adverb clause: *Anywhere you go,* you will still find most people care about others.

Prepositional phrase: *After a long Saturday of work,* Sarah did not feel like going out.

Complement: *Most interesting to me* was an electronic display of the battlefield. (complement of the verb *was*)

Direct object: *Our report* I gave to the editor; my opinion I kept to myself. (object of the verb *gave*)

Vary Subject-Verb Order You can vary sentence beginnings by reversing the usual subject-verb order.

Original: The mystery guest is here at last.

Inverted: Here at last is the mystery guest.

Grammar in Your Writing

As you review the three longest paragraphs in your draft, examine the length and pattern of each sentence to look for ways to improve variety. Change sentence lengths, alter sentence beginnings, and invert subject-verb order to add interest to your writing.

STUDENT MODEL: **Jonathan Chan, Royersford, PA**

True Friend

Late one Thursday night in July, my sister and I were packing for our upcoming trip to youth camp. This was my first time attending the camp, but it would be my older sister Phoebe's third experience. Everything was running smoothly until my mother called from downstairs, "Don't forget to grab a sleeping bag from my closet!" Our mother never dreamed such a simple statement would start a desperate dash by both of us to seize the most coveted sleeping bag in our household.

Jonathan's use of dialogue helps to make this opening scene more real and vivid.

The night-sky blue, extra long, brand new, one hundred percent fleece sleeping bag with a built-in pillow was one-of-a-kind. By comparison, the old sleeping bag, with a broken zipper and a small hole forming at the bottom, looked even worse. Phoebe and I reached for the beautiful new bag at the exact same moment. Insulting remarks sailed from our lips as we each grabbed it. Our stomps and yells attracted our parents to the fight scene. I began to argue that I had reached the bag first, when my sister simply let go, returned to her room, and slammed the door. She was so thoroughly angry we did not speak again that night.

The detailed description of the sleeping bag helps to establish the conflict.

As the weekend progressed, our relationship did not improve. Even worse, she had shared the story with her friends. Phoebe's words were so moving, they convinced her friends to embark on a personal voyage to "get me." As a result, I spent the getaway with a target on my back.

Here, the conflict intensifies.

As the skinny new kid at the camp, terror struck my heart when I heard a rumor about the plot against me. By Sunday morning, the plan, "Operation Little Brother," was all set. My sister's friends were on a mission.

Jonathan uses specific details to paint a picture of the problem he faces.

I was shooting hoops in the gym that morning when my sister's friends appeared. I looked frantically for an escape but was quickly surrounded. The assailants closed to within inches of me when a familiar voice echoed through the emptiness of the open gymnasium. My sister walked calmly between her friends and me and said, "Do not bother him or you will feel the wrath of Phoebe." I was in awe. With this statement, "Operation Little Brother" came to an abrupt end. The sister I was feuding with had just saved me. Her friends never bothered me again.

The dialogue and description help to convey the drama of the moment and make it seem real.

On the trip home I asked her to explain her unlikely action. She simply replied, "I still don't like you, but I would dislike myself even more if I ever abandoned a friend in trouble." Since then, I have often modeled my actions to emulate my sister's behavior that day. I have learned that even when I am angry, I must stand up for my friends. My sister has taught me many things, but the most important lesson is how to be a true friend.

Jonathan concludes by drawing an important lesson from his experience.

Editing and Proofreading

Check your draft for errors in grammar, spelling, and punctuation.

Focus on dates and facts. Review your manuscript to make sure you have provided accurate factual information. Capitalize the proper names of people or places, and use correct punctuation when including dates.

Spiral Review
Earlier in the unit, you learned about **simple and compound sentences** (p. 796) and **complex and compound-complex sentences** (p. 826). Check your narrative to be sure you have used these grammatical forms correctly.

Publishing and Presenting

Consider one of the following ways to share your writing:

Present an oral narrative. Mark up a copy of your autobiographical narrative, underlining any thoughts or conversations that you believe your audience would enjoy. As you present your narrative to your class, emphasize those passages. Be sure to pace the presentation of actions to accommodate changes in time or mood. When you are done, gracefully accept your classmates' applause and praise.

Post your essay. With your classmates, create a bulletin board display of the narratives. Have each writer supply a short comment about the event or idea that inspired his or her writing.

Reflecting on Your Writing

Writer's Journal Jot down your answers to this question:

How did writing about events help you to understand them better?

Rubric for Self-Assessment

Use the following criteria to evaluate the effectiveness of your essay.

Criteria	Rating Scale
PURPOSE/FOCUS Clearly presents a narrative that develops real experiences and events; engages and orients the reader by setting out a problem, a situation, or an observation	*not very* .... *very* 1 2 3 4
ORGANIZATION Creates a smooth progression of experiences or events; sequences events so they build to create a coherent whole; presents a strong conclusion that follows from and reflects on events in the narrative	1 2 3 4
DEVELOPMENT OF IDEAS/ELABORATION Establishes one or more clear points of view; clearly introduces a narrator and characters; effectively uses narrative techniques, such as dialogue, pacing, description, reflection, and multiple plot lines	1 2 3 4
LANGUAGE Uses precise words and phrases, telling details, and sensory language to convey a vivid picture of experiences, events, settings, and characters	1 2 3 4
CONVENTIONS Demonstrates command of the conventions of standard English in writing	1 2 3 4

SELECTED RESPONSE

Common Core State Standards

RL.9-10.1, RL.9-10.3, RL.9-10.4, RL.9-10.5, RL.9-10.6; W.9-10.10; L.9-10.4.a, L.9-10.5.a

[For full standards wording, see the chart in the front of this book.]

I. Reading Literature

Directions: *This excerpt from* Bullfinch's Mythology *tells part of the tale of Jason and the Golden Fleece. King Pelias has ordered Jason to obtain the Golden Fleece. In the land of Colchis, Jason marries Medea, a sorceress and daughter of the king, Aeetes. Aeetes owns the Golden Fleece and promises it to Jason if he plows a field with fire-breathing oxen, sows a field with dragon teeth, and defeats the sleepless dragon that guards the Golden Fleece. Read the excerpt, and then answer the questions that follow.*

The brazen-footed bulls rushed in, breathing fire from their nostrils that burned up the herbage as they passed. The sound was like the roar of a furnace, and the smoke like that of water upon quick-lime. Jason advanced boldly to meet them. His friends, the chosen heroes of Greece, trembled to behold him. Regardless of the burning breath, he soothed their rage with his voice, patted their necks with fearless hand, and adroitly slipped over them the yoke, and compelled them to drag the plough. The Colchians were amazed; the Greeks shouted for joy. Jason next proceeded to sow the dragon's teeth and plough them in. And soon the crop of armed men sprang up, and, wonderful to relate! no sooner had they reached the surface than they began to brandish their weapons and rush upon Jason. The Greeks trembled for their hero, and even she who had provided him a way of safety and taught him how to use it, Medea herself, grew pale with fear. Jason for a time kept his <u>assailants</u> at bay with his sword and shield, till, finding their numbers overwhelming, he resorted to the charm which Medea had taught him, seized a stone and threw it in the midst of his foes. They immediately turned their arms against one another, and soon there was not one of the dragon's brood left alive. The Greeks embraced their hero, and Medea, if she dared, would have embraced him too.

It remained to lull to sleep the dragon that guarded the fleece, and this was done by scattering over him a few drops of a preparation which Medea had supplied. At the smell he relaxed his rage, stood for a moment motionless, then shut those great round eyes, that had never been known to shut before, and turned over on his side, fast asleep. Jason seized the fleece and with his friends and Medea accompanying, hastened to their vessel before Aeetes the king could arrest their departure, and made the best of their way back to Thessaly, where they arrived safe, and Jason delivered the fleece to Pelias, and dedicated the *Argo* to Neptune.

1. **Part A** The story of Jason, as shown in this excerpt, contains which of the following **archetypal plot patterns?**

   A. magical transformation
   B. trickster prank
   C. heroic quest
   D. disguised identity

   Part B Which detail from the excerpt best demonstrates this plot pattern?

   A. Jason marries Medea.
   B. Jason faces a series of difficult tasks.
   C. Jason tames the bulls.
   D. Jason uses a magical potion.

2. Which aspect of the **historical and cultural context** of ancient Greece does this excerpt most clearly reveal?

   A. Magical potions were frequently used by ordinary people.
   B. Agriculture was important and most ancient Greeks were familiar with farm tools and activities.
   C. The ancient Greeks condemned the taking of life, whether human or animal.
   D. The ancient Greeks did not undertake long journeys.

3. **Part A** Which **epic hero** character trait does Jason most clearly display in this excerpt?

   A. bravery
   B. obedience
   C. charm
   D. pride

   Part B Which detail from the excerpt best shows this trait?

   A. "Jason delivered the fleece to Pelias, and dedicated the *Argo* to Neptune."
   B. "They immediately turned their arms against one another"
   C. "Jason advanced boldly to meet them"
   D. "before Aeetes the king could arrest their departure"

4. In what key way does an **epic simile** differ from a regular simile?

   A. Epic similes do not describe sounds, but regular similes do.
   B. Epic similes use *as,* and regular similes use *like.*
   C. Epic similes are shorter and less elaborate than regular similes.
   D. Epic similes are longer and more elaborate than regular similes.

5. What does it mean to start a story ***in medias res?***

   A. The story begins with a prologue that provides background information.
   B. The story begins without background information and with the action already underway.
   C. The story begins at the end of the action and then goes back in time to show how events unfolded.
   D. The story begins entirely with dialogue.

6. If this excerpt contained a **flashback,** what information would it most likely provide?

   A. stories of Jason's earlier feats
   B. the meaning of symbols in Greek mythology
   C. a timeline of Greek history
   D. details from Medea's childhood

7. What is the meaning of the underlined word *assailants* as it is used in the excerpt?

   A. friends
   B. bulls
   C. sailors
   D. attackers

Timed Writing

8. Write a **contemporary interpretation** of this excerpt. Your interpretation should be a retelling of the story that either uses modern settings and details or describes events from the point of view of a minor character. Be sure to reread the passage before you write your contemporary interpretation.

GO ON

II. Reading Informational Text

Directions: *Read the passages. Then, answer each question that follows.*

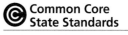

Common Core State Standards

RI.9-10.1; L.9-10.1, L.9-10.3, L.9-10.4.a
[For the full wording of the standards, see the standards chart in the front of your textbook.]

Encyclopedia Entry

Bill of Rights The Bill of Rights is the name for the first ten amendments to the Constitution of the United States of America. Some delegates to the Constitutional Convention believed that certain individual rights had to be protected from government interference. The Bill of Rights defines those protections. James Madison played a crucial role in the creation and ratification, or confirmation, of the document, which was officially adopted in 1791.

Biography

James Madison (1751–1836) was born in Port Conway, Virginia. He attended the College of New Jersey, which is now Princeton University. After he graduated in 1771, he began his political career. Madison eventually went on to become the fourth president of the United States. However, his major contribution to the country came before his presidency. He served as a delegate to the Constitutional Convention of 1787, drafting much of the document of the Constitution. In addition, he was a <u>proponent</u> and author of the Bill of Rights, which eventually tipped the scale for ratification of the Constitution.

Public Document

Bill of Rights

Amendment I: Congress shall make no law respecting an establishment of religion, or prohibiting the free exercise thereof; or abridging the freedom of speech, or of the press; or the right of the people peaceably to assemble, and to petition the government for a redress of grievances.

1. Part A Which of the following is true of James Madison?

A. He single-handedly wrote the entire Constitution and Bill of Rights.
B. He began his political career while attending Princeton University.
C. His major contribution to the country came before his presidency.
D. He was president from 1751–1836.

Part B Which sentence from the passage best indicates this accomplishment?

A. "He served as a delegate to the Constitutional Convention of 1787.... In addition, he was a proponent and author of the Bill of Rights."
B. "After he graduated in 1771, he began his political career."
C. "Madison eventually went on to become the fourth president of the United States."
D. "Some delegates...believed that certain individual rights had to be protected from government interference."

2. What is the best synonym for the underlined word *proponent?*

A. antagonist
B. advocate
C. critic
D. creator

3. What rights are protected by Amendment I of the Bill of Rights?

A. freedom to bear arms
B. freedom of dress
C. protection from unnecessary search
D. freedom of speech and the press

III. Writing and Language Conventions

Directions: *Read the passage. Then, answer each question that follows.*

(1) I had been looking forward to Nana's visit for months. (2) She came all the way to California from Ohio every August, and we always had so much fun together. (3) Each time I saw Nana, I learned something new. (4) She taught me to fish, to cook, and to sew. (5) A week before she was expected, my cousin invited me to come with his family to Yellowstone National Park. (6) I had never been there before, and I couldn't believe I had the chance to go. (7) Only after the phone call did I realize that the trip was the exact same week Nana was coming. (8) I had to make a decision. (9) In the end, I weighed the pros and cons, and I told my cousin that I couldn't go. (10) I saw Nana only twice a year. (11) Besides, Yellowstone will always be there for me to visit. (12) I saw Nana. (13) I knew I had made the right decision.

1. Which of the following is a **compound sentence?**
   A. sentence 1
   B. sentence 2
   C. sentence 3
   D. sentence 4

2. What is the **sentence structure** of sentence 5?
   A. simple
   B. compound
   C. complex
   D. compound-complex

3. What is the **sentence structure** of sentence 8?
   A. simple
   B. compound
   C. complex
   D. compound-complex

4. Which of these sentences is a **compound-complex sentence?**
   A. sentence 9
   B. sentence 10
   C. sentence 11
   D. sentence 12

5. Which revision correctly combines sentences 12 and 13 with an identifying **adverb clause?**
   A. I saw Nana; I knew I had made the right decision.
   B. The right decision to see Nana had been made.
   C. I saw Nana, and I knew I had made the right decision.
   D. As soon as I saw Nana, I knew I had made the right decision.

CONSTRUCTED RESPONSE

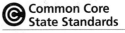

RL.9-10.2, RL.9-10.3, RL.9-10.5, RL.9-10.6, RL.9-10.9; W.9-10.7, W.9-10.9.a; SL.9-10.3, SL.9-10.4; L.9-10.1
[For full standards wording, see the chart in the front of this book.]

Directions: *Follow the instructions to complete the tasks below as required by your teacher.*

As you work on each task, incorporate both general academic vocabulary and literary terms you learned in Parts 1 and 2 of this unit.

Writing

TASK 1 Literature [RL.9-10.5; W.9-10.9.a]

Analyze a Literary Form

Write an essay in which you explain how the Odyssey *exemplifies the epic form.*

- Introduce the *Odyssey* and briefly summarize the story it tells.
- Set up a clear organization in which you explain the literary elements that are common to the epic form. Consider the form's structures, character types, plot patterns, and types of language, including figures of speech.
- Cite passages and details from the *Odyssey* to illustrate each epic element you discuss.
- Write a conclusion that follows logically from the ideas you share in the body of your essay.

TASK 2 Literature [RL.9-10.9; L.9-10.1]

Analyze an Author's Interpretation of Source Material

Write an essay in which you analyze how an author from Part 2 of this unit draws on and transforms a theme or topic from an older work.

- Select a work from Part 2 of this unit that interprets, draws upon, or makes an allusion to an older work of literature.
- Organize your ideas in an outline that compares the two works.
- Begin your essay by introducing the selection you chose and briefly summarizing its content. Then, explain the source work, summarizing its content and explaining how it is used in the later work.
- Explain how the source material enriches the modern selection. In particular, analyze how the material influences the plot, characters, meaning, or tone of the work you chose.
- Cite strong and thorough textual evidence from both works to support your ideas.
- Provide a strong conclusion that summarizes how references to the older work make your chosen selection more understandable and enjoyable.
- Use a variety of simple, complex, and compound sentences.

TASK 3 Literature [RL.9-10.6; W.9-10.9.a]

Analyze Cultural Perspective

Write an essay in which you analyze the cultural perspective conveyed in a literary work from Part 2 of this unit. The work must have been written outside the United States.

Part 1

- Choose a work and reread it. Take notes as you review.
- Use your notes to write a summary of the work and to explain the cultural perspective it expresses.
- Answer the following question: How does the cultural experience or perspective influence the selection's content and contribute to the overall meaning and tone of the work?

Part 2

- Write an essay in which you explain the theme or message of the work and show with specific examples how that message is influenced by the author's cultural perspective.
- Establish and maintain a formal style and an objective tone.
- Provide a concluding statement that follows from and supports the explanation you have presented.

Speaking and Listening

TASK 4 Literature [RL.9-10.3; SL.9-10.4]

Analyze a Complex Hero

Deliver an oral report in which you analyze a heroic character in a work of literature from Part 2 of this unit.

- Introduce the character and explain how the character's actions, dialogue, and interactions with other characters convey heroic qualities.
- Show how the character develops over the course of the work, analyzing how events and relationships with other characters reinforce the character's heroism.
- Cite specific examples from the work to show whether the character's actions suggest a hero's quest or a universal theme.
- Present your information and supporting evidence clearly, concisely, and logically so that your audience can understand your ideas.
- Employ correct grammar and an appropriate speaking style.

TASK 5 Literature [RL.9-10.2; SL.9-10.3, SL.9-10.4]

Analyze Theme

Deliver a presentation in which you analyze the theme in a literary work from Part 2 of this unit and consider whether it is universal.

- Explain which work you chose, and provide at least two interesting facts about its author or the culture it represents.
- Briefly summarize the work, and state the theme it expresses. Cite specific details from the work that support your interpretation.
- Discuss whether the theme the work expresses is universal—one shared by people across time and from different cultures. Cite specific details.
- Add interest to your presentation by including visuals, such as photographs or drawings.
- Explain or define terms with which your audience may not be familiar. Present information clearly, concisely, and logically so that listeners can follow your reasoning.
- Conclude with a summarizing statement.

Research

TASK 6 Literature [RL.9-10.2; W.9-10.7; W.9-10.9.a]

Do heroes have responsibilities?

In Part 2 of this unit, you have read about heroes. Now you will conduct a short research project on a local hero. Your hero might be a classmate, a neighbor, or even a family member or friend. Use both the texts you have read in Part 2 and your research to reflect on and write about this unit's Big Question. Review the following guidelines before you begin your research:

- Focus your research on one local hero.
- Gather information from at least two reliable sources. If possible, conduct an interview with your hero or with someone who can speak reliably about his or her achievements.
- Take notes as you gather information.
- Cite your sources accurately and thoroughly.

When you have completed your research, write an essay in response to the Big Question. Discuss how your initial ideas have changed or been reinforced. Support your response with examples from the literature you have read and the research you have conducted.

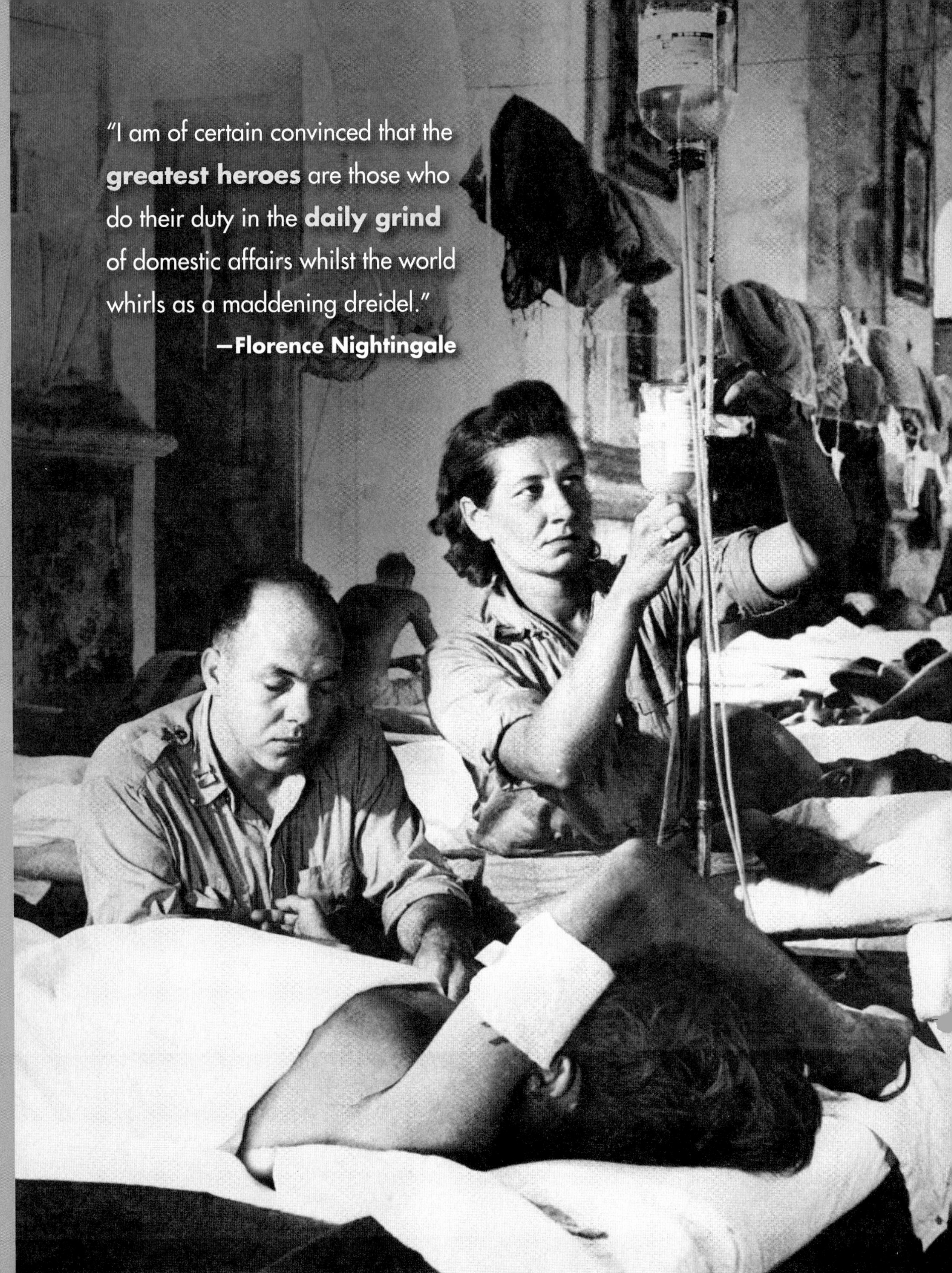

"I am of certain convinced that the **greatest heroes** are those who do their duty in the **daily grind** of domestic affairs whilst the world whirls as a maddening dreidel."

—Florence Nightingale

PART 3
TEXT SET DEVELOPING INSIGHT

DEFINING HEROISM

How do we define a hero? Is he or she someone who is stronger and braver than others? Is he or she someone we admire and want to emulate? Is the hero simply the person who does the right thing consistently or when no one else will? The selections that follow explore heroes of different kinds and examine the roles they play in our individual lives and in our culture. As you read each text, consider how it speaks to the Big Question for this unit: **Do heroes have responsibilities?**

◀ CRITICAL VIEWING Which, if any, of the people in this photograph is a hero? Explain your position.

CLOSE READING TOOL

Use the **Close Reading Tool** to practice the strategies you learn in this unit.

READINGS IN PART 3

from the Ramayana

retold by R. K. Narayan

Background: *As an adult, Rama is about to inherit the throne from his father when evil plots result in his banishment from the kingdom. For fourteen years, he wanders in exile with his wife, Sita, and his brother, Lakshmana. During this time, Sita is kidnapped by the evil giant Ravana, chief of a group of rakshasas, or demons. His name means "He who makes the universe scream." Rama sets out to rescue Sita with the help of Hanuman, the monkey god, and a huge battle ensues. This selection opens as the battle is reaching its climax.*

Rama and Ravana in Battle

Every moment, news came to Ravana of fresh disasters in his camp. One by one, most of his commanders were lost. No one who went forth with battle cries was heard of again. Cries and shouts and the wailings of the widows of warriors came over the chants and songs of triumph that his courtiers arranged to keep up at a loud pitch in his assembly hall. Ravana became restless and abruptly left the hall and went up on a tower, from which he could obtain a full view of the city. He surveyed the scene below but could not stand it. One who had spent a lifetime in destruction, now found the gory spectacle intolerable. Groans and wailings reached his ears with deadly clarity. . . . This was too much for him. He felt a terrific rage rising within him, mixed with some admiration for Rama's valor. He told himself, "The time has come for me to act by myself again."

◀ **intolerable** (in täl′ər ə bəl) *adj.* impossible to put up with; unbearable

He hurried down the steps of the tower, returned to his chamber, and prepared himself for the battle. He had a ritual bath and performed special prayers to gain the benediction of Shiva; donned his battle dress, matchless armor, armlets, and crowns. He had on a protective armor for every inch of his body. . . .

◀ **benediction** (ben′ə dik′shən) *n.* goodwill or blessing

When he emerged from his chamber, his heroic appearance was breathtaking. He summoned his chariot, which could be drawn by horses or move on its own if the horses were hurt or killed. People stood aside when he came out of the palace and entered his chariot. "This is my resolve," he said to himself: "Either that woman Sita, or my wife Mandodari, will soon have cause to cry and roll in the dust in grief. Surely, before this day is done, one of them will be a widow."

The gods in heaven noticed Ravana's determined move and felt that Rama would need all the support they could muster. They requested Indra to send down his special chariot for Rama's use. When the chariot appeared at his camp, Rama was deeply impressed with the magnitude and brilliance of the vehicle. . . .

Rama fastened his sword, slung two quivers full of rare arrows over his shoulders, and climbed into the chariot.

The beat of war drums, the challenging cries of soldiers, the trumpets, and the rolling chariots speeding along to confront each other, created a deafening mixture of noise. While Ravana had instructed his charioteer to speed ahead, Rama very gently ordered his chariot driver, "Ravana is in a rage; let him perform all the antics he desires and exhaust himself. Until then be calm; we don't have to hurry forward. Move slowly and calmly, and you must strictly follow my instructions; I will tell you when to drive faster."

Ravana's assistant and one of his staunchest supporters, Mahodara—the giant among giants in his physical appearance—begged Ravana, "Let me not be a mere spectator when you confront Rama. Let me have the honor of grappling with him. Permit me to attack Rama."

This illustration depicts an earlier episode in the *Ramayana*. Here, Rama's ally Hanuman, the monkey god, has enlarged himself to serve as a bridge for Rama's army.

"Rama is my sole concern," Ravana replied. "If you wish to engage yourself in a fight, you may fight his brother Lakshmana."

Noticing Mahodara's purpose, Rama steered his chariot across his path in order to prevent Mahodara from reaching Lakshmana. Whereupon Mahodara ordered his chariot driver, "Now dash straight ahead, directly into Rama's chariot."

The charioteer, more practical-minded, advised him, "I would not go near Rama. Let us keep away." But Mahodara, **obstinate** and intoxicated with war fever, made straight for Rama. He wanted to have the honor of a direct encounter with Rama himself in spite of Ravana's advice; and for this honor he paid a heavy price, as it was a moment's work for Rama to destroy him, and leave him lifeless and shapeless on the field. Noticing this, Ravana's anger mounted further. He commanded his driver, "You will not slacken now. Go." Many ominous signs were seen now—his bowstrings suddenly snapped; the mountains shook; thunders rumbled in the skies; tears flowed from the horses' eyes; elephants with decorated foreheads moved along dejectedly. Ravana, noticing them, hesitated only for a second, saying, "I don't care. This mere mortal Rama is of no account, and these omens do not concern me at all." Meanwhile, Rama paused for a moment to consider his next step; and suddenly turned towards the armies supporting Ravana, which stretched away to the horizon, and destroyed them. He felt that this might be one way of saving Ravana. With his armies gone, it was possible that Ravana might have a change of heart. But it had only the effect of spurring Ravana on; he plunged forward and kept coming nearer Rama and his own doom.

◀ **obstinate** (äb′stə nət) *adj.* unreasonably determined; unyielding; stubborn

ABOUT THE RETELLER

R. K. Narayan (1906–2001)

R. K. Narayan was born in the city of Madras in southern India. He was one of nine children in a middle-class family. After briefly working as a teacher, he became a writer. In 1960, his novel *The Guide* won India's highest literary honor.

Within a career that spanned nearly seventy years, Narayan wrote more than fifteen novels—as well as collections of short stories and essays. His works skillfully combine Western plots and themes with Indian subject matter.

Close Reading Activities

READ

Comprehension

Reread all or part of the text to help you answer the following questions.

1. Who are the two key players in the battle?
2. Why are they fighting?
3. As the excerpt begins, which side is winning?
4. How do the gods help Rama?
5. What does Rama do to Ravana's armies?

Research: Clarify Details This selection may include references that are unfamiliar to you. Choose at least one unfamiliar detail, and briefly research it. Then, explain how the information you learned from research sheds light on an aspect of the text.

Summarize Write an objective summary of the text. Remember that an objective summary is free from opinion and evaluation.

Language Study

Selection Vocabulary The following passages appear in the excerpt from the *Ramayana*. Identify a synonym for each boldface word. Then, use each word in a sentence of your own.

- One who had spent a lifetime in destruction, now found the gory spectacle **intolerable.**
- He had a ritual bath and performed special prayers to gain the **benediction** of Shiva; donned his battle dress, matchless armor, armlets, and crowns.
- But Mahodara, **obstinate** and intoxicated with war fever, made straight for Rama.

Diction and Style Study the passage from the epic that appears below. Then, answer the questions that follow.

> One who had spent a lifetime in destruction, now found the gory spectacle intolerable. Groans and wailings reached his ears with deadly clarity. . . . This was too much for him. He felt a terrific rage rising within him, mixed with some admiration for Rama's valor.

1. **(a)** Choose a synonym that the writer could have used in place of *spectacle*. **(b)** Explain the differences in connotations between the synonym and *spectacle*. **(c)** Given its connotations, why do you think the author chose *spectacle* rather than a synonym? Explain.
2. **(a)** What does the word *terrific* often mean in general usage? **(b)** How does its meaning here suggest both terror and immensity? Explain.

Conventions Read this passage from the epic. Identify each sentence as simple or compound. Then, explain how the author's use of varied sentence structures makes the dialogue believable.

> "I don't care. This mere mortal Rama is of no account, and these omens do not concern me at all."

Academic Vocabulary

The following words appear in blue in the instructions and questions on the facing page.

chaos **rationality** **embodiment**

Categorize the words by deciding whether you know each one well, know it a little bit, or do not know it at all. Then, use a print or online dictionary to look up the definitions of the words you are unsure of or do not know at all.

Literary Analysis

Reread the identified passages. Then, respond to the questions that follow.

Focus Passage 1 *(p. 862)*
The beat of war drums…to drive faster."

Key Ideas and Details

1. What is happening on the battlefield as Rama arrives in his chariot?
2. What instructions does Rama give to his charioteer?

Craft and Structure

3. **(a) Distinguish:** In the first sentence, which words create an image of the **chaos** and din of battle? **(b) Interpret:** How does the mood of the passage shift as Rama enters the scene? **(c) Analyze:** Cite specific word choices that create this abrupt shift in mood.
4. **Analyze:** What attitude toward Ravana is suggested by Rama's use of the word *antics* and the notion that Ravana will soon "exhaust himself"? Explain.

Integration of Knowledge and Ideas

5. **(a) Distinguish:** Identify details throughout the excerpt that relate to caution or to heedlessness. **(b) Connect:** Explain how the epic associates goodness with calm and **rationality** and evil with disorder and impulsiveness.

Focus Passage 2 *(p. 863)*
The charioteer, more…his own doom.

Key Ideas and Details

1. **(a)** What does Mahodara do, despite the charioteer's advice? **(b)** What is his motivation? **(c)** What happens to Mahodara as a result?
2. **(a)** What omens warn Ravana of his peril? **(b)** How does Ravana react to the omens? **(c)** What qualities in his character do these reactions reveal? Explain.

Craft and Structure

3. **Interpret:** Which details used to describe Mahodara suggest that violence is like both a drug and an illness? Explain.
4. **(a)** Why does Rama destroy Ravana's armies? **(b) Analyze:** What attitude toward the value of life does this action suggest? **(c) Connect:** How does this detail remind the reader that Rama is the **embodiment** of a god?

Integration of Knowledge and Ideas

5. **Analyze:** In what ways does Ravana's dismissal of omens suggest that in his battle with Rama he is at odds with creation itself? Explain.

Archetype

An **archetype** is a character, image, situation, or type of plot that appears in the literature of all cultures and eras. Reread the selection, and note its presentation of archetypes.

1. **(a)** What qualities do the main characters exhibit? **(b)** How do these qualities reflect the archetypes of good and evil? Explain.
2. **(a)** What archetypal situations are depicted in the selection? Explain. **(b)** How is the situation itself an example of an archetype? Explain.
3. **Defining Heroism: (a)** What personal qualities does an archetypal hero possess? **(b)** In what ways is Rama an archetypal hero? Explain, citing details from the selection to support your response.

RL.9-10.1, RL.9-10.2, RL.9-10.3, RL.9-10.4, RL.9-10.5, RL.9-10.6, RL.9-10.10; L.9-10.4, L.9-10.4.d, L.9-10.6
[For full standards wording, see the chart in the front of this book.]

DISCUSS

From Text to Topic **Write and Discuss**

Write a quick response to the passage. Then, share and discuss your response and the passage with a small group of classmates.

> Every moment, news came ... act by myself again." *(p. 861)*

QUESTIONS FOR DISCUSSION

1. Why might Ravana admire Rama?
2. Does Ravana seem wholly evil in this passage? Why or why not?
3. What might Ravana, in his rage, represent?

WRITE

Writing to Sources **Informative Text**

Assignment
Write a **comparison-and-contrast essay** in which you discuss the similarities and differences between Rama and Ravana, and explore what each character means in the epic's presentation of good versus evil.

Prewriting and Planning Reread the excerpt, looking for descriptions of each character's thoughts, feelings, actions, and words. Record your notes in a two-column chart.

Drafting Select an organizational structure, such as the block method or the point-by-point method. If you choose the block method, discuss all of your ideas about Rama and then all of your ideas about Ravana. If you choose the point-by-point method, discuss one idea at a time as it relates to each character.

- Clearly state a central idea or thesis early in your essay.
- Include sufficient and varied evidence, such as explanations, details from the epic, and direct quotations, to support your ideas.
- Use signal words and phrases to clarify your comparisons and contrasts. Signal words include transitional expressions, such as *similarly, however, on the other hand, likewise,* and *conversely.*
- End your draft with a memorable conclusion that follows logically from your central idea.

Revising Reread your essay, examining the textual evidence you have used to support your analysis. Review the direct quotations you have chosen, and make sure each is the best choice to illustrate and reinforce your comparisons.

Editing and Proofreading Review your draft to make sure you have avoided errors in grammar, usage, and mechanics. Check that you have maintained an appropriate academic style throughout your essay. Be sure that any paraphrases accurately reflect the original text.

CONVENTIONS
Check your essay for the overuse of a basic subject-verb pattern. Add interest by revising some sentences to begin with prepositional phrases. Set off an introductory prepositional phrase of four or more words with a comma.

RESEARCH

Research Investigate the Topic

Rama as Hero Rama is an important figure in Indian culture, and the *Ramayana* is the main account of his life and journey. In this excerpt, we see one episode from Rama's life, in which he is heroic and associated with good. However, not all elements of Rama's story show him in a heroic light.

Assignment

Conduct research to learn about Rama's story and to assess his overall portrayal as a hero working on the side of good. Consult various literary analyses, and read further about his adventures in the *Ramayana*. Carefully identify your sources. Share your findings in a **research report.**

PREPARATION FOR ESSAY

You may use the knowledge you gain during this research assignment to support your claims in an essay you will write at the end of this section.

Gather Sources Locate authoritative print and electronic sources. Secondary sources, such as commentaries and literary analyses, will give you insight into the topic. You may wish to revisit the original excerpt to identify the qualities that you believe make Rama a hero. Then, look for these qualities in other parts of Rama's story. Find sources that feature expert authors and up-to-date information.

Take Notes Use an organized note-taking strategy as you gather information.

- If you are conducting research on the Internet, use the Bookmark feature to organize Web sites you visit frequently to keep them easily accessible.
- As you work through a variety of sources, notice whether any are markedly different from the others in content or presentation. For example, a source may be disorganized, inappropriate in tone, or factually inaccurate. If so, omit that source from consideration, as it is not credible.
- Make sure you record all the source information you need while you have the source in hand. Making a photocopy of a copyright page and pages with direct quotations can save you time later.
- Label your notes with the name of the source for easy reference.

Synthesize Multiple Sources Assemble data from your sources, and organize them into a cohesive report. Follow accepted conventions to create a Works Cited list of all sources you use in your essay. See the Citing Sources pages in the Introductory Unit of this textbook for additional guidance.

Organize and Present Ideas Review your report for accuracy, clarity, and the correct uses of conventions. Then, create presentation notes that identify the most important points you want to convey to listeners. Use your presentation notes to deliver a summary of your findings to the class.

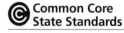

Common Core State Standards

W.9-10.2a–f, W.9-10.4, W.9-10.5, W.9-10.7, W.9-10.8, W.9-10.9, W.9-10.9.a; SL.9-10.1, SL.9-10.1.a, SL.9-10.2, SL.9-10.4, SL.9-10.6; L.9-10.3.a

[For full standards wording see the chart in the front of this book.]

Perseus

Edith Hamilton

King Acrisius [a kris′ ē əs] of Argos had only one child, a daughter, Danaë [dan′ ā ē]. She was beautiful above all the other women of the land, but this was small comfort to the King for not having a son. He journeyed to Delphi to ask the god if there was any hope that some day he would be the father of a boy. The priestess told him no, and added what was far worse: that his daughter would have a son who would kill him.

The only sure way to escape that fate was for the King to have Danaë instantly put to death—taking no chances, but seeing to it himself. This Acrisius would not do. His fatherly affection was not strong, as events proved, but his fear of the gods was. They visited with terrible punishment those who shed the blood of **kindred**. Acrisius did not dare slay his daughter. Instead, he had a house built all of bronze and sunk underground, but with part of the roof open to the sky so that light and air could come through. Here he shut her up and guarded her.

◀ **kindred** (kin′drid) *n.* people to whom one is related by blood

So Danaë endured, the beautiful,
To change the glad daylight for brass-bound walls,
And in that chamber secret as the grave
She lived a prisoner. Yet to her came
Zeus in the golden rain.

As she sat there through the long days and hours with nothing to do, nothing to see except the clouds moving by overhead, a mysterious thing happened, a shower of gold fell from the sky and filled her chamber. How it was revealed to her that it was Zeus who had visited her in this shape we are not told, but she knew that the child she bore was his son.

For a time she kept his birth secret from her father, but it became increasingly difficult to do so in the narrow limits of that bronze house and finally one day the little boy—his name was Perseus—was discovered by his grandfather. "Your child!" Acrisius cried in great anger. "Who is his father?" But when Danaë answered proudly, "Zeus," he would not believe her. One thing only he was sure of, that the boy's life was a terrible danger to his own. He was afraid to kill him for the same reason that had kept him from killing her, fear of Zeus and the Furies who pursue such murderers. But if he could not kill them outright, he could put them in the way of tolerably certain death. He had a great chest made, and the two placed in it. Then it was taken out to sea and cast into the water.

In that strange boat Danaë sat with her little son. The daylight faded and she was alone on the sea.

When in the carven chest the winds and waves
Struck fear into her heart she put her arms,
Not without tears, round Perseus tenderly
She said, "O son, what grief is mine.
But you sleep softly, little child,
Sunk deep in rest within your cheerless home,
Only a box, brass-bound. The night, this darkness visible,
The scudding waves so near to your soft curls,
The shrill voice of the wind, you do not heed,
Nestled in your red cloak, fair little face."

Through the night in the tossing chest she listened to the waters that seemed always about to wash over them. The dawn came, but with no comfort to her for she could not see it. Neither could she see that around them there were islands rising high above the sea, many islands. All she knew was that presently a wave seemed to lift them and carry them swiftly on and then, retreating, leave them on something solid and motionless. They had made land; they were safe from the sea, but they were still in the chest with no way to get out.

Fate willed it—or perhaps Zeus, who up to now had done little for his love and his child—that they should be discovered by a good man, a fisherman named Dictys. He came upon the great box and broke it open and took the pitiful cargo home to his wife who was as kind as he. They had no children and they cared for Danaë and Perseus as if they were their own. The two lived there many years, Danaë content to let her son follow the fisherman's humble trade, out of harm's way. But in the end more trouble came. Polydectes [pol i dek′ tēz], the ruler of the little island, was the brother of Dictys, but he was a cruel and ruthless man. He seems to have taken no notice of the mother and son for a long time, but at last Danaë attracted his attention. She was still radiantly beautiful even though Perseus by now was full grown, and Polydectes fell in love with her. He wanted her, but he did not want her son, and he set himself to think out a way of getting rid of him.

There were some fearsome monsters called Gorgons who lived on an island and were known far and wide because of their deadly power. Polydectes evidently talked to Perseus about them; he probably told him that he would rather have the head of one of them than anything else in the world. This seems practically certain from the plan he devised for killing Perseus. He announced that he was about to be married and he called his friends together for a celebration, including Perseus in the invitation. Each guest, as was customary, brought a gift for the bride-to-be, except Perseus alone. He had nothing he could give. He was young and proud and keenly **mortified**. He stood up before them all and did exactly what the King had hoped he would do, declared that he would give him a present better than any there. He would go off and kill Medusa and bring back her head as his gift. Nothing could have suited the King better. No one in his senses would have made such a proposal. Medusa was one of the Gorgons,

> And they are three, the Gorgons, each with wings
> And snaky hair, most horrible to mortals.
> Whom no man shall behold and draw again
> The breath of life,

for the reason that whoever looked at them were turned instantly into stone. It seemed that Perseus had been led by his angry pride into making an empty boast. No man unaided could kill Medusa.

mortified (môrt′ ə fīd′) *adj.* extremely embarrassed

And they are three, the Gorgons, each with wings And snaky hair, most horrible to mortals.

But Perseus was saved from his folly. Two great gods were watching over him. He took ship as soon as he left the King's hall, not daring to see his mother first and tell her what he intended, and he sailed to Greece to learn where the three monsters were to be found. He went to Delphi, but all the priestess would say was to bid him seek the land where men eat not Demeter's golden grain, but only acorns. So he went to Dodona, in the land of oak trees, where the talking oaks were which declared Zeus's will and where the Selli lived who made their bread from acorns. They could tell him, however, no more than this, that he was under the protection of the gods. They did not know where the Gorgons lived.

When and how Hermes and Athena came to his help is not told in any story, but he must have known despair before they did so. At last, however, as he wandered on, he met a strange and beautiful person. We know what he looked like from many a poem, a young man with the first down upon his cheek when youth is loveliest, carrying, as no other young man ever did, a wand of gold with wings at one end, wearing a winged hat, too, and winged sandals. At sight of him hope must have entered Perseus' heart, for he would know that this could be none other than Hermes, the guide and the giver of good.

This radiant personage told him that before he attacked Medusa he must first be properly equipped, and that what he needed was in the possession of the nymphs of the North. To find the nymphs' abode, they must go to the Gray Women who alone could tell them the way. These women dwelt in a land where all was dim and shrouded in twilight. No ray of sun looked ever on that country, nor the moon by night. In that gray place the three women lived, all gray themselves and withered as in extreme old age. They were strange creatures, indeed, most of all because they had but one eye for the three, which it was their custom to take turns with, each removing it from her forehead when she had had it for a time and handing it to another.

All this Hermes told Perseus and then he unfolded his plan. He would himself guide Perseus to them. Once there Perseus must keep hidden until he saw one of them take the eye out of her forehead to pass it on. At that moment, when none of the three could see, he must rush forward and seize the eye and refuse to give it back until they told him how to reach the nymphs of the North.

He himself, Hermes said, would give him a sword to attack Medusa with—which could not be bent or broken by the Gorgon's scales, no matter how hard they were. This was a wonderful gift, no doubt, and yet of what use was a sword when the creature to be struck by it could turn the swordsman into stone before he was within striking distance? But another great deity was at hand to help. Pallas Athena stood beside Perseus. She took off the shield of polished bronze which covered her breast and held it out to him. "Look into this when you attack the Gorgon," she said. "You will be able to see her in it as in a mirror, and so avoid her deadly power."

Now, indeed, Perseus had good reason to hope. The journey to the twilight land was long, over the stream of Ocean and on to the very border of the black country where the Cimmerians dwell, but Hermes was his guide and he could not go astray. They found the Gray Women at last, looking in the wavering light like gray birds, for they had the shape of swans. But their heads were human and beneath their wings they had arms and hands. Perseus did just as Hermes had said, he held back until he saw one of them take the eye out of her forehead. Then before she could give it to her sister, he snatched it out of her hand. It was a moment or two before the three realized they had lost it. Each thought one of the others had it. But Perseus spoke out and told them he had taken it and that it would be theirs again only when they showed him how to find the nymphs of the North. They gave him full directions at once; they would have done anything to get their eye back. He returned it to them and went on the way they had pointed out to him. He was bound, although he did not know it, to the blessed country of the Hyperboreans [hī per bō′ rē anz], at the back of the North Wind, of which it is said: "Neither by ship nor yet by land shall one find the wondrous road to the gathering place of the Hyperboreans." But Perseus had Hermes with him, so that the road lay open to him, and he reached that host of happy people who are always banqueting and holding joyful revelry. They showed him great kindness: they welcomed him to their feast, and the maidens dancing to the sound of flute and lyre paused to get for him the gifts he sought. These were three: winged sandals, a magic wallet which would always become the right size for whatever was to be carried in it, and, most important of all, a cap which made the wearer invisible. With these and Athena's shield and Hermes' sword Perseus was ready for the Gorgons. Hermes knew where they lived, and leaving the happy land the two flew back across Ocean and over the sea to the Terrible Sisters' island.

◀ **revelry** (rev′ əl rē) *n.* noisy merrymaking

By great good fortune they were all asleep when Perseus found them. In the mirror of the bright shield he could see them clearly, creatures with great wings and bodies covered with golden scales and hair a mass of twisting snakes. Athena was beside him now as well as Hermes. They told him which one was Medusa and that was important, for she alone of the three could be killed; the other two were immortal. Perseus on his winged sandals hovered above them, looking, however, only at the shield. Then he aimed a stroke down at Medusa's throat and Athena guided his hand. With a single sweep of his sword he cut through her neck and, his eyes still fixed on the shield with never a glance at her, he swooped low enough to seize the head. He dropped it into the wallet which closed around it. He had nothing to fear from it now. But the two other Gorgons had awakened and, horrified at the sight of their sister slain, tried to pursue the slayer. Perseus was safe; he had on the cap of darkness and they could not find him.

So over the sea rich-haired Danaë's son,
Perseus, on his winged sandals sped,
Flying swift as thought.
In a wallet of silver,
A wonder to behold,
He bore the head of the monster,

While Hermes, the son of Maia,
The messenger of Zeus,
Kept ever at his side.

On his way back he came to Ethiopia and alighted there. By this time Hermes had left him. Perseus found, as Hercules was later to find, that a lovely maiden had been given up to be devoured by a horrible sea serpent. Her name was Andromeda and she was the daughter of a silly vain woman,

That starred Ethiop queen who strove
To set her beauty's praise above
The sea-nymphs, and their power offended.

She had boasted that she was more beautiful than the daughters of Nereus, the Sea-god. An absolutely certain way in those days to draw down on one a wretched fate was to claim superiority in anything over any deity;[1] nevertheless people were perpetually doing so. In this case the punishment for the arrogance the gods detested fell not on Queen Cassiopeia [kas´ ē ō pē´ ə], Andromeda's mother, but on her daughter. The Ethiopians were being devoured in numbers by the serpent; and, learning from the oracle that they could be freed from the pest only if Andromeda were offered up to it, they forced Cepheus [sē´ fəs], her father, to consent. When Perseus arrived the maiden was on a rocky ledge by the sea, chained there to wait for the coming of the monster. Perseus saw her and on the instant loved her. He waited beside her until the great snake came for its prey; then he cut its head off just as he had the Gorgon's. The headless body dropped back into the water; Perseus took Andromeda to her parents and asked for her hand, which they gladly gave him.

With her he sailed back to the island and his mother, but in the house where he had lived so long he found no one. The fisherman Dictys' wife was long since dead, and the two others, Danaë and the man who had been like a father to Perseus, had had to fly and hide themselves from Polydectes, who was furious at Danaë's refusal to marry him. They had taken refuge in a temple, Perseus was told. He learned also that the King was holding a banquet in the palace and all the men who favored him were gathered there. Perseus instantly saw his opportunity. He went straight to the palace and entered the hall. As he stood at the entrance, Athena's shining buckler on his breast, the silver wallet at his side, he drew the eyes of every man there. Then before any could look away he held up the Gorgon's head; and at the sight one and all, the cruel King and his servile courtiers, were turned into stone. There they sat, a row of statues,

1. **deity** (dē´ ə tē) *n.* a god.

each, as it were, frozen stiff in the attitude he had struck when he first saw Perseus.

When the islanders knew themselves freed from the tyrant it was easy for Perseus to find Danaë and Dictys. He made Dictys king of the island, but he and his mother decided that they would go back with Andromeda to Greece and try to be reconciled to Acrisius, to see if the many years that had passed since he had put them in the chest had not softened him so that he would be glad to receive his daughter and grandson. When they reached Argos, however, they found that Acrisius had been driven away from the city, and where he was no one could say. It happened that soon after their arrival Perseus heard that the King of Larissa, in the North, was holding a great athletic contest, and he journeyed there to take part. In the discus-throwing when his turn came and he hurled the heavy missile, it swerved and fell among the spectators. Acrisius was there on a visit to the King, and the discus struck him. The blow was fatal and he died at once.

So Apollo's oracle was again proved true. If Perseus felt any grief, at least he knew that his grandfather had done his best to kill him and his mother. With his death their troubles came to an end. Perseus and Andromeda lived happily ever after. Their son, Electryon, was the grandfather of Hercules.

Medusa's head was given to Athena, who bore it always upon the aegis, Zeus's shield, which she carried for him.

ABOUT THE RETELLER

Edith Hamilton (1867–1963)

Edith Hamilton was a groundbreaking educator who helped found the Bryn Mawr School in Baltimore, the first college preparatory school for women. She taught a generation of young women not to limit their goals simply because they were not men.

After leaving Bryn Mawr, Hamilton began writing articles about ancient Greece, which she later turned into a book entitled *The Greek Way* (1930). Her other books include *The Roman Way* (1932) and *Mythology* (1942), which are both beautifully crafted retellings of ancient myths.

Close Reading Activities

READ

Comprehension

Reread all or part of the text to help you answer the following questions.

1. What fate does the priestess at Delphi predict for King Acrisius?
2. What does Acrisius do to try to avoid this fate?
3. How does Perseus find the Gorgons?
4. What does Perseus do to Polydectes?
5. What happens to Acrisius in the end?

Research: Clarify Details This myth may include references that are unfamiliar to you. Choose at least one unfamiliar detail, and briefly research it. Then, explain how the information you learned from research sheds light on an aspect of the myth.

Summarize Write an objective summary of the myth. Remember that an objective summary is free from opinion and evaluation.

Language Study

Selection Vocabulary The phrases at right appear in the myth. Define each boldface word and identify a synonym. Then, write a paragraph in which you use all three boldface words correctly.

- the blood of **kindred**
- young and proud and keenly **mortified**
- banqueting and holding joyful **revelry**

Literary Analysis

Reread the identified passage. Then, respond to the questions that follow.

Focus Passage *(pp. 873–874)*
By great good fortune ... ever at his side.

Key Ideas and Details

1. **(a)** How is Medusa different from the other Gorgons? **(b) Summarize:** Explain the equipment that Perseus uses and the actions he takes to kill Medusa.

Craft and Structure

2. **Connect:** What does the stanza of poetry represent? Explain. **(b) Analyze:** What quality does the inclusion of poetry bring to the retelling of this ancient story? Explain your analysis.

Integration of Knowledge and Ideas

3. **Evaluate:** Is Perseus' slaying of Medusa heroic? Why or why not?

The Hero's Quest

The hero's quest is an archetypal, or **universal**, plot structure. In a classic quest tale the hero undertakes a journey for something of great value; faces and overcomes obstacles; receives a boon, or benefit, that helps others; and returns home changed.

1. **(a)** What object of great value does Perseus seek? **(b)** What obstacles does he encounter? **(c)** How do these obstacles test his character?
2. **(a)** What aid does Perseus receive? **(b)** What boon or benefit does he carry home?
3. **Defining Heroism:** Is Perseus truly heroic as we might define the term today? Explain why or why not, citing evidence from the text.

DISCUSS • RESEARCH • WRITE

From Text to Topic **Group Discussion**

Discuss the following passage with a group of classmates. Take notes during the discussion. Contribute your own ideas, and support them with examples from the text.

> He had nothing he could give. He was young and proud and keenly mortified. He stood up before them all and did exactly what the King had hoped he would do, declared that he would give him a present better than any there. He would go off and kill Medusa and bring back her head as his gift.

Research **Investigate the Topic**

Heroes in Greek Mythology Greek mythology is **rife** with heroes like Perseus who accomplish great feats with the help of gods and goddesses.

Assignment

Conduct research to learn about another hero or heroine from Greek mythology. Consult retellings of Greek myths and literary analyses of Greek heroes. Gather information about the hero, his or her strengths and weaknesses, and textual details that reveal those qualities. Once you have gathered your information, compare the hero you researched with Perseus. Use your analysis of the two heroic figures to prepare a **poster** that combines text with images.

Writing to Sources **Argument**

Perseus is one of the many heroes of ancient Greece whose motivations and actions may seem questionable to modern readers.

Assignment

Write a **response to literature** in which you analyze the character of Perseus, determine whether he displays true heroism, and effectively state and defend your position. Follow these steps:

- Explain the criteria you used to assess whether someone is truly heroic. Then, show how Perseus does or does not meet that criteria.
- Develop your position thoroughly, but also take into account at least one differing opinion. Supply evidence that explains the strengths and limitations of both interpretations.
- Write a conclusion that makes logical sense, given the argument you have laid out, and briefly restates the points you have made.

QUESTIONS FOR DISCUSSION

1. In what ways does Perseus combine the qualities of an ordinary person with those of a hero? Explain.
2. Assess Perseus' plan for killing Medusa. Is it sensible? Why or why not?

PREPARATION FOR ESSAY

You may use the results of this research project in an essay you will write at the end of this section.

ACADEMIC VOCABULARY

Academic terms appear in blue on these pages. If these words are not familiar to you, use a dictionary to find their definitions. Then, use them as you speak and write about the text.

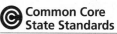

Common Core State Standards

RL.9-10.1, RL.9-10.2, RL.9-10.3, RL.9-10.4, RL.9-10.5, RL.9-10.6; W.9-10.1.a, W.9-10.1.b, W.9-10.1.e, W.9-10.4, W.9-10.7, W.9-10.9, W.9-10.9.a; SL.9-10.1, SL.9-10.4

[For full standards wording, see the chart in the front of this book.]

The Washwoman

Isaac Bashevis Singer

Our home had little contact with Gentiles.[1] The only Gentile in the building was the janitor. Fridays he would come for a tip, his "Friday money." He remained standing at the door, took off his hat, and my mother gave him six groschen.[2]

Besides the janitor there were also the Gentile washwomen who came to the house to fetch our laundry. My story is about one of these.

She was a small woman, old and wrinkled. When she started washing for us, she was already past seventy. Most Jewish women of her age were sickly, weak, broken in body. All the old women in our street had bent backs and leaned on sticks when they walked. But this washwoman, small and thin as she was, possessed a strength that came from generations of peasant forebears. Mother would count out to her a bundle of laundry that had accumulated over several weeks. She would lift the unwieldy pack, load it on her narrow shoulders, and carry it the long way home. She lived on Krochmalna Street too, but at the other end, near the Wola section. It must have been a walk of an hour and a half.

She would bring the laundry back about two weeks later. My mother had never been so pleased with any washwoman. Every piece of linen sparkled like polished silver. Every piece was neatly ironed. Yet she charged no more than the others. She was a real find. Mother always had her money ready, because it was too far for the old woman to come a second time.

Laundering was not easy in those days. The old woman had no faucet where she lived but had to bring in the water from a pump. For the linens to come out so clean, they had to be scrubbed thoroughly in a washtub, rinsed with washing soda, soaked, boiled in an enormous pot, starched, then ironed. Every piece was

1. **Gentiles** (jen´ tīlz) *n.* any persons not Jewish; here, specifically Christians.
2. **groschen** (grō´ shən) *n.* Austrian cent or penny.

The Oldest Inhabitant, 1876, Julian Alden Weir, Butler Institute of American Art, Youngstown, Ohio handled ten times or more. And the drying! It could not be done outside because thieves would steal the laundry. The wrung-out wash had to be carried up to the attic and hung on clotheslines. In the winter it would become as brittle as glass and almost break when touched. And there was always a to-do with other housewives and washwomen who wanted the attic clothesline for their own use. Only God knows all the old woman had to endure each time she did a wash!

She could have begged at the church door or entered a home for the penniless and aged. But there was in her a certain pride and love of labor with which many Gentiles have been blessed. The old woman did not want to become a burden, and so she bore her burden.

My mother spoke a little Polish, and the old woman would talk with her about many things. She was especially fond of me and used to say I looked like Jesus. She repeated this every time she came, and Mother would frown and whisper to herself, her lips barely moving, "May her words be scattered in the wilderness."

The woman had a son who was rich. I no longer remember what sort of business he had. He was ashamed of his mother, the washwoman, and never came to see her. Nor did he ever give her a groschen. The old woman told this without **rancor**. One day the son was married. It seemed that he had made a good match. The wedding took place in a church. The son had not invited the old mother to his wedding, but she went to the church and waited at the steps to see her son lead the "young lady" to the altar.

rancor ▶ (raŋ′ kər) *n.* bitter hate

The story of the faithless son left a deep impression on my mother. She talked about it for weeks and months. It was an affront not only to the old woman but to the entire institution of motherhood. Mother would argue, "Nu, does it pay to make sacrifices for children? The mother uses up her last strength, and he does not even know the meaning of loyalty."

And she would drop dark hints to the effect that she was not certain of her own children: Who knows what they would do some day? This, however, did not prevent her from dedicating her life to us. If there was any delicacy in the house, she would put it aside for the children and invent all sorts of excuses and reasons why she herself did not want to taste it. She knew charms that went back to ancient times, and she used expressions she had inherited from generations of devoted mothers and grandmothers. If one of the children complained of a pain, she would say, "May I be your ransom and may you outlive my bones!" Or she would say, "May I be the **atonement** for the least of your fingernails." When we ate she used to say, "Health and marrow in your bones!" The day before the

atonement ▶ (ə tōn′ mənt) *n.* act of making up for a wrongdoing or an injury new moon she gave us a kind of candy that was said to prevent parasitic worms. If one of us had something in his eye, Mother would lick the eye clean with her tongue. She also fed us rock candy against coughs, and from time to time she would take us to be blessed against the evil eye. This did not prevent her from studying *The Duties of the Heart, The Book of the Covenant,* and other serious philosophic works.

But to return to the washwoman. That winter was a harsh one. The streets were in the grip of a bitter cold. No matter how much we heated our stove, the windows were covered with frostwork and decorated with icicles. The newspapers reported that people were dying of the cold. Coal became dear. The winter had become so severe that parents stopped sending children to cheder,[3] and even the Polish schools were closed.

At first she swayed, as though she were about to fall under the load.

On one such day the washwoman, now nearly eighty years old, came to our house. A good deal of laundry had accumulated during the past weeks. Mother gave her a pot of tea to warm herself, as well as some bread. The old woman sat on a kitchen chair trembling and shaking, and warmed her hands against the teapot. Her fingers were gnarled from work, and perhaps from arthritis too. Her fingernails were strangely white. These hands spoke of the stubbornness of mankind, of the will to work not only as one's strength permits but beyond the limits of one's power. Mother counted and wrote down the list: men's undershirts, women's vests, long-legged drawers, bloomers, petticoats, shifts, featherbed covers, pillowcases, sheets, and the men's fringed garments. Yes, the Gentile woman washed these holy garments as well.

The bundle was big, bigger than usual. When the woman placed it on her shoulders, it covered her completely. At first she swayed, as though she were about to fall under the load. But an inner obstinacy seemed to call out: No, you may not fall. A donkey may permit himself to fall under his burden, but not a human being, the crown of creation.

It was fearful to watch the old woman staggering out with the enormous pack, out into the frost, where the snow was dry as salt and the air was filled with dusty white whirlwinds, like goblins dancing in the cold. Would the old woman ever reach Wola?

3. **cheder** (khā´ dər) religious school.

She disappeared, and Mother sighed and prayed for her.

Usually the woman brought back the wash after two or, at the most, three weeks. But three weeks passed, then four and five, and nothing was heard of the old woman. We remained without linens. The cold had become even more intense. The telephone wires were now as thick as ropes. The branches of the trees looked like glass. So much snow had fallen that the streets had become uneven, and sleds were able to glide down many streets as on the slopes of a hill. Kindhearted people lit fires in the streets for vagrants[4] to warm themselves and roast potatoes in, if they had any to roast.

For us the washwoman's absence was a catastrophe. We needed the laundry. We did not even know the woman's address. It seemed certain that she had collapsed, died. Mother declared she had had a premonition, as the old woman left our house that last time, that we would never see our things again. She found some old torn shirts and washed and mended them. We mourned, both for the laundry and for the old, toil-worn woman who had grown close to us through the years she had served us so faithfully.

More than two months passed. The frost had subsided, and then a new frost had come, a new wave of cold. One evening, while Mother was sitting near the kerosene lamp mending a shirt, the door opened and a small puff of steam, followed by a gigantic bundle, entered. Under the bundle tottered the old woman, her face as white as a linen sheet. A few wisps of white hair straggled out from beneath her shawl. Mother uttered a half-choked cry. It was as though a corpse had entered the room. I ran toward the old woman and helped her unload her pack. She was even thinner now, more bent. Her face had become more gaunt, and her head shook from side to side as though she were saying no. She could not utter a clear word, but mumbled something with her sunken mouth and pale lips.

After the old woman had recovered somewhat, she told us that she had been ill, very ill. Just what her illness was, I cannot remember. She had been so sick that someone had called a doctor, and the doctor had sent for a priest. Someone had informed the son, and he had contributed money for a coffin and for the funeral. But the Almighty had not yet wanted to take this pain-racked soul to Himself. She began to feel better, she became well, and as soon as she was able to stand on her feet once more, she resumed her washing. Not just ours, but the wash of several other families too.

"I could not rest easy in my bed because of the wash," the old woman explained. "The wash would not let me die."

---

4. **vagrants** (vā′ grənts) *n.* people who wander from place to place, especially those without regular jobs.

"With the help of God you will live to be a hundred and twenty," said my mother, as a benediction.

"God forbid! What good would such a long life be? The work becomes harder and harder . . . my strength is leaving me . . . I do not want to be a burden on anyone!" The old woman muttered and crossed herself, and raised her eyes toward heaven.

Fortunately there was some money in the house and Mother counted out what she owed. I had a strange feeling: the coins in the old woman's washed-out hands seemed to become as worn and clean and pious as she herself was. She blew on the coins and tied them in a kerchief. Then she left, promising to return in a few weeks for a new load of wash.

◀ **pious** (pī´ əs) *adj.* having or showing religious devotion

But she never came back. The wash she had returned was her last effort on this earth. She had been driven by an indomitable will to return the property to its rightful owners, to fulfill the task she had undertaken.

And now at last her body, which had long been no more than a shard[5] supported only by the force of honesty and duty, had fallen. Her soul passed into those spheres where all holy souls meet, regardless of the roles they played on this earth, in whatever tongue, of whatever creed. I cannot imagine paradise without this Gentile washwoman. I cannot even conceive of a world where there is no recompense for such effort.

---

5. **shard** (shärd) fragment or broken piece.

ABOUT THE AUTHOR

Isaac Bashevis Singer (1904–1991)

Storytelling always had an important place in Isaac Bashevis Singer's life. He grew up in the city of Warsaw in what is now Poland. Singer's father was a rabbi, a teacher of the Jewish faith and laws. Advice-seekers streamed through the family home, telling their stories as the fascinated young Singer listened and observed.

Fleeing persecution against Jews, Singer left Poland for New York City in 1935. In New York, Singer began to make a name for himself as a writer. He set many of his tales in the world of European Jewry he had left. Ironically, as he wrote, World War II devastated that world. Villages like the one of his birth were wiped off the face of the Earth even as Singer brought them to life on the page.

Close Reading Activities

READ

Comprehension

Reread all or part of the text to help you answer the following questions.

1. How is the washwoman different from the narrator and his family?
2. Why is the washwoman's job so difficult?
3. Why does the washwoman take so long with the last bundle of wash?

Research: Clarify Details This essay may include references that are unfamiliar to you. Choose at least one unfamiliar detail, and briefly research it. Then, explain how the information you learned from research sheds light on an aspect of the essay.

Summarize Write an objective summary of the essay. Remember that an objective summary is free from opinion and evaluation.

Language Study

Selection Vocabulary The following passages appear in "The Washwoman." Define each boldface word. Then, use each word in a new sentence.

- The old woman told this without **rancor.**
- Or she would say, "May I be the **atonement** for the least of your fingernails."
- ...the coins in the old woman's washed-out hands seemed to become as worn and clean and **pious** as she herself was.

Literary Analysis

Reread the identified passage. Then, respond to the questions that follow.

Focus Passage *(p. 881)*

On one such day...ever reach Wola?

Key Ideas and Details

1. **(a)** In what state is the washwoman when she arrives at the author's home? **(b) Infer:** What has she endured to get there, and how is that situation more difficult when she leaves? Explain.

Craft and Structure

2. **(a)** Cite specific details with which the author describes the washwoman's hands. **(b)** In Singer's eyes, what do the washwoman's hands symbolize?
3. **Analyze:** How does the detailed list of laundry items add power to the portrayal of the washwoman?

Integration of Knowledge and Ideas

4. **Synthesize:** In the author's eyes, how does the washwoman **exemplify** the idea that a human being is "the crown of creation"? Explain.

Characterization

Characterization is the art of portraying a character. In **direct characterization,** the author tells the reader what a character is like. In **indirect characterization,** the author gives clues about a character. Reread the essay, noting what you learn about the washwoman and how you learn it.

1. **(a)** Identify two examples of direct characterization of the washwoman. **(b)** Identify two examples of indirect characterization of the washwoman—for example, descriptions of her appearance and behavior.
2. Using your responses to question 1 as examples, explain how direct and indirect characterization **align** in Singer's portrayal.

DISCUSS • RESEARCH • WRITE

From Text to Topic **Partner Discussion**

Discuss the following passage with a partner. Take notes during the discussion. Contribute your own ideas, and support them with examples from the text.

> A donkey may permit himself to fall under his burden, but not a human being, the crown of creation.

QUESTIONS FOR DISCUSSION

1. What does the contrast between the beast of burden and "the crown of creation" suggest about the washwoman?
2. Does the washwoman's effort make her heroic or merely human? Explain.

Research **Investigate the Topic**

Fleeing Persecution Like many other Polish Jews, Isaac Bashevis Singer fled his homeland to escape persecution.

Assignment

Conduct research about Singer and other Polish Jews and their **emigration** from Poland in the years leading up to World War II. Consult news reports, interviews, historical documents, personal essays, and firsthand accounts. Consider whether these stories are examples of heroism. Take careful notes, and identify all sources you use. Share your findings in an **oral presentation.**

PREPARATION FOR ESSAY

You may use the results of this research project in an essay you will write at the end of this section.

Writing to Sources **Narrative**

"The Washwoman" provides a small window into the life of the washwoman. Singer reveals a great deal about her character at the end of her life. He also gives clues about events that brought her to where she is at the time of his narrative.

Assignment

Write a **short story** in which you describe the washwoman's life in her earlier years. Use clues about her past to shape your narrative and make it consistent with Singer's essay. Follow these steps:

- Consider how Singer describes the washwoman, and make her character consistent in your story.
- Identify a conflict that initiates the plot of your story, and develop it clearly through the rising action, climax, falling action, and resolution.
- Use dialogue and description as well as precise words and phrases to convey a vivid picture of the washwoman's life.

ACADEMIC VOCABULARY

Academic terms appear in blue on these pages. If these words are not familiar to you, use a dictionary to find their definitions. Then, use them as you speak and write about the text.

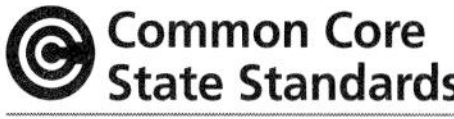

RI.9-10.1, RI.9-10.2, RI.9-10.4, RI.9-10.5, RI.9-10.10; W.9-10.3, W.9-10.3.a–e, W.9-10.4, W.9-10.7; SL.9-10.1, SL.9-10.4

[For full standards wording, see the chart in the front of this book.]

from THE HERO'S ADVENTURE

from The Power of Myth

Joseph Campbell and Bill Moyers

MOYERS: Why are there so many stories of the hero in mythology?

CAMPBELL: Because that's what's worth writing about. Even in popular novels, the main character is a hero or heroine who has found or done something beyond the normal range of achievement and experience. A hero is someone who has given his or her life to something bigger than oneself.

MOYERS: So in all of these cultures, whatever the local costume the hero might be wearing, what is the deed?

CAMPBELL: Well, there are two types of deed. One is the physical deed, in which the hero performs a courageous act in battle or saves a life. The other kind is the spiritual deed, in which the hero learns to experience the supernormal range of human spiritual life and then comes back with a message.

The usual hero adventure begins with someone from whom something has been taken, or who feels there's something lacking in the normal experiences available or permitted to the members of his society. This person then takes off on a series of adventures beyond the ordinary, either to recover what has been lost or to discover some life-giving elixir. It's usually a cycle, a going and a returning.

◄ **elixir** (i lik´sər) *n.* substance that is believed to prolong or give life

But the structure and something of the spiritual sense of this adventure can be seen already anticipated in the puberty or initiation rituals of early tribal societies, through which a child is compelled to give up its childhood and become an adult—to die, you might say, to its infantile personality and psyche and come back as a responsible adult. This is a fundamental psychological transformation that everyone has to undergo. We are in childhood in a condition of dependency under someone's protection and supervision for some fourteen to twenty-one years—and if you're going on for your Ph.D., this may continue to perhaps thirty-five. You are in no

◄ **psyche** (sī´kē) *n.* consciousness or mind

way a self-responsible, free agent, but an obedient dependent, expecting and receiving punishments and rewards. To evolve out of this position of psychological immaturity to the courage of self-responsibility and assurance requires a death and a resurrection. That's the basic motif of the universal hero's journey—leaving one condition and finding the source of life to bring you forth into a richer or mature condition.

motif ▶
(mō tēf′) *n.* repeated element or idea that has thematic importance, especially in a work of art, literature, or music

MOYERS: So even if we happen not to be heroes in the grand sense of redeeming society, we still have to take that journey inside ourselves, spiritually and psychologically.

CAMPBELL: That's right. Otto Rank in his important little book *The Myth of the Birth of the Hero* declares that everyone is a hero in birth, where he undergoes a tremendous psychological as well as physical transformation, from the condition of a little water creature living in a realm of amniotic fluid into an air-breathing mammal which ultimately will be standing. That's an enormous transformation, and had it been consciously undertaken, it would have been, indeed, a heroic act. And there was a heroic act on the mother's part, as well, who had brought this all about.

MOYERS: Then heroes are not all men?

CAMPBELL: Oh, no. The male usually has the more conspicuous role, just because of the conditions of life. He is out there in the world, and the woman is in the home. But among the Aztecs, for example, who had a number of heavens to which people's souls would be assigned according to the conditions of their death, the heaven for warriors killed in battle was the same for mothers who died in childbirth. Giving birth is definitely a heroic deed, in that it is the giving over of oneself to the life of another.

MOYERS: Don't you think we've lost that truth in this society of ours, where it's deemed more heroic to go out into the world and make a lot of money than it is to raise children?

CAMPBELL: Making money gets more advertisement. You know the old saying: if a dog bites a man, that's not a story, but if a man bites a dog, you've got a story there. So the thing that happens and happens and happens, no matter how heroic it may be, is not news. Motherhood has lost its novelty, you might say.

MOYERS: That's a wonderful image, though—the mother as hero.

CAMPBELL: It has always seemed so to me. That's something I learned from reading these myths.

MOYERS: It's a journey—you have to move out of the known, conventional safety of your life to undertake this.

CAMPBELL: You have to be transformed from a maiden to a mother. That's a big change, involving many dangers.

MOYERS: And when you come back from your journey, with the child, you've brought something for the world.

CAMPBELL: Not only that, you've got a life job ahead of you. Otto Rank makes the point that there is a world of people who think that their heroic act in being born qualifies them for the respect and support of their whole community.

MOYERS: But there's still a journey to be taken after that.

CAMPBELL: There's a large journey to be taken, of many trials.

MOYERS: What's the significance of the trials, and tests, and ordeals of the hero?

CAMPBELL: If you want to put it in terms of intentions, the trials are designed to see to it that the intending hero should be really a hero. Is he really a match for this task? Can he overcome the dangers? Does he have the courage, the knowledge, the capacity, to enable him to serve?

ABOUT THE AUTHORS

Joseph Campbell (1904–1987)

At the age of seven, Joseph Campbell attended Buffalo Bill's Wild West show and became enamored with all things Native American. His curiosity led him to the studies of anthropology and English literature. Through those disciplines, Campbell formed his grand understanding of the hero, which he shared in his acclaimed book, *The Hero with a Thousand Faces.* Campbell and Bill Moyers spent hours in videotaped conversation about Campbell's ideas concerning mythology and heroism. PBS broadcast *Joseph Campbell and The Power of Myth with Bill Moyers* the year after Campbell's death.

Bill Moyers (b. 1934)

A publisher, a writer, a press secretary, a presidential assistant, a deputy director of the Peace Corps, and a broadcast journalist, Bill Moyers has expanded the tradition of television journalism to include not only political discussion but also conversations with some of the world's leading thinkers. Moyers worked for both CBS and PBS starting in the 1970s, and continues to work for PBS. He has won more than thirty Emmy awards and was inducted into the Television Hall of Fame in 1995.

Close Reading Activities

READ

Comprehension

Reread all or part of the text to help you answer the following questions.

1. Why does Joseph Campbell believe there are so many stories about heroes?
2. How does Campbell define a hero?
3. What are the two types of deeds that make up the hero's journey?

Research: Clarify Details This interview may include unfamiliar references. Choose at least one unfamiliar detail, and briefly research it. Then, explain how the information you learned sheds light on an aspect of the interview.

Summarize Write an objective summary of the interview, one that is free from opinion and evaluation.

Language Study

Selection Vocabulary The phrases at right appear in the interview. Define each boldface word. Then, explain why each word is a strong choice that precisely expresses the speaker's meaning.

- to discover some life-giving **elixir**
- its infantile personality and **psyche**
- the basic **motif** of the universal hero's journey

Literary Analysis

Reread the identified passage. Then, respond to the questions that follow.

Focus Passage *(pp. 888–889)*

MOYERS: Don't you think ... many dangers.

Key Ideas and Details

1. What comparison do the speakers make between motherhood and the traditional hero's journey?

Craft and Structure

2. **(a)** What **colloquial,** or common, saying does Campbell cite? **(b) Interpret:** What does this saying mean? Explain.
3. **Analyze:** How does the saying Campbell cites relate to his larger point about the general perception of motherhood? Explain.

Integration of Knowledge and Ideas

4. **Synthesize:** In Campbell's view, how does the selflessness of the hero, described earlier in the interview, relate to the heroic task of motherhood? Explain, citing details from the text.

Archetypal Narrative Patterns

Archetypal narrative patterns are storytelling structures that appear in literature from around the world. For example, a pattern of three is common in folk tales from all over the world. Reread the interview, and take notes on the archetypal patterns the speakers define.

1. **(a)** According to Campbell, what motivates the hero to undertake the journey? **(b)** What are the steps along the way? **(c)** How is the hero's journey cyclical? Explain.
2. **Defining Heroism:** In Campbell's view, why does the heroic journey require trials and tests? Explain.

DISCUSS • RESEARCH • WRITE

From Text to Topic **Debate**

Consider whether you agree or disagree with Otto Rank's idea of the "heroic act in being born," referred to below, and then debate your **stance** with classmates. Be sure you respond to other debater's points. Then, add your own ideas, supporting them with examples from the text.

> Otto Rank makes the point that there is a world of people who think that their heroic act in being born qualifies them for the respect and support of their whole community.

QUESTIONS FOR DISCUSSION

1. Is the sheer act of being born heroic?
2. Should a heroic act qualify a person for the respect and support of the whole community?

Research **Investigate the Topic**

Origin Stories Joseph Campbell states that the hero is always "someone from whom something has been taken." This state of loss is sometimes referred to as a hero's "origin story."

Assignment

Conduct research about the "origin story" of a hero from literature, film, television, or another narrative source. Consult critical writings and the works in which the hero appears. Consider how the hero's story you research follows the universal pattern Campbell describes. Take organized notes, and document your sources. Share your findings in a **multimedia presentation.**

PREPARATION FOR ESSAY

You may use the results of this research project in an essay you will write at the end of this section.

Writing to Sources **Argument**

In their discussion of the idea of "the mother as hero," Campbell and Moyers briefly consider why a heroic perception of motherhood is not common throughout society.

Assignment

Write a **persuasive essay** in which you explain whether you think motherhood meets Campbell's definition of the heroic journey. Follow these steps:

- Reread the interview, and take notes about Campbell's definition of the heroic journey.
- Consider how motherhood does or does not fit that pattern.
- Present your claims clearly, and develop them with strong supportive evidence from the text and your own observations.

ACADEMIC VOCABULARY

Academic terms appear in blue on these pages. If these words are not familiar to you, use a dictionary to find their definitions. Then, use them as you speak and write about the text.

Common Core State Standards

RI.9-10.1, RI.9-10.2, RI.9-10.4, RI.9-10.5, RI.9-10.6, RI.9-10.8; W.9-10.1, W.9-10.1.a, W.9-10.4, W.9-10.7; SL.9-10.1, SL.9-10.1.a, SL.9-10.1.c, SL.9-10.5; L.9-10.4, L.9-10.6

[For full standards wording, see the chart in the front of this book.]

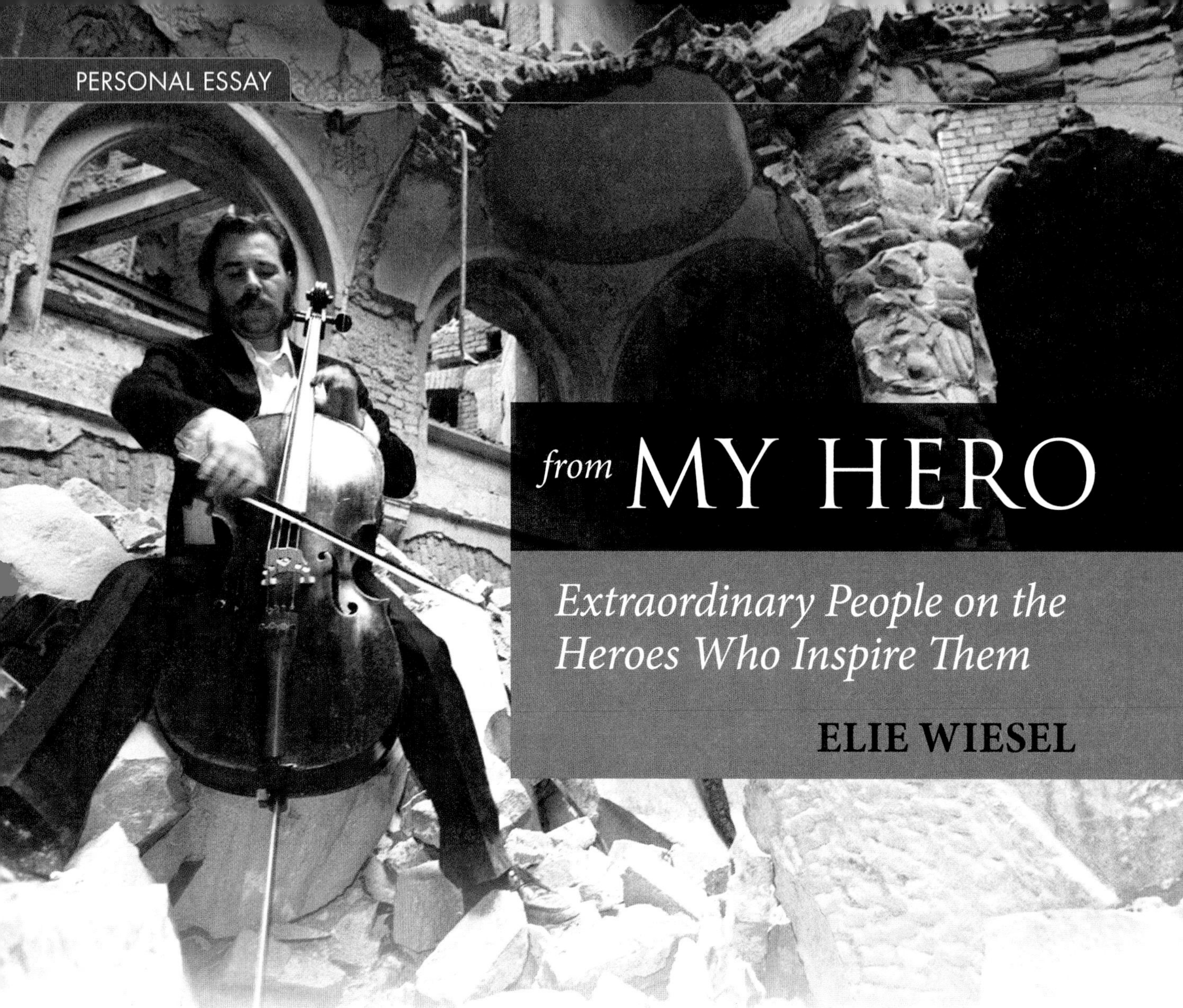

from MY HERO

Extraordinary People on the Heroes Who Inspire Them

ELIE WIESEL

Cellist Vedran Smailovic playing Strauss in the bombed National Library in Sarajevo

I am deeply skeptical about the very concept of the hero for many reasons and I am uncomfortable with what happens in societies where heroes are worshipped. As Goethe[1] said, "blessed is the nation that doesn't need them."

To call someone a hero is to give that person tremendous power. Certainly that power may be used for good, but it may also be used to destroy individuals.

1. **Goethe** (gö′tə) Johann Wolfgang von Goethe (1749–1832), famous German Romantic writer and philosopher.

Which societies have proven to be the most fertile fields for the creation of heroes, and have devised the most compelling reasons for hero worship? Dictatorships. Stalin and Hitler[2] were worshipped as gods by millions. It was idolatry, or worse, blind faith. Anyone who questioned the gods, knew too much, or rebelled in any way was finished.

Even if we do not worship our heroes, they may cow us. It takes a certain amount of confidence and courage to say, "I can do something. I can change this and make a difference." But if you, as a writer, think, "What are my words next to those of my hero, Shakespeare?" then something is lost for those who need your help and your voice. Excessive humility is no virtue if it prevents us from acting.

So we need to be very careful of those we put on a pedestal, and choose only those who embody those qualities that reflect the very best of human nature. But even that is a dangerous game. What do we do with a hero who has done something less than heroic?

◀ **embody** (em bäd′ē) *v.* represent or personify

None of our forefathers was perfect. Moses[3] is probably the single most important figure in the Bible besides Abraham. He was a teacher, the leader of the first liberation army, a legislator. Without him there is no Jewish religion at all. Yet of the many things he is called in the Bible, he is never called a hero, perhaps because he did not always behave heroically. He began his public career by killing an Egyptian; later, he failed to identify himself as a Jew. For these reasons and others, he is prevented from entering the Promised Land with the people he has led there. Is Moses a hero?

Is a hero a hero twenty-four hours a day, no matter what? Is he a hero when he orders his breakfast from a waiter? Is he a hero when he eats it? What about a person who is not a hero, but who has a heroic moment? In the Bible, God says "there are just men for life and there are also just men for an hour." Is a just man for an hour a hero? The definition itself and the question of who deserves the title are slippery at best.

I do believe in the heroic act, even in the heroic moment. There are different heroisms for different moments in time. Sometimes just to make a child smile is an act of heroism.

In my tradition, a hero is someone who understands his or her own condition and limitations and, despite them, says, "I am not alone in the world. There is somebody else out there, and I want that

2. **Stalin** (stä′lin) **and Hitler** dictators in the USSR and Germany, respectively, during World War II.

3. **Moses** Old Testament figure who led the Hebrew people out of slavery in Egypt.

surmount ▶ (sər mount′) *v.* triumph over; overcome

person to benefit from my sacrifice and self-control." This is why one of the most heroic things you can do is to **surmount** anger, and why my definition of heroism is certainly not the Greek one, which has more to do with excelling in battle and besting one's enemies.

My heroes are those who stand up to false heroes. If I had to offer a personal definition of the word, it would be someone who dares to speak the truth to power. I think of the solitary man in Tiananmen Square[4], who stood in front of a column of tanks as they rolled in to quash a peaceful protest, and stopped them with his bare hands. In that moment, he was standing up against the entire Chinese Communist Party. I think of the principal cellist of the Sarajevo[5] Opera Orchestra, who sat in the crater formed by a mortar shell blast and played for twenty-two days—one day to commemorate each one of his neighbors killed in a bread line on the same spot—while all around him, bullets whistled and bombs dropped. Those people were heroes.

Maybe heroes can simply be those people who inspire us to become better than we are. In that case, I find my heroes among my friends, family, and teachers. My mother and father's respect and love for learning had a great influence on me, and my son's generosity and humility continue to inspire me.

recalcitrant ▶ (ri kal′si trənt) *adj.* stubbornly defying control or authority

It was my grandfather who allowed me—who obliged me—to love life, to assume it as a Jew, and indeed to celebrate it for the Jewish people. He led a perfectly balanced life. He knew how to work the land, impose respect on tavern drunks, and break **recalcitrant** horses, but he was also devoted to his quest for the sacred. He told wonderful stories of miracle makers, of unhappy princes, and righteous men in disguise.

When I was a child, my heroes were always anonymous wanderers. They experienced the wonder of the wider world and brought it to me in my small village. These men were masters. A master must give himself over to total anonymity, dependent on the goodness of strangers, never sleeping or eating in the same place twice. Someone who wanders this way is a citizen of the world. The universe is his neighborhood. It is a concept that resonates with me to this day.

In fact, it is to one of those wanderers that I owe my constant drive to question, my pursuit of the mystery that lies within knowledge and the darkness hidden within light. I would not be the man, the Jew, I am today if a disconcerting vagabond—an anti-hero—had not accosted me on the street in Paris one day to tell

4. **Tiananmen** (tyen′ə men) **Square** large city square in Beijing, China, and site of a famous protest during the late 1980s.
5. **Sarajevo** (sar′ə yä′vō) capital city in Bosnia and Herzegovenia, and the cite of a major battle in the Bosnian War for independence.

me I knew nothing. This was my teacher Shushani Rosenbaum. He said he spoke thirty languages, and there wasn't a country he hadn't visited. He looked like a beggar.

I was his best student, so he tried to destroy my faith by demonstrating the fragility of it. This was his chosen role: the troublemaker, the agitator. I gave him my reason and my will, and he shook my inner peace, destroyed everything I felt to be certain. Then he built me back up with words that banished distance and obstacles. Learning this way was a profoundly disturbing experience, but a life-changing one. I have never stopped questioning and challenging what I believe to be true. I speak of him as a disciple speaks of his master, with tremendous gratitude, and his is the advice I give to young people: "Always question."

I find my heroes among my friends, family, and teachers.

In Hebrew there is no word for hero, but there is one that comes close, based on the word for justice: *tzaddik*. A *tzaddik* is a "righteous man," someone who overcomes his instincts . . .: jealousy, envy, ambition, the desire to hurt someone else—anything, essentially, that you want to do very much.

There is a story about a *tzaddik* that says a great deal to me about the character of the true hero. A man came to Sodom to preach against lies, thievery, violence, and indifference. No one listened, but he would not stop preaching. Finally someone asked him, "Why do you continue when you see that it is of no use?" He said, "I must keep speaking out. In the beginning, I thought I had to shout to change them. Now I know I must shout so that they cannot change me."

ABOUT THE AUTHOR

Elie Wiesel (b. 1928)

Winner of the Nobel Peace Prize in 1986, Elie Wiesel is a survivor of Auschwitz and Buchenwald, concentration and death camps established by Nazi Germany during World War II. He was born in Romania in 1928 and was deported along with the rest of his family to Auschwitz in 1944. Wiesel and his two older sisters survived the camps, but his parents and younger sister did not. After the Allied troops liberated Buchenwald in 1945, Wiesel went to Paris where he returned to school and began to write. His most famous book, *Night,* a memoir published in 1958, tells of his experiences in the camps.

Wiesel immigrated to the United States in 1956 and became a U.S. citizen in 1963. He was appointed chairman of the President's Commission on the Holocaust, which recommended building the United States Holocaust Memorial Museum in Washington, D.C. That project was completed in 1993.

Close Reading Activities

READ

Comprehension

Reread all or part of the text to help you answer the following questions.

1. Why does Wiesel hesitate to call someone a hero?
2. According to Wiesel, what types of societies have been most apt to create heroes?
3. In Wiesel's point of view, why is the choosing of heroes a "dangerous game"?
4. What is a *tzaddik*?

Research: Clarify Details This essay may include references that are unfamiliar to you. Choose at least one unfamiliar detail, and briefly research it. Then, explain how the information you learned from research sheds light on an aspect of the essay.

Summarize Write an objective summary of the essay. Remember that an objective summary is free from opinion and evaluation.

Language Study

Selection Vocabulary The following passages appear in the essay. For each boldface word, add, delete, or change the prefix or suffix—or both—to create a new word. Identify each new word's part of speech and use it in a sentence.

- So we need to ... choose only those who **embody** those qualities that reflect the very best of human nature.
- This is why one of the most heroic things you can do is to **surmount** anger....
- He knew how to work the land, impose respect on tavern drunks, and break **recalcitrant** horses....

Literary Analysis

Reread the identified passage. Then, respond to the questions that follow.

Focus Passage *(pp. 893–894)*
In my tradition ... Those people were heroes.

Key Ideas and Details

1. According to Wiesel, what is one of the most heroic things a person can do?
2. **(a)** What is Wiesel's personal definition of *hero*? **(b) Connect:** What examples does Wiesel give to illustrate this definition?

Craft and Structure

3. **(a) Distinguish:** How are the sentences that introduce and end the second paragraph similar? **(b) Analyze:** Which elements in the paragraph's interior sentences reveal the author's thought process and suggest that he is working through an idea? Explain.

Integration of Knowledge and Ideas

4. **Synthesize:** Why is Wiesel comfortable with the idea of the heroic moment but not with the idea of heroism? Explain, citing details from the text.

Argumentation

In **argumentation,** a writer presents and defends a position or claim and arrives at a conclusion based on logical reasoning and evidence.

1. **(a)** What claim does Wiesel state in his first paragraph? **(b)** Cite two pieces of evidence he uses to support that claim. **(c)** Cite two related ideas Wiesel uses to develop that claim and explain his line of reasoning.
2. **Defining Heroism:** What conclusion about heroism does Wiesel **ultimately** draw?

DISCUSS • RESEARCH • WRITE

From Text to Topic **Group Discussion**

Discuss the following passage with a group of classmates. Listen closely and build on one another's ideas. Support your own ideas with examples from the text.

> Is a hero a hero twenty-four hours a day, no matter what? Is he a hero when he orders his breakfast from a waiter? Is he a hero when he eats it? What about a person who is not a hero, but who has a heroic moment?

QUESTIONS FOR DISCUSSION

1. Why does Wiesel ask these questions?
2. How do you answer each of these questions? How might Wiesel answer these questions?
3. How do these questions clarify the problem Wiesel sees in defining heroism?

Research **Investigate the Topic**

False Heroes To **underscore** the **ambiguity** and possible dangers of hero worship, Elie Wiesel mentions dictators such as Stalin and Hitler who manipulated and devastated entire populations.

Assignment

Conduct research about one of the false heroes Wiesel mentions, and determine the role hero worship played in the figure's rise to power. Keep careful track of your sources, noting titles, authors, and publication information. Share your findings in an **informal presentation.**

PREPARATION FOR ESSAY

You may use the results of this research project in an essay you will write at the end of this section.

Writing to Sources **Explanatory Text**

In this essay, Elie Wiesel presents and supports his definition of the idea of heroism.

Assignment

Write a **definition essay**—one in which you define an abstract idea—about heroism. Follow these steps:

- Review the text to isolate the various definitions that Wiesel provides of the *hero* or *heroism*. Synthesize these ideas to arrive at your own understanding of the concept.
- State your definition in a thesis statement. Take your readers through your thought process, ordering ideas logically and providing meaningful transitions from section to section.
- Include strong supporting evidence, including examples from Wiesel's text as well as your own observations.

ACADEMIC VOCABULARY

Academic terms appear in blue on these pages. If these words are not familiar to you, use a dictionary to find their definitions. Then, use them as you speak and write about the text.

Common Core State Standards

RI.9-10.1, RI.9-10.2, RI.9-10.3, RI.9-10.4, RI.9-10.5, RI.9-10.6; W.9-10.2, W.9-10.2.a, W.9-10.2.b, W.9-10.4, W.9-10.7, W.9-10.9; SL.9-10.1, SL.9-10.4; L.9–10.4.b

[For full standards wording, see the chart in the front of this book.]

Of Altruism, Heroism and Nature's Gifts in the Face of Terror

Natalie Angier

For the wordless, formless, expectant citizens of tomorrow, here are some postcards of all that matters today:

Minutes after terrorists slam jet planes into the towers of the World Trade Center, streams of harrowed humanity crowd the emergency stairwells, heading in two directions. While terrified employees scramble down, toward exit doors and survival, hundreds of New York firefighters, each laden with 70 to 100 pounds of lifesaving gear, charge upward, never to be seen again.

As the last of four hijacked planes advances toward an unknown but surely populated destination, passengers huddle together and plot resistance against their captors, an act that may explain why the plane fails to reach its target, crashing instead into an empty field outside Pittsburgh.

Hearing of the tragedy whose dimensions cannot be charted or absorbed, tens of thousands of people across the nation storm their local hospitals and blood banks, begging for the chance to give blood, something of themselves to the hearts of the wounded—and the heart of us all—beating against the void.

altruism ▶ (al′tro͞o iz′əm) *n.* interest in others' well-being that is unselfishly motivated

Altruism and heroism. If not for these twin radiant badges of our humanity, there would be no us, and we know it. And so, when their vile opposite threatened to choke us into submission last Tuesday, we rallied them in quantities so great we surprised even ourselves.

Nothing and nobody can fully explain the source of the emotional genius that has been everywhere on display. Politicians have cast it as evidence of the **indomitable** spirit of a rock-solid America; pastors have given credit to a more celestial source. And while biologists in no way claim to have discovered the key to human nobility, they do have their own spin on the subject. The altruistic impulse, they say, is a nondenominational[1] gift, the birthright and defining characteristic of the human species.

◀ **indomitable** (in däm′i tə bəl) *adj.* impossible to subdue or discourage

As they see it, the roots of altruistic behavior far predate *Homo sapiens*, and that is why it seems to flow forth so readily once tapped. Recent studies that model group dynamics suggest that a spirit of cooperation will arise in nature under a wide variety of circumstances.

"There's a general trend in evolutionary biology toward recognizing that very often the best way to compete is to cooperate," said Dr. Barbara Smuts, a professor of anthropology at the University of Michigan, who has published papers on the evolution of altruism. "And that, to me, is a source of some solace and comfort."

Moreover, most biologists concur that the human capacity for language and memory allows altruistic behavior—the desire to give, and to sacrifice for the sake of others—to flourish in measure far beyond the cooperative spirit seen in other species.

With language, they say, people can learn of individuals they have never met and feel compassion for their suffering, and honor and even emulate their heroic deeds. They can also warn one another of any selfish cheaters or malign tricksters lurking in their midst.

"In a large crowd, we know who the good guys are, and we can talk about, and ostracize, the bad ones," said Dr. Craig Packer, a professor of ecology and evolution at the University of Minnesota. "People are very concerned about their reputation, and that, too, can inspire us to be good."

Oh, better than good.

"There's a grandness in the human species that is so striking, and so profoundly different from what we see in other animals," he added. "We are an amalgamation of families working together. This is what civilization is derived from."

At the same time, said biologists, the very conditions that encourage heroics and selflessness can be the source of profound barbarism as well. "Moral behavior is often a within-group phenomenon," said Dr. David Sloan Wilson, a professor of biology at the State University of New York at Binghamton. "Altruism is practiced within your group, and often turned off toward members of other groups."

1. **nondenominational** not connected to a particular religion.

The desire to understand the nature of altruism has occupied evolutionary thinkers since Charles Darwin, who was fascinated by the apparent existence of altruism among social insects. In ant and bee colonies, sterile female workers labor ceaselessly for their queen, and will even die for her when the nest is threatened. How could such seeming selflessness evolve, when it is exactly those individuals that are behaving altruistically that fail to breed and thereby pass their selfless genes along?

By a similar token, human soldiers who go to war often are at the beginning of their reproductive potential, and many are killed before getting the chance to have children. Why don't the stay-at-homes simply outbreed the do-gooders and thus bury the altruistic impulse along with the casualties of combat?

The question of altruism was at least partly solved when the British evolutionary theorist William Hamilton formulated the idea of inclusive fitness: the notion that individuals can enhance their reproductive success not merely by having young of their own, but by caring for their genetic relatives as well. Among social bees and ants, it turns out, the sister workers are more closely related to one another than parents normally are to their offspring; thus it behooves the workers to care more about current and potential sisters than to fret over their sterile selves.

The concept of inclusive fitness explains many brave acts observed in nature. Dr. Richard Wrangham, a primatologist at Harvard, cites the example of the red colobus monkey. When they are being hunted by chimpanzees, the male monkeys are "amazingly brave," Dr. Wrangham said. "As the biggest and strongest members of their group, they undoubtedly could escape quicker than the others." Instead, the males jump to the front, confronting the chimpanzee hunters while the mothers and offspring jump to safety. Often, the much bigger chimpanzees pull the colobus soldiers off by their tails and slam them to their deaths.

Their courageousness can be explained by the fact that colobus monkeys live in multimale, multifemale groups in which the males are almost always related. So in protecting the young monkeys, the adult males are defending their kin.

accrued ▶ (ə kro͞od′) *v.* regularly added or increased

Yet, as biologists are learning, there is more to cooperation and generosity than an investment in one's nepotistic patch of DNA.[2] Lately they have **accrued** evidence that something like group selection encourages the evolution of traits beneficial to a group, even when members of the group are not related.

In computer simulation studies, Dr. Smuts and her colleagues modeled two types of group-living agents that would behave like herbivores: one that would selfishly consume all the food in a given patch before moving on, and another that would consume resources modestly rather than greedily, thus allowing local plant food to regenerate.

---

2. **nepotistic patch of DNA** blood relatives.

Researchers had assumed that cooperators could collaborate with genetically unrelated cooperators only if they had the cognitive capacity to know goodness when they saw it.

But the data suggested otherwise. "These models showed that under a wide range of simulated environmental conditions you could get selection for prudent, cooperative behavior," Dr. Smuts said, even in the absence of cognition or kinship. "If you happened by chance to get good guys together, they remained together because they created a mutually beneficial environment."

This sort of win-win principle, she said, could explain all sorts of symbiotic arrangements, even among different species—like the tendency of baboons and impalas to associate together because they use each other's warning calls.

Add to this basic mechanistic selection for cooperation the human capacity to recognize and reward behaviors that strengthen the group—the tribe, the state, the church, the platoon—and selflessness thrives and multiplies. So, too, does the need for group identity. Classic so-called minimal group experiments have shown that when people are gathered together and assigned membership in arbitrary groups, called, say, the Greens and the Reds, before long the members begin expressing amity for their fellow Greens or Reds and animosity toward those of the wrong "color."

"Ancestral life frequently consisted of intergroup conflict," Dr. Wilson of SUNY said. "It's part of our mental heritage."

Yet he does not see conflict as inevitable. "It's been shown pretty well that where people place the boundary between us and them is extremely flexible and strategic," he said. "It's possible to widen the moral circle, and I'm optimistic enough to believe it can be done on a worldwide scale."

Ultimately, though, scientists acknowledge that the evolutionary framework for self-sacrificing acts is overlaid by individual choice. And it is there, when individual firefighters or office workers or airplane passengers choose the altruistic path, that science gives way to wonder.

Dr. James J. Moore, a professor of anthropology at the University of California at San Diego, said he had studied many species, including many different primates. "We're the nicest species I know," he said. "To see those guys risking their lives, climbing over rubble on the chance of finding one person alive, well, you wouldn't find baboons doing that." The horrors of last week notwithstanding, he said, "the overall picture to come out about human nature is wonderful."

"For every 50 people making bomb threats now to mosques," he said, "there are 500,000 people around the world behaving just the way we hoped they would, with empathy and expressions of grief. We are amazingly civilized."

True, death-defying acts of heroism may be the province of the few. For the rest of us, simple humanity will do.

Close Reading Activities

READ

Comprehension

Reread all or part of the text to help you answer the following questions.

1. What events does Angier describe at the beginning of the article?
2. According to Angier, what did many people do after hearing the news of those events?
3. What is "inclusive fitness"?

Research: Clarify Details This article may include references that are unfamiliar to you. Choose at least one unfamiliar detail, and briefly research it. Then, explain how the information you learned from research sheds light on an aspect of the article.

Summarize Write an objective summary of the article. Remember that an objective summary is free from opinion and evaluation.

Language Study

Selection Vocabulary The following passages appear in the article. Define each boldface word. Then, use all the boldface words in a paragraph.

- **Altruism** and heroism. If not for these twin radiant badges of our humanity, there would be no us....
- Politicians have cast it as evidence of the **indomitable** spirit of a rock-solid America....
- Lately they have **accrued** evidence that something like group selection encourages the evolution of traits beneficial to a group....

Literary Analysis

Reread the identified passage. Then, respond to the questions that follow.

Focus Passage *(pp. 898–899)*

Altruism and heroism ... solace and comfort."

Key Ideas and Details

1. What, according to Angier, are the "twin badges of our humanity"?
2. What have recent studies shown about a spirit of cooperation in nature? Explain.

Craft and Structure

3. **(a) Distinguish:** Cite two charged, or emotional, terms Angier uses in the first two paragraphs to rename her topics. **(b) Analyze:** How does her diction change when she turns to scientific content? **(c) Draw Conclusions:** What does her diction suggest about a scientific perspective versus a political, social, or personal one? Explain.

Integration of Knowledge and Ideas

4. **Generalize:** Why might a scientist, or anyone, find the idea that "the best way to compete is to cooperate" comforting? Explain.

Structure

The **structure** of a work is the way in which it is organized. A logical structure will help readers better understand connections among ideas. Reread the article, and take notes about its structure.

1. **(a)** Which paragraphs **comprise** the introduction? **(b)** How does the introduction **establish** a foundation for the entire article?
2. **Defining Heroism: (a)** At what point does the conclusion begin? **(b)** How does the conclusion relate directly to the introduction? Explain.

DISCUSS • RESEARCH • WRITE

From Text to Topic **Write and Share**

Write a quick response to the passage, and then share your writing with a partner. Discuss your ideas and your partners' responses to both the passage and to your ideas.

> "For every 50 people making bomb threats now to mosques," he said, "there are 500,000 people around the world behaving just the way we hoped they would, with empathy and expressions of grief. We are amazingly civilized."
>
> True, death-defying acts of heroism may be the province of the few. For the rest of us, simple humanity will do.

QUESTIONS FOR DISCUSSION

1. What does Angier mean by "simple humanity"?
2. Is "simple humanity" enough? Why or why not?

Research **Investigate the Topic**

9/11 Relief Efforts Natalie Angier uses the events of September 11, 2001, to frame her explanation of altruism, heroism, and human nature.

Assignment
Conduct research to learn about relief efforts that occurred in the aftermath of the events of September 11, 2001. Relate the information you learn to the findings about altruism and heroism Angier describes in her article. Examine newspaper articles, history books, and Web sites. Take clear notes, and carefully document your sources. Share your findings in a **research report.**

PREPARATION FOR ESSAY

You may use the results of this research project in an essay you will write at the end of this section.

Writing to Sources **Informative Text**

In her conclusion, Angier explains that the qualities of altruism and heroism are more **prevalent** in humans than in other species.

Assignment
Write an **article or blog post** in which you discuss altruistic behavior you may have observed in your school, your community, or another setting. Explain how the behavior you observed demonstrates some of the qualities Angier describes in her essay. Follow these steps:

- Using Angier's essay as a model, begin with an engaging introduction that sets up a foundation for the rest of your discussion.
- Organize your ideas logically, using clear transitions to connect your ideas.
- Write a conclusion in which you reflect upon the information you introduced and developed earlier in the essay.

ACADEMIC VOCABULARY

Academic terms appear in blue on these pages. If these words are not familiar to you, use a dictionary to find their definitions. Then, use them as you speak and write about the text.

Common Core State Standards

RI.9-10.1, RI.9-10.2, RI.9-10.3, RI.9-10.4, RI.9-10.5, RI.9-10.6; W.9-10.2, W.9-10.2.a, W.9-10.2.c, W.9-10.2.f, W.9-10.4, W.9-10.6, W.9-10.7, W.9-10.9; SL.9-10.1

[For full standards wording, see the chart in the front of this book.]

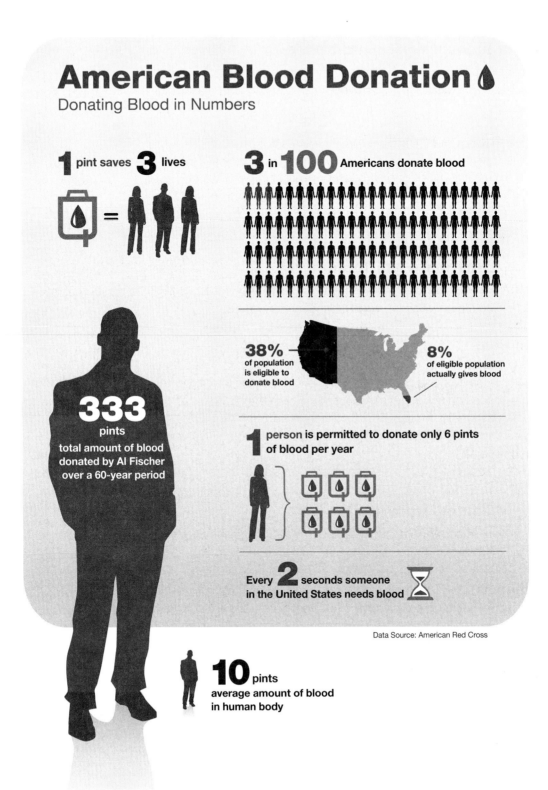

American Blood Donation

Donating Blood in Numbers

1 pint saves **3** lives

3 in **100** Americans donate blood

38% of population is eligible to donate blood

8% of eligible population actually gives blood

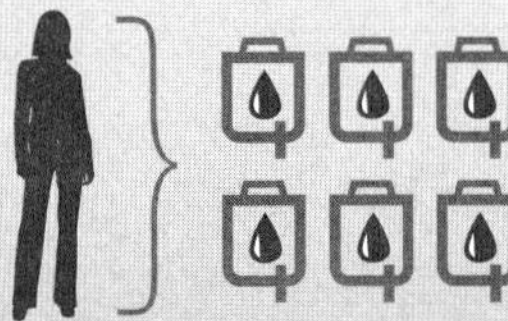

333 pints total amount of blood donated by Al Fischer over a 60-year period

1 person is permitted to donate only 6 pints of blood per year

Every **2** seconds someone in the United States needs blood

Data Source: American Red Cross

10 pints average amount of blood in human body

Close Reading Activities

READ • RESEARCH

Comprehension

Look at the graphic closely, and reread the captions and labels. Then, answer the following questions.

1. For every 100 Americans, how many donate blood?
2. How many lives can a single pint of blood save?

Critical Analysis

Key Ideas and Details

1. **(a) Analyze:** Explain the persuasive message this graphic conveys: What do the makers of this infographic want readers to think and to do? **(b) Connect:** In what ways does the information, both visual and verbal, about the demand for donated blood add urgency to the message? Explain.

Craft and Structure

2. **Analyze:** What **distinct** information is conveyed in each of the six main sections of the graphic? Explain.
3. **(a)** What information does the image of the United States convey? **(b) Interpret:** Explain how this graphic **underscores** the importance of blood donation for those who are eligible to give.

Integration of Knowledge and Ideas

4. **(a) Synthesize:** What information is conveyed by the large and small images of a person? **(b) Analyze:** How does this information **implicitly** argue that Al Fischer is a hero? Explain. **(c) Evaluate:** Is this argument well supported and convincing? Explain.
5. **(a) Make a Judgment:** Is blood donation a heroic activity? Explain your position. **(b) Connect:** How might the various authors in this section answer that question? Explain, citing specific examples and evidence from the texts.

Research Investigate the Topic

Blood Banks Conduct research about the history of blood banks in the United States and how they are run and operated today. Consult authoritative sources, including Web sites run by government agencies and reputable nonprofit organizations. After you have gathered your data, write a **summary** of your findings, and explain how this topic relates to the ideas about heroism presented in this section.

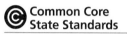

Common Core State Standards

RI.9-10.1, RI.9-10.2, RI.9-10.8; W.9-10.7

[For full standards wording, see the chart in the front of this book.]

ACADEMIC VOCABULARY

Academic terms appear in blue on these pages. If these words are not familiar to you, use a dictionary to find their definitions. Then, use them as you speak and write about the infographic.

PREPARATION FOR ESSAY

You may use the results of this research project in an essay you will write at the end of this section.

Assessment: Synthesis

Speaking and Listening: Group Discussion

Heroism and Responsibility The texts in this section vary in genre, length, style, and perspective. However, all of them share stories of heroes and the deeds they perform or reflect on what it means to be a hero. These ideas are all related to the Big Question addressed in this unit: **Do heroes have responsibilities?**

Assignment

Conduct discussions. With a small group of classmates, conduct a discussion about issues of heroism and responsibility. Refer to the texts in this section, other texts you have read, your personal experience, and research you have conducted to support your ideas. Begin your discussion by addressing the following questions:

- What is a hero?
- Is there a difference between a hero and someone who performs a heroic act?
- What responsibilities do heroes have to society, to other people, and to themselves?
- What makes people choose the heroic path?
- Are all heroes good? Are heroes good all the time?

Summarize and present your ideas. After you have fully explored the topic, summarize your discussion, and present your findings to the class as a whole.

▲ Refer to the selections you read in Part 3 as you complete the activities on this assessment.

Criteria for Success

✓ **Organizes the group effectively**
Appoint a group leader and a timekeeper. The group leader should present the discussion questions. The timekeeper should make sure the discussion takes no longer than twenty minutes.

✓ **Maintains focus of discussion**
As a group, stay on topic and avoid straying into other subject areas.

✓ **Involves all participants equally and fully**
Treat all participants equally and with respect. Allow everyone a chance to speak, and encourage reluctant group members to contribute.

✓ **Works together as a group**
Listen to one another's ideas, and make connections among different speaker's points. Work to arrive at a consensus.

USE NEW VOCABULARY

As you speak and share ideas, work to use the vocabulary words you have learned in this unit. The more you use new words, the more you will "own" them.

Writing: **Narrative**

Heroism and Responsibility Fictional heroes are often exceptional characters who may have enhanced abilities or skills. They may be professional heroes who devote their lives and skills to helping others. By contrast, a hero in everyday life may be an otherwise ordinary person who happens to perform a selfless task.

Common Core State Standards

W.9-10.3, W.9-10.3.a–e, W.9-10.4; SL.9-10.1, SL.9-10.1.a–d; L.9-10.2.c

[For full standards wording, see the chart in the front of this book.]

Assignment

Write a **reflective essay** about a real person whom you consider to be a hero. Describe why this person is heroic and how he or she carries out responsibilities. Include an example of a heroic incident you have witnessed your subject perform as a way to frame your essay. As you write, draw on the selections you have read in this section and the research you have completed.

Criteria for Success

Purpose/Focus

✓ **Makes connections to larger ideas**

Compare the heroism of the person you are describing with examples from the texts you have read. Draw parallels or point out meaningful differences.

✓ **Engages the audience with significant details**

Involve your reader by focusing on colorful or moving incidents.

Organization

✓ **Builds a clear progression of ideas**

Structure your ideas so that they flow logically and smoothly from sentence to sentence, paragraph to paragraph, and section to section.

Development of Ideas/Elaboration

✓ **Uses narrative techniques effectively**

Include elements such as dialogue, pacing, and description to create vivid pictures of characters and situations.

✓ **Concludes with purpose and reflection**

Provide a conclusion that restates earlier details and offers a meaningful insight.

Language

✓ **Uses description effectively**

Describe scenes, settings, and people clearly so that readers can visualize them.

Conventions

✓ **Eliminates errors**

Check your essay to eliminate errors in grammar, spelling, and punctuation.

WRITE TO EXPLORE

Before writing, brainstorm for ideas about heroism. Brainstorming may lead you to new insights that you can then explore in your essay.

Writing to Sources: **Argument**

Heroism and Responsibility The related readings in this section present a range of ideas about heroism and responsibility. They raise questions, such as the following, about the concept of the hero:

- What makes a hero heroic?
- What responsibilities does a hero have, and for how long does he or she have them?
- What happens if a hero fails to live up to his or her reputation or responsibilities?
- Does a hero perform only good deeds?

Focus on the question that intrigues you the most, and then complete the following assignment.

Assignment

Write an **argumentative essay** in which you state and defend a claim about the concepts of heroism and responsibility. Build evidence for your claim by synthesizing ideas about heroism from two or more texts in this section. Present, develop, and support your ideas with examples and details from the texts.

INCORPORATE RESEARCH

The research you have conducted in this section may provide support for your position. Review the notes you took, and incorporate any relevant facts or details into your essay.

Prewriting and Planning

Examine texts. Make a list of the texts you have read in this section, and describe your understanding of each. Then, look for connected ideas among the texts, your ideas, and the research you conducted.

Gather information to arrive at a claim. Use a chart like the one shown to develop your claim. Though you may refine or change your claim, the working version will help you to establish your focus.

Focus Question: Does a hero perform only good deeds?

Text	Passage	Notes
"My Hero: Extraordinary People on the Heroes Who Inspire Them"	[Moses] began his public career by killing an Egyptian; later, he failed to identify himself as a Jew.	A person many consider a hero had committed murder and denied his heritage. He is never called a hero in the Bible because of these deeds.
"Perseus"	Perseus kills the sea serpent, rescuing Andromeda and sparing the Ethiopians from being devoured by it.	Perseus resorts to violence, but as a result he eliminates a great evil.
Example Claim: Heroes may not always be good. They should be judged by their motivations in general and not solely on their actions.		

Consider opposing viewpoints. As you lay out your argument, anticipate disagreements. Explain why your ideas are convincing, and provide evidence to support your assertions.

Drafting

Structure an organized argument. Review the textual evidence you have chosen to support your claim. Use those ideas to form the points of your argument, and sequence them so that each idea leads clearly and logically to the next.

Distinguish separate claims. Explain why your position is different from other interpretations with which you are familiar. Support your explanation with strong reasoning and accurate evidence.

Frame and connect ideas. Consider grabbing your reader's attention with a controversial statement. Then, explain how that statement relates to your claim. Carefully use words, phrases, and clauses to make clear connections between sentences, paragraphs, and whole sections of your essay.

Revising and Editing

Check for coherence. Review your draft to be sure that your argument flows logically from beginning to end. If any parts of the essay feel out of place, move, rewrite, or eliminate that section.

Check style and tone. Be sure that you have used language appropriate for your subject and audience. Review your essay, and replace any questionable word choices with more appropriate alternatives.

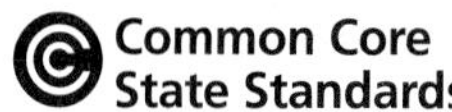

W.9-10.1, W.9-10.1a–e, W.9-10.4, W.9-10.5, W.9-10.9; L.9-10.3.a

[For full standards wording, see the chart in the front of this book.]

CITE RESEARCH CORRECTLY

You may find supporting evidence in nontraditional sources such as a piece of music or film. Consult a reputable style guide for tips on formatting these citations. See the Citing Sources pages in the Introductory Unit of this textbook for additional guidance.

Self-Evaluation Rubric

Use the following criteria to evaluate the effectiveness of your essay.

Criteria	Rating Scale			
	not very .... *very*			
PURPOSE/FOCUS Introduces a precise claim and distinguishes the claim from (implied) alternate or opposing claims; provides a concluding section that follows from and supports the argument presented	1	2	3	4
ORGANIZATION Establishes a logical organization; uses words, phrases, and clauses to link the major sections of the text, create cohesion, and clarify relationships among claims, reasons, and evidence, and between claims and counterclaims	1	2	3	4
DEVELOPMENT OF IDEAS/ELABORATION Develops the claim and counterclaims fairly, supplying evidence for each while pointing out the strengths and limitations of both	1	2	3	4
LANGUAGE Establishes and maintains a formal style and an objective tone	1	2	3	4
CONVENTIONS Attends to the norms and conventions of the discipline	1	2	3	4

Independent Reading

Titles for Extended Reading

In this unit, you have read texts in a variety of genres. Continue to read on your own. Select works that you enjoy, but challenge yourself to explore new authors and works of increasing depth and complexity. The titles suggested below will help you get started.

INFORMATIONAL TEXT

Joan of Arc
by Mary Gordon

This **biography** tells the remarkable story of the short life of a fifteenth-century peasant turned warrior named Joan. After hearing a voice she believed was God's, she left her family and home behind to lead the French army to victory over the British.

The Carolina Way
by Dean Smith and Gerald Bell with John Kilgo

Dean Smith, the coach of the University of North Carolina men's basketball team for almost 40 years, shares his strategies for leadership, teamwork, and winning with integrity in this **nonfiction** book.

The Story of Science: Newton at the Center
by Joy Hakim — EXEMPLAR TEXT

An examination of the accomplishments and lives of several scientists, this work of **nonfiction** includes interesting stories and facts that present some engaging aspects of science.

Nelson Mandela
by Laaren Brown and Lenny Hort

This **biography** of Nelson Mandela describes his struggles against the unjust government of South Africa and how he survived 27 years as a political prisoner. It also documents his rise to become president of his country as South Africa emerged from the dark ages of apartheid.

LITERATURE

Fathers and Sons
by Ivan Turgenev — EXEMPLAR TEXT

This 1862 **novel** set in Russia delves into the gap that has grown between a generation of parents and children who differ greatly in their philosophies. As the young demand social change, the old cling desperately to tradition.

Revolutionary Petunias and Other Poems
by Alice Walker — EXEMPLAR TEXT

Known for her bold honesty and poetic language, Walker crafts a collection of **poetry** that explores the similarities between revolution and love.

The Odyssey
by Homer
Translated by Robert Fagles — EXEMPLAR TEXT

When the hero Odysseus begins his voyage home after the Trojan War, he has no idea his travels will lead him to seductive goddesses, man-eating monsters, and vengeful gods. Read this **epic tale** to decide for yourself if Odysseus is the ultimate hero.

ONLINE TEXT SET

SPEECH
There Is a Longing
Chief Dan George

SHORT STORY
The Man to Send Rain Clouds
Leslie Marmon Silko

POEM
There Is No Word for Goodbye
Mary Tall Mountain

Preparing to Read Complex Texts

Attentive Reading As you read literature on your own, bring your imagination and questions to the text. The questions shown below and others that you ask as you read will help you learn and enjoy literature even more.

Reading Literature/ Informational Text

10. By the end of grade 9, read and comprehend literature, including stories, dramas, poems, and literary nonfiction in the grades 9–10 text complexity band proficiently, with scaffolding as needed at the high end of the range.

When reading texts from the oral tradition, ask yourself...

Comprehension: **Key Ideas and Details**

- Who are the main characters in this text, and what conflicts or struggles do they face?
- From what culture does this text come? What elements of the culture do I see in the text? For example, do I notice beliefs, foods, traditions, or settings that have particular meaning for the people of this culture?
- Do any aspects of this text seem familiar to me? For example, do any characters, settings, or events in the plot remind me of those in other stories I have read or films I have seen?

Text Analysis: **Craft and Structure**

- What type of text is this: an epic, a myth, a tale, or a legend? What types of characters, events, and ideas do I expect to find?
- Is this text a retelling by a modern author? If so, does the author change the text for modern readers?
- What do I notice about the language, including descriptions and dialogue? Does the language reflect values or customs related to the cultural or historical context of the text?
- Does the text include symbols? If so, do they have special meanings in the original culture of the text? Do they also have meanings in modern life?
- Does the text include patterns of events or repetitions of statements or images? If so, which ones? What is the effect?

Connections: **Integration of Knowledge and Ideas**

- How does this text round out the picture of the culture I might get from a nonfiction source, such as an encyclopedia entry?
- Does this text express universal ideas or values—those that are common to people in many different cultures and time periods?
- How does this text compare to similar texts I have read?
- If I were researching this culture for a report, would I include passages from this text? If so, what would those passages show?

Resources

For example, at the beginning of "The Necklace" (p. 332), Maupassant directly characterizes Madame Loisel: "She was one of those pretty, charming young women. . . ."

In ***indirect characterization,*** an author provides clues about a character by describing what a character looks like, does, and says, as well as how other characters react to him or her. It is up to the reader to draw conclusions about the character based on this indirect information.

The most effective indirect characterizations usually result from showing characters acting or speaking.

See also ***Character.***

CLIMAX The ***climax*** of a story, novel, or play is the high point of interest or suspense. The events that make up the rising action lead up to the climax. The events that make up the falling action follow the climax.

See also ***Conflict, Plot,*** and ***Anticlimax.***

COMEDY A ***comedy*** is a literary work, especially a play, that has a happy ending. Comedies often show ordinary characters in conflict with society. These conflicts are resolved through misunderstandings, deceptions, and concealed identities, which result in the correction of moral faults or social wrongs. Types of comedy include *romantic comedy,* which involves problems among lovers, and the *comedy of manners,* which satirically challenges the social customs of a sophisticated society. Comedy is often contrasted with tragedy, in which the protagonist meets an unfortunate end.

COMIC RELIEF ***Comic relief*** is a technique that is used to interrupt a serious part of a literary work by introducing a humorous character or situation.

CONFLICT A ***conflict*** is a struggle between opposing forces. Characters in conflict form the basis of stories, novels, and plays.

There are two kinds of conflict: external and internal. In an ***external conflict,*** the main character struggles against an outside force. This force may be another character, as in Richard Connell's "The Most Dangerous Game" (p. 214), in which Rainsford struggles with General Zaroff. The outside force could also be the standards or expectations of a group, such as the family prejudices that Romeo and Juliet struggle against. Their story (p. 806) shows them in conflict with society. The outside force may be nature itself, a person-against-nature conflict. The two men who are trapped by a fallen tree in Saki's "The Interlopers" (p. 270) face such a conflict.

An ***internal conflict*** involves a character in conflict with himself or herself. In "Checkouts" (p. 82), two young people who meet by chance in a supermarket agonize over whether they should speak to each other.

See also ***Plot.***

CONNOTATION The ***connotation*** of a word is the set of ideas associated with it in addition to its explicit meaning.

See also ***Denotation.***

CONSONANCE ***Consonance*** is the repetition of final consonant sounds in stressed syllables with different vowel sounds, as in *hat* and *sit.*

CONTEMPORARY INTERPRETATION A ***contemporary interpretation*** is a literary work of today that responds to and sheds new light on a well-known, earlier work of literature. Such an interpretation may refer to any aspect of the older work, including plot, characters, settings, imagery, language, and theme. Edna St. Vincent Millay's poem "An Ancient Gesture" (p. 1128), for example, provides a modern perspective on the characters Penelope and Odysseus in the *Odyssey.*

COUPLET A ***couplet*** is a pair of rhyming lines, usually of the same length and meter. In the following couplet from a poem by William Shakespeare, the speaker comforts himself with the thought of his love:

> For thy sweet love remember'd such wealth brings
>
> That then I scorn to change my state with kings.

See also ***Stanza.***

DENOTATION The ***denotation*** of a word is its dictionary meaning, independent of other associations that the word may have. The denotation of the word *lake,* for example, is an inland body of water. "Vacation spot" and "place where the fishing is good" are connotations of the word *lake.*

See also ***Connotation.***

DESCRIPTION A ***description*** is a portrait in words of a person, a place, or an object. Descriptive writing uses sensory details, those that appeal to the senses: sight, hearing, taste, smell, and touch. Description can be found in all types of writing. Rudolfo Anaya's essay "A Celebration of Grandfathers" (p. 444) contains descriptive passages.

DIALECT ***Dialect,*** the form of language spoken by people in a particular region or group, may involve changes

Literary Terms

ACT See ***Drama.***

ALLEGORY An ***allegory*** is a story or tale with two or more levels of meaning—a literal level and one or more symbolic levels. The events, setting, and characters in an allegory are symbols for ideas and qualities.

ALLITERATION ***Alliteration*** is the repetition of initial consonant sounds. Writers use alliteration to give emphasis to words, to imitate sounds, and to create musical effects. In the following line from Edgar Allan Poe's "The Raven" (p. 710), there is alliteration of the *w* sound: Once upon a midnight dreary, while I pondered weak and weary, . . .

ALLUSION An ***allusion*** is a reference to a well-known person, place, event, literary work, or work of art. In O. Henry's "The Gift of the Magi" (p. 260), the title and details of the story refer to the biblical account of the Magi, wise men who brought gifts to the baby Jesus.

ANALOGY An ***analogy*** makes a comparison between two or more things that are similar in some ways but otherwise unalike.

ANECDOTE An ***anecdote*** is a brief story about an interesting, amusing, or strange event told to entertain or to make a point. In the excerpt from "A Lincoln Preface" (p. 500), Carl Sandburg tells anecdotes about Abraham Lincoln. See also ***Narrative***.

ANTAGONIST An ***antagonist*** is a character or force in conflict with a main character, or protagonist.

ANTICLIMAX Like a climax, an ***anticlimax*** is a turning point in a story. However, an anticlimax is always a letdown. It's the point at which you learn that the story will not turn out the way you had expected. In Thayer's "Casey at the Bat" (p. 696), the anticlimax occurs when Casey strikes out instead of hitting a game-winning run.

ARCHETYPE An ***archetype*** is a type of character, detail, image, or situation that appears in literature throughout history. Some critics believe that archetypes reveal deep truths about human experience.

ARGUMENT See ***Persuasion.***

ASIDE An ***aside*** is a short speech delivered by a character in a play in order to express his or her true thoughts and feelings. Traditionally, the aside is directed to the audience and is presumed to be inaudible to the other actors.

ASSONANCE ***Assonance*** is the repetition of vow sounds followed by different consonants in two or mo stressed syllables. Assonance is found in the phrase " and weary" in Edgar Allan Poe's "The Raven" (p. 710).

ATMOSPHERE See ***Mood.***

AUTOBIOGRAPHY An ***autobiography*** is a form nonfiction in which a writer tells his or her own life s An autobiography may tell about the person's whole l or only a part of it. An example of an autobiography i excerpt from *A White House Diary* (p. 104).

See also ***Biography*** and ***Nonfiction.***

See also ***Oral Tradition.***

BIOGRAPHY A ***biography*** is a form of nonfiction in which a writer tells the life story of another perso Biographies have been written about many famous p historical and contemporary, but they can also be wr about "ordinary" people. An example of a biography excerpt from *Arthur Ashe Remembered* (p. 508).

See also ***Autobiography*** and ***Nonfiction.***

BLANK VERSE ***Blank verse*** is poetry written in unrhymed iambic pentameter lines. This verse form widely used by William Shakespeare.

See also ***Meter.***

CHARACTER A ***character*** is a person or an anim takes part in the action of a literary work. The main acter, or protagonist, is the most important characte story. This character often changes in some importa as a result of the story's events. In Richard Connell's Most Dangerous Game" (p. 214), Rainsford is the ma character and General Zaroff is the antagonist, or ch who opposes the main character.

Characters are sometimes classified as round or flat dynamic or static. A ***round character*** shows many c ent traits—faults as well as virtues. A *flat characte* only one trait. A *dynamic character* develops and gro during the course of the story; a static character doe change.

See also ***Characterization*** and ***Motivation.***

CHARACTERIZATION ***Characterization*** is the creating and developing a character. In ***direct chara zation,*** the author directly states a character's traits to the pronunciation, vocabulary, and sentence structure of standard English. An example from Mark Twain's "The Invalid's Story" (p. 362) is a character's use of the term *yourn* for *yours*.

DIALOGUE A ***dialogue*** is a conversation between characters that may reveal their traits and advance the action of a narrative. In fiction or nonfiction, quotation marks indicate a speaker's exact words, and a new paragraph usually indicates a change of speaker. Following is an exchange between the narrator and his frail younger brother, Doodle, in "The Scarlet Ibis" (p. 384):

> "Aw, come on Doodle," I urged. "You can do it. Do you want to be different from everybody else when you start school?"
>
> "Does it make any difference?"

Quotation marks are not used in a *script*, the printed copy of a play. Instead, the dialogue follows the name of the speaker, as in this example from Chekhov's *The Inspector General* (p. 970):

> **DRIVER.** Oh, yes, he's a good one, this one.

DICTION ***Diction*** refers to an author's choice of words, especially with regard to range of vocabulary, use of slang and colloquial language, and level of formality. These lines from Ernest Lawrence Thayer's poem "Casey at the Bat" (p. 696) are an example of colloquial, informal diction: "It looked extremely rocky for the Mudville nine that day; / The score stood two to four; with but an inning left to play."

See also ***Connotation*** and ***Denotation.***

DIRECT CHARACTERIZATION
See ***Characterization.***

DRAMA A ***drama*** is a story written to be performed by actors. The script of a drama is made up of ***dialogue***—the words the actors say—and ***stage directions,*** which are comments on how and where action happens.

The drama's ***setting*** is the time and place in which the action occurs. It is indicated by one or more sets, including furniture and backdrops, that suggest interior or exterior scenes. *Props* are objects, such as a sword or a cup of tea, that are used onstage.

At the beginning of most plays, a brief ***exposition*** gives the audience some background information about the characters and the situation. Just as in a story or novel, the plot of a drama is built around characters in conflict.

Dramas are divided into large units called ***acts,*** which are divided into smaller units called scenes. A long play may include many sets that change with the ***scenes,*** or it may indicate a change of scene with lighting.

See also ***Dialogue, Genre, Stage Directions,*** and ***Tragedy.*** *Romeo and Juliet* (p. 806) is a long play in five acts.

DRAMATIC IRONY See ***Irony.***

DRAMATIC MONOLOGUE A ***dramatic monologue*** is a poem in which a character reveals himself or herself by speaking to a silent listener.

DRAMATIC POETRY ***Dramatic poetry*** is poetry that utilizes the techniques of drama. The dialogue used in Edgar Allan Poe's "The Raven" (p. 710) makes it dramatic dialogue. A ***dramatic monologue*** is a poem spoken by one person, addressing a silent listener.

END RHYME See ***Rhyme.***

EPIC An ***epic*** is a long narrative poem about the deeds of gods or heroes. Homer's *Odyssey* (p. 1044) is an example of epic poetry. It tells the story of the Greek hero Odysseus, the king of Ithaca.

An epic is elevated in style and usually follows certain patterns. The poet begins by announcing the subject and asking a Muse—one of the nine goddesses of the arts, literature, and sciences—to help. An *epic hero* is the larger-than-life central character in an epic. Through behavior and deeds, the epic hero displays qualities that are valued by the society in which the epic originated.

See also ***Epic Simile*** and ***Narrative Poem.***

EPIC SIMILE An ***epic simile,*** also called ***Homeric simile,*** is an elaborate comparison of unlike subjects. In this example from the *Odyssey* (p. 1044), Homer compares the bodies of men killed by Odysseus to a fisherman's catch heaped up on the shore:

> Think of a catch that fishermen haul in to a
> half-moon bay
>
> in a fine-meshed net from the whitecaps of the sea:
> how all are poured out on the sand, in throes
> for the salt sea,
>
> twitching their cold lives away in Helios' fiery air:
> so lay the suitors heaped on one another.

See also ***Figurative Language*** and ***Simile.***

EPIPHANY An ***epiphany*** is a character's sudden flash of insight into a conflict or situation. At the end of Judith

Ortiz Cofer's story "American History" (p. 240), for example, the central character experiences an epiphany.

ESSAY An ***essay*** is a short nonfiction work about a particular subject. While classification is difficult, four types of essays are sometimes identified.

A *descriptive essay* seeks to convey an impression about a person, place, or object. In "A Celebration of Grandfathers" (p. 444), Rudolfo Anaya describes the cultural values that his grandfather and other "old ones" from his childhood passed down.

A *narrative essay* tells a true story. In "The Washwoman" (p. 26), Isaac Bashevis Singer tells of his childhood in Poland.

An *expository essay* gives information, discusses ideas, or explains a process. In "Single Room, Earth View" (p. 468), Sally Ride explains what it is like to be in outer space.

A *persuasive essay* tries to convince readers to do something or to accept the writer's point of view. Pete Hamill's "Libraries Face Sad Chapter" (p. 530) is a persuasive essay.

See also ***Description, Exposition, Genre, Narration, Nonfiction,*** and ***Persuasion.***

EXPOSITION ***Exposition*** is writing or speech that explains a process or presents information. In the plot of a story or drama, the exposition is the part of the work that introduces the characters, the setting, and the basic situation.

EXTENDED METAPHOR In an ***extended metaphor,*** as in regular metaphor, a writer speaks or writes of a subject as though it were something else. An extended metaphor sustains the comparison for several lines or for an entire poem.

See also ***Figurative Language*** and ***Metaphor.***

EXTERNAL CONFLICT See ***Conflict.***

FALLING ACTION See ***Plot.***

FANTASY A ***fantasy*** is highly imaginative writing that contains elements not found in real life. Examples of fantasy include stories that involve supernatural elements, stories that resemble fairy tales, and stories that deal with imaginary places and creatures.

See also ***Science Fiction.***

FICTION ***Fiction*** is prose writing that tells about imaginary characters and events. The term is usually used for novels and short stories, but it also applies to dramas and narrative poetry. Some writers rely on their imaginations alone to create their works of fiction. Others base their fiction on actual events and people, to which they add invented characters, dialogue, and plot situations.

See also ***Genre, Narrative,*** and ***Nonfiction.***

FIGURATIVE LANGUAGE ***Figurative language*** is writing or speech not meant to be interpreted literally. It is often used to create vivid impressions by setting up comparisons between dissimilar things.

Some frequently used figures of speech are ***metaphors, similes,*** and ***personifications.***

See also ***Literal Language.***

FLASHBACK A ***flashback*** is a means by which authors present material that occurred earlier than the present tense of the narrative. Authors may include this material in a character's memories, dreams, or accounts of past events.

FOIL A ***foil*** is a character who provides a contrast to another character. In *Romeo and Juliet* (p. 806), the fiery temper of Tybalt serves as a foil to the good nature of Benvolio.

FOOT See ***Meter.***

FORESHADOWING ***Foreshadowing*** is the use in a literary work of clues that suggest events that have yet to occur. This technique helps create suspense, keeping readers wondering about what will happen next.

See also ***Suspense.***

FREE VERSE ***Free verse*** is poetry not written in a regular pattern of meter or rhyme. Like Whitman's "I Hear America Singing" (p. 750), however, it may use parallelism and various sound devices.

GENRE A ***genre*** is a category or type of literature. Literature is commonly divided into three major genres: poetry, prose, and drama. Each major genre is in turn divided into smaller genres, as follows:

1. Poetry: Lyric Poetry, Concrete Poetry, Dramatic Poetry, Narrative Poetry, and Epic Poetry
2. Prose: Fiction (Novels and Short Stories) and Nonfiction (Biography, Autobiography, Letters, Essays, and Reports)
3. Drama: Serious Drama and Tragedy, Comic Drama, Melodrama, and Farce

See also ***Drama, Poetry,*** and ***Prose.***

HAIKU The ***haiku*** is a three-line verse form. The first and third lines of a haiku each have five syllables. The second line has seven syllables. A haiku seeks to convey a single vivid emotion by means of images from nature.

HOMERIC SIMILE See ***Epic Simile.***

HYPERBOLE A ***hyperbole*** is a deliberate exaggeration or overstatement. In Mark Twain's "The Notorious Jumping Frog of Calaveras County," the claim that Jim Smiley would follow a bug as far as Mexico to win a bet is a hyperbole. As this example shows, hyperboles are often used for comic effect.

IAMB See ***Meter.***

IDIOM An ***idiom*** is an expression that is characteristic of a language, region, community, or class of people. *Idiomatic expressions* often arise from figures of speech and therefore cannot be understood literally. In "The Invalid's Story" (p. 362), for example, a character uses the idiom *throw up the sponge,* meaning "surrender."

See also ***Dialect.***

IMAGE An ***image*** is a word or phrase that appeals to one or more of the five senses—sight, hearing, touch, taste, or smell. Writers use images to re-create sensory experiences in words.

See also ***Description.***

IMAGERY ***Imagery*** is the descriptive or figurative language used in literature to create word pictures for the reader. These pictures, or images, are created by details of sight, sound, taste, touch, smell, or movement.

INDIRECT CHARACTERIZATION
See ***Characterization.***

INTERNAL See ***Conflict.***

INTERNAL RHYME See ***Rhyme.***

IRONY ***Irony*** is the general term for literary techniques that portray differences between appearance and reality, or expectation and result. In ***verbal irony,*** words are used to suggest the opposite of what is meant. In ***dramatic irony,*** there is a contradiction between what a character thinks and what the reader or audience knows to be true. In *irony of situation,* an event occurs that directly contradicts the expectations of the characters, the reader, or the audience.

LEGEND See ***Oral Tradition.***

LITERAL LANGUAGE ***Literal language*** uses words in their ordinary senses. It is the opposite of ***figurative language.*** If you tell someone standing on a diving board to jump in, you speak literally. If you tell someone on the street to jump in a lake, you are speaking figuratively.

See also ***Figurative Language.***

LYRIC POEM A ***lyric poem*** is a highly musical verse that expresses the thoughts, observations, and feelings of a single speaker.

MAIN CHARACTER See ***Character.***

METAPHOR A ***metaphor*** is a figure of speech in which one thing is spoken of as though it were something else. Unlike a simile, which compares two things using *like* or *as,* a metaphor implies a comparison between them. In "Dreams" (p. 621), Langston Hughes uses a metaphor to show what happens to a life without dreams:

> . . . if dreams die
>
> Life is a broken-winged bird
>
> That cannot fly.

See also ***Extended Metaphor*** and ***Figurative Language.***

METER The ***meter*** of a poem is its rhythmical pattern. This pattern is determined by the number and types of stresses, or beats, in each line. To describe the meter of a poem, you must scan its lines. Scanning involves marking the stressed and unstressed syllables, as shown with the following two lines from "I Wandered Lonely as a Cloud" by William Wordsworth (p. 622):

> Ĭ wán|deřed lońe|lÿ ás| ă clóud
>
> Thăt floáts | ŏn hígh| o'ĕr váles| ănd hílls.

As you can see, each strong stress is marked with a slanted line (´) and each unstressed syllable with a horseshoe symbol (˘). The stressed and unstressed syllables are then divided by vertical lines (|) into groups called ***feet.*** The following types of feet are common in English poetry:

1. *Iamb:* a foot with one unstressed syllable followed by a stressed syllable, as in the word "again"
2. *Trochee:* a foot with one stressed syllable followed by an unstressed syllable, as in the word "wonder"
3. *Anapest:* a foot with two unstressed syllables followed by one strong stress, as in the phrase "on the beach"
4. *Dactyl:* a foot with one strong stress followed by two unstressed syllables, as in the word "wonderful"
5. *Spondee:* a foot with two strong stresses, as in the word "spacewalk"

Depending on the type of foot that is most common in them, lines of poetry are described as ***iambic, trochaic, anapestic,*** and so forth.

Lines are also described in terms of the number of feet that occur in them, as follows:

1. *Monometer:* verse written in one-foot lines
   All things
   Must pass
   Away.
2. *Dimeter:* verse written in two-foot lines
   Thomas | Jefferson
   What do | you say
   Under the | gravestone
   Hidden | away?

   —Rosemary and Stephen Vincent Benét,
   "Thomas Jefferson, 1743–1826"
3. *Trimeter:* verse written in three-foot lines
   I know | not whom | I meet
   I know | not where | I go.
4. *Tetrameter:* verse written in four-foot lines
5. *Pentameter:* verse written in five-foot lines
6. *Hexameter:* verse written in six-foot lines
7. *Heptameter:* verse written in seven-foot lines

Blank verse, used by Shakespeare in *Romeo and Juliet* (p. 806), is poetry written in unrhymed iambic pentameter.

Free verse, used by Walt Whitman in "I Hear America Singing" (p. 750), is poetry that does not follow a regular pattern of meter and rhyme.

MONOLOGUE A ***monologue*** in a play is a speech by one character that, unlike a ***soliloquy,*** is addressed to another character or characters. An example from Shakespeare's *Romeo and Juliet* (p. 806) is the speech by the Prince of Verona in Act 1, Scene i, lines 72–94.

See also ***Soliloquy.***

MONOMETER See ***Meter.***

MOOD ***Mood,*** or ***atmosphere,*** is the feeling created in the reader by a literary work or passage. The mood is often suggested by descriptive details. Often the mood can be described in a single word, such as lighthearted, frightening, or despairing. Notice how this passage from Edgar Allan Poe's "The Cask of Amontillado" (p. 60) contributes to an eerie, fearful mood:

> "The niter!" I said; "see, it increases. It hangs like moss upon the vaults. We are below the river's bed. The drops of moisture trickle among the bones. Come, we will go back ere it is too late."

See also ***Tone.***

MORAL A ***moral*** is a lesson taught by a literary work, especially a fable—many fables, for example, have a stated moral at the end. It is customary, however, to discuss contemporary works in terms of the themes they explore, rather than a moral that they teach.

MOTIVATION ***Motivation*** is a reason that explains or partially explains why a character thinks, feels, acts, or behaves in a certain way. Motivation results from a combination of the character's personality and the situation he or she must deal with. In "Checkouts" (p. 82), the main character is motivated by conflicting feelings.

See also ***Character*** and ***Characterization.***

MYTH A ***myth*** is a fictional tale that describes the actions of gods and heroes or explains the causes of natural phenomena. Unlike legends, myths emphasize supernatural rather than historical elements. Many cultures have collections of myths, and the most familiar in the Western world are those of the ancient Greeks and Romans. "Perseus" (p. 1225) is a retelling of a famous ancient Greek myth.

See also ***Oral Tradition.***

NARRATION ***Narration*** is writing that tells a story. The act of telling a story in speech is also called narration. Novels and short stories are fictional narratives. Nonfiction works—such as news stories, biographies, and autobiographies—are also narratives. A narrative poem tells a story in verse.

See also ***Anecdote, Essay, Narrative Poem, Nonfiction, Novel,*** and ***Short Story.***

NARRATIVE A ***narrative*** is a story told in fiction, nonfiction, poetry, or drama.

See also ***Narration.***

NARRATIVE POEM A ***narrative poem*** is one that tells a story. "Casey at the Bat" (p. 696) is a humorous narrative poem about the last inning of a baseball game. Edgar Allan Poe's "The Raven" (p. 710) is a serious narrative poem about a man's grief over the loss of a loved one.

See also ***Dramatic Poetry, Epic,*** and ***Narration.***

NARRATOR A ***narrator*** is a speaker or character who tells a story. The writer's choice of narrator determines the story's ***point of view,*** which directs the type and amount of information the writer reveals.

When a character in the story tells the story, that character is a *first-person narrator.* This narrator may be a major character, a minor character, or just a witness. Readers see only what this character sees, hear only what he or she hears, and so on. The first-person narrator may or may not be reliable. We have reason, for example, to be suspicious of the first-person narrator of Edgar Allan Poe's "The Cask of Amontillado" (p. 60).

When a voice outside the story narrates, the story has a *third-person narrator.* An omniscient, or all-knowing, third-person narrator can tell readers what any character thinks and feels. For example, in Guy de Maupassant's "The Necklace" (p. 332), we know the feelings of both Monsieur and Madame Loisel. A limited third-person narrator sees the world through one character's eyes and reveals only that character's thoughts. In James Thurber's "The Secret Life of Walter Mitty" (p. 128), the narrator reveals only Mitty's experiences and feelings.

See also ***Speaker.***

NONFICTION ***Nonfiction*** is prose writing that presents and explains ideas or that tells about real people, places, ideas, or events. To be classified as nonfiction, a work must be true. "Single Room, Earth View" (p. 468) is a nonfictional account of the view of Earth from space.

See also ***Autobiography, Biography,*** and ***Essay.***

NOVEL A ***novel*** is a long work of fiction. It has a plot that explores characters in conflict. A novel may also have one or more subplots, or minor stories, and several themes.

NOVELLA A ***novella*** is a work of fiction that is longer than a short story but shorter than a novel.

OCTAVE See ***Stanza.***

ONOMATOPOEIA ***Onomatopoeia*** is the use of words that imitate sounds. *Whirr, thud,* and *hiss* are examples.

ORAL TRADITION The ***oral tradition*** is the passing of songs, stories, and poems from generation to generation by word of mouth. Many folk songs, ballads, fairy tales, legends, and myths originated in the oral tradition.

See also ***Myth.***

OXYMORON An ***oxymoron*** is a combination of words, or parts of words, that contradict each other. Examples are "deafening silence," "honest thief," "wise fool," and "bittersweet." This device is effective when the apparent contradiction reveals a deeper truth, as in Act 2, Scene ii, line 184, of *Romeo and Juliet* (p. 806) when Juliet bids goodbye to Romeo: "Parting is such *sweet sorrow.*"

PARADOX A ***paradox*** is a statement that seems contradictory but actually may be true. Because a paradox is surprising, it catches the reader's attention.

PARALLELISM See ***Rhetorical Devices.***

PENTAMETER See ***Meter.***

PERSONIFICATION ***Personification*** is a type of figurative language in which a nonhuman subject is given human characteristics. William Wordsworth personifies daffodils when he describes them as "Tossing their heads in sprightly dance" (p. 626).

See also ***Figurative Language.***

PERSUASION ***Persuasion*** is writing or speech that attempts to convince the reader to adopt a particular opinion or course of action. An ***argument*** is a logical way of presenting a belief, conclusion, or stance. A good argument is supported with reasoning and evidence.

PLOT ***Plot*** is the sequence of events in a literary work. In most novels, dramas, short stories, and narrative poems, the plot involves both characters and a central conflict. The plot usually begins with an ***exposition*** that introduces the setting, the characters, and the basic situation. This is followed by the ***inciting incident,*** which introduces the central conflict. The conflict then increases during the ***development*** until it reaches a high point of interest or suspense, the ***climax.*** All the events leading up to the climax make up the ***rising action.*** The climax is followed by the ***falling action,*** which leads to the ***denouement,*** or ***resolution,*** in which a general insight or change is conveyed.

POETRY ***Poetry*** is one of the three major types of literature, the others being prose and drama. Most poems make use of highly concise, musical, and emotionally charged language. Many also make use of imagery, figurative language, and special devices of sound such as rhyme. Poems are often divided into lines and stanzas and often employ regular rhythmical patterns, or meters. However, some poems are written out just like prose, while others are written in free verse.

See also ***Genre.***

POINT OF VIEW See ***Narrator.***

PROSE ***Prose*** is the ordinary form of written language. Most writing that is not poetry, drama, or song is considered prose. Prose is one of the major genres of literature and occurs in two forms: fiction and nonfiction.

See also ***Fiction, Genre,*** and ***Nonfiction.***

PROTAGONIST The protagonist is the main character in a literary work.

See also ***Antagonist*** and ***Character.***

PUN A ***pun*** is a play on words involving a word with two or more different meanings or two words that sound alike but have different meanings. In *Romeo and Juliet* (p. 806), the dying Mercutio makes a pun involving two meanings of the word *grave,* "serious" and "burial site": "Ask for me tomorrow, and you shall find me a grave man" (Act 3, Scene i, lines 92–93).

QUATRAIN A ***quatrain*** is a stanza or poem made up of four lines, usually with a definite rhythm and rhyme scheme.

REPETITION ***Repetition*** is the use of any element of language—a sound, a word, a phrase, a clause, or a sentence—more than once.

Poets use many kinds of repetition. Alliteration, assonance, rhyme, and rhythm are repetitions of certain sounds and sound patterns. A refrain is a repeated line or group of lines. In both prose and poetry, repetition is used for musical effects and for emphasis.

See also ***Alliteration, Assonance, Rhyme,*** and ***Rhythm.***

RESOLUTION See ***Plot.***

RHETORICAL DEVICES ***Rhetorical devices*** are special patterns of words and ideas that create emphasis and stir emotion, especially in speeches or other oral presentations. ***Parallelism,*** for example, is the repetition of a grammatical structure in order to create a rhythm and make words more memorable. In his "I Have a Dream" speech (p. 542), Martin Luther King, Jr., uses parallel statements beginning, "I have a dream that . . ."

Other common rhetorical devices include *restatement,* expressing the same idea in different words, and *rhetorical questions,* questions with obvious answers.

RHYME ***Rhyme*** is the repetition of sounds at the ends of words. ***End rhyme*** occurs when the rhyming words come at the ends of lines, as in "The Desired Swan Song" by Samuel Taylor Coleridge:

> Swans sing before they die—'twere no bad thing
> Should certain persons die before they sing.

Internal rhyme occurs when the rhyming words appear in the same line, as in the first line of Edgar Allan Poe's "The Raven" (p. 710):

> Once upon a midnight *dreary,* while I pondered, weak and *weary,*

Exact rhyme involves the repetition of words with the same vowel and consonant sounds, like *ball* and *hall. Slant rhyme* involves the repetition of words that sound alike but do not rhyme exactly, like *grove* and *love.*

See also ***Repetition*** and ***Rhyme Scheme.***

RHYME SCHEME A ***rhyme scheme*** is a regular pattern of rhyming words in a poem. The rhyme scheme of a poem is indicated by using different letters of the alphabet for each new rhyme. In an *aabb* stanza, for example, line 1 rhymes with line 2 and line 3 rhymes with line 4. William Wordsworth's poem "I Wandered Lonely as a Cloud" (p. 622) uses an *ababcc* rhyme pattern:

> I wandered lonely as a cloud a
> That floats on high o'er vales and hills, b
> When all at once I saw a crowd, a
> A host, of golden daffodils; b
> Beside the lake, beneath the trees, c
> Fluttering and dancing in the breeze. c

Many poems use the same pattern of rhymes, though not the same rhymes, in each stanza.

See also ***Rhyme.***

RHYTHM ***Rhythm*** is the pattern of *beats,* or *stresses,* in spoken or written language. Some poems have a very specific pattern, or meter, whereas prose and free verse use the natural rhythms of everyday speech.

See also ***Meter.***

RISING ACTION See ***Plot.***

ROUND CHARACTER See ***Character.***

SATIRE A ***satire*** is a literary work that ridicules the foolishness and faults of individuals, an institution, society, or even humanity in general.

SCENE See ***Drama.***

SCIENCE FICTION ***Science fiction*** is writing that tells about imaginary events involving science or technology. Many science-fiction stories are set in the future. Arthur C. Clarke's "If I Forget Thee, Oh Earth . . ." (p. 162) is set on the moon after a nuclear disaster on Earth.

See also ***Fantasy.***

SENSORY LANGUAGE ***Sensory language*** is writing or speech that appeals to one or more of the senses.

See also ***Image.***

SESTET See ***Stanza.***

SETTING The ***setting*** of a literary work is the time and place of the action. Time can include not only the historical period—past, present, or future—but also a specific year, season, or time of day. Place may involve not only the geographical place—a region, country, state, or town—but also the social, economic, or cultural environment.

In some stories, setting serves merely as a backdrop for action, a context in which the characters move and speak. In others, however, setting is a crucial element.

See also ***Mood.***

SHORT STORY A *short story* is a brief work of fiction. In most short stories, one main character faces a conflict that is resolved in the plot of the story. Great craftsmanship must go into the writing of a good story, for it has to accomplish its purpose in relatively few words.

See also ***Fiction*** and ***Genre.***

SIMILE A ***simile*** is a figure of speech in which the words *like* or *as* are used to compare two apparently dissimilar items. The comparison, however, surprises the reader into a fresh perception by finding an unexpected likeness. In "Dream Deferred" (p. 620), Langston Hughes uses the simile "Does it dry up/like a raisin in the sun?" to discuss a dream deferred.

SOLILOQUY A ***soliloquy*** is a long speech expressing the thoughts of a character alone on stage. In William Shakespeare's *Romeo and Juliet* (p. 806), Romeo gives a soliloquy after the servant has fled and Paris has died (Act V, Scene iii, lines 74–120).

See also ***Monologue.***

SONNET A ***sonnet*** is a fourteen-line lyric poem, usually written in rhymed iambic pentameter. The *English,* or *Shakespearean,* sonnet consists of three quatrains (four-line stanzas) and a couplet (two lines), usually rhyming *abab cdcd efef gg.* The couplet usually comments on the ideas contained in the preceding twelve lines. The sonnet is usually not printed with the stanzas divided, but a reader can see distinct ideas in each. See the Sonnet 30 by William Shakespeare on page 754.

The *Italian,* or *Petrarchan,* sonnet consists of an octave (eight-line stanza) and a sestet (six-line stanza). Often, the octave rhymes *abbaabba* and the sestet rhymes *cdecde.* The octave states a theme or asks a question. The sestet comments on or answers the question.

See also ***Lyric Poem, Meter,*** and ***Stanza.***

SOUND DEVICES A ***sound device*** is a technique used by a poet to emphasize the sound relationships among words in order to create musical and emotional effects and emphasize a poem's meaning. These devices include ***alliteration, consonance, assonance, onomatopoeia,*** and ***rhyme.***

SPEAKER The ***speaker*** is the imaginary voice assumed by the writer of a poem. In many poems, the speaker is not identified by name. When reading a poem, remember that the speaker within the poem may be a person, an animal, a thing, or an abstraction. The speaker in the following stanza by Emily Dickinson is a person who has died:

> Because I could not stop for Death—
>
> He kindly stopped for me—
>
> The Carriage held but just Ourselves—
>
> And Immortality.

STAGE DIRECTIONS ***Stage directions*** are notes included in a drama to describe how the work is to be performed or staged. These instructions are printed in italics and are not spoken aloud. They are used to describe sets, lighting, sound effects, and the appearance, personalities, and movements of characters.

See also ***Drama.***

STANZA A ***stanza*** is a repeated grouping of two or more lines in a poem that often share a pattern of rhythm and rhyme. Stanzas are sometimes named according to the number of lines they have—for example, a ***couplet,*** two lines; a ***quatrain,*** four lines; a ***sestet,*** six lines; and an ***octave,*** eight lines.

STATIC CHARACTER See ***Character.***

STYLE ***Style*** refers to an author's unique way of writing. Elements determining style include diction; tone; characteristic use of figurative language, dialect, or rhythmic devices; and syntax, or typical grammatical structures and patterns.

See also ***Diction*** and ***Tone.***

SURPRISE ENDING A ***surprise ending*** is a conclusion that violates the expectations of the reader but in a way that is both logical and believable.

O. Henry's "The Gift of the Magi" (p. 260) and Guy de Maupassant's "The Necklace" (p. 332) have surprise endings. Both authors were masters of this form.

SUSPENSE ***Suspense*** is a feeling of uncertainty about the outcome of events in a literary work. Writers create suspense by raising questions in the minds of their readers.

SYMBOL A ***symbol*** is anything that stands for something else. In addition to having its own meaning and reality, a symbol also represents abstract ideas. For example, a flag is a piece of cloth, but it also represents the idea of a country. Writers sometimes use conventional symbols like flags. Frequently, however, they create symbols of their own through emphasis or repetition. In James Hurst's "The Scarlet Ibis" (p. 384), for example, the ibis symbolizes the character named Doodle. Both are beautiful and otherworldly.

TALL TALE A ***tall tale*** is a type of folk tale that contains some or all of these features: humor, hyperbole, far-fetched situations, highly imaginative language, and a hero who performs outrageous feats. Tall tales originated during the development of the American frontier and are a particularly American form of folk tale. "Pecos Bill: The Cyclone" (p. 1218) is an example of a tall tale.

THEME A ***theme*** is a central message or insight into life revealed through a literary work.

The theme of a literary work may be stated directly or implied. When the theme of a work is implied, readers think about what the work suggests about people or life.

Archetypal themes are those that occur in folklore and literature across the world and throughout history. Ill-fated love, the theme of *Romeo and Juliet* (p. 806), is an example of such a theme.

TONE The ***tone*** of a literary work is the writer's attitude toward his or her audience and subject. The tone can often be described by a single adjective, such as *formal* or *informal, serious* or *playful, bitter* or *ironic.* When O. Henry discusses the young couple in "The Gift of the Magi" (p. 260), he uses a sympathetic tone.

See also ***Mood.***

TRAGEDY A ***tragedy*** is a work of literature, especially a play, that results in a catastrophe, a disaster or great misfortune, for the main character, or *tragic hero.* In ancient Greek drama, the main character was always a significant person—a king or a hero—and the cause of the tragedy was a *tragic flaw,* or weakness, in his or her character. In modern drama, the main character can be an ordinary person, and the cause of the tragedy can be some evil in society itself. Tragedy not only arouses fear and pity in the audience but also, in some cases, conveys a sense of the grandeur and nobility of the human spirit.

Shakespeare's *Romeo and Juliet* (p. 806) is a tragedy. Romeo and Juliet both suffer from the tragic flaw of impulsiveness. This flaw ultimately leads to their deaths.

See also ***Drama.***

UNDERSTATEMENT An ***understatement*** is a figure of speech in which the stated meaning is purposely less than (or "under") what is really meant. It is the opposite of ***hyperbole,*** which is a deliberate exaggeration.

UNIVERSAL THEME A ***universal theme*** is a message about life that can be understood by most cultures. Many folk tales and examples of classic literature address universal themes such as the importance of courage, the effects of honesty, or the danger of greed.

VERBAL IRONY See ***Irony.***

VILLANELLE A ***villanelle*** is a nineteen-line lyric poem written in five three-line stanzas and ending in a four-line stanza. It uses two rhymes and repeats two refrain lines that appear initially in the first and third lines of the first stanza. These lines then appear alternately as the third line of subsequent three-line stanzas and, finally, as the last two lines of the poem.

VISUAL ESSAY A ***visual essay*** is an exploration of a topic that conveys its ideas through visual elements as well as language. Like a standard essay, a visual essay presents an author's views of a single topic. Unlike other essays, however, much of the meaning in a visual essay is conveyed through illustrations or photographs.

VOICE ***Voice*** is a writer's distinctive "sound" or way of "speaking" on the page. It is related to such elements as word choice, sentence structure, and tone. It is similar to an individual's speech style and can be described in the same way—fast, slow, blunt, meandering, breathless, and so on.

Voice resembles ***style,*** an author's typical way of writing, but style usually refers to a quality that can be found throughout an author's body of work, while an author's voice may sometimes vary from work to work.

See also ***Style.***

Tips for Discussing Literature

As you read and study literature, discussion with other readers can help you understand, enjoy, and develop interpretations of what you read. Use the following tips to practice good speaking and listening skills while participating in group discussions of literature.

- ## Understand the purpose of your discussion

  When you discuss literature, your purpose is to broaden your understanding and appreciation of a work by testing your own ideas and hearing the ideas of others. Stay focused on the literature you are discussing, and keep your comments relevant to that literature. Starting with one focus question will help keep your discussion on track.

- ## Communicate effectively

  Effective communication requires thinking before speaking. Plan the points that you want to make, and decide how you will express them. Organize these points in logical order, and cite details from the work to support your ideas. Jot down informal notes to help keep your ideas focused.

  Remember to speak clearly, pronouncing words slowly and carefully so that others can understand your points. Also, keep in mind that some literature touches readers deeply—be aware of the possibility of counterproductive emotional responses, and work to control them. Negative emotional responses can also be conveyed through body language, so work to demonstrate respect in your demeanor as well as in your words.

- ## Encourage everyone to participate

  While some people are comfortable participating in discussions, others are less eager to speak up in groups. However, everyone should work to contribute thoughts and ideas. To encourage the entire group's participation, try the following strategies:

  - If you enjoy speaking, avoid monopolizing the conversation. After sharing your ideas, encourage others to share theirs.
  - Try different roles. For example, have everyone take turns being the facilitator or host of the discussion.
  - Use a prop, such as a book or gavel. Pass the prop around the group, allowing whomever is holding the prop to have the floor.

- ## Make relevant contributions

  Especially when responding to a short story, a poem, or a novel, avoid simply summarizing the plot. Instead, consider *what* you think might happen next, *why* events take place as they do, or *how* a writer provokes a response in you. Let your ideas inspire deeper thought or discussion about the literature.

- ## Consider other ideas and interpretations

  A work of literature can generate a wide variety of responses in different readers—and that can make your discussions exciting. Be open to the idea that many interpretations can be valid. To support your own ideas, point to the events, descriptions, characters, or other literary elements in the work that produced your interpretation. To consider someone else's ideas, decide whether details in the work support the interpretation he or she presents. Be sure to convey your criticism of the ideas of others in a respectful and supportive manner.

- ## Ask questions and extend the contributions of others

Get in the habit of asking questions to help you clarify your understanding of another reader's ideas. You can also use questions to call attention to possible areas of confusion, to points that are open to debate, or to errors.

In addition, offer elaboration of the points that others make by providing examples and illustrations. To move a discussion forward, pause occasionally to summarize and evaluate tentative conclusions reached by the group members. Then, continue the discussion with a fresh understanding of the material and ideas you have already covered.

- ## Manage differing opinions and views

Each participant brings his or her own personality, experiences, ideas, cultural background, likes and dislikes to the experience of reading, making disagreement almost inevitable. As differences arise, be sensitive to each individual's point of view. Do not personalize disagreements, but keep them focused on the literature or ideas under discussion.

When you meet with a group to discuss literature, use a chart like the one shown to analyze the discussion.

Work Being Discussed:	
Focus Question:	
Your Response:	Another Student's Response:
Supporting Evidence:	Supporting Evidence:

Literary Criticism

Criticism is writing that explores the meaning and techniques of literary works, usually in order to evaluate them. Writing criticism can help you think through your experience of a work of literature and can also help others deepen their own understanding. All literary criticism shares similar goals:

- ***Making Connections*** within or between works, or between a work of literature and its context
- ***Making Distinctions*** or showing differences between elements of a single work or aspects of two or more works
- ***Achieving Insights*** that were not apparent from a superficial reading
- ***Making a Judgment*** about the quality or value of a literary work

Critics use various ***theories of literary criticism*** to understand, appreciate, and evaluate literature. Some theories focus on the context of the work while others focus on the work itself. Sometimes critics combine one or more theories. These charts show a few examples of the many theories of criticism:

Focus on Contexts	
Human Experience	**Mythic Criticism** Explores universal situations, characters, and symbols called archetypes as they appear in a literary work.
Culture and History	**Historical Criticism** Analyzes how circumstances or ideas of an era influence a work
Author's Life	**Biographical Criticism** Explains how the author's life sheds light on the work

Focus on the Work Itself
Formal Criticism Shows how the work reflects characteristics of the genre, or literary type, to which it belongs

Examples of Literary Theories in Action

- ***Mythic Criticism:*** discussing how Robert Frost's "The Road Not Taken," p. 395, explores the archetypal situation of choice at a fork in the road
- ***Historical Criticism:*** showing how American frontier life led to the use of exaggeration in "Pecos Bill: The Cyclone," p. 733
- ***Biographical Criticism:*** showing that Edgar Allan Poe's loss of his parents at an early age influenced the theme of "The Raven," p. 382
- ***Formal Criticism:*** showing how "The Scarlet Ibis," p. 129, displays short-story elements like plot, setting, character, symbol, and theme

Literary Movements

Our literary heritage has been shaped by a number of literary movements, directions in literature characterized by shared assumptions, beliefs, and practices. This chart shows, in chronological order, some important literary movements. While these movements developed at particular historical moments, all of them may still influence individual writers working today.

Movement	Beliefs and Practices	Examples
Classicism Europe during the Renaissance (c. 1300–1650)	• Looks to classical literature of ancient Greece and Rome as models • Values logic, clarity, balance, and restraint • Prefers "ordered" nature of parks and gardens	the clarity and restraint of Robert Frost's verse ("The Road Not Taken," p. 395)
Romanticism Europe during the late 1700s and the early 1800s	• Rebels against Classicism • Values imagination and emotion • Focuses on everyday life	the celebration of the natural world in Rachel Carson's writings ("Silent Spring," p. 254)
Realism Europe and America from the mid–1800s to the 1890s	• Rebels against Romanticism's search for the ideal • Focuses on everyday life	the faithful rendering of Pueblo life in Leslie Marmon Silko's fiction ("The Man to Send Rain Clouds,")
Naturalism Europe and America during the late 1800s and early 1900s	• Assumes people cannot choose their fate but are shaped by psychological and social forces • Views society as a competitive jungle	the portrayal of characters as victims of social pressures and psychology in Guy de Maupassant's fiction ("The Necklace," p. 686)
Modernism Worldwide between 1890 and 1945	• In response to WWI, questions human reason • Focuses on studies of the unconscious and the art of primitive peoples • Experiments with language and form	the experiments with language in E. E. Cummings's poetry ("maggie and milly and molly and may,")
Post-Modernism Worldwide after 1945; still prevalent today	• Includes an eclectic mix of styles, such as parody, magical realism, and dark humor. • Often rebels against reason.	the magical realism in Isabel Allende's fiction ("Uncle Marcos,")

Tips for Improving Reading Fluency

When you were younger, you learned to read. Then, you read to expand your experiences or for pure enjoyment. Now, you are expected to read to learn. As you progress in school, you are given more and more material to read. The tips on these pages will help you improve your reading fluency, or your ability to read easily, smoothly, and expressively.

Keeping Your Concentration

One common problem that readers face is the loss of concentration. When you are reading an assignment, you might find yourself rereading the same sentence several times without really understanding it. The first step in changing this behavior is to notice that you do it. Becoming an active, aware reader will help you get the most from your assignments. Practice using these strategies:

- Cover what you have already read with a note card as you go along. Then, you will not be able to reread without noticing that you are doing it.
- Set a purpose for reading beyond just completing the assignment. Then, read actively by pausing to ask yourself questions about the material as you read.
- Use the Reading Strategy instruction and notes that appear with each selection in this textbook.
- Stop reading after a specified period of time (for example, 5 minutes) and summarize what you have read. To help you with this strategy, use the Reading Check questions that appear with each selection in this textbook. Reread to find any answers you do not know.

Reading Phrases

Fluent readers read phrases rather than individual words. Reading this way will speed up your reading and improve your comprehension. Here are some useful ideas:

- Experts recommend rereading as a strategy to increase fluency. Choose a passage of text that is neither too hard nor too easy. Read the same passage aloud several times until you can read it smoothly. When you can read the passage fluently, pick another passage and keep practicing.
- Read aloud into a tape recorder. Then, listen to the recording, noting your accuracy, pacing, and expression. You can also read aloud and share feedback with a partner.
- Use the *Prentice Hall Listening to Literature* audiotapes or CDs to hear the selections read aloud. Read along silently in your textbook, noticing how the reader uses his or her voice and emphasizes certain words and phrases.

Understanding Key Vocabulary

If you do not understand some of the words in an assignment, you may miss out on important concepts. Therefore, it is helpful to keep a dictionary nearby when you are reading. Follow these steps:

- Before you begin reading, scan the text for unfamiliar words or terms. Find out what those words mean before you begin reading.
- Use context—the surrounding words, phrases, and sentences—to help you determine the meanings of unfamiliar words.
- If you are unable to understand the meaning through context, refer to the dictionary.

Paying Attention to Punctuation

When you read, pay attention to punctuation. Commas, periods, exclamation points, semicolons, and colons tell you when to pause or stop. They also indicate relationships between groups of words. When you recognize these relationships you will read with greater understanding and expression. Look at the chart below.

Punctuation Mark	Meaning
comma	brief pause
period	pause at the end of a thought
exclamation point	pause that indicates emphasis
semicolon	pause between related but distinct thoughts
colon	pause before giving explanation or examples

Using the Reading Fluency Checklist

Use the checklist below each time you read a selection in this textbook. In your Language Arts journal or notebook, note which skills you need to work on, and chart your progress each week.

Reading Fluency Checklist
❑ Preview the text to check for difficult or unfamiliar words.
❑ Practice reading aloud.
❑ Read according to punctuation.
❑ Break down long sentences into the subject and its meaning.
❑ Read groups of words for meaning rather than reading single words.
❑ Read with expression (change your tone of voice to add meaning to the word).

Reading is a skill that can be improved with practice. The key to improving your fluency is to read. The more you read, the better your reading will become.

Types of Writing

Good writing can be a powerful tool used for many purposes. Writing can allow you to defend something you believe in or show how much you know about a subject. Writing can also help you share what you have experienced, imagined, thought, and felt. The three main types of writing are argument, informative/explanatory, and narrative.

Argument

When you think of the word *argument*, you might think of a disagreement between two people, but an argument is more than that. An argument is a logical way of presenting a belief, conclusion, or stance. A good argument is supported with reasoning and evidence.

Argument writing can be used for many purposes, such as to change a reader's point of view or opinion or to bring about an action or a response from a reader.

There are three main purposes for writing a formal argument:

- to change the reader's mind
- to convince the reader to accept what is written
- to motivate the reader to take action, based on what is written

The following are some types of argument writing:

Advertisements An advertisement is a planned message meant to be seen, heard, or read. It attempts to persuade an audience to buy a product or service, accept an idea, or support a cause. Advertisements may appear in print, online, or in broadcast form.

Several common types of advertisements are public-service announcements, billboards, merchandise ads, service ads, and political campaign literature.

Persuasive Essay A persuasive essay presents a position on an issue, urges readers to accept that position, and may encourage a specific action. An effective persuasive essay

- Explores an issue of importance to the writer
- Addresses an issue that is arguable
- Uses facts, examples, statistics, or personal experiences to support a position
- Tries to influence the audience through appeals to the readers' knowledge, experiences, or emotions
- Uses clear organization to present a logical argument

Forms of persuasion include editorials, position papers, persuasive speeches, grant proposals, advertisements, and debates.

Informative/Explanatory

Informative/explanatory writing should rely on facts to inform or explain. Informative/explanatory writing serves some closely related purposes: to increase readers' knowledge of a subject, to help readers better understand a procedure or process, or to provide readers with an enhanced comprehension of a concept. It should also feature a clear introduction, body, and conclusion. The following are some examples of informative/explanatory writing:

Cause-and-Effect Essay A cause-and-effect essay examines the relationship between events, explaining how one event or situation causes another. A successful cause-and-effect essay includes

- A discussion of a cause, event, or condition that produces a specific result
- An explanation of an effect, outcome, or result
- Evidence and examples to support the relationship between cause and effect
- A logical organization that makes the explanation clear

Comparison-and-Contrast Essay A comparison-and-contrast essay analyzes the similarities and differences between or among two or more things. An effective comparison-and-contrast essay

- Identifies a purpose for comparison and contrast
- Identifies similarities and differences between or among two or more things, people, places, or ideas
- Gives factual details about the subjects
- Uses an organizational plan suited to the topic and purpose

Descriptive Writing Descriptive writing creates a vivid picture of a person, place, thing, or event. Most descriptive writing includes

- Sensory details—sights, sounds, smells, tastes, and physical sensations
- Vivid, precise language
- Figurative language or comparisons
- Adjectives and adverbs that paint a word picture
- An organization suited to the subject

Types of descriptive writing include descriptions of ideas, observations, travel brochures, physical descriptions, functional descriptions, remembrances, and character sketches.

Problem-and-Solution Essay A problem-and-solution essay describes a problem and offers one or more solutions to it. It describes a clear set of steps to achieve a result. An effective problem-and-solution essay includes

- A clear statement of the problem, with its causes and effects summarized for the reader
- The most important aspects of the problem
- A proposal of at least one realistic solution
- Facts, statistics, data, or expert testimony to support the solution
- A clear organization that makes the relationship between problem and solution obvious

Research Writing Research writing is based on information gathered from outside sources. A research paper—a focused study of a topic—helps writers explore and connect ideas, make discoveries, and share their findings with an audience. An effective research paper

- Focuses on a specific, narrow topic, which is usually summarized in a thesis statement
- Presents relevant information from a wide variety of sources
- Uses a clear organization that includes an introduction, body, and conclusion
- Includes a bibliography or works-cited list that identifies the sources from which the information was drawn

Other types of writing that depend on accurate and insightful research include multimedia presentations, statistical reports, annotated bibliographies, and experiment journals.

Workplace Writing Workplace writing is probably the format you will use most after you finish school. In general, workplace writing is fact-based and meant to communicate specific information in a structured format. Effective workplace writing

- Communicates information concisely
- Includes details that provide necessary information and anticipate potential questions
- Is error-free and neatly presented

Common types of workplace writing include business letters, memorandums, résumés, forms, and applications.

Narrative

Narrative writing conveys experience, either real or imaginary, and uses time to provide structure. It can be used to inform, instruct, persuade, or entertain. Whenever writers tell a story, they are using narrative writing. Most types of narrative writing share certain elements, such as characters, a setting, a sequence of events, and, often, a theme. The following are some types of narration:

Autobiographical Writing Autobiographical writing tells a true story about an important period, experience, or relationship in the writer's life. Effective autobiographical writing includes

- A series of events that involve the writer as the main character
- Details, thoughts, feelings, and insights from the writer's perspective
- A conflict or an event that affects the writer
- A logical organization that tells the story clearly
- Insights that the writer gained from the experience

Types of autobiographical writing include autobiographical sketches, personal narratives, reflective essays, eyewitness accounts, and memoirs.

Short Story A short story is a brief, creative narrative. Most short stories include

- Details that establish the setting in time and place
- A main character who undergoes a change or learns something during the course of the story
- A conflict or a problem to be introduced, developed, and resolved
- A plot, the series of events that make up the action of the story
- A theme or message about life

Types of short stories include realistic stories, fantasies, historical narratives, mysteries, thrillers, science-fiction stories, and adventure stories.

Writing Friendly Letters

WRITING HANDBOOK

Writing Friendly Letters

A friendly letter is much less formal than a business letter. It is a letter to a friend, a family member, or anyone with whom the writer wants to communicate in a personal, friendly way. Most friendly letters are made up of five parts:

- ✔ the heading
- ✔ the salutation, or greeting
- ✔ the body
- ✔ the closing
- ✔ the signature

The purpose of a friendly letter is often one of the following:

- ✔ to share personal news and feelings
- ✔ to send or to answer an invitation
- ✔ to express thanks

Model Friendly Letter

In this friendly letter, Betsy thanks her grandparents for a birthday present and gives them some news about her life.

11 Old Farm Road
Topsham, Maine 04011

April 14, 20—

The **heading** includes the writer's address and the date on which he or she wrote the letter.

Dear Grandma and Grandpa,

Thank you for the sweater you sent me for my birthday. It fits perfectly, and I love the color. I wore my new sweater to the carnival at school last weekend and got lots of compliments.

The weather here has been cool but sunny. Mom thinks that "real" spring will never come. I can't wait until it's warm enough to go swimming.

School is going fairly well. I really like my Social Studies class. We are learning about the U.S. Constitution, and I think it's very interesting. Maybe I will be a lawyer when I grow up.

When are you coming out to visit us? We haven't seen you since Thanksgiving. You can stay in my room when you come. I'll be happy to sleep on the couch. (The TV is in that room!!)

Well, thanks again and hope all is well with you.

The **body** is the main part of the letter and contains the basic message.

Love,

Betsy

Some common **closings** for personal letters include "Best Wishes," "Love," "Sincerely," and "Yours Truly."

Writing Business Letters

Formatting Business Letters

Business letters follow one of several acceptable formats. In **block format,** each part of the letter begins at the left margin. A double space is used between paragraphs. In **modified block format,** some parts of the letter are indented to the center of the page. No matter which format is used, all letters in business format have a heading, an inside address, a salutation or greeting, a body, a closing, and a signature. These parts are shown and annotated on the model business letter below, formatted in modified block style.

Model Business Letter

In this letter, Yolanda Dodson uses modified block format to request information.

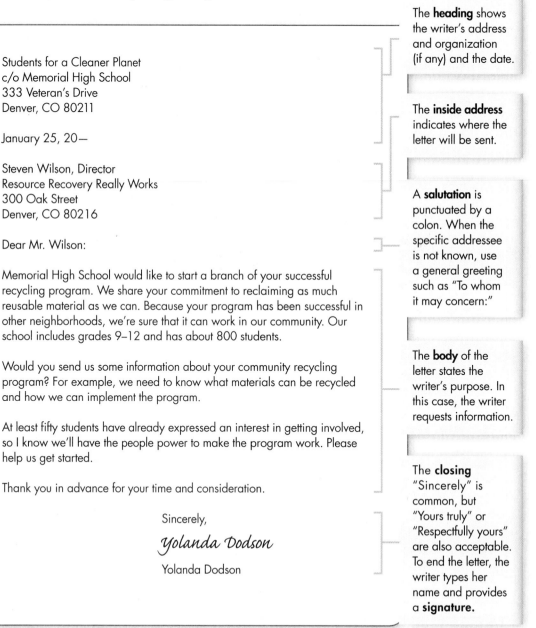

Students for a Cleaner Planet
c/o Memorial High School
333 Veteran's Drive
Denver, CO 80211

January 25, 20—

The **heading** shows the writer's address and organization (if any) and the date.

Steven Wilson, Director
Resource Recovery Really Works
300 Oak Street
Denver, CO 80216

The **inside address** indicates where the letter will be sent.

Dear Mr. Wilson:

A **salutation** is punctuated by a colon. When the specific addressee is not known, use a general greeting such as "To whom it may concern:"

Memorial High School would like to start a branch of your successful recycling program. We share your commitment to reclaiming as much reusable material as we can. Because your program has been successful in other neighborhoods, we're sure that it can work in our community. Our school includes grades 9–12 and has about 800 students.

Would you send us some information about your community recycling program? For example, we need to know what materials can be recycled and how we can implement the program.

At least fifty students have already expressed an interest in getting involved, so I know we'll have the people power to make the program work. Please help us get started.

Thank you in advance for your time and consideration.

The **body** of the letter states the writer's purpose. In this case, the writer requests information.

Sincerely,

Yolanda Dodson

Yolanda Dodson

The **closing** "Sincerely" is common, but "Yours truly" or "Respectfully yours" are also acceptable. To end the letter, the writer types her name and provides a **signature.**

Writing a Résumé

A résumé summarizes your educational background, work experiences, relevant skills, and other employment qualifications. It also tells potential employers how to contact you. An effective résumé presents the applicant's name, address, and phone number. It follows an accepted résumé organization, using labels and headings to guide readers.

A résumé should outline the applicant's educational background, life experiences, and related qualifications using precise and active language.

Model Résumé

With this résumé, James, a college student, hopes to find a full-time job.

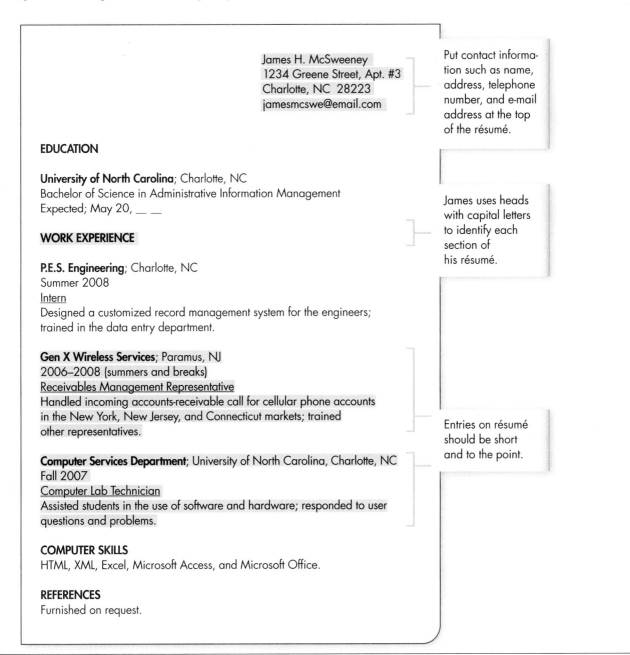

James H. McSweeney
1234 Greene Street, Apt. #3
Charlotte, NC 28223
jamesmcswe@email.com

Put contact information such as name, address, telephone number, and e-mail address at the top of the résumé.

EDUCATION

University of North Carolina; Charlotte, NC
Bachelor of Science in Administrative Information Management
Expected; May 20, __ __

WORK EXPERIENCE

James uses heads with capital letters to identify each section of his résumé.

P.E.S. Engineering; Charlotte, NC
Summer 2008
Intern
Designed a customized record management system for the engineers; trained in the data entry department.

Gen X Wireless Services; Paramus, NJ
2006–2008 (summers and breaks)
Receivables Management Representative
Handled incoming accounts-receivable call for cellular phone accounts in the New York, New Jersey, and Connecticut markets; trained other representatives.

Entries on résumé should be short and to the point.

Computer Services Department; University of North Carolina, Charlotte, NC
Fall 2007
Computer Lab Technician
Assisted students in the use of software and hardware; responded to user questions and problems.

COMPUTER SKILLS
HTML, XML, Excel, Microsoft Access, and Microsoft Office.

REFERENCES
Furnished on request.

Rules of Debate

A **debate** is a structured contest based on a formal discussion of opinion. In essence, it is a battle of intellect and verbal skill. The goal is mastering the art of persuasion. Who can best express, argue, and support opinions on a given topic? Who can best refute an argument, showing that the opponent's points are invalid? Which team, in the end, can convince the judges that their argument is the most sound?

Teams

A **formal debate** is conducted with two teams—an Affirmation team and a Negative team. As the names suggest, the Affirmation team is responsible for presenting the "pro" side of an issue, while the Negative team presents the "con" side of the issue. Each team has a main purpose and will offer both constructive and rebuttal speeches, practicing the art of persuasion and debate.

Affirmation team The Affirmation team as a whole carries the burden of proof for the debate. They must prove there is a problem. To do so, they need to cite credible sources, include relevant details, and present and support valid points. Each team member has a specific job. The first speaker has the most responsibility. He or she must

- define the issue or problem
- introduce the team line—a one-line summary of the team's position on the issue
- identify the point of the argument each speaker will discuss

The remaining team members have the job of presenting and supporting the main points of the argument.

Negative team Though the Negative team does not carry the burden of proof, the team must show that there is no problem or that the Affirmation team's solutions are invalid. Though their purpose is to rebut an argument, the rebuttal technique calls for a formation of their own argument. They must argue against the Affirmation team. To construct their argument, they must use—like the Affirmation team—credible sources, relevant details, and valid points. They should incorporate any available statistics, pertinent facts, or applicable testimonies to bolster their argument. Even though the first speaker of the Affirmation team lays out each point of the argument, the Negative team speakers cannot address points that have not been thoroughly discussed by an Affirmation team member.

Structure

Just like most other contests, debates have a set structure. Debates are divided into halves. The first half begins with the constructive speeches from both teams, which last ten minutes each.

After the first half, there is a short intermission. Then, the second half begins with the Negative team. This half is reserved for the rebuttal speeches, which last five minutes each and include rebuttals and refutations. This is each team's chance to rebuild their arguments that the other team broke down (rebuttal), and put forth evidence to show the other team is wrong (refutation). Although the Negative team begins the argument in the second half, every debate begins and ends with the Affirmation team.

Structure of Debate

1st Half: Constructive Speeches (10 minutes each)	**2nd Half: Rebuttal Speeches** (5 minutes each)
1st Affirmative Team Speaker	1st Negative Team Speaker
1st Negative Team Speaker	1st Affirmative Team Speaker
2nd Affirmative Team Speaker	2nd Negative Team Speaker
2nd Negative Team Speaker	2nd Affirmative Team Speaker
3rd Affirmative Team Speaker	3rd Negative Team Speaker
3rd Negative Team Speaker	3rd Affirmative Team Speaker

Speeches—Content, Organization, and Delivery

Debate speeches are the result of practicing the art of persuasion. To be effective, speakers must include pertinent content, use clear and logical organization, and have a powerful delivery. These combined elements make a strong speech.

Content Debates often focus on concrete issues that can be proved or disproved. The basis for a debate speech is its content. The Affirmation team should first determine their position. They should be sure to include any facts and/or statistics that concretely support the argument. Speech writers should cite specific instances and occurrences that solidify their position. Writers might also include testimonies or ideas from professionals. Finally, the Affirmation team needs to propose possible solutions to the problem or issue and examine the costs and effects of those solutions.

Though the Negative team does not have to state a position—their position is automatically the opposing position—they still need to include facts, statistics, testimony, and descriptions of specific instances or occurrences to make their counterpoints. They need to analyze the Affirmation team's proposed solutions and explain why they will not work. In essence, the Negative team must construct an argument around the Affirmation team's argument.

Organization Debate speeches are organized like other speeches and essays. They should have an introduction, transitions, body, and conclusion. The speeches should have clear main points and supporting details for those points. Because a debate is a structured discussion, there will be a specific order of points and the speakers who present them must be identified. Speakers can use note cards to help them stick to the planned organization, but they should only use brief notes, never reading directly from the cards.

Delivery The manner in which a speech is delivered can make or break the argument. The impression the speaker makes on the audience, including the judges, is key. To make a good impression, the speaker must present the material with confidence. He or she can portray confidence by forming a connection with the audience through eye contact, glancing away only briefly to consult notes. A speaker should focus on his or her voice, varying the tone, volume, and pace appropriately. Body movements should not include fidgeting or nervous movement. They should only be used if they are deliberate and help express or underscore a point. Finally, speakers should be concise, focusing on vivid and clear word choice and using words that emphasize the point.

Scoring

Debates are scored much like other contests. Each side is judged on the content and delivery of their speeches. Judges contemplate different elements of content and delivery in order to determine the number of points to give each team. They might ask themselves the questions in the chart below in order to determine the score.

Finally, judges look at the observation of debate etiquette. Speakers are expected to be mature and respectful of their opponents. Speakers should never attack an opponent, but instead should attack the argument. Judges will deduct points for personal attacks.

Scoring Criteria

Content	Delivery
Were arguments convincing?	Were speakers able to speak extemporaneously?
Were arguments supported with credible, valid and relevant reasons?	Were body movements deliberate and effective?
Were refutations and rebuttals effective?	Did speakers make a connection with the audience?
Were speakers confident and knowledgeable?	Did speakers stay within their time limits?

Grammar, Usage, and Mechanics Handbook

Parts of Speech

Nouns A noun names a person, place, or thing. Common nouns name any one of a class of people, places, or things. Proper nouns name specific people, places, or things.

Common Noun	***Proper Noun***
city	Washington, D.C.

Use *apostrophes* with nouns to show ownership. Add an apostrophe and *s* to show the **possessive case** of most singular nouns. Add just an apostrophe to show the possessive case of plural nouns ending in *s* or *es*. Add an apostrophe and s to show the possessive case of plural nouns that do not end in *s* or *es*.

Pronouns A **pronoun** is a word that stands for a noun or for a word that takes the place of a noun.

A **personal pronoun** refers to (1) the person speaking, (2) the person spoken to, or (3) the person, place, or thing spoken about.

	Singular	***Plural***
First Person	I, me, my, mine	we, us, our, ours
Second Person	you, your, yours	you, your, yours
Third Person	he, him, his, she, her, hers, it, its	they, them, their, theirs

A **reflexive pronoun** ends in *-self* or *-selves* and adds information to a sentence by pointing back to a noun or pronoun earlier in the sentence.

As I said these words I busied *myself* among the pile of bones of which I have before spoken.

—"The Cask of Amontillado," p. 82

An **intensive pronoun** ends in *-self* or *-selves* and simply adds emphasis to a noun or a pronoun in the same sentence.

The best playground, however, was the dark alley *itself*.

—"Rules of the Game," p. 64

Demonstrative pronouns (*this, these, that,* and *those*) direct attention to a specific person, place, or thing.

These are the juiciest pears I have ever tasted.

A **relative pronoun** begins a subordinate (relative) clause and connects it to another idea in the sentence.

The poet *who* wrote "Fire and Ice" is Robert Frost.

The poet *whom* I admire is Frost.

An **interrogative pronoun** is used to begin a question. The five interrogative pronouns are *what, which, who, whom, whose*.

An **indefinite pronoun** refers to a person, place, or thing, often without specifying which one.

Some of the flowers were in bloom.

Everybody chose something.

Verbs A **verb** is a word that expresses time while showing an action, a condition, or the fact that something exists.

An **action verb** indicates the action of someone or something. An action verb is **transitive** if it directs action toward someone or something named in the same sentence.

Marcos accepted their bouquets . . .

—"Uncle Marcos,"

An action verb is **intransitive** if it does not direct action toward something or someone named in the same sentence.

"He nodded and smiled a lot."

—"American History," p. 448

A **linking verb** is a verb that connects the subject of a sentence with a noun or pronoun that renames or describes the subject. All linking verbs are intransitive.

Life *is* a broken-winged bird . . .

—"Dreams," p. 348

A **helping verb** is a verb that can be added to another verb to make a verb phrase.

Nor *did* I suspect that these experiences could be part of a novel's meaning.

Adjectives An **adjective** describes a noun or a pronoun or gives a noun or a pronoun a more specific meaning. Adjectives answer these questions:

What kind?	*blue* lamp, *large* tree
Which one?	*this* table, *those* books
How many?	*five* stars, *several* buses
How much?	*less* money, *enough* votes

The articles *the, a,* and *an* are adjectives. *An* is used before a word beginning with a vowel sound.

A noun may sometimes be used as an adjective.

diamond necklace *summer* vacation

Adverbs An **adverb** modifies a verb, an adjective, or another adverb. Adverbs answer the questions *Where? When? In what way?* or *To what extent?*

He could stand *there*. (modifies verb *stand*)

He was *blissfully* happy. (modifies adjective *happy*)

It ended *too* soon. (modifies adverb *soon*)

Prepositions A **preposition** relates a noun or a pronoun that appears with it to another word in the sentence.

the scene *before* the end stood *near* me

Conjunctions A **conjunction** connects other words or groups of words. A **coordinating conjunction** connects similar kinds or groups of words.

mother *and* father   simple *yet* stylish

Correlative conjunctions are used in pairs to connect similar words or groups of words.

both Sue *and* Meg   *neither* he *nor* I

A **subordinating conjunction** connects two complete ideas by placing one idea below the other in rank or importance.

You would know him *if* you saw him.

Interjections An **interjection** expresses feeling or emotion and functions independently of a sentence.

"*Oh*, my poor, poor, Mathilde!"
—"The Necklace," p. 686

Sentences, Phrases, and Clauses

Sentences A **sentence** is a group of words with a subject and a predicate. Together, these parts express a complete thought.

I closed my eyes and pondered my next move.
— "Rules of the Game," p. 64

A **fragment** is a group of words that does not express a complete thought.

The Swan Theater in London

A **run-on** is two or more complete sentences run together without punctuation.

A **direct object** is a noun or pronoun that receives the action of a transitive verb.

An **indirect object** is a noun or pronoun that appears with a direct object and names the person or thing that something is given to or done for.

The Four Structures of Sentences There are two kinds of clauses: independent and subordinate. These can be used to form four basic sentence structures: *simple, compound, complex,* and *compound-complex.*

A **simple sentence** consists of a single independent clause.

A **compound sentence** consists of two or more independent clauses.

The clauses in a compound sentence can be joined by a comma and a coordinating conjunction (*and, but, for, not, or, so, yet*) or by a semicolon (;).

A **complex sentence** consists of one independent clause and one or more subordinate clauses.

The independent clause in a complex sentence is often called the *main clause* to distinguish it from the subordinate clause or clauses.

A **compound-complex sentence** consists of two or more independent clauses and one or more subordinate causes.

Phrases A **phrase** is a group of words, without a subject and a verb, that functions in a sentence as one part of speech.

A **prepositional phrase** is a group of words that includes a preposition and a noun or a pronoun that is the object of the preposition.

outside my window   below the counter

An **adjective phrase** is a prepositional phrase that modifies a noun or a pronoun by telling *what kind* or *which one.*

The wooden gates *of that lane* stood open.

An **adverb phrase** is a prepositional phrase that modifies a verb, an adjective, or an adverb by pointing out *where, when, in what way,* or *to what extent.*

". . . I could sleep without closing my eyes . . ."
—"The Most Dangerous Game," p. 24

An **appositive phrase** is a noun or pronoun with modifiers, placed next to a noun or a pronoun to add information and details.

"It is a very great pleasure and honor to welcome Mr. Sanger Rainsford, *the celebrated hunter,* to my home."
—"The Most Dangerous Game," p. 24

A **participial phrase** is a participle with its modifiers or complements. The entire phrase acts as an adjective.

"Try the settee," said Holmes, *relapsing into his armchair . . .*
—"The Red-headed League,"

A **gerund phrase** is a gerund with modifiers or a complement, all acting together as a noun.

The baying of the hounds drew nearer, . . .
—"The Most Dangerous Game," p. 24

An **infinitive phrase** is an infinitive (*to* and a verb) with modifiers, complements, or a subject, all acting together as a single part of speech.

I continued, as was my wont, *to smile in his face,* . . .
—"The Cask of Amontillado," p. 82

Clauses A **clause** is a group of words with a subject and a verb.

An **independent clause** has a subject and a verb and can stand by itself as a complete sentence.

A **subordinate clause** has a subject and a verb but cannot stand by itself as a complete sentence; it can only be part of a sentence.

An **adjective clause** is a subordinate clause that modifies a noun or a pronoun by telling *what kind* or *which one.*

Walter Mitty stopped the car in front of the building *where his wife went to have her hair done.*
—"The Secret Life of Walter Mitty,"

An **adverb clause** modifies a verb, an adjective, an adverb, or a verbal by telling *where, when, in what way, to what extent, under what condition,* or *why.*

The hunter shook his head several times, *as if he was puzzled.*
—"The Most Dangerous Game," p. 24

A **noun clause** is a subordinate clause that acts as a noun.

. . . I discovered *that the intoxication had worn off* . . .
—"The Cask of Amontillado," p. 82

Parallelism involves using similar grammatical structures to express similar ideas. Sentences with parallel structure contain repeated grammatical patterns or repeated types of phrases or clauses within a sentence.

Marguerite has a great love *for art, for children,* and *for teaching.*

The Four Principal Parts of Verbs

Tenses are formed from principal parts and helping verbs.

A verb has four **principal parts:** the present, the present participle, the past, and the past participle.

Pronoun Case The **case** of a pronoun is the form it takes to show its use in a sentence. There are three pronoun cases: nominative, objective, and possessive.

The **nominative case** is used to rename the subject of the sentence. The nominative case pronouns are *I, you, he, she, it, we, you, they.*

As the subject: *She* is brave.

Renaming the subject: The leader is *she.*

The **objective case** is used as the direct object, indirect object, or object of the preposition. The objective case pronouns are *me, you, him, her, us, you, them.*

As a direct object: Our manager praised her.

As an indirect object: Give him the new product.

As an object of the preposition: The coach gave pointers to me.

The **possessive case** is used to show ownership. The possessive pronouns are *my, you, his, her, its, our, their, mine, yours, his, hers, its, ours, theirs.*

Subject and Verb Agreement A singular verb must be used with a singular subject; a plural verb must be used with a plural subject.

Reegan is going home now.

Many *storms are* the cause of beach erosion.

In a sentence with combined singular and plural subjects, the verb should agree with the subject closest to it.

Either the *cats* or the *dog is* hungry.

Neither *Angie* nor her *sisters were* present.

Antecedents are the nouns (or the words that take the place of nouns) to which pronouns refer.

A personal pronoun must agree with its antecedent in number and gender. *Number* indicates whether a pronoun is singular or plural.

Some pronouns and nouns also indicate one of three *genders:* masculine, feminine, or neuter.

Use a singular personal pronoun to refer to two or more singular antecedents joined by *or* or *nor.*

Use a plural personal pronoun to refer to two or more antecedents joined by *and.*

Degrees of Comparison Most adjectives and adverbs have different forms to show degrees of comparison.

The three degrees of comparison are the *positive,* the *comparative,* and the *superlative.*

Use the comparative degree to compare two people, places, or things. Use the superlative degree to compare three or more people, places, or things.

Use *more* or *most* to form the comparative and superlative degrees of all modifiers with three or more syllables.

Memorize the irregular comparative and superlative forms of certain adjectives and adverbs.

The most commonly used irregular modifiers are listed in the following chart. Notice that some modifiers differ only in the positive degree. For instance, the modifiers *bad, badly,* and *ill* all have the same comparative and superlative forms (*worse, worst*).

Capitalization and Punctuation

Capitalization Capitalize the first word of a sentence and also the first word in a quotation if the quotation is a complete sentence.

I said to him, "My dear Fortunato, you are luckily met."
—"The Cask of Amontillado," p. 82

Capitalize all proper nouns and adjectives.

O. Henry Ganges River Great Wall of China

Capitalize a person's title when it is followed by the person's name or when it is used in direct address.

Madame Dr. Mitty General Zaroff

Capitalize titles showing family relationships when they refer to a specific person, unless they are preceded by a possessive noun or pronoun.

Uncle Marcos Granddaddy Cain

Capitalize the first word and all other key words in the titles of books, periodicals, poems, stories, plays, paintings, and other works of art.

Odyssey "I Wandered Lonely as a Cloud"

Punctuation

End Marks Use a **period** to end a declarative sentence, an imperative sentence, an indirect question, and most abbreviations.

Mr. Jabez Wilson laughed heavily.
—"The Red-headed League,"

Use a **question mark** to end a direct question, an incomplete question, or a statement that is intended as a question.

"What do you expect me to do with that?"
—"The Necklace," p. 686

Use an **exclamation mark** after a statement showing strong emotion, an urgent imperative sentence, or an interjection expressing strong emotion.

Free at last! Free at last!
Thank God almighty, we are Free at last!
—"I Have a Dream," p. 242

Commas Use a **comma** before the coordinating conjunction to separate two independent clauses in a compound sentence.

All at once . . . she came upon a superb diamond necklace, and her heart started beating with overwhelming desire.
—"The Necklace," p. 686

Use commas to separate three or more words, phrases, or clauses in a series.

My brothers and I would peer into the medicinal herb shop, watching old Li dole out onto a stiff sheet of white paper the right amount of insect shells, saffron-colored seeds, and pungent leaves for his ailing customers.
—"Rules of the Game," p. 64

Use commas to separate adjectives of equal rank. Do not use commas to separate adjectives that must stay in a specific order.

The big cottonwood tree stood apart from a small group of winterbare cottonwoods which grew in the wide, sandy arroyo.
—"The Man to Send Rain Clouds,"

His present turned out to be a box of intricate plastic parts.
—"Rules of the Game," p. 64

Use a comma after an introductory word, phrase, or clause.

When Marvin was ten years old, his father took him through the long, echoing corridors . . .
—"If I Forget Thee, Oh Earth . . . ," p. 258

Use commas to set off parenthetical and nonessential expressions.

An evil place can, so to speak, broadcast vibrations of evil.
—"The Most Dangerous Game," p. 24

Use commas with places, dates, and titles.

Poe was raised in Richmond, Virginia.
On September 1, 1939, World War II began.
Dr. Martin Luther King, Jr., was born in 1929.

Use a comma to set off a direct quotation, to prevent a sentence from being misunderstood, and to indicate the omission of a common verb in a sentence with two or more clauses.

Michele said, "I'm going to the game tonight."

Faulty: She stifled the sob that rose to her lips and lay motionless.

Revised: She stifled the sob that rose to her lips, and lay motionless.

In the *Odyssey,* the Cyclops may symbolize brutishness; the Sirens, knowledge.

Semicolons Use a **semicolon** to join independent clauses that are not already joined by a conjunction.

The lights of cities sparkle; on nights when there was no moon, it was difficult for me to tell the Earth from the sky. . . .
—"Single Room, Earth View,"

Use a semicolon to join independent clauses separated by either a conjunctive adverb or a transitional expression.

Edward Way Teale wrote nearly thirty books; moreover, he was also an artist and a naturalist.

Use semicolons to avoid confusion when independent clauses or items in a series already contain commas.

Unable to afford jewelry, she dressed simply; but she was as wretched as a *déclassée,* for women have neither caste nor breeding—in them beauty, grace, and charm replace pride of birth.
—"The Necklace," p. 686

Colons Use a **colon** in order to introduce a list of items following an independent clause.

The authors we are reading include a number of poets: Robert Frost, Lewis Carroll, and Emily Dickinson.

Use a colon to introduce a formal quotation.

I have a dream that one day this nation will rise up and live out the true meaning of its creed: "We hold these truths to be self-evident; . . ."
—"I Have a Dream," p. 242

Quotation Marks A **direct quotation** represents a person's exact speech or thoughts and is enclosed in quotation marks.

"This great nation will endure as it has endured, will revive and will prosper," said President Franklin D. Roosevelt.
—"First Inaugural Address," p. 284

An **indirect quotation** reports only the general meaning of what a person said or thought and does not require quotation marks.

I went up to her, put my arms around her, and said something to her.

—from *A White House Diary,* p. 440

Always place a comma or a period inside the final quotation mark.

"There," he said, "there's something for you."

—"The Necklace," p. 686

Place a question mark or an exclamation mark inside the final quotation mark if the end mark is part of the quotation; if it is not part of the quotation, place it outside the final quotation mark.

"That pig will devour us, greedily!"

—"The Golden Kite, the Silver Wind,"

Have you ever read the poem "Dreams"?

Use single quotation marks for a quotation within a quotation.

" 'But,' said I, 'there would be millions of red-headed men who would apply.' "

—"The Red-headed League,"

Use quotation marks around the titles of short written works, episodes in a series, songs, and titles of works mentioned as parts of a collection.

"I Hear America Singing" "Pride"

Dashes Use **dashes** to indicate an abrupt change of thought, a dramatic interrupting idea, or a summary statement.

The streets were lined with people—lots and lots of people—the children all smiling, placards, confetti, people waving from windows.

—from *A White House Diary,* p. 440

Parentheses Use **parentheses** to set off asides and explanations only when the material is not essential or when it consists of one or more sentences.

One last happy moment I had was looking up and seeing Mary Griffith . . . (Mary for many years had been in charge of altering the clothes which I purchased) . . .

—from *A White House Diary,* p. 440

Hyphens Use a **hyphen** with certain numbers, after certain prefixes, with two or more words used as one word, and with a compound modifier coming before a noun.

seventy-six Post-Modernist

Apostrophes Add an **apostrophe** and *-s* to show the possessive case of most singular nouns.

Thurmond's wife the playwright's craft

Add an apostrophe to show the possessive case of plural nouns ending in *-s* and *-es.*

the sailors' ships the Wattses' daughter

Add an apostrophe and *-s* to show the possessive case of plural nouns that do not end in *-s* or *-es.*

the children's games the people's friend

Use an apostrophe in a contraction to indicate the position of the missing letter or letters.

You'll be lonely at first, they admitted, but you're so nice you'll make friends fast.

—"Checkouts," p. 96

Glossary of Common Usage

among, between: *Among* is usually used with three or more items. *Between* is generally used with only two items.

Among the poems we read this year, Margaret Walker's "Memory" was my favorite.

Mark Twain's "The Invalid's Story" includes a humorous encounter *between* the narrator and a character named Thompson.

around: In formal writing, *around* should not be used to mean *approximately* or *about.* These usages are allowable, however, in informal writing or in colloquial dialogue.

Shakespeare's *Romeo and Juliet* had its first performance in *approximately* 1595.

Shakespeare was *about* thirty when he wrote this play.

as, because, like, as to: The word *as* has several meanings and can function as several parts of speech. To avoid confusion, use *because* rather than *as* when you want to indicate cause and effect.

Because Cyril was interested in the history of African American poetry, he decided to write his report on Paul Laurence Dunbar.

Do not use the preposition *like* to introduce a clause that requires the conjunction as.

Dorothy Parker conversed *as* she wrote—wittily.

The use of *as to* for *about* is awkward and should be avoided.

Rosa has an interesting theory *about* E. E. Cummings's unusual typography in his poems.

Glossary

GLOSSARY

PRONUNCIATION KEY

Symbol	Sample Words	Symbol	Sample Words
a	at, tap, mat	ȯi	oil, toy, royal
ā	ate, rain, break	ȯu	out, now, sour
ä	car, father, heart	u	mud, ton, trouble
ch	chew, nature, such	ʉ	her, sir, word
e	end, feather, said	’l	cattle, paddle, cuddle
ē	sea, steam, piece	’n	sudden, hidden, sweeten
ə	ago, pencil, lemon	ŋ	ring, anger, pink
i	it, stick, gym	sh	shell, mission, fish
ī	nice, lie, sky	th	thin, nothing, both
ō	no, oat, low	*th*	then, mother, smooth
ô	all, law, taught	zh	vision, treasure, seizure
o͝o	look, would, pull	yo͝o	cure, furious
o͞o	boot, drew, tune	yo͞o	cute, few, use

Academic vocabulary appears in blue type.

A

abash (ə bash´) *v.* embarrass

accentuate (ak sen´ cho͞o āt´) *v.* emphasize a particular feature of something or make something more noticeable

accentuated (ak sen´ cho͞o āt´ id) *v.* emphasized; heightened the effect of

accept (ak sept´) *v.* 1. regard with approval or recognize as valid; 2. take something that is given

accrued (ə kro͞od´) *v.* regularly added or increased

adversary (ad´ vər ser´ ē) *n.* person who opposes or fights against another

advocate 1. (ad´ və kāt´) *v.* speak or write in support of ; 2. (ad´ və kit) *n.* a person who pleads another's cause; someone who speaks or writes in support of something

afflicted (ə flik´ tid) *adj.* suffering or sickened

aggregate (ag´ rə git) *adj.* gathered together into a whole; taken as one

align (ə līn´) *v.* match up with; bring into agreement

allegedly (ə lej´ id lē) *adv.* questionably true; supposedly

aloofness (ə lo͞of´ nəs) *n.* emotional distance

altruism (al´ tro͞o iz´ əm) *n.* interest in others' well-being that is unselfishly motivated

ambiguities (am´ bə gyo͞o´ ə tēz) *n.* statements or events whose meanings are unclear

ambiguity (am´ bə gyo͞o´ ə tē) *n.* state or quality of being indefinite; vagueness

ambiguous (am big´ yo͞o əs) *adj.* having more than one meaning; able to be interpreted in different ways

amicably (am´ i kəb lē) *adv.* in a friendly manner

analyze (an´ ə līz´) *v.* study or examine something in detail to learn more about it

ancestry (an´ ses´ trē) *n.* one's line of descent or family lineage

anonymous (ə nän´ ə məs) *adj.* without a known or an acknowledged name

antagonize (an tag´ ə nīz´) *v.* make an enemy of

antic (an´ tik) *adj.* wildly playful

apex (ā´ peks´) *n.* highest point; peak

appreciate (ə prē´ shē āt´) *v.* be aware of the value of something

ardor (är´ dər) *n.* passion; enthusiasm

arduous (är´ jo͞o əs) *adj.* difficult; laborious

argument (är´ gyo͞o mənt) *n.* 1. discussion in which there is disagreement; dispute; 2. line of reasoning; reasons offered for or against something

articulate 1. (är tik´ yo͞o lāt´) *v.* express; 2. (är tik´yo͞o lit) *adj.* able to express oneself clearly

articulated (är tik´ yo͞o lā´ tid) *v.* expressed clearly

assertions (ə sʉr´ shənz) *n.* positive statements; declarations

asserts (ə sʉrtz´) *v.* declares; affirms

assimilated (ə sim´ ə lāt´ id) 1. *v.* took in or absorbed; 2. *adj.* having been taken in fully

assuage (ə swāj´) *v.* calm; pacify

atonement (ə tōn´ mənt) *n.* act of making up for a wrongdoing or an injury

augmenting (ôg ment´ iŋ) *v* increasing; enlarging

authentic (ô then´ tik) *adj* genuine

aware (ə wer´) *adj.* having knowledge or a sense of situations, facts, or ideas

B

background (bak´ ground´) *n.* facts or circumstances that cause or explain something

bafflement (baf´ əl mənt) *n.* puzzlement; bewilderment

balmy (bäm´ ē) *adj.* having the qualities of balm; soothing, mild, pleasant

barren (bar´ ən) *adj.* empty; having little or no vegetation

barrier (bar´ ē ər) *n.* obstacle; something that prevents passage or hinders

battle (bat´ 'l) 1. *n.* hostile encounter between two opposing forces; 2. *v.* fight or struggle

beguiling (bē gī´ liŋ) *v.* tricking; charming

bemusing (bē myo͞o´ ziŋ) *v.* stupefying; confusing

benediction (ben´ ə dik´ shən) *n.* goodwill or blessing

benevolently (bə nev´ ə lənt´ lē) *adv.* in a well-meaning way

bereft (bē reft´) *adj.* deprived

bias (bī´əs) *n.* mental leaning or inclination; partiality

bilingual (bī liŋ´ gwəl) *adj.* using two languages

blight (blīt) *n.* something that destroys or prevents growth

bravado (brə vä´ dō) *n.* pretended courage or defiant confidence

C

calculating (kal´ kyo͞o lāt´ iŋ) *v.* determining by using mathematics

candor (kan´ dər) *n.* sharp honesty or frankness in expressing oneself

caption (kap´ shən) *n.* brief, descriptive information that accompanies an image, such as an illustration or a photograph

cascade (kas kād´) *n.* small steep waterfall; anything suggesting such a waterfall

chaos (kā´ äs´) *n.* total confusion; disorder

character (kar´ ək tər) *n.* combined qualities (intellectual, moral, etc.) that make a person unique

characterize (kar´ ək tər īz´) *v.* describe something by stating its main qualities

choices (choi´ səz) *n.* alternatives, a variety of possibilities from which a person can make a selection

clarify (klar´ ə fī´) *v.* make something more clear or understandable

class (klas) *n.* group of people considered as a unit according to economic, occupational, or social status

colloquial (kə lō´ kwē əl) *adj.* conversational, ordinary or familiar

communication (kə myo͞o´ ni kā´ shən) *n.* sharing of information or ideas

compelling (kəm pel´ iŋ) *adj.* irresistibly or keenly interesting or attractive; captivating

compensation (käm´ pən sā´ shən) 1. *n.* anything that makes up for a loss, damage, or debt; 2. mechanism by which an individual seeks to make up for a real or imagined defect

compete (kəm pēt´) *v.* try to win against an opponent; strive to outdo another

competition (käm´ pə tish´ ən) *n.* contest or match; rivalry

composition (käm´ pə zish´ ən) *n.* arrangement of elements in a work of art

comprehend (käm´ prē hend´) *v.* understand

comprehension (käm´ prē hen´ shen) *n.* understanding; ability to understand something

comprise (kəm prīz´) *v.* make up; form

concept (kän´ sept´) *n.* idea; notion

concessions (kən sesh´ ənz) *n.* things given or granted as privileges

concise (kən sīs´) *adj.* brief and to the point

conduct (kän´ dukt´) *n.* way that one acts; behavior

confines (kän´ fīnz´) *n.* regions within a border; limits

conformity (kən fôr´ mə tē) *n.* acting or thinking in accordance with accepted customs, rules, or attitudes

connection (kə nek´ shən) *n.* joining of two or more things or ideas

consider (kən sid´ ər) *v.* think about in order to understand or decide

consult (kən sult´) *v.* look at or refer to for information

contempt (kən tempt´) *n.* disdain; scorn

contradictory (kän´ trə dik´ tə rē) *adj.* asserting the opposite

controversy (kän´ trə vʉr´ sē) *n.* lengthy, often public discussion of a question in which opposing opinions clash; debate or argument

cooperate (kō äp´ ər āt´) *v.* work together to achieve a common goal

counteract (kount´ ər akt´) *v.* act against or in opposition to

credentials (kri den´ shəlz) *n.* documents showing one's right to exercise power; qualifications

creed (krēd) *n.* statement of belief

critical (krit´ i kəl) *adj.* important; crucial

critique (kri tēk´) *n.* critical analysis of a subject

crystallize (kris´ təl īz´) *v.* take shape or definite form

culture (kul´ chər) *n.* ideas, customs, skills, and arts of a group of people living in a particular time and place

cunning (kun´ iŋ) *adj.* skilled in deception

curtailed (kər tāld´) *v.* cut short; reduced

D

daunting (dônt´ iŋ) *adj.* intimidating

defaulted (dē fôl´ tid) *v.* 1. failed to do something or be somewhere when required or expected; 2. failed to make payment when due

defend (dē fend´) *v.* 1. protect against attack; 2. support, maintain, or justify

deferred (dē furd´) *adj.* put off until a future time

defiance (dē fī´ əns) *n.* open, bold resistance to authority

defrauded (dē frôd´ ed) *v.* cheated

degenerate (dē jen´ ər āt´) *v.* grow worse

dejection (dē jek´ shən) *n.* lowness of spirits; depression

delirium (di lir´ ē əm) *n.* mental disturbance marked by confusion, disturbed speech, and hallucinations

demonstrative (di män´ strə tiv) *adj.* showing feelings openly

demure (di myo͞or´) *adj.* modest

depicted (dē pikt´ id) *v.* represented in a drawing, painting, sculpture, or other work of art

depicts (dē pikts´) *v.* represents in a drawing, painting, sculpture, or other work of art

depravity (dē prav´ ə tē) *n.* crookedness; corruption

depreciate (dē prē´ shē āt´) *v.* reduce in value

determine (dē tur´ mən) *v.* cause something to happen in a certain way; control

detract (dē trakt´) *v.* take something desirable away; make inferior

devastation (dev´ ə stā´ shən) *n.* destruction

differences (dif´ ər ən səs) *n.* qualities that make people or things not the same

differentiate (dif´ ər en´ shē āt´) *v.* distinguish between items or ideas

dilapidated (də lap´ ə dāt´ id) *adj.* broken down

discerning (di surn´ iŋ) *adj.* having good judgment or understanding

disclosed (dis klōzd´) *v.* revealed; made known

discreet (di skrēt´) *adj.* careful about what one says or does; prudent; keeping silent or preserving confidences when necessary

discreetly (di skrēt´ lē) *adv.* without drawing attention

discrepancy (di skrep´ ən sē) *n.* difference; being in disagreement

discriminate (di skrim´ i nāt´) *v.* 1. recognize differences; 2. show partiality (in favor of) or prejudice (against)

discuss (di skus´) *v.* consider a topic in writing or in conversation

disgrace (dis grās´) *n.* loss of respect, honor, or esteem; shame

disheveled (di shev´ əld) *adj.* untidy

dishevelment (di shev´ əl mənt) *n.* disorder; messiness

dismal (diz´ məl) *adj.* causing gloom or misery

dispatched (di spachd´) *v.* finished quickly

disperse (di spurs´) *v.* breakup and scatter in all directions; spread about; distribute widely

disproportionately (dis´ prə pôr´ shə nət lē) *adv.* in a way that is out of proportion or unfair

dissemble (di sem´ bəl) *v.* conceal under a false appearance; disguise

disseminating (di sem´ ə nāt´ iŋ) *v.* spreading far and wide

dissension (di sen´ shən) *n.* disagreement; difference of opinion

distinct (di stiŋkt´) *adj.* seen or understood as different or separate from others

distinction (di stiŋk´ shən) *n.* difference

diverged (dī vurjd´) *v.* branched out in different directions

domestic (dō mes´ tik) *adj.* having to do with the home, house, or family

duration (do͞o rā´ shən) *n.* length of time that something lasts

E

effective (e fek´ tiv) *adj.* producing a definite or desired result

elaborate (ē lab´ ə rāt´) *v.* develop in detail

elevated (el´ ə vāt´ id) *adj.* raised; from above

elixir (i lik´ sər) *n.* substance that is believed to prolong or give life

eloquence (el´ ə kwəns) *n.* speech or writing that is graceful and persuasive

embellishes (em bel´ ish əz) *v.* improves; adds decoration

embodiment (em bäd´ i mənt) *n.* representation of an idea in visible form

embody (em bäd´ ē) *v.* represent or personify

emigration (em´ i grā´ shən) *n.* leaving of one's place of residence or country to live elsewhere

empathy (em´ pə thē) *n.* ability to understand and share someone else's feelings

emphasize (em´ fə sīz´) *v.* give special force or prominence to; stress

empirical (em pir´ i kəl) *adj.* based on observations and experiments rather than theory

emulate (em´ yo͞o lāt´) *v.* imitate (a person or thing admired)

enamored (en am´ ərd) *v.* filled with love and desire; charmed

endeavor (en dev´ ər) *n.* earnest attempt or effort

enjoined (en joind´) *v.* directed or ordered to do something

enthralled (en thrôld´) *v.* held as in a spell; captivated

entrenched (en trencht´) *adj.* securely established; unmovable

enumerated (ē no͞o´ mər āt´ id) *v.* named one by one; specified, as in a list

equity (ek´ wit ē) *n.* quality of being equal or fair; fairness; justice

establish (ə stab´ lish) *v.* 1. set up; 2. prove; demonstrate

estimation (es´ tə mā´ shən) *n.* opinion; judgment

eulogy (yo͞o´ lə jē) *n.* speech in honor of someone who has died

evidence (ev´ ə dəns) *n.* anything that helps prove that something is true or not true

exchange (eks chānj´) 1. *n.* act of trading; 2. *v.* trade with another

exodus (eks´ ə dəs) *n.* departure from an area in large numbers

exemplify (eg zem´ plə fī´) *v.* show or illustrate by example

exile (ek´ sīl´) *v.* banish

explicit (eks plis´ it) *adj.* clearly and directly stated

F

fact (fakt) *n.* event or circumstance that has actually happened or is true

faltered (fôl´ tərd) *v.* acted hesitantly; showed uncertainty

famine (fam´ in) *n.* severe shortage of food

feasible (fē´ zə bəl) *adj.* capable of being done or carried out; practicable; possible

feeling (fēl´ iŋ) *n.* emotion

fertile (furt´ 'l) *adj.* rich in nutrients that promote growth

fester (fes´ tər) *v.* become infected; form pus

fickle (fik´ əl) *adj.* changeable

findings (fin´ diŋz) *n.* discoveries; results of an inquiry

formidable (fôr´ mə də bəl) *adj.* causing fear or dread

fortitude (fort´ ə to͞od´) *n.* strength of mind that lets one encounter danger or bear pain or adversity with courage

forum (fôr´ əm) *n.* assembly or situation that provides an opportunity for open discussion

fray (frā) *n.* noisy fight

futile (fyo͞ot´ 'l) *adj.* useless; hopeless

futility (fyo͞o til´ ə tē) *n.* quality of having no result or effect; uselessness

G

gallant (gal´ ənt) *adj.* brave and noble

grievance (grēv´ əns) *n.* injustice; complaint

grotesque (grō tesk´) *adj.* having a strange, bizarre design; shocking or offensive

H

hallowed (hal´ ōd) *adj.* sacred

haughty (hôt´ ē) *adj.* arrogant

hero (hir´ ō) *n.* person who is admired for brave or noble actions

honesty (än´ is tē) *n.* quality of being truthful

humble (hum´ bəl) *adj.* modest; having humility

I

ideals (ī dē´ əlz) *n.* 1. perfect forms, as of virtue, beauty, etc.; 2. guiding principles

identify (ī den´ tə fī´) *v.* recognize as being a particular person or thing

ignorance (ig´ nə rəns) *n.* lack of knowledge or education

illuminate (i lo͞o´ mə nāt´) *v.* make clear; explain

illustrate (il´ ə strāt´) *v.* 1. show clearly; 2. provide explanatory or decorative drawings

imitate (im´ i tāt´) *v.* copy the actions of another

immaculate (i mak´ yə lit) *adj.* perfectly correct or clean; without flaw, fault, or error

imminent (im´ ə nənt) *adj.* likely to happen soon

implicit (im plis´ it) *adj.* suggested or understood though not plainly expressed

implicitly (im plis´ it lē) *adv.* in a way that is understood without being clearly stated

implied (im plīd´) *adj.* suggested or understood without being directly expressed

imposition (im´ pə zish´ ən) *n.* introduction of something such as a rule, tax, or punishment

incognito (in´ käg nēt´ ō´) *adj.* with true identity unrevealed or disguised; under an assumed name

incongruity (in´ kän gro͞o´ i tē) *n.* state of being incompatible, inharmonious, or inconsistent

incredulity (in´ krə do͞o´ lə tē) *n.* unwillingness or inability to believe

indiscretion (in´ di skresh´ ən) *n.* action or remark that shows bad judgment and may offend someone

individuality (in´ də vij´ o͞o al´ ə tē) *n.* state of being one of a kind

indolently (in´ də lənt lē) *adv.* lazily; idly

indomitable (in däm´ i tə bəl) *adj.* impossible to subdue or discourage

inevitable (in ev´ i tə bəl) *adj.* certain to happen; incapable of being avoided

infallibility (in fal´ ə bil´ ə tē) *n.* condition of being unlikely to fail

information (in´ fər mā´ shən) *n.* facts or knowledge

informed (in fôrmd′) 1. *v.* gave someone information; 2. *adj.* having much knowledge, information, or education

insidious (in sid′ ē əs) *adj.* characterized by craftiness and betrayal

insight (in′ sīt′) *n.* clear understanding of the true inner nature of something

interaction (in′ tər ak′ shən) *n.* action on each other; reciprocal action or effect

instigates (in′ stə gātz′) *v.* urges on; stirs up

instinct (in′ stiŋkt′) *n.* inborn or natural behavior or response

intentions (in ten′ shənz) *n.* aims, ends, or purposes of someone's action or behavior

intercession (in′ tər sesh′ ən) *n.* act of pleading on another's behalf

intermission (in′ tər mish′ ən) *n.* any kind of break from an ongoing action; more specifically, a break during a performance

interpret (in tʉr′ prət) *v.* understand or explain the meaning of a concept or an idea

interpretation (in tʉr′ prə tā′ shən) *n.* explanation of the meaning of a concept or an idea

intimate (in′ tə mət) *adj.* private or personal

intolerable (in täl′ ər ə bəl) *adj.* impossible to put up with; unbearable

involvement (in välv′ mənt) *n.* 1. state of being included in something; 2. state of being engaged as a participant

issue (ish′ o͞o) *n.* subject for debate or discussion

J

jibed (jībd) *v.* changed direction

justice (jus′ tis) *n.* quality of fairness and impartiality; lawfulness; righteousness

K

kindred (kin′ drid) *n.* people to whom one is related by blood

L

lament (lə ment′) *v.* express deep sorrow; mourn

lamentable (lam′ en tə bəl; *often* lə men′ tə bəl) *adj.* distressing; sad

lexicon (lek′ si kän′) *n.* special vocabulary of a particular subject

literal (lit′ ər əl) *adj.* based on the actual words in their ordinary meaning; not figurative or symbolic

loathsome (lōth′ səm) *adj.* disgusting; detestable

lofty (lôf′ tē) *adj.* very high; noble

M

maladies (mal′ ə dēz) *n.* diseases

malodorous (mal ō′ dər əs) *adj.* having a bad smell

martial (mär′ shəl) *adj.* military; warlike

maudlin (môd′ lin) *adj.* tearfully and foolishly sentimental

meaning (mē′ niŋ) *n.* what is expressed, referred to, or understood; significance

mediate (mē′ dē āt′) *v.* attempt to bring about agreement between people who disagree

medium (mē′ dē əm) *n.* particular means of communicating information and news, such as a newspaper or a television broadcast

melancholy (mel′ ən käl′ ē) *adj.* sad; gloomy

metaphysical (met′ ə fiz′ i kəl) *adj.* spiritual; beyond the physical

minimize (min′ i mīz′) *v.* reduce in degree or importance

momentous (mō men′ təs) *adj.* very important

monotone (män′ ə tōn′) *n.* uninterrupted repetition of the same tone; utterance of successive syllables or words without change of pitch or key

monotonous (mə nät′ ′n əs) *adj.* unvarying; dull and uniform

morality (mō ral′ i tē) *n.* code of conduct; principles that a person uses to decide whether behavior is right or wrong

moribund (môr′ i bund′) *adj.* slowly dying

mortified (mort′ ə fīd′) *adj.* extremely embarrassed

motif (mō tēf′) *n.* repeated element or idea that has thematic importance, especially in a work of art, literature, or music

multitude (mul′ tə to͞od′) *n.* large number of people or things, especially when gathered together or considered as a unit

N

naive (nä ēv′) *adj.* unsophisticated

noteworthy (nōt′ wʉr′ *th*ē) *adj.* deserving of notice; outstanding

O

objective (əb jek′ tiv) *adj.* without bias; not influenced by personal feelings

obligation (äb′ li gā′ shən) *n.* something that must be done out of a sense of duty or as a result of law or tradition

oblivion (ə bliv′ ē ən) *n.* forgetfulness; state of being unconscious or unaware

obscures (əb skyo͝orz′) *v.* conceals; hides

obstinate (äb′ stə nət) *adj.* unreasonably determined; unyielding; stubborn

ominous (äm′ ə nəs) *adj.* threatening

oppression (ə presh′ ən) *n.* 1. keeping others down by the unjust use of power; 2. feeling of being weighed down with worries or problems

P

pallor (pal′ ər) *n.* unnatural paleness

palpable (pal′ pə bəl) *adj.* able to be felt; easily perceived

palpitating (pal′ pə tāt′ iŋ) *adj.* beating rapidly; throbbing

paradoxical (par′ ə däk′ si kəl) *adj.* seemingly full of contradictions

pensive (pen´ siv) *adj.* deeply thoughtful

penury (pen´ yo͞o rē) *n.* extreme poverty

pernicious (pər nish´ əs) *adj.* causing great injury or ruin

pervade (pər vād´) *v.* exist or be present throughout

perverse (pər vʉrs´) *adj.* different from what is considered right or reasonable

picturesque (pik´ chər esk´) *adj.* like or suggesting a picture; lovely to look at; attractive and interesting

pious (pī´ əs) *adj.* having or showing religious devotion

plundered (plun´ dərd) *v.* took goods by force; looted

poignant (poin´ yənt) *adj.* emotionally touching

pondered (pän´ dərd) *v.* thought deeply about

pose (pōz) *v.* put forward or propose, as in a question or a solution

precariously (prē ker´ ē əs lē) *adv.* in a risky way; insecurely

preceded (prē sēd´ əd) *v.* came before in time, place, order, rank, or importance

precluded (prē klo͞od´ əd) *v.* prevented

predominant (prē däm´ ə nənt) *adj.* having greater frequency, strength, or influence

prejudice (prej´ ə dis) *n.* strong opinion, often formed without good reason

presumed (prē zo͞omd´) *adj.* accepted as true, lacking proof to the contrary; supposed

pretentious (prē ten´ shəs) *adj.* grand in a showy way

prevail (prē vāl´) *v.* gain the advantage or mastery; be victorious; triumph

prevalence (prev´ ə ləns) *n.* state of being prevalent or happening often

prevalent (prev´ ə lənt) *adj.* widely existing

prime (prīm) *n.* in mathematics, any number greater than 1 that is not evenly divisible by any number other than 1 and itself

privations (prī vā´ shənz) *n.* state of being deprived of what is needed to survive

procure (prō kyoor´) *v.* get; obtain

prodigy (präd´ ə jē) *n.* person, especially a child, of extraordinary talent or ability

profound (prō found´) *adj.* deep; intense

profoundly (prō found´ lē) *adv.* deeply

progression (prō gresh´ ən) *n.* series of events that builds; sequence or succession

provocative (prə väk´ ə tiv) *adj.* exciting; stimulating

prudence (pro͞o´ dəns) *n.* sensible and careful attitude that makes you avoid some risks

psyche (sī´ kē) *n.* consciousness or mind

pungent (pun´ jənt) *adj.* producing a sharp smell

purged (pʉrjd) *v.* cleansed

R

rancor (raŋ´ kər) *n.* bitter hate

rationality (rash´ ə nal´ ə tē) *n.* quality of relying on reason or logic rather than emotion

react (rē´ akt´) *v.* act in response to something, such as an event, influence, etc.

realm (relm) *n.* area; region

reasoning (rē´ zən iŋ) *n.* process of drawing inferences or forming conclusions from known or assumed facts

recalcitrant (ri kal´ si trənt) *adj.* stubbornly defying control or authority

recoiling (ri koil´ iŋ) *v.* staggering back

relationship (ri lā´ shən ship´) *n.* connection between or among two or more people or things

remnants (rem´ nənts) *n.* what is left over; remainders

reprieve (ri prēv´) *n.* temporary relief or escape

requiem (rek´ wē əm) *n.* musical service in honor of the dead

research (rē´ sʉrch) 1. *n.* careful study in a field of knowledge; 2. *v.* perform careful study

resolution (rez´ ə lo͞o´ shən) *n.* 1. part of a narrative in which the plot is concluded; 2. solving or termination of a conflict; 3. decision about an action to take or not take

respite (res´ pit) *n.* rest; relief

respond (ri spänd´) *v.* reply or react

responsibility (ri span´ sə bil´ ə tē) *n.* 1. state of being accountable; 2. particular burden, task, or service a person or group is obliged to carry or fulfill

retort (ri tort´) *n.* sharp or clever reply

retribution (re´ trə byo͞o´ shən) *n.* payback; punishment for a misdeed

revelry (rev´ əl rē) *n.* noisy merrymaking

revered (ri vird´) *adj.* regarded with great respect and awe

reverie (rev´ ə rē) *n.* dreamy thinking and imagining

rife (rīf) *adj.* plentiful; prevalent

rifled (rī´ fəld) *v.* ransacked and robbed; searched quickly through a cupboard or drawer

S

sallow (sal´ ō) *adj.* of a sickly, pale-yellowish hue

scourge (skʉrj) *n.* instrument for inflicting punishment

scruples (skro͞o´ pəlz) *n.* misgivings about something one feels is wrong

senses (sens´ əz) 1. *n.* faculties of sight, hearing, touch, taste, and smell; 2. *v.* becomes aware of

sensory (sen´ sər ē) *adj.* relating to the senses of sight, sound, taste, touch, or smell

serve (sʉrv) *v.* perform duties or take on responsibilities for the benefit of others or for a higher purpose

siege (sēj) *n.* encirclement of a fortified place by an opposing armed force intending to take it

signaled (sig´ nəld) *v.* indicated or provided information

similarity (sim′ ə ler′ ə tē) *n.* state of being alike

skeptics (skep′ tiks) *n.* people who doubt accepted ideas

solicitude (sə lis′ ə to͞od′) *n.* state of being concerned; anxiety

solidarity (säl′ ə dar′ ə tē) *n.* unity based on common interests or purpose

sources (sôr′ sez) *n.* people, books, documents, etc. that provide information

squelching (skwelch′ iŋ) *v.* suppressing; silencing

stance (stans) *n.* attitude taken toward a particular situation or idea; position

standard (stan′ dərd) 1. *n.* basis for comparison; idea or thing by which other things are evaluated; 2. *adj.* normal; average

statistics (stə tis′ tiks) *n.* science of collecting, analyzing, and using mathematical data

status (stat′ əs) *n.* position or rank in relation to others

stirs (stʉrz) *v.* evokes; calls up

stout (stout) *adj.* sturdy

strategy (strat′ ə jē) *n.* plan or action

subjective (səb jek′ tiv) *adj.* modified or affected by personal views, experience, or background

subsided (səb sīd′ əd) *v.* settled down; became less active or intense

surmount (sər mount′) *v.* triumph over; overcome

survival (sər vī′ vəl) *n.* state of continuing to exist

symmetrical (si me′ tri kəl) *adj.* capable of being divided into identical halves

T

telegraph (tel′ ə graf′) *n.* apparatus or system that converts a coded message into electric impulses and sends it to a distant receiver

temporal (tem′ pə rəl) *adj.* having to do with time

trace (trās) *v.* describe the origins of something or the way it developed

transgression (trans gresh′ ən) *n.* wrongdoing; sin

treble (treb′ əl) *n.* high-pitched voice or sound

trundle (trun′ dəl) *v.* roll along

U

ultimately (ul′ tə mit lē) *adv.* finally; at last; in the end

underscores (un′ dər skôrz′) *v.* emphasizes

understanding (un′ dər stan′ diŋ) 1. *n.* ability to grasp meaning; ability to think or learn; 2. *adj.* having or characterized by comprehension, sympathy, etc.

unique (yo͞o nēk′) *adj.* one of a kind

universal (yo͞o′ nə vʉr′ səl) *adj.* existing everywhere

unwieldy (un wēl′ dē) *adj.* awkward; clumsy

usurped (yo͞o sʉrpt′) *v.* took power without right

V

values (val′ yo͞oz) *n.* moral principles or standards held by an individual or a group

vial (vī′ əl) *n.* small bottle containing medicine or other liquids

vigilant (vij′ ə lənt) *adj.* watchful and alert

visionary (vizh′ ən er′ ē) *adj.* having or marked by foresight and imagination

vivid (viv′ id) *adj.* 1. noticeably bright or intense, as of color, light, etc.; 2. strongly distinct; clear

volumes (väl′ yo͞omz) *n.* 1. books; 2. books that are either part of a set or combined into one; 3. organized sets of issues of a periodical published during a fixed period of time

voluminously (və lo͞o′ mə nəs lē) *adv.* fully; in great volume

W

wail (wāl) *n.* lament; cry of deep sorrow

war (wôr) *n.* 1. armed conflict between nations; 2. continuing state of hostility between individuals or groups

warp (wôrp) *v.* twist; distort

wayward (wā′ wərd) *adj.* headstrong

wisdom (wiz′ dəm) *n.* ability to make good judgments based on knowledge and experience

woeful (wō′ fəl) *adj.* full of sorrow

woes (wōz) *n.* great sorrows

writhing (rīth′ iŋ) *adj.* twisting; turning

Spanish Glossary

El vocabulario de Gran Pregunta aparece en **azul**.

A

abash / avergonzar *v.* apenar

accentuate / acentuar *v.* enfatizar una característica particular de algo o hacer que una cosa sea más notable

accentuated / acentuó *v.* enfatizó; realzó el efecto de

accept / aceptar *v.* recibir algo que se da

accrued / acumulado *v.* agregado o incrementado regularmente

adversary / adversario *s.* persona que se opone o lucha contra otra

advocate / defender *v.* escribir o hablar en defensa o apoyo de algo o alguien

afflicted / afligió *v.* que sufrió o padeció de

aggregate / agregado *adj.* juntado como un todo; global

align / alinear *v.* juntar con; estar de acuerdo con algo

allegedly / supuestamente *adv.* posiblemente cierto; no comprobado

aloofness / retraimiento *s.* calidad de estar distante o apartado

altruism / altruismo *s.* interés en el bienestar de otro sin que haya de por medio ningún beneficio personal

ambiguities / ambigüedades *s.* declaraciones o eventos cuyos significados no son claros

ambiguity / ambigüedad *s.* estado o cualidad de ser indefinido; vago

ambiguous / ambiguo *adj.* que tiene más de un significado

amicably / amigablemente *adv.* de manera amigable o amistosa

analyze / analizar *v.* examinar o estudiar en detalle para aprender más

ancestry / ascendencia *s.* la línea de la que uno desciende o conjunto de antepasados de una persona

anonymous / anónimo *adj.* que no tiene nombre conocido o nombre que se reconozca

antagonize / contrariar *v.* enemistar

antic / bufonesco *adj.* ridículo; absurdo

apex / cima *s.* punto más alto; cumbre

appreciate / apreciar *v.* reconocer el valor de algo

ardor / ardor *s.* pasión; entusiasmo

arduous / arduo *adj.* difícil; laborioso

argument / discusión *s.* intercambio de ideas cuando hay un desacuerdo

articulate / articular 1. v. expresar; 2. *adj.* capaz de expresarse claramente

articulated / articulado. *v.* claramente expresado

assertions / afirmaciones *s.* declaraciones positivas; aseveraciones

asserts / afirma *v.* declara; asevera

assimilated / asimiló *v.* ingirió o absorbió

assimilated / asimilado *adj.* algo o alguien que ha sido completamente absorbido

assuage / apaciguar *v.* calmar; sosegar

atonement / desagravio *s.* acción de enmendar algún agravio o perjuicio

augmenting / aumentando *v.* incrementando; haciendo más grande

authentic / auténtico *adj.* genuino; verdadero

aware / consciente *adj.* saber algo por haberlo experimentado o por haber sido informado de ello

B

background / antecedentes *s.* hechos o circunstancias que causan o explican algo

bafflement / desconcierto *s.* perplejidad; dificultad de comprensión

balmy / balsámico *adj.* que tiene las cualidades del bálsamo; apacible, suave, agradable

barren / árido *adj.* desértico; que tiene poca o ninguna vegetación

barrier / barrera *s.* obstáculo que previene o dificulta el paso

battle / batalla *s.* encuentro hostil entre dos fuerzas opuestas

battle / batallar *v.* pelear o luchar

beguiling / cautivar *v.* engañar; encantar

bemusing / desconcertante *v.* dejar perplejo; dejar confundido

benediction / bendición *s.* buena voluntad o bendición

benevolently / benévolamente *adv.* de manera bien intencionada

bereft / desprovisto *adj.* despojado, privado de

bias / predisposición *s.* inclinación o tendencia mental; parcialidad

bilingual / bilingüe *adj.* que usa dos idiomas

blight / plaga *s.* algo que destruye o impide el crecimiento

bravado / fanfarronería *s.* valentía falsa o jactancia desafiante

C

calculating / calculando *v.* determinando por medio de las matemáticas

candor / franqueza *s.* marcada honestidad o sinceridad al expresarse

caption / subtítulo *s.* información breve y descriptiva que acompaña una imagen, tales como una ilustración o una fotografía

cascade / cascada *s.* pequeño salto de agua empinado; cualquier cosa que se asemeje a un salto de agua

chaos / caos *s.* confusión total; desorden

character / carácter *s.* cualidades que hacen única a una persona

characterize / caracterizar *v.* describir expresando las cualidades principales de una persona o cosa

choices / alternativas *s.* opciones; una variedad de posibilidades entre las cuales una persona puede escoger

clarify / aclarar *v.* hacer que algo sea más claro y comprensible

class / clase *s.* grupo de personas consideradas como una unidad de acuerdo a su condición económica, ocupacional o social

colloquial / coloquial *adj.* conversacional, informal o familiar

communication / comunicación *s.* intercambio de información

compelling / irresistible *adj.* extremadamente interesante o atractivo; cautivador

compensation / compensación 1. *s.* cualquier cosa que paga por una pérdida, daño o deuda; 2. mecanismo por el cual un individuo busca minimizar un defecto real o imaginario

compete / competir *v.* tratar de ganarle a un oponente; esforzarse por superar a otro

competition / competencia *s.* rivalidad; acción de competir

composition / composición *s.* arreglo de elementos en una obra de arte

comprehend / comprender *v.* entender

comprehension / comprensión *s.* acción de entender algo

comprehension / comprensión *s.* entendimiento

comprise / componerse de *v.* conformar; formar

concept / concepto *s.* idea; noción

concessions / concesiones *s.* cosas otorgadas o cedidas como privilegios

concise / conciso *adj.* breve y directo

conduct / conducta *s.* la forma en la que uno actúa; comportamiento

confines / confines *s.* zona encerrada por fronteras; límite

conformity / conformidad *s.* actuar de acuerdo a las costumbres, reglas o actitudes aceptadas

connection / conexión *s.* unión de dos o más cosas o ideas

consider / considerar *v.* pensar acerca de algo para entender o tomar una decisión

consult / consultar *v.* mirar o referirse a algo para obtener información

contempt / desprecio *s.* desdén o menosprecio

contradictory / contradictorio *adj.* que afirma lo contrario

controversy / controversia *s.* discusión de un asunto en el que chocan las opiniones divergentes

cooperate / cooperar *v.* trabajar juntos para lograr un objetivo común

counteract / contrarrestar *v.* actuar en oposición a; neutralizar

credentials / credenciales *s.* documento que muestra el derecho que se tiene de ejercer poder; certificación

creed / credo *s.* declaración de creencias

critical / crítico *adj.* importante; crucial

critique / crítica *s.* análisis crítico de un tema

crystallize / cristalizar *v.* tomar forma definitiva

culture / cultura *s.* ideas, costumbres, habilidades y arte de un grupo de personas que viven en un lugar y tiempo determinados

cunning / astuto *adj.* que tiene habilidad para engañar

curtailed / restringió *v.* acortó; redujo

D

daunting / amedrentador *adj.* intimidante

defaulted / incumplió *v.* dejó de hacer algo o no compareció en alguna parte cuando era requerido o esperado; faltó a un pago a su vencimiento

defend / defender *v.* proteger contra ataques

deferred / difirió *v.* postergó a una fecha futura

defiance / desafío *s.* franca y descarada resistencia a la autoridad

defrauded / estafó *v.* enganó

degenerate / degenerar *v.* empeorar

dejection / desaliento *s.* desánimo; depresión

delirium / delirio *s.* disturbio mental cuyos síntomas incluyen la confusión, problemas para hablar y alucinaciones

demonstrative / demostrativo *adj.* que muestra los sentimientos abiertamente

demure / reservado *adj.* modesto

depicted / representado *v.* recreado en un dibujo, pintura, escultura o en cualquier obra de arte

depicts / representa *v.* recrea en un dibujo, pintura, escultura o en cualquier obra de arte

depravity / depravación *s.* deshonestidad; corrupción

depreciate / depreciar *v.* disminuir su valor

determine / determinar *v.* ocasionar que algo ocurra de cierta forma

detract / restar *v.* quitar algo deseable; hacer inferior

devastation / devastación *s.* destrucción

differences / diferencias *s.* características que hacen que las cosas sean disímiles; maneras en que las cosas no son iguales

differentiate / diferenciar *v.* percibir o expresar diferencias entre dos o más cosas

dilapidated / desmoronado *adj.* ruinoso

discerning / perspicaz *adj.* tener buen juicio o comprensión

disclosed / divulgó *v.* reveló; hizo público

discreet / discreto *adj.* cuidadoso con lo que dice o hace; prudente; que calla o mantiene confidencias cuando es necesario

discreetly / discretamente *adv.* sin llamar la atención

discrepancy / discrepancia *s.* diferencia; desacuerdo

discriminate / discriminar *v.* distinguir las diferencias entre las cosas; actuar en contra de alguien por prejuicio

discuss / discutir *v.* hablar sobre algo

disgrace / deshonra *s.* pérdida del respeto, honor, o estima; vergüenza

disheveled / desordenado *adj.* desarreglado

dishevelment / desorden *s.* desarreglo; desaseo

dismal / melancólico *adj.* que ocasiona tristeza o desolación

dispatched / despachó *v.* terminó con prontitud

disperse / dispersar *v.* romper y desparramar en todas direcciones; esparcir; distribuir ampliamente

disproportionately / desproporcionadamente *adv.* fuera de toda proporción o injusto

dissemble / disimular *v.* ocultar la verdad; fingir

disseminating / diseminando *v.* esparciendo o regando por todas partes

dissension / disensión *s.* desacuerdo; diferencia de opinión

distinct / distinto *adj.* visto o comprendido como algo diferente o separado de los demás

distinction / distinción *s.* diferencia

diverged / bifurcó *v.* ramificó en diferentes direcciones

domestic / doméstico *adj.* que tiene que ver con hogar, casa o familia

duration / duración *s.* el tiempo en que algo continúa o permanece

E

effective / efectivo *adj.* que produce un resultado definido o deseado

elaborate /elaborar *v. desarrollar* en detalle

elevated / elevado *adj.* alzado; a una altura superior

elixir / elixir *s.* sustancia que se cree que da vida o la prolonga

eloquence / elocuencia *s.* elegancia y persuasión en el discurso o la escritura

embellishes / adorna *v.* mejora; agrega decoración

embodiment / encarnación *s.* representación de una idea en forma visible

embody / encarnar *v.* representar o personificar

emigration / emigración *s.* dejar uno su lugar de residencia o país para ir a vivir a otro lado

empathy / empatía *s.* capacidad de comprender y compartir los sentimientos de otra persona

emphasize / enfatizar *v.* dar importancia a algo; subrayar

empirical / empírico *adj.* basado en observaciones y experimentos en lugar de teorías

emulate / emular *v.* imitar

enamored / enamoró *v.* lleno de amor y deseo; encantado

endeavor / intento *s.* tentativa o esfuerzo formal

enjoined / ordenó *v.* se le obligó o mandó a hacer algo

enthralled / embelesó *v.* mantuvo como hechizado; cautivó

entrenched / arraigado *adj.* firmemente establecido; que mantiene su posición, ideas o actitud con firmeza

enumerated / enumeró *v.* nombró uno a uno; especificó, como en una lista

equity / equidad *s.* la cualidad de ser igual o justo; justicia; imparcialidad

establish / establecer *v.* 1. probar; demostrar 2. crear

estimation / estimación *s.* opinión; juicio

eulogy / panegírico *s.* discurso en honor a alguien que ha muerto

evidence / evidencia *s.* información utilizada para apoyar o probar la verdad o el valor de una idea

exchange / intercambio *s.* acción de comerciar algo

exchange / intercambiar *v.* comerciar

exemplify / ejemplificar *v.* mostrar o ilustrar con un ejemplo

exile / exiliar *v.* desterrar

exodus / éxodo *s.* partida o emigración de un lugar de gran número de personas

explicit / explícito *adj.* expresado con claridad

F

fact / hecho *s.* suceso o circunstancia que ha pasado realmente o que es verdadero

faltered / titubeó *v.* actuó de forma vacilante; mostró incertidumbre; flaqueó; se acobardó

famine / hambruna *s.* escasez severa de alimentos

feasible / factible *adj.* capaz de hacerse o realizarse; viable; posible

feeling / sentimiento *s.* emoción

fertile / fértil *adj.* rico en nutrientes que promueven el crecimiento

fester / enconar *v.* infectar; formar pus

fickle / voluble *adj.* cambiante

findings / hallazgos *s.* descubrimientos; resultados de una investigación

formidable / formidable *adj.* que causa temor o asombro

fortitude / fortaleza *s.* fuerza mental que permite que uno se enfrente a peligros o permite soportar dolor o adversidad con valentía

forum / fórum *s.* asamblea o situación que provee una oportunidad para llevar a cabo una discusión abierta acerca de un tema

fray / refriega *s.* pelea escandalosa

futile / fútil *adj.* inútil; sin remedio

futility / inutilidad *s.* cualidad de no dar resultado o tener efecto; cualidad de inútil

G

gallant / gallardo *adj.* valiente y noble

grievance / agravio *s.* circunstancia injusta que da motivo para sentir resentimiento; queja

grotesque / grotesco *adj.* que tiene un diseno extrano, raro; extrano o inusual de manera tal que resulta repugnante u ofensivo

H

hallowed / santificado *adj.* sagrado

haughty / altanero *adj.* arrogante

hero / héroe *s.* alguien a quien se admira por sus acciones valientes o nobles

honesty / honestidad *s.* cualidad de ser sincero

humble / humilde *adj.* modesto; que tiene humildad

I

ideals / ideales *s.* 1. formas perfectas tales como virtud, belleza, etc.; 2. principios que guian

identify / identificar *v.* describir lo que es una persona o cosa

ignorance / ignorancia *s.* falta de conocimiento o educación

illuminate / iluminar *v.* aclarar; explicar

illustrate / ilustrar *v.* 1. mostrar claramente; 2. proveer dibujos para explicar algo o para decorar

imitate / imitar *v.* copiar las acciones de otro

immaculate / impecable *adj.* en perfectas condiciones; sin defectos, faltas o errores

imminent / inminente *adj.* que probablemente ocurrirá pronto

implicit / implícito *adj.* sugerido o entendido pero que no ha sido expresado directamente

implicitly / implícitamente *adv.* de una manera que se entiende sin haber sido expresado directamente

implied / sobreentendido *adj.* sugerido o dado a entender sin haber sido expresado directamente

imposition / imposición *s.* introducción de algo como una norma, impuesto o castigo

incognito / incógnito *adj.* que oculta su verdadera identidad; que asume otro nombre para no ser reconocido

incongruity / incongruencia *s.* algo incompatible, inarmónico o inconsistente

incredulity / incredulidad *s.* renuencia o incapacidad para creer

indiscretion / indiscreción *s.* acción o comentario que demuestra falta de tacto y que puede ofender a alguien

individuality / individualidad *s.* estado de ser diferente de los demás; originalidad

indolently / indolentemente *adv.* con pereza; ociosamente

indomitable / indomable *adj.* imposible de someter o reprimir

inevitable / inevitable *adj.* que va a ocurrir con certeza; incapaz de ser evitado

infallibility / infalibilidad *s.* condición de que no puede fallar

information / información *s.* hechos o conocimientos sobre algo

informed / informado *adj.* que tiene mucho conocimiento, información o educación

informed / informó *v.* le dio información a alguien

insidious / insidioso *adj.* que se caracteriza por su astucia y traición

insight / percepción *s.* conocimiento profundo de la verdadera naturaleza interior de algo

interaction / interacción *s.* acción del uno sobre el otro; acción o efecto recíproco

instigates / instiga *v.* fomenta; promueve

instinct / instinto *s.* conducta o respuesta con la que se nace

intentions / intenciones *s.* objetivos o propósitos de una acción

intercession / intercesión *s.* acción de abogar por otra persona

intermission / intermedio *s.* cualquier tipo de interrupción de alguna acción continua; más específicamente, una pausa durante una presentación

interpret / interpretar *v.* entender o explicar el significado de algo

interpretation / interpretación *s.* explicación del significado de algo

intimate / íntimo *adj.* privado o personal

intolerable / intolerable *adj.* que no se puede resistir; insoportable

involvement / participación *s.* 1. estar incluido en algo; 2. tomar parte en algo

issue / asunto *s.* tema para debate o discusión

J

jibed / viró *v.* cambió de dirección

justice / justicia *s.* cualidad de equidad e imparcialidad; ley; rectitud

K

kindred / parientes *s.* personas a las que uno está relacionado por vínculos de sangre

L

lament / lamentar *v.* expresar profunda tristeza; penar

lamentable / lamentable *adj.* angustioso; penoso

lexicon / léxico *s.* vocabulario especial de un tema en particular

literal / literal *adj.* basado en el significado común de las palabras, no en sentido figurado ni simbólico

loathsome / odioso *adj.* repugnante; detestable

lofty / elevado *adj.* muy alto; noble

M

maladies / dolencias *s.* enfermedades

malodorous / maloliente *adj.* que tiene mal olor

martial / marcial *adj.* de corte militar

maudlin / llorón *adj.* lloroso y tontamente sentimental

meaning /significado *s.* lo que es expresado, representado o comprendido; sentido

mediate / mediar *v.* interceder para que las partes que están en desacuerdo lleguen a un acuerdo

medium / medio *s.* manera particular de comunicar información y noticias a la gente, como un periódico o un programa de televisión

melancholy / melancolía *s.* tristeza; pesimismo

metaphysical / metafísico *adj.* espiritual; que traspasa lo físico

minimize / minimizar *v.* reducir en grado o en importancia

momentous / trascendental *adj.* muy importante

monotone / monotonía *s.* repetición ininterrumpida de un mismo tono; pronunciación de sílabas o palabras sucesivas sin cambiar el tono o tonalidad

monotonous / monótono *adj.* repetición constante del mismo tono; hablar sin cambiar de entonación

morality / moralidad *s.* código de conducta; principios que una persona utiliza para definir si un comportamiento es correcto o no

moribund / moribundo *adj.* que muere lentamente

mortified / avergonzado *adj.* extremadamente humillado

motif / motivo *s.* elemento o idea repetida que tiene una importancia temática, especialmente en una obra de arte, en la literatura o en la música

multitude / multitud *s.* gran cantidad de personas o cosas, especialmente cuando se juntan o se consideran una unidad

N

naive / ingenuo *adj.* poco sofisticado; inocente

noteworthy / notable *adj.* digno de ser notado; sobresaliente

O

objective / objetivo *adj.* imparcial; que no está influenciado por sentimientos personales

obligation / obligación *s.* algo que debe hacerse por deber o como resultado de una ley o tradición

oblivion / olvido *s.* falta de memoria; condición de estar inconsciente o inadvertido de lo que ocurre

obscures / oscurece *v.* oculta; esconde

obstinate / obstinado *adj.* decidido de una manera irrazonable; terco; inflexible

ominous / siniestro *adj.* amenazante

oppression / opresión *s.* sensación de estar agobiado o reprimido por preocupaciones, problemas o el uso injusto del poder

P

pallor / palidez *s.* lividez poco natural

palpable / palpable *adj.* capaz de sentirse; percibido con facilidad

palpitating / palpitante *adj.* que late rápidamente; que pulsa

paradoxical / paradójico *adj.* aparentemente lleno de contradicciones

pensive / pensativo *adj.* que reflexiona profunda o seriamente

penury / penuria *s.* extrema pobreza

pernicious / pernicioso *adj.* que causa gran perjuicio o ruina; destructivo

pervade / impregnar *v.* existir o estar presente de manera total

perverse / perverso *adj.* distinto de lo que se considera correcto o razonable

picturesque / pintoresco *adj.* que sugiere o que se parece a una pintura; hermoso a la vista

pious / piadoso *adj.* que tiene o muestra fervor religioso

plundered / saqueó *v.* que tomó mercancías por la fuerza; robó

poignant / conmovedor *adj.* que suscita emociones

pondered / sopesó *v.* consideró profundamente

pose / plantear *v.* presentar o proponer, como por ejemplo una pregunta o una solución

precariously / precariamente *adv.* de forma insegura

preceded / precedió *v.* que estaba antes en tiempo, lugar, orden, rango o importancia

precluded / impidió *v.* imposibilitó

predominant / predominante *adj.* que tiene influencia dominante sobre otros

prejudice / prejuicio *s.* opinión fuerte a menudo formada sin una buena razón

presumed / supuesto *adj.* dado por sentado; aceptado como cierto, a falta de prueba de lo contrario; asumido

pretentious / pretencioso *adj.* magnífico de manera ostentosa

prevail / prevalecer *v.* obtener la ventaja o el dominio; salir victorioso; triunfar

prevalence / prevalencia *s.* el estado de ser prevalente o de que pase con frecuencia

prevalent / prevalente *adj.* frecuente, persistente

prime / número primo *s.* en las matemáticas, cualquier número mayor que 1 que es divisible sólo por 1 o por sí mismo

privations / privaciones *s.* falta o escasez de las cosas que se necesitan para sobrevivir

procure / procurar *v.* lograr; obtener

prodigy / prodigio *s.* persona, por lo general un niño, que posee una habilidad o un talento extraordinarios

profound / profundo *adj.* hondo; intenso

profoundly / profundamente *adv.* intensamente

progression / progresión *s.* una serie de sucesos, secuencia o sucesión

provocative / provocativo *adj.* excitante; estimulante

prudence / prudencia *s.* actitud racional y cuidadosa; economía

psyche / psique *s.* conciencia o mente

pungent / acre *adj.* que produce un olor penetrante

purged / depuró *v.* purificó

R

rancor / rencor *s.* odio implacable

rationality / racionalidad *s.* cualidad de depender de la razón o de la lógica en lugar de las emociones

react / reaccionar *v.* actuar en respuesta a algo, por ejemplo un suceso, influencia etc.

realm / reino *s.* área, terreno

reasoning / razonamiento *s.* proceso de hacer inferencias o sacar conclusiones de datos conocidos o asumidos

recalcitrant / recalcitrante *adj.* que desafía la autoridad o control en forma terca y obstinada

recoiling / retrocediendo *v.* dando marcha atrás

relationship / relación *s.* conexión entre dos o más personas o cosas

remnants / remanentes *s.* sobrantes; restos

reprieve / respiro *s.* descanso o alivio temporal

requiem / réquiem *s.* composición musical en honor a los muertos

research / investigación *s.* estudio profundo en algún campo del conocimiento

research / investigar *v.* realizar estudio profundo

resolution / resolución *s.* solución o culminación de un conflicto

resolution / clímax *s.* parte de una narrativa en la cual se resuelve el conflicto o la trama

respite / respiro *s.* descanso; alivio

respond / responder *v.* contestar o reaccionar

responsibility / responsabilidad *s.* 1. obligación de responder ante ciertos actos; 2. una tarea o un servicio que una persona o grupo debe cumplir

retort / réplica *s.* respuesta cortante o astuta

retribution / castigo *s.* restitución; escarmiento por una falta cometida

revelry / parranda *s.* fiesta ruidosa

revered / venerado *adj.* tratado con gran respeto y admiración

reverie / ensueño *s.* pensamiento e imaginación sonadora

rife / abundante *adj.* lleno; repleto

rifled / desvalijó *v.* saqueó y robó; buscó rápidamente en un armario o gaveta

S

sallow / amarillento *adj.* de color enfermizo, pálido macilento

scourge / azote *s.* instrumento para imponer un castigo

scruples / escrúpulos *s.* dudas sobre algo que uno siente que es incorrecto

senses / sentidos *s.* la vista, el oído, el olfato, el gusto, el tacto

senses / siente *v.* está consciente de

sensory / sensorial *adj.* relativo a los sentidos de la vista, oído, gusto, tacto y olfato

serve / servir *v.* desempeñar deberes o tomar responsabilidades para el beneficio de otros o para un propósito mayor

siege / asedio *s.* un área cercada por una fuerza enemiga armada

signaled /señaló *v.* indicó o dio información

similarity / similitud *s.* condición de ser parecidos

skeptics / escépticos *s.* gente que no cree o duda de ideas aceptadas por otros

solicitude / desvelo *s.* estado de estar preocupado por algo; ansiedad

solidarity / solidaridad *s.* unidad generada a partir de un interés o propósito en común

sources / fuentes *s.* personas, libros, documentos etc. que dan información

squelching / silenciar *v.* suprimir o callar

stance / postura *s.* actitud tomada frente a una situación o idea en particular; posición

standard / estándar 1. *s.* base de comparación; idea o cosa que sirve para evaluar otras; 2. *adj.* normal; promedio

statistics / estadísticas *s.* ciencia de recoger, analizar y usar datos matemáticos

status / estatus *s.* posición o rango con relación a otros

stirs / provoca *v.* evoca; despierta

stout / sólido *adj.* robusto

strategy / estrategia *s.* plan o acción

subjective / sujetivo *adj.* afectado por puntos de vista o experiencias personales

subsided / disminuyó *v.* se calmó; se volvió menos activo o intenso

surmount / superar *v.* triunfar sobre algo; vencer

survival / supervivencia *s.* condición de continuar existiendo

symmetrical / simétrico *adj.* que puede ser dividido en dos partes iguales

T

telegraph / telégrafo *s.* aparato o sistema que utiliza un código para convertir mensajes en impulsos eléctricos y transmitirlos a distancia

temporal / temporal *adj.* que tiene que ver con el tiempo

trace / rastrear *v.* describir el origen de algo o la forma en que fue desarrollado

transgression / transgresión *s.* infracción; pecado

treble / tiple *s.* voz o sonido muy agudo

trundle / rodar con dificultad *v.* avanzar en ruedas lentamente

U

ultimately / últimamente *adv.* finalmente; por fin; al final

underscore / enfatizar *v.* subrayar

understanding / entendimiento *s.* capacidad de comprender el significado de algo; capacidad para pensar o aprender; comprensión

understanding / comprensivo *adj.* que se caracteriza por su simpatía y tolerancia

unique / único *adj.* exclusivo

universal / universal *adj.* que existe en todas partes

unwieldy / abultado *adj.* incómodo; torpe

usurped / usurpó *v.* tomó poder sin tener derecho

V

values / valores *s.* principios morales o estándares aceptados por un individuo o grupo

vial / frasco *s.* envase pequeno que contiene medicamento u otros líquidos

vigilant / vigilante *adj.* atento y alerto

visionary / visionario *adj.* que tiene gran imaginación y visión del futuro

vivid / vívido *adj.* 1. muy brillante o intenso, como por ejemplo cuando se habla del color, la luz etc.; 2. que se distingue de forma intensa, claro

volumes / volúmenes *s.* conjunto de números de una publicación periódica dentro de un tiempo determinado, usualmente un año; 2. libros

voluminously / voluminosamente *adv.* completamente; de gran volumen

W

wail / gemido *s.* lamento; grito de profundo dolor

war / guerra *s.* 1. conflicto armado entre naciones; 2. estado continuo de hostilidad entre grupos o individuos

warp / torcer *v.* retorcer; distorsionar

wayward / rebelde *adj.* obstinado; desobediente

wisdom / sabiduría *s.* capacidad de emitir buenos juicios con base en el conocimiento y la experiencia

woeful / afligido *adj.* lleno de dolor

woes / aflicciones *s.* grandes tristezas

writhing / retorcer *v.* contorsionar; serpentear

Index of Skills

Literary Analysis

Comprehension Skills

Writing

Applications

Process

Rubrics for Self-Assessment

Speaking and Listening

Activities

Strategies

Research

Activities

Strategies

Language Conventions

Vocabulary

Assessment

Index of Authors and Titles

The following authors and titles appear in the print and online versions of Pearson Literature.

Additional Selections: Author and Title Index

The following authors and titles appear in the Online Literature Library.

Acknowledgments

Grateful acknowledgment is made to the following for copyrighted material:

The Academy of American Poets "Emily Dickinson Poetfans" by Sharyn Moore from *http://poets.org/viewmedia.php/prmMID/19605.* Copyright © 1997-2007 by The Academy of American Poets. Used by permission of the Academy of American Poets.

American Broadcasting Companies, Inc. "No. 42 Jackie Robinson" by John Nadel from *http://abcnews.go.com/Sports/wireStory?id=3044174.* Copyright © 2007 ABCNews Internet Ventures. Used courtesy of ABC News.

American Psychological Association (APA) "Majority Responses to Standard and Comparison Lines on Successive Trials" by Solomon Asch, in Psychological Monographs. Copyright © 2012. The American Psychological Association.

Arte Publico Press, Inc. "A Voice" by Pat Mora from *Communion* by Pat Mora. Copyright © 1991 Arte Publico Press—University of Houston. Used by permission of the publisher.

Ballantine Books "New Road Chicken Pies" from *The Book Lover's Cookbook* by Shaunda Kennedy Wenger and Janet Kay Jensen. Copyright © 2003 by Shaunda Kennedy Wenger and Janet Kay Jensen. Used by permission of Ballantine Books, a division of Random House, Inc.

Bantam Doubleday Dell Publishing "Tell Me a Riddle" by Tillie Olsen from *Delta Book, Doubleday.* "Things Fall Apart" by Chinua Achebe from *Anchor Books, Doubleday.* All rights reserved.

Susan Bergholz Literary Services "Twister Hits Houston" from *My Wicked Wicked Ways* by Sandra Cisneros. Copyright © 1987 by Sandra Cisneros. Published by Third Woman Press and in hardcover by Alfred A. Knopf. From *A Celebration of Grandfathers* by Rudolfo Anaya. Copyright © 1983 by Rudolfo Anaya. First published in New Mexico Magazine, March 1983. "My English" by Julia Alvarez from *Something to Declare* by Julia Alvarez. Published by Plume, an imprint of Penguin Group (USA), in 1999 and originally in hardcover by Algonquin Books of Chapel Hill. Copyright © 1998 by Julia Alvarez. Used by permission of Third Woman Press and Susan Bergholz Literary Services, New York, NY and Lamy, NM. All rights reserved.

Gary I. Blackwood From *The Shakespeare Stealer* by Gary I. Blackwood. Copyright © 2003 by Gary I. Blackwood. Used by permission of the author.

Tyroneca Booker "The Day of the Storm" by Ty Booker from *Katrina, In Their Own Words* edited by Richard Louth. All works copyrighted © 2006 by the individual authors. Southeastern Louisiana Writing Project, Publisher. Southeastern Louisiana University, Hammond, Louisiana, 70402. Used by permission of Tyroneca Booker.

Georges Borchardt, Inc. "The Glass Menagerie" by Tennessee Williams. Copyright © 1945, renewed 1973 by The University of the South. Reprinted by permission.

Brandt & Hochman Literary Agents, Inc. "The Most Dangerous Game" from *The Most Dangerous Game* by Richard Connell. Copyright © 1924 by Richard Connell. Copyright renewed © 1952 by Louise Fox Connell. "Sonata For Harp and Bicycle" from *The Green Flash and Other Tales of Horror* by Joan Aiken. Copyright © 1957, 1958, 1959, 1960, 1965, 1968, 1969, 1971 by Joan Aiken. Used by permission of Brandt & Hochman Literary Agents, Inc. Any copying or redistribution of the text is expressly forbidden.

Brooks Permissions "The Assassination of John F. Kennedy" by Gwendolyn Brooks in *Words of Protest, Words of Freedom.* Copyright © 2012. Reprinted by consent of Brooks Permissions.

Curtis Brown, Ltd. "Uncoiling" by Pat Mora. First appeared in *Daughters of the Fifth Sun*, published by Riverhead Press. Copyright © 1995. Used by permission of Curtis Brown, Ltd.

The Bukowski Agency "The Jade Peony" by Wayson Choy. First published in the *UBC Alumni Chronicle*, Vol. 34, No. 4, Winter 1979. Copyright by Wayson Choy 1977. The novel *The Jade Peony*, based on this story, is published in the United States by The Other Press. Used by permission of The Bukowski Agency.

Jonathan Clowes Ltd. "The Red-headed League" from *The Adventures of Sherlock Holmes* by Sir Arthur Conan Doyle. Copyright © 1996 Sir Arthur Conan Doyle Copyright Holders. Used by kind permission of Jonathan Clowes Ltd., London, on behalf of Andrea Plunket, the Administrator of the Sir Arthur Conan Doyle Copyrights.

Don Congdon Associates, Inc. "The Golden Kite, the Silver Wind" by Ray Bradbury from *Epoch*, February 1953. Copyright © 1953 by Epoch Associates; renewed 1981 by Ray Bradbury. Used by permission of Don Congdon Associates, Inc.

Catherine Costello "There is No Word For Goodbye" by Mary Tall Mountain from *There Is No Word for Goodbye: Poems by Mary Tall Mountain.* Copyright © 1994 by Tall Mountain Estate. Used by permission of Catherine Costello. All rights reserved.

Dell Publishing, a div of Random House, Inc. From *The Giant's House* by Elizabeth McCracken, copyright © 1996 by Elizabeth McCracken. Used by permission of The Dial Press/Dell Publishing, a division of Random House, Inc.

Dunow Carlson Lerner Agency "Desiderata" by Elizabeth McCracken from *http://www.randomhouse.com/boldtype/0397/mccracken/.* Copyright © 1996 by Elizabeth McCracken. Used by permission of Dunow Carlson Lerner Agency.

Stephen Edwards "Rock Climbing Equipment and Techniques" by Stephen Edwards from *http://alumnus.caltech.edu/~sedwards/climbing/techniques.html.* Used by permission of Stephen Edwards.

Faber and Faber Limited "The Horses" by Edwin Muir from *Collected Poems by Edwin Muir*, copyright © 1960 by Willa Muir. "Macavity: The Mystery Cat" by T. S. Eliot from *Old Possum's Book of Practical Cats* by T. S. Eliot. Copyright © 1939 by T. S. Eliot and renewed 1967 by Esme Valerie Eliot. Used by permission of Faber and Faber Limited.

Farrar, Straus & Giroux, LLC "Prologue and Epilogue" by Derek Walcott from *The Odyssey: A Stage Version* by Derek Walcott. Copyright © 1993 by Derek Walcott. "The Washwoman" by Isaac Bashevis Singer from *A Day of Pleasure* by Isaac Bachevis Singer. Copyright © 1969 by Isaac Bashevis Singer. "Part 1: The Adventures of Odysseus" and "Part 2: The Return of Odysseus" from *The Odyssey* by Homer, translated by Robert Fitzgerald. Copyright © 1961, 1963 by Robert Fitzgerald. Copyright renewed 1989 by Benedict R. C. Fitzgerald, on behalf of the Fitzgerald children. Used with permission of Farrar, Straus and Giroux, LLC.

Folkways Music Publishers "Instead of an Elegy" by G.S. Fraser in *Of Poetry and Power: Poems Occasioned by the Presidency and by the Death of John F. Kennedy.* Copyright © 1965. Folkways Music Publishers, Inc.

Graywolf Press "Fifteen" from *The Way It Is: New and Selected Poems* by William Stafford. Copyright © 1966, 1998 by the Estate of William Stafford. Used by permission of Graywolf Press, Saint Paul, MN.

Greenwillow Books "Sally Ann Thunder Ann Whirlwind Crockett" by Caron Lee Cohen. Text copyright © 1985. Greenwillow Books.

Harcourt Education Limited "The Girl Who Can" by Ama Ata Aidoo from *Opening Spaces: An Anthology of Contemporary African Women's Writing*, edited by Yvonne Vera. Used by permission of Harcourt Education.

Harcourt, Inc. "The Writer" from *The Mind-Reader* by Richard Wilbur. Copyright © 1971 by Richard Wilbur. "Women" by Alice Walker from *Revolutionary Petunias & Other Poems*, copyright © 1970 and renewed 1998 by Alice Walker. From *A Lincoln Preface*, copyright 1953 by Carl Sandburg and renewed 1981 by Margaret Sandburg, Janet Sandburg, and Helga Sandburg Crile. "Macavity: The Mystery Cat" from *Old Possum's Book of Practical Cats* by T. S. Eliot. Copyright 1939 by T. S. Eliot and renewed 1967 by Esme Valerie Eliot. "Ithaca" by Constantine Cavafy from *The Complete Poems of Cavafy.* English translation copyright © 1961 and renewed 1989 by Rae Dalven. Used by permission of Harcourt, Inc. This material may not be reproduced in any form or by any means without the prior written permission of the publisher.

HarperCollins Publishers, Inc. "Summer" from *Brown Angels: An Album of Pictures and Verse* by Walter Dean Myers. Copyright © 1993 by Walter Dean Myers. Used by permission of HarperCollins Publishers.

Harvard University Press "Much madness is divinest sense" from *The Poems of Emily Dickinson*, Thomas H. Johnson, ed., Cambridge, Mass.: The Belknap Press of Harvard University Press, Copyright © 1951, 1955, 1979, 1983 by the President and Fellows of Harvard College. Used by permission of the publishers and the Trustees of Amherst College. Reprinted by permission of the publishers and the Trustees of Amherst College from *The Poems of Emily Dickinson*, Thomas H. Johnson, ed., Cambridge, Mass.: The Belknap Press of Harvard University Press, Copyright (c) 1951, 1955, 1979, 1983 by the President and Fellows of Harvard College.

David Hilbun "Hope" by David Hilbun from *Katrina, In Their Own Words* edited by Richard Louth. All works copyrighted © 2006 by the individual authors. Southeastern Louisiana Writing Project, Publisher. Southeastern Louisiana University, Hammond, Louisiana, 70402. Used by permission of David Hilbun.

Helmut Hirnschall "There is a Longing . . ." by Chief Dan George & Helmut Hirnschall from *My Heart Soars.* Copyright © 1974 by Chief Dan George and Helmut Hirnschall. Used by permission of Helmut Hirnschall.

The Barbara Hogenson Agency, Inc. "The Secret Life of Walter Mitty" by James Thurber from *My World—And Welcome To It.* Copyright © 1942 by James Thurber. Copyright © renewed 1970 by Rosemary A. Thurber. Used by permission from The Barbara Hogenson Agency, Inc.

Henry Holt and Company, Inc. "Talk" by Harold Courlander and George Herzog from *The Cow-Tail Switch and Other West African Stories* by Harold Courlander and George Herzog, © 1947, 1974 by Harold Courlander. "Fire and Ice" by Robert Frost from *The Poetry of Robert Frost*, edited by Edward Connery Lathem. Copyright © 1951 by Robert Frost. Used by permission of Henry Holt and Company, LLC.

Houghton Mifflin Company, Inc. "Siren Song" from *Selected Poems, 1965-1975* by Margaret Atwood. Copyright © 1976 by Margaret Atwood. Excerpt from "A Fable for Tomorrow" from *Silent Spring* by Rachel Carson. Copyright © 1962 by Rachel I. Carson, renewed 1990 by Roger Christie. "All Watched Over by Machines of Loving Grace" from *The Pill Versus the Springhill Mine Disaster* by Richard Brautigan. Copyright © 1968 by Richard Brautigan. Used by permission of Houghton Mifflin Company. All rights reserved.

James Hurst "The Scarlet Ibis" by James Hurst, published in *The Atlantic Monthly*, July 1960. Copyright © 1988 by James Hurst. Used by permission of the author.

Hyperion From the book THE GEEKS SHALL INHERIT THE EARTH by Alexandra Robbins. Reprinted by permission of Hyperion. All rights reserved.

International Creative Management, Inc. "Libraries Face Sad Chapter" by Pete Hamill from *www.petehamill.com.* Copyright © 2002 by Pete Hamill. Used by permission of International Creative Management, Inc.

Japan Publications, Inc. "Temple bells die out" by Basho; and "Dragonfly catcher" and "Bearing no flowers" by Chiyojo, translated by Daniel C. Buchanan, from *One Hundred Famous Haiku* by Daniel C. Buchanan. Copyright © 1973 by Japan Publications. Used by permission of Japan Publications, Inc.

President Lyndon B. Johnson Address Before a Joint Session of Congress November 27th, 1963 by President Lyndon B. Johnson.

Lyndon B. Johnson Library From *A White House Diary* by Lady Bird Johnson. Used with permission of the Lyndon B. Johnson Library.

The Estate of Dr. Martin Luther King, Jr. c/o Writer's House LLC "I Have a Dream" by Dr. Martin Luther King, Jr. from *The Words Of Martin Luther King, Jr.* Copyright © 1963 Martin Luther King Jr., copyright renewed © 1991 Coretta Scott King. Used by arrangement with The Heirs to the Estate of Martin Luther King Jr., c/o Writers House as agent for the proprietor New York, NY.

Knopf Doubleday Publishing Group, a division of Random House LLC Excerpt(s) from "The Hero's Adventure," in THE POWER OF MYTH by Joseph Campbell, copyright © 1988 by Apostrophe S Productions, Inc. and Bill Moyers and Alfred Van der Marck Editions, Inc. for itself and the estate of Joseph Campbell. Used by permission of Doubleday, an imprint of the Knopf Doubleday Publishing Group, a division of Random House LLC. All rights reserved.

Alfred A. Knopf, a division of Random House, Inc. "Pecos Bill: The Cyclone" from *Pecos Bill: Texas Cowpuncher* by Harold W. Felton, illustrated by Aldren A. Watson, copyright © 1949 by Alfred A. Knopf, a division of Random House, Inc. Copyright © renewed 1976 by Harold W. Felton. "Dreams" from *The Collected Poems of Langston Hughes* by Langston Hughes. Copyright © 1994 by The Estate of Langston Hughes. "The News" from *Conscientious Objections* by Neil Postman, copyright © 1988 by Neil Postman. "Dream Deferred" from *The Collected Poems of Langston Hughes* by Langston Hughes. Copyright © 1994 by The Estate of Langston Hughes. Used by permisson of Alfred A. Knopf, a division of Random House, Inc.

Learned Hand "I Am An American Day" address by Learned Hand. New York City, May 21, 1944.

Little, Brown and Company, Inc. "Pyramus and Thisbe" and "Perseus" from *Mythology* by Edith Hamilton. Copyright © 1942 by Edith Hamilton; Copyright © renewed 1969 by Dorian Fielding Reid and Doris Fielding Reid. Used by permission of Little Brown & Company.

Liveright Publishing Corporation "maggie and milly and molly and may" by E. E. Cummings from *Complete Poems, 1904-1962* by E.E. Cummings, edited by George J. Frimage. Copyright © 1956, 1984, 1991 by the Trustees for the E. E. Cummings Trust. Used by permission of Liveright Publishing Corporation.

Andrew MacAndrew "The Necklace" by Guy de Maupassant, translated by Andrew MacAndrew, from *Boule de Suif and Selected Stories* by Guy de Maupassant, New York, NAL, 1964, pp. 143-151. Translation copyright © 1964 by Andrew MacAndrew. Used by permission of Marie-Christine MacAndrew.

Massachusetts Institute of Technology "Team Builds 'Sociable' Robot" by Elizabeth A. Thompson from *Massachusetts Institute of Technology News Office February 14, 2001, http://web.mit.edu/newsoffice/2001/kismet-0214.html.* Copyright © 2001. Used by permission of MIT News Office.

John McPhee "Arthur Ashe Remembered" by John McPhee, first published in *The New Yorker*, March 1, 1993. Used by permission of the author.

Methuen Publishing, Ltd. "The Inspector-General" from *The Sneeze: Plays and Stories* by Anton Chekhov, translated and adapted by Michael Frayn, published by Methuen Drama. Originally from An Awl in a Sack by Anton Chekhov, 1885. Used by permission of Methuen Publishing, Ltd.

Edna St. Vincent Millay Society "An Ancient Gesture" by Edna St. Vincent Millay from *Collected Poems*, HarperCollins. Copyright © 1954, 1982 by Norma Millay Ellis. All rights reserved. Used by permission of Elizabeth Barnett, literary executor.

MIT Press *The High Price of Materialism* by Tim Kasser. Copyright © 2002. Reprinted with permission of MIT Press. "Table: Fragile Self-Worth" by Tim Kasser in *The High Price of Materialism.* Copyright © 2003. MIT Press. Reprinted with permission of MIT Press.

NASA Johnson Space Center "Launch Schedule 101/ NASA's Shuttle and Rocket Missions" from *www.nasa.gov/missions/highlights/schedule101.html.* "Robotics Education Project" by Staff from *http://robotics.arc.nasa.gov/.* Copyright © National Aeronautics and Space Administration.

Charles Neider "The Invalid's Story" by Mark Twain from *The Complete Sketches and Tales of Mark Twain*, edited by Charles Neider: Copyright © 1977 by Charles Neider. Used by permission of Charles Neider.

The New York Times, 09/18/2001. "Of Altruism, Heroism, and Nature's Gifts in the Face of Terror" by Natalie Angier. Copyright © 2001. The New York Times. All rights reserved. Used by permission and protected by the Copyright Laws of the United States. The printing, copying, redistribution, or retransmission of this Content without express written permission is prohibited.

The New York Times, 3/30/2008. "The Case for Fitting In" by David Berreby. Copyright © 2008. New York Magazine. The New York Times. All rights reserved. Used by permission and protected by the Copyright Laws of the United States. The printing, copying, redistribution, or retransmission of this Content without express written permission is prohibited.

The New York Times Syndication Sales Corp. Headquarters "World Trade Center Movie Review" by Rebecca Murray from *http://movies.about.com/od/worldtradecenter/fr/wtcreview080806.htm.* Copyright © 2007 by Rebecca Murray. Used with permission of About, Inc., a part of The New York Times Company. All rights reserved.

NJ TRANSIT Port Jervis & Pascack Valley Lines from *MTA Train Schedule: Metro-North Railroad.* Copyright © 2006 NJ Transit. Used by permission of NJ TRANSIT.

Northwestern University Press "Sonnets on Love XIII" from *Sonnets on Love and Death* by Jean de Sponde translated by David R. Slavitt. English translation copyright © 2001 by David R. Slavitt. Published 2001. Evanston: Northwestern University Press, 2001. Used by permission of Northwestern University Press. All rights reserved. http://www.nupress.northwester.edu.

W. W. Norton & Company, Inc. "The War Against the Trees" from *The Collected Poems* by Stanley Kunitz. Copyright © 2000 by Stanley Kunitz. Used by permission of W. W. Norton & Company, Inc.

Naomi Shihab Nye "Daily" by Naomi Shihab Nye from *Hugging The Jukebox* by Naomi Shihab Nye. Copyright © 1982 All rights reserved. Used by permission of the author.

Orchard Books, an imprint of Scholastic Inc. "Checkouts" adapted from *A Couple of Kooks and Other Stories About Love* by Cynthia Rylant. Published by Scholastic Inc./Orchard Books. Copyright © 1990 by Cynthia Rylant. Used by permission of Scholastic, Inc.

Oxford University Press, Canada "Siren Song" by Margaret Atwood from *Selected Poems 1966-1984.* Copyright © Margaret Atwood 1990. Used by permission of Oxford University Press Canada.

Oxford University Press, Inc. "The Horses" by Edwin Muir from *Collected Poems* by Edwin Muir. Copyright © 1960 by Willa Muir. Used by permission of Oxford University Press, Inc.

Oxford University Press (US) "Americans in the Depression" by Eric Rauchway in *The Great Depression and the New Deal: A Very Short Introduction.* Copyright © 2009. Oxford University Press. Reprinted with permission.

Penguin Group (USA) Inc. & Wallace Literary Agency, Inc. "Rama and Ravana in Battle," from *The Ramayana* by R. K. Narayan, copyright © 1972 by R. K. Narayan. Used by permission.

The Penguin Press "Play Hard; Play Together; Play Smart" by Dean Smith and Gerald D. Bell with John Kilgo from *The Carolina Way: Leadership Lessons From A Life In Coaching.* Copyright © 2004 by Dean E. Smith. Used by permission of The Penguin Press, a division of Penguin Group (USA) Inc.

Playbill Magazine "On Summer" by Lorraine Hansberry, reprinted from *Playbill Magazine*, June 1960. Copyright © Playbill, Inc. All rights reserved. Used by permission of Playbill, Inc.

Portfolio (A Penguin Company) "The Only Thing We Have to Fear" from *Nothing to Fear: Lessons in Leadership from FDR*, by Alan Axelrod. Copyright © 2003 by Alan Axelrod. Used by permission of Portfolio, an imprint of Penguin Group (USA) Inc.

Psychology Today "My Possessions, Myself" by Russell Belk. Copyright © 1988. *Psychology Today.*

G.P. Putnam Sons From "Rules of the Game" from *The Joy Luck Club* by Amy Tan. Copyright © 1989 by Amy Tan. Used by permission of G.P. Putnam Sons, a division of Penguin Putnam, Inc.

Random House Group, Ltd. & Simon & Schuster, Inc. "Blues Ain't No Mockin Bird" from *Gorilla, My Love* by Toni Cade Bambara. Copyright

© 1971 by Toni Cade Bambara. "New Directions" from *Wouldn't Take Nothing For My Journey Now* by Maya Angelou. Copyright © 1993 by Maya Angelou. Used by permission of Random House, Inc. From *The Complete Short Stories of Ernest Hemingway* by Ernest Hemingway. Copyright renewed © 1966 by Mary Hemingway. All rights reserved.

Dr. Sally K. Ride c/o The Washington Speakers Bureau "Single Room, Earth View" by Sally Ride, published in the April/May 1986 issue of *Air & Space/Smithsonian Magazine*, published by The Smithsonian Institution. Used by permission of Dr. Sally K. Ride.

Riverhead Books "Carry Your Own Skis" by Lian Dolan, from *Satellite Sisters' Uncommon Sense* by Julie, Liz & Sheila Dolan and Monica & Lian Dolan. Copyright © 2001 by Satellite Sisters LLC. Used by permission of Riverhead Books, an imprint of Penguin Group (USA) Inc.

Scovil Chichak Galen Literary Agency, Inc. "If I Forget Thee, Oh Earth…" from *Expedition to Earth* by Arthur C. Clarke. Copyright © 1953, 1970 by Arthur C. Clarke; Copyright 1951 by Columbia Publications, Inc. Used by permission of the author and the author's agents, Scovil Chichak Galen Literary Agency, Inc.

Simon and Schuster "Blue Nines and Red Words" by Daniel Tammet in *Born on a Blue Day.* Copyright © 2009. Simon and Schuster, Inc. "The Concept of Heroes" by Elie Wiesel in *My Hero: Extraordinary People and the Heroes Who Inspire Them.* Copyright © 2007. Simon and Schuster, Inc.

The Supreme Court of Ohio "A Hero in Our Midst" by Justice Paul E. Pfeifer from *www.sconet.state.oh.us/Justices/pfeifer/column/2006/jp091306.asp.* Copyright © 2006 The Supreme Court of Ohio. Used by permission of The Supreme Court of Ohio.

Literary Estate of May Swenson "Analysis of Baseball" by May Swenson from *American Sports Poems* by R. R. Knudson and May Swenson. Copyright © 1989. Orchard Press. Used with permission of The Literary Estate of May Swenson.

University of California, Davis "Poultry Fact Sheet No. 35: Incubating Eggs in Small Quantities" by Ursula K. Abbott, Ralph A. Ernst, and Francine A. Bradley from *http://animalscience.ucdavis.edu/Avian/pubs.htm.* Used by permission of University of California, Davis.

The University of Georgia Press "American History" from *The Latin Deli: Prose and Poetry* by Judith Ortiz Cofer. Copyright © 1992 by Judith Ortiz Cofer. Used by permission of The University of Georgia Press.

University Press of New England "The Talk" by Gary Soto from *A Summer Life* by Gary Soto. Copyright © 1990 by University Press of New England, Hanover, NH. Reprinted with permission.

Viking Penguin, Inc. "Old Man of the Temple" from *Under The Banyan Tree* by R. K. Narayan. Copyright © 1985 by R. K. Narayan. Used by permission of Viking Penguin, a division of Penguin Group (USA) Inc.

Villard Books From *Big Kiss* by Henry Alford, copyright © 2000 by Henry Alford. Used by permission of Villard Books, a division of Random House, Inc.

Vital Speeches of the Day "Glory and Hope" by Nelson Mandela, from *Vital Speeches of the Day,* June 1, 1994. Used by permission of Vital Speeches of the Day.

Wesleyan University Press "Slam, Dunk, & Hook" from *Magic City* by Yusef Komunyakaa. Copyright © 1992 by Yusef Komunyakaa. Used by permission of Wesleyan University Press.

West End Press "Women on the Breadlines" from *Harvest: Collected Stories* by Meridel LeSueur. Reprinted with the permission of The Permissions Company, Inc., on behalf of West End Press, Albuquerque, New Mexico, www.westendpress.org.

Writer's House, LLC "Meciendo" by Gabriela Mistral ("Rocking"), translated by Doris Dana from *Selected Poems Of Gabriela Mistral,* translated and edited by Doris Dana. Copyright © 1961, 1964, 1970, 1971 by Doris Dana. Used by permission of Writer's House, LLC.

The Wylie Agency, Inc. "The Man to Send Rain Clouds" from *Storyteller* by Leslie Marmon Silko. Copyright © 1981 by Leslie Marmon Silko. Used by permission of The Wylie Agency, Inc.

Credits

Photo locators denoted as follows: Top (T), Center (C), Bottom (B), Left (L), Right (R), Background (Bkgd)

Cover Filip Fuxa/Shutterstock

xliv-xlv Thomas Owen Jenkins/Shutterstock; 9 Colin Mcconnell/ ZUMAPRESS/Newscom; 17 Cargo/Imagezoo/Getty Images; 22 The New York Times/Redux Pictures; 26 (B) Kathleen Brown/CORBIS, (B) istock-photo; 29 iStockphoto; 31 Sovfoto/Eastfoto; 43 (Bkgd) Hulton Archive/ Getty Images Inc., (CB) Jane Burton/© Dorling Kindersley,(CR) The Imperial War Museum London,(TC) Getty Images; 50 Bettmann/ CORBIS; 52 (BL) Culver Pictures/The Art Archive at Art Resource, NY, (border)Webeye/iStockphoto; 54 Wadsworth Atheneum Museum of Art / Art Resource, NY/ARS; 55 Robert Maass/CORBIS; 57 De Agostini Picture Library/Getty Images; 62 Mark Mainz/Getty Images Entertainment/Getty Images; 64 ©Andrea Danti/Shutterstock; 66 ©sabi-no.parente/Fotolia; 69 ©Perrush/Shutterstock; 70 Getty Images; 71 ©zhuda/Shutterstock; 73 Mary Grace Long /Asia Images/ Getty Images; 74 Bettmann/Corbis; 80 Bettmann/CORBIS; 82 iStockphoto; 89 © Holton Collection / SuperStock; 94 (CL) Cynthia Rylant,(CR) Nana Kofi Acquah Photography; 96 ©Brian A Jackson/Shutterstock; 97 ©06photo/ Shutterstock; 99 (CBR) NASA / Photo Researchers, Inc., (TCR) Frank Zullo/Photo Researchers, Inc.; 100 ©Paul Smith/Alamy; 104 Space Telescope Science Institute / NASA / Photo Researchers, Inc.; 105 NASA / Science Source; 126 Douglas Menuez/Stockbyte/Getty Images; 128 ©Morales/age fotostock/SuperStock; 131 ©Biosphoto /BIOS;Bios - Auteurs (droits geres),Huguet Pierre; 138 Two Boys in a Punt, 1915 - Cover Illustration, Popular Magazine N.C. Wyeth (1882–1945) Oil on Canvas, 37-1/2 x 26 1/2, Private Collection, Photography courtesy of Brandywine River Museum;144 (BR) The Granger Collection, New York,(TR) Comstock Images/Getty Images; 146 (BC) ©Ocean/ Corbis,(Bkgd) Shutterstock; 149 (CR) Shutterstock,(R) ©Marek/Fotolia; 151 George Marks/Retrofile; 152 Shutterstock; 153 AP Photo/Ramon Espinosa; 156 ©trendywest/Shutterstock; 158 ©trendywest/ Shutterstock; 162 ©1xpert/Fotolia; 165 (TC) ©ZUMA Press, Inc./ Alamy,(TR) ©Pictorial Press Ltd / Alamy; 168 (BR) ©Geraint Lewis/ Alamy,(Bkgd) ©Petr Vaclavek/Shutterstock; 171 ©Petr Vaclavek/ Shutterstock; 172 ©Petr Vaclavek/Shutterstock; 174 ©Petr Vaclavek/ Shutterstock; 175 ©Geraint Lewis/Alamy; 178 Donald Reilly / The New Yorker Collection /cartoonbank; 184 (BR) Mark Mainz/Getty Images Entertainment/Getty Images,(CL) Jeff Janowski/Getty Images,(CR) Bettmann/CORBIS,(TR) ©Georgios Kollidas/Fotolia; 186 ©Images/ Corbis; 194 ©Brian Velenchenko/Corbis; 201 ©jovannig/Fotolia; 206 Bettmann/ Corbis; 208 (Bkgd) ©Steve Lovegrove/Shutterstock,(L,R,B) ©Jo Ann Snover/Shutterstock,(C) ©Bettmann/CORBIS; 211 (C) ©selit-bul/Fotolia,(TL) ©Steve Lovegrove/Shutterstock; 216 AP Photo/Udo Weitz; 218 (C) ©faysal/Shutterstock,(Bkgd) ©pio3/Fotolia; 220 ©with-God/Fotolia; 222 (Bkgd) ©smarques27/Fotolia,(TC) ©Artur Marciniec/ Fotolia; 230 Jim Cooper/ Bio Photo Source/ AP Images; 232 ©Sylvain Legare/Shutterstock; 234 George Steinmetz/Corbis; 235 The Granger Collection; 240 Bettmann/ Corbis; 241 Bob Adelman/ Magnum Photos; 242 ©Hulton-Deutsch Collection/CORBIS; 244 ©Bettmann/CORBIS; 245 ©Bill Perry/Fotolia; 247 © Hulton-Deutsch Collection/CORBIS; 252 (CL) FIONA HANSON/ AP/Wide World Photos,(CR) Photofest; 254 ©Ttphoto/ Shutterstock; 256 Ed Freeman / Stone / Getty Images; 258 (B) ©Mopic/ Fotolia,(CR) NASA; 260 (BL) NASA; 261 ©1xpert/Fotolia; 283 ©INTERFOTO/Alamy; 284 Underwood & Underwood/CORBIS; 287 Getty Images, Inc.; 288 Bettmann/CORBIS; 289 © Oscar White/CORBIS; 294 ©Bettmann/CORBIS; 298 ©Bettmann/CORBIS; 301 ©Bettmann/CORBIS; 303 MPI/Archive Photos/Getty Images; 305 Library of Congress, Prints & Photographs Division, FSA/OWI Collection, [LC-DIG-fsa-8b29516];308 Archive Holdings Inc./Getty Images; 315 Nancy R. Schiff/Hulton Archive/Getty Images; 318 ©Corbis; 324 (BCR) © Sophie Bassouls/ Sygma/Corbis,(CR) HANDOUT/KRT/Newscom; 326 ©Daumier, Honore (188-79)/Musee d'Orsay, Paris, France/The Bridgeman Art Library; 334 Cheron Bayna; 338 kelly bowden/Flickr/Getty Images; 346 (BL) Hulton Archive/Getty Images Inc.,(TL) Hulton Archive/Getty Images; 347 The Jacob and Gwendolyn Lawrence Foundation / Art Resource, NY; 348 Oronzo Montedoro/Getty Images; 349 Feti, Domenico c. 1589–1624 ascribed to A Learned Man, oil on canvas 98 x 73.5 cm350 ©MPH/ Fotolia; 352 ©ivan kmit/Shutterstock; 358 The Granger Collection, New York,(BL) Bettmann/Corbis,(BCL) David Snodgress/Bloomington Herald-Times/Associated Press,(TCL) Oscar White/CORBIS,(TL) The Bells of Rostov, 1983 (oil on canvas), Chepik, Sergei (b.1953) / Private Collection, Roy Miles Fine Paintings / The Bridgeman Art Library International; 359 The Bells of Rostov, 1983 (oil on canvas), Chepik, Sergei (b.1953) / Private Collection, Roy Miles Fine Paintings / The Bridgeman Art Library International; 361 Christie's Images / Artists Rights Society/ Superstock; 362 The New York Public Library / Art Resource, NY; 364 Greg Paprocki/Photodisc/Getty Images; 366 Images/Corbis; 368 Copyright © 1977 by Jane Zalben. First appeared in The Jabberwocky, published by F. Warne. Reprinted by permission of Curtis Brown, Ltd.; 369 Copyright © 1977 by Jane Zalben. First appeared in The Jabberwocky, published by F. Warne. Reprinted by permission of Curtis Brown, Ltd.; 372 Tyler Stableford/The Image Bank/Getty Images; 376 (BL) The Granger Collection, New York,(BCL) AP World Wide Photos,(TCL) The Granger Collection, New York,(TL) Associated Press; 377 iStockphoto/Thinkstock; 378 The Granger Collection, New York; 381 ©James Thew/Fotolia; 382 ©Deuceswild/Fotolia; 394 (BL) The Granger Collection, New York,(BCL) ©Georgios Kollidas/Fotolia,(TCL) Library of Congress,(TL) Eric Schaal/Time Life Pictures/ Getty Images; 395 Martin Ruegner/Photographer's Choice RF/Getty Images; 396 ©ksysha/Fotolia; 398 Eileen Tweedy/The Art Archive at Art Resource, NY; 400 ©javar-man/Fotolia; 404 (BL) ©Georgios Kollidas/Fotolia,(BCL) AP World Wide Photos,(CL) The Granger Collection, New York,(TCL) The Granger Collection, New York; 406 (TL) Ron Brown/ SuperStock,408 Ron Levine/ Lifesize/Getty Images; 428 ©JP Laffont/Sygma/CORBIS; 432 ©Bettmann/CORBIS; 433 ©Bettmann/CORBIS; 434 ©Bettmann/CORBIS; 440 Everett Collection/Newscom; 441 Lisa Svara / istockphoto; 443 Bettmann/ Corbis; 444 Bettmann/ Corbis; 445 Hulton Archive/Stringer/ Getty; 448 ©Albright-Knox Art Gallery/CORBIS; 451 © Josef Scaylea/ CORBIS; 453 bpk, Berlin/Heinrich Hohl/Art Resource, NY; 455 ©Bettmann/CORBIS; 460 ©Everett Collection Inc/Alamy; 463 ©Associated Press; 465 ©GL Archive/Alamy; 468 Art Rickerby / Time & Life Pictures / Getty Images; 469 CL Bettmann/CORBIS,(CR) Bettmann/ Corbis; 470 (CL) Wally McNamee / CORBIS,(CR) Keystone/ Hulton Archive/ Getty images; 476 (CL) Najlah Feanny-Hicks/Corbis,(TR) ©Everett Collection Inc/Alamy; 478 ©Images/Corbis; 487 Bettmann/ CORBIS; 492 ©The Gallery Collection/Corbis; 493 (BR) 20th Century Fox Film Corp/ Everett Collection,(BCR) 20th Century Fox/ Photofest,(TCR) The Kobal Collection at Art Resource, NY,(TR) The Koball Collection at Art Resource, NY; 498 Portrait of Queen Elizabeth I of England, known as the Sieve Portrait, c. 1575, by Frederico Zuccaro (1540–1609) Source: Art Resource,499 Lebrecht Music and Arts Library/Alamy Images; 500 Andrea Pistolesi/ Getty Images; 502 Jon Arnold Images/Masterfile Corporation; 504 (CR) The Kobal Collection at Art Resource, NY,(TR) The Kobal Collection at Art Resource, NY; 505 ©Banauke/Fotolia; 508 The Koball Collection at Art Resource, NY; 512 Alinari/Art Resource, NY;516 © 20th Century Fox Film Corp. All rights reserved. Courtesy: Everett Collection; 522 Dorling Kindersley, Inc.;525© 20th Century Fox Film Corp. All rights reserved; 528 The Kobal Collection at Art Resource, NY; 529 The Kobal Collection at Art Resource, NY; 531 20th Century Fox/Photofest; 536 The Kobal Collection at Art Resource, NY; 540 20th Century Fox/ Photofest; 543 20th Century Fox/ Photofest;544 AKG Images; 550 Araldo de Luca/Corbis; 553 (BL) TM and

Copyright © 20th Century Fox Film Corp; 559 The Kobal Collection at Art Resource, NY; 564 The Kobal Collection at Art Resource, NY;567 © 2th Century Fox Film Corp. All rights reserved. Courtesy: Everett Collection; 568 © 20th Century Fox Film Corp. All rights reserved. Courtesy: Everett Collection; 569 The Kobal Collection at Art Resource, NY; 574 Private Collecton/Bridgeman Art Library, London/New York; 578 (BC) Mary Evans Picture Library/MARK FURNESS / The Image Works,(BCL) Mary Evans Picture Library/The Image Works,(CR) The Kobal Collection at Art Resource, NY; 579 (BC) MGM/ Photofest,(BR) Paramount Pictures/ Photofest,(CL) The Everett Collection; 580 (BC) ArenaPal / Topham / The Image Works,(CL) ArenaPal / Topham / The Image Works,(CR) Royal Shakespeare Theatre/Lebre / Lebrecht Music & Arts; 581 (BL) Tristram Kenton/Lebrecht Music / Lebrecht Music & Arts,(BR) Neale Osborne/Lebrecht Music & / Lebrecht Music & Arts,(CL) Royal Shakespeare Theatre/ Lebrecht Music & Arts,(CR) Maremagnum/ Getty Images; 585 Rod Planck/Photo Researchers, Inc.; 591 20th Century Fox/Photofest; 596 20th Century Fox/ Photofest; 604 20th Century Fox/ Photofest; 609 Barry Gregg/ Corbis; 611 (BR) The Kobal Collection at Art Resource, NY; 611 (CL) Barry Gregg/ Corbis; 616 The Kobal Collection at Art Resource,NY; 618 20th Century Fox/ Everett Collection; 620 The Granger Collection, New York; 625 20th Century Fox Film Corp/ Everett Collection; 626 The Kobal Collection at Art Resource, NY; 638 (CL) Archivo Iconografico, S.A/Corbis,(CR) Georgios Kollidas/ Fotolia; 640 Thisbe, John William Waterhouse/The Bridgeman Art Library, London/New York; 641 iStockphoto; 642 Thisbe and the Lioness, from 'The Children's Hour: Stories from the Classics', published by the Waverley Book Company (colour litho), Brock, Charles Edmund (1870-1938) / Private Collection, / The Bridgeman Art Library International; 643 Helmut Meyer zur Capellen/zefa/Corbis; 644 Everett Collection; 646 The Granger Collection, New York; 648 Everett Collection; 650 Sygma/Corbis;674 ©lynea/Shutterstock; 679 ©lynea/ Fotolia; 681 Bettmann/ Corbis; 686(Bkgd)ussr/iStockphoto,(T) FINBARR O'REILLY/Reuters/Landov; 690 DeAgostini/SuperStock; 693 Time & Life Pictures/Getty Images; 696 ©silver-john/Shutterstock; 698 ©silver-john/ Shutterstock; 699 Jeff Janowski/Getty Images; 702 ©Gena/Fotolia,(TCR) ©Scanrail/Fotolia,(BCL) ©Denis Gladkiy/Fotolia,(BCR) ©Coccinella/ Fotolia,(BL) ©pzAxe/Fotolia,(BR) ©Oleksandr Moroz/Fotolia,(CL) ©Pavlo Vakhrushev/Fotolia,(CR) ©steamroller/Fotolia,(TCL) ©Pixel Embargo/ Fotolia,(TL) ©deusexlupus/Fotolia,(TR) ©ras-slava/Fotolia; 710 Gunilla Lundström/NordicPhotos/age fotostock; 716 Matthew Diffee / The New Yorker Collection /cartoonbank; 722 Charles Barry, University of Santa Clara. With permission of the author.; 724 ©Corbis; 740 ©Burstein Collection/CORBIS; 746 Robert Harding Images/Masterfile Corp.; 746 (TR) Masterfile; 747 Pearson Education; 748 ADV/ Shutterstock; 749 Clara/ Shutterstock; 750 Georgy Markov/ Shutterstock; 753 Christie's Images/SuperStock; 756 (B) ©National Gallery, London/Art Resource, NY,(Bkgd) ©Viktoriya/Shutterstock,(CR) ©Araldo de Luca/Corbis; 760 Mary Evans Picture Library/EDWIN WALLACE/Everett Collection; 767 Mary Evans Picture Library/EDWIN WALLACE/Everett Collection; 770 ©Mary Evans Picture Library/Alamy; 773 Illustrations by N.C. Wyeth from THE ODYSSEY OF HOMER, translated by George Herbert Palmer. Copyright 1929 by N.C. Wyeth; copyright renewed (c) 1957 by Carolyn Wyeth. Reprinted by permission of Houghton Mifflin Harcourt Publishing Company. All rights reserved.; 778 Illustrations by N.C. Wyeth from THE ODYSSEY OF HOMER, translated by George Herbert Palmer. Copyright 1929 by N.C. Wyeth; copyright renewed (c) 1957 by Carolyn Wyeth. Reprinted by permission of Houghton Mifflin Harcourt Publishing Company. All rights reserved.; 782 New York Public Library/ Art Resource, NY; 787 Mary Evans Picture Library; 792 Stapleton Collection/Corbis; 800 Serov, Valentin Aleksandrovich (1865-1911)/ Tretyakov Gallery, Moscow, Russia/RIA Novosti/The Bridgeman Art Library; 805 Scala/Art Resource, NY; 806 Araldo de Luca/ CORBIS; 809 Mary Evans Picture Library/EDWIN WALLACE/Everett Collection; 810 ©Mary Evans Picture Library/Alamy; 814 Bridgeman Art Library; 816 Mary Evans Picture Library/EDWIN WALLACE/Everett Collection ; 823 Erich Lessing / Art Resource, NY; 828 (BL) The Granger Collection,(BCL) Comstock Images/ Getty Images,(L) Bassouls Sophie/ CORBIS Sygma,(CL) Time Life Pictures/ Getty Images; 830 John Roddam Spencer Stanhope/The Bridgeman Art Library/Getty Images; 832 (c) RMN-Grand Palais/Art Resource, NY; 834 Perry Mastrovito/ CORBIS, 836 John Miller/Robert Harding Picture Library/Alamy; 842 AP Photo/Max Photo; 843 Ted Steshinsky/Corbis; 858 ©Hulton-Deutsch Collection/ CORBIS; 860 (C) ©Steve Vidler/Alamy,(Border) ©appujee/Fotolia; 862 (BC) ©Svetlana Nikolaeva/Fotoli,(Border) ©appujee/Fotolia; 863 Marilyn Silverstone / Magnum Photos; 868 Erich Lessing / Art Resource, NY; 871 Scala / Art Resource, NY; 875 Time Life Pictures/Getty Images; 878 Archives Charmet/The Bridgeman Art Library International; 883 Robert Maass/ Corbis; 886 ©John Kuss/Corbis; 888 ©John Kuss/Corbis; 889 (BR) Writer Pictures/Associated Press,(CR) Mathew Cavanaugh/ Associated Press; 892 MICHAEL EVSTAFIEV/AFP/Getty Images; 895 ©ZUMA Press, Inc./Alamy; 898 2001 The Record (Bergen Co. NJ)/Getty Images; 904 (T,C,R,B)©liravega/Fotolia,(TR) ©Matthew Cole/Fotolia, (BR)©raven/Fotolia, (B) ©Roman Sotola/Fotolia; 910 AP World Wide Photos.